A Guide to the Mammals of China

EDITORS

ANDREW T. SMITH

AND

YAN XIE

A Guide to the Mammals of China

CONTRIBUTING AUTHORS

Robert S. Hoffmann
Darrin Lunde
John MacKinnon
Don E. Wilson
W. Chris Wozencraft

ILLUSTRATOR

Federico Gemma

HONORARY EDITOR

Professor Wang Sung

PRINCETON UNIVERSITY PRESS PRINCETON AND OXFORD

Published by Princeton University Press, 41 William Street, Princeton, New Jersey 08540
In the United Kingdom: Princeton University Press, 3 Market Place, Woodstock, Oxfordshire OX20 1SY

Library of Congress Cataloging-in-Publication Data
A guide to the mammals of China/Andrew T. Smith and Yan Xie, editors; Robert S. Hoffmann … [et al.], contributing authors; illustrator Federico Gemma.
p. cm.
Includes bibliographical references and index.
ISBN 978-0-691-09984-2 (hardcover: alk.paper) 1. Mammals—China—Identification. I. Smith, Andrew T., 1946- II. Xie, Yan, 1967-
QL729.C5G85 2008
599.0951--dc22
2007020625
British Library Cataloging-in-Publishing Data is available

This book has been composed in Cheltenham Light and Gil Sans
Printed on acid-free paper.
nathist.press.princeton.edu
Printed in Malaysia
10 9 8 7 6 5 4 3 2 1

To Harriet, Yanlin, Sally, Sakiko, Monica, Kate, and Julie
for their continual support and understanding

Contents

Species Plates

Figures

Maps

Habitat Illustrations

Preface

A Guide to the Mammals of China is an outgrowth of the desire of the Biodiversity Working Group (BWG) of the China Council for International Cooperation in Environment and Development (CCICED) to offer a comprehensive guide to the mammalian fauna of China. Despite the fact that the 556 species of mammal in China represent over 10 percent of all mammals on Earth, this fauna had not previously been systematically or comprehensively catalogued. Our goal was to bring together for the first time a thorough compilation of the systematics, identification, distribution, natural history, and conservation status of this remarkable and diverse mammalian fauna. One of our coauthors, John MacKinnon, earlier produced a guide to the birds of China (MacKinnon and Phillipps 2000). Covering over 1,300 species, that volume was translated into Chinese by the BWG and distributed widely to managers of protected areas and biodiversity practitioners across China. We hope that *A Guide to the Mammals of China* similarly can be used by managers, conservation biologists, border officials, and enforcement personnel throughout China to help protect and preserve the country's rich mammal biodiversity.

The stimulus to write this book was the existence of an unpublished work on China's mammals written by the Chinese BWG cochair, Professor Wang Sung. This comprehensive work, written several years previously, remained untranslated and unpublished, thus unavailable to the world's mammalogists. To make available the vast amount of data in this treatment, *A Guide to the Mammals of China* was born. The first step was to translate the text into English (approximately 300 pages of typescript). We then assembled a team to expand the information with current literature, against the background of contemporary mammalian systematics. Within the international team on the BWG were several mammalogists who had worked in China for many years (Robert Hoffmann, John MacKinnon, and Andrew Smith), and others (Don Wilson and Chris Wozencraft, also with considerable China field experience) had either participated directly in some BWG meetings or been hosted in China by the BWG. Additionally, Wilson had served as editor of the previous edition of *Mammal Species of the World* and was in the process (with DeeAnn Reeder) of producing the third edition of that authoritative reference (Wilson and Reeder 2005). Hoffmann, Wozencraft, and Smith were contributing authors to various chapters of that edition. The addition of Darrin Lunde, with his extensive experience working with the small mammals of southeast Asia, completed our team to handle the species accounts.

One of the major projects undertaken by the BWG was the creation of the China Species Information Service (CSIS). This project, largely the outgrowth of Xie Yan's efforts and supported by Wang Sung and John MacKinnon, established the database and maps used herein. The final piece in forming our team was to enlist Federico Gemma from Rome to draw the color plates. Smith had worked with Federico on other projects concerning the IUCN Species Survival Commission Species Information Service and knew that his background in mammalogy (working with rabbits) and artistry made him ideally suited for our project.

Along the way we all came to realize that the vastness of China, coupled with a paucity of information on many of its mammal species, made our efforts almost Sisyphean. While we strove to make this volume as complete and accurate as possible, we know that each account and each map should best be treated as a work in progress—much remains to be learned of the distribution, systematics, and natural history of Chinese mammals. Thus, we hope that this book engenders a new enthusiasm for the study of Chinese mammals, especially in their natural and wild state.

Andrew Smith, Tempe, and Xie Yan, Beijing

Contributors

Federico Gemma
Viale Marconi 19
Rome 00146
Italy
f.gemma@quipo.it
www.federicogemma.it

Robert S. Hoffmann
Division of Mammals
Department of Vertebrate Zoology
National Museum of Natural History
Smithsonian Institution—MRC-108
Washington, DC 20013
USA
hoffmann@si.edu

Darrin Lunde
Department of Mammalogy
American Museum of Natural History
Central Park West at 79th Street
New York, NY 10024-5192
USA
lunde@amnh.org

John R. Mackinnon
11 Leycroft Close
Canterbury CT2 7LD
United Kingdom
arcbc_jrm@hotmail.com

Andrew T. Smith
School of Life Sciences
Box 874501
Arizona State University
Tempe, AZ 85287-4501
USA
a.smith@asu.edu

Wang Sung
Institute of Zoology
Chinese Academy of Sciences
Datunlu, Andingmenwai
Beijing 100101
People's Republic of China
wangs@panda.ioz.ac.cn

Don E. Wilson
Division of Mammals
Department of Vertebrate Zoology
National Museum of Natural History
Smithsonian Institution—MRC-108
Washington, DC 20013
USA
wilsond@si.edu

W. Chris Wozencraft*
Division of Natural Sciences
Bethel College
1001 West McKinley Avenue
Mishawaka, IN 46545
USA
wozencc@bethel-in.edu

Xie Yan
Institute of Zoology
Chinese Academy of Sciences
Datunlu, Andingmenwai
Beijing 100101
People's Republic of China
xieyan@public3.bta.net.cn

*deceased

A Guide to the Mammals of China

Introduction

Andrew T. Smith and Xie Yan

China is a magnificent country and one of the most diverse on Earth. Its size ranks fourth among the world's nations (9,596,960 km^2), and it is home to over 1.3 billion people. The topography of China ranges from the highest elevation on Earth (Mt. Everest or Chomolungma; 8,850 m) to one of the lowest (Turpan Pendi; 154 m below sea level). Chinese environments include some of Earth's most extensive and driest deserts (the Taklimakan and Gobi) and its highest plateau (the Tibetan Plateau or "Roof of the World"). Habitats range from tropical to boreal forest, and from extensive grasslands to desert. This wide variety of habitats has contributed greatly to the richness of China's mammal fauna. Additionally, the geographic location of China, at the suture zone between the Palaearctic and Indo-Malayan biogeographic regions (Hoffmann 2001), further contributes to the country's mammal diversity. Overall, more than 10 percent of the world's species of mammal live in China (556/5,416; total count from Wilson and Reeder 2005). Twenty percent (109/556) of China's mammals are endemic, and one of these is among the most recognizable of the world's mammals, the Giant Panda. In their analysis of megadiversity countries, Mittermeier et al. (1997) consider China to have the third highest diversity of mammals among all countries (following Brazil and Indonesia).

China's Geography and Mammalian Biogeography

There have been many attempts to describe China's diverse landscape (reviewed in MacKinnon and Hicks 1996; MacKinnon et al. 1996; Xie et al. 2004a). Conventionally, China has been divided into three major physical geographic regions: the Tibetan (Qinghai-Xizang) Plateau, northwest arid China, and eastern monsoon China (map 4).

The Tibetan Plateau is one of the highest and most remote landscapes on Earth. The plateau averages between 3,000 and 5,000 m in elevation and encompasses roughly a quarter of China. The word "plateau" is a misnomer, as this area is crisscrossed by numerous impressive mountain chains, such as the Anyemaqin Shan, Bayan Har Shan, and Tanggula Shan, and many smaller spur ranges. Nevertheless, approximately 70 percent of the plateau is composed of alpine meadow or semisteppe vegetation. The Qaidam Basin, an interesting area of tectonic collapse, is found at the northern extreme of the plateau at an elevation of only 2,600 m (MacKinnon and Hicks 1996).

The arid northwest encompasses about 30 percent of China and represents an eastern extension of the great Eurasian deserts and grasslands. One of the world's most desolate deserts, the Taklimakan (translation: "those who go in do not come out alive") lies north of the Tibetan Plateau and the Kunlun range. The cooler Dzungarian Basin, China's second-largest desert, lies in the far northwest. Various smaller deserts extend to the east, increasingly interspersed with semidesert and temperate steppe grasslands. Finally, the rocky Gobi Desert occupies the northern part of China and extends into Mongolia. Two of Asia's major mountain ranges break up this barren expanse in the northwest: the Tian Shan and the Altai. One can stand below sea level in Turpan Pendi and clearly see the snow-capped top of Bogda Feng (in a spur of the Tian Shan) at 5,445 m (MacKinnon and Hicks 1996).

Eastern monsoon China comprises about 45 percent of the country but is home to roughly 95 percent of China's human population. This land is crossed by major rivers that originate on the Tibetan Plateau, most notably the Huang He (Yellow River) and the Yangtze. Almost all of the arable land has been converted to agriculture, and much of the original forest habitat has been destroyed. Most of this landscape is low in elevation and consists of broad alluvial valleys, coastal plains, and modest ancient mountain ranges. The south is seasonably humid, and the plains are punctuated by dramatic limestone pillars. The climate becomes increasingly temperate toward the north, with deciduous trees giving way to expansive coniferous forests in the far northeast (MacKinnon and Hicks 1996).

These physical geographical regions, however, do not adequately define the major biogeographic divisions in China (maps 3, 4, and 5; Xie et al. 2004a). Biogeographically, China's flora and fauna have been affected by both historical factors (their derivation from two formerly isolated biogeographic realms—the Palaearctic and the Indo-Malayan) and their relative ability to colonize new habitats.

The southern boundary of the Palaearctic realm in China and adjacent countries was analyzed by Hoffmann (2001), particularly with regard to the distribution of mammals. He found extreme compression of the zone of overlap between the Palaearctic and Indo-Malayan realms along the southern boundary of western China, as this region is defined by high altitudinal relief. In contrast, in areas of low relief (such as in eastern central China), the zonation is determined more by latitude than altitude, and there is a broad latitudinal band of overlap between forms that originated from the Palaearctic and Indo-Malayan realms (Hoffmann 2001). In the south this zone extends from about 28° N on the coast to roughly 25 ° N in the area in northern Yunnan where the three great rivers (Yangtze, Mekong, Salween) lie in close proximity. The northern edge of this zone essentially follows the Yangtze River from the east coast to the area where the three great rivers come together (Hoffmann 2001). This description contrasts with previous opinions that the southern limit of the Palaearctic in China largely corresponds to the latitude of the Huang He in eastern China (about 30° N; Corbet 1978; Corbet and Hill 1992).

A sensitive and objective approach to understanding the zoogeography of Chinese mammals has been developed recently by Xie et al. (2004a). They defined 124 biogeographic units in China based on a comprehensive suite of factors (altitude, landform, climate, vegetation, hydrology, etc.) and then overlaid maps of 171 diagnostic mammal species on these units. A statistical analysis identified aggregations of biogeographic units based on mammal distributions, and this information was used to create cluster dendrograms. This analysis produced a classification of the boundaries dividing the mammal fauna at different spatial scales across China. A similar analysis was performed on 509 representative plant species.

The biogeographical divisions of mammals and plants in China determined by the methodology outlined above contrast significantly with the commonly used physical geographical regions for China (map 4). Additionally, there are distinctive differences between the biogeographical divisions using the plant and mammal data. Four major biogeographical divisions occur in China based on vegetation: northeast, southeast, southwest, and northwest. These in turn can be broken down into 8 subareas and 27 regions (table 1; maps 3 and 4). Compared with the physical geographical regions, the major divisions based on plants separate the arid northwest into a western and eastern section, and eastern monsoonal China into a northern and southern part. The southwest China biogeographical region for plants is basically similar to the Tibetan Plateau physical geographic region, although both the northern and southern boundaries of the biogeographical region are found farther south than the physical geographical region (table 1; map 4; Xie et al. 2004a).

There are three major biogeographical divisions for mammals (map 5; Xie et al. 2004a). As for plants, the mammals have distinctive western and eastern distributions in the arid northwest geographical region; the divisional boundary for mammals occurs farther west than that for plants (map 4). The mammals also separate eastern monsoonal China into northern and southern areas, and the boundary for mammals is further south than that for plants. In the large arc from northwest to southeast China, there is a single mammal biogeographical boundary compared with two for plants (map 4). Mammals in the interior drainage area on the Tibetan Plateau have northern affinities. The southeastern plateau region shows a continuous extension in faunal affinities to the southeast, maintaining a mammal fauna more similar to that of monsoonal southeastern China.

In northwest China the montane forests and grasslands of the Tian Shan and Altai mountains clearly are distinct from the surrounding

Table 1. China Biogeographic Divisions (from Xie et al. 2004a)

Area	Subareas	Regions
I. Northeast China	Ia. Nei Mongol steppe and northeast China plain	1. Greater Xing'an mountains
		2. Northeast China plain
		3. Nei Mongol arid and desert grassland
		4. Ordos Plateau arid and desert grassland
	Ib. Lesser Xing'an and Changbai mountains	5. East of Northeast China
	Ic. North China	6. North China
		7. Huangtu Plateau forest grassland and arid grassland
II. Southeast China	IIa. Central China	8. Huaibei Plain and plains of the middle and lower Yangtze River
		9. Qinling and Daba mountain mixed forest
		10. Sichuan Basin agriculture
	IIb. Highlands and plains in the south to Yangze River	11. Southeast China hills and basins evergreen broadleaf forest
		12. Yangtze River southern bank evergreen broadleaf forest
		13. Yunnan-Guizhou Plateau evergreen broadleaf forest.
	IIc. Coast and islands of South China	14. South to Nan Ling evergreen broadleaf forest
		15. South Yunnan tropical monsoon forest
		16. Hainan and Leizhou Peninsula tropical rainforest and monsoon forest
		17. Taiwan island evergreen broadleaf forest and monsoon forest
		18. South China Sea islands tropical rainforest
III. Southwest China	IIIa. Southeast and south of Tibetan Plateau	19. South Sichuan and Yunnan Plateau evergreen broadleaf forest
		20. East Tibet and West Sichuan incisive hill coniferous forest and alpine meadow
		21. Himalaya mountains
	IIIb. Central and northern Tibetan Plateau	22. Northeast Tibetan Plateau
		23. West and central Tibetan Plateau
IV. Northwest China		24. Alashan Plateau temperate desert
		25. East Tian Shan temperate desert
		26. North Xinjiang
		27. Tarim Basin and Kunlun mountains

arid landscape. The Altai (F3; map 5) shows clear ties to the fauna of Russia's boreal forest. As a result, Zhang and Zhou (1978) biogeographically linked the Altai with the Greater Xing'an mountains of northeast China. However, more than twice as many Altai mammals occur simultaneously in the Tian Shan mountains and the arid Dzungarian Basin as in the Greater Xing'an mountains (Xie et al. 2004a).

In northeast China there are distinct differences in vegetation between the Greater and Lesser Xing'an mountains (regions 1 and 5; map 3), whereas mammal distributions are similar between these ranges, and the area can be classified as a single region (region A; map 5).

Overall, the analysis of Xie et al. (2004a) demonstrates that the ability to colonize varies between plants and animals, producing distinctive differences in the cluster analysis and the designation of major biogeographic areas in China. While plant distributions tend to be closely tied to prevailing environmental conditions, mammals generally exhibit broader geographic tolerance. Additionally, mammal distributions appear to be truncated by major rivers and mountain chains, whereas these do not appear to be as stringent barriers to plant distributions. Thus plant divisions appear to be more reliable than those of mammals as a general descriptor of China's biogeography (table 1; map 3).

History of Chinese Mammalogy, by Wang Sung

Pre–People's Republic of China

In ancient times knowledge about animals was primarily obtained from human activities, such as hunting and fishing. As early as the Shang dynasty (ca. 1500 BC), over 100 words existed for various kinds of birds (such as chickens), mammals (such as sheep, horses, cattle, and pigs), fish, and insects. By the Tang dynasty (AD 600–900), when culture and exploration in China were ascendant, knowledge of mammals was widespread (Schafer 1963).

During the most active time of natural history exploration (the mid–late 1800s and early 1900s), China's culture was more introspective. Most explorations in China at that time were conducted by scientists from Europe or North America (John Anderson, Roy Chapman Andrews, M. Berezovski, Douglas Carruthers, Père Armand David, George Forrest, Walter Granger, P. M. Heude, Pyotr Kozlov, Clifford Pope, G. Potanin, Nikolai Przewalski, Vsevolod Roborovski, Arthur de Carle Sowerby, Robert Swinhoe, and Walter Zappey to name a few; Allen 1938, 1940; Rayfield 1976). A quick look in this book at the names of scientific authorities for the majority of Chinese mammal species and subspecies bears witness to the prevalence of Western scientists in the initial determination of the Chinese mammal fauna. Indeed, most of the type specimens from these expeditions remain deposited in the major museums of the United States and Europe, a factor that hampers systematic mammalogy in China to this day.

Toward the end of this era (the 1920s and 1930s), some Chinese mammalogists became involved in the study of the Chinese fauna, including Shou Zhenhuang, Fu Tongsheng, Liu Chengzao, and Peng Hongshou. The publication of Glover Allen's *The Mammals of China and Mongolia* (1938, 1940) provided a benchmark capturing the results of these early investigations. Allen's treatise continues to inform, and it provided essential information used by the authors of this book.

Early People's Republic of China Period (1949–1966)

Chinese mammalogy began in earnest in the early 1950s, upon the founding of the PRC. The Chinese Academy of Sciences (CAS) was founded in late 1949 after the advent of the PRC, followed shortly by the establishment of the Institute of Zoology (IOZ) under the CAS in 1951. It was immediately recognized that mammalogy was a field that had received minimal attention in the past. To rectify this, Shou Zhenhuang, an experienced zoologist who had studied abroad throughout the 1930s and 1940s, was appointed to found the Mammalogical Research Division of the IOZ. As one of the leading zoologists in China, he had published the first scientific paper about Chinese ichthyology and was the author of *Birds of Hopei Province* (1936), the only ornithological monograph published before the PRC was founded. Shou recruited young students for the Mammal Division and established a mammal collection, beginning with materials from old institutions in Beijing and the former Heude Museum in Shanghai. He also developed the mammalogical portion of the institutional library (including important international journals, e.g., *Journal of Mammalogy, Zoological Record, Biological Abstracts, Proceedings of the Zoological Society of London, Annals and Magazine of Natural History,* as well as significant reference books, e.g., Allen's *Mammals of China and Mongolia* [1938, 1940], Miller's *Mammals of Western Europe* [1912], Ellerman and Morrison-Scott's *Checklist of Palaearctic and Indian Mammals* [1951]), despite the extreme difficulty in amassing foreign currency needed to purchase them.

Most important, Shou initiated field surveys and ecological research. A five-year plan, the

Mammalogical Faunal Survey, began in 1953 in northeastern China (Heilongjiang, Jilin, Liaoning, and eastern Nei Mongol), a minimally disturbed area that still contained large expanses of virgin forest. This survey covered much of the Lesser Xing'an mountains (1953), Greater Xing'an mountains (1954), Changbai Shan mountains (1955), and the Liaodong Peninsula, Songhuajiang-Liaohe Delta, and Sanjiang Plain (1956–57). Involved in the field survey team were the majority of the Mammal Division of IOZ/CAS, headed by Peng Hongshou (1953–57) together with Zhu Jing (1954), Yang Hefang (1953), Wang Sung (1954–56), Zhang Jie (1954), and Li Xueren (1954–56). While the main survey was being conducted in the northeast, other mammalian surveys began in other areas (southern Yunnan, Hainan, Guangxi, Sichuan, Xizang, Gansu, Qinghai, Guangxi), many of which remained productive until they were terminated during the Cultural Revolution.

As the IOZ's Mammal Division developed, it became the center of mammalogical research in China. A number of young colleagues from universities and institutions were sent to IOZ/CAS for further study under Shou's supervision, including Li Guiyuan (Sichuan Agricultural University), Yang Anfeng (Peking University), He Hong'en (from Hunan), Zhang Luanguang (Beijing Normal University), Chen Jun (Lanzhou University), Zheng Changlin (from Xining, Qinghai), Wu Delin (Kunming Institute of Zoology), and Xu Munong (Shandong Normal University). These young scientists eventually became some of the leading mammalogists in China.

In parallel additional zoological institutions were established, such as the Kunming Institute of Zoology (KIZ) in the late 1950s (headed by Pan Qinghua) and the Northwest Plateau Institute of Biology (NWPIB) in Xining in 1966 (headed by Xia Wuping), as well as some local institutions in Shaanxi, Xinjiang, and Guangdong. Research staff from these institutions and university teachers conducted a large number of field surveys and research projects in various regions. Thus, mammalian collections were further developed not only at the IOZ/CAS, but also in different locations throughout China.

Over 10,000 mammal specimens were collected during the Mammalogical Faunal Survey, and these constituted the first mammalian collection in China at IOZ/CAS. The final results of the five-year survey were compiled and published as *Report on Mammalian Survey in Northeastern China* (1958), now regarded as a milestone of early Chinese mammalogy. It was followed by publication of *The Economical Fauna–Mammalia* (1962) and *Illustrated Books of Animals–Mammalia* (1963). These are the earliest publications about the mammalian fauna written and compiled by Chinese mammalogists.

At this time it was difficult for Chinese mammalogists to catalog incoming specimens because nearly all the type specimens were housed in foreign collections, and most of the relevant literature was in either English or Russian. The language barrier was formidable for younger scientists. Although universities offered courses in Russian, no English courses would become available for another two decades.

The first international collaboration involving Chinese mammalogists also occurred during the 1950s. A Joint Survey on Agro-Biological Resources with the former East Germany was conducted in northeastern and northern China over a four-month period in 1956. Shou and Klaus Zimmerman (Museum für Naturkunde der Humboldt-Universitat in Berlin) were the coleaders of the zoological group (mammals and birds), and Wang Sung was the Chinese academic secretary for the joint survey team. Specimens were mainly sent to the Museum für Naturkunde, except for a small number that were deposited at the IOZ/CAS. The results of the mammalian survey were published in the 1960s in East Germany by Zimmermann.

A second international collaboration involved a special animal ecology course for graduates sponsored by the Northeast Normal University under a Sino-Soviet cooperative agreement on education in 1957–58. Fu Tongsheng, a famous zoologist in China who had formerly studied in France, was the head of the program. A. P. Kuziakin, a professor from Moscow Normal College, was invited to Changchun, Jilin, to develop the first team of Chinese graduate students majoring in animal ecology. Students from normal universities and colleges from each province were included to become broadly trained in vertebrate zoology, including mammalogy. This cohort became active instructors and researchers upon returning to their own regions throughout China.

Throughout this period Chinese mammalogy was developing a distinctive personality above and beyond that of faunal surveys, collections, and systematic research. Studies on population dynamics of rodents that were initiated in Dailing (Lesser Xing'an mountain area) linked rodent pest control with prevention of deforestation of pine plantations following large-scale logging. This activity was led by Shou and carried out by Xia Wuping, who became a pioneer of mammalian ecology in China. Xia ultimately developed projects concerning rodent ecology and their control in the steppes of northern China, and he was later appointed as the deputy head of the Department of Animal Ecology of the IOZ, under Shou. This research direction was further linked with epidemiological research. Specifically, disease control and rodent control were carried out by the epidemiological sector from the central to local levels. Some epidemiologists became interested in mammalian taxonomy and published a number of survey results.

China also developed an expertise in captive breeding of mammals to harvest for fur and body parts for traditional Chinese medicine (TCM). This activity was initiated with captive breeding of fur-bearing mammals, most notably the Red Fox, upon the founding of the PRC. Because this specific project was not highly successful, external trade sectors of the government founded the Institute of Fur-bearing Animals in Zuojia, Jilin Province, in the late 1950s. This institute formed the prototype for fur-bearing mammal breeding centers in China. Following this, many deer-breeding centers were founded, sponsored by TCM communities and designed to meet the demands of the TCM market. This trend has continued and now includes facilities housing musk deer (since the late 1950s for the production of musk) and bears (since the 1980s for the production of bear bile), each providing a critical ingredient for TCM.

A Critical Period for China: 1966–1976

From 1966 to 1976 a massive political movement, the Cultural Revolution, brought Chinese mammalogy to a screeching halt. This movement prevented progress in every aspect of Chinese life—economic, industrial, agricultural, cultural, education, and scientific. All scientific research and all education in research institutions and universities were terminated. The publication of scientific journals and books was largely suspended for many years. During this period Chinese mammalogists became increasingly isolated from the international community, particularly with regard to systematic studies.

It was particularly disturbing that some activities just nearing completion were suddenly terminated, such as the manuscript for *A Synopsis of Chinese Mammals,* which included a species key, species accounts, and maps of all the mammals recorded from China at that time. This collective work, initiated and organized by Wang Sung, was never published. However, the manuscript was eventually printed and used as a teaching resource for the Wildlife Department of the North East Forestry College, and as the identification reference for the epidemiology sectors. We had this work translated into English, and its contents provided much of the data for this book.

Only a few fields of scientific research were given special permission to restart during the Cultural Revolution. One of these research programs was the compilation of the series *Fauna Sinica*—over 100 volumes, 9 of which would focus on mammals. As neither new field surveys nor specimen collection were allowed, and existing specimens required for the compilation of *Fauna Sinica* were far from sufficient, work on the mammal portion of this project was difficult. Nevertheless, the initiative of *Fauna Sinica* had a positive influence on Chinese science during this critical time, as it promoted the study of regional fauna and flora when the majority of other scientific programs had been stopped.

Current Developments: Late 1970s to the Present

For a long time, there had been very few contacts between China and the international science community. Between the 1950s and 1970s, for example, there were only a few joint projects between China and the former USSR and East Germany. In the late 1970s, however, a new era of international collaboration began with the Qinghai–Tibetan Plateau International

Symposium, sponsored by the CAS and held in Beijing. Conservationists and zoologists (S. Dillon Ripley, Smithsonian Institution; Peter Jackson, World Conservation Union (IUCN); Richard Mitchell, United States Fish and Wildlife Service, George Schaller, New York Zoological Society; and others) were invited to visit Beijing to attend the symposium. This momentous occasion allowed the first contact between Chinese and Western mammalogists since the new open policy was initiated. Attendees were permitted to visit CAS institutions, including the IOZ in Beijing, where they interacted with Chinese mammalogists, among them Wang Sung, Zhu Jing, and Gao Yaoting.

At almost the same time, a joint team from IUCN and Worldwide Fund For Nature (WWF), headed by Sir Peter Scott (WWF president and chair of IUCN's Species Survival Commission (SSC/IUCN) and accompanied by Lee Talbot (director general of IUCN) and Charles de Haes (director general of WWF), visited China. The State Council Environment Protection Bureau (EPB), headed by Li Chaobai and Qu Geping, hosted the delegation, and a team that included representatives from the CAS and the Ministry of Forestry met with the group. As a result of the visit, a memorandum of mutual understanding of cooperation between China and IUCN-WWF was signed by Scott and Qu Geping, deputy head of the EPB, including the following proposals: (1) China would send Zhang Shuzhong, another deputy head of the EPB, and Wang Sung from the CAS, as observers to the Convention on International Trade in Endangered Species of Wild Fauna and Flora, 2nd Convention of the Parties (CITES COP 2), held in Costa Rica; (2) China's National Conservation Strategy would be formulated under the coordination of the EPB, headed by Qu; and (3) the Wolong Panda Project would be initiated. The Panda Project was first bilateral cooperative project for wildlife research and conservation endorsed by the PRC and was initiated to protect one of China's most charismatic and endangered species, the Giant Panda. This project was ultimately funded by WWF and carried out by George Schaller, Hu Jinchu, Pan Wenshi, and Zhu Jing.

The new era of international communication and cooperation for Chinese mammalogy was solidified with the founding of the Mammalogical Society of China (MSC) in 1979. Zhou Mingzhen, a well-known paleontologist and director of the Institute of Vertebrate Palaeontology and Palaeo-anthropology at the CAS, was elected the founding president, and Xia Wuping, Huang Wenji, and Wang Sung were elected as vice presidents. The MSC sponsored publication of the journal *Acta Theriologica Sinica*, the first issue of which appeared in 1981. This journal became an important tool for communication and exchange between Chinese mammalogists and their international colleagues.

Another early activity undertaken by the MSC was to sponsor the first Chinese symposium on primatology, held in Kunming. This activity led to the establishment of a Primate Center in Kunming, and since then Kunming has become the focal point for primate research, conservation, and breeding programs in China.

The MSC began international institutional exchanges beginning with the Sino-Japanese Symposium on Mammalogy in 1983, held in Hefei, Anhui Province. This event, coordinated by Wang Sung and Kazuo Wada, was cosponsored by the Japanese Society of Mammalogy and attended by 17 mammalogists. During the symposium, a joint project on Tibetan macaques between Kyoto University and Anhui University was initiated. This project, under the leadership of Wada and Wang Qishan, was effectively carried out for several years on Huang Shan mountain, Anhui Province.

A larger gathering, the Asian-Pacific Symposium on Mammalogy, was held in Beijing in 1988. This symposium was jointly sponsored by the MSC and the American Society of Mammalogists (ASM), and cochaired by Wang Sung and Andrew Smith. Attending the symposium were over 200 participants from China and 184 participants from about 30 other countries. This was the first large-scale contact between Chinese and Western mammalogists and thus should be regarded as a landmark of international cooperation and communication in mammalogy. At the meeting Don Wilson, then president of the American Society of Mammalogists, presented Xia Wuping with honorary membership in the ASM. Wang Sung joined Xia Wuping as the only two Chinese mammalogists so honored, with his election to honorary membership in 1998. Symposium participants visited the IOZ/CAS in Beijing, and, during extended pre- or postsymposium tours of China, they visited local institutions and their mammalian collections. This event greatly enhanced international contacts, communications, and cooperation.

China has now hosted several major international meetings relevant to mammalogy: the 19th International Congress on Primatology (2003) and the 19th International Congress of Zoology (2004) were held in Beijing. Interactions and cooperative research of Chinese mammalogists with international mammalogists is increasing as a result.

Specimens from 50 years of mammalian surveys are now housed throughout China in significant systematic collections. Three collections contain over 10,000 specimens: the Institute of Zoology, CAS, Beijing (early 1950s to present; approximately 25,000 specimens); Kunming Institute of Zoology, CAS, Kunming (late 1950s to present); and Northwest Plateau Institute of Biology, CAS, Xining, Qinghai (late 1950s to present). Small, more or less well-preserved mammalian collections of no more than 5,000 specimens are housed in the following regional institutions: Zoology Division, Guangdong Institute of Entomology, Guangzhou, Guangdong; Shaanxi Institute of Zoology, Xi'an, Shaanxi; Xinjiang Institute of Geography and Biology, CAS, Urumqi, Xinjiang; Shanghai Museum of Natural History, Shanghai (formerly the Heude Museum and Asiatic Society Natural History Museum); School of Life Science, Fudan University, Shanghai; Zhejiang University, Hangzhou, Zhejiang; Sichuan Epidemic Center, Chengdu, Sichuan; Xinjiang Epidemic Center, Urumqi, Xinjiang; Southwest Agriculture University, Ya'an, Sichuan; School of Wildlife Management, Northeast Forestry University, Harbin, Heilongjiang; Beijing Museum of Natural History, Beijing; Heilongjiang Museum of Natural History, Harbin, Heilongjiang. The majority of these institutions are no longer actively collecting specimens.

With the establishment of mammalogical collections in China, there has been increased activity in the naming of new species and subspecies, with type specimens remaining in China. Numerous provincial and regional guides along with specialized taxonomic treatments of the mammals of China have now been published. And for the first time major references of Chinese mammals have been made available: *The Distribution of Mammalian Species in China* (1997), coordinated by Zhang Yongzu and the CITES Management Authority of China; *The Mammalian of China* (1999), by Sheng Helin, Noriyuki Ohtaishi, and Lu Houji; *China Red Data Book of Endangered Animals: Mammalia* (1998), edited by Wang Sung; *A Dictionary of Mammalian Names: Latin, Chinese, English* (2001), edited by Wang Sung, Xie Yan, and Wang Jiajun; and *A Complete Checklist of Mammal Species and Subspecies in China: A Taxonomic and Geographic Reference* (2003), by Wang Yingxiang; and *China Species Red List* (2004), edited by Wang Sung and Xie Yan. We relied heavily on all of these sources for the production of this book.

In summary, the scientific study of mammals in China has a rather short history that began in the early 1950s. A major achievement during this half century was the identification of China's mammal fauna. Initially, communication with the international community was infrequent. Additionally, Chinese mammalogists faced difficulties at the beginning due to the unavailability of collections for study and a lack of comparative sources for systematic reviews. Recent developments have produced hope that more complete data on China's mammals may become available. Because of the current desire to conserve wildlife and biological diversity, studies in cell biology, molecular biology, genetics, population ecology, behavior, and conservation biology are increasing throughout China. Unfortunately, the increase in molecular research has resulted in a decline in traditional mammalogy research. Young students are more interested in laboratory research than in field work. As a result, there have been fewer additions to mammalian specimen collections in recent decades, and mammalian taxonomy is a low priority. Field biology as a whole in China is weak, and, except for some selected species, little is known about the natural history of most of China's mammals. The resulting scientific gap not only influences the development of an integrated biological science program in China, but also seriously impacts biodiversity conservation. We hope that this book brings increased attention to mammalian systematics in China.

Mammalian Conservation

The mammals of China have been seriously threatened by a variety of anthropogenic causes. Few Chinese landscapes appear today as they occurred in the past; there has been an extreme loss of natural habitat, and natural habitats have increasingly become fragmented and isolated from one another. Chinese mammals have been harvested or poached heavily and unsustainably for food, products, and the pet trade. Native species have been subject to widespread poisoning campaigns. Additionally, the presence of alien invasive species, pollution, and litter has degraded many natural habitats. We fear that finding many Chinese mammals in the regions indicated on our distribution maps may not be possible today. One of our motivations for writing this guide is to attract attention to the Chinese mammal fauna so that effective conservation measures can be enacted.

The government of China understands the gravity of biodiversity loss. China is signatory to most major conservation conventions, such as the Convention on International Trade in Endangered Species (CITES; 1981), the Convention on Wetlands (Ramsar; 1992), the World Heritage Convention (1985), and the Convention on Biological Diversity (CBD; 1993). China has hosted a large number of major conservation workshops and congresses. The China Council for International Cooperation in Environment and Development (CCICED) has served as a model organization linking Chinese and international specialists in order to address issues of conservation and sustainable development. These efforts, however, often fall short in their implementation, resulting in ongoing threats to China's mammal diversity.

A first step in any conservation agenda is to recognize those species most in need of protection. We have listed the threatened species categorization for Chinese mammals using four separate criteria, in this order: China (national) Species Red List, China State Key Protected Animal List, CITES Appendix designation, and IUCN (global) Red List. We also present additional conservation information, when available, for each species. The instruments used for categorizing threatened species each have distinctive characteristics and notations, as given below.

IUCN Red List

The IUCN Red List presents the global status for a species using five independent quantitative criteria: (A) Population Reduction (measured as declines in population over time); (B) Geographic Range (extent of occurrence or area of occupancy); (C) Small Population and Decline; (D) Very Small, or Restricted Population; and (E) Quantitative Analysis. Within each of these main criteria are additional refined criteria (see IUCN 1994; 2001). Threatened species may qualify under any of these criteria for a listing as Critically Endangered (CR), Endangered (E), or Vulnerable (VU). Additionally, species can be listed as Near Threatened (NT), of Least Concern (LC), Extinct (EX), or Extinct in the Wild (EW). Some species cannot be listed because they are Data Deficient (DD). The above listing criteria and categories follow from IUCN (2001), an updated revision of the original quantitative Red List categories and criteria (IUCN 1994). There are small but significant differences in how these two listing procedures operate (for example, the 1994 category for Near Threatened is portrayed as Least Concern/near threatened; LC/nt). We do not present the stand-alone global IUCN category for Least Concern. We identify which criteria (ver 2.3 1994 or ver 3.1 2001) were followed for each assessment listed, as not all Chinese species have yet been assessed using the new criteria. The IUCN Red List is one of the most respected indicators of the threatened status of species (de Grammont and Cuarón 2006; Rodrigues et al. 2005).

China Species Red List

To complement the IUCN global Red Listing process, and to allow countries and regions to develop their own conservation priorities, IUCN undertook a process to develop a parallel mechanism for listing threatened species at national levels (Gardenfors 2001; Gardenfors et al. 2001; IUCN 2003). These quantitative criteria take into consideration the extent of a species' range within a host country and other applications to tailor the IUCN Red Listing process to national levels. These criteria were followed in an ambitious effort to Red List all of China's mammals (Wang and Xie 2004). These evaluations include two additional categories: Regionally Extinct (RE), for those species that are now extinct in China although they exist elsewhere in the world; and Not Applicable (NA), for those species that are distributed at the margin of China and for which data are lacking (even though there may be sufficient data for a global assessment). All of China's mammals were assessed against these regional criteria (Wang and Xie 2004); the only species for which we do not present a China Species Red List category are those whose taxonomy has changed since the workshops were held to produce the China Species Red List.

China State Key Protected Animal List

Each Chinese mammal species is listed on the State Key Protected Animal List as a Category I or a Category II species. This national schedule of protected fauna is heavily skewed toward charismatic megafauna and is primarily composed of primates, carnivores, marine mammals, and ungulates. The representation on this list is not truly indicative of the overall threat across all taxa of mammals in China. The formulation of this list was initiated by the Chinese Endangered Species Scientific Commission and authorized by the Ministry of Forestry. Inclusion of species on the list was derived by consensus at an interactive workshop comprised of species specialists from throughout China. The State Key Protected Animal List was finalized soon after the People's Congress issued China's Wildlife Law in 1989.

Convention on International Trade in Endangered Species of Wild Fauna and Flora—CITES

Those species of mammal believed to be negatively affected by trade are listed in CITES appendixes. The Appendix I classification incorporates those mammals that would be threatened with extinction if traded. Trade in specimens of these species is permitted only in exceptional circumstances. Appendix II includes species not necessarily threatened with extinction, but for which trade must be controlled in order to avoid utilization incompatible with their survival (CITES 2006).

China's Protected Area System

Biodiversity conservation can take many forms, but one of the most recognizable is the establishment of nature reserves and protected areas, coupled with their effective management, to ensure that a decline in biodiversity does not occur. Thus, protected areas remain one of the best ways for governments to ensure biodiversity preservation, as well as serving as magnets for eco-tourists who desire to observe native species. Initially, few areas were protected, but the Chinese government has recently stepped up efforts to protect areas rich in biodiversity. Currently over 2,000 protected areas have been established in China, encompassing 14.4–18% of China's land area (see map 6); most of these were established after 1980, many after 1995 (Xie et al. 2004b). These sites are variously catalogued as nature reserves, scenic landscapes, historic sites, nonhunting zones, and forest parks. Over 10 different ministries or administrations are responsible for the management of these areas in mainland China (not including Taiwan and Hong Kong), including the State Forestry Administration, Ministry of Agriculture, Ministry of Water Conservation, Ministry of Construction, Ministry of Geology and Mineral Resources, Ministry of Land Resources, State Oceanic Administration, and State Environmental Protection Agency. Other protected areas are administered at the provincial, county, or township level. The decision to protect species-rich areas in China stems from the belief that these lands will help define the national culture, assist in economic development among rural people, and provide destinations for tourists. Their function is to promote the retention of natural capital, provide flood control, and preserve biodiversity. A full review of the Chinese protected area system is available in MacKinnon et al. (1996) and Xie et al. (2004b).

In spite of the positive strides made in protected-area management in China, more work needs to be done to ensure that these lands will continue to support mammalian biodiversity. China's protected areas are mainly found in the sparsely populated west. Many protected areas in China are small and isolated, minimizing their effectiveness in the preservation of biodiversity. Often they are poorly managed and insufficiently funded; in some instances key programs have been initiated that are actually counterproductive to the preservation of biodiversity (such as poisoning native wildlife). Incursions and poaching by people living outside of protected areas jeopardize their success. Nevertheless, the protected-area system in China has great potential to protect mammalian biodiversity. With improved management, China's protected areas can become sites in which the study and viewing of mammals are enhanced.

How to Use This Book

We present available data on the systematics, distribution, and natural history of the 556 species of mammal found in China. The order of presentation follows the higher-level classification (from order to family to subfamily) as outlined in *Mammal Species of the World*, third edition (Wilson and Reeder 2005). Genera (within a family or subfamily) and species (within a genus) are alphabetized within a taxon. All taxa are identified by both their scientific and common names in English. Chinese names are given in both character and pinyin format. We have given a single English common name for each species, basically following the naming convention used in Wilson and Reeder (2005). Many species are known by more than one common name, but we believe that the application of a single name will, over time, eliminate confusion and enhance the ability of mammalogists to communicate.

We present brief descriptions at each level of classification, followed by a cascade of keys that can be used to discriminate forms within hierarchical levels. Information given for each species includes distinctive characteristics, distribution, natural history, comments (if any), conservation status, and any relevant references. The depth of treatment reflects the information available for each species.

Distinctive Characteristics

Standard specimen measurements are given for each species, when available. These include head and body length (HB); tail length (T); length of hind foot (HF); ear length (E); and greatest length of skull (GLS) (Fig. 1). Bat measurements include forearm length (FA) (Fig. 2), shoulder height (SH) is presented for most larger mammals. These measurements are given in mm, unless otherwise stated for large mammals. Body mass (Wt) is given when available. The dental formula for a species (or taxon) is presented as the upper canines (C), incisors (I), premolars (P), and molars (M)/lower canines (c), incisors (i), premolars (p), and molars (m), followed by the total number of teeth (e.g., 2.0.3.3/1.0.2.3 = 28). Individual teeth are noted as being uppers with capital letters or lowers with lowercase letters, each followed by the tooth number for that tooth type. For example, the third upper incisor = I3; and the second lower premolar = m2. In some rodent groups (fig. 3 and 4), and for some insectivores, we have used a slightly different notation (clarified when introduced in the text).

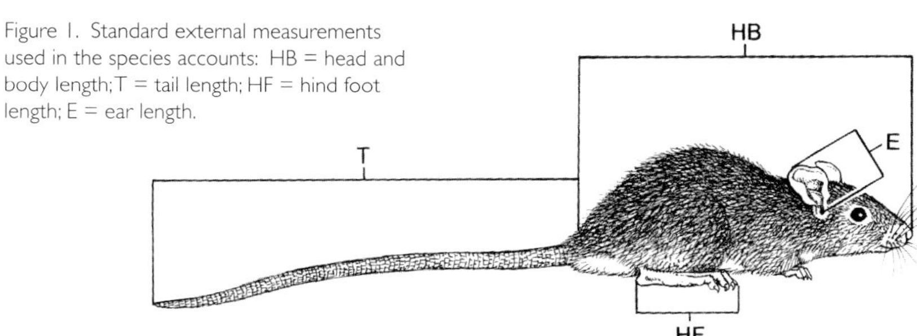

Figure 1. Standard external measurements used in the species accounts: HB = head and body length; T = tail length; HF = hind foot length; E = ear length.

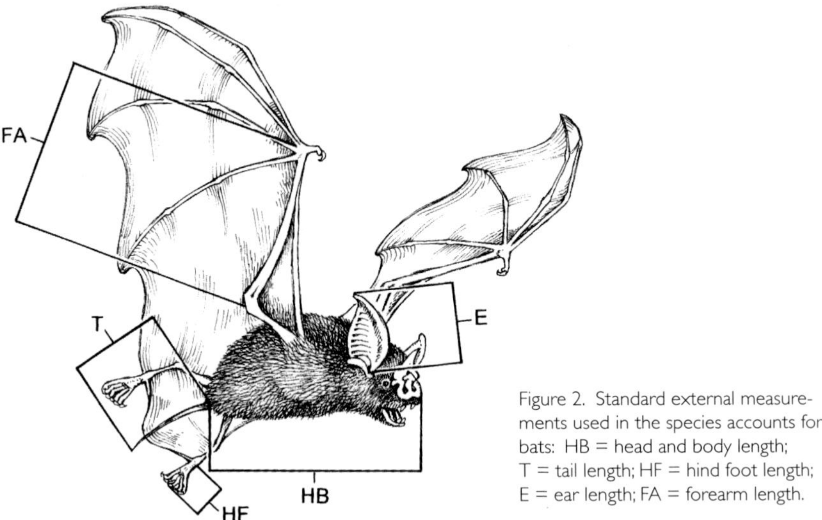

Figure 2. Standard external measurements used in the species accounts for bats: HB = head and body length; T = tail length; HF = hind foot length; E = ear length; FA = forearm length.

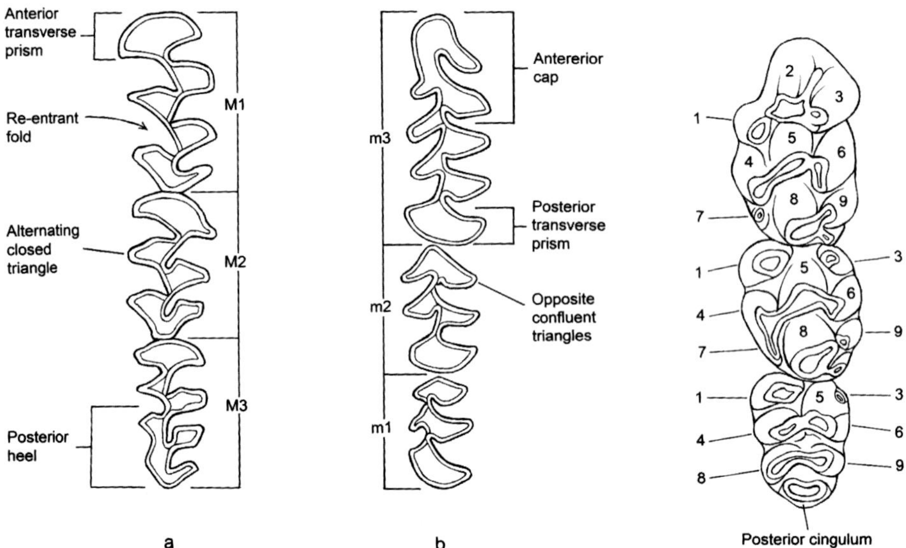

Figure 3. Molar occlusal patterns of a typical volelike rodent illustrating descriptive terms used in the text. Note that the molars of the upper toothrow (a) are numbered M1–M3 from anterior to posterior, whereas in the lower toothrow (b), the teeth are numbered m1–m3 from posterior to anterior.

Figure 4. Upper molar toothrow (M1–M3) of a typical murid rodent illustrating Miller's (1912) cusp numbering scheme. The three rows of cusps on each tooth are numbered sequentially from the lingual to the labial side. Drawn from Musser (1981; fig. 1).

A description of the appearance of each species and its distinctive characteristics (including descriptions of skull features) follows. Plates, including drawings of 384 species (69 percent of Chinese mammals), accompany these descriptions. Our artist, Federico Gemma, examined specimens from the Institute of Biology, Chinese Academy of Sciences, Beijing, as well as the American Museum of Natural History, New York, and Smithsonian Institution, National Museum of Natural History, Washington, DC, to capture the color and nuances of each species; only a few drawings depict species that were not represented in these collections. He also visited the Beijing Zoo collection, which contains most of the large mammal species found in China. Additionally, authors made available to Gemma original photographs, other printed material, and Internet sources to assist with his depiction of species.

Distribution

A brief description of the distribution in China is given for each species, along with its range outside of China or the statement that the form is endemic to China. Often multiple subspecies are found in China, and we present these (in alphabetic order) along with a general description of the geographic range the subspecies occupies. The determination of subspecies for many species in China is problematic; in the interest of aiding further taxonomic inquiry, we incorporated subspecies, relying heavily on the treatments in Wilson and Reeder (2005) and Wang (2003), as well as original literature. In cases where there were discrepancies (and there were many of these), we issue cautionary comments.

Every species description is accompanied by a map of its distribution in China. In a few cases we present separate maps of the historical and contemporary distribution of a species; otherwise the maps depict the original range of the species in China before any potential recent contraction of the range due to anthropogenic factors (see Mammalian Conservation). Each map portrays the actual localities (dots) where a species has been found (or collected) in China. We present the maps in this manner, rather than as shaded range maps, for several reasons. First, the topography of China is so varied that any attempt to shade in a distributional range would inevitably be misleading of the area(s) the species actually inhabits. Second, dot maps, such as we present, give a gestalt for how well known or represented the species is in China; for example, common species are represented by hundreds of dots and tend to be very well understood, whereas those portrayed by only a few localities are generally poorly known.

The localities presented on maps were derived from data from the China Species Information Service. Data in CSIS were gathered using a variety of sources and recorded at the county level. The primary data included original locations from specimens housed at major mammal collections in China (Institute of Zoology, CAS) and the United States (American Museum of Natural History; National Museum of Natural History), as well as published locality records from Chinese scientific surveys, journal articles, and Chinese provincial and regional mammal guides (see References). All data added to CSIS were cross-referenced to their source, so that in verifying maps each author had available the data source for each locality. The original data entered for each map could have been corrupted for a number of reasons; including misidentification of specimens and out-of-date nomenclature. Thus, every map was reviewed carefully and frequent modifications were made (for example, moving a subspecies from one species to another to reflect current taxonomic understanding, which we could do with a single command because of the database structure within CSIS). We believe that these maps portray the distribution of all mammal species in China in the most accurate form possible at the present time, although some of these distributions may need further definition.

Natural History

While information on the natural history of many Chinese mammals is fragmentary, some species are among the most widely recognized on Earth. We focus on the habitat requirements, mode of life, diet, and reproduction for each species, drawing from a variety of sources.

Comments

Frequently it was necessary to explain variants or deviations in our systematic treatment. Some scientific names that are well established in the historical literature have been changed recently, and these are mentioned. Often there are differences of opinion regarding the taxonomy of a species—either with different subspecies or synonyms, or by combining or splitting the species in a manner different from that found in our treatment—and these cases have been documented.

Conservation Status

We list the conservation status as determined by the China Species Red List analysis, the category from the China State Key Protected Animal List, the appropriate CITES Appendix, and the IUCN global Red List analysis. Not all species have been categorized using all four of these criteria; we include only those that have been so evaluated. Details of each of these forms for assessing conservation status are found above.

References

Key references, if available, are listed for each species. We utilized a wide variety of sources in compiling most accounts, and general regional or national sources are normally not listed in the reference section for a particular species—instead, this section highlights primarily the recent journal literature available on the species. Our bibliography, however, is comprehensive and treats all sources consulted even if they are not directly referenced in the text. Importantly, these sources include Chinese regional and provincial guides to mammals. Throughout the text cited literature references take the form of (Wang 2004); no comma separates the author and the year of publication. Each scientific name is followed by the name of the author(s) and the year in which it was described. These references are not placed in parentheses if the genus and species are unchanged. However, a species originally named by its author in a genus different from the one in which it is currently placed has parentheses surrounding the author and date. A comma separates the author from the date of publication (such as Liang, 1877) when the citation refers to the naming authority for a taxon.

Additional Material

Appendixes review those marine mammals that are found off the coast of China but are not included as a part of the Chinese fauna (appendix I), those species whose distributional ranges appear very close to the Chinese border and may eventually be found in China (appendix II), and those mammal species that have been introduced into China (appendix III).

Acknowledgments

Financial assistance for this project was provided by the China Council for International Cooperation in Environment and Development, from funds made available by the governments of Norway and Sweden. We also received support from Arizona State University, Bethel College, the National Museum of Natural History (Smithsonian Institution), and the American Museum of Natural History. The assistance of staff in the Beijing office of the Biodiversity Working Group was invaluable, including Wu Lihui, Yin Songxia, Du Youmei, Du Youcai, Li Shengbiao, and Du Langhua. The administration and staff of the CAS Institute of Zoology mammal collection in Beijing were very helpful, and it is a pleasure to acknowledge their support. We benefited also from the mammal collections at the American Museum of Natural History, National Museum of Natural History (Smithsonian Institution), and the Chicago Field Museum (with thanks to Larry Heaney and Bruce Patterson). We appreciate the consultation and advice given by many of our colleagues, which greatly enriched our accounts: Alexei Abramov, William Bleisch, Thomas Geissmann, Colin Groves, Richard Harris, Mike Hoffmann, Charlotte Johnston, John Lamoreux, Richard Thorington, and Wang Yingxiang. William Bleisch and Richard Harris kindly reviewed selected color plates and range maps. We thank Erin Gibbon, Hayley Ivins, Mary Boise, and Scott Holtz for their assistance with the manuscript. Scott also manually cross-checked all the bibliographic citations against original sources, a time-consuming but crucial task. Brenda Flores assisted with the final formatting of many of the range maps. We are grateful to the following for their assistance in translating scientific research papers: Eileen

Westwig (Russian, French, and German); Margarita Uvaydov (Russian); and Julie Wozencraft, Chien Hsun Lai, Yu Xiang, Zhang Jingshuo, and Zhou Jiang (Chinese). We appreciate the talents of Patricia Wynne, who drew figures 1–4, and the unidentified Chinese artist(s) who drew figures 5–15 (these were composed during the Cultural Revolution when it was politically incorrect to bring attention to oneself by signing artwork). The ASU School of Life Sciences Visualization Center, in particular Jacob Sahertian, Allyson Moskovits, and Sabine Deviche, helped format the baseline map of China, prepared various black-and-white figures for publication, and assisted with the final preparation of the color maps. Larry Heaney and Harriet Smith kindly edited selected portions of the manuscript. Finally, we are indebted to the talented and supportive staff at Princeton University Press. Robert Kirk guided and encouraged our efforts, and the completed project is a direct result of his vision. We are also grateful for the meticulous attention that Terri O'Prey, Dimitri Karetnikov, and Anita O'Brien brought to this project.

Map 1

Administrative provinces and autonomous regions of China.

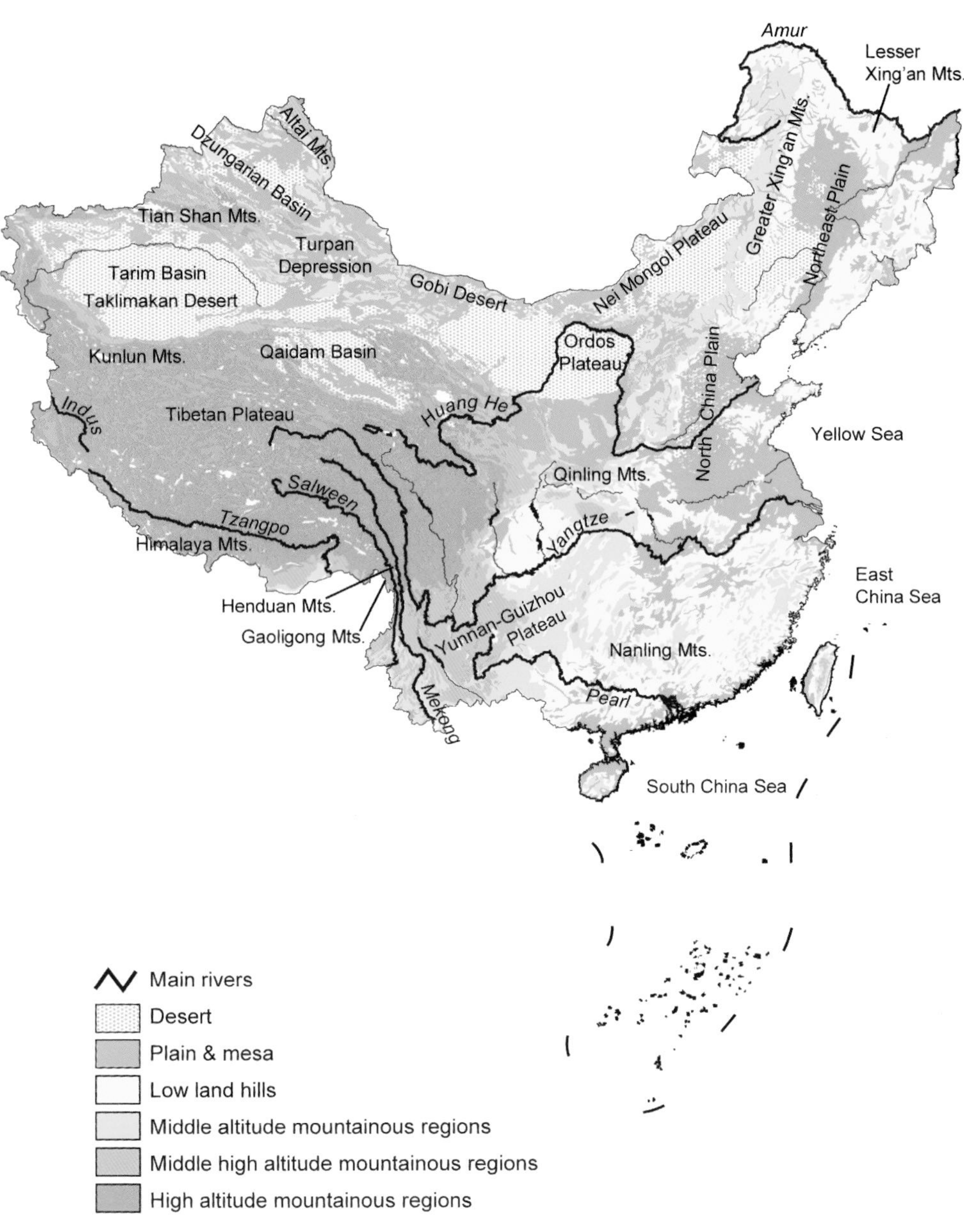

Map 2

Major rivers and landforms of China. Background highlights major topographic regions. Generated from the China Species Information Service.

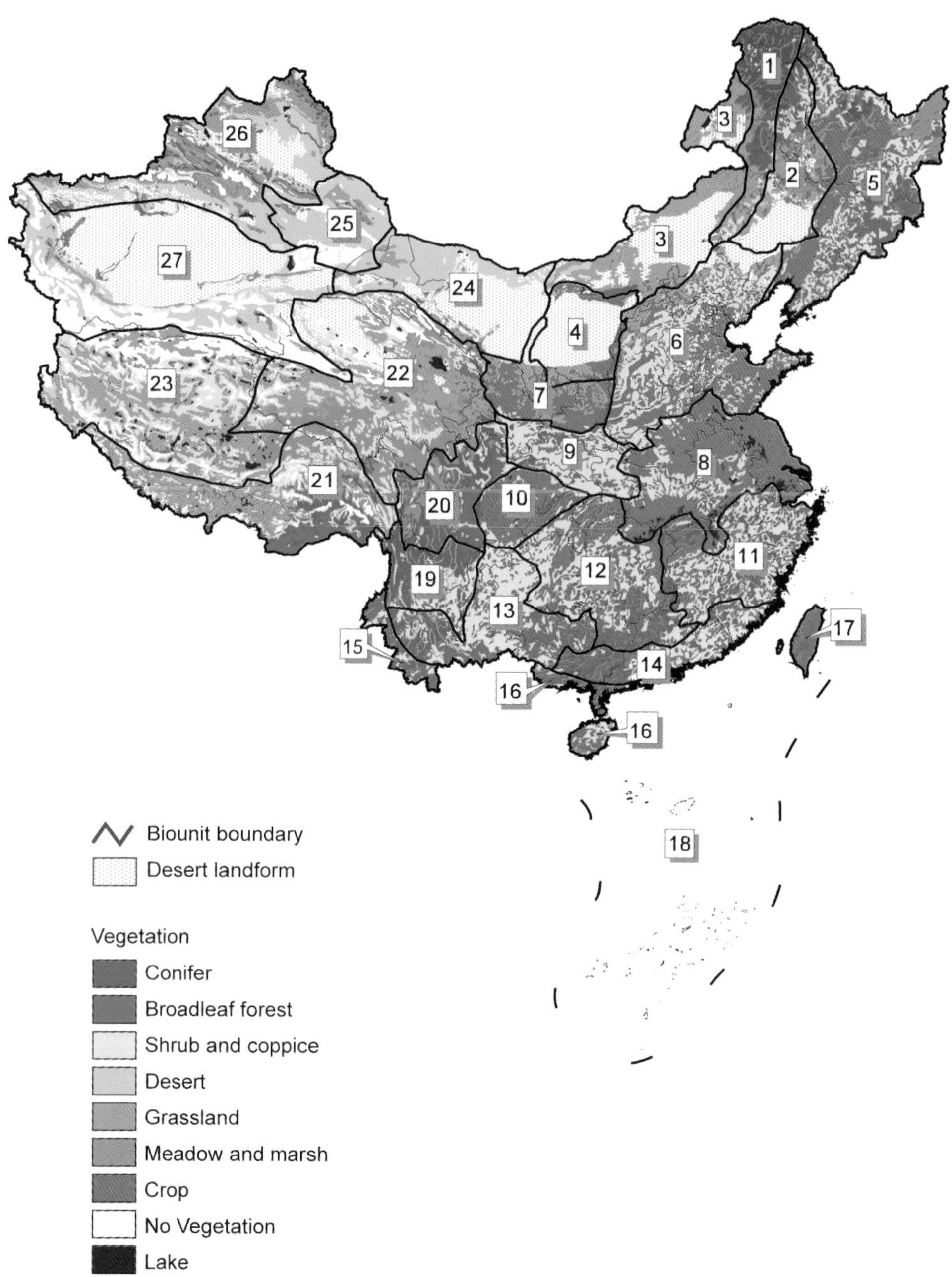

Map 3

Biogeographic regions of China. The 27 biogeographic regions based on vegetative characteristics of China (following Xie et al. 2004a) are portrayed. Regions 1–7 = Northeast China Vegetational Area; Regions 8–18 = Southeast China Vegetational Area; Regions 19–23 = Southwest China Vegetational Area; Regions 24–27 = Northwest China Vegetational Area (table 1). Background highlights vegetational zones across China. Generated from the China Species Information Service.

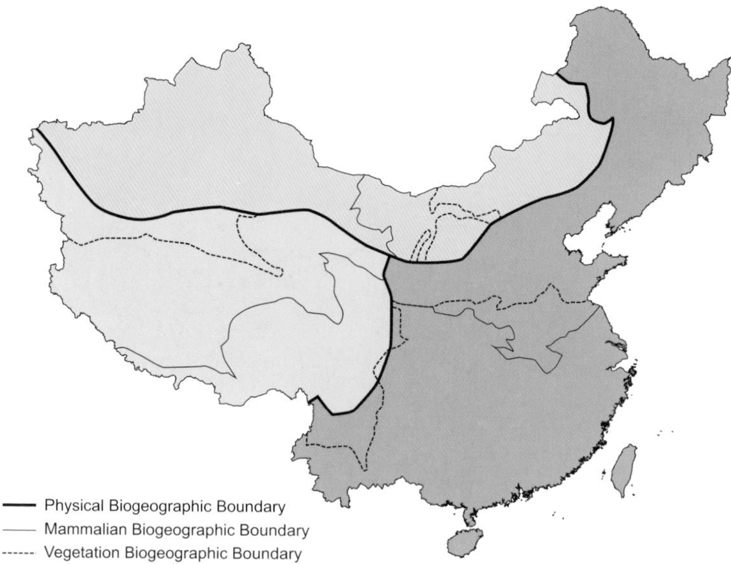

Map 4

China's physical geographic regions and major biotic divisions. The three physical geographic regions in China are shaded (salmon = Northwest Arid China; blue = Tibetan Plateau; purple = Eastern Monsoon China). The biotic divisions based on vegetation and mammal distributions are compared (following Xie et al. 2004a). Generated from the China Species Information Service.

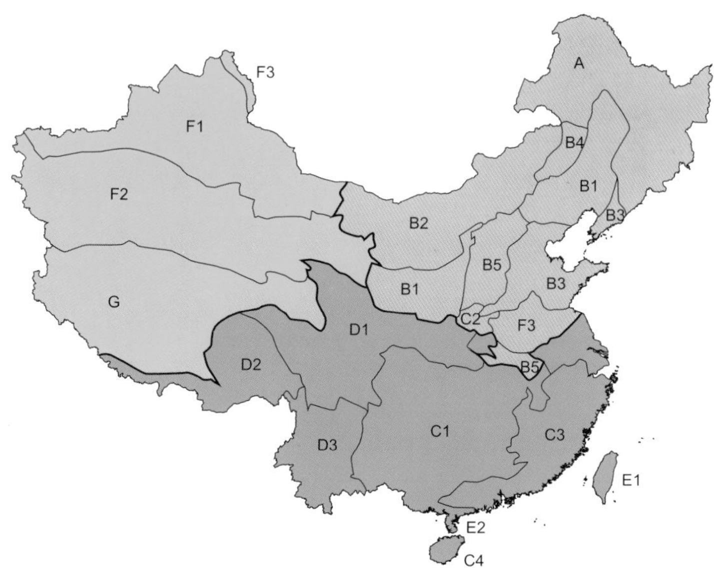

Map 5

Mammalian biogeographic divisions and regions of China. The major mammalian biogeographic divisions (thick lines; blue = Northeast; green = Southeast; pink = West) and regions (thin lines) are portrayed. Unit designations from Xie et al. 2004a. Generated from the China Species Information Service.

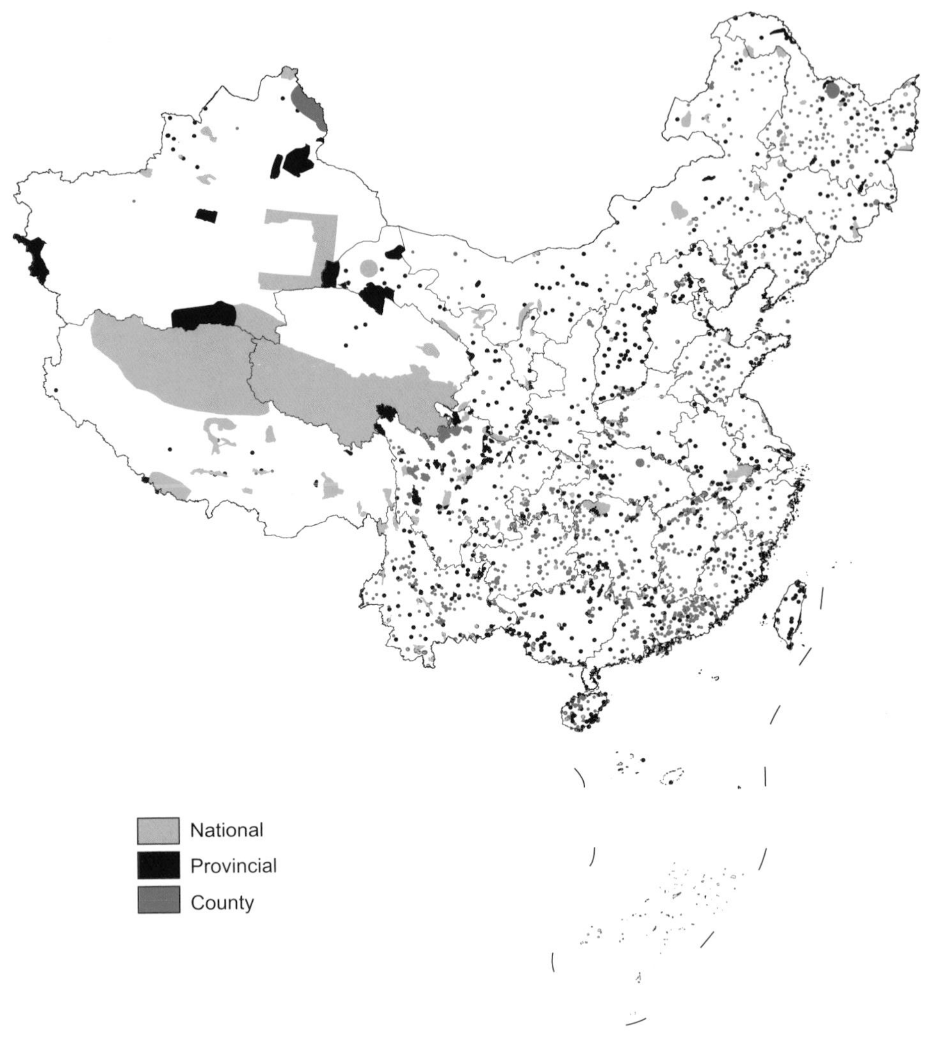

Map 6

Protected areas of China. National, provincial, and county-level protected areas are portrayed (from Xie et al. 2004b). Shaded polygons = gazetted protected areas; dot localities = ungazetted protected areas (area not portrayed). Generated from the China Species Information Service.

Habitat 1. Tian Shan grassland and forest; Xinjiang (Andrew Smith)

Habitat 2. Tamarisk riparian habitat; Xinjiang (Andrew Smith)

Habitat 3. Bogda Feng from Turpan Depression; Xinjiang (Andrew Smith)

Habitat 4. Gobi Desert habitat; Gansu (Andrew Smith)

Habitat 5. Nei Mongol grasslands; Nei Mongol (Jingle Wu)

Habitat 6. Tibetan Plateau grasslands; Qinghai (Andrew Smith)

Habitat 7. Tibetan Plateau wetlands; Qinghai (Andrew Smith)

Habitat 8. Upper Yangtze River; Qinghai (Andrew Smith)

Habitat 9. Juniper forest, Tibetan Plateau; Qinghai (Andrew Smith)

Habitat 10. Bamboo forest, Dujiangyan Longqi-Hongkou Reserve; Sichuan (Andrew Smith)

Habitat 11. Coniferous forest, Juizhaigou; Sichuan (John MacKinnon)

Habitat 12. Forest understory, Dahonggou Creek, Sichuan (W. Chris Wozencraft)

Habitat 13. Wolong Nature Reserve, Sichuan (Andrew Smith)

Habitat 14. Karst forest; Maolan Protected Area; Guizhou (John MacKinnon)

Habitat 15. Xishuangbanna National Nature Reserve; Yunnan (Xie Yan)

Habitat 16. Mengla forest; Yunnan (W. Chris Wozencraft)

Habitat 17. Damingshan Nature Reserve; Guangxi (John MacKinnon)

Habitat 18. Hainan forest; Hainan (John MacKinnon)

Habitat 19. Mangrove habitat; Hainan (John MacKinnon)

Habitat 20. Mixed forest, Changbai Shan Nature Reserve; Jilin (Xie Yan)

Habitat 21. Mixed conifer forest, Changbai Shan Nature Reserve; Jilin (John MacKinnon)

Habitat 22. Northern tundra, Changbai Shan Nature Reserve; Jilin (John MacKinnon)

Habitat 23. Northern coniferous forest, Changbai Shan Nature Reserve; Jilin (John MacKinnon)

Habitat 24. Grassland and forest edge, Changbai Shan Nature Reserve; Jilin (John MacKinnon)

Habitat 25. Forest understory, Mudangjiang; Heilongjiang (John MacKinnon)

1. Northern Tree Shrew
Tupaia belangeri Page 158
北树鼩 Beishuqu
HB 160–195; T 150–190; HF 36–45; E 12–20; GLS 41–49; Wt 110–185 g.

2. Pygmy Slow Loris
Nycticebus pygmaeus Page 160
倭蜂猴 Wo Fenghou
HB 210–260; T 10; GLS < 55; Wt 250–800 g.

3. Bengal Slow Loris
Nycticebus bengalensis Page 159
蜂猴 Feng Hou
HB 260–380; T 22–25; E 20–25; GLS 61–68; Wt 1–2 kg.

4. Chinese Pangolin
Manis pentadactyla Page 388
穿山甲 Chuanshanjia
HB 423–920; T 280–350; HF 65–85; E 20–26; GLS 72–94; Wt 2.4–7 kg.

5. Asiatic Brush-Tailed Porcupine
Atherurus macrourus Page 274
帚尾豪猪 Zhouwei Haozhu
HB 345–525; T 139–228; HF 64–75; E 30–36; GLS 83–120; Wt 2–4 kg.

6. Malayan Porcupine
Hystrix brachyura Page 274
豪猪 Hao Zhu
HB 558–735; T 80–115; HF 75–93; E 25–38; GLS 131–146; Wt 10–18 kg.

1
2
3
4
5
6

1. Stump-Tailed Macaque
Macaca arctoides Page 161
短尾猴 Duanwei Hou
HB 485–650; T 45–50; HF 145–177; GLS 120–157; Wt 7 kg (male), 5 kg (female)

2. Assam Macaque
Macaca assamensis Page 161
熊猴 Xiong Hou
HB 515–665; T 170–250; HF 155–175; E 35–37; GLS 131–159; Wt 6–12 kg (male), 5 kg (female).

3. Rhesus Macaque
Macaca mulatta Page 163
猕猴 Mi Hou
HB 430–600; T 150–320; HF 140–167; GLS 95–122; Wt 7–10 kg (male), 5–6 kg (female).

4. Northern Pig-Tailed Macaque
Macaca leonina Page 162
北豚尾猴 Beitunwei Hou
HB 440–620; T 120–180; GLS 111–142; Wt 11–14 kg.

5. Tibetan Macaque
Macaca thibetana Page 163
藏酋猴 Zangqiu Hou
HB 490–710; T 60–100; GLS 121–168; Wt 10–25 kg.

1
2
3
4
5

1. Gray Snub-Nosed Monkey
Rhinopithecus brelichi Page 165
黔金丝猴 Qian Jinsihou
HB 640–690; T 700–850; GLS 100–130;
Wt 15 kg (male), 8 kg (female).

2. Golden Snub-Nosed Monkey
Rhinopithecus roxellana Page 165
川金丝猴 Chuan Jinsihou
HB 520–780; T 570–800; GLS 104–135;
Wt 15–17 kg (male), 6.5–10 kg (female).

3. Black Snub-Nosed Monkey
Rhinopithecus bieti Page 164
滇金丝猴 Dian Jinsihou
HB 740–830; T 510–720; GLS 104–135;
Wt 17 kg (male), 12 kg (female).

1
2
3

1. Nepal Gray Langur
Semnopithecus schistaceus Page 166
长尾叶猴 Changwei Yehou
HB 620–790; T 690–1,030; GLS 120–145; Wt 9–24 kg (male), 7.5–18 kg (female).

2. Shortridge's Langur
Trachypithecus shortridgei Page 168
戴帽叶猴 Daimao Yehou
HB 1,090–1,600; SH 500–700; T 70–120; HF 190–200; GLS 190; Wt 17–40 kg.

3. François' Langur
Trachypithecus francoisi Page 167
黑叶猴 Hei Yehou
HB 520–710; T 700–900; GLS 84–97; Wt 9–9.5 kg.

4. Phayre's Leaf-Monkey
Trachypithecus phayrei Page 167
菲氏叶猴 Feishi Yehou
HB 550–710; T 600–800; HF 168–180; E 33; GLS 91–107; Wt 6–9 kg.

1
2
3
4

1. Black Crested Gibbon
Nomascus concolor (a, female; b, male) Page 170
黑长臂猿 Hei Changbiyuan
HB 430–540; HF 150–165; GLS 90–115; Wt 7–8 kg.

2. Hainan Gibbon
Nomascus hainanus (female) Page 171
海南长臂猿 Hainan Changbiyuan
Wt 7–8 kg.

3. Northern White-Cheeked Gibbon
Nomascus leucogenys (a, female; b, male) Page 171
白颊长臂猿 Baijia Changbiyuan
Wt 7–9 kg.

4. Hoolock Gibbon
Bunopithecus hoolock (a, female; b, male) Page 169
白眉长臂猿 Baimei Changbiyuan
HB 600–900; HF 140–153; GLS 93–99; Wt 6–8.5 kg.

5. White-Handed Gibbon
Hylobates lar Page 170
白掌长臂猿 Baizhang Changbiyuan
HB 450–600; HF130–155; E 33–37; GLS 93–110; Wt 3.9–7 kg.

1b
1a
2
3b
3a
4a
5
4b

1. Northern Chinese Flying Squirrel
Aeretes melanopterus Page 174
沟牙鼯鼠 Gouya Wushu
HB 275–355; T 275–362; HF 47–63; E 21–40;
GLS 61–66

2. Hairy-Footed Flying Squirrel
Belomys pearsoni Page 174
毛耳飞鼠 Mao'er Feishu
HB 160–260; T 102–158; HF 31–47; E 31–40;
GLS 40–44.

3. Particolored Flying Squirrel
Hylopetes alboniger Page 176
黑白飞鼠 Heibai Feishu
HB 175–247; T 180–185; HF 36–45; E 27–34;
GLS 41–52.

4. Indochinese Flying Squirrel
Hylopetes phayrei Page 176
海南低泡飞鼠 Hainandipao Feishu
HB 144–173; T 128–159; HF 32–35; E 23–25;
GLS 36–42.

5. Siberian Flying Squirrel
Pteromy volans Page 180
小飞鼠 Xiao Feishu
HB 156–198; T 100–122; HF 31–37; E 15–16;
GLS 38–42; Wt 75–130 g.

6. Complex-Toothed Flying Squirrel
Trogopterus xanthipes Page 181
复齿鼯鼠 Fuchi Wushu
HB 200–300; T 260–270; HF 56–60; E 30;
GLS 55–61.

1
2
3
4
5
6

1. **Red and White Giant Flying Squirrel**
   Petaurista alborufus Page 177
   红白鼯鼠 Hongbai Wushu
   HB 350–580; T 430–615; HF 78–90; E47–59; GLS 78–83.

2. **Spotted Giant Flying Squirrel**
   Petaurista elegans Page 178
   白斑小鼯鼠 Baiban Xiaowushu
   HB 296–375; T 347–405; HF 59–68; E 44–45; GLS 62–65.

3. **Hodgson's Giant Flying Squirrel**
   Petaurista magnificus Page 178
   栗褐鼯鼠 Lihe Wushu
   HB 359–420; T 415–480; HF 72–78; E 41–43; GLS 65–74.

4. **Red Giant Flying Squirrel**
   Petaurista petaurista Page 179
   红背鼯鼠 Hongbei Wushu
   HB 398–520; T 375–630; HF 63–100; E 35–50; GLS 63–78; Wt 1596–2450 g.

5. **Indian Giant Flying Squirrel**
   Petaurista phillipensis Page 179
   霜背大鼯鼠 Shuangbei Dawushu
   HB 410–610; T 550–691; HF 65–90; E 45–47; GLS 65–82.

6. **Chinese Giant Flying Squirrel**
   Petaurista xanthotis Page 180
   灰鼯鼠 Hui Wushu
   HB 325–430; T 294–350; HF 65–80; E 43–50; GLS 65–70; Wt 700–1,200 g.

1
2
3
4
5
6

1. **Pallas's Squirrel**
Callosciurus erythraeus Page 183
赤腹松鼠 Chifu Songshu
HB 175–240; T 146–267; HF 41–55; E 18–23; GLS 48–56; Wt 280–420 g.

2. **Irrawaddy Squirrel**
Callosciurus pygerythrus Page 184
蓝腹松鼠 Lanfu Songshu
HB 190–230; T 110–220; HF 43–48; E 17–20; GLS 49–52.

3. **Anderson's Squirrel**
Callosciurus quinquestriatus Page 184
五纹松鼠 Wuwen Songshu
HB 200–222; T 180–210; HF44–55; E 18–23; GLS 50–55; Wt 258–315 g.

4. **Perny's Long-Nosed Squirrel**
Dremomys pernyi Page 186
珀氏长吻松鼠 Poshichangwen Songshu
HB 170–230; T 156–180; HF 43–54; E 19–28; GLS 46–55; Wt 160–225 g.

5. **Red-Hipped Squirrel**
Dremomys pyrrhomerus Page 186
红腿长吻松鼠 Hongtuichangwen Songshu
HB 195–210; T 140–162; HF 50–55; E 22–24; GLS 55–58.

6. **Asian Red-Cheeked Squirrel**
Dremomys rufigenis Page 187
红颊长吻松鼠 Hongjiachangwen Songshu
HB 170–228; T 130–180; HF 44–54; E 23–25; GLS 46–51; Wt 210–335 g.

7. **Black Giant Squirrel**
Ratufa bicolor Page 173
巨松鼠 Ju Songshu
HB 360–430; T 400–510; HF 84–91; E 30–38; GLS 71–77; Wt 1,300–2,300 g

8. **Eurasian Red Squirrel**
Sciurus vulgaris Page 181
松鼠 Songshu
HB 178–260; T 159–215; HF 25–70; E 33–36; GLS 44–48; Wt 200–480 g.

1
2
3
4
5
6
7
8

1. Himalayan Marmot
Marmota himalayana Page 191
喜马拉雅旱獭 Ximalaya Hanta
HB 475–670; T 125–150; HF 76–100; E 23–30; GLS 96–114; Wt 4,000–9,215 g

2. Long-Tailed Marmot
Marmota caudata Page 190
长尾旱獭 Changwei Hanta
HB 426–570; T 185–275; HF 63–92; E 18–30; GLS 87–105; Wt 4,100–4,600 g.

3. Indochinese Ground Squirrel
Menetes berdmorei Page 187
线松鼠 Xian Songshu
HB 162–210; T 130–175; HF 40–47; E 18–22; GLS 45–51; Wt 213 g.

4. Forrest's Rock Squirrel
Sciurotamias forresti Page 192
侧纹岩松鼠 Cewen Yansongshu
HB 194–250; T 130–180; HF 47–54; E 25–27; GLS 54–60.

5. Père David's Rock Squirrel
Sciurotamias davidianus Page 192
岩松鼠 Yansongshu
HB 190–250; T 125–200; HF 45–59; E 20–28; GLS 52–58.

1
2
3
4
5

1. Alashan Ground Squirrel
Spermophilus alashanicus Page 193
阿拉善黄鼠 Alashan Huangshu
HB 190–210; T 55–76; HF 33–37; E 8–10; GLS 45–48; Wt 192–224 g.

2. Brandt's Ground Squirrel
Spermophilus brevicauda Page 194
阿尔泰黄鼠 Aertai Huangshu
HB 165–210; T 31–50; HF 29–38; E 5–9; GLS 42–47; Wt 143–436 g.

3. Daurian Ground Squirrel
Spermophilus dauricus Page 194
达乌尔黄鼠 Dawu'er Huangshu
HB 165–268; T 40–75; HF 30–39; E 5–10; GLS 42–50; Wt 154–264 g.

4. Long-Tailed Ground Squirrel
Spermophilus undulatus Page 195
长尾黄鼠 Changwei Huangshu
HB 210–315; T 100–140; HF 45–50; E 10–11; GLS 46–56; Wt 250–580 g.

5. Siberian Chipmunk
Tamias sibiricus Page 196
花鼠 Hua Shu
HB 120–165; T 90–130; HF 28–40; E 13–20; GLS 34–48; Wt 78–102 g.

6. Swinhoe's Striped Squirrel
Tamiops swinhoei Page 189
隐纹松鼠 Yinwen Songshu
HB 140–164; T 67–116; HF 28–35; E 9–16; GLS 31–41.

7. Maritime Striped Squirrel
Tamiops maritimus Page 188
倭松鼠 Wo Songshu
HB 105–134; T 80–115; HF 25–30; E 9–17; GLS 36–38.

1
2
3
4
5
6
7

1. Eurasian Beaver
Castor fiber Page 197
河狸 He Li
HB 600–1,000; T length 215–300; breadth 102–127; HF 160–170; E 35–40; GLS 125–151; Wt 17–30 kg.

2. Gobi Jerboa
Allactaga bullata Page 200
巨泡五趾跳鼠 Jupaowuzhi Tiaoshu
HB 115–145; T 165–200; HF 56–62; E 31–38; GLS 30–35; Wt 80–93 g.

3. Small Five-Toed Jerboa
Allactaga elater Page 200
小五趾跳鼠 Xiaowuzhi Tiaoshu
HB 90–115; T 144–185; HF 46–55; E 29–39; GLS 25–29; Wt 54–73 g (male); 44–59 g (female).

4. Mongolian Five-Toed Jerboa
Allactaga sibirica Page 201
五趾跳鼠 Wuzhi Tiaoshu
HB 130–170; T 180–230; HF 67–76; E 41–57; GLS 36–47; Wt 82–140 g.

5. Dwarf Fat-Tailed Jerboa
Pygeretmus pumilio Page 202
小地兔 Xiao Ditu
HB 90–125; T 121–185; HF 47–52; E 20–30; GLS 24–28; Wt 27–65 g.

1
2
3
4
5

1. Five-Toed Pygmy Jerboa
Cardiocranius paradoxus Page 203
五趾心颅跳鼠 Wuzhixinlu Tiaoshu
HB 45–60; T 59–78; HF 22–27; E 5–6; GLS 21–25; Wt 7–12 g.

2. Thick-Tailed Pygmy Jerboa
Salpingotus crassicauda Page 203
肥尾心颅跳鼠 Feiweixinlu Tiaoshu
HB 41–54; T 93–105; HF 20–23; E 6–10; GLS 23–24; Wt 10–14 g.

3. Koslov's Pygmy Jerboa
Salpingotus kozlovi Page 204
三趾心颅跳鼠 Sanzhixinlu Tiaoshu
HB 43–56; T 110–126; HF 24–27; E 9–12; GLS 22–28; Wt 7–12 g.

4. Northern Three-Toed Jerboa
Dipus sagitta Page 204
三趾跳鼠 Sanzhi Tiaoshu
HB 101–155; T 145–190; HF 52–67; E 13–24; GLS 30–36; Wt 56–117 g.

5. Andrews' Three-Toed Jerboa
Stylodipus andrewsi Page 205
蒙古羽尾跳鼠 Mengguyuwei Tiaoshu
HB 113–130; T 136–150; HF 50–59; E 16–18; GLS 31–34; Wt 60 g.

6. Thick-Tailed Three-Toed Jerboa
Stylodipus telum Page 205
羽尾跳鼠 Yuwei Tiaoshu
HB 104–133; T 140–165; HF 50–54; E 15–21; GLS 30–33; Wt 70–90 g.

7. Long-Eared Jerboa
Euchoreutes naso Page 206
长耳跳鼠 Chang'er Tiaoshu
HB 80–95; T 144–185; HF 41–49; E 37–47; GLS 29–31; Wt 24–38 g.

1
2
3
4
5
6
7

1. Long-Tailed Birch Mouse
Sicista caudata Page 206
长尾蹶鼠 Changwei Jueshu
HB 59–67; T 96–115; HF 16–18; E 13; GLS 19–21; Wt 8 g.

2. Chinese Birch Mouse
Sicista concolor Page 207
蹶鼠 Jue Shu
HB 51–76; T 86–109; HF 17–18; E 11–14; GLS 19–20; Wt 5–8 g.

3. Southern Birch Mouse
Sicista subtilus Page 207
草原蹶鼠 Caoyuan Jueshu
HB 59–73; T 79–84; HF 14–17; E 11–15; GLS 18–21; Wt 12–13 g.

4. Tian Shan Birch Mouse
Sicista tianshanica Page 207
天山蹶鼠 Tianshan Jueshu
HB 67–73; T 99–114; HF 16–19; E 11–15; GLS 18–21; Wt 9–14 g.

5. Chinese Jumping Mouse
Eozapus setchuanus Page 208
四川林跳鼠 Sichuan Lintiaoshu
HB 70–100; T 115–144; HF 26–31; E 11–15; GLS 21–24; Wt 15–20 g.

6. Striped Field Mouse
Apodemus agrarius Page 252
黑线姬鼠 Heixian Jishu
HB 80–113; T 72–115; HF 19–22; E 12–15; GLS 24–28; Wt 29–38 g.

7. Chevrier's Field Mouse
Apodemus chevrieri Page 253
高山姬鼠 Gaoshan Jishu
HB 88–110; T 83–105; HF 22–25; E 14–16; GLS 26–30.

8. South China Field Mouse
Apodemus draco Page 254
中华姬鼠 Zhonghua Jishu
HB 87–106; T 80–102; HF 20–23; E 15–17; GLS 24–28.

9. Large-Eared Field Mouse
Apodemus latronum Page 255
大耳姬鼠 Da'er Jishu
HB 92–107; T 100–120; HF 25–27; E 18–21; GLS 28.0–30.

10. Korean Field Mouse
Apodemus peninsulae Page 255
大林姬鼠 Dalin Jishu
HB 80–118; T 75–103; HF 21–23; E 14–17; GLS 25–29.

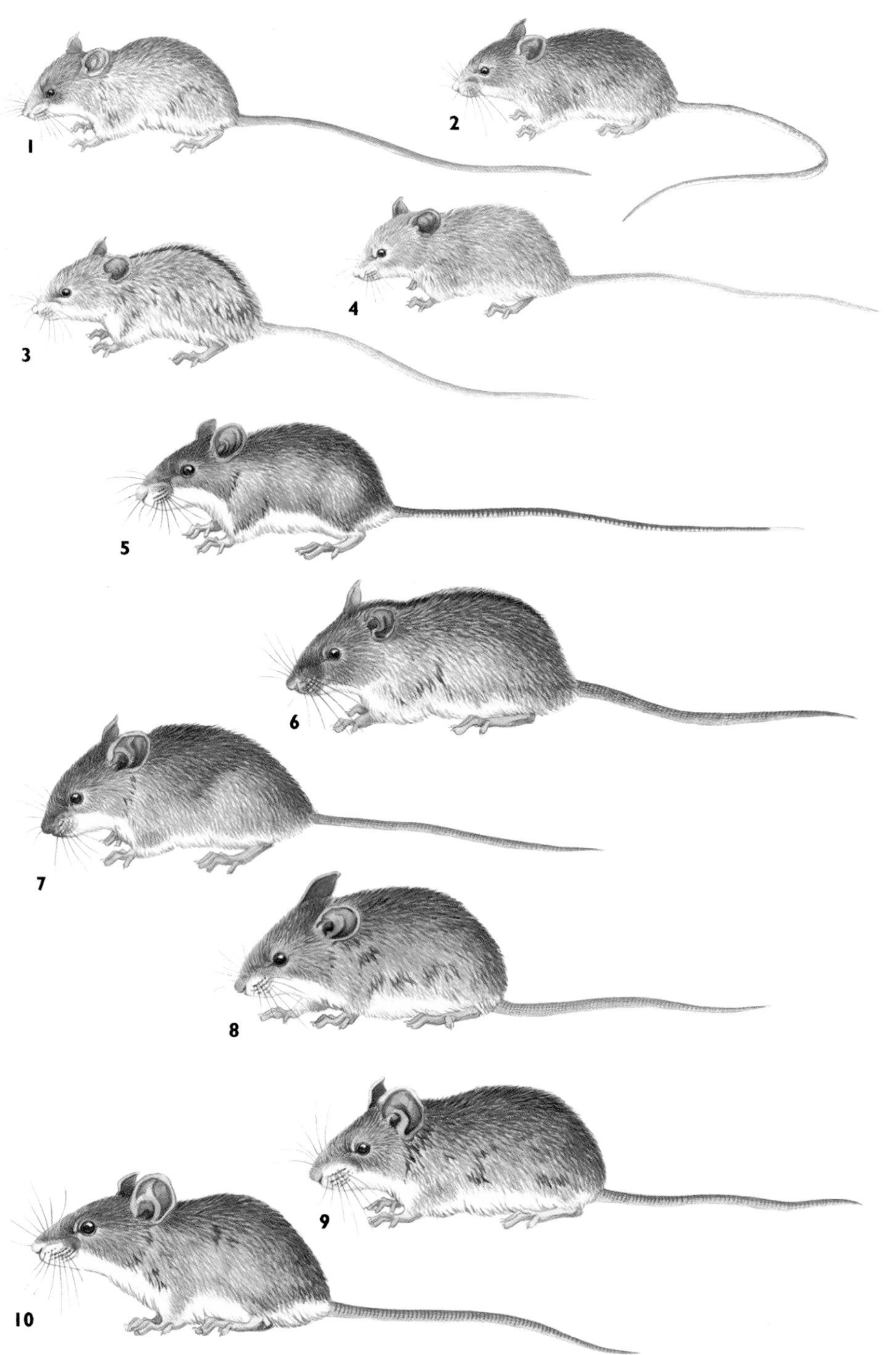
1
2
3
4
5
6
7
8
9
10

1. Chinese Zokor
Eospalax fontanierii Page 210
中华鼢鼠 Zhonghua Fenshu
HB 155–245; T 40–62; HF 25–38; GLS 41–49; Wt 150–620 g.

2. Rothschild's Zokor
Eospalax rothschildi Page 210
罗氏鼢鼠 Luoshi Fenshu
HB 149–172; T 29–37; HF 23–31; GLS 33–44; Wt 164–440 g.

3. Smith's Zokor
Eospalax smithii Page 210
斯氏鼢鼠 Sishi Fenshu
HB 162–255; T 34–39; HF 25–33; GLS 42–51; Wt 180–460 g.

4. Steppe Zokor
Myospalax aspalax Page 211
草原鼢鼠 Caoyuan Fenshu
HB 140–233; T 48–69; HF 28–36; GLS 38–48; Wt 225–422 g.

5. North China Zoker
Myospalax psilurus Page 211
东北鼢鼠 Dongbei Fenshu
HB 200–270; T 35–55; HF 25–37; GLS 43–52; Wt 185–400 g.

1

2

3

4

5

1. Chinese Dormouse
Chaetocauda sichuanensis Page 197
四川毛尾睡鼠 Sichuanmaowei Shuishu
HB 90–91; T 92–102; HF 18–19; E 17–19; GLS 26–27; Wt 24–36 g.

2. Forest Dormouse
Dryomys nitedula Page 197
林睡鼠 Lin Shuishu
HB 85–120; T 75–115; HF 19–24; E 13–19; GLS 25–28; Wt 36–61 g.

3. Chinese Pygmy Dormouse
Typhlomys cinereus Page 208
猪尾鼠 Zhuwei Shu
HB 67–90; T 100–138; HF 19–23; E 14–17; GLS 21–25; Wt 15–32 g.

4. Lesser Bamboo Rat
Cannomys badius Page 212
小竹鼠 Xiao Zhushu
HB 175–215; T 54–67; HF 27–32; E 5–11; GLS 44–53; Wt 210–340 g.

5. Hoary Bamboo Rat
Rhizomys pruinosus Page 213
银星竹鼠 Yinxing Zhushu
HB 240–345; T 90–130; HF 40–50; E 13–20; GLS 56–71; Wt 1,500–2,500 g.

6. Chinese Bamboo Rat
Rhizomys sinensis Page 213
中华竹鼠 Zhonghua Zhushu
HB 216–380; T 50–96; HF 38–60; E 15–19; GLS 58–87; Wt 1,875–1,950 g.

7. Large Bamboo Rat
Rhizomys sumatrensis Page 214
大竹鼠 Da Zhushu
HB 381–480; T 141–192; HF 50–68; E 25–28; GLS 80–88; Wt 2,150–4,000 g.

1
2
3
4
5
6
7

1. Silver Mountain Vole
Alticola argentatus Page 216
银色高山䶄 Yinse Gaoshanping
HB 94–115; T 30–33; HF 18–20; E 14–15; GLS 24.5–27; Wt 25–40 g.

2. Stoliczka's Mountain Vole
Alticola stoliczkanus Page 218
斯氏高山䶄 Sishi Gaoshanping
HB 100–121; T 14–24; HF 20–23; GLS 25–28.

3. Flat-Headed Mountain Vole
Alticola strelzowi Page 218
扁颅高山䶄 Bianlu Gaoshanping
HB 104–135; T 33–47; HF 19–22; E 14.5–26; GLS 25–30.

4. Eurasian Water Vole
Arvicola amphibius Page 219
水䶄 Shui Ping
HB 145–185; T 90–110; HF 28–32; E 14–15; GLS 34–42; Wt 130–270 g.

5. Northern Red-Backed Vole
Myodes rutilus Page 235
红背䶄 Hongbei Ping
HB 95–100; T 25–27; HF 18–20; E 14–19.

6. Gray Red-Backed Vole
Myodes rufocanus Page 235
棕背䶄 Zongbei Ping
HB 100–122; T 27–35; HF 17–20; E 15–19.

7. Shanxi Red-Backed Vole
Myodes shanseius Page 235
山西绒鼠 Shanxi Rongshu
HB 105–106; T 25–30; HF 20–21; E 13–15.

1
2
3
4
5
6
7

1. Eastern Mole Vole
Ellobius tancrei Page 220
鼹形田鼠 Yanxing Tianshu
HB 95–131; T 8–20; HF 19–24; E 0; GLS 24–36; Wt 30–88 g.

2. Yellow Steppe Vole
Eolagurus luteus Page 221
黄兔尾鼠 Huang Tuweishu
HB 105–195; T 12–22; HF 19–21; E 5–9; GLS 28–32.

3. Przewalski's Steppe Vole
Eolagurus przewalskii Page 222
普氏兔尾鼠 Pushi Tuweishu
HB 125–130; T 11–15; HF 19–22; E 7.

4. Sichuan Chinese Vole
Eothenomys chinensis Page 223
中华绒鼠 Zhonghua Rongshu
HB 101–125; T 63–76; HF 19–24; E 12–15.

5. Southwest Chinese Vole
Eothenomys custos Page 224
西南绒鼠 Xi'nan Rongshu
HB 81–105; T 35–59; HF 16.5–20; E 12–14.

6. Père David's Chinese Vole
Eothenomys melanogaster Page 224
黑腹绒鼠 Heifu Rongshu
HB 87–108; T 21–42; HF 15–17; E 10–12.

7. Eva's Vole
Caryomys eva Page 219
洮州绒鼠 Taozhou Rongshu
HB 83–100; T 46–60; HF 15–18; E 10.5–13; GLS 21–24.5.

8. Inez's Vole
Caryomys inez Page 220
苛岚绒鼠 Kelan Rongshu
HB 87–94; T 32–42; HF 15–16; E 10–12; GLS 23–24.

1
2
3
4
5
6
7
8

1. Steppe Vole
Lagurus lagurus Page 226
草原兔尾鼠 Caoyuan Tuweishu
HB 80–120; T 7–19; HF 15; E 5.

2. Mandarin Vole
Lasiopodomys mandarinus Page 228
棕色田鼠 Zongse Tianshu
HB 97–113; T 20–27; HF 15–18; E 7–12; GLS 24–26.

3. Brandt's Vole
Lasiopodomys brandtii Page 227
布氏田鼠 Bushi Tianshu
HB 110–130; T 22–30; HF 18–24; E 9–12; GLS 25–30; Wt 55–84 g.

4. Wood Lemming
Myopus schisticolor Page 236
林旅鼠 Linlü Shu
HB 75–100; T 14–15; HF 16–17; E 11–14; GLS 25–28.

5. Duke Of Bedford's Vole
Proedromys bedfordi Page 238
沟牙田鼠 Gouya Tianshu
HB 75–100; T 14–15; HF 16–17; E 11–14; GLS 25–28

6. Irene's Mountain Vole
Neodon irene Page 237
高原松田鼠 Gaoyuan Songtianshu
HB 80–108; T 22–40; HF 15–19; E 11–13.

7. Blyth's Mountain Vole
Phaiomys leucurus Page 238
白尾松田鼠 Baiwei Songtianshu
HB 98–128; T 26–35; HF 16–19; E 10–13.

8. Sichuan Vole
Volemys millicens Page 239
四川田鼠 Sichuan Tianshu
HB 83–95; T 46–53; HF 18–18.5; E 14; GLS 23.7–24.7.

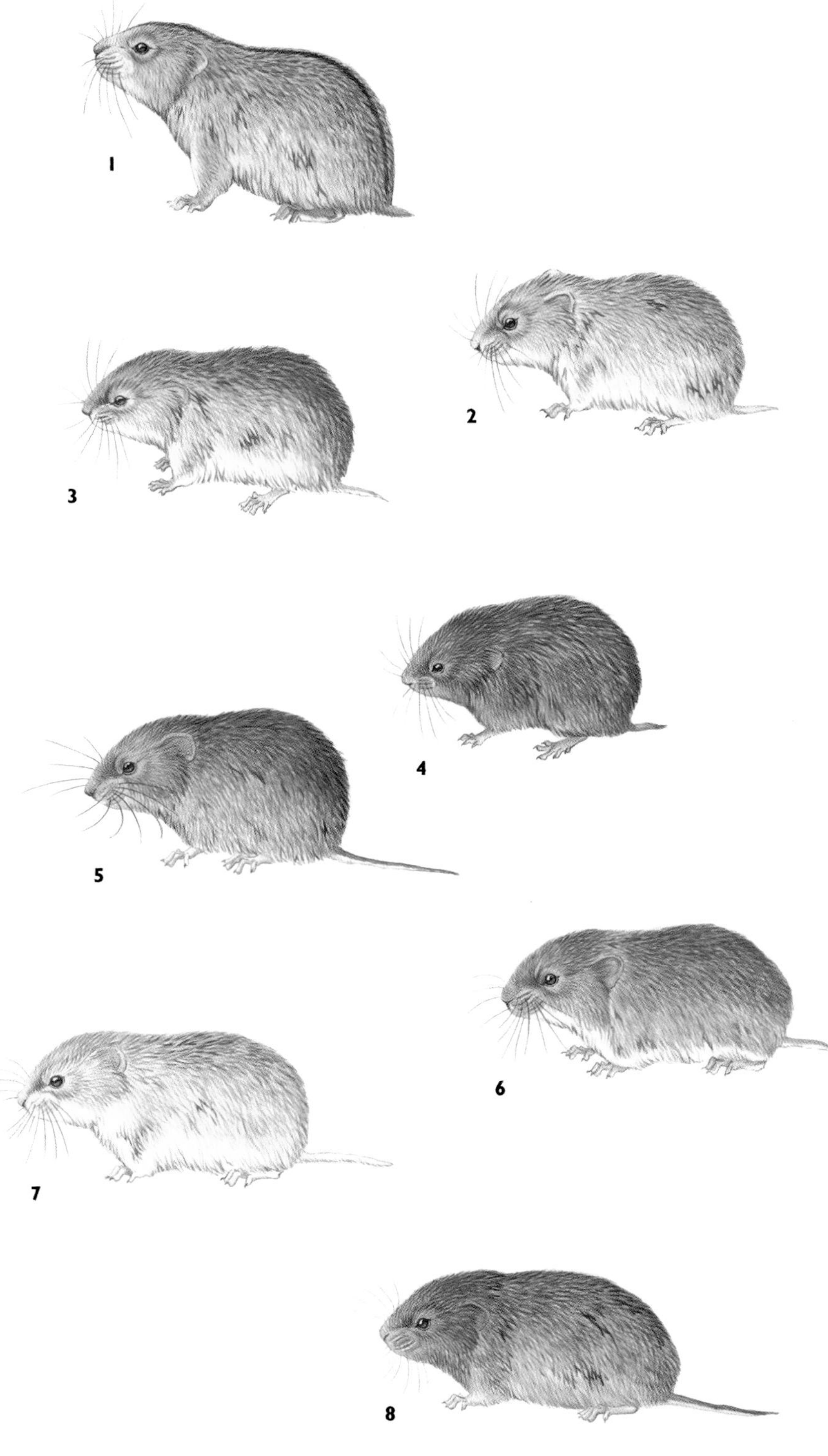
1
2
3
4
5
6
7
8

1. Reed Vole
Microtus fortis Page 230
东方田鼠 Dongfang Tianshu
HB 120–139; T 48–67; HF 22–25; E 13–15.

2. Narrow-Headed Vole
Microtus gregalis Page 231
狭颅田鼠 Xialu Tianshu
HB 89–122; T 21–32; HF 15–18; E 9–12; GLS 25–27.

3. Clarke's Vole
Microtus clarkei Page 230
克氏田鼠 Keshi Tianshu
HB 114–134; T 62–67; HF 19–21; E 12–15.

4. Lacustrine Vole
Microtus limnophilus Page 232
经营田鼠 Jingying Tianshu
HB 88–118; T 32–44; HF 20–21; E 13–14; GLS 26–28.

5. Maximowicz's Vole
Microtus maximowiczii Page 232
莫氏田鼠 Moshi Tianshu
HB 116–155; T 37–60; HF 18–22; E 12–16.6.

6. Mongolian Vole
Microtus mongolicus Page 233
蒙古田鼠 Menggu Tianshu
HB 119–132; T 28–38; HF 17–19; E 13–14.

7. Common Vole
Microtus arvalis Page 229
普通田鼠 Putong Tianshu
HB 102–132; T 32–40; HF 14–19; E 14–15; GLS 27–29.5.

8. Social Vole
Microtus socialis Page 234
社田鼠 She Tianshu
HB 92–100; T 20–25; HF 17–18.

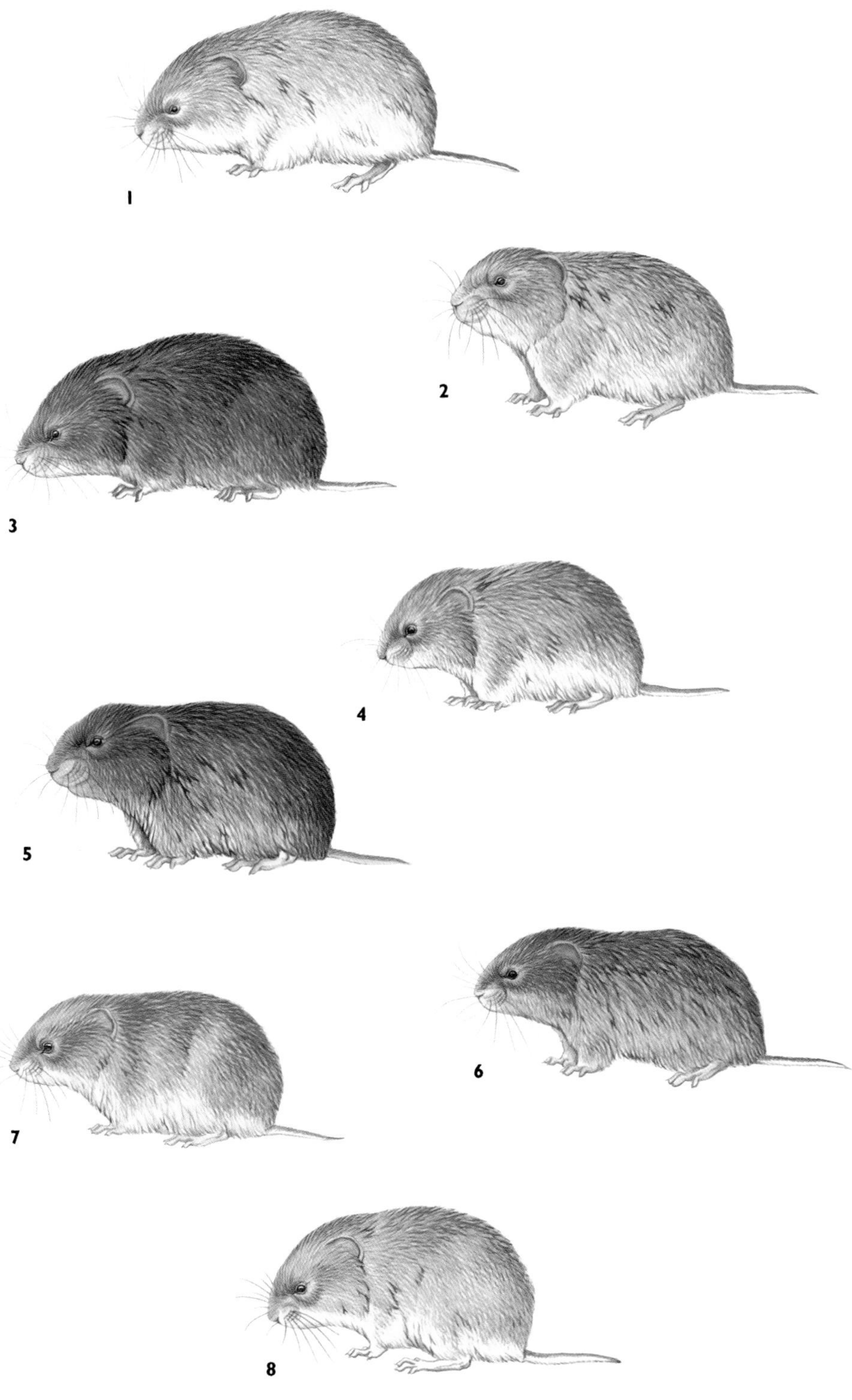
1
2
3
4
5
6
7
8

1. Mongolian Hamster
Allocricetulus curtatus Page 240
无斑短尾仓鼠 Wuban Duanweicangshu
HB 85–130; T 18–25; HF 14–20; E 11–17; GLS 27–33; Wt 30–70 g.

2. Gansu Hamster
Cansumys canus Page 241
甘肃仓鼠 Gansu Cangshu
HB 100–170; T 77–111; HF 17–24; E 15–23; GLS 32–40; Wt 61–120 g.

3. Greater Long-Tailed Hamster
Tscherskia triton Page 247
大仓鼠 Da Cangshu
HB 142–220; T 69–106; HF 20–25; E 17–24; GLS 36–42; Wt 92–241 g.

4. Desert Hamster
Phodopus roborovskii Page 246
小毛足鼠 Xiao Maozushu
HB 61–102; T 6–11; HF 9–12; E 10–13; GLS 19–23; Wt 10–20 g.

5. Campbell's Hamster
Phodopus campbelli Page 246
坎氏毛足鼠 Kanshi Maozushu
HB 76–105; T 4–14; HF 12–18; E 13–15; GLS 22–26; Wt 23 g.

6. Black-Bellied Hamster
Cricetus cricetus Page 245
原仓鼠 Yuan Cangshu
HB 200–300; T 28–60; HF 28–36; E 22–32; GLS 44–52; Wt 290–425 g.

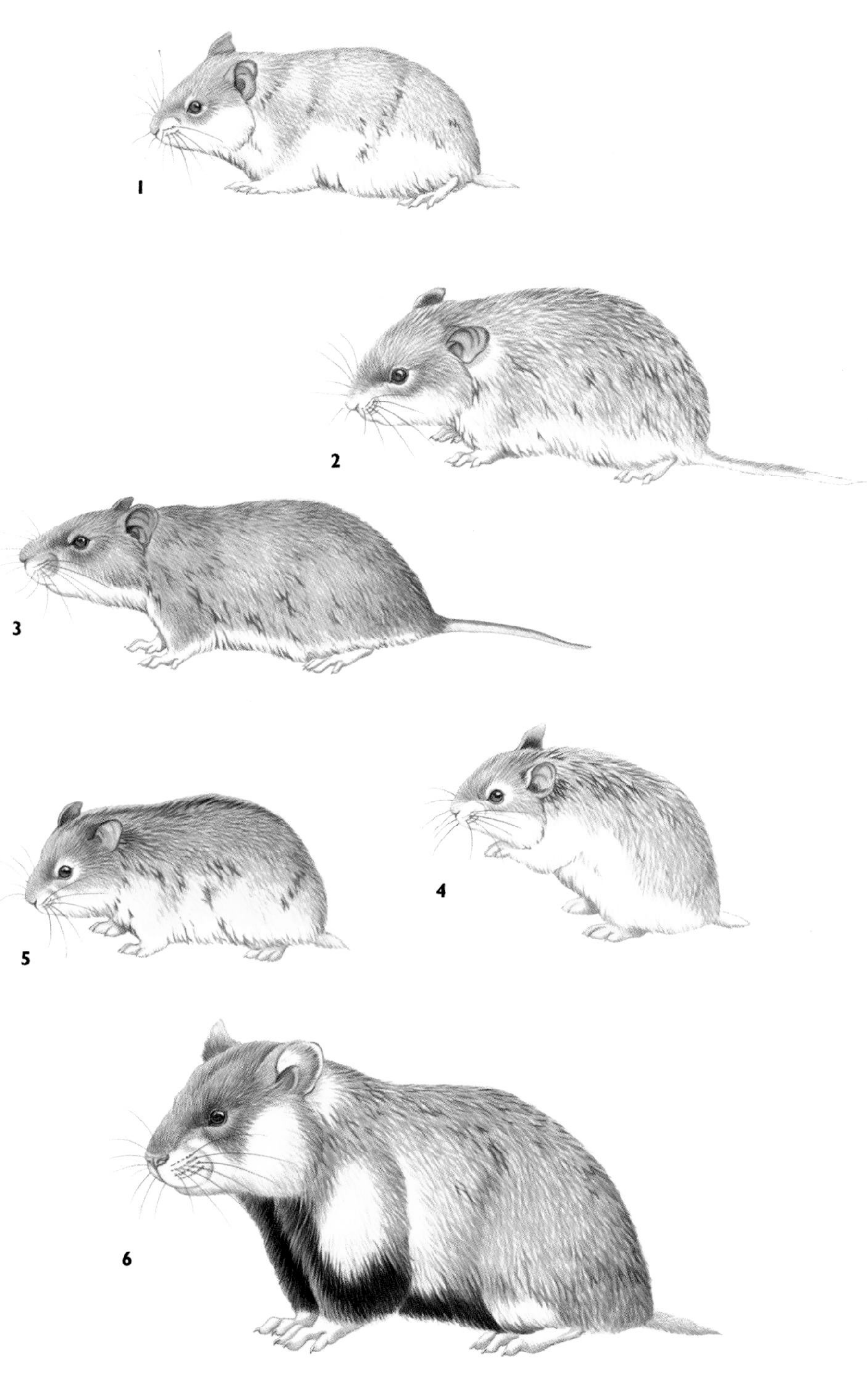
1
2
3
4
5
6

1. Striped Dwarf Hamster
Cricetulus barabensis Page 242
黑线仓鼠 Heixian Cangshu
HB 72–116; T 15–26; HF 13–19; E 14–17; GLS 22–28; Wt 20–35 g.

2. Kam Dwarf Hamster
Cricetulus kamensis Page 243
康藏仓鼠 Kangzang Cangshu
HB 88–112; T 51–64; HF 17–18; E 16–18; GLS 27–29; Wt 20–40 g.

3. Lama Dwarf Hamster
Cricetulus lama Page 243
藏南仓鼠 Zangnan Cangshu
HB 86–103; T 40–50; HF 15–18; E 14–18; GLS 26–28; Wt 24–39 g.

4. Long-Tailed Dwarf Hamster
Cricetulus longicaudatus Page 243
长尾仓鼠 Changwei Cangshu
HB 80–135; T 35–48; HF 15–21; E 15–20; GLS 25–31; Wt 15–50 g.

5. Gray Dwarf Hamster
Cricetulus migratorius Page 244
灰仓鼠 Hui Cangshu
HB 85–120; T 23–39; HF 15–18; E 15–21; GLS 22–31; Wt 31–58 g.

6. Tibetan Dwarf Hamster
Cricetulus tibetanus Page 245
藏仓鼠 Zang Cangshu
HB 103; T 30–37; HF 17–18; E 15–16; GLS 23.5–25.4.

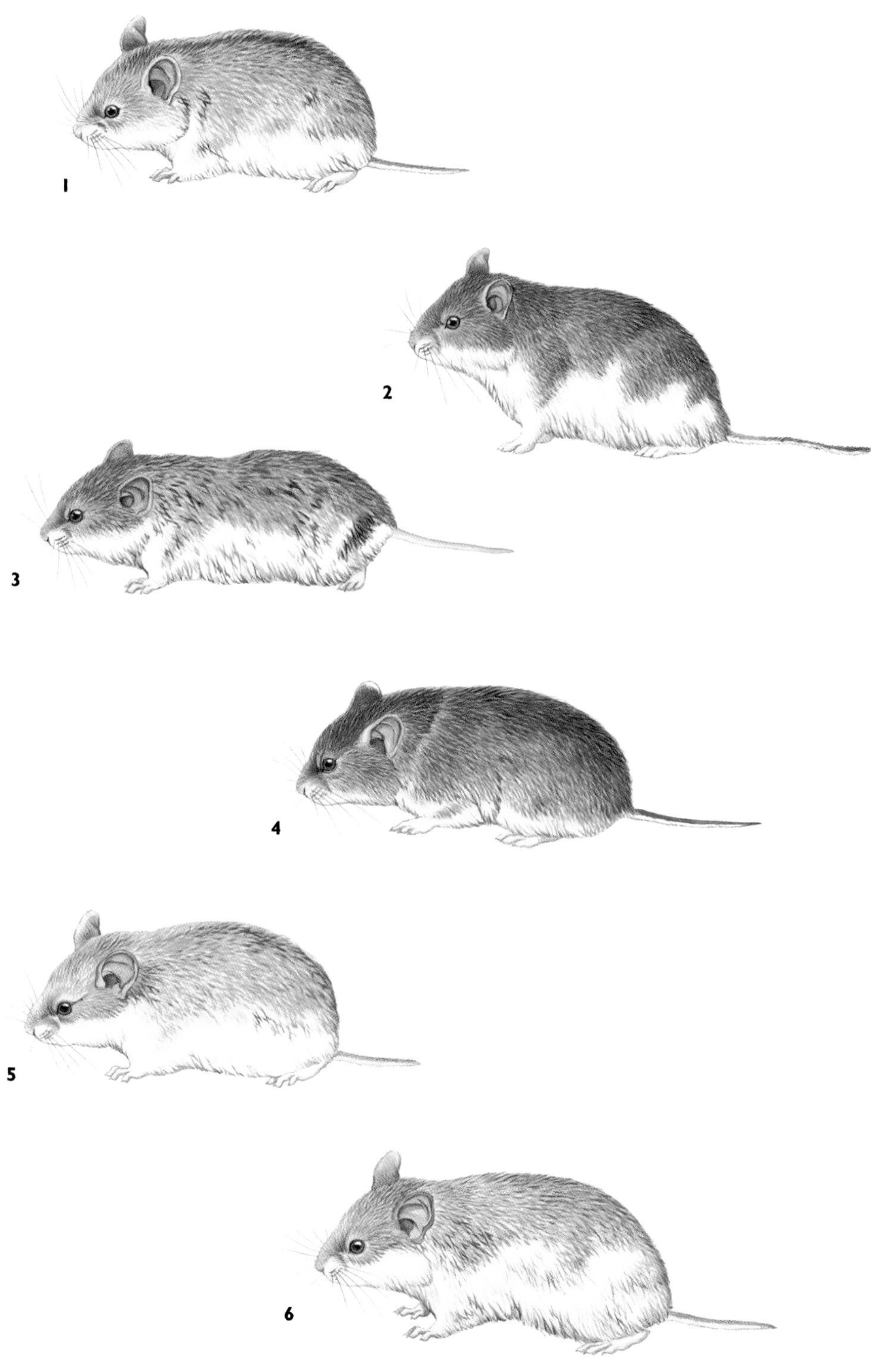
1
2
3
4
5
6

1. **Przewalski's Gerbil**
Brachiones przewalskii Page 248
短耳沙鼠 Duan'er Shashu
HB 67–103; T 56–78; HF 22–24; E 6–9; GLS 24–29; Wt 12–42 g.

2. **Libyan Gerbil**
Meriones libycus Page 249
红尾沙鼠 Hongwei Shashu
HB 100–180; T 108–180; HF 31–38; E 11–22; GLS 36–42; Wt 56–155 g.

3. **Mid-Day Gerbil**
Meriones meridanus Page 250
子午沙鼠 Ziwu Shashu
HB 95–134; T 84–120; HF 25–34; E 10–19; GLS 31–36; Wt 30–60 g.

4. **Tamarisk Gerbil**
Meriones tamariscinus Page 250
柽柳沙鼠 Chengliu Shashu
HB 135–190; T 115–150; HF 32–39; E 15–21; GLS 36–44; Wt 60–180 g.

5. **Mongolian Gerbil**
Meriones unguiculatus Page 251
长爪沙鼠 Changzhua Shashu
HB 97–132; T 85–106; HF 24–32; E 13–15; GLS 30–36.

6. **Great Gerbil**
Rhombomys opimus Page 251
大沙鼠 Da Shashu
HB 150–185; T 130–160; HF 36–47; E 12–19; GLS 39–45; Wt 169–275 g.

2
1
4
3
5
6

1. Greater Bandicoot Rat
Bandicota indica Page 257
板齿鼠 Banchi Shu
HB 188–328; T 190–280; HF 46–60; E 25–33;
GLS 48.6–63.6; Wt 500–1,000 g.

2. Bower's White-Toothed Rat
Berylmys bowersi Page 258
青毛硕鼠 Qingmao Shuoshu
HB 236–285; T 249–292; HF 48–61; E 32–36;
GLS 52–58.5; Wt up to 420 g.

3. Indomalayan Tree Mouse
Chiropodomys gliroides Page 259
笔尾树鼠 Biwei Shushu
HB 81–101; T 105–134; HF 18–22; E 16–20;
GLS 23.5–26; Wt 20–33 g.

4. Millard's Dacnomys
Dacnomys millardi Page 260
大齿鼠 Dachi Shu
HB 228–290; T 308–335; HF 50–56; E 25–29;
GLS 60.

5. Yunnan Hadromys
Hadromys yunnanensis Page 260
云南壮鼠 Yunnan Zhuangshu
HB 123–140; T 114–132; HF 24–27; E 15–20;
GLS 32–33; Wt 41–77 g.

6. Lesser Marmoset Rat
Hapalomys delacouri Page 261
小狨鼠 Xiao Rongshu
HB 123–136; T 140–160; HF 22–24; E 14–15;
GLS 32–34.

7. Edward's Leopoldamys
Leopoldamys edwardsi Page 261
小泡巨鼠 Xiaopao Jushu
HB 210–290; T 264–315; HF 42–58; E 28–32;
GLS 54–58; Wt 230–480 g.

8. Harvest Mouse
Micromys minutus Page 262
巢鼠 Chao Shu
HB 55–68; T 54–79; HF 14–16; E 10; GLS < 20 mm;
Wt 5–7 g.

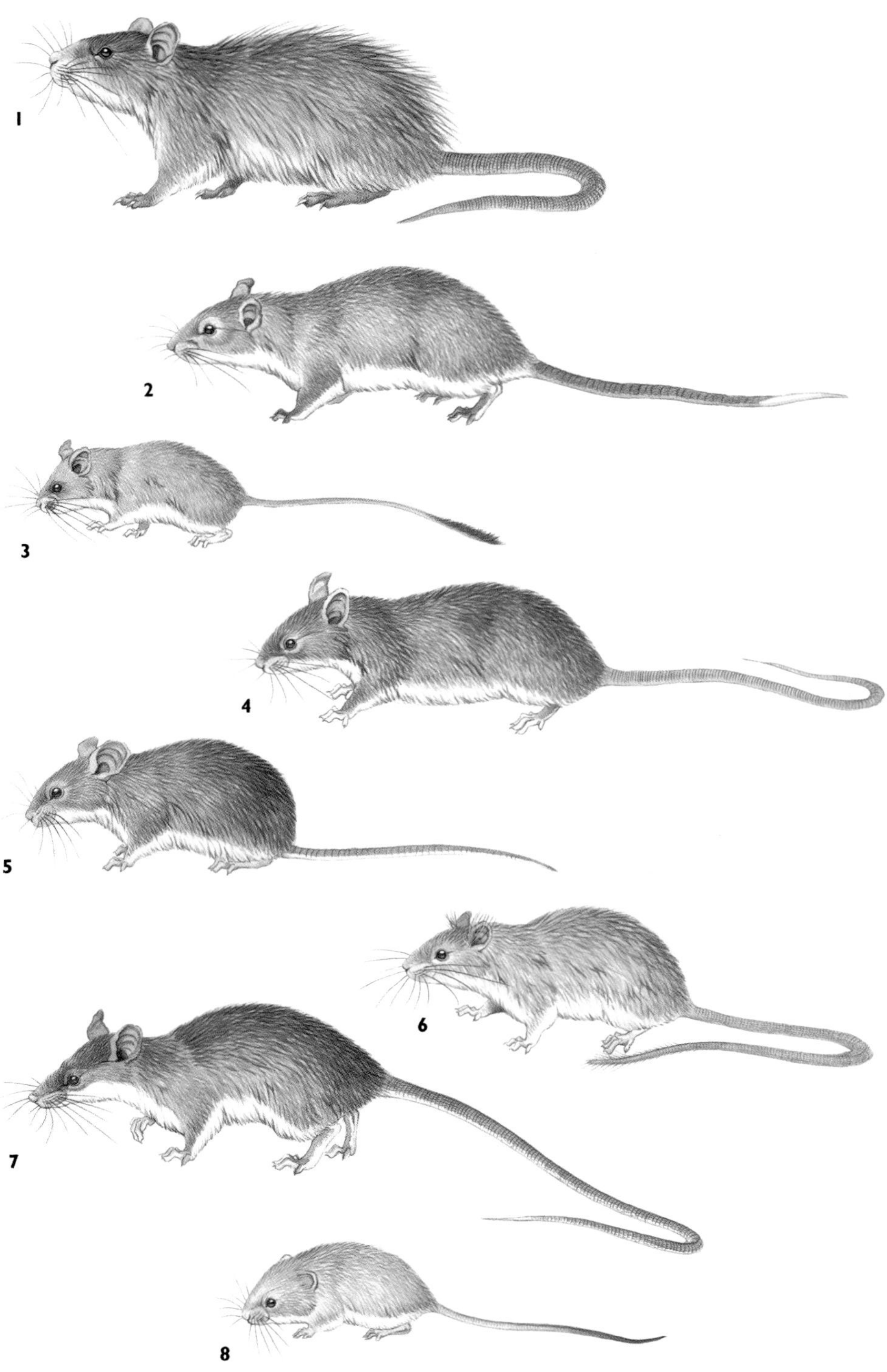
1
2
3
4
5
6
7
8

1. Ryukyu Mouse
Mus caroli Page 263
琉球小家鼠 Liuqiu Xiaojiashu
HB 72–95; T 75–95; HF 15–19; E 12–14; GLS 19–20.5; Wt 11.5–19.5 g.

2. Short-Tailed Bandicoot Rat
Nesokia indica Page 264
印度地鼠 Yindu Dishu
HB 150–194; T 110–129; HF 23–37; E 16–22; GLS 36–42; Wt 137–203 g.

3. Anderson's Niviventer
Niviventer andersoni Page 265
安氏白腹鼠 Anshi Baifushu
HB 150–198; T 194–269; HF 31–40; E 22–28; GLS 39–46.

4. Confucian Niviventer
Niviventer confucianus Page 266
北社鼠 Bei Sheshu
HB 116–173; T 154–255; HF 28–35; E 21–25; GLS 31.5–38 rarely up to 43.

5. Smoke-Bellied Niviventer
Niviventer eha Page 267
灰腹鼠 Hui Fushu
HB 112–130; T 165–195; HF 28–31; E 17–19; GLS 29–33

6. Sichuan Niviventer
Niviventer excelsior Page 268
川西白腹鼠 Chuanxi Baifushu
HB 127–175; T 190–213; HF 31–33; E 22–27; GLS 38.1–41.3.

7. Indomaylayan Niviventer
Niviventer fulvescens Page 268
针毛鼠 Zhenmao Shu
HB 131–172; T 160–221; HF 30–34; E 17–23; GLS 32–40; Wt 60–135 g.

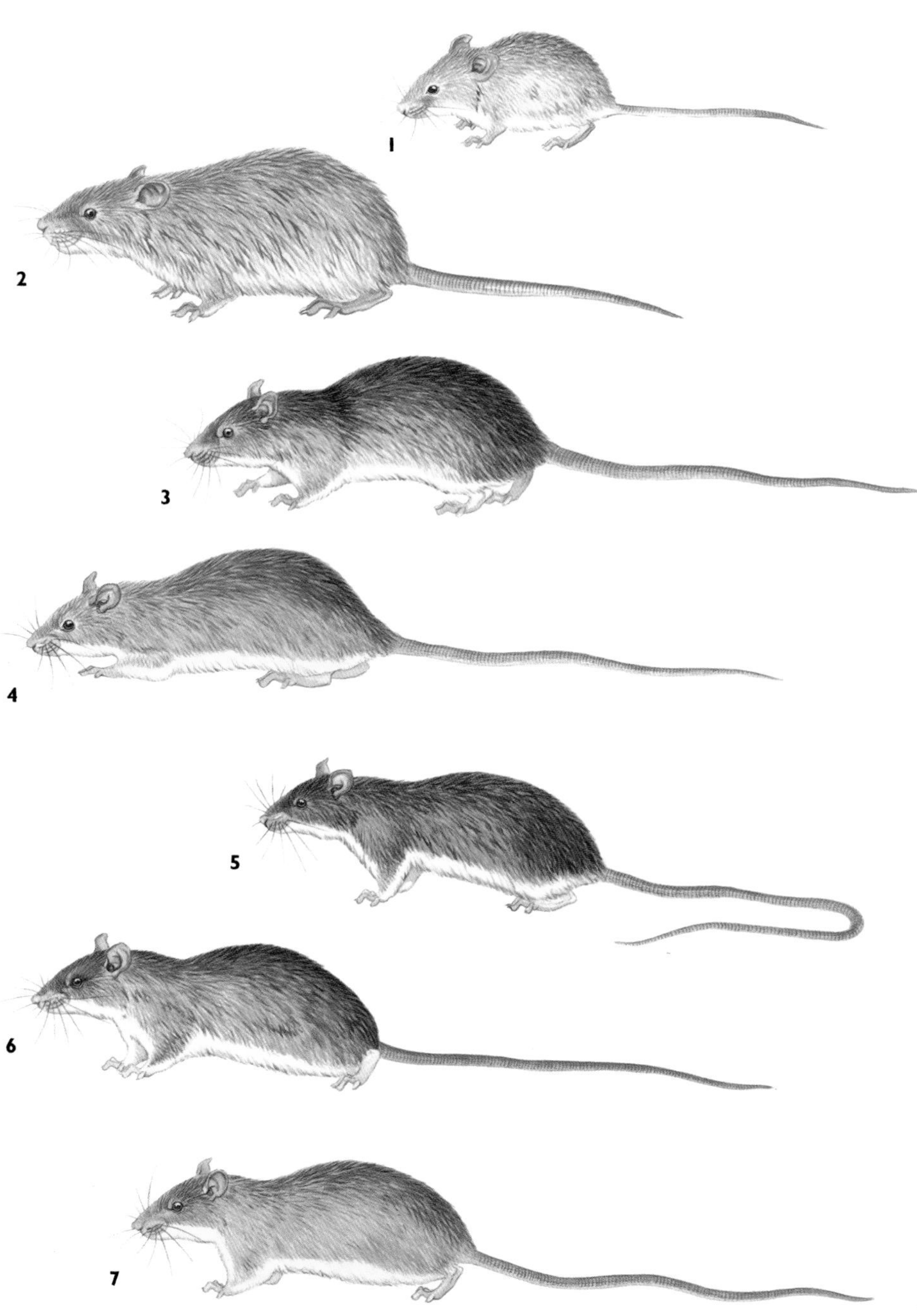
1
2
3
4
5
6
7

1. Losea Rat
Rattus losea Page 270
黄毛鼠 Huangmao Shu
HB 120–185; T 128–175; HF 24–32; E 18–21; GLS 33–40; Wt 22–90 g.

2. White-Footed Indochinese Rat
Rattus nitidus Page 271
大足鼠 Dazu Shu
HB 148–180; T 135–206; HF 32–36; E 21; GLS 34–44; Wt 114–136.

3. Indochinese Forest Rat
Rattus andamanensis Page 269
黑缘齿鼠 Heiyuan Chishu
HB 128–185; T 172–222; HF 32–36; E 20–25; GLS 40–43; Wt 125–155.

4. Oriental House Rat
Rattus tanezumi Page 272
黄胸鼠 Huangxiong Shu
HB 105–215; 120–230; HF 26–35; E 17–23; GLS 38–44.

5. Himalayan Rat
Rattus pyctoris Page 272
拟家鼠 Ni Jiashu
HB 140–165; T 135–178; HF 32–34; E 20–25.

6. Indomalayan Vandeleuria
Vandeleuria oleracea Page 272
长尾攀鼠 Changwei Panshu
HB 61–90; T 92–110; HF 17–18; E 11–16; GLS 19–22.6.

7. Vernay's Climbing Mouse
Vernaya fulva Page 273
滇攀鼠 Dian Panshu
HB 58–75; T 120–133; HF 18–18.5; E 17; GLS 20–22.3.

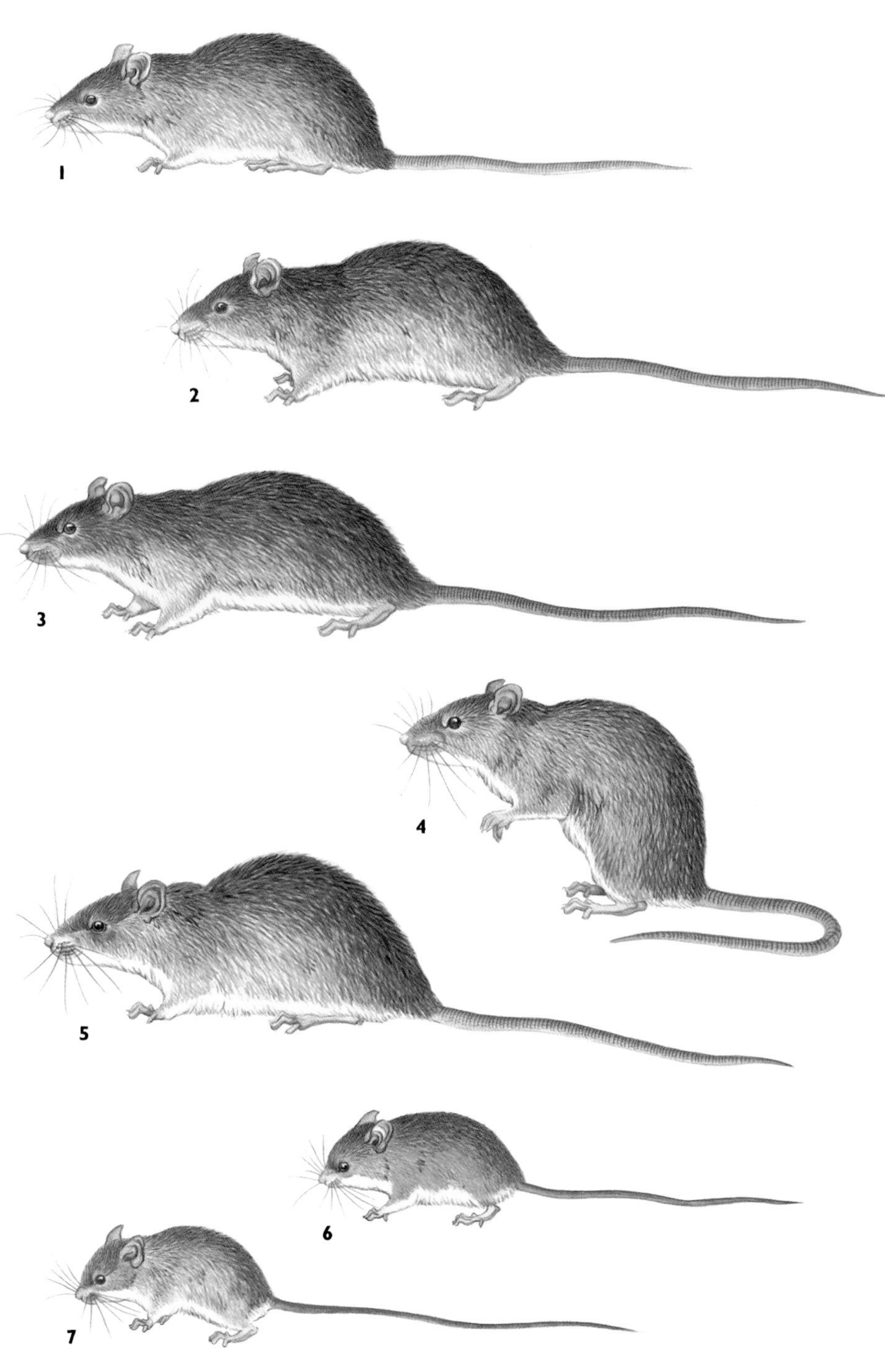
1
2
3
4
5
6
7

1. Plateau Pika
Ochotona curzoniae Page 278
高原鼠兔 Gaoyuan Shutu
HB 140–192; HF 28–37; E 18–26; GLS 39–44;
Wt 130–195 g.

2. Daurian Pika
Ochotona dauurica Page 279
达乌尔鼠兔 Dawu'er Shutu
HB 150–200; HF 27–33; E 16–26; GLS 39–45;
Wt 110–150 g.

3. Chinese Red Pika
Ochotona erythrotis Page 279
红耳鼠兔 Hong'er Shutu
HB 181–285; HF 32–42; E 32–39; GLS 48–51;
Wt 184–352 g.

4. Glover's Pika
Ochotona gloveri Page 280
川西鼠兔 Chuanxi Shutu
HB 160–220; HF 31–36; E 31–39; GLS 43–53;
Wt 140–300 g.

5. Ili Pika
Ochotona iliensis Page 282
伊犁鼠兔 Yili Shutu
HB 203–204; HF 42–43; E 36–37; GLS 45–48;
Wt 217–250 g.

6. Koslov's Pika
Ochotona koslowi Page 282
柯氏鼠兔 Keshi Shutu
HB 220–240; HF 38–42; E 16–20; GLS 40–47;
Wt 150–180 g.

7. Large-Eared Pika
Ochotona macrotis Page 283
大耳鼠兔 Da'er Shutu
HB 150–204; HF 30–33; E 27–36; GLS 34–45;
Wt 142–190 g.

8. Moupin Pika
Ochotona thibetana Page 286
藏鼠兔 Zang Shutu
HB 140–180; HF 24–32; E 17–23; GLS 36–42;
Wt 72–136 g

1
2
3
4
5
6
7
8

1. Yunnan Hare
Lepus comus Page 287
云南兔 Yunnan Tu
HB 322–480; T 95–110; HF 98–130; E 97–135; GLS 84–95; Wt 1,800–2,500 g.

2. Woolly Hare
Lepus oiostolus Page 289
高原兔 Gaoyuan Tu
HB 400–580; T 65–125; HF 102–140; E 105–155; GLS 84–100; Wt 2,000–4,250 g.

3. Chinese Hare
Lepus sinensis Page 290
华南兔 Huanan Tu
HB 350–450; T 40–57; HF 81–111; E 60–82; GLS 67–93; Wt 1,025–1,938 g.

4. Mountain Hare
Lepus timidus (a, summer coat; b, winter coat) Page 291
雪兔 Xue Tu
HB 452–620; T 50–75; HF 135–165; E 80–110; GLS 87–106; Wt 2,140–2,700 g.

5. Tolai Hare
Lepus tolai Page 291
托氏兔 Tuoshi Tu
HB 400–590; T 72–110; HF 110–127; E 83–120; GLS 80–88; Wt 1,650–2,650 g.

6. Yarkand Hare
Lepus yarkandensis Page 292
塔里木兔 Talimu Tu
HB 285–430; T 55–86; HF 90–110; E 90–110; GLS 76–88; Wt 1,100–1,900 g.

1
2
3
4a
4b
5
6

1. Amur Hedgehog
Erinaceus amurensis Page 293
东北刺猬 Dongbei Ciwei
HB 158–287; T 17–42; HF 34–54; E 16–26; GLS 47–58; Wt 600–1,000 g.

2. Long-Eared Hedgehog
Hemiechinus auritus Page 294
大耳猬 Da'er Wei
HB 170–230; T 18–28; HF 32–39; E 31–40; GLS 44–48; Wt 280–500 g.

3. Daurian Hedgehog
Mesechinus dauuricus Page 294
达乌尔猬 Da'wu'er Wei
HB 175–250; T 14–15; E 25–29; GLS 52; Wt 500 g.

4. Hugh's Hedgehog
Mesechinus hughi Page 295
林猬 Lin Wei
HB 155–200.

5. Hainan Gymnure
Neohylomys hainanensis Page 296
海南新毛猬 Hainanxin Maowei
HB 132–147; T 36–43; HF 24–29; E 17–22; GLS 33–36; Wt 52–70 g.

6. Shrew Gymnure
Neotetracus sinensis Page 296
鼩猬 Qu Wei
HB 91–125; T 56–78; HF 21–36; GLS 27–32.

7. Short-Tailed Gymnure
Hylomys suillus Page 296
毛猬 Maowei
HB 120–150; T 19; HF 23–25; GLS 31–33.

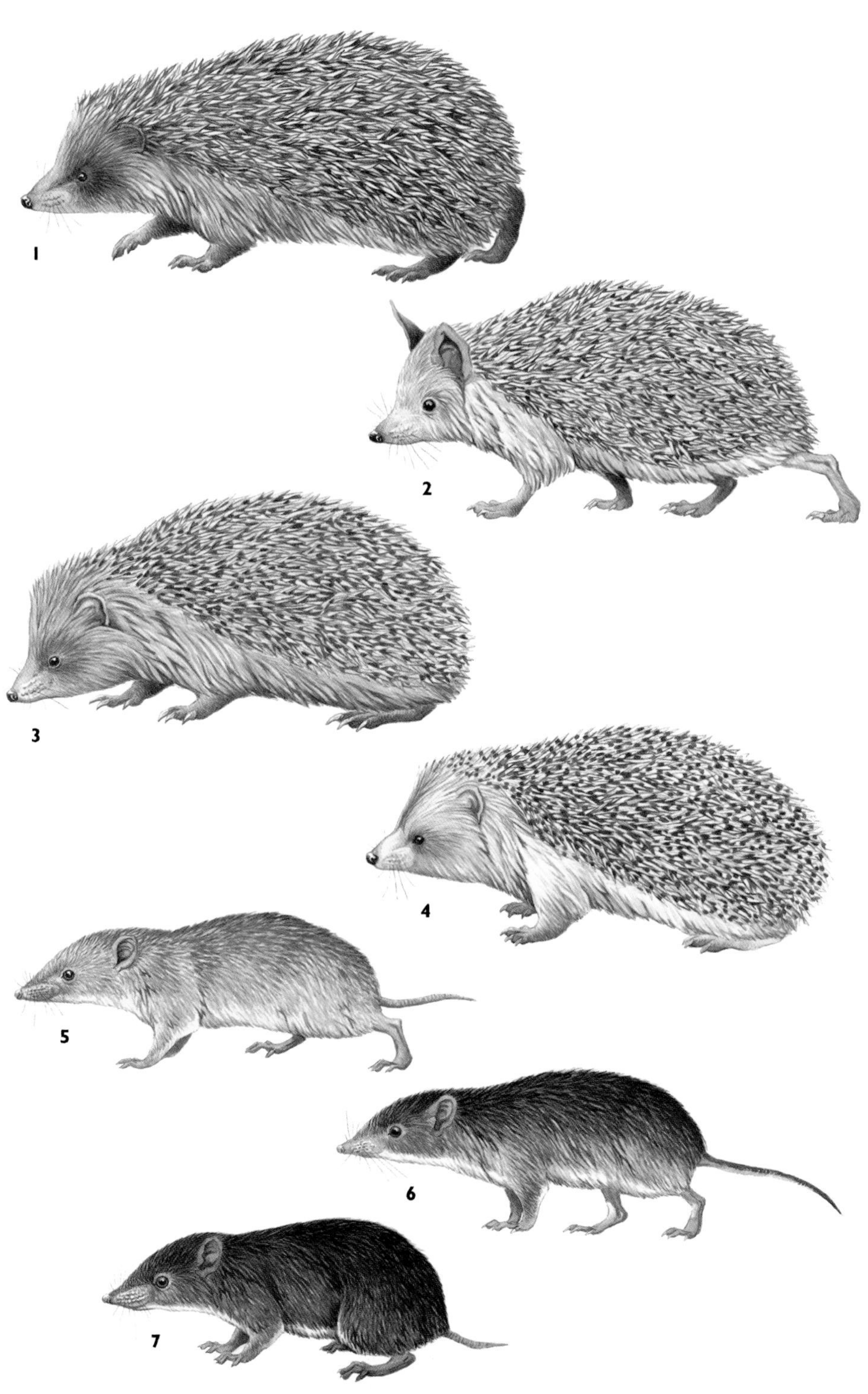
1
2
3
4
5
6
7

1. Asian Gray Shrew
Crocidura attenuata Page 298
灰麝鼩 Hui Shequ
HB 60–89; T 41–60; HF 11–16; E 7–13; GLS 18–22; Wt 6–12 g.

2. Southeast Asian Shrew
Crocidura fuliginosa Page 299
长尾大麝鼩 Changweida Shequ
HB 72–105; T 62–89; HF 15–19; E 10; GLS 22–25; Wt 13 g.

3. Ussuri White-Toothed Shrew
Crocidura lasiura Page 300
大麝鼩 Da Shequ
HB 68–104; T 28–47; HF 15–23.

4. Chinese White-Toothed Shrew
Crocidura rapax Page 300
华南中麝鼩 Huananzhong Shequ
HB 56–70; T 38–47; HF 11–13; GLS 17.4–18.3.

5. Asian Lesser White-Toothed Shrew
Crocidura shantungensis Page 301
山东小麝鼩 Shandong Xiaoshequ
HB 51–65; T 35–43; HF 10–13; GLS 15.5–17.

6. Etruscan Shrew
Suncus etruscus Page 303
小臭鼩 Xiao Chouqu
HB 43–53; T 20–31; HF 6–9; E 4.5–6; GLS 13–14; Wt 2–3 g.

7. Asian House Shrew
Suncus murinus Page 303
臭鼩 Chouqu
HB 119–147; T 60–85; HF 19–22; GLS 30.

8. Chinese Mole Shrew
Anourosorex squamipes Page 304
短尾鼩 Duanwei Qu
HB 74–110; T 8–19; HF 11–16; E 0; GLS 23–26.

9. Asiatic Short-Tailed Shrew
Blarinella quadraticauda Page 306
黑齿鼩鼱 Heichi Qujing
HB 65–81; T 40–60; HF 13–16; GLS 20–22.

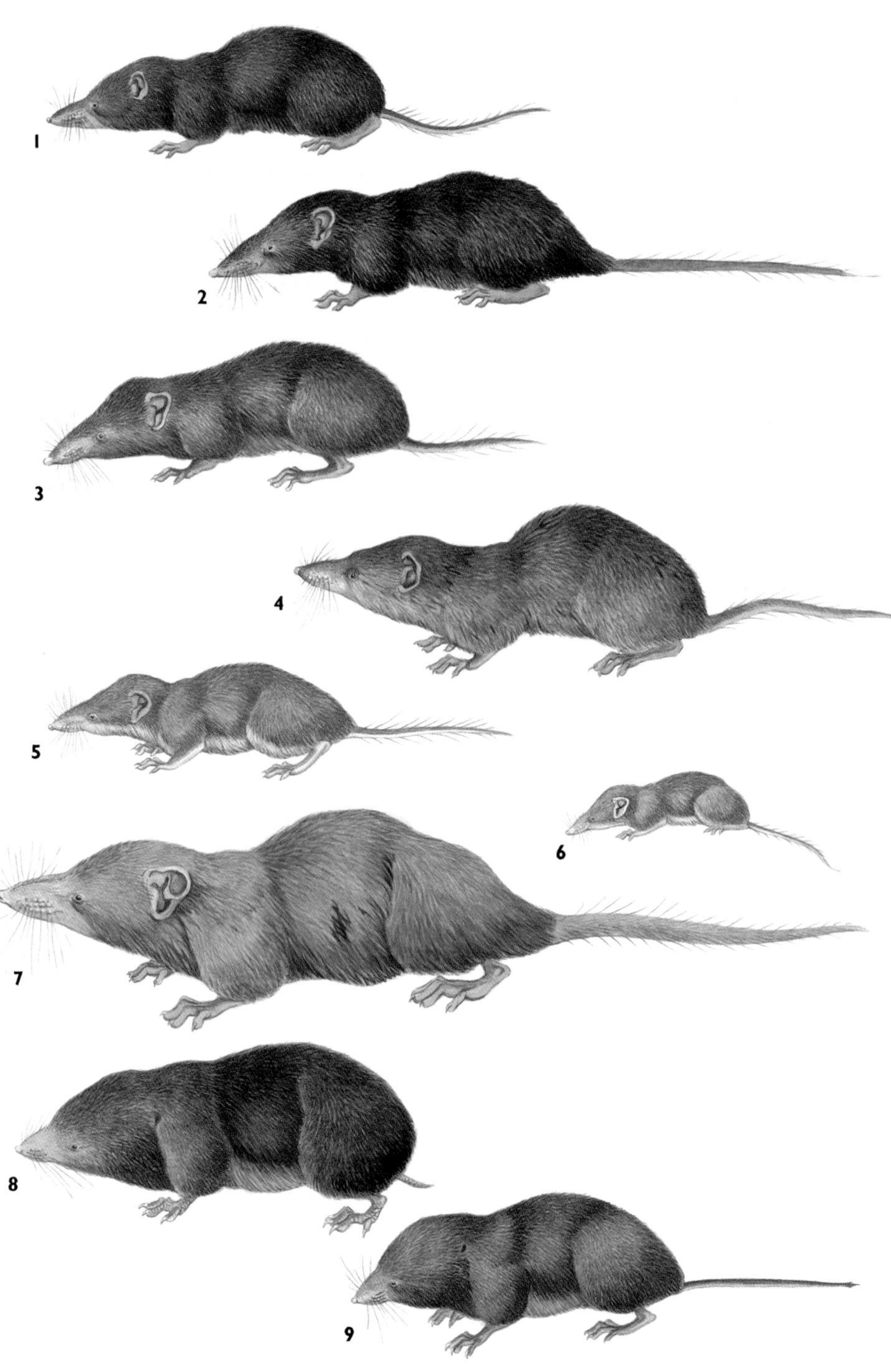
1
2
3
4
5
6
7
8
9

1. Himalayan Water Shrew
Chimarrogale himalayica Page 306
喜马拉雅水鼩 Ximalaya Shuiqu
HB 115–132; T 79–112; HF 17–30; E 0; GLS 25–28; Wt 23–56 g.

2. Chinese Water Shrew
Chimarrogale styani Page 307
斯氏水鼩 Sishi Shuiqu
HB 96–108; T 61–85; HF 20–23; GLS 23–25.

3. Elegant Water Shrew
Nectogale elegans Page 311
蹼麝鼩 Pu Shequ
HB 90–115; T 100–104; HF 25–27; GLS 25–27.

4. Eurasian Water Shrew
Neomys fodiens Page 312
水鼩鼱 Shui Qujing
HB 69–94; T 44–80; HF 17–21; Wt 8–26 g

5. Lesser Striped Shrew
Sorex bedfordiae Page 314
小纹背鼩鼱 Xiaowenbei Qujing
HB 50–72; T 48–66; HF 11–15; GLS 17–19.

6. Laxmann's Shrew
Sorex caecutiens Page 314
中鼩鼱 Zhong Qujing
HB 52–65; T 30–38; HF 11–13.

7. Stripe-Backed Shrew
Sorex cylindricauda Page 315
纹背鼩鼱 Wenbei Qujing
HB 67–77; T 55–62; HF 15–16; GLS 17–21.

8. Large-Toothed Siberian Shrew
Sorex daphaenodon Page 316
栗齿鼩鼱 Lichi Qujing
HB 48–76; T 25–39; HF 10–13.

9. Chinese Highland Shrew
Sorex excelsus Page 316
云南鼩鼱 Yunnan Qujing
HB 60–73; T 44–51; HF 16–13; GLS 18–20; Wt 5–10 g.

10. Slender Shrew
Sorex gracillimus Page 316
细鼩鼱 Xi Qujing
HB 48–52; T 37–43; HF 10–11; GLS < 17.

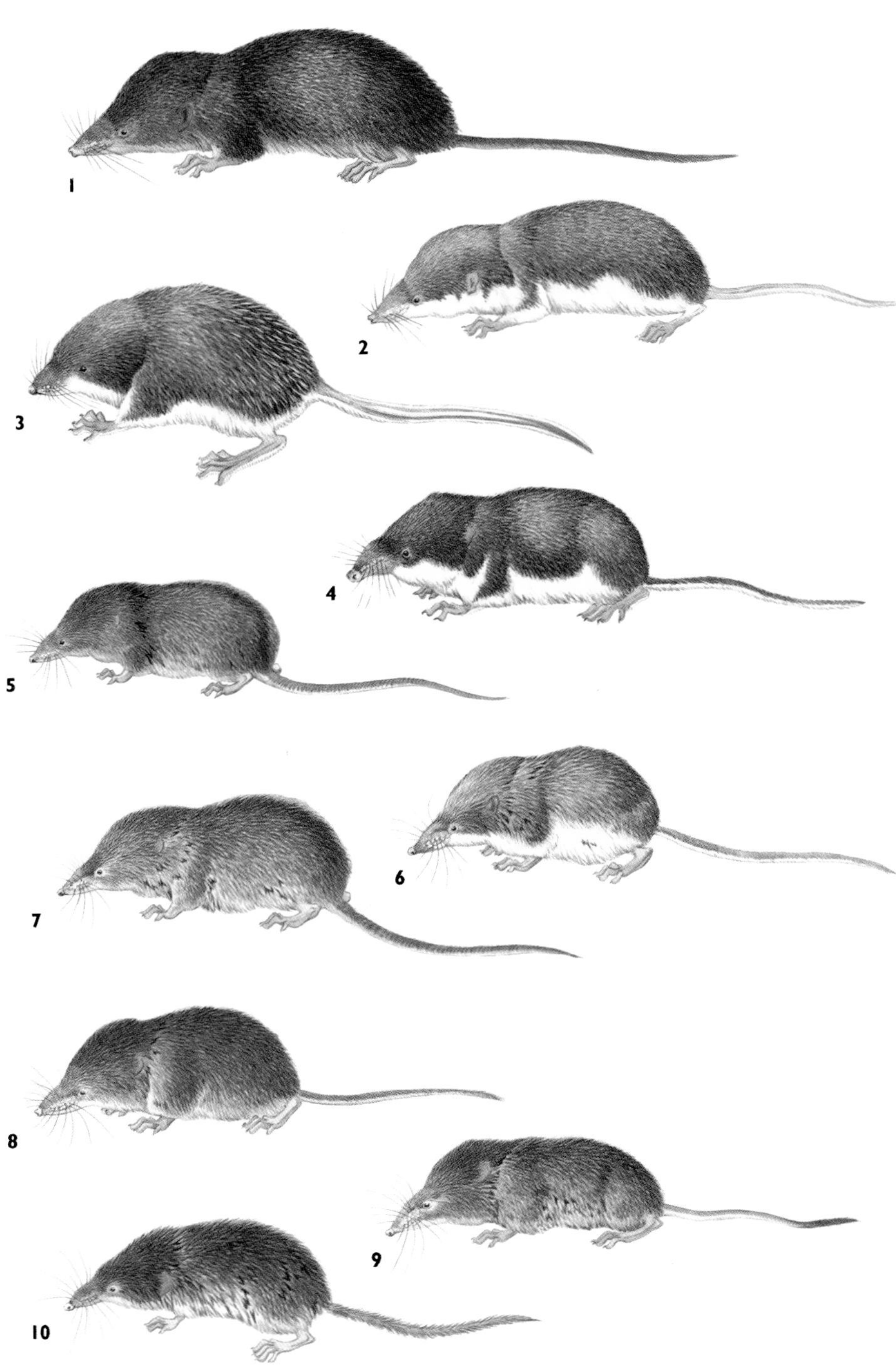
1
2
3
4
5
6
7
8
9
10

1. Ussuri Shrew
Sorex mirabilis Page 318
大鼩鼱 Da Qujing
HB 74–97; T 63–73; HF 16–18; Wt 11–14 g.

2. Chinese Shrew
Sorex sinalis Page 319
陕西鼩鼱 Shaanxi Qujing
HB 64–85; T 49–68; HF 13–17; GLS 20–22.

3. Tundra Shrew
Sorex tundrensis Page 319
苔原鼩鼱 Taiyuan Qujing
HB 60–85; T 22–36; Wt 5–10 g.

4. De Winton's Shrew
Chodsigoa hypsibia Page 308
川西长尾鼩 Chuanxi Changweiqu
HB 73–99; T 60–80; HF 15–18; GLS 19–22.

5. Lamulate Shrew
Chodsigoa lamula Page 308
甘肃长尾鼩 Gansu Changweiqu
HB 54–75; T 43–66; HF 11–16; GLS 17–19.

6. Smith's Shrew
Chodsigoa smithii Page 309
缺齿鼩 Quechi Qu
HB 72–96; T 92–108; HF 16–19; GLS 21–23.

7. Hodgson's Red-Toothed Shrew
Episoriculus caudatus Page 310
长尾鼩鼱 Changwei Qujing
HB 58–74; T 48–69; HF 12–16; GLS 17–19.

8. Long-Tailed Red-Toothed Shrew
Episoriculus leucops Page 311
印度长尾鼩 Yindu Changwiequ
HB 53–81; T 58–83; HF 12–19; GLS 18–21.

9. Long-Tailed Mountain Shrew
Episoriculus macrurus Page 311
缅甸长尾鼩 Miandian Changweiqu
HB 47–73; T 76–101; HF 14–18; GLS 17–19.

10. Himalayan Shrew
Soriculus nigrescens Page 320
大爪长尾鼩 Dazhua Changweiqu
HB 70–94; T 32–48; HF 12–17; GLS 20–23; Wt 17.5–25.5 g.

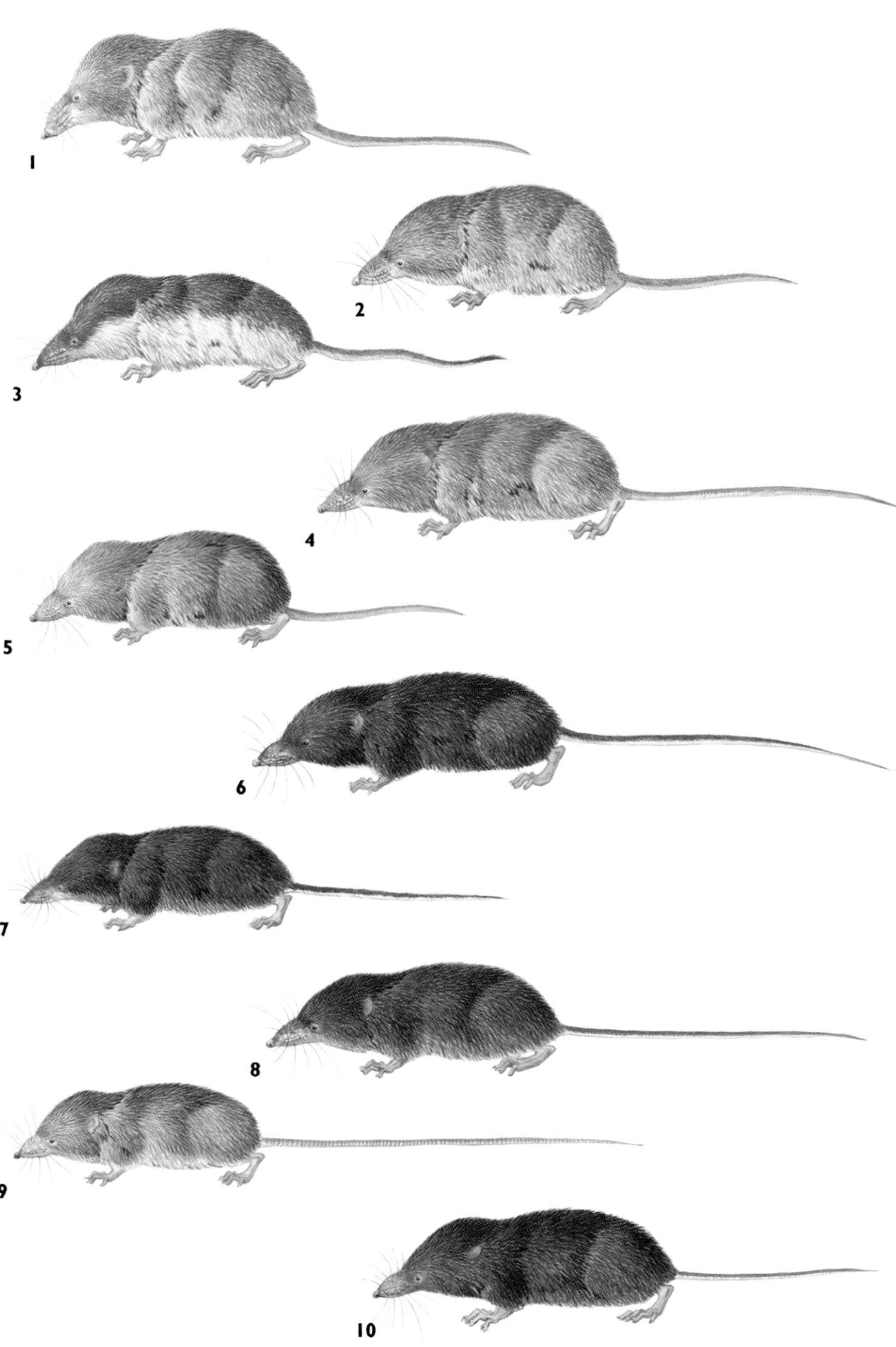
1
2
3
4
5
6
7
8
9
10

1. Long-Nosed Mole
Euroscaptor longirostris Page 323
长吻鼹 Changwen Yan
HB 90–145; T 11–25; HF 14–23; E 0; GLS 30–33.

2. Insular Mole
Mogera insularis Page 324
华南缺齿鼹 Huanan Quechiyan
HB 87–137; T 3–14; HF 5–18; E 0; GLS 27–33.

3. Large Mole
Mogera robusta Page 324
大缺齿鼹 Da Quechiyan
HB 170–220; T 19–23; HF 22–24; E 0; GLS 37–48

4. White-Tailed Mole
Parascaptor leucura Page 325
白尾鼹 Baiwei Yan
HB 100–112; T 10–15; HF 15–16; E 0; GLS 27–30.

5. Gansu Mole
Scapanulus oweni Page 321
甘肃鼹 Gansu Yan
HB 108–136; T 37–41; HF 14–20; E 0; GLS 27–32.

6. Short-Faced Mole
Scaptochirus moschatus Page 325
麝鼹 She Yan
HB 100–126; T 14–23; HF 15–19; E 0; GLS 30–36.

7. Long-Tailed Mole
Scaptonyx fusicaudus Page 325
长尾鼩鼹 Changwei Quyan
HB 72–90; T 26–45; HF 17; E 0; GLS 23; Wt 12 g.

8. Chinese Shrew Mole
Uropsilus soricipes Page 327
鼩鼹 Qu Yan
HB 66–80; T 50–69; HF 14–17; GLS 20–21.5.

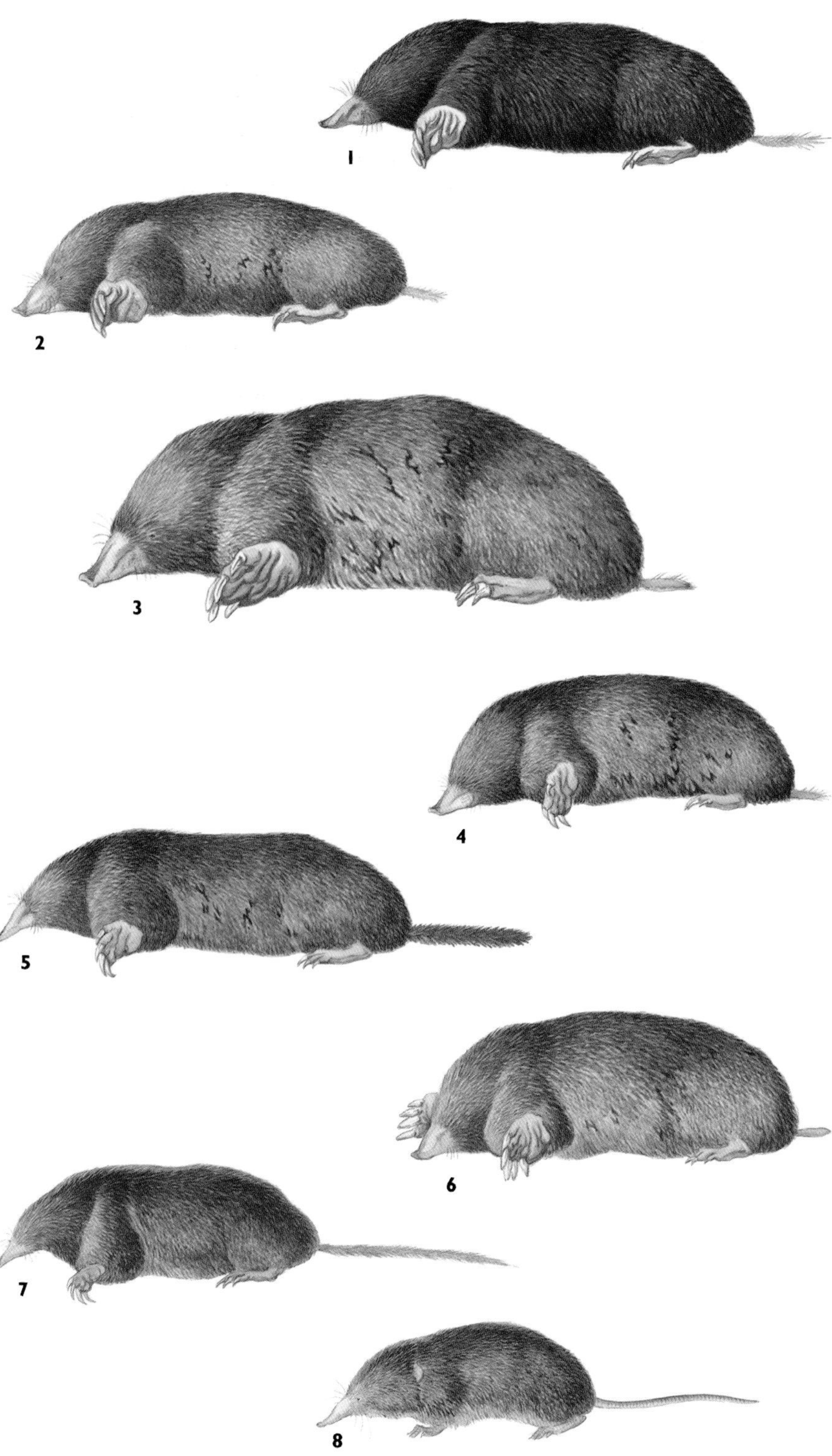
1
2
3
4
5
6
7
8

1. Greater Short-Nosed Fruit Bat
Cynopterus sphinx Page 329
犬蝠 Quanfu
HB 80–90; T 7–12; HF 16–19; E 18–21; FA 66–83; GLS 30–35.

2. Ryukyu Flying Fox
Pteropus dasymallus Page 332
琉球狐蝠 Liuqiu Hufu
HB 186–227; HF 40–55; E 20–28; FA 124–1411; GLS 60–65.

3. Blanford's Fruit Bat
Sphaerias blanfordi Page 334
布氏球果蝠 Bushiqiu Guofu
HB 80–90; HF 11–12; E 16–20; FA 50–61; GLS 27–28.

4. Leschenault's Rousette
Rousettus leschnaultii Page 333
棕果蝠 Zong Guofu
HB 95–120; T 10–18; HF 19–24; E 18–24; FA 80–99; GLS 34–40.

5. Lesser Dawn Bat
Eonycteris spelaea Page 330
长舌果蝠 Changshe Guofu
HB 80–130; T 11–23; HF 17–24; E 17–24; FA 61–73; GLS 35–37.

1
2
3
4
5

1. Black-Bearded Tomb Bat
Taphozous melanopogon Page 350
黑髯墓蝠 Heiran Mufu
HB 67–86; T 20–32; HF 8–15; E 16–23; FA 55–68; GLS 19.4–21.9.

2. Greater False Vampire Bat
Megaderma lyra Page 349
印度假吸血蝠 Yindu Jiaxixuefu
HB 70–95; T 0; HF 14–20; E 31–45; FA 56–72; GLS 30.

3. Intermediate Horseshoe Bat
Rhinolophus affinis Page 336
中菊头蝠 Zhong Jutoufu
HB 58–63; T 20–35; HF 11–13; E 15–21; FA 46–56; GLS 22–24.

4. Greater Horseshoe Bat
Rhinolophus ferrumequinum Page 337
马铁菊头蝠 Matie Jutoufu
HB 56–79; T 25–44; HF 10–14; E 18–29; FA 53–64; GLS 21–25.

5. Shortridge's Horseshoe Bat
Rhinolophus shortridgei Page 342
短翼菊头蝠 Duanyi Jutoufu
HB 51–59; T 18–25; HF 9; E 16–20; FA 39–43; GLS 16.8–18.7.

6. Woolly Horseshoe Bat
Rhinolophus luctus Page 338
大菊头蝠 Da Jutoufu
HB 75–95; T 36–61; HF 16–18; E 28–44; FA 58–81; GLS 28–33.

7. Big-Eared Horseshoe Bat
Rhinolophus macrotis Page 338
大耳菊头蝠 Da'er Jutoufu
HB 47–51; T 12–32; HF 9–10; E 18–27; FA 39–48; GLS 20.

8. Pearson's Horseshoe Bat
Rhinolophus pearsonii Page 340
皮氏菊头蝠 Pishi Jutoufu
HB 61–68; T 16–29; HF 12–13; E 23–29; FA 47–56; GLS 24.

9. Chinese Rufous Horseshoe Bat
Rhinolophus sinicus Page 342
中华菊头蝠 Zhonghua Jutoufu
HB 43–53; T 21–30; HF 7–10; E 15–20; FA 43–56; GLS 18–23.

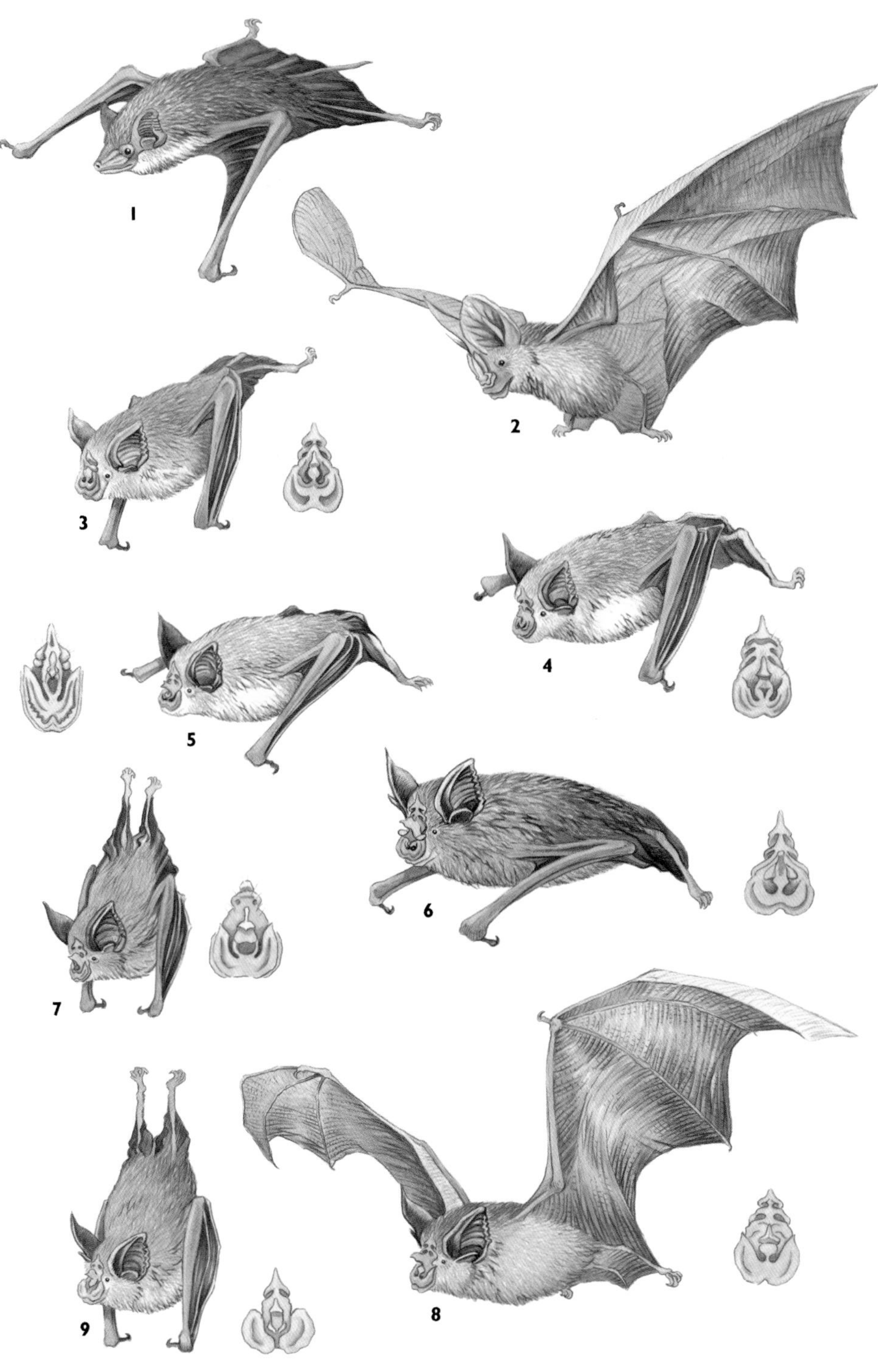
1
2
3
4
5
6
7
8
9

1. Stoliczka's Asian Trident Bat
Aselliscus stoliczkanus Page 345
三叶蹄蝠 Sanye Tifu
HB 40–50; T 30–40; HF 9–10; E 10–14; FA 39–44; GLS 16.

2. East Asian Tailless Leaf-Nosed Bat
Coelops frithii Page 345
无尾蹄蝠 Wuwei Tifu
HB 38–50; T 0; HF 5–9; E 11–15; FA 35–42; GLS 16.

3. Great Leaf-Nosed Bat
Hipposideros armiger Page 346
大蹄蝠 Da Tifu,
HB 80–110; T 48–70; HF 13–17; E 26–35; FA 82–99; GLS 31–33.

4. Intermediate Leaf-Nosed Bat
Hipposideros larvatus Page 347
中蹄蝠 Zhong Tifu
HB 74–78; T 37–44; HF 10–15; E 23–26; FA 56–69; GLS 23.

5. Pomona Leaf-Nosed Bat
Hipposideros pomona Page 348
双色蹄蝠 Shuangse Tifu
HB 36–52; T 28–35; HF 6–9; E 18–25; FA 38–43; GLS 17–18.

6. Pratt's Leaf-Nosed Bat
Hipposideros pratti Page 348
普氏蹄蝠 Pushi Tifu
HB 91–110; T 50–62; HF 15–22; E 33–38; FA 75–90; GLS 28–35.

7. Wrinkle-Lipped Free-Tailed Bat
Chaerephon plicatus Page 352
犬吻蝠 Quanwenfu
HB 65–75; T 30–40; HF 9–12; E 16–21; FA 40–50; GLS 18–21.

8. East Asian Free-Tailed Bat
Tadarida insignis Page 352
宽耳犬吻蝠 Kuan'er Quanwenfu
HB 84–94; T 48–60; HF 10–15; E 31–34; FA 57–65; GLS 22–24.

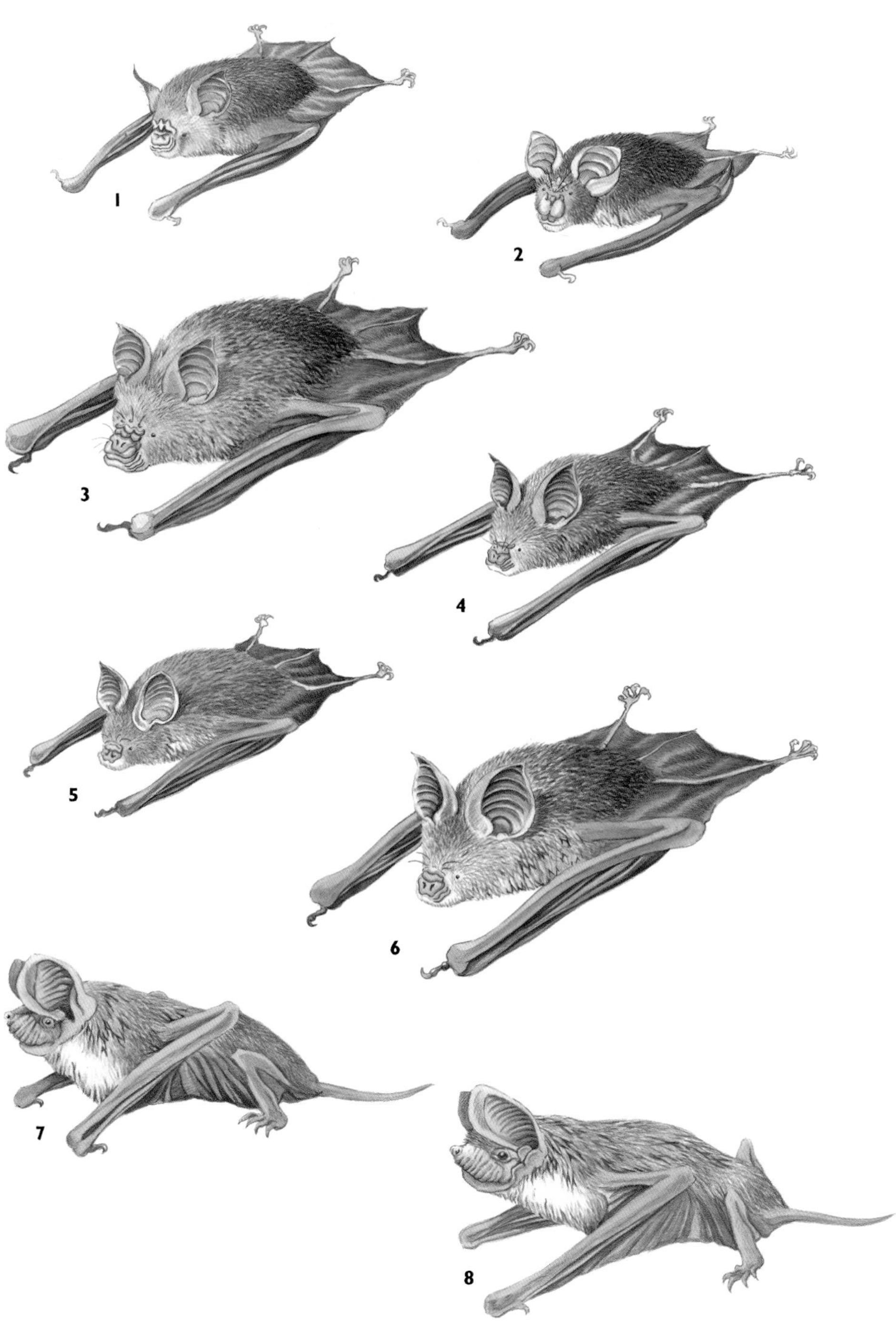
1
2
3
4
5
6
7
8

1. Bronze Sprite
Arielulus circumdatus Page 355
大黑伏翼 Da Heifuyi
HB 95; T 40; HF 10; E 15; FA 41–44; GLS 15–16.

2. Eastern Barbastelle
Barbastella leucomelas Page 355
宽耳蝠 Kuan'erfu
HB 47–51; T 40–47; HF 7–8; E 15–17; FA 38–45; GLS 14–16.

3. Gobi Big Brown Bat
Eptesicus gobiensis Page 356
戈壁北棕蝠 Gebi Beizongfu
HB 57–65; T 40–45; HF 9–10; E 10–15; FA 38–42; GLS 16.

4. Northern Bat
Eptesicus nilssonii Page 357
北棕蝠 Beizongfu
HB 54–64; T 35–50; HF 10–12; E 13–18; FA 37–44; GLS 14–16.

5. Common Serotine
Eptesicus serotinus Page 357
大棕蝠 Da Zongfu
HB 70–80; T 52–58; HF 10–18; E 14–18; FA 49–57; GLS > 20.

6. Chinese Pipistrelle
Hypsugo pulveratus Page 359
灰伏翼 Hui Fuyi
HB 44–47; T 37–38; HF 7–8; E 12–14; FA 33–36; GLS 14–15.

7. Great Evening Bat
Ia io Page 360
南蝠 Nanfu
HB 89–104; T 61–83; HF 13–18; E 22–29; FA 71–80; GLS 27.

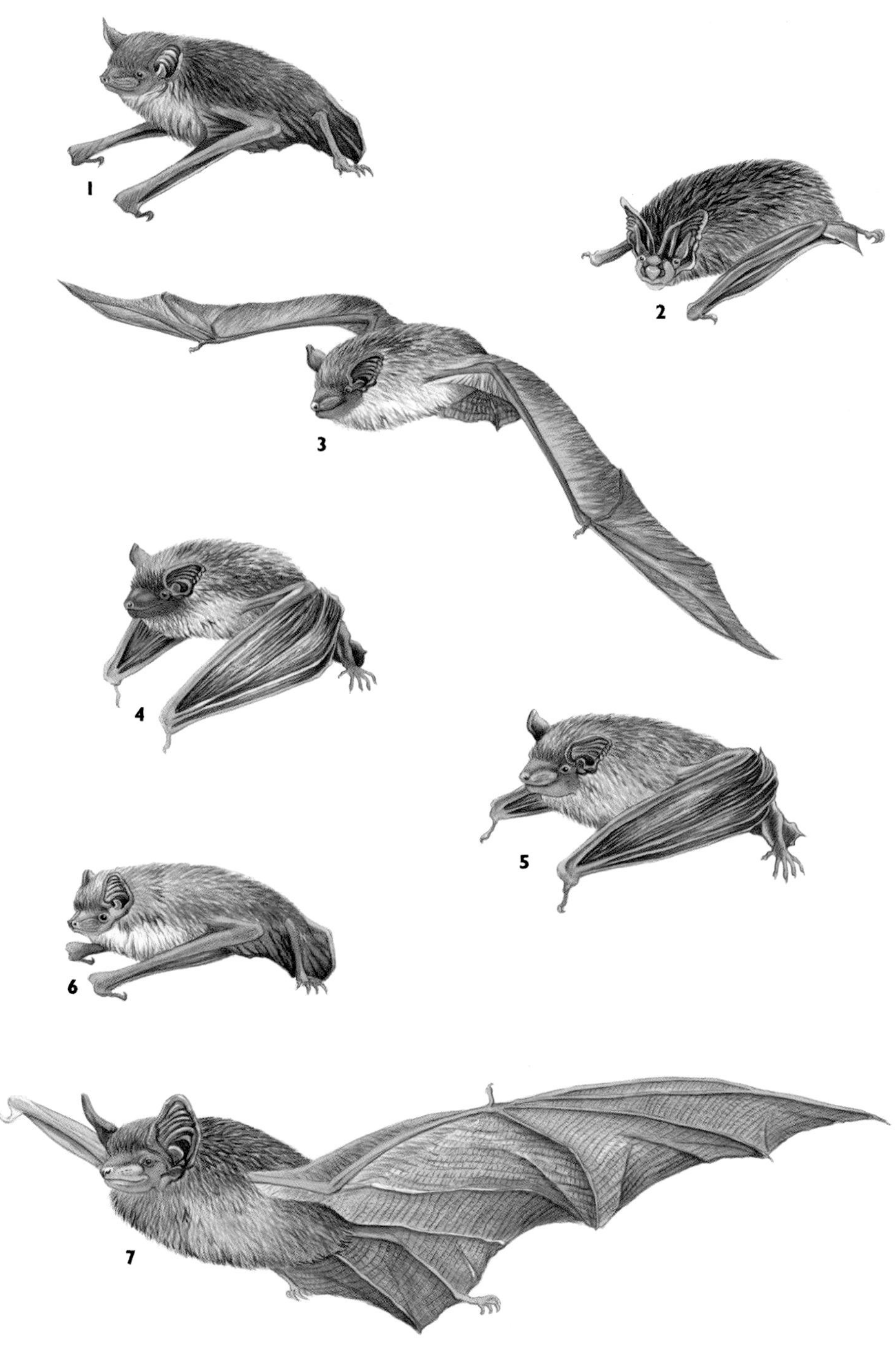
1
2
3
4
5
6
7

1. Birdlike Noctule
Nyctalus aviator Page 361
大山蝠 Da Shanfu
HB 80–106; T 45–62; HF 12–17; E 16–23; FA 58–64.

2. Noctule
Nyctalus noctula Page 361
褐山蝠 He Shanfu
HB 60–82; T 41–61; HF 12–14; E 16–21; FA 47–60; GLS 17–19.4.

3. Japanese Pipistrelle
Pipistrellus abramus Page 362
东亚伏翼 Dongya Fuyi
HB 38–60; T 29–45; HF 6–10; E 8–13; FA 31–36; GLS 12.2–13.4.

4. Kelaart's Pipistrelle
Pipistrellus ceylonicus Page 363
锡兰伏翼 Xilan Fuyi
HB 45–64; T 30–45; HF 6–11; E 9–14; FA 33–42; GLS 14.7–15.8; Wt 9–10 g.

5. Indian Pipistrelle
Pipistrellus coromandra Page 364
印度伏翼 Yindu Fuyi
HB 34–49; T 22–39; HF 3–8; E 7–14; FA 25–35; GLS 10.6–11.9.

6. Javan Pipistrelle
Pipistrellus javanicus Page 364
爪哇伏翼 Zhaowa Fuyi
HB 40–55; T 26–40; HF 3–8; E 5–15; FA 30–36.

7. Mount Popa Pipistrelle
Pipistrellus paterculus Page 365
棒茎伏翼 Bangjing Fuyi
HB 42–48; T 31–38; HF 6–7; E 10–13; FA 29–34; GLS 13–14.

8. Brown Long-Eared Bat
Plecotus auritus Page 366
褐长耳蝠 He Chang'erfu
HB 40–45; T 48–50; HF 7–8; E 39–41; FA 36–46; GLS 16.5–18.8.

9. Gray Long-Eared Bat
Plecotus austriacus Page 366
灰长耳蝠 Hui Chang'erfu
HB 41–58; T 37–55; HF 7–10; E 37–42; FA 37–45.

1
2
3
4
5
6
7
8
9

1. Harlequin Bat
Scotomanes ornatus Page 367
斑蝠 Banfu
HB 64–85; T 52–66; HF 12–15; E 19–23; FA 50–62; GLS 20.

2. Greater Asiatic Yellow House Bat
Scotophilus heathii Page 368
大黄蝠 Da Huangfu
HB 67–93; T 43–71; HF 9–15; E 13–21; FA 55–66; GLS 21–26.

3. Lesser Bamboo Bat
Tylonycteris pachypus Page 369
扁颅蝠 Bianlufu
HB 34–46; T 26–33; HF 5–7; E 9–10; FA 25–29; GLS 11.

4. Greater Bamboo Bat
Tylonycteris robustula Page 370
褐扁颅蝠 He Bianlufu
HB 40–44; T 26–31; HF 5–6; E 8–11; FA 26–29; GLS 11.8–12.5.

5. Asian Particolored Bat
Vespertilio sinensis Page 371
东方蝙蝠 Dongfang Bianfu
HB 58–80; T 34–54; HF 9–16; E 14–21; FA 43–55; GLS 17.3–18.

6. Szechwan Myotis
Myotis altarium Page 373
西南鼠耳蝠 Xinan Shu'erfu
HB 55–60; T 48–50; HF 11–12; E 22–24; FA 42–46; GLS 15–16.

7. Lesser Mouse-Eared Myotis
Myotis blythii Page 373
狭耳鼠耳蝠 Xia'er Shu'erfu
HB 65–89; T 53–81; HF 11–17; E 19–22; FA 53–70; GLS 21–23.

8. Far Eastern Myotis
Myotis bombinus Page 374
远东鼠耳蝠 Yuandong Shu'erfu
HB 41–52; T 38–45; HF 8–12; E 14–19; FA 37–42; GLS 14.

9. Large Myotis
Myotis chinensis Page 374
中华鼠耳蝠 Zhonghua Shu'erfu
HB 91–97; T 53–58; HF 16–18; E 20–23; FA 64–69; GLS 23.

10. David's Myotis
Myotis davidii Page 375
须鼠耳蝠 Xu Shu'erfu
HB 41–44; T 30–43; HF 7–9; E 12–15; FA 31–35.

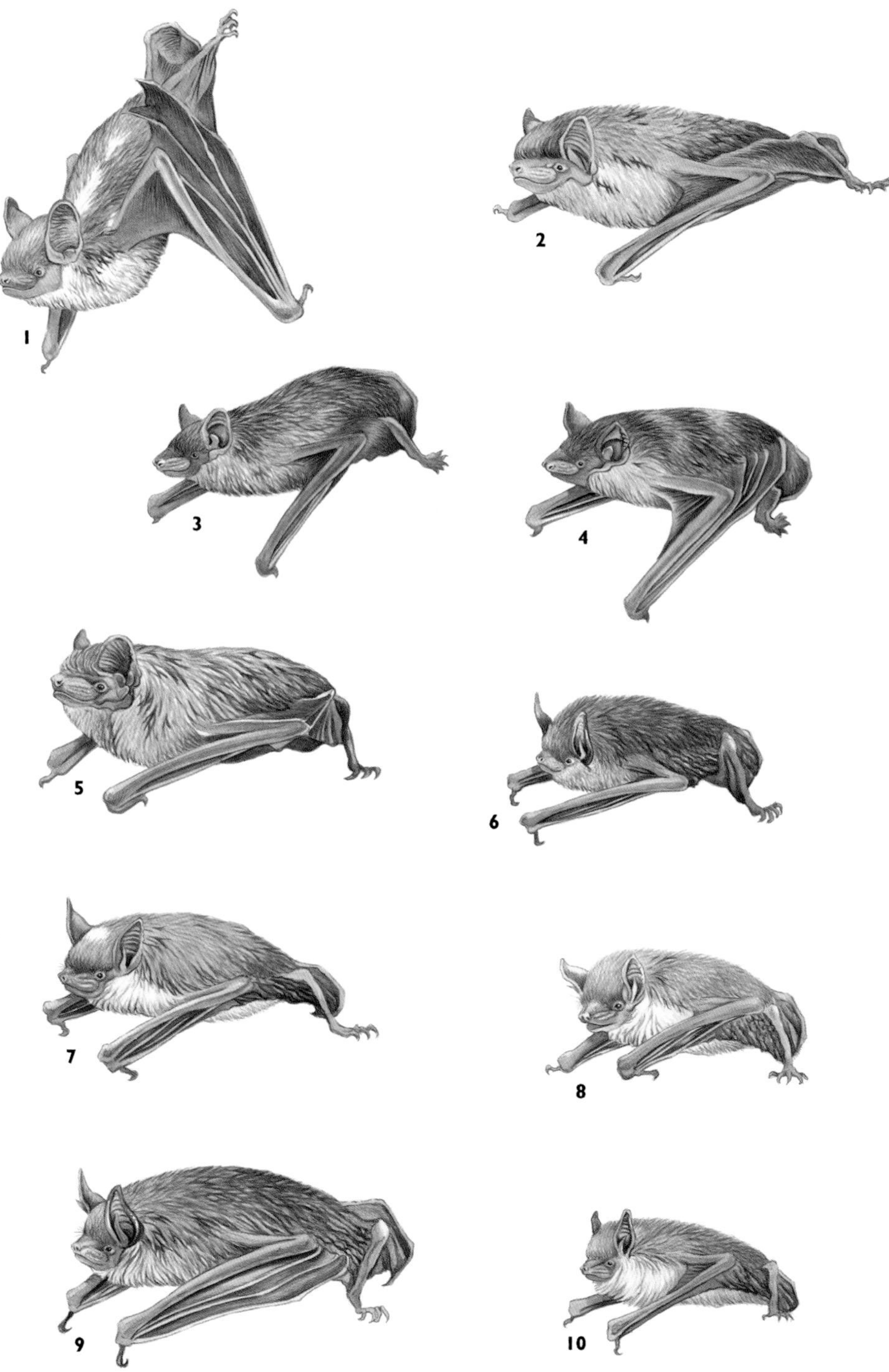
1
2
3
4
5
6
7
8
9
10

1. Daubenton's Myotis
Myotis daubentonii Page 375
水鼠耳蝠 Shui Shu'erfu
HB 44–58; T 27–41; HF 9–12; E 11–15; FA 34–39; GLS 14.

2. Hodgson's Myotis
Myotis formosus Page 376
绯鼠耳蝠 Fei Shu'erfu
HB 45–70; T 43–52; HF 10–12; E 16–17; FA 45–50.

3. Fraternal Myotis
Myotis frater Page 377
长尾鼠耳蝠 Changwei Shu'erfu
HB 43–57; T 38–47; HF 7–12; E 11–14; FA 36–42; GLS 13.5.

4. Horsfield's Myotis
Myotis horsfieldii Page 377
郝氏鼠耳蝠 Haoshi Shu'erfu
HB 49–59; T 34–42; HF 7–11; E 13–15; FA 36–42.

5. Ikonnikov's Myotis
Myotis ikonnikovi Page 377
伊氏鼠耳蝠 Yishi Shu'erfu
HB 36–52; T 30–38; HF 7–9; E 11–13; FA 30–36; GLS 12.7.

6. Burmese Whiskered Myotis
Myotis montivagus Page 378
山地鼠耳蝠 Shandi Shu'erfu
HB 56–62; T 42–48; HF 9–10; E 14–16; FA 40–49.

7. Peking Myotis
Myotis pequinius Page 379
北京鼠耳蝠 Beijing Shu'erfu
HB 62; T 42; HF 12; E 18; FA 48–50.

8. Rickett's Big-Footed Myotis
Myotis pilosus Page 380
大足鼠耳蝠 Dazu Shu'erfu
HB 65; T 45–54; HF 15–17; E 15–18; FA 53–56; GLS 21.

9. Himalayan Whiskered Myotis
Myotis siligorensis Page 380
高颅鼠耳蝠 Gaolu Shu'erfu
HB 40–41; T 25–38; HF 6–8; E 8–13; FA 31–36; GLS 13.

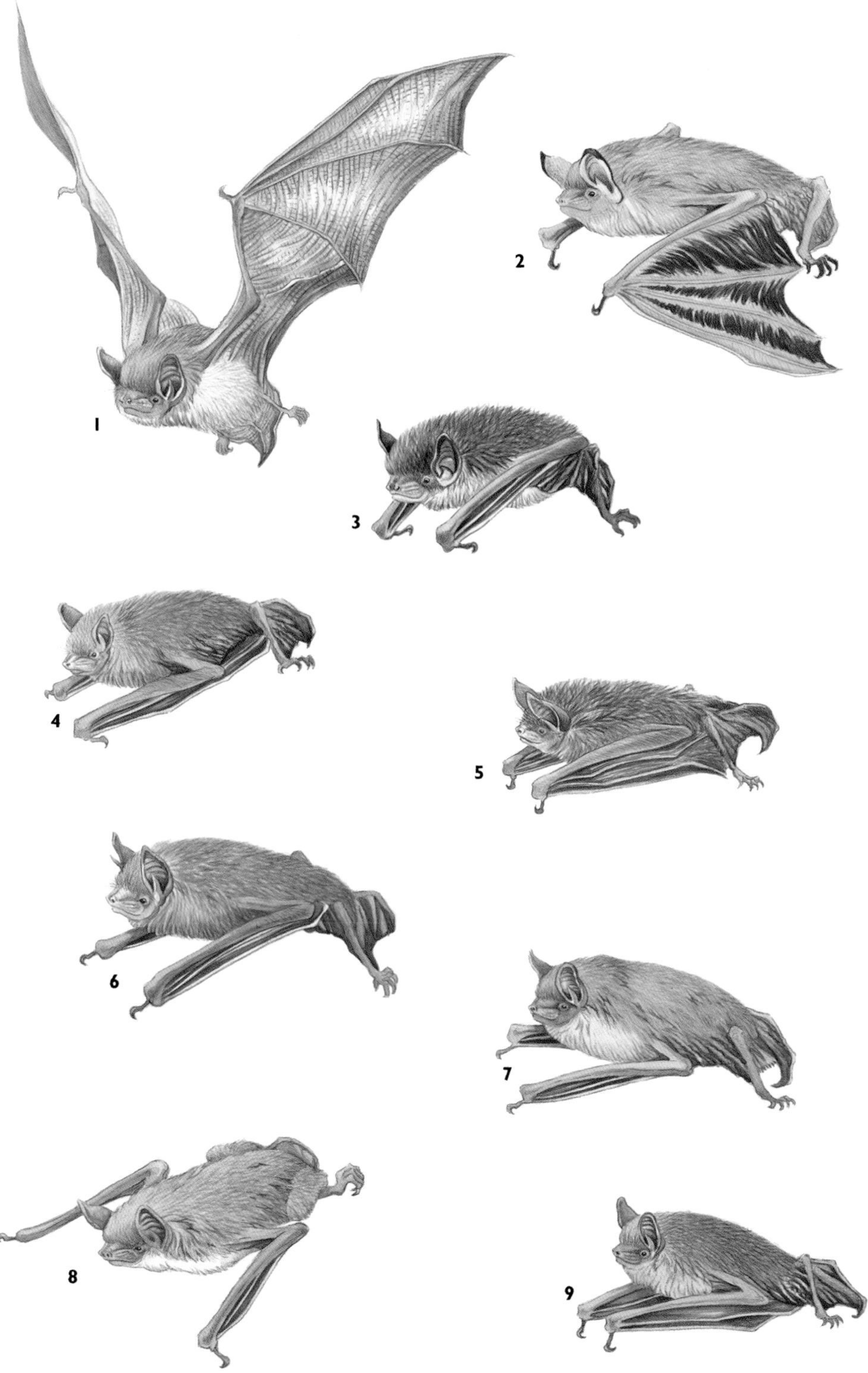
1
2
3
4
5
6
7
8
9

1. Lesser Hairy-Winged Bat
Harpiocephalus harpia Page 382
毛翼管鼻蝠 Maoyi Guanbifu
HB 60–75; T 40–50; HF 11–14; E 17–18; FA 44–50; GLS 23.

2. Little Tube-Nosed Bat
Murina aurata Page 383
小管鼻蝠 Xiao Guanbifu
HB 33–35; T 29–31; HF 7–8; E 10–12; FA 28–32; GLS 15.6–15.9.

3. Round-Eared Tube-Nosed Bat
Murina cyclotis Page 384
圆耳管鼻蝠 Yuan'er Guanbifu
HB 38–50; T 32–42; HF 7–10; E 12–15; FA 30–35.

4. Dusky Tube-Nosed Bat
Murina fusca Page 384
暗色管鼻蝠 Anse Guanbifu
HB 58; T 34; HF 8; E 18; FA 40; GLS 17.

5. Hutton's Tube-Nosed Bat
Murina huttoni Page 384
中管鼻蝠 Zhong Guanbifu
HB 47–50; T 31–39; HF 6–10; E 16–18; FA 29–38; GLS 15–18.

6. Greater Tube-Nosed Bat
Murina leucogaster Page 385
白腹管鼻蝠 Baifu Guanbifu
HB 47–49; T 35–45; HF 9–10; E 14–15; FA 40–43; GLS 18–19.

7. Schreiber's Long-Fingered Bat
Miniopterus schreibersii Page 381
长翼蝠 Changyifu
HB 67–78; T'50–62; HF 9–12; E 12–14; FA 47–50; GLS 15.7–17.2.

8. Hardwicke's Woolly Bat
Kerivoula hardwickii Page 386
哈氏彩蝠 Hashi Caifu
HB 39–55; T 35–43; HF 5–10; E 11–15; FA 31–36; GLS 15.

9. Painted Woolly Bat
Kerivoula picta Page 386
彩蝠 Caifu
HB 40–48; T 43–48; HF 4–8; E 13–16; FA 31–38; GLS 15.

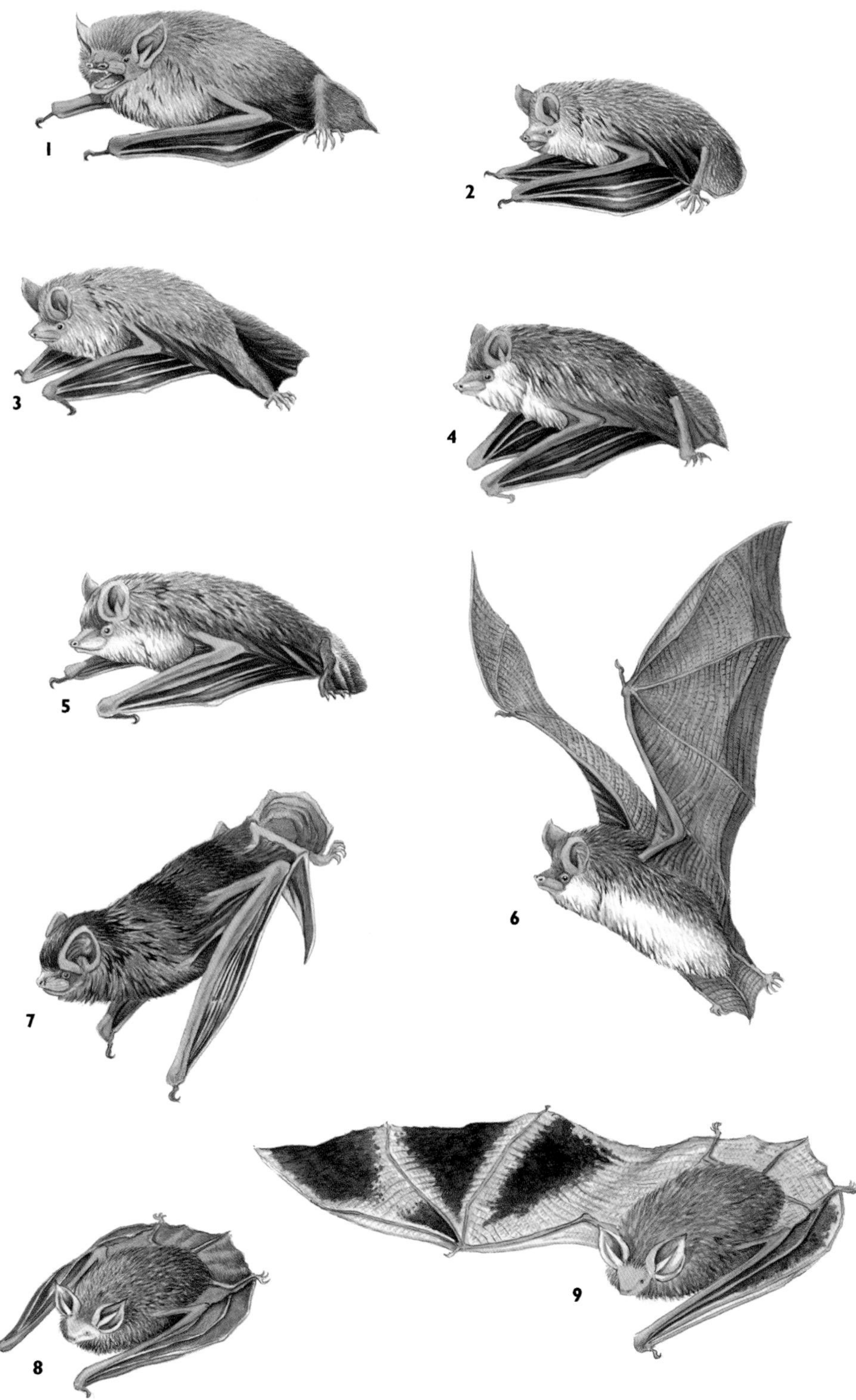
1
2
3
4
5
6
7
8
9

1. Asian Golden Cat
Catopuma temminckii Page 391
金猫 Jinmao
HB 710–1,050; T 400–560; HF 165–180; E 60–70; GLS 98–131; Wt 9–16 kg.

2. Chinese Mountain Cat
Felis bieti Page 392
漠猫 Mo Mao
HB 600–850; T 290–350; E 58–67; GLS 94–100; Wt 5.5–9 kg.

3. Jungle Cat
Felis chaus Page 394
丛林猫 Conglin Mao
HB 580–760; T 218–270; HF 108–145; E 45–80; GLS 100–120; Wt 5–9 kg.

4. Pallas' Cat
Felis manul Page 395
兔狲 Tusun
HB 450–650; T 210–350; HF 120–140; E 40–50; GLS 82–92; Wt 2.3–4.5 kg.

5. Lynx
Lynx lynx Page 397
猞猁 She Li
HB 800–1,300; T 110–250; HF 225–250; E 80–95; GLS 145–160; Wt 18–38 kg.

6. Marbled Cat
Pardofelis marmorata Page 397
云猫 Yunmao
HB 400–660; T 450–560; HF 115–120; E 35–40; GLS 79–91; Wt 3–5.5 kg.

7. Leopard Cat
Prionailurus bengalensis Page 398
豹猫 Baomao
HB 360–660; T 200–370; HF 80–130; E 35–55; GLS 75–96; Wt 1.5–5 kg.

1
2
3
4
5
6
7

1. Clouded Leopard

Neofelis nebulosa Page 399
云豹 Yun Bao
HB 700–1,080; T 550–915; HF 200–225; E 45–60; GLS 150–200; Wt 16–32 kg.

2. Leopard

Panthera pardus Page 401
豹 Bao
HB 1,000–1,910; T 700–1,000; HF 220–245; E 63–75; GLS 175–221; Wt 37–90 kg.

3. Tiger

Panthera tigris (a, *P. t. altaica*; b, *P. t. amoyensis*) Page 402
虎 Hu
HB 140–280 cm; T 910–1,100; HF 234–420; E 95–130; GLS 252–333; Wt 90–306 kg.

4. Snow Leopard

Uncia uncia Page 403
雪豹 Xue Bao
HB 1,100–1,300; T 800–1,000; HF 265; E 61; GLS 155–173; Wt 38–75 kg.

1
2
3a
3b
4

1. Owston's Palm Civet
Chrotogale owstoni Page 406
长颌带狸 Changhe Daili
HB 400–660; T 350–490; HF 70–90; GLS 102–113; Wt 2.4–3.4 kg.

2. Binturong
Arctictis binturong Page 407
熊狸 Xiong Li
HB 522–900; T 520–890; HF 100–135; E 45–65; GLS 113–155; Wt 9–14 kg.

3. Small-Toothed Palm Civet
Arctogalidia trivirgata Page 408
小齿狸 Xiaochi Li
HB 440–600; T 510–690; HF 74–80; E 38–42; GLS 100–118; Wt 2–2.5 kg.

4. Common Palm Civet
Paradoxurus hermaphroditus Page 409
椰子狸 Yezi Li
HB 470–570; T 470–560; HF 67–85; E 42–58; GLS 90–118; Wt 2.4–4 kg.

5. Masked Palm Civet
Paguma larvata Page 409
花面狸 Huamian Li
HB 400–690; T 350–600; HF 65–120; E 40–60; GLS 100–130; Wt 3–7 kg.

6. Spotted Linsang
Prionodon pardicolor Page 410
斑灵猫 Ban Lingmao
HB 350–400; T 300–375; HF 60–68; E 30–35; GLS 65–75; Wt 4.1–8 kg.

7. Large Indian Civet
Viverra zibetha Page 412
大灵猫 Da Lingmao
HB 500–950; T 380–590; HF 90–145; E 35–65; GLS 135–150; Wt 3.4–9.2 kg.

8. Small Indian Civet
Viverricula indica Page 413
小灵猫 Xiao Lingmao
HB 500–610; T 280–390; HF 65–120; E 25–43; GLS 90–105; Wt 1.6–4 kg.

1
2
3
4
5
6
7
8

1. Wolf
Canis lupus Page 416
狼 Lang
HB 1,000–1,600; T 330–550; HF 200–250; E 90–120; GLS 214–250; Wt 28–40 kg.

2. Dhole
Cuon alpinus Page 418
豺 Chai
HB 880–1,130; T 400–500; HF 70–90; E 95–105; GLS 150–170; Wt 10–20 kg.

3. Raccoon Dog
Nyctereutes procyonoides Page 419
貉 He
HB 450–660; T 160–220; HF 75–120; E 35–60; GLS 100–130; Wt 3–6 kg.

4. Corsac Fox
Vulpes corsac Page 420
沙狐 Sha Hu
HB 450–600; T 240–350; HF 90–120; E 50–70; GLS 95–118; Wt 1.8–2.8 kg.

5. Tibetan Fox
Vulpes ferrilata Page 421
藏狐 Zang Hu
HB 490–650; T 250–300; HF 110–140; E 52–63; GLS 138–150; Wt 3.8–4.6 kg.

6. Red Fox
Vulpes vulpes Page 421
赤狐 Chi Hu
HB 500–800; T 350–450; HF 115–155; E 74–102; GLS 130–150; Wt 3.6–7 kg.

1
2
4
3
5
6

1. Red Panda
Ailurus fulgens Page 448
小熊猫 Xiaoxiongmao
HB 510–730; T 370–480; HF 95–115; E 50–80; GLS 100–120; Wt 2.5–5 kg.

2. Giant Panda
Ailuropoda melanoleuca Page 423
大熊猫 Daxiongmao
HB 1,500–1,800; T 120–150; HF 140–200; E 70–110; GLS 280–300; Wt 85–125 kg.

3. Sun Bear
Helarctos malayanus Page 423
马来熊 Malaixiong
HB 1,000–1,400; T 30–70; HF 180–210; E 40–60; GLS 230–290; Wt 25–65 kg.

4. Brown Bear
Ursus arctos Page 425
棕熊 Zongxiong
HB 1,150–1,190; T 80–130; HF 190–280; E 100–170; GLS 250–380; Wt 125–225 kg.

5. Asian Black Bear
Ursus thibetanus Page 426
黑熊 Heixiong
HB 1,160–1,750; T 50–160; HF 190–340; E 115–180; GLS 206–413; Wt 54–240 kg.

1
2
3
4
5

1. Northern Fur Seal
Callorhinus ursinus (a, male; b, female) Page 428
海狗 Hai Gou
HB 1.4–2.5 m; Wt 175–275 kg (males) 30–50 (females)

2. Steller's Sea Lion
Eumetopias jubatus (a, male; b, female) Page 428
北海狮 Bei Haishi
HB 2.3–3.3 m; GLS 325–400; Maximum Wt 350 kg (females), 1,120 kg (males).

3. Bearded Seal
Erignathus barbatus Page 429
髯海豹 Ran Haibao
HB 2.1–2.3 m; Wt 200–250 kg.

4. Spotted Seal
Phoca largha Page 430
斑海豹 Ban Haibao
HB 1.4–1.7 m; GLS 218; Wt 85–150 kg.

5. Ringed Seal
Pusa hispida Page 431
环斑海豹 Huanban Haibao
HB 1.4–1.5 m; Wt 45–90 kg.

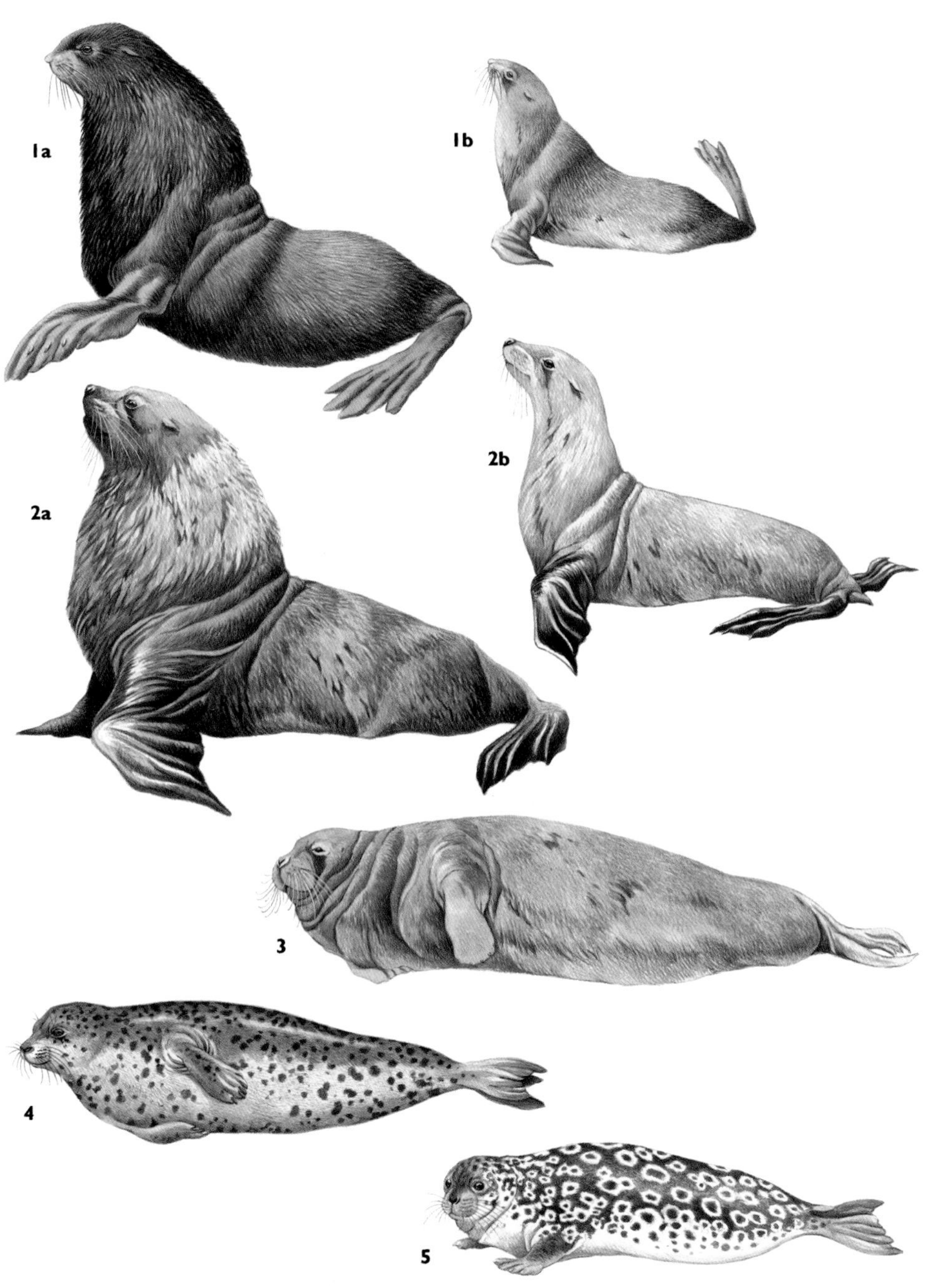
1a
1b
2a
2b
3
4
5

1. Small Indian Mongoose
Herpestes javanicus Page 415
红颊獴 Hongjia Meng
HB 250–370; T 240–270; HF 50–65; E 12–27; GLS 66–77; Wt 0.6–1.2 kg.

2. Crab-Eating Mongoose
Herpestes urva Page 415
食蟹獴 Shixie Meng
HB 360–520; T 240–336; HF 80–102; E 20–30; GLS 88–100; Wt 1–2.3 kg.

3. Asian Small-Clawed Otter
Aonyx cinerea Page 432
小爪水獭 Xiaozhua Shuita
HB 400–610; T 290–350; HF 75–95; E 20–25; GLS 84–94; Wt 2–4 kg.

4. Eurasian Otter
Lutra lutra Page 433
水獭 Shui Ta
HB 490–840; T 243–440; HF 88–125; E 15–30; GLS 90–120; Wt 2.5–9 kg.

5. Smooth-Coated Otter
Lutrogale perspicillata Page 434
江獭 Jiang Ta
HB 650–750; T 400–450; HF 100–140 mm; E 20–30; GLS 122–128; Wt 5–12 kg.

6. Wolverine
Gulo gulo Page 436
貂熊 Diaoxiong
HB 675–780; T 180–195; HF 180–195; E 45–55; GLS 140–165; Wt 6.5–14 kg.

1
2
3
4
5
6

1. Hog Badger
Arctonyx collaris Page 435
猪獾 Zhu Huan
HB 317–740; T 90–220; HF 55–135; E 21–45;
GLS 80–140; Wt 9.7–12.5 kg.

2. Asian Badger
Meles leucurus Page 440
狗獾 Gouhuan
HB 495–700; T 130–205; HF 85–110; E 35–50;
GLS 110–128; Wt 3.5–9 kg.

3. Chinese Ferret Badger
Melogale moschata Page 441
鼬獾 You Huan
HB 305–430; T 115–215; HF 45–65; E 20–40;
GLS 70–84; Wt 0.5–1.6 kg.

4. Yellow-Throated Marten
Martes flavigula Page 437
青鼬 Qing You
HB 325–630; T 250–480; HF 70–130; E 24–53;
GLS 90–103; Wt 0.8–2.8 kg.

5. Beech Marten
Martes foina Page 438
石貂 Shi Diao
HB 340–480; T 220–330; HF 45–100; E 18–25;
GLS 75–90; Wt 0.8–1.6 kg.

6. Sable
Martes zibellina Page 439
紫貂 Zi Diao
HB 340–460; T 110–180; HF 60–90; E 32–50;
GLS 68–85; Wt 0.4–1.1 kg.

1
2
3
4
5
6

1. Mountain Weasel
Mustela altaica Page 443
香鼬 Xiang You
HB 105–270; T 66–162; HF 22–47; E 11–28
GLS 36–50; Wt 80–280 g.

2. Yellow-Bellied Weasel
Mustela kathiah Page 445
黄腹鼬 Huangfu You
HB 205–334; T 65–182; HF 22–46; E 12–21;
GLS 43–54; Wt 168–250 g.

3. Least Weasel
Mustela nivalis Page 446
伶鼬 Ling You
HB 130–190 ; T 20–53; HF 16–25; E 9–13;
GLS 27–37; Wt 28–70 g.

4. Siberian Weasel
Mustela sibirica Page 446
黄鼬 Huang You
HB 220–420; T 120–250; HF 45–65; E 15–25;
GLS 50–72; Wt 500–1,200 g.

5. Back-Striped Weasel
Mustela strigidorsa Page 447
纹鼬 Wen You
HB 275–340; T 145–205; HF 47–54; E 20–23;
GLS 57–65; Wt 443–1,200 g.

6. Steppe Polecat
Mustela eversmanii Page 445
艾鼬 Ai You
HB 315–460; T 90–200; HF 45–68; E 15–35;
GLS 62–73; Wt 460–1,198 g.

7. Marbled Polecat
Vormela peregusna Page 447
虎鼬 Hu You
HB 300–400; T 150–210; HF 24–88; E 15–30;
GLS 52–65; Wt 370–700 g.

1
3
2
4
5
6
7

1. Asian Elephant
Elephas maximus Page 156
亚洲象 Yazhou Xiang
HB 5.5–6.5 m; SH 3.2 m (male), 2.5 m (female); T 1.2–1.5 m; Wt 4,160 kg (male), 2,720 kg (female).

2. Horse (Przewalski's Horse)
Equus caballus Page 449
野马 Yema
HB 180–280 cm; SH 120–146 cm; T 38–60 cm (without hair); E 140–180; SL 471–540; Wt 200–350 kg.

3. Kulan
Equus hemionus Page 450
蒙古野驴 Menggu Yelu
HB 200–220 cm; SH 126–130 cm; T 43–48 cm; HF 58; E 178; GLS 489–544; Wt 200–260 kg.

4. Kiang
Equus kiang Page 450
藏野驴 Zang Yelu
HB 182–214 cm; SH 132–142 cm; T 32–45 cm; HF 41–54 cm; E 220; GLS 473–547; Wt 250–400 kg.

1
2
3
4

1. Wild Boar
Sus scrofa Page 452
野猪 Ye Zhu
HB 900–1,800; SH 590–1,090; T 200–300; HF 250–350; E 114; GLS 295–350; Wt 50–200 kg.

2. Bactrian Camel
Camelus bactrianus Page 453
双峰驼 Shuangfeng Tuo
HB 3.2–3.5 m; SH 1.6–1.8 m; Wt 450–680 kg.

3. Java Mouse-deer
Tragulus javanicus Page 453
小鼷鹿 Xiao Xilu
HB 430–500; SH 350; T 65–80; E 35–50; GLS 92–103; Wt 2.5–4.5 kg.

1
2
3

1. Forest Musk Deer
Moschus berezovskii Page 455
林麝 Lin She
HB 630–800; SH < 500; T 40; GSL 102–146; Wt 6–9 kg.

2. Alpine Musk Deer
Moschus chrysogaster Page 455
马麝 Ma She
HB 800–900; SH 500–600; T 40–70; HF 270 GSL 140–170; Wt 9.6–13 kg.

3. Black Musk Deer
Moschus fuscus Page 456
黑麝 Hei She
SH < 500; GLS < 150; Wt 8 kg.

4. Siberian Musk Deer
Moschus moschiferus Page 457
原麝 Yuan She
HB 650–900; SH 560–610; T 40–60; GLS 130–160; Wt 8–12 kg.

1
2
3
4

1. Eurasian Elk
Alces alces Page 458
驼鹿 Tuo Lu
HB 2.0–2.9 m; SH 1.7–2.1 m; T 7–10 cm;
Wt 320–450 kg (male), 275–375 kg (female).

2. Reindeer
Rangifer tarandus (a, summer coat male; b, winter coat female) Page 459
驯鹿 Xun Lu
HB 1.2–2.2 m; SH 94–127 cm; T 7–21 cm;
Wt 91–272 kg.

3. Siberian Roe
Capreolus pygargus (a, winter coat male; b, summer coat female) Page 459
西伯利亚狍 Xiboliya Pao
HB 95–140 cm; SH 65–95 cm; T 20–40; E 128–140;
GLS 210–250; Wt 20–40 kg.

1
2a
2b
3a
3b

1. Red Deer
Cervus elaphus (a, winter coat male; b, summer coat female) Page 461
马鹿 Ma Lu
HB 165–265 cm; SH 100–150 cm; T 10–22 cm; GLS 40–45 cm; Wt 75–240 kg.

2. White-Lipped Deer
Przewalskium albirostris Page 465
白唇鹿 Baichun Lu
HB 155–210 cm; SH 120–140 cm (male), 115 cm (female); T 100–130; HF 330–520; E 210–280; GLS 340–404; Wt 180–230 kg (male), < 180 kg (female).

3. Eld's Deer
Rucervus eldii Page 466
坡鹿 Po Lu
HB 150–170 cm; SH 120–130 cm; T 220–250; E 136–170; HF 350–400; GLS 290; Wt 64–100 kg.

4. Sika Deer
Cervus nippon (a, summer coat female; b, winter coat male) Page 461
梅花鹿 Meihua Lu
HB 105–170 cm; SH 64–110 cm; T 80–180; GLS 260–290; Wt 40–150 kg.

5. Sambar
Rusa unicolor Page 466
水鹿 Shui Lu
HB 180–200 cm; SH 140–160 cm; T 250–280; E 180–220; GLS 370–390; Wt 185–260 kg.

1a
1b
2
3
4a
4b
5

1. Père David's Deer
Elaphurus davidianus Page 463
麋鹿 Mi Lu
HB 150–200 cm; SH 114 cm; T 500; GLS 400–420; Wt 135 kg.

2. Tufted Deer
Elaphodus cephalophus Page 462
毛冠鹿 Maoguan Lu
HB 85–170 cm; SH 49–72 cm; T 70–130; HF 440; E 80; GLS 166–190; Wt 15–28 kg.

3. Chinese Water Deer
Hydropotes inermis Page 467
獐 Zhang
HB 89–103 cm; SH 45–57 cm; T 60–70; GLS 150–170; Wt 14–17 kg.

4. Hog Deer
Axis porcinus Page 460
豚鹿 Tun Lu
HB 140–150 cm; SH 65–72 cm; T 17.5–21 cm; E 16–18 cm; Wt 70–110 kg.

1
3
2
4

1. Red Muntjac
Muntiacus muntjak Page 464
赤麂 Chi Ji
HB 98–120 cm; SH 50–72 cm; T 170–200; GLS 176–220; Wt 17–40 kg.

2. Reeve's Muntjac
Muntiacus reevesi Page 465
小麂 Xiao Ji
HB 64–90 cm; SH 40–49 cm; T 86–130; HF 210–223; E 85; GLS 146–164; Wt 11–16 kg.

3. Black Muntjac
Muntiacus crinifrons Page 464
黑麂 Hei Ji
HB 98–132 cm; SH 62–78 cm; T 165–240; HF 280; E 105; GLS 200–235; Wt 21–28.5 kg.

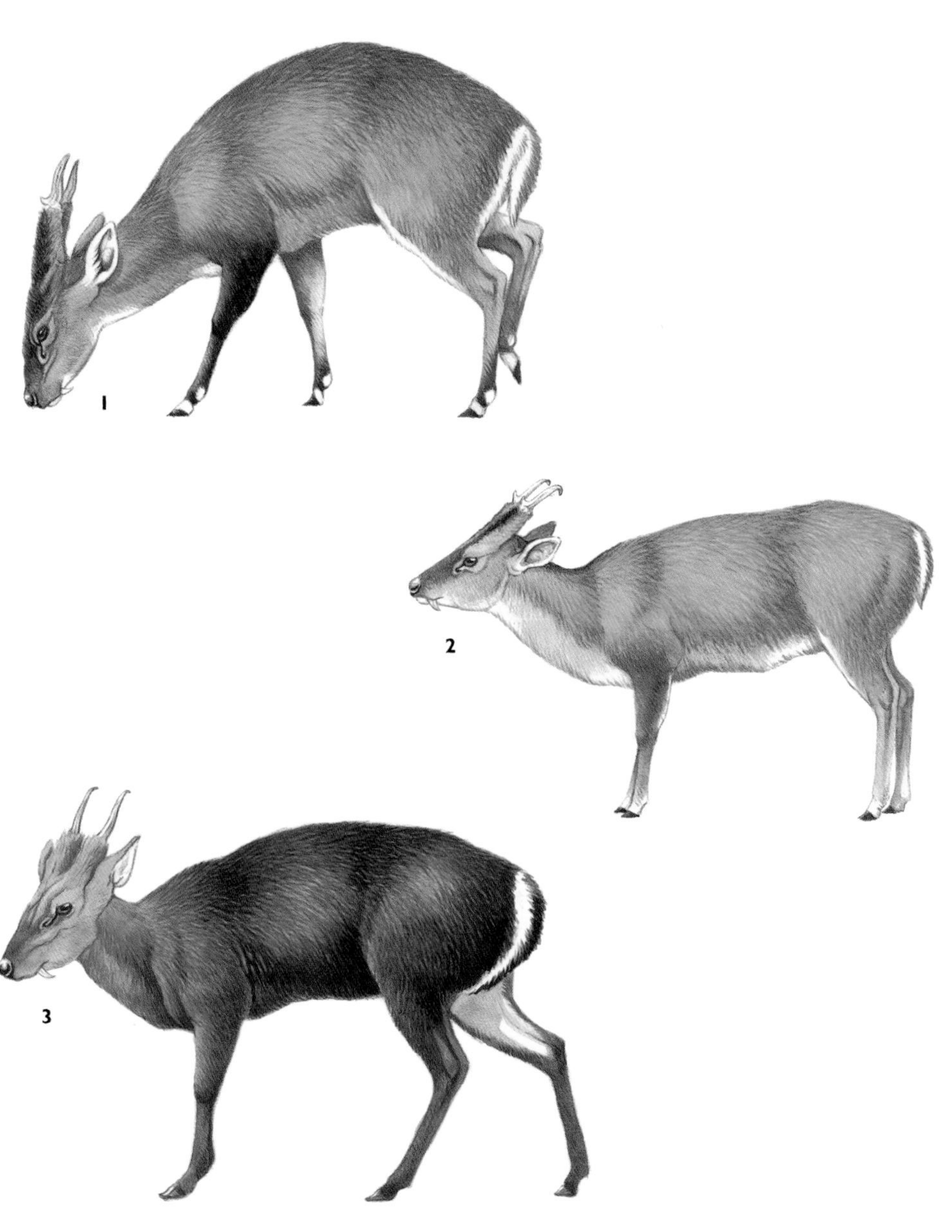
1
2
3

1. Tibetan Antelope
Pantholops hodgsonii (a, male; b, female) Page 479
藏羚 Zang Ling
HB 100–140 cm; SH 79–94; T 130–140; E 120–150; GLS 216–278; Wt 24–42 kg.

2. Goitered Gazelle
Gazella subgutturosa Page 468
鹅喉羚 E' hou Ling
HB 88–109 cm; SH 60–70 cm; T 120–175; GLS 170–215; Wt 29–42 kg.

3. Mongolian Gazelle
Procapra gutturosa Page 470
黄羊 Huang Yang
HB 108–160 cm; SH 54–84 cm; T 50–120; E 97; GLS 220–270; Wt 25–45 kg.

4. Tibetan Gazelle
Procapra picticaudata Page 470
藏原羚 Zang Yuanling
HB 91–105 cm; SH 54–65 cm; T 80–100; GLS 170–190; Wt 13–16 kg.

5. Przewalski's Gazelle
Procapra przewalskii Page 471
普氏原羚 Pushi Yuanling
HB 109–160 cm; SH 50–70 cm; T 70–120; GLS 185–220; Wt 17–32 kg.

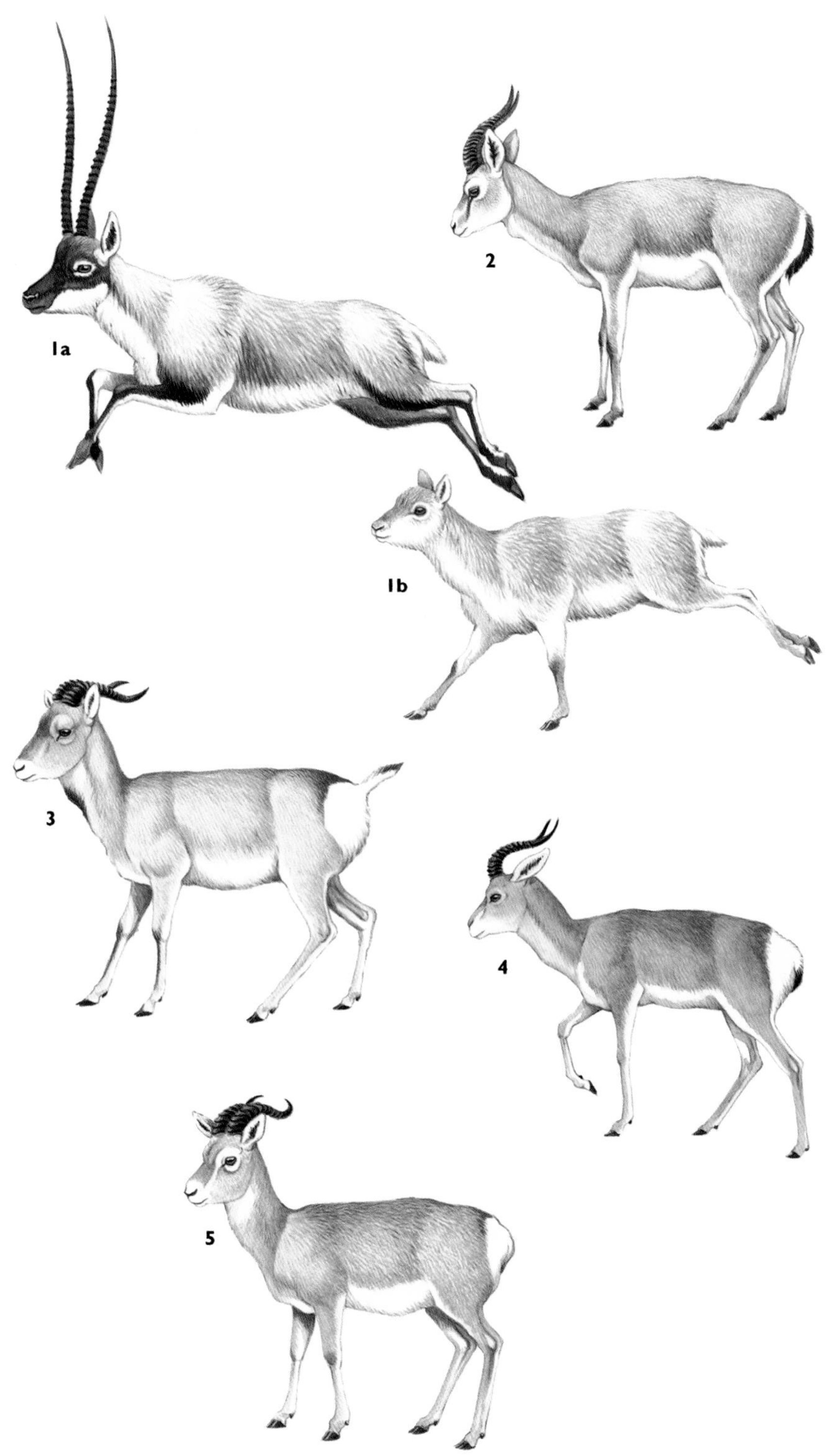
1a
2
1b
3
4
5

1. Steppe Saiga
Saiga tatarica Page 471
赛加羚羊 Saijia Lingyang
HB 100–140 cm; SH 60–80 cm; T 60–120; GLS 190–240; Wt 26–69 kg.

2. Gaur
Bos frontalis Page 472
野牛 Ye Niu
HB 250–330 cm; SH 165–220 cm; T 70–105 cm; E 30–35 cm; GLS 500; Wt 650–1,500 kg.

3. Yak
Bos grunniens Page 473
野牦牛 Ye Maoniu
HB 305–380 cm; SH 170–200 cm (males), 137–156 cm (females); T 100 cm; GLS 50 cm; Wt 535–821 kg (male), 306–338 kg (female).

4. Takin
Budorcas taxicolor (a, and b, contrasting color phases) Page 474
羚牛 Ling Niu
HB 170–220 cm; SH 107–140 cm; T 100–216; HF 267–444; E 101–149; GLS 350–460; Wt 250–600 kg.

1
2
3
4a
4b

1. Himalayan Thar
Hemitragus jemlahicus Page 477
喜马拉雅塔尔羊 Ximalaya Ta'eryang
HB 130–170 cm; SH 62–106 cm; T 90–120; Wt 50–108 kg.

2. Argali
Ovis ammon Page 479
盘羊 Panyang
Male: HB 180–200 cm; SH 110–125 cm; T 10–18; HF 43–50; E 10–15; GLS 290–360; Wt 95–140 kg rarely up to 180 kg.

3. Siberian Ibex
Capra sibirica Page 475
北山羊 Bei Shanyang
HB 115–170 cm; SH 65–105 cm; T 100–200; GLS 230–306; Wt 80–100 kg (male), 30–50 kg (female).

4. Blue Sheep
Pseudois nayaur Page 480
岩羊 Yanyang
Male: HB 120–165 cm; SH 69–91 cm; T 130–200; E 90–130; HF 70–100 cm; GLS 198–258; Wt 50–70 kg.

1
2
3
4

1. Red Goral
Naemorhedus baileyi Page 477
红斑羚 Hong Banling
HB 930–1,070; SH 570–610; T 80–100; E 95–106; HF 200–250; GLS 168–199; Wt 20–30 kg.

2. Long-Tailed Goral
Naemorhedus caudatus Page 477
中华鬣羚 Zhonghua Lieling
HB 1,060–1,200; SH 690–750; T 130–160; E 130–170; HF 270–320; Wt 32–42 kg.

3. Chinese Serow
Capricornis milneedwardsii Page 475
甘南鬣羚 Gannan Lieling
HB 140–170 cm; SH 90–100 cm; T 115–160; E 175–205; GLS 280–320; Wt 85–140 kg.

1
2
3

1. Dugong
Dugong dugon Page 157
儒艮 Rugen
HB 2.4–4.0 m; Wt 230–1,000 kg.

2. Yangtze River Dolphin
Lipotes vexillifer Page 483
白暨豚 Baiji Tun
HB to 2.2 m (males), to 2.5 m (females);
Wt 135–160 kg (males), 240 kg (females).

3. Indo-Pacific Humpback Dolphin
Sousa chinensis (a, white form;
b, spotted form) Page 482
中华白海豚 Zhonghuabai Haitun
HB 2.5 m; GLS 575; Wt 250 kg.

4. Finless Porpoise
Neophocaena phocaenoides Page 483
江豚 Jiang Tun
HB 1.0–2.3 m; Wt 25–50 kg.

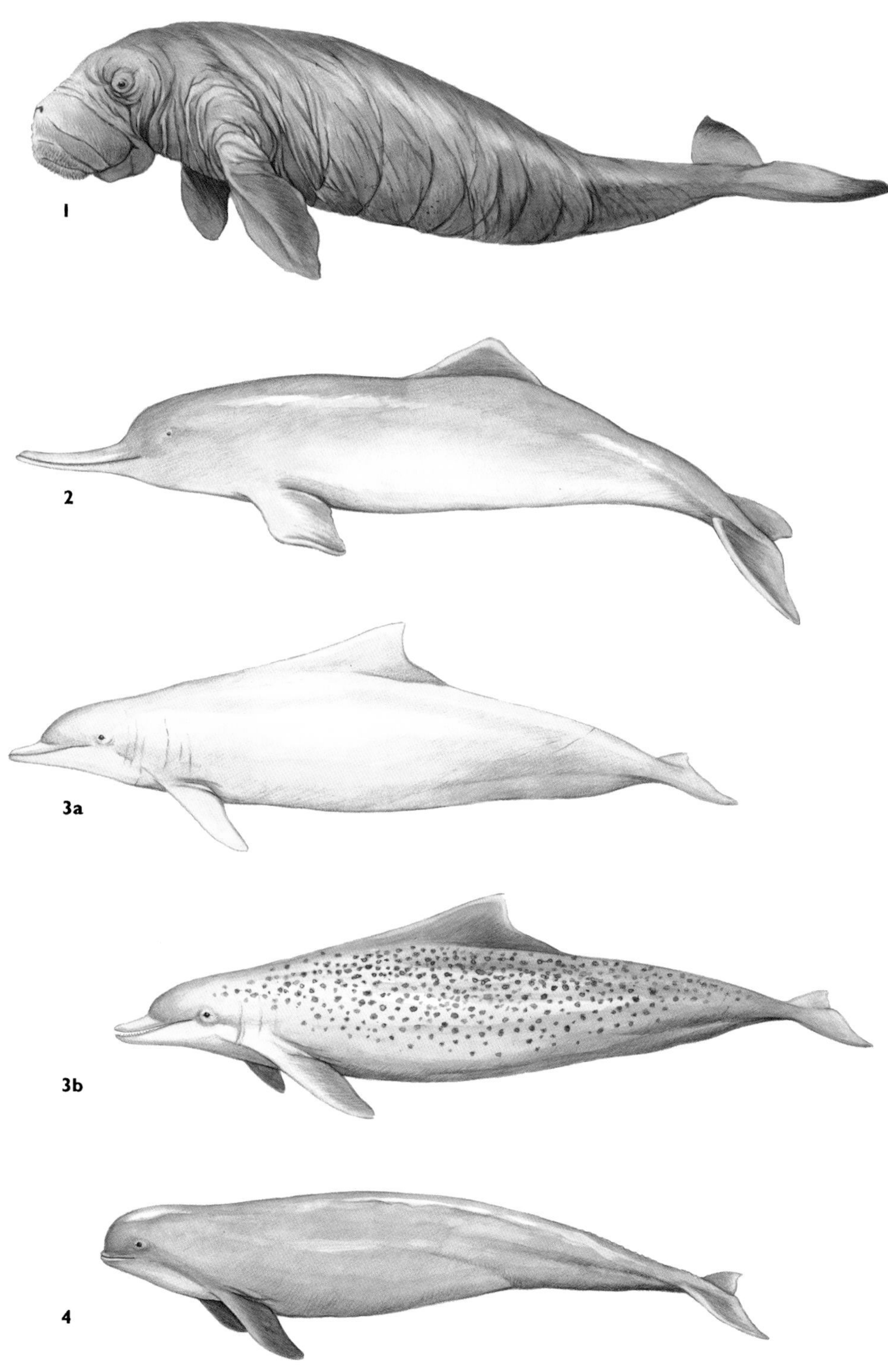
1
2
3a
3b
4

Taxonomic Descriptions

CLASS MAMMALIA

The Mammals

哺乳类 Burulei

Andrew T. Smith

Mammals belong to the class Mammalia, subphylum Vertebrata, phylum Chordata, kingdom Animalia. In spite of considerable variation in morphological structure among mammals, there is a suite of unique characteristics that define the class. Pelage, or hair, is present in at least some stage of development of all mammals. It completely covers the bodies of most species, although it may be restricted to specific areas in some forms or occur only during embryonic development in others (such as cetaceans). All young mammals are nourished with milk provided from mammary glands. A muscular diaphragm separates the lungs from the posterior body cavity. Mammals possess a four-chambered heart with only a left aortic arch (the right aortic arch is lost during development). Red blood cells lack nuclei at maturity in most species. And all mammals have three middle-ear bones (malleus, incus, and stapes), and a single (dentary) bone comprises the lower jaw. The jaw articulates with the squamosal bone of the cranium. The roof of the brain (the neopallium) in mammals is proportionately larger than in other vertebrates, and the midbrain has become divided into four prominences (the *corpora quadrigemina*), which integrate sight and hearing. Additionally, nearly all mammals are viviparous (except monotremes), quadrupedal (except bats, some bipedal species, and those aquatic forms that have developed front flippers and lost their hind limbs), and have an external ear opening surrounded by a well-developed pinna (although the pinna may be reduced or absent in some aquatic species). Mammals are primarily endothermic, maintaining relatively high and constant body temperatures most of the time. Consequently, many of their adaptations revolve around the necessity to acquire significant amounts of food. Thus, most mammals have heterodont dentition, with teeth specialized to their diet in nature.

Mammals evolved from a lineage of primitive synapsid reptiles. The pathway to modern mammals, passing through successive radiations of pelycosaurs, therapsids, and cynodonts, is complex. Mammal-like traits evolved in many of these lineages, and contemporary findings are still sorting out those that led directly to mammals. Some of the most important fossil records of these early mammal-like creatures have been discovered in China–such as the small shrew-like animal the size of a paper clip recently described from Yunnan Province and dated to 195 million years ago in the Early Jurassic (Luo 2001). Many of the forms formerly attributed to being mammals at this time ("Mesozoic mammals" such as triconodonts [Morganucodontidae], docodonts, symmetrodonts [Kuehneotheriidae], and the hotly debated Allotheria [multituberculates]) may have been Mammaliaformes and not true mammals. The monophyletic pathway to the lineage describing true mammals apparently passes through the symmetrodont lineage (whether they are considered true mammals or not), and forms representing true mammals appeared about 200 million years ago (Cifelli 2001). Thus the first two-thirds of mammalian history coincide with the tenure of dinosaurs. While many consider the last 65 million years of Earth history (the Cenozoic) as the age of mammals, the major branches of the mammalian evolutionary tree diverged during this early period (Wyss 2001). Eventually the three major branches of living mammals (monotremes, marsupials, and placentals) appeared and diversified in the exciting diversity of mammals found on Earth today.

The current (third) edition of *Mammal Species of the World* portrays living mammals as represented by 5,416 species in 1,229 genera in 29 orders (Wilson and Reeder 2005). Attempts to organize the higher categories of mammals have been varied, and an explosion of recent molecular and paleontological investigations has led to significant alterations in our efforts to characterize the phylogenetic relationships of mammals since the previous edition (Wilson and Reeder 1993). We follow the order of presentation of mammals in the third edition to describe the 556 mammals species in 14 orders that are found in China.

ORDER PROBOSCIDEA
Family Elephantidae

Genus *Elephas*—Elephants

长鼻目 Changbi Mu; 象科 Xiang Ke

象属 Xiang Shu—象 Xiang

Andrew T. Smith and John MacKinnon

The elephants are unmistakable. Current systematic work places elephants in the Afrotheria. There are two genera of elephants, one in Africa (*Loxodonta*) currently with two recognized species (Shoshani 2005), and one in Asia (*Elephas*) whose range includes China. The Asian Elephant is distinguished from the African forms by having smaller ears and a single lip on the end of its trunk, compared with two lips in African elephants. Dental formula: 1.0.3.3/0.0.3.3 = 26 (but tusk usually absent in female *Elephas*).

Key to the Chinese Orders of Mammalia

1.a.	Hind limbs absent; forelimbs paddlelike; tail greatly expanded laterally, flukelike; body largely hairless	2
b.	Both fore and hind limbs present; tail not as above; body usually covered with hair, sometimes sparsely, or with scaly plates	3
2.a.	Nostrils (or single nostril) located at top of head	Cetacea
b.	Nostrils located toward tip of snout	Sirenia
3.a.	Dorsal surface covered with hard scales; a few hairs present at the base of each scale, and sparse pelage covers underparts and other scaleless areas	Pholidota
b.	Dorsal and ventral surfaces (except tail and feet) lack visible scales, being covered with hairs either densely or sparsely	4
4.a.	Forelimbs modified to form wings	Chiroptera
b.	Forelimbs not winglike, consist of standard limb and foot elements of various shapes	5
5.a.	Nose modified into long proboscis (trunk)	Proboscidea
b.	Nose not modified into long proboscis	6
6.a.	Feet possess hooves	7
b.	Feet possess claws or nails	8
7.a.	Feet possess odd number of toes	Perissodactyla
b.	Feet possess even number of toes	Artiodactyla
8.a.	Feet possess flattened nails; digits on forefeet long, separated	Primates
b.	Feet possess pointed (blunt to sharp) claws	9
9.a.	Incisors (anterior teeth) in upper and lower jaws separated from premolar and molar ("cheek") teeth by a large, toothless gap (diastema)	10
b.	No large diastema present in either upper or lower jaws	11
10.a.	Behind enlarged incisors in upper jaw are a pair of very small, blunt, peglike teeth	Lagomorpha
b.	Not as above; single upper incisors	Rodentia
11.a.	Canines prominent, conical, long; cheek teeth never tritubercular or quadritubercular	Carnivora
b.	Canines usually indistinct; if large, not conical; cheek teeth tritubercular or quadritubercular	12
12.a.	Appearance squirrel-like, tail long and bushy; habits largely arboreal; lacks long vibrissae	Scandentia
b.	Not squirrel-like; fur short and soft or formed into spines	13
13.a.	Fur short and soft; zygomatic arch absent, incomplete, or weakly developed	Soricomorpha
b.	Fur long, may have long sharp spines over dorsal surface; zygomatic arch strongly developed	Erinaceomorpha

Asian Elephant PLATE 50
Elephas maximus Linnaeus, 1758 MAP 1
亚洲象 Yazhou Xiang

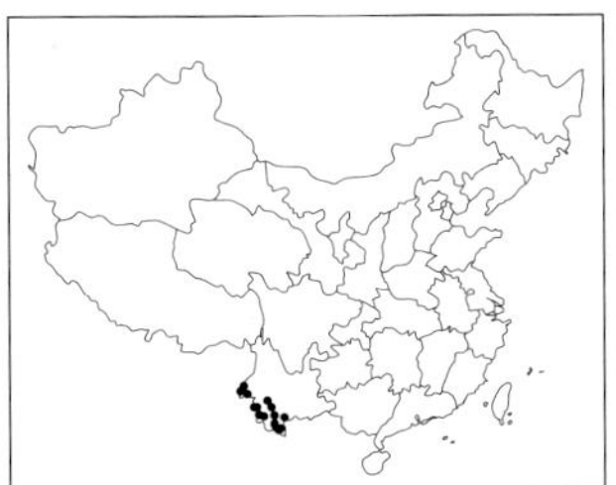
MAP 1. ASIAN ELEPHANT, *Elephas maximus*

Distinctive Characteristics: HB 5.5–6.5 m; SH 3.2 m (male), 2.5 m (female); T 1.2–1.5 m; Wt 4,160 kg (male), 2,720 kg (female). Uniquely large mammal with long proboscis, large triangular ears, thick gray skin with only a few bristly hairs (especially as tail tuft and on infants). Males have large ivory tusks; tusks of females at most protrude a few cm. Large rounded flat feet.

Distribution: There is evidence that elephants once ranged widely over much of S China, including Fujian, Guangdong, and Guangxi. Records indicate that they disappeared from S Fujian and N Guangdong during the 12th century (Song dynasty) but held on in Guangxi into the 17th century (Ming dynasty). The species is now confined to Xishuangbanna Prefecture of S Yunnan; extending to the Indian subcontinent including Sri Lanka, through Indochina, Malay Peninsula, Sumatra, and NE Borneo.

Natural History: The Asian Elephant inhabits lowland and hill forests (generally at elevations < 1,000 m) in evergreen and semievergreen tropical zone, often with bamboos. Eats a wide range of vegetation with a strong preference for grasses and palms. Raids fields of rice, sugar cane, bananas, and papayas. May consume over 200 kg of vegetation per day. Diurnal and nocturnal, but usually rests at midday. Lives in small matriarchal family herds. Males solitary, or two or three males may travel together. Several female-led families may congregate at favored salt licks and mud wallows. Herds visit water every day. Various low rumbling sounds and loud trumpeting vocalizations are used to maintain social contact. Males have large tusks used in fighting and defense, to move obstacles in the forest, and to excavate mineral-rich earth at salt licks. Single young (rarely twins) weighing about 100 kg are born at intervals of several years. Gestation lasts 18–22 months.

Conservation Status: Rare, restricted, and endangered by poaching and loss of habitat; also persecuted by farmers for raiding crops. While poaching continues, a ban on this activity is strictly enforced. There is evidence that the Chinese population has grown from approximately 100 in the 1970s, to 180 in the 1980s, to perhaps 150–250 by the mid-1990s (Duckworth and Hedges 1998). However, the sex ratio increasingly favors females, and an increasing percentage of males are tuskless because poaching is changing the gene pool. China RL—EN A1acd. China Key List—I. CITES—I. IUCN RL—EN A1cd ver. 2.3 (1994).

References: Duckworth and Hedges (1998); Feng and Zhang (2005); Gao (1981); Li and Wang (2003); Santiapillai and Jackson (1990); Sukumar (1989); Zhang and Wang (2003).

ORDER SIRENIA
Family Dugongidae
Genus *Dugong*—Dugongs
海牛目 **Hainiu Mu;** 儒艮科 **Rugen Ke**
儒艮属 **Rugen Shu**—儒艮 **Rugen**

Andrew T. Smith

These large herbivorous marine mammals are also in the Afrotheria. The order contains three families (one extinct) totaling five species and is characterized by paddlelike forelimbs, heavy bones, no hind limbs, and no dorsal fin. The dugongs (Dugongidae) can be distinguished from the other living family, the manatees (Trichechidae), by possessing an incisor (versus no functional incisors in manatees) and a notched tail (versus a spoon-shaped tail), and lacking nails on their flippers (versus flippers with nails in two of the three manatee species). The Chinese representative is in the monotypic Dugongidae.

Dugong
PLATE 61
Dugong dugon (Müller, 1776) MAP 2
儒艮 **Rugen**

Distinctive Characteristics: HB 2.4–4 m; Wt 230–1,000 kg. Body fusiform and hind limbs absent; head round; tail a deeply notched fluke with a crescent shape; forelimbs paddlelike and without nails. The short hair is distributed sparsely over the body, with the exception of dense bristles on the muzzle. Rostrum tip flat; nasal cavity quite large and positioned in middle of the skull; mandible thick; two incisors in upper jaw, those of males long and protruding. Dental formula: 2.0.3.3/3.1.3.3 = 36, although all the teeth are not present at once; premolars and first pair of molars are gradually lost as animals age. Skeletal structure extremely dense and heavy.

Distribution: East China and South China seas, at Guangdong, Behai City (Guangxi), Hainan, and Dashufang in S Taiwan; extending to the coasts of the Indian Ocean and SW Pacific Ocean.

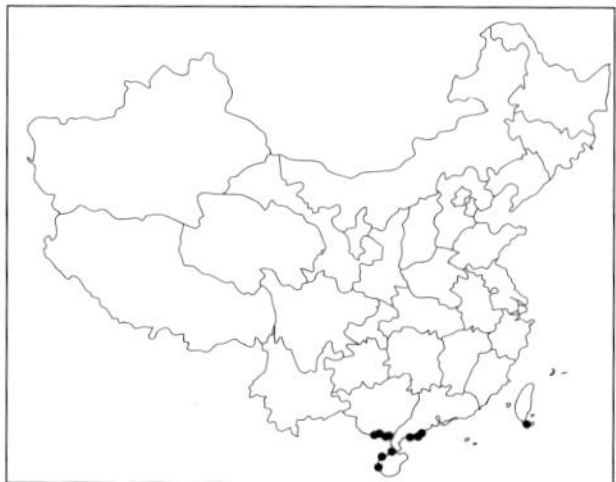

MAP 2. DUGONG, *Dugong dugon*

Natural History: Live in small groups in shallow coastal waters, although they can sometimes be found in deeper offshore waters. Most animals remain submerged for several minutes at a time, surfacing for a short time to breathe. Dugongs are not built for speed. They are herbivorous, subsisting largely on sea grass. Reproductive season primarily from June to September but may extend throughout the year. Males fight for access to females in a polygynous mating system. Gestation lasts 12–14 months. The single offspring is weaned at about 18 months but may remain with its mother for several years.

Conservation Status: While there may be up to 100,000 dugongs in the wild, they are endangered in China. The Taiwanese population is believed to have been extirpated; there have been no recent sightings on the island. The mainland population is very poorly known. In the mid-1980s, Wang and Sun (1986) stated that dugongs mostly occurred along the coast of Guanxi and W Guangdong, and rarely the coasts of Dianbai and Yangjang counties, Guangdong, in addition to the west coast of Hainan Island. However, most recent sightings have come only from Hainan (Marsh et al. 2002), although even there coastal development and harbor construction have eliminated key seagrass beds, causing dugongs to disappear. While dugongs have historically occurred in the Pearl River estuary, none have been seen in recent years in spite of intensive research on dolphins in this area. China RL—CR A1c; B1ab(i,iii)c + 2ab(i,iii)c; C; D; E. China Key List—I. CITES—I. IUCN RL—VU A1cd ver. 2.3 (1994).

References: Husar (1978); Marsh et al. (2002); Wang and Sun (1986); Zhou et al. (2003).

ORDER SCANDENTIA
Family Tupaiidae

Genus *Tupaia*—Tree Shrews
树鼩目 Shuqu Mu; 树鼩科 Shuqu Ke
树鼩属 Shuqu Shu—树鼩 Shuqu

Andrew T. Smith

In the annals of mammalogy, few other taxa have proved to be as difficult to classify as the Scandentia. They have been included with the Macroscelididae in the insectivore suborder Menotyphla, and within the primate suborder Prosimii. Most recent treatments consider these forms to represent an independent taxon most closely allied with the orders Primates, Dermoptera, and Chiroptera. These squirrel-like animals are distributed across SE Asia. Dental formula: 2.1.3.3/3.1.3.3 = 38; with large incisors, caniform; small canines; and broad upper molars. The facial region lacks long vibrissae and possesses large eyes. There are 5 genera and 20 species in the Scandentia; only a single species occurs in China (one of 15 species in the genus *Tupaia*). Stone (1995) reviews the conservation status of tree shrews.

Northern Tree Shrew

PLATE 1
MAP 3

Tupaia belangeri (Wagner, 1841)
北树鼩 Beishuqu

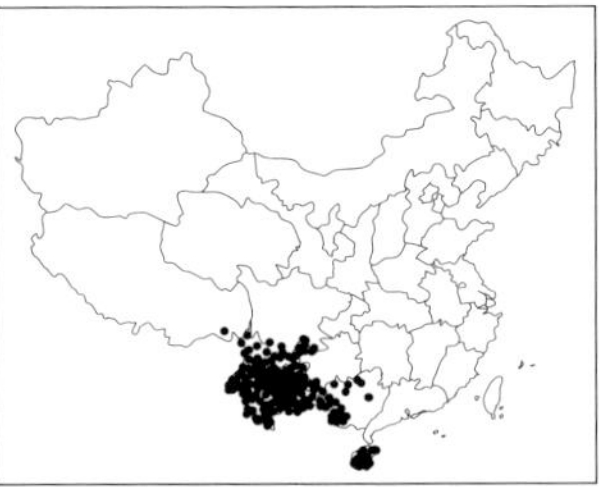

MAP 3. NORTHERN TREE SHREW, *Tupaia belangeri*

Distinctive Characteristics: HB 160–195; T 150–190; HF 36–45; E 12–20; GLS 41–49; Wt 110–185 g. Pelage olive green to dense brown; shoulder with faint vertical stripes. Tail bicolored, olive brown above and whitish underneath; tail hairs long, and overall the tail has the appearance of being flat. All five toes developed on feet; claws strong and sharp. The rostrum is elongated, and the ears are short and rounded. 2N = 62 (Wang 1987).

Distribution: S China; extending south through Thailand, Myanmar, India, Cambodia, Laos, Vietnam, and associated coastal islands. Eight subspecies in China: (1) *T. b. chinensis* Anderson, 1879; Yunnan, SW Sichuan; (2) *T. b. gaoligongensis* Wang, 1987; NW Yunnan; (3) *T. b. lepcha* Thomas, 1922; S Xizang; (4) *T. b. modesta* Allen, 1906; Hainan; (5) *T. b. tonquinia* Thomas, 1925; SW Guangxi; (6) *T. b. versurae* Thomas, 1922; SE Xizang; (7) *T. b. yaoshanensis* Wang, 1987; E Guangxi; (8) *T. b. yunalis* Thomas, 1914; SE Yunnan, S Guizhou.

Natural History: Occupies tropical to subtropical forests from low elevations up to 3,000 m. Lives in tree holes (not of its own making). Arboreal and primarily crepuscular, but may be active at any time. Omnivorous, feeding on fruits and seeds in addition to insects, small vertebrates, and bird eggs. Territorial. Mates from March through August. Estrus lasts approximately 10 days, and gestation about one and a half months. Females produce one or two litters of two to four young per year. As tree shrews are nonrodent, primatelike, small mammals, there is increasing interest in using them to establish models for medical and biological research (Cao et al. 2003).

Comments: *T. glis* is found south of 10° N; *belangeri* has been attributed to *glis* in some earlier treatments. The two forms are sympatric in S Thailand, confirming that they should be recognized as separate species.

Conservation Status: China RL—LC.

References: Cao et al. (2003); Wang (1987); Zou et al. (1987).

Order Primates—Primates

灵长目 Lingzhang Mu 灵长类 Lingzhanglei

John MacKinnon

The order Primates includes humankind and its nearest relatives, including apes, monkeys, lemurs, and lorises. Most species have five digits on each limb, usually with an opposable first digit and mostly with flattened nails rather than claws. Brain is well developed. Uterus bifurcate and only two pectoral mammae are present. Primates have two sets of teeth, the deciduous juvenile set being later replaced by permanent adult teeth. Upper canines, especially in males, are generally tusk-shaped. Molars with blunt cusps. There are two suborders of Primates, the

Key to the Chinese Families of Primates

1.a. Size small (adult weight < 2 kg); tail short; eye socket confluent with temporal fossa; second hind toe has long grooming claw — Lorisidae

b. Size medium to large; forelegs shorter than or about equal length to hind legs; normal stance quadrupedal with long to short tail — Cercopithecidae

c. Size medium; forelegs much longer than hind legs; normal posture hanging by arms with spine vertical; tail absent — Hylobatidae

Strepsirrhini with seven families, one of which (Lorisidae) is found in China; and the Haplorrhini with eight families, two of which (Cercopithecidae, Hylobatidae) are found in China (Groves 2001; 2005). The status of primate research in China has been reviewed by Ji and Jiang (2004). The systematics of Asian primates has been outlined by Brandon-Jones et al. (2004).

Family Lorisidae—Lorises

懒猴科 Lanhou Ke—懒猴 Lanhou

Lorises are compact small nocturnal primates with flat faces and large reflective eyes. Arms and legs slender and about equal in length. They have short tails, and their short ears are covered in fur. Second digit of forearm is reduced; second digit of hind leg possesses a claw. Rostrum long. Dental formula: 2.1.3.3/2.1.3.3 = 36. Upper incisors are small and separated from each other to form a comb. Upper canine is long, but lower canine resembles incisors. Molar cusps arranged in a "W" pattern. Originally called Loridae, but the commonly used form Lorisidae was conserved by Opinion 1995 of the International Commission on Zoological Nomenclature. The Lorisidae contains five genera and a total of nine species; most forms are African, but two genera occur in Asia, of which only *Nycticebus* reaches China.

Genus *Nycticebus*—Slow Lorises

蜂猴属 Fenghou Shu—蜂猴 Fenghou

Nycticebus differs significantly from other genera of Lorisidae, bearing a compact form and with short limbs. The central pair of upper incisors is relatively large, and the first premolar is canine-shaped and longer than other premolars; anterior and posterior cusps on outer side of molars are very conspicuous; protocones on inner side are also large. Short thick fur; vestigial tail; grasping hands. Of three species, two occur in China (Ji and Jiang 2004).

Bengal Slow Loris PLATE 1

Nycticebus bengalensis (Lacépède, 1800) MAP 4

蜂猴 Feng Hou

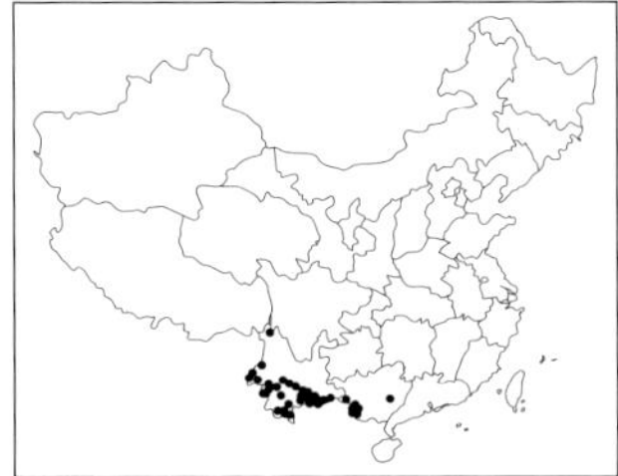

MAP 4. BENGAL SLOW LORIS, *Nycticebus bengalensis*

Distinctive Characteristics: HB 260–380; T 22–25; E 20–25; GLS 61–68; Wt 1–2 kg. Medium-sized nocturnal primate with very fluffy pelage. Dark brown stripe down back, short fluffy tail, and broad flat face with large eyes and moist rhinarium. General color varies from whitish to pale yellowish brown. The big toe on the hind foot is set apart from the other toes, allowing for greater gripping power. Second digit on hands is reduced in size, and second toe has a long curved claw used for scratching (fig. 5). The Bengal Slow Loris is much larger, paler, and has a more pronounced dark dorsal stripe than the Pygmy Slow Loris, also found in S China.

Distribution: Occurs only in tropical regions of S Yunnan (Xishuangbanna and Lincang) and S Guangxi; extending to NE India and Indochina.

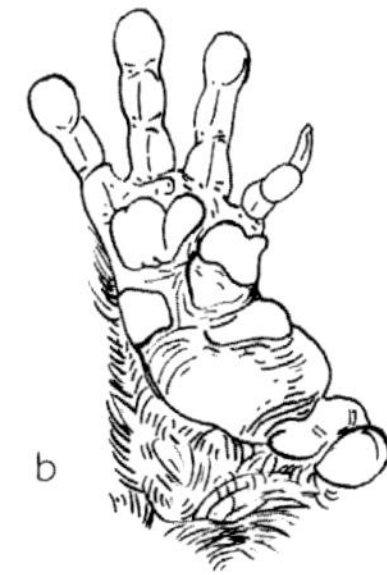

Figure 5. Feet of the Bengal Slow Loris showing the reduced second digit and enlarged and separated big toe (a = front foot; b = hind foot).

Key to the Chinese Species of *Nycticebus*

1.a. Size larger (adults > 800 gm); hair thick and fluffy; color brown with blackish dorsal stripe *Nycticebus bengalensis*

b. Size smaller (adults < 600 gm); hair thinner and less fluffy; color orange brown with thin brown dorsal stripe becoming pale on crown *Nycticebus pygmaeus*

Natural History: Inhabits tropical forest, scrub, bamboo thickets, and orchards. Occurs in both evergreen and deciduous formations. Feeds mostly on large insects such as katydids and crickets, but also eats fruits and some young leaves and buds. Occasionally catches small birds, lizards, or larger prey. Strictly nocturnal. Mostly seen alone, moving slowly and cautiously within the canopy or in small trees. Can walk quite fast when crossing the ground from one tree to another. Sleeps by day curled up in a ball in dense vegetation or tree hole. Both sexes are territorial and mark territories with urine. Ranges of different sexes overlap, and animals may engage in social grooming. The large eyes possess pronounced tapeta lucida, giving the animal excellent night vision. The animal stalks prey by slow, stealthy movements, then grabs with front paws in a fast and accelerating move followed by a bite. Second digit on each hind foot has an elongated toilet claw used for grooming; other digits have flat nails. Estrous females emit a loud whistle that attracts males. Gestation lasts about six months. Single young, or rarely twins, cling on their mother for about three months but may be "parked" on a branch while their mother forages alone.
Conservation Status: China RL—EN A2cd; B1ab(iii). China Key List—I. CITES—II. IUCN RL—DD ver 2.3 (1994).
References: Groves (1971; 1998).

Pygmy Slow Loris

PLATE I
MAP 5

Nycticebus pygmaeus Bonhote, 1907
倭蜂猴 Wo Fenghou

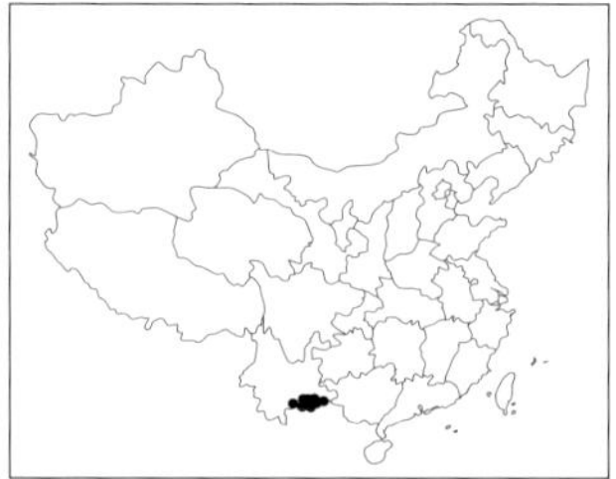

MAP 5. PYGMY SLOW LORIS, *Nycticebus pygmaeus*

Distinctive Characteristics: HB 210–260; T 10; GLS < 55; Wt 250–800 g. Small rufous-orange-colored loris. In winter, grayer, with light dark dorsal stripe and curly hair; in summer, without dark dorsal stripe and with little curly hair. 2N = 50.
Distribution: Only recorded in SE Yunnan, however, it is unclear if these are locally wild-caught animals or animals brought into the country from Vietnam in the wildlife trade; extending into NE Laos, Vietnam, and E Cambodia to east of the Mekong River.

Natural History: Inhabits low-lying evergreen forest, secondary forest, and scrub. Diet consists of insects, fruits, young leaves, and presumably small vertebrates. Also known to gouge trees and eat the resulting gum exudate. Behavior similar to that of the Bengal Slow Loris.
Comments: There has been significant confusion with records assigned to *N. intermedius*, although it is now considered to be the winter form of *N. pygmaeus*. However, it is possible that another form, not yet described, is sympatric with the Pygmy Slow Loris.
Conservation Status: China RL—EN A2cd; B1ab(iii); D. China Key List—I. CITES—II. IUCN RL—VU A1cd ver 2.3 (1994).
References: Groves (1971; 1998); Tan and Drake (2001).

Family Cercopithecidae—Old World Monkeys and Baboons

猴科 Hou Ke—猴类 Houlei

The suborder Haplorrhini is commonly divided into three infraorders containing the tarsiers, New World monkeys (Platyrrhini), and Old World monkeys (Catarrhini), respectively. The catarrhine lineage is further divided into two superfamilies: the Cercopithecoidea and the Hominoidea. Within the Cercopithecoidea is the single family Cercopithecidae, containing two subfamilies, the Cercopithecinae and Colobinae, and representatives of both are found in China. In some treatments these subfamilies are treated as separate families. The Cercopithecidae are medium-large apes and monkeys, with tails and limbs equal in length or hind limbs slightly longer than fore limbs. Dental formula: 2.1.2.3/2.1.2.3 = 32; middle pair of incisors larger than lateral pair; canines of male usually tusk-shaped; premolar with a pair of cusps, molar with two pairs, but rear of last molar with an additional cusp, thus five.

Subfamily Cercopithecinae—Old World Monkeys

猴亚科 Hou Yake—猴类 Houlei

The Cercopithecinae represents the main branch of Old World monkeys, including many African genera such as mangabeys, baboons, and guenons. Of 10 total genera, only one, *Macaca* (the macaques), reaches Asia. Quadrupedal, omnivorous monkeys with both arboreal and terrestrial abilities. Tails long to short. Socially, most live in large multimale groups; weakly territorial.

Key to the Chinese Subfamilies of Cercopithecidae

1.a.	Tail < HB length; with cheek pouch	Cercopithecinae
b.	Tail > HB length; no cheek pouch	Colobinae

Key to the Chinese Species of *Macaca*

1.a.	Tail < 100 mm; superior margins of orbits confluent, forming strong superciliary arch	2
b.	Tail > 100 mm; superior margins of orbits not usually confluent and superciliary arch weak	3
2.a.	Color dark brown above, off-white ventrally, thick and woolly; skull narrow; glans short	*Macaca thibetana*
b.	Color brown above, ventrally paler but little contrast and not woolly; skull short and broad with sagital crest; glans slender	*Macaca arctoides*
3.a.	Hairs on crown normal; face short	4
b.	Hairs on crown form circular cap; face long	5
4.a.	Dorsal hair and tail orange contrasting with otherwise brown pelage; tail not shaggy	*Macaca mulatta*
b.	Dorsal hair dark brown; tail blackish with shaggy hair	*Macaca cyclopis*
5.a.	Hair on crown short, forming dark cap; tail sparsely haired	*Macaca leonina*
b.	Hair on crown long and brown; tail well haired	*Macaca assamensis*

Genus *Macaca*—Macaques

猕猴属 Mihou Shu—猕猴 Mihou

Macaques are highly intelligent, versatile monkeys. They are to varying degrees adapted to terrestrial life with their quadrupedal stance and reduced tail length. They usually jump to the ground to flee predators rather than stay in the canopy. Some species can swim. They live in large multimale groups. Females show a bright red face and ischial swellings to indicate oestrus. Diet is omnivorous, and most are wily crop raiders. Typical pelage color is agouti brown. Possess cheek pouches. Upper canines of males strong, with a groove on the labial surface. Of 21 species of *Macaca*, 6 occur in China. A seventh species, the Long-tailed Macaque (*M. fascicularis*), has been introduced into Hong Kong and now ranges feral there where it hybridizes with *M. mulatta*. The evolutionary phylogeny of *Macaca* using chromosomes and molecular techniques has been investigated by Tosi et al. (2000; 2003).

Stump-Tailed Macaque

PLATE 2

Macaca arctoides

(Geoffroy Saint-Hilaire, 1831) MAP 6

短尾猴 Duanwei Hou

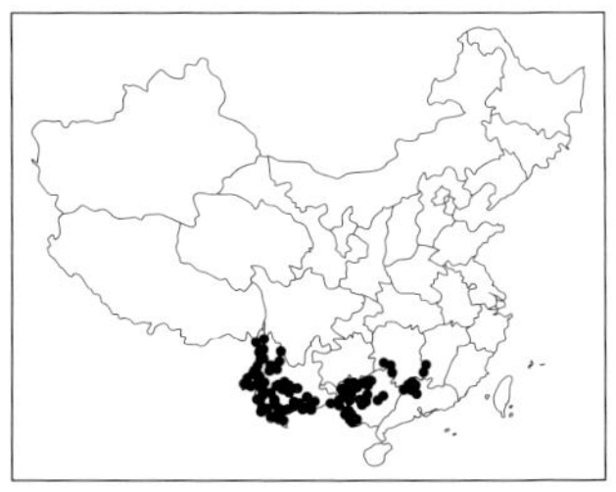

MAP 6. STUMP-TAILED MACAQUE, *Macaca arctoides*

Distinctive Characteristics: HB 485–650; T 45–50; HF 145–177; GLS 120–157; Wt 7 kg (male), 5 kg (female). Pelage is dark brown, varying from blackish to reddish. The face is bare and reddish brown in color, becoming bright red when excited or in oestrus. Tail is very short (ca. 10% of HB length), so short that the species sits on its tail. Skull is comparatively wide and has pronounced brow ridges.

Distribution: SW China, generally south of 30° latitude; extending to Bhutan, Assam, Myanmar, Indochina to N Malay Peninsula. Two subspecies in China: (1) *M. a. brunneus* Anderson, 1871; Yunnan; (2) *M. a. melli* (Matschie, 1912); Guizhou, Guangxi, Guangdong, Fujian.

Natural History: Occurs in upland forests in mountainous regions. Feeds on fruits, seeds, insects, small vertebrates, and young leaves. Regularly raids crops for maize, rice, and potatoes. As in other macaques, has cheek pouches to carry food while foraging. Lives in multimale groups of up to 50 individuals, occupying very large ranges and sometimes moving from one hill range to another. Female face and bare skin around ischial callosities become red during oestrus. Mating is baboon-style with male grasping the female's legs with his feet. Single births occur at about one- to two- year intervals. Males form affiliations with infants and sometimes care for them.

Conservation Status: China RL—VU A2cd + 3cd. China Key List—II. CITES—II. IUCN RL—VU A1cd ver 2.3 (1994).

References: Fooden (1990); Wu (1995)

Assam Macaque

PLATE 2

Macaca assamensis (M'Clelland, 1840) MAP 7

熊猴 Xiong Hou

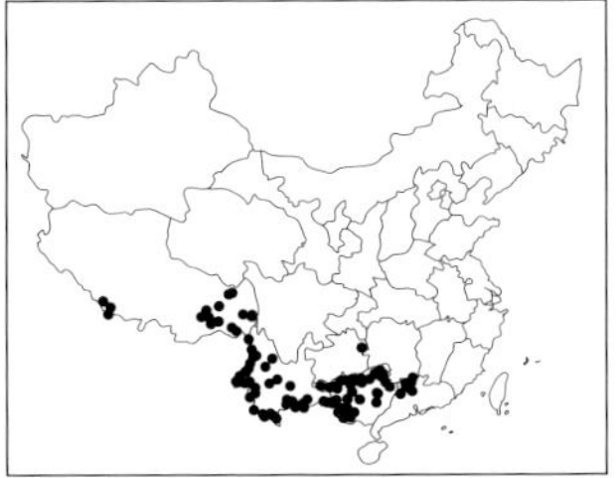

MAP 7. ASSAM MACAQUE, *Macaca assamensis*

Distinctive Characteristics: HB 515–665; T 170–250; HF 155–175; E 35–37; GLS 131–159; Wt 6–12 kg (male),

5 kg (female). A brown, short-tailed macaque with bare brown face. Distinguished from the Rhesus Macaque by gray rather than rufous hindquarters and hair extending up to callosities. Distinguished from Northern Pig-tailed Macaque (but not from Rhesus) by its hairy, pendulous tail. Slightly smaller, longer-tailed, and paler than the Tibetan Macaque. Tail much longer than the Stump-tailed Macaqueis. Sagittal crest of skull conspicuous; face long, nose flat.
Distribution: SW and S China; extending to E Himalayas, Bangladesh, Bhutan, and Assam through Myanmar and through N Indochina as far south as Tenassarim and W Thailand. Three subspecies in China: (1) *M. a. assamensis* (M'Clelland, 1940); Yunnan and SE Xizang; (2) *M. a. coolidgei* Osgood, 1932; Yunnan, SW Guangxi; Guizhou, Guangdong; (3) *M. a. pelops* (Hodgson, 1840); SW Xizang.
Natural History: Occurs in both evergreen and deciduous forests in hill and mountain terraine. Feeds on fruits, young leaves, insects, and small vertebrates. Typical diurnal, quadrupedal macaque. Lives in small groups of 10–15 animals usually with only one adult male per group; sexually dimorphic. Travels mostly on ground and spends long periods resting and grooming on ground or rocky terrain, but feeds mostly in trees and bushes. Has large cheek pouches for carrying food while foraging. Female posterior becomes red during oestrus. Single births occur at about one-year intervals.
Conservation Status: China RL—VU A2cd + 3cd. China Key List—I. CITES—II. IUCN RL—VU A1cd ver 2.3 (1994).
References: Fooden (1982).

Formosan Rock Macaque

Macaca cyclopis (Swinhoe, 1863) MAP 8
台湾猴 Taiwan Hou

MAP 8. FORMOSAN ROCK MACAQUE, *Macaca cyclopis*

Distinctive Characteristics: HB 360–450; T 260–456; GLS 96–117; Wt 4–5 kg. Typical pink-faced macaque with a medium-length tail and grayish brown pelage. Similar to Rhesus Macaque, but grayer with dark tail. Some rufous on crown. Head round, face flat; cheek teeth smaller than those of Rhesus Macaque.
Distribution: Taiwan (most common in NE and SW parts). Endemic.
Natural History: Mostly confined to main mountain chain and wild coastlines. Eats fruits, leaves, seeds, insects, crustaceans, and small vertebrates. Diurnal and quadrupedal; lives in small to medium-sized, multimale groups containing up to 60 individuals. Due to population reduction in recent years, most groups are small and may contain only a single male. Habits similar to those of other macaques. Red perineum swells in oestrous females. Reaches maturity at five to six years. Single young are born and stay with their mother for about two years.
Conservation Status: China RL—EN B1ab(i,iii). China Key List—I. CITES—II. IUCN RL—VU A1cd ver 2.3 (1994).
References: Masui et al. (1986).

Northern Pig-Tailed Macaque

Macaca leonina (Blyth, 1863) PLATE 2 MAP 9
北豚尾猴 Beitunwei Hou

MAP 9. NORTHERN PIG-TAILED MACAQUE, *Macaca leonina*

Distinctive Characteristics: HB 440–620; T 120–180; GLS 111–142; Wt 11–14 kg. Powerful stocky macaque with short, sparsely haired tail. Tail is normally pendulous but held erect at times of high excitement. General color an agouti brown. Sexual dimorphism is high, and males have a broad ruff of grayish hair around face with a concave dark patch on their crown caused by shorter vertical hairs. The bare face is generally pink, but bluish above the eyes; males give threat signals by raising their eyebrows to give a blue flash. Supraorbital crest of skull inconspicuous; posterior margin of last upper molar has small cusp.
Distribution: W Yunnan (Chinese records from Xizang are probably misidentified Rhesus Macaques); extending to N Indochina and Bangladesh to Assam as far north as Brahmaputra River.
Natural History: Inhabits tropical and subtropical evergreen and semievergreen forests in hilly terrain. Eats fruits, leaves, shoots, and some insects, small animals, and eggs. Lives in large multimale troops, often of 30 or more animals, which range over very large home ranges of many square kilometers. Troops feed in trees but travel mostly on the ground. Dispersed groups maintain contact with low hoots and grunts. When alarmed, animals drop from trees and flee on ground. The species is a serious and wily crop raider especially of maize fields. Males can be aggressive and have been known to kill dogs. A single young is produced following a gestation of 171 days.
Comments: Included with *M. nemestrina* in many accounts.

Conservation Status: China RL–EN A1cd; B1ab(i, iii); D. China Key List–I (as *M. nemestrina*). CITES–II. IUCN RL–VU A1cd ver 2.3 (1994).
References: Fooden (1975); Groves (2001).

Rhesus Macaque

PLATE 2
MAP 10

Macaca mulatta (Zimmerman, 1780)
猕猴 Mi Hou

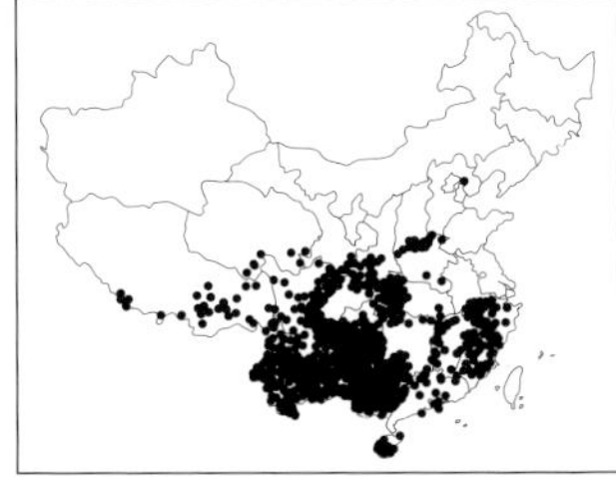

MAP 10. RHESUS MACAQUE, *Macaca mulatta*

Distinctive Characteristics: HB 430–600; T 150–320; HF 140–167; GLS 95–122; Wt 7–10 kg (male), 5–6 kg (female). Medium-sized brown macaque with moderate sexual dimorphism. Pelage light agouti brown with contrasting orange tinge on cap, lower back, and base of tail. Tail medium length and not very fluffy. Cranium relatively round, without sagittal crest.
Distribution: From the eastern valleys of the Tibetan Plateau to the east coast, Hainan Island, and as far north as Beijing in the east; introduced into Hong Kong; extending to N Indochina, N Thailand, N India, and Afghanistan. Six subspecies, many of them dubious (see Comments), have been described in China: (1) *M. m. brevicaudatus* (Elliot, 1913); Hainan; (2) *M. m. lasiotus* (Gray, 1868); N Yunnan, W Sichuan, S Gansu, NE Qinghai; (3) *M. m. littoralis* (Elliot, 1909); Anhui, Zhejiang, Jiangxi, Fujian, Hunan, Hubei, Guizhou; (4) *M. m. siamica* Kloss, 1917; Yunnan (except N); (5) *M. m. tcheliensis* (Milne-Edwards, 1872); N Henan, Shanxi; (6) *M. m. vestita* (Milne-Edwards, 1892); S and SE Xizang.
Natural History: Inhabits forests, woodlands, coastal scrub, and rocky areas with scrub and trees. Feeds on fruits, leaves, shoots, insects and small vertebrates, and eggs. Lives in large multimale troops of up to 50 animals. Troops occupy large to small home ranges, depending upon the suitability of habitat. In areas where monkeys are provisioned such as S Hainan and Guangdong, high densities and considerable overlap of group ranges can occur. Noisy squabbles over food, females, dominance, or territory are accompanied by barking and fear squeals. Animals are quite terrestrial but also feed in trees. On Hong Kong where *M. fascicularis* has also been introduced, mixed-species groups and hybridization have occurred.
Comments: Fooden (2000) concluded that no subspecies were recognizable, but Melnick et al. (1993) detected distinct eastern and western clades based on mitochondrial DNA such that Rhesus from the east were more similar to Formosan and Japanese macaques than to Rhesus from the west. This division is approximately at the Brahmaputra River. Certainly Chinese Rhesus from Xizang (*vestita*) are larger, darker, and grayer than Rhesus from the rest of China (forms previously identified as *brevicaudatus, siamica, littoralis, lasiotus*, and *tcheliensis*; Groves 2005), all of which should probably be referred to as *mulatta*.
Conservation Status: China RL–VU A2cd. China Key List–II. CITES–II. IUCN RL–LR/nt ver 2.3 (1994).
References: Fooden (2000); Jiang et al. (1991); Melnick et al. (1993); Pan et al. (1993); Peng et al. (1993); Qu et al. (1993).

Tibetan Macaque

PLATE 2
MAP 11

Macaca thibetana (Milne-Edwards, 1870)
藏酋猴 Zangqiu Hou

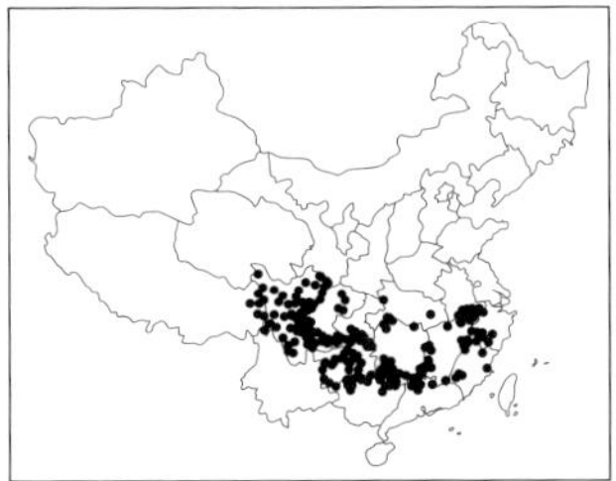

MAP 11. TIBETAN MACAQUE, *Macaca thibetana*

Distinctive Characteristics: HB 490–710; T 60–100; GLS 121–168; Wt 10–25 kg. Large, stocky, short-tailed macaque. Hair is long and thick; dark brown on back and paler buff-white ventrally. The bare face is generally pink, but red in adult females. Skull narrower and longer than that of *M. arctoides*.
Distribution: Wide ranging across C, SE China. Endemic. Three subspecies: (1) *M. t. huangshanensis* Jiang and Wang, 1999; Anhui; (2) *M. t. quizhouensis* Jiang and Wang, 1999; Guizhou; (3) *M. t. thibetana* (Milne-Edwards, 1870); W Sichuan, NE Yunnan.
Natural History: Inhabits tropical and subtropical forests of mountainous regions up to 3,000 m. Eats fruits, young leaves, insects and small birds, and eggs. Lives in large multimale troops. A single dominant male leads in defense and arbitrates disputes. Low levels of aggression are expressed among group members, and females display consistently high levels of affiliative behavior based on kinship. Troops travel both through trees and on ground. Food is collected mostly in trees, but increasingly monkeys exposed to tourists have learned to pester visitors for food and eat off the ground. Breeding occurs throughout the year, primarily between January and August, and concentrated in March and April. Females, on average, become sexually active in their fourth year. Generally a single young is born every two years; gestation is approximately 70 days. Males deliver a significant proportion of the parental care of young. The thick coat enables the species to survive the extremes of winter weather in the mountains.

Conservation Status: Widespread, but shy where persecuted. There are large groups of Tibetan macaques in Emei Mountain of Sichuan and Huang Shan Mountain of Anhui. China RL—VU A1cd. China Key List—II. CITES—II. IUCN RL—LR/cd ver 2.3 (1994).
References: Berman et al. (2004); Cui and Zhao (1999); Fooden (1983); Fooden et al. (1994); Jiang et al. (1996); Xiong (1998).

Subfamily Colobinae—Leaf Eating Monkeys

疣猴亚科 **Youhou Yake**—疣猴 **Youhou**

The Colobinae are the leaf-eating specialists among the Old World monkeys. These animals are typically rather arboreal with arms nearly as long as their legs, and the ability to travel through trees in a semibrachiating manner. They have long intestines and sacculated stomachs for digesting cellulose. All species have long tails that are used for balance. Socially, colobines live in single-male groups or aggregations of such groups. Some species are strongly territorial. Of 10 genera, 3 occur in China.

Genus *Rhinopithecus*—Snub-nosed Monkeys

仰鼻猴属 **Yangbihou Shu**—仰鼻猴 **Yangbihou**

Rhinopithecus is a specialized group of colobines. Three species occur in China. All species have a sacculated stomach that allows them to digest very coarse and woody materials. This allows them to live at higher altitudes and in harsher environments than other primates, where they occur in huge aggregate troops sometimes numbered in hundreds of animals together. They are large monkeys and have a special upturned form of nose and small lappets at the side of their mouth. All three Chinese species were formerly classed as a single species, but the differences between them are too great for this arrangement to stand (Li et al. 2004). The fourth species of *Rhinopithecus*, the Tonkin Snub-nosed Monkey (*R. avunculus*), lives not far over the Chinese border in N Vietnam but has a very limited range and appears never to have occurred in China, although it has been found in trade consignments crossing the border destined for Chinese kitchens. Another species of the related genus *Pygathrix* is the Douc Langur, which has been recorded from Hainan in the 19th century. The record is probably erroneous, but even if the species did formerly occur there it is clear that it does not today.

Black Snub-Nosed Monkey

Rhinopithecus bieti Milne-Edwards, 1897 — PLATE 3, MAP 12

滇金丝猴 **Dian Jinsihou**

MAP 12. BLACK SNUB-NOSED MONKEY, *Rhinopithecus bieti*

Distinctive Characteristics: HB 740–830; T 510–720; GLS 104–135; Wt 17 kg (male), 12 kg (female). Large monkey with very long tail. Back, sides, sides of limbs, hands, feet, and tail all grayish black. Cheeks, ears, side of neck, ventrum, and inner sides of limbs white. Bare facial skin is pink with black patch on bluish nose. Lips are deep reddish pink. Infants are white and become yellowish before turning gray. Adult male has long hair on back and crown.
Distribution: SW China; confined to montane forests of Yun Ling mountains in NW Yunnan and extreme SE Xizang to west of Yangtze River and east of Mekong River. Endemic.

Key to the Chinese Genera of Colobinae

1.a.	Size very large; tail long; nose vertically compressed. Nasal bones reduced; nasal tip and nostrils anodal. Rostrum short; muzzle massive. Male with lateral lappets on mouth. Sexual dimorphism very marked. Infants colored like adults. Facial skin at least partially blue	*Rhinopithecus*
b.	Size large; tail long and slender; pelage pale; infant color whitish	*Semnopithecus*
c.	Size small to medium; tail long; infants orange to yellow	*Trachypithecus*

Key to the Chinese Species of *Rhinopithecus*

1.a.	Outer arms, legs, and base of tail not gray/black	*Rhinopithecus roxellana*
b.	Outer arms, legs, and base of tail gray/black	2
2.a.	Belly gray, chest rufous, bare skin around eyes blue	*Rhinopithecus brelichi*
b.	Belly whitish, chest buff, bare skin around eyes pink, lips reddish	*Rhinopithecus bieti*

Natural History: The Black Snub-nosed Monkey lives in high-altitude evergreen conifer forests and mixed conifer and oak forests from 3,400 to 4,100 m altitude. Eats mostly lichens, supplemented by bark, leaves, bamboo, acorns, and some berries. Has a sacculated stomach to assist in the breakdown of cellulose, allowing this species to eat tough and woody materials available in these forests through the winter. Live in large bands, up to 200 animals, composed of many smaller unimale groups. The bands break into smaller units, groups, and some all male groups during the breeding season. Survives severe winters and deep snow. Long, dense hair is also an adaptation to cold, damp local conditions. Animals are mostly arboreal and agile for their size, making great leaps and some semibrachiation. They feed and travel on the ground above the treeline. Groups proceed in single file and spend roughly a third of their time feeding actively and a third resting. Groups have large home ranges and may take several years to exploit their entirety. They move to lower altitudes in severe winter weather. Vocalizations consist mainly of soft murmurs; loud calls are heard only infrequently. Menstrual cycle is 26 days, and frequency of breeding peaks in spring and autumn. A single young is born. Females reach maturity in four to five years; males in five to six years.
Comments: Classified as *Pygathrix* in earlier treatments. The form *beiti* was first considered an independent species on morphological grounds by Peng et al. (1988) and confirmed using mtDNA sequences by Wang et al. (1997).
Conservation Status: China RL—EN A1cd; B1ab(i, iii); F. China Key List—I. CITES—I (as *Pygathrix*). IUCN RL—EN C2a ver 2.3 (1994).
References: Ding and Zhao (2004); Kirkpatrick and Long (1994); Kirkpatrick (1995); Long (1992); Long et al. (1994); Ma et al. (1989); Wang et al. (1997); Wu (1994).

Gray Snub-Nosed Monkey

PLATE 3
Rhinopithecus brelichi (Thomas, 1903) MAP 13
黔金丝猴 Qian Jinsihou

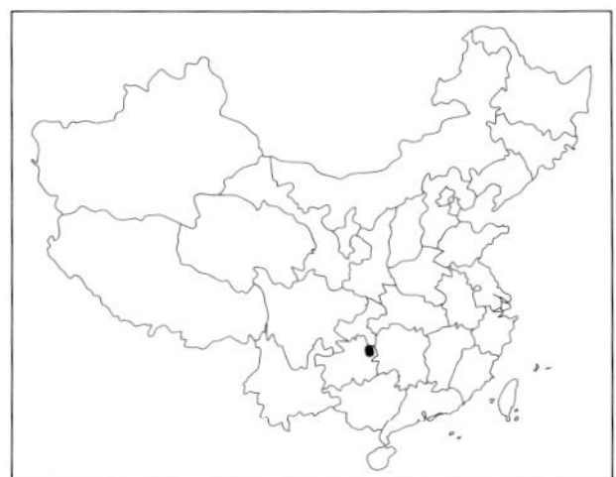

MAP 13. GRAY SNUB-NOSED MONKEY, *Rhinopithecus brelichi*

Distinctive Characteristics: HB 640–690; T 700–850; GLS 100–130; Wt 15 kg (male), 8 kg (female). Large, long-tailed monkey with dark pelage and blue face. Males are much larger than females and more brightly colored. Crown blackish with pale rufous central spot and centrally parted, ears with whitish tuft of hair. Facial skin blue with pinkish above eyes and around mouth. Sometimes has pink lappet at corner of mouth. Fringe of hair around face grayish. Rest of pelage dark blackish gray with a chestnut band across chest, on back, and on upper forearms. Nipples and scrotum are white in contrast to the darker body, and the penis is black. Tail black with whitish tip.
Distribution: Guizhou; confined to mountain forests on and around Fanjing Mountain in the Wuling range. Endemic.
Natural History: Lives in mixed deciduous and evergreen broadleaf forests at moderate altitudes between 1,500 and 2,200 m. Like the other *Rhinopithecus* species, this is a folivorous monkey living in huge troops that consist of aggregations of several subgroups that periodically break up and recombine. Subgroups are generally unimale or all male in composition. A wide range of flowers, shoots, twigs, bark, lichens, and fruits are consumed.
Comments: Classified as *Pygathrix* in earlier treatments.
Conservation Status: China RL—EN A1ac; B1ab(i, ii, iii); E. China Key List—I. CITES—I (as *Pygathrix*). IUCN RL—EN C2b ver 2.3 (1994).
References: Bleisch et al. (1993); Bleisch (1995).

Golden Snub-Nosed Monkey

PLATE 3
Rhinopithecus roxellana
(Milne-Edwards, 1870) MAP 14
川金丝猴 Chuan Jinsihou

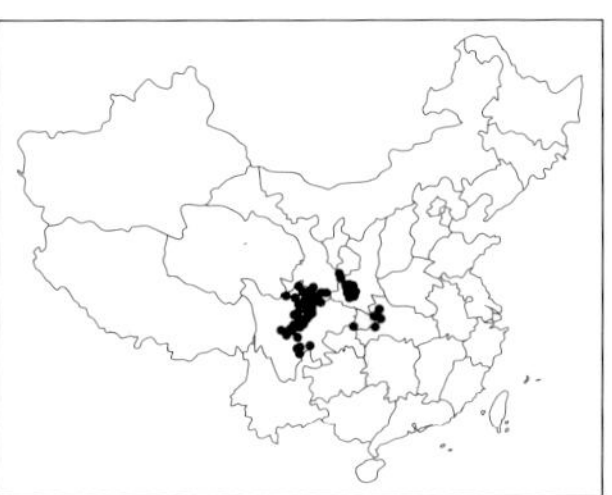

MAP 14. GOLDEN SNUB-NOSED MONKEY, *Rhinopithecus roxellana*

Distinctive Characteristics: HB 520–780; T 570–800; GLS 104–135; Wt 15–17 kg (male), 6.5–10 kg (female). A large long-tailed monkey with golden yellow pelage, long hair, and bluish face. Adult male much larger than female and has upturned nose and pink lappets at corner of mouth. Races vary in coloration: *R. r. roxellana* in Sichuan is darker, *R. r. qinlingensis* is bright golden, and *R. r. hubeiensis* is paler. Nasal bones very reduced; interorbital region wide; distance between bilateral temporal sutures large.
Distribution: C China. Endemic. Three subspecies: (1) *R. r. hubeiensis* Wang, Jiang, and Li, 1998; Shennongjia region of W Hubei; (2) *R. r. qinlingensis* Wang, Jiang, and Li, 1998; Qinling mountains of Shaanxi; (3) *R. r. roxellana* (Milne-Edwards, 1870); Sichuan to S Gansu.

Natural History: Inhabits subalpine conifer forests from 2,000 to 3,500 m, descending into broadleaf and mixed forests in winter months. Strongly prefers to live in primary (undisturbed) forests. Feeds on a wide variety of tree leaves, hemlock shoots, tree bark, some fruits, a few insects, and especially the cabbage lichens that festoon the tree branches in these damp, cold forests. Primarily arboreal, although it occasionally descends to the ground. Lives in very large troops reaching a hundred or more animals. These seem to be composed of several subgroups that may disperse and reform in irregular patterns. The smaller family subgroups are composed of 5–10 individuals with a single adult male and form the primary social unit within this species. Groups range over many square kilometers. Most females first breed at age five, and males do not become reproductively competent until the age of six and a half. Mating occurs in the fall with births occurring six months later in the spring.
Comments: Classified as *Pygathrix* in earlier treatments.
Conservation Status: China RL–VU A1c. China Key List–I. CITES–I (as *Pygathrix*). IUCN RL–VU C2a ver 2.3 (1994).
References: Kirkpatrick et al. (1999); Li et al. (2000a); Li (2001; 2004); Liang et al. (2000); Qi et al. (2004); Wang et al. (1998).

Genus *Semnopithecus*—Sacred Langurs

长尾叶猴属 Changweiyehou Shu—
长尾叶猴 Changweiyehou

The sacred langurs are larger, longer legged, and more terrestrial than the closely related *Trachypithecus* (lutungs) and live in larger multimale groups. Once classified with *Trachypithecus* within the genus *Presbytis*. The young are born white and gradually assume darker adult coloration. Calls tend to be discrete barks. Of seven species in the genus, only one occurs in China.

Nepal Gray Langur

PLATE 4
MAP 15

Semnopithecus schistaceus Hodgson, 1840
长尾叶猴 Changwei Yehou

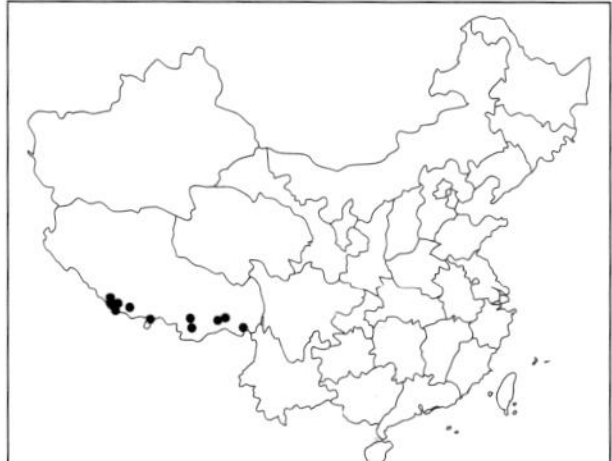

MAP 15. NEPAL GRAY LANGUR, *Semnopithecus schistaceus*

Distinctive Characteristics: HB 620–790; T 690–1,030; GLS 120–145; Wt 9–24 kg (male), 7.5–18 kg (female). Large rangy langur with long hind legs and tail held high when running across ground. Color pale gray to cream; back, tail, and outside of thighs darkest. Ears and almost bare face black. Hair of forehead forms a fringe over the brow. Himalayan race *achilles* is a darker gray than *lania*.
Distribution: S Xizang; ranging to N Pakistan, Nepal, Sikkim, Bhutan, N Myanmar. Two subspecies in China: (1) *S. s. achilles* (Pocock, 1928); S Xizang; (2) *S. s. lania* (Elliot, 1909); recorded only from Chunhuan (Chumbi) River, S Xizang.
Natural History: Occurs in high forests and mountain scrub of the Himalayas up to over 5,000 m. Omnivorous diet consists of leaves, fruits, and some insects and vertebrates. More terrestrial than most other leaf monkeys, but also feeds in trees where it shows considerable agility and occasional semibrachiation and spectacular leaping. Lives in small to large troops of up to 25 animals formed as single male or multimale units with adult males acquiring a harem of females. Groups show much allo-grooming behavior. Single births are the norm. Gestation is 168–200 days, and weaning takes up to 20 months. Mothers may allow other females to hold or care for their young.
Comments: The forms *achilles* and *lania* were formerly treated as subspecies of *S. entellus*.
Conservation Status: Scarce and limited in distribution within China, but able to escape persecution in rugged mountain terrain. China RL–EN A2c; B1ab(i, iii). China Key List–I. CITES–I. IUCN RL–LR/nt ver 2.3 (1994) (as *Semnopithecus entellus schistaceus*).
References: Hrdy (1974); Sugiyama (1965).

Genus *Trachypithecus*—Lutungs

乌叶猴属 Wuyehou Shu—乌叶猴 Wuyehou

Trachypithecus and *Semnopithecus* are similar genera, and formerly both were classified within the genus *Presbytis*. *Trachypithecus* young are born golden, then fade to pale yellow before assuming adult coloration. Groups usually contain a single male or represent associations of two single-male groups. Male territorial calls are harsh and repetitive. More arboreal than *Semnopithecus*. Of 17 species of *Trachypithecus*, 5 occur in China, although some authors lump *poliocephalus* (synonym *leucocephalus*) within *francoisi* (Wang 2003). There are doubtful claims of the Golden Langur, *T. geei*, occurring in Yunnan, however this form most definitely never occurred in China and has a small and well-defined distribution along Bhutan's southern border with India.

Tenasserim Lutung

MAP 16

Trachypithecus barbei (Blyth, 1847)
缅甸乌叶猴 Miandian Wuyehou

Distinctive Characteristics: HB 520–620; T 600–880; Wt 6–9 kg. Back brown, nearly black; legs and tail paler dark gray with no black on distal part; underparts pale (gray). There is an asymmetrical white patch on the skin of the inside of the thigh of females. The upright crown hair forms a distinct crest. There are sparse white hairs on the upper lip and blacking hairs on the lower lip, and the lips are

Key to the Chinese Species of *Trachypithecus*

1.a.	Pelage of back and body black	2
b.	Pelage of back and body not black	3
2.a.	Head and neck creamy white	*Trachypithecus poliocephalus*
b.	Head all black of back with some white only in cheeks	*Trachypithecus francoisi*
3.a.	Pelage all gray/brown, pale blue skin around eyes, and white patch on muzzle	*Trachypithecus phayrei*
b.	Pelage pale brown to gray, face black, no pale eye patch	4
4.a.	Crown gray, eyes yellow	*Trachypithecus shortridgei*
b.	Crown brown, eyes brown	*Trachypithecus barbei*

bluish black in coloration; the face has a soft violet coloration.
Natural History: Gives birth to one offspring at a time. Its natural history is likely similar to that of other lutungs.

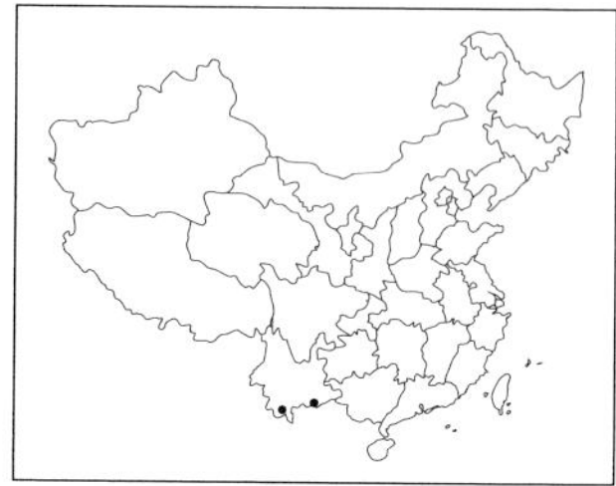

MAP 16. TENASSERIM LUTUNG, *Trachypithecus barbei*

Distribution: A few records exist from Yunnan (Hekou and Xishuangbanna); extending to Myanmar and N Indochina.
Comments: The distinctiveness of *barbei* has been substantiated by molecular analysis (Geissmann et al. 2004)
Conservation Status: Very rare and poorly known. Must be locally endangered in China, although NE (not evaluated) for either the Chinese national or IUCN global Red Lists. CITES II.
References: Geissmann et al. (2004); Groves (2001).

François' Langur

PLATE 4 MAP 17

Trachypithecus francoisi (Pousargues, 1898)
黑叶猴 **Hei Yehou**

MAP 17. FRANÇOIS' LANGUR, *Trachypithecus francoisi*

Distinctive Characteristics: HB 520–710; T 700–900; GLS 84–97; Wt 9–9.5 kg. Elegant black leaf monkey with long tail and hair on crown forming pointed crest. Adults all black or may have white cheek fringes. Infant is orange, fading to yellow.
Distribution: Guangxi and Guizhou; extending to N Vietnam, C Laos.
Natural History: Confined to limestone outcrops with forest or scrub in monsoon evergreen rainforest habitats. Seems to prefer steep slopes and deep valleys with complex topography. Occurs at low elevations. Lives in single-male troops. Eats leaves and some fruits. Uses caves for shelter and giving birth. Moves slowly and rests for most of the day in sparsely vegetated areas. Behavior similar to that of other leaf monkeys.
Comments: Many treatments include the form *poliocephalus* (herein regarded as distinct) as a synonym.
Conservation Status: Rare, restricted range, fragmentation, and narrow habitat combined with persecution by farmers and hunters have made this species vulnerable. Its primary threat is the tradition of using the species to make a medicated wine. In Fusui Nature Reserve in SW Guangxi, the local population declined by over 50% between 1995 and 2000 due to severe loss of habitat (Hu et al. 2004). There are encouraging signs that hunting of this species is being controlled (Li et al. 2005). China RL—EN A2cd + 3cd. China Key List—I. CITES—II. IUCN RL—VU A1cd + 2cd; C2a ver 2.3 (1994).
References: Hu et al. (2004); Li (1993); Li et al. (2005a); Nadler (1996).

Phayre's Leaf-Monkey

PLATE 4 MAP 18

Trachypithecus phayrei (Blyth, 1847)
菲氏叶猴 **Feishi Yehou**

Distinctive Characteristics: HB 550–710; T 600–800; HF 168–180; E 33; GLS 91–107; Wt 6–9 kg. A medium-sized gray or pale brown leaf monkey with darker hands, feet, and head, and with conspicuous bluish white eyerings and whitish muzzle patch. Tail same color as back. Infant is orange.
Distribution: SW China; extending to NE India, Bangladesh, Myanmar, N Thailand, N Laos, and N Vietnam. Two subspecies in China: (1) *T. p. crepuscula* (Elliot, 1909); S and SW Yunnan; (2) *T. p. shanicus* (Wroughton, 1917); Salween River valley, Yunnan, in drier forest.

Natural History: Inhabits lowland and hill forests including deciduous forest. Feeds mostly on leaves and shoots with some seeds, and fond of visiting salt licks. Females routinely disperse from family groups, and males are primarily philopatric. Females display a linear dominance hierarchy and appear more likely to squabble over food than expected.

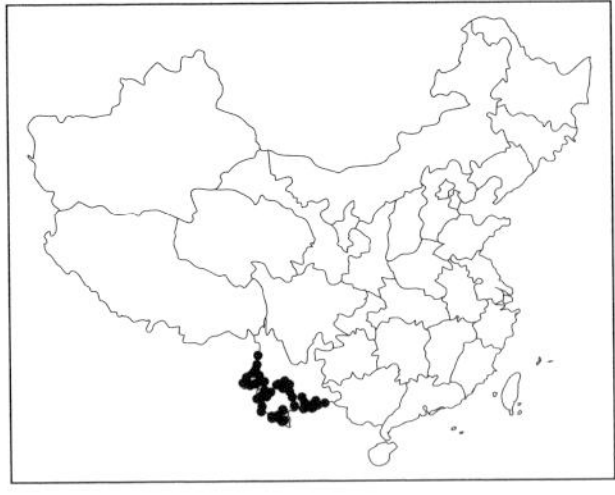

MAP 18. PHAYRE'S LEAF-MONKEY, *Trachypithecus phayrei*

Comments: Considered by some authors to be a race of the Dusky Leaf Monkey (*Trachypithecus obscurus*); see Brandon-Jones et al. (2004).
Conservation Status: Limited distribution and persecuted in China, but widespread elsewhere. China RL—EN A1c; B1ab(I,iii). China Key List—I. CITES—II.
References: Borries et al. (2004); Brandon-Jones et al. (2004); He and Yang (1982); Koenig et al. (2004).

White-Headed Langur

PLATE 4

Trachypithecus poliocephalus
(Pousargues, 1898)

MAP 19

白头叶猴 Baitou Yehou

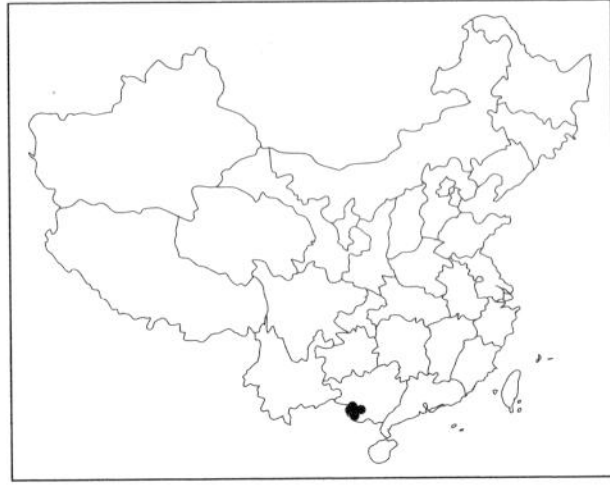

MAP 19. WHITE-HEADED LANGUR, *Trachypithecus poliocephalus*

Distinctive Characteristics: HB 520–710; T 700–900; Wt 6–9.5 kg. Graceful black langur with white head and neck and yellowish central crest. Tail basally black, but almost white at tip. Infant is golden.
Distribution: S Guangxi; also on Cat Ba Island, Vietnam. The form *T. p. leucocephalus* Tan, 1955 in Guangxi is isolated from and differs in color from the Vietnam form and may warrant separate specific status.
Natural History: Lives on limestone outcrops with scrub or forest cover, sometimes sympatric with *T. francoisi*. Stone caves on cliffs are used as sleeping sites. Lives in single-male troops, and group size ranges from 4 to16 individuals. White-headed Langurs rest more than half of daylight hours, and percentage of time engaged in play behavior increases with habitat quality. Leafy vegetation accounts for more than 90% of annual diet. White-headed Langurs require high-quality habitat for successful reproduction.
Comment: Has been treated as a synonym of *T. francoisi*, although these forms are distinct and may overlap geographically.
Conservation Status: Habitat of the White-headed Langur is deteriorating and becoming increasingly fragmented; only 200 km^2 in 16 patches remain of its preferred habitat (Huang et al. 2002). Additionally, they have been subject to a high level of poaching (Lu 2000). Overall, their population has declined dramatically in recent years. China RL—EN A2cd + 3cd; C2a(i). China Key List—I. CITES—II. IUCN RL—CR A2cd; C2ab ver. 2.3 (1994).
References: Huang et al. (1995); Huang et al. (2002); Huang et al. (2003); Li and Ma (1980); Li and Rogers (2004a; b); Li et al. (2003); Lu and Li (1991); Lu (2000); Nadler (1996).

Shortridge's Langur

PLATE 4

Trachypithecus shortridgei
(Wroughton, 1915)

MAP 20

戴帽叶猴 Daimao Yehou

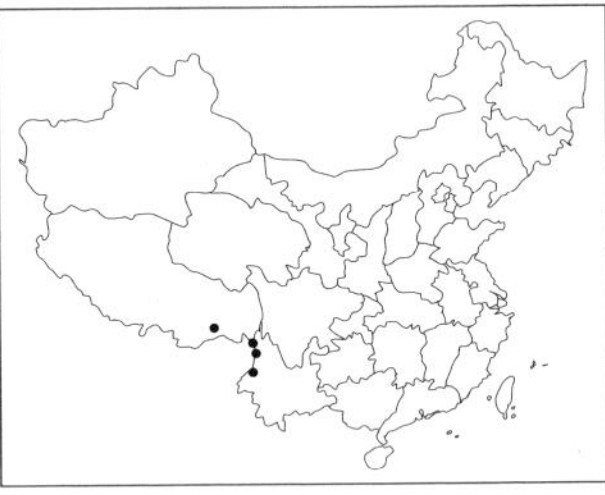

MAP 20. SHORTRIDGE'S LANGUR, *Trachypithecus shortridgei*

Distinctive Characteristics: HB 1,090–1,600; SH 500–700; T 70–120; HF 190–200; GLS 190; Wt 17–40 kg. Silvery gray color, hands and feet darker gray, tail darkening toward tip. Legs slightly paler gray, underside more so. Facial skin shiny black, eyes startlingly yellow-orange. Narrow black brow band ending laterally in upward-pointed "spikes." Similarly, cheek whiskers at each corner of the mouth ending in downward-pointed spikes. Infant is orange.
Distribution: SE Xizang, and as the far west as the Gong Shan mountains along Yunnan border on west side of Salween River; extending to N Myanmar east of Chindwin River.
Natural History: Occupies dense, humid monsoon, evergreen broadleaf forests at low elevations (1,200–1,600 m).
Comments: Formerly included as a subspecies of Capped Langur (*T. pileatus*), but appearance and vocalizations are quite different. Some authors suggest inclusion under Tenasserim Lutung (*T. barbei*). It is possible that *T. pileatus* occurs in SE Xizang in the border dispute zone with Assam (Medog).
Conservation Status: Rare and restricted in China; it is estimated that no more than 500–600 occur in

China. China RL–EN A2cd; C2a(i). China Key List–I. CITES–I. IUCN RL–EN A1cd, C2a ver 2.3 (1994) as *Trachypithecus pileatus shortridgei.*

Family Hylobatidae—Gibbons and Siamangs

长臂猿科 Changbiyuan Ke—长臂猿 Changbiyuan

Hylobatids are small to medium-sized "Lesser Apes." All species have no tail, but some have a pubic tuft. Forelimbs are very long, hanging below the knees. Upper canines of both males and females well developed and tusk-shaped. Animals travel in a suspensory brachiation mode of arm swinging, although they can walk bipedally if they need to cross open ground. Gibbons are regarded as frugivorous with a strong association with fig fruits, but up to half the diet may be composed of leaves. Social system is generally one of small territorial monogamous families. Families patrol and defend their territories from neighbors with loud chorus calls given in early morning. Some species are sexually dichromatic, males being dark and females light colored. Four genera of gibbons are recognized (molecular evidence in Roos and Geissmann 2001), three of which occur in China. These forms are anatomically very similar and were all formerly included in *Hylobates*. The division between the genera is largely based on chromosome number and call pattern rather than morphology (*Bunopithecus* 2N = 38; *Hylobates* 2N = 44; *Nomascus* 2N = 52).

Genus *Bunopithecus (monotypic)*

白眉长臂猿属 Baimei Changbiyuan Shu

Hoolock Gibbon

PLATE 5
Bunopithecus hoolock (Harlan, 1834) MAP 21
白眉长臂猿 Baimei Changbiyuan

Distinctive Characteristics: HB 600–900; HF 140–153; GLS 93–99; Wt 6–8.5 kg. Males and females about the same size. Typical gibbon with very long arms used to hang and brachiate beneath branches. No tail, but male has long genital tassle; opposable but short thumb; curved fingers act as hooks in suspensory hanging. Female has small throat sac that helps to amplify territorial calls. Fur is dense and woolly. Male is blackish brown with white brows and buff-colored beard and genital tuft. Female is beige or buffy gray with dark brown cheeks and ventral area. Eyebrows are white, as is narrow edge to blackish face and a stripe beneath the eyes and across ridge of nose, giving face a skull-like appearance. Young are whitish at birth, but resemble male pelage after a few months.
Distribution: SW Yunnan, W of Salween River only; extending to Assam, Bangladesh, and Myanmar. Chinese subspecies: *B. h. leuconedys* Groves, 1967; distributed between the Chindwin River in Myanmar and the Salween River in China.

MAP 21. HOOLOCK GIBBON, *Bunopithecus hoolock*

Natural History: Inhabits a wide range of evergreen and semievergreen forest types from tropical to subtropical hill forest. Eats fruits supplemented by young leaves and occasionally flowers and insects. Lives in small monogamous family groups. Strongly territorial with home ranges from 14 to 55 ha per family. Larger ranges may occur in poor habitat. Almost totally arboreal. Territorial duet calls are given frequently in early morning in summer, and later and less frequently in winter. Calls consist of loud wailing cries rising and falling in pitch and last about 15 minutes per session, and no sex-specific phrases are evident. Families sleep curled on large branches of emergent trees. Usually only one young born at a time at two- to three-year intervals.
Conservation Status: China RL–CR A2cd; D. China Key List–I. CITES–I. IUCN RL–EN A1cd ver 2.3 (1994).
References: Ma and Wang (1986); Ma et al. (1988).

Genus *Hylobates*—Gibbons

长臂猿属 Changbiyuan Shu—长臂猿 Changbiyuan

Of seven species of *Hylobates*, only one occurs in China.

Key to the Chinese Genera of Hylobatidae

1.a.	Color creamy to dark brown with white hands and feet and white facial ring around naked black face; 2N = 44	*Hylobates*
b.	Hands and feet not white	2
2.a.	Color creamy (female) or dark brown (male) with broad outsweeping white or cream brows; 2N = 38	*Bunopithecus*
b.	Brows not contrastingly pale; 2N = 52	*Nomascus*

Key to the Chinese Species of *Nomascus*

1.a. Male black with crest and contrasting white cheeks; female pale with dark crown patch and some white in cheeks, but no dark chest patch — *Nomascus leucogenys*
b. Male all black; female pale with dark crown patch and dark chest patch — *Nomascus concolor*
c. Male all black; female with slight or no dark on chest and with whitish muzzle — *Nomascus hainanus*

White-Handed Gibbon

PLATE 5
MAP 22

Hylobates lar (Linnaeus, 1771)
白掌长臂猿 Baizhang Changbiyuan

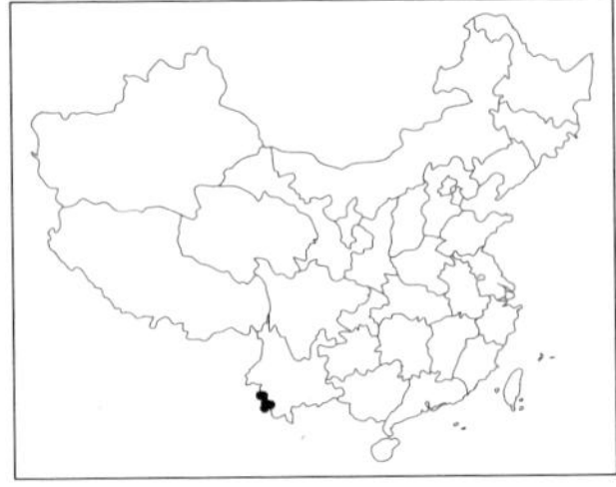

MAP 22. WHITE-HANDED GIBBON, *Hylobates lar*

Distinctive Characteristics: HB 450–600; HF 130–155; E 33–37; GLS 93–110; Wt 3.9–7 kg. Small gibbon with no genital tuft or throat sac, white hands and feet, and clean white margin around black face. Various color forms occur from dark chocolate to pale buff, but these are not related to gender. Long arms and curved fingers, typical of all gibbons.
Distribution: Only a tiny distribution in the tropical zone of SW Yunnan between the Salween and Mekong rivers; extending to E Myanmar through W Indochina to Malay Peninsula and N Sumatra. Chinese subspecies: *H. l. yunnanensis* Ma and Wang, 1986.
Natural History: Inhabits tropical evergreen and semievergreen rainforests. Eats mostly fruits (especially strangler figs) supplemented by leaves, buds, and some insects. Typical gibbon, living in small monogamous family units. Highly arboreal and territorial, defending territories with vocal "great calls" and aggressive chases and occasional fights. Travels in swift bursts of suspensory brachiation, feeding in many sites each day and sleeping on large branches or forks in the high canopy. Shy of water, and drinks from tree holes or rain on branches rather than visiting streams. Loud territorial chorus given at dawn and early morning consists of duet with males giving many barks and whoops and females giving the "great call" of prolonged wailing notes rising and falling in pitch. Normally only one infant is born at intervals of two to three years.
Comments: The White-handed Gibbon has a small overlap zone with the Black Crested Gibbon, which ranges to the north. The form *yunnanensis* is very similar to and probably synonymous with the form *carpenteri* found in N Thailand.
Conservation Status: Very rare and restricted in China. Locally endangered, though quite common in other parts of its range outside of China. China RL—CR A2cd; D. China Key List—I. CITES—I. IUCN RL—LR/nt; *H. l. yunnanensis* CR C2a; D ver 2.3 (1994).
References: Ma and Wang (1986); Ma et al. (1988).

Genus *Nomascus*—Gibbons

黑长臂猿属 Hei Changbiyuan Shu

Of five species of *Nomascus*, three occur in China (Groves and Wang 1990).

Black Crested Gibbon

PLATE 5
MAP 23

Nomascus concolor (Harlan, 1826)
黑长臂猿 Hei Changbiyuan

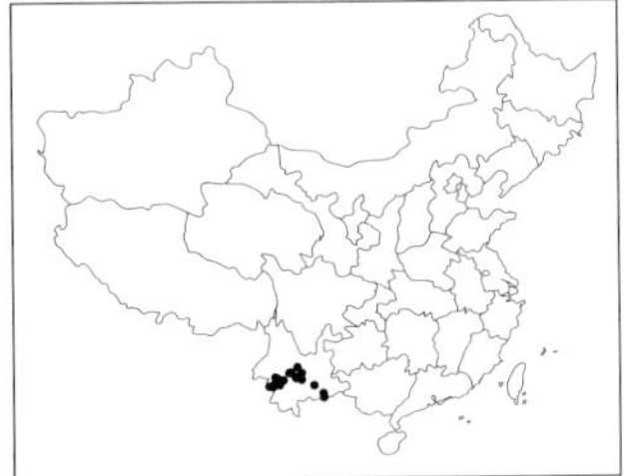

MAP 23. Black Crested Gibbon, *Nomascus concolor*

Distinctive Characteristics: HB 430–540; HF 150–165; GLS 90–115; Wt 7–8 kg. Largish gibbon. Male is all black; female is yellow, orange, or beige brown with black crown and often a dark patch on ventral region. Both sexes have blackish face and pronounced hair crest on crown. Races supposedly differ in the shape of the dark crown patch of females: *concolor* has small diamond-shaped patch, *jingdongensis* has round patch with trailing nape line, and *furvogaster* has large patch over entire crown with nape band.
Distribution: Yunnan and SW Guangxi; extending to N Vietnam between Red and Black rivers. Four subspecies in China: (1) *N. c. concolor* (Harlan, 1826); Yunnan (east of Black River); (2) *N. c. furvogaster* Ma and Wang, 1986; Yunnan, between Salween and Mekong rivers; (3) *N. c. jingdongensis* Ma and Wang, 1986; between Mekong and Black rivers; (4) *N. c. nasutus* Kunkel d'Herculais, 1884; Guangxi.
Natural History: Found in evergreen and semievergreen forests between 500 and 3,000 m. Eats mostly fruit, but supplemented with leaves, buds, and insects. As found in other gibbons, the social structure consists of small territorial family groups with three to six individuals, but some with two females; home ranges 44–200 ha. Highly arboreal; suspensory brachiation locomotion and early morning territorial duets. Call sessions last 10–13 minutes with female

giving the "great call" commencing with long notes, becoming faster and higher pitched as a series of barks to a climax followed by twitters. Male adds booms, staccato notes, and modulated phrases to the chorus. Subadults may join in. One young is born at a time at intervals of several years.
Comments: The forms *furvogaster* and *jingdongensis* are very similar to the nominate subspecies, and many authors consider these subdivisions dubious.
Conservation Status: Becoming increasingly rare. Form *nasutus* extirpated. Vulnerable to hunting, pet trade, and habitat destruction and fire. Main strongholds are in Ailao and Wuliang mountains. China RL—EN A1abcd; B1ab(i,ii,iii,iv,v); C2a(i); E. China Key List—I. CITES—I. IUCN RL—EN A1cd; C2a; *N. c. concolor* EN A1cd; C2a; *N. c. furvogaster* CR A2cd; B2a; *N. c. jingdongensis* CR C2b ver 2.3 (1994).
References: Bleisch and Chen (1991); Dao (1993); Geissmann (1989; 1995); Ma et al. (1988); Ma and Wang (1986).

Hainan Gibbon

Nomascus hainanus (Thomas, 1892) MAP 24
海南长臂猿 Hainan Changbiyuan

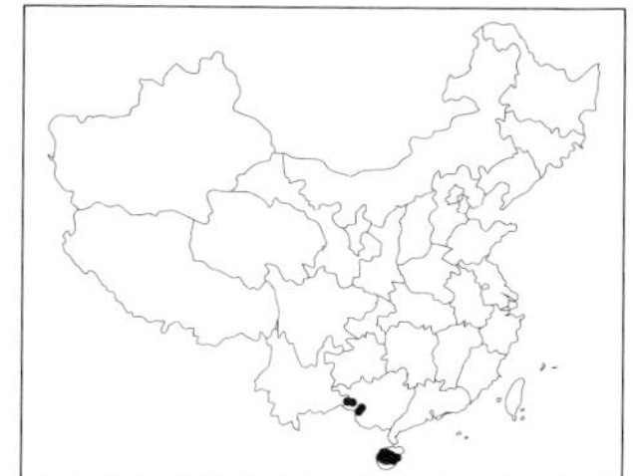

MAP 24. HAINAN GIBBON, *Nomascus hainanus*

Distinctive Characteristics: Wt 7–8 kg. Males and females same size. Largish gibbon, standing about 60 cm tall. Male is almost entirely black with sometimes a brownish tinge on chest and ventrum. Female is yellowish, orange, or beige brown with a blackish cap and pale ventrum. Infants are born with a light coat, like that of females. At one year of age young turn dark, like males, but later only females will change again to a light coat color.
Distribution: S China, including Hainan Island; extending to NE Vietnam east of the Red River. The nominate subspecies occupies Hainan. Additional specimens are known from N Vietnam and maybe formerly extended into SE Yunnan and Guangxi. A third form from NE Vietnam awaits description.
Natural History: As in the Black Crested Gibbon, with which it was formerly classified. Differs by uttering unique vibrato-type notes in the female territorial "great call." Lives in tropical evergreen rainforest where it obtains all its food, sleeps, and gives birth in treetops. Formerly occupied lowlands, but now confined to 800–1,200 m. Favorite foods include fleshy fruits but will also eat animals and young leaves. Small family breeding groups of the Hainan Gibbon defend territories against other such families. Females give birth to a single infant in alternate years, and young are carried by their mother for about two years.
Comments: Formerly classified in *Hylobates*. Has been regarded as a race of *N. concolor*, but differing in pelage, call, and shape of bacculum. Relations with mainland races are unclear, and assignment of these specimens is also unclear. Possibly should be referred to as *N. nasutus*, but the type specimen of *nasutus* is missing, and it is not known whether the now extinct Guangxi populations or populations in N Vietnam are all conspecific.
Conservation Status: Extremely precarious. Extinct over most of former range. It is believed that as many as 2,000 Hainan Gibbons inhabited the island in the 1950s, however in 2003 only 13 animals were documented in Bawangling Nature Reserve. China RL—CR A1abcd; B1ab(i,ii,iii,iv,v); C2a(i); E. China Key List—I. CITES—I. IUCN RL—CR B1ab(iii,v); C2a(ii)b; D ver 3.1 (2001) as *Nomascus nasutus hainanus*.
References: Chan and Fellowes (2003); Haimoff (1984).

Northern White-Cheeked Gibbon

PLATE 5
Nomascus leucogenys Ogilby, 1840 MAP 25
白颊长臂猿 Baijia Changbiyuan

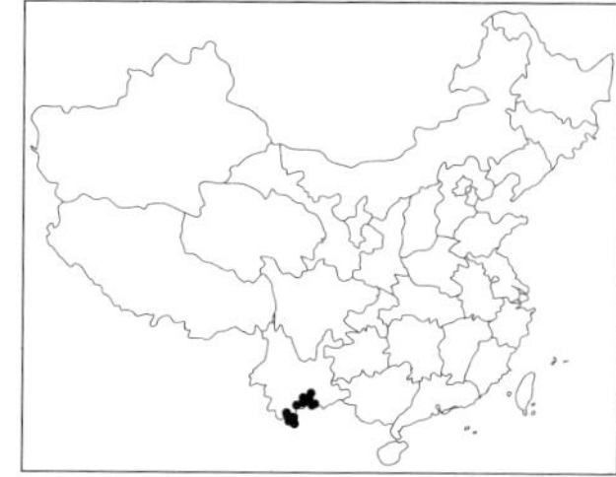

MAP 25. NORTHERN WHITE-CHEEKED GIBBON, *Nomascus leucogenys*

Distinctive Characteristics: Wt 7–9 kg. Largish gibbon. Male is black except for white cheek patches that connect under black chin and extend over the ears. Crown hair raised to form crest. Females are dark to light buff or creamy orange often suffused with tan, gray, or black with a black crown patch. Crown hair not raised as in male. Females are sometimes larger than males.
Distribution: S Yunnan; extending to N and S Laos, C and N Vietnam (west of Black River). In Yunnan the species is restricted to the southern parts of Xishuangbanna to the east of the Mekong River. A few families remain in Mengla County.
Natural History: As in the Black Crested Gibbon, with which this species was formerly classified. Songs in this species are given as duets between males and females, and the calls are highly dimorphic between the genders.
Conservation Status: Rare and endangered. Extinct in much of its original and recent range (e.g., Mengyang and Menglun). Found only in remote parts of Mengla and Shangyong nature reserves. Vulnerable to hunting, pet trade, and forest clearance. China RL—CR A2cd; D. China Key List—I. CITES—

I. IUCN RL—DD; *N. l. leuogenys* EN A1cd; 2cd ver 2.3 (1994).
References: DePutte (1982); Ma et al. (1988); Ma and Wang (1986); Yang and Xu (1988).

ORDER RODENTIA—Rodents

啮齿目 Niechi Mu—鼠类 Shulei

Darrin Lunde, Andrew T. Smith, and Robert S. Hoffmann

Rodents occur in nearly every habitat type present in China—from the high altitudes of the Himalayas and the Tibetan Plateau to tropical rainforests, grasslands, dry deserts, agricultural fields, villages, cities, and even ships in port. They exploit terrestrial, arboreal, subterranean, and aquatic habitats. Some rodents are strictly herbivorous, but most are omnivorous, feeding on a wide variety of plants, fungi, insects, and small vertebrates. Often highly fecund, most rodents have an incredible capacity to populate their environment. Altogether there are more species of rodent in China than any other group (192 of 2,277 species recognized worldwide; Carleton and Musser 2005), and their impact on both the environment and society is enormous. They may be important agricultural pests, disease vectors, seed dispersers and seed predators, laboratory animals, keystone species, ecosystem engineers, and sources of food for wildlife and sometimes even for humans.

Rodents are distinguished by a single set of large, ever-growing, chisel-like upper and lower incisor teeth. The rootless incisors are used for gnawing and enable them to gain access to a wide range of foods (lagomorphs are similar in this regard, but they have a second set of peglike upper incisors just behind the first set). Gnawing maintains a chisel edge at the tips of the incisors because the anterior side of each incisor is covered with hard enamel that wears down more slowly than the softer dentine behind it. Canines are absent, leaving a long gap or diastema between the incisors and the cheek teeth. The cheek teeth may be rooted and cuspidate or unrooted, ever growing, and flat crowned. Dental formula: 1.0.0–2.3/1.0.0–1.3 = 16–22.

The many convergences among species and the great number of species have made the systematics of rodents volatile and complex. They have also been aligned with a diversity of higher taxa within the mammals. Currently both morphological and molecular evidence places the rodents with the lagomorphs in the Glires (Douzery and Huchon 2004). Five suborders of Rodentia are recognized (reviewed in Carleton and Musser 2005), four of which are represented in China (encompassing 9 of 33 rodent families): (1) Sciuromorpha (Sciuridae, Gliridae); (2) Castorimorpha (Castoridae); (3) Myomorpha (Dipodidae, Platacanthomyidae, Spalacidae, Cricetidae, Muridae); and (4) Hystricomorpha (Hystricidae).

Family Sciuridae—Squirrels

松鼠科 Songshu Ke—松鼠 Songshu

Robert S. Hoffmann and Andrew T. Smith

This family of rodents is extremely diverse in many aspects of its biology. It includes both arboreal and terrestrial forms, and very small (mouse-size) to large (dog-size) species. Dentition is typically rodentlike;

Key to the Chinese Families of Rodentia

1.a.	Mandibles U-shaped in ventral view; body covered with quills	Hystricidae
b.	Mandibles V-shaped in ventral view; no quills on body	2
2.a.	Tail a broad flattened paddle	Castoridae
b.	Tail not a broad flat paddle	3
3.a.	Tail completely covered with long hairs, bushy	4
b.	Tail not completely covered with long hairs, not bushy	5
4.a.	Postorbital processes of skull long and pointed	Sciuridae
b.	Skull lacks postorbital processes	Gliridae
5.a.	Eyes minute and completely covered with skin	Spalacidae
b.	Eyes large or small but never completely covered with skin	6
6.a.	Bony palate with large foramina between first upper molars	Platacanthomyidae
b.	Bony palate lacks large foramina between first upper molars	7
7.a.	Hind legs elongated for hopping; mandible with large foramen on angular process	Dipodidae
b.	Hind legs not greatly elongated; mandible lacks large foramen on angular process	8
8.a.	Cusps on occlusal surface of first and second molars arranged in triserial rows or else transverse lophs separated by enamel	Muridae
b.	Cusps on occlusal surface of first and second molars arranged in biserial rows or else as triangular or rhombic dental leaves	Cricetidae

dental formula: 1.0.1–2.3/1.0.1.3 = 20–22. Rooted cheek-teeth range from brachydont to hypsodont, the occlusal surface usually with large cusps and ridges; P3 reduced or absent; postorbital processes of frontals and jugal bones well developed in most species. The skull is usually domed, and the auditory bullae are not excessively inflated. Sciurids possess five digits on their hind feet and four on their forefeet (the thumb is diminutive but present). The tail is well haired, but tail hairs are of variable length, longer on arboreal and shorter on terrestrial species (McLaughlin 1984).

There are three broadly defined types of sciurids: flying squirrels, tree squirrels, and ground squirrels. The mostly nocturnal flying squirrels possess a furred gliding membrane (patagium) that extends between the limbs, as well as horizontally arranged hairs on the tails of small species (although not on *Petaurista*). Styliform cartilage extends from the wrist to add support to the patagium. Tree squirrels have rounded heads with prominent eyes and sharp curved claws on their feet—traits they share with the gliding forms. Most tree squirrels, however, are diurnally active. The primarily diurnal ground squirrels have relatively flatter heads and straight claws. While living in burrows, they lack the extreme adaptations for life underground as found in some fossorial mammals.

Sciurids are found worldwide except for Australia, Madagascar, southern South America, and the extensive African and Arabian deserts. The family is comprised of 51 genera and 278 species; of these, 16 genera and 43 species are represented in China. The classification of the Sciuridae has been unsettled; a large variety of subfamilies and tribes with varying composition have been proposed over the years (Thorington and Hoffmann 2005). The monophyly of the flying squirrels has been both supported and questioned (Thorington and Hoffmann 2005). Historically, most classifications have recognized two subfamilies: Pteromyinae, the flying squirrels; and Sciurinae, consisting of several tribes of arboreal and terrestrial squirrels. Recent molecular studies, however, have rejected this two subfamily classification (Herron et al. 2004; Mercer and Roth 2003; Steppan et al. 2004). These analyses converge and strongly suggest that the Sciuridae is divided into five subfamilies (Ratufinae, Sciurillinae, Sciurinae, Callosciurinae, Xerinae), four of which are found in China. In this scheme, the flying squirrels are represented as one of two tribes within the Sciurinae (Thorington and Hoffmann 2005).

Subfamily Ratufinae

Genus *Ratufa*—Giant Squirrels

巨松鼠亚科 Jusongshu Yake; 巨松鼠属 Jusongshu Shu—巨松鼠 Jusongshu

Size large, habits arboreal; tail longer than HB length; skull robust; rostrum short, nasal length about half that of zygomatic breadth; frontal long and broad; postorbital process stout; occipital region depressed; posterior edge of bony palate terminates at anterior margin of posterior molars; first upper premolar absent, dental formula: 1.0.1.3/1.0.1.3 = 20. Three pairs of mammae. This subfamily is represented by a single genus, *Ratufa*, all forms occurring in SE Asia from S India to Hainan Island, and four species, one of which is found in China.

Black Giant Squirrel

PLATE 8
MAP 26

Ratufa bicolor (Sparrmann, 1778)
巨松鼠 Ju Songshu

Distinctive Characteristics: HB 360–430; T 400–510; HF 84–91; E 30–38; GLS 71–77; Wt 1,300–2,300 g. The Black Giant Squirrel is appropriately named, since the entire dorsal surface is covered by black fur, as is the entire tail; ears with tufts. The nose and muzzle are white, and the ventral surface is buffy to rusty yellow, as is the small eyering. This species is highly variable throughout its range.

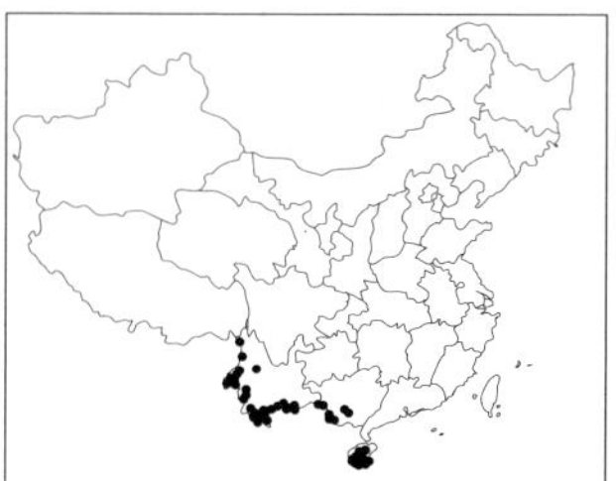

MAP 26. BLACK GIANT SQUIRREL, *Ratufa bicolor*

Distribution: S Yunnan, S Guanxi, Hainan Island; extending to E Nepal, Assam (India), Myanmar, Thailand, Laos, Cambodia, and Vietnam, south through the Malay Peninsula to Java and Bali. Two subspecies in China: (1) *R. b. gigantea* (McClelland, 1839); S Guangxi, S Yunnan, E Xizang; (2) *R. b. hainana* Allen, 1906; Hainan Island; *stigmosa* Thomas, 1923 a synonym.

Natural History: Black Giant Squirrels are arboreal and natives of tropical forests. On Hainan Island they are said to live high in the forest. They generally perch with their tail hanging down. They venture onto the ground only to chase another squirrel, or, during the breeding season, to follow a female. At other times they are solitary or paired. Vocalization is a harsh short chatter. They are excellent climbers, able to leap 6 m or more. Their diet includes fruits, nuts, bark of some trees and shrubs, insects, and bird's eggs. Tree holes are used as shelters, and during the breeding period they construct large nests of leaves and branches. Here the young are born and raised. May breed twice each year (in spring and fall), and gestation lasts 28–35 days. Litter size may consist of one to three young.

Conservation Status: China RL—VU A1cd. China Key List—II. CITES—II.

Subfamily Sciurinae—True Squirrels

松鼠亚科 Songshu Yake—松鼠 Songshu

The Sciurinae is comprised of 20 genera and 81 species, of which 7 genera and 14 species are represented in China. The Sciurinae can be divided into two tribes: Sciurini (tree squirrels) and Pteromyini (flying squirrels). The phylogeny of flying squirrels has recently been reviewed by Thorington et al. (2002). The Chinese fauna contains only a single species in the Sciurini, *Sciurus vulgaris*; all others represent the Pteromyini.

Genus *Aeretes* (monotypic)

沟牙鼯鼠属 Gouyawushu Shu

Northern Chinese Flying Squirrel

PLATE 6
Aeretes melanopterus
(Milne-Edwards, 1867)
MAP 27
沟牙鼯鼠 Gouya Wushu

MAP 27. NORTHERN CHINESE FLYING SQUIRREL, *Aeretes melanopterus*

Distinctive Characteristics: HB 275–355; T 275–362; HF 47–63; E 21–40; GLS 61–66. Not distinctively different from other large flying squirrels in form. No slender tufted hairs at base of ears. Sandy brown or dusky dorsal pelage soft, long, and loose; tail brown, no black tip; feet black; ventrum pale buff to whitish, hairs shorter than on dorsum; edges of gliding membranes black dorsally; face and throat gray; upper incisors broad, grooved on anterior surface. M3 smaller than P4, M1, and M2; crown of P4 subequal to that of M1 in size; P3 invisible from a lateral view; crown of molars complicated. Rostrum short, upper branch of anterior maxilla terminates about 2 mm short of posterior margin of nasal, so not in the same plane; anterior margin of palate has a short pointed process.
Distribution: Two isolated populations in C China. Endemic. Two subspecies: (1) *A. m. melanopterus* (Milne-Edwards, 1867); Hebei; *sulcatus* (Howell, 1927); Eastern tombs, a synonym; (2) *A. m. szechuanensis* Wang, Tu and Wang, 1966; C and NE Sichuan, S Gansu.
Natural History: Occupies mountainous forests. Information on the biology of this species is apparently very scarce.
Conservation Status: China RL—EN A1ac. IUCN RL—LR/nt ver 2.3 (1994).

Genus *Belomys* (monotypic)

毛耳飞鼠属 Maoerfeishu Shu

Hairy-Footed Flying Squirrel

PLATE 6
Belomys pearsonii (Gray, 1842)
MAP 28
毛耳飞鼠 Mao'er Feishu

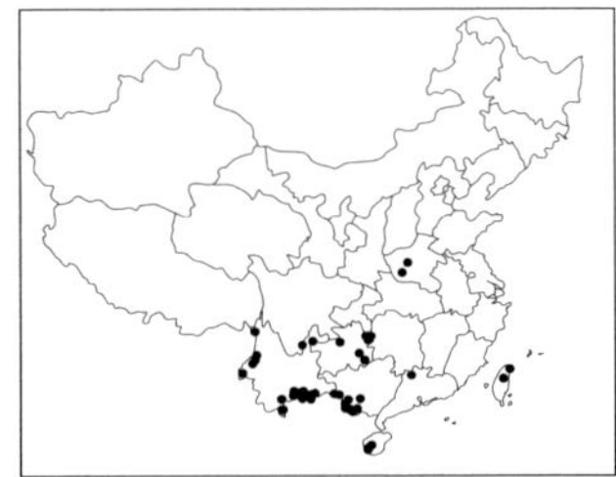

MAP 28. HAIRY-FOOTED FLYING SQUIRREL, *Belomys pearsonii*

Distinctive Characteristics: HB 160–260; T 102–158; HF 31–47; E 31–40; GLS 40–44. Small flying squirrels with relatively large ears sporting threadlike black tufted hairs at their base. Tail relatively short and bushy; dorsal surface of patagium blackish, contrasting strongly with dark reddish brown of the dorsal pelage. Ventral patagium dark yellow-orange merging with the hoary, dark gray at base, ventral pelage. Three pairs of mammae. Frontal narrow, orbits long, foramen magnum small, auditory bullae large,

Key to the Chinese Subfamilies of Sciuridae

1.a.	Body size very large, HB length and tail length > 300; arboreal; first upper premolar absent	Ratufinae
b.	Not as above	2
2.a.	Tail short, generally < HB length, generally not very bushy; terrestrial	Xerinae
b.	Tail generally ≥ HB length, generally bushy; mostly arboreal forms	3
3.a.	Tail flattened or round and with well-defined membrane (patagium) between limbs, or with a very bushy tail and pronounced ear tufts	Sciurinae
b.	Tail moderately bushy; most forms arboreal; no ear tufts or patagium	Callosciurinae

Key to the Chinese Genera of Sciurinae

1.a. Lacks gliding membrane (patagium) and calcar Tribe Sciurini, *Sciurus*
b. Possesses gliding membrane (patagium) and styliform process Tribe Pteromyini, 2
2.a. Size small, HB plus tail < 500 mm; GLS < 52 mm 3
b. Size large, HB plus tail > 500 mm; GLS > 52 mm 5
3.a. Threadlike black tufted hairs present around base of ears; tail bushy, not flattened; structure of upper and lower molar dentition complex, irregular tubercles present *Belomys*
b. Threadlike black tufted hairs absent around base of ears; tail flattened and featherlike; structure of upper and lower dentition regular 4
4.a. Eight mammae; two horizontal dental ridges present on anterior and posterior margin of M3; incisive foramen long, its length ≥ breadth of interpterygoid foramen *Pteromys*
b. Six mammae; one horizontal dental ridge present on anterior and posterior margin of M3; incisive foramen short, its length clearly < breadth of interpterygold foramen *Hylopetes*
5.a. Threadlike black tufted hairs present around base of ears, crown of P4 clearly > M1; P3 very small, concealed in anterior interior angle of P4 *Trogopterus*
b. Threadlike black tufted hairs around base of ears absent; crown of P4 slightly < M1; P3 lies at anterior end or interior inner angle of P4 6
6.a. Upper incisors broad, with longitudinal groove present at middle of labial surface; crown of M3 < M1 and M2; tail thick, nearly flattened *Aeretes*
b. Upper incisors narrow, their labial surfaces lack grooves; crown of M3 equal to M1 and M2 *Petaurista*

Key to the Chinese Species of *Hylopetes*

1.a. Throat white, the color extending forward onto the cheek below the eye to form a "half collar"; dorsal color dark gray; ventral pelage gray or off-white. Larger; HB length 175–247 mm; tail pelage full, rounded *Hylopetes alboniger*
b. Throat white, but not spreading forward to cheek; does not form a "half collar"; dorsal pelage russet; ventral pelage white. Smaller; HB length 144–173 mm; tail well-haired, but flattened *Hyloptes phayrei*

distance between left and right auditory bullae equal to the greatest breadth of interpterygoid foramen; incisive foramen small, clearly narrower than interpterygoid foramen; cheek tooth row short, crowns of teeth low, complex tubercles present; crown of P4 largest, larger than M1 and M2; P3 very small, in internal angle before P4, nearly hidden; M1 and M2 slightly square, four tubercles present plus a small accessory tubercle in middle, irregularly positioned. 2N = 38.

Distribution: SE China and offshore islands; extending to Vietnam, Thailand, and N Myanmar, and west in the Himalayas to E Nepal. Three subspecies in China: (1) *B. p. blandus* Osgood, 1932; Yunnan, Guizhou, Guangxi, Hainan, Guangdong; (2) *B. p. kaleensis* (Swinhoe, 1863); Taiwan; (3) *B. p. trichotis* Thomas, 1908; Yunnan.

Natural History: Occurs in dense subtropical and mixed forests at altitudes of 500–2,400 m in the southern part of its range; to the north, lives in mixed broadleaf forest. Reported to feed on leaves and fruits, and in the north or at higher latitudes on oak leaves, but prefers needles of cedar and pine. Almost nothing else is known of its habits.

Comments: The closest relative to *Belomys is Trogopterus xanthipes* (Thorington et al. 2002), and some consider them congeneric (Corbet and Hill 1992). However, the ranges of the two species overlap broadly in SE China; while *xanthipes* extends farther north.

Conservation Status: China RL—NT; although it nearly met the criteria for VU A1cd. IUCN RL—LR/nt ver 2.3 (1994).

References: Mitchell (1977); Thorington et al. (2002).

Genus *Hylopetes*—Flying Squirrels

箭尾飞鼠属 Jianweifeishu Shu—箭尾飞 Jianweifeishu

Size small, HB plus tail length less than 500 mm; tail wide and sometimes flattened, feather-shaped; six mammae. Incisive foramen small, its length not more than width of interpterygoid foramen; auditory bullae large, but smaller than *Petaurista* in proportion, its length less than distance from anterior margin of auditory bullae to posterior margin of M3; auditory bullae relatively far apart from each other, width of basioccipital much exceeds that of interpterygoid foramen; foramen magnum large; P3 slender anterior to P4; P4 as large as M1 and M2, crown of cheek teeth normally structured, possesses orderly transverse and longitudinal dental ridge, not forming irregular surface; P4 possesses a longitudinal dental ridge inside and three transverse dental ridges outside; M1 and M2 possess a longitudinal ridge and two lophs; M3 possesses a longitudinal ridge and a loph. Distributed in tropical and subtropical zones of SE Asia. Of the nine species of *Hylopetes*, two occur in China.

Particolored Flying Squirrel

PLATE 6
MAP 29

Hylopetes alboniger (Hodgson, 1836)
黑白飞鼠 **Heibai Feishu**

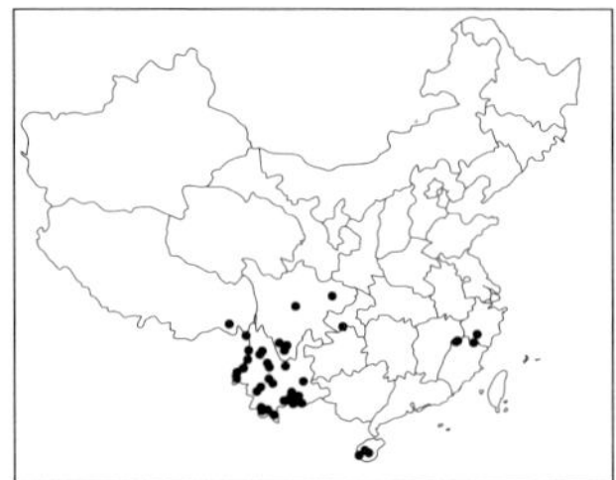

MAP 29. PARTICOLORED FLYING SQUIRREL, *Hylopetes alboniger*

Distinctive Characteristics: HB 175–247; T 172–227; HF 36–45; E 27–36; GLS 41–52. Throat white, extending as gray forward onto the cheek below the eye and behind the ears to form a "half-collar." Both sides of the ears are covered with minute black hairs. Dorsal color dark rufous brown shading into blackish on the limbs, dorsal surface of gliding membranes, and underside of tail; ventral color white to creamy (except tail). Tail not strongly flattened, as in *H. phayrei*. 2N = 38.
Distribution: SE China; extending broadly across SE Asia from the Himalayas to S Vietnam. Three subspecies in China: (1) *H. a. chianfengensis* Wang and Lu, 1966; Hainan; (2) *H. a. leonardi* (Thomas, 1921); NW Yunnan; (3) *H. a. orinus* (Allen, 1940); Yunnan, Sichuan, Guizhou, Guangxi, Zhejiang.
Natural History: The Particolored Flying Squirrel is much smaller than most other Chinese flying squirrels. They are arboreal and nocturnal, and nest in hollow trees, primarily in oak and rhododendron forests at middle to high elevation (1,500–3,400 m). *Hylopetes* and *Petaurista* are equally abundant in these forests. Nests consist of a ball of oak leaves and ferns lined with fine grasses. At night the squirrel's presence can be detected by a high-pitched trill, or a repeated "scree" vocalization. The diet consists of fruits, nuts, leaves, and buds. The breeding season runs from April through mid-June, and there are two or three young born each litter.
Conservation Status: China RL—NT; although it nearly met the criteria for VU A1cd. IUCN RL—EN A1c ver 2.3 (1994).
References: Mitchell (1977).

Indochinese Flying Squirrel

PLATE 6
MAP 30

Hylopetes phayrei (Blyth, 1859)
海南低泡飞鼠 **Hainandipao Feishu**

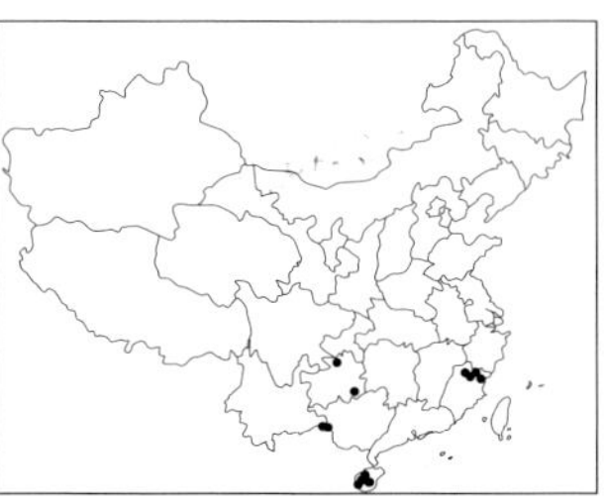

MAP 30. INDOCHINESE FLYING SQUIRREL, *Hylopetes phayrei*

Distinctive Characteristics: HB 144–173; T 128–159; HF 32–35; E 23–25; GLS 36–42. Smallest flying squirrel in China. No slender tufted hairs at the base of the ear; tail flattened, dorsal pelage russet. Cheeks white, extending behind the ears. Ventral pelage generally white tinged with yellow. Auditory bullae more than 20% of GLS, compared with *H. alboniger* whose bullae are less than 20% of GLS.
Distribution: Hainan Island, Guizhou, Guangxi, and Fujian. Endemic. Chinese subspecies: *H. p. electilus* (Allen, 1925).
Natural History: Occupies lower montane forests and mixed deciduous forests. These flying squirrels remain in hollow trees during the day and forage at night. *H. alboniger* and *H. phayrei* occur sympatrically on Hainan Island.
Conservation Status: China RL—VU A1c.
Comments: The form *electilus* may only occur on Hainan, although it is similar to mainland forms and adoption of additional subspecific notation in China may be unnecessary.

Genus *Petaurista*—Giant Flying Squirrels

鼯鼠属 **Wushu Shu**—鼯鼠 **Wushu**

This genus contains the largest forms in the tribe Pteromyini, HB plus tail length clearly more than 500 mm, and the largest more than 1,000 mm; no slender tufted hairs at the base of ears; tail length close to or surpasses HB length, tail narrow, rounded, slightly broader in one or two northern species. Three pairs of mammae. Skull broad; GLS mostly greater than 60 mm, frontal in interorbital region noticeably concave; sutures on frontal, parietal, and interparietal obsolete; postorbital process robust, its margin perpendicular to longitudinal axis of cranium; parietal possesses evident longitudinal ridge; orbital processes on upper margin of zygoma opposite the postorbital processes of the frontal; incisive foramen short, crown of molars complex, wrinkles present on inside posterior angular from P4 to M3; crown of P4 subequal to M1 in size; P3 very robust, lies in inner anterior part of P4, visible from outside of dentition.

Key to the Chinese Species of *Petaurista*

1.a.	Dorsal pelage light (gray or dusky), pale brown at base of ears	2
b.	Dorsal pelage not gray or dusky, not pale brown at base of ears	3
2.a.	Ventral pelage whitish brown; upper side of feet orange; size small, GLS < 65 mm	*Petaurista caniceps*
b.	Ventral pelage gray, upper sides of feet dusky; size large, GLS > 65 mm	*Petaurista xanthotis*
3.a.	Size small, tail length < 400 mm; dorsal pelage with large white spots	*Petaurista elegans*
b.	Size large, tail length > 400 mm; dorsal pelage without large white spots	4
4.a.	Cheek and side of head white	*Petaurista alborufus*
b.	Cheek and side of head not white	5
5.a.	Entire tail black (not tipped with black)	*Petaurista philippensis*
b.	Tail lighter but with dark or black tip	6
6.a.	Dorsal surface solid red (no yellow shoulder patch nor dark stripe on back)	*Petaurista petaurista*
b.	Yellow shoulder patches, broad dark brown stripe from head to base of tail	*Petaurista magnificus*

Occurs primarily in the Indo-Malayan realm, extending to the Palaearctic. Seven of the eight recognized species occur in China. This genus has presented numerous systematic problems, and the treatment below represents a hypothesis rather than a definitive description of these forms. Recent molecular data are beginning to unravel the true relationships among these taxa (Yu et al. 2006).

Red and White Giant Flying Squirrel

PLATE 7

Petaurista alborufus (Milne-Edwards, 1870) MAP 31

红白鼯鼠 Hongbai Wushu

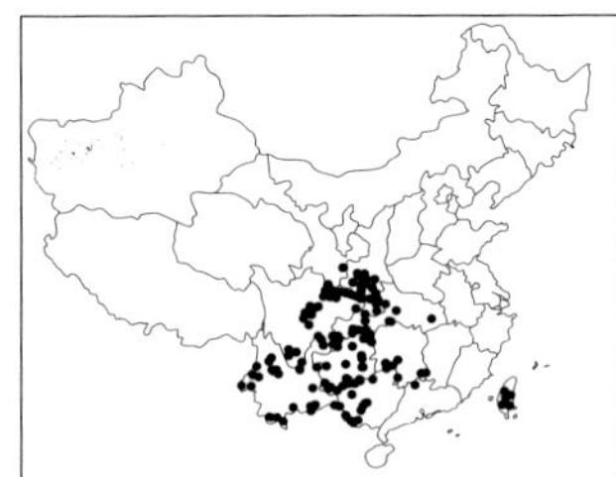

MAP 31. RED AND WHITE GIANT FLYING SQUIRREL, *Petaurista alborufus*

Distinctive Characteristics: HB 350–580; T 430–615; HF 78–90; E 47–59; GLS 78–83. Largest species in the genus, with a thick glossy pelage. Characterized by a large area of light speckling formed by mixture of wholly white or light russet hairs with maroon hairs on the dorsum; throat white; ventral pelage pinkish brown; base of tail possesses pinkish brown or off-white rings. Skull robust, with a strongly developed triangular postorbital process.

Distribution: Found throughout C and S China, including Taiwan; extending into Myanmar. Four subspecies in China: (1) *P. a. alborufus* (Milne-Edwards, 1870); W Sichuan, Gansu (hairs of feet red; a large area of light speckling on dorsum slightly russet tinged); (2) *P. a. castaneus* Thomas, 1923; E Sichuan, Hubei, Guizhou, Yunnan (hairs of feet black; tail base possesses pinkish brown rings; distal 2/3 of tail russet); (3) *P. a. lena* Thomas, 1907; Taiwan (smallest form); (4) *P. a. ochraspis* Thomas, 1923; Yunnan, Guangxi (hairs of feet red; speckling on dorsum lighter than in *P. a. alborufus*; tail base possesses nearly white rings; 2/3 of tail end nearly black).

Natural History: The Red and White Giant Flying Squirrel has rarely been collected, and little is known of its natural history. It inhabits dense hillside forests in mountainous terrain where nests are normally located high in tree hollows, although they may also occupy niches in limestone cliffs. In Taiwan it occurs in both hardwood and coniferous forests, preferring hardwood forest. Ranges from 800–3,500 m in elevation, but is most commonly found between 2,000 and 3,000 m. Nocturnal, it covers the home range by climbing high in trees and gliding distances of up to 400 m. Diet consists of acorns, other nuts, fruits, and leafy vegetation, as well as insects, larvae, and perhaps bird's eggs. The reproductive rate is low, most likely with litters of one or two young. It has been observed sympatric with *Hylopetes alboniger, P. phillipensis,* and *Trogopterus xanthipes.*

Conservation Status: China RL—LC.

Comments: Recent karyological studies have indicated that the Taiwanese form (*lena*) seems to be primitive when compared with mainland forms and could even be categorized as an independent species (Oshida et al. 2000). Chinese *Petaurista* from Qinghai and Gansu attributed to *alborufus* probably represent *P. xanthotis.*

References: Lee et al. (1993a); Oshida et al. (2000).

Gray-Headed Flying Squirrel

Petaurista caniceps (Gray, 1842) MAP 32

灰头小鼯鼠 Huitou Xiaowushu

Distinctive Characteristics: HB 300–370; T 360–400; HF 61–67; E 45–50; GLS 62–65. Size small. Dorsal pelage gray or dusky, pale brown at base of ears; ventral pelage whitish brown, throat pure white; upper side of feet orange; tail tip black. Lack of dorsal spots distinguishes this form from the similar *P. elegans.*

Distribution: South C China; extending to Nepal and Myanmar. Three subspecies recognized in China: (1) *P. c. clarkei* Thomas, 1922; Yunnan, Sichuan, Guizhou; (2) *P. c. gorkhali* (Lindsey, 1929); S Xizang; (3) *P. c. sybilla* Thomas and Wroughton, 1916; Yunnan, S. Sichuan. In addition, two apparently distinguishable but undescribed forms occur in Guangxi and Hunan, and Hubei, Shaanxi, and Gansu (Wang 2003). The ranges of *P. c. clarkei* and *P. c. sybilla* overlap *P. elegans* in Yunnan and Sichuan, and perhaps also E Nepal (Corbet and Hill 1992), supporting the view that these forms are distinct species.

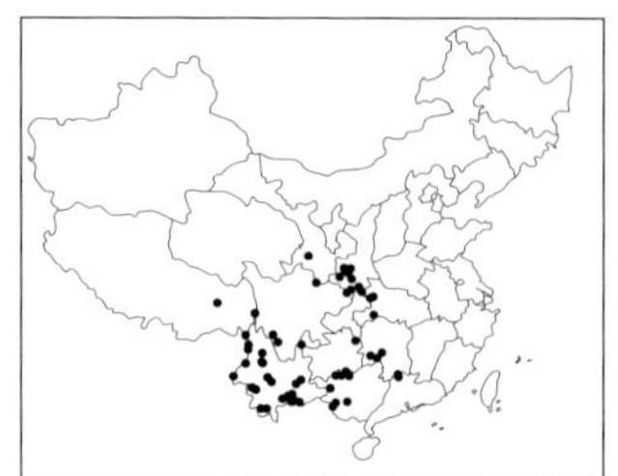

MAP 32. GRAY-HEADED FLYING SQUIRREL, *Petaurista caniceps*

Natural History: Occupies oak rhododendron forests from 2,100 to 3,600 m and temperate and alpine coniferous biotopes from 3,000 to 3,600 m. These squirrels are strictly arboreal and nocturnal and feed on rhododendron leaves, buds, and fir cones. Although pairs gave been sighted in oak and fir forests 30–40 m above the ground, they usually occur singly. Nest in hollow oak trees or build a nest of ferns in tall rhododendron and fir trees. These squirrels can be located at night by their continuous cries. Little information is available regarding their breeding habits. Females usually give birth to one, but sometimes two, young. A lactating female was collected in October.
Comments: Regarded as a full species by Corbet and Hill (1992) and Wang (2003), although treated as a subspecies of *P. elegans* by Thorington and Hoffmann (2005).
Conservation Status: China RL—LC.
References: Mitchell (1977).

Spotted Giant Flying Squirrel

PLATE 7
MAP 33

Petaurista elegans (Müller, 1840)
白斑小鼯鼠 Baiban Xiaowushu

MAP 33. SPOTTED GIANT FLYING SQUIRREL, *Petaurista elegans*

Distinctive Characteristics: HB 296–375; T 347–405; HF 59–68; E 44–45; GLS 62–65. Size small; dorsal pelage dark gray, dark yellow, or russet tinged, with many white-tipped hairs giving it a frosted or spotted appearance; gliding membranes darker reddish orange; tail color same as dorsum; rump and base of tail dark rufous and unspotted; lateral margin of gliding membrane to back of feet dark rufous-brown; inside of ear bases and orbits russet; ventral pelage bright orange-brown.
Distribution: South C China; extending to Myanmar, Vietnam, and Laos. Chinese subspecies: *P. e. marica* Thomas, 1912; Yunnan, Guangxi; *punctatus* (Gray, 1846) a synonym.
Natural History: The Spotted Giant Flying Squirrel is apparently a species of mountain forests where it is found in tall trees, but also often in rhododendron scrub and on rock cliffs. In the Himalayas it has been found to be quite common between 3,000 and 4,000 m. Nests in hollows in fir trees (*Abies spectabilis*), breeding just before the rainy season.
Comments: See comments under *P. caniceps*, which has been treated as a subspecies of *P. elegans* by some authors.
Conservation Status: China RL—LC.
References: Lekagul and McNeely (1977); Medway (1969).

Hodgson's Giant Flying Squirrel

PLATE 7
MAP 34

Petaurista magnificus (Hodgson, 1836)
栗褐鼯鼠 Lihe Wushu

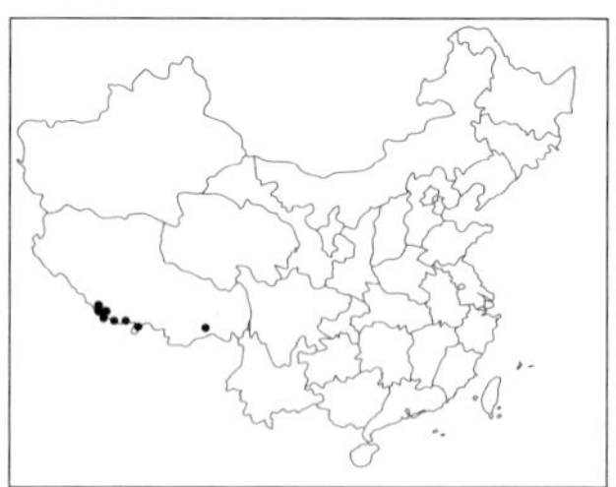

MAP 34. HODGSON'S GIANT FLYING SQUIRREL, *Petaurista magnificus*

Distinctive Characteristics: HB 359–420; T 415–480; HF 72–78; E 41–43; GLS 65–74; Wt 1,350 g. Size large; dorsal pelage dark brown or russet with a dark brown to blackish stripe running from head to base of tail, contrasting strongly with yellow patches on shoulders, bordered laterally by deep russet sides and gliding membranes; underparts and feet are light rufous and tail is deep brown at base, shading into rufous for most of its length, with a small black tip; feet black.
Distribution: S Xizang; extending into Nepal, Sikkim, and Bhutan.
Natural History: This species lives in evergreen and broadleaf forests from the lowlands up to 3,000 m; it seems to prefer deciduous forests. It is about 25% larger than *P. elegans*, with which it shares the same habitat. They are chiefly nocturnal and arboreal, and

feed on leaves, buds, and flowers of rhododendrons and trees, fruits, and even grass. Hodgson's Giant Flying Squirrel is highly vocal, uttering a deep monotonous booming call when emerging at dusk. At dusk these squirrels can be seen gliding 60–100 m from oaks to the rhododendron below, landing in a short upward arc at the end of the glide. They occupy nests with a round entrance at heights of 5–15 m above the ground. Here they make nests using moss and other soft materials. Reproductive habit not known, except that only mothers occupy nests with their young.
Conservation Status: China RL–NA. IUCN RL–LR/nt ver 2.3 (1994).
References: Shrestha (1981).

Red Giant Flying Squirrel

PLATE 7
MAP 35

Petaurista petaurista (Pallas, 1776)
红背鼯鼠 Hongbei Wushu

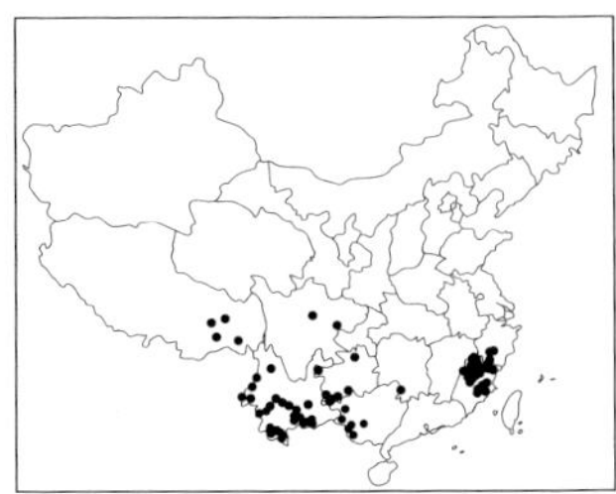

MAP 35. RED GIANT FLYING SQUIRREL, *Petaurista petaurista*

Distinctive Characteristics: HB 398–520; T 375–630; HF 63–100; E 35–507; GLS 63–78; Wt 1,596–2,450 g. Large, bright-red squirrel. Dorsal pelage russet, white tipped, and dark gray at the base, giving a grizzled appearance; ventral pelage light brown, not gray at base; tail color the same as the back, with dark brown to black tip; ear pinnae, around eyes and lower jaw dark brown, very noticeable; ear thin and nearly hairless. Postorbital process very large, perpendicular to axis of braincase; frontal bone deeply depressed.
Distribution: Across S China; extending widely along the Himalayas from Afghanistan, Pakistan, India, and Nepal through Myanmar and Thailand and south into Sumatra, Java, Borneo, and Malaysia. Two subspecies in China: (1) *P. p. albiventer* Gray, 1834; Yunnan; (2) *P. p. rufipes* Allen, 1925; Sichuan, Fujian, Guangxi, and Guangdong.
Natural History: Red Giant Flying Squirrels occupy evergreen broadleaf and coniferous forests between 1,500 and 2,400 m elevation. These squirrels build nests in hollows of tall trees or on cliff crannies. They are primarily nocturnal and vocalize mainly at dusk. They are generally associated in pairs, both with and without young. Diet consists of young fir and pine cones, fruit, leaves, and shoots. Limited evidence indicates that two young are produced.
Comments: *P. p. rufipes* Sody, 1949 from Sumatra is preoccupied by *P. p. rufipes* Allen, 1925 from China. *P. p. rufipes* Allen, 1925 was provisionally included in *P. philippensis* by Corbet and Hill (1992). The form *albiventer* may prove to be distinct; Yu et al. (2006) consider *albiventer* from N Pakistan to be independent. Molecular data further indicate that the form *grandis* (herein associated with *philippensis*) may best fit within *P. petaurista* (Yu et al. 2006).
Conservation Status: China RL–VU A1cd.
References: Medway (1969); Yu et al. (2006).

Indian Giant Flying Squirrel

PLATE 7
MAP 36

Petaurista philippensis (Elliot, 1839)
霜背大鼯鼠 Shuangbei Dawushu

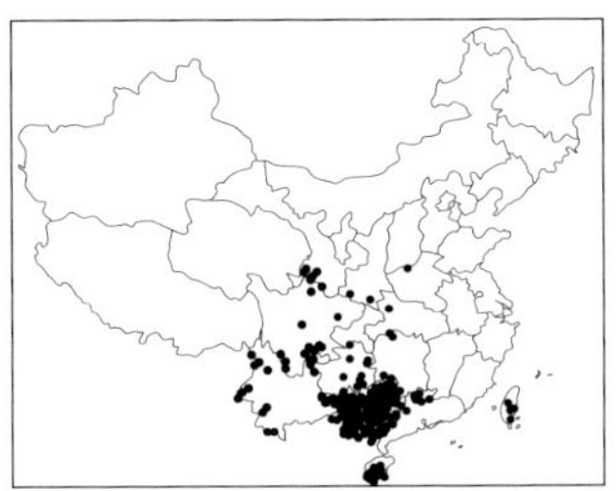

MAP 36. INDIAN GIANT FLYING SQUIRREL, *Petaurista philippensis*

Distinctive Characteristics: HB 410–610; T 550–691; HF 65–90; E 45–47; GLS 65–82. Second-largest species in the genus; entire dorsal pelage dark maroon to black, with white tips, so whole dorsum shows a gray hue; ventral pelage russet to buff, somewhat sparse; tail very long, all black; ears black, but with conspicuous red front surface.
Distribution: S China including Hainan and Taiwan; extending to Thailand, Myanmar, India, Sri Lanka, and the Indochinese peninsula. Five subspecies in China: (1) *P. p. grandis* (Swinhoe, 1863); Taiwan; (2) *P. p. hainana* Allen, 1925; Hainan Island; (3) *P. p. nigra* Wang, 1981; NW Yunnan; (4) *P. p. rubicundus* Howell, 1927; Sichuan, Shaanxi; (5) *P. p. yunanensis* (Anderson, 1875); Yunnan.
Natural History: On Hainan the Indian Giant Flying Squirrel has been found only in large patches of forest, where it was considered abundant. On Taiwan it is most abundant in hardwood compared with coniferous forest, and is most commonly found between 500 and 2,000 m elevation. Diet is broad in Taiwan and includes 30 plant species. Primarily eats young and mature leaves (74% of the diet). They are seasonal breeders in Taiwan, with peaks in spring and fall. About half of all females become pregnant in each breeding season. Litter size is normally one, although occasionally a second young will be produced.
Comments: Wang (2003) includes the forms *grandis, hainana, nigra,* and *yunanensis* in *Petaurista albiventer*—a taxon most include as a subspecies of *P. petaurista* (see Thorington and Hoffmann 2005). Wang also includes the form *rubicundus* in *P. sybilla* (herein *P. caniceps sybilla*). This fluid arrangement of subspecies within the genus indicates how poorly known these forms are, and this may result in misidentifications and inaccurate mapping of these forms. See Corbet and Hill (1992) for a recent effort to allocate

names among these groups. Finally, recent molecular data have been presented that indicate the forms *hainana* and *yunanensis* may be independent, and that *grandis* should be aligned with *P. petaurista* (Yu et al. 2006).
Conservation Status: China RL—LC.
References: Kuo and Lee (2003); Lee et al. (1993a; 1993b); Yu et al. (2006).

Chinese Giant Flying Squirrel

PLATE 7
MAP 37

Petaurista xanthotis (Milne-Edwards, 1872)
灰鼯鼠 Hui Wushu

MAP 37. CHINESE GIANT FLYING SQUIRREL, *Petaurista xanthotis*

Distinctive Characteristics: HB 325–430; T 294–350; HF 65–80; E 43–50; GLS 65–70; Wt 700–1,200 g. Pelage grayish yellow, soft, and loose; dorsum dark, with black underfur, guard hairs black at base, with white to buff tips; large orange spot behind black-tipped, round ears, otherwise lateral base of ears bright russet; throat white, remainder of ventrum grayish, due to black underfur and white tips of guard hairs; feet black but legs and outer margins of gliding membranes orange; upper side of feet dusky. Tail long, covered with long sparse black-and orange-tipped hairs; sharp contrast between light ventrum and dark underbase of tail. Cheek teeth are more complex than in any other *Petaurista*.
Distribution: Restricted to C China; Gansu, Sichuan, Yunnan, Qinghai, Xizang, and Shanxi. Endemic. Three subspecies: (1) *P. x. buechneri* (Matschie, 1907); between Gansu and Sichuan; (2) *P. x. filchnerinae* (Matschie, 1907); Gansu; (3) *P. x. xanthotis* (Milne-Edwards, 1872); Sichuan.
Natural History: Natural history information on this species is scarce, although records indicate that its range and numbers are extensive in spruce forest habitat at elevations of about 3,000 m in the highlands of western China. Nocturnally active and nests in burrows in trees. Diet consists of young shoots and leaves, as well as pine nuts. This species has been commonly collected for the fur trade, many specimens being secured in winter—evidence that the species does not hibernate. Reproduction occurs in summer; litter size is small, averaging two young.
Comments: Formerly included in *P. leucogenys* (of Japan), but see Corbet and Hill (1992).
Conservation Status: China RL—LC.
References: McKenna (1962).

Genus *Pteromys*—Northern Flying Squirrels

飞鼠属 Feishu Shu—飞鼠 Feishu

Size small. Skull has a large rounded braincase with a short rostrum; orbits large, a small gap present on anterior portion of postorbital process; projecting ridgelike in the central temporal fossa; incisive foramen large, its length equal to interpterygoid foramen breadth at least; auditory bullae highly inflated, its diameter equal to distance between anterior margin of auditory bullae and posterior margin of M_3; P_3 very small, before P_4, visible from lateral side; P_4 similar to M_1 and M_2, crown composed of an inside longitudinal ridge and three outside horizontal ridges; M_3 similar to M_1 and M_2 in size, but only two horizontal ridges between anterior and posterior margins; eight mammae. Distributed in broadleaf forests of the Palaearctic realm. There are two species in the genus, one of which is found in China.

Siberian Flying Squirrel

PLATE 6
MAP 38

Pteromys volans (Linnaeus, 1758)
小飞鼠 Xiao Feishu

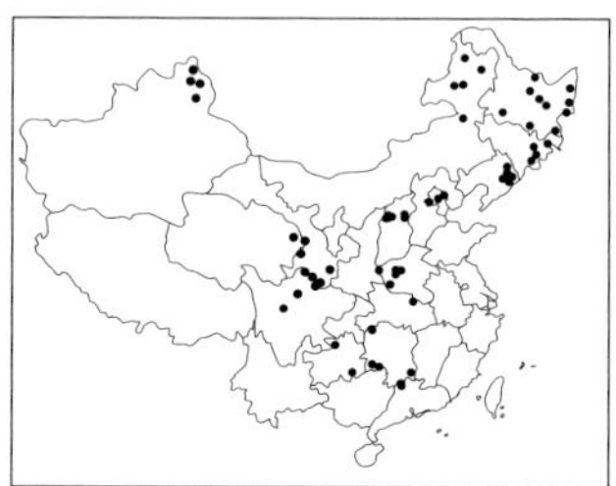

MAP 38. SIBERIAN FLYING SQUIRREL, *Pteromys volans*

Distinctive Characteristics: HB 156–198; T 100–122; HF 31–37; E 15–16; GLS 38–42; Wt 75–130 g. Size small with short dense (soft and silky) closely fitting body hairs. Dorsal pelage dusky and usually darker than ventral surface; ventral pelage whitish to buffy; feet white ventrally, brown dorsally. Hair on tail grows in an arrowhead pattern; tail flattened, lateral tail hairs longer, grayish black at the tip. Eyes black and large. Structure of cheek teeth very regular; no complex lophs on crown.
Distribution: NW China and NE China extending down into C China; extending from Hokkaido and Sakhalin across Siberia to Scandinavia. Four subspecies in China: (1) *P. v. arsenjevi* Ognev, 1935; NE Nei Mongol, Heilongjiang, Jilin, Liaoning; (2) *P. v. buechneri* Satunin, 1903; Shanxi, Gansu, Ningxia, Qinghai; (3) *P. v. turovi* Ognev, 1929; Xinjiang; (4) *P. v. wulungshanensis* (Mori, 1939); Hebei, Beijing, Henan, Shanxi.
Natural History: This species characteristically inhabits the boreal evergreen forests of the Old World from Scandinavia to eastern Siberia, including the fir forests of N China up to 2,500 m. Also frequents mature birch forests. Nests are constructed in hollows in trees, and they also construct dreys (leaf nests high in trees). Most Siberian Fying Squirrels occupy

several nests, which they change frequently. They do not hibernate and are strictly nocturnal. Individuals are highly mobile, often moving up to 300 m per night. Diet consists of nuts, pine seeds, buds, shoots, leaves, berries, alder and birch catkins, and occasional bird's eggs and nestlings, mushrooms, and insects. They collect large food stores. Small litters of one to four young are produced in early spring.
Conservation Status: China RL–VU A1cd. IUCN RL–LR/nt ver 2.3 (1994).
References: Hanski et al. (2000).

Genus *Sciurus*—Tree Squirrels

松鼠属 Songshu Shu—松鼠 Songshu

Habits typically arboreal, form slender; tail long, its length more than half HB length. Some species grow long tufted hairs on their ears in winter. Interorbital region faintly concave, posterior margin of nasal nearly in the same line as premaxilla, cranium protruding, temporal ridge low and weak. Dental formula: 1.0.2.3/1.0.1.3 = 22; first upper premolar very small, rod shaped; a small cusp often present between second upper premolar and second and third cusps outside of first and second molars, prominent when viewed from sides, its surface possess two lophlike processes; baculum spoonlike, a small process present at right side. Broadly distributed in both Palaearctic and Nearctic realms; of 28 species in the genus, a single species occurs in China.

Eurasian Red Squirrel

Sciurus vulgaris Linnaeus, 1758 — PLATE 8, MAP 39
松鼠 Songshu

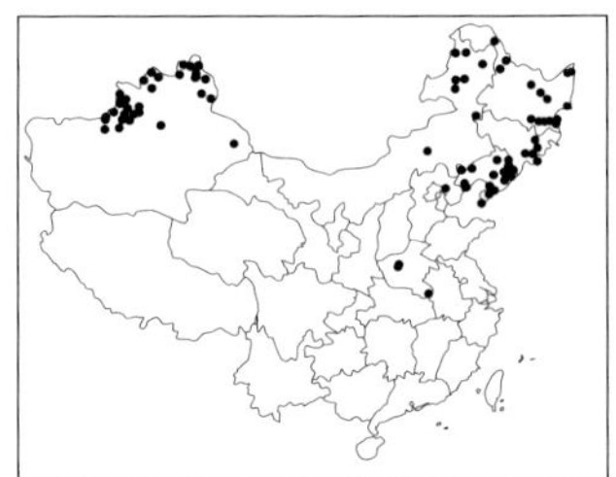

MAP 39. EURASIAN RED SQUIRREL, *Sciurus vulgaris*

Distinctive Characteristics: HB 178–260; T 159–215; HF 25–70; E 33–36; GLS 44–48; Wt 200–480 g. In winter pelage, long tufts of upright hair grow on the ears; in summer, the ears are not tufted, but the tail hairs are very long and bushy. Two color phases occur: winter pelage gray or brown on dorsum, whitish on venter; summer pelage black or brownish black on dorsum, whitish at venter. Eight mammae. Skull possesses a short rostrum and rounded zygomatic arches; nasals are narrow at the base and wider anteriorly.
Distribution: NW and NE China; extending across the forested regions of the Palaearctic, from Iberia and Great Britain east to the Kamchatka Peninsula and Sakhalin Island. Four subspecies in China: (1) *S. v. altaicus* Serebrennikov, 1928; NW Xinjiang, W Nei Mongol; (2) *S. v. chiliensis* Sowerby, 1921; Hebei, Henan, Shanxi, Shaanxi, Yunnan; (3) *S. v. exalbidus* Pallas, 1778; Xinjiang; (4) *S. v. mantchuricus* Thomas, 1909; Heilongjiang, Jilin, Liaoning, E Nei Mongol.
Natural History: The Eurasian Red Squirrel occupies northern evergreen forests where it is diurnally active. Does not hibernate. Diet consists largely of conifer seeds, acorns, fungi, bark, and sap tissue. Individuals store food in larder hoards (hollow trees), or a scatter hoards (buried in shallow holes or under surface litter). They maintain home ranges 2–10 ha in size that usually overlap. Both sexes also build one or more dreys within their home ranges. The peak of mating activities is early spring (January–March) followed by birth of first litters (March–May), or later (July–September). Litter size ranges from one to eight. Young are weaned after 7–10 weeks and are independent at 10–16 weeks.
Conservation Status: China RL–NT; although it nearly met the criteria for VU A2cd + 3cd. IUCN RL–NT ver 3.1 (2001).

Genus *Trogopterus* (monotypic)

复齿鼯鼠属 Fuchiwushu Shu

Complex-Toothed Flying Squirrel

Trogopterus xanthipes (Milne-Edwards, 1867) — PLATE 6, MAP 40
复齿鼯鼠 Fuchi Wushu

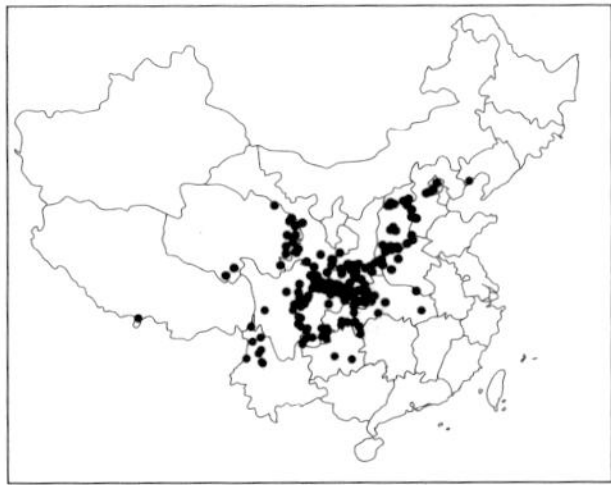

MAP 40. COMPLEX-TOOTHED FLYING SQUIRREL, *Trogopterus xanthipes*

Distinctive Characteristics: HB 200–300; T 260–270; HF 56–60; E 30; GLS 55–61. Size medium, dorsal pelage light reddish buff, dark gray at base; ventral pelage light gray at base, russet at tips; lateral margin of gliding membrane and central ventral side bright brown. Tail slightly shorter than HB length and slightly flattened. Long black hairs predominate on the tip of the tail. A prominent characteristic is the tuft of slender black hairs around the base of the ears. Skull structure not unusual; length of upper cheek dentition surpasses one quarter of GLS, P4 large, its crown larger than those of molars, small P3 hidden in upper inside angle of P4, invisible from outside; crowns of upper and lower cheek dentition have complicated wrinkled dental ridge; upper incisors small, lack longitudinal groove. 2N = 38.

Distribution: Widely distributed across C China. Endemic.
Natural History: Closely associated with forest habitats, in particular temperate forests. Feeds from the canopy of oaks and pines, primarily eating oak leaves. Apparently nests in caves that provide a stable microclimate for this species, and glides between cliff faces and nearby trees. Nocturnal. Litter size ranges from one to four, gestation is 78–89 days, and sexual maturity is attained at 22 months of age.
Comments: Closely related to *Belomys*.
References: Wang (1985a).
Conservation Status: China RL–VU A1cd. IUCN RL–EN A1cd ver 2.3 (1994).

Subfamily Callosciurinae—Oriental Tree Squirrels

丽松鼠亚科 **Lisongshu Yake—丽松鼠 Li Songshu**

Generalized diurnal squirrels, most forms arboreal. Tails moderately bushy; no distinctive ear tufts. Dental formula: 1.0.2.3/1.0.1.3 = 22. The Callosciurinae is comprised of 14 genera and 64 species; of these, 4 genera and 15 species occur in China.

Genus *Callosciurus*—Beautiful Tree Squirrels

丽松鼠属 **Lisongshu Shu—丽松鼠 Lisongshu**

Habits typically arboreal, similar to *Sciurus* in size and form, no tufts of hair on ears; tail long, no stripes on dorsum. *Callosciurus* effectively fills the tree squirrel niche in southern Asian tropical forests that is occupied by *Sciurus* in Holarctic forests. Two or three pairs of mammae. Skull profile similar to *Sciurus*, but smaller; rostrum short and broad; postorbital process robust, curved downward externally; interorbital constriction approximately equal to breadth of rostrum, greater than length of nasal; coronoid process of mandible well developed. Baculum unusual; the body and edge portion are separated from each other. *Callosciurus* is comprised of 15 species, 6 of which live in China.

Gray-Bellied Squirrel

Callosciurus caniceps (Gray, 1842) MAP 41

金背松鼠 **Jinbei Songshu**

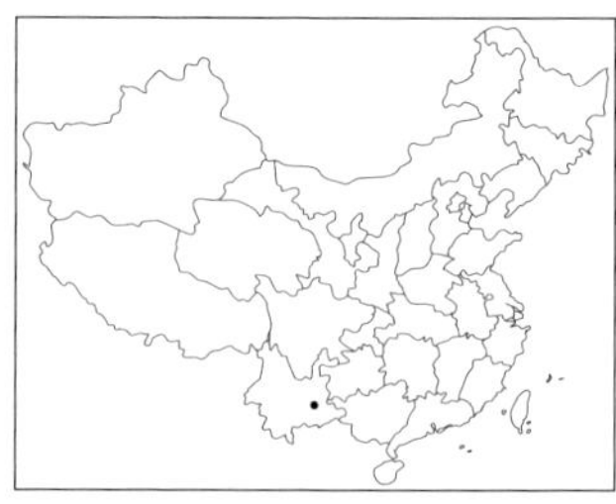

MAP 41. GRAY-BELLIED SQUIRREL, *Callosciurus caniceps*

Distinctive Characteristics: HB 194–391; T 156–242; HF 49–54; E 19–23; GLS 50–56; Wt 227–270 g. Dorsum dark brown, ventral pelage silvery gray; tail gray with a distinct black tip.

Key to the Chinese Genera of Callosciurinae

1.a.	Black and/or white lines on back	2
b.	No black and/or white lines on back	3
2.a.	HB $>$ 150 mm; nasal bones long; coronoid process of mandible poorly developed	*Menetes*
b.	HB $<$ 150 mm; nasal bones short; coronoid process of mandible well developed	*Tamiops*
3.a.	Dorsal pelage light, often olive-gray; two pairs of mammae; nasal bones short	*Callosciurus*
b.	Dorsal pelage dark, often agouti; base of tail or thigh orangish; three pairs of mammae; nasal bones long	*Dremomys*

Key to the Chinese Species of *Callosciurus*

1.a.	Lateral black stripes wide, running from base of forelimbs to base of hindlimbs	2
b.	No lateral dark stripes	3
2.a.	Ventral pelage orange	*Callosciurus phayeri*
b.	Ventral pelage with broad median stripe running from belly to vent	*Callosciurus quinquestriatus*
3.a.	Distinct or indistinct red hip patch	4
b.	No red hip patch	5
4.a.	Ventral pelage maroon; baculum long and thin	*Callosciurus erythraeus*
b.	Ventral pelage gray, intergrading to cream or buff; baculum short and thick	*Callosciurus pygerythmus*
5.a.	Ventral pelage plain silvery gray, feet and legs gray; distributed west of Mekong river	*Callosciurus caniceps*
b.	Ventral pelage violet-gray; feet and legs agouti; distributed east of Mekong River	*Callosciurus inornatus*

Distribution: Yunnan; extending into Thailand, Myanmar, and the Malay Peninsula. Chinese form the nominate subspecies.
Natural History: This squirrel is well adapted to the presence of people; it may be found in plantations, cultivated areas, second growth, and gardens, as well as forest. In natural habitats it seems to prefer dense dipterocarp forests with thick brushy vegetation. It may be found up to 2,500 m but is usually found at lower elevations. The Gray-bellied Squirrel is normally arboreal, although it sometimes descends to the ground to pick up food, which it then carries into a tree and eats. The alarm call is loud and repetitive. Diet consists of fruit and some insects. The spherical nest is built on the upper branches of a bush or small tree. The home range is small compared with other arboreal squirrels and does not change in size seasonally. There are two to four young in a litter.
Comments: In the past many have considered *C. caniceps* a subspecies of *C. erythraeus*, which in turn has at least 80 synonyms (Corbet and Hill 1992; Thorington and Hoffmann 2005).
Conservation Status: China RL—VU D2.
References: Moore and Tate (1965); Medway (1969); Saiful et al. (2001).

Pallas's Squirrel

PLATE 8
MAP 42

Callosciurus erythraeus (Pallas, 1779)
赤腹松鼠 Chifu Songshu

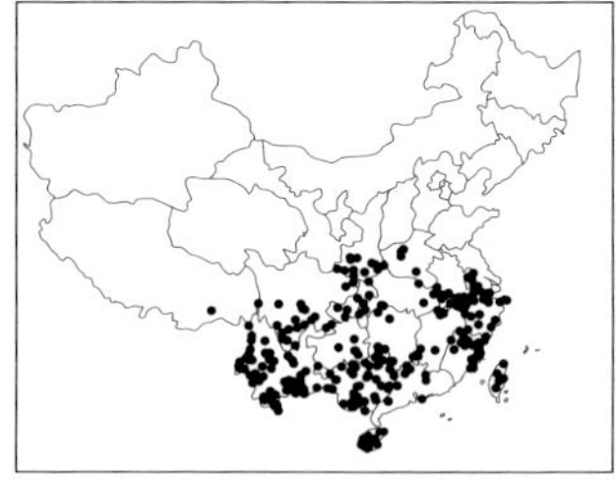

MAP 42. PALLAS'S SQUIRREL, *Callosciurus erythraeus*

Distinctive Characteristics: HB 175–240; T 146–267; HF 41–55; E 18–23; GLS 48–56; Wt 280–420 g. The pelage characteristics of this widespread species are highly variable. Dorsal pelage olive gray; ventral pelage a rich red, maroon, brown, or buffy; an olive or olive-gray line is present at midline in some forms; ear same color as dorsum. The tail shows diffuse banding, flecked with black and tan, and is sometimes black tipped. Baculum long and thin. Skull broad; interorbital constriction about 17–19 mm, slightly more than a third of GLS.
Distribution: Widely distributed in SE China, including Hainan and Taiwan; extending to India, Myanmar, Thailand, Malay Peninsula, Indochina. Nine subspecies in China, but see Wang (2003) who recognized 19 forms: (1) *C. e. bonhotei* (Robinson and Wroughton, 1911); E and S Sichuan; (2) *C. e. castaneoventris* (Gray, 1842); Guandong, Guangxi, S Hunan, S Guizhou, SE Yunnan, Hainan Island; (3) *C. e. centralis* (Bonhote, 1901); Taiwan; (4) *C. e. gloveri* (Thomas, 1921); W Sichuan, NW Yunnan, SE Xizang; (5) *C. e. gordoni* (Anderson, 1871); W Yunnan; (6) *C. e. hendeei* Osgood, 1932; S Yunnan; (7) *C. e. michianus* (Robinson and Wroughton, 1911); SW Yunnan; (8) *C. e. ningpoensis* (Bonhote, 1901); Zhejiang and Fujian; (9) *C. e. styani* (Thomas, 1894); Jiangsu, N Zhejiang, Anhui, Henan, Hubei.
Natural History: Pallas's Squirrel mainly inhabits tropical and subtropical forests at low elevations, although it may be found in subalpine coniferous forests or in a mix of conifers and broadleaf trees at altitudes above 3,000 m. Primarily active at dawn and dusk, they are very active jumping among trees. They make leaf nests high in trees that are used throughout the year; underground nests may be made during winter. Individuals maintain traditional home ranges, although these are more fixed in the case of females; males and young animals are more likely to shift home ranges seasonally in response to population density or varying food availability. Highly vocal, including a variety of antipredator calls that elicit predator-specific antipredator behavior. Males produce two types of mating vocalizations: precopulatory calls and postcopulatory calls. Postcopulatory calls may last up to 17 minutes and allow males to efficiently guard their mate without interruption. Feed on different kinds of nuts, berries, insects, even bird's eggs and fledglings. Reproductive rate low; only litter sizes of two have been reported.
Comments: The large number of subspecies does not necessarily reflect true isolation of unique populations; rather there appears to be considerable morphological and color variation across the species range.
Conservation Status: China RL—LC.
References: Setoguchi (1991); Tamura (1995); Yo et al. (1992).

Inornate Squirrel

MAP 43

Callosciurus inornatus (Gray, 1867)
印支松鼠 Yinzhi Songshu

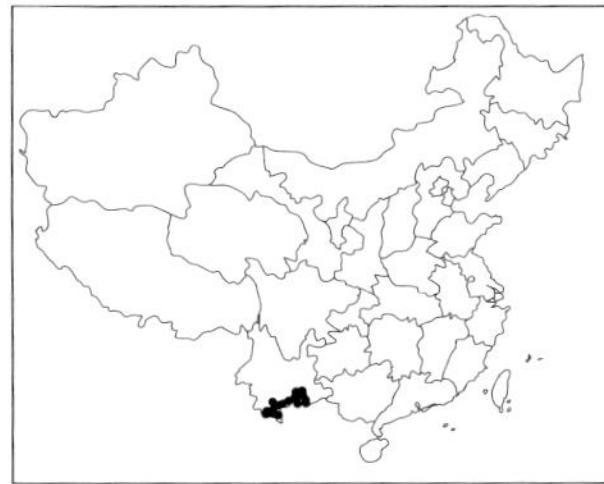

MAP 43. INORNATE SQUIRREL, *Callosciurus inornatus*

Distinctive Characteristics: HB 218–291; T 176–210; HF 46–49; E 20–22; GLS 51–52. Ventral pelage light violet-gray from chin to wrists and ankles; chin almost invariably bluish gray; dorsal pelage agouti, with two or three light bands on individual hairs, and deep olive in color; ears and feet same as dorsal pelage. The tail is colored dorsally the same as the dorsal pelage, and often black-tipped. Baculum short and robust. *C. inornatus* is smaller than *C. e. hendeei*,

with which it is almost completely sympatric (see above); comparatively, *inornatus* lacks the lighter color markings on the hip of *hendeei*; also the feet and forelegs are colored like the dorsum instead of being noticeably more gray.
Distribution: S Yunnan, extending into Laos and Vietnam.
Natural History: This species has been reported from a variety of habitats: scrub, degraded evergreen forest, and pristine evergreen forest.
Comments: *C. inornatus* has been included as a subspecies of *C. erythraeus* but is likely more closely allied with *caniceps*.
Conservation Status: China RL—VU A1cd; B1ab(iii).

Phayre's Squirrel
Callosciurus phayrei (Blyth, 1855) MAP 44
非氏松鼠 Feishi Songshu

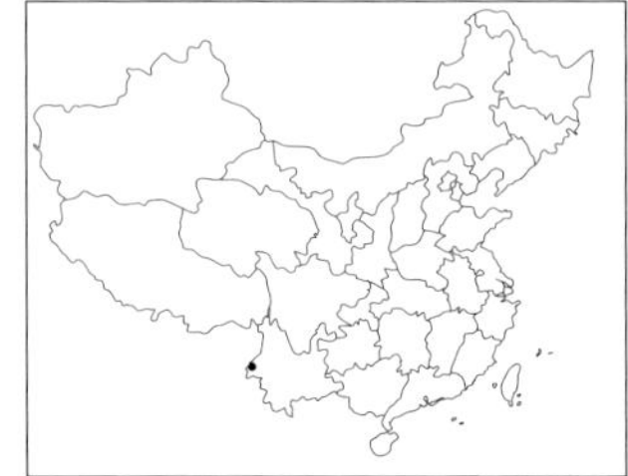

MAP 44. PHAYRE'S SQUIRREL, *Callosciurus phayrei*

Distinctive Characteristics: HB 190–220; T 160–210; HF 50–54; GLS 46–54. This species has a distinctive color pattern: a diffuse lateral dark stripe as wide as 1 cm runs from the base of the forelimbs to the base of the hindlimbs separating the dorsal and ventral pelage. The rostrum, ears, crown, and side of the neck are agouti gray like the dorsum. The ventral pelage varies from rich orange to very pale orange but is never red or gray. All four feet are yellowish buff to pale orange. The tail is black-tipped, and a bright yellow 12–15 mm wide stripe runs ventrally down the tail. The baculum is short and robust.
Distribution: W Yunnan; extending into Myanmar.
Natural History: This species appears to inhabit the rainforest vegetation area from the mouth of the Salween River northward. Phayre's Squirrel is apparently the medium-sized tree squirrel in these tropical deciduous forests
Conservation Status: China RL—NA.
References: Moore and Tate (1965).

Irrawaddy Squirrel
PLATE 8
Callosciurus pygerythrus
(Geoffroy Saint-Hilaire, 1831) MAP 45
蓝腹松鼠 Lanfu Songshu
Distinctive Characteristics: HB 190–230; T 110–220; HF 43–48; E 17–20; GLS 49–52; Wt 230–300. Dorsum dark olive-brown. The light bluish gray ventral pelage is not uniform, as these colors grade into cream and orange-buff. Pale red patch on hip. Tail gray and with an evident black tip. Front legs and all feet are grayer than the back. Baculum short and stout. Skull narrow, frontal breath less than 1/3 of occipital-nasal length; auditory bullae small, usually less than 9.2 mm.

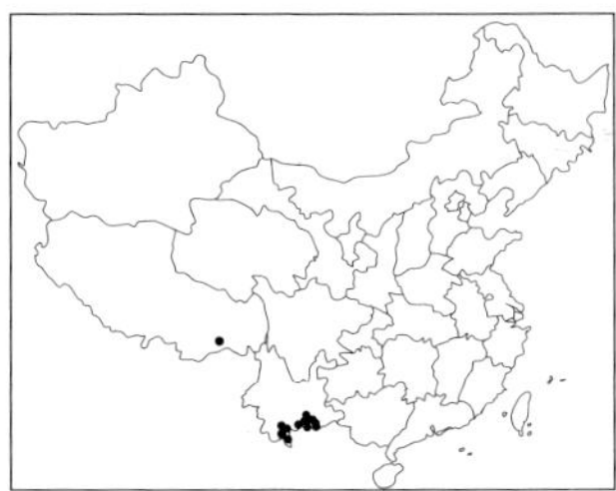

MAP 45. IRRAWADDY SQUIRREL, *Callosciurus pygerythrus*

Distribution: Yunnan; extending into Myanmar, Nepal, India. Chinese subspecies: *C. p. stevensi* (Thomas, 1908).
Natural History: Primarily occupies rainforest habitat at 600–1,300 m elevation. Often found in cane shrubs at forest edge or in banana plantations. Lives in the holes of trees. Throughout its range *pygerythrus* is sympatric with a larger species of tree squirrel; in China, *C. erythraeus*. Normally solitary, although sometimes seen moving in pairs, and diurnally active. Diet consists of flower buds of bananas or other fruit, but also insects. Reproduces once each year, and litter size averages three or four young.
Comments: This species exhibits seasonal changes in pelage color (see Moore and Tate (1965).
Conservation Status: China RL—NA. IUCN RL—VU A1cd ver 2.3 (1994).
References: Moore and Tate (1965).

Anderson's Squirrel
PLATE 8
Callosciurus quinquestriatus
(Anderson, 1871) MAP 46
五纹松鼠 Wuwen Songshu

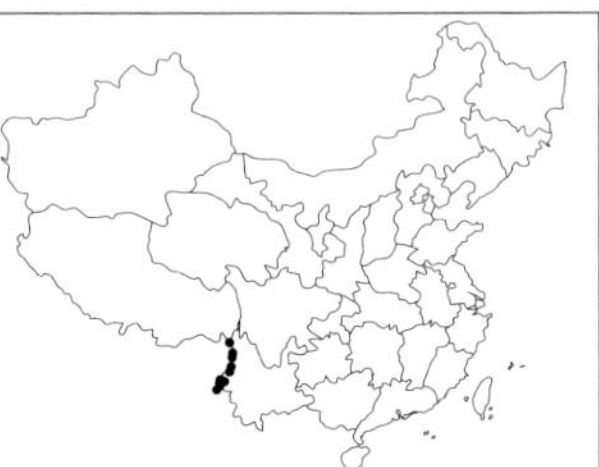

MAP 46. ANDERSON'S SQUIRREL, *Callosciurus quinquestriatus*

Distinctive Characteristics: HB 200–222; T 180–210; HF 44–55; E 18–23; GLS 50–55; Wt 258–315 g. Dorsum a grizzled olive-brown or olive-yellow, but with a rufous tint. Ventral pelage white, but marked with one to three black or nut-black midline or lateral stripes; one of these runs along the midline of the chest from the belly to the vent. These stripes are separated by white, and one is apparent when viewed from the

side, distinctly dividing the ventral and dorsal pelage. The chin and throat are gray. The tail is the same color as the dorsum, but with black and rufous annulations and tipped in black. Skull similar to *Callosciurus erythraeus*; anterior part of nasal much inflated, posterior part narrower; interorbital region broad, often more than 1/3 of occipital-nasal length.
Distribution: Yunnan; extending into Myanmar. Three subspecies in China: (1) *C. q. imarius* Thomas, 1926; Yunnan-Myanmar border region; (2) *C. q. quinquestriatus* (Anderson, 1871); SW Yunnan; (3) *C. q. sylvester* Thomas, 1926; W Yunnan.
Natural History: This species occurs primarily in mountain forests above about 1,000 m but can also be found in the lowlands. It lives alone or in small family groups. Nests are built of twigs, and placed on the outer branches of small trees. Diet consists of vegetation and a fair proportion of insects. One female pregnant with a single embryo was recorded in March.
Comments: At one time *quinquestriatus* was included in *C. erythraeus*, but it is clearly distinct and broadly sympatric with *erythraeus* in Yunnan, thus its treatment here as an independent species (see also Thorington and Hoffmann 2005).
Conservation Status: China RL—VU D2. IUCN RL—VU A1cd ver 2.3 (1994).
References: Medway (1969).

Genus *Dremomys*—Red-cheeked Squirrels

长吻松鼠属 Changwensongshu Shu—长吻松鼠 Changwen Songshu

Habits semiarboreal; tail hairs not fluffed out, ears lack tufted hairs; some species possess reddish marks on venter and cheeks; most prominent character of skull is long, narrow rostrum, tapering forward from base; frontal and orbital regions often shorter than 30% of GLS, nasal length more than width of interorbital constriction; skull round and convex; dental formula: 1.0.2.3/1.0.1.3 = 22, first upper premolar not much reduced, equal to second upper premolar and molars in height; shaft of baculum slightly curved, but not forming an obtuse angle, edge portion curved backwards from shaft, base large but anterior extremity tapering, upper side flattened and process lacking. Of six species of *Dremomys*, five occur in China.

Red-Throated Squirrel

Dremomys gularis Osgood, 1932 MAP 47
橙喉长吻松鼠 Chenhouchangwen Songshu

MAP 47. RED-THROATED SQUIRREL, *Dremomys gularis*

Distinctive Characteristics: HB 187–230; T 145–180; HF 42–50; E 23–26; GLS 58. Similar to *D. pyrrhomerus* and *D. rufigenis*, but chin, throat, and neck a rich ochraceous tawny in abrupt contrast to other underparts; ventral pelage dark blue-gray; flank patch obsolescent and reduced to a narrow line; entire ventral side of tail red.
Distribution: Yunnan; extending into Vietnam.
Natural History: The type specimen was collected at high elevation (2,500–3,000 m) from Mount Fan Si Pan, near Chapa Tonkin, Vietnam. It was the only *Dremomys* found at this high altitude, but it was found in company with *Tamiops swinhoei olivaceus*, microtines, and other species having affinities with northern mammals. Little else is known of its ecology.
Comments: This distinctive species has in the past been included in *pyrrhomerus* or *rufigenis*, but their diagnostic characters are constant, leading Corbet and Hill (1992) to justify their specific rank.
Conservation Status: China RL—NT; although it nearly met the criteria for VU B1ab(i, ii, iii).
References: Osgood (1932).

Key to the Chinese Species of *Dremomys*

1.a.	Ventral surface of tail solid rich red	2
b.	Ventral surface of tail not solid red	4
2.a.	Ventral surface dark gray, with some admixture of white	*Dremomys gularis*
b.	Ventral surface light grayish white	3
3.a.	Prominent orange-red spots on external surface of thigh; cheeks not bright orange-red	*Dremomys pyrrhomerus*
b.	No bright orange spot on external thigh; cheeks bright orange red	*Dremomys rufigenis*
4.a.	Ventral surface whitish to light gray, ventral surface of tail reddish at base turning to russet or isabelline toward tip	*Dremomys pernyi*
b.	Throat and ventral surface dusky orange, ventral surface of tail black with a mixture of orange hairs	*Dremomys lokriah*

Orange-Bellied Himalayan Squirrel

Dremomys lokriah (Hodgson, 1836) MAP 48

橙腹长吻松鼠 Chenfuchangwen Songshu

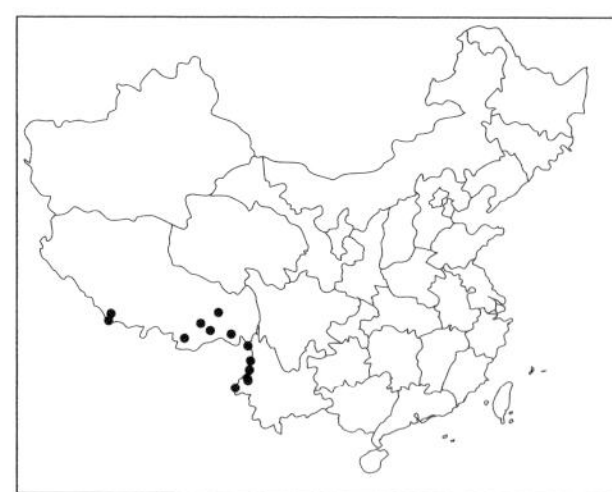

MAP 48. ORANGE-BELLIED HIMALAYAN SQUIRREL, *Dremomys lokriah*

Distinctive Characteristics: HB 165–205; T 135–220; HF 38–48; E 15–24; GLS 46–53; Wt 150–240 g. A dark rufous brown animal; back of ear with white spots; ventral pelage orange to buffy; ventral side of tail black with a mixture of orange hairs, although not red.
Distribution: Xizang and Yunnan; extending into Myanmar, Bhutan, Nepal, India. Four subspecies in China: (1) *D. l. lokriah* (Hodgson, 1836); S Xizang (Mt. Everest region); (2) *D. l. macmillani* Thomas and Wroughton, 1916; SE Xizang; (3) *D. l. motuoensis* Cai and Zhang, 1980; SE Xizang; (4) *D. l. subflaviventris* Thomas, 1922; E Yunnan.
Natural History: The Orange-bellied Himalayan Squirrel lives in a variety of habitats from 1,500 to 3,400 m elevation. Occupies oak-rhododendron forests to subtropical forests at lower elevations, and conifer forests at high elevations. Strictly diurnal, and nests in tree hollows close to the ground. The nest consists of fern and oak leaves, with a lining of fine grasses. Frequently comes to the ground to search for fruits, nuts, and plant materials. A favorite food is mistletoe (*Usnea longissima*). In the eastern Himalayas, individuals have been seen feeding on the fruits of *Pandanus furcatus*. Insects are also an important part of the diet. Utters loud sharp squeaky vocalizations, which are often repeated. Young are born from May to August in litters of two to five young. Lactating females have been seen in May, June, and August.
Conservation Status: China RL—NT; although it nearly met the criteria for VU B1ab(i, ii, iii).
References: Abe (1971); Mitchell (1977).

Perny's Long-Nosed Squirrel

Dremomys pernyi (Milne-Edwards, 1867) PLATE 8 MAP 49

珀氏长吻松鼠 Poshichangwen Songshu

Distinctive Characteristics: HB 170–230; T 156–180; HF 43–54; E 19–28; GLS 46–55; Wt 160–225 g. Dorsum olive-brown; ventral pelage buffy-white; ventral and dorsal side of tail reddish at base, other parts russet or isabelline. This is a fairly distinct, large northern species distinguished by its lighter gray dorsal pelage and tail. Venter is white from chin to anus, while anal area and inner sides of hindlimbs are bright rusty brown; yellow tufts behind ears. Lacks red markings on chin and throat. 2N = 38.
Distribution: Throughout C and SE China, including Taiwan; extending into Vietnam, Myanmar, and India. Seven subspecies in China: (1) *D. p. calidior* Thomas, 1916; Fujian, Jiangxi, Zhejiang, Anhui; (2) *D. p. flavior* Allen, 1912; Yunnan, Guangxi; (3) *D. p. howelli* Thomas, 1922; SW Yunnan; (4) *D. p. modestus* Thomas, 1916; Guizhou, S Hunan, Guangxi, Guangdong; (5) *D. p. owstoni* (Thomas, 1908); Taiwan; (6) *D. p. pernyi* (Milne-Edwards, 1867); W Sichuan, NW Yunnan, S Gansu, S Shaanxi; (7) *D. p. senex* Allen, 1912; Hubei, N Guizhou.

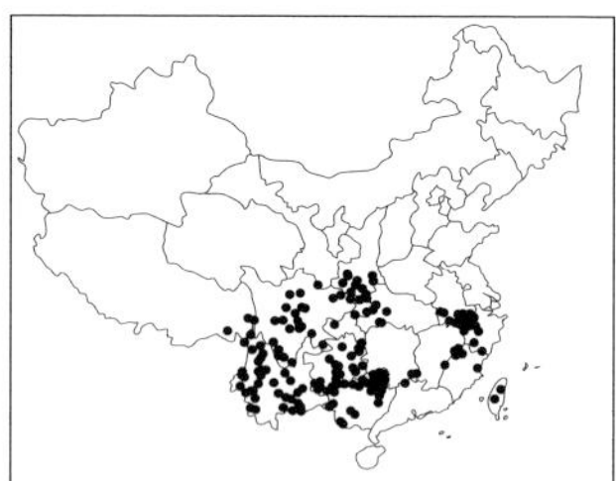

MAP 49. PERNY'S LONG-NOSED SQUIRREL, *Dremomys pernyi*

Natural History: Typically found in forest uplands from 2,000 to 3,500 m in elevation, where they live in evergreen broadleaf trees and conifers. They are diurnal and primarily terrestrial (commonly seen running along fallen tree trunks). Highly vocal; they utter cries that have great power and resonance.
Comments: This species replaces *lokriah* in the east and is sympatric with it in N Myanmar and Assam; in C and E China, *pernyi* and *pyrrhomerus* in some manner seem to share this vast area. The ranges of the *lokriah, pernyi*, and *rufigenis* seem to overlap broadly in upper Myanmar.
Conservation Status: China RL—LC.
References: Moore and Tate (1965); Thomas (1922a).

Red-Hipped Squirrel

Dremomys pyrrhomerus (Thomas, 1895) PLATE 8 MAP 50

红腿长吻松鼠 Hongtuichangwen Songshu

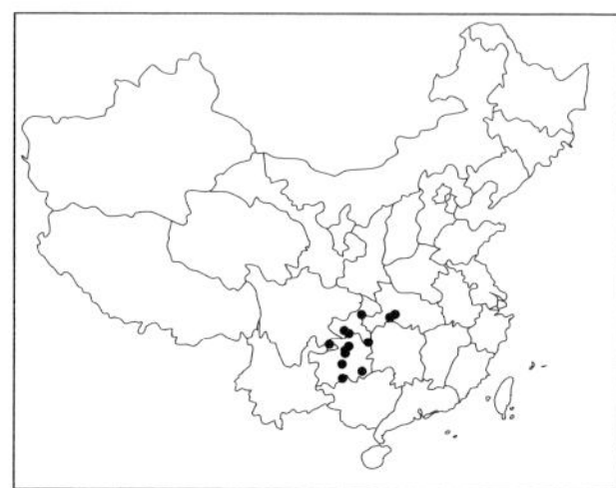

MAP 50. RED-HIPPED SQUIRREL, *Dremomys pyrrhomerus*

Distinctive Characteristics: HB 195–210; T 140–162; HF 50–55; E 22–24; GLS 55–58. Evident reddish spots present on thigh; cheek and sides of neck not conspicuously reddish. Dorsum olive-gray, venter, gray, and white, yellowish spots behind eyes; tail is white-grizzled above and brilliant red below.

Distribution: Central S China and Hainan Island. Endemic. Three subspecies: (1) *D. p. melli* Matschie, 1922; Guangxi, Hunan, Guangdong, Fujian, Anhui; (2) *D. p. pyrrhomerus* (Thomas, 1895); Sichuan, Guizhou, Hubei; (3) *D. p. ruidonensis* Allen, 1906; Hainan.
Natural History: These squirrels are apparently, almost entirely terrestrial, and live in holes in the rocky habitats. During the winter months they are infrequently active. The species seems to have a very spotty distribution.
Comments: Some older treatments include *pyrrhomerus* in *D. rufigenis*, with which it is broadly sympatric.
Conservation Status: China RL—NT; although it nearly met the criteria for VU A2cd + 3cd.

Asian Red-Cheeked Squirrel

PLATE 8
MAP 51

Dremomys rufigenis (Blanford, 1878)
红颊长吻松鼠 Hongjiachangwen Songshu

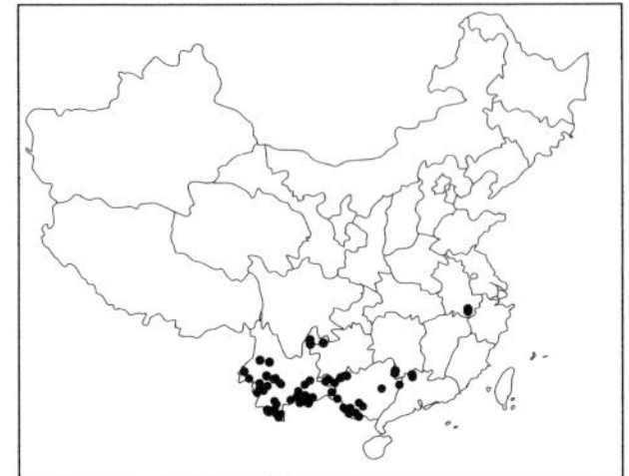

MAP 51. ASIAN RED-CHEEKED SQUIRREL, *Dremomys rufigenis*

Distinctive Characteristics: HB 170–228; T 130–180; HF 44–54; E 23–25; GLS 46–51; Wt 210–335 g. No reddish spots on thigh; pelage of cheeks is red; the ventral surface of the tail is a rich red; the throat is not red, and vental pelage is grayish white.
Distribution: S China; extending into Vietnam, Thailand, Laos, peninsular Malaysia, Myanmar, and India. Three subspecies in China: (1) *D. r. opimus* Thomas, 1916; W Yunnan; (2) *D. r. ornatus* Thomas, 1914; Yunnan, SW Guangxi; (3) *D. r. rufigenis* (Blanford, 1878); SW Yunnan.
Natural History: This is a semiterrestrial foothills species, generally found at less than 1,500 m elevation.
Comments: Formerly included *pyrrhomerus*.
Conservation Status: China RL—NT; although it nearly met the criteria for VU A2cd.

Genus *Menetes* (monotypic)

线松鼠属 Xiansongshu Shu—线松鼠 Xiansongshu

Indochinese Ground Squirrel

PLATE 9
MAP 52

Menetes berdmorei (Blyth, 1849)
线松鼠 Xian Songshu

Distinctive Characteristics: HB 162–210; T 130–175; HF 40–47; E 18–22; GLS 45–51; Wt 213 g. Body dusky, dorsum with blackish brown and buffy short stripes; ventral pelage buffy white. Skull long and narrow, rostrum long, nasal length more than width of interorbital constriction, slightly slanting forward, frontal narrow, postorbital process short and minute; coronoid process of mandible short and blunt. Dental formula: 1.0.2.3/1.0.1.3 = 22; first upper premolar conspicuous; baculum slender, about 11 mm, a process present on anterior portion of shaft, the edge projecting backward from the process.
Distribution: S Yunnan; extending into Vietnam, Cambodia, Laos, and Thailand and to C Myanmar. Chinese subspecies: *M. b. consularis* Thomas, 1914.

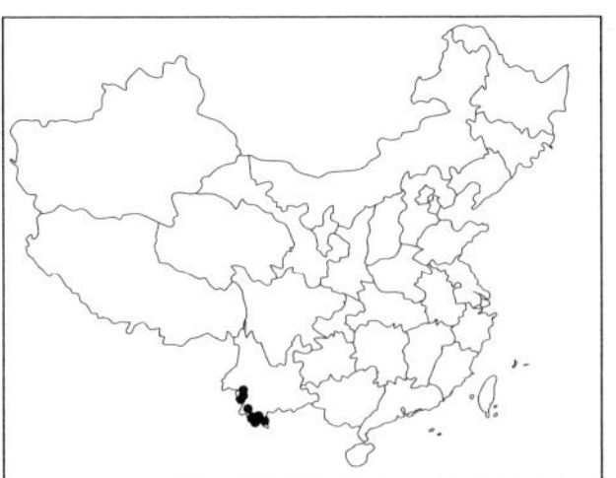

MAP 52. INDOCHINESE GROUND SQUIRREL, *Menetes berdmorei*

Natural History: This squirrel forages on the ground in forests and along the forest edge; it also frequents cultivated areas. Lives at elevations up to 1,200 m. Known to enter rice and corn fields to dig up and eat the planted grain. Often caught in traps baited with bananas. Although this species spends most of its time on the ground, occasionally it may be seen running along railings or up and down slanting or broken bamboos, but never far from the ground.
Conservation Status: China RL—NA.
References: Moore and Tate (1965).

Genus *Tamiops*—Asiatic Striped Squirrels

花松鼠属 Huasongshu Shu—花松鼠 Huasongshu

Size smallest of Asian Sciuridae; chipmunklike. Tufted white hairs present on ears; dorsum with dark and light longitudinal stripes; pelage highly variable in color; tail narrow; skull similar to *Callosciurus*, but smaller, rear of rostrum smooth, length of nasal less than interorbital constriction; skull round and convex, zygomatic plate projecting obliquely upward, forms an obtuse angle with the zygomatic arch; first upper premolar present, but very small. Dental formula: 1.0.2.3/1.0.1.3 = 22; length of baculum about 5 mm, shaft curved at an obtuse angle in middle, edge portion curved at base, tapering backward, with a small process above anterior edge; three pairs of mammae. Of four species in *Tamiops*, three occur in China. Some authors have considered all four *Tamiops* to be conspecific as *T. mcclellandi*; Moore and Tate (1965) and Thorington and Hoffmann (2005) have separated them, although it must be considered that these forms are difficult to define and therefore are tentative.

Key to the Chinese Species of *Tamiops*

1.a. Medial pair of light stripes faint, lateral pair bright. Pale stripe under eye continuous with lateral light stripe on back *Tamiops mcclellandi*

b. Medial pair of light stripes faint, lateral pair either of equal intensity or not bright. Pale stripe under eye not continuous with lateral light stripe on back 2

2.a. All four light stripes of equal intensity; long fluffy pelage, ventor whitish; usually larger *Tamiops swinhoei*

b. Medial pair of light stripes faint, lateral pair not bright but distinct; pelage short, venter bright buff; usually smaller *Tamiops maritimus*

Maritime Striped Squirrel

PLATE 10
MAP 53

Tamiops maritimus (Bonhote, 1900)
倭松鼠 Wo Songshu

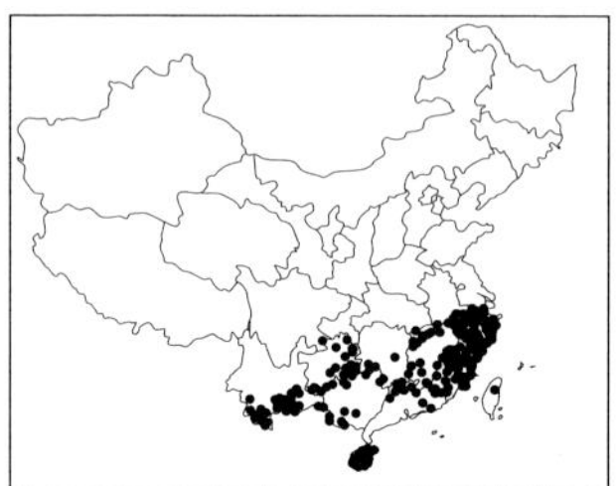

MAP 53. MARITIME STRIPED SQUIRREL, *Tamiops maritimus*

Distinctive Characteristics: HB 105–134; T 80–115; HF 25–30; E 9–17; GLS 36–38. Dorsal pelage short and olive-gray; ventral pelage buffy; lateral light stripes short and narrow, dusky-white. Medial pair of light stripes faint, lateral pair more distinct, but not as pronounced as in *mcclellandi*. Pale stripe under eye not continuous with other light stripe on back. Pelage short; ventral pelage buffy. 2N = 38.
Distribution: SE China; extending to Vietnam and Laos. Four subspecies in China: (1) *T. m. bopinglingensis* Hong and Wang, 1984; Fujian; (2) *T. m. formosanus* (Bonhote, 1900); Taiwan; (3) *T. m. hainanus* Allen, 1906; Hainan Island, Guangxi, S Yunnan; (4) *T. m. maritimus* (Bonhote, 1900); Fujian.
Natural History: This is a relatively low-altitude species occupying the SE coastal region of China. In Taiwan, however, it is most common at elevations between 2,000 and 3,000 m. On mainland China it occurs in two general forest types, evergreen broadleaf forest with evergreen oaks, laurels, and *Pinus massoniana* in secondary stands, and mixed mesophytic forest. Diet includes the very specialized habit of robbing nectar from ginger plants (*Alpina kwangsiensis*). Highly arboreal, it is known to make long leaps between trees. Its characteristic vocalization sounds like a "cluck" or short "chirrup."
Comments: Has been included in *T. swinhoei* in many treatments; here it is considered independent following Thorington and Hoffmann (2005). The Mekong River largely separates *maritimus* to the east and *swinhoei* to the west in the area of Xishuangbanna.
Conservation Status: China RL—LC.
References: Deng et al. (2004); Moore and Tate (1965); Yu (1994).

Himalayan Striped Squirrel

MAP 54

Tamiops mcclellandii (Horsfield, 1840)
明纹花松鼠 Mingwenhua Songshu

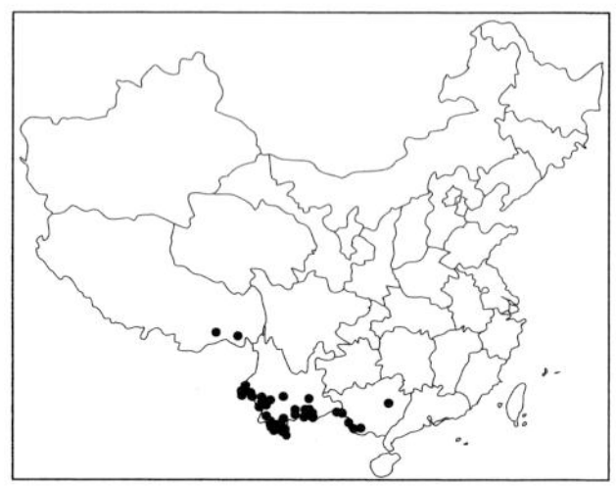

MAP 54. HIMALAYAN STRIPED SQUIRREL, *Tamiops mcclellandii*

Distinctive Characteristics: HB 100–125; T 86–120; HF 27–32; E 15–22; GLS 30–34; Wt 27–51g. Dorsum olive yellow, possesses three brownish black or grayish black longitudinal stripes separated by buffy longitudinal stripes; the medial pair of light stripes are faint, the lateral pair bright. There is a pale stripe under the eye that is continuous with the lateral light stripe on the back. Pelage short; ventral pelage ochraceous; tail tip black.
Distribution: S China; extending to Nepal, India, Myanmar, Thailand, Cambodia, Laos, and Vietnam, to the S Malay Peninsula. Three subspecies in China: (1) *T. m. collinus* Moore, 1958; Yunnan; (2) *T. m. inconstans* Thomas, 1920; Yunnan; (3) *T. m. mcclellandii* (Horsfield, 1840); Xizang.
Natural History: Himalayan Striped Squirrels are commonly found high in tropical-subtropical forest trees above 1,700 m elevation. They are also found in association with humans in fruit trees and coconut palm plantations. While they usually occur in mountains above 700 m, they occur also in low plains in the southern part of their range. They are generally seen alone or in pairs. They are rarely seen on the ground, preferring to run up and down tree trunks. The dorsal stripes serve as camouflage when the squirrels are on the bark of a tree; when frightened they often spread

themselves out against the bark to heighten the effect. They use holes in trees for shelter, and they often move through the trees by making long leaps. The diet consists of insects and some fruit and vegetable matter, including mistletoe. Vocalization is a harsh "chick." They are sometimes sympatric with *Dremomys lokriah*.
Conservation Status: China RL–LC.
References: Moore and Tate (1965).

Swinhoe's Striped Squirrel

PLATE 10
MAP 55

Tamiops swinhoei (Milne-Edwards, 1874)
隐纹松鼠 Yinwen Songshu

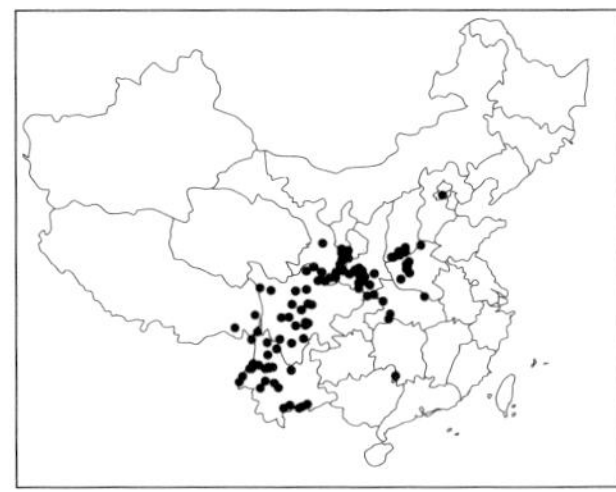

MAP 55. SWINHOE'S STRIPED SQUIRREL, *Tamiops swinhoei*

Distinctive Characteristics: HB 140–164; T 67–116; HF 28–35; E 9–16; GLS 31–41; Wt 67–90 g. Dorsal pelage long and soft, olive-brown or olive-gray in color; five dark stripes, the central one black; lateral stripes brown or same color as body hairs; four light dorsal stripes, olive-yellow, olive-gray, even buffy; ventral pelage whitish. Pale stripe under the eye not continuous with the barely discernible lateral light stripe on the dorsum. Although there is considerable overlap, *swinhoei* is usually larger than other species of *Tamiops*.
Distribution: C China; extending to N Myanmar and N Vietnam. Eight subspecies in China: (1) *T. s. chingpingensis* Lu and Qyan, 1965; W Yunnan; (2) *T. s. clarkei* Thomas, 1920; Yunnan (upper Yangtze River valley); (3) *T. s. forresti* Thomas, 1920; Yunnan (Lichiang range); (4) *T. s. olivaceus* Osgood, 1932; S Yunnan; (5) *T. s. russeolus* Jacobi, 1923; Sichuan, Yunnan (between upper Yangtze and Mekong rivers); (6) *T. s. spencei* Thomas, 1921; NW Yunnan, SE Xizang; (7) *T. s. swinhoei* (Milne-Edwards, 1874); Sichuan, N Yunnan; (8) *T. s. vestitus* Miller, 1915; Beijing, Hebei, Henan, Shaanxi, Shanxi, Gansu, Ningxia, Hubei, NE Sichuan.
Natural History: The range of this species does not overlap the range of *T. mcclellandii* to any significant extent. However, at points where the two ranges meet, there are significant differences in elevation between the two, *mcclellandii* occupying tropical habitat between 300 and 600 m, while *swinhoei* is most common in evergreen broadleaf trees or conifers at elevations between 2,500 and 3,000 m. This squirrel is almost exclusively arboreal, living in holes in trees, although they can be found on the ground. It is known to take long jumps between trees. The call uttered by Swinhoe's Stripped Squirrel is high pitched, like that of a bird. They are primarily active at dawn and dusk. Diet consists of young shoots, fruits, and insects.
Comments: Has included *maritimus* in many treatments.
Conservation Status: China RL–LC.
References: Moore and Tate (1965).

Subfamily Xerinae—Afro-Asian Ground Squirrels

非洲地松鼠亚科 Feizhoudisongshu Yake—
非洲地松鼠 Feizhoudisongshu

The subfamily Xerinae consists of 15 genera and 128 species, divided into three tribes: Xerini, Protoxerini, and Marmotini. The Xerini are confined to Africa, with the exception of *Spermophilopsis*, which extends into Central Asia (but not as far as China), while all representatives of the Protoxerini are found in Africa. All Chinese Xerinae are placed in the tribe Marmotini; 4 genera and 13 species are represented in China.

Genus *Marmota*—Marmots

旱獭属 Hanta shu—旱獭 Hanta

Size large, habits terrestrial; body stout; tail short, tip flat; ears short and round; limbs stout; forefeet, four toes, pollex reduced, middle digit on forefeet longest, fore limbs with robust claws modified for burrowing; hind feet, five toes; female five pairs of teats; skull robust, nearly triangle-shaped; skull low and flat, skull height subequal to the distance between anterior margin of premaxilla and premolars; orbits long, postorbital process robust, slightly curved externally downward; sagittal crest well developed, anterior portion branches off to link with postorbital

Key to the Chinese Genera of Xerinae

1.a.	Size large, HB > 350 mm	*Marmota*
b.	Size smaller, HB < 300 mm	2
2.a.	Size very small, HB < 165	*Tamias*
b.	Size larger, HB > 165	3
3.a.	Hairs on tail short, not bushy	*Spermophilus*
b.	Hairs on tail long, bushy	*Sciurotamias*

Key to the Chinese Species of *Marmota*

1.a.	Tail long, with terminal hairs averages half of HB length	*Marmota caudata*
b.	Tail short, with terminal hairs averages < half of HB length	2
2.a.	Dorsum light brown or light rusty, not mixed with black	*Marmota sibirica*
b.	Dorsum not brown, mixed with black and light brown	3
3.a.	Ventral pelage buffy or light brown, rostrum blackish brown; ears usually russet	*Marmota himalayana*
b.	Ventral pelage drab or dark russet; rostrum dark brown; ears generally sandy yellow	*Marmota baibacina*

process; occipital ridge conspicuously elevated; mastoid process on occipital well developed; palate longer than half of GLS; incisors robust, anterior surface yellowish; first upper premolar large, crown about half of second premolar; third molar largest; lower molars with two lateral cusps. Dental formula: 1.0.2.3/1.0.1.3 = 22. Baculum similar to *Spermophilus*, form nearly S-shaped, tip edged by irregular denticles. The molecular phylogeny of the marmots has been reviewed by Steppan et al. (1999). Diurnally active; all forms hibernate. Occurs in Asia, Europe, and North America. Of 14 species, 4 occur in China.

Gray Marmot

Marmota baibacina Kastschenko, 1899 MAP 56
灰旱獭 Hui Hanta

MAP 56. GRAY MARMOT, *Marmota baibacina*

Distinctive Characteristics: HB 460–650; T 130–154; HF 74–99; E 22–30; GLS 83–100; Wt 4,250–6,500 g. Size similar to *Marmota caudata*, tail short, less than 1/3 of HB length; dorsum buffy or sandy yellow, sprinkled with black or dark blackish brown; ventral pelage dusty or dark russet; ears sandy yellow; rostrum dark brown; skull broader and sagittal crest more robust than in *caudata*; rear margin of foramen magnum round; second upper premolar slightly larger than the former molar. 2N = 38.

Distribution: Xinjiang; extending into Mongolia, Russia, Kyrgystan, and Kazakhstan. Chinese subspecies: *M. b. centralis* (Thomas, 1909).

Natural History: Preferred habitats include montane steppe spreading over low mountains with gentle slopes. Fewer live in stony mountain steppes strewn with boulders, or the alpine zone. Where the Gray Marmot lives in sympatry with the Siberian Marmot, the Gray Marmot occupies only tips of ridges characterized by alpine vegetation while the Siberian Marmot inhabits productive highland valleys. This species, like most marmots, is highly social and lives in colonies with many burrows. Summer and winter burrows are usually separate; winter burrows are deeper, while summer burrows are just as long, but not as deep; both types may hold 2–3 marmots, but in winter, up to 10. Marmots eat a wide variety of food plants, which vary with season. Early spring foods include *Artemisia frigida;* by late spring and early summer their diet consists mainly of grasses; and by late summer, herbaceous vegetation. Mating begins in early May and ends by the beginning of June. Gestation lasts 40 days. Hibernation is initiated at different times in different places, from August to October, and appears influenced by local weather and food resources. Enemies include large raptors, wolves, and other smaller predators such as foxes, steppe polecats, and Pallas' cats.

Comments: Formerly included in *M. bobac*, but these forms are considered sister species.

Conservation Status: China RL—LC.

References: Rogovin (1992).

Long-Tailed Marmot

PLATE 9

Marmota caudata
(Geoffroy Saint-Hilaire, 1844) MAP 57
长尾旱獭 Changwei Hanta

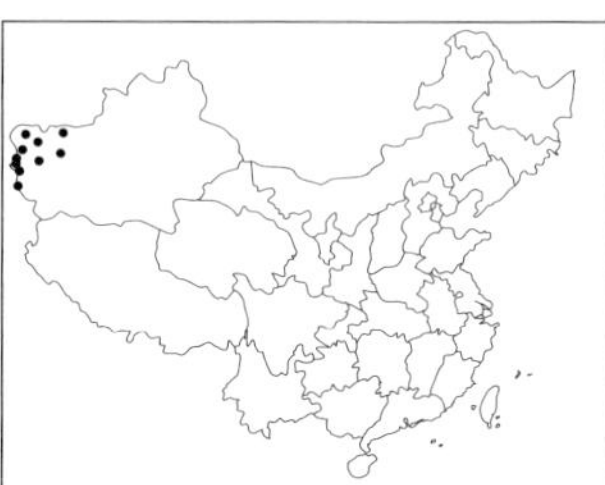

MAP 57. LONG-TAILED MARMOT, *Marmota caudata*

Distinctive Characteristics: HB 426–570; T 185–275; HF 63–92; E 18–30; GLS 87–105; Wt 4,100–4,600 g. Form stout; tail longest within *Marmota*, with terminal hairs up to half of HB length and black at the tip. Whole body orange or pale brown; ventral pelage essentially colored the same as the dorsum, with no evident boundary. Postorbital process strongly curved out and down; dorsal rim of foramen magnum semicircular; crown of second upper premolar subequal to that of the previous two molars.

Distribution: Xinjiang (Tian Shan mountains); extending throughout Central Asia, Afghanistan, Pakistan, and N India. Chinese subspecies: *M. c. aurea* (Blanford, 1875).
Natural History: The Long-tailed Marmot is a montane animal; it inhabits the zone of coniferous forests but also penetrates the alpine zone, chiefly on open stony stretches, although it does not avoid forests. This species is less common in feather-grass and fescue areas, and it is uncommon in semidesert tracts with shrub cover (winter-fat, sagebrush); it shuns saline soils. The animal prefers dry, clifflike mountain slopes covered mainly by short grasses, or at lower elevations, stands of junipers up to 3–4 m high. Like other marmots, it is strictly diurnal. Emerges from burrow shortly after sunrise, when the ground surface has begun to warm. If disturbed by an intruder, it utters a call that resembles a bird call, which is unique to this species. Diet consists of the leaves and stems of various grasses, and legumes, which it prefers. Frequently found in monogamous situations consisting of one adult male and one adult female, although social groups of up to seven adults may be formed. When multiple females share a common home range, only a single adult female lactates and weans young. Litters of two to five are seen outside burrows by late April or early May. Shortly after the young emerge, adults begin to molt, ending by mid- or late August. Two weeks after the end of molt, they enter their burrow to begin hibernation, about mid-September.
Conservation Status: China RL—LC. CITES—III (India). IUCN RL—LR/nt ver 2.3 (1994).
References: Blumstein and Arnold (1998).

Himalayan Marmot

PLATE 9
MAP 58

Marmota himalayana (Hodgson, 1841)
喜马拉雅旱獭 Ximalaya Hanta

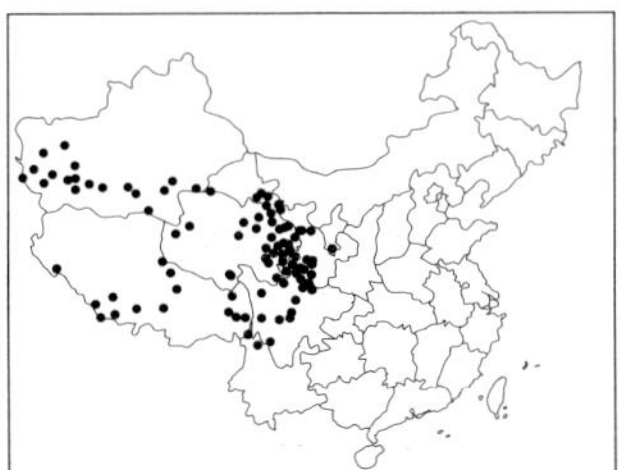

MAP 58. HIMALAYAN MARMOT, *Marmota himalayana*

Distinctive Characteristics: HB 475–670; T 125–150; HF 76–100; E 23–30; GLS 96–114; Wt 4,000–9,215 g. Form stout; tail very short—less than twice HF length. Dorsum grass-yellow or buffy, sprinkled with many irregular black spots; ventral pelage buffy or light brown; ears dark yellow or russet; rostrum often with black or blackish brown spots. Skull large; dorsal rim of foramen magnum semioval; structure of teeth shows no evident difference from *Marmota baibacina*.
Distribution: C to W China; extending to Nepal, India. Two subspecies in China: (1) *M. h. himalayana* (Hodgson, 1841); S Xizang; (2) *M. h. robusta* (Milne-Edwards, 1871); Qinghai, Xizang, W Sichuan, Yunnan, Gansu, Xinjiang.
Natural History: Inhabits upland grassland from 3,750 to 5,200 m (up to 5,670 m). This species is adapted to alpine meadows and desert conditions with very low rainfall, typically inhabiting steep bush-dotted slopes. Himalayan Marmots live in small or large colonies, depending on local resources, and feed on grasses by preference, although they also consume roots, leaves of herbaceous plants, and seeds. They excavate unusually deep burrows, which are shared by colony members during hibernation. Females give birth toward the end of hibernation, with litter size reported to be 2–11 (average = 7 at low density; 4.8 at high density), born from April to July. Gestation is one month, and young are generally weaned at 15 days of age. Young normally remain with their family, and females become reproductively active only in their second spring.
Comments: In the early literature, *M. sibirica*, *M. himalayana*, and *M. baibacina* have all been considered subspecies of *Marmota bobak* (see Thorington and Hoffmann 2005).
Conservation Status: China RL—LC. CITES—III (India).
References: Huang et al. (1986).

Tarbagan Marmot

MAP 59

Marmota sibirica (Radde, 1862)
草原旱獭 Caoyuan Hanta

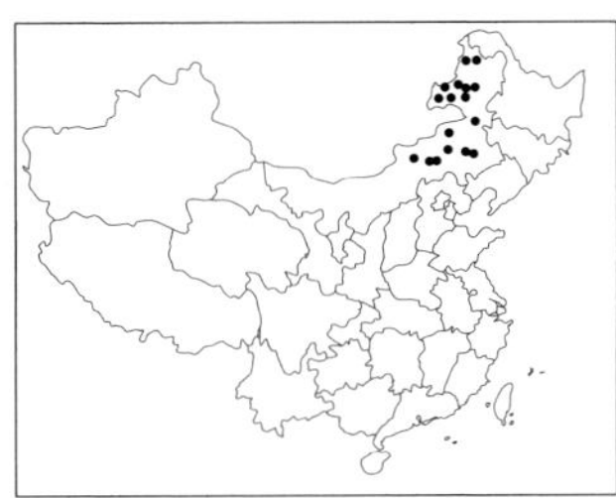

MAP 59. TARBAGAN MARMOT, *Marmota sibirica*

Distinctive Characteristics: HB 360–495; T 112–121; HF 72–82; GLS 80–104; Wt 5,000 g. Size slightly smaller than other species; dorsum light brown or light rusty, sprinkled with light whitish yellow; ventral pelage brown; rostrum and top of forehead dark brown; ears light orange; tail dark brown without black hue. Frontal flat behind, not concave; postorbital process robust, lateral side of anterior zygomatic arch clearly lozenge-shaped; rear margin of foramen magnum round; crown of second upper premolar equal to that of first molar, but less than that of the last two molars. 2n = 38.
Distribution: Nei Mongol, Heilongjiang; extending across Mongolia and Russia (Siberia, Tuva, Transbaikalia). Only one subspecies is generally accepted; *M. sibirica caliginosus* Bannikov and Skalon, 1949.
Natural History: The Tarbagan Marmot resembles the Bobac Marmot of E Europe and C Asia in mode

of life and habits. Both species are highly colonial, and their primary habitat is steppe grasslands. Marmots of all ages forage on grasses, but also on 10–15 species of herbs and a few woody plants such as sagebrush. Autumn hibernation is initiated in September but is influenced by summer food conditions and fall weather. Both Bobac and Tarbagan marmots hibernate in groups of 5–20 in a single burrow. Enemies include wolves, red foxes, and several species of large eagles and hawks. The Tarbagan Marmot may carry and transmit bubonic plague and is therefore subject to stringent control measures in many parts of its range. Mating begins in April, after it has aroused from hibernation. Gestation lasts 40–42 days. Young appear above ground in June; typical litter size is four to six, occasionally eight. Molting of winter hair in adults occurs about 2.5–3 weeks after the birth of young.
Conservation Status: China RL–LC.
References: Rogovin (1992).

Genus *Sciurotamias*—Rock squirrels

岩松鼠属 Yansongshu Shu—岩松鼠 Yansongshu

Medium-sized bushy-tailed squirrels. Habits terrestrial, rostrum long, but not longer than *Dremomys*, postorbital process reduced, skull low and flat, zygomatic plate not elevated. Both species of *Sciurotamias* are restricted to China.

Père David's Rock Squirrel

PLATE 9

Sciurotamias davidianus (Milne-Edwards, 1867)

MAP 60

岩松鼠 Yansongshu

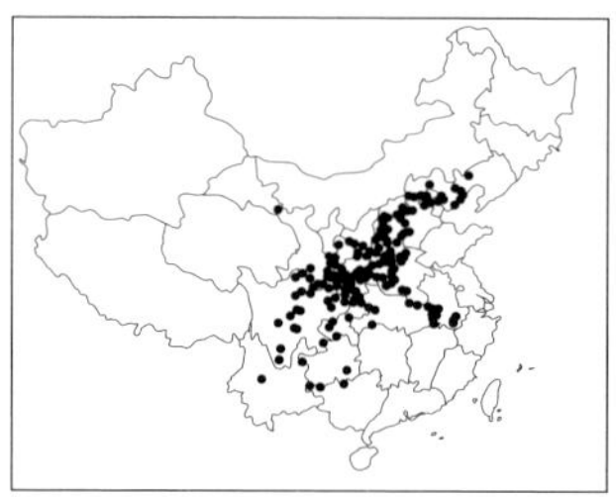

MAP 60. PÈRE DAVID'S ROCK SQUIRREL, *Sciurotamias davidianus*

Distinctive Characteristics: HB 190–250; T 125–200; HF 45–59; E 20–28; GLS 52–58. Dorsum olive gray; ventral pelage yellowish-white or ochraceous. No pale stripe on side. A dark line crosses the cheek. Soles of feet densely haired. Dental formula: 1.0.2.3/1.0.1.3 = 22, first upper molar present; baculum arched, edge projecting like a spoon in front of body. Skull wide and flattened, bullae small.
Distribution: Throughout C China. Endemic. Three subspecies: (1) *S. d. consobrinus* (Milne-Edwards, 1868–1874); W Sichuan; NE Yunnan; NW Guizhou; (2) *S. d. davidianus* (Milne-Edwards, 1867); Liaoning, Hebei, Beijing, Tianjin, Henan, Shanxi, Shaanxi, Gansu, Ningxia, Shandong, N Sichuan; (3) *S. d. saltitans* Heude, 1898; Hubei, NE Guizhou, Sichuan, Chongqing, Henan, Anhui.
Natural History: Père David's Rock Squirrels favor rocky terrain and make dens in deep crevices between rocks. They show great agility, and while capable of climbing trees, apparently rarely do so. They do not hibernate. Known to collect and eat seeds that they carry in large cheek pouches. They are particularly adept at scatter hoarding the large acorns of the oak *Quercus liatungensis*. They may reach high densities in places and may constitute an agricultural pest on occasion.
Conservation Status: China RL–LC.
References: Wang and Ma (1999).

Forrest's Rock Squirrel

PLATE 9

Sciurotamias forresti (Thomas, 1922)

MAP 61

侧纹岩松鼠 Cewen Yansongshu

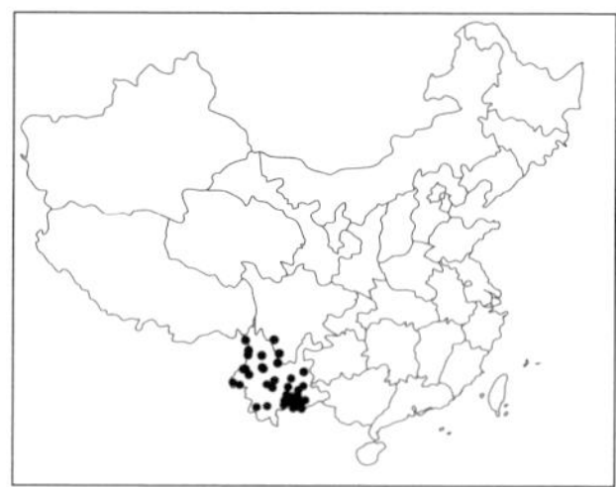

MAP 61. FORREST'S ROCK SQUIRREL, *Sciurotamias forresti*

Distinctive Characteristics: HB 194–250; T 130–180; HF 47–54; E 25–27; GLS 54–60. Dorsum of head and body dark grayish brown, hairs ringed with black and buff. On the side a narrow white line runs from shoulder to hip; the dark line running below the white matches the back in color, turning ochraceous below and on the venter; ears buffy brown; sides of head, throat, and sides also ochraceous; ventral

Key to *Sciurotamias*

1.a. No pale stripe on side; dental formula: 1.0.2.3/1.0.1.3 = 22, first upper molar present; baculum arched, edge projecting like a spoon in front of body — *Sciurotamias davidianus*
b. Side of body with light stripe running from shoulder back toward rump; dental formula: 1.0.1.3/1.0.1.3 = 20; baculum flat and straight — *Sciurotamias forresti*

surface like sides, but paler, and with white patch from chin to chest. Dental formula: 1.0.1.3/1.0.1.3 = 20; baculum flat and straight, its edge extending into a V shape into the sides in the anterior of the shaft. Soles of hind feet almost naked.

Distribution: Yunnan, S Sichuan. Endemic.

Natural History: This species has a very restricted distribution in NW Yunnan where it occupies scrub-clad cliffs at about 3,000 m in elevation. Its biology is likely similar to that of its sister species, *Sciurotamias davidianus*.

Comments: This species has frequently been allocated to its own genus, *Rupestes*.

Conservation Status: China RL–LC. IUCN RL–VU A1c ver 2.3 (1994).

References: Thomas (1922a).

Genus *Spermophilus*—Ground Squirrels

黄鼠属 Huangshu Shu—黄鼠 Huangshu

Size small, habits burrowing; eyes large, ears small, limbs and tail short, claws robust; pollices on fore feet reduced; cheek pouch present, females with five pairs of mammae (chest two, abdomen three). Back of skull mostly curved, rostrum robust; auditory bullae large and convex; anterior portion of zygomatic arch narrow, skull tending slightly toward triangle shape, modified for burrowing; postorbital process not very robust; occipital ridge present; angular process of mandible clearly turned inward; upper molars with evident longitudinal ridge, structure of teeth similar to *Sciurus*. Dental formula: 1.0.2.3/1.0.1.3 = 22; first upper premolar large. Baculum short, about 3–6 mm long; shaft generally slightly curved, base expanded but gradually tapering forward; edge convex with small denticles, a small process present in front of the shaft. Of 41 species of *Spermophilus* occurring across Asia, Europe, and North America, 6 are found in China. In much of the older literature, this genus is referred to as *Citellus*.

Alashan Ground Squirrel

PLATE 10
MAP 62

Spermophilus alashanicus Büchner, 1888

阿拉善黄鼠—Alashan Huangshu

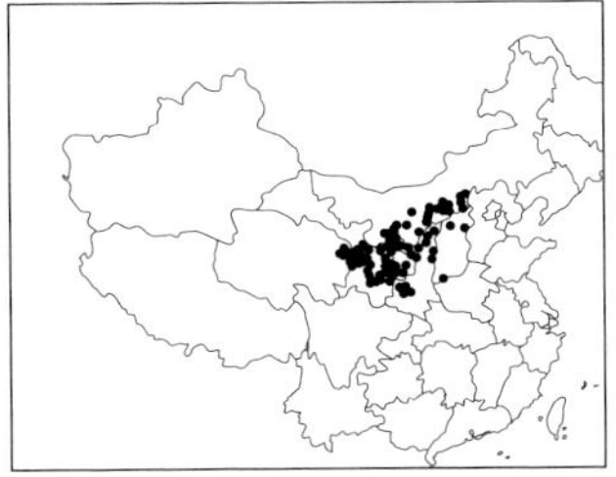

MAP 62. ALASHAN GROUND SQUIRREL, *Spermophilus alashanicus*

Distinctive Characteristics: HB 190–210; T 55–76; HF 33–37; E 8–10; GLS 45–48; Wt 192–224 g. A pale form; summer pelage light russet to distinctly pinkish buff. Winter pelage lighter and more yellow. Has a distinctive eyering, and a light brown spot is positioned below the eye and separated from the ring by a whitish stripe running from the base of the ear to the muzzle. Tail colored as the back, but rusty red beneath. Auditory bullae much longer than broad; interorbital distance usually greater than 9 mm.

Distribution: Central N China; Ningxia, Gansu, Qinghai, Nei Mongol. Endemic.

Natural History: This species lives in the deserts of C China but also is found in grasslands at the edge of the Gobi. Its preferred habitat appears to be dry sandy areas; locally its common name translates to "sand rat." Occupies single sloping burrows; no dirt mounds surround burrow entrances. The Alashan Ground Squirrel lives in small scattered groups. Diurnal. Hibernates like other *Spermophilus*. The species feeds on a variety of herbs and other plants, including cultivated grains. Vocalizations consist of frequently uttered high-pitched squeaks. Litter size ranges from one to nine, normally three to six; parturition most likely in June.

Comments: In the past this taxon was considered a subspecies of *S. dauricus*, but Orlov and Davaa (1975) provided evidence that the two are separate species.

Key to the Chinese Species of *Spermophilus*

1.a.	Tail > 100 mm	*Spermophilus undulatus*
b.	Tail < 90 mm	2
2.a.	Distinctive black banding near distal end of tail	3
b.	Tail lacking black hair	4
3.a.	No spots on back; distinct white line from muzzle to ear	*Spermophilus dauricus*
b.	Faint light spotting on back; no distinctive markings on face	*Spermophilus ralli*
4.a.	Tail > 55 mm	*Spermophilus alashanicus*
b.	Tail < 55 mm	5
5.a.	Light spots on back; no rusty spot beneath eye	*Spermophilus brevicauda*
b.	No spots on back; rusty spot beneath eye; rostrum shorter	*Spermophilus pallidicauda*

Conservation Status: China RL–LC.
References: Chen (1991); Orlov and Davaa (1975).

Brandt's Ground Squirrel

PLATE 10
MAP 63

Spermophilus brevicauda Brandt, 1843
阿尔泰黄鼠 Aertai Huangshu

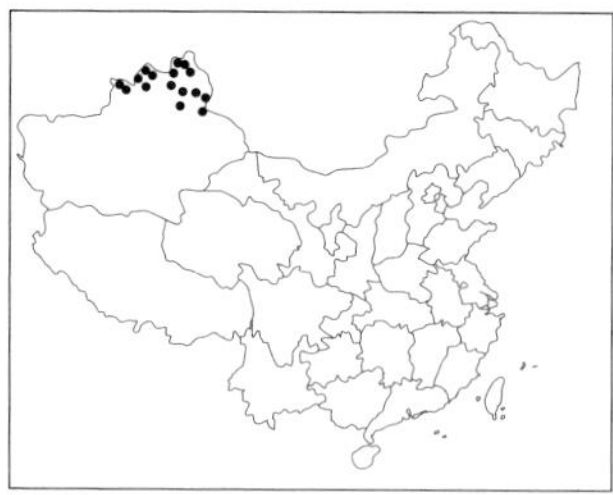

MAP 63. BRANDT'S GROUND SQUIRREL, *Spermophilus brevicauda*

Distinctive Characteristics: HB 165–210; T 31–50; HF 29–38; E 5–9; GLS 42–47; Wt 143–436 g. Size smaller than some other *Spermophilus*; tail short, about 1/5 of HB length. Hind metatarsal russet; dorsum ochraceous, with distinctive small light spots; tail rusty in some forms to light yellow in others. Noticeable rust-colored patches above and below their light eyerings. Skull round; anterior gap on postorbital process minute; nasal small and short; auditory bullae broader than long.
Distribution: N Xinjiang; extending into Kazakhstan. Three subspecies in China: (1) *S. b. brevicauda* Brandt, 1843; NW Xinjiang (Altai mountains); (2) *S. b. carruthersi* (Thomas, 1912); NE Xinjiang; (3) *S. b. iliensis* (Belyaev, 1945), NW Xinjiang; region of Ili River.
Natural History: This taxon is very poorly known but appears to inhabit dry steppes and semidesert brushlands. Its range, as presently understood, is restricted to NW Xinjiang, while *S. alashanicus* is found in the Alashan Desert, from Nei Mongol on the north to Gansu on the south, and *S pallidicauda* is restricted to NE Gansu and Nei Mongol. These three closely related *Spermophilus* are allopatric in distribution. Chiefly vegetarian, they climb and dig in order to obtain whatever is in season, enjoying the young shoots of certain shrubs as well as tulip bulbs and wild onions. They may be either solitary or communal, and they spend much time in their burrows, in which they hibernate if the temperature is low enough, or aestivate if the summer heat becomes too high. Burrows are normally constructed at the base of shrubs. They rarely stand upright on their hind legs (like other *Spermophilus*), and their alarm call is a very quiet squeek.
Comments: Previously considered a subspecies of *S. erythrogenys*, but a phylogeny based on molecular sequence data separates *brevicauda* from *erythrogenys*, *pallidicauda*, and *alashanicus* (Harrison et al. 2003). This species has also been linked taxonomically with *S. major*, and we believe that specimens attributed to *major* in Xinjiang are actually *brevicauda*.
Conservation Status: China RL–LC.
References: Harrison et al. (2003).

Daurian Ground Squirrel

PLATE 10
MAP 64

Spermophilus dauricus Brandt, 1843
达乌尔黄鼠 Dawu'er Huangshu

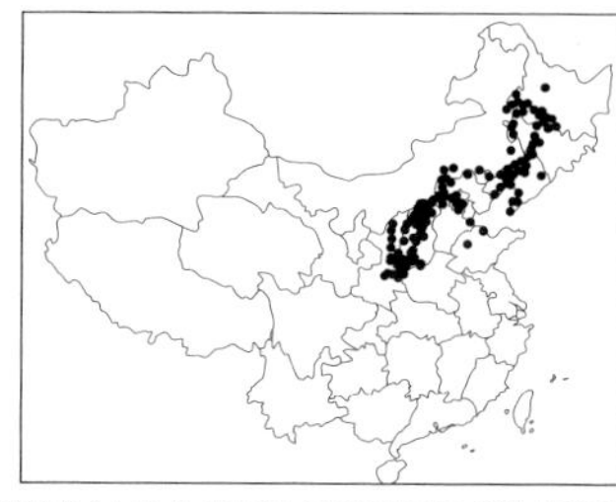

MAP 64. DAURIAN GROUND SQUIRREL, *Spermophilus dauricus*

Distinctive Characteristics: HB 165–268; T 40–75; HF 30–39; E 5–10; GLS 42–50; Wt 154–264 g. Size small; tail short, about a fifth to a third of HB length; fore palms naked; hind palms covered with hairs; whole body buffy or gray russet, no light spots on dorsum. Tip of tail light yellow, with a distinctive black-brown preterminal band. A light eyering extends to the ear. Summer pelage relatively short and coarse; winter pelage significantly longer and softer. Longitudinal axis of auditory bullae longer than transverse axis; no hollow behind incisive socket on palatal surface of premaxilla; posterior edge of nasals slender. 2N = 36.
Distribution: NE China; extending into Mongolia and Russia (Transbaikalia). Two subspecies in China: (1) *S. d. mongolicus* (Milne-Edwards, 1867); Hebei, Beijing, Tianjin, Henan, Shandong; (2) *S. d. ramosus* (Thomas, 1909); Jilin, Heilongjiang, Liaoning, E Nei Mongol, Shanxi.
Natural History: This ground squirrel occupies open plains or deserts. It is considered a characteristic species of the northern edge of the Gobi in extreme N Mongolia and the adjacent borders of Siberia. It apparently does not extend far into the Gobi but follows around the northeastern edge to reappear in Chinese territory along the borders of Hebei and adjacent Nei Mongol. It is strictly diurnal and lives in dense colonies where it constructs relatively simple burrows, generally with only two entrances. Tunnels normally extend a maximum of 2 m, although some may reach as far as 6–8 m in length. A single nest, lined with grass, is normally found at a depth of 50 cm. Hibernates over winter. These ground squirrels feed on various herbs and other plants, including grain fields. Single litters of two to nine young are produced in spring.
Conservation Status: China RL–LC.
References: Wang et al. (1992).

Pallid Ground Squirrel

MAP 65

Spermophilus pallidicauda Satunin, 1903
内蒙黄鼠 Neimeng Huangshu
Distinctive Characteristics: HB 198–233; T 35–53; HF 36–41; E 5–9; GLS 42–46. This is a pale species characterized by its short tail that is uniformly

yellow-straw-white, except for the middle of the upper three-fourths, which is rust-colored. The dorsum is pinkish buff to straw-sand in color. Tail solid whitish yellow. A weakly defined white line runs from the vibrissae on the cheek to the ear. Eyelids are white, but there is a rusty spot beneath each eye. Underside is white, faintly tinged with buffy. In the summer pelage the coloring becomes more sandy and less buffy. The skull is unusual in that the rostrum is quite short, while the zygomatic arches abruptly flare out just at the base of the rostrum.
Distribution: Nei Mongol and E Xinjiang; extending into Mongolia. Considered monotypic by Thorington and Hoffmann (2005).

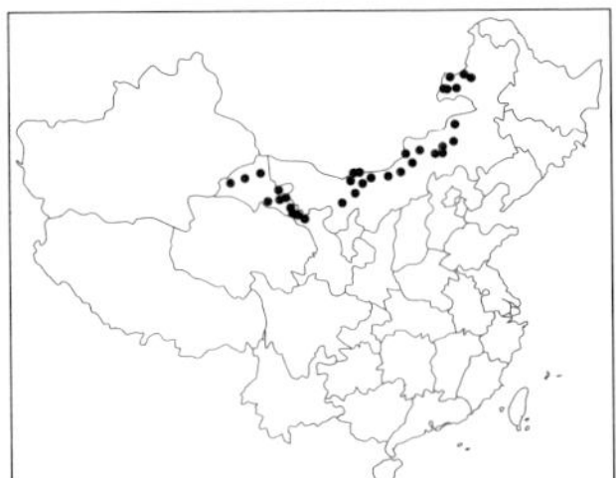

MAP 65. PALLID GROUND SQUIRREL, *Spermophilus pallidicauda*

Natural History: This species has a wide distribution in the grasslands of the Gobi and adjacent areas. Colonial and diurnally active.
Comments: Formerly included in *S. erythrogenys*, from which it differs in chromosome number and DNA sequences (Harrison et al. 2003).
Conservation Status: China RL—LC.

Tian Shan Ground Squirrel

Spermophilus ralli (Kuznetsov, 1948) MAP 66
天山黄鼠 Tianshan Huangshu

MAP 66. TIAN SHAN GROUND SQUIRREL, *Spermophilus ralli*

Distinctive Characteristics: HB 200–240; T 60–75; HF 33–42; GLS 47–50; Wt 290–405 g. Summer pelage is gray-brown to light yellow on the back, with lighter sides; ventrally yellow-gray. Light spots on the back are indistinct. Winter pelage is lighter and grayer. Dorsal surface of tail is rusty to light yellow; end of tail characterized by a band of dark coloration with a yellowish white tip. There are no facial markings around the eye.
Distribution: W. Xinjiang; extending into Kazakhstan.
Natural History: A meadow-dwelling ground squirrel. Burrow diameter averages 6 cm, and there are many openings close together and clumped. Diurnal, yet not active during the hottest part of the day. Often stands erect next to it burrow; highly vocal. Diet consists of grass, green vegetation, and insects. Hibernates from between August/September and the end of February/beginning of March. Reproduces in spring following emergence. Litter size averages three to seven young born after a 25–27 day gestation.
Comments: A sister species, *S. relictus*, is found in the western extension of the Tian Shan mountains.
Conservation Status: China RL—NA.

Long-Tailed Ground Squirrel

Spermophilus undulatus (Pallas, 1778) MAP 67
长尾黄鼠 Changwei Huangshu

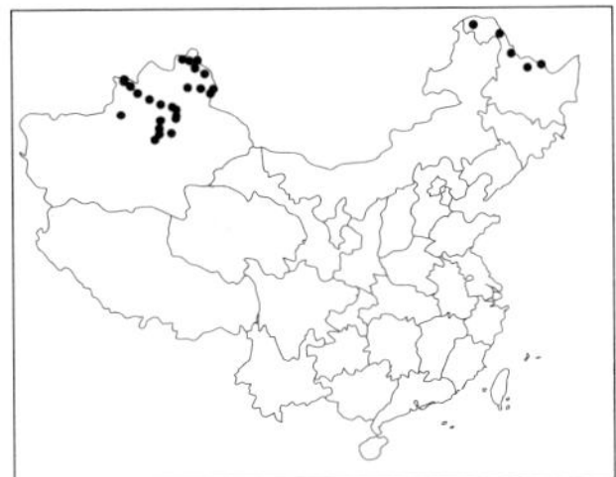

MAP 67. LONG-TAILED GROUND SQUIRREL, *Spermophilus undulatus*

Distinctive Characteristics: HB 210–315; T 100–140; HF 45–50; E 10–11; GLS 46–56; Wt 250–580 g. Size large; tail long, more than a third of HB length. Upper parts with russet or dusky black-brown patterning; sides a gray-straw or yellow; underparts orange, reddish brown, or brown; sides and extremity of tail tinged with white or yellowish white. Winter pelage much lighter. Skull large; no indentation in front of supraorbital process; base of incisive alveolus on premaxilla concave; nasal at premaxilla as broad as posterior portion of nasal; rear roots of second and third upper molars robust.
Distribution: Extreme NW and NE China; extending into Kazakhstan, Russia,and Mongolia. Four subspecies in China: (1) *S. u. altaicus* (Brandt, 1841); Altai and Sayan mountains; (2) *S. u. eversmanni* (Brandt, 1841); Xinjiang (Altai mountains); (3) *S. u. menzbieri* Ognev, 1937; N Heilongjiang; (4) *S. u. stramineus* (Obolenskii, 1927); Xinjiang (Tian Shan mountains).
Natural History: This large ground squirrel typically occurs in thinly wooded savannahs and grassy steppes bordering the Gobi Desert. In addition to grasslands, they occupy bushy terrain among oaks and white or black beech groves, alpine meadows, and wet areas along river valleys. Lives in colonies with a labyrinth of burrows. Burrows are characteristically 8–13 cm in diameter and surrounded by a

large mound of soil (up to 2 m in diameter and 40 cm high). Diurnally active; although most active at dawn and dusk. The alarm call is soft and unlike that of most other ground squirrels–it more closely resembles the call of a chipmunk. Diet consists of green vegetation and seeds, but also insects. Before hibernating makes a store of vegetation to utilize following arousal. Hibernates from October until late March/mid-April. Reproduces once per year in spring; litters of three to nine young are produced following a 30-day gestation.
Conservation Status: China RL–LC.

Genus *Tamias*—Chipmunks

花鼠属 Huashu Shu—花鼠 Huashu

Size small, pelage thick, dorsum with five brown or brownish black longitudinal stripes; skull, in contrast to *Tamiops*, narrow, long, low, and flat, rostrum gradually tapering forward; nasal length more than width of interorbital constriction, zygomatic arch slender, approaching palate, infraorbital foramen round. Dental formula: 1.0.2.3/1.0.1.3 = 22, teeth in lower dentition gradually enlarged from front to back; baculum about 5 mm, gradually tapering forward from base, extremity slightly curved upward. Four pairs of mammae; well-developed internal cheek pouches. Of 25 species, all but 1 occupies the Nearctic realm, the single species that occurs in China.

Siberian Chipmunk

Tamias sibiricus (Laxmann, 1769) PLATE 10 MAP 68
花鼠 Hua Shu

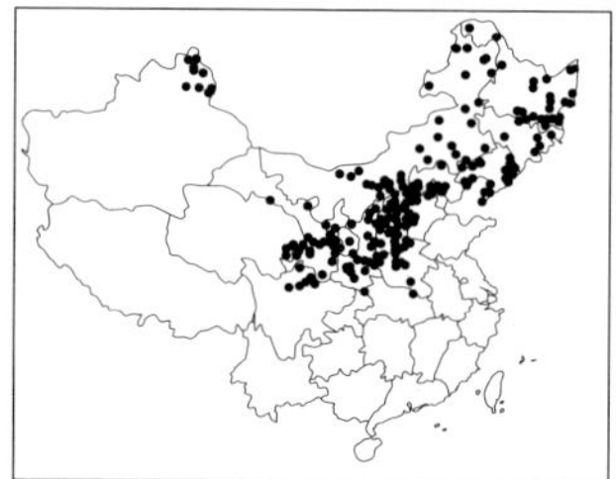

MAP 68. SIBERIAN CHIPMUNK, *Tamias sibiricus*

Distinctive Characteristics: HB 120–165; T 90–130; HF 28–40; E 13–20; GLS 34–48; Wt 78–102 g. Dorsum russet, five conspicuous brown or brownish black stripes, ventral buffy white.
Distribution: NW China, C China; extending to NE China; extending to N European and Siberian Russia to Sakhalin, including Kazakhstan, Mongolia, Korea, Japan (Hokkaido Island). Six subspecies in China: (1) *E. s. albogularis* Allen, 1909; Gansu, Qinghai, Ningxia, Sichuan; (2) *T. s. lineatus* (Siebold, 1824); Heilongjiang; (3) *T. s. ordinalis* Thomas, 1908; Shanxi, Shaanxi, Ningxia; (4) *T. s. orientalis* (Bonhote, 1899); Jilin, Liaoning; (5) *T. s. senescens* Miller, 1898; Heibei, Shanxi, Henan; (6) *T. s. sibiricus* (Laxmann, 1769); Xinjiang, Nei Mongol.
Natural History: Nests and burrows near tree roots. Diet consists of pine nuts and young shoots and leaves of vegetation. In summer and fall also eats flowers, mushrooms, and occasionally insects. Hibernates from September to March/April. In late summer constructs large winter stores, carrying seeds back to nest in their cheek pouches. Diurnally active, with activity concentrated in the early morning. Tends to run along the ground, but also ascends trees. Siberian Chipmunks utter a "chirping" vocalization when alarmed. Females enter hibernation first, followed by males; this order may allow males to know where females are for mating upon emergence in early spring. They normally produce a single litter of four to six young each year, although there are reports of two litters in some populations.
Conservation Status: China RL–LC.
References: Kawamichi (1996).

Family Gliridae—Dormice

日本睡鼠科 Ribenshuishu Ke—
日本睡鼠 Ribenshuishu

Andrew T. Smith

Most dormice resemble small squirrels with soft thick fur, a heavily furred tail, and large eyes, although some are mouselike. One of their unique traits is their ability to regenerate the tail. Forefeet with four digits; hindfeet with five. Underside of feet and digits naked; toes have short curved claws. Generally arboreal, they store food in nests made in tree holes and add fat prior to entering hibernation in winter. Dental formula: 1.0.1.3/1.0.1.3 = 20 (compared to 16 in spiny dormice); incisors sharply pointed. Possess well-developed zygomatic arches, no postorbital processes, and relatively large auditory bullae. The Gliridae represents an old and distinctive family among the rodents and appears to be a sister clade to that containing the Sciuridae and Aplodontidae within the Sciuromorpha (Montgelard et al. 2003; Holden 2005). Of 9 genera and 28 species within the Gliridae (Holden 2005), 2 genera are found in China, the monospecific *Chaetocauda* and 1 of 3 species of *Dryomys*. This family is sometimes referred to as Myoxidae.

Key to the Chinese Genera and Species of Gliridae

1.a.	Black mask on face; tail distichous; incisive foramina short	*Dryomys nitedlula*
b.	No black mask on face; tail round; incisive foramina long	*Chaetocauda sichuanensis*

Chinese Dormouse PLATE 15 MAP 69
Chaetocauda sichuanensis Wang, 1985
四川毛尾睡鼠 Sichuanmaowei Shuishu

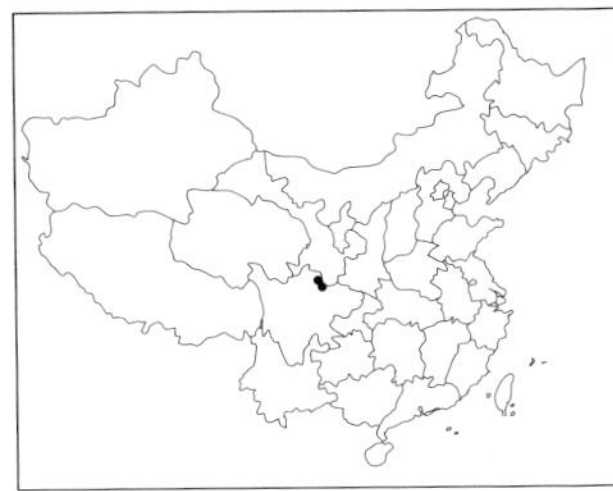

MAP 69. CHINESE DORMOUSE, *Chaetocauda sichuanensis*

Distinctive Characteristics: HB 90–91; T 92–102; HF 18–19; E 17–19; GLS 26–27; Wt 24–36 g. Dark chestnut around the large eyes; vibrissae long (up to 31 mm). Tail round (tail hairs not flattened as in the Forest Dormouse); the tail tip is covered with dense hairs forming a club shape. Incisive foramen long, its posterior edge reaching beyond the middle of the first molar. Surface of upper incisor deeply grooved in the center, forming a V-shaped notch on the cutting edge.
Distribution: N Sichuan. Endemic.
Natural History: Occurs in subalpine forest with mixed coniferous and broadleaf trees. Constructs nests in trees generally at a height of 3–3.5 m; nest diameter = 12 cm. Diet consists of green plants. Nocturnal. Breeds in May and produces litters of four young.
Comments: Listed as *Dryomys* in some treatments; this poorly known species is represented by only five specimens.
Conservation Status: China RL—EN A1c; B1ab(iii). IUCN RL—EN B1 + 2c ver 2.3 (1994) (as *Dryomys sichuanensis*).
References: Wang (1985b).

Forest Dormouse PLATE 15 MAP 70
Dryomys nitedula (Pallas, 1778)
林睡鼠 Lin Shushu

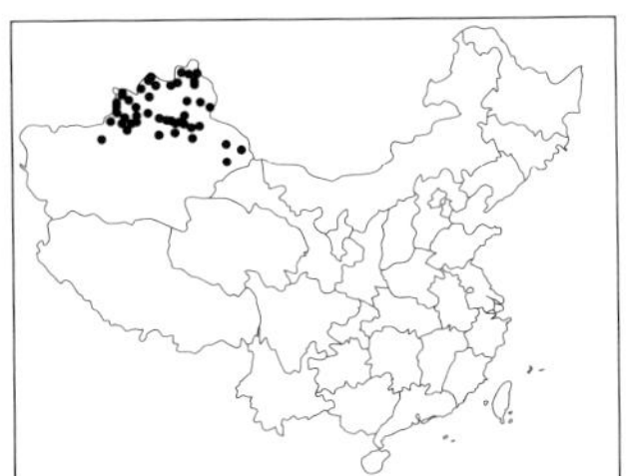

MAP 70. FOREST DORMOUSE, *Dryomys nitedula*

Distinctive Characteristics: HB 85–120; T 75–115; HF 19–24; E 13–19; GLS 25–28; Wt 36–61 g. Dorsal pelage gray-brown; a distinct dark blackish patch extends from the region around the eye and below the ear anteriorly, but not to the end of the nose; tail flat and covered with long light brown hair; ears rounded and short; feet naked. The skull is long in profile; no crest appears on the cranium; the rostrum is narrow; nasals extend beyond the incisors; auditory bullae rounded and moderately large; incisive foramen short. 2N = 48.
Distribution: NW Xinjiang; extending across Central Asia to as far west as Switzerland. Two subspecies in China: (1) *D. n. angelus* (Thomas, 1906); W Xinjiang; (2) *D. n. milleri* Thomas, 1912; N Xinjiang.
Natural History: Lives in broadleaf forests and mixed conifers but prefers oak. Nests in trees, with an entrance on one side, lined with moss, feathers, and hair, constructed in tree holes or niches in trees. In winter may make underground nests, in which they hibernate. Primarily nocturnal; an excellent climber. Diet consists of nuts, seeds, and fruit, but also may include insects and larvae; stores food. Utters a variety of vocalizations: soft melodic calls, clicks, snarling, hissing, and whistling sounds when excited or threatened. Litter size is small (generally three or four young, but as many as seven). Two litters are produced in a breeding season that extends throughout summer.
Conservation Status: China RL—EN A2c + 3c. IUCN RL—LR/nt ver 2.3 (1994).

Family Castoridae

Genus *Castor*—Beavers

河狸科 Heli Ke; 河狸属 Heli Shu—河狸 Heli

Andrew T. Smith

Beavers are very large rodents adapted to aquatic habitats; guard hairs dense; ears with valves; tail large and flat, ovate, covered with large scales; hind feet possess complete webs, fourth toe with double nails, forefeet small, armed with robust claws. Suture between zygoma and maxilla broad, preorbital fossa small; basioccipital slightly concave; incisors robust, deeply pigmented, modified for cutting branches and stripping tree bark; each side of upper and lower jaws possesses four cheek teeth. Dental formula: 1.0.1.3/1.0.1.3 = 20; occlusal surface broad, outer side of each molar possess a deep concave fold, inner side three deep concave folds. While the Castoridae has traditionally been allied with the Sciuromorpha, recent analyses place it in the Castorimorpha along with the Heteromyidae and Geomyidae (Carleton and Musser 2005). The single genus occurs in aquatic habitats throughout the Holarctic. Of two species, one occurs in China (Helgen 2005).

Eurasian Beaver PLATE 11 MAP 71
Castor fiber Linnaeus, 1758
河狸 He Li
Distinctive Characteristics: HB 600–1,000; T length 215–300, breadth 102–127; HF 160–170; E 35–40; GLS 125–151; Wt 17–30 kg. There is essentially no sexual dimorphism in size. Head round, limbs short; each foot possesses five toes; hairs long, whole body

brown, feet black; hind foot webs complete (fig. 6), tail large, flat, and ovate; adapted to aquatic life; incisors robust, able to eat branches; anal gland present, enlarged in males.

Distribution: N Xinjiang; extending across N Eurasia. Chinese subspecies: *C. f. birulai* Serebrennikov, 1929.

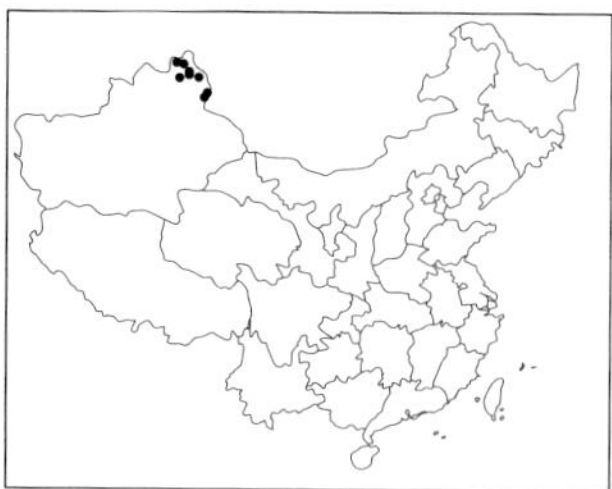

MAP 71. EURASIAN BEAVER, *Castor fiber*

Natural History: Eurasian Beavers inhabit rivers and lakes where they make dams and create ponds, although in Xinjiang they frequently use underground nests in lieu of building dams. These dams, ranging between 5 and 30 m in length, regulate water levels and stream flows. Lodges are dug into banks or by constructing a lodge in ponds by piling branches held together by mud; entrances to lodges are through an underwater passage. Has a strictly herbivorous diet consisting of aquatic plants, tubers, and trees (preferring willows and aspen). Beavers are social animals, living in small family groups. They communicate by slapping their tail on the water surface, whistling, or through deposits from their scent glands. In Xinjiang, normally 1–2 km separate lodges. Sexual maturity is reached in three years (occasionally two); gestation is 103–108 days; and litter size ranges from one to six (normally two or three). One litter is born annually. Their thick waterproof fur was formerly considered precious, leading to heavy exploitation.

Conservation Status: The Chinese subspecies of the Eurasian Beaver (*C. f. birulai*) is one of the rarest and least known aquatic mammals in China. In the 1970s it was believed that only 100 animals remained in fewer than 20 family groups. Currently, only one substantial population is known, at the Buergan River Beaver Reserve along the Xinjiang-Mongolian border—a narrow strip 50 km long and only 500 m wide. Here the population is estimated to be only 500 animals, and only 700 may live in all of China. Firewood gathering has depleted much of the forest on which the beavers need to subsist; heavy grazing pressure has further reduced vegetation needed by beavers. China RL—EN A1bcd. China Key List—I. IUCN RL—NT (in the Ural mountains, *Castor fiber pohlei* is considered VU D1 ver 3.1 (2001)).

References: Sheng et al. (1990); Wong (1994).

Family Dipodidae—Jerboas, Birch Mice, and Jumping Mice

跳鼠科 Tiaoshu Ke—跳鼠 Tiaoshu

Andrew T. Smith

This family comprises a variety of long-tailed, primarily saltatorial rodents, and many of the morphological specializations within the family are related to this form of locomotion. The family is composed of six subfamilies, all of which occur in China (Allactaginae, Cardiocraniinae, Dipodinae, Euchoreutinae, Sicistinae, Zapodinae). In many treatments the first four of these subfamilies are united within the Dipodidae (the jerboas), with the latter two allocated to the Zapodidae. Contemporary evidence indicates that these forms are more similar than previously believed and represent a distinct clade within the Myomorpha (Klingener 1984; Holden and Musser 2005; Michaux et al. 2001). All forms hibernate seasonally. Jerboas possess numerous convergent adaptations with the New World family Heteromyidae. Cheek teeth rooted. Dental formula: 1.0.0–1.3/1.0.0.3 = 16–18.

Subfamily Allactaginae—Four-and Five-toed Jerboas; Fat-tailed Jerboas

五趾跳鼠亚科 Wuzhitiaoshu Yake—
五趾跳鼠 Wuzhitiaoshu

The largest jerboas, with long ears that when turned forward extend beyond the tip of the nose in most

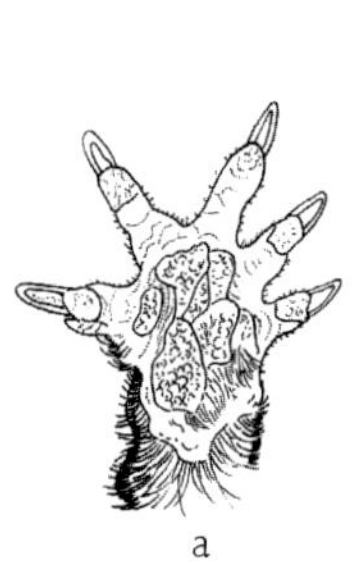

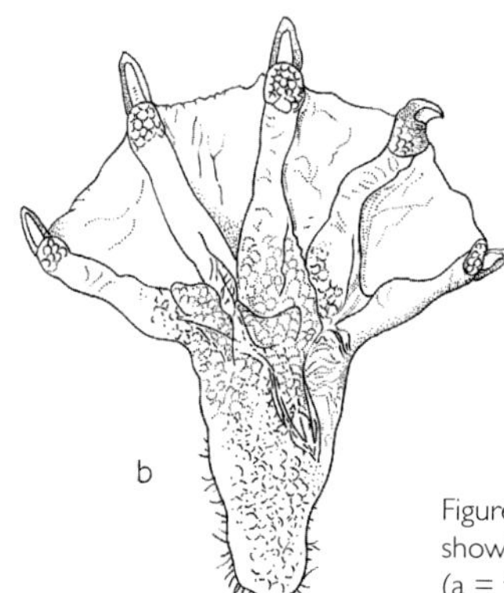

Figure 6. Feet of the Eurasian Beaver showing the large webbed hind foot (a = front foot; b = hind foot).

Key to the Chinese Subfamilies of Dipodidae

1.a.	Mouselike, with thin, sparsely haired, untufted tails; hind feet < 1/3 of HB length	2
b.	Head large, tail long and with terminal tuft and/or fat, hind feet > 40% of HB length	3
2.a.	Forelimbs short, hind foot shorter than GLS, not adapted for saltatorial locomotion; upper incisors yellow, not grooved	Sicistinae
b.	Hind limbs long, hind foot noticeably longer than GLS, adapted for saltatorial locomotion; upper incisors red, grooved	Zapodinae
3.a.	Ears very large, about half HB length	Euchoreutinae
b.	Ears no longer than head, or shorter	4
4.a.	Size small, HB length < 65 mm; mastoid process of skull excessively inflated	Cardiocraniinae
b.	Size large, HB length much > 65 mm; mastoid process of skull not excessively inflated	5
5.a.	Hind limbs with five toes, three middle toes long, lateral two toes very short; ears long, approximately equal to or longer than GLS	Allactaginae
b.	Hind limbs with only three middle toes, lateral two toes absent; ears short, approximately half of GLS	Dipodinae

Key to the Chinese Genera of Allactaginae

1.a.	Ear pinnae long, when turned forward extend to tip of nose or beyond; small premolar present	*Allactaga*
b.	Ear pinnae short, when turned forward do not extend to tip of nose; premolar absent	*Pygeretmus*

species; eyes large. Hind limbs three or four times longer than forelimbs, and the hindfoot with five toes (fig. 7). The three central metatarsals are fused into a cannon bone, and the outer two toes are vestigial (they do not touch the ground, and their tips do not reach the base of the three middle toes). The tail is long and slender, far longer than the head and body; long hairs on the tip of the tail mostly grow laterally, forming a compressed white and black tuft of hairs. The auditory bullae are not obviously inflated in most species. Has one small upper premolar. Contains three genera, two of which occur in China.

Genus *Allactaga*—Four-and Five-toed Jerboas

五趾跳鼠属 **Wuzhitiaoshu Shu**
五趾跳鼠 **Wuzhitiaoshu**

Typical jerboas. Genus occurs throughout N and E Eurasia; 11 species, 5 of which occur in China.

Balikun Jerboa

Allactaga balikunica Xia and Feng, 1964 MAP 72
游跳鼠 **You Tiaoshu**

MAP 72. BALIKUN JERBOA, *Allactaga balikunica*

Distinctive Characteristics: HB 115–132; T 165–190; HF 57–61; E 31–36; GLS 30–33; Wt 65–80 g. Dorsum yellow-brown-gray, with black stripes. Base of hairs gray, middle of hairs yellow, and tips dark brown.

Figure 7. Comparison of the toe pattern of a five-toed jerboa (*Allactaga sibirica*; a) and a three-toed jerboa (*Dipus sagitta*; b).

Key to the Chinese Species of *Allactaga*

1.a.	Small size, HB length < 115 mm; shape of skull relatively short and broad, and GLS < 30 mm	*Allactaga elater*
b.	Size larger, HB length > 115 mm; shape of skull relatively long and narrow, and GLS > 30 mm	2
2.a.	GLS > 35 mm; auditory bullae not inflated; upper incisors strongly procumbent	3
b.	GLS < 35 mm; auditory bullae inflated; upper incisors not strongly procumbent	4
3.a.	Size smaller, HB length < 170 mm; tail length < 230 mm	*Allactaga sibirica*
b.	Size larger, HB length > 180 mm; tail length > 230 mm	*Allactaga major*
4.a.	Narrow black line present at basal part of distal tail tuft	*Allactaga balikuncia*
b.	Broad white median line present at basal part of distal tail tuft	*Allactaga bullata*

Darker coloration on rump, and sides tending toward grayish white. Venter, arms, and inside of legs pure white, while the back of foot is sandy yellowish gray. Tail with weakly developed darker tufted hairs, base of ventral side without white hairs. Skull arched, and base of the skull rounded. Incisors extend beyond the nasals; nasal bones are short. Upper extension of the zygomatic arch vertical; auditory bullae inflated and with little separation.

Distribution: Balikun region, Xinjiang; extending into Mongolia.

Natural History: Occupies rocky sandy areas with sparse vegetation. Diet consists of green leaves of plants, grass seeds, roots, shoots, and insects. Lives alone in burrows. Is a good jumper. Nocturnal. Reproduction has been reported in May; some indication that it may breed twice per year; litter size one to three young.

Comments: Closely related to *Allactaga bullata*, and considered a subspecies in Wang (2003). *A. nataliae* a synonym (Sokolov et al. 1981).

Conservation Status: China RL—LC.

References: Xia and Feng (1964); Sokolov et al. (1981).

Gobi Jerboa

PLATE 11
MAP 73

Allactaga bullata Allen, 1925
巨泡五趾跳鼠 Jupaowuzhi Tiaoshu

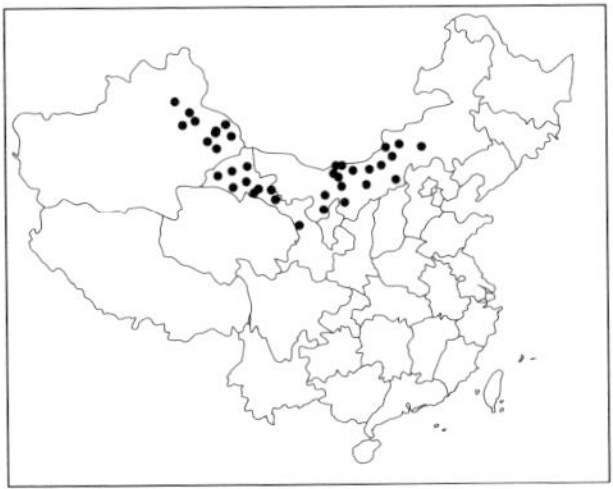

MAP 73. GOBI JERBOA, *Allactaga bullata*

Distinctive Characteristics: HB 115–145; T 165–200; HF 56–62; E 31–38; GLS 30–35; Wt 80–93 g. Similar to *Allactaga siberica* in color; pelage light, the entire dorsal pelage as well as the outer sides of the thigh grayish buff; ventral surface, forearms, hind limbs, and upper lip pure white to the roots of the hairs; there is a prominent hip stripe on the outside posterior half of the thigh; lighter and slightly more reddish than *A. balikuncia*. Tail covered with well-developed tufted hairs, base of ventral surface of tufts white, black portion of inner surface with a white median longitudinal stripe, the distal 20 mm of tail pure white (in *A. balikuncia* the broad white median line is replaced by a narrow black line at the basal part of the tuft). Auditory bullae very large (nearly three times the volume as *A. sibirica*), nearly meeting anteriorly; upper incisors somewhat procumbent.

Distribution: E Xinjiang, W Nei Mongol, N Gansu; extending into Mongolia.

Natural History: Occupies open sandy desert characterized by saltworts, ephedra, and desert bushes. Lives alone in relatively simple unplugged burrows that extend up to 60 cm in length. Burrows contain well-defined nest chambers without bedding. Burrows are readily visible, due to the contrast of light sand against a background substrate of dark gravel. Considered one of the most "desert loving" of the Gobi rodents. Eats green vegetation, roots, seeds, and insects (grasshoppers and beetles). Nocturnal. Breeds once or twice each year between May and August; litter size one to three young.

Conservation Status: China RL—LC. IUCN RL—LR/nt ver 2.3 (1994).

Small Five-Toed Jerboa

PLATE 11
MAP 74

Allactaga elater (Lichstenstein, 1828)
小五趾跳鼠 Xiaowuzhi Tiaoshu

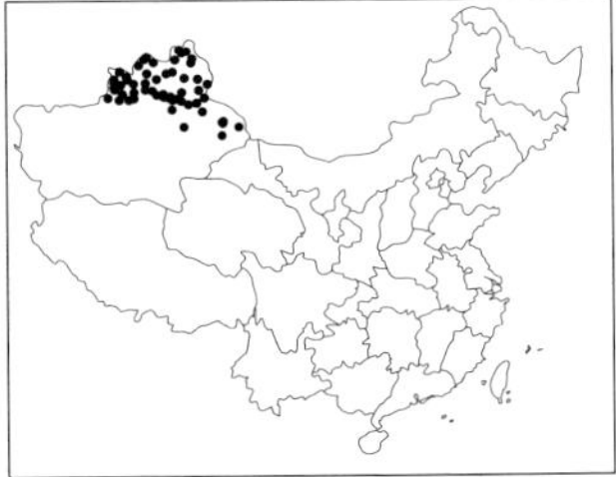

MAP 74. SMALL FIVE-TOED JERBOA, *Allactaga elater*

Distinctive Characteristics: HB 90–115; T 144–185; HF 46–55; E 29–39; GLS 25–29; Wt 54–73 g (male); 44–59 g (female). Small size but with long tail, large ears, and large hind feet. Dorsum dark to dusky gray; sides

a light dusty yellow. Neck, chest, and belly snow white. Long vibrissae. The dark portion of the tail flag is black, and the tip pure white. A whitish line divides the tail flag along the medial surface to the tip of the flag in most specimens. Hind feet with five well-developed toes that are widely separate and sport comblike structures. Front feet are significantly smaller, and claws are markedly shorter than in *Allactaga sibirica*. The long ears nearly close to form a tube near the base. Nasals half the length of the suture between frontal and parietal bones; upper incisors not obviously procumbent; diameter of upper premolars obviously less than that of last molar.
Distribution: N Xinjiang (Dzungarian Basin); species extends across Iranian Plateau and to the Caucasus. Chinese subspecies: *A. e. dzungariae* Thomas, 1912.
Natural History: Occupies deserts and semidesert habitats, shunning sandy expanses and preferring clay and gravel substrates or desert grasslands. Never found in areas of dense vegetation, it does commonly occur in areas sparsely vegetated with wormwood (*Artemisia maritima*). Constructs burrows that can be shallow or up to 60 cm deep; burrows are always plugged, and very little dirt is piled at the entrance so they are difficult to locate. Burrows may extend up to 138 cm in length, and a spherical nest chamber is centrally located. May occupy up to four different types of burrows: winter, summer, reproduction, and temporary. May dig burrows in hard ground with the aid of their incisors. Solitary. While primarily nocturnal, can be seen foraging several hours before sunset and after sunrise. Diet consists of underground roots and stems, as well as leaves, seeds, and insects. Can jump up to 2.4 m in a single hop. Reproductive season extends from April to July; females may produce one to three litters of two to eight young during this period. First litters average 4.5 young; second litters, 3.7 young. Young males and some females attain sexual maturity at 3–3.5 months of age.
Conservation Status: China RL—LC.
References: Bekenov and Myrzabekov (1977); Colak and Yigit (1998).

Great Jerboa

Allactaga major Kerr, 1792 MAP 75
大五趾跳鼠 Dawuzhi Tiaoshu

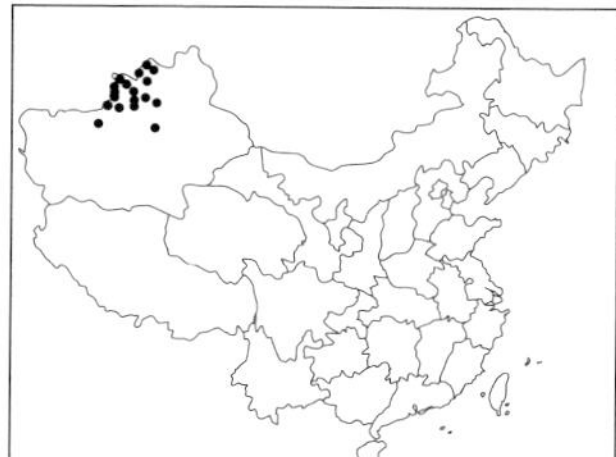

MAP 75. GREAT JERBOA, *Allactaga major*

Distinctive Characteristics: HB 180–263; T 230–308; HF 80–98; E 50–64; GLS 41–47; Wt 280–420 g. Largest Chinese jerboa, with soft silky fur. Dorsally brown-gray with a tinge of cinnamon to sandy yellow-gray; sides lighter and yellower. Dramatic white band extends across hip. Ventrally, pure white from throat to chest and belly. Tail with conspicuous white flag. Skull broad; rostrum massive; upper incisors slant forward.
Distribution: N Xinjiang; extending into W Kazakhstan, S Russia, and Ukraine.
Natural History: Occupies deserts, semidesert, and steppe habitats with firm soil (density increases as soil becomes firmer and more open). Primarily nocturnal, but frequently crepuscular. Can run at extremely high speeds (40–50 km/hr). Solitary. Occupies four different types of burrow: permanent summer burrows (up to 2 m deep, no obvious soil mounds on surface, females with a nest chamber); temporary summer burrows occupied during the day; temporary summer burrows occupied at night; and winter burrows (100–250 cm deep). Diet consists of seeds and tulip bulbs. Two–three litters of three to six young produced each year.
Conservation Status: China RL—LC.
Comments: Called *A. jaculus* (a junior synonym) in much of the literature.
References: Naumov and Lobachev (1975).

Mongolian Five-Toed Jerboa

PLATE 11
Allactaga sibirica (Forster, 1778) MAP 76
五趾跳鼠 Wuzhi Tiaoshu

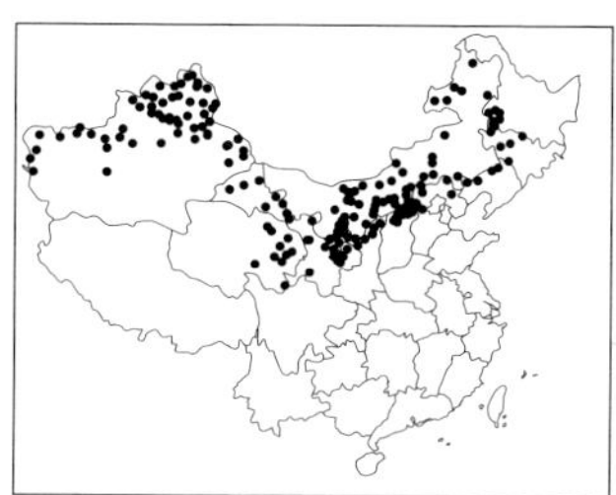

MAP 76. MONGOLIAN FIVE-TOED JERBOA, *Allactaga sibirica*

Distinctive Characteristics: HB 130–170; T 180–230; HF 67–76; E 41–57; GLS 36–47; Wt 82–140 g. Dorsal pelage variable, mostly dark pale brown with dusty ripples, or sandy yellow; ventral pelage white; thigh with a large white spot; tip of the muzzle and back of the nose dark brown; ears as long as the head; tail pale russet, tip of tail well furred and white, with a broad and distinctive black band; first toe longer than fifth toe. Auditory bullae small and widely separated; width of rostrum less than in *Allactaga major*, upper incisors obviously procumbent.
Distribution: Occurs in desert regions of N China; extending from Central Asia, across Mongolia and S Russia into the Baikal region. Five subspecies in China: (1) *A. s. altorum* Ognev, 1946; W Xinjiang (Tian Shan mountains and Pamir Plateau); (2) *A. s. annulata* (Milne-Edwards, 1867); Nei Mongol, Hebei, N Shanxi, Shaanxi, Ningxia, N Gansu, Qinghai; (3) *A. s. semideserta* Bannikov, 1947; E Xinjiang

(Dzungarian Basin); (4) *A. s. sibirica* (Forster, 1778); Heilongjiang, Jilin, Hebei; (5) *A. s. suschkini* Satunin, 1900; N Xinjiang.
Natural History: Found in open gravelly and clay desert habitats, as well as mountain and desert grasslands (avoids mountainous country). Solitary and nocturnal, although it may be crepuscular in spring and autumn. Reported to jump in bounds of up to 2 m. Its permanent burrows are less complex than those of *A. major*. Burrows extend approximately 5 m in length at a depth of 35–65 cm and have one to three openings. Hibernates from September to April in soft nests constructed in its burrow. Temporary burrows, in contrast, are shorter (60–120 cm long) and shallower (20–30 cm deep). In spring it is reported to live primarily off of bulbs of *Gagea uniflora*, although it is also reported to be the most carnivorous of jerboas, eating insects, locusts, and beetles. It also includes leaves, stems, and seeds in its diet. Breeding begins in April or May, and one or two litters may be born in an extended breeding season. Litters normally consist of two to five young, although litters of eight or nine have been reported.
Conservation Status: China RL—LC.
References: Naumov and Lobachev (1975).

Genus *Pygeretmus*—Fat-tailed Jerboa

肥尾跳鼠属 Feiweitiaoshu Shu—
肥尾跳鼠 Feiweitiaoshu

Compared to jerboas in the genus *Allactaga*, ears are shorter and without a premolar. Of three species in the genus, all confined to Central Asia, only one is present in China.

Dwarf Fat-Tailed Jerboa

PLATE 11
MAP 77

Pygeretmus pumilio (Kerr, 1792)
小地兔 Xiao Ditu

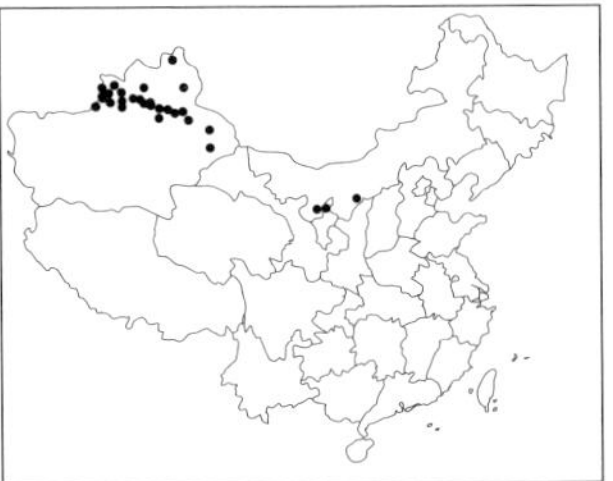

MAP 77. DWARF FAT-TAILED JERBOA, *Pygeretmus pumilio*

Distinctive Characteristics: HB 90–125; T 121–185; HF 47–52; E 20–30; GLS 24–28; Wt 27–65 g. Pelage similar to *Allactaga sibirica* in color, but much more variant; tail tuft not as prominent, the black portion narrow when viewed from the sides, white tip narrow (only 10–15 mm); a broad white stripe across the hip. Skull short and broad; zygomatic breadth 18–22.3 mm; interorbital constriction about 1/3 the greatest length of the skull; vertical branch of zygomatic arch slender; auditory bullae not inflated.
Distribution: NW China; extending into Mongolia and west across Central Asia to NE Iran. Two subspecies in China: (1) *P. p. aralensis* (Ognev, 1948); Dzungarian Basin, Xinjiang; (2) *P. p. potanini* (Vinogradov, 1926); N. Ningxia, SW Nei Mongol.
Natural History: Inhabits clay and gravel deserts and semideserts, preferring hollows and dry ancient river beds. Tends to be associated with succulent vegetation, primarily of the family Chenopodiaceae. Diet is primarily herbivorous and in summer primarily consists of succulents. Stores fat in its tail as a reserve during times of food scarcity. Individuals occupy separate but extensively overlapping home ranges. Day burrows consist of single narrow tunnels (100–180 cm long and 60–75 cm deep). These burrows may have one or two entrances, which are plugged and inconspicuous when viewed from above. Additionally, animals utilize from three to five shelter burrows (25–45 cm deep) during their nightly activities; entrances are conspicuous and not plugged. Two to three litters with two to five young are produced each year.
Conservation Status: China RL—LC.
References: Rogovin et al. (1996).

Subfamily Cardiocraniinae—Dwarf Jerboas

心颅跳鼠亚科 Xinlutiaoshu Yake—
心颅跳鼠 Xinlutiaoshu

Small jerboas with small tubular ears and tails without tufted hairs. Auditory bullae excessively inflated, about half as long as GLS. Skull heart-shaped. Possess one small upper premolar. Hind feet are elongated but show no sign of fusion of the metatarsals as in other jerboa subfamilies. Subfamily comprises two genera and seven species distributed across Asia; three species representing both genera occur in China.

Key to the Chinese Genera of Cardiocraniinae

1.a.	Tail not more than one and a half times HB length; hind feet with five toes	*Cardiocranius*
b.	Tail about twice HB length; hind feet with three toes	*Salpingotus*

Genus *Cardiocranus* (monotypic)

五趾心颅跳鼠属 Wuzhixinlutiaoshu Shu

Five-Toed Pygmy Jerboa

PLATE 12
MAP 78

Cardiocranius paradoxus Satunin, 1903
五趾心颅跳鼠 Wuzhixinlu Tiaoshu

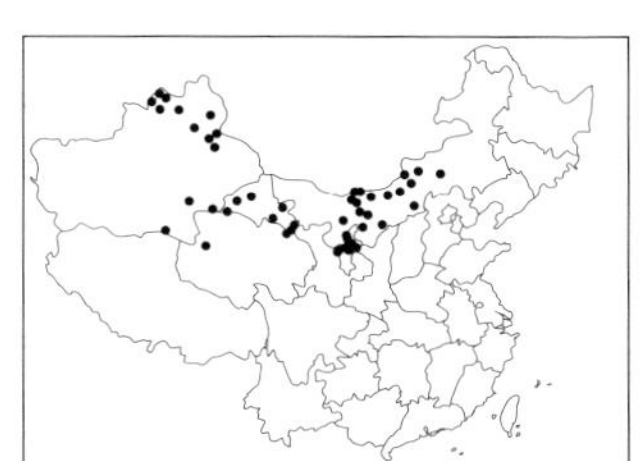

MAP 78. FIVE-TOED PYGMY JERBOA, *Cardiocranius paradoxus*

Distinctive Characteristics: HB 45–60; T 59–78; HF 22–27; E 5–6; GLS 21–25; Wt 7–12 g. Large head with small eyes; ears short and tubular; base of tail may have a thickened fat layer. Dorsum dusky grayish buff to ochraceous; ventral pelage pure white; narrow rusty-yellow stripes present between dorsum and venter. The fifth (outermost) toe is about 4 mm shorter than the fourth toe, and the innermost toe is vestigial; soles of hind feet with a bristle pad of stiff hairs. Metatarsals not aligned for jumping, as in most other jerboas. Enormous auditory bullae; zygomatic breadth 10.7–12.5 mm; broad area on anterior half of zygomatic arch gradually tapered; no backward-pointing process on inferior margin of middle zygomatic arch; front of incisors has a longitudinal groove.
Distribution: Xinjiang, Gansu, Ningxia, Nei Mongol; extending into Mongolia, Tuva, and E Kazakhstan.
Natural History: Inhabits burrows in rocky desert or sand hills, generally occupying those initially dug by other species. Nocturnal. Possesses obvious body fat deposits in summer, when tail may reach a diameter of 8 mm. Diet primarily seeds and grains. Reproduces once each year. Ecology poorly known.
Conservation Status: China RL—LC. IUCN RL—VU A1c ver 2.3 (1994).
References: Naumov and Lobachev (1975).

Genus *Salpingotus*—Three-toed Pygmy Jerboas

三趾心颅跳鼠属 Sanzhixinlutiaoshu Shu—
三趾心颅跳鼠 Sanzhixinlutiaoshu

Small jerboas with large heads; hind limbs with three toes and palms with highly developed long brushes. Of six species found throughout Central Asia, two occur in China. 2N = 46.

Thick-Tailed Pygmy Jerboa

PLATE 12
MAP 79

Salpingotus crassicauda Vinogradov, 1924
肥尾心颅跳鼠—Feiweixinlu Tiaoshu

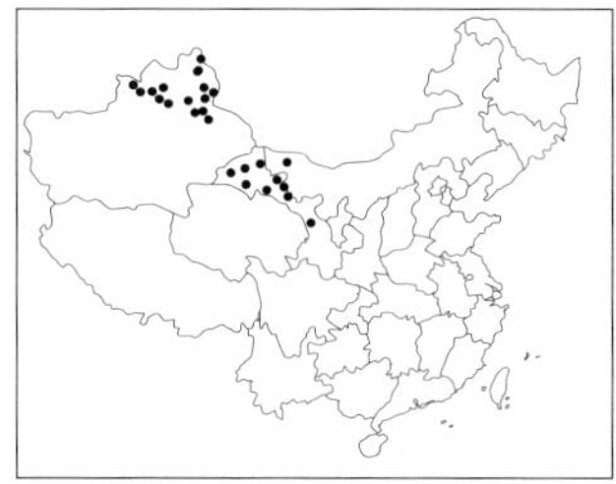

MAP 79. THICK-TAILED PYGMY JERBOA, *Salpingotus crassicauda*

Distinctive Characteristics: HB 41–54; T 93–105; HF 20–23; E 6–10; GLS 23–24; Wt 10–14 g. Dorsal pelage light sandy yellow; ventral pelage white. Nearly a quarter of the base of the tail greatly inflated; tail wholly covered with short hairs, longer at the tip, but not formed into a tuft; hind feet small with a thick, brushlike pad beneath the hind toes. Skull short and small; zygomatic breadth about 11.6 mm; zygomatic process well developed but small, posterior portion curved; broad anterior portion of zygomatic arch contrasts with narrow posterior portion; bullae enormous.
Distribution: N Xinjiang, W Nei Mongol, N Gansu; extending into S and SW Mongolia and E Kazakhstan.
Natural History: Occupies sandy areas with stabilized vegetation. Inhabits two distinct types of burrow: simple and temporary, and composite and permanent (extending up to 3 m in length with plugged entrances). Prefers insects without a hard chitinous integument, seeds, and green vegetation in its diet. May breed only in spring with an average litter size of 2.7 young. Ecology poorly known.
Conservation Status: China RL—LC. IUCN RL—VU A1c ver 2.3 (1994).
References: Naumov and Lobachev (1975).

Key to the Chinese Species of *Salpingotus*

1.a. Tail slender, > 110 mm; anterior half to one-third of tail not obviously inflated; tail wholly covered with short dense hair and sparse long hairs, longer at tip forming a tuft — *Salpingotus koslovi*
b. Tail < 105 mm; anterior half to one-third of tail swollen; tail wholly covered with short hairs, longer only at tip and not forming a tuft — *Salpingotus crassicauda*

Koslov's Pygmy Jerboa PLATE 12
Salpingotus kozlovi Vinodradov, 1922 MAP 80
三趾心颅跳鼠 Sanzhixinlu Tiaoshu

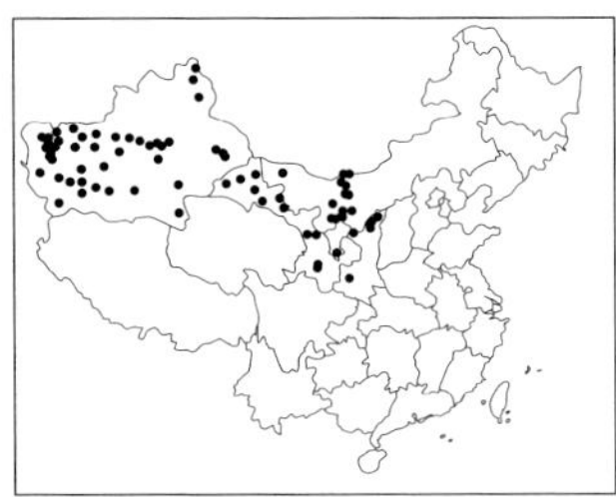

MAP 80. KOSLOV'S PYGMY JERBOA, *Salpingotus kozlovi*

Distinctive Characteristics: HB 43–56; T 110–126; HF 24–27; E 9–12; GLS 22–28; Wt 7–12 g. Dorsal pelage silky, sandy with scattered gray; head less gray than dorsum; base of dorsal pelage light yellowish gray; sides light; ventral pelage white to pale yellowish. Tail covered with scattered long hairs, tip with long hairs formed into a tuft; pad of stiff hairs under hind foot. Skull stout with large auditory bullae that project far behind the occiput; a process on the middle zygomatic arch points backward and extends beyond the optic foramen when viewed from the sides.
Distribution: NW China; extending into S and SE Mongolia. Two subspecies in China: (1) *S. k. kozlovi* Vinogradov, 1922; N Xinjiang, W Nei Mongol, NW Shaanxi, NW Gansu, Ningxia; (2) *S. k. xiangi* Hou and Jiang, 1994; S Xinjiang.
Natural History: Lives in sandy areas, generally overgrown with tamarisk and saxaul. Diet consists of green vegetation and seeds; also eats insects. Nocturnal, but sometimes also crepuscular. Reproduces in April–May; litter size three to five young. Ecology poorly known.
Conservation Status: China RL—LC. IUCN RL—LR/nt ver 2.3 (1994).

Subfamily Dipodinae—Three-toed Jerboas
跳鼠亚科 Tiaoshu Yake—跳鼠 Tiaoshu

Medium to small jerboas; skull mostly broad; ears short, when turned forward reach just to the eyes; hind limbs with three toes resulting from the fusion of the three central metatarsals into a cannon bone and the loss of digits one and five (fig. 7); palms with well-developed brush; tail slender and longer than head and body; tail with tufted hairs, except in *Stylodipus* (tail hairs arranged featherlike); auditory bullae inflated, inner anterior portions nearly touching. Occurs in deserts and grasslands from Europe, Africa, and Asia within the Palaearctic realm. Of four genera, two occur in China.

Genus *Dipus* (monotypic)
三趾跳鼠属 Sanzhitiaoshu Shu

Northern Three-Toed Jerboa PLATE 12
Dipus sagitta (Pallas, 1773) MAP 81
三趾跳鼠 Sanzhi Tiaoshu

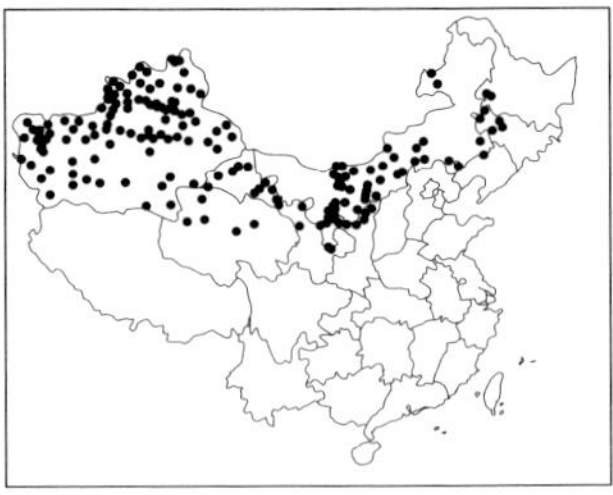

MAP 81. NORTHERN THREE-TOED JERBOA, *Dipus sagitta*

Distinctive Characteristics: HB 101–155; T 145–190; HF 52–67; E 13–24; GLS 30–36; Wt 56–117 g. Pelage sandy brown to rusty brown dorsally; white ventrally; a distinct white stripe originates at the tail and extends forward over the hip. Hind feet with long white hairs, only three toes (central three metatarsals have fused to form a cannon bone; fig. 7), and a stiff brush of hair forms a pad beneath the toes; tail tufted with a white tip extending beyond a black band. Outer surface of upper incisors yellow and with a longitudinal median grove; upper premolars well developed, their diameter equal to that of smaller cusps; the bullae are large and rounded; mastoid process slightly inflated.
Distribution: Across arid regions of N China; extending into Iran and the Caucasus and east into NE Manchuria. Seven subspecies in China: (1) *D. s. aksuensis* Wang, 1964; Xinjiang; (2) *D. s. deasyi* Barrett-Hamilton 1900; Xinjiang; (3) *D. s. fuscocanus* Wang, 1964; Xinjiang; (4) *D. s. lagopus* Lichtstenstein, 1823; NW Xinjiang; (5) *D. s. sagitta* (Pallas, 1773); NW Xinjiang (Dzungarian Basin); (6) *D. s. sowerbyi* Thomas, 1908; Jilin, Liaoning, Nei Mongol, Shaanxi; (7) *D. s. zaissanensis* Selevin, 1934; N Xinjiang.
Natural History: Inhabits high sandy deserts and semidesert, generally between 1,000 and 1,300 m but as high as 3,000 m (in the Altai). Solitary, and occupies three burrow types: permanent summer burrows

Key to the Chinese Genera of Dipodinae

1.a. Tail with black-white or brown-white tuft of hairs at tip; upper incisors yellow; premolars present in upper jaw — *Dipus*
b. Tail without black-white or brown-white tuft of hairs at tip; upper incisors white; upper premolars small or absent — *Stylodipus*

(1–5 m long, 50–150 cm deep); temporary summer burrows; and hibernation burrows. Permanent burrows can contain three to five chambers. Burrows are sealed during the day and sometimes marked with a distinctive pyramid of sand; wind may blow this sand away and the entrance may become difficult to locate. Normally bounds 10–15 cm, however when agitated may jump 120–140 cm. Nocturnal. Eats seeds, leaves, roots, and even insects. Hibernates for long periods, normally from November to March. Mating season peaks from March to May, during which females produce two or three litters of two to eight (generally three or four) young; gestation lasts 25–30 days.
Conservation Status: China RL—LC.
References: Mi et al. (1998); Naumov and Lobachev (1975); Wang (1964).

Genus *Stylodipus*—Three-toed Jerboas

羽尾跳鼠属 Yuweitiaoshu Shu—羽尾跳鼠 Yuweitiaoshu

Species of this genus were long considered members of *Jaculus*. Hairs on hind toes and sides of palms shorter than in *Dipus*; brush not erect; hairs on palms black or brown; tail tip lacks tuft of black and white hairs; hairs on distal half of tail arranged gradually longer along side axis in a "featherlike" formation; terminal hairs dark and without white tip; ears short; white spots behind ears; mastoid process of skull rather inflated when viewed from back; upper premolars vestigial, with diameter far smaller than smallest molar cusp, or upper premolars absent. The three species in the genus are restricted to Central Asia; two species occur in China.

Andrews' Three-Toed Jerboa

PLATE 12
MAP 82

Stylodipus andrewsi Allen, 1925
蒙古羽尾跳鼠 Mengguyuwei Tiaoshu

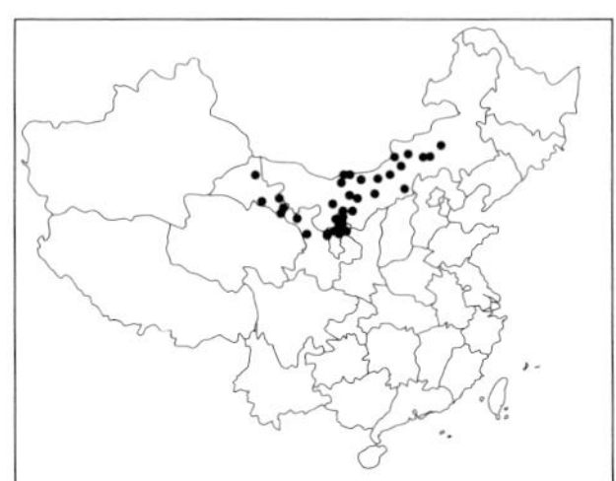

MAP 82. ANDREWS' THREE-TOED JERBOA, *Stylodipus andrewsi*

Distinctive Characteristics: HB 113–130; T 136–150; HF 50–59; E 16–18; GLS 31–34; Wt 60 g. Dorsum straw gray, crown gray with whitish spots present over the eye and a characteristic white spot behind the ear. A white stripe runs across the hip, and the entire venter is pure white. The tail is thick with subcutaneous adipose tissue and covered with straw-gray hair that gradually increase in length toward the distal end forming a flat feather; the distal 30 mm of the tail is black. Of the three digits, the middle one is the longest; the sole of the hind foot is hairy with a brushlike pad beneath the toes. Differs from *S. telum* in having upper premolars; also the tympanic bullae are significantly larger, and the rostral region and nasals are longer.
Distribution: Nei Mongol, N Gansu, Ningxia; extending into Mongolia.
Natural History: Inhabits semidesert, grass beach, and grassland habitats, and even enters coniferous and shrub forests. Diet consists of green vegetation and seeds. Nocturnal. Breeds once each year; litter size two to four young. Ecology poorly known.
Conservation Status: China RL—LC.
Comments: Has been included in *Stylodipus telum* by many authors. *Scirtopoda* a synonym in some treatments.

Thick-Tailed Three-Toed Jerboa

PLATE 12
MAP 83

Stylodipus telum (Lichtenstein, 1823)
羽尾跳鼠 Yuwei Tiaoshu

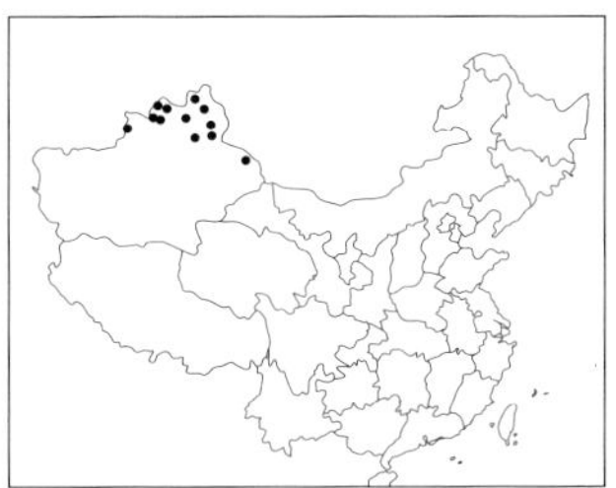

MAP 83. THICK-TAILED THREE-TOED JERBOA, *Stylodipus telum*

Distinctive Characteristics: HB 104–133; T 140–165; HF 50–54; E 15–21; GLS 30–33; Wt 70–90 g. In summer dorsum light grayish yellow; this background is conspicuously darkened by black flecks created by guard hairs with completely black-gray tips; sides light straw and also conspicuously darkened by small blackish-gray flecks; a white stripe extends across the hip; top of head dull and dark colored. Premolar absent in adults, and tympanic bullae inflated but smaller than in *S. andrewsi*.
Distribution: N Xinjiang; extending into Kazakhstan, Uzbekistan, Turkmenistan, E Ukraine, and to the N Caucasus. Chinese subspecies: *S. t. karelini* (Selewin, 1934).
Natural History: Found in desert and mountainous grassland where it is not exclusively confined to

Key to the Chinese Species of *Stylodipus*

1.a.	Small upper premolar present; large tympanic bullae	*Stylodipus andrewsi*
b.	Upper premolar absent; small tympanic bullae	*Stylodipus telum*

sandy areas; prefers clay substrate to shifting sands. Lives in association with saltbush and *Artemisia*, also extending into pine forests. Does not hop like most jerboas, rather its gait more closely resembles that of a gerbil. Solitary and nocturnal. Occupies a permanent burrow (100–270 cm long; 20–120 cm deep) with multiple entrances each sealed with a plug. Home ranges of males and females equivalent; those of the same sex do not overlap, while those of males and females overlap considerably. Shelter burrows are often used by several individuals. Diet consists of seeds, bulbs, and green vegetation; does not construct food caches. Breeds twice each year, with peaks in the spring and autumn; litter size two to four young.
Conservation Status: China RL–LC.
Comments: Some Chinese specimens of *S. andrewsi* may be identified as *S. telum*; in China, *telum* is confined to Xinjiang. *Scirtopoda* a synonym in some treatments.
References: Heske et al. (1995).

Subfamily Euchoreutinae

Genus *Euchoreutes* (monotypic)

长耳跳鼠亚科 Chang'ertiaoshu Yake;
长耳跳鼠属 Chang'ertiaoshu Shu

Long-Eared Jerboa

PLATE 12
MAP 84

Euchoreutes naso Sclater, 1891
长耳跳鼠 Chang'er Tiaoshu

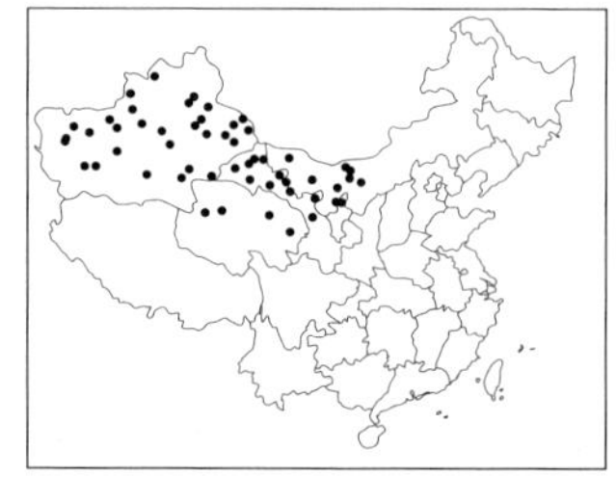

MAP 84. LONG-EARED JERBOA, *Euchoreutes naso*

Distinctive Characteristics: HB 80–95; T 144–185; HF 41–49; E 37–47; GLS 29–31; Wt 24–38 g. This subfamily is represented by a single unmistakable species, set apart by its large ears. Medium in size compared with other members of the family. Dorsum sandy yellow, base of hairs gray; sides and ventral pelage wholly white. Head long and slender, rostrum pointed, eyes small, vibrissae long (normally longer than half of HB length); central three metatarsals partially fused with the middle toe slightly longer than adjacent toes and the two lateral toes short; tuft of long hair on tip of tail well developed, but growing all around shaft of tail rather than forming a flat "flag" as in true jerboas; tail white, including tip, with a black band set back from the tip. Skull greatly expanded posteriorly; auditory bullae greatly inflated; the upper branch of zygomatic arch extends sharply downward. Incisors very narrow and white, and the premolar circular and with a crown area only about a quarter the size of the first molar.
Distribution: Across arid regions of NW China; extending N into Mongolia. Three subspecies in China: (1) *E. n. alashanicus* Howe, 1928; W Nei Mongol, N Ningxia, Gansu, N Qinghai; (2) *E. n. naso* Sclater, 1891; W Xinjiang; (3) *E. n. yiwuensis* Ma and Li, 1979; E. Xinjiang.
Natural History: An inhabitant of sandy desert regions; usually found in sand hills on the edge of desert oases or in sandy valleys with sparse vegetation. Diet is primarily green plants, but may also contain insects and lizards. Breeds in early spring; litter size two to six young.
Conservation Status: China RL–LC. IUCN RL–EN A1c ver 2.3 (1994).
References: Ma and Li (1979).

Subfamily Sicistinae

Genus *Sicista*—Birch Mice

蹶鼠亚科 Jueshu Yake; 蹶鼠属 Jueshu Shu—
蹶鼠 Jueshu

This subfamily contains a single genus. The 13 species are distributed in forests and meadows across the northern Palaearctic; 4 species are found in China. This is a small mouselike form with a long and semiprehensile tail. Although they do not possess the specializations of long legs or feet found throughout the Dipodidae, they still move about primarily by jumping. They also readily climb vegetation using their outer toes to grasp limbs and curling their tails around branches for support. Interparietal breadth about twice its length; posterior margin of palate extends behind molars and projects outward at the middle; occlusal surface of molars not concave.

Long-Tailed Birch Mouse

PLATE 13
MAP 85

Sicista caudata Thomas, 1907
长尾蹶鼠 Changwei Jueshu

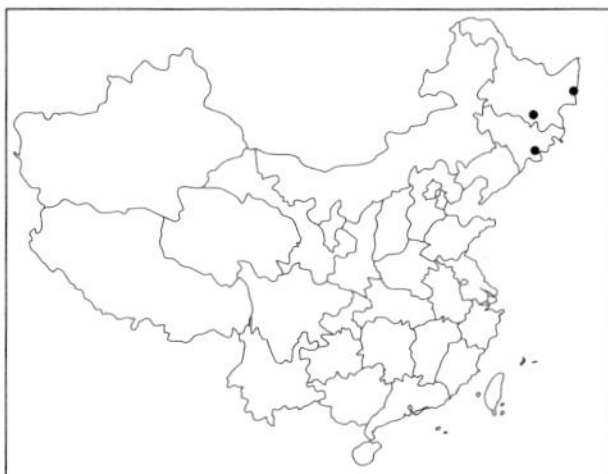

MAP 85. LONG-TAILED BIRCH MOUSE, *Sicista caudata*

Distinctive Characteristics: HB 59–67; T 96–115; HF 16–18; E 13; GLS 19–21; Wt 8 g. Dorsally relatively light grayish brown with a tinge of yellow; along dorsal spine sparse black-brown tipped hair; sides more

Key to the Chinese Species of *Sicista*

1.a.	Distinct or indistinct stripe running along dorsal spine	2
b.	No black longitudinal stripes along spine	3
2.a.	Faint stripe of sparse black-brown tipped hairs present along dorsal spine	*Sicista caudata*
b.	Conspicuous longitudinal black stripe extending down middle of spine from head to base of tail	*Sicista subtilis*
3.a.	Dorsally dark russet sprinkled with black hairs	*Sicista concolor*
b.	Dorsally yellowish straw gray with lighter flanks, white chin and throat	*Sicista tianshanica*

yellow, in part sprinkled with gray. Ventrally a dirty whitish with yellowish tinge. Long tail uniform pale yellowish gray. Back of skull rounded; zygomatic arch widest in the middle; premolars large. 2N = 50.
Distribution: Heilongjiang and Jilin; extending to Sakhalin Island, Russia.
Natural History: Occupies conifer and mixed broadleaf forests. All aspects of this species are poorly known.
Conservation Status: China RL–DD. IUCN RL–EN B1 + 2c ver 2.3 (1994).
Comments: Sometimes referred to as *S. concolor*.

Chinese Birch Mouse

PLATE 13 MAP 86

Sicista concolor (Büchner, 1892)
蹶鼠 Jue Shu

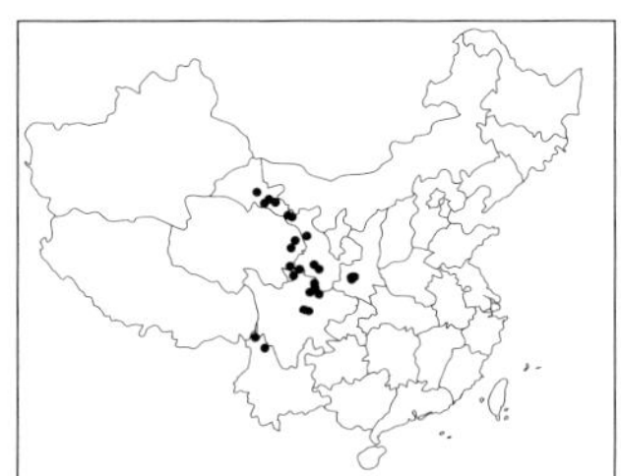

MAP 86. CHINESE BIRCH MOUSE, *Sicista concolor*

Distinctive Characteristics: HB 51–76; T 86–109; HF 17–18; E 11–14; GLS 19–20; Wt 5–8 g. Dorsum dark russet, sprinkled with black hairs; no black longitudinal stripes along spine. Ventral pelage gray-white. Tail very long and same color as back, with underside lighter. Back and front feet with short white hair; palms bare. Upper incisors orange (and grooved), while lower incisors are white.
Distribution: Gansu, E Qinghai, Shaanxi, Sichuan, Yunnan; extending south into India. Nominate subspecies occurs in China.
Natural History: Occupies temperate forest edge, shrubs, and grassland habitats. Constructs a neatly woven ball of grass as a nest, located in crevices or bushes. Diet consists of green vegetation, berries, and seeds. Nocturnal; hibernates in underground burrows. Vocalization a high-pitched whistle. Believed to produce a single litter of three to six young annually.
Conservation Status: China RL–NT; although it nearly met the criteria for VU A1c.

Southern Birch Mouse

PLATE 13 MAP 87

Sicista subtilis (Pallas, 1773)
草原蹶鼠 Caoyuan Jueshu

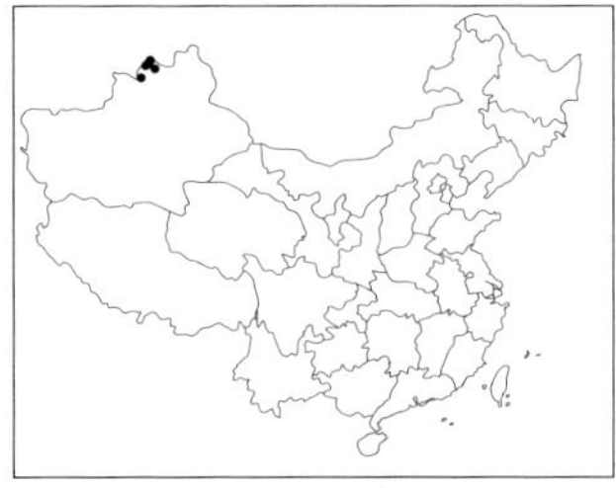

MAP 87. SOUTHERN BIRCH MOUSE, *Sicista subtilis*

Distinctive Characteristics: HB 59–73; T 79–84; HF 14–17; E 11–15; GLS 18–21; Wt 12–13 g. Dorsally deep grayish straw brown to pale gray with yellowish straw tinge; longitudinal black stripe extends down middle of spine from hear to base of tail (more conspicuous on back than on head); yellowish straw gray bands lie adjacent to stripe on either side. Whitish ventrally, with intermittent grayish or slightly strawish tinge; tail brownish gray dorsally, whitish underneath. Skull oval in form with elevated frontal and parietal bones; infraorbital foramina broad.
Distribution: N Xinjiang; extending into Kazakhstan, Russia, and to E Austria. Nominate subspecies occurs in China.
Natural History: Occupies grassland steppe, extending into semidesert regions. Can be found in birch woods dominated by grassy meadows. Primarily nocturnal, although it can be found active at any time of day or night. Diet consists of green vegetation and insects. Poorly known.
Conservation Status: China RL–NA. IUCN RL–LR/nt ver 2.3 (1994).

Tian Shan Birch Mouse

PLATE 13 MAP 88

Sicista tianshanica (Salensky, 1903)
天山蹶鼠 Tianshan Jueshu

Distinctive Characteristics: HB 67–73; T 99–114; HF 16–19; E 11–15; GLS 18–21; Wt 9–14 g. Pelage uniformly colored, lacking black spinal stripe; dorsally yellowish straw gray; flanks lighter with more straw hues. Ventrally dull whitish gray with a light tinge of straw. Chin and throat white. Skull elongated, compared with *S. subtilis*. 2N = 32–34.
Distribution: N Xinjiang; extending into Kazakhstan.

Natural History: Found in forested regions, in rocks of meadows at 2,500–3,000 m. Primarily nocturnal but can also be seen active during the day. Its main shelter type is holes in rotten stumps. A single litter of three to six young is produced.

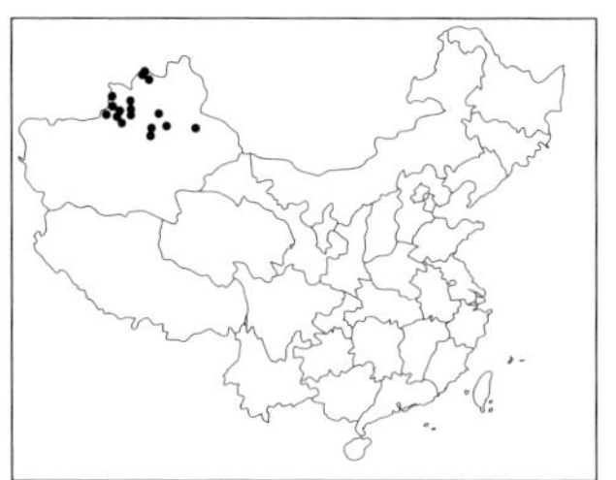

MAP 88. TIAN SHAN BIRCH MOUSE, *Sicista tianshanica*

Conservation Status: China RL–LC.

Subfamily Zapodinae

Genus *Eozapus*—Jumping Mice

林跳鼠亚科 Lintiaoshu Yake; 林跳鼠属 Lintiaoshu Shu—林跳鼠 Lintiaoshu

The subfamily Zapodinae comprises three genera and five species, most of which are distributed widely across North America. The only Asian form is the monotypic genus *Eozapus*, which is endemic to China. The Zapodinae all have long hind limbs, modified for saltitorial locomotion, and long tails.

Chinese Jumping Mouse

PLATE 13
MAP 89

Eozapus setchuanus (Pousargues, 1896)
四川林跳鼠 Sichuan Lintiaoshu

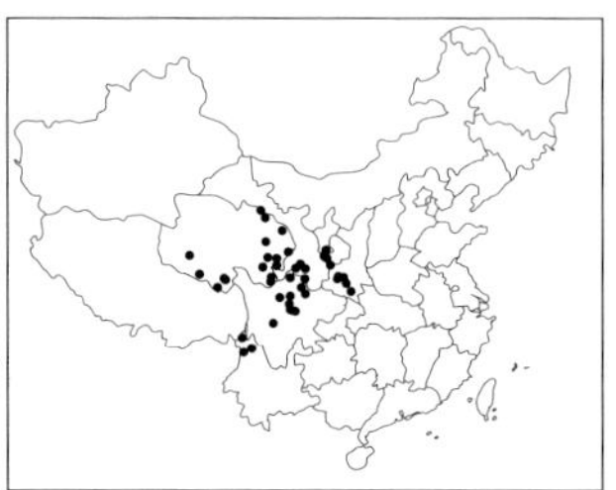

MAP 89. CHINESE JUMPING MOUSE, *Eozapus setchuanus*

Distinctive Characteristics: HB 70–100; T 115–144; HF 26–31; E 11–15; GLS 21–24; Wt 15–20 g. Tawny ochraceous dorsally, with a darker and sharply defined dorsal area from the forehead to the tail; sides light, pale reddish brown. Ventrally white, but with an evident pale brown 5 mm wide longitudinal stripe in *E. s. setchuanus*, whereas *E. s. vicinus* has a wholly white belly with no ventral stripe. The tail is long and thinly haired, distinctly bicolored with dusky above and pure white below; tip white. The interparietal breadth is up to three times its length; auditory bullae large; palate long. Occlusal surface of molars clearly concave.

Distribution: C China. Endemic. Two subspecies: (1) *E. s. setchuanus* (Pousargues, 1896); W Sichuan, NW Yunnan, SW Qinghai; (2) *E. s. vicinus* (Thomas, 1912); S Gansu, E Qinghai, S Shaanxi, Ningxia.

Natural History: Found at high elevations in mountainous regions, where it primarily occupies shrub-steppe or meadow habitats, although it may be found in spruce forests. Diet primarily consists of green plants.

Conservation Status: China RL–VU A1c. IUCN RL–VU A1c ver 2.3 (1994).

Family Platacanthomyidae

Genus *Typhlomys*—Spiny Dormice

刺山鼠科 Cishanshu Ke; 猪尾鼠属 Zhuweishu Shu—猪尾鼠 Zhuweishu

Andrew T. Smith

This is a small and unique family, currently composed of only two genera (*Platacanthomys* and *Typhlomys*) and three species (only one of which is found in China). These rodents closely resemble dormice (family Gliridae), with which they have frequently been aligned. They may be distinguished from the dormice, however, by their number of teeth (dental formula: 1.0.0.3/1.0.0.3 = 16; compared with 20 for glirids), the presence of large foramina in the palate between the toothrows, and their distinctive tail (the distal two-thirds of the tail is covered with long hairs resembling a bottlebrush). The first lower and upper molar is small compared to the second and third molars. The fifth digit on the front feet sports a rudimentary thumb with a nail.

The Platacanthomyidae appears to represent an assemblage that is recognizable back as far as the early Miocene, and which may have had its origins in a primitive yet unknown Asian stock of cricetids as far back as the Eocene or Oligocene (Carleton and Musser 1984; Musser and Carleton 2005). This family is also the first of six recognized in the Superfamily Muroidea, a clade represented in China by four families: Platacanthomyidae, Spalacidae, Cricetidae, Muridae (Michaux et al. 2001; Musser and Carleton 2005).

Chinese Pygmy Dormouse

PLATE 15
MAP 90

Typhlomys cinereus Milne-Edwards, 1877
猪尾鼠 Zhuwei Shu

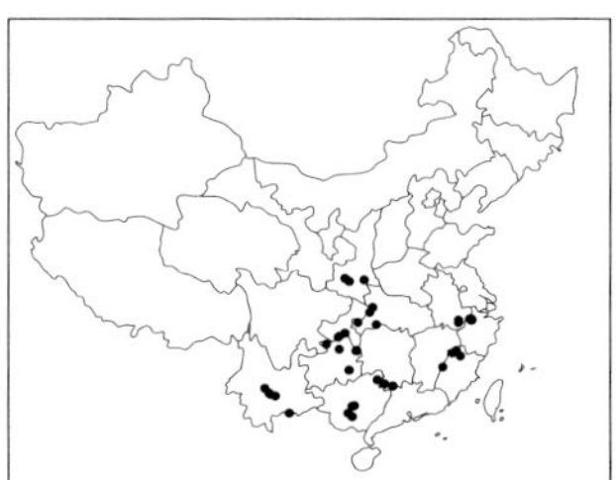

MAP 90. CHINESE PYGMY DORMOUSE, *Typhlomys cinereus*

Distinctive Characteristics: HB 67–90; T 100–138; HF 19–23; E 14–17; GLS 21–25; Wt 15–32 g. Mouselike with prominent, nearly naked ears. The long hairy tail has rings of scales closest to the body, while the long hairs on the distal two-thirds ends in a white brushlike tuft. Vibrissae long and white. The short pelage is uniformly dark mouse gray dorsally, while the ventral surface is grayish with hairs tipped with white. Zygomatic plate relatively narrow and tilted upward; rostrum straight and extends beyond the level of upper incisors; auditory bullae small.
Distribution: SE China. Endemic. Four subspecies: (1) *T. c. cinereus* Milne-Edwards, 1877; Fujian, Jiangxi, Zhejiang, Anhui; (2) *T. c. daoloushanensis* Wang and Li, 1996; S Sichuan, N Guizhou, SW Hubei, S Shaanxi, SE Gansu; (3) *T. c. guangxiensis* Wang and Chen, 1996; Guangxi; (4) *T. c. jingdongensis* Wu and Wang, 1984; Yunnan.
Natural History: Occupies subtropical forests at altitudes of 360–1,570 m. While a burrowing form, there is no evidence that it is a "blind mouse" as would be indicated by its Latin name *Typhlomys*. Subsists on a diet of leaves, stems, fruits, and seeds. Little is known of its reproduction. Although possessing four pairs of mammae, reported litter sizes are small (ranging from two to four).
Conservation Status: China RL—LC.
References: Wang et al. (1996); Wu and Wang (1984).

Family Spalacidae—Bamboo-rats and Zokors

鼹形鼠科 Yanxingshu Ke—鼹形鼠 Yanxingshu

Andrew T. Smith

This family comprises murid rodents that are all fossorial or subterranean, and each is characterized by specific and extreme morphological, physiological, and behavioral specializations associated with this way of life. Currently the Spalacidae is composed of four subfamilies (Myospalacinae, Rhizomyinae, Spalacinae, Tachyoryctinae), the first two of which occur in China. Historically, however, forms ascribed to these different subfamilies have been treated in a number of different ways systematically; the Chinese subfamilies have often been presented as independent families (Myospalacidae, Rhizomyidae). These classifications have been based on the assumption of evolutionary convergence of morphological traits shared by these taxa. However, recent molecular evidence, bolstered by a reanalysis of molar morphology, indicates that each of these four subfamilies represents a monophyletic clade that is a sister-group to all other murid rodents (Jansa and Weksler 2004; Steppan et al. 2004). It has further been hypothesized that this clade diverged early (in the middle- to-late Oligocene) from ancestral muroid stock. Dental formula: 1.0.0.3/1.0.0.3 = 16. A full review of the Spalacidae is available in Musser and Carleton (2005).

Subfamily Myospalacinae—Zokors

鼢鼠亚科 Fenshu Yake—鼢鼠 Fenshu

Stocky medium-sized rodents with a conical tail whose length is 25% or less of HB length. The pelage is soft and thick, covering the eyes and vestigial pinnae (in the species accounts no ear lengths are given as these are rarely measured). Nasals extend beyond the premaxillary. Incisors thick and large; molars not rooted and continuously growing. Front feet are strongly built with recurved digits—the center three claws being three times or more the length of hind claws. The Myospalacinae is divided into two genera, *Eospalax* and *Myospalax*, both found in China (Musser and Carleton 2005).

Genus *Eospalax*—Zokors

中华鼢鼠属 Zhonghua Fenshu Shu—鼢鼠 Fenshu

These zokors have consistently been clustered together because of the many similarities that they share, in addition to their morphological adaptations to a fossorial way of life (Lawrence 1991). Skull

Key to the Chinese Subfamilies of Spalacidae

1.a.	Occur in steppe or open habitat; ear pinnae < 3 mm; nasals extend beyond premaxillary	Myospalacinae
b.	Occur in bamboo forest; ear pinnae > 7 mm; nasals do not extend beyond premaxillary	Rhizomyinae

Key to the Chinese Genera of Myospalacinae

1.a.	Lambdoidal ridge thin; occipital shield extends posterior to lambdoidal crest; optic foramen large	*Eospalax*
b.	Lambdoidal ridge broad; occipital shield even with lambdoidal crest; optic foramen small	*Myospalax*

Key to Chinese Species of *Eospalax*

1.a.	Orbital ridge overhanging; posterior border of nasals notched	2
b.	Orbital rim not overhanging; posterior border of nasals transverse	*Eospalax smithii*
2.a.	Strong, powerfully built forepaws	*Eospalax fontanierii*
b.	Narrow and comparatively delicate forepaws	*Eospalax rothschildi*

characteristics include a convex occipital shield, long incisive foramina about half included within the maxillae, and a rostrum that in profile forms a straight line continuous with the plane of the brain case. *Eospalax* contains only these three species, all confined to China (Musser and Carleton 2005).

Chinese Zokor

PLATE 14
Eospalax fontanierii (Milne-Edwards, 1867) MAP 91
中华鼢鼠 Zhonghua Fenshu

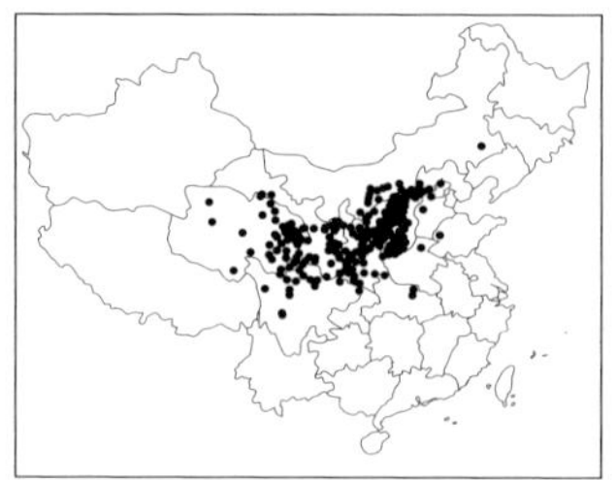

MAP 91. CHINESE ZOKOR, *Eospalax fontanierii*

Distinctive Characteristics: HB 155–245; T 40–62; HF 25–38; GLS 41–49; Wt 150–620 g. Dorsal pelage a dark rust; grayish black base of hairs usually not concealed. Ventral pelage grayish black with reddish tips; a prominent white blaze on the forehead; tail nearly naked. Skull flat and broad; posterior border of nasals notched; orbital rim overhanging; sagittal crest well developed; supraoccipital bone slightly extending backward from lambdoidal crest to turn downward. 2N = 60.
Distribution: Broadly distributed in C to NE China. Endemic. Three subspecies: (1) *E. f. baileyi* (Thomas, 1911); Gansu, Qinghai; (2) *E. f. cansus* (Lyon, 1907); Gansu, Ningxia, Shaanxi, Sichuan, Hubei, Anhui; (3) *E. f. fontanierii* (Milne-Edwards, 1867); Shanxi, Hebei, Henan, Shandong.
Natural History: The Chinese Zokor occupies steppe grasslands. Fossorial; constructs an elaborate burrow system with characteristic domes of loose dirt piled near entrances. Burrows may extend up to 100 m in length and contain large food-storage areas (34 × 18 × 23 cm; holding 2.4–4.5 kg of vegetation; the largest stores may reach 30 kg). Food-finding tunnels range 8–13 cm below the surface, while pathway tunnels may reach a depth of 25–48 cm; the greatest burrow depths reach 180–240 cm. Zokors primarily eat roots and stems. They are often considered a pest, although recent analyses have highlighted the important role that the Chinese Zokor plays in the ecosystem; as ecosystem engineers they increase local environmental heterogeneity at the landscape level, aid in the formation, aeration, and mixing of soil, and enhance infiltration of water into the soil, thus curtailing erosion. They are also a major link in the food chain, and their loss (should populations be poisoned) leads to a cascading loss of many other species. Reproduction begins in early spring, and one to three litters of one to seven young (generally two or three) are produced.
Comments: Fan and Shi (1982) considered the three subspecies to be independent, but Li and Chen's (1987; 1989) molecular analyses concluded that they should be treated together. Includes the form *rufescens*, which has sometimes been aligned with *baileyi* or *cansus*. Formerly treated as *Myospalax*.
Conservation Status: China RL—LC. IUCN RL—VU A1d ver 2.3 (1994) (as *Myospalax fontanierii*).
References: Fan and Gu (1981); Fan and Shi (1982); Li and Chen (1987; 1989); Wang and Li (1993); Wang et al. (1993); Zhang and Liu (2003); Zhang et al. (2003a).

Rothschild's Zokor

PLATE 14
Eospalax rothschildi Thomas, 1911 MAP 92
罗氏鼢鼠—Luoshi Fenshu

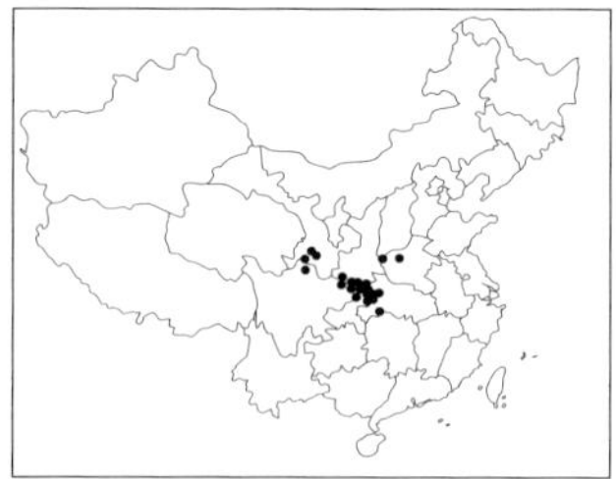

MAP 92. ROTHSCHILD'S ZOKOR, *Eospalax rothschildi*

Distinctive Characteristics: HB 149–172; T 29–37; HF 23–31; GLS 33–44; Wt 164–440 g. Dorsal pelage grayish brown with red-tipped fur and a white blaze above the head in some specimens. Tail is hairy and bicolored, grayish yellow above and white beneath. Ventral pelage light grayish brown. Compared with other zokors, the claws are relatively slender and light. The skull is small, heavy, and rounded; rostrum is elongated and rectangular in shape; the zygomatic arch flares to the outside and is strongly built; posterior border of nasals notched; orbital rim overhanging; bullae are small and low; and a narrow gap occurs between the front incisors. 2N = 58.
Distribution: C China. Endemic. Two subspecies: (1) *E. r. hubeinensis* Li and Chen, 1989; Hubei, S Shaanxi; (2) *E. r. rothschildi* Thomas, 1911; S Gansu, S Shaanxi, N Sichuan.
Natural History: Occupies forest, scrub, and grassland habitat; may occur in cropland. Generally found between 1,000 and 3,000 m in elevation. Favors soft soil in which it constructs complicated burrows. Diet is broad, including grasses, roots, and occasionally crops. Reproduction begins in April; one litter of between one to five young produced annually.
Comments: Formerly treated as *Myospalax*.
Conservation Status: China RL—LC. IUCN RL—LR/nt ver 2.3 (1994) (as *Myospalax fontanierii*).
References: Li and Chen (1989).

Smith's Zokor

PLATE 14
Eospalax smithii Thomas, 1911 MAP 93
斯氏鼢鼠 Sishi Fenshu

Distinctive Characteristics: HB 162–255; T 34–39; HF 25–33; GLS 42–51; Wt 180–460 g. Dorsal pelage dark brown minutely tipped with cinnamon; back of head

dark gray to velvety black; dark brown around ears; long black and white vibrissae. May sport a white blaze on forehead. Ventral pelage grayish brown washed with cinnamon. Orbital margin not conspicuous or overhanging; interorbital region narrower than in other zokors; posterior portion of nasal flat; temporal ridges close to form a midline sagittal crest.
Distribution: Gansu, Ningxia, N Sichuan, and W Shaanxi. Endemic.

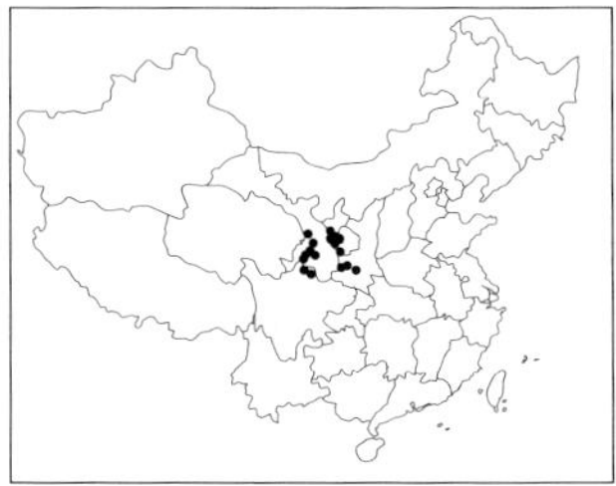

MAP 93. SMITH'S ZOKOR, *Eospalax smithii*

Natural History: Primarily lives in steppe and open fields, grasslands, and occasionally cropland. Prefers wet soft soil in which it constructs complicated burrows with separate living and storage areas. Diet consists primarily of grasses. Two litters are produced between May and September (with a breeding peak of June–July). Litter size two to four, with as many as eight young.
Comments: Formerly treated as *Myospalax*.
Conservation Status: China RL—NT; although it nearly met the criteria for VU A1bc. IUCN RL—LC/nt ver 2.3 (1994) (as *Myospalax smithii*).
References: Qin (1991).

Genus *Myospalax*—Zokors

鼢鼠属 Fenshu Shu—鼢鼠 Fenshu

Myospalax also forms a distinctive grouping of zokors marked by skull features (Lawrence 1991; Musser and Carleton 2005). The narrow, flat, and sharply truncate occipital surface is markedly different from the skulls in the genus *Eospalax*. There are three species within *Myospalax*, two of which extend into China, and one of which (*Myospalax myospalax*) occurs close to the Xinjiang border and may eventually be included in the Chinese mammal fauna.

Steppe Zokor

PLATE 14
MAP 94

Myospalax aspalax (Pallas, 1776)
草原鼢鼠 Caoyuan Fenshu

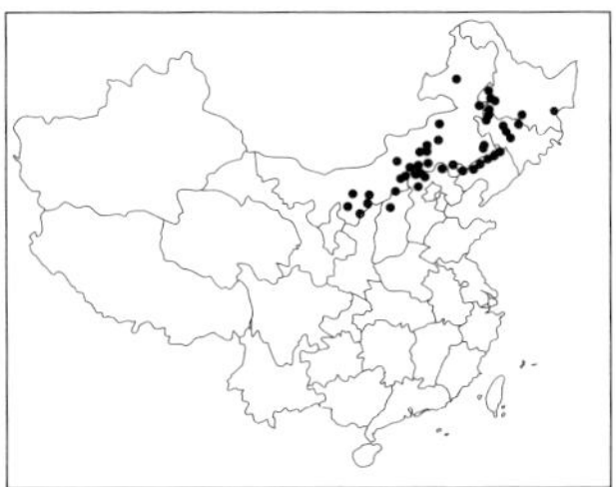

MAP 94. STEPPE ZOKOR, *Myospalax aspalax*

Distinctive Characteristics: HB 140–233; T 48–69; HF 28–36; GLS 38–48; Wt 225–422 g. Dorsum grayish yellow tinged with light brown; base of dorsal pelage gray; lip white; forehead sometimes with white spots; ventral pelage grayish white; tail and upper side of hind feet covered with short white hairs. Skull slopes steeply downward at lambdoidal crest, when viewed from the side, crest of skull obliquely straight line; nasals flat, posterior portion narrow, nearly in the same line with frontal; upper molars resemble each other, although the first is larger, and the second and third respectively smaller. 2N = 62.
Distribution: E Nei Mongol, N Hebei, S Heilongjiang, W Jilin, N Shanxi, and W Liaoning; extending north into Russia and Mongolia.
Natural History: Found in rich, dark, soft soil habitats on open steppe or farmland. Spacing between burrow entrances 1–3 m; diameter of the mound of soil demarcating burrows is 50–70 cm. Burrows reach a depth of 30–50 cm but may extend to 2 m deep in winter. Diet normally consists of underground roots. Breeds in May–June, with young from a single litter of two to five young appearing in July.
Comments: Member of the *M. myospalax* group, and earlier treated as a subspecies of *M. myospalax*. For comparison, chromosome number of *M. myospalax* differs significantly (2N = 44).
Conservation Status: China RL—LC.

North China Zoker

PLATE 14
MAP 95

Myospalax psilurus (Milne-Edwards, 1874)
东北鼢鼠 Dongbei Fenshu

Distinctive Characteristics: HB 200–270; T 35–55; HF 25–37; GLS 43–52; Wt 185–400 g. Dorsal pelage reddish gray; cheeks and forehead ashy fawn; there is a small white blaze on the back of the head; tail and hind feet nearly naked with only sparse white bristles. Ventral pelage gray. Skull stocky and similar to

Key to Chinese Species of *Myospalax*

1.a. Tail and hind feet covered with short white hairs	*Myospalax aspalax*
b. Tail and hind feet nearly naked	*Myospalax psilurus*

M. aspalax; lambdoidal crest on posterior portion of skull truncate; nasal broad anteriorly and pointed posteriorly; infraorbital foramen wide and short. 2N = 64.
Distribution: Throughout NE China from Gansu to Heilongjiang; extending to Mongolia and Russia (Amur region).
Natural History: Occupies grasslands and agricultural fields at low elevations (but some populations may extend up to 1,400 m). Males and females live separately in extensive and complicated burrows that may extend as long as 40 m. Mounds of dirt outside of entrances may extend 40–59 cm in diameter and reach a height of 8–15 cm. Normal tunnels are 10 cm in diameter and run 10–50 cm below the surface. However, these zokors construct two or three special burrows to store food that reach depths of 90 cm; more than 350 g of food may be stored in each compartment. Their diet primarily consists of roots but may include insects. One litter of two to five young is produced in the April–June reproductive season.

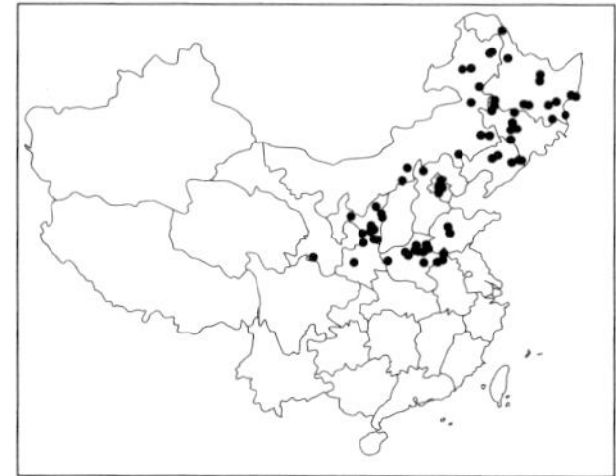

MAP 95. NORTH CHINA ZOKOR, *Myospalax psilurus*

Comments: In the *M. myospalax* species-group; the form *epsilanus* is a synonym.
Conservation Status: China RL–LC. IUCN RL–LC/nt ver 2.3 (1994) (as *M. epsilanus*).

Subfamily Rhizomyinae—Bamboo Rats

竹鼠亚科 Zhushu Yake—竹鼠 Zhushu

The bamboo rats are solidly built animals with clear adaptations to fossorial life and a diet of bamboo shoots. Their skull is stout, the zygomatic arch thick and extroverted (nearly triangle-like), and the sagittal and lambdoidal crests conspicuous. The auditory bullae are flattened, and the nasals do not extend beyond the premaxillary. The length of the upper diastema is significantly longer than the dentary diastema. Their short tail is sparsely haired and lacks scales (instead, it is covered with soft wrinkled skin). Ear pinnae small. Dental formula: 1.0.0.3/1.0.0.3 = 16. The Rhizomyinae is divided into two genera, *Cannomys* and *Rhizomys*, both of which occur in China (see Flynn 1990).

Genus *Cannomys* (monotypic)

小竹鼠属 Xiaozhushu Shu—小竹鼠 Xiaozhushu

Lesser Bamboo Rat

PLATE 15
MAP 96

Cannomys badius (Hodgson, 1841)
小竹鼠 Xiao Zhushu

MAP 96. LESSER BAMBOO RAT, *Cannomys badius*

Distinctive Characteristics: HB 175–215; T 54–67; HF 27–32; E 5–11; GLS 44–53; Wt 210–340 g (Chinese specimens appear to be smaller than the species in other parts of its range). Dorsally red-brown to grayish brown soft dense pelage. Occasionally with white bands on the top of the head and on the throat. Ventral pelage lighter and less thick. Tail sparsely haired. Compared with bamboo rats of the genus *Rhizomys*, the skull has a longer rostum and larger bullae; the sagittal crest is long and prominent; the first molar is largest, the third the smallest. 2N = 60.
Distribution: E Yunnan; extending into E Nepal, N India, Bhutan, SE Bangladesh, Myanmar, Thailand, Laos, Cambodia, and NW Vietnam. Chinese subspecies: *C. b. castaneus* (Blyth, 1843).
Natural History: Lives primarily in bamboo thickets in mountainous areas in the tropical-subtropical zone (300–950 m elevation); can occur in brush and other broadleaf vegetation. Excavate extensive burrows (tunnels may reach 58 m in length and 60 cm in depth) with a spacious sleeping chamber. Burrows are normally plugged when occupied. Lesser Bamboo Rats emerge in the evening to feed on young roots and shoots, primarily of bamboo. They reach sexual maturity at one year of age and produce litters of two to five young. Gestation is 40–43 days, and the naked young are slow to develop; weaning occurs at about eight weeks.
Conservation Status: China RL–NA.
References: He et al. (1991).

Key to the Chinese genera of Rhizomyinae

1.a.	Ear length ≤ 11 mm and completely hidden in pelage; smooth footpads; body mass < 800 g	*Cannomys*
b.	Ear length >13 mm and projecting above pelage; granular footpads; body mass > 1,500 g	*Rhizomys*

Genus *Rhizomys*—Bamboo Rats

竹鼠属 Zhushu Shu—竹鼠 Zhushu

This genus comprises three large stocky burrowing rodents, all of which are found in China. The tails are short and naked, and the short ears protrude above the fur. Upper incisors are nearly perpendicular, slanting inward; molar tooth surface broad, orange in color.

Hoary Bamboo Rat

PLATE 15
MAP 97

Rhizomys pruinosus Blyth, 1851
银星竹鼠 Yinxing Zhushu

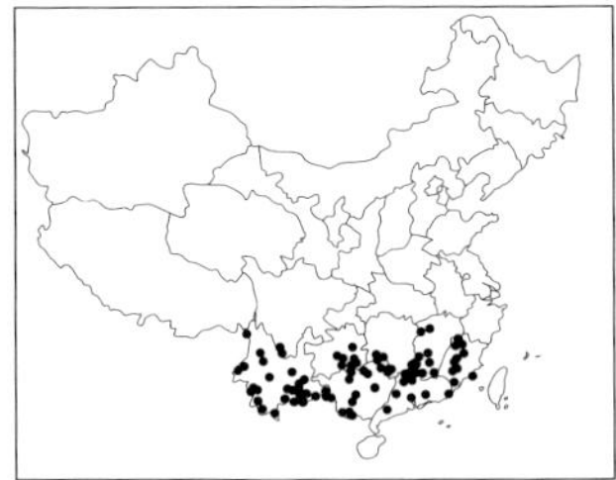

MAP 97. HOARY BAMBOO RAT, *Rhizomys pruinosus*

Distinctive Characteristics: HB 240–345; T 90–130; HF 40–50; E 13–20; GLS 56–71; Wt 1,500–2,500 g. Pelage grayish brown to chocolate brown, darker dorsally than the belly; interspersed dorsal guard hairs are white at the tip, yielding a grizzled appearance; tail nearly hairless. Skull is broad and flattened; rostrum wide; zygomatic arch large and wide; occipital condyles prominent; sagittal crest lyre-shaped.
Distribution: Widespread throughout S China (S of Yangtze River); extending to NE India, E Myanmar, Thailand, Laos, Cambodia, Vietnam, and N Malay Peninsula. Three subspecies in China: (1) *R. p. latouchei* Thomas, 1915; Guizhou, Guangxi, Hunan, Guangdong, Fujian; (2) *R. p. pruinosus* Blyth, 1851; W Yunnan; (3) *R. p. senex* Thomas, 1915; S Yunnan.
Natural History: Lives in bamboo thickets or bunch beard grass, generally at low elevations. When sympatric with the Chinese Bamboo Rat, Hoary Bamboo Rat normally lives lower than 1,000 m, with *R. sinensis* found higher. Lives alone in relatively simple burrows with a single entrance marked with a mound, tunnel, nest (12 × 32 cm), toilet, and predator escape hole. Nests are lined with grass and bamboo. Comes out to feed at night, primarily on roots and stems of bamboo and beard grass, although roots of other plants are occasionally harvested. Has been reported to breed year-round, but peak reproductive seasons are November–December and March–June. During breeding, males relocate to the burrow system of a female. Following a 22-day gestation, they produce litters of one to five altricial young. Weaning occurs 56–78 days following birth.
Conservation Status: China RL—LC.
References: Xu (1984).

Chinese Bamboo Rat

PLATE 15
MAP 98

Rhizomys sinensis Gray, 1831
中华竹鼠 Zhonghua Zhushu

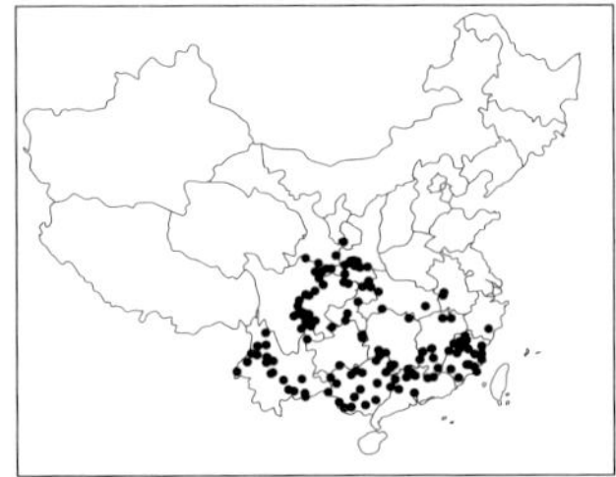

MAP 98. CHINESE BAMBOO RAT, *Rhizomys sinensis*

Distinctive Characteristics: HB 216–380; T 50–96; HF 38–60; E 15–19; GLS 58–87; Wt 1,875–1,950 g. Fur soft, dorsum and sides brownish gray, darker on forehead and side of face. Ventral pelage sparsely haired. Occipital high and oblique; upper incisors nearly perpendicular with maxilla, not procumbent; the single thin sagittal crest is not as high as in *R. sumatrensis* and not lyre-shaped as in *R. pruinosus*. The skull of *sinensis* is not as deep as that of *R. pruinosus*, and the zygomatic arch is thinner and more triangular.
Distribution: Throughout SE China; extending into N Myanmar and Vietnam. Five subspecies in China: (1) *R. s. davidi* Thomas, 1911; NE Guangdong, Hunan, S Guizhou, Fujian, Jiangxi, Zhejiang, Anhui, SW Hubei; (2) *R. s. pediculus* Wang, 2002; W Yunnan; (3) *R. s. sinensis* Gray, 1831; E Guangdong, Guangxi, Yunnan; (4) *R. s. vestitus* Milne-Edwards, 1871; W Sichuan, S Gansu, S Shaanxi, N Hubei; (5) *R. s. wardi* Thomas, 1921; NW Yunnan.
Natural History: Occupies bamboo thickets, generally at high elevations, but may also occupy pine forests. Burrows are constructed in soft soils in which they live a solitary existence (except to mate). Each home range is marked by four to seven external mounds of dirt marking the plugged entrances, each of which may be 50–80 cm in diameter and 20–40 cm

Key to Chinese Species of *Rhizomys*

1.a.	Heel pads joined; tail length > 140 mm; tail with pink tip; pelage sparse and harsh; pinnae length > 20 mm	*Rhizomys sumatrensis*
b.	Heel pads separate; tail length < 140 mm; pelage soft; ear pinnae < 20 mm	2
2.a.	Dark brown dorsal pelage soft and intermixed with long white guard hairs	*Rhizomys pruinosus*
b.	Light brownish gray and lacking projecting guard hairs	*Rhizomys sinensis*

high. Burrows may extend up to 45 m in length and to depths of 20–30 cm below the surface. A den (20–25 cm diameter) is lined with bamboo leaves, and all burrow systems have an escape tunnel. Most burrows are occupied for about a year, after which the occupant shifts to a new site because of depletion of food resources. Their diet consists primarily of roots and shoots of bamboo; most foraging occurs on the surface. Litters of two to four (but as many as eight) can be produced in all seasons (reproduction peaking in spring). Young are naked at birth and not weaned until three months of age.

Comments: Wang (2003) lists *wardi* as an independent species.

Conservation Status: China RL–LC.

References: He (1984).

Large Bamboo Rat

Rhizomys sumatrensis (Raffles, 1821) PLATE 15 MAP 99

大竹鼠 Da Zhushu

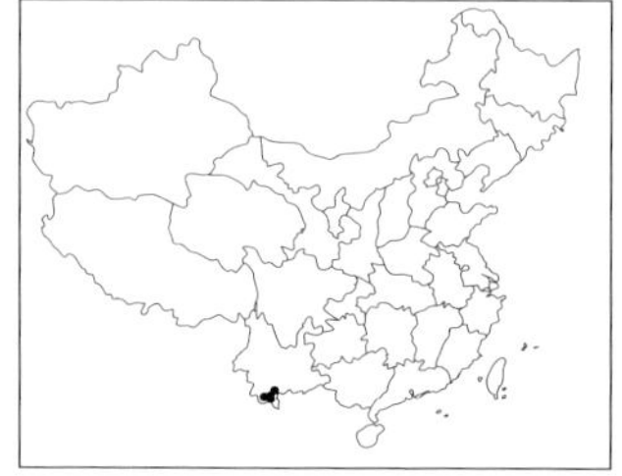

MAP 99. LARGE BAMBOO RAT, *Rhizomys sumatrensis*

Distinctive Characteristics: HB 381–480; T 141–192; HF 50–68; E 25–28; GLS 80–88; Wt 2,150–4,000 g. Dorsal pelage light brown with long, coarse guard hairs, giving a shaggy appearance; hair very sharp; crown and cheeks reddish; darker hairs form a triangle on the forehead; tail long and naked with a pink tip; feet large with sturdy long claws. Ventral pelage slightly lighter than dorsum and sparsely haired so that belly skin is visible. Two posterior sole pads joined. Skull large and sturdy, with a pronounced zygomatic arch; upper incisors stout and somewhat procumbent; sagittal crest pronounced; first upper molar slightly smaller than second upper molar. 2N = 50.

Distribution: S Yunnan; extending to Myanmar, Vietnam, Cambodia, Laos, Thailand, Malay Peninsula, and Sumatra. Chinese subspecies: *R. s. cinereus* M'Clelland, 1842.

Natural History: Lives in bamboo thickets in areas of soft soil. Its solitary burrows are shorter than those of other bamboo rats, reaching a length of 9 m dug to a depth of 1 m. Large mounds mark the one to six burrow entrances. Emerges at night, when it may climb bamboo. Diet primarily bamboo, although it may eat other roots or cultivated plants. Known to grind its molars noisily or to utter harsh grunts. Reproductive activity is biseasonal (February–April; August–October). Litters of three to five young are born after a 22-day gestation in an underground nest. Lifespan is four years.

Conservation Status: China RL–NA.

Family Cricetidae—Cricetid Rodents

仓鼠科 Cangshu Ke—仓鼠 Cangshu

Darrin Lunde and Andrew T. Smith

A very large family of rodents united in possessing a biserial arrangement of molar cusps, with the retention of a longitudinal connection between them, and in the formation of a discrete anterocone/anteroconid on the first molars. Of six subfamilies, two occur in China: the Arvicolinae (voles, lemmings, and water voles) and the Cricetinae (hamsters).

Subfamily Arvicolinae—Voles, Lemmings, Water Voles

平亚科 Ping Yake—鼾类 Pinglei

Darrin Lunde

A diverse group of primarily herbivorous rodents including voles and lemmings. Most are terrestrial and make elaborate runways through vegetation or just below the surface of the ground. One species occurring in China is strictly fossorial (*Ellobius*) and one is amphibious (*Arvicola*). Nests are made underground or in rocky crevices and other sheltered places. They are active year round, day and night. Nearly all members are stocky in build with short limbs, a short tail, and reduced ears and eyes. The skull is generally robust with a short rostrum, broad zygoma, fairly large auditory bullae, forward-placed eye orbits, and tall flat-crowned molars.

On the skull, the morphology of the posterior palate may be of a simple or complex form. In the simple form the palate ends as a transverse shelf at about the level of the anterior face of the third upper molar. This shelf may or may not have a central median spine, but when present it is never extended dorsolaterally to form an inner border with the lateral pits (i.e., the lateral pits appear as inward-directed C shapes). In the complex form the palate ends with a median spine that extends dorsolaterally to form the inner borders of the lateral pits (i.e., the lateral pits

Key to the Chinese Subfamilies of Cricetidae

1.a.	Large internal cheek pouches present; molars cuspidate	Cricetinae
b.	Large internal cheek pouches absent; molars hypsodont and with a prismatic pattern	Arvicolinae

Key to the Chinese Genera of Arvicolinae

1.a. Ear pinnae vestigial and < 4 mm high; upper incisors strongly procumbent and protruding outside the mouth. The anterior surfaces of the incisors lack pigmentation and are pure white — *Ellobius*

b. Ear pinnae > 4 mm high; upper incisors not strongly procumbent and not protruding outside the mouth. The anterior surfaces of the incisors are pigmented yellowish orange — 2

2.a. Lower incisors rooted on the lingual side of the molar toothrow; molar toothrows strongly divergent posteriorly, M3 with four transverse prisms — *Myopus*

b. Lower incisor rooted on the labial side of the molar toothrow; molar toothrows roughly parallel, M3 with only one transverse prism — 3

3.a. Posterior margin of palate ends as a simple transverse shelf at about the level of the anterior face of M3 — 4

b. Posterior margin of the palate ends with a median spine that is elongated and inclined dorsally, forming a connection with the inner borders of the posterio-lateral pits — 7

4.a. Dorsal pelage pale grayish brown; M3 with a very shallow first labial fold and an elongated posterior heel — *Alticola*

b. Dorsal pelage dark brown or dark reddish brown; M3 with a fairly deep first labial fold. Posterior heel not especially long and thin — 5

5.a. Dorsal pelage usually with a distinct reddish swath in contrast with the grayish sides; triangles of the molars rounded, not angular — *Myodes*

b. Dorsal pelage dark brown or dark reddish brown but not in sharp contrast with grayish sides; triangles of molars acute, not rounded — 6

6.a. M1 and M2 tending to have alternating and closed triangles that lack a posteriol-ingual angle — *Caryomys*

b. M1 and especially M2 tending to have opposite confluent triangles and with some species possessing a posterio-lingual angle — *Eothenomys*

7.a. Upper incisors with obvious grooves on their anterior surface — *Proedromys*

b. Upper incisors smooth, lacking grooves on their anterior surface — 8

8.a. First lower molar (m3) with only three alternating closed triangles ahead of the posterior transverse prism, the fourth and fifth triangles being fused with the anterior cap — 9

b. First lower molar (m3) with more than three (usually five) alternating closed triangles ahead of the posterior transverse prism. The base of the anterior most triangle may be broadly fused with the anterior cap or may be closed and isolated — 11

9.a. Size large, in adults HB > 145, HF > 25, GLS > 34; tail laterally compressed as an adaptation to an amphibious lifestyle — *Arvicola*

b. Size small, in adults HB < 145, HF < 25, GLS < 34; tail not noticeably compressed laterally — 10

10.a. GLS > 28 mm; incisive foramina narrow to a point posteriorly — *Phaiomys*

b. GLS < 28 mm; incisive foramina narrowing only slightly and not ending in a posterior point — *Neodon*

11.a. Dorsal pelage with a prominent, dark brown mid-dorsal stripe — *Lagurus*

b. Adults lack any trace of a mid-dorsal stripe — 12

12.a. Tail very short, < the length of the hind foot. Folds of molars very deep and wide, cutting off series of alternating triangles connected at their very tips. Posterior heel of M3 long and thin, without folds — *Eolagurus*

b. Tail generally longer than the length of the hind foot. Folds of molars not particularly wide, and if cutting off alternating triangles, these are more solidly connected to each other. Posterior heel of M3 not particularly elongated, often with folds — 13

13.a. Claw on the thumb, front claws elongated, plantar surfaces of feet densely furred. M3 with only two folds on the lingual side, anterior-labial margin of molars concave. Cap of first lower molar (m3) with only one angle on the lingual side — *Lasiopodomys*

b. Nail on the thumb, front claws not particularly elongated, plantar surfaces of feet not densely furred. M3 with at least three folds on the lingual side, anterior-labial margin of molars angular. Cap of first lower (m3) molar with angles on both the labial and lingual sides — 14

14.a. M2, and sometimes M1, with a large posterio-lingual triangle that is broadly confluent with the opposite labial triangle, forming a V-shaped posterior lamina — *Volemys*

b. M2 with three alternating triangles posterior to the transverse prism. If there is a fourth triangle on the posterio-lingual side, it is small and not directly opposite nor confluent with the last labial triangle — *Microtus* are completely closed O shapes). In the accounts below, these basic palate morphologies are referred to as the "simple type" and "complex type."

The molars may be rooted in adults or unrooted, and persistently growing throughout life, but in either case their occlusal surfaces are characterized by complex patterns of enamel folds and triangles, the morphology of which is of diagnostic importance. The first upper molar typically consists of an anterior transverse prism followed by four alternating triangles; the second, an anterior transverse prism followed by three alternating triangles. The third upper molar is variable and can be used to diagnose genera and species. On the lower molars the occlusal pattern is reversed, with the triangles lying ahead of a posterior transverse prism and with the toothrow ending with a cap on the anterior face of the first lower molar. For this reason the upper molars are numbered from anterior to posterior (the posteriormost upper molar is M3), but the lower molars are numbered from posterior to anterior (the posteriormost lower molar, the "third" molar, is m1; see fig. 3).

Molar occlusal patterns can be described in terms of the numbers of reentrant folds and the numbers of "triangles" cut off by these folds. The triangles of the lingual and labial sides of each molar may be arranged in an alternating pattern, with the bases of the triangles tending to be "closed" or cut off by a reentrant angle of enamel, or they may be arranged nearly opposite each other, in which case the bases of the triangles will tend to be open or confluent. In some cases the distinction between an open or closed triangle is subject to interpretation, and there may even be a gradual transition from alternating closed triangles at one end of the toothrow, to opposite and confluent triangles at the other end of the same toothrow. Of particular diagnostic importance are the enamel folding patterns of the anterior cap of the first lower molar (m3) and posterior heel of the third upper molar (M3) (fig. 3).

Of 28 genera of Arvicolinae, 15 can be found in China. Following is a key to the genera of Chinese voles. Although helpful for narrowing down genera, determinations made using these diagnostic keys should be checked against the accounts of genera and species.

Genus *Alticola*—Mountain Voles

高山鼠平属 Gaoshanping Shu—
高山鼠平 Gaoshanping

Pale grayish brown voles of open rocky mountain habitats. Skull with a simple palate and rootless evergrowing molars. M3 consists of an anterior transverse prism that is usually open and confluent with the posterior fields (but in *A. macrotis* it is completely closed). The first labial fold is very shallow, but the second labial fold and all of the lingual folds are characteristically deep and broad. There are usually two, but sometimes only one, deep folds on the lingual side of M3, depending on the species, but in all the tooth ends in a characteristically long narrow posterior heel. Of 12 species, 6 occur in China.

Silver Mountain Vole

PLATE 16
MAP 100

Alticola argentatus (Severtzov, 1879)
银色高山鼠平 Yinse Gaoshanping

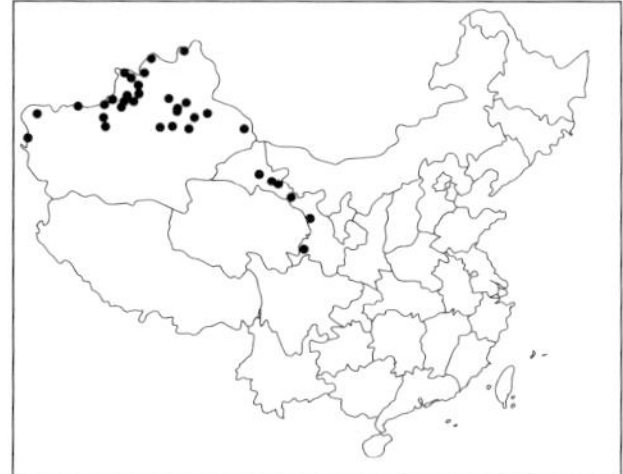

MAP 100. SILVER MOUNTAIN VOLE, *Alticola argentatus*

Distinctive Characteristics: HB 94–115; T 30–33; HF 18–20; E 14–15; GLS 24.5–27; Wt 25–40 g. Dorsal pelage usually some shade of straw brown with grayish mixtures. The dorsal pelage color pales along the sides and gradually blends into the grayish white ventral pelage. Unlike *A. barakshin* and *A. semicanus*,

Key to the Chinese Species of *Alticola*

1.a.	Anterior transverse prism of M3 completely closed and isolated	*Alticola macrotis*
b.	Anterior transverse prism of M3 not closed, confluent with posterior fields	2
2.a.	Skull dorso-ventrally compressed; much flatter than it is wide	*Alticola strelzowi*
b.	Skull not dorso-ventrally compressed; only slightly flatter than it is wide	3
3.a.	Tail very short, < 20% HB length; M3 with only one fold on the lingual side	4
b.	Tail not very short, about 1/3 HB length; M3 with two or sometimes three folds on the lingual side	5
4.a.	Length of bullae > 8 mm	*Alticola barakshin*
b.	Length of bullae about 7 mm	*Alticola stoliczkanus*
5.a.	Ventral pelage grayish white, lacking buffy or pale reddish tones and not so sharply demarcated from dorsal pelage	*Alticola argentatus*
b.	Ventral pelage buffy white and sometimes with pale reddish tones. Ventral pelage sharply demarcated from dorsal pelage	*Alticola semicanus*

the ventral pelage of this species lacks reddish tones. Tail about 1/3 HB length and covered in white or pale brown hairs. The upper surface of the tail may be slightly browner than the underside, but it is never distinctly bicolored. Dorsal surfaces of hands and feet white or grayish white. M3 with two reentrant folds on the lingual side.
Distribution: N Xinjiang and Gansu; extending southwest through E Kazakhstan, Kyrgyzstan, and Tajikistan to NW India, NW Pakistan and N Afghanistan. Five subspecies are expected to occur in China: (1) *A. a. argentatus* (Severtzov, 1879); eastern slopes of the Pamir Plateau; (2) *A. a. phasma* Miller, 1912; eastern side of the Karakorum; (3) *A. a. subluteus* Thomas, 1914; Saur, Tarbagatai, and Altai mountains of N Xinjiang; (4) *A. a. tarasovi* Rossolimo and Pavlinov, 1992; may occur on the E slopes of Kok Shaal Tau, W Tian Shan mountains; (5) *A. a. worthingtoni* Miller, 1906; Tian Shan.
Natural History: Lives among boulders and eroding rocky outcrops in alpine grasslands and shrub lands at altitudes between 1,500 and 3,500 m. Diurnal and strictly herbivorous. Eats green grass when available and dried grass through winter. Tunnels under rocks and in rocky crevices where it builds a spherical nest about 20–25 cm in diameter. Cuts and dries plants on sunny rocks during the day and drags the hay into the nest for the night. Emits a high-pitched piping sound. Breeds twice each year, usually between April and August. Average litter size four or five young.
Comments: Often included as a synonym of *A. roylei*, but now considered a separate species. Specimens mapped from Nei Mongol (Zhang et al. 1997, Zhao et al. 1981) are probably *A. semicanus* (see Rossolimo et al. 1994: 90; Musser and Carleton 2005).
Conservation Status: China RL—LC. IUCN RL—LR/nt ver 2.3 (1994).
References: Musser and Carleton (2005); Rossolimo (1989); Rossolimo and Pavlinov (1992); Rossolimo et al. (1994).

Gobi Altai Mountain Vole

Alticola barakshin Bannikov, 1947 MAP 101
阿尔泰高山鼾 **Aertai Gaoshanping**

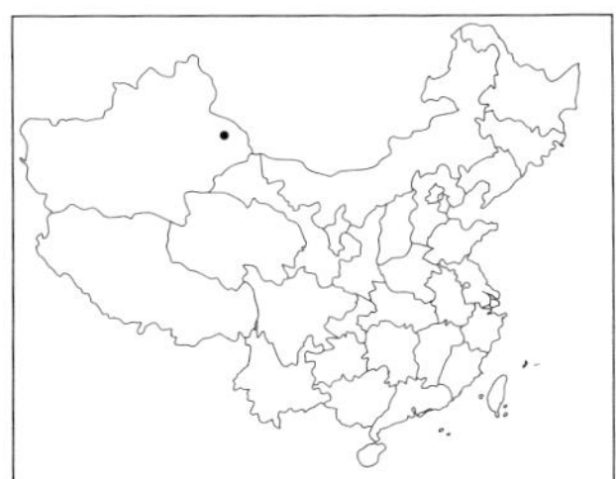

MAP 101. GOBI ALTAI MOUNTAIN VOLE, *Alticola barakshin*

Distinctive Characteristics: HB 100–125; T 18–26; HF 17–21; E 15–19; GLS 27–30; Wt 31–40 g. Dorsal pelage variable in color, but usually brownish gray with some dull reddish tones on the upper back and sides. Ventral pelage grayish white with a pale orange wash. Tail very short and indistinctly bicolored, pale brown above and white below. Dorsal surfaces of hands and feet white or grayish white. M3 with only one fold on the lingual side (a characteristic shared with *A. stoliczkanus*).
Distribution: One record from E Tian Shan mountains, Xinjiang. Occurs at low to middle altitudes throughout the Gobi and Mongol Altai of S Mongolia and the Tuva region of Russia.
Natural History: Reported from rocky brush-covered hill slopes where they seem to favor stands of juniper. Herbivorous. A female captured in June was lactating and had six placental scars.
Comments: Formerly included in *A. stoliczkanus*. See Musser and Carleton (2005).
Conservation Status: China RL—NA.
References: Hou et al. (1995); Rossolimo and Pavlinov (1992); Rossolimo et al. (1994).

Large-Eared Mountain Vole

Alticola macrotis (Radde, 1862) MAP 102
大耳高山鼾 **Da'er Gaoshanping**

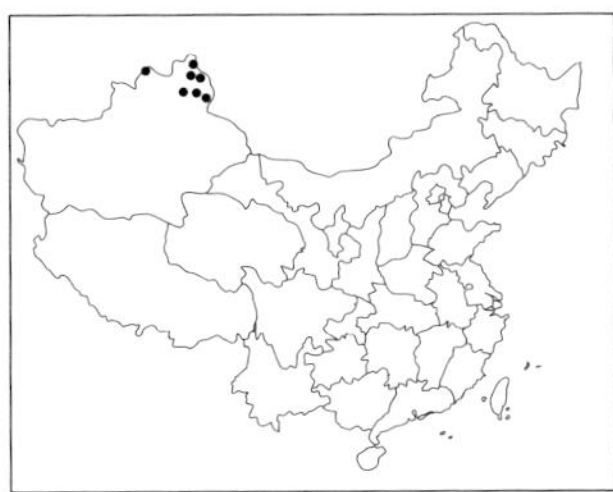

MAP 102. LARGE-EARED MOUNTAIN VOLE, *Alticola macrotis*

Distinctive Characteristics: HB 100–125; T 21–29; HF 15–17; E 13–16; GLS 25.5–28.0; Wt 36–40 g. Dorsal pelage dark gray brown with scattered long black hairs. Ventral pelage white. Tail short and distinctly bicolored, dark brown above, white below. Skull with very small auditory bullae, molars with a rather thick layer of enamel and more rounded salient angles compared to other members of the genus. M3 usually with the anterior prism completely closed and isolated (in all other Chinese *Alticola* the anterior prism is confluent with the posterior fields) and with three well-developed lingual folds.
Distribution: N Xinjiang (Tarbagatai and Altai mountains); extending eastward through S Siberia to the vicinity of Lake Baikal. Chinese subspecies: *A. m. vinogradovi* Rasorenova, 1933.
Natural History: Lives in conifer forest and mixed deciduous/conifer forest on rocky mountain slopes.
Conservation Status: China RL—LC.
References: Wang and Yong (1981).

Mongolian Mountain Vole

Alticola semicanus (Allen, 1924) MAP 103
半白高山鼾 **Banbai Gaoshanping**
Distinctive Characteristics: HB 104–140; T 24–35; HF 19–23; E 15–21; GLS 27–31. A large mountain vole. Dorsal pelage buffy gray with scattered black hairs.

Ventral pelage buffy white and sharply demarcated from the dorsal pelage. There is often a yellowish red stripe at the border between the dorsal and ventral pelage. Tail covered with white hairs and in stark contrast with the rather dark color of the dorsal pelage. Skull slightly flattened compared to most other *Alticola* (except *A. strelzowi*), with rather long auditory bullae (ca. 8.5 mm) and a slight depression in the interorbital region. M3 with two lingual folds.
Distribution: Nei Mongol. Range includes most of Mongolia and adjacent parts of S Russia.

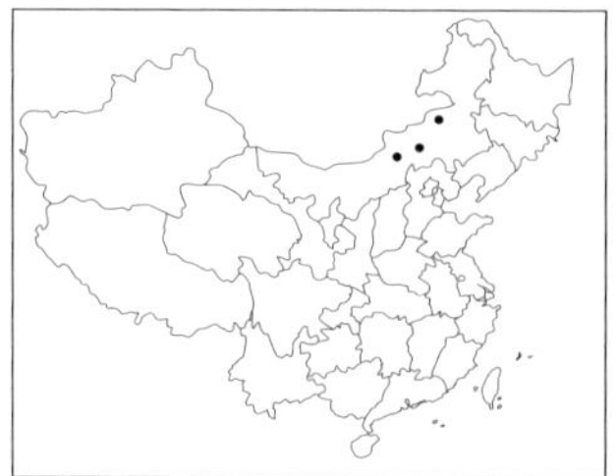

MAP 103. MONGOLIAN MOUNTAIN VOLE, *Alticola semicanus*

Natural History: Inhabits rocky meadow outcrops. Mainly nocturnal, but also active at times during the day. Strictly herbivorous. Lives under rocks and boulders leaving large quantities of banana-shaped droppings near the entrances to its hole.
Comments: Sometimes considered conspecific with *A. argentatus* or as a subspecies of *A. macrotis* but is now generally regarded a distinct species.
Conservation Status: China RL—LC.
References: Rossolimo and Pavlinov (1992); Rossolimo et al. (1994).

Stoliczka's Mountain Vole

PLATE 16
MAP 104

Alticola stoliczkanus (Blanford, 1875)
斯氏高山鼾 Sishi Gaoshanping

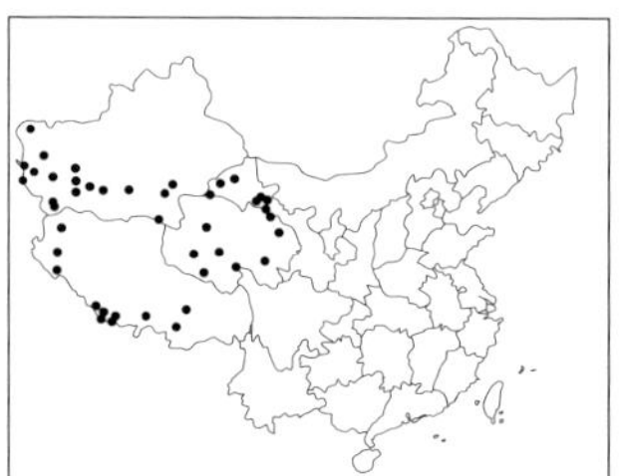

MAP 104. STOLICZKA'S MOUNTAIN VOLE, *Alticola stoliczkanus*

Distinctive Characteristics: HB 100–121; T 14–24; HF 20–23; GLS 25–28. Dorsal pelage pale brownish gray, often with a hint of reddish brown and sharply demarcated from the pale grayish white ventral pelage. Tail very short and covered in pure white hairs. Skull similar to *A. barakshin* in that M3 has only one fold on the lingual side, but the bullae of this species are smaller (ca. 7 mm).
Distribution: Tibetan Plateau (Xizang and S Xinjiang) and adjoining high mountain regions of Qinghai and Gansu; extending into N India and Nepal. Two subspecies in China: (1) *A. s. lama* (Barret-Hamilton, 1900); N margin of Tibetan Plateau; (2) *A. s. stoliczkanus* (Blanford, 1875); Tibetan Plateau and adjoining mountainous regions of Qinghai and Gansu.
Natural History: Inhabits arid and semiarid grassland and scrubland between the upper limits of coniferous forest and the edge of snow line. Diurnal. Eats grass and alpine herbs. Breeds twice each year between April and August. Litter size four or five.
Comments: Following Rossolimo and Pavlinov (1992), we regard *stracheyi* a synonym of this species, although Feng et al. (1986), Wang (2003), and others consider it a valid species. See discussion in Musser and Carleton (2005).
Conservation Status: China RL—LC.
References: Agrawal (2000); Feng et al. (1986); Rossolimo and Pavlinov (1992); Rossolimo et al. (1994).

Flat-Headed Mountain Vole

PLATE 16
MAP 105

Alticola strelzowi (Kastchenko, 1899)
扁颅高山鼾 Bianlu Gaoshanping

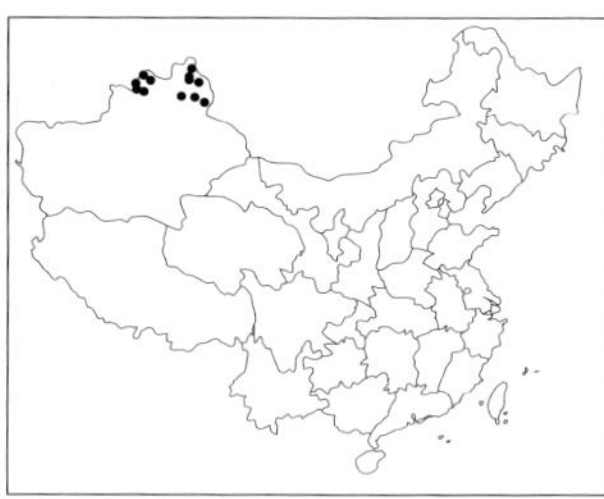

MAP 105. FLAT-HEADED MOUNTAIN VOLE, *Alticola strelzowi*

Distinctive Characteristics: HB 104–135; T 33–47; HF 19–22; E 14.5–26; GLS 25–30. Dorsal pelage variable but generally grayish brown. Ventral pelage grayish white. Tail relatively long for the genus, usually white but sometimes with a faint brownish tinge on the dorsal surface. Dorsal surfaces of hands and feet white. Skull extremely flat, much flatter than it is wide.
Distribution: N Xinjiang; extending from Kazakhstan to NW Mongolia. Chinese subspecies: *A. s. strelzowi* (Kastchenko, 1899).
Natural History: Inhabits rocky slopes and eroding outcrops with narrow cavities and crevices. Constructs piles of stone and debris at the entrance to its crevice. Diurnal. Eats grass stems and seeds. Stores vegetation in crevices for consumption through winter. There are at least three litters per breeding season, and specimens with 7–11 embryos have been reported.
Conservation Status: China RL—LC.
References: Ma et al. (1987); Musser and Carleton (2005); Pavlinov and Rossolimo (1987).

Genus *Arvicola*—Water Voles

水鼠平属 Shuping Shu—水鼠平 Shuping

A very large brown semiaquatic vole. Skull large and massively built, palate complex, molars rootless and ever growing. Of three species of *Arvicola*, only one is found in China

Eurasian Water Vole

PLATE 16
MAP 106

Arvicola amphibius (Linnaeus, 1758)
水鼠平 Shui Ping

MAP 106. EURASIAN WATER VOLE, *Arvicola amphibius*

Distinctive Characteristics: HB 145–185; T 90–110; HF 28–32; E 14–15; GLS 34–42; Wt 130–270 g. A large semiaquatic vole. Dorsal pelage thickly furred, variable in color, but usually some shade of dark brown with long black guard hairs scattered throughout. Pelage color somewhat paler brown on the cheeks and along the sides of the body and blending into the buffy brown ventral pelage. Tail entirely dark brown and covered in short stiff hairs. Dorsal surfaces of hands and feet dark brown and bearing long claws. Flank glands measuring about 20 × 10 mm are most conspicuous in males. The skull is large and massively built, with prominent squamosal ridges. M3 simplified and consisting of an anterior prism followed by only two, or sometimes three, alternate closed triangles and a posterior heel. First lower molar (m3) consists of a posterior transverse prism ahead of which there are only three alternating closed triangles and an anterior cap.
Distribution: N Xinjiang; extending across the Palearctic. Two subspecies in China: (1) *A. a. kuznetzovi* Ognev, 1933; N parts of Tarbagatai, Jeminay, Tacheng, Habahe, and Burjin of Taragatai area; (2) *A. a. scythicus* Thomas, 1914; N parts of Jiayr and Tian Shan mountains.
Natural History: Inhabits moist meadows, weedy riverbanks and lakeshores, and upriver swamps. May also occur in irrigated farmland and villages. May be active at any time, but is most active at dawn and dusk. Feeds primarily on succulent vegetation, but also consumes some insects, mollusks, and small fish. Lives in complex burrows that are usually not deeper than 1 m. Males mark territories with flank gland secretions. Reproduction occurs during the warmer months of the year and may begin as early as February in mild years. Gestation period is 21 days. Females produce two to four litters per year. Average litter size between four and six young.
Comments: The names *amphibius* and *terrestris* have been used interchangeably for this species, but the former is strictly correct. See discussion in Musser and Carleton (2005).
Conservation Status: China RL–LC.
References: Panteleyev (2000).

Genus *Caryomys*—Montane Forest Voles

绒鼠平属 Rongping Shu—绒鼠平 Rongping

Small dark brown voles similar to *Eothenomys*, and once included as a subgenus within it, but now regarded a distinct genus based on karyological data (see discussion in Musser and Carleton 2005). The skulls of both *Eothenomys* and *Caryomys* have a simple palate and usually rootless and persistently growing molars. The molars of *Caryomys* have alternating, well-rounded triangles that are closed at their base. M1 and M2 lack posterio-lingual angles and the posterior heel of M3 is simple and U-shaped. In contrast, most members of the *Eothenomys melanogaster* species group have nearly opposite, broadly confluent triangles and prominent posterio-lingual angles on M1 and M2. Members of the *E. chinensis* group, however, have folding patterns on M1 and M2 that are similar to *Caryomys*, but these are distinguished as *Eothenomys* by a complex posterior heel to M3. Among members of the *E. chinensis* species group, the posterior heel has deep folds on both the lingual and labial sides, whereas in *Caryomys* the posterior heel is a simple, unfolded U shape. Females have only four mammae (two inguinal pairs). The two species of *Caryomys* are endemic to China.

Eva's Vole

PLATE 17
MAP 107

Caryomys eva (Thomas, 1911)
洮州绒鼠 Taozhou Rongshu

Distinctive Characteristics: HB 83–100; T 46–60; HF 15–18; E 10.5–13; GLS 21–24.5. Dorsal pelage dark reddish brown. Ventral pelage dark gray with buff brown tips. Tail less than half HB length, dark brown above, paler brown below, but not distinctly bicolored. Dorsal surfaces of hands and feet dark brown. M3 consists of an anterior prism followed by one set of nearly opposite and usually broadly confluent lingual and labial triangles and a simple and relatively short

Key to the Chinese species of *Caryomys*

1.a.	Dorsal pelage dark reddish brown; tail longer, ca. 50–60 mm	*Caryomys eva*
b.	Dorsal pelage dull buff brown; tail shorter, ca. 30–40 mm	*Caryomys inez*

U-shaped posterior heel. First lower molar (m3) consists of a posterior prism ahead of which are four alternating closed triangles and a fifth lingual triangle confluent with the anterior cap.
Distribution: Mountains of N Sichuan, S Gansu and adjoining Shaanxi, and Hubei. Endemic. Two subspecies: (1) *C. e. alcinous* (Thomas, 1911); Daxue and Qionglai mountains of N Sichuan; (2) *C. e. eva* (Thomas, 1911); range outside N Sichuan.

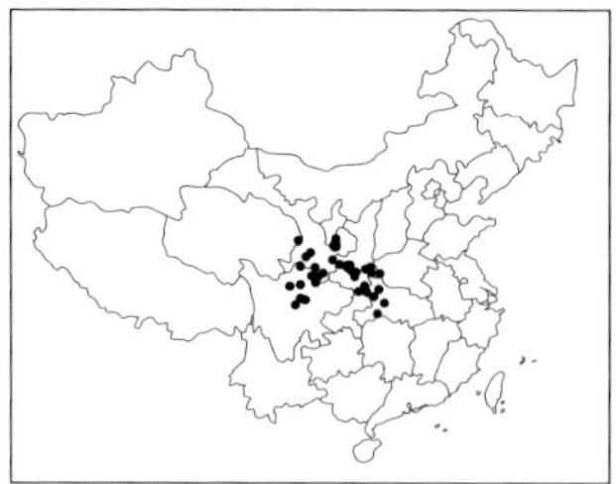

MAP 107. EVA'S VOLE, *Caryomys eva*

Natural History: Mountain forests, and particularly damp mossy forest at altitudes between about 2,600 and 4,000 m. Appears to fill the ecological niche of *Eothenomys* at higher elevations. Feeds on seeds, buds, young leaves, bark, and grass.
Comments: Sometimes regarded a species of *Eothenomys*, but see Ma and Jiang (1996) for the validity of the genus.
Conservation Status: China RL–LC.
References: Kaneko (1992); Ma and Jiang (1996).

Inez's Vole

Caryomys inez (Thomas, 1908) PLATE 17
苛岚绒鼠 Kelan Rongshu MAP 108

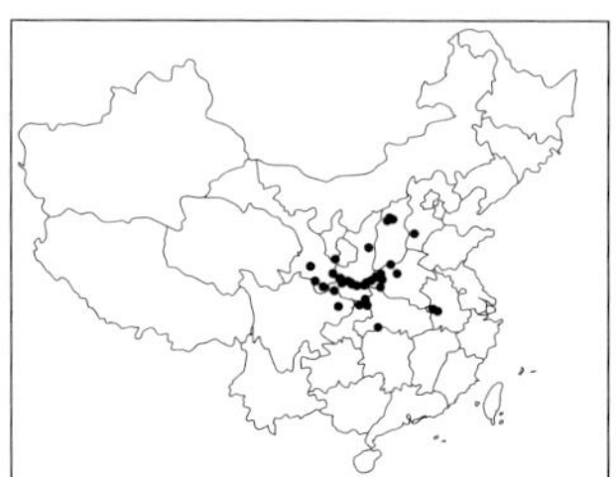

MAP 108. INEZ'S VOLE, *Caryomys inez*

Distinctive Characteristics: HB 87–94; T 32–42; HF 15–16; E 10–12; GLS 23–24. Dorsal pelage uniform dull buff brown. Ventral pelage pale buff. Tail more than half HB length, bicolored, dark brown above, paler brown below. Dorsal surfaces of hands and feet brown. Ears small, only slightly projecting above the fur. Molar pattern similar to that of *C. eva*, but with the posterior heel of M3 more elongated and sometimes with an incipient fold on the labial side.
Distribution: SE Shaanxi eastward through Shanxi. Endemic. Two subspecies: (1) *C. i. inez* (Thomas, 1908); N part of range; (2) *C. i. nux* (Thomas, 1910); S part of range.
Natural History: Inhabits overgrown wooded gullies and ravines between 500 and 2,000 m elevation, where it burrows in loose soil. Reproduction occurs from March to October. One female was reported to have two embryos.
Comments: See comments for *C. eva*.
Conservation Status: China RL–LC.
References: Kaneko (1992); Ma and Jiang (1996).

Genus *Ellobius*—Mole Voles

鼹形田鼠属 Yanxingtianshu Shu—
鼹形田鼠 Yanxingtianshu

A fossorial form highly specialized for subterranean life. Fur short and velvety, small eyes, ears vestigial. The long white incisors protrude outside of the mouth and extend far forward of the nasal bones. Skull with complex palate and rooted molars. Third molars (upper and lower) very much reduced, much smaller than the second molars. Of five species of *Ellobius*, only one occurs in China.

Eastern Mole Vole

Ellobius tancrei Blasius, 1884 PLATE 17
鼹形田鼠 Yanxing Tianshu MAP 109

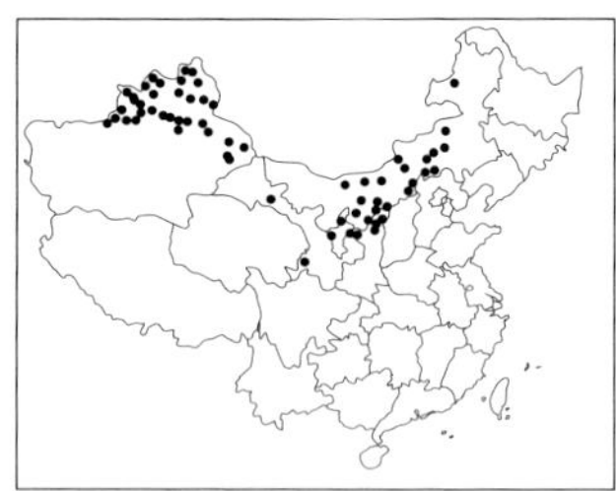

MAP 109. EASTERN MOLE VOLE, *Ellobius tancrei*

Distinctive Characteristics: HB 95–131; T 8–20; HF 19–24; E 0; GLS 24–36; Wt 30–88 g. A fossorial vole highly adapted to life underground. Dorsal pelage soft, velvety, and highly variable in coloration from dark grayish brown to pale sandy brown. Ventral pelage ranges from dark grayish brown to nearly pure white. Face and top of head with a distinctive dark brown patch between the eyes and ears. Tail short and covered in gray-based sandy brown hairs but with a short tuft of grayish white hairs at the tip. Hands and feet covered in white hairs and somewhat broadened, but otherwise not much specialized for digging and having very small claws. Ear pinnae reduced to an inconspicuous fleshy ridge about 4 mm high. Skull dorsoventrally compressed; zygomatic arches wide and posteriorly divergent; auditory bullae with very small external apertures; rostrum short and narrow, with small incisive foramina. The pure white, ungrooved incisors are very long and straight and extend far forward of the nasals. Molar occlusal surfaces highly

simplified and consisting of a series of very weak and well-rounded angles, but these rarely extend far enough inward to define closed fields. Third molars (upper and lower) very much reduced, about half the size of the second molars.
Distribution: N Xinjiang through Mongolia to Nei Mongol and extending south to S Gansu and Shaanxi; extending westward into E Turkmenistan, Uzbekistan, and E Kazakhstan. Five subspecies in China: (1) *E. t. albicatus* Thomas, 1912; Hami region; (2) *E. t. coenosus* Thomas, 1912; Tian Shan mountains; (3) *E. t. larvatus* Allen, 1924; W Nei Mongol; (4) *E. t. orientalis* Allen, 1924; E Nei Mongol; (5) *E. t. tancrei* Blasius, 1884; Altai mountains.
Natural History: Inhabits steppes, semideserts, and grasslands, especially in moist valleys and near the banks of lakes and streams. Sometimes found in oasis farmlands. Feeds on the underground parts of plants and especially starch bulbs and tubers. Fossorial "head-lift diggers," they use their incisors and skull to loosen and shovel dirt. Lives in a complex burrow system including food storage and nest chambers. Long burrow passages are 5–6 cm in diameter and usually lie at depths between 10 and 40 cm, while nest and food storage chambers descend to depths of 50–70 cm. They are active day and night but spend little time outside their burrows during the day. At night, however, they may range quite far from their burrows. Extremely timid, they may emit a birdlike chirp when frightened. Reproduction typically occurs between April and September. Males and females reach reproductive maturity at about 90 days. Gestation period is about 26 days, and females have their first litter at about five months of age and may have as many as six or seven litters of three to four or five to seven, depending on environmental conditions. Offspring remain in their underground nest until they are weaned at about 60 days of age. The interval between litters is 34–36 days.
Comments: Substantial geographic variation is reflected in the recognition of at least five subspecies from China; see Thomas (1912b) and Allen (1924) for detailed descriptions of each. Briefly, there is a trend toward smaller size and paler pelage coloration from west to east. Formerly included in *E. talpinus*.
Conservation Status: China RL—LC.
References: Allen (1924); Musser and Carleton (2005); Stein (2000); Thomas (1912b).

Genus *Eolagurus*—Steppe Voles

东方兔尾鼠属 Dongfangtuweishu Shu—
东方兔尾鼠 Dongfangtuweishu

Pale sandy yellow, short-tailed voles of desert steppes. Skull with a complex palate and rootless, ever-growing molars. Similar to *Lagurus* but distinguished by larger size, the absence of a mid-dorsal stripe in the adult pelage, and a relatively high and convex cranium among other characteristics. There are two species of *Eolagurus*, and they both occur in China.

Yellow Steppe Vole

Eolagurus luteus (Eversmann, 1840) PLATE 17
黄兔尾鼠 Huang Tuweishu MAP 110

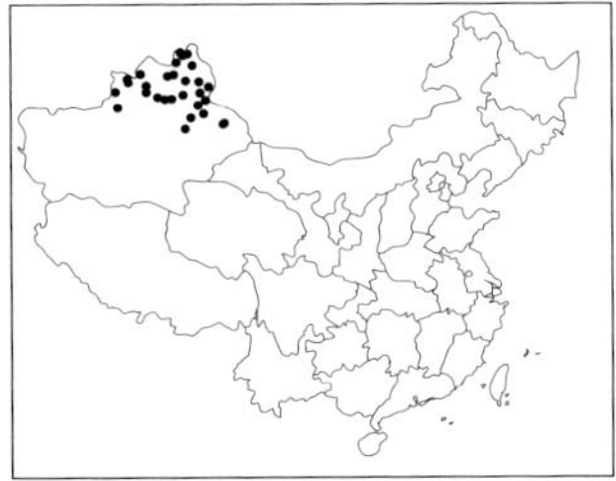

MAP 110. YELLOW STEPPE VOLE, *Eolagurus luteus*

Distinctive Characteristics: HB 105–195; T 12–22; HF 19–21; E 5–9; GLS 28–32. Dorsal pelage pale sandy brown, occasionally with darker tinges on the back of the head and around the eyes. Sides pale sandy yellow and blending into the pale yellow ventral pelage (pure white in *E. przewalskii*). Dorsal surfaces and soles of hands and feet furred yellow brown. Pollex of forelimb with a small pointed claw (large and obtuse claw in *E. przewalskii*). Juveniles may exhibit a faint mid-dorsal stripe, but this is absent in adults. In lateral view the skull is well domed, dipping downward over the occiput and nasals. This species is distinguished from *E. przewalskii* by its smaller bullae, which do not extend ventrally beyond the occlusal plane of the molar tooth-row; and by mastoid processes that do not protrude beyond the level of the occipital condyles.
Distribution: N Xinjiang; extending from E Kazakhstan to W Mongolia.
Natural History: Inhabits dry steppes and semideserts. In spring and summer occurs at lower altitudes, where it will remain until the grass is all dried,

Key to the Chinese Species of *Eolagurus*

1.a. Ventral pelage pale yellow; thumb with small pointed claw; auditory bullae not extending ventrally beyond the occlusal plane of the molar toothrow; mastoid processes not protruding below the levels of the occipital condyles *Eolagurus luteus*

b. Ventral pelage white; thumb with a large obtuse claw; auditory bullae extending below the level of the occlusal surface of the molars; mastoid processes protruding beyond the level of the occipital condyles *Eolagurus przewalskii*

at which time it will move up to higher altitudes to feed on montane grass through winter. Diurnal. Feeds on roots, tubers, and seeds in the vicinity of holes and emerges for only very short periods of time. Once the food around the hole has been depleted, will move on to a new hole or dig a new one. Reproduction occurs in the summer months, producing at least three litters of about six to nine young per litter. The young are sexually mature within three to four weeks. Population sizes and the extent of the distribution of the species may fluctuate greatly from year to year. In years of abundance the species may be distributed across all of N Xinjiang, reaching densities of 1,000–3,000 per hectare. When populations crash, however, the species is rare and restricted to just a few localities with very favorable conditions. Disease transmission is a problem during high population years.
Comments: The two species of *Eolagurus* are sometimes included within the genus *Lagurus*; however, Gromov and Polyakov (1992) summarized the morphological distinctions between the two.
Conservation Status: China RL—LC. IUCN RL—LR/cd ver 2.3 (1994).
References: Gromov and Polyakov (1992); Shubin (1974); Prof. Ma Yong (personal communication, January 2004).

Przewalski's Steppe Vole

Eolagurus przewalskii (Büchner, 1889) PLATE 17 MAP 111
普氏兔尾鼠 Pushi Tuweishu

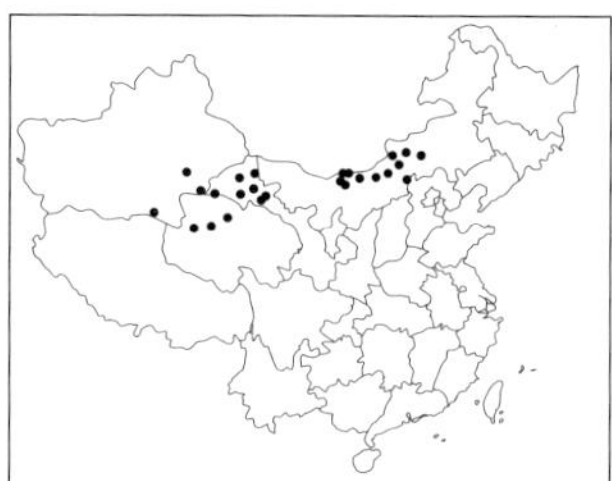
MAP 111. PRZEWALSKI'S STEPPE VOLE, *Eolagurus przewalskii*

Distinctive Characteristics: HB 125–130; T 11–15; HF 19–22; E 7. Dorsal pelage pale sandy brown; sides brighter yellow and blending into the generally pure white ventral pelage, although there may occasionally be some gray-based hairs on the middle of the chest and abdomen. Tail very short, buff above, white below. Feet, including the soles, well covered with pure white fur and a fringe of somewhat stiffened hairs along their outer margins. Pollex of forelimb with a large obtuse claw (small and pointed in *E. luteus*). Skull similar to *E. luteus* in being well domed, but distinguished by possessing larger bullae, which are inflated below the level of the occlusal surface of the molars, and by mastoid processes protruding beyond the level of the occipital condyles.
Distribution: S Xinjiang through N Qinghai and N Gansu; extending through Mongolia to C Nei Mongol.
Natural History: Inhabits montane meadows and riverbanks. Diurnal, feeds on grass, roots, tubers, and seeds. Burrows are complex with three to seven openings and as many as three storage chambers, and three nests per burrow system. Excavated burrow systems also have one to three enlarged chambers in addition to the usual nests and storage areas. Reproduction occurs between May and August; females give birth to about three litters of three to eight young each.
Conservation Status: China RL—LC.
Comments: See notes for *E. luteus*. Sometimes treated as a subspecies of *E. luteus*.
References: Gromov and Polyakov (1992); Zhao (1984).

Genus *Eothenomys*—Chinese Voles

绒鼠属 Rongshu Shu—绒鼠 Rongshu

Dark-colored forest voles; pelage often has a vague brassy sheen. Skull with a simple palate and usually rootless, ever-growing molars. The genus can be divided into two species groups: the *melanogaster* group (*cachinus, melanogaster, miletus*) and the *chinensis* group (*chinensis, wardi, proditor, custos, olitor*). Among members of the *melanogaster* species group, the triangles of the molars tend to be opposite and confluent (although alternating triangles with closed bases are sometimes present toward the anterior of the toothrow); the first fold on the labial side of M3 tends to be deep enough to meet the first reentrant fold from the lingual side to cut off an island of dentine; and the second and third upper molars each have a posterio-internal triangle so that following the anterior prism M1 has five angles and M2 four (i.e., one more angle than usual for the arvicolinae). Among members of the *chinensis* species group, the triangles of the molars tend to be alternating and closed; the first fold on the labial side of M3 is very shallow (similar to *Caryomys* and *Alticola*); the second and third upper molars lack a posterio-internal triangle. For both the *melanogaster* and *chinensis* species groups, the number of folds on M3 were frequently used to diagnose species; however, it is now known that these characters are subject to intraspecific variation. Nonetheless, in combination with other characters the number of folds on the lingual side of the upper M3 (give or take a fold) is still useful for the diagnosis of species. Females with only four mammae (two inguinal pairs). Phylogeny and historical biogeography discussed by Luo et al. (2004a). All of the eight known species of *Eothenomys* are found in China.

Kachin Chinese Vole

Eothenomys cachinus (Thomas, 1921) MAP 112
克钦绒鼠 Keqin Rongshu
Distinctive Characteristics: A large-bodied member of the *melanogaster* species group. Dorsal pelage somewhat tawny brown. Ventral pelage grayish with pale buff to ochraceous washes. Tail relatively long,

Key to the Chinese Species of *Eothenomys*

1.a. M1 and M2 with posterio-lingal triangles so that posterior to the anterior prism there are five triangles on M1 and four triangles on M2 — *melanogaster* species group, 2
   b. M1 and M2 usually lack posterio-lingual triangles so that posterior to the anterior prism there are four triangles on M1 and three triangles on M2 — *chinensis* species group, 4
2.a. Size small, HB usually < 100 mm, tail usually < 40 mm. M3 tending to have three folds on the lingual side, but the third is often only weakly developed (especially in Eastern China and Taiwan) — *Eothenomys melanogaster*
   b. Size large, HB usually > 100 mm, tail usually > 40 mm. M3 tending to have three well-developed folds on the lingual side — 3
3.a. Range restricted to areas west of the Salween River. M3 tends to have three folds on the labial side — *Eothenomys cachinus*
   b. Range restricted to areas east of the Salween River. M3 tends to have only two folds on the labial side — *Eothenomys miletus*
4.a. HB usually > 100 mm, tail usually > 60 mm, M3 tending to have three or four folds on the lingual side — 5
   b. HB usually < 100 mm, tail usually < 60 mm, M3 tending to have four or fewer folds on the lingual side — 6
5.a. Known from the highlands of C Sichuan. Size smaller; length of auditory bullae ranges between 6.6 and 8.4 mm — *Eothenomys chinensis*
   b. Range restricted to a small area between the Mekong and Salween rivers. Size smaller; length of auditory bullae ranges between 6.2 an d 7.4 mm — *Eothenomys wardi*
6.a. Size very small, HB < 100 mm, tail < 40 mm — *Eothenomys olitor*
   b. Size larger — 7
7.a. M3 tending to have three or more lingual folds — *Eothenomys custos*
   b. M3 tending to have only two well-developed lingual folds — *Eothenomys proditor*

much longer than in any other member of the *melanogaster* species group (but shorter than in *E. chinensis*). M3 usually with three folds on the lingual side. Similar to *E. miletus* but geographically isolated. Both species tend to have three folds on the lingual side of M3, but *E. cachinus* also tends to have three folds on the labial side compared to only two in *E. miletus*.
Distribution: Yunnan west of Salween River valley; extending to adjacent NE Myanmar.

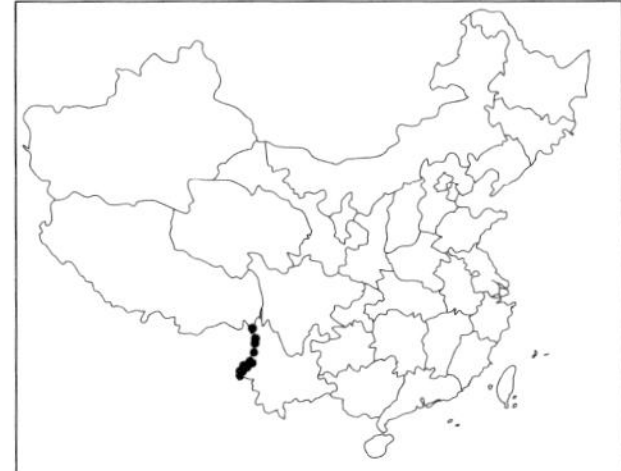

MAP 112. KACHIN CHINESE VOLE, *Eothenomys cachinus*

Natural History: Known from dense montane forest between 2,300 and 3,200 m, where it seems to favor steep slopes and stream banks.
Comments: Previously regarded a subspecies of *E. melanogaster*, *E. miletus*, or *E. mucronatus*. See discussion in Musser and Carleton (2005). Wang (2003) regarded the forms occurring in Guizhou as an undescribed subspecies. Includes *confinii* Hinton, 1922, although Wang (2003) regarded this taxon a subspecies of *E. miletus*.
Conservation Status: China RL—LC.
References: Anthony (1941); Thomas (1921); Wang (2003).

Sichuan Chinese Vole

PLATE 17
MAP 113

Eothenomys chinensis (Thomas, 1891)
中华绒鼠 Zhonghua Rongshu

MAP 113. SICHUAN CHINESE VOLE, *Eothenomys chinensis*

Distinctive Characteristics: HB 101–125; T 63–76; HF 19–24; E 12–15. A large-bodied member of the *chinensis* species group. The tail is more than half of HB length, the longest of all the *Eothenomys*. Dorsal pelage grayish brown. Ventral pelage slate gray and with a characteristic pinkish buff wash in the center of the abdomen. Tail dark brown above, slightly

paler below. Dorsal surfaces of the hands and feet grayish brown. M3 usually has four folds on the lingual side.
Distribution: Known only from the vicinity of Omei Shan Mountain, Sichuan. Endemic.
Natural History: Recorded between 1,500 and 3,000 m.
Conservation Status: China RL–LC.
References: Kaneko (1996); Thomas (1912c).

Southwest Chinese Vole

PLATE 17
Eothenomys custos (Thomas, 1912) MAP 114
西南绒鼠 Xi'nan Rongshu

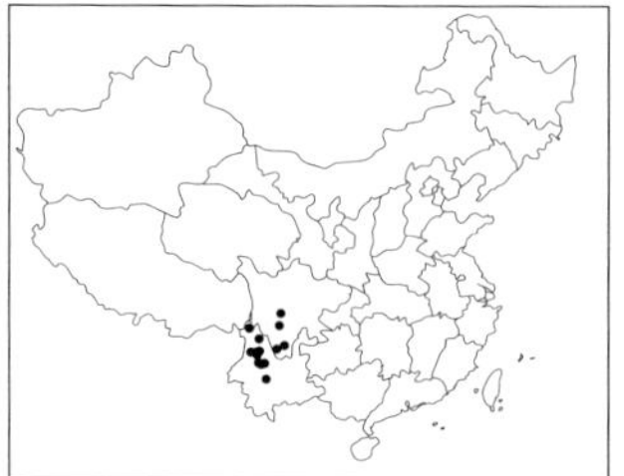

MAP 114. SOUTHWEST CHINESE VOLE, *Eothenomys custos*

Distinctive Characteristics: HB 81–105; T 35–59; HF 16.5–20; E 12–14. A member of the *chinensis* species group, similar to *E. chinensis* and *E. wardi*, but averaging smaller and with a shorter tail. Dorsal pelage dark brown. Ventral pelage grayish. Tail bicolored dark brown above, whitish below. Dorsal surfaces of hands and feet dark brown with a few pale hairs. M3 with three or four folds on the lingual side.
Distribution: NW Yunnan, C Sichuan. Endemic. Wang (2003) recognized five subspecies: (1) *E. c. cangshanensis* Wang and Li, 2000; Yunnan (Cang Mountain of Dali); (2) *E. c. custos* (Thomas, 1912); NW Yunnan; (3) *E. c. hintoni* Osgood, 1932; W Sichuan; (4) *E. c. ninglangensis* Wang and Li, 2000; N Yunnan, S Sichuan; (5) *E. c. rubellus* (Allen, 1924); N Yunnan.
Natural History: Inhabits montane forests between 2,500 and 4,800 m, where it is especially common along stream banks. Also found in scrub, bamboo, and open and rocky meadows. Reproduction occurs from early summer to late fall.
Conservation Status: China RL–LC.
References: Kaneko (1996); Thomas (1912c); Yang (1985).

Père David's Chinese Vole

PLATE 17
Eothenomys melanogaster (Milne-Edwards, 1871) MAP 115
黑腹绒鼠 Heifu Rongshu

Distinctive Characteristics: HB 87–108; T 21–42; HF 15–17; E 10–12. A small-bodied member of the *melanogaster* group. Dorsal pelage dark brown, often very nearly black. Ventral pelage slate gray, sometimes washed with buff or brown. Tail short to medium in length, dark brown above, paler below. Individuals from Sichuan and Yunnan average smaller than those from E China. Populations from W China tend to have two or three reentrant folds on the lingual side of M3, whereas individuals from E China and Taiwan are more consistently two-folded.

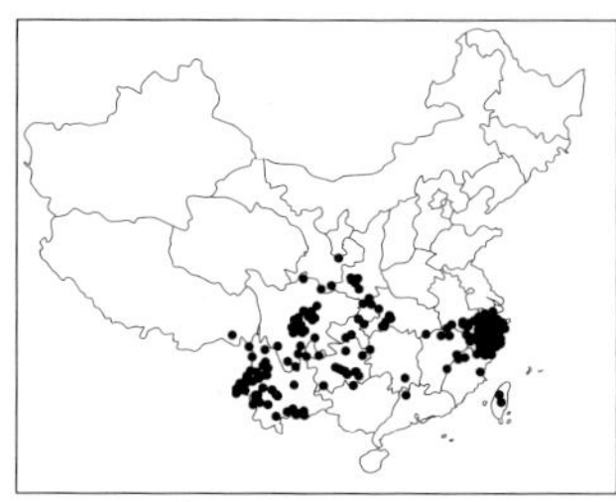

MAP 115. PÈRE DAVID'S CHINESE VOLE, *Eothenomys melanogaster*

Distribution: Widespread through the highlands of S China from E Xizang to S Jiangsu and Taiwan. Wang (2003) recognized six subspecies: (1) *E. m. chenduensis* Wang and Li, 2000; Sichuan (Chengdu); (2) *E. m. colurnus* (Thomas, 1911); E Sichuan east to Anhui and south to Guangdong; (3) *E. m. kanoi* Tokuda, 1937; Taiwan; (4) *E. m. libonotus* Hinton, 1923; W Yunnan, SE Xizang; (5) *E. m. melanogaster* (Milne-Edwards, 1871); W Sichuan, S Gansu, SW Shaanxi; (6) *E. m. mucronatus* (Allen, 1912); SW Sichuan.
Natural History: Common in pine/rhododendron forest between 700 and 3,000 m. Breeds in February–March, and then again in September–October, with populations reaching peaks in May–June and September–October. Average home range for males is 417 m^2; for females, 469 m^2. Home ranges of same-sex individuals overlap, indicating no territoriality in the species.
Comments: Our definition of *E. melanogaster* follows Musser and Carleton (2005) and includes the following as synonyms: *aurora, bonzo, chenduensis, colurnus, eleusis, kanoi, libonotus, mucronatus, yingjiangensis*. Ye et al. (2002) listed *yingjiangensis* as a subspecies of *E. eleusis*, and Kaneko (2002) used *mucronatus* as the oldest name for taxa identified as *E. miletus*. See comments in Musser and Carleton (2005).
Conservation Status: China RL–LC.
References: Bao and Zhuge (1986); Kaneko (2002); Musser and Carleton (2005); Yu (1993; 1994; 1995).

Yunnan Chinese Vole

Eothenomys miletus (Thomas, 1914) MAP 116
大绒鼠 Da Rongshu

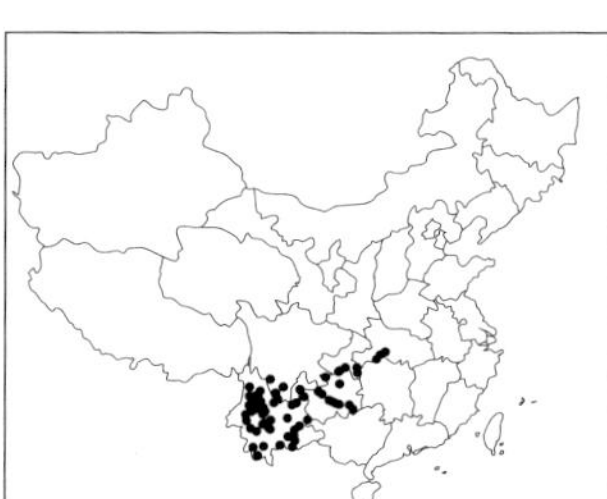

MAP 116. YUNNAN CHINESE VOLE, *Eothenomys miletus*

Distinctive Characteristics: HB 110–120; T 40–50; HF 18–21; E 12–15. The largest member of the *melanogaster* species group. Dorsal pelage soft long and thick, rich dark reddish brown, blending into the blue-gray ventral pelage. M3 usually has three folds on the lingual side. Occurs together with *E. melanogaster* over much of its range, but *E. miletus* is usually larger and has a much higher cranium. May also be confused with *E. cachinus*, the only other member of the *melanogaster* species group, but see that account for distinguishing characteristics.
Distribution: Known from the mountains of S Sichuan and Yunnan east of the Salween River valley. Endemic. According to Zhang et al. (1997), the species also occurs in Guizhou, but Musser and Carleton (2005) point out that these records need verification. Wang (2003) recognized two subspecies: *E. m. miletus* and *E. m. confinii*, but we regard *confinii* as a synonym of *Eothenomys cachinus*.
Natural History: Occurs in montane forests.
Comments: See discussion in Musser and Carleton (2005).
Conservation Status: China RL—LC.
References: Kaneko (2002) (as *E. mucronatus*); Musser and Carleton (2005); Ye et al. (2002).

Black-Eared Chinese Vole

Eothenomys olitor (Thomas, 1911) MAP 117
昭通绒鼠 Zhaotong Rongshu

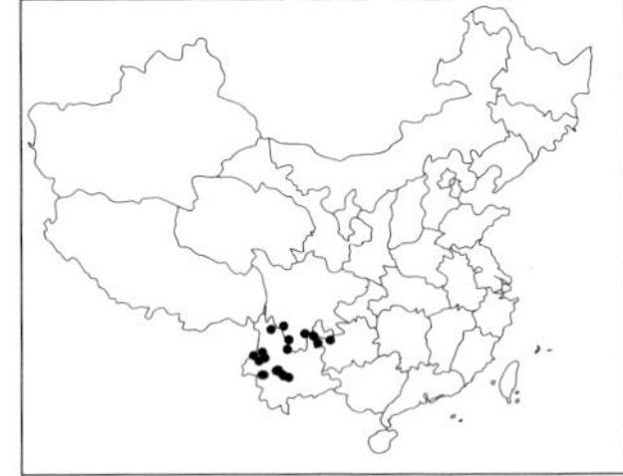

MAP 117. BLACK-EARED CHINESE VOLE, *Eothenomys olitor*

Distinctive Characteristics: HB 80–92; T 29–39; HF 14–17; E 9–11. The smallest member of the *chinensis* group and the smallest of all *Eothenomys*. Similar to *E. melanogaster*, but smaller. Dorsal Pelage dark brown to nearly black. Ventral pelage slate gray. Tail and feet dark brown. Skull small and somewhat dorsal ventrally flattened compared to others in the genus. M3 usually has three folds on the lingual side. Compared to other species of *Eothenomys, E. olitor* has a rather large first fold on the lingual side of M2.
Distribution: Yunnan between the Salween and Mekong rivers, Ailao mountains to the east of the Mekong, and the type locality (Zhaotong) in extreme NE Yunnan. Also known from points in S Sichuan and W Guizhou adjacent to the type locality. Endemic. Two subspecies: (1) *E. o. hypolitor* Wang and Li, 2000; W Yunnan (Yingjiang); (2) *E. o. olitor* (Thomas, 1911); NE Yunnan (Zhaotong area).
Natural History: Known from montane habitats between 1,800 and 3,350 m.
Conservation Status: China RL—LC.
References: Kaneko (1996); Lu et al. (1965); Ye et al. (2002).

Yulong Chinese Vole

Eothenomys proditor Hinton, 1923 MAP 118
玉龙绒鼠 Yulong Rongshu

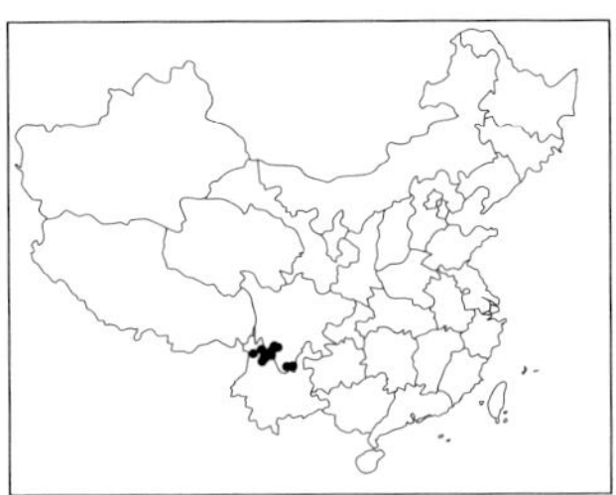

MAP 118. YULONG CHINESE VOLE, *Eothenomys proditor*

Distinctive Characteristics: HB 105–115; T 26–34; HF 17–20; E 12–13. A large member of the *chinensis* species group. Dorsal pelage dark brown over the back, reddish brown over the rump, blending along the sides into the slate gray ventral pelage. Tail dark brown above, paler below, feet dark brown. M3 is distinctive in that it most commonly has only two folds on the lingual side.
Distribution: Restricted to the border region between Sichuan and Yunnan. Endemic.
Natural History: Inhabits meadows and rocky areas between 2,500 and 4,200 m. Reproductive activity from spring to fall.
Conservation Status: China RL—VU D2.
References: Kaneko (1996).

Ward's Chinese Vole

Eothenomys wardi (Thomas, 1912) MAP 119
德钦绒鼠 Deqin Rongshu

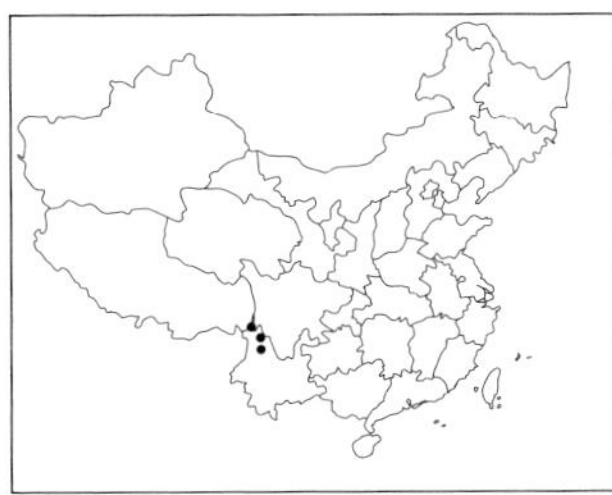

MAP 119. WARD'S CHINESE VOLE, *Eothenomys wardi*

Distinctive Characteristics: HB 110–107; T 59–66; HF 19–20; E 14–15. A member of the *chinensis* species group and somewhat similar to *E. chinensis*, but much smaller and with a shorter tail, shorter hind

feet, and much smaller auditory bullae. According to Kaneko (1996), bullar length in *E. chinensis* ranges between 6.6 and 8.4 mm, but in *E. wardi* it ranges between 6.2 and 7.4 mm. M3 usually has four folds.
Distribution: Extreme NW Yunnan in the Mekong and Salween river valleys. Endemic.
Natural History: Stream banks in forest, open and rocky meadows between 2,400–4,250 m. Reproduction from early summer to late fall.
Comments: Formerly included in *E. chinensis*. See summary in Musser and Carleton (2005).
Conservation Status: China RL–LC.
References: Kaneko (1996); Musser and Carleton (2005); Thomas (1912c).

Genus *Lagurus* (monotypic)

兔尾鼠属 Tuweishu Shu

Voles with a distinctive black stripe along the midline of the back. Skull with complex palate and rootless ever-growing molars. Females with eight mammae.

Steppe Vole

PLATE 18
MAP 120

Lagurus lagurus (Pallas, 1773)
草原兔尾鼠 Caoyuan Tuweishu

MAP 120. STEPPE VOLE, *Lagurus lagurus*

Distinctive Characteristics: HB 80–120; T 7–19; HF 15; E 5. Dorsal pelage pale grayish buff with a dark blackish stripe extending along the midline of the back. Ventral pelage buffy white. Tail short and colored like the dorsal pelage. The dorsal and much of the ventral surfaces of the hands and feet are covered with buffy gray fur. Skull somewhat flattened in profile and with widely flared zygomatic arches that are broadest anteriorly. M3 consists of an anterior prism followed by three alternating closed triangles and a posterior heel; the posterior heel may have slight indentations on both the lingual and labial sides. First lower molar (m3) consists of a posterior transverse prism ahead of which are five alternate closed triangles and a very distinctive anterior cap having deep folds on both the lingual and labial sides that cut off two opposite confluent triangles.
Distribution: NW Xinjiang; extending into Mongolia and through Kazakhstan to Ukraine. Chinese subspecies: *L. l. altorum* Thomas, 1912.
Natural History: Inhabits rocky steppes and semideserts up to 2,800 m. May also occur in grasslands, agricultural areas, and along the edges of roads and canals, but generally avoids areas with brushy undergrowth. Feeds on green grasses and legumes in warmer months, roots and tubers through winter. Diurnal, but most active in early morning and late evening. Constructs a system of burrows extending to about 90 cm below the surface and with two to three entrances. A spherical grass-lined nest chamber is situated about halfway down the burrow system. Males and females live together in the same burrow until the appearance of young, at which time the males move to a nearby burrow. Reproduction occurs from April until October, with a peak in summer months. Estrous cycle is 7 days, gestation 20 days. Females may have as many as six litters per year. Litter size usually varies from four to eight, depending on precipitation levels. Young reach sexual maturity at four to six weeks, and population densities may reach 30–50 per hectare.
Conservation Status: China RL–LC.
References: Fan (1984); Formozov (1966); Shubin (1972).

Genus *Lasiopodomys*—Brandt's Voles

毛足田鼠属 Maozutianshu Shu—
毛足田鼠 Maozutianshu

Voles modified for a semifossorial life: tail very short, ears shortened, barely projecting above fur, foreclaws slightly enlarged, upper incisors fairly proodont. Skull with a complex palate. In profile the skull is similar to *Microtus*, but with an abrupt and fairly distinctive downward dip at about the level of the anterior roots of the zygomatic arches. Molars rootless and

Key to *Lasiopodomys*

1.a. Dorsal pelage sharply demarcated from ventral pelage. Anteriormost triangles of the second lower molar tend to be opposite and broadly confluent at their bases — *Lasiopodomys fuscus*
b. Dorsal pelage not sharply demarcated from ventral pelage. Anteriormost triangles of the second lower molar tend to be alternate and closed at their bases — 2
2.a. Dorsal pelage pale sandy brown. Skulls of adult specimens with longitudinal crest present in interorbital space — *Lasiopodomys brandtii*
b. Dorsal pelage usually dark grayish brown. Skulls of adult specimens lack a longitudinal crest in the interorbital space — *Lasiopodomys mandarinus*

ever-growing. The reentrant folds of the molars are very long and acute. Third upper molar consists of two posterior transverse prisms and an anterio-external prism. The first lower molar consists of a posterior transverse loop ahead of which are four alternating triangles that are closed at their bases, and an anterior cap with a deep reentrant fold on the lingual side. The labial side of the anterior cap, however, usually lacks any trace of an indentation. All three species of the genus occur in China.

Brandt's Vole

PLATE 18
Lasiopodomys brandtii (Raddle, 1861) MAP 121
布氏田鼠 Bushi Tianshu

Distinctive Characteristics: HB 110–130; T 22–30; HF 18–24; E 9–12; GLS 25–30; Wt 55–84 g. A very distinctive pale vole with a short tail. Dorsal pelage pale buffy yellow or "sand colored" with admixtures of black hairs. Sides of face below ear lack mixtures of black hairs and appear brighter yellow. The color of the dorsal pelage blends along the sides into the buffy gray ventral pelage. Tail monocolored pale sandy brown. Dorsal surfaces of hands and feet covered in pale buffy white fur, claws on all digits of hands and feet long and sharp. Skull with wide flaring zygoma, adults with a prominent median bony crest in the interorbital region. M3 consists of an anterior prism followed by three alternating and completely closed triangles and a simple posterior heel. First lower molar (m3) consists of a posterior prism ahead of which are five alternating closed triangles and a simple anterior cap. 2N = 34.

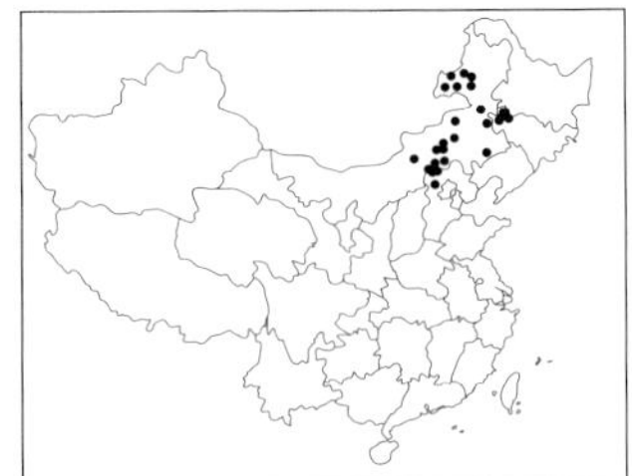

MAP 121. BRANDT'S VOLE, *Lasiopodomys brandtii*

Distribution: Nei Mongol, Jilin, Hebei; extending into Mongolia and Russia.

Natural History: Inhabits dry grasslands to altitudes of about 2,000 m. Strictly herbivorous, eating the green grasses around their burrows through the warmer months and storing dried grass in nest chambers for winter. Strictly diurnal, they emerge from their burrows only after the sun has become sufficiently warm and bright. Live in large colonies and constructs both simple and complex burrows at depths of 14–24 cm. Entrances to burrows are 3–5 cm across and are surrounded conspicuous mounds of dirt. Simple burrows have 2–5 exit holes and dirt mounds about 4 cm high and 10–25 cm across. Simple burrows lack storerooms and nest chambers and are usually occupied by a single young vole. Complex burrows have 4–12 exit holes and dirt mounds 6–12 cm high and 40–80 cm across. Complex burrows may have as many as two nests and four storage chambers and are usually occupied by this many older voles. Overall, complex burrows are 10–30 m long and cover an area of 8–23 m^2. Emits a high-pitched and sharp trill sharp warning whistle when danger is sensed. Reproduction occurs from mid-March to September, giving four or five litters of 6–8 young each; however, under favorable conditions there may be as many as 12–15 young per litter.

Comments: Sometimes included in the genus *Microtus* (subgenus *Phaiomys*).

Conservation Status: This species has been considered an agricultural pest and subjected to widespread poisoning campaigns. China RL—LC.

References: Allen (1940); Formozov (1966); Zhang et al. (2003a); Zhong et al. (1999).

Smokey Vole

Lasiopodomys fuscus (Büchner, 1889) MAP 122
青海田鼠 Qinghai Tianshu

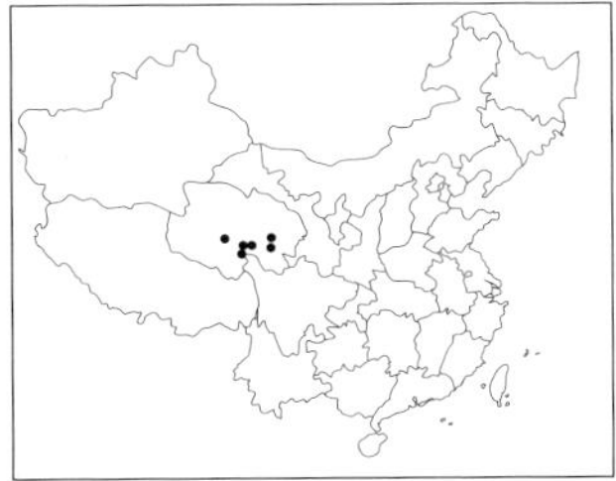

MAP 122. SMOKEY VOLE, *Lasiopodomys fuscus*

Distinctive Characteristics: HB 110–150; T 22–31; HF 18–22; E 14–19; GLS 26–32; Wt 30–58 g. Dorsal pelage grayish brown and rather sharply demarcated along the sides from the gray buff ventral pelage. Tail bicolored, brown above, buff below. Dorsal surfaces of hands and feet grayish buff. Readily distinguished from the other two species in the genus by its rather sharply demarcated dorsal-ventral pelage. The second lower molar of all members of the genus consists of a posterior prism ahead of which are four alternating triangles. In *L. brandtii* and *L. mandarinus*, these triangles are usually closed at their bases, but in *L. fuscus* the two anterior triangles have a tendency to be opposite and broadly confluent at their base.

Distribution: S Qinghai. Endemic.

Natural History: Inhabits moist meadows in high mountain grasslands between 3,700 and 4,800 m.

Comments: Previously included in *Pitymys leucurus*, but separated out by Zheng and Wang (1980).

Conservation Status: China RL—LC. IUCN RL—LR/nt ver 2.3 (1994).

References: Hoffmann (1996); Zheng and Wang (1980).

Mandarin Vole

Lasiopodomys mandarinus (Milne-Edwards, 1871) PLATE 18 MAP 123
棕色田鼠 Zongse Tianshu

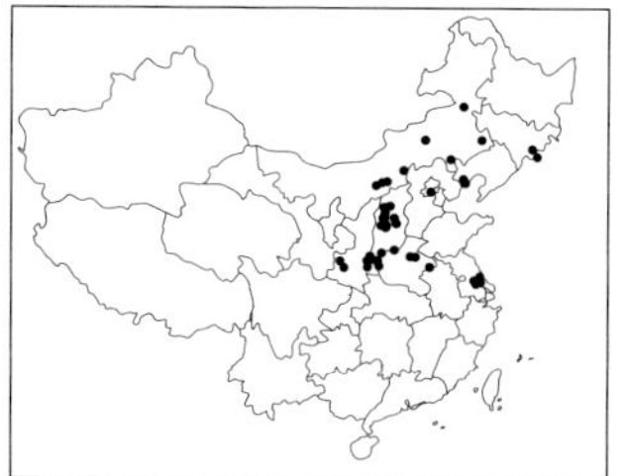

MAP 123. MANDARIN VOLE, *Lasiopodomys mandarinus*

Distinctive Characteristics: HB 97–113; T 20–27; HF 15–18; E 7–12; GLS 24–26. Dorsal pelage ranges from pale reddish brown (chestnut) to dark grayish brown. Ventral pelage ranges from light buff brown to dark gray brown. On paler specimens the tail is a uniform buff color, but on dark specimens the tail is bicolored grayish brown above and buff below; the dorsal surfaces of the hands and feet likewise range from buff to grayish brown. Paler-colored individuals of this species may be difficult to distinguish from *L. brandtii* because the two are similar in overall cranial and dental morphology.
Distribution: NE and C China; extending into Mongolia, Russia, and Korea. Wang (2003) recognizes three subspecies: (1) *L. m. faeceus* (Allen, 1924); W Liaoning, Hebei, Beijing, C Shandong, N Jiangsu, N Anhui; (2) *L. m. johannes* (Thomas, 1910); Shanxi (Kelan of NW Taiyuan); (3) *L. m. mandarinus* (Milne-Edwards, 1871); Central S Nei Mongol, S Shanxi, N Henan).
Natural History: Inhabits rocky mountain steppe up to 3,000 m. Usually found away from woods but near water sources. Especially common in dense brush along the banks of lakes, rivers, and streams. Feeds on the underground parts of plants.Highly social and lives in extended family groups. Members occupy a common burrow to which they remain strongly attached. In summer groups consist of one breeding male for every one to two breeding females plus the young of one to three generations. Total number of individuals per burrow averages 8.7, but ranges between 3 and 22. Reproduction occurs between March and August, yielding litters of two to four young.
Conservation Status: China RL—LC.
References: Allen (1940); Smorkatcheva (1999); Zorenko et al. (1994).

Genus *Microtus*—Voles

田鼠属 Tianshu Shu—田鼠 Tianshu

Typical voles not especially modified for subterranean life. Skull with complex palate and rootless ever-growing molars. M3 with an anterior prism followed by a small outer triangle, a larger inner triangle, and a smaller outer triangle, all of which are normally closed. M3 ends in a C-shaped posterior heel with the upper portion of the "C" forming a longer inner projection than the lower. First lower molar (m3) with a posterior prism ahead of which there are three inner and two outer triangles, all normally closed and ending in an anterior loop of variable outline. Females with eight mammae. Of 62 species, 12 occur in China.

Field Vole

Microtus agrestis (Linnaeus, 1761) MAP 124
黑田鼠 Hei Tianshu

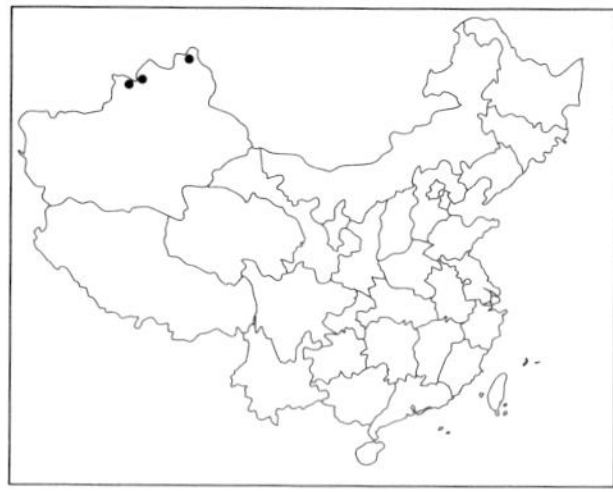

MAP 124. FIELD VOLE, *Microtus agrestis*

Distinctive Characteristics: HB 109; T 44; HF 18.5; E 13; GLS 26–28. Dorsal pelage dark grayish brown. Ventral pelage gray based with buff gray tips. Tail bicolored brownish black above, white below. Dorsal surfaces of feet grayish white; hind feet with six plantar pads. Winter pelage brighter, more ochraceous. M2 with two triangles, a larger and a smaller, on the lingual side of the tooth just behind the anterior prism. Most Chinese *Microtus* have only one large closed triangle on the lingual side of M2 (but see account for *M. clarkei*). M3 consists of an anterior prism followed by three alternating closed triangles and C-shaped posterior heel, with the upper arm of the "C" extending further lingually than the lower arm. First lower molar (m3) with a posterior transverse prism ahead of which are at least five or rarely six alternating closed triangles and an anterior cap with indentations on both the lingual and labial sides.
Distribution: Highlands surrounding the Dzungarian Basin of N Xinjiang; ranging across the Palaearctic from W Europe to Lake Baikal. Two subspecies in China: (1) *M. a. arcturus* Thomas, 1912; Xinjiang (Barlik Hill of W Dzungarian Basin); (2) *M. a. mongol* Thomas, 1911; Xinjiang (Altai mountains).
Natural History: Inhabits moist and densely vegetated meadows, lakeshores, and river edges. Uncommon in agricultural areas. Herbivorous and prefers green grass when available, but also consumes stored roots, bulbs, and bark through the winter. Active at all times, but most active in early morning and late evening. Digs a short burrow approximately 20–30 cm in length and leading to a small, round, grass-lined nest measuring 35–38 cm long and 23–27 cm high. Leading from the nest chamber are several short exit tunnels and one or two passages 5–10 cm long leading to small food storage chambers. Burrows are usually dug under some form of cover

Key to the Chinese Species of *Microtus*

1.a.	Range restricted to Taiwan	*Microtus kikuchii*
b.	Does not occur on Taiwan	2
2.a.	Skull laterally compressed, interorbital breadth about 3 mm	*Microtus gregalis*
b.	Skull not laterally compressed, interorbital breadth > 4 mm	3
3.a.	M2 with two lingual triangles behind the anterior prism	4
b.	M2 with only one lingual triangle behind the anterior prism	5
4.a.	Hind foot with six plantar pads. Posteriormost triangles of M2 tending to be alternate and closed at their bases	*Microtus agrestis*
b.	Hind foot with five plantar pads. Posteriormost triangles of M2 tending to be opposite and confluent at their bases	*Microtus clarkei*
5.a.	Size small, HB < 100 mm, tail < 25 mm. Auditory bullae very large in absolute size and relative to the length of the skull: GLS < 27 mm, length of bullae > 8 mm	*Microtus socialis*
b.	Size larger, HB > 100 mm, tail > 25 mm, GLS > 25 mm, but bullae small, usually < 8 mm	6
6.a.	Pelage pale brownish gray and rather muted overall. Anterior cap of first lower molar with deep folds on both the lingual and labial sides	*Microtus ilaeus*
b.	Pelage not conspicuously pale, but rather a darker, more reddish brown. Anterior cap with a deep fold on the lingual side only. A shallow fold may be present on the labial side of the cap, but it is rarely very deep	7
7.a.	First lower molar with five well-formed triangles ahead of the posterior prism. The fifth triangle is broadly confluent with the anterior cap. Anterior cap with an indentation on the lingual side, but with the labial side convex. Species' ranges restricted to the western half of China	8
b.	First lower molar with five well-formed triangles ahead of the posterior transverse prism. The base of the fifth triangle is closed and not confluent with the anterior cap. Anterior cap with indentations on both the lingual and labial sides. Species' ranges restricted to the eastern half of China	10
8.a.	Interpterygoid fossa tends to extend forward of the anterior margin of M3. Posterior heel of M3 with a small triangle on the labial side (these characters highly variable)	*Microtus arvalis*
b.	Interpterygoid fossa does not extend forward of the anterior margin of M3. Posterior heel of M3 lacks a small triangle on the labial side or if present it is very weakly developed (these characters highly variable)	9
9.a.	Larger size (GLS 29–32 mm). Pelage more reddish brown	*Microtus oeconomus*
b.	Smaller size (GLS 26–28 mm). Pelage more yellowish brown	*Microtus limnophilus*
10.a.	Size very large. HB > 120 mm, tail > 1/3 HB and usually close to 1/2. GLS > 28 mm	*Microtus fortis*
b.	Size somewhat smaller	11
11.a.	Anterior cap of first lower molar usually has obvious indentations on both the lingual and labial side (these characters highly variable)	*Microtus maximowiczii*
b.	Anterior cap of first lower molar with a fairly well-defined indentation on the lingual side, but usually convex or with only a very weak indentation on the labial side (these characters highly variable)	*Microtus mongolicus*

such as root masses, bushes, stumps, or piles of twigs. Alarm call consists of a staccato *tucktucktuck-tucktuck*. Females reach sexual maturity after 40 days of age, males after 45 days; females are polyestrous with a postpartum estrus cycle and a 21-day gestation period. Reproduction occurs from April to September, with females giving two to four litters of about three offspring each, but ranging anywhere between one and seven depending on conditions. Populations fluctuate over a cycle of three to four years. In high population years females outnumber males 5:1, however during population lows the percentage of females to males is roughly equal. Young are born naked and blind; by day 4 some hairs are visible, and by day 6 there is a juvenile coat of gray-black hairs. Eyes open by day 9 or 10; by day 11 they begin feeding for themselves, and weaning occurs at day 14.

Conservation Status: China RL—LC.

References: Krapp and Niethammer (1982); Ognev (1964).

Common Vole

PLATE 19
MAP 125

Microtus arvalis (Pallas, 1778)

普通田鼠 Putong Tianshu

Distinctive Characteristics: HB 102–132; T 32–40; HF 14–19; E 14–15; GLS 27–29.5. Dorsal pelage from light buffy brown to dark brownish gray; ventral pelage gray based with buffy gray tips. Tail bicolored,

brownish black above, white below; tail with a slight terminal pencil. Dorsal surfaces of hands and feet drab brown with silvery white hairs; hind feet with six plantar pads. M3 consists of an anterior prism followed by three alternating closed triangles and a complex posterior heel that usually has a small angular projection on the labial side and a deep anterior and shallower posterior folds on the lingual side. The first lower molar consists of a posterior prism ahead of which are five alternating triangles and an anterior heel. The anterior cap has folds on both the lingual and labial sides.
Distribution: C and N Xinjiang, N Gansu (Hexizoulang); extending westward through Europe. Chinese subspecies: *M. a. obscurus* (Eversmann, 1841).

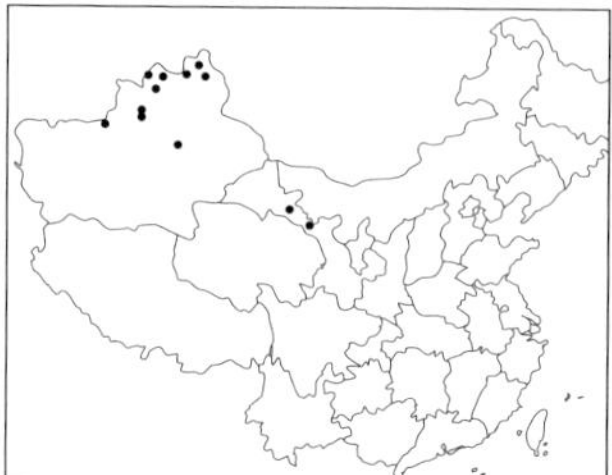
MAP 125. COMMON VOLE, *Microtus arvalis*

Natural History: Lives in a wide variety of open habitats including moist meadows, forest steppe, moist forest, and sometimes agricultural areas. Eats a variety of green plants supplemented with seeds and insects in summer and roots and bark through winter. Active at all times, but more so when dark. Groups of related individuals inhabit one nest—a grass-lined chamber about 10–20 cm in diameter at a depth of up to 20–30 cm. Four to six exit burrows extend from the nest chamber, and from smaller chambers for food storage and special latrine rooms for the accumulation of excrement. May also dig temporary burrows in the area surrounding the nesting burrow, and the entire surface outside the nest is marked by trails. Makes use of special feeding stations where it is less visible to predators. When populations reach high levels and when an area's resources are depleted, will migrate to outlying areas. Alarm call consists of a high-pitched single syllable. A fecund species, females are capable of breeding as early as two weeks following birth. Gestation lasts 19–21 days, with females producing about seven litters of 5 offspring yearly, but ranging between 1 and 13 offspring depending on conditions. Under favorable conditions reproduction may continue through the winter months, albeit at lower rates.
Conservation Status: China RL—LC.
References: Niethammer and Krapp (1982); Sokolov and Bashenina (1994).

Clarke's Vole

PLATE 19
MAP 126

Microtus clarkei (Hinton, 1923)
克氏田鼠 **Keshi Tianshu**

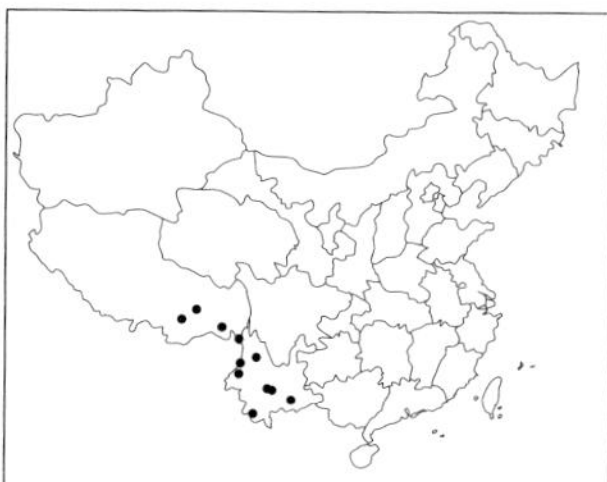
MAP 126. CLARKE'S VOLE, *Microtus clarkei*

Distinctive Characteristics: HB 114–134; T 62–67; HF 19–21; E 12–15. Externally very similar to *M. fortis*, but with the dorsal pelage less yellow and more of a warm reddish brown; hairs of ventral pelage dark gray with silver tips. Tail brown above, dirty white below. Dorsal surfaces of hands and feet dirty white; soles of hind foot with only five plantar pads instead of the usual six for the genus. M2 with two folds on both the lingual and labial sides and forming opposite confluent triangles at the posterior margin of the tooth.
Distribution: Mountainous regions of W and S Yunnan, SE Xizang; extending to N Myanmar.
Natural History: Known from coniferous forests and alpine meadows at elevations between 3,400 and 4,290 m.
Comments: Sometimes included in the genus *Volemys*. See discussion in Musser and Carleton (2005).
Conservation Status: China RL—LC. IUCN RL—LR/nt ver 2.3 (1994) (as *Volemys clarkei*).
References: Hinton (1923); Musser and Carleton (2005).

Reed Vole

PLATE 19
MAP 127

Microtus fortis Büchner, 1889
东方田鼠 **Dongfang Tianshu**

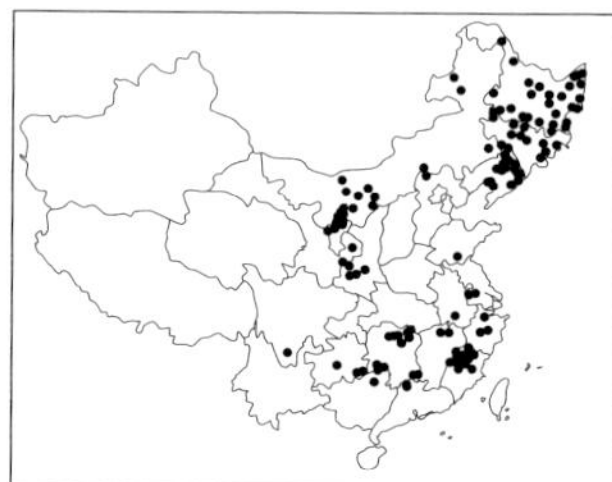
MAP 127. REED VOLE, *Microtus fortis*

Distinctive Characteristics: HB 120–139; T 48–67; HF 22–25; E 13–15. A large and relatively long-tailed species of *Microtus*. Dorsal pelage dark reddish brown, sides somewhat buff brown and blending into the grayish ventral pelage. Tail bicolored, dark brown above, whitish below. Dorsal surfaces of hands and feet light brown; hind feet with only five plantar pads (but a rudimentary sixth pad may sometimes be present). M3 with three folds on each side, posterior heel forming a "C" with the upper arm of the "C" extending further lingually than the lower arm. First lower molar with four folds on the lingual side, three on the labial side, the anterior cap with a notch on the lingual side only.

Distribution: Widespread throughout temperate China; extending into Russia and Korea. Five subspecies in China: (1) *M. f. calamorum* Thomas, 1902; Jiangsu, Shanghai, Anhui, Zhejiang, Jiangxi, Hunan, Hubei; (2) *M. f. dolichocephalus* Mori, 1930; Liaoning, Jilin, Nei Mongol; (3) *M. f. fortis* Buchner, 1889; Shaanxi, S Nei Mongol; (4) *M. f. fujianensis* Hong, 1981; Fujian; (5) *M. f. pelliceus* Thomas, 1911; Heilongjiang, Jilin, NE Nei Mongol.

Natural History: Common to wet environments, especially lakeshores, riverbanks, and streams surrounded by heavy vegetation. Although favoring waterside habitats, they may invade adjacent agricultural areas and undeveloped lands when overcrowded or forced out by rising water levels in spring and early summer. However, these migrations never exceed 5 km, and with the subsidence of water levels they will return to their favored lakeshore and riverbank habitats. The species is also known to inhabit marshy parts of steppe and forests to altitudes of about 2,000 m. There are distinct seasonal changes in diet. During the growing season feeds predominantly on grass stems and leaves. During the fall begins to store grasses and grain for use through winter, at which time may also feed on roots, bark, and the pith of reeds; however, at all times leaves appear to represent the most favored parts of the plants. Active day and night, is slow moving on land but an excellent swimmer. These voles dig burrows of varying extent and to varying depths depending on the local conditions. In well-drained soils burrows are dug to a depth of about 10–15 cm and overall length of 120–150 cm. Passages branching from the main corridor may lead to dead ends, storage rooms, or nest chambers, and there are numerous escape tunnels to the surface throughout. Under heavy cover or in very wet areas burrows may be shallower and may even take the form of open ruts on the ground's surface. In damp areas, such as along overgrown riverbanks and lake-shores, these voles will construct a large spherical (25– 30 cm diameter) nest above ground. Often found right next to the water, five or six nests sometimes occur in close proximity with obvious paths leading to the nests. Reproduction occurs from April to November with up to six litters of five offspring per litter in favorable years. Gestation lasts about 20 days, and the interval between litters is 40–45 days. Females reach sexual maturity by 3.5–4 months, with males maturing a little later.

Conservation Status: China RL—LC.

References: Guo et al. (1997); Wu et al. (1996a; 1998).

Narrow-Headed Vole

PLATE 19
MAP 128

Microtus gregalis (Pallas, 1779)
狭颅田鼠 Xialu Tianshu

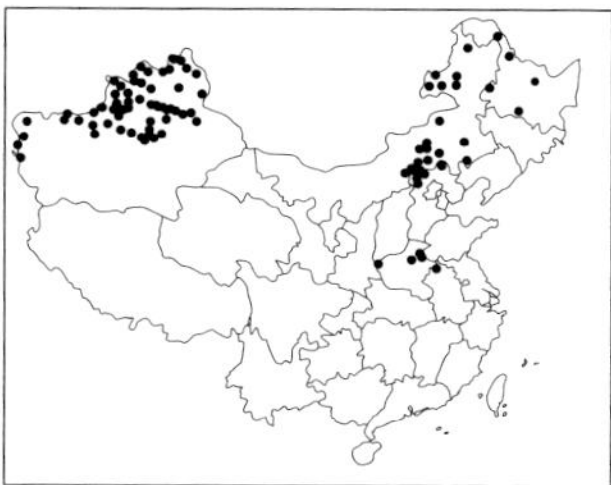

MAP 128. NARROW-HEADED VOLE, *Microtus gregalis*

Distinctive Characteristics: HB 89–122; T 21–32; HF 15–18; E 9–12; GLS 25–27. Dorsal pelage pale yellow-buff, lighter along the sides and blending into the grayish buff ventral pelage. In winter the dorsal pelage is a brighter ochraceous red. Tail may be monocolored yellow-buff or bicolored dark brown above and yellow buff below. Dorsal surfaces of hands and feet brownish white. This species is readily distinguished from all other *Microtus* occurring in China by its long and laterally narrowed skull; the greatest length of the skull is nearly twice that of the zygomatic breadth (12.6–14.0 mm). Dental pattern similar to that of *M. arvalis*. M3 consists of an anterior prism followed by three alternating closed triangles and a simple posterior heel with a weak reentrant fold on the lingual side only. First lower molar consists of a posterior prism ahead of which are five alternating closed triangles and an anterior cap with folds on both the lingual and labial sides.

Distribution: NW Xinjiang and the Aur area of NE China; widely distributed throughout the Palearctic. Five subspecies in China: (1) *M. g. angustus* Thomas, 1908; Hebei, Nei Mongol (Baochang, S Xilin Gol Meng); (2) *M. g. dolguschini* Afanasiev, 1939; NW Xinjiang; (3) *M. g. raddei* (Poljakov, 1881); Nei Mongol; (4) *M. g. ravidulus* Miller, 1899; W Xinjiang; (5) *M. g. sirtalaensis* Ma, 1966; Nei Mongol (from the N bank of the Hailar River to Morgele River of Xilin Gol Meng).

Natural History: Inhabits dry steppe and grassy meadows up to altitudes of about 4,000 m. Consumes both the exposed and underground parts of a variety of plants but prefers legumes and cereals. Active at all times but especially toward evening and at night. Lives in complex burrows at depths of 10–25 cm. One burrow may have as many as 10 or more openings as well as up to 5 nest chambers and storage chambers. Its narrow cranium is apparently an adaptation to life in narrow burrows and cracks in frozen ground. About five litters are produced per season; the number of young per litter varies through the year. Reproduction occurs during the warmer months. The first litter of the season usually consists of only two young, but litters of 7–9 offspring per litter are more common. Litters of up to 12 offspring have been recorded.

Conservation Status: China RL—LC.

References: Gromov and Polyakov (1992).

Kazakhstan Vole

Microtus ilaeus Thomas, 1912 MAP 129

伊犁田鼠 Yili Tianshu

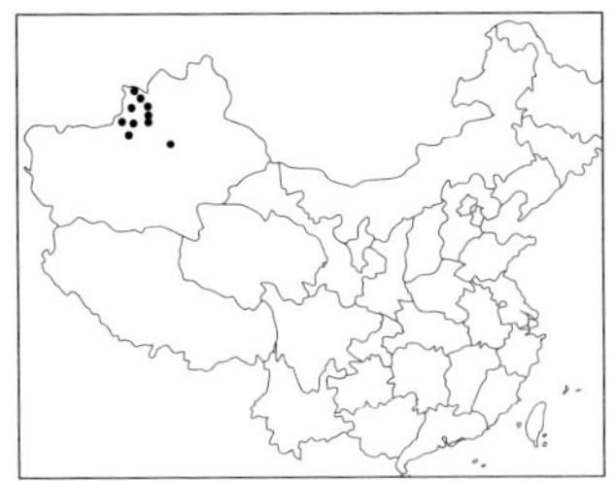

MAP 129. KAZAKHSTAN VOLE, *Microtus ilaeus*

Distinctive Characteristics: HB 100–127; T 32–48; HF 17–20; E 12; GLS 29. Dorsal pelage pale grayish brown. Ventral pelage buffy gray. Tail pale brown above, white below. Dorsal surfaces of hands and feet white. Anterior cap of first lower molar with deep folds on both the lingual and labial sides.
Distribution: Tian Shan mountains of N Xinjiang; extending west to Uzbekistan.
Natural History: Inhabits forest, forest-steppe, and scrub meadow.
Conservation Status: China RL—LC.
References: Thomas (1912a).

Taiwan Vole

Microtus kikuchii Kuroda, 1920 MAP 130

台湾田鼠 Taiwan Tianshu

MAP 130. TAIWAN VOLE, *Microtus kikuchii*

Distinctive Characteristics: HB 95–120; T 68–85; HF 20–25; E 12–15; GLS 27.8–30.5. Dorsal pelage warm reddish brown, sides somewhat brighter, almost fulvus brown and blending into the grayish orange ventral pelage; tail rather long for the genus, bicolored dark brown above, whitish below; dorsal surfaces of hands and feet light brown to nearly white. M3 consists of an anterior prism followed by three alternating closed triangles and a posterior heel with an especially deep fold on the lingual side and a second posterio-lingual indentation. The first lower molar consists of a posterior prism ahead of which are five alternating closed triangles and an anterior cap with indentations on both the labial and lingual sides.
Distribution: Taiwan. Endemic.
Natural History: Inhabits highland forest.
Comments: Sometimes treated as a species of *Volemys*. See discussion in Musser and Carleton (2005).
Conservation Status: China RL—LC. IUCN RL—VU B1 + 2c ver 2.3 (1994) (as *Volemys kikuchii*).
References: Kaneko (1987); Lawrence (1982); Yu (1993; 1994; 1995).

Lacustrine Vole

Microtus limnophilus Büchner, 1889 PLATE 19 MAP 131

经营田鼠 Jingying Tianshu

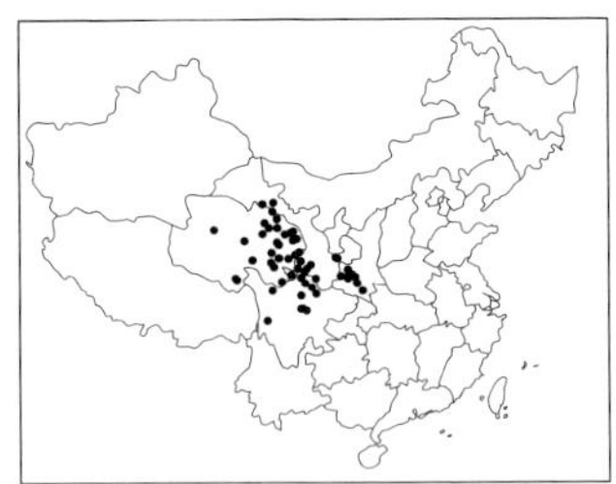

MAP 131. LACUSTRINE VOLE, *Microtus limnophilus*

Distinctive Characteristics: HB 88–118; T 32–44; HF 20–21; E 13–14; GLS 26–28. Dorsal pelage distinctly yellow, individual hairs gray at the base, pale buff terminally. Ventral pelage gray based with white tips and imparting an overall bluish gray effect. Tail bicolored, buffy brown above, white below. Dorsal surfaces of hands and feet buffy white. The molar enamel pattern is similar to that seen in *M. arvalis* but differing in the morphology of the first lower molar, which consists of the usual posterior transverse prism anterior to which there are two outer and two inner, alternating closed triangles, with the fifth triangle (on the lingual side) confluent with the anterior loop. Females with eight mammae: two pectoral pairs, two abdominal pairs.
Distribution: N Sichuan and E Qinghai through Gansu to S Shaanxi. Limits of geographic range uncertain; a likely endemic.
Natural History: Saline desert and alpine meadows.
Conservation Status: China RL—LC.
References: Malygin et al. (1990).

Maximowicz's Vole

Microtus maximowiczii (Schrenk, 1859) PLATE 19 MAP 132

莫氏田鼠 Moshi Tianshu

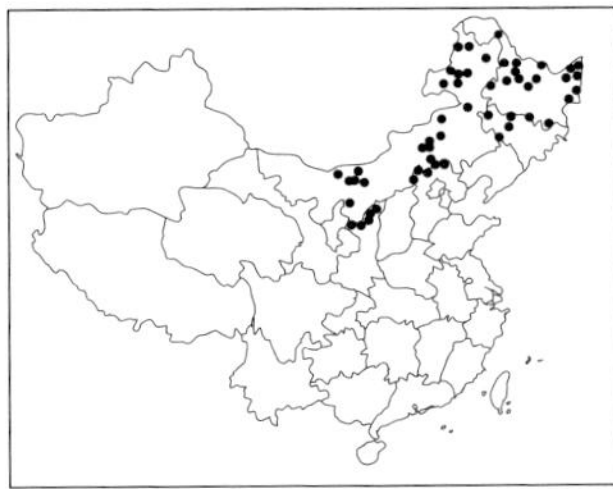

MAP 132. MAXIMOWICZ'S VOLE, *Microtus maximowiczii*

Distinctive Characteristics: HB 116–155; T 37–60; HF 18–22; E 12–16.6. A large vole (but smaller than *M. fortis*) resembling *M. oeconomus* externally, but having a more complex first lower molar. Dorsal pelage dark blackish brown with ochraceous specks; paler brown along the sides, gradually blending into the dark grayish white ventral pelage. Tail monocolored dark brown or bicolor brown above, white below. Dorsal surfaces of hands and feet brownish white; hind foot with six plantar pads. Although similar to *M. oeconomus* externally, the species can usually be distinguished by the first lower molar, the anterior loop of which has obvious indentations on both the labial and lingual sides.
Distribution: NE China; extending into Mongolia and S Russia.
Natural History: Occupies densely vegetated mountain foothills and riverbanks. Especially active in early morning and late evening. Digs burrows in dense vegetation, leaving obvious heaps of discarded soil around the entrance to its burrow with mounds 50–100 cm across and 15–20 cm high. The passage to the burrow is only 20–30 cm long and leads directly to a round, 35 cm-diameter nest chamber that is about 25 cm high. Constructs special food storage chambers, which it fills with roots and bulbs before winter. Reproduction little known; females with seven and nine embryos have been reported.
Conservation Status: China RL–NE.

Mongolian Vole

Microtus mongolicus (Radde, 1861) PLATE 19 MAP 133
蒙古田鼠 Menggu Tianshu

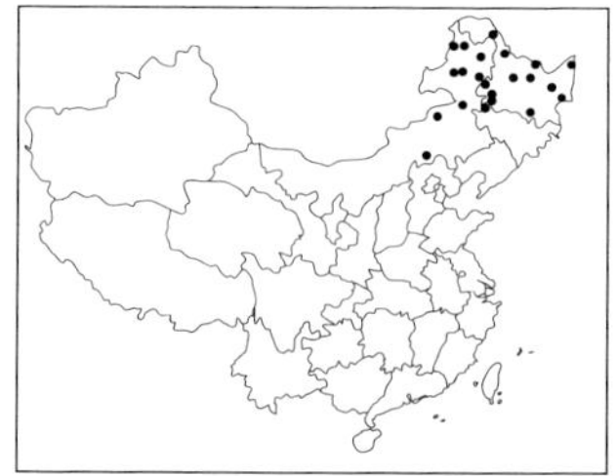

MAP 133. MONGOLIAN VOLE, *Microtus mongolicus*

Distinctive Characteristics: HB 119–132; T 28–38; HF 17–19; E 13–14. Dorsal pelage dark reddish brown, sides lighter and blending into the gray ventral pelage. Tail distinctly bicolored, dark brown above, buff below. Dorsal surfaces of hands and feet with mixtures of brown and silvery white hairs. M3 consists of an anterior prism followed by four alternating triangles and a posterior heel with three folds on both the lingual and labial sides. First lower molar consists of a posterior transverse prism ahead of which there are usually five alternating closed triangles and an anterior cap. The anterior cap has a weak fold on the lingual side, but the labial side is either convex or only very weakly indented. In some cases the anterior lingual triangle may be broadly confluent with the anterior cap.
Distribution: NE China; extending into Mongolia and Russia.
Natural History: Little known.
Comments: Specimens reported as *M. arvalis* from NE China (Zhang et al. 1997) are now recognized as this species.
Conservation Status: China RL–LC.

Root Vole

Microtus oeconomus (Pallas, 1776) MAP 134
根田鼠 Gen Tianshu

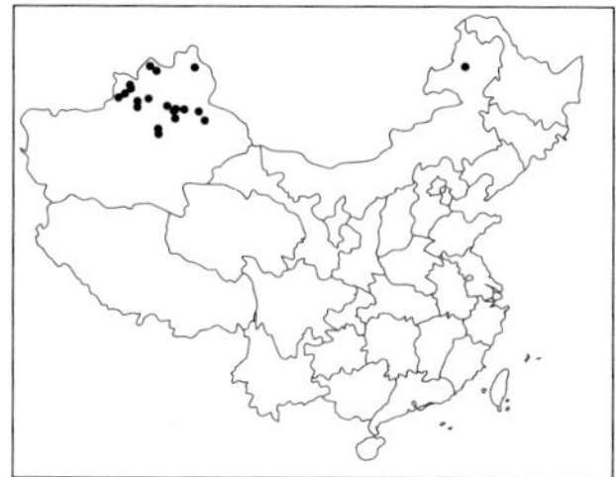

MAP 134. ROOT VOLE, *Microtus oeconomus*

Distinctive Characteristics: HB 102–122; T 32–49; HF 16–18; E 12–16; GLS 29–32. Dorsal pelage reddish brown. Ventral pelage yellowish brown; tail bicolored, dark brown above, white below. Dorsal surfaces of feet silvery; hind foot with six plantar pads. M3 with three folds on both the lingual and labial sides, the posterior heel forming a "C" with the upper arm of the "C" extending further lingually than the lower arm. First lower molar usually with four lingual and three labial folds; the anterior lingual triangle (the fifth triangle counting forward from the posterior prism) is often broadly confluent with the anterior loop; the anterior cap with a small notch on the lingual side, but well rounded on the labial side.
Distribution: N Xinjiang and N Nei Mongol; ranging across the Holarctic.
Natural History: Inhabits dense vegetation along the edges of lakes, streams, and marshes. Swims well and is most active late in the day and at night. Digs its burrow into the bases of vegetation clumps, and tunnel systems are often extensive. Feeds on succulent grasses. Litter size large, ranging from 2 to 11 young. Produce multiple (2–5) litters per year, and young reach sexual maturity at six weeks of age.
Comments: Traditional morphological characters used to distinguish *M. oeconomus* from *M. limnophilus* are apparently not useful for separating putative Chinese populations, and the existence of true *M. oeconomus* in China needs to be confirmed by karyological analysis. See Courant et al. (1999). Allen (1940) and Ognev (1964) both used *ratticeps* for this species, and this may indeed be the correct name. See discussion in Musser and Carleton (2005).
Conservation Status: China RL–LC.
References: Courant et al. (1999); Ognev (1964).

Social Vole PLATE 19
Microtus socialis (Pallas, 1773) MAP 135
社田鼠 She Tianshu

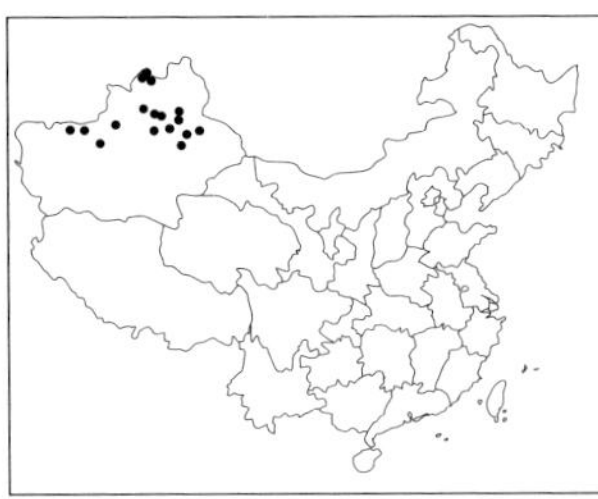

MAP 135. SOCIAL VOLE, *Microtus socialis*

Distinctive Characteristics: HB 92–100; T 20–25; HF 17–18. A small, light-colored vole with a very short tail. Dorsal pelage pale buffy brown, sides paler and yellower. Ventral pelage gray based with pale buff tips; tail indistinctly bicolored buffy brown above, somewhat paler buff below; dorsal surfaces of feet buffy white; hind foot with five plantar pads.
Distribution: NW Xinjiang; extending across the Palaearctic. Chinese subspecies: *C. s. gravesi* Goodwin, 1934.
Natural History: Specimens from the type series of the subspecies occurring in China (*C. s. gravesi*) were collected in scattered clumps of grass near small springs at the base of an escarpment. The animals were active most of the day, lived in burrows, and fed on succulent grass bases. According to the collector they were rather localized and not very abundant.
Conservation Status: China RL—LC.
References: Goodwin (1934).

Genus *Myodes*—Red-Backed Voles

红背鼠属 Hongbeishu Shu—红背鼠 Hongbeishu

Most species with a reddish dorsal pelage. Skull with simple palate. Molars rootless when young, but two roots develop with age (except for *Myodes shanseius*). Triangles of upper molars rounded and tending to be closed, or nearly so. M3 with two folds on the labial side (or sometimes a very weakly developed third), and either two or three folds on the lingual side. First lower molar with five closed triangles ahead of the posterior prism. Females with eight mammae: one pectoral pair, one axillary pair, and two inguinal pairs. Earlier systematists commonly listed red-backed voles under the genera *Evotomys* or *Clethrionomys*; however, Carleton et al. (2003) and Musser and Carleton (2005) have convincingly shown that *Myodes* is the appropriate genus name. Phylogeny and historical biogeography discussed by Cook et al. (2004). Of 12 species of *Myodes*, 4 occur in China.

Tian Shan Red-Backed Vole
Myodes centralis (Miller, 1906) MAP 136
灰棕背䶄 Huizongbei Ping

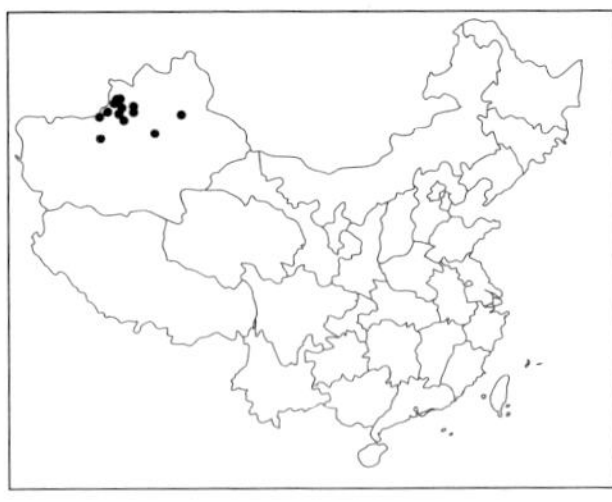

MAP 136. TIAN SHAN RED-BACKED VOLE, *Myodes centralis*

Distinctive Characteristics: HB 85–112; T 35–59; HF 17–19; E 14. Dorsal pelage generally dark brown with only a hint of red, but varying from light brown on top of the head to dark grayish brown over the rump. Sides of face and body grayish brown with a slight yellow tinge, blending into the buffy gray underparts. Tail bicolored, dark brown above, white below. Dorsal surfaces of hands and feet brownish white. M3 usually with three lingual and two labial folds. Distinguished from other species of *Myodes* occurring in China by the lack of a conspicuously reddish dorsal pelage.
Distribution: NW Xinjiang (Tian Shan mountains); extending westward into Kazakhstan and Kyrgyzstan.
Natural History: Occurs in montane forest. Eats grain and to a lesser extent grassy vegetation.
Comments: See generic account. Some Chinese authors still use *frater* for this species.
Conservation Status: China RL—LC.
References: Musser and Carleton (2005).

Key to the Chinese Species of *Myodes*

1.a.	Dorsal pelage rich reddish brown	2
b.	Dorsal pelage dark brown with only a hint of red	*Myodes centralis*
2.a.	Molars rooted in adults	3
b.	Molars rootless and ever-growing even in adults	*Myodes shanseius*
3.a.	M3 with three deep folds on the lingual side. Size smaller, HB usually < 100 mm	*Myodes rutilus*
b.	M3 usually with two folds, or rarely a weakly developed third fold on the lingual side. Size larger, HB usually > 100 mm	*Myodes rufocanus*

Gray Red-Backed Vole

PLATE 16
MAP 137

Myodes rufocanus (Sundevall, 1846)
棕背䶄 Zongbei Ping

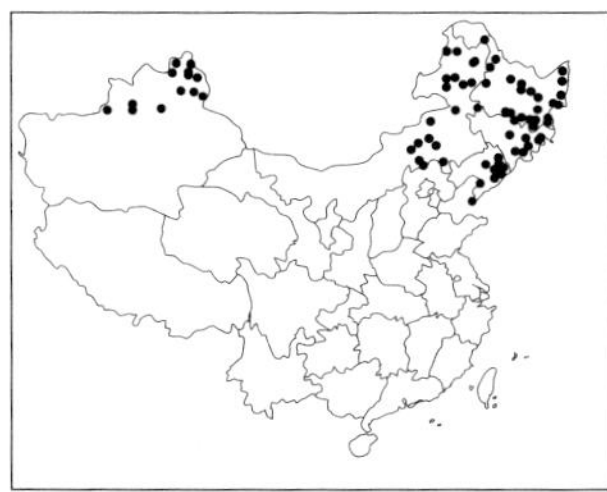

MAP 137. GRAY RED-BACKED VOLE, *Myodes rufocanus*

Distinctive Characteristics: HB 100–122; T 27–35; HF 17–20; E 15–19. Dorsal pelage rich reddish brown from crown to rump; sides of face and flanks distinctly and contrastingly gray, sometimes with a slight mixture of buffy hairs where the gray sides meet the reddish back. Hairs of ventral pelage gray based with buffy white tips, appearing grayish overall. Tail blackish brown above, grayish white below. Dorsal surfaces of the hands and feet pale grayish brown. The winter pelage is considerably brighter and more yellowish dorsally and whiter ventrally. M3 has two or sometimes a weakly developed third fold on the labial side and two folds, or very rarely a weakly developed third fold, on the lingual side.

Distribution: N Xinjiang east through Mongolia to NE China; extending across the Palearctic. Two subspecies in China: (1) *M. r. changbaishanensis* (Jiang, Ma, and Luo, 1993); Jilin, Liaoning; (2) *M. r. irkutensis* (Ognev, 1924); Xinjiang to Nei Mongol and Heilongjiang.

Natural History: Inhabits forests and woodlands. Commonly found among fallen trees and in dense underbrush. Eats green leaves, shoots, and to a lesser extent seeds. Active day and night, but primarily nocturnal. Breeding season generally April–October with breeding peaks in spring and fall (warmer climates) or summer (cooler climates). Most breeding females give birth to two to four litters per season. Gestation 18–19 days, litter size four to seven, newborns weigh about 2 g and are weaned after about 17 days; sexual maturity attained between 30 and 60 days.

Comments: See generic account. Specimens identified as *regulus* from China are this species: *M. regulus* is endemic to the Korean Peninsula (see discussion in Musser and Carleton 2005).

Conservation Status: China RL—LC.

References: Jiang et al. (1993); Kaneko (1990); Kaneko et al. (1998); Musser and Carleton (2005).

Northern Red-Backed Vole

PLATE 16
MAP 138

Myodes rutilus (Pallas, 1779)
红背䶄 Hongbei Ping

Distinctive Characteristics: HB 95–100; T 25–27; HF 18–20; E 14–19. Dorsal pelage deep reddish brown from crown to rump; muzzle, sides of face, and flanks ochraceous brown; hairs of ventral pelage gray based with white tips, appearing grayish overall. Tail well furred, reddish brown above, pale buff below. Dorsal surfaces of hands and feet brownish white. Winter pelage brighter and more yellow. M3 usually with three well-developed folds on the lingual side and two folds, or sometimes a weakly developed third fold, on the labial side. Superficially similar to *M. rufocanus*, with which it is often sympatric, but *M. rutilus* is smaller and more richly colored. The length of the upper molar toothrow ranges between ca. 4.5 and 4.8 mm compared to ca. 5.8–6.1 mm in *M. rufocanus*; and whereas *M. rutilus* tends to have three folds on the lingual side of M3, *M. rufocanus* tends to have only two.

Distribution: N Xinjiang through Mongolia to NE China; ranging across the Holarctic from N Scandinavia to NE Canada. Two subspecies in China: (1) *M. r. amurensis* (Schrenk, 1859); NE China; (2) *M. r. rutilus* (Pallas, 1779); Xinjiang.

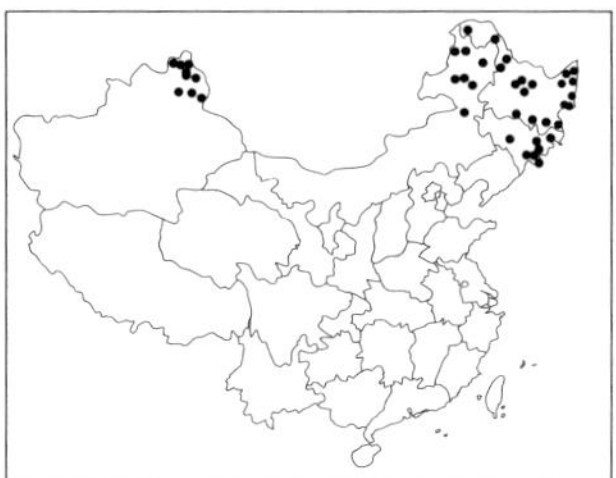

MAP 138. NORTHERN RED-BACKED VOLE, *Myodes rutilus*

Natural History: Inhabits forests and woodlands where it is more commonly found among fallen trees and in dense underbrush. Eats green vegetation and shoots and to a lesser extent seeds. Active day and night but primarily nocturnal. Make burrows either in the ground (generally under tree roots, stones, or shrubs) or arboreally (in tree holes or the forks of limbs). Nests comprise moss or grass clippings. Known to make a variety of vocalizations, including chattering, squeaking, and barking. Females reach sexual maturity at four months of age, and gestation is short (17–20 days). Two or three litters of 1–11 young are produced annually.

Conservation Status: China RL—LC.

Shanxi Red-Backed Vole

PLATE 16
MAP 139

Myodes shanseius (Thomas, 1908)
山西绒鼠 Shanxi Rongshu

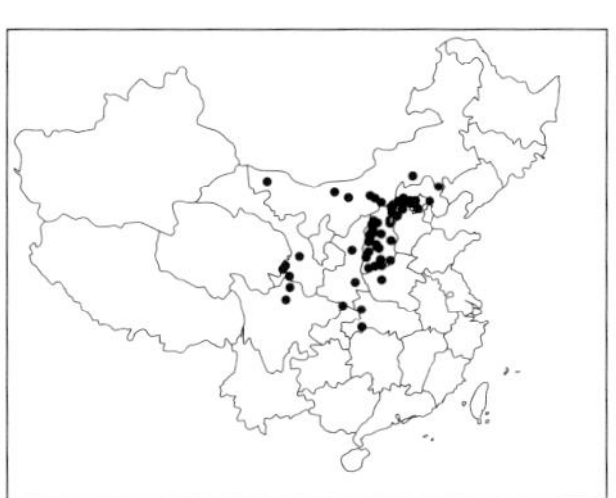

MAP 139. SHANXI RED-BACKED VOLE, *Myodes shanseius*

Distinctive Characteristics: HB 105–106; T 25–30; HF 20–21; E 13–15. Similar to *M. rufocanus* (and sometimes regarded a subspecies), but with the reddish area of the back tending to be less rufous, and with the sides more ochraceous gray and lacking the contrastingly grayish sides so characteristic of *M. rufocanus*. Dorsal pelage dull reddish brown, hairs of the sides gray based with pale ochraceous tips. Ventral pelage gray based with buff tips, appearing grayish buff overall. Tail brown above, whitish below. Dorsal surfaces of hands and feet brownish white. M3 similar to *M. rufocanus* in usually having only two folds on the lingual side. Unlike the other members of the genus, *M. shanseius* have entirely rootless molars as adults.
Distribution: N Sichuan and S Gansu through N Shanxi, N Shaanxi, and Hebei to Beijing and into C Nei Mongol. Endemic.
Natural History: Inhabits forests and woodlands. Eats green vegetation, shoots, and to a lesser extent seeds. Primarily nocturnal.
Comments: Often regarded as a subspecies of *M. rufocanus*, and as a species of *Eothenomys*, not *Myodes*; see discussion in Musser and Carleton (2005).
Conservation Status: China RL—LC.
References: Musser and Carleton (2005).

Genus *Myopus* (monotypic)

林旅鼠属 Linlüshu Shu

Small, thick-set rodents with soft dense fur that is red along the back and gray along the sides. Although resembling short-tailed voles externally, they share a number of cranial and dental traits with the true lemmings (diverging molar toothrows, third upper molar with three transverse prisms, among other characteristics) and were at one time regarded a subgenus of the true lemmings (genus *Lemmus*).

Wood Lemming

PLATE 18
MAP 140

Myopus schisticolor (Lilljeborg, 1844)
林旅鼠 Linlü Shu

MAP 140. WOOD LEMMING, *Myopus schisticolor*

Distinctive Characteristics: HB 75–100; T 14–15; HF 16–17; E 11–14; GLS 25–28. Red-backed, gray-sided lemmings of coniferous taiga forest. May be confused with Red-Backed Voles (*Myodes*), but unambiguously distinguished cranially and dentally. Skull with a simple palate, zygomatic arches broad and boxy. Molars rootless and ever growing. The lower incisor remains rooted on the lingual side of the molars (in all other Microtine rodents occurring in China, the root of the lower incisor passes to the labial side of the dentary under m2 and m3). M3 unlike in any other Chinese Arvicoline in having four transverse prisms. Molars large, with the toothrow extending back very near to the large bullae. Overall a dull slate gray lemming with a narrow wash of reddish brown hairs extending from the top of the head and along the upper back. This wash of reddish brown fur increases in intensity and in the extent to which it covers the dorsal pelage such that the lower back and rump are almost entirely bright reddish brown. The sides of the muzzle, face, and body are a dull slate gray, the individual hairs dull slate gray with silver gray tips. Entirely black hairs are scattered throughout the dorsal pelage. Ventral pelage slate gray, similar in overall appearance to the coloration along the sides but somewhat lighter. Dorsal surfaces of the feet grayish brown, pads naked. Tail moderately haired, grayish brown above, pale gray below.
Distribution: Extreme NE China; ranging across the entire coniferous taiga zone from Scandinavia to Kamchatka. Chinese subspecies: *M. s. saianicus* Hinton, 1914.
Natural History: Inhabits taiga forest, where it primarily lives in moss habitats. Constructs its burrows and runways in moss, and moss makes up the majority of its diet. Nocturnal. Breeding occurs primarily during summer, and litters of one to six young are produced at 25-day intervals. Sexual maturity occurs at one month of age.
Conservation Status: Rare in collections, but Emelyanova (1994) found them to be the dominant small mammal species in NE Siberia. China RL—LC. IUCN RL—NT ver 3.1 (2001).
References: Emelyanova (1994).

Genus *Neodon*—Mountain Voles

松田鼠属 Songtianshu Shu

Similar to *Microtus* externally and in the conformation of the skull, but differing in the morphology of the first lower molar, which has only three closed triangles anterior to the posterior prism, the fourth and fifth generally being broadly confluent with each other and the anterior cap. In *Microtus* there are always at least five closed triangles ahead of the posterior prism. Females with eight mammae. The genus was previously referred to under the name *Pitymys*. All four species occur in China.

Forrest's Mountain Vole

MAP 141

Neodon forresti Hinton, 1923
云南松田鼠 Yunnan Songtianshu

Distinctive Characteristics: HB 100–134; T 36–43; HF 17–20; E 13–15. A large species of *Neodon*. Similar to *N. irene*, but larger and with a longer, darker brown pelage. Dorsal pelage dark brown, ventral pelage gray washed with grayish white. Tail bicolored, brown above, white below. Dorsal surfaces of hands and feet grayish white.

Key to the Chinese Species of *Neodon*

1.a.	Anterior cap of the first lower molar (m3) with lingual and labial folds	*Neodon sikimensis*
b.	Anterior cap of first lower molar with a weakly developed lingual fold and virtually nonexistent labial fold	2
2.a.	Size large, HB averages 120 mm	*Neodon forresti*
b.	Size small, HB usually < 100 mm	3
3.a.	Dorsal pelage dark brown. Anterior cap of first lower molar (m3) lacks any trace of an indentation on the labial margin	*Neodon irene*
b.	Dorsal pelage pale brown. Anterior cap of first lower molar (m3) with a slight indentation on the labial margin	*Neodon juldaschi*

Distribution: NW Yunnan and adjacent N Myanmar.
Natural History: Rocky alpine meadows between 3,350 and 3,650 m

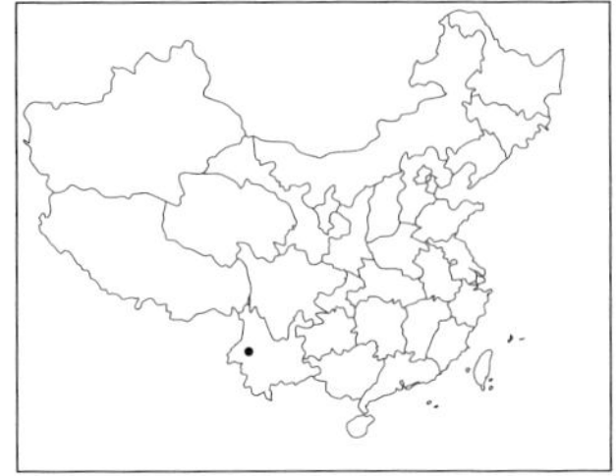

MAP 141. FORREST'S MOUNTAIN VOLE, *Neodon forresti*

Comments: Morphologically closely related it *N. irene* and sometimes treated as a subspecies of it; see discussion in Musser and Carleton (2005).
Conservation Status: China RL—VU D2.
References: Hinton (1923).

Irene's Mountain Vole

Neodon irene (Thomas, 1911) PLATE 18 MAP 142
高原松田鼠 Gaoyuan Songtianshu

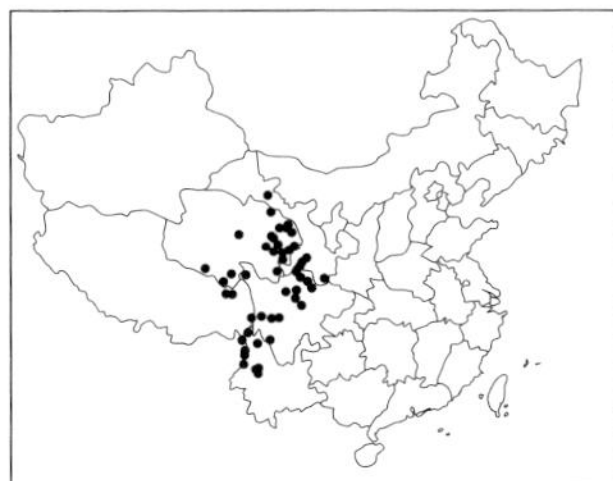

MAP 142. IRENE'S MOUNTAIN VOLE, *Neodon irene*

Distinctive Characteristics: HB 80–108; T 22–40; HF 15–19; E 11–13. Dorsal pelage dark grayish brown, a somewhat brighter ochraceous brown along the sides and blending into the dark gray ventral pelage. Tail bicolored, brownish above, whitish below; dorsal surfaces of hands and feet brownish white.
Distribution: High mountains of E Qinghai, S Gansu, W Sichuan, NE Xizang; NW Yunnan. Endemic.
Natural History: Alpine meadows and shrubby mountainsides. A female specimen collected in August had three nearly mature embryos.
Comments: Sometimes included as a synonym of *N. sikkimensis*, but the two do not appear to be sympatric and are distinguishable based on size and tooth morphology. See comments in Musser and Carleton (2005).
Conservation Status: China RL—LC.
References: Lawrence (1982).

Juniper Mountain Vole

Neodon juldaschi (Severtzov, 1879) MAP 143
帕米尔松田鼠 Pami'er Songtianshu

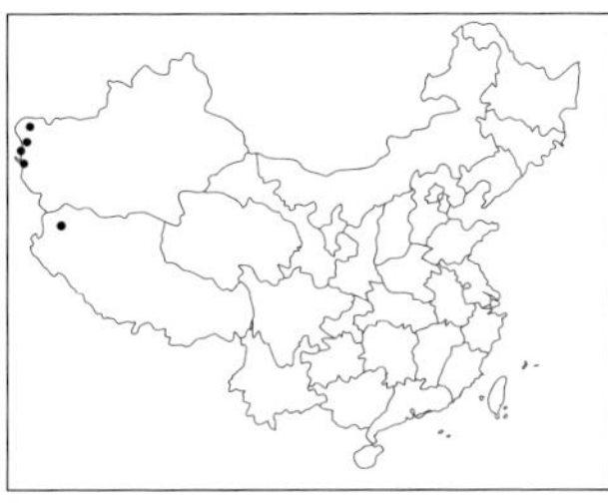

MAP 143. JUNIPER MOUNTAIN VOLE, *Neodon juldaschi*

Distinctive Characteristics: HB 83–105; T 29–39; HF 15–17; E 11–14. Dorsal pelage pale brown ventral pelage grayish brown. Tail bicolored, pale brown above, silvery white below.
Distribution: NW Xizang, SW Xinjiang; extending into Pakistan, NE Afghanistan, E Tajikistan and SW Kyrgyzstan.
Natural History: Inhabits mountane steppe above 3,000 m. Herbivorous; known to make winter stores.
Conservation Status: China RL—LC.
References: Roberts (1997).

Sikkim Mountain Vole

Neodon sikimensis (Horsfield, 1841) MAP 144
锡金松田鼠 Xijin Songtianshu
Distinctive Characteristics: HB 97–119; T 30–52; HF 17–22; E 11–16. A dark brown vole very similar to *N. irene*, but distinguished dentally. See the account of *N. irene*.
Distribution: S Xizang; extending through the Himalaya of Nepal, NE India, and Bhutan.

Natural History: Inhabits alpine meadows and dense vegetation growing at the edges of rhododendron and coniferous forest between 2,100 and 3,700 m. Eats green vegetation and seeds to a lesser extent. Pregnant females reported with two or three embryos.

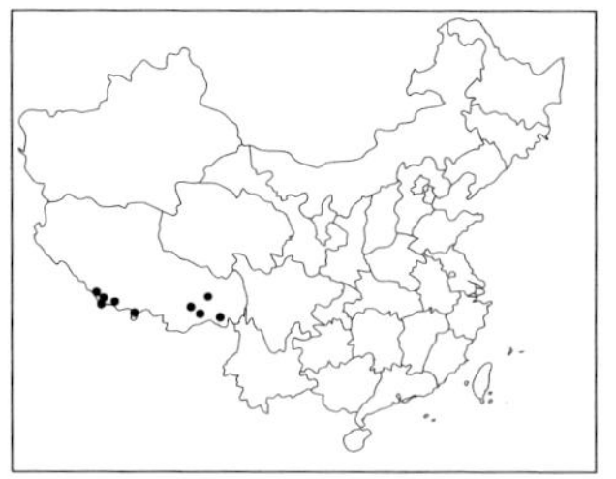

MAP 144. SIKKIM MOUNTAIN VOLE, *Neodon sikimensis*

Conservation Status: China RL–LC.
References: Abe (1971); Agrawal (2000); Gruber (1969).

Genus *Phaiomys* (monotypic)

白尾松田鼠属 Baiwei Songtianshu Shu

Blyth's Mountain Vole

PLATE 18
MAP 145

Phaiomys leucurus (Blyth, 1863)
白尾松田鼠 Baiwei Songtianshu

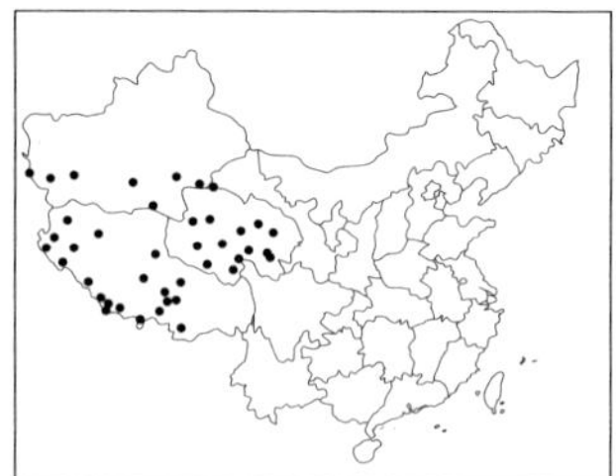

MAP 145. BLYTH'S MOUNTAIN VOLE, *Phaiomys leucurus*

Distinctive Characteristics: HB 98–128; T 26–35; HF 16–19; E 10–13. Dorsal pelage pale yellowish brown, paler along the sides and blending into the yellowish gray ventral pelage. Tail a monocolored yellowish brown. Dorsal surfaces of hands and feet pale yellowish white. Adaptations to a semifossorial life include short ears and elongated claws. Molar enamel pattern reduced, similar to that of *Arvicola* in that the first lower molar (m3) has only three closed alternating triangles ahead of the posterior transverse prism and an anterior loop with indentations on the lingual and labial sides. Posterior margin of palate with a medial bony bridge joining the mesopterogoid fossa and separating two lateral pits.
Distribution: Tibetan Plateau; extending south along the Himalayan massif to NW India.
Natural History: High-altitude grassy habitats, especially along watercourses. Strictly herbivorous. Lives in colonies, digs deep burrows, especially in the banks of streams and lakes. The uterus of one specimen contained seven embryos.
Comments: Sometimes included in the genus *Pitymys, Neodon* or *Microtus*; see discussion in Musser and Carleton (2005).
Conservation Status: China RL–LC.
References: Agrawal (2000); Hoffmann (1996); Zheng and Wang (1980).

Genus *Proedromys* (monotypic)

沟牙田鼠属 Gouyatianshu Shu

Duke of Bedford's Vole

PLATE 18
MAP 146

Proedromys bedfordi Thomas, 1911
沟牙田鼠 Gouya Tianshu

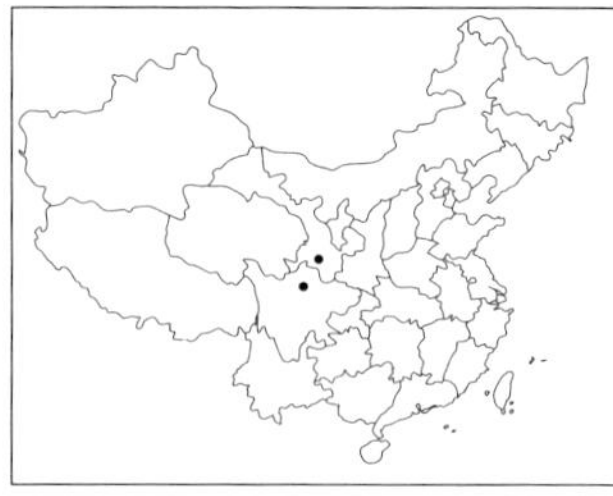

MAP 146. DUKE OF BEDFORD'S VOLE, *Proedromys bedfordi*

Distinctive Characteristics: HB 75–100; T 14–15; HF 16–17; E 11–14; GLS 25–28. Dorsal pelage with long dull brown hairs, ventral pelage grayish white. Tail well haired, brown above and dull white below. Hands and feet dull white. The skull is robust, strongly curved in profile and with well-developed postorbital squamosal projections. Posterior palate with a median process sloping upward to join the mesopterogoid and separating the lateral pits. Molars rootless and persistently growing. Upper incisors broad strongly recurved and grooved on their anterior face—a distinctive trait among microtine rodents. Occlusal pattern of last upper molar very simple, the inner side with only one reentrant fold. Females with eight mammae, two pectoral pairs and two inguinal pairs.
Distribution: Recent specimens known from only two localities in S Gansu and N Sichuan. Endemic.
Natural History: Mountain forests; the two known specimens were collected at 2,440 and 2,550 m.
Comments: Known from only two Recent specimens collected in C China. The genus is also known from Pleistocene remains and was apparently once more widespread.
Conservation Status: China RL–VU D2. IUCN RL–LR/nt ver 2.3 (1994).
References: Thomas (1911); Wang et al. (1966); Zheng and Li (1990).

Genus *Volemys*—Voles

川田鼠属 Chuantianshu Shu—川田鼠 Chuantianshu

Similar to *Microtus*, but distinguished by its smooth cranium, slim dentary with a low ramus, inflated auditory bullae, and long tail relative to HB length. The second upper molar has a large posterio-lingual

Key to *Volemys*

1.a. HB < 100 mm. A posterio-lingual triangle present on the second molar only — *Volemys millicens*
b. HB usually > 100 mm. Both the first and second upper molars have posterio-lingual triangles confluent with the last labial triangle — *Volemys musseri*

triangle confluent with the opposite labial triangle and forms an inverted chevron-shaped lamina. Both of the two known species occur in China.

Sichuan Vole

PLATE 18
MAP 147

Volemys millicens (Thomas, 1911)
四川田鼠 Sichuan Tianshu

MAP 147. SICHUAN VOLE, *Volemys millicens*

Distinctive Characteristics: HB 83–95; T 46–53; HF 18–18.5; E 14; GLS 23.7–24.7. Dorsal pelage dark brown. Ventral pelage grayish. Tail grayish brown above, white below. Dorsal surfaces of hands and feet white. Similar to *Volemys musseri* but smaller and with posterio-lingual triangles on the second upper molar only.
Distribution: Known from six specimens from the type locality in the mountains of NW Sichuan. Endemic.
Natural History: Known from forests above 4,000 m.
Comments: Sometimes treated as a species of *Microtus*.
Conservation Status: China RL–VU A1ac.
References: Lawrence (1982; as *Microtus millicens*).

Marie's Vole

MAP 148

Volemys musseri (Lawrence, 1982)
马瑟川田鼠 Masechuan Tianshu

MAP 148. MARIE'S VOLE, *Volemys musseri*

Distinctive Characteristics: HB 90–129; T 47–70; HF 18–23; GLS 24.5–27.5. Dorsal pelage dark brown. Ventral pelage dark gray with a pale buff wash. Tail bicolored, dark brown above, buff white below. Dorsal surfaces of hands and feet buffy. Similar to *V. millicens* but larger and with posterio-lingual triangles on the first and second upper molars.
Distribution: W Sichuan (Qionglai Shan range, 2,318–3,660 m). Endemic.
Natural History: Collected from rocks and cliffs in alpine meadows.
Comments: Originally described as a species of *Microtus*.
Conservation Status: China RL–DD.
References: Lawrence (1982).

Subfamily Cricetinae—Hamsters

仓鼠亚科 Cangshu Yake—仓鼠 Cangshu

Andrew T. Smith and Robert S. Hoffmann

Form stout; tail short, the greatest length not more than HB length; covered with dense hairs; with large internal cheek pouches; pinnae short and densely furred. No evident bony ridge in the skull of most species; anterior portion of nasal extends beyond labial of incisors; occipital condyle on the same vertical plane with occipital plane, or slightly protruding backward; cranium not evidently inflated. Dental formula: 1.0.0.3/1.0.0.3 = 16; occlusal surface of molar crown with conical cusps arranged in double longitudinal rows separated by a deep groove, when worn, form a joined transverse ridge. The taxonomic arrangement within the Cricetinae has been fluid, with significant movement of subspecies among taxa and lack of understanding of species limits; a full revision is needed (Musser and Carleton 2005). Of seven genera of Cricetinae, six occur in China. The Cricetinae represents a monophyletic clade that appears to be the sister taxon to Arvicolinae, with a divergence date of 16.3–18.8 mya (Michaux et al. 2001; Steppan et al. 2004).

Genus *Allocricetulus*—Hamsters

短尾仓鼠属 Duanweicangshu Shu—
短尾仓鼠 Duanweicangshu

Allocricetulus has been included frequently within *Cricetulus*, although their cranial morphology apparently is more similar to that of *Cricetus*. In any case, as with many of the hamster genera, a comprehensive systematic revision is necessary (Musser and Carleton 2005). Both species of *Allocricetulus* occur in China.

Key to the Chinese Genera of Cricetinae

1.a. Ventral pelage solid black; body mass > 250 g — *Cricetus*
b. Ventral pelage white or gray, not black; body mass < 250 g — 2
2.a. Tail length < 14 mm; soles of feet densely haired — *Phodopus*
b. Tail length > 14 mm; soles of feet naked or sparsely haired — 3
3.a. Tail long > 65 mm — 4
b. Tail short < 65 mm — 5
4.a. Tail shaggy, distal half white; claws white; claw on first digit on hind foot nail-like — *Cansumys*
b. Tail not shaggy, brown for full length; claws not white and none nail-like — *Tscherskia*
5.a. Long hairs cover most of tail, almost forming a cone — *Allocricetulus*
b. Tail without long hairs — *Cricetulus*

Key to the Species of *Allocricetulus*

1.a. Chest without a brown spot, back yellow-gray. 2N = 20 — *Allocricetulus curtatus*
b. Brown spot on chest, dorsally dark gray or reddish brown. 2N = 26 — *Allocricetulus eversmanni*

Mongolian Hamster

PLATE 20
MAP 149

Allocricetulus curtatus (Allen, 1925)
无斑短尾仓鼠 Wuban Duanweicangshu

MAP 149. MONGOLIAN HAMSTER, *Allocricetulus curtatus*

Distinctive Characteristics: HB 85–130; T 18–25; HF 14–20; E 11–17; GLS 27–33; Wt 30–70 g. Tail short, near or slightly longer than hind foot; tail appears conical as basal hairs grow out long and nearly reach the tail tip. All dorsal surfaces a pale buffy gray, almost light cinnamon; ventrally white extending up the sides and including thighs, forearms, and cheeks; no dark patch on chest. Skull round with a short broad rostrum; zygomatic arch thin and clearly expanded outward; interorbital region not narrow; interparietal highly reduced, its width four to five times its length; incisive foramina reaches anterior margin of first upper molar; interpterygoid foramen very shallow, its anterior end behind the posterior margin of third upper molar; auditory bullae more inflated than in *eversmanni*. 2N = 20.
Distribution: N C China; Nei Mongol, Ningxia, Gansu, Xinjiang; extending into Mongolia.
Natural History: An obligate species of sand dune habitats in grasslands or semidesert. Eats seeds and sometimes insects. Constructs very simple, short burrows with only a few entrances; caches seeds in burrows to eat over winter. Active in early evening and night. Reproduction begins in April, and two or three litters of four to nine young are produced each year.
Comments: Closely related to and often included in *A. eversmanni*.
Conservation Status: China RL—LC.
References: Ma et al. (1978); Sokolov and Orlov (1980).

Eversman's Hamster

MAP 150

Allocricetulus eversmanni (Brandt, 1859)
短尾仓鼠 Duanwei Cangshu

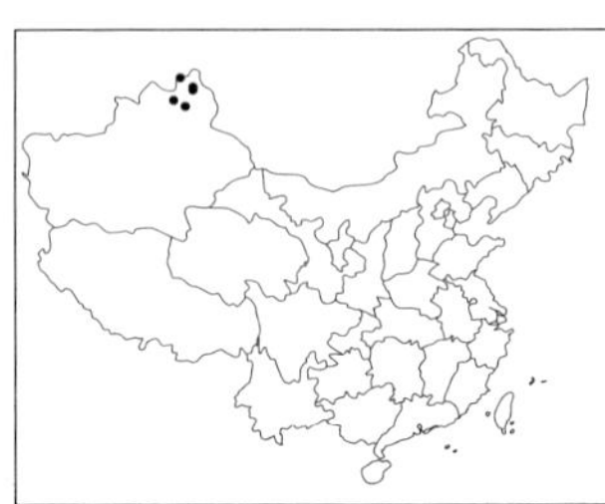

MAP 150. EVERSMAN'S HAMSTER, *Allocricetulus eversmanni*

Distinctive Characteristics: HB 93–115; T 17–28; HF 15–18; E 12–16; GLS 30–33; Wt 36–60 g. Size medium; tail very short, near or slightly longer than hind foot; dorsal pelage sandy ochre or brown, with dark gray base; darker than in *E. curtatus*; sides and ventral pelage grayish white—white at tip and light gray at base; white below neck and on underside of hind feet and tail. A prominent dark patch is found on the chest. Long hairs grow out to cover most of tail. Skull without evident bony ridge, no supraorbital ridge and parietal ridge; jaw region broader than in *curtatus*; zygomatic arch thin, clearly expanded outward;

incisive foramen does not reach the first molar; auditory bullae small. 2N = 26.
Distribution: N Xinjiang; extending into Kazakhstan. Chinese subspecies: *A. e. belajwi* (Argyropulo, 1933).
Natural History: Occurs in grasslands and semidesert habitats, but also known to occur in woody areas. Eats vegetation, seeds, insects, and a variety of small vertebrates (lizards, nestling birds, young squirrels, etc.). Nocturnal. Constructs a simple burrow system that goes straight down (or slightly slanting) to a maximum depth of 30 cm. There is a nest at the end of the burrow, and often branches radiate from the burrow at that point. Often can be found living in burrows constructed by other mammals. Solitary and aggressive. Reproduction begins in April, and two or three litters of four to six young are produced; reproduction can also take place in winter.
Conservation Status: China RL—LC.
References: Ma et al. (1987).

Genus *Cansumys* (monotypic)

甘肃仓鼠属 Ganshucangshu Shu

Gansu Hamster

Cansumys canus Allen, 1928 PLATE 20 MAP 151
甘肃仓鼠 Gansu Cangshu

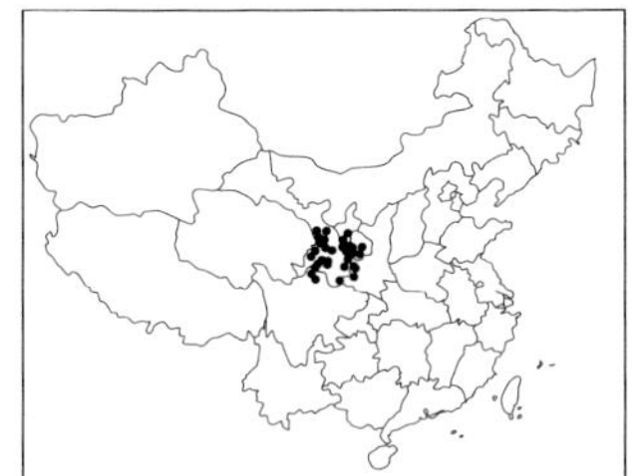

MAP 151. GANSU HAMSTER, *Cansumys canus*

Distinctive Characteristics: HB 100–170; T 77–111; HF 17–24; E 15–23; GLS 32–40; Wt 61–120 g. Tail shaggy at the base; distal half white. Dorsal pelage thick and dense, a hoary gray color. Possesses a conspicuous white patch on the cheek and at the base of the ears; white under the neck; ears dark brown and black inside. Feet delicate with long fore toes; claws white; digit of hind foot short and flattened (almost nail-like). Skull arches upward; auditory bullae large and rounded (unlike other cricetids); supraorbital ridges are raised and prominent; rostrum longer than in *Cricetulus* or *Tscherskia*. The tooth rows diverge slightly in front, and the molars are extremely hypsodont, unlike any other hamsters. Significantly smaller than *T. triton*. 2N = 24.
Distribution: C China (S Gansu, SW Ningxia, E Shaanxi). Endemic.
Natural History: Poorly known. The Gansu Hamster was originally described as an arboreal form (unlike other hamsters); this contention is supported by its morphology—the delicate feet and nail-like claw, coupled with the shaggy pelage (especially the tail). It is found in mountainous habitats, generally between 1,000 and 1,400 m elevation. Occupies deciduous forests. In spite of its arboreal habits, it can be found on the ground even nesting in rocks. Nocturnal, and primarily active in spring and summer. Diet consists of leaves and even grasses. LS = 6–8.
Comments: Earlier this form was considered a subspecies of *Cricetulus triton* (thus also of *Tscherskia triton*). The subspecies *ningshanensis* from S Shaanxi was originally described by Song (1985) as a subspecies of *Tscherskia*; others have included this form in *Cansumys*. Musser and Carleton (2005) clarify that there are few similarities between *ningshanensis* and *canus*, whereas it is clearly more similar to *Tscherskia* (where it is treated herein).
Conservation Status: China RL—LC.
References: Musser and Carleton (2005); Ross (1988); Wang and Xu (1992).

Genus *Cricetulus*—True Hamsters

仓鼠属 Cangshu Shu—仓鼠 Cangshu

Mouselike in appearance, but with short tail. Feet white and sparsely haired (fig. 8), ears long and delicate, white-bellied, and with a slender skull. All eight species of *Cricetulus* live in China.

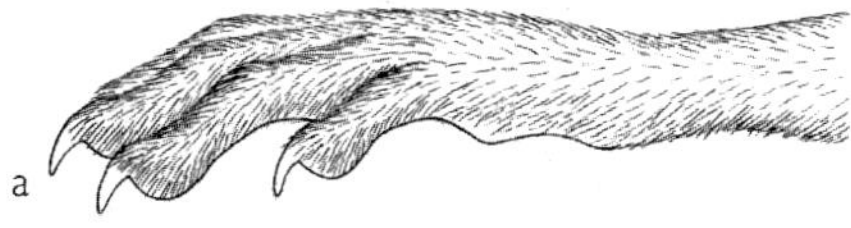

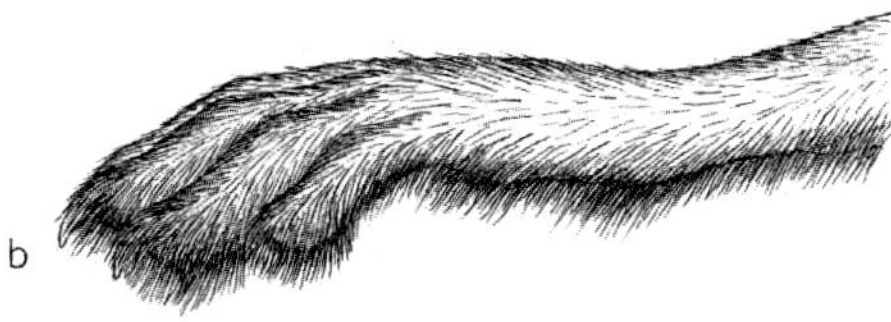

Figure 8. Comparison of the feet of dwarf hamsters of the genus *Cricetulus* (naked or sparsely haired; a) and genus *Phodopus* (generously haired; b).

Key to the Chinese Species of *Cricetulus*

1.a.	Tail short, generally < 30 mm	2
b.	Tail longer, generally > 30 mm	3
2.a.	Ears blackish	*Cricetulus barabensis*
b.	Ears gray with dark brown spot in middle of ear	*Cricetulus sokolovi*
3.a.	Auditory bullae large, tall, and round	*Cricetulus longicaudatus*
b.	Auditory bullae small	4
4.a.	Tail > 50 mm; black blaze extends down thighs	*Cricetulus kamensis*
b.	Tail < 50 mm; no black blaze extending down thighs	5
5.a.	Molars with distinct folding pattern	*Cricetulus alticola*
b.	Molars without distinct folding pattern	6
6.a.	Tail > 40 mm	*Cricetulus lama*
b.	Tail < 40 mm	7
7.a.	Ears short; dusky brown with white edge	*Cricetulus tibetanus*
b.	Ears larger	*Cricetulus migratorius*

Ladak Hamster

Cricetulus alticola Thomas, 1917 MAP 152
高山仓鼠 Gaoshan Cangshu

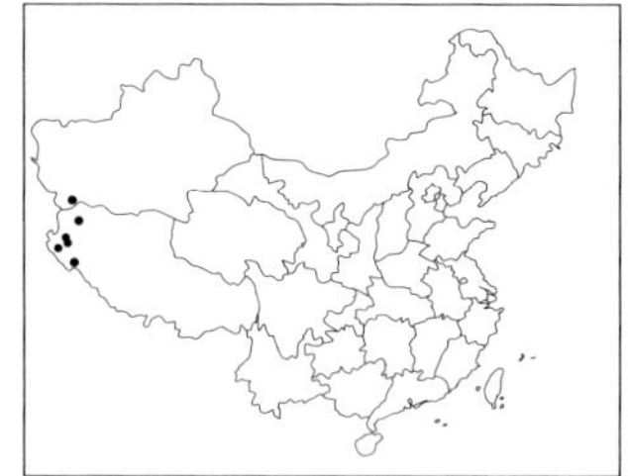

MAP 152. LADAK HAMSTER, *Cricetulus alticola*

Distinctive Characteristics: HB 80–98; T 36–42; HF 15–18; E 13–16; GLS 25–28; Wt 22–48 g. Dorsal pelage gray-yellow brown. There are no spots on the back, and the boundary between the dorsal and ventral pelage is indistinct, more like a wavy line along the side; thigh gray. Tail short, light brown on top and white underneath. Bullae small. First upper molar with a distinctive enamel folding pattern. 2N = 22.
Distribution: SW Xinjiang, NW Xizang; extending into W Nepal and India (Kashmir and Ladakh).
Natural History: Occupies coniferous and birch forests to desert steppe, shrubland, swampy meadow, and highland meadow–obviously a very broad niche. Normally found at elevations ranging from 3,100 to 5,200 m. Primarily nocturnal but can also be active during the day. Diet consists of grass seed, grains, and insects. Reproduction occurs from May to August, with a peak in June and July. Littter size ranges from 5 to 10 young (7–8 being most common).
Comments: Often considered a subspecies of *C. kamensis* as *C. alticola tibetanus*.
Conservation Status: China RL–LC.
References: Lim and Ross (1992).

Striped Dwarf Hamster

PLATE 21
Cricetulus barabensis (Pallas, 1773) MAP 153
黑线仓鼠 Heixian Cangshu

Distinctive Characteristics: HB 72–116; T 15–26; HF 13–19; E 14–17; GLS 22–28; Wt 20–35 g. Size small, tail averages about 30% length of HB; dorsal pelage light grayish brown, a faint black longitudinal stripe along dorsal mid-line; ears blackish and rimmed with white edge. Ventral pelage gray; hairs tipped with white. Skull without supraorbital ridge; zygomatic arch thin and convex outward; rostrum short, interorbital region broad; interparietal normal to excessively low and flat; antero-external angle of parietal pointed and long, its extremity hooked inward; incisive foramina do not reach anterior margin of first upper molar; interpterygoid foramen very deep, its anterior extremity reaching the posterior margin of third upper molar; bullae large. 2N = 20–24

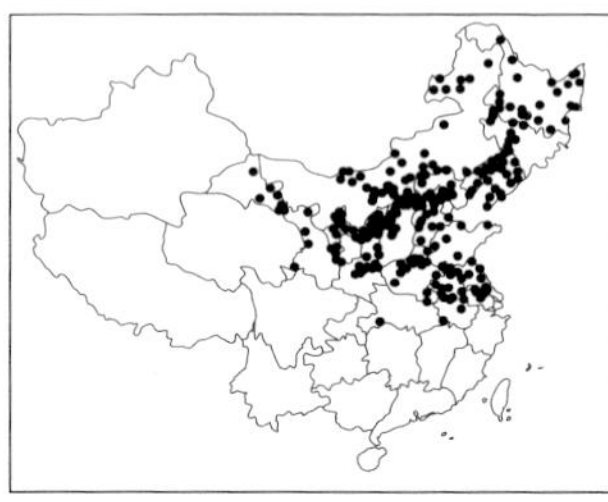

MAP 153. STRIPED DWARF HAMSTER, *Cricetulus barabensis*

Distribution: C to NW China; extending into Russia (S Siberia), Mongolia, and Korea. Six subspecies in China: (1) *C. b. fumatus* Thomas, 1909; SE Heilongjiang, Jilin, Nei Mongol; (2) *C. b. griseus* (Milne-Edwards, 1867); Liaoning, Nei Mongol, Hebei, Beijing, Tianjin, Shandong, Henan, Shanxi; (3) *C. b. manchuricus* Mori, 1930; E Heilongjiang; (4) *C. b. obscurus*

(Milne-Edwards, 1867); Nei Mongol, Ningxia, E Gansu, N Shaanxi, Shanxi; (5) *C. b. pseudogriseus* Orlov and Iskhakova, 1975; (6) *C. b. xinganensis* Wang, 1980; N Heilongjiang, NE Nei Mongol.
Natural History: Inhabits arid country, although it adapts to and is commonly found in croplands. Occupies a simple burrow system with two or three entrances; the circular opening has a diameter of 2–3 cm. The burrow runs to 1 m in length at a depth of 10–50 cm, and four or five branches end in nest or food storage areas. Nests are lined with grass. About four to five individuals (a maximum of eight) occupy each burrow. Most active in the first half of the night. Diet consists of grains and legumes, and these seeds are stored in caches. Hibernates over-winter, emerging in February–March. Reproduction peaks in March and April, and again in autumn. May breed two to five times each year, producing large litters (range 1–10; average 6–7).
Comments: The status of various subspecies is unclear. While most *barabensis* have a 2N = 20, *griseus* 2N = 22, and *pseudogriseus* 2N = 24; these differences have led some to erect these latter two forms to independent status. Representatives of *C. b. obscurus* may be assignable to *C. sokolovi* (see that account).
Conservation Status: China RL—LC.
References: Zhang (1986); Zhu and Qin (1991).

Kam Dwarf Hamster

PLATE 21
Cricetulus kamensis (Satunin, 1903) MAP 154
康藏仓鼠 Kangzang Cangshu

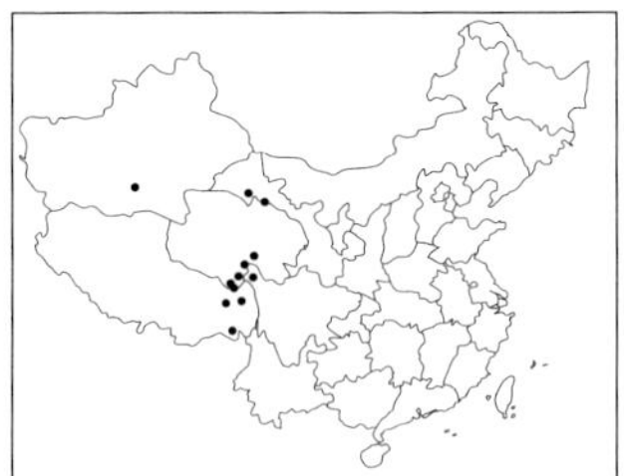

MAP 154. KAM DWARF HAMSTER, *Cricetulus kamensis*

Distinctive Characteristics: HB 88–112; T 51–64; HF 17–18; E 16–18; GLS 27–29; Wt 20–40 g. Dorsal pelage dark brownish gray, but may have black spots or streaks on the back; ventral pelage grayish white, dark at base, white at tip; tail with dark narrow stripe above, wholly white below and at tip, thick and covered with long guard hairs; sides of body with wavelike appearance formed by contrasting colors of dorsal and ventral pelage; black coloration extends down upper part of hind leg. Skull slightly convex, so that dorsal side of skull arched; incisive foramina short, not reaching anterior edge of first upper molar; antero-external angle of the parietal round and blunt; auditory bullae small; interparietal not excessively low and flat.
Distribution: C China. Endemic. Two subspecies: (1) *C. k. kamensis* (Satunin, 1903); E Xizang, S Qinghai; (2) *C. k. kozlovi* (Satunin, 1903); N Qinghai, NW Kansu, S Xinjiang.
Natural History: Lives in high mountain grasslands, shrubby marshes, and open steppe at high elevations (3,300–4,100 m). Active day and night. Eats grains, grass seeds, and insects. Constructs a simple burrow 50 cm deep in which it stores grain on which to feed during winter. Reproduces from May to August, primarily during June and July. Litter size ranges from 5 to 10, normally 7–8.
Comments: Musser and Carleton (2005) and Wang and Zheng (1973) consider the forms *lama* and *tibetanus* (as *alticola tibetanus*) synonyms.
Conservation Status: China RL—LC.
References: Feng et al. (1986); Thomas and Hinton (1922); Wang and Zheng (1973).

Lama Dwarf Hamster

PLATE 21
Cricetulus lama Bonhote, 1905 MAP 155
藏南仓鼠 Zangnan Cangshu

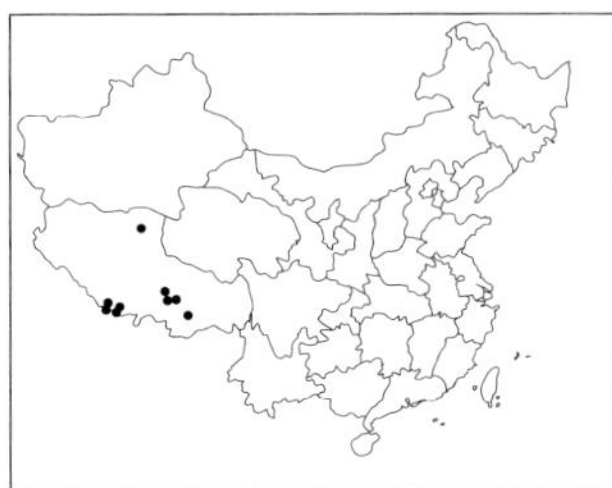

MAP 155. LAMA DWARF HAMSTER, *Cricetulus lama*

Distinctive Characteristics: HB 86–103; T 40–50; HF 15–18; E 14–18; GLS 26–28; Wt 24–39 g. Pelage light and similar to *kamesnis*, but without any dark dorsal fur; not as striking as *C. kamensis*. No black on upper thigh, as in *kamensis*. Tail shorter than *kamensis*, averaging less than half of HB length; bicolored, dark on top and white underneath. The white fur on side is shorter than in *kamensis*, there is no wavy line on the side, and it is grayer.
Distribution: S Xizang. Endemic.
Natural History: Believed to be similar to that of *kamensis*.
Comments: Included in *kamensis* in many treatments.
Conservation Status: China RL—LC.

Long-Tailed Dwarf Hamster

PLATE 21
Cricetulus longicaudatus (Milne-Edwards, 1867) MAP 156
长尾仓鼠 Changwei Cangshu
Distinctive Characteristics: HB 80–135; T 35–48; HF 15–21; E 15–20; GLS 25–31; Wt 15–50 g. Size small, near *Cricetulus barabensis* or slightly larger. Dorsal color sandy yellow or dark brownish gray, ventral pelage grayish white with hairs, grayish black at base, white at tip; sides of body have a nearly horizontal sharp line formed by contrasting colors of dorsal and ventral pelage. Tail slender, long; obviously longer

than hind foot, about 33% length of HB or even longer; dark on top and white underneath. Backs of feet pure white; ears dark with white rim. Cranium low, so that dorsal side of skull slightly convex or tending to smooth; rostrum narrow and long; no supraorbital ridge, occipital condyle not protruding behind occipital plane; incisive foramina long, reaching beyond anterior margin of first upper molar; interpterygoid foramen deep, its anterior extremity reaches third upper molar; auditory bullae large, tall, and round. 2N = 24.
Distribution: N C China; extending to Kazakhstan and Russia (Tuva, Altai regions). Two subspecies in China: (1) *C. l. chiumalaiensis* Wang and Zheng, 1973; S Qinghai, Xizang; (2) *C. l. longicaudatus* (Milne-Edwards, 1867); Nei Mongol, Hebei, Beijing, Tianjin, N Henan, Shanxi, Shaanxi, Gansu, Ningxia, Qinghai, N Xinjiang; *nigrescens* Allen, 1925, a synonym.

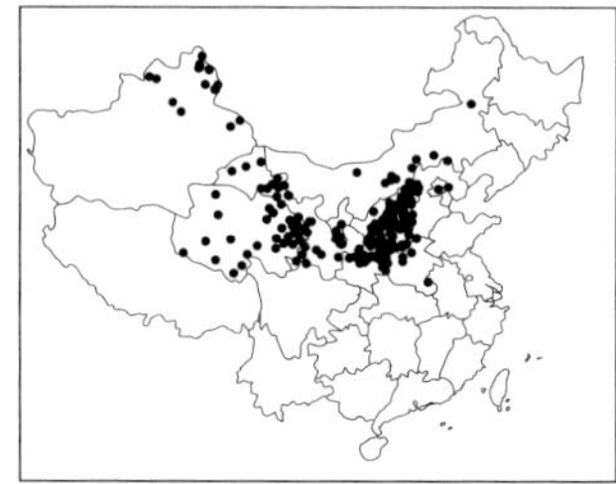

MAP 156. LONG-TAILED DWARF HAMSTER, *Cricetulus longicaudatus*

Natural History: Inhabits desert country to shrubland to forests and alpine meadows. It occupies shallow burrows often constructed under rocks that extend horizontally beneath the surface. Constructs food stores and grass-lined nests. Sometimes occupies burrows built by other small mammals. Eats vegetation and insects. Nocturnal. At least two litters of four to nine young are produced each year, beginning in March or April.
Conservation Status: China RL—LC.

Gray Dwarf Hamster

Cricetulus migratorius (Pallas, 1773) PLATE 21 MAP 157
灰仓鼠 Hui Cangshu

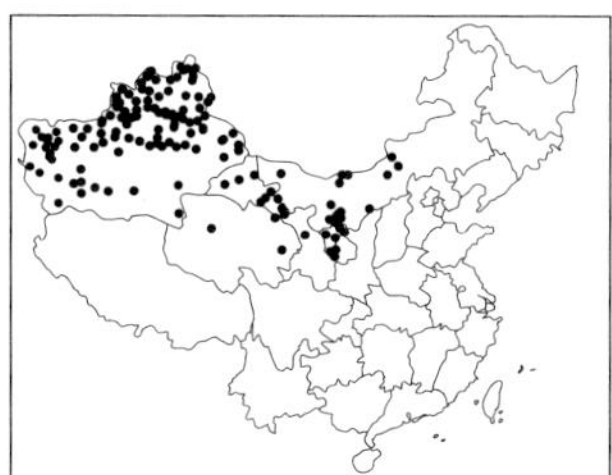

MAP 157. GRAY DWARF HAMSTER, *Cricetulus migratorius*

Distinctive Characteristics: HB 85–120; T 23–39; HF 15–18; E 15–21; GLS 22–31; Wt 31–58 g. Size medium, tail about 30% length of HB and fully furred; ears large. Dorsal pelage sandy brownish gray; ventral pelage sometimes with gray base of hairs, the rest of the hairs white. Dorsal skull low and flat; rostrum narrow, zygomatic arch slightly thickened without supraorbital ridge and parietal ridge; interparietal normal, excessively low and flat; auditory bullae very small, low, and flat; incisive foramina short, terminates before the first upper molar. 2N = 22.
Distribution: NE China; extending to Mongolia, Kazakhstan, Russia, Central Asia, Middle East, and SE Europe. Three subspecies in China: (1) *C. m. caesius* Kashkarov, 1923; Xinjiang, Nei Mongol, Gansu, Ningxia, N Qinghai; (2) *C. m. coerulescens* Severtzov, 1897; Xinjiang (Pamir Plateau); (3) *C. m. fulvus* Blanford, 1875; Xinjiang (Tarim Basin).
Natural History: Lives in desert and semidesert habitats, extending into grasslands and alpine meadows. Constructs a burrow system that runs as deep as 1.5 m with several food storage and nesting chambers. Nocturnal or crepuscular; does not hibernate. Eats seeds, green vegetation, and insects. Produces up to three litters of 1–13 young (average 6–7) each year following a 19-day gestation period.
Conservation Status: China RL—LC. IUCN RL—LR/nt ver 2.3 (1994).
References: Yan and Zhong (1984).

Sokolov's Dwarf Hamster

Cricetulus sokolovi Orlov and Malygin, 1988 MAP 158
索氏仓鼠 Suoshi Cangshu

MAP 158. SOKOLOV'S DWARF HAMSTER, *Cricetulus sokolovi*

Distinctive Characteristics: HB 77–114; T 18–32; HF 13–18; E 13–19; GLS 23–26. Dorsal pelage gray with a brownish-yellow or walnut hue; lighter in tone than *C. barabensis pseudogriseus*. There is an evident mid-line dorsal dark stripe that runs from the nape of the neck to the base of the tail; this stripe is most prominent in young animals and gradually fades to a shadow in the oldest animals. Ventrally a light gray, with a distinct separation between the dorsal and ventral pelage. Ears are the same color as the dorsum, but with a dark brown spot in the middle of the ear. Tail is similarly colored on top as the dorsum, but lighter underneath without a sharp separation in color. Feet are white and the toes tend to curl up; that is, the feet are not flat. 2N = 20.

Distribution: Nei Mongol; extending into Mongolia.
Natural History: Lives in shrubby habitat in sandy areas. Burrows are normally constructed under desert shrubs. Reproduction begins in mid-May, and two or three litters of four to nine young may be produced annually.
Comments: Specimens originally attributed to *C. barbarensis obscurus* from Mongolia and Nei Mongol are now assigned to *sokolovi* upon meeting the necessary chromosomal or pelage characteristics.
Conservation Status: China RL—DD.
References: Orlov and Malygin (1988).

Tibetan Dwarf Hamster

PLATE 21

Cricetulus tibetanus
Thomas and Hinton, 1922 MAP 159
藏仓鼠 Zang Cangshu

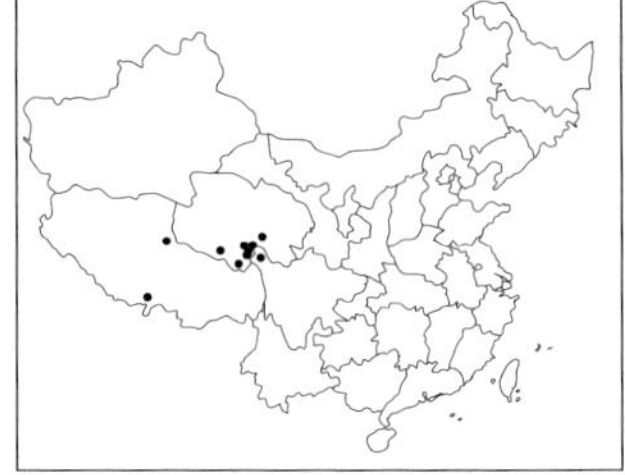

MAP 159. TIBETAN DWARF HAMSTER, *Cricetulus tibetanus*

Distinctive Characteristics: HB 103; T 30–37; HF 17–18; E 15–16; GLS 23.5–25.4. Dorsal pelage a nearly uniform ochraceous, fading to a lighter sandy color toward the forehead, cheek, and neck. Ears are a contrasting dusky brown, with a narrow edge of white on the tips and a small tuft of white at their base. Tail is bicolored, pure white below and dusky on top. Ventrally white, as are the backs of the feet.
Distribution: Central S Qinghai to C Xizang. Endemic.
Natural History: Believed to be similar to that of *C. kamensis.*
Comments: Included in *kamenis* in many treatments.
Conservation Status: China RL—DD.
References: Thomas and Hinton (1922).

Genus *Cricetus* (monotypic)

原仓鼠属 Yuancangshu Shu

Black-Bellied Hamster

PLATE 20

Cricetus cricetus (Linnaeus, 1758) MAP 160
原仓鼠 Yuan Cangshu

Distinctive Characteristics: HB 200–300; T 28–60; HF 28–36; E 22–32; GLS 44–52; Wt 290–425 g. Largest species in the Cricetinae; form stout, tail short, equal to or longer than hind foot; foot palms haired posteriorly and naked anteriorly; cheek pouch present; eight mammae. Dorsal pelage brown, ventral pelage uniform black; head and sides of body with three or four conspicuous light spots. Four pairs of mammae. Skull robust with well-developed supraorbital ridge and parietal ridge, interparietal very reduced, occipital plane slants obliquely to rear; rostrum very broad, cranium narrow; rostral breadth more than half breadth of cranium; interorbital region very narrow, zygomatic arch noticeably expanded outward; zygomatic plate broad, jugal bone very short and minute; incisors broad and long; first, second, and third molars gradually decreasing in size, with three, two, and two pairs of cusps, respectively. 2N = 22.
Distribution: N Xinjiang; extending to Russia, Kazakhstan, and across Europe to Belgium. Chinese subspecies: *C. c. fuscidorsis* Argyropulo, 1932.
Natural History: Lives in dry grassland to forest meadow habitats, generally at low elevation. Constructs an elaborate burrow system up to 2 m in depth, containing multiple entrances (5–10) and chambers for nesting and food storage (in summer these are 30–60 cm deep). Hibernates; nocturnal or crepuscular. Diet consists of seeds and tubers; food caches may be extensive, with a total weight of up to 65 kg. Large litters of 3–15 are born following a 20-day gestation; multiple litters can be produced each year beginning in spring. Young may mature and breed in their summer of birth.

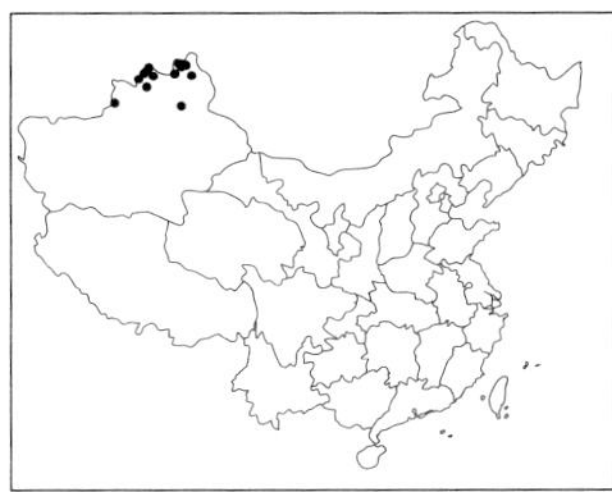

MAP 160. BLACK-BELLIED HAMSTER, *Cricetus cricetus*

Conservation Status: China RL—NT; although it nearly met the criteria for VU A2d + 3d.

Genus *Phodopus*—Dwarf Hamsters

毛足鼠属 Maozushu Shu—毛足鼠 Maozushu

Form short, feet broad and short; entire palm and lower side of toes densely covered with white hairs, no foot pads visible (fig. 8); tail very short, not longer than hind foot; eight mammae; with large internal cheek pouches; skull normal, convex above, interorbital region broad, without supraorbital ridge, cranium not narrow, auditory bullae low and small; zygomatic plate very narrow; structure of molars normal; first, second, and third upper molars, respectively, with three, two, and two pairs of cusps, as also with lower molars. Two of the three species of *Phodopus* occur in China.

Key to the Chinese Species of *Phodopus*

1.a. Dorsum with a thin, black mid-dorsal stripe, different colors of dorsal and ventral pelage intergrade, forming a wavelike pattern on the sides of the body; 2N = 28 *Phodopus campbelli*

b. Dorsum lacks black mid-dorsal stripe, different colors of dorsal and ventral pelage do not intergrade but form sharp border on sides of body; 2N = 34 *Phodopus roborovskii*

Campbell's Hamster

PLATE 20
MAP 161

Phodopus campbelli (Thomas, 1905)
坎氏毛足鼠 Kanshi Maozushu

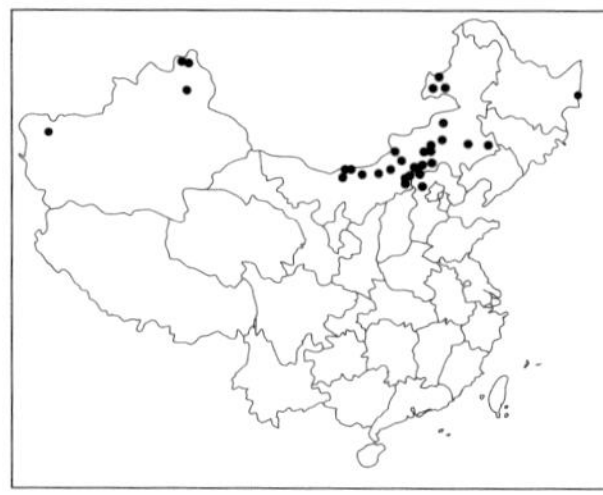

MAP 161. CAMPBELL'S HAMSTER, *Phodopus campbelli*

Distinctive Characteristics: HB 76–105; T 4–14; HF 12–18; E 13–15; GLS 22–26; Wt 23 g. Size small, dorsal pelage dark gray tinged with pale brown, with a black mid-dorsal stripe from the nape of the neck to the base of the tail; ventral pelage gray at base, white at tip; colors on the sides intergrade, yielding a wavelike pattern on the lateral pelage. Tail extremely short; palms covered with white hairs. Skull short and rounded; posterior extremity of incisive foramina reach the anterior edges of first molars, its length more than length of upper molar dentition; auditory bullae small. 2N = 28.
Distribution: Across N China (Heilongjiang, Nei Mongol, Xinjiang); extending to Russia (Transbaikalia), Mongolia, Kazakhstan.
Natural History: Occurs in grasslands, semidesert, and desert; more likely to be found living on soils with a firmer substrate than *P. roborovskii*. Burrows (4–6 vertical entrances) lead to a nest chamber as deep as 1 m (but normally shallower) and food caches of seeds. May occupy burrows of *Meriones*, rather than digging their own. Diet primarily seeds, but known to consume insects. Nocturnal or crepuscular; do not hibernate. Breeds from April to October, producing three or four litters of four to eight young following a 20–22 day gestation period. Juveniles may become reproductively active in their first year.
Comments: Often included in *P. sungorus*.
Conservation Status: China RL—LC.
References: Ross (1995).

Desert Hamster

PLATE 20
MAP 162

Phodopus roborovskii (Satunin, 1903)
小毛足鼠 Xiao Maozushu

Distinctive Characteristics: HB 61–102; T 6–11; HF 9–12; E 10–13; GLS 19–23; Wt 10–20 g. Slightly smaller than *Phodopus campbelli*; HB length generally < 90 mm. Dorsal pelage light sandy brown, dark gray at base; venter sides and feet including entire palms covered with wholly white hairs; the different colors of dorsal and ventral pelage not intergrading, but form a distinct line along the sides. Rostral portion of skull short, cranium convex; incisive foramina short, shorter than length of upper dentition, and terminating before first molar; auditory bullae very low and small; molar cusps less developed than *P. campbelli*, crown of teeth smaller.
Distribution: Across N China; extending to Mongolia, Russia (Tuva), and Kazakhstan.

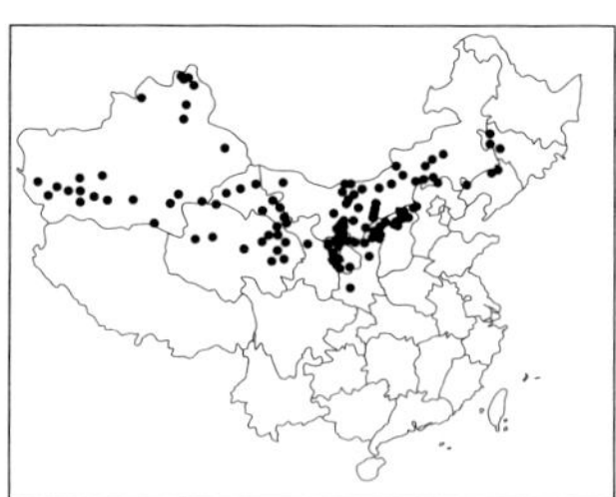

MAP 162. DESERT HAMSTER, *Phodopus roborovskii*

Natural History: Occurs in sandy deserts and grasslands; avoids areas with clay soil or those overgrown with shrubby vegetation. Burrows with a single opening (4 cm diameter) are dug between sand dunes or at their edge. Burrows extend 90 cm deep and contain a single nest and two or three food caches. Eats seeds (often filling their cheek pouches); also known to consume green vegetation and insects. Nocturnal; does not hibernate. Reproduces from March to September (or even later). Up to four litters ranging from three to nine young are born following a 20-day gestation. Young of the year may become reproductively active.
Comments: Includes *bedfordiae* (Thomas, 1908).
Conservation Status: China RL—LC.
References: Ross (1994).

Genus *Tscherskia* (monotypic)

大仓鼠属 Dacangshu Shu

Greater Long-Tailed Hamster

PLATE 20
MAP 163

Tscherskia triton (de Winton, 1899)

大仓鼠 Da Cangshu

Distinctive Characteristics: HB 142–220; T 69–106; HF 20–25; E 17–24; GLS 36–42; Wt 92–241 g. Larger than largest species of *Cricetulus*; tail long, about half HB length. Dorsal pelage pale brownish gray; ventral pelage gray at base, white at tip. Tail dark brown to tip; long hare at the base only. Skull robust and not arched, bony ridge well developed, nasals very narrow, with evident supraorbital, parietal and occipital ridges; roots of upper incisors extending backward along alveolus merging into a convex auditory bulla; incisive foramina do not reach anterior margin of first upper molar; interpterygoid foramen very deep, its anterior end extends to the posterior margin of the third upper molar; auditory bullae round; occipital condyle clearly protruding behind occipital plane. 2N = 28.

Distribution: C to NE China; extending to E Russia, Korea. Five subspecies in China: (1) *T. t. collinus* (Allen, 1925); Shaanxi, Shanxi; (2) *T. t. fuscipes* (Allen, 1925); Heilongjiang, Jilin, Liaoning, Nei Mongol; (3) *T. t. incanus* (Thomas, 1908); Shaanxi, Shanxi; (4) *T. t. ningshaanensis* Song, 1985; S Shaanxi; (5) *T. t. triton* (de Winton, 1899); Hebei, Beijing, Shandong, Jiangsu, Henan, Shanxi, Shaanxi, Anhui, Zhejiang.

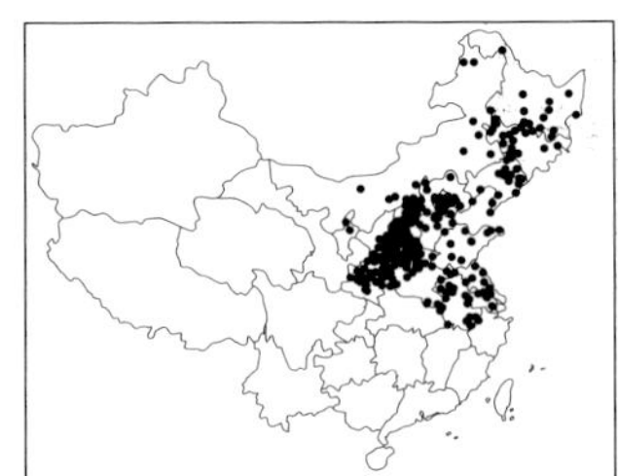

MAP 163. GREATER LONG-TAILED HAMSTER, *Tscherskia triton*

Natural History: Generally found in open xeric areas where it constructs deep vertical burrows in which it caches vast quanties of seed in a large storage chamber. Occasionally known to harvest leaves. Primarily nocturnal, although can be seen active during the day. Life expectancy about one year (tends to waste away following breeding). Reproductive season May–August, but extending to September in some areas. Breed two or three times and generally produce litters of 8–10 young.

Comments: Commonly included in *Cricetulus*, but its morphology is sufficiently distinctive to warrant independent status. The form *ningshaanensis* has been included with *Cansumys canus*.

Conservation Status: Has been considered an agricultural pest. China RL–LC.

References: Wang and Xu (1992); Zhang et al. (1997); Zhu and Qin (1991).

Family Muridae—Old World Rats and Mice

鼠科 Shu Ke—鼠类 Shulei

Andrew T. Smith and Darrin Lunde

The Muridae, with 730 species, is the largest family of mammals. Murids lack longitudinal enamel crests on their molars, a characteristic that defines the Cricetidae. Molecular evidence also separates the Muridae from its sister taxon within the Muroidea, the Cricetidae, and the date of divergence has been established at about 24 mya (Michaux et al. 2001; Steppan et al. 2004). Morphological and molecular data clearly differentiate the Muridae into five subfamilies, two of which occur in China (Michaux et al. 2001; Musser and Carleton 2005; Steppan et al. 2004).

Subfamily Gerbillinae—Gerbils

沙鼠亚科 Shashu Yake—沙鼠 Shashu

Andrew T. Smith and Robert S. Hoffmann

Form ratlike, but tending toward saltatorial habits and less obviously specialized than jerboas; hind foot has slight tendency toward elongation, tail very long, hair cover dense, auditory bullae of skull well developed; cranium very wide, rostrum narrow; nasals extend intero-anteriorly above incisors; zygomatic plate protrudes forward; zygomatic arch not evidently expanded outward; two pairs of palatine foramina, behind the anterior pair of the larger one there is a pair of minute ones between tooth rows; coronoid process of mandible very short and small; angular process

Key to the Chinese Subfamilies of Muridae

1.a. Lacrimal enlarged and forming a ledge over the anterior margin of the orbit; mesopterygoid fossa narrowly V-shaped; mandible perforated by foramen high on ascending ramus; angular process of mandible deflected laterally — Gerbillinae

b. Lacrimal not enlarged to form a margin over the orbit; mesopterygoid fossa broadly U-shaped; mandible not perforated by foramina; angluar process of mandible not deflected laterally — Murinae

Key to the Chinese Genera of Gerbillinae

1.a. Labial surface of upper incisors with two small longitudinal grooves — *Rhombomys*
b. Labial surface of upper incisors with a single small longitudinal groove — 2
2.a. Ears very short, about a third the length of hind foot with claws; rostral portion of skull short, jugal bone diverge very widely; cranium well developed, so that skull triangular — *Brachiones*
b. Ears normal, about half length of hind foot with claws; skull not triangular; rostral portion of skull reduced, jugal bone not widely spreading — *Meriones*

narrow; condylar process tall and large. Labial surface of upper incisors with longitudinal grooves; surface of tooth crown smooth without protuberant cusps; rather transverse oval or lozenge dentine rings are separated by interoexternal notch; first upper molar with three rings, second with two rings, third small with one or two rings.

Habits typically sand-dwelling and burrowing. Occurs in the Palaearctic realm, including central and western Asia and Africa. The Gerbillinae represents a well established clade (Carleton and Musser 1984; Pavlinov et al. 1990) that diverged from its sister taxa within the Muridae (Murinae, Deomyinae) in the early Miocene (Michaux et al. 2001; Steppan et al. 2004). Fossil gerbils date back to the late Miocene (Wessels 1998). Of 16 genera currently known, 3 are found in China, mainly occurring in NW and N China. All Chinese species are in the tribe Gerbillini, subtribe Rhombomyina (Musser and Carleton 2005). Pavlinov et al. (1990) comprehensively reviewed all aspects of the biology of the Gerbillinae.

Genus *Brachiones* (monotypic)

短耳沙鼠属 Duan'ershashu Shu

Przewalski's Gerbil

PLATE 22
MAP 164

Brachiones przewalskii (Büchner, 1889)
短耳沙鼠 Duan'er Shashu

Distinctive Characteristics: HB 67–103; T 56–78; HF 22–24; E 6–9; GLS 24–29; Wt 12–42 g. Size small, ears short, body hairs short; forelimbs with well-developed claws, slightly adapted to subterranean living habits; hind soles completely covered with hairs. Dorsal pelage sandy or light grayish; ventral pelage wholly white. Tail lightly colored and pointed. Skull short and broad, slightly triangular; rostrum short, nasal short and narrow; frontal broad, interorbital region not obviously narrowed; palatine foramina short, especially the posterior pair; posterior portion of cranium broad, auditory bullae well developed; upper incisor extending straight, not curved backward; labial surface with a longitudinal groove.

Distribution: Arid lands of NW China. Endemic. Three subspecies: (1) *B. p. arenicolor* (Miller, 1900); Xinjiang (W Tarim Basin); (2) *B. p. callichrous* Heptner, 1934; Nei Mongol; (3) *B. p. przewalskii* (Büchner, 1889); Xinjiang, Gansu.

Natural History: Prefers semipermanent sand dunes overgrown with shrubs or close to wooded areas. Burrow system is quite simple compared with that of most gerbils; the opening is about 4.5 cm in diameter, and the tunnels run no deeper than 60 cm. They occur at characteristically lower density than other gerbils.

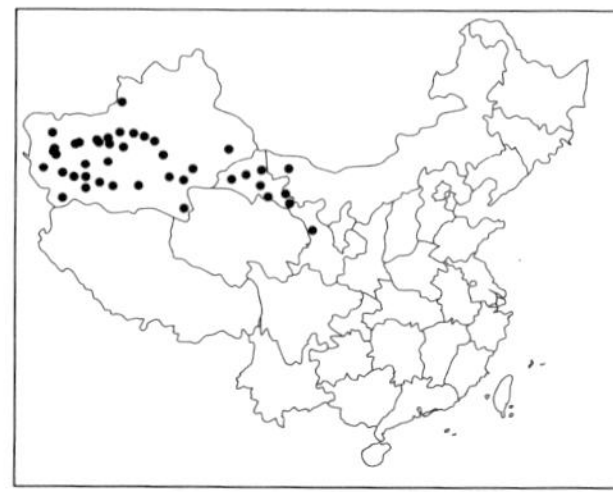

MAP 164. PRZEWALSKI'S GERBIL, *Brachiones przewalskii*

Comments: Closely related to *Meriones*–in fact, appears like a specialized relative of *Meriones*.

Conservation Status: China RL–LC.

Genus *Meriones*—Gerbils

沙鼠属 Shashu Shu—沙鼠 Shashu

Form ratlike, ears normal or somewhat enlarged; tail long, near HB length, covered with longer hairs; hind limbs and hind feet slightly elongate, soles mostly covered with hairs, naked near ankles; claws on forefeet normal or somewhat elongate. Posterior portion of skull enlarged, auditory bullae generally well developed, but small in some species; anterior portion of zygomatic arch broad; weak or robust supraorbital ridge present; anterior palatine foramina long, posterior palatine foramina short or absent. Labial surface of upper incisors with a small longitudinal groove; crowns of upper molars high, without protruding cusps, instead lozenge dentine rings separated by intero-external notch; first, second, and third molars, respectively, with three, two and one dentine rings; third molar sometimes with slight notch. The 17 species of *Meriones* occur in Central and SW Asia and N Africa; five species live in China.

Key to the Chinese Species of *Meriones*

1.a. Soles of hind feet brown with long dark spots, size large, auditory bullae small, average < 27% of GLS — *Meriones tamariscinus*
b. Soles of hind feet grayish white or yellowish white, no long dark spots; size small, auditory bullae large, average not < 30% of GLS — 2
2.a. Soles of hind feet with naked portion near hind ankles; GLS > 36 mm — 3
b. Soles of hind feet without naked portion; GLS generally < 36 mm — 4
3.a. Tail blackish brown above, pale brown below, tail length ≥ HB length — *Meriones libycus*
b. Tail pale brown both above and below, tail length clearly < HB length — *Meriones chengi*
4.a. Base of ventral pelage gray, claws grayish black; auditory bullae length about 31% of GLS — *Meriones unguiculatus*
b. Base of ventral pelage white, claws white or buffy; auditory bullae length 33% of GLS or larger — *Meriones meridianus*

Cheng's Gerbil

Meriones chengi Wang, 1964 MAP 165
郑氏沙鼠 Zhengshi Shashu

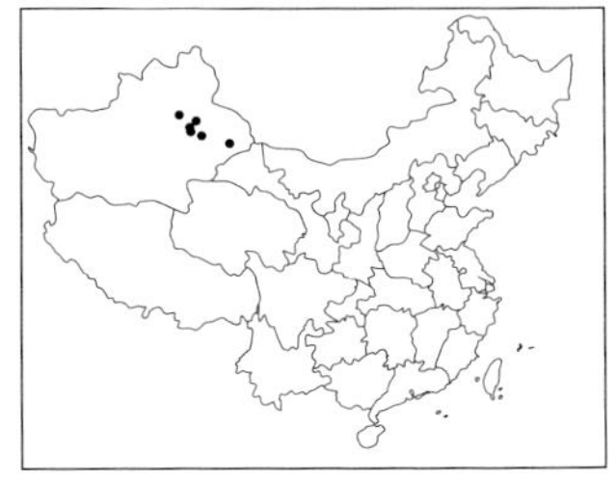

MAP 165. CHENG'S GERBIL, *Meriones chengi*

Distinctive Characteristics: HB 131–150; T 88–117; HF 31–34; E 17; GLS 36–38. Size medium, somewhat larger than *Meriones meridianus*, but smaller than *M. libycus*. Soles covered with hairs, with a narrow naked stripe near ankles; hind feet with black claws; tail length about 3/4 of HB length; tail pale brown both above and below and terminally tufted; dorsal pelage dark brown, darker than in *M. meridianus*, grayish black at base; ventral pelage wholly white, with light gray base of hairs at middle. Skull somewhat larger than that of *M. meridianus*, frontal and interorbital region broad; meatus especially well developed, its length 37% of GLS; supraorbital ridge conspicuous.
Distribution: E Xinjiang (Turpan Basin). Endemic.
Natural History: Inhabits mountainous regions and semidesert or xeric grasslands, normally above 1,000 m elevation. A highly social species, they construct many burrows characteristically at the base of shrubs.
Comments: Thought to be most closely related to *M. meridianus*.
Conservation Status: China RL—LC. IUCN RL—CR C2b ver. 2.3 (1994).

Libyan Gerbil

Meriones libycus Lichtenstein, 1823 PLATE 22 MAP 166
红尾沙鼠 Hongwei Shashu

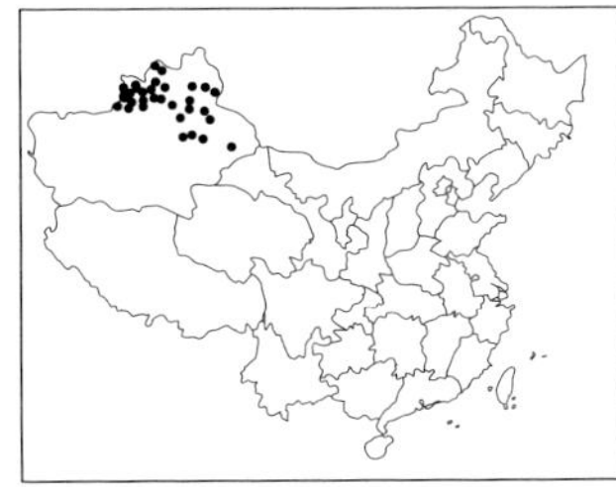

MAP 166. LIBYAN GERBIL, *Meriones libycus*

Distinctive Characteristics: HB 100–180; T 108–180; HF 31–38; E 11–22; GLS 36–42; Wt 56–155 g. Tail as long as HB; hind soles only partly covered with hairs, so with naked area; claws dark; dorsal pelage grayish brown, darker than in *Meriones meridianus*; ventral pelage white at tip, gray at base; tail with pale brown hairs, but nutbrown or black at about 1/3 portion near extremity. Supraorbital ridge well developed, extending laterally; auditory bullae large, its length 33–35% of GLS; antero-external side of auditory meatus inflated into an evident small tympanic bulla.
Distribution: NW China; extending west to Middle East (Saudi Arabia, Jordan, Iraq, Syria, Iran, Afghanistan) and to N Africa (Egypt). Two subspecies in China: (1) *M. l. aquilo* Thomas, 1912; N Xinjiang; (2) *M. l. turfanensis* (Satunin, 1903); Xinjiang (Tarim Basin).
Natural History: Occupies desert habitat, generally in areas with stabilized dunes. Becomes most abundant in unflooded river plains. Frequently occupies the burrows of *Rhombomys* in areas of sympatry. Where they construct their own burrows, these are less complicated than those of *Rhombomys*, while being more complicated than those of most other gerbils. Between 10 and 60 burrow entrances may characterize a territory. Burrows consist of two layers: the upper one utilized for food storage, and

the deeper one (1–1.5 m below the surface) holds the nest chamber. This species often lives socially in burrow systems, with smaller dispersed groups occurring during summer, but larger groups (25–30 individuals) forming in winter. Libyan Gerbils are highly mobile, frequently changing burrows or even migrating should forage conditions deteriorate. They are usually diurnal but can be seen active at any time of day or night. Diet consists primarily of seeds, and burrow caches may weigh up to 10 kg. Reproductively active year-round, except during the hottest summer months. Multiple litters of five to six young are produced each year.
Comments: In much of the literature, *erythrearus* a synonym.
Conservation Status: China RL—LC.
References: Naumov and Lobachev (1975).

Mid-Day Gerbil

PLATE 22
MAP 167

Meriones meridianus (Pallas, 1773)
子午沙鼠 Ziwu Shashu

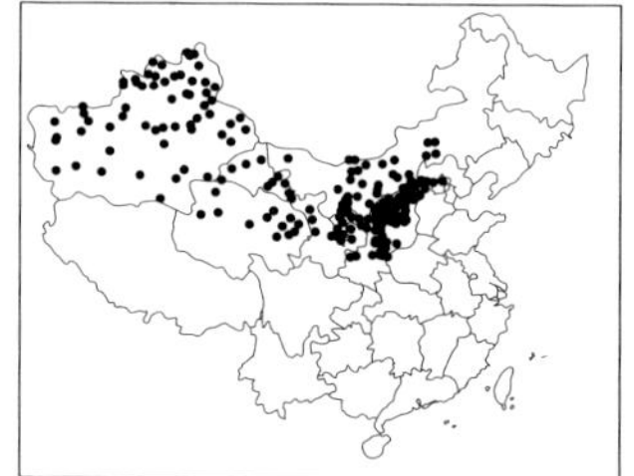
MAP 167. MID-DAY GERBIL, *Meriones meridianus*

Distinctive Characteristics: HB 95–134; T 84–120; HF 25–34; E 10–19; GLS 31–36; Wt 30–60 g. Medium in size; tail length similar to HB length; hind feet covered with dense hairs, soles with no naked portion, claws white; dorsal pelage light grayish yellow, drab or dark brown, grayish black at base; ventral pelage wholly white, with pale brown narrow stripe at chest; tail dark pale brown to bright ochraceous above, slightly lighter below. Auditory bullae of skull large, its length about 33% or more of GLS; antero-external side of meatus with small convex tympanic bullae; palatal foramina long.
Distribution: N C China to NW China; extending to Mongolia, Afghanistan, Iran, and the Caucasus region. Seven subspecies in China: (1) *M. m. buechneri* Thomas, 1909; Xinjiang (Dzungarian Basin); (2) *M. m. cryptorhinus* (Blanford, 1875); Xinjiang (Tarim Basin); (3) *M. m. jei* Wang, 1964; Xinjiang (Turpan Basin); (4) *M. m. lepturus* (Büchner, 1889); Xinjiang (Tarim Basin); (5) *M. m. muleiensis* Wang, 1981; Xinjiang (Dzungarian Basin); (6) *M. m. penicilliger* (Heptner, 1933); W Xinjiang; (7) *M. m. psammophilus* (Milne-Edwards, 1871); Gansu, Qinghai, N Shanxi, N Shaanxi, NW Hebei, Nei Mongol, Ningxia, E Xinjiang.
Natural History: The Mid-day Gerbil is the most desert-adapted of all gerbils. It occupies sandy terrain with different degrees of soil stabilization, preferring brushy habitats characterized by thorn scrub under which it constructs its burrows. Primarily nocturnal (in contrast with *M. unguiculatus*); it is only active during the day in winter. It is unclear how it was given the common name Mid-day Gerbil. Colonial. Burrows are dug under roots of plants and may be simple to fairly complicated. Winter burrows extend to a depth of 2 m or more, and their length ranges up to 4 m. Diet consists mainly of seeds and fruits of desert plants, although it is also known to consume leafy vegetation. Stores are small, usually less than 800 g. Reproduction is spread out over the year, although the intensity drops off during summer and during November and December. Litter size ranges from 1 to 12, averaging about 6 young.
Conservation Status: China RL—LC.
References: Naumov and Lobachev (1975); Song and Liu (1984).

Tamarisk Gerbil

PLATE 22
MAP 168

Meriones tamariscinus (Pallas, 1773)
柽柳沙鼠 Chengliu Shashu

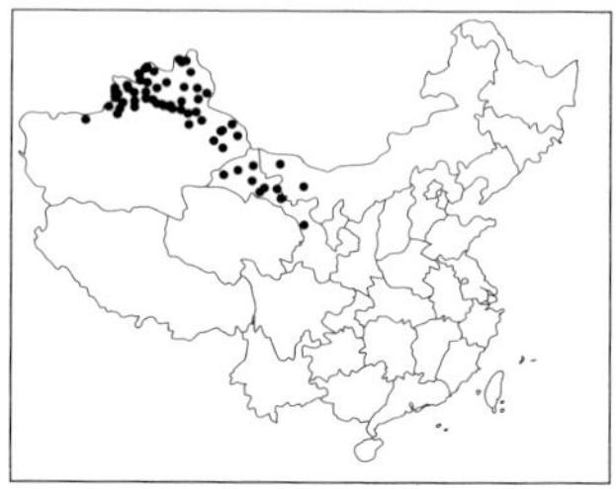
MAP 168. TAMARISK GERBIL, *Meriones tamariscinus*

Distinctive Characteristics: HB 135–190; T 115–150; HF 32–39; E 15–21; GLS 36–44; Wt 60–180 g. Size large; dorsal pelage rusty brown, ventral pelage wholly white; tail sharply bicolored, dark brown above, white below; soles of hind feet with long dark brown spots; soles of hind feet entirely covered with hairs; claws nearly white. GLS longer than in *Meriones meridianus*; auditory bullae of skull smaller than that of other gerbils, its length averaging 27% of GLS; antero-external side of meatus without small convex tympanic bullae; labial surface of upper incisor with a longitudinal groove.
Distribution: NW China; extending into Kazakhstan and across Central Asia to N Caucasus. Two subspecies in China: (1) *M. t. jaxartensis* (Ognev and Heptner, 1928); N Xinjiang; (2) *M. t. satschouensis* (Satunin, 1903); W Gansu, NW Nei Mongol, Xinjiang.
Natural History: Occupies desert and semidesert where its preferred habitat is grass and bush-covered sandy areas. Highest densities are in dry river courses, but it can also occupy saline marshes, areas avoided by other gerbils. Maximum population densities are less than those of other gerbils, normally ranging from 20 to 30 per ha. Burrows are dug under tree roots and bushes and normally consist of only two to four entrances. Burrows can extend up to 6 m in length. Nests of plant stems and bird feathers are constructed at depths of 50 cm (summer) to 250 cm

(winter). Tamarisk Gerbils are primarily nocturnal. They are wide ranging and have been known to move up to 1.5 km. Their diet consists of green parts of plants, although they also eat fruits, insects, and even small rodents. Their food caches may weigh up to 4.5 kg. Reproduction can occur year-round, although reproductive activity is diminished in winter. Litter size ranges from one to eight (usually four or five).

Conservation Status: China RL—LC.

References: Naumov and Lobachev (1975).

Mongolian Gerbil

PLATE 22

Meriones unguiculatus

(Milne-Edwards, 1867)

MAP 169

长爪沙鼠 Changzhua Shashu

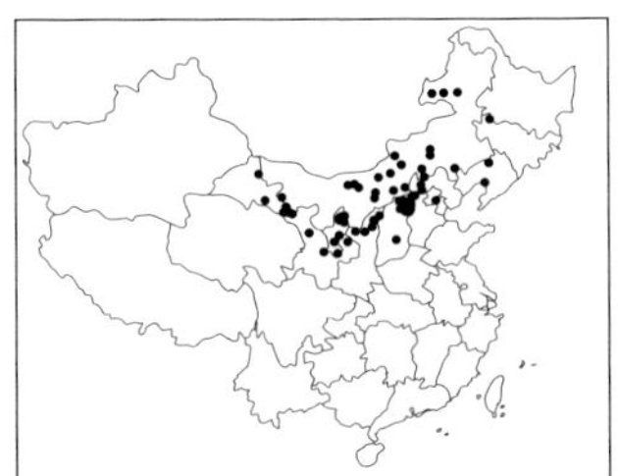

MAP 169. MONGOLIAN GERBIL, *Meriones unguiculatus*

Distinctive Characteristics: HB 97–132; T 85–106; HF 24–32; E 13–15; GLS 30–36. Size slightly smaller than size of other gerbils; tail shorter (70–90%) than HB. Soles of hind feet entirely covered with hairs, claws grayish black; ear pinnae exposed; dorsal pelage grayish brown, ventral pelage gray at base, white at tip, so presents dull white appearance, different from other species in China; tail sharply bicolored, dark grayish brown above, pale-brown below, tail extremity with black tufts of hairs. Auditory bullae, while large, is smaller than in *Meriones meridianus*, about 31% of GLS; antero-external side of meatus without small tympanic bullae; upper incisors with a conspicuous longitudinal grove. 2N = 44.

Distribution: Central N China (Nei Mongol, Liaoning, Hebei, N Shanxi, N Shaanxi, E Gansu, Ningxia); extends into Mongolia and Russia (Transbaikalia). Only the nominate subspecies occurs in China.

Natural History: Lives in semidesert, sandy steppe, or grassland habitat; not found in mountainous terrain. Can occur in areas with compact soils. Active during both day and night, although primarily diurnal during winter. Density is quite variable over its range, but it can occur at extremely high densities under some conditions. Colonial, its normal social unit is the family group. Families live together and mutually defend their burrow system, and all members contribute to gathering food stores (which can weigh as much as 20 kg). Burrow structure is not complicated. Burrows can extend 5–6 m in length and have nest chambers situated at 45 cm in depth (summer) or 150 cm in depth (winter). Diet consists of seeds and greens, but also consumes fruits of desert plants. Peak reproduction extends from February until September, LS 2–11 (average about 6).

Conservation Status: China RL—LC.

References: Ågren et al. (1989a; 1989b); Gulotta (1971); Naumov and Lobachev (1975); Qin (1984).

Genus *Rhombomys* (monotypic)

大沙鼠属 Dashashu Shu

Great Gerbil

PLATE 22

Rhombomys opimus (Lichtenstein, 1823)

MAP 170

大沙鼠 Da Shashu

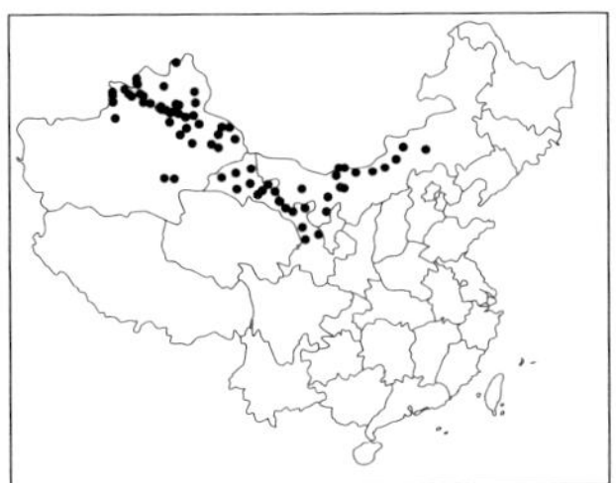

MAP 170. GREAT GERBIL, *Rhombomys opimus*

Distinctive Characteristics: HB 150–185; T 130–160; HF 36–47; E 12–19; GLS 39–45; Wt 169–275 g. Size large, tail length near or somewhat less than HB length. Dorsal pelage ochraceous tinged with light grayish—color most vivid over the rump and lighter over the shoulders; ventral pelage dull white; chin white; tail rusty brown both above and below, sprinkled with black long hairs near extremity; ears well furred. Skull evidently more robust than that of *Meriones;* rostrum stout, auditory bullae not excessively inflated; supraorbital ridge evident posteriorly, forming a temporal ridge, turned laterally at interparietal; anterior palatine foramina short, not reaching anterior edge of first molar, posterior palatine foramina minute or absent. Labial surface of upper incisor with two longitudinal grooves, the outer one deeper, the inner one more shallow; first molar with three transverse rows of oval dentine rings; second molar with two rings; last molar distinctly bilobed. 2N = 40.

Distribution: NW China; extending to Mongolia, Kazakhstan, Afghanistan, Iran, and Pakistan. Four subspecies in China: (1) *R. o. giganteus* (Büchner, 1889); Xinjiang; (2) *R. o. nigrescens* (Satunin, 1903); Nei Mongol, Gansu, Ningxia; (3) *R. o. opimus* (Lichtenstein, 1823); N Xinjiang (Dzungarian Basin); (4) *R. o. pevzovi* Heptner, 1939; W Gansu, Nei Mongol, SE Xinjiang.

Natural History: Occupies desert to semidesert habitat and is most successful in dry river beds dominated by shrubby vegetation. Diurnal; most active at dawn. Constructs large entrance holes to a very elaborate burrow system that consists of long deep tunnels, nest and food storage chambers. In winter the nest chambers may be as deep as 2.5 m. The continuous occupancy of these burrows, coupled

with the ongoing removal of soil, yields large depressions up to a meter deep and many meters in diameter. Feeds on succulent bushes (such as *Salsola*). Vegetation is often stored underground, but occasionally haypiles are constructed on the surface that range in size from 2 to 3 m in diameter and up to 1 m in height. Foraging can radically alter the local vegetative landscape, and in some situations it is considered a pest and controlled. These animals live in family groups, and multiple families (up to three) may occupy a single burrow system, although these families may remain behaviorally intolerant of each other. A family may also occupy multiple burrow systems. When predators are sighted, repetitive alarm calls are uttered coupled with foot-drumming. Great Gerbils are highly mobile, and they may migrate distances of up to 10 km. Reproduction is possible year-round, although the intensity diminishes in summer. Litter size ranges from 1 to 14 (usually 4–7).
Conservation Status: China RL—LC.
References: Naumov and Lobachev (1975); Zhou et al. (2000).

Subfamily Murinae—Murine Rodents

鼠亚科 Shu Yake—鼠类 Shulei

Darrin Lunde

A subfamily of 126 genera and 561 species confined to the Old World (excepting introductions), where they range throughout much of Europe, Africa, Asia, and Australia. Murine rodents, or typical rats and mice, are characterized by a suite of external, cranial, postcranial, dental, reproductive, and arterial characteristics as discussed in Carleton and Musser (1984) and Musser and Carleton (2005); however, it is a series of derived dental characteristics that is most important in defining the subfamily. Specifically, molar cusps t1 and t4 are present on the lingual border of M1 forming two chevron-shaped lamina; both upper and lower molars lack longitudinal enamel crests between lamina; and cusps on the lower molars are positioned opposite one another (Musser and Carleton 2005) (see fig. 4). Seventeen genera occur in China.

Genus *Apodemus*—Field Mice

姬鼠属 Jishu Shu—姬鼠 Jishu

Small, soft-furred mice of open grassy fields, croplands, woods, and forest edges. Dorsal pelage usually yellowish brown to reddish brown. One species has a mid-dorsal stripe. Ventral pelage white or grayish white. Tail more or less equal to or slightly shorter than HB length and bicolored dark brown above and pale below. Dorsal surfaces of hands and feet pale brownish white. Skull rather generalized. A posterio-internal cusp (t7) is retained on the first and second upper molars—a trait shared in common with *Micromys* and *Vandeleuria*. The genus is Palaearctic in distribution and contains 21 species, of which 8 occur in China. These can be divided into two species groups following Musser et al. (1996): the *Apodemus* group (*agrarius, chevrieri, peninsulae, latronum, draco, semotus*); and the *Sylvaemus* group (*uralensis, pallipes*). One of the principal morphological differences distinguishing these two groups is that members of the first exhibit prominent supraorbital ridges whereas in members of the second the supraorbital region is smoothly rounded. Females usually have four pairs of mammae, but one species occurring in China (*A. latronum*) has only three pairs.

Striped Field Mouse

Apodemus agrarius (Pallas, 1771) PLATE 13 MAP 171
黑线姬鼠 Heixian Jishu

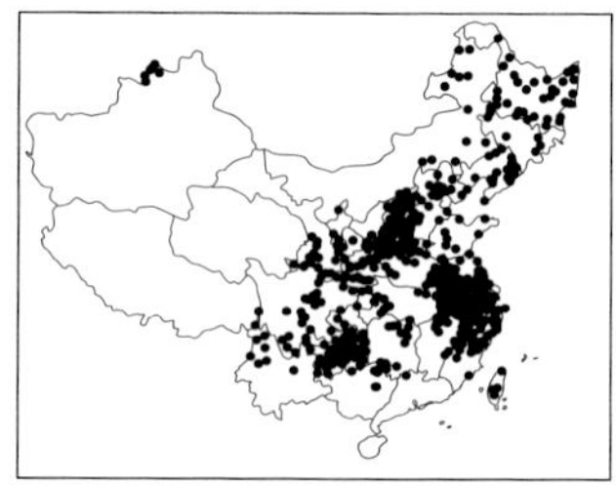

MAP 171. STRIPED FIELD MOUSE, *Apodemus agrarius*

Distinctive Characteristics: HB 80–113; T 72–115; HF 19–22; E 12–15; GLS 24–28; Wt 29–38 g. Dorsal pelage yellowish brown to pale reddish brown and often with a thin blackish brown mid-dorsal stripe, but this is less distinct among individuals from the southern part of the range and may be little more than a faint mid-dorsal darkening; pelage becoming somewhat brighter yellow brown along the sides. Ventral pelage grayish white and fairly well demarcated from the dorsal pelage but not forming a sharp line. Tail approximately equal to or shorter than HB length, dark brown above, paler below. Ears not differing in color from the surrounding parts of head and shoulders. Females with four pairs of mammae (two pectoral pairs, two abdominal pairs). Skull with supraorbital ridges extending along the lateral margins of frontals and onto the parietals. First upper molar often with two lingual roots; second upper molar usually lacks an anterio-external cusp (t3) or tiny if present; third upper molar lacks cusp t8 (or coalesced with cusp t5) and appears to have only two lingual lobes.
Distribution: W Yunnan to N Heilongjiang and Taiwan, with a disjunctive population in NW Xinjiang; extending into Siberia and Korea. The population in Xinjiang is continuous with European populations (Musser and Carleton 2005). Wang (2003) recognized four subspecies in China: (1) *A. a. agrarius* (Pallas, 1771); NW China (Xinjiang); (2) *A. a. insulaemus* Tokuda, 1941; Taiwan; (3) *A. a. mantchuricus* (Thomas, 1898); NE China; (4) *A. a. ningpoensis* (Swinhoe, 1870); S China.

Key to the Chinese Genera of Murinae

1.a.	First toe of hind foot semi-opposable and with a flattened nail instead of a claw	2
b.	First toe of hind foot not opposable and with a claw	6
2.a.	Fifth finger and fifth toe with a flattened nail instead of a claw	*Vandeleuria*
b.	Fifth finger and fifth toe each with a claw	3
3.a.	HF > 25, GLS > 35	*Chiromyscus*
b.	HF < 25, GLS < 35	4
4.a.	Tail approximately twice the length of HB; interorbital region of skull with longitudinal depression	*Vernaya*
b.	Tail longer than HB but considerably less than twice so, skull lacks depression in interorbital region	5
5.a.	HF ≥ 22, GLS > 30; first molars with three rows of three almost perfectly symmetrical teeth	*Hapalomys*
b.	HF ≤ 22, GLS < 30; cusps of first molars not symmetrically aligned	*Chiropodomys*
6.a.	Small mouselike species, HF < 30, GLS < 30	7
b.	Large ratlike species, HF usually > 30, GLS usually > 30	9
7.a.	Size very small (HF ≤ 16, GLS < 20), tail prehensile	*Micromys*
b.	Size generally larger, tail not prehensile	8
8.a.	First upper molar more than half the length of the molar toothrow and with the posterio-lingual cusp (t7) absent	*Mus*
b.	First upper molar not exceeding half the length of the molar toothrow and with the posterio-lingual cusp (t7) present	*Apodemus*
9.a.	Incisors white or pale yellow	10
b.	Incisors deep yellow or orange	11
10.a.	Lower incisors narrower than upper incisors	*Berylmys*
b.	Lower incisors broader than upper incisors	*Nesokia*
11.a.	Molars high crowned; zygomatic plate of skull with a jutting anterior spine and deeply concave anterior margin	*Hadromys*
b.	Molars not especially high crowned, zygomatic plate of skull more or less convex, without a jutting anterior spine and without a deeply concave anterior margin	12
12.a.	Dorsal pelage sharply demarcated from ventral pelage, zygoma attached high on braincase	13
b.	Dorsal pelage gradually blends into ventral pelage, zygoma attached low on braincase	16
13.a.	HB > 250, GLS > 50	13
b.	HB < 250, GLS < 50	15
14.a.	Molar toothrow < 11 mm	*Leopoldamys*
b.	Molar toothrow > 11 mm	*Dacnomys*
15.a.	HF > 40, incisive foramina of skull short	*Maxomys*
b.	HF < 40, incisive foramina of skull long	*Niviventer*
16.a.	Upper incisors broad, > 4 mm across	*Bandicota*
b.	Upper incisors narrower, < 4 mm across	*Rattus*

Natural History: Occurs in agricultural areas, grassy fields, and open woodland habitats, usually below 1,000 m. Eats seeds and some insects. Diurnal. Reproduction occurs between March and November with peaks between April and May and July through October. Litter size ranges from 1 to 10, averaging 5–6.
Comments: Some authors recognize *A. a. pallidior* as a valid subspecies, but we follow Liu et al. (1991; 2002) in regarding this name a synonym of *A. a. mantchuricus*, while still recognizing that there is much more taxonomic work that needs to be done within the group.
Conservation Status: China RL—LC.
References: Liu et al. (1991; 2002); Musser et al. (1996); Suzuki et al. (2003); Wang (1985c); Wang et al. (1994); Yang and Lu (1998); Zhang (1989); Zhao and Lu (1986).

Chevrier's Field Mouse

PLATE 13
Apodemus chevrieri (Milne-Edwards, 1868) MAP 172
高山姬鼠 Gaoshan Jishu

Distinctive Characteristics: HB 88–110; T 83–105; HF 22–25; E 14–16; GLS 26–30. Closely related to and very much resembling *A. agrarius*, but distinguished by larger size and complete absence of a mid-dorsal stripe.

Key to the Chinese Species of *Apodemus*

1.a.	Interorbital region smooth, lacking any trace of supraorbital ridges	2
b.	Interorbital region with supraorbital ridges	3
2.a.	Known from N Xinjiang, GLS < 26 mm	*Apodemus uralensis*
b.	Known from S Xinjiang, GLS > 26 mm	*Apodemus pallipes*
3.a.	First upper molar usually with two lingual roots, second upper molar lacks cusp t3, third upper molar has two internal lobes	4
b.	First upper molar usually with only one lingual root, second upper molar with cusp t3 present, third upper molar with three internal lobes	5
4.a.	Blackish brown mid-dorsal stripe usually present, HF 22 mm or less	*Apodemus agrarius*
b.	Blackish brown mid-dorsal stripe absent, HF 22 mm or more	*Apodemus chevrieri*
5.a.	Ears very dark brown, much darker than the surrounding parts of the head and shoulders	6
b.	Ears not much darker than the surrounding parts of the head and shoulders	*Apodemus peninsulae*
6.a.	Size larger, HF 25–27 mm	*Apodemus latronum*
b.	Size smaller, HF 20–23 mm	7
7.a.	Restricted to the highlands of Taiwan	*Apodemus semotus*
b.	Restricted to mainland China, does not occur on Taiwan	*Apodemus draco*

Distribution: Yunnan, Sichuan, Guizhou, Chongqing, W Hubei, S Shaanxi, S Gansu, and one record from Hunan. Endemic. Wang (2003) notes two unnamed subspecies from Yunnan.
Natural History: Occurs in agricultural areas, grassy fields, and open woodland habitats between 1,800 and 2,300 m. Eats seeds primarily, but also consumes insects. Diurnal.
Comments: Previously regarded as a subspecies of *A. agrarius*.

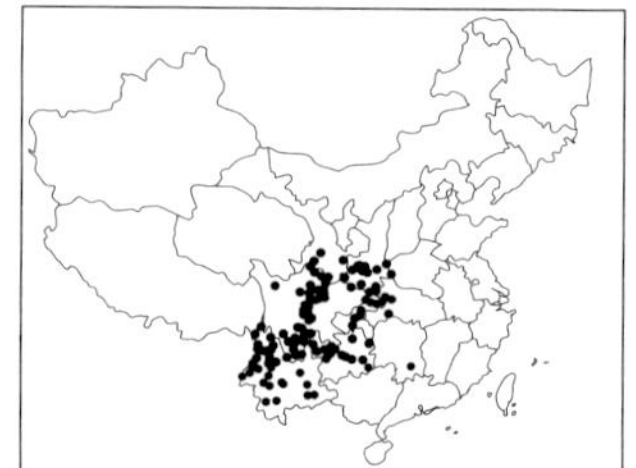

MAP 172. CHEVRIER'S FIELD MOUSE, *Apodemus chevrieri*

Conservation Status: China RL—LC.
References: Liu et al. (2002); Musser et al. (1996); Suzuki et al. (2003); Wang (1985c).

South China Field Mouse

PLATE 13
MAP 173

Apodemus draco (Barrett-Hamilton, 1900)
中华姬鼠 Zhonghua Jishu

Distinctive Characteristics: HB 87–106; T 80–102; HF 20–23; E 15–17; GLS 24–28. Dorsal pelage pale reddish brown and becoming somewhat brighter yellow brown along the sides. Ventral pelage grayish white, fairly well demarcated from dorsal pelage but not forming a sharp line. Tail equal to or slightly longer than HB length, dark brown above, paler below. Ears dark blackish brown, much darker than the surrounding parts of the heads and shoulders. Females with four pairs of mammae (two pectoral pairs, two abdominal pairs). Skull with well-defined supraorbital ridges, but these rarely extend onto the parietals; first upper molar usually with only one lingual root, rarely two; second upper molar usually has an anterio-external cusp; third upper molar clearly exhibits cusp t8 and thus appears to have three lingual lobes.
Distribution: E Xizang and Yunnan extending east to Fujian and northeast to Hebei; extending to Myanmar and NE India. Two subspecies in China: (1) *A. a. draco* (Barrett-Hamilton, 1900); eastern part of range; (2) *A. d. orestes* Thomas, 1911; western part of range.

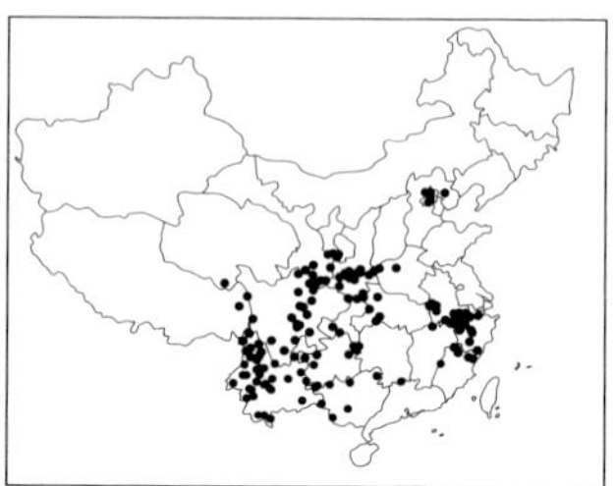

MAP 173. SOUTH CHINA FIELD MOUSE, *Apodemus draco*

Natural History: Inhabits wooded areas up to ca. 3,000 m. Approximate home range for adult males 4,000–5,000 m^2; females 2,200–2,600 m^2.
Comments: The taxon *orestes* was regarded as a distinct species of *Apodemus* by Corbet and Hill (1992) and Jiang and Wang (2000), but Musser and Carleton (2005) and Liu et al. (2002) included it as a synonym of *A. draco*. Dr. Yukibumi Kaneko is currently revising the East Asian *Apodemus* and expects to resolve the status of *orestes*.
Conservation Status: China RL—LC.

References: Chen et al. (1996); Jiang and Wang (2000); Liu et al. (2002); Musser et al. (1996); Musser and Carleton (2005); Suzuki et al. (2003); Wu et al. (1987).

Large-Eared Field Mouse

Apodemus latronum Thomas, 1911 PLATE 13 MAP 174
大耳姬鼠 Da'er Jishu

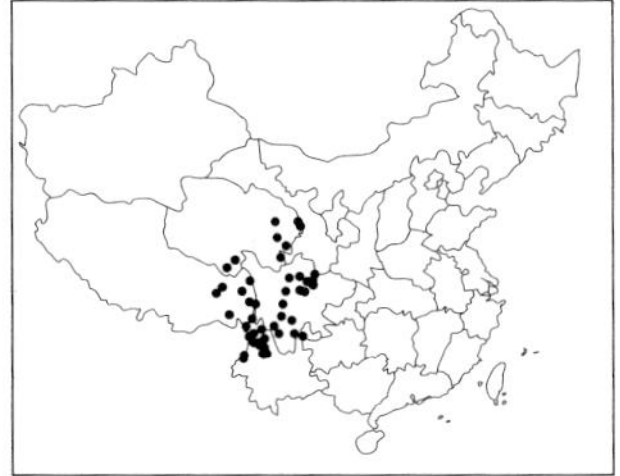

MAP 174. LARGE-EARED FIELD MOUSE, *Apodemus latronum*

Distinctive Characteristics: HB 92–107; T 100–120; HF 25–27; E 18–21; GLS 28–30. Dorsal pelage dark brown, becoming somewhat brighter reddish brown along the sides. Ventral pelage grayish white, indistinctly demarcated from dorsal pelage. Tail approximately equal to HB length, dark brown above, paler below. Ears dark blackish brown, much darker than the surrounding parts of the heads and shoulders. Females with three pairs of mammae (one pectoral pair, two abdominal pairs). Skull with well-defined supraorbital ridges, but these rarely extend onto the parietals. First upper molar with either one or two lingual roots; second upper molar usually has an anterio-external cusp; third upper molar with three lingual lobes. Similar to *A. draco*, and some authors consider it a subspecies of this taxon; but *A. latronum* is larger and has longer ears, and longer hind feet, and is further distinguished as being the only China species with just three pairs of mammae.
Distribution: E Xizang, N Yunnan, Sichuan, E Qinghai; extending to N Myanmar.
Natural History: Occurs in alpine forests and adjacent meadows from about 2,700 to 4,000 m.
Comments: Feng et al. (1986) treated *latronum* as a subspecies of *A. draco*.
Conservation Status: China RL—LC.
References: Chen et al. (1996); Liu et al. (2002); Musser et al. (1996); Suzuki et al. (2003).

Himalayan Field Mouse

Apodemus pallipes (Barrett-Hamilton, 1900) MAP 175
帕氏姬鼠 Paishi Jishu
Distinctive Characteristics: HB 72–110; T 70–110; HF 19–22; E 14–18; GLS 27–28.5. Dorsal pelage ranges from pale buffy brown to drab brownish gray. Ventral pelage grayish white and fairly well demarcated from the dorsal pelage. Tail approximately equal to or slightly longer than HB length, bicolored brown above, whitish below. Dorsal surfaces of hands and feet pale buffy brown. Skull lacks any trace of supraorbital ridges. Similar to *A. uralensis* but larger and with a paler dorsum and more white on the under parts.
Distribution: Distribution centered in the Pamirs and extending into the Hindu Kush and Himalayas. Range in China marginal, restricted to SW Xizang.

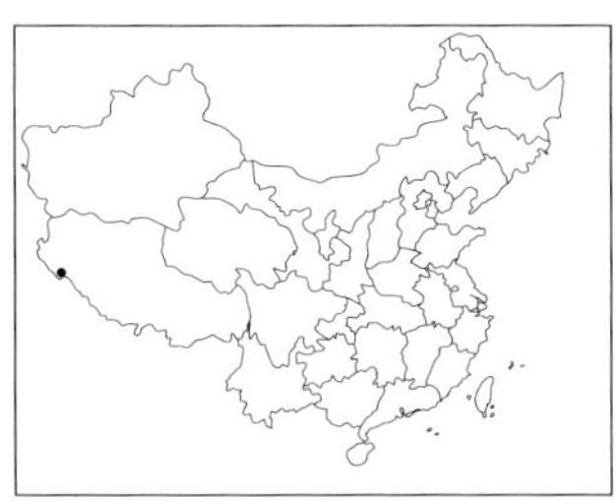

MAP 175. HIMALAYAN FIELD MOUSE, *Apodemus pallipes*

Natural History: Occurs in coniferous and rhododendron forests. Altitudinal range 1,465–3,965 m, with most records from above 2,440 m (Musser and Carleton 2005).
Comments: Previously included as a synonym of *A. uralensis* but recognized as a distinct species by Mezhzherin (1997a; 1997b). Musser and Carleton (2005) provisionally allocate the Tibetan *bushengensis* Zheng, 1979 to this species. Wang (2003) included *bushengensis* under *A. wardi* (Wroughton, 1908)—a taxon Musser and Carleton (2005) regard as a junior synonym of *A. pallipes*.
Conservation Status: China RL—LC.
References: Feng et al. (1986); Mezhzherin (1997a; 1997b); Musser and Carleton (2005); Zheng (1979).

Korean Field Mouse

Apodemus peninsulae (Thomas, 1907) PLATE 13 MAP 176
大林姬鼠 Dalin Jishu

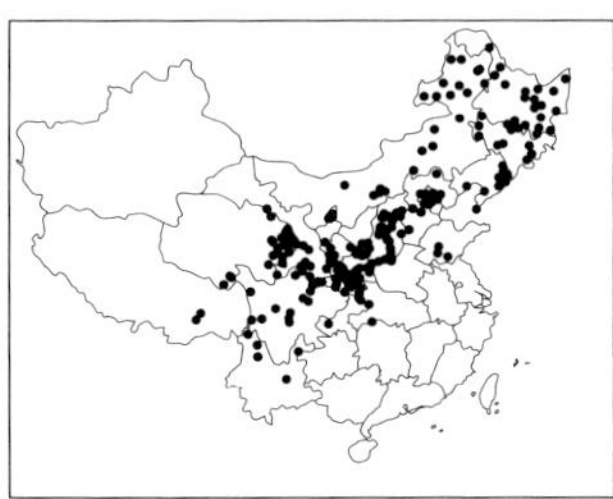

MAP 176. KOREAN FIELD MOUSE, *Apodemus peninsulae*

Distinctive Characteristics: HB 80–118; T 75–103; HF 21–23; E 14–17; GLS 25–29. Dorsal pelage pale reddish brown, becoming somewhat paler yellow brown along the sides. Ventral pelage grayish white, fairly well demarcated from the dorsal pelage but not forming a distinct line. Tail approximately equal to or somewhat shorter than HB length. Ears not differing in color from the surrounding parts of head and shoulders. Females with four pairs of mammae (two pectoral pairs, two abdominal pairs). Skull with supraorbital ridges, but these rarely extend onto the

parietals. First upper molar usually with only one medial root but sometimes two; second upper molar usually has an anterio-external cusp; third upper molar with three lingual lobes.
Distribution: Throughout much of China excepting the xeric western regions and the eastern lowlands; extending to S Siberia and Korea. Wang (2003) recognized three subspecies in China: (1) *A. p. praetor* Miller, 1914; Heilongjiang, Jilin, Liaoning, Nei Mongol; (2) *A. p. qinghaiensis* Feng, Zheng, and Wu, 1983; Qinghai, Sichuan, Gansu, Yunnan, Shaanxi, Ningxia, SE Xizang; (3) *A. p. sowerbyi* Jones, 1956; Shanxi, Hebei, Beijing, Shandong, Henan. A fourth, unnamed subspecies delimited from Yunnan has been recognized by Wang (2003).
Natural History: Favors brushy growth and woodlands.
Comments: Records of this species from Xinjiang are probably *A. uralensis*. The form *tscherga* is a synonym.
Conservation Status: China RL—LC.
References: Feng et al. (1983); Koh and Lee (1994); Liu et al. (2002); Musser et al. (1996); Musser and Carleton (2005); Suzuki et al. (2003);

Taiwan Field Mouse

Apodemus semotus Thomas, 1908 MAP 177
台湾姬鼠 Taiwan Jishu

MAP 177. TAIWAN FIELD MOUSE, *Apodemus semotus*

Distinctive Characteristics: HB 82.5–100; T 100–119; HF 23–25.5; E 15–17; GLS 29; Wt 18.5–39 g. Very similar to *A. draco* of the mainland. The only other species of *Apodemus* occurring on Taiwan is *A. agrarius*, but this species has a very distinctive mid-dorsal stripe and occurs at elevations below 1,000 m.
Distribution: Taiwan. Endemic.
Natural History: A habitat generalist reported from grass-land, broadleaf and coniferous forests, bamboo, and subalpine shrubs from 1,800 to 3,200 m. Favors microhabitats with dense ground cover but is sometimes captured in houses. Capable of breeding year-round, but there are two peak breeding seasons: April–May and September–October. Breeding is most frequent in the fall. Mean litter size about 3.5 (range 2–6).
Comments: Sometimes regarded a subspecies of *A. draco*.
Conservation Status: China RL—LC. IUCN RL—LR/nt ver 2.3 (1994).
References: Adler (1996); Huang et al. (1997); Liu et al. (2002); Musser et al. (1996); Musser and Carleton (2005); Yu (1993; 1994; 1995).

Herb Field Mouse

Apodemus uralensis (Pallas, 1811) MAP 178
小眼姬鼠 Xiaoyan Jishu

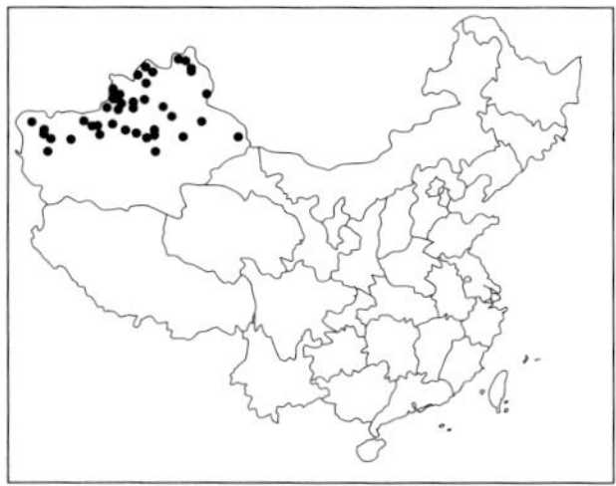

MAP 178. HERB FIELD MOUSE, *Apodemus uralensis*

Distinctive Characteristics: HB 85–102; T 83–97; HF 18–22; E 14–16; GLS 23.5–25. Dorsal pelage pale sandy brown to pale reddish brown. Ventral pelage sharply demarcated, white but with the grayish under fur showing through. Tail bicolored, brown above and white below. Dorsal surfaces of hands and feet white. Among Chinese *Apodemus* only *A. uralensis* and *A. pallipes* have a smooth interorbital region lacking any trace of a supraorbital ridge, but *A. uralensis* is distinguished by its smaller size.
Distribution: NW China (Xinjiang); extending to C Europe. Chinese subspecies: *A. u. nankiangensis* Wang, 1964.
Natural History: Forest edges and open areas bordering forests.
Comments: Reported as *A. sylvaticus nankiangensis* and *A. sylvaticus tscherga*, but the use of the name *sylvaticus* has since been restricted to populations in Europe and W Russia. The taxon *nankiangensis* is more appropriately associated with *A. uralensis*, and *tscherga* is a synonym of *A. penninsulae*; nonetheless, specimens reported as *A. sylvaticus tsherga* from Xinjiang by Ma et al. (1987) are actually *A. uralensis*. See Musser and Carleton (2005).
Conservation Status: China RL—LC.
References: Mezhzherin (1997a; 1997b); Ma et al. (1987); Musser and Carleton (2005); Suzuki et al. (2003); Wang (1964).

Genus *Bandicota*—Bandicoot Rats

板齿鼠属 Banchishu Shu—板齿鼠 Banchishu

Large, shaggy burrowing rats. The dorsal pelage ranges from pale grayish brown to almost black and is marked with numerous black guard hairs projecting above the fur along the midline of the back; the ventral pelage is usually grayish white. Scantily haired tail thick and more or less equal to HB length. Skull massively built, with prominent supraorbital ridges, robust zygoma, large bullae, and broad incisors. The molar cusps are broadly fused to form a series of transverse lamina. Bandicoot rats are often found in association with human degraded habitats and are especially common near water. They are similar to the Norway Rat (*Rattus norvegicus*) but are distinguished by wider upper incisors. Of three species of bandicoots, only one is found in China.

Greater Bandicoot Rat

PLATE 23
MAP 179

Bandicota indica (Bechstein, 1800)
板齿鼠 Banchi Shu

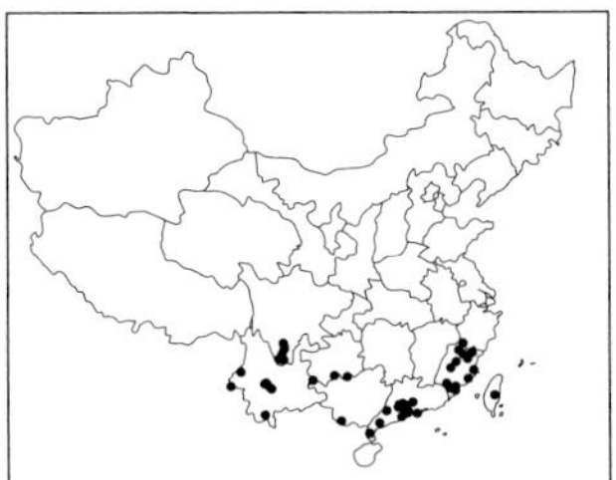

MAP 179. GREATER BANDICOOT RAT, *Bandicota indica*

Distinctive Characteristics: HB 188–328; T 190–280; HF 46–60; E 25–33; GLS 48.6–63.6; Wt 500–1,000 g. A very large, coarse-haired rat. Dorsal pelage shaggy; dark blackish brown with long coarse black guard hairs along the midline of the back; sides brownish gray. Ventral pelage dark brownish gray. Tail thickened, somewhat shorter than HB length, monocolored dark brown to almost black and covered in short stiff bristles. Dorsal surfaces of hands and feet dark blackish brown, but the claws are pale brown and strongly developed for digging. Females with six pairs of mammae (one pectoral pair, two postaxillary pairs, one abdominal pair, two inguinal pairs).
Distribution: S China (Yunnan and S Sichuan to Fujian); Taiwan; extending throughout mainland S and SE Asia and Sri Lanka. Introduced to Java and parts of the Malay Peninsula. Wang (2003) recognized four subspecies in China: (1) *B. i. eloquens* (Kishida, 1926); Taiwan; (2) *B. i. mordax* Thomas, 1916; SW Yunnan; (3) *B. i. nemorivaga* (Hodgson, 1836); S Sichuan to E Fujian and Guangdong; (4) *B. i. sonlaensis* Dao, 1975; SE Yunnan.
Natural History: A synanthropic species occurring in fields, villages, and cities, they prefer to be near water and are especially common in lowland rice fields. Feeds on mollusks, crabs, fish, fruits, tubers, rice, sugar cane, and other crops. Insects, earthworms, and leaves make up a small part of the diet. Nocturnal. Constructs elaborate burrows in stream banks, paddy dikes, and at the edges of fields. Spends the day in its burrow, emerging after dusk to feed throughout the night. Often searches for prey near water but returns to a particular feeding place to consume it. Typical litter size between five and seven. Offspring sexually mature at 170 days. Many authors have described this species as being particularly ferocious when captured.
Conservation Status: China RL—LC.
References: Adler (1995); Agrawal (2000); Aplin et al. (2003); Chakraborty and Chakraborty (1999); Musser and Brothers (1994).

Genus *Berylmys*—White-toothed Rats

硕鼠属 Shuoshu Shu—硕鼠 Shuoshu

Large rats with a short and crisp, iron gray-colored dorsal pelage, which is sharply demarcated from the pure white ventral pelage. Females with four or five pairs of mammae. In dorsal view the braincase has a characteristic triangular shape. The enamel of the incisors tends to be white or very pale yellow, unlike the dark orange of most other Murids. Molars with some of the cusps normally typical of the murinae either absent or merged to form featureless, almost noncuspidate laminae. All four species of *Berylmys* occur in China.

Berdmore's White-Toothed Rat

MAP 180

Berylmys berdmorei (Blyth, 1851)
大炮硕鼠 Dapao Shuoshu

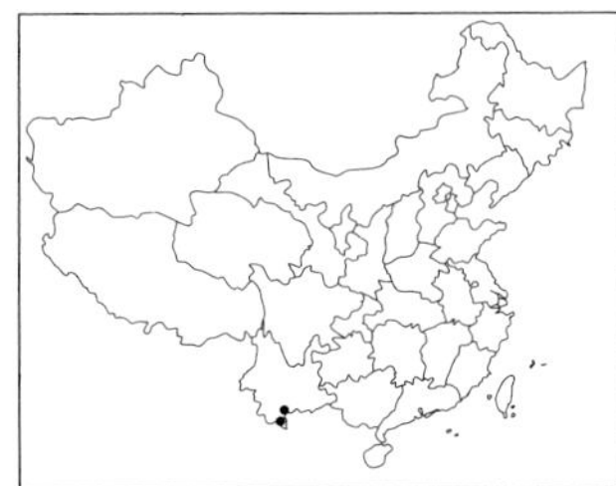

MAP 180. BERDMORE'S WHITE-TOOTHED RAT, *Berylmys berdmorei*

Distinctive Characteristics: HB 175–255; T 134–192; HF 36–46; E 23–29; GLS 42; Wt 118–235. Dorsal

Key to Chinese Species of *Berylmys*

1.a.	HF < 50 mm	2
b.	HF > 50 mm	3
2.a.	Tail usually < HB length and monocolored brown	*Berylmys berdmorei*
b.	Tail equal to or > HB length, the distal third white at the tip	*Berylmys manipulus*
3.a.	White of tail restricted to tip; females with four pairs of mammae	*Berylmys bowersi*
b.	White more or less covering distal half of tail; females with five pairs of mammae	*Berylmys mackenziei*

pelage iron gray. Ventral pelage pure white. Tail shorter than HB length, entirely dark brown above from base to tip, underside of tail ranges from solid brown to mottled grayish white speckled with black. Dorsal surfaces of hands and feet grayish white. Females with five pairs of mammae (one pectoral pair, two postaxillary pairs, two inguinal pairs).
Distribution: S Yunnan (Xishuangbanna); extending from S Myanmar to S Vietnam.
Natural History: Inhabits forests from near sea level to at least 1,400 m, but most common in upland areas where it is reported to favor swampy areas. Occasionally an agricultural pest, but generally avoids human habitations. Terrestrial and nocturnal, spends the day in its burrow.
Conservation Status: China RL—NA.
References: Aplin et al. (2003); Musser and Newcomb (1983); Musser and Carleton (2005); Yang and Wu (1979).

Bower's White-Toothed Rat

Berylmys bowersi (Anderson, 1879) PLATE 23 MAP 181
青毛硕鼠 Qingmao Shuoshu

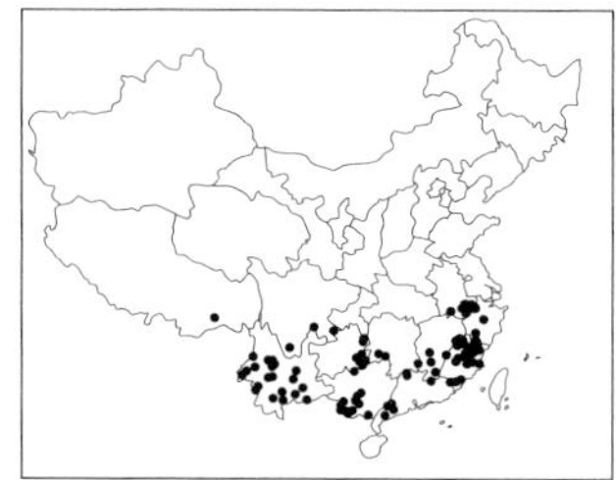

MAP 181. BOWER'S WHITE-TOOTHED RAT, *Berylmys bowersi*

Distinctive Characteristics: HB 236–285; T 249–292; HF 48–61; E 32–36; GLS 52–58.5; Wt up to 420 g. The largest species of *Berylmys*. Dorsal pelage dull brownish gray. Ventral pelage pure white. Tail slightly longer than HB length, usually entirely dark brown with a white tip, rarely monocolored brown. Dorsal surfaces of hands and feet dark brown, but digits and sides of feet white. Females with only four pairs of mammae (one pectoral pair, one postaxillary pair, two inguinal pairs).
Distribution: S China from Yunnan and S Sichuan to Zhejiang and Fujian; extending from NE India to Vietnam and south to the Malay Peninsula and N Sumatra.
Natural History: Nocturnal and predominantly terrestrial, although a capable climber. Spends the day in its burrow. Most common in primary forest between 1,000 and 1,600 m, but may also occur in secondary forest and scrub. Primarily a forest rat, but also found in cultivated fields and scrub along the margins of forest. Largely vegetarian, mostly eating fruits and vegetables but also some insects and land mollusks. Digs a large burrow among rocks, holes in fallen logs, along forest streams and paths, and at the base of trees. Typical litter size two to five.
Comments: Feng et al. (1986) identified a sample from SE Xizang, but it is not clear if this represents this species or *B. mackenziei*. See comments in Musser and Carleton (2005).
Conservation Status: China RL—LC.
References: Agrawal (2000); Aplin et al. (2003); Musser and Newcomb (1983); Musser and Carleton (2005).

Mackenzie's White-Toothed Rat

Berylmys mackenziei (Thomas, 1916) MAP 182
白齿家鼠 Baichi Jiashu

MAP 182. MACKENZIE'S WHITE-TOOTHED RAT, *Berylmys mackenziei*

Distinctive Characteristics: HB 233–272; T 248–262; HF 50–61; E 27–31; GLS 50.5–57.7; Wt 265 g. Similar to *B. bowersi*, but smaller and with white more or less covering the distal half of the tail; dorsal surfaces of the hind feet dark brown, but digits and sides of feet white; hands white, without a blaze of brown hairs on the dorsal surface; five pairs of mammae (one pectoral pair, two postaxillary pairs, two inguinal pairs).
Distribution: Known from a single specimen (USNM 255354) collected in C Sichuan (Omei Shan Mountain); otherwise known from NE India to S Vietnam.
Natural History: A highland species; the only specimen known from China was collected at 2,000 m.
Comments: The single specimen from Sichuan is larger and darker than typical examples of the species (see Musser and Newcomb 1983). More specimens need to be collected to determine if it represents a separate species.
Conservation Status: China RL—VU D2.
References: Musser and Newcomb (1983).

Manipur White-Toothed Rat

Berylmys manipulus (Thomas, 1916) MAP 183
小泡硕鼠 Xiaopao Shuoshu

Distinctive Characteristics: HB 135–185; T 140–187; HF 33–40; E 23–25; GLS 36.2–42.7. Similar to *B. berdmorei*, but smaller; this is the smallest species in the genus. Tail equal to or slightly longer than HB length, and with the distal 1/2 to 1/3 entirely white; dorsal surfaces of hands and feet white; five pairs of mammae (one pectoral pair, two post-axillary pairs, two inguinal pairs). Skull with incisors slightly proodont, pale yellowish orange; bullae very small.
Distribution: Range in China apparently restricted to Yunnan west of Salween River; extending from NE India to N Myanmar.

Natural History: Oak scrub forest and upland rainforests to at least 1,800 m. Avoids agricultural areas and human habitations. Eats plants, insects, and earthworms. Terrestrial, burrow dweller.

MAP 183. MANIPUR WHITE-TOOTHED RAT, *Berylmys manipulus*

Conservation Status: China RL–NA.
References: Agrawal (2000); Musser and Newcomb (1983).

Genus *Chiromyscus* (monotypic)

费氏树鼠属—Feishishushu Shu

Indochinese Chiromyscus

Chiromyscus chiropus (Thomas, 1891) MAP 184
费氏树鼠 Feishi Shushu

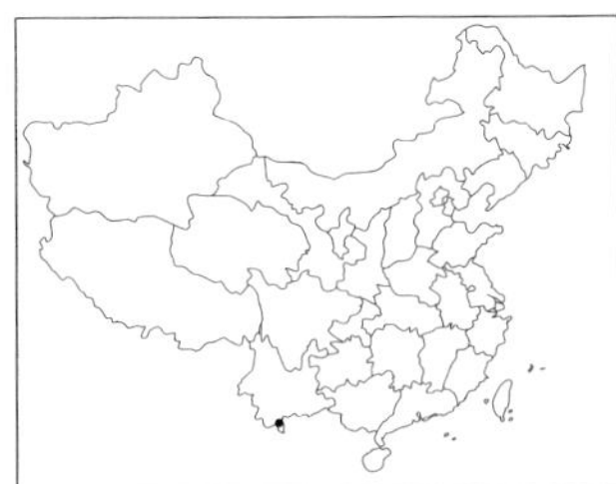

MAP 184. INDOCHINESE CHIROMYSCUS, *Chiromyscus chiropus*

Distinctive Characteristics: HB 138–160; T 200–233; HF 27–29; E 19–20; GLS 38.6. A monotypic genus similar to *Niviventer*, but with a nail instead of a claw on the first digit of each hind foot. The skull is also very similar to *Niviventer* but is distinguished in having more prominent shelflike supraorbital ridges. Dorsal pelage orange-brown and with an ochraceous lateral line along the margin with the ventral pelage. Ventral pelage sharply demarcated, creamy white. Tail bicolored, brown above, whitish below. Broad dark brown rings encircle each eye.
Distribution: S Yunnan (Xishuangbanna); extending from Myanmar to Vietnam.
Natural History: An arboreal species favoring deciduous forest.
Comments: Distribution in China is marginal. The species is very similar to *Niviventer langbianis* but has nails instead of claws on each big toe. See Musser and Carleton (2005).
Conservation Status: China RL–DD.
References: Marshall (1977a); Musser (1981); Musser and Carleton (2005).

Genus *Chiropodomys*—Tree Mice

笔尾树鼠属 Biweishushu Shu—笔尾树鼠 Biweishushu

Small arboreal mice with short, broad face, soft woolly fur, and a long tufted tail. The first digit of each hand is short and bears a broad nail; the first digit of each foot with a thick fleshy pad and an embedded nail. Of six species of *Chiropodomys*, one occurs in China.

Indomalayan Tree Mouse

PLATE 23
Chiropodomys gliroides (Blyth, 1856) MAP 185
笔尾树鼠 Biwei Shushu

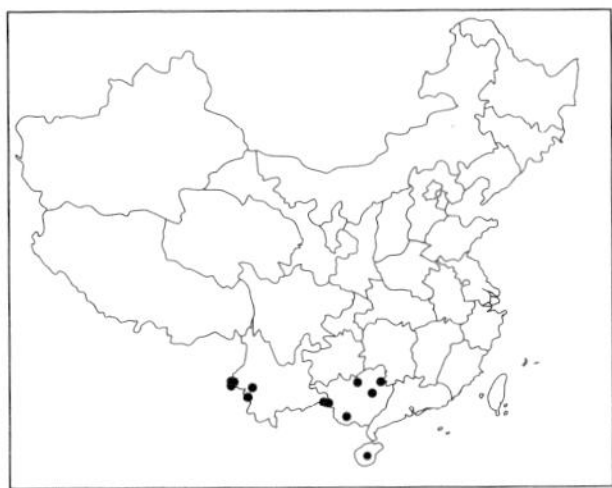

MAP 185. INDOMALAYAN TREE MOUSE, *Chiropodomys gliroides*

Distinctive Characteristics: HB 81–101; T 105–134; HF 18–22; E 16–20; GLS 23.5–26; Wt 20–33 g. A small arboreal mouse with a short rostrum and large eyes surrounded by a dark ring of black fur. Dorsal pelage soft and fluffy, pale reddish brown; whiskers very long and extending well beyond the ears when laid flat. Ventral pelage pure creamy white, sharply demarcated from dorsal pelage. Tail grayish brown and with a tuft of longer hairs at the tip (hairs ca. 3.5 mm). Dorsal surfaces of hands white, feet white with a brown blaze; first digit of foot bears a flattened nail and is opposable. Females with two pairs of inguinal mammae.
Distribution: S China, from W Yunnan to Hainan Island; extending from NE India to Vietnam and south to Bali.
Natural History: Inhabits primary and secondary forest from near sea level to ca. 2,600 m. Primarily herbivorous, but the composition of diet not completely known. Nocturnal and arboreal, but sometimes descends to the ground. Nests in hollow parts of trees. Uses woody lianas as runways through dense understory vegetation. The species seems to be more common in forest with an understory of bamboo, but also occurs in areas completely devoid of bamboo. Litter size averages two. Polyestrus with each estrus period lasting about 1 day and an estrus cycle lasting a minimum of 7 days; gestation

approximately 20 days. There is apparently no restricted breeding season, and pregnancies occur throughout the year.
Comments: Corbet and Hill (1992) and Musser and Carleton (2005) treat *C. jingdongensis* Wu and Deng, 1984, as a synonym of this species, but Zhang et al. (1997) and Wang (2003) continue to regard it as a separate species.
Conservation Status: China RL—VU A2c + 3c.
References: Musser (1979); Musser and Carleton (2005); Wu and Deng (1984).

Genus *Dacnomys* (monotypic)

大齿鼠属 Dachishu Shu

Millard's Dacnomys

PLATE 23
MAP 186

Dacnomys millardi Thomas, 1916
大齿鼠 Dachi Shu

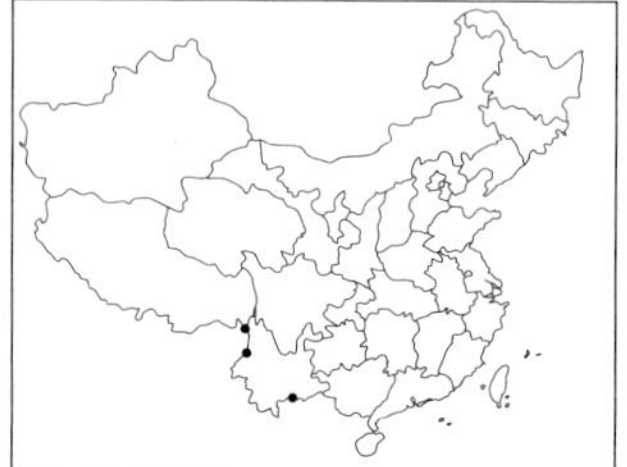

MAP 186. MILLARD'S DACNOMYS, *Dacnomys millardi*

Distinctive Characteristics: HB 228–290; T 308–335; HF 50–56; E 25–29; GLS 60. A giant long-tailed rat similar in size to *Leopoldamys*, but with the demarcation between the dorsal and ventral pelage not as sharp. Skull with very large molars and tiny bullae. Pelage short and thin, dark grayish brown flecked with buff dorsally, becoming paler along the sides and blending into the pale brownish white ventral pelage; the individual hairs of the ventral pelage are grayish brown at the base with dull creamy white tips except on the throat; axillary and inguinal regions where the hairs are pure creamy white to their bases; tail unicolored brown, sparsely haired; dorsal surfaces of hands and feet pale brown with white digits; eight mammae (one pectoral pair, one postaxillary pair, two inguinal pairs). Skull large long and narrow, with prominent supraorbital ridges; auditory bullae very small in relation to the overall size of the skull. Molars hypsodont and exceptionally large.
Distribution: S and W Yunnan; extending from E Nepal to NW Vietnam. Wang (2003) recognized two subspecies from China: *D. millardi ingens* Osgood, 1932; and *D. m. wroughtoni* Thomas, 1922; however, there are still too few specimens available to adequately assess geographic variation in this species.
Natural History: Inhabits highland forests above 1,000 m.
Comments: This genus is known from only a few museum specimens.
Conservation Status: China RL—NT; although it nearly meets the criteria for VU A2c + 3c.
References: Agrawal (2000); Li et al. (1987); Musser (1981); Musser and Carleton (2005); Osgood (1932).

Genus *Hadromys*—Hadromys

壮鼠属 Zhuangshu Shu—壮鼠 Zhuangshu

Large, stout-bodied rats with soft, thick, grayish brown fur and large rounded ears. The skull has a short rostrum and is remarkably convex in lateral view and has especially broad incisors. Of two *Hadromys* species, one occurs in China.

Yunnan Hadromys

PLATE 23

Hadromys yunnanensis
Yang and Wang, 1987

MAP 187

云南壮鼠 Yunnan Zhuangshu

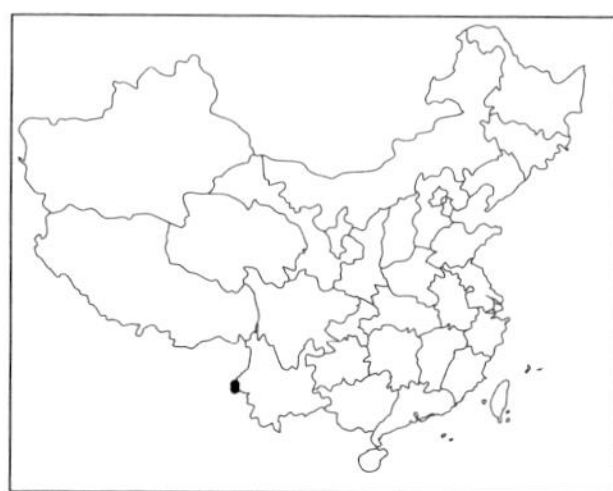

MAP 187. YUNNAN HADROMYS, *Hadromys yunnanensis*

Distinctive Characteristics: HB 123–140; T 114–132; HF 24–27; E 15–20; GLS 32–33; Wt 41–77 g. Fur soft and dense; dorsal pelage dark grayish brown sprinkled with black and either yellow or white, becoming reddish over the back and rump and with a yellow ochre patch on the cheek. Ventral pelage pure white. Tail shorter than HB length, dorsal surface of tail brown underside white. Hands and feet long and slender; four pairs of mammae (one pectoral pair, one postaxillary pair, two inguinal pairs).
Distribution: Known only from Ruili County, W Yunnan. Endemic.
Natural History: Terrestrial. Occurs between 970 and 1,300 m elevation.
Comments: Previously described and reported as a subspecies of *Hadromys humei*, but now regarded as a separate species (Musser and Carleton 2005; Wang 2003).
Conservation Status: China RL—VU D2.
References: Musser (1987); Yang and Wang (1987).

Genus *Hapalomys*—Marmoset Rats

狨鼠属 Rongshu Shu—狨鼠 Rongshu

Arboreal mice with a long soft pelage and a long tail ending in a tuft of hairs. The big toe is opposable and bears a flat nail instead of a claw. The ears are conspicuously fringed with very long fine hairs. Females with four pairs of mammae. Skull with a short rostrum; cusp pattern on the first upper and lower molars unique in consisting of three neat rows of three cusps each. Only one of two species of *Haplomys* occurs in China.

Lesser Marmoset Rat

Hapalomys delacouri Thomas, 1927 — PLATE 23, MAP 188

小狨鼠 Xiao Rongshu

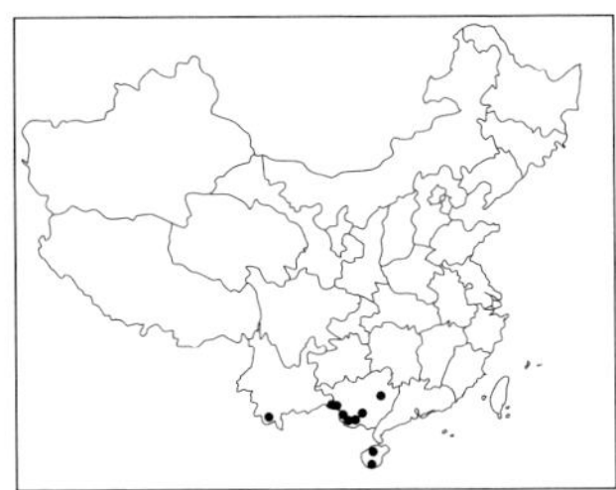

MAP 188. LESSER MARMOSET RAT, *Hapalomys delacouri*

Distinctive Characteristics: HB 123–136; T 140–160; HF 22–24; E 14–15; GLS 32–34. Dorsal pelage ochraceous brown, hairs long and soft. Ventral pelage pure white, sharply demarcated from dorsal pelage; tail slightly longer than HB length, pale brown near the base, darker brown toward the tip, ending in short tuft of hair approximately 6 mm long. Ears conspicuously fringed with very long fine hairs that are more than twice the length of the pinnae; vibrissae long, extending to the shoulders when laid back against the body; four pairs of mammae (one pectoral, one postaxillary, two inguinal); hands and feet short and broad; the thumb is fully opposable and bears a nail instead of a claw. Skull with a short broad rostrum and a wide braincase with prominent supraorbital ridges, appearing somewhat square-shaped overall. The first upper and first lower molars each have three rows of three cusps that are almost perfectly symmetrical from front to back and side to side.

Distribution: S Yunnan, Guangxi, and Hainan Island; extending to N Laos and Vietnam. Wang (2003) recognized two subspecies in China: (1) *H. d. delacouri* Thomas, 1927; mainland part of range; (2) *H. d. marmosa* Allen, 1927; Hainan .

Natural History: Highly arboreal and probably restricted to bamboo habitats between 1,200 and 1,500 m.

Comments: Specimens of *H. longicaudatus* reported from Yunnan by Wang (2003) are probably this species.

Conservation Status: China RL—EN A1bc. IUCN RL—LR/nt ver 2.3 (1994).

References: Musser (1972).

Genus *Leopoldamys*—Leopoldamys

长尾大鼠属 Changweidashu Shu—
长尾大鼠 Changweidashu

Large, long-tailed rats with short, sleek fur. Dorsal pelage brown to grayish brown. Ventral pelage pure white and sharply demarcated. Tail indistinctly bicolored, dark brown above, creamy white below. Dorsal surfaces of hands and feet brownish white. Skull long and narrow and with the squamosal roots of zygomatic arches set high on the sides of the braincase. Incisive foramina short and wide and ending just before the first molars; posterior margin of bony palate at the level of the third upper molars; mesopterygoid fossa as wide as palate; bullae very small compared to the large skull. One of four species of *Leopoldamys* lives in China.

Edward's Leopoldamys

Leopoldamys edwardsi (Thomas, 1882) — PLATE 23, MAP 189

小泡巨鼠 Xiaopao Jushu

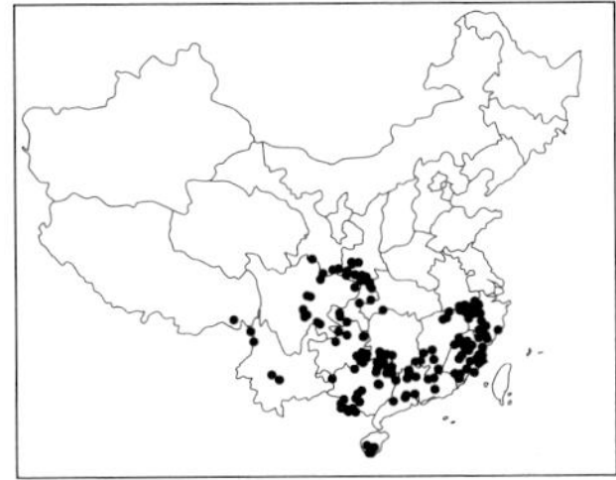

MAP 189. EDWARD'S LEOPOLDAMYS, *Leopoldamys edwardsi*

Distinctive Characteristics: HB 210–290; T 264–315; HF 42–58; E 28–32; GLS 54–58; Wt 230–480 g. Very large rats with a long tail, long ears, and fairly short, sleek fur. Dorsal pelage brown to grayish brown. Ventral pelage pure white and sharply demarcated. Tail indistinctly bicolored, dark brown above, creamy white below. Dorsal surfaces of hands and feet brownish white.

Distribution: E Xizang and Yunnan north to S Gansu and east to Zhejiang and Hainan Island; extending west to India and south to Indochina, Myanmar, and Thailand. Wang (2003) recognized four subspecies in China: (1) *L. e. edwardsi* (Thomas, 1882); SE China (Guizhou to Zhejiang and Guangdong; (2) *L. e. gigas* (Satunin, 1903); C China (Sichuan, S Gansu, S Shaanxi, Hubei); (3) *L. e. hainanensis* (Xu and Yu, 1985); Hainan; (4) *L. e. milleti* (Robinson and Kloss, 1922); S Yunnan (see comment below).

Natural History: Inhabits lowland and montane forests. Omnivorous. Primarily nocturnal and terrestrial but will climb short distances for food.

Comments: Taxonomic status of Hainan Island populations uncertain; see discussion in Musser and Carleton (2005). *Leopoldamys milleti* (Robinson and Kloss, 1922) was listed as a subspecies of *L. edwardsi* from S Yunnan by Wang (2003) and others, but Musser and Carleton (2005) elevate this taxon to full species and document it only from the Langbian highlands of S Vietnam.

References: Lunde and Son (2001); Musser and Carleton (2005); Xu and Yu (1985).

Genus *Maxomys*—Maxomys

刺鼠属 Chishu Shu—刺鼠 Chishu

Medium-sized, short furred, reddish orange forest rats. The dorsal pelage is usually spinous in the Chinese species, bright orange red, and sharply demarcated from the creamy white ventral pelage. Tail about as long as HB length; the base is brown above and white below, but the tip is entirely white. Hind foot long and slender. Skull with squamosal roots of zygomatic arches set high on the side of the braincase; incisive foramina short and wide, ending well in front of the first molars; posterior margin of palate at level of the posterior margin of the third upper molars; mesopterygoid fossa as wide as palate; bullae relatively small. Of 17 species of *Maxomys*, only 1 occurs in China.

Indomalayan Maxomys

Maxomys surifer (Miller, 1900) MAP 190

红刺鼠 Hong Cishu

Distinctive Characteristics: HB 160–226; T 160–227; HF 40–47; E 24–28; GLS 43.3–47; Wt 90–230 g. Dorsal pelage bright reddish orange with admixtures of black guard hairs, becoming paler along the sides and forming a sharp line of demarcation with the pure white ventral pelage. Hind foot nearly five times as long as it is wide, with small smooth plantar pads. Females with four pairs of mammae (one pectoral pair, one postaxillary pair, two inguinal pairs).
Distribution: S Yunnan (Xishuangbanna); extending across Indochina, Thailand, and Myanmar.

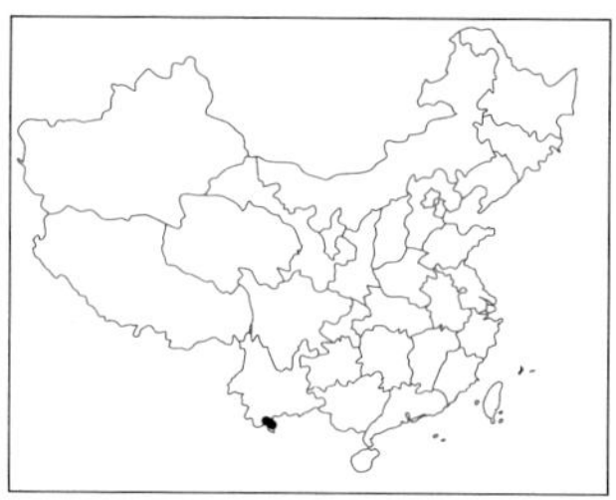

MAP 190. INDOMALAYAN MAXOMYS, *Maxomys surifer*

Natural History: Cursorial rats adapted for life on tropical rainforest floors. Lives in burrows on the forest floor. Nocturnal and omnivorous feeding on roots, fallen fruits, insects, and small vertebrates. Litter size typically ranges between two and five.
Conservation Status: China RL—LC.
References: Wu et al. (1996b).

Genus *Micromys* (monotypic)

巢鼠属 Chaoshu Shu

Harvest Mouse

PLATE 23

Micromys minutus (Pallas, 1771) MAP 191

巢鼠 Chao Shu

Distinctive Characteristics: HB 55–68; T 54–79; HF 14–16; E 10; GLS < 20 mm; Wt 5–7 g. Tiny field mice of the Palaearctic realm. The dorsal pelage is reddish brown above and ventral pelage gray based with dull white tips. The tail is prehensile, allowing it to climb easily through tall grassy vegetation. Tail bicolored, dark brown above, slightly paler below. Head short and rounded, with a very short muzzle. Hind foot with a claw on the hallux (in *Vandeleuria* there is a nail). Skull tiny, molars characterized by the presence of a posterio-internal cusp (t7). Females with four pairs of mammae.
Distribution: Throughout China wherever suitable lowland grassy habitats exist; extending across the Palaearctic. Wang (2003) recognized at least seven subspecies in China: (1) *M. m. erythrotis* (Blyth, 1856); SE Xizang; (2) *M. m. pianmaensis* Peng, 1981; Yunnan; (3) *M. m. pygmaeus* (Milne-Edwards, 1872); Sichuan to Guangdong and Fujian; (4) *M. m. shenshiensis* Li, Wu, and Shao, 1965; S Shaanxi; (5) *M. m. takasagoensis* Tokuda, 1941; Taiwan; (6) *M. m. ussuricus* (Barrett-Hamilton, 1899); Heilongjiang, Jilin, Liaoning, Nei Mongol; 7) *M. m. zhenjiangensis* Huang, 1989; Jiangsu, Zhejiang, Anhui, Hubei. Additional unnamed forms from Xinjiang, Guangdong, and central N China have been recognized (see Wang 2003).

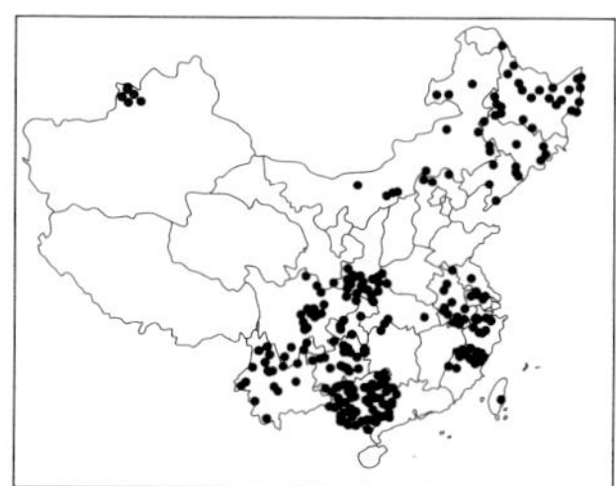

MAP 191. HARVEST MOUSE, *Micromys minutus*

Natural History: Inhabits tall grass fields, rice fields, bamboo stands, and other weedy areas. Eats seeds, green vegetation, and some insects. Active day or night. Constructs a special nest during the breeding season consisting of a tightly woven ball of plant fibers suspended on tall stems about 100–130 cm above the ground and about 60–130 mm in diameter. Typical litter sizes range between five and nine. Home range approximately 400 m^2 for males; 350 m^2 for females.
Comments: Wang (2003) recognized three additional but unnamed subspecies.
Conservation Status: China RL—LC. IUCN RL—LR/nt ver 2.3 (1994).
References: Trout (1978); Wang (2003).

Genus *Mus*—Old World Mice

小鼠属 Xiaoshu Shu—小鼠 Xiaoshu

Small terrestrial mice including both wild and synanthropic species. Of the 38 species currently allocated to the genus, only 4 occur in China (not including *Mus musculus*, the introduced house mouse). The fur of Chinese species may be soft or stiff and ranges from dark gray to pale yellowish brown dorsally, and

Key to the Chinese Species of *Mus*

1.a.	Dorsal pelage bluish gray; eyes very small; least interorbital breadth of skull > 4 mm	*Mus pahari*
b.	Dorsal pelage reddish brown; eyes not especially small, least interorbital breadth of skull < 4 mm	2
2.a.	Tail bicolored, but not sharply; upper incisors strongly recurved (opisthodont)	*Mus cookii*
b.	Tail usually sharply bicolored; upper incisors not strongly recurved (pro-odont)	3
3.a.	Tail length approximately equals HB length; skull with short nasal bones such that the incisors are visible in dorsal view; upper incisors dark orange	*Mus caroli*
b.	Tail length < HB length; skull with long nasal bones such that the incisors are occluded in dorsal view; upper incisors pale orange or yellow	*Mus cervicolor*

dark gray to white ventrally. Females with five pairs of mammae (one pectoral, two postaxillary, two inguinal). The genus may be distinguished from all other genera of small mice occurring in China by details of the molars: the first upper molar slightly exceeds half the length of the entire molar tooth-row and lacks a posterio-internal cusp. Most of the species occurring in China are to some extent associated with human-modified habitats, being most common in rice fields and scrubby habitats around villages.

Ryukyu Mouse

Mus caroli Bonhote, 1902 PLATE 24 MAP 192

琉球小家鼠 Liuqiu Xiaojiashu

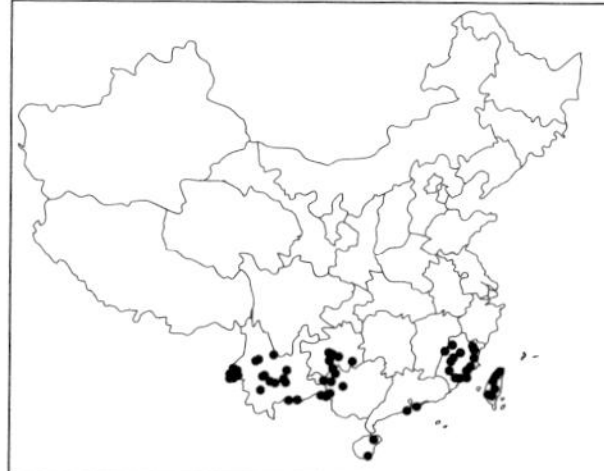

MAP 192. RYUKYU MOUSE, *Mus caroli*

Distinctive Characteristics: HB 72–95; T 75–95; HF 15–19; E 12–14; GLS 19–20.5; Wt 11.5–19.5. Dorsal pelage grayish brown, fur rather stiff. Ventral pelage grayish white. Tail equal to or slightly shorter than HB length, sharply bicolored dark brown above, paler below. Dorsal surfaces of hands and feet pale brown. Upper incisors dark orange. Similar to *M. cervicolor*, but with a longer tail that is sharply bicolored.
Distribution: Yunnan, Guizhou, Guangxi, Guangdong; Fujian, Hainan Island, Hong Kong, and Taiwan; extending south to Vietnam, Cambodia, Laos, and Thailand. Likely introduced to Sumatra, Java, Flores, and other smaller islands of Indonesia.
Natural History: Common in and around rice fields, grassy areas, scrub, and secondary growth. Burrows are typically constructed in rice-paddy dikes and usually have two entrances leading to a central chamber. Burrow entrances are left open and are usually marked by small mounds of freshly dug soil. The species is primarily nocturnal, but it is not unusual for them to emerge from their burrows for brief periods during the day.
Conservation Status: China RL—LC.
References: Adler (1995); Aplin et al. (2003); Macholán (2001); Marshall (1977a; 1997b); Musser and Newcomb (1983); Musser and Carleton (2005)

Fawn-Colored Mouse

Mus cervicolor Hodgson, 1845 MAP 193

仔鹿小鼠 Zilu Xiaoshu

Distinctive Characteristics: HB 61–80; T 67–88; HF 14–19; E 13–15; GLS 20.5–24.5; Wt 8–17.5 g. Dorsal pelage very soft and orange-brown to brownish gray. Ventral pelage creamy white with pale gray bases. Tail shorter than HB and distinctly bicolored, dark brown above and white below. Dorsal surfaces of hands and feet white. Similar to *M. caroli,* with which it is often sympatric, but distinguished by its smaller size and shorter tail.
Distribution: Known from only two localities in Yunnan—Anning in the east and Ruili in the west; extending from N India and Nepal east through Myanmar, Laos, Cambodia, and N Vietnam. Likely inadvertently introduced to Sumatra and Java.

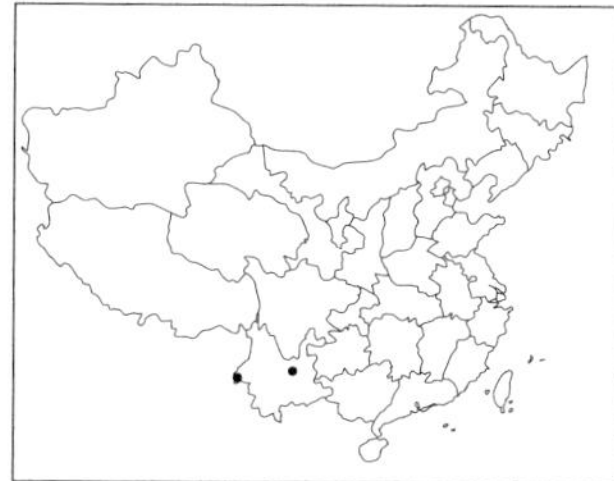

MAP 193. FAWN-COLORED MOUSE, *Mus cervicolor*

Natural History: Occurs in secondary growth, grass, brush, rice fields, and other agricultural areas.
Conservation Status: China RL—NA.
References: Aplin et al. (2003); Marshall (1977a; 1997b); Musser and Newcomb (1983).

Cook's Mouse

Mus cookii Ryley, 1914 MAP 194
丛林小鼠 Conglin Xiaoshu

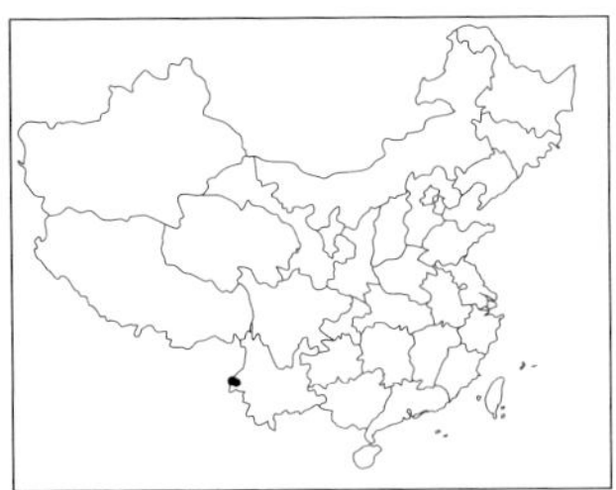

MAP 194. COOK'S MOUSE, *Mus cookii*

Distinctive Characteristics: HB 77–96; T 83–91; HF 19.5; E 15; GLS 24–25; Wt 16.5–23. Dorsal pelage with a stiff texture, dark grayish brown. Ventral pelage grayish white. Tail shorter than HB length, brown above, paler below. Dorsal surfaces of hands and feet grayish white. Upper incisors pale orange. Resembles *M. caroli*, but larger and without a sharply bicolored tail and pale orange upper incisors.
Distribution: Yunnan, west of the Salween River; extending from Nepal to Myanmar and south to Thailand, Laos, and Vietnam.
Natural History: Reported from upland rice fields and other disturbed habitats.
Comments: Reported as *M. famulus cookii* by Zhang et al. (1997).
Conservation Status: China RL—NA.
References: Aplin et al. (2003); Marshall (1977a; 1997b).

Indochinese Shrewlike Mouse

Mus pahari Thomas, 1916 MAP 195
锡金小鼠 Xijin Xiaoshu

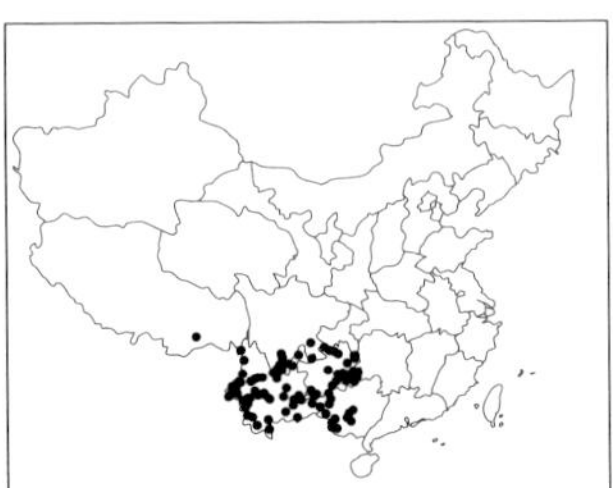

MAP 195. INDOCHINESE SHREWLIKE MOUSE, *Mus pahari*

Distinctive Characteristics: HB 88–103; T 88–90; HF 21–23; E 15–17; GLS 24–26; Wt 21–24 g. A long-nosed, shrewlike mouse with small eyes and short ears. Dorsal pelage dark blue-gray, spiny in adults, ventral pelage silver gray. Tail longer than HB, bicolored dark brown above, white below. Dorsal surfaces of hands and feet white. Skull more elongated compared to other species of *Mus*.
Distribution: SE Xizang, Yunnan, S Sichuan, Guizhou, Guangxi; extending from NE India through N Myanmar to Thailand, Laos, Vietnam, and Cambodia. Three subspecies in China: (1) *M. p. gairdneri* (Kloss, 1920); Yunnan; (2) *M. p. jacksoniae* (Thomas, 1921); Guangxi, Guizhou, Sichuan; (3) *M. p. pahari* Thomas, 1916; SE Xizang.
Natural History: Little known; builds a grass nest but does not burrow. Strictly nocturnal and terrestrial. Feeds on insects.
Comments: This species was treated under the name *Leggada cookii meator* in Allen (1940).
Conservation Status: China RL—LC.
References: Allen (1927); Marshall (1977a; 1997b); Wu et al. (1996b).

Genus *Nesokia*—Short-tailed Bandicoot Rats

地鼠属 Dishu Shu—地鼠 Dishu

Short-tailed, burrowing rats similar to *Bandicota*, but with larger hands, longer claws, and more forward-projecting upper incisors that are only slightly pigmented or completely white. The skull has very short and narrow incisive foramina, and the bony palate ends well anterior to the posterior margin of the bony palate. Females with four pairs of mammae. One of the two species of *Nesokia* is distributed in China.

Short-Tailed Bandicoot Rat

PLATE 24
Nesokia indica (Gray, 1830, in 1830–1835) MAP 196
印度地鼠 Yindu Dishu

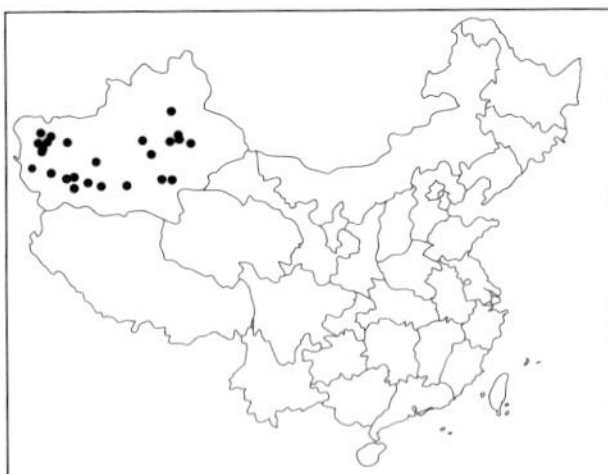

MAP 196. SHORT-TAILED BANDICOOT RAT, *Nesokia indica*

Distinctive Characteristics: HB 150–194; T 110–129; HF 23–37; E 16–22; GLS 36–42; Wt 137–203 g. A stocky rat with a broad head, short snout, and short rounded ears. The incisor teeth are very broad and with the lower set wider than the upper set. Dorsal pelage thick and shaggy, grayish brown with orange across the shoulders. Ventral pelage pale gray. Tail very short and thinly furred. Females with four pairs of mammae (one pectoral pair, one abdominal pair, and two inguinal pairs). 2N = 42.
Distribution: Full range extends from NE Egypt through the Arabian Peninsula and eastward to NW China (Xinjiang). Wang (2003) recognized two subspecies in China: (1) *N. i. brachyura* Büchner, 1889; Xinjiang (Lop Nur, Korla, and Yuli); (2) *N. i. scullyi* Wood-Mason, 1876; Xinjiang (W Sangzhu and Hetian area).
Natural History: Inhabits mountainous areas where it is especially common in agricultural areas. A highly fossorial species, it digs extensive burrows in

firm, damp soil using its large teeth; feeds on underground bulbs and succulent grass roots. Adults are solitary and aggressive and rarely emerge above ground. Reproduction occurs throughout the year, but litter size is low and probably close to four young per litter.

Conservation Status: China RL—LC.

References: Aplin et al. (2003); Musser and Brothers (1994); Musser and Carleton (2005); Roberts (1997).

Genus *Niviventer*—Niviventer

白腹鼠属 Baifushu Shu—白腹鼠 Baifushu

Medium-sized rats having a yellowish brown to reddish brown or brownish gray spinous dorsal pelage and a sharply demarcated creamy white ventral pelage. The tail is about the same length as HB or somewhat longer and may be monocolored or bicolored. Females with four pairs of mammae. Skull with squamosal roots of the zygomatic arches set high on the sides of the braincase; incisive foramina extend almost to the first molars; posterior margin of the bony palate ends at the level of the posterior margin of the third upper molars; mesopterygoid fossa as wide as palate; bullae relatively small. Of 17 species of *Niviventer*, 10 occur in China.

Anderson's Niviventer

Niviventer andersoni (Thomas, 1911)
安氏白腹鼠 Anshi Baifushu

PLATE 24
MAP 197

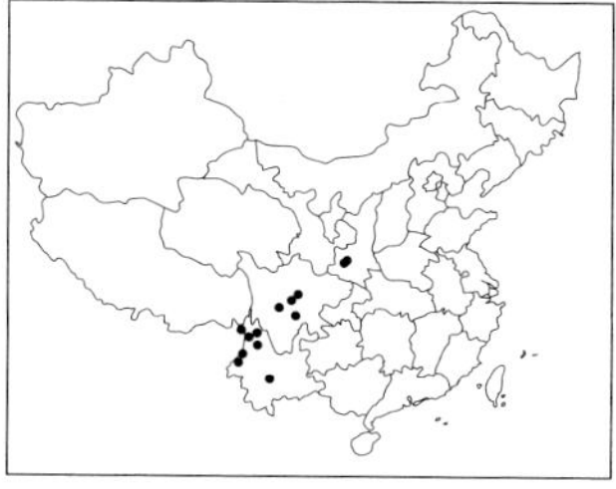

MAP 197. ANDERSON'S NIVIVENTER, *Niviventer andersoni*

Distinctive Characteristics: HB 150–198; T 194–269; HF 31–40; E 22–28; GLS 39–46. Dorsal pelage long and soft, dark grayish brown with mixtures of black hairs mid-dorsally, brighter ochraceous brown along the sides of cheeks neck and body. Ventral pelage creamy white and sharply demarcated from the dorsal pelage. There is a contrastingly blackish area extending from the base of the vibrissae back to and around the eye and part way to the base of the ear. Tail longer than HB; bicolored, dark brown above but becoming progressively paler towards the tip so that the terminal third is white. The underside of the tail is pale brownish white. There is a slight tuft of longer hairs at the tip of the tail. Dorsal surfaces of hands

Key to the Chinese Species of *Niviventer*

1.a.	Endemic to Taiwan	2
b.	Does not occur on Taiwan	3
2.a.	Larger (GLS > 40), and with reddish brown fur. Occurs at altitudes below 2,000 m	*Niviventer coninga*
b.	Smaller (GLS < 40), and with dark grayish brown fur. Occurs at altitudes above 2,000 m	*Niviventer culturatus*
3.a.	Size large, GLS usually > 38 mm; molar toothrow usually > 7 mm	4
b.	Size not so large, GLS usually < 38 mm; molar toothrow usually < 7 mm	5
4.a.	Larger (molar toothrow > 7.2 mm) and with dorsal pelage more grayish brown; hairs toward the tip of the tail not noticeably longer	*Niviventer andersoni*
b.	Smaller (molar toothrow < 7.2 mm) and with dorsal pelage more reddish brown; hairs toward the tip of the tail noticeably longer	*Niviventer excelsior*
5.a.	Dorsal pelage soft and dense, never spiny; ventral pelage gray based; females with three pairs of mammae	6
b.	Dorsal pelage not so soft and fluffy, often with spines; ventral pelage without gray-based hairs; females with four pairs of mammae	7
6.a.	Size larger (HB > 134, GLS >35)	*Niviventer brahma*
b.	Size smaller (HB < 134, GLS < 35)	*Niviventer eha*
7.a.	Tail always monocolored brown	*Niviventer langbianis*
b.	Tail usually white on the ventral surface	8
8.a.	Skull long, ears large	*Niviventer tenaster*
b.	Skull shorter, ears not so large	9
9.a.	Pelage brighter, more yellow brown or orange brown; hairs of the tail not longer toward the tip	*Niviventer fulvescens*
b.	Pelage duller, grayer; tail hairs slightly longer toward the tip	*Niviventer confucianus*

and feet usually dark brown, but digits and sides of the feet are whitish. Resembles *N. excelsior*, with which it is sympatric, but distinguished by its darker dorsal pelage and larger size. In *N. andersoni* the molar toothrow length ranges between 7.2 and 8.3 mm, while in *N. excelsior* it is less than 7.2 mm (Musser and Chiu 1979).
Distribution: Along the eastern edge of the Tibetan Plateau and Himalayas (E Xizang, Yunnan, Sichuan, Shaanxi, and perhaps N Guizhou). Endemic.
Natural History: Little known beyond the fact that it inhabits high montane forest at altitudes between approximately 2,000 and 3,000 m.
Comments: Specimens reported as *Niviventer andersoni* or *N. coxingi andersoni* from Taiwan, SE China, or any other locality well outside of the geographic range described in this account are not *N. andersoni*. On Taiwan they probably represent the large-bodied *N. coninga*; elsewhere they likely represent *N. tenaster* or large-bodied *N. fulvescens*, or an undescribed species misidentified as *N. andersoni* (Musser and Lunde, ms). Wang (2003) lists *Niviventer andersoni lushuiensis* Wu and Wang, subsp. nov., 2002; but this has yet to be published with a diagnosis and identification of holotype.
Conservation Status: China RL—LC.
References: Feng et al. (1986); Musser and Chiu (1979); Musser (1981); Musser and Carleton (2005); Wang (2003).

Brahman Niviventer

Niviventer brahma (Thomas, 1914) MAP 198
梵鼠 Fan Shu

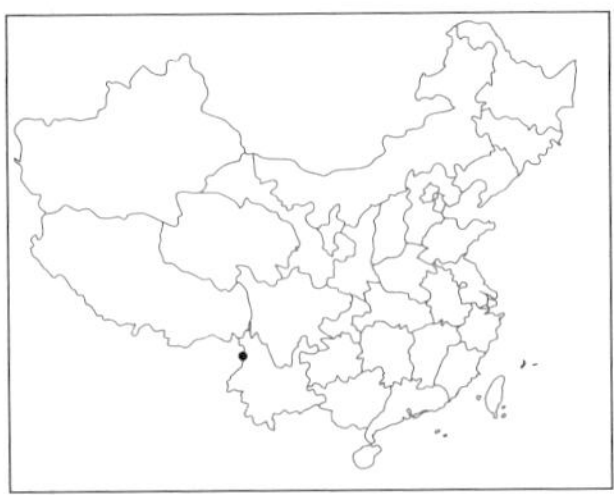

MAP 198. BRAHMAN NIVIVENTER, *Niviventer brahma*

Distinctive Characteristics: HB 136–155; T 201–237; HF 31–34; E 20–25; GLS 35.8–38.1. A beautiful *Niviventer* with long, soft, thick fur. Dorsal pelage bright orange brown to yellow brown with mixtures of very long black guard hairs, face with dark blackish brown patches extending from the tip of the nose to just behind the ears. The bright fulvous orange sides are sharply demarcated from the gray-based white ventral pelage, and there is usually a streak or patch of buff brown fur along the midline of the chest. Tail long, about 1.5 times HB length, and more-or-less uniform brown in color; the underside is usually slightly paler brown, but the tail is never distinctly bicolored. Tail tipped with a little brush of hair; dorsal surfaces of hands and feet brownish gray with pale brown fingers and toes. Females with three pairs of mammae (one postaxillary pair, one abdominal pair, and one inguinal pair).
Distribution: Yunnan west of Salween River (NW Gaoligong mountains); extending to NE India and N Myanmar.
Natural History: Inhabits cool, damp, high-altitude forests. Terrestrial.
Comments: Of the several species of *Niviventer* occurring within the range of *N. brahma*, *N. fulvescens* and *N. eha* are the most likely to be confused with it. The tail of *N. fulvescens* is proportionally shorter, averaging about the same length as HB. *N. eha* exhibits a tail and head and body proportions similar to that of *N. brahma*, but *N. eha* is much smaller overall.
Conservation Status: China RL—VU D2.
References: Musser (1970; 1973a; 1981).

Confucian Niviventer

PLATE 24
Niviventer confucianus
(Milne-Edwards, 1871) MAP 199
北社鼠 Bei Sheshu

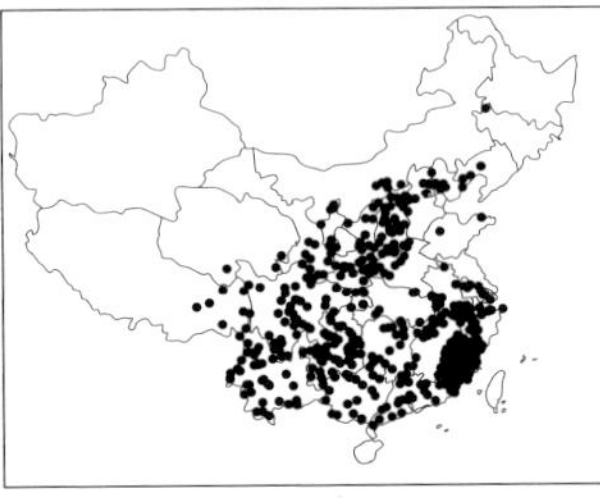

MAP 199. CONFUCIAN NIVIVENTER, *Niviventer confucianus*

Distinctive Characteristics: HB 116–173; T 154–255; HF 28–35; E 21–25; GLS 31.5–38, rarely up to 43. Dorsal pelage may be soft or spiny and ranging in color from reddish brown to dull brownish gray with an area of brighter ochraceous brown along the sides. Ventral pelage pale yellowish white, sharply demarcated from the dorsal pelage. There is sometimes a buffy spot on the center of the chest. Tail only slightly longer than head and body, dark brown above, whitish below, tip completely white. Individuals are sometimes difficult to distinguish from *N. fulvescens*. Where the two species occur together, *N. confucianus* is usually darker and has a narrower rostrum.
Distribution: Common throughout the highlands of S, C, and E China, but absent from Hainan and Taiwan; extending to N Myanmar, NW Thailand, and NW Vietnam. Wang (2003) recognized eight subspecies from China, but the status of these needs to be reassessed: (1) *N. c. chihliensis* (Thomas, 1917); N Hebei, Beijing, Tianjin, Liaoning; (2) *N. c. confucianus* (Milne-Edwards, 1871); much of S China south of Yangtze River, from Sichuan and Yunnan eastward to Jiangsu and Guangdong; (3) *N. c. deqinensis* Deng and Wang, 2000; NW Yunnan; (4) *N. c. mentosus* (Thomas, 1916); S and SE Xizang; (5) *N. c. naoniuensis* (Zhang and Zhao, 1984); Jilin; (6) *N. c. sacer*

(Thomas, 1908); much of N China north of Yangtze River, from Gansu, N Sichuan, eastward to Shandong and Jiangsu; (7) *N. c. yajiangensis* Deng and Wang, 2000; W Sichuan between Yalong and Dadu rivers; (8) *yushuensis* (Wang and Zheng, 1981); SW Qinghai, NW Sichuan, E Xizang.
Natural History: An abundant species occurring in all kinds of habitats from primary forest to cultivated land.
Comments: Specimens reported from Hainan are actually *N. tenaster*, and those from Taiwan are *N. culturatus*, which in the past was treated as a subspecies of *N. confucianus*. There exists considerable geographic variation between populations of *N. confucianus*, but the significance of this is still difficult to determine. Deng et al. (2000) recognized ten subspecies, but one of these (*lotipes*) represents *N. tenaster* and another, *culturatus*, is now recognized as a valid species (Musser and Carleton 2005). Eight subspecies are listed in the distribution section above, but the status of these needs to be tested in the context of a systematic revision. *N. confucianus* is very similar to, and easily confused with *N. fulvescens*; however, *N. confucianus* is larger, darker gray brown, and has large ears. The terminal portion of the tail is usually white all around, while in *N. fulvescens* the tail is usually brown all the way to the tip along the dorsal surface. The skull of *N. confucianus* is larger, with larger bullae and a longer molar tooth-row (5.6–6.9 mm in *N. confucianus* compared to 5.7–5.8 mm in *N. fulvescens*).
Conservation Status: China RL—LC.
References: Deng et al. (2000); Musser and Chiu (1979); Musser (1981); Musser and Carleton (2005); Osgood (1932); Wang and Zheng (1981); Zhang and Zhao (1984).

Spiny Taiwan Niviventer

Niviventer coninga (Swinhoe, 1864) MAP 200
台湾白腹鼠 Taiwan Baifushu

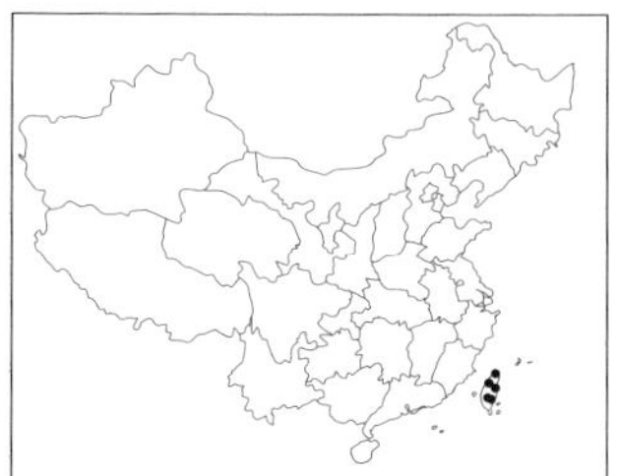

MAP 200. SPINY TAIWAN NIVIVENTER, *Niviventer coninga*

Distinctive Characteristics: HB 140–205; T 174–262; HF 30–37; E 22–29; GLS 39–49; Wt 108–176 g. A large bodied species with a reddish brown to yellow brown spiny pelage. Ventral pelage creamy white. Tail slightly shorter than HB, bicolored dark brown above, paler below. Similar to *N. culturatus*, but larger.
Distribution: Taiwan. Endemic.
Natural History: Found in broadleaf forest, forest edge, and scrub growth; restricted to altitudes below 2,000 m.
Comments: Wang (2003) and many other authors refer to this species by the name *coxingi*; but see Corbet and Hill (1992: 364) for an explanation of why *coninga* is the appropriate name.
Conservation Status: China RL—LC. IUCN RL—LR/nt ver 2.3 (1994) (as *N. coxingi*).
References: Adler (1995; 1996); Aoki and Tanaka (1941); Yu (1993; 1994; 1995).

Soft-Furred Taiwan Niviventer

Niviventer culturatus (Thomas, 1917) MAP 201
台湾社鼠 Taiwan Sheshu

MAP 201. SOFT-FURRED TAIWAN NIVIVENTER, *Niviventer culturatus*

Distinctive Characteristics: HB 130–150; T 170–200; HF 29–35; E 23–25; GLS 37–39. Dorsal pelage dark grayish brown, sharply demarcated from the creamy white ventral pelage. Tail bicolored, brown above, creamy white below; the terminal portion is entirely white. Dorsal surfaces of hands and feet brown, but the digits and sides are white. Face rather grayish, but with dark patches in front of and just behind the eyes.
Distribution: Taiwan. Endemic.
Natural History: Favors primary hemlock forests but may also be found in secondary habitats. Normally restricted to highlands between 2,000 and 3,000 m in elevation. Usually found in association with large logs on the forest floor.
Comments: Previously regarded as a subspecies of *N. confucianus*, but now considered a separate species.
Conservation Status: China RL—LC. IUCN RL—NR/nt ver 2.3 (1994).
References: Adler (1996); Aoki and Tanaka (1941); Musser and Carleton (2005); Yu (1993; 1994; 1995); Yu et al. (1996).

Smoke-Bellied Niviventer

PLATE 24
Niviventer eha (Wroughton, 1916) MAP 202
灰腹鼠 Hui Fushu

Distinctive Characteristics: HB 112–130; T 165–195; HF 28–31; E 17–19; GLS 29–33. A small *Niviventer* with a long tail (ca. 1.5 × HB). Dorsal pelage long, soft and fluffy, without spines, dull brownish orange in color, sides somewhat brighter orange; individual hairs of ventral pelage gray-based with dull grayish white tips, giving the ventral pelage an overall grayish white or "smoky" appearance; ears dark brown and with conspicuous brownish black tuft of hair at the front base of each. There may also be an indistinctly marked extension of brown fur from the

eyering to the vibrissae, but this patch does not extend as far as the nose. Tail long, brownish black above, slightly paler below but not distinctly bicolored; the hairs of the tail increase in length distally to form a small brush at the tip. Hind feet long and slender, their dorsal surfaces dark brown, but with the fingers and toes brownish white. Females with three pairs of mammae: one postaxillary pair, one abdominal pair, and one inguinal pair.
Distribution: S Xizang, W and C Yunnan (Gaoligong and Ailao mountains); extending to Nepal, NE India, and N Myanmar. Wang (2003) recognized two subspecies in China: (1) *N. e. eha* (Wroughton, 1916); Xizang; (2) *N. e. ninus* (Thomas, 1922); Yunnan and perhaps ranging into adjacent Sichuan and Guizhou.

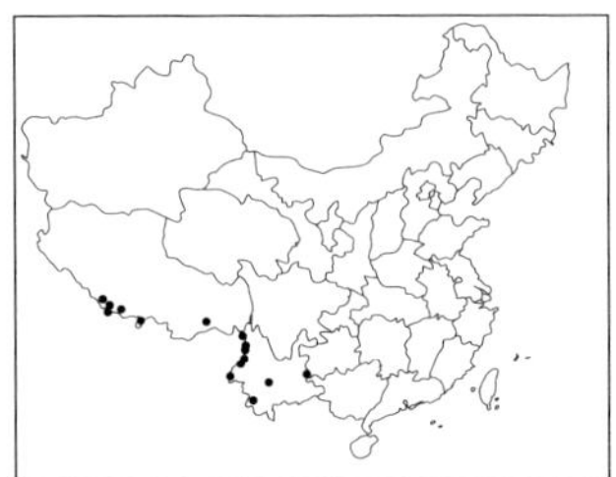

MAP 202. SMOKE-BELLIED NIVIVENTER, *Niviventer eha*

Natural History: Inhabits cool, damp temperate forests characterized by conifers and rhododendrons. Altitudinal range approximately 2,500–3,300 m. Eats insects and especially larvae mostly, but also some fruits and starchy roots. Predominantly terrestrial.
Conservation Status: China RL—LC.
References: Abe (1971); Anthony (1941); Gruber (1969); Musser (1970).

Sichuan Niviventer

Niviventer excelsior (Thomas, 1911) PLATE 24 MAP 203
川西白腹鼠 Chuanxi Baifushu

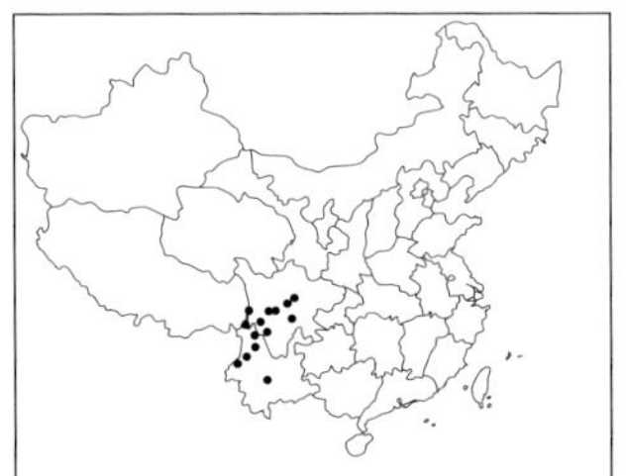

MAP 203. SICHUAN NIVIVENTER, *Niviventer excelsior*

Distinctive Characteristics: HB 127–175; T 190–213; HF 31–33; E 22–27; GLS 38.1–41.3. A large species of *Niviventer* similar to *N. andersoni* but a little smaller. Dorsal pelage dull grayish brown, a somewhat richer orange brown along the sides and sharply demarcated from the pure white ventral pelage. Tail longer than HB, bicolored, dark brown above, pale brownish white below; the terminal portion (1/2–1/4) is entirely white and tufted. Dorsal surfaces of hands and feet brown, fingers and toes brownish white. There is a faint dark brown patch extending forward from the eye to the base of the vibrissae. Skull with the postorbital regions only slightly beaded, and the edges of the braincase convex and smooth.
Distribution: SW Sichuan, NW Yunnan, one record from Ailao Mountain in C Yunnan (Wang 2003). Endemic.
Natural History: Little known beyond the fact that it inhabits high-elevation montane forests.
Comments: Wang (2003) lists *Niviventer excelsior tengchongensis* Deng and Wang, subsp. nov. 2002; an apparent *nomen nudum*.
Conservation Status: China RL—LC.
References: Musser and Chiu (1979).

Indomaylayan Niviventer

Niviventer fulvescens (Gray, 1847) PLATE 24 MAP 204
针毛鼠 Zhenmao Shu

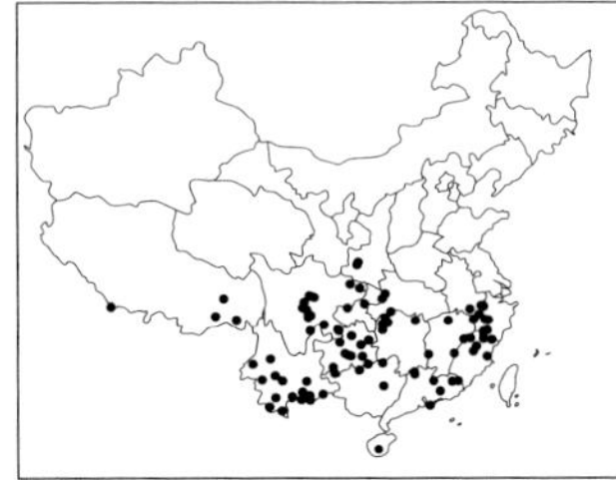

MAP 204. INDOMALAYAN NIVIVENTER, *Niviventer fulvescens*

Distinctive Characteristics: HB 131–172; T 160–221; HF 30–34; E 17–23; GLS 32–40; Wt 60–135 g. Dorsal pelage highly variable even within populations, ranging from dull ochraceous brown to bright fulvous orange. Ventral pelage yellowish white and sharply demarcated. Tail averages slightly longer than HB and is usually bicolored, dark brown above and whitish along the entire length of the underside. Occasionally, individuals will have a monocolored brown tail.
Distribution: Widely distributed throughout S China, including Hainan Island; extending from N Pakistan to Indochina and south to Sumatra, Java, and Bali. Wang (2003) recognized two subspecies from China: (1) *N. f. fulvescens* (Gray, 1847); SE Xizang, Yunnan, Guizhou, Hunan; (2) *N. f. huang* (Bonhote, 1905); Guangxi, Guangdong, Hainan, Jiangxi, Fujian, Zhejiang, Anhui, Henan, Shaanxi, Gansu, Sichuan, Hong Kong, Macao.
Natural History: A common rat favoring all kinds of forest habitats, but also occurring in scrub, bamboo, and agricultural areas near forest. They are predominantly terrestrial, but it is not at all uncommon to find them climbing vines. They are omnivorous and feed on seeds, berries, insects, and probably some green vegetation.
Conservation Status: China RL—LC.
References: Abe (1971; 1983).

Indochinese Arboreal Niviventer

Niviventer langbianis
(Robinson and Kloss, 1922) MAP 205
南洋鼠 Nanyang Shu

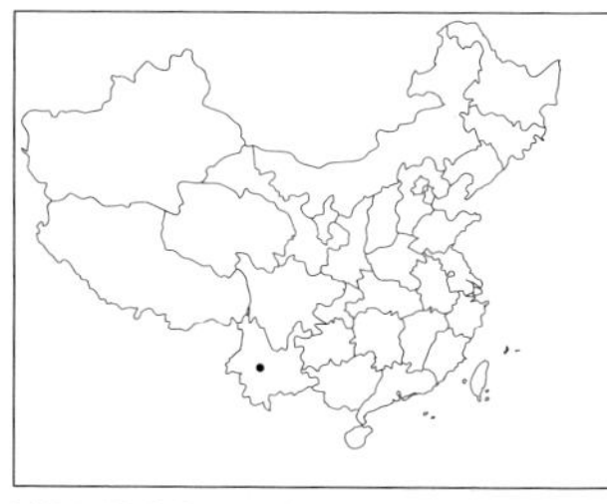

MAP 205. INDOCHINESE ARBOREAL NIVIVENTER, *Niviventer langbianis*

Distinctive Characteristics: HB 131–162; T 154–199; HF 29–33; E 19–22; GLS 33–40; Wt 58–98 g. Dorsal pelage yellowish to reddish brown with dark brown spines and with an indistinct fringe of buffy hairs at the sharply demarcated border of the dorsal and ventral pelage. Ventral pelage white. Tail monocolored brown. Dorsal surfaces of hands and feet pale brown to white, sometimes with a dark brown patch.
Distribution: Reported from a single marginal locality in Yunnan; extending throughout Indochina, Thailand, Myanmar, and NE India.
Natural History: Occurs in evergreen forests where it is usually spottily distributed, being fairly common in some forests and seemingly absent from similar habitats within its range. The species is primarily arboreal, although it is sometimes trapped on the ground.
Comments: Listed as *Rattus cremoriventer indosinicus* in Zhang et al. (1997), and as *Niviventer cremoriventer indosinicus* in Wang (2003). The species occurs from areas just over the Chinese border in Vietnam (Lunde et al. 2003a) and Laos (specimens collected by Lunde) and is very likely to be more widespread in S China. Specimens of *N. langbianis* are often misidentified as *N. confucianus* in museum collections, and surveys of existing collections may uncover additional records of *N. langbianis* from China.
Conservation Status: China RL—NA.
References: Musser (1973b).

Indochinese Mountain Niviventer

Niviventer tenaster (Thomas, 1916) MAP 206
缅甸山鼠 Miandian Shanshu

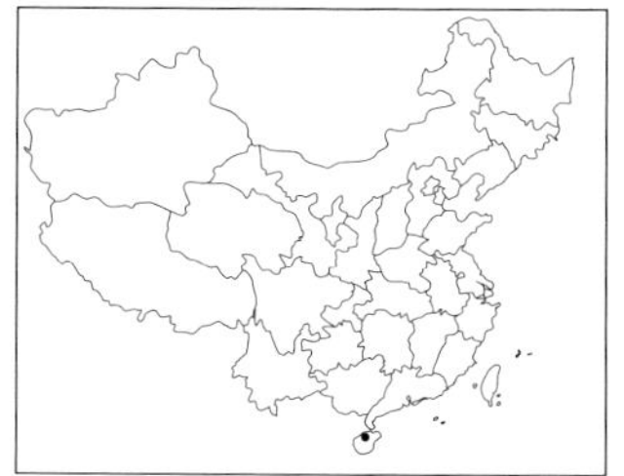

MAP 206. INDOCHINESE MOUNTAIN NIVIVENTER, *Niviventer tenaster*

Distinctive Characteristics: HB 120–189; T 174–234; HF 32–35; E 23–26; GLS 37–42; Wt 53–140 g. Dorsal pelage yellowish brown interspersed with dark brown spines. Ventral pelage white and sharply demarcated. Dorsal surface of the tail brown but often with a mottled white tip; ventral surface of tail paler brown but not sharply demarcated. Ears conspicuously large for the genus.
Distribution: Hainan Island; extending from Myanmar through Thailand and Laos to Vietnam and south to Cambodia.
Natural History: Montane forest.
Conservation Status: China RL—DD.
References: Lunde and Son (2001).

Genus *Rattus*—Old World Rats

家鼠属 Jiashu Shu—家鼠 Jiashu

A diverse genus of Old World rats perhaps best known for its human commensal species. The pelage may be soft or coarse and ranges in color through shades of gray, red, yellow, orange, brown, and black. The ventral pelage may be white or gray. Cranially the genus exhibits very prominent ridges extending along the sides of the braincase; squamosal roots set low on the braincase; a bony palate that extends posterior to the molar toothrow; a mesopterygoid fossa that is narrow in relation to the bony palate and large foramina within each pterygoid fossae. They are omnivorous, eating a wide variety of plants and animals, and highly adaptable. Of 66 species of *Rattus*, 7 occur in China.

Indochinese Forest Rat

PLATE 25
MAP 207

Rattus andamanensis (Blyth, 1860)
黑缘齿鼠 Heiyuan Chishu

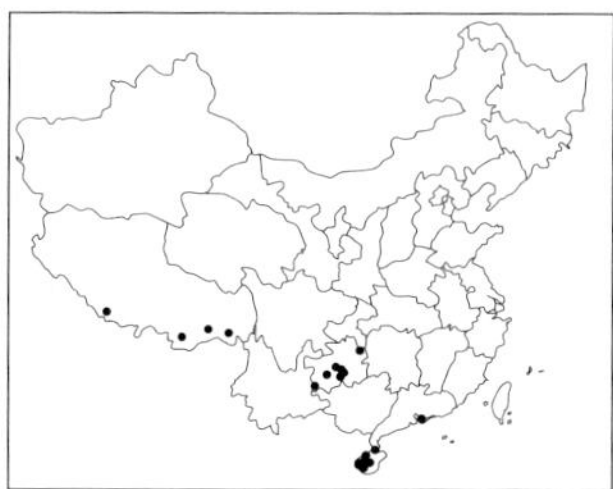

MAP 207. INDOCHINESE FOREST RAT, *Rattus andamanensis*

Distinctive Characteristics: HB 128–185, T 172–222, HF 32–36, E 20–25, GLS 40–43; Wt 125–155. A large *Rattus* with a long, thick pelage. Dorsal pelage varying shades of brown with mixtures of pale brown-and black-tipped hairs and with conspicuous long black guard hairs along much of the midline of the back. Other species of *Rattus* may have long black guard hairs in the dorsal pelage, but these tend to be restricted to the rump. Ventral pelage sharply demarcated from the dorsal pelage, hairs pure creamy white or rarely with small spots of grayish based hairs. Tail much longer than HB and a uniform dark brown. Dorsal surfaces of the feet dark brown. Six pairs of mammae: three pectoral and three inguinal. Skull

Key to the Chinese Species of *Rattus*

1.a. Range in China restricted to small islands in the South China Sea. Size very small, HF < 23 mm. Females with four pairs of mammae *Rattus exulans*
b. Occurs on mainland China and Taiwan. Size larger, HF > 23 mm. Females with five or six pairs of mammae 2
2.a. Hands and feet covered with short white hairs, giving a lustrous pearly white sheen, tail usually shorter than HB. First upper molar with cusp t3 absent or very reduced 3
b. Hands and feet grayish brown or grayish white, but usually without a lustrous sheen; tail usually equal to or considerably longer than HB. First upper molar with cusp t3 present 4
3.a. Size very large, HF > 40 mm *Rattus norvegicus*
b. Not so large, HF < 40 mm *Rattus nitidus*
4.a. Size small, HF < 32 mm *Rattus losea*
b. Size larger, HF > 32 mm 5
5.a. Size somewhat larger, GLS > 45 mm; prominent guard hairs along entire length of back; skull with fairly broad rostrum *Rattus andamanensis*
b. Size somewhat smaller, GLS < 45 mm; prominent guard hairs generally restricted to rump; skull with fairly narrow rostrum 6
6.a. Females with six pairs of mammae *Rattus pyctoris*
b. Females with five pairs of mammae *Rattus tanezumi*

robust, with a broad rostrum, large molars, but with comparatively small bullae.
Distribution: S China; extending into Indochina, Thailand, Myanmar, and NE India. Chinese subspecies: *R. a. koratensis* Kloss, 1919.
Natural History: Most often found in agricultural areas, scrub, and around houses.
Comments: *R. andamanensis* is the oldest available name for the species previously identified as either *R. sikkimensis* or *R. remotus*; see Musser and Carleton (2005).
Conservation Status: China RL—LC.
References: Musser and Carleton (2005); Musser and Newcomb (1985); Musser and Heaney (1985).

Pacific Rat

Rattus exulans (Peale, 1848) MAP 208
缅鼠 Mian Shu

MAP 208. PACIFIC RAT, *Rattus exulans*

Distinctive Characteristics: HB 91–140; T 100–115; HF 22–23; E 15–17.5; GLS 28–33; Wt 43–55 g. A small species with a grayish brown dorsal pelage and pale gray ventral pelage. Tail much longer than HB and monocolored dark brown. Females with four pairs of mammae (one pectoral pair, one postaxial pair, two inguinal pairs).

Distribution: Widespread throughout SE Asia, but range in China restricted to Taiwan and Yongxing Island of Xisha archipelago, South China Sea. Chinese subspecies: *R. e. concolor* (Blyth, 1859).
Natural History: Closely associated with human habitations, they are only rarely found far from villages. They are highly arboreal, climbing through brush, low trees, and on the walls and roofs of houses. Constructs a nest in roof thatch or elevated about 20 cm above the ground in dense grass.
Conservation Status: China RL—DD.
References: Aplin et al. (2003); Motokawa et al. (2001a); Musser and Newcomb (1983).

Losea Rat

PLATE 25
Rattus losea (Swinhoe, 1871) MAP 209
黄毛鼠 Huangmao Shu

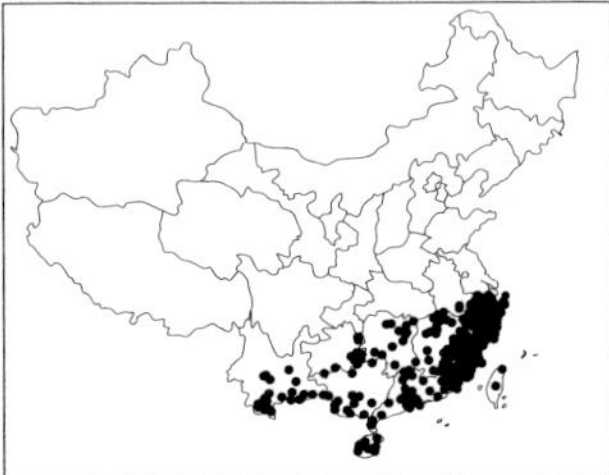

MAP 209. LOSEA RAT, *Rattus losea*

Distinctive Characteristics: HB 120–185; T 128–175; HF 24–32; E 18–21; GLS 33–40; Wt 22–90 g. A relatively small-sized species of *Rattus* with a soft, dense pelage lacking obvious spines. Dorsal pelage varying shades of dull gray-brown with mixtures of pale brown-and black-tipped hairs, becoming somewhat paler along the sides and blending into the gray-based buffy brown ventral pelage without a clear line of demarcation. The inguinal region and underside of the chin are often pure white. Tail approximately equal to HB length or somewhat shorter, monocolored brown or only very slightly paler brown below. Dorsal surfaces of the hands and feet brown. Females with five pairs of mammae (one pectoral pair, one abdominal pair, three inguinal pairs). Skull small and stocky, with a short wide rostrum, high braincase, and relatively large bullae.

Distribution: SE China (Fujian, Guangdong, Jiangxi, Hainan) and Taiwan; extending into Indochina and Thailand. Wang (2003) recognized three subspecies in China: (1) *R. l. exiguus* Howell, 1927; continental China; (2) *R. l. losea* (Swinhoe, 1871); Taiwan; (3) *R. l. sakeratensis* Gyldenstolpe, 1917; Hainan Island.

Natural History: Inhabits grass, scrub, mangroves, cultivated fields, and other human-modified areas from sea level up to about 1,000 m. Terrestrial. Studies in Vietnam suggest that population sizes may fluctuate in relation to the availability of field crops.

Conservation Status: China RL—LC.

References: Adler (1995); Aoki and Tanaka (1938); Aplin et al. (2003); Musser and Newcomb (1985).

White-Footed Indochinese Rat

Rattus nitidus (Hodgson, 1845) PLATE 25 MAP 210

大足鼠 Dazu Shu

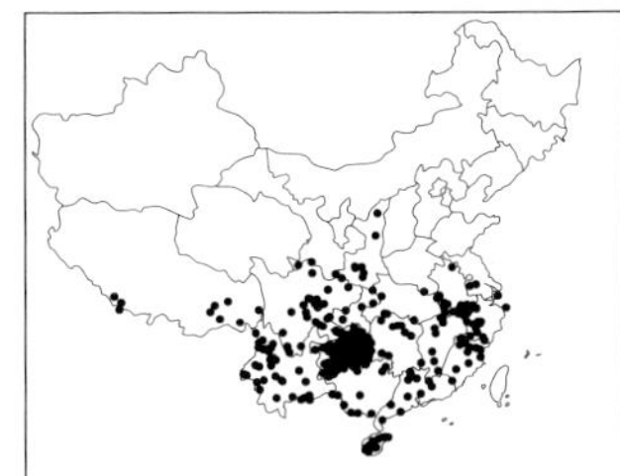

MAP 210. WHITE-FOOTED INDOCHINESE RAT, *Rattus nitidus*

Distinctive Characteristics: HB 148–180; T 135–206; HF 32–36; E 21; GLS 34–44; Wt 114–136 g. A medium-sized species of *Rattus* with a short, thick pelage. Dorsal pelage varying shades of brown but generally dark grayish brown with mixtures of pale brown-and black-tipped hairs, becoming somewhat paler gray along the sides and blending into the dull grayish color of the ventral pelage. Tail approximately equal to or somewhat shorter than HB, monocolored brown or slightly paler brown on the underside. Dorsal surfaces of hands and feet a lustrous pearly white. Females with six pairs of mammae (one pectoral pair, two postaxillary pairs, one abdominal pair, two inguinal pairs). Skull with long rostrum, cusp t3 of each first upper molar is absent or greatly diminished.

Distribution: Widespread across C and SE China including Hainan Island; extending across mainland SE Asia from N India through Nepal, Bhutan, Myanmar, and N Thailand to Vietnam.

Natural History: The natural habitat of this species appears to be the disturbed habitats along the courses of streams and rivers; however, in areas where agricultural habitats and villages are not overrun with *Rattus rattus*, this species will readily occupy these habitats as well. The species is a major agricultural pest in China, infesting all kinds of agricultural areas including rice, wheat, corn, and potato fields. Terrestrial and active day and night. Breeding occurs between March and November, with peaks in March–April and August–September. Litter size ranges from 4 to 15 but averages about 8, with females producing two or three litters per year.

Conservation Status: China RL—LC.

References: Aplin et al. (2003); Zeng et al. (1996a; 1996b; 1999).

Brown Rat

Rattus norvegicus (Berkenhout, 1769) MAP 211

褐家鼠 He Jiashu

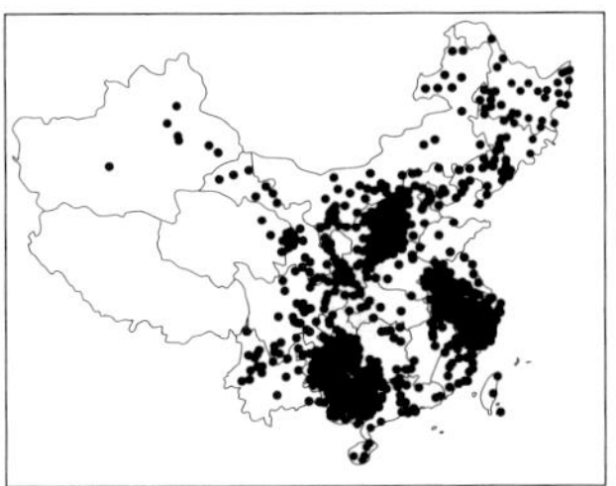

MAP 211. BROWN RAT, *Rattus norvegicus*

Distinctive Characteristics: HB 205–260; T 190–250; HF 38–50; E 19–26; GLS 45–55; Wt 230–500 g (rarely up to 1 kg). A large *Rattus*. Dorsal pelage varying shades of brown with mixtures of pale brown-and black-tipped hairs, becoming somewhat paler along the sides and blending into the gray ventral pelage without a clear line of demarcation. Some pure white hairs may be present in the axillary region. Tail always shorter than HB, indistinctly bicolored, dark brown above, grayish white below. Dorsal surfaces of feet white, sometimes with a pearly luster not unlike that of *R. nitidus*. Females with six pairs of mammae (one pectoral pair, two postaxillary pairs, one abdominal pair, two inguinal pairs). First upper molar lacks cusp t3. 2N = 42.

Distribution: Original distribution comprised N China, SE Siberia, and Japan, but it has been since introduced worldwide. Wang (2003) listed five subspecies from China: (1) *R. n. caraco* (Pallas, 1778); Heilongjiang, Jilin, E Nei Mongol; (2) *R. n. humiliatus* (Milne-Edwards, 1868); Liaoning, Hebei, Beijing, Tianjin, Shandong, N Anhui, N Jiangsu; (3) *R. n. norvegicus* (Berkenhout, 1769); coastal SE China; (4) *R. n. socer* Miller, 1914; Gansu, Ningxia, Qinghai, Nei Mongol, Shaanxi, Hubei, Sichuan, Yunnan, Guizhou, Hunan, Guangxi, Fujian, Jiangxi, Zhejiang, S Anhui, S Jiangsu; (5) *R. n. suffureoventris* Kuroda, 1952; Hong Kong, Taiwan.

Natural History: In China the species is more common in colder climates at higher latitudes. At southern latitudes it is restricted to habitats modified

by humans and especially in association with water (sewers, ports, and warehouses). Terrestrial and an excellent swimmer.
Conservation Status: China RL–LC.
References: Aplin et al. (2003); Wu (1982).

Himalayan Rat

PLATE 25
MAP 212

Rattus pyctoris (Hodgson, 1845)
拟家鼠 Ni Jiashu

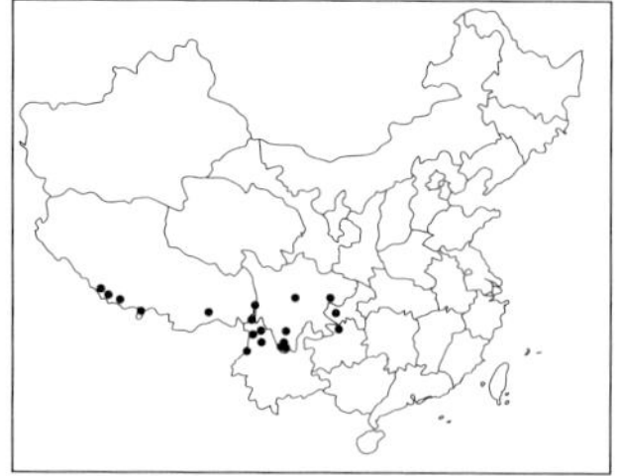

MAP 212. HIMALAYAN RAT, *Rattus pyctoris*

Distinctive Characteristics: HB 140–165; T 135–178; HF 32–34; E 20–25. A small-sized species of *Rattus* with dense, shaggy fur. Dorsal pelage dull grayish brown, paler along the sides and sharply demarcated, blending into the buffy white ventral pelage. Hairs of ventral pelage buffy white but with patches of gray-based hairs sometimes present on the chest or throat. Tail approximately equal to HB length or somewhat longer, dark brown above, paler brown below, especially near the base of the tail. Dorsal surfaces of feet dusky white, lacking the pearly luster seen in *R. nitidus* and *R. norvegicus*. Females with six pairs of mammae. First upper molar with reduced anterolabial cusp (t3) relative to the adjacent two cusps; this cusp is usually absent or undetectable in most samples of *R. norvegicus* and *R. nitidus* but prominent in all other species of *Rattus*.
Distribution: S China (Yunnan, Sichuan, Guangdong); extending westward to SE Kazakhstan and Iran.
Natural History: A montane species generally occurring at altitudes above 1,200 m to approximately 4,250 m.
Comments: *R. pyctoris* is the oldest available name for specimens previously identified as *R. turkestanicus* or *R. rattoides* (Musser and Carleton 2005). Allen's *celsus* also represents this species (Allen 1926, 1940).
Conservation Status: China RL–LC.
References: Allen (1940; as *R. losea celsus*); Caldarini et al. (1989).

Oriental House Rat

PLATE 25
MAP 213

Rattus tanezumi Temminck, 1844
黄胸鼠 Huangxiong Shu
Distinctive Characteristics: HB 105–215; 120–230; HF 26–35; E 17–23; GLS 38–44. A medium-sized species of *Rattus* with a short, coarse pelage. Dorsal pelage varying shades of brown with mixtures of pale brown-and black-tipped hairs; hairs of ventral pelage gray-based with buffy white tips, ventral pelage not sharply demarcated from dorsal pelage. Tail longer than HB, monocolored brown or slightly paler along the underside near the base. Feet whitish on the sides and on the fingers but with distinctive dark grayish brown patches in the center. Similar to *Rattus rattus*, but with a shorter tail relative to HB.
Distribution: Widespread in SE China, including Hainan Island and Taiwan. Populations in Xinjiang are invasive. Natural range extends from E Afghanistan to NE India and China, Korea, Indochina south to Isthmus of Kra, but the species has been widely introduced throughout Asia.

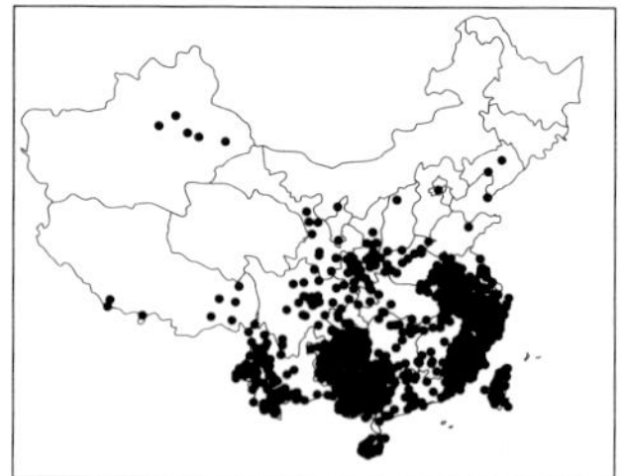

MAP 213. ORIENTAL HOUSE RAT, *Rattus tanezumi*

Natural History: Most commonly found in and around villages and agricultural areas, where they are equally at home on the ground or climbing through the rafters of houses.
Comments: Most specimens identified as *Rattus rattus* from China are *R. tanezumi* (formerly known as the "Asia form" of *Rattus rattus*). In China, true *Rattus rattus* is an invasive species restricted to cities, harbors, and ships in port. Wang's (2003) *R. yunnanensis* is included in this species.
Conservation Status: China RL–LC.
References: Aplin et al. (2003); Xie et al. (2001).

Genus *Vandeleuria*—Vandeleuria

长尾攀鼠属 Changweipanshu Shu—长尾攀鼠 Changweipanshu

Small orange climbing mice with a long tail and with the first and fifth digits of both the hands and feet partially opposable and lacking claws. Skull fairly narrow across the frontals, the least interorbital breadth being less than 4 mm. Upper incisors narrow with pale yellow enamel. A posterio-internal cusp (t7) is retained. One of three species of *Vandeleuria* occurs in China.

Indomalayan Vandeleuria

PLATE 25
MAP 214

Vandeleuria oleracea (Bennett, 1832)
长尾攀鼠 Changwei Panshu
Distinctive Characteristics: HB 61–90; T 92–110; HF 17–18; E 11–16; GLS 19–22.6. Dorsal pelage dull rusty brown to bright reddish brown. Ventral pelage pure creamy white. Tail uniform brown and very long, averaging 1.5 times HB length and appearing naked. The first and fifth digits of the hands and feet are

shorter than the third and fourth and bear a flattened nail. Females with four pairs of mammae (two thoracic pairs and two inguinal pairs).
Distribution: Yunnan; extending to India, Sri Lanka, Nepal, Myanmar, Thailand, Vietnam, and probably south throughout Indochina. Wang (2003) recognized two subspecies in China: (1) *V. o. dumeticola* (Hodgson, 1845); W Yunnan; (2) *V. o. scandens* Osgood, 1932; S Yunnan.

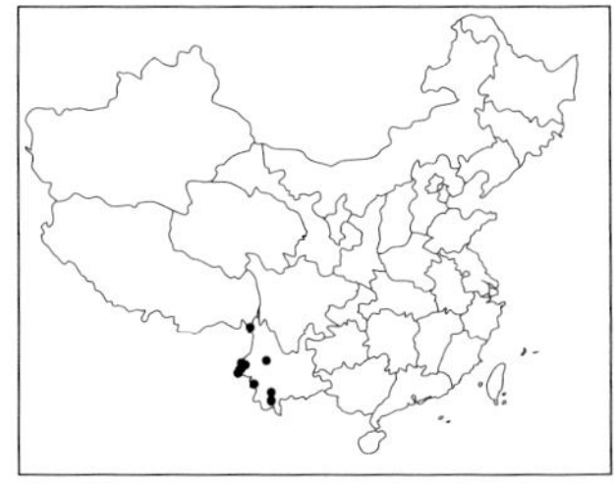

MAP 214. INDOMALAYAN VANDELEURIA, *Vandeleuria oleracea*

Natural History: Arboreal and strictly nocturnal. Eats fruits, buds, and flowers. A very agile denizen of thick vegetation, it occurs in understory trees, shrubs, and dense grassy vegetation, and even in piles of brush. Builds a grass nest along slender branches several meters above the ground. Litter size three to six.
Conservation Status: China RL—VU A1c.
References: Agrawal (2000); Allen (1940); Osgood (1932); Prakash et al. (1995a; 1995b).

Genus *Vernaya* (monotypic)

滇攀鼠属 Dianpanshu Shu

Vernay's Climbing Mouse

PLATE 25
MAP 215

Vernaya fulva (Allen, 1927)
滇攀鼠 Dian Panshu

Distinctive Characteristics: HB 58–75; T 120–133; HF 18–18.5; E 17; GLS 20–22.3. A small arboreal mouse with an exceptionally long tail about twice HB length. Externally similar to *Vandeleuria*, but with a much longer tail and with pointed claws on all digits except the thumb. Dorsal pelage rich orange brown, brighter fulvous along the sides. Ventral pelage gray-based with white tips, but only the white shows so the ventral pelage appears pale buffy white. Tail dark brown above, slightly paler below, but not distinctly bicolored. Skull with short rostrum and a conspicuous longitudinal depression extending from the posterior of the nasals through the interorbital region and onto the frontals. There are often two unossified vacuities in the interorbital region. Incisive foramina extend posteriorly to just past the anterior face of the first molars.
Distribution: W Yunnan, C and N Sichuan, S Gansu, SW Shaanxi; extending into N Myanmar.

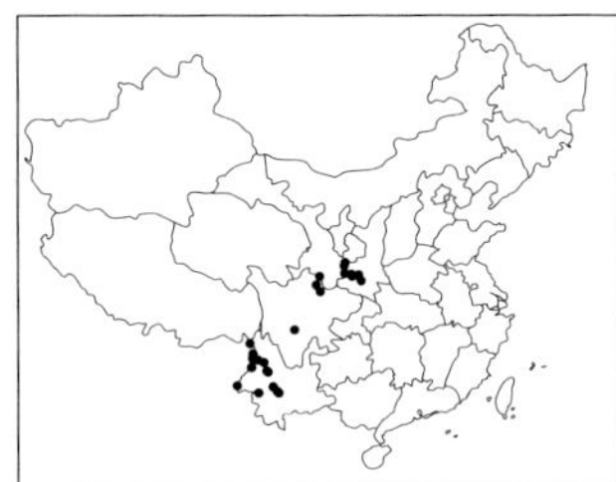

MAP 215. VERNAY'S CLIMBING MOUSE, *Vernaya fulva*

Natural History: Arboreal. Specimens collected between 2,100 and 2,700 m elevation.
Comments: *V. foramena* Wang, Hu, and Chen, 1980, is now considered a synonym of *V. fulva*.
Conservation Status: China RL—EN A1c. IUCN RL—VU C2a ver 2.3 (1994).
References: Allen (1927); Anthony (1941); Li and Wang (1995); Wang et al. (1980).

Family Hystricidae—Old World Porcupines

豪猪科 Haozhu Ke—豪猪 Haozhu

Andrew T. Smith

Form stout, whole body covered with round or flat quills; tail also has quills or stiff hairs; fore and hind feet with five digits, without long claws. Nasal cavity large, frontal larger than parietal, median area of zygomatic arch formed by jugal; occipital ridge evident; angular process of mandible not obliquely outward or behind occipital condyle; auditory bullae small. Dental formula: 1.0.1.3/1.0.1.3 = 20; molar crowns flat with transverse folds of enamel surrounding islands of dentine. Occurs widely throughout the Indo-Malayan realm, southern Palaearctric realm, and most portions of Africa. The family comprises three genera, of which two occur in China.

Key to the Chinese Genera of Hystricidae

1.a. Tail longer than twice length of hind foot, ending in tufts of quills, "beaded" in structure; longest quills on dorsum only about 75 mm, flattened, mostly brown, a few white tipped *Atherurus*
b. Tail shorter than twice length of hind foot, tip of tail with tubular "rattle" quills; longest quills on dorsum and hind quarters much > 75 mm *Hystrix*

Genus *Atheurus*—Brush-tailed Porcupines

帚尾豪猪属 Zhouweihaozhu Shu—帚尾豪猪 Zhouweihaozhu

Size small, body long, limbs stout, ears short and round; extremity of tail covered with white tufted quills, posterior portion of quills possess many "beaded" knobs; quills on dorsum flat, grooved above; quills on belly soft and fine. Distribution disrupted; occurs in both Indo-Malayan and African realms; of two species, only one occurs in China.

Asiatic Brush-Tailed Porcupine

PLATE 1
MAP 216

Atherurus macrourus (Linnaeus, 1758)

帚尾豪猪 Zhouwei Haozhu

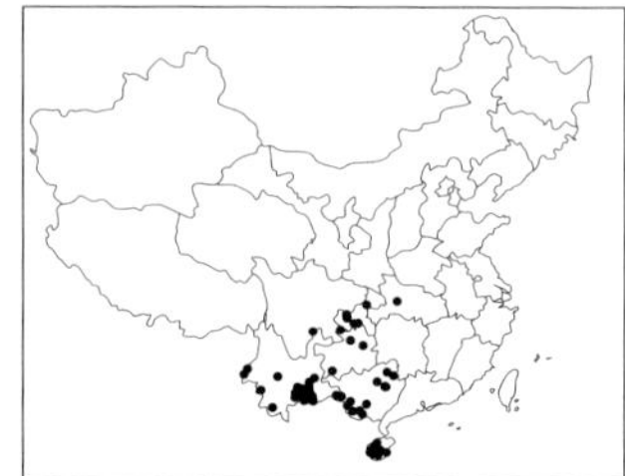

MAP 216. ASIATIC BRUSH-TAILED PORCUPINE, *Atherurus macrourus*

Distinctive Characteristics: HB 345–525; T 139–228; HF 64–75; E 30–36; GLS 83–120; Wt 2–4 kg. A small porcupine with a long, scaly tail that ends in a brush of white bristles over 20 cm in length. Quills grooved. Has two laterally placed mammae. Nasal narrow and short, less than 30% of GLS, posterior portion just 3–4 mm longer than posterior margin of premaxilla; preorbital fossa smaller than temporal fossa; molars completely rooted. 2N = 54.
Distribution: Central S China; extending to India, Myanmar, Thailand, Laos, Vietnam, Malaysia, and Sumatra. Two subspecies in China: (1) *A. m. hainanus* Allen, 1906; Hainan Island; (2) *A. m. macrourus* (Linnaeus, 1758); Sichuan, Guizhou, Yunnan, Hubei, Hunan, Guangxi.
Natural History: Occupies dense forests where it constructs and occupies burrows. These burrows may connect and hold up to three individuals. May favor rocky areas. Nocturnal and generally terrestrial, but known to climb trees. Diet consists of roots, tubers, and green plants. One (sometimes two) precocial young is born following a 100–110-day gestation. Two litters may be produced per year. Young leave the nest after about one week, the time it takes for their quills to harden.
Conservation Status: China RL—VU A2cd + 3cd.

Genus *Hystrix*—Old World Porcupines

豪猪属 Haozhu Shu—豪猪 Haozhu

Form larger and stouter than *Atherurus;* tail short, less than 115 mm; sides and chest with flat quills; quills on hind quarters and tail round. Nasal broad and long, more than 30% of GLS, posterior portion over 15 mm longer than posterior margin of premaxilla; preorbital fossa subequal to temporal fossa in size; molars partially rooted. Structure of upper molars conspicuously different from *Atherurus*. Occurs broadly in S Europe, S Asia, and N Africa. Consists of eight species, one of which occurs in China.

Malayan Porcupine

PLATE 1
MAP 217

Hystrix brachyura Linnaeus, 1758

豪猪 Hao Zhu

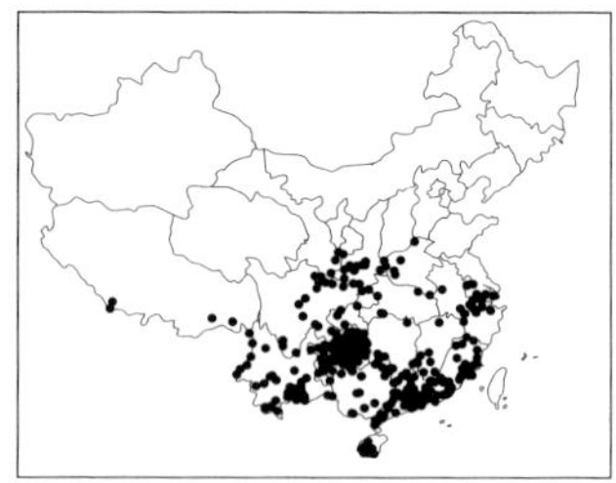

MAP 217. MALAYAN PORCUPINE, *Hystrix brachyura*

Distinctive Characteristics: HB 558–735; T 80–115; HF 75–93; E 25–38; GLS 131–146; Wt 10–18 kg. Heavy-set porcupine with very small eyes and ears. Median area between frontal and anterior dorsum quills with light brown base and white upper side forms white stripes; neck possesses a white stripe; body dark brown; quills on dorsum square at anterior portion and round at posterior portion, base and tip of quills white, middle part brown. Tail with peculiar tubular quills with hollow tip and extending 20–30 cm in length; these rattle when tail is shaken. Has three laterally paired mammae. Nasal long and broad, longer than half of the GLS; skull with inflated pneumatic cavities. 2N = 60.
Distribution: Broadly distributed across SE China including Hainan Island; extending into Nepal, India (Sikkim and Assam), Myanmar, Thailand, Indochina, Malasia, Sumatra, Borneo. Four subspecies in China: (1) *H. b. hodgsoni* (Gray, 1847); Xizang; (2) *H. b. papae* Allen, 1927; Hainan; (3) *H. b. subcristata* Swinhoe, 1870; Yunnan, Sichuan, Chongqing, Guizhou, Hunan, Guangxi, Guangdong, Hong Kong, Fujian, Jianxi, Zhejiang, Shanghai, Jiangsu, Anhui, Henan, Hubei, Shaanxi, Gansu; (4) *H. b. yunnanensis* Anderson, 1878; Yunnan. The boundaries between these forms (except *papae*) are likely to intergrade, and thus subspecific designations are likely to be arbitrary.
Natural History: Occupies forests and open fields where large burrows are dug into banks and under rocks. These burrows may be occupied by family groups that emerge at night and forage together along well-defined runways. Diet consists of roots, tubers, bark, vegetation, and fallen fruit. Although these porcupines do not "throw" their quills, when in danger they can forcefully hurl themselves backward and drive their quills into their enemy. When alarmed they rattle their tail quills, snort, and stomp

their feet. Following a gestation of about 110 days, two (sometimes three) precocial young are born. Two litters may be produced per year.
Conservation Status: China RL—VU A2cd + 3cd. IUCN RL—VU A1d ver 2.3 (1994).

ORDER LAGOMORPHA—Pikas, Rabbits, and Hares
兔形目 **Tuxing Mu—**鼠兔类 **Shutu Lei,** 兔类 **Tulei**

Andrew T. Smith

The most characteristic feature separating lagomorphs from rodents is the presence of a second, peglike upper incisor that sits behind the large anterior incisor. A single layer of enamel coats the front incisors, in contrast to the double layer in rodents. Canines absent. Dental formula: 2.0.3.2–3/1.0.2.3 = 26–28, with a long postincisor diastema. Because the distance along the upper cheek dentition is wider than that of the lower cheek dentition, lagomorphs chew in a side-to-side motion to ensure full occlusion on one side, then the other. Lagomorph means "hare-shaped"—thus signifying a characteristic posture (more pronounced in leporids than pikas). Generally with large hind feet, large ears, and small tails. Produce two types of fecal pellets (round hard and viscous soft dark), and engage in coprophagy of the soft feces.

Lagomorphs were once classified as Duplicidentata in the Rodentia, but it is clear that they represent an independent lineage at the ordinal level. Over the years the lagomorphs have been aligned with a number of orders within the Mammalia; currently it is felt once again that they are most closely related to rodents, within a clade termed Glires (Douzery and Huchon 2004). Recent molecular and paleontological evidence indicates that the lagomorphs split from the rodents as long ago as the Cretaceous—between 65 and 100 mya. Lagomorphs are found worldwide, with the exception of Australia, Oceania, and southern South America, although they have been widely introduced into these regions. Includes two families, Ochotonidae and Leporidae, both represented in China.

Family Ochotonidae
Genus *Ochotona*—Pikas
鼠兔科 **Shutu Ke;** 鼠兔属 **Shutu Shu—**鼠兔 **Shutu**

Small, egg-shaped, with soft, dense pelage; ears short and round; tail concealed (and usually not included in standard measurements); forefeet (with five digits) shorter than hind feet (four digits); side of frontal with no supraorbital processes; large foramen present on lateral sides of nasals; posterior extension of zygomatic arch extends almost to the anterior margin of auditory bullae. Dental formula: 2.0.3.2/1.0.2.3 = 26.

Pikas are diurnal, nonhibernating, generalized herbivores. Some species occur in rock and talus environments; these generally are long-lived, live in low-density populations with low turnover, and have low reproductive rates. Other species construct burrows and live in meadow or steppe environments; these usually live at high densities with high turnover and are short-lived, and have high reproductive rates (Smith et al. 1990).

The Ochotonidae apparently originated in Asia; paleontological and molecular evidence indicates that it split from the Leporidae in the early Oligocene. At one time the family was particularly diverse (there are 25 fossil genera) and distributed throughout North America, Asia, and Africa. Currently there are 30 species of pika, all in a single genus *Ochotona*. Two species occur in the mountains of western North America, the remainder in Asia. China is home to 24 species of pika, the most of any country; 12 of these are endemic to China. Recent systematic studies of *Ochotona* in China include Feng and Zheng (1985), Niu (2002), Niu et al. (2001), Niu et al. (2004), Smith et al. (1990), Yu et al. (1997), and Yu et al. (2000). The status and conservation of *Ochotona* has been reviewed by Smith et al. (1990).

Alpine Pika
Ochotona alpina (Pallas, 1773) MAP 218
高山鼠兔 **Gaoshan Shutu**

Distinctive Characteristics: HB 152–235; HF 26–35; E 17–26; GLS 41–54; Wt 226–360 g. A large pika, although some Chinese forms are smaller than those outside of China. In summer dorsal pelage dark or cassia brown; flanks have a rust-red tinge. Underneath light brown or light whitish yellow. In winter dorsal pelage pale grayish brown, head and anterior dorsum tinged with yellow. The skull is stoutly built but long and narrow. Incisive foramen and palatal foramen completely separated; frontal low and flat, with no oval alveolus above; parietal slightly

Key to the Chinese Families of Lagomorpha

1.a. Size small, HB length < 285 mm; short ears rounded, < 40 mm; tail concealed; skull without supraorbital process; two pairs of upper premolars — Ochotonidae

b. Size large, HB length > 300 mm; ear pinnae long (> 60 mm); hind limbs significantly longer than forelimbs; tail short but evident; skull with supraorbital processes and highly fenestrated; three pairs of upper premolars — Leoporidae

Key to the Chinese Species of *Ochotona*

1.a.	Incisive foramen and palatal foramen separate (although they may merge in young individuals)	2
b.	Incisive foramen and palatal foramen combined into a single foramen	10
2.a.	Frontal with no small oval foramen above	3
b.	Frontal with two small oval foramina above	9
3.a.	Ears small and round, length averaging < 23 (17–26)	4
b.	Ears well-developed, length averaging > 28 (28–35)	7
4.a.	Winter-spring pelage a striking silvery color	*Ochotona argentata*
b.	Winter-spring pelage brown-gray tone	5
5.a.	Interorbital region narrow, its breadth < breadth in middle of nasal; neck below ears with brown or reddish spot	*Ochotona pallasi*
b.	Interorbital width > breadth in middle of nasal; neck below ears lacks any spot	6
6.a.	Skull short and round	*Ochotona hyperborea*
b.	Skull stoutly built, but long and narrow	*Ochotona alpina*
7.a.	Color light, dorsal pelage in summer sandy yellow; dorsal side of ears tinged with light brown; no light spots behind ear	*Ochotona ladacensis*
b.	Color dark, dorsal pelage in summer grayish brown to tea brown; dorsal side of ears tinged with grayish black or rusty brown; light spots behind ear	8
8.a.	Pelage from rostrum to frontal rusty ochraceous or bright reddish brown; dorsal side of ears grayish black; anterior portion of nasal conspicuously inflated	*Ochotona rutila*
b.	Pelage from rostrum to frontal tinged with rusty yellow; dorsal side of ears chestnut or orange.	*Ochotona muliensis*
9.a.	In summer dorsal pelage bright red constrasting sharply with pure white ventor; rostral portion of skull short and broad; nasals short	*Ochotona erythrotis*
b.	Summer dorsal pelage orange or pale brown only at rostrum, frontal and dorsal side of ears; rostral portion of skull narrow and long; nasals long	*Ochotona gloveri*
10.a.	Ears large, > 26 mm	11
b.	Ears small-medium, < 26 mm	14
11.a.	Mass > 200 g; restricted range in Tian Shan mountains	*Ochotona iliensis*
b.	Mass < 200 g	12
12.a.	Frontal with no small oval foramen above	*Ochotona himalayana*
b.	Frontal with small oval foramina above	13
13.a.	Ear well furred; skull strongly arched	*Ochotona macrotis*
b.	Ear sparsely furred; skull weakly arched	*Ochotona roylei*
14.a.	HB length > 200; skull strongly arched; zygomatic breadth 25–27 mm	*Ochotona koslowi*
b.	HB length < 200; skull weakly arched or flat; zygomatic breadth < 23 mm	15
15.a.	Skull moderately arched; extremities of toes usually hidden in fur	16
b.	Skull flat; extremities of toes naked	17
16.a.	Area around rostrum blackish brown; auditory bullae small	*Ochotona curzoniae*
b.	Area around rostrum dull white; auditory bullae well developed and conspicuously inflated	*Ochotona dauurica*
17.a.	Margin of the foramen resulting from combining the incisive and palatal foramen violin-shaped	18
b.	Margin of the foramen resulting from combining the incisive and palatal foramen pear-shaped or club-shaped	20
18.a.	Pelage black (melanistic)	*Ochotona nigritia*
b.	Pelage dark brown, rufous brown	19
19.a.	Back of ear black; head and neck a brilliant rufous brown; dark brown dorsum extending to venter	*Ochotona gaoligongensis*
b.	Dark gray spots behind ears; may form a dorsal collar extending onto the face; both dorsal and ventral pelage blackish brown or dark reddish brown	*Ochotona forresti*
20.a.	Skull conspicuously narrow and fragile; auditory bullae elongated and convex	*Ochotona thomasi*
b.	Skull flattened, but not as narrow or fragile; auditory bullae not elongated	21

21.a. Dorsal side of skull slightly swollen — *Ochotona nubrica*
b. Dorsal side of skull not swollen — 22
22.a. Auditory bullae large; skull pear-shaped — *Ochotona cansus*
b. Auditory bullae small; skull not pear-shaped — 23
23.a. Dorsal pelage tea brown; narrow interorbital space; narrow braincase — *Ochotona thibetana*
b. Dorsal pelage dark brown or chestnut tinged with conspicuous black; broad interorbital space; broad braincase — *Ochotona huangensis*

protruding anteriorly, and posteriorly forming an oblique slope with interparietal; no fenestrae are present in the frontals; zygomatic arch thick and large; lambdoidal crest of skull well developed; diastema usually larger than upper dentition length. 2N = 42.
Distribution: NW and NE China. Two subspecies in China: (1) *O. a. cinereofusca* (Schrenk, 1858); Heilongjiang; extending into Russia; (2) *O. a. nitida* Hollister, 1912; N Xinjiang; extending into Kazakhstan, Russia, and Mongolia.

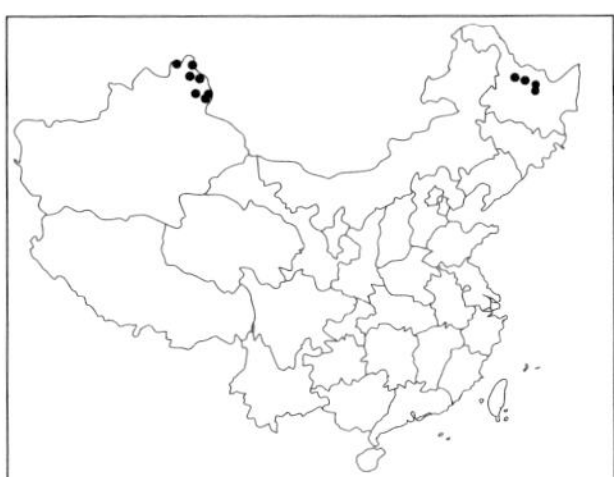

MAP 218. ALPINE PIKA, *Ochotona alpina*

Natural History: Inhabits rocky regions and crevices in forested regions at elevations greater than 2,000 m; may occupy old moss-covered scree or lacunae under tree roots. A generalized herbivore; may feed on mosses, pine nuts, and branches of trees. Constructs large haypiles (up to 30 kg/ha of vegetation may be cached). Lives in family territories (an adult pair and their young) at low density (10–12/ha). Frequently vocalizes (long-calls or songs given by males during mating season; territorial calls, alarm calls). Produces two litters averaging three young.
Comments: Formerly included *O. hyperborea*, but the forms are distinctive and they overlap in several areas. The assignment of subspecies between *O. hyperborea* and *O. alpina* still causes considerable confusion. Formerly included *O. argentata*, herein considered an independent form. Also, closely related to *O. pallasi*, and some assignments of subspecies between these species have been debated.
Conservation Status: China RL—LC.
References: He (1958); Hollister (1912); Ma et al. (1987); Wang and Yang (1983).

Silver Pika

Ochotona argentata Howell, 1928 — MAP 219
宁夏鼠兔 Ningxia Shutu

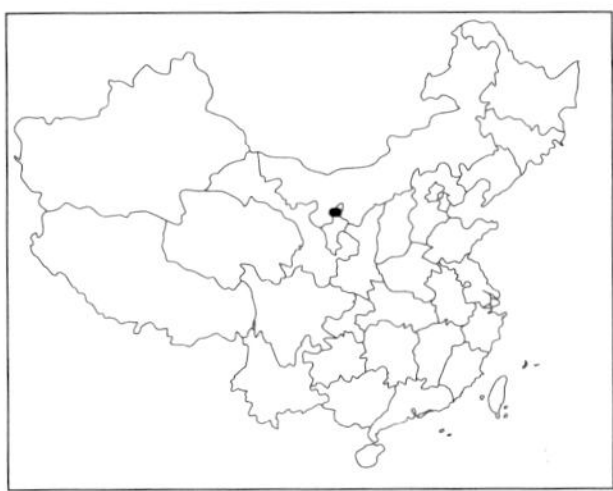

MAP 219. SILVER PIKA, *Ochotona argentata*

Distinctive Characteristics: HB 208–235; HF 31–35; E 22–25; GLS 48–52; Wt 176–236 g. In winter the dorsum is a striking silvery color, the hairs being a pale steel gray with fine black tips. Feet white above and grayish below. Ventral pelage white tinged with buffy. Summer pelage is bright rusty red, similar with *O.rutila* and *O. macrotis*. Compared with the skull of *O. alpina*, the orbit is markedly larger, and the posterior palatal foramen are longer. 2N = 38.
Distribution: Known only from the Helan Shan mountains in Ningxia, where its range is extremely restricted to a 2 × 1.5 km ridge-top area. Endemic.
Natural History: A rock-dwelling pika in forested areas. Its shelters include artificial rock slides around mines; also may be found living inside mines as far as 20 m from the entrance. A generalized herbivore, it constructs a typical pika haypile. The Silver Pika is relatively unvocal in comparison with *O. pallasi* and *O. alpina*.
Comments: This form has been included as a subspecies of *O. alpina* and of *O. pallasi* (as *O. p. helanshanensis*, a junior synonym), but it is distinctive in morphology, chromosome number, molecular characteristics, and acoustic attributes.
Conservation Status: Its habitat has been greatly impacted within its restricted distributional range. China RL—VU D2. IUCN RL—CR A2cd ver 2.3 (1994).
References: Formozov (1997); Formozov et al. (2004); Howell (1928).

Gansu Pika

Ochotona cansus Lyon, 1907 — MAP 220
间颅鼠兔 Jianlu Shutu
Distinctive Characteristics: HB 116–165; HF 22–29; E 14–24; GLS 33–39; Wt 50–99 g. In summer dorsal

pelage dark russet, tea brown, or dark brown to dull-grayish buff (there is considerable variation throughout the geographic range); a light stripe from the chest to abdomen is somewhat inconspicuous. Ventral pelage light white, generally tinged with buffy. Winter pelage is uniformly grayish russet. Skull proportionally large, although skull shorter, zygomatic arch and interorbital width narrower than in *O. thibetana,* with which it is frequently compared. Incisive foramen and palatal foramen combine into one foramen; frontal bone low and flat, with no alveolus above; parietal slightly convex; posterior processes of zygomatic arch nearly parallel; profile of skull pear-shaped, broader than that of *O. thomasi*; auditory bullae well developed.

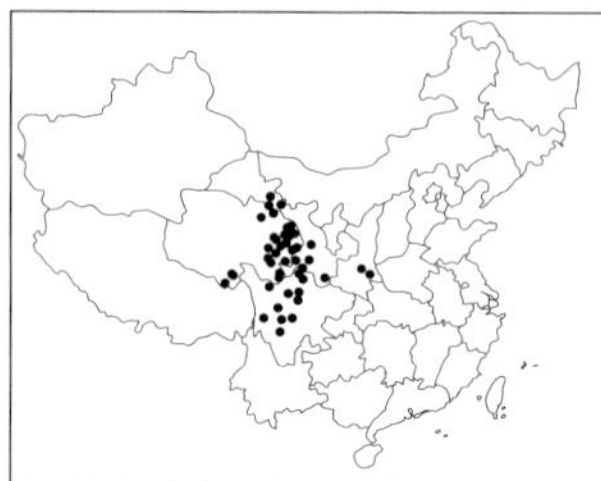

MAP 220. GANSU PIKA, *Ochotona cansus*

Distribution: Highlands of C China. Endemic. Five subspecies: (1) *O. c. annectens* Miller, 1911; Gansu, N Sichuan, W Qinghai; (2) *O. c. cansus* Lyon, 1907; Gansu, Qinghai, NW Sichuan; (3) *O. c. morosa* Thomas, 1912; Shaanxi; (4) *O. c. sorella* Thomas, 1908; Ningqu, Shanxi; (5) *O. c. stevensi* Osgood, 1932; Hengduan mountains, W Sichuan.
Natural History: Occupies open areas within shrublands adjoining alpine meadow, primarily inhabiting the *Potentilla fruticosa* and *Caragana jubata* zone at 2,700–3,800 m. Constructs simple burrows with few openings. A generalized herbivore. Lives in family groups composed of an adult pair and their young in a communal burrow system. Mating system monogamous. Most behavioral interactions affiliative and expressed among family members. Four distinct vocalizations are given: male-only long calls (or songs), short calls (territorial and antipredator function), whines, and trills. May spend twice as much time surface active as the Plateau Pika. Produces three litters of up to six young.
Comments: Originally this form was included in the distinctive *O. roylei*. More recently it has been assigned commonly to *O. thibetana*. These two species, however, are distinctive and sympatric over much of their range. There has been considerable difficulty in assigning some subspecies between these two forms. Here we include the form *annectens* contra Hoffmann and Smith (2005), who followed several earlier treatments that included it in *dauurica*; recent molecular analyses align *annectens* with *cansus*, and it could represent an independent form (Niu et al. 2004; Yu et al. 2000).

Conservation Status: China RL—LC. IUCN RL—LC; *O. c. morosa* DD; *O. c. sorella*: EN A2d ver 2.3 (1994).
References: Jiang and Wang (1991); Niu et al. (2004); Su (2001); Yu et al. (2000).

Plateau Pika

PLATE 26
MAP 221

Ochotona curzoniae (Hodgson, 1858)
高原鼠兔 Gaoyuan Shutu

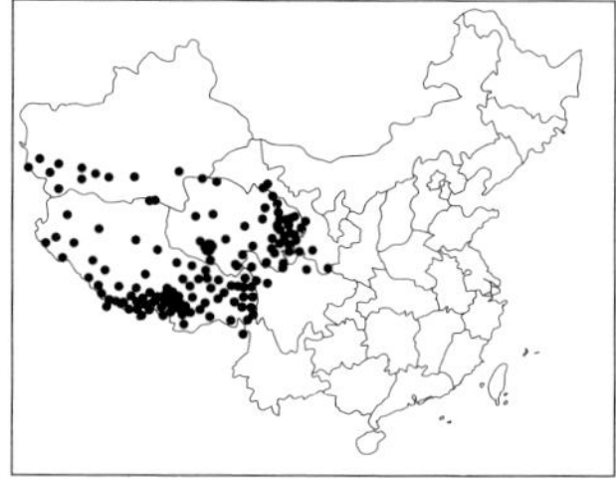

MAP 221. PLATEAU PIKA, *Ochotona curzoniae*

Distinctive Characteristics: HB 140–192; HF 28–37; E 18–26; GLS 39–44; Wt 130–195 g. In summer, dorsal pelage sandy brown or dark sandy russet; ventral pelage sandy yellow or grayish white; dorsal side of ears rust-colored, with white margin. In winter, dorsal pelage light, sandy yellow or yellowish white, softer and longer than summer pelage. The nose has a blackish tip with the same color extending to and ringing the lips. Feet with hairy soles and long black claws on fore and hind feet. The medium-sized skull is greatly arched, and the frontal is obviously convex; the interorbital region is moderately narrow. Incisive foramen and palatal foramen combined into one foramen; auditory bullae small. 2N = 46.
Distribution: Tibetan Plateau of S Xinjiang, Qinghai, Xizang, and W Sichuan; extending into N Nepal and N India.
Natural History: Lives in burrows in open alpine meadow, meadow-steppe, or desert-steppe at high elevations (3,000–5,000 m). Strictly herbivorous; may store vegetation during late summer to use as food over winter. The Plateau Pika is highly social, living in well-defined and defended family burrow system territories. Family groups are composed of either an adult pair (monogamy), a male with multiple females (polygyny), or multiple males and female(s) (polyandry) along with their young from sequential litters born during the breeding season. Affiliative social interactions (such as allogrooming, nose rubbing, sitting side-by-side) are expressed frequently within family groups, primarily among siblings of all ages and their father. They utter six different calls: the long call (or song) given only by adult males during the mating season; the soft and repetitive short call given mostly by adult females when predators have been sighted; and whines, trills, muffles, and transition calls given primarily by young animals. Young tend to remain in their family burrow system throughout their summer of birth, and dispersal—when it occurs—is normally only a short distance.

The population density of the Plateau Pika increases throughout the summer with the addition of each weaned litter to family groups and may approach over 300 animals/ha. Rate of mortality during winter is high, leading to a dispersal shuffle in early spring of surviving animals into the variable mating systems on individual family burrow system territories. Three to five litters of two to eight young are born during the summer.

Comments: This form has been treated as a subspecies of *O. dauurica*, but they are clearly independent. The form *melanostoma* is a synonym.

Conservation Status: The high density of Plateau Pikas and the burrows that they construct make this a keystone species in the Tibetan alpine meadow ecosystem. Nearly all predators rely on pikas for food, and their burrows serve as nesting habitat for a variety of birds and lizards. The burrowing activity also decreases erosion (allowing the soil to absorb more water during the heavy monsoon rains) and increases the rate of nutrient cycling on the meadows. Nevertheless, the Plateau Pika has been labeled as a pest species and poisoned over much of its geographic range (over 200,000 km^2 in Qinghai Province in recent years). China RL—LC.

References: Dobson et al. (1998; 2000); Lai and Smith (2003); Smith and Foggin (1999); Smith et al. (1986); Smith and Wang (1991); Su (2001); Zhang et al. (2002).

Daurian Pika

PLATE 26
MAP 222

Ochotona dauurica (Pallas, 1776)
达乌尔鼠兔 Dawu'er Shutu

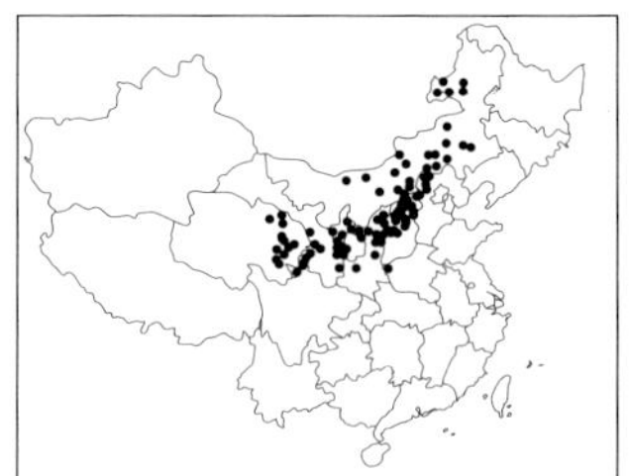

MAP 222. DAURIAN PIKA, *Ochotona dauurica*

Distinctive Characteristics: HB 150–200; HF 27–33; E 16–26; GLS 39–45; Wt 110–150 g. Summer pelage yellowish brown to straw gray dorsally, ventral surface whitish with a buffy collar that continues posteriorly onto the chest. Winter pelage uniformly a pale sandy yellow, grayish russet, or sandy brown. Ears with a clear white margin, dorsal side of ears blackish brown (no rust-colored patch as in *O. curzoniae*). Pads at the ends of the toes are concealed in dense hair of the sole (unlike the exposed toes of *O. pallasi*). Incisive foramen and palatal foramen combined into one foramen; frontal slightly convex, with no oval alveolus; nasal narrow and long, posterior portion somewhat narrow; auditory bullae large; dorsal surface of skull slightly arched. 2N = 50.

Distribution: Gobi Desert south to northern (xeric) reaches of the Tibetan Plateau; also extends north through the Gobi Desert of Mongolia and Russia. Two subspecies in China: (1) *O. d. bedfordi* Thomas, 1908 (includes *shaanxiensis* Xu and Wang, 1992); Shanxi, N Shaanxi, Ningxia, Henan; (2) *O. d. dauurica* (Pallas, 1776); Nei Mongol, Liaoning, N Hebei.

Natural History: Occupies desert grassland, often selecting low-lying fertile areas, where populations may be subject to flooding. Inhabits burrows. A generalized herbivore; gathers large haypiles that attract both domestic and wild ungulates as a food source. Ecology very similar to that of the Plateau Pika. Lives in territorial family groups of breeding adults and young of the year; family burrow systems may possess as many as 15–20 entrances. Populations can reach high, but fluctuating, densities. Very social, with amicable behaviors including allogrooming, sitting in contact, huddling, and boxing. Three discrete vocalizations (long call—primarily uttered by males—short calls, and trills). Several large litters (of up to 11 young) are produced each season.

Comments: In the past has included *O. curzoniae*. The form *annectens* has often been included in *dauurica*, but herein it is included within *cansus*.

Conservation Status: Considered an agricultural pest and poisoned, yet is a keystone species for biodiversity throughout its range. China RL—LC.

References: Zhang et al. (2001).

Chinese Red Pika

PLATE 26
MAP 223

Ochotona erythrotis (Büchner, 1890)
红耳鼠兔 Hong'er Shutu

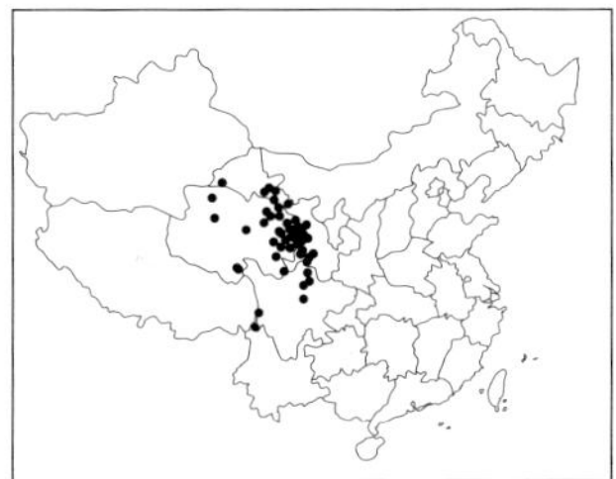

MAP 223. CHINESE RED PIKA, *Ochotona erythrotis*

Distinctive Characteristics: HB 181–285; HF 32–42; E 32–39; GLS 48–51; Wt 184–352 g. One of the flashiest pikas—in summer dorsal pelage bright rusty red throughout, in contrast with the pure white belly, chin, legs, and feet. The large red ears are thin and sparsely furred. In winter the species becomes a drab pale gray dorsally and ventrally, although the ears retain their reddish coloration. The incisive foramen and palatal foramen are separated; the skull is evenly and slightly arched; frontal with two oval alveoli above; posterior cranium slightly oblique; sagittal crest conspicuous; rostrum short and broad; nasal conspicuously short; auditory bullae large.

Distribution: NE edge of the Tibetan Plateau; Qinghai, Gansu, Sichuan. Endemic.

Natural History: Inhabits rock faces and crags; found commonly along the Huang He. May live in adobe walls. Primarily found above 2,000 m. Generalized

herbivore; stores vegetation for the winter. Constructs simple burrows that extend only 1–2 m in length; has not been reported to be vocal. Produces two litters of three to seven young between May and August.
Comments: Formerly included *O. gloveri*; and some have assigned it to *O. rutila*.
Conservation Status: China RL–LC.
References: Zheng (1989).

Forrest's Pika

Ochotona forresti Thomas, 1923 MAP 224
灰颈鼠兔 Huijing Shutu

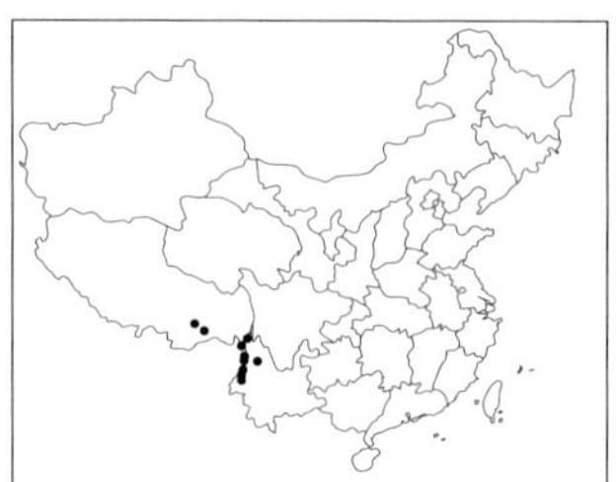

MAP 224. FORREST'S PIKA, *Ochotona forresti*

Distinctive Characteristics: HB 155–185; HF 27–30; E 18–23; GLS 37–41; Wt 110–148 g. In summer both dorsal and ventral pelage blackish brown or dark reddish brown; dark gray spots form behind each ear—in some forming a dorsal collar and extending onto the face, but the forehead remains brown; dorsal side of ears light chestnut with well-defined white edge. Winter pelage grayish brown dorsally, only slightly lighter ventrally. Fore claws significantly longer than in *O. thibetana*; feet dull white. Skull more arched (convex) than *O. thibetana*. Incisive foramen and palatal foramen combined into one, mostly with a wavelike margin, so its profile violin-shaped; when viewed from front, nasals narrow and rectangular; interorbital region broad.
Distribution: NW Yunnan and SE Xizang; extending into NW Myanmar, NE India, and Bhutan.
Natural History: Inhabits a mix of broadleaf forests and conifers, coniferous forests, and shrub thickets at high altitudes (2,600–4,400 m) along the eastern Himalayan massive. Very little is known about this species. It is thought to be a burrowing pika and a generalized herbivore.
Comments: A form that has generated considerable taxonomic confusion over the years—*forresti* has been included in *O. pusilla, O. roylei,* and *O. thibetana*, it may be closely related to *O. erythrotis*, and it may include *O. gaoligongensis, O. nigritia*.
Conservation Status: China RL–NT; although it nearly met the criteria for VU A2c + 3c. IUCN RL–LR/nt ver 2.3 (1994).
References: Thomas (1923).

Gaoligong Pika

Ochotona gaoligongensis
Wang, Gong, and Duan, 1988 MAP 225
高黎贡鼠兔 Gaoligong Shutu

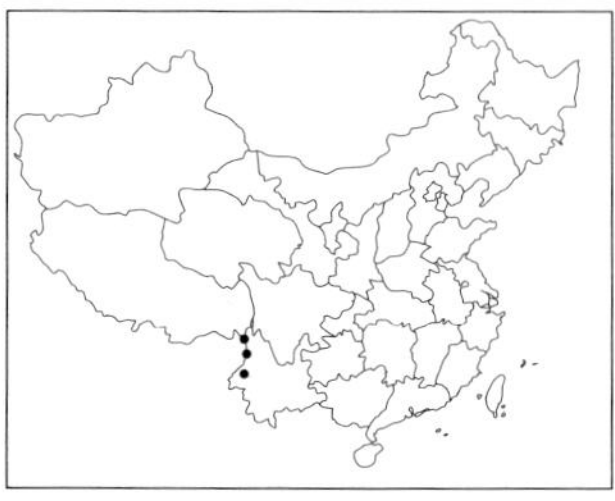

MAP 225. GAOLIGONG PIKA, *Ochotona gaoligongensis*

Distinctive Characteristics: HB 165–170; HF 28–30; E 20–21; GLS 38–39. Head and neck brilliant rufous-brown; dorsum dull rufous-black; back of ear black. Skull flattened in profile; palatal-incisive foramen violin-shaped; vacuities lacking at anterior end of frontals; nasal bone long and broad posteriorly; large bullae.
Distribution: Restricted range in the Gaoligong Shan mountains, NW Yunnan. Endemic (although it may occur across the border into Myanmar).
Natural History: Lives in talus and rocky habitat in forested areas at 3,000 m. Very little is known about this pika. It is likely to be a generalized herbivore.
Comments: Likely a sister species of *O. forresti*, or even a synonym.
Conservation Status: China RL–EN A1c; B1ab(iii). IUCN RL–DD ver 2.3 (1994).
References: Wang et al. (1988).

Glover's Pika

Ochotona gloveri Thomas, 1922 PLATE 26 MAP 226
川西鼠兔 Chuanxi Shutu

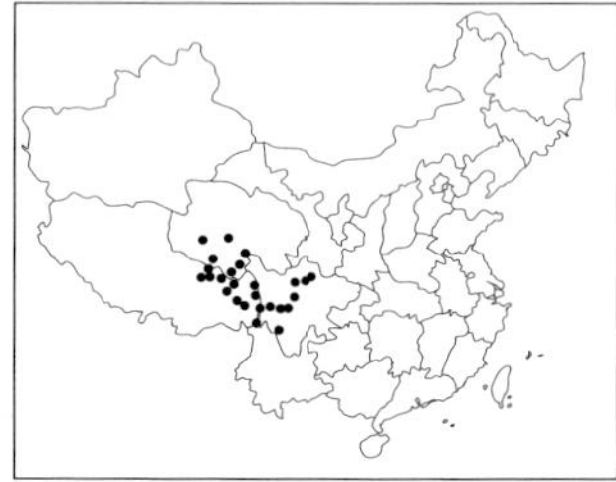

MAP 226. GLOVER'S PIKA, *Ochotona gloveri*

Distinctive Characteristics: HB 160–220; HF 31–36; E 31–39; GLS 43–53; Wt 140–300 g. Summer pelage tea brown, grayish brown, grayish russet, or grayish brown dorsally; head from rostrum to frontal orange or pale brown (in *brookei*, tip of nose orange rufous with light gray patches above eyes, like a mask; in *gloveri*, cheek dark gray and rostrum smoky yellow); venter and upper side of feet grayish white, dull gray, or white; large, thinly haired ears light chestnut,

orange brown, or orange. Winter pelage similar to summer pelage but slightly lighter. Incisive foramen and palatal foramen separated or adjoined; frontal slightly protruding, with two oval alveoli above; parietal clearly slanted obliquely backward so the dorsal side of skull arch-shaped. Compared with *O. erythrotis*, rostrum narrower and longer; nasal longer; auditory bullae smaller.
Distribution: Eastern third of Tibetan Plateau. Endemic. Three subspecies: (1) *O. g. brookei* Allen, 1937 (includes *kamensis*); SW Qinghai, NE Xizang; (2) *O. g. calliceps* Pen et al. 1962; NW Yunnan, E Xizang; (3) *O. g. gloveri* Thomas, 1922; W Sichuan.
Natural History: Inhabits talus and rocky clefts at high elevations (3,500–4,200 m), but it may also occur as low as 1,700 m in Sichuan. Can be found living commensally in adobe walls of villages and lamaseries. A generalized herbivore; constructs prominent haypile. Appears to be a typical rock-dwelling pika. Few details known of its biology.
Comments: Formerly included in *O. erythrotis* and *O. rutila*. Based on molecular evidence, Niu (2004) believes *brookei* should be independent and a sister species of *O. muliensis*.
Conservation Status: China RL–LC.
References: Allen (1937); Niu et al. (2004); Pen et al. (1962); Thomas (1922b).

Himalayan Pika

Ochotona himalayana Feng, 1973 MAP 227
喜马拉雅鼠兔 Ximalaya Shutu

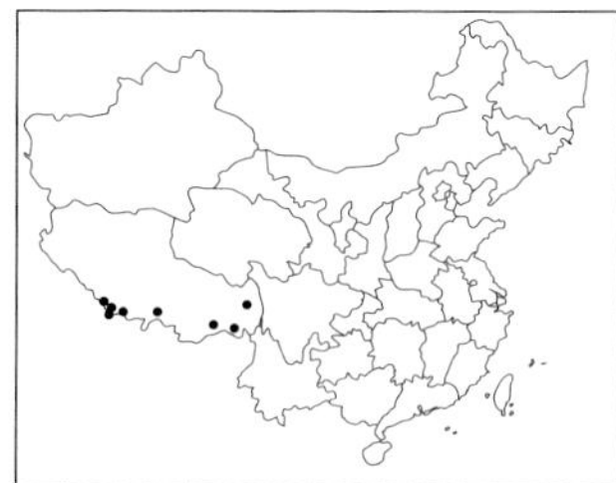

MAP 227. HIMALAYAN PIKA, *Ochotona himalayana*

Distinctive Characteristics: HB 140–186; HF 28–32; E 26–30; GLS 41–45; Wt 120–175 g. Dorsal pelage dark tea brown, dorsal side of neck and shoulders tinged with rufous-brown or dark brown spots; buffy spots present behind ears, white margin of ears obscure; ventral pelage grayish yellow; upper side of feet grayish yellow or tinged with white. Incisive foramen and palatal foramen combined into one foramen, frontal with no oval alveolus above; interorbital region broad; posterior margin of nasal obviously exceeds anterior margin of orbit; orbit well-developed, its longitudinal diameter longer than diastema; posterior portion of parietal conspicuously oblique downward; skull arch-shaped when viewed from the side.
Distribution: Lives along northern flank of Himalayas; Xizang. Endemic.
Natural History: Occupies rocky habitats (cracks in walls, precipices, and talus) along coniferous forest margins at high altitudes (2,400–4,200 m). Generalized herbivore. Active primarily at dawn and dusk. Litter size ranges from three to four. A poorly known pika.
Comments: Has been considered a synonym of *O. rutilla*; its independent status has been confirmed by molecular studies.
Conservation Status: China RL–LC.
References: Feng (1973); Yu et al. (2000).

Tsing-Ling Pika

Ochotona huangensis (Matschie, 1908) MAP 228
黄河鼠兔 Huanghe Shutu

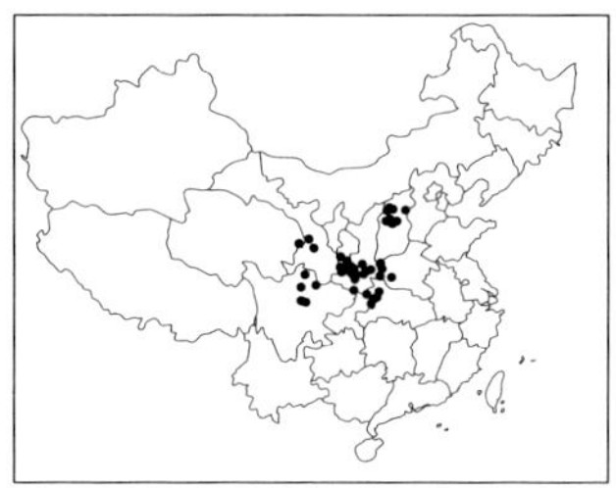

MAP 228. TSING-LING PIKA, *Ochotona huangensis*

Distinctive Characteristics: HB 125–176; HF 23–32; E 16–24; GLS 36–41; Wt 52–108 g. Summer pelage dark brown or chestnut, dorsum tinged with conspicuous black; throat collar very pale buffy, extending as a short buffy median line to the lower chest; ears with white margin; ventral pelage drab or light ocherous. Winter pelage mostly grayish. Dorsal side of skull low and flat; interorbital space and braincase broad; bullae small; skull height similar to that of *O. thibetana*.
Distribution: Mountains of C China. Endemic.
Natural History: Inhabits montane mix of conifers and broadleaf trees, birch forest, coniferous forest, and shrub meadow, occasionally grasslands, usually at elevations of less than 2,700 m (but may extend up to 4,000 m). Generalized herbivore. Constructs complicated burrows, and is believed to adopt most of the normal life-history suite characteristic of burrowing pikas; otherwise poorly known.
Comments: Formerly treated as a subspecies of *O. thibetana*; its independent status has been confirmed based on morphological and molecular distinctiveness. The forms *syrinx* and *xunhuanensis* are synonyms. Broadly sympatric with *O. thibetana*.
Conservation Status: China RL–LC. IUCN RL–EN A2d as *O. thibetana huangensis* ver 2.3(1994).
References: Yu and Zheng (1992b); Yu et al. (1997); Yu et al. (2000).

Northern Pika

Ochotona hyperborea (Pallas, 1811) MAP 229
东北鼠兔 Dongbei Shutu
Distinctive Characteristics: HB 150–204; HF 22–33; E 17–22; GLS 38–43; Wt 122–190 g. In summer dorsal

pelage bright russet with some darkening with black hairs in the middle of the back; sides and belly lighter; ears grayish with a narrow white rim; in *coreana*, rostrum with black stripes above. In winter pelage grayer with a mixture of pale ochraceous and black dorsally, and dull whitish-clay ventrally. The skull is shorter and more rounded than that of the Alpine Pika; no fenestrae are present in the frontals; the incisive foramina are completely separated from the anterior palatal foramen; auditory bullae relatively wide and flat; cranium is less flexed posteriorly. 2N = 40.

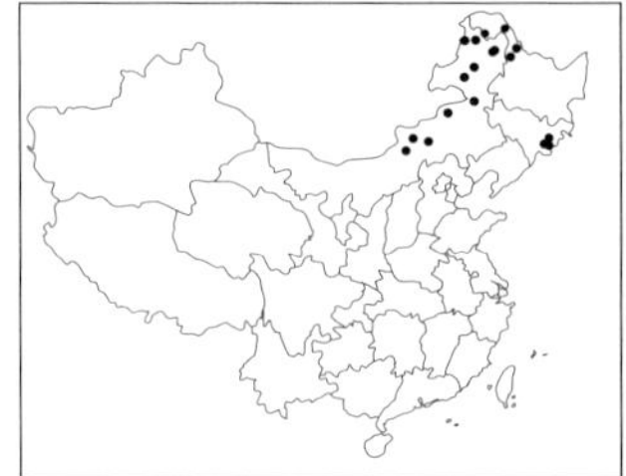

MAP 229. NORTHERN PIKA, *Ochotona hyperborea*

Distribution: NE China; extending from the Ural mountains in Russia east to Sakhalin Island and Kamchatka Peninsula, and to Hokkaido Island, Japan. Two subspecies in China: (1) *O. h. coreana* Allen and Andrews, 1913; Jilin; (2) *O. h. mantchurica* Thomas, 1909; NE Nei Mongol, N Heilongjiang.
Natural History: A characteristic rock-dwelling pika, although it may also occupy crevices under fallen logs and in moss banks, sometimes in the shadow of forest; *coreana* may occur as low as 1,000 m. A generalized herbivore; known to construct a large haypile. Adult male/female pairs defend large territories on which they are sedentary; territories are large, thus population density is low. Social contact between the male and female is limited. Young disperse to fill vacancies in nearby territories. Vocalizations are loud and sharp; a long call (or song) is given by adult males, both genders utter the short call used to advertise territory occupancy and as an antipredator warning. Generally two litters with three or four young are produced each summer, although characteristically only one litter will be weaned successfully.
Comments: Formerly included in *O. alpina*; smaller than *alpina* generally, especially when sympatric; however, Chinese subspecies tend to be the largest within the *hyperborea* complex, particularly when they do not occur sympatrically with *alpina*.
Conservation Status: China RL—LC.
References: Allen and Andrews (1913); He (1958); Thomas (1909).

Ili Pika

PLATE 26
Ochotona iliensis Li and Ma, 1986 MAP 230
伊犁鼠兔 Yili Shutu

Distinctive Characteristics: HB 203–204; HF 42–43; E 36–37; GLS 45–48; Wt 217–250 g. A large pika; brightly colored with large rusty red spots on the forehead and crown, as well as on the sides of the neck; dorsally gray; ears well furred and edges lined with rufous. Incisive and palatal foramen widely confluent, forming a single pear-shaped opening; vomer completely discovered. No foramen present in anterior frontals.
Distribution: Inhabits a restricted geographic range in two spurs of the Tian Shan mountains, Xinjiang. Endemic.

MAP 230. ILI PIKA, *Ochotona iliensis*

Natural History: Prefers slightly sloping rock walls containing gaps or holes, where it makes its den; generally occurs between 2,800 and 4,000 m. Generalized herbivore; stores vegetation in haypiles. A nonvocal pika. Individually territorial and lives at low population density; social interactions uncommon. While normally diurnal, also can be active at night. Litter size unknown, but assumed small; apparently only one or two litters born each breeding season.
Conservation Status: Population declining and highly fragmented. Surveys in 2002 and 2003 failed to find any Ili Pikas in over 50% of the localities where they had been recorded a decade earlier (Li and Smith 2005). China RL—EN A2abc; C2a(i). IUCN RL—VU D1 + 2 ver 2.3 (1994).
References: Li and Ma (1986); Li and Zhao (1991); Li et al. (1991a; 1991b); Li (1997); Li and Smith (2005).

Koslov's Pika

PLATE 26
Ochotona koslowi (Büchner, 1894) MAP 231
柯氏鼠兔 Keshi Shutu

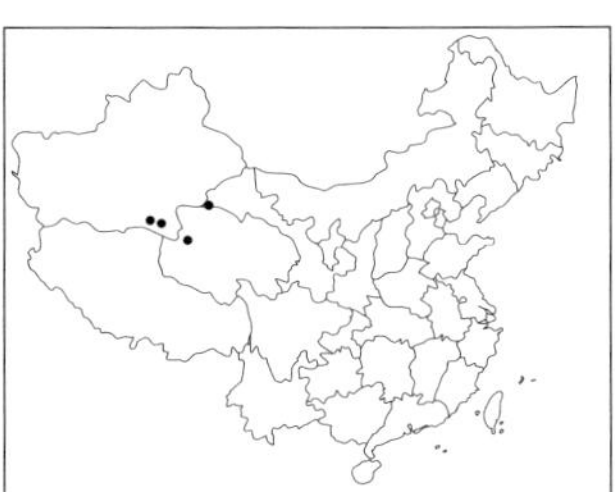

MAP 231. KOSLOV'S PIKA, *Ochotona koslowi*

Distinctive Characteristics: HB 220–240; HF 38–42; E 16–20; GLS 40–47; Wt 150–180 g. In summer dorsum ochraceous pink; dorsal side of ears

yellowish white or buffy, with white margin; ventral pelage yellowish white or grayish white. Pelage long and thick. In winter pelage slightly lighter, a yellowish white. Skull large and strongly arched; frontal with no oval alveolus above; dorsal side of frontal more convex than in *O. curzoniae*; zygomatic arch extending outward; interorbital region narrow; rostrum obviously short; nasal relatively short and wide.
Distribution: Vicinity of Kunlun mountains near the junction of Qinghai, Xizang, and Xinjiang. Endemic.
Natural History: Constructs burrows in smooth sandy soils in basins or mountain valleys at high elevations (4,200–4,800 m). Vegetative habitat throughout its range characterized as high-cold grassland type (Moorcroft sedge, *Carex moocroftii*; purple flower needlegrass, *Stipa purpurea*). Generalized herbivore. Favored plants include falcate crazyweed (*Oxytropis falcate*), rock jasmine (*Androsace acrolasia*), and creeping false tamarisk (*Myricaria prostrata*). Behavior typical of burrowing pikas; lives in communal family groups. Burrows are generally shallow (extending to a depth of only 30–40 cm). Lives in colonies at high density (burrow density 44–152 per ha). Females possess eight teats; the first pair anterior to the forelimbs. Limited data available on reproduction, but litters of four to eight have been recorded.
Conservation Status: Following its original description, nearly 100 years passed before being rediscovered (Zheng 1986). China RL—EN B1ab(i, ii, iii). IUCN RL—EN B1 + 2abd ver 2.3 (1994).
References: Zheng (1986).

Ladak Pika

Ochotona ladacensis (Günther, 1875) MAP 232
拉达克鼠兔 Ladake Shutu

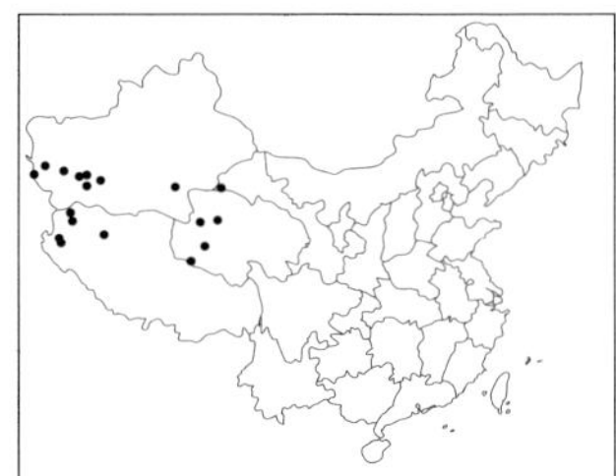

MAP 232. LADAK PIKA, *Ochotona ladacensis*

Distinctive Characteristics: HB 180–229; HF 34–40; E 24–33; GLS 47–51; Wt 190–288 g. In summer dorsal pelage sandy yellowish brown, head with brown, pale brown, or reddish brown spots; dorsal side of ear light brown or orange-brown; underparts gray or light yellowish white. In winter dorsal pelage ochraceous. Skull large and arched; incisive foramen and palatal foramen separated; frontal with no oval alveolus above, slightly protruding at middle; interorbital region narrow; sides of zygomatic arches almost parallel; auditory bullae small.
Distribution: Along N and W edge of the Tibetan Plateau (primarily Kunlun mountains); SW Xinjiang, E Qinghai, N and W Xizang; extending into Kashmir.
Natural History: A burrowing pika that occupies barren (normally xeric) alpine valleys in high mountains (4,200–5,400 m). Digs huge holes under gravel, beside shrubs, or in meadows. Generalized herbivore. May feed on roots of cushion plants (*Primula*) in winter; its long incisors may be an adaptation for this foraging niche. Vocal, social, and lives in family groups with well-defined territories. Poorly known species.
Comments: Originally included in *O. curzoniae*; overall, larger than *curzoniae*, with which it is broadly sympatric.
Conservation Status: China RL—LC.

Large-Eared Pika

PLATE 26
Ochotona macrotis (Günther, 1875) MAP 233
大耳鼠兔 Da'er Shutu

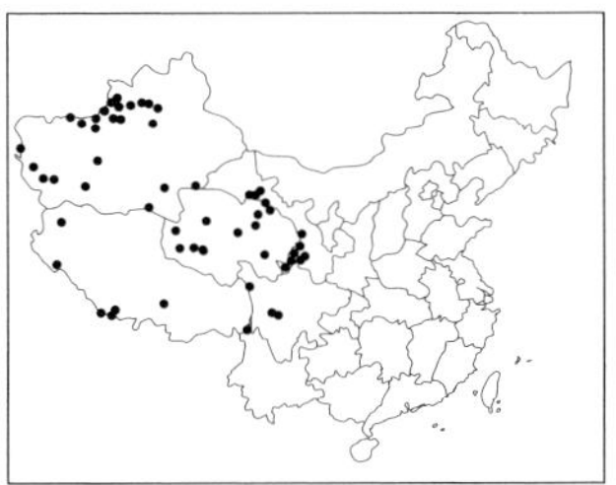

MAP 233. LARGE-EARED PIKA, *Ochotona macrotis*

Distinctive Characteristics: HB 150–204; HF 30–33; E 27–36; GLS 34–45; Wt 142–190 g. Summer pelage pale brownish gray with an ochre tinge (in *macrotis*, head and shoulders with smoky yellow or brown spots; *wollastoni* without any brown spots); ventral pelage white to grayish white; feet white with toe pads exposed. In winter dorsal pelage pale gray with smoky yellow highlights. Ears inside more thickly clad than in *O. roylei*. Incisive foramen and palatal foramen combined into one foramen; frontal with oval alveoli above; interorbital region broad; size of auditory bullae and general shape of skull similar to *O. roylei*. 2N = 62.
Distribution: Found in high mountain ranges across W China (Sichuan, Yunnan, Xizang, Qinghai, Gansu, Xinjiang); distributional range includes where these mountains (Tian Shan, Pamir, Hindu Kush, Himalaya) extend outside of China. Three subspecies in China: (1) *O. m. chinensis* Thomas, 1911; Sichuan; (2) *O. m. macrotis* (Günther, 1875), includes *baltina*; Chinese range except that of *chinensis* and *wollastoni*; (3) *O. m. wollastoni* Thomas and Hinton, 1922; Mt. Everest (Chomolangma) region; S Xizang.
Natural History: Inhabits rocky landscapes at high elevations (up to 6,400 m); where sympatric with *O. roylei*, occupies the higher elevational range. Generalized herbivore. May not store vegetation into a haypile like some pika species. Lives at low density

in territories occupied by a pair of breeding adults and their young. Long-lived. Development of vocal behavior weak; occasional alarm or territorial calls uttered. Usually two small litters, averaging three young, produced per year.
Comments: In earlier accounts included in *O. roylei*, but clearly distinctive.
Conservation Status: China RL—LC.
References: Kawamichi (1971); Thomas and Hinton (1922).

Muli Pika

Ochotona muliensis Pen and Feng, 1962 MAP 234
木里鼠兔 **Muli Shutu**

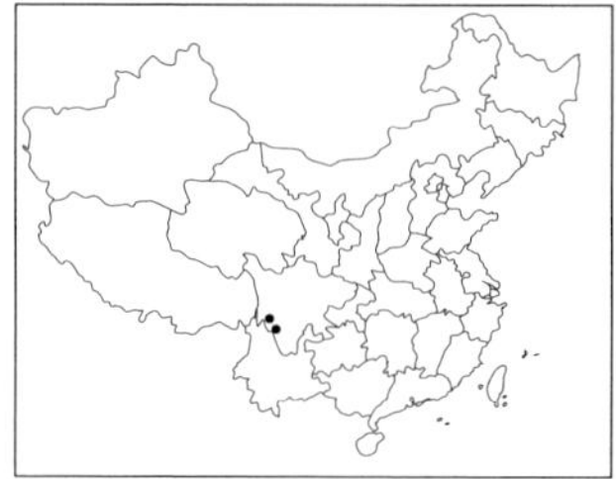

MAP 234. MULI PIKA, *Ochotona muliensis*

Distinctive Characteristics: HB 222; HF 35; E 30–35; GLS 50–51; Wt 235 g. In summer, dorsum grayish brown (brighter and grayer than in *O. gloveri*); rostrum and eye regions tinged with buffy; dorsal side of ears chestnut or orange red; light spots behind ear and around tail region; chin, ventor, and inguinal region grayish white; upper side of feet grayish white. Skull stout; posterior extremity of incisive foramen and anterior extremity of palatal foramen adjoined; frontal with no alveolus above; relatively short nasals; rostrum broad; posterior processes of zygomatic arches almost parallel; interorbital region clearly broad.
Distribution: SW Sichuan. Endemic.
Natural History: Inhabits grassy slopes and rocky clefts at the margins of dense coniferous forests at high elevation (3,600 m). Generalized herbivore. Poorly known pika.
Comments: Originally described as a subspecies of *O. gloveri*, and some consider it to be a junior synonym of *gloveri*.
Conservation Status: China RL—VU D2. IUCN RL—DD ver 2.3 (1994).
References: Formozov (1997); Pen et al. (1962).

Black Pika

Ochotona nigritia Gong and Wang, 2000 MAP 235
黑鼠兔 **Hei Shutu**
Distinctive Characteristics: HB 153–160; HF 27–28; E 17–18; GLS 37–39. Distinguished from all other pikas by its especially dark coloration. In summer dorsal pelage dark blackish with patch of brownish-umber on head and sides of cheek; ventor pure blackish. In winter pelage pure black dorsally and ventrally. Incisive and palatal foramen completely confluent and pear-shaped; skull flattened in profile but with a prominent braincase; no small oval foramina on anterior of the frontal; auditory bullae large.
Distribution: Known only from Pianma, Lushui County, W Yunnan; elevation 3,200 m. Endemic.
Natural History: Nothing is known about the ecology of this species.

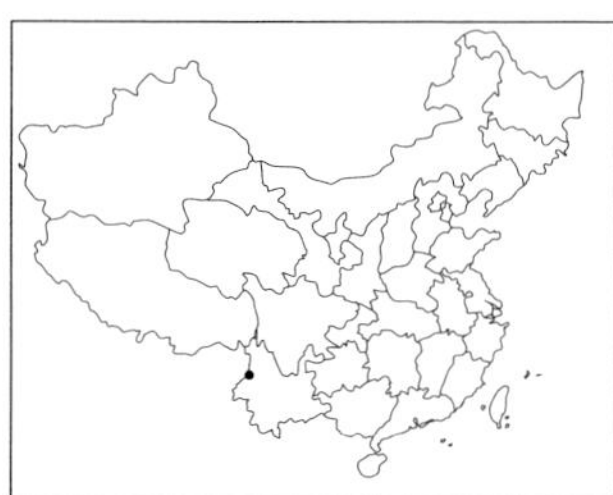

MAP 235. BLACK PIKA, *Ochotona nigritia*

Comments: This recently described form appears to be closely related to *O. forresti*, and it may represent a melanistic form of *forresti*.
Conservation Status: China RL—EN C2a(i, ii).
References: Gong et al. (2000).

Nubra Pika

Ochotona nubrica Thomas, 1922 MAP 236
奴布拉鼠兔 **Nubula Shutu**

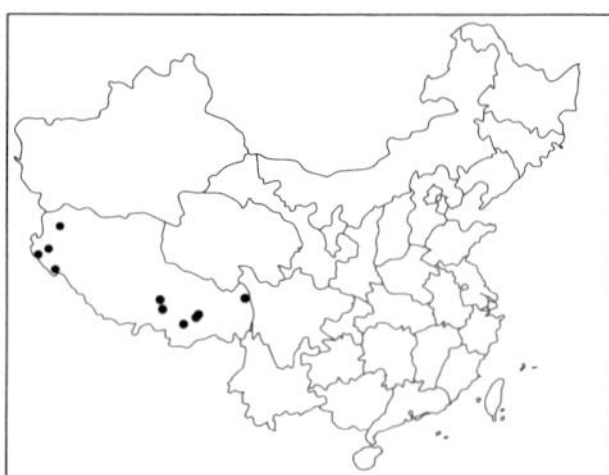

MAP 236. NUBRA PIKA, *Ochotona nubrica*

Distinctive Characteristics: HB 140–184; HF 27–35; E 21–27; GLS 37–43; Wt 96–135 g. Dorsum gray to brownish red with black hairs interspersed throughout the coat (the pelage is less saturated in the west and darkens toward the east; overall pelage less saturated than the Moupin Pika); base of all hairs charcoal black; flanks straw-gray; ventral surface dull white to yellowish; ear patches dull buffy whitish, ears blackish behind with white edges; feet brownish gray. Skull flat, but slightly swollen dorsally, and relatively narrow; broad interorbital and short rostrum; palatal foramen widely expanded posteriorly; bullae small and narrow.
Distribution: Mountains of S Xizang; extending south into the Himalayas (Ladakh, Nepal). Two subspecies in China: (1) *O. n. lhasaensis* Feng and Kao, 1974, *lama* a synonym; E Xizang; (2) *O. n. nubrica* Thomas, 1922, *aliensis* a synonym; W Xizang.

Natural History: Found in alpine desert habitat at 3,000–4,500 m, where it constructs burrows in shrubby habitat (*Caragana, Salix, Lonicera*). Generalized herbivore. Social, lives in well-defined family group territories. Biology poorly known.
Comments: This form has generated taxonomic confusion, having been assigned at one time or another to *O. pusilla*, *O. roylei*, and *O. thibetana*.
Conservation Status: China RL—LC.
References: Feng and Kao (1994); Thomas (1922b); Yu and Zheng (1992a).

Pallas's Pika

Ochotona pallasi (Gray, 1867) MAP 237
蒙古鼠兔 Menggu Shutu

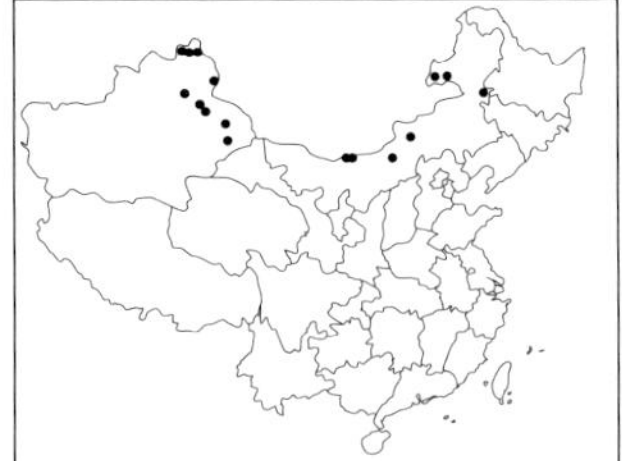

MAP 237. PALLAS'S PIKA, *Ochotona pallasi*

Distinctive Characteristics: HB 160–220; HF 27–36; E 18–23; GLS 42–50; Wt 174–254 g. In summer dorsal pelage sandy yellow or sandy yellowish brown; sides of neck below ears brown or reddish brown spots; ventral pelage dull gray or tinged with yellowish; upper side of feet creamy yellow, and toe pads bare and black (in contrast with the heavily furred feet of sympatric *O. dauurica*). In winter dorsum light gray or grayish yellow; underparts grayish white. Skull somewhat arched; incisive foramen and palatal foramen completely separated; frontal with no oval alveolus above; orbit well developed; interorbital region narrow; auditory bullae large. 2N = 38.
Distribution: Distributed discontinuously in the N Gobi Desert region; extending into Mongolia, Kazakhstan, and Russia. Three subspecies in China: (1) *O. p. hamica* Thomas, 1912; E Xinjiang (Karlik Shan mountains); (2) *O. p. pricei* Thomas, 1911; NE Xinjiang; (3) *O. p. sunidica* Ma, Lin, and Li, 1980; N Nei Mongol.
Natural History: Pallas's Pika appears intermediate between obligate rock-dwelling and burrowing species of pika. They inhabit desert steppe and montane grass-land, living in rocky clefts or burrowing (burrows are characterized with many entrances). Generalized herbivores; construct large haypiles. Populations may have variable densities—some reaching 100/ha. They are relatively long-lived (up to four years of age). Mating system polygynous, and aggressive encounters between neighboring adult males frequent. Within a family territory adult males and females interact rarely and construct separate haypiles. While vocal, there is considerable variation among subspecies; *O. p. pricei* does not utter the long call that is characteristic of so many pika species. In late summer *O. p. pricei* collects stones that they use to close burrow entrances before the onset of winter. Many large litters (1–12 young) produced each season. Young may mature and breed in summer of birth. Gestation is 25 days.
Comments: This form has been referred to commonly as *O. pricei* in the Russian literature. Yu et al. (2000) assigned the form *helanshanensis* (the junior synonym to *O. argentata*) as a subspecies of *pallasi.*
Conservation Status: China RL—LC. IUCN RL—LC; *O. p. hamica* CR A1a + 2d; *O. p. sunidica* EN A2d ver 2.3 (1994).
References: Ma et al. (1980); Thomas (1922b).

Royle's Pika

Ochotona roylei (Ogilby, 1839) MAP 238
灰鼠兔 Hui Shutu

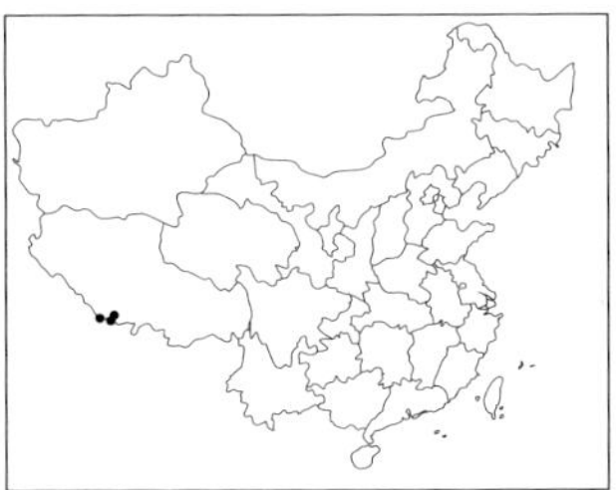

MAP 238. ROYLE'S PIKA, *Ochotona roylei*

Distinctive Characteristics: HB 155–204; HF 25–34; E 26–32; GLS 41–46; Wt 130–180 g. Summer dorsal pelage iron gray, dark gray, or dark grayish brown; head, front, and shoulders with pale brown or reddish highlights to bright chestnut; dorsal side of ear dark grayish brown, and hairs in ear short and sparse (compared to the heavily furred ears of *O. macrotis*); ventral summer pelage light white, grayish white, or dark gray; upper side of foot white or dull white, sometimes tinged with buffy. In winter ventral pelage lighter, gray. Skull slightly arched, less so than *O. macrotis*; rostrum short and bullae small; incisive foramen and palatal foramen combined into one foramen; frontal with two oval alveoli above; frontal and anterior portion of parietal somewhat convex.
Distribution: Mountainous regions of S Xizang; extending west along Himalayan massif to Kashmir. Chinese subspecies: *O. roylei nepalensis* Hodgson, 1841.
Natural History: Inhabits talus areas in humid hilly country characterized by rhododendrons, deodar, or spruce forests. Generally found at lower elevations (3,500–4,500 m) than *O. macrotis*. May invade rock wall huts of local people. Generalized herbivore. Caching behavior less well developed than in most pikas, but more likely to construct haypiles than *O. macrotis*. Lives in family territories composed of an adult male, adult female, and their offspring. Highly vocal, although most calls uttered are faint and difficult to hear. Can give a piercing whistle, however. Generally active at dawn and dusk. One to two litters averaging three young are produced.

Comments: Formerly included, at one time or another, the forms *macrotis, cansus, forresti, himalayana,* and *nubrica*. The form *angdawai* is a synonym of *O. r. nepalensis*.
Conservation Status: China RL—LC.
References: Kawamichi (1971); Thomas and Hinton (1922).

Turkestan Red Pika

Ochotona rutila (Severtzov, 1873) MAP 239
红鼠兔 Hong Shutu

MAP 239. TURKESTAN RED PIKA, *Ochotona rutila*

Distinctive Characteristics: HB 196–230; HF 36–39; E 27–29; GLS 46–53; Wt 220–320 g. In summer dorsal pelage bright reddish brown; dorsal side of ears grayish black; neck behind ears with white spots sometimes forming a yellowish white collar; venter ochraceous or white, but with a rusty red transverse stripe on the chest. In winter dorsum pale brown and ventral pelage light ochraceous or white. Skull large and moderately arched; incisive foramen and palatal foramen not combined into one foramen; frontal with no oval alveolus above; anterior portion of nasal conspicuously inflated; nasal generally longer than middle slot of frontal; interorbital constriction wide. 2N = 62.
Distribution: Mountains of W Xinjiang; species occurs mostly outside of China, where it is found sporadically in the mountains of Central Asia.
Natural History: A rock-dwelling pika that prefers the cover of large boulders at moderate elevations (normally not found higher than 3,000 m). Generalized herbivore. Caches vegetation in haypiles like most pikas; most foraging occurs within talus rather than far from the talus-vegetation edge. Lives at low density on large family territories composed of an adult pair and their young (during the reproductive season). Most affiliative social interactions are among family members, and some (but not all) juveniles overwinter with their parents. In fall, male and female partners rarely interact, even while continuing to share the same territory. The Turkestan Red Pika is silent compared with most pikas; it has no song, no typical alarm call, and vocalizations are not used for communication among family members. Normally two litters averaging about four young produced each season. Young do not become reproductively active in their summer of birth.
Comments: *O. erythrotis* has occasionally been incuded in *O. rutila*.
Conservation Status: China RL—LC.

Moupin Pika

PLATE 26
Ochotona thibetana (Milne-Edwards, 1871) MAP 240
藏鼠兔 Zang Shutu

Distinctive Characteristics: HB 140–180; HF 24–32; E 17–23; GLS 36–42; Wt 72–136 g. In summer dorsal pelage tea brown, reddish brown, dark brown, or sandy brown; a well-marked buffy collar extends across the coat and continues down the middle line of the belly; otherwise ventral pelage dull gray, dull grayish yellow, ochraceous, and white; ears dark brown, their edged narrowly bordered in white; sole of feet moderately furred. In winter dorsal coat buffy to dull brown. Larger than *O. cansus*, although still a small form. Incisive foramen and palatal foramen combine into one foramen; frontal bone low and flat with no oval alveolus above; parietal not convex, so cranium low; auditory bullae relatively small; posterior processes of zygomatic arches nearly parallel; profile of skull broader than that of *O. cansus*.

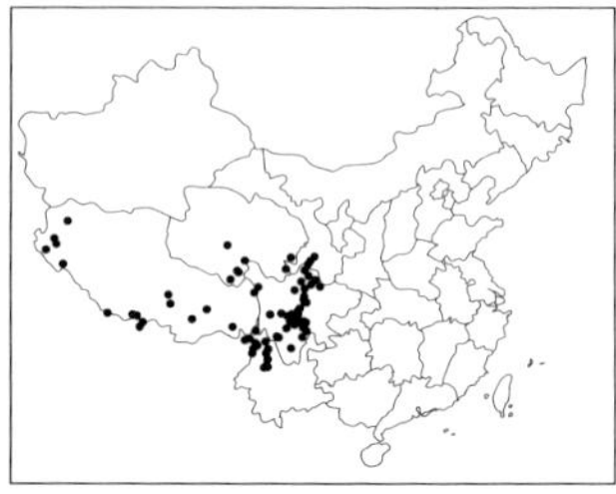

MAP 240. MOUPIN PIKA, *Ochotona thibetana*

Distribution: Primarily mountains of E Tibetan Plateau and their eastern extensions, south along Himalayan massif; extending to N Myanmar, Bhutan, Sikkim. Three subspecies in China: (1) *O. t. nangqenica* Zheng, Liu, and Pi, 1980; Xizang; (2) *O. t. sacraria* Thomas, 1923; W Sichuan; (3) *O. t. thibetana* (Milne-Edwards, 1871), *hodgsoni* and *zappeyi* are synonyms; S Qinghai, W Sichuan, SE Xizang, NW Yunnan.
Natural History: A burrowing pika that characteristically inhabits rhododendron and bamboo forests at moderate elevations (can be found as low as 1,800 m) to high-elevation subalpine forests. Can occupy rocky areas under forest cover. Generalized herbivore. Stores vegetation into haypiles. A social, burrowing pika. Can be active at night. Litter size one to five.
Comments: *O. cansus* has commonly been included in *O. thibetana*, but is now considered independent. In addition, various treatments have included *O. forresti*, *O. huangensis*, and several forms now attributed to *O. nubrica*.
Conservation Status: China RL—LC.

Thomas's Pika

Ochotona thomasi Argyropulo 1948 MAP 241
狭颅鼠兔 Xialu Shutu

Distinctive Characteristics: HB 105–165; HF 22–29; E 17–22; GLS 33–37; Wt 45–110 g. In summer dorsal pelage russet; underparts light white or tinged with yellow. In winter dorsum mouse-gray with conspicuously black tips of hairs. Skull fragile, and narrower,

smaller, and flatter than any other pika; incisive foramen and palatal foramen combined into one foramen; frontal with no oval foramen above; cranium relatively broader anteriorly, so profile of cranium oval; auditory bullae convex and elongated.
Distribution: E Qilian mountains along boundary of Qinghai and Gansu, E Qinghai, NW Sichuan. Endemic.

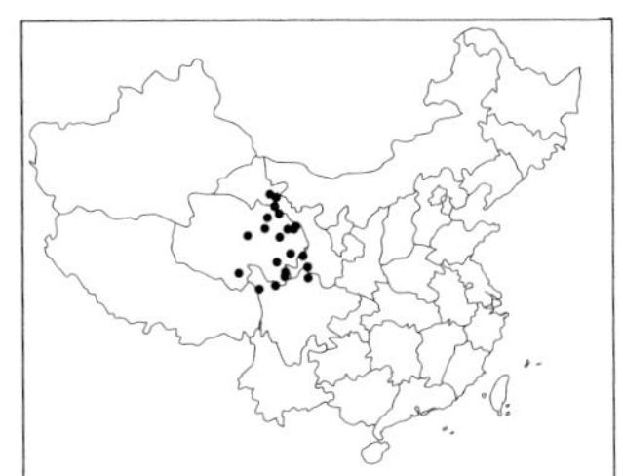

MAP 241. THOMAS'S PIKA, *Ochotona thomasi*

Natural History: Inhabits hilly shrub forest (rhododendron, *Salix, Caragana jubata, Potentilla fruticosa*) at elevations of 3,400–4,020 m. Generalized herbivore. Not well known; ecology believed to be similar to *O. cansus*.
Conservation Status: China RL—NT; although it nearly met the criteria for VU A2c + 3C. IUCN RL—LR/nt ver 2.3 (1994).

FAMILY LEPORIDAE—Rabbits and Hares

兔科 Tu Ke—兔类 Tulei

Medium-sized, "hare-shaped," nonhibernating generalized herbivores. Ears long, with short tail. Digits 4-4, but first digit tends to be reduced on both forefoot and hind foot. Skull highly arched and pronouncedly fenestrated; zygomatic arch well developed; auditory bullae oval and convex; pronounced supraorbital process; three upper molars, third column-shaped, second upper premolar (P3) and third upper premolar (P4) molariform. Dental formula usually: 2.0.3.3/1.0.2.3 = 28.

Found worldwide, except Australia, Oceania, and southern South America, areas to which leporids have been successfully introduced. The family is comprised of 11 genera, many of them monotypic and threatened with extinction; 61 species overall. Only *Lepus*, the true hares and the most successful of leporids, is represented in China. The conservation and status of *Lepus* has been reviewed by Flux and Angermann (1990).

Genus *Lepus*—Hares

兔属 Tu Shu—兔类 Tulei

Of the leporids, *Lepus* are the largest forms and have the longest ears and very long hind feet. Supraorbital process highly developed. Young are precocial at birth. Dental formula: 2.0.3.3/1.0.2.3 = 28. All *Lepus* are 2N = 48. Recently Luo (1988), Xiang (2004), and Wu et al. (2005; using molecular data) reviewed the hares of China. Of 32 species of hare, 10 occur in China, 2 of which are endemic.

Yunnan Hare

PLATE 27
MAP 242

Lepus comus Allen, 1927

云南兔 Yunnan Tu

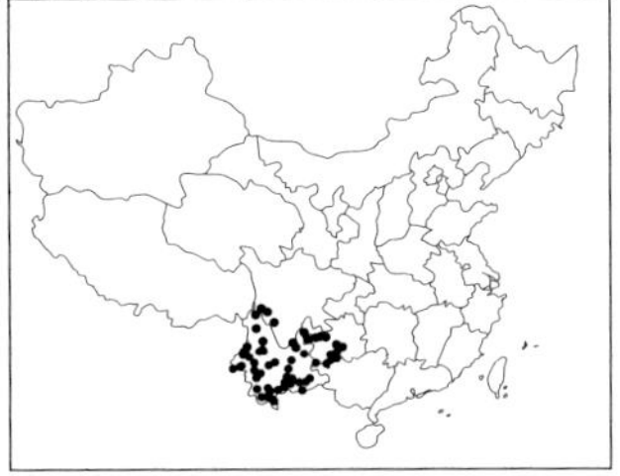

MAP 242. YUNNAN HARE, *Lepus comus*

Distinctive Characteristics: HB 322–480; T 95–110; HF 98–130; E 97–135; GLS 84–95; Wt 1,800–2,500 g. A medium-sized hare. Dorsal fur soft, long, and flat; dorsal pelage grayish pale brown or dark gray. Posterior portion of hip vaguely gray, and an ochraceous buff extends on the flanks, forelegs, and to the outer side of the hind legs. A whitish band extends from the muzzle to the base of the ear, including an arch over the eye. Top of ears black, inside of ears pale gray. Tail brownish above and without a distinct stripe, light gray tinged with yellow below. Ventral pelage white. Skull slender; supraorbital process low, flat, and not flared upward. Nasals relatively short and posterior portion of nasals broad. When worn the upper incisor is V-shaped and filled with cement; when unworn, Y-shaped. 2N = 48.
Distribution: Central S China; also recorded in N Myanmar. Three subspecies in China: (1) *L. c. comus* Allen, 1927; W Yunnan; (2) *L. c. peni* Wang and Luo, 1985; E Yunnan, W Guizhou, SW Sichuan; (3) *L. c. pygmaeus* Wang and Feng, 1985; Yunnan.
Natural History: Inhabits montane meadows and shrubs at middle elevations (1,300–3,200 m); prefers warm and wet habitats; may move into forest edges or open forests. Diet consists of forbes and shrubs. There are reports that each adult has three burrows, and that those of males are smaller, shallower, and straighter than those of females. They are active during the day but primarily forage at night. Breeding normally begins in April, with the first of two or three litters appearing in May. Litter size one to four young (generally two).
Comments: Formerly included as a subspecies of *Lepus oiostolus*, with which it is thought to be closely related (Wu et al. 2005; Xiang 2004).
Conservation Status: China RL—NT; although it nearly met the criteria for VU A2cd + 3cd.
References: Gao and Feng (1964); Wang et al. (1985); Wu et al. (2005); Xiang (2004).

Key to the Chinese Species of *Lepus*

1.a. Ear length < length of hind foot	2
b. Ear length ≥ length of hind foot	6
2.a. Ear length averages < 100 mm	3
b. Ear length averages > 100 mm	4
3.a. Tips of ear with black triangle marking, supraorbital process minute, bullae small, tail generally < 55 mm	*Lepus sinensis*
b. Tail generally > 60 mm	*Lepus coreanus*
4.a. Dorsal pelage dark, ears ochraceous, supraorbital process small and anterior branch minute, palatal bridge broad, auditory bullae not inflated	*Lepus mandshuricus*
b. Dorsal pelage light, ear tips black, supraorbital process heavy, palatal bridge narrow, bullae inflated	5
5.a. Tail all white in both summer and winter; supraorbital process with small anterior extension, turns all white in winter (except ear tips)	*Lepus timidus*
b. Tail with broad black/dark brown stripe above, supraorbital process well developed, winter pelage gray sandy-brown	*Lepus tibetanus*
6.a. Auditory bullae inflated and round, width ≥ distance between bullae	7
b. Auditory bullae small, width < distance between bullae	8
7.a. Tail with brown/black dorsal stripe, ear tips black, supraorbital process triangular and well developed	*Lepus tolai*
b. Tail smoke gray without dorsal stripe, ear tips not black, supraorbital process low	*Lepus yarkandensis*
8.a. Pelage thick and curly, rostrum long and narrow, supraorbital process well developed and triangular	*Lepus oiostolus*
b. Pelage soft, rostrum short and broad, supraorbital process small and flat	9
9.a. Tail brown above with no distinct stripe, ears usually > 95 mm, suborbital process low and flat—not flared upward, upper incisor V-shaped when worn	*Lepus comus*
b. Tail with brown/black dorsal stripes, ears short (usually < 95 mm), suborbital process warped upward, upper incisor with Y-shaped groove	*Lepus hainanus*

Korean Hare

Lepus coreanus Thomas, 1892 MAP 243

高丽兔 Gaoli Tu

Distinctive Characteristics: HB 425–490; T 60–75; HF 108–122; E 73–79; GLS 82–86; Wt 1,700 g. Medium-sized hare with thick pelage. Dorsal fur grayish yellow with brown hair tips; head same color as back. Tail light brown on top and at tip. Underneath, pure white.

Distribution: Widespread in Korean peninsula, extending N into S Jilin.

Natural History: Apparently known in China from a single specimen, but is common throughout the Korean Peninsula where it occupies lowland and mountainous habitats.

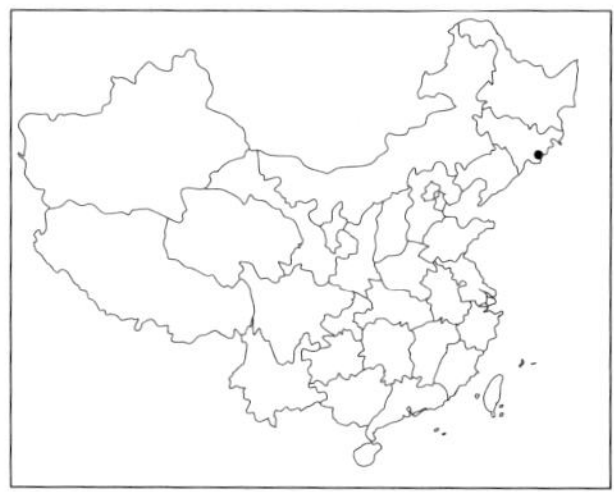

MAP 243. KOREAN HARE, *Lepus coreanus*

Conservation Status: Common in neighboring Korea. China RL–LC.

Comments: This form has generated significant taxonomic confusion. It has formerly been included in *Lepus sinensis*, *L. brachyurus*, and *L timidus*, and some believe that it is most closely allied with *L. mandshuricus*. The molecular analysis of Koh et al. (2001) clearly shows that *coreanus* is an independent species when compared with *sinensis* and *mandshuricus*.

References: Jones and Johnson (1965); Kim and Kim (1974); Koh et al. (2001).

Hainan Hare

Lepus hainanus Swinhoe, 1870 MAP 244

海南兔 Hainan Tu

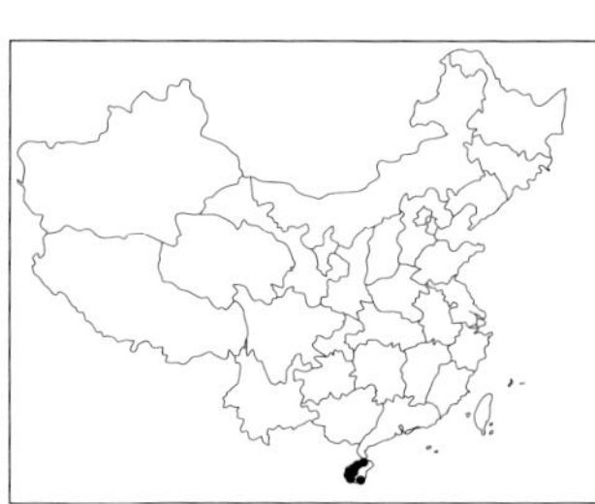

MAP 244. HAINAN HARE, *Lepus hainanus*

Distinctive Characteristics: HB 350–394; T 45–70; HF 76–96; E 76–98; GLS 73–84; Wt 1,250–1,750 g. A small hare. Pelage soft, color bright; dorsal pelage pale brown tinged with chestnut brown and black; sides of body mixed with pale brown and brownish white; chin and ventral pelage pure white; tail with brownish black stripes above, white below; feet pale brown with white marks; a whitish ring circles the eye and extends back toward the base of the ear and anteriorly toward the muzzle; winter pelage brighter than summer pelage. Cranium rounded, supraorbital process warped upward; auditory bullae small; rostrum short and broad. The Y-shaped groove on the front of upper incisors tends to be filled with cement.
Distribution: Hainan Island; greatest density in the NW and SW parts of the island. Endemic.
Natural History: Inhabits shrub forest and short grass-lands in the low-lying plains; they do not live in the mountains. A shy animal. Primarily active before midnight, with activity level dropping after midnight; occasionally seen active during the day. They have never been observed burrowing.
Comments: At one time considered a subspecies of *Lepus peguensis* (Burmese Hare).
Conservation Status: Extirpated from much of its former range, most likely due to habitat destruction and unsustainable harvest. China RL—VU A2cd + 3cd; B1ab(iii). China Key List—II. IUCN RL—VU A1ac ver 2.3 (1994).
References: Lazell et al. (1995); Xu et al. (1983).

Manchurian Hare

Lepus mandshuricus Radde, 1861 MAP 245
东北兔 Dongbei Tu

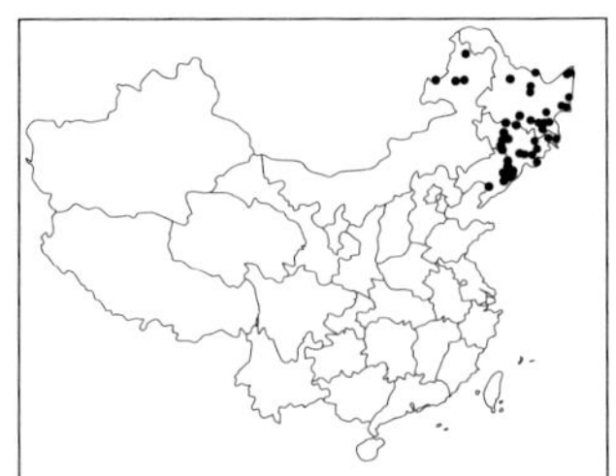

MAP 245. MANCHURIAN HARE, *Lepus mandshuricus*

Distinctive Characteristics: HB 410–540; T 50–80; HF 110–145; E 75–118; GLS 79–89; Wt 1,400–2,600 g. Pelage soft, long, and thick. Dorsal pelage grayish black to blackish brown to rust brown; breast, flanks, and legs cinnamon; ears ochraceous; neck dull rust brown. Belly whitish, and tail blackish brown above, dull white below. In winter appears lighter, with some individuals ash gray. Frequently includes melanistic (black) individuals, and these have been misidentified and assigned as *L. melainus*. Supraorbital process not warped upward and anterior branch minute; palatal bridge broad; auditory bullae laterally compressed and not inflated.
Distribution: NE China (NE Nei Mongol, Heilongjiang, and Jilin); extending into Russia and perhaps N Korea.
Natural History: Mainly inhabits coniferous and broadleaf forests, particularly where tall Mongolian oaks occur with an undergrowth of Manchurian hazelnuts, at altitudes between 300 and 900 m. Does not like open valleys or grasslands, and shies away from human habitation. Is replaced by *L. tolai* (Tolai Hare) in areas cleared of forest, and can be sympatric with *L. timidus*. Feeds on bark and twigs of willow, linden, maple, wide apple, birch, and elm, as well as various shrubs, herbs, and fallen fruit. Appears to represent the Old World equivalent of the Snowshoe Hare (*L. americanus*) in North America. A very shy animal, it is presumably solitary. Does not bed down in lairs in the open; rather it settles in holes in tree trunks. Nocturnal, but also active at dawn. Litter size small, usually only one or two and occasionally as large as five. Breeding begins in April, with young first appearing in May.
Comments: Formerly included in *L. brachyurus* (Japanese Hare). Melanistic forms have been designated as *L. melainus*.
Conservation Status: China RL—LC.
References: Angermann (1966); Loukashkin (1943).

Woolly Hare

Lepus oiostolus Hodgson, 1840 PLATE 27 MAP 246
高原兔 Gaoyuan Tu

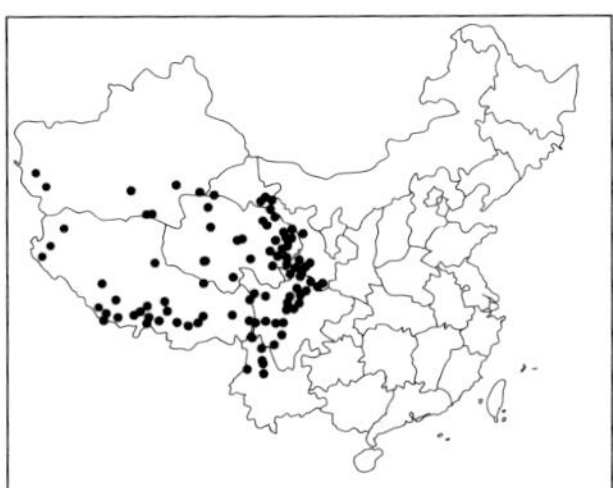

MAP 246. WOOLLY HARE, *Lepus oiostolus*

Distinctive Characteristics: HB 400–580; T 65–125; HF 102–140; E 105–155; GLS 84–100; Wt 2,000–4,250 g. A stocky hare. Pelage thick and soft, tips of hairs mostly curved so that dorsal pelage is wavelike and curly. Ears largest of the Chinese hares; dark at tip. Dorsal pelage sandy yellow, light pale brown, dark yellowish brown, and tea brown; hip with a large, silvery gray, dull gray, lead gray, or brownish gray spot, obviously different from the color of dorsal pelage. Bushy tail white above except for a brown-gray narrow stripe on the dorsal surface, and white below. There is a whitish ring around the eye. Muzzle elongated and narrow; anterior and posterior branch of supraorbital process well developed and triangular in shape; supraorbital process clearly warped upward; auditory bullae small. Anterior groove on upper incisors is simple and deep, V-shaped, and filled with cement.

Distribution: Across C and W highlands of China; extending into Ladakh, Nepal, and Sikkim.
Natural History: Found primarily in upland grasslands of various types, montane meadows, shrub meadow, and alpine cold desert generally at elevations above 3,000 m to as high as 5,300 m. SE populations inhabit montane coniferous and broad-leafed mixed forests. Primarily eats grasses and herbaceous plants. Shy and solitary, although they may be seen foraging in small groups during the mating season. Activity is usually confined to a restricted area, where the same individual can be seen night after night. While primarily nocturnal, they can be seen active during the day. Will rest in quiet, low areas exposed to the sun but sheltered from the wind during the day. Molts only once per year. Breeding begins in April and produces two litters of four to six young.
Comments: Several authors, including Wang (2003) recognize several subspecies of *O. oiostolus*; herein these forms (*grahami, kozlovi, przewalskii, qinghaiensis, qusongensis,* and *sechuenensis*) are considered synonyms, as they appear to be continuously distributed throughout the species range. The form *przewalskii* has been assigned to *L. capensis* (= *L. tolai*) in some treatments. Molecular analyses cluster *L. oiostolus* with *L. comus* (Wu et al. 2005; Xiang 2004).
Conservation Status: China RL—LC.
References: Cai and Feng (1982); Gao and Feng (1964); Wu et al. (2005); Xiang (2004).

Chinese Hare

Lepus sinensis Gray, 1832 — PLATE 27, MAP 247
华南兔 Huanan Tu

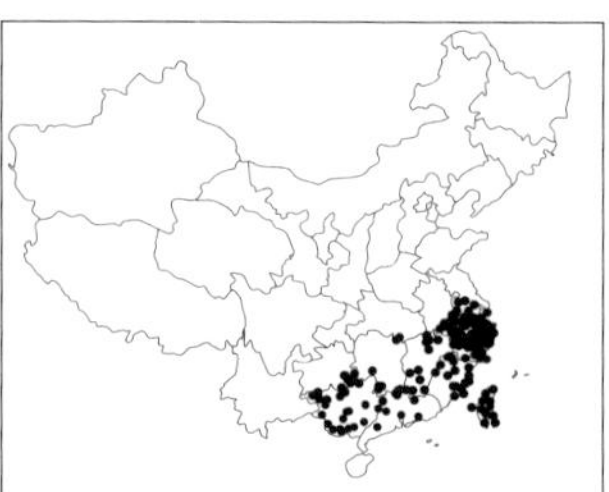

MAP 247. CHINESE HARE, *Lepus sinensis*

Distinctive Characteristics: HB 350–450; T 40–57; HF 81–111; E 60–82; GLS 67–93; Wt 1,025–1,938 g. A small hare with short ears. Overall, the animal has a rather uniform but rich color, with short straight and sometimes course fur. Dorsum and head sandy pale brown, dark pale brown, or grayish yellow, often with chestnut or rufous tones; tail color same russet as the back. Underside ochraceous buff, not contrasting sharply with the backside. Tips of the ears have black triangular markings; a ring is present around eyes. Winter pelage yellowish, mixed with black-tipped hairs. Supraorbital process minute, its anterior branch only a minute proterberance; auditory bullae small; nasals elongate. Groove on anterior face of upper incisors indistinct and not filled with cement. 2N = 48.
Distribution: SE China and Taiwan; extends into N Vietnam. Two subspecies in China: (1) *L. s. formosus* Thomas, 1908; Taiwan; (2) *L. s. sinensis* Gray, 1832; SE China.
Natural History: Lives in open edge grassland habitat and scrubby vegetation in hill country. Can occur up to 4,000–5,000 m in bamboo. Eats leafy plants, other green shoots, and twigs. Does not dig its own burrow, rather utilizes those made by other animals. Occupied burrows usually have a smooth opening, and pellets are piled outside the entrance. Nocturnal, although can be seen active during the day. Females breed from April until August, giving birth within their burrows. Litter size averages three precoital young.
Comments: Formerly included *L. coreanus* in several treatments; herein this form is considered independent.
Conservation Status: China RL—LC.

Desert Hare

Lepus tibetanus Waterhouse, 1841 — MAP 248
藏兔 Zang Tu

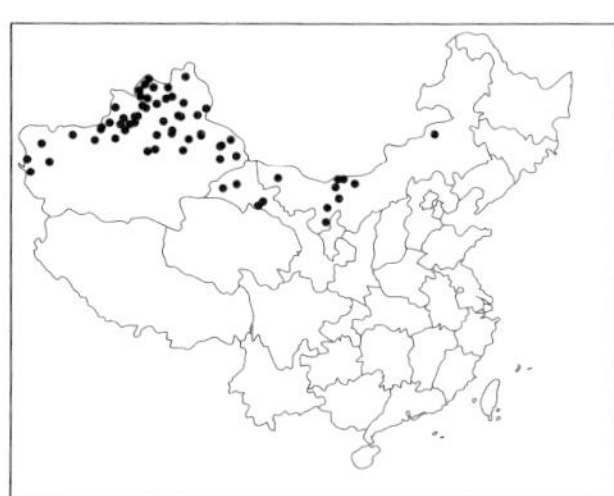

MAP 248. DESERT HARE, *Lepus tibetanus*

Distinctive Characteristics: HB 401–480; T 87–109; HF 109–135; E 81–110; GLS 84–92; Wt 1,625–2,500 g. A slender-bodied hare with a relatively small head. Dorsal pelage sandy yellow or drab tinged with blackish; hip grayish and outside of hind leg and forefeet white; ears wide with tufted hairs anteriorly, tip of ear black-brown; tail with black-brown dorsal stripes; eye surrounded by light ring. Underparts pale yellow to white. In winter, pelage thick and a grayer sandy-brown color. Relatively long premaxilary and short nasal bones; supraorbital process warped upward; auditory bullae inflated; zygomatic arch broad; incisors procumbent.
Distribution: Across NW China; extending into S Siberia and west into Pakistan and Afghanistan. Two subspecies in China: (1) *L. t. centrasiaticus* Satunin, 1907; E. Xinjiang, Gansu, W Nei Mongol; (2) *L. t. pamirensis* Günther, 1875; Xinjiang.
Natural History: Occupies desert, semidesert, and steppe, where it is found in grassland or shrubby habitats on the slopes of river banks; does not occupy alpine grasslands, although it may extend into the subalpine belt (3,500–4,000 m). Eats herbaceous

plants, seeds, berries, roots, and twigs. Mainly active at dusk but can also be seen during the day. Does not construct its own burrow. Breeds up to three times each year; litter size 3–10.
Comments: This form has had a checkered taxonomic history. It was considered a distinct species until the 1930s. It was then united with *L. europaeus* and *L. tolai* into a single species, and then placed as a subspecies of *L. capensis* along with *tolai*. Xiang (2004) retains *pamirensis* within the *L. capensis* complex, and assigns *centrasiaticus* to *L. tolai* (see also Wu et al. 2005).
Conservation Status: China RL—LC.
References: Qui (1989); Shou (1962); Wu et al. (2005); Xiang (2004).

Mountain Hare

PLATE 27
MAP 249

Lepus timidus Linnaeus, 1758
雪兔 Xue Tu

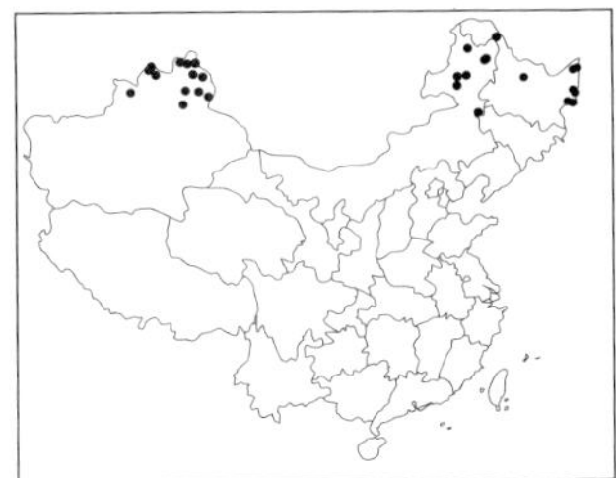

MAP 249. MOUNTAIN HARE, *Lepus timidus*

Distinctive Characteristics: HB 452–620; T 50–75; HF 135–165; E 80–110; GLS 87–106; Wt 2,140–2,700 g. Large hare. Pelage straight and coarse; ears short, obviously shorter than hind feet; tail short and usually all white in summer and winter. Summer pelage brown, pale brown, or ochre-pale brown, dorsal hairs light brown or dull gray above, light grayish white below; winter pelage wholly white except for black-tipped ears. Has eight mammae. Palatal bridge narrow; fore and hind branches of supraorbital process slender and slightly warped upward; size of auditory bullae medium, inflated, and round.
Distribution: NW and NE China; species extends across Palearctic from Scandinavia to E Siberia and Hokkaido. Four subspecies in China: (1) *L. t. mordeni* Goodwin, 1933; Heilongjiang; (2) *L. t. sibiricorum* Johanssen, 1923; N Xinjiang; (3) *L. t. timidus* Linnaeus, 1758; N Xinjiang; (4) *L. t. transbaikalicus* Ognev, 1929; E Nei Mongol.
Natural History: Inhabits coniferous forest of subarctic zone, in particular grass habitats in open pine, birch, and juniper forests or along rivers. Eats twigs, buds, and bark of birch, juniper, poplar, and willow; also palatable berries, grasses, and clovers when available. Tends to forage in a fixed area. Is more social than other hares and often gathers to feed in the same place in groups of 20–100. May live in pairs. Nocturnal, yet may show increased daylight activity in summer when nights are short. Lifespan may extend 8–10 years. Molts twice per year; the spring molt is quite extended. May burrow 1–2 m into hillsides or lie in a shallow depression under vegetation for cover. In winter may burrow into the snow to a depth of 100–120 cm. Mating begins in early spring, and first litters normally appear in May. Produces one or two litters of three to six precoital young. Gestation about 50 days.
Conservation Status: China RL—LC. China Key List—II.
References: Loukashkin (1943).

Tolai Hare

PLATE 27
MAP 250

Lepus tolai Pallas, 1778
托氏兔 Tuoshi Tu

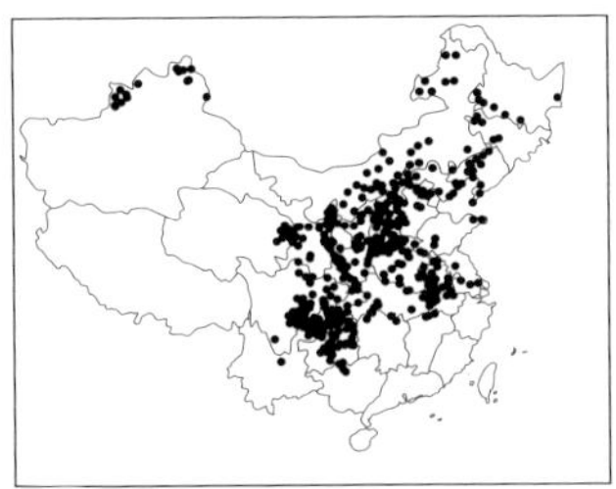

MAP 250. TOLAI HARE, *Lepus tolai*

Distinctive Characteristics: HB 400–590; T 72–110; HF 110–127; E 83–120; GLS 80–88; Wt 1,650–2,650 g. Coloration is variable across the species range in China. Dorsal pelage sandy yellow, pale brown, dusty yellow, sandy gray mixed with dark brown and laurel red stripes; hip grayish to ochraceous (southern forms); tail with broad black or blackish brown stripe above, wholly white below and at sides; eye surrounded by a grayish white area (ochraceous in southern forms) tending back to the base of the ear and forward toward the muzzle; tip of ears black. Ventral pelage pure white. Nasal long and broad; supraorbital process well developed, almost triangular, slightly low, and flat or warped upward; auditory bullae generally round and large; palatal bridge narrow; rostrum short and broad.
Distribution: NW, C, and NE China; species extends from Central Asia across S Siberia and Mongolia. Six subspecies in China: (1) *L. t. aurigineus* Hollister, 1912; N Jiangxi, Anhui, Hubei, S Shaanxi, Sichuan, N Guizhou; (2) *L . t. cinnamomeus* Shamel, 1940; SW Sichuan, N Yunnan; (3) *L. t. huangshuiensis* Luo, 1982; Qinghai; (4) *L. t. lehmanni* Severtzov, 1873; Xinjiang; (5) *L. t. swinhoei* Thomas, 1894; from Heilongjiang, Jilin, Liaoning, and Nei Mongol southward to Hebei, Beijing, Henan, Shaanxi, Shanxi, Shandong; (6) *L. t. tolai* Pallas, 1778; Nei Mongol, Gansu.
Natural History: Occupies grassland and forest meadows (never true forests); prefers tall grass or shrubby areas for the cover they provide. Generally found at lower elevations (600–900 m). Eats grass, roots, and herbaceous plants. Nocturnal. Does not burrow (except to give birth) but creates a shallow depression using its front paws for resting; the depth of these depressions is shallower during hot weather

and deeper when it is cold and windy. They may remain motionless and hide in their depression for as long as possible before running from approaching danger. Utilizes fixed (and restricted) routes while foraging. Reproduces two or three times each year; litter size two to six young.
Comments: Formerly included in *L. capensis* or *L. europaeus* or *L. tibetanus*. Has included the form *przewalskii*, which we have assigned to *L. oiostolus*. The molecular analysis of Xiang (2004) separates the form *swinhoei* as an independent species. See also comments under *tibetanus*.
Conservation Status: China RL–LC.
References: Luo (1981; 1982); Xiang (2004).

Yarkand Hare

PLATE 27
MAP 251

Lepus yarkandensis Günther, 1875
塔里木兔 Talimu Tu

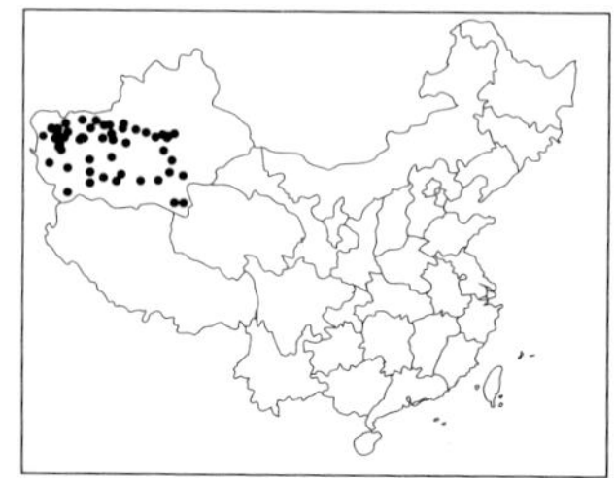

MAP 251. YARKAND HARE, *Lepus yarkandensis*

Distinctive Characteristics: HB 285–430; T 55–86; HF 90–110; E 90–110; GLS 76–88; Wt 1,100–1,900 g. Somewhat small, pelage short and straight; dorsal pelage sandy brown mixed with many grayish black stripes; ears relatively long, tips not black; tail light smoke gray or similar to dorsal pelage, white or creamy yellowish white along the sides and below. Ventral pelage wholly white. Winter pelage lighter, light sandy brown above. Skull somewhat small, nasal narrow, and posterior portion of nasal flat and straight; supraorbital process low flat or slightly warped upward; palatal bridge narrow; well-developed auditory bullae (round and tall). Upper incisors with deep V-shaped groove, filled with cement. 2N = 48.
Distribution: Tarim Basin, S Xinjiang. Endemic.
Natural History: Inhabits internal basins and various desert sites, largely in tamarisk and poplar forests along the margins of rivers. Frequently uses reed vegetation along rivers for cover. Active from dawn until midmorning, then again in the late afternoon; may also forage at night. Hides in shallow depressions under vegetation during the day. Utilizes traditional routes while foraging, and these routes can be as long as 1–2 km. Significant genetic subdivision occurs among isolated populations throughout the Tarim basin. Breeding begins in February and may extend seven or eight months; two or three litters of two to five young produced annually.
Conservation Status: While locally common, may be of conservation concern because of habitat patchiness, habitat loss, and unsustainable harvest. China RL–VU A1cd. China Key List–II. IUCN RL–LC/nt ver 2.3 (1994).
References: Gao (1983); Li et al. (2005b).

ORDER ERINACEOMORPHA
Family Erinaceidae—Hedgehogs and Gymnures
猬目 Wei Mu; 猬科 Wei Ke—刺猬 Ciwei

Robert S. Hoffmann and Darrin Lunde

Although previously included in the order Insectivora along with the moles and shrews, the hedgehogs and gymnures are now thought to represent a separate, distantly related clade—the Erinaceomorpha (Asher et al. 2002, Hutterer 2005, Stanhope et al. 1998). The hedgehogs belong to the subfamily (Erinaceinae) and are most easily recognized by a dorsal covering of protective quills. The Gymnures (Galericinae) lack quills but have the ability to secrete an offensive scent for protection. In all the fore and hind limbs possess five toes (but some genera outside China have four toes); eyes and ears well developed; rostrum long and somewhat pointed; skull robust, sutures distinct in contrast to the Soricomorpha; zygomatic arch well developed; postorbital region prominently constricted; postorbital process either minute or absent; first pair of incisor teeth in upper jaw longest, canines very small but well developed and two-rooted; posterior premolars possess well-developed odontoid process laterally, crown of first and second molar teeth quadrate, four robust cusps and a small cusp present at middle; number of teeth is 36–44. Found throughout Asia, Europe, and Africa; habits terrestrial. Contains two subfamilies: Erinaceinae and Galericinae (sometimes known as the Hylomyinae), both of which are represented in China (Hutterer 2005). Corbet (1988) provides an in-depth review of the family.

Key to the Chinese Subfamilies of Erinaceidae

1.a.	Size small; HB length < 160 mm; pelage may be soft or stiff, but lacking spines; number of teeth 40–44	Galericinae
b.	Size larger; HB length > 160 mm; in adults, 200+ mm; pelage coarse, with strong sharp spines on dorsal surface; number of teeth 36	Erinaceinae

Key to the Chinese Genera of Erinaceinae

1.a. Ears very large, protruding well above spines on head. Ventral pelage sparse and soft. No spineless mid-dorsal area on top of head. Surface of spines faintly grooved. Rostrum narrow, anterior upper incisors slender, close together at base *Hemiechinus*

b. Ears smaller, not, or only slightly, projecting above head spines. Ventral pelage coarse and usually dark, brownish at least in part. Rostrum broad; anterior upper incisors robust, farther apart at base; surface of spines not grooved 3

2.a. Ears about equal in height to dorsal spines or somewhat longer; no wholly white spines present among darker ones *Mesechinus*

b. Ears short, do not project above spines. Narrow spineless mid-dorsal area on top of head. Ventral pelage coarse, mostly dark brown; wholly white spines present among darker ones *Erinaceus*

Subfamily Erinaceinae—Hedgehogs

猬亚科 Ciwei Yake—刺猬 Ciwei

Dorsal surface covered in a distinctive coat of stiff spines; nose elongated; neck and tail short and posture crouched giving these animals a distinctly compact appearance. The Erinaceinae comprises 5 genera and 16 species; of these, 3 genera and 4 species occur in China.

Genus *Erinaceus*—Eurasian Hedgehogs

刺猬属 Ciwei Shu—刺猬 Ciwei

Dorsal surface covered with sharp, stiff, smooth quills, size large, hind feet with halluces well developed; ears short, not longer than quills on top of head. Dental formula: 3.1.3.3/2.1.2.3 = 36. Broadly distributed in Europe and Asia. Of four species of *Erinaceus*, one occurs in China.

Amur Hedgehog

Erinaceus amurensis Schrenk, 1859

东北刺猬 Dongbei Ciwei

PLATE 28
MAP 252

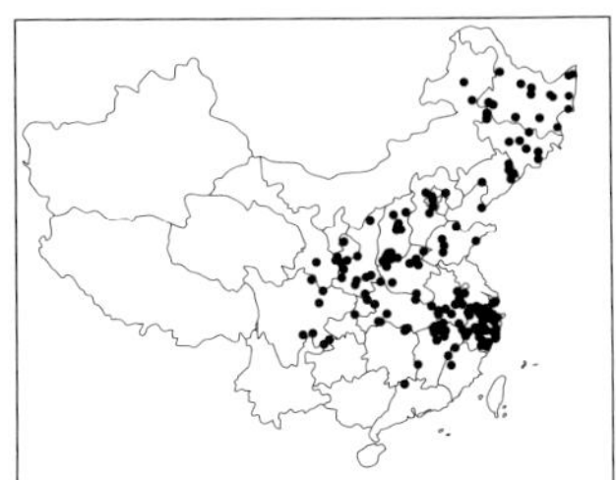

MAP 252. AMUR HEDGEHOG, *Erinaceus amurensis*

Description: HB 158–287; T 17–42; HF 34–54; E 16–26; GLS 47–58; Wt 600–1,000 g. Head, dorsum and sides covered with long, pointed spines; tail very short. Ventral hair consistently light, and face usually light. Quills on dorsum have two kinds of colors, one wholly white, the other with white or yellowish brown basal and terminal bands, and brown or dark brown middle band, producing an overall light brownish gray dorsal color, including limbs and side. Spines on top of head separated by a narrow bare space. Skull obviously more massive than *E. europaeus*; a hedgehog of larger size. Basisphenoid depressed to V-shape, alisphenoid not fused to stapes orifice.

Distribution: C and E China; extending to Russia and Korea. Three subspecies in China: (1) *E. a. amurensis* Schrenk, 1859; Nei Mongol, Heilongjiang, Jilin, Liaoning; (2) *E. a. dealbatus* Swinhoe, 1870; Nei Mongol, Beijing, Hebei, Shandong, Henan, Shanxi, Jiangsu, Anhui, Hubei; (3) *E. a. kreyenbergi* Matschie, 1907; Shanghai, Zhejiang, Anhui, Jiangxi, Hunan, Hubei.

Natural History: This species occupies a variety of habitats, including villages and city parks, all kinds of croplands, deciduous forest and shrublands, mesic steppes and woodland steppes, and montane terrain, lower-level coniferous forests, and subalpine habitats. It does not live in dark taiga forests in northern Manchuria. The Amur Hedgehog, like others, is nocturnal, and forages on ground-dwelling invertebrates, especially fly larvae. In turn, it is said by Chinese sources to be preyed on by the sable (*Martes zibellina*), but the Russian literature does not support this claim. Hibernates in winter, entering torpor in October and emerging in spring. There are one or two litters per year; four to six young per litter.

Comments: Once thought a subspecies of *E. europaeus*.

Conservation Status: China RL—LC.

References: Corbet (1988).

Genus *Hemiechinus*—Desert Hedgehogs

大耳猬属 Da'erwei Shu—大耳猬 Da'erwei

Size small; ears large, clearly projecting above the surrounding spines; ventral pelage soft; surface of spines faintly grooved; hind feet with halluces small; rostrum narrow; upper first incisors somewhat slender, closer together at base than *Mesechinus*; number of teeth is 36; *dauuricus* and *hughi* were once included in this genus but were later placed in *Mesechinus* by Frost et al. (1991) because of concordance with the character of *Mesechinus*. Distributed from North Africa eastward through the Near East and Central Asia to Mongolia, N and W China, and southward to Pakistan and NW India. Of two species of *Hemiechinus*, one lives in China.

Long-Eared Hedgehog

PLATE 28
MAP 253

Hemiechinus auritus (Gmelin, 1770)
大耳猬 Da'er Wei

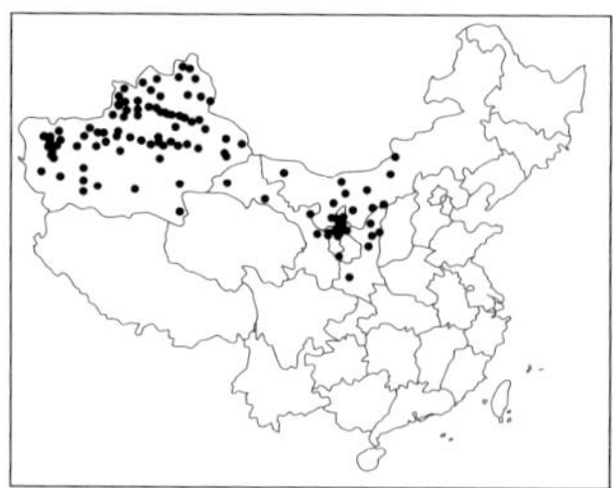

MAP 253. LONG-EARED HEDGEHOG, *Hemiechinus auritus*

Description: HB 170–230; T 18–28; HF 32–39; E 31–40; GLS 44–48; Wt 280–500 g. Size small; ears large and pale, projecting above quills. Dorsum sandy beige; forehead, cheeks, and upper part of head pale rusty; ventral pelage soft and fine; surface on spines faintly grooved; squamosal and basisphenoid expanded; interorbital region of skull narrow, V-shaped bulge present on frontal; lambdoidal crest not projecting up and backward, so occipital condyle and foramen magnum are visible from top of skull; basioccipital slightly triangular.
Distribution: N C and NE China; extending to Mongolia, Ukraine, Libya, W Pakistan. Two subspecies in China: (1) *H. a. aegyptius* (E. Geoffroy, 1803); Nei Mongol, E Gansu, Ningxia, Shaanxi, N Sichuan; (2) *H. a. auritus* (Gmelin, 1770); Xinjiang, Gansu.
Natural History: The Long-eared Hedgehog inhabits semiarid steppes and shrublands throughout its broad geographic range. It also occurs in croplands of various sorts but is less tolerant of true desert conditions. It feeds mainly on insects and other invertebrates, but frogs, snakes, lizards, and small mammals are also taken, as well as both wild and cultivated fruits, such as melons. Like other hedgehogs, this species is entirely nocturnal. They dig their own burrows with their long-clawed forefeet in many substrates (sand, clay, rocky) as daytime refuges, in which a single litter of four to seven young is born during the warm season. By October, they retire to their burrows and hibernate until the coming of spring. Little is known of predation on this seemingly well-protected animal, but there is evidence that it is killed and eaten by small carnivores such as foxes, and by raptors such as the Eurasian Eagle Owl.
Comments: Wang (2003) used *alaschanicus* for the eastern subspecies, but *aegypticus* is the appropriate name (Hutterer 2005).
Conservation Status: China RL—NT; although it nearly met the criteria for VU A2cd + 3cd.
References: Corbet (1988).

Genus *Mesechinus*—Steppe Hedgehogs

林猬属 Linwei Shu—刺猬 Ciwei

Two species of this genus were formerly placed in *Hemiechinus*. Frost et al. (1991) argued that many characteristics were in accord with those of *Mesechinus*, especially the shape of the suprameatal fossa. The suprameatal fossa of *Erinaceus* is large, broad, and deep with a C-shaped rim, while that of *Hemiechinus* is large, broad, and deep with a U-shaped rim. *Mesechinus*, in contrast, has a small, narrow, and shallow suprameatal fossa with a U-shaped rim. Basisphenoid inflation of *Mesechinus* is intermediate between that of *Hemiechinus* and of *Erinaceus*. Ears equal in length to quills or slightly longer; hind feet with halluces small; no dorsal quills nearly wholly white. Both species of *Mesechinus* occur in China.

Daurian Hedgehog

PLATE 28
MAP 254

Mesechinus dauuricus (Sundevall, 1842)
达乌尔猬 Da'wu'er Wei

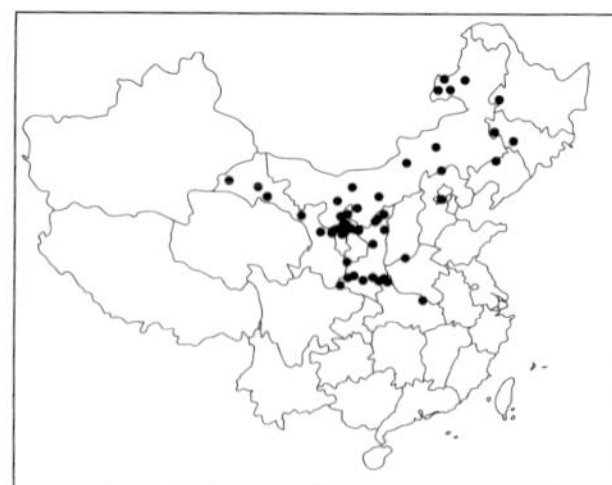

MAP 254. DAURIAN HEDGEHOG, *Mesechinus dauuricus*

Description: HB 175–250; T 14–15; E 25–29; GLS 52; Wt 500 g. Ears projecting above spines on head; no wholly white spines among darker ones. Size slightly larger than *Erinaceus* and *Hemiechinus*. Dorsal pelage rather coarse; surface of spines not grooved,

Key to *Mesechinus*

1.a. Ears project somewhat above dorsal spines; small papillae on surface of spines. In China, known only from NE Manchuria and N C China, but widespread in adjacent Mongolia and Transbaikalia — *Mesechinus dauuricus*
b. Ears short; do not project above spines; no surface papillae on spines. Known only from C China; Sichuan, Henan, Shanxi, and Shaanxi — *Mesechinus hughi*

but covered with small papillae, 3–5 mm at the end; penis spines long and slender, some with hooks; dorsum light brown. Lambdoidal crest of skull robust, but not projecting up and backward, so the occipital condyle and foramen magnum are visible from the back of the skull; interorbital region broad, no bulge on frontal; basioccipital evidently trapeziform; third premolars three-rooted. Dental formula: 3.1.3.3/2.1.2.3 = 36.
Distribution: N C China; extending to Mongolia and Russia (Amur Basin). Two subspecies in China: (1) *M. d. dauuricus* (Sundevall, 1842); Nei Mongol, N Hebei, Shaanxi, Shanxi, Ningxia, Gansu; (2) *M. d. manchuricus* (Mori, 1926); Heilongjiang, Jilin, Liaoning.
Natural History: Inhabits grassland habitat in the dry steppe zone. Diet includes small mammals, lizards, and insects. Hibernates. Produces litters of three to seven young in late spring to early summer.
Comments: Sometimes included in *Hemiechinus*.
Conservation Status: China RL—VU A2cd.
References: Corbet (1988); Frost et al. (1991); Gould (1995).

Hugh's Hedgehog

Mesechinus hughi (Thomas, 1908) PLATE 28 MAP 255
林猬 Lin Wei

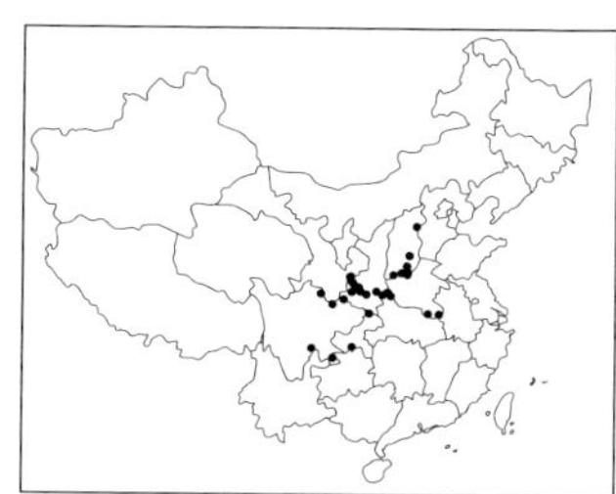

MAP 255. HUGH'S HEDGEHOG, *Mesechinus hughi*

Description: HB 155–200. Ears shorter than spines; spines and pelage dark, white ring present at tip of darker spines. Pelage on spineless area coarser than *M. dauuricus*, darker brown; spines smooth. Ear bones not expanded; lambdoidal crest of skull prominently projecting up and backward, so the occipital condyle and foramen magnum are not visible from the back of the skull; sagittal and occipital crests are nearly perpendicular; basioccipital trapezoid-shaped. Tooth formula apparently not described; probably similar to *M. dauurica*.
Distribution: Occupies C China. Endemic. Three subspecies: (1) *M. h. hughi* (Thomas, 1908); S Shaanxi, Sichuan; (2) *M. h. miodon* (Thomas, 1908); Shaanxi, Gansu; (3) *M. h. sylvaticus* (Ma, 1964); known only from Zhongtiao mountain region of Shanxi.
Natural History: A very poorly known species, and very rare in museum collections. The species occurs in sympatry with *E. amurensis* in the Chingling mountains in Shaanxi Province, where both inhabit low-elevation coniferous forest and subalpine habitats.
Comments: Wang (2003) considers *miodon* an independent form.
Conservation Status: China RL—VU A2cd. IUCN RL—VU B1 + 2c ver 2.3 (1994).
References: Corbet (1988); Ma (1964).

Subfamily Galericinae—Gymnures

毛猬亚科 Maowei Yake—毛猬 Maowei

Pelage without stiff spines, with most forms appearing small and shrewlike. Tail nearly bare. The Galericinae is also known as Hylomyinae (Frost et al. 1991). Galericinae contains five genera, of which three occur in China.

Genus *Hylomys*—Gymnures

毛猬属 Maowei Shu—毛猬 Maowei

Appearance shrewlike to ratlike, but size variable; rostrum sharp, ears well developed, tail short; pelage on the body surface hairy; canines large; four upper premolars. At one time *Hylomys* was considered to include *Neohylomys* and *Neotetracus*; Frost et al. (1991) held that the difference between the three genera was insufficient to support independent generic status (see also Hutterer 2005). Of three species of *Hylomys*, one occurs in China.

Key to the Chinese Genera of Galericinae

1.a. Size small, HB length 120–150 mm; tail very short, about 10–15% of HB length; upper canine teeth well developed, larger than adjacent incisors and premolars (four upper, four lower) *Hylomys*
b. Size small, as above, but tail longer, equal to or more than 30% of HB length; upper canine smaller, only three lower premolars 2
2.a. Tail about 30% of HB length; upper canine teeth only slightly larger than adjacent incisors and premolars (four upper, three lower). Known only from Hainan Island *Neohylomys*
b. Tail about 50% of HB length; upper canine teeth no larger than adjacent incisors and premolars (usually three upper and three lower) *Neotetracus*

Short-Tailed Gymnure

PLATE 28
MAP 256

Hylomys suillus Müller, 1840
毛猬 Maowei

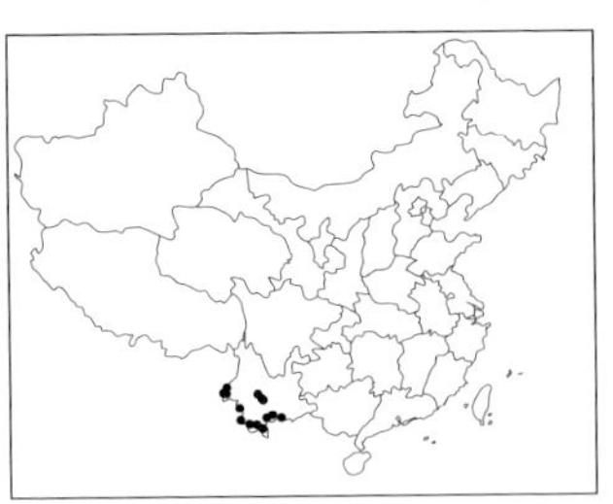

MAP 256. SHORT-TAILED GYMNURE, *Hylomys suillus*

Description: HB 120–150; T 19; HF 23–25; GLS 31–33. Appearance ratlike, slightly stouter, rostrum pointed. Hairs rusty black, ventral pelage buffy, lighter than dorsal; dorsum sometimes shows faint black lines; four mammae, one pair inguinal, one pair thoracic. Tail short, subequal to hind foot length and shorter than other species of *Hylomys*, about 10–15% of HB length. Ears short, about 10% of HB length. Distinguished from rodents of similar size and shape in lacking paired, curving, chisel-shaped teeth at front of mouth; have instead paired, nearly straight, conical incisor teeth at front of mouth, separated by a distinct space. Upper canine larger than adjacent teeth; upper and lower fourth premolars present. Dental formula: 3.1.4.3/3.1.4.3 = 44 (this is the primitive tooth pattern found in the earliest placental mammals).
Distribution: SE Yunnan; extending through Indochina and peninsular Malaysia. Two subspecies in China: (1) *H. s. microtinus* Thomas, 1925; SE Yunnan; (2) *H. s. peguensis* Blyth, 1859; frontier region between Yunnan and Myanmar.
Natural History: Appears to be confined to hill and mountain forests with dense understory and ground litter. Reported to form runways and burrows, but may climb up into shrubs, perhaps foraging for fruits such as *Ficus* and *Melastoma*. However, its main foods are obtained from ground litter and the soil: arthropods (insects, etc.), snails, and earthworms. A pregnant female with two embryos was caught in late February at an altitude of 500 m. Others report litter sizes of three to six, and altitudinal ranges up to 3,500 m. Litter size and breeding season probably vary with season and altitude.
Conservation Status: China RL—VU B1ab(i, ii, iii).
References: Corbet (1988); Ruedi et al. (1994); Ruedi and Fumagalli (1996).

Genus *Neohylomys* (monotypic)

Hainan Gymnure

PLATE 28
MAP 257

Neohylomys hainanensis
Shaw and Wong, 1959
海南新毛猬 Hainanxin Maowei

Description: HB 132–147; T 36–43; HF 24–29; E 17–22; GLS 33–36; Wt 52–70 g. Tail longer than in *H. suillus*; tail about 30% of HB length, evidently longer than hind feet. Only three lower premolars, rather than four, as in *H. suillus*. Form hedgehoglike, slightly stouter, rostrum pointed; pelage on body surface normal; first upper canine somewhat enlarged. Dental formula: 3.1.4.3/3.1.3.3 = 42; but variable in individuals, sometimes one premolar in upper jaw absent, or one more premolar in lower jaw present; skull stout, postorbital process and lambdoidal crest well developed; size slightly larger than *H. suillus*. Hairs mouse gray, lighter than *H. suillus*, tinged with yellowish brown, black lines on anterior midback faintly present.
Distribution: Hainan Island. Endemic.

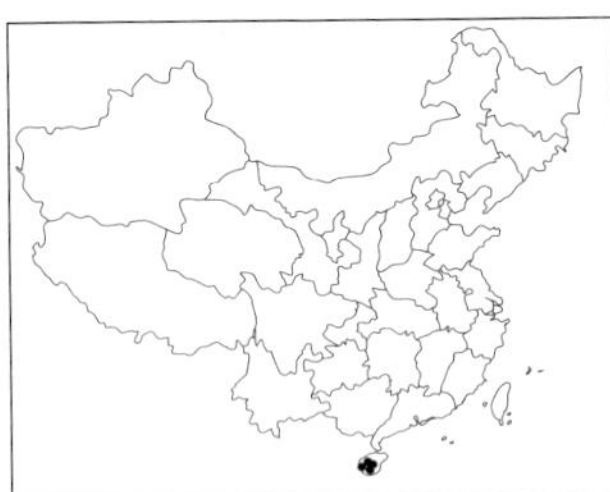

MAP 257. HAINAN GYMNURE, *Neohylomys hainanensis*

Natural History: Described as "volelike" and known to construct burrows. Occupies tropical rainforest and subtropical forest. Very poorly known.
Comments: Frost et al. (1991) included *hainanensis* in *Hylomys*.
Conservation Status: China RL—EN B1ab(i, ii, iii). IUCN RL—EN B1+ 2c ver 2.3 (1994).
References: Corbet (1988); Jenkins and Robinson (2002).

Genus *Neotetracus* (monotypic)

Shrew Gymnure

PLATE 28
MAP 258

Neotetracus sinensis Trouessart, 1909
鼩猬 Qu Wei

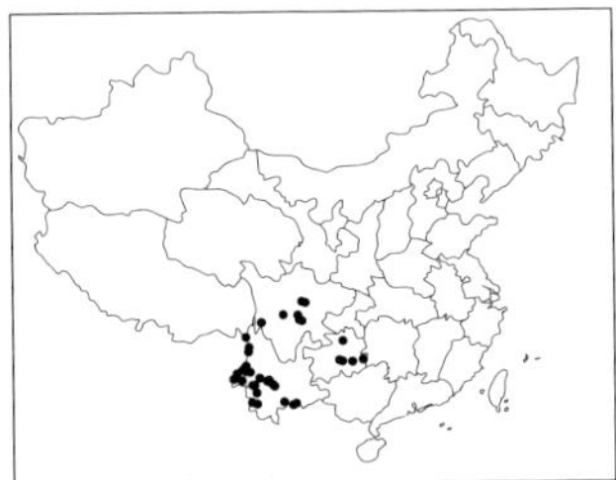

MAP 258. SHREW GYMNURE, *Neotetracus sinensis*

Description: HB 91–125; T 56–78; HF 21–36; GLS 27–32. Shrewlike in appearance; tail longer than in either of the other two gymnures; only three upper premolars, rather than four, as in the other species. Tail about 50% of HB length; ears long, about 15% of HB length. Dorsum a dull olive brown; ventral pelage gray, tinged with light yellow. Rostrum short,

postorbital process robust and projecting. Dental formula: 3.1.3.3/3.1.3.3 = 40; first canines not larger than adjacent teeth, three premolars on each side (a few with either two or four).
Distribution: Central S China; extending to Myanmar, Vietnam. Three subspecies in China: (1) *N. s. cuttingi* Anthony, 1941; W Yunnan; (2) *N. s. fulvescens* Osgood, 1932; S Yunnan; (3) *N. s. sinensis* Trouessart, 1909; Sichuan, Yunnan, Guizhou.
Natural History: This species inhabits subtropical ever-green forest at higher altitudes (1,500–2,700 m) than *H. suillus*. These forms appear to be allo- to parapatric in distribution. *N. sinensis* has been found both close to and away from streams. They are probably also ground foragers that subsist on forest floor invertebrates (ants, caterpillars, earthworms), and vegetable matter. The species occurs "in run-ways and burrows along the moss- and fern-covered banks edging the trail and under logs, rocks, or any other good cover. Rodents, shrews, and shrew-moles used the same runways." (Anthony 1941).
Comments: Frost et al. (1991) included *sinensis* in *Hylomys*.
Conservation Status: China RL–LC. IUCN RL–LR/nt ver 2.3 (1994).
References: Anthony (1941); Corbet (1988).

ORDER SORICOMORPHA—Shrews and Moles
鼩鼱目 Qujing Mu—鼩鼱 Qujing

Robert S. Hoffmann and Darrin Lunde

Shrews and moles were formerly included in the order "Insectivora" along with tenrecs, golden moles, solenodons, and hedgehogs, but recent evidence suggests this to be a paraphyletic clade. Taxa previously united within an all-inclusive "Insectivora" are now generally regarded as constituting three orders in two clades: an African clade including the tenrecs and golden moles (order Afrosoricida), and a Holarctic clade including the hedgehogs and gymnures (order Erinaceomorpha) and the shrews, moles, and allies (order Soricomorpha; see Hutterer 2005 and references therein). Following Hutterer (2005) the Soricomorpha comprises four families–Nesophontidae, Solenodontidae, Soricidae, and Talpidae; the latter two are represented in China. Shrews and moles are rarely observed in the wild, and most of what is known of their natural history comes from trapping data. Stone (1995) comprehensively covers the conservation and status of Eurasian species.

Family Soricidae—Shrews
鼩鼱科 Qujing Ke—鼩鼱 Qujing

Size small, many smaller than most mice; pelage fine and thick; head and rostrum pointed; body and limbs slender and claws very small; a few aquatic species have fringes of hairs or webs on toes; eyes small; ears short but visible. Lateral scent glands present. Skull long and narrow; most sutures fused; zygomatic arch incomplete; no auditory bulla. Main characteristics of tooth structure include elongated upper and lower first incisors; upper incisors procumbent, with a downward hooked apex followed by an elongated cusp or talon; lower incisors projecting straight forward. Second and third upper incisors and canine teeth much reduced in size and either unicuspid in shape or absent altogether. Premolar 1 is absent, and premolars 2 and 3 are either reduced to unicuspids or absent. In the mandible, incisor 2 is unicuspid; incisor 3, canine; and lower premolars 1, 2, and 3 are absent, only premolar 4 being retained followed by molars 1 through 3. Tooth formulas vary among genera. In this account of the family Soricidae we depart from the traditional dental formulae of incisor, canine, premolar, and molar. Instead we use a special "unicuspid" tooth category for incisors, canine, and premolar teeth that are so reduced it is difficult to determine their origins. This approach follows Dannelid (1998) (except we refer to the reduced teeth as unicuspids while Dannelid prefers "antemolars"). Using this system (which we will hereafter refer to as the unicuspid dental formula), dental formulas vary only in the numbers of unicuspid teeth, simplifying identification. Thus, within the family all genera have one upper incisorform tooth, from two to five upper unicuspid teeth, one premolarifom tooth, and three molars. In the lower dentition there is one incisorform tooth, one or two unicuspid teeth, one premolarifom tooth, and three molars. Crowns of upper molars have W-shaped ectolophs. M3 smaller than other molars. Condyloid processes of mandibles with two condyles doubly articulated to skull; condylar shape varies among subfamilies (Repenning 1967; Yates 1984).

Key to the Chinese Families of Soricomorpha

1.a. Skull with zygomatic arches absent; auditory bullae absent; condyloid process of mandible with two condyles forming a double articulation; first pair of upper incisors procumbent and composed of an anterior hooklike apex, and a posterior unicuspid-like talon ... Soricidae

b. Skull with zygomatic arches present; auditory bullae present; condyloid process of mandible with one articulation; first pair of upper incisors either small or large, flattened, projecting straight downward, and not divided into apex and talon ... Talpidae

Key to the Chinese Subfamilies of Soricidae

1.a. Cusps of teeth (except *Anourosorex* and *Chimarrogale*) chestnut red; fourth lower premolar with posterolingual basin; articular condyles of mandible merged on labial side forming a pronounced lingual notch — Soricinae
b. Cusps of teeth white; fourth lower premolar lacks posterio-lingual basin; articular condyles of mandible merged on lingual side, forming a pronounced labial notch — Crocidurinae

Key to the Chinese Genera of Crocidurinae

1.a. Four unicuspid teeth in upper jaw — *Suncus*
b. Three unicuspid teeth in upper jaw — *Crocidura*

Mainly insectivorous, terrestrial, and plantigrade, but some develop arboreal, semiaquatic, or semisubterranean habits. Shrews have high metabolic rates and are active both day and night. They are rarely observed in the wild, and what little is known of the natural history of individual species has been inferred from trapping data. Of three subfamilies, two occur in China: Soricinae and Crocidurinae.

Subfamily Crocidurinae—Crocidurinae Shrews

麝鼩亚科 Shequ Yake—麝鼩 Shequ

The Crocidurinae is characterized by having the articular facets of the mandibular condyle separated, but not widely, and often merged along the lingual side; fourth lower premolar lacks a posterolingual basin; mental foramen located below the anterior root of m1; tooth pigment absent. The Crocidurinae are distributed in Asia, Europe, and Africa, in the Palaeo-tropical zone. Of nine genera, two occur in China.

Genus *Crocidura*—White-toothed Shrews

麝鼩属 Shequ Shu—麝鼩 Shequ

Size typical of Soricidae; three unicuspids in upper jaw. Unicuspid dental formula: 1.3.1.3/1.1.1.3 = 28. Distributed in Asia, Africa, and Europe; most species concentrated in tropical and subtropical zones; a few species occur in northern Europe. Of the 172 species of *Crocidura*, 11 are known from China. Many species of *Crocidura* are very similar in external morphology, differing mainly in size and the relative length of tail, and the hairyness of the tail. Examination of cleaned skulls and morphometric and molecular analysis are usually necessary to definitively identify species. Some currently recognized species probably represent complexes of more than one species, and given the historical undersampling of shrews in general, and *Crocidura* in particular, it is likely that many additional species remain to be discovered.

Asian Gray Shrew

PLATE 29
MAP 259

Crocidura attenuata Milne-Edwards, 1872
灰麝鼩 Hui Shequ

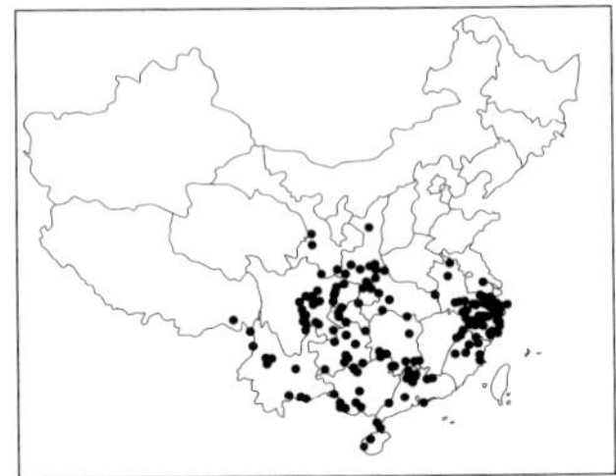

MAP 259. ASIAN GRAY SHREW, *Crocidura attenuata*

Distinctive Characteristics: HB 66–89; T 41–60; HF 13–16; E 7–13; GLS 19–22; Wt 6–12 g. Tail relatively short (usually between 60–70% of HB length); hind foot usually less than 16 mm. Dorsal pelage smoky brown to dark grayish black, gradually merging into dark gray on ventrum, summer pelage darker; tail dark drown above and lighter below, but the contrast is not strong. Throughout its range it is often the most commonly captured shrew.
Distribution: Widespread in SE China; extending to India (Assam, Sikkim), Nepal, Bhutan, Myanmar, Thailand, Vietnam, peninsular Malaysia. Three subspecies are tentatively recognized in China: (1) *C. a. attenuata* Milne-Edwards, 1872; Jiangsu, Zhejiang, Anhui, Jiangxi, Hubei, Hunan, Sichuan, Yunnan, Guangdong, Guanxi, Gansu, Hainan Island; (2) *C. a. grisea* Howell, 1926; Fujian; (3) *C. a. rubricosa* Anderson, 1877; Yunnan, Guizhou.
Natural History: A common shrew found in all kinds of habitats: lowland rainforest, bamboo forest, herbaceous vegetation, scrub, and montane forest to altitudes approaching 3,000 m. Little is known about breeding in this species, but litter sizes of four and five have been noted.
Comments: Once included the form *tanakae*, which is treated independently here following Motokawa et al. (2001b) and Hutterer (2005).
Conservation Status: China RL—LC.

Key to the Chinese Species of *Crocidura*

1.a.	Size medium or small; HB length < 70 mm; GLS < 20 mm; hind foot < 14 mm	2
b.	Size large; HB length > 70 mm; GLS > 20 mm; hind foot > 14 mm	8
2.a.	Occurring in Xinjiang	3
b.	Not occurring in Xinjiang	4
3.a.	Restricted to xeric areas of W Xinjiang; pelage paler	*Crocidura gmelini*
b.	Occurring in more mesic areas of Xinjiang; dorsal pelage darker	*Crocidura sibirica*
4.a.	Pelage dark grayish brown, especially in summer	5
b.	Pelage lighter, pale grayish brown	6
5.a.	Size larger; HB length 66; T 47–50; GLS 17	*Crocidura indochinensis*
b.	Size smaller; HB length 55–65; T 35–42; GLS 15–17	*Crocidura wuchihensis*
6.a.	Size smaller; GLS 16–17.3; tail densely covered with hair, bristles on most of tail	*Crocidura shantungensis*
b.	Size larger, GLS > 17.5; tail less densely haired, long bristles only on basal two-thirds	7
7.a.	Dorsal pelage paler, grayish; tail bicolored; skull with distinct sagittal crest	*Crocidura vorax*
b.	Dorsal pelage darker, brownish; tail indistinctly bicolored; skull with indistinct sagittal crest	*Crocidura rapax*
8.a.	Tail long, more than half HB length	9
b.	Tail short, about 45% of HB length	*Crocidura lasiura*
9.a.	Size smaller, HB 70–79 mm; GLS 20–21.5 mm, hind foot around 14 mm	10
b.	Size larger, HB 79–105 mm; GLS 22–25 mm or more, hind foot 15–19 mm	*Crocidura fuliginosa*
10.a.	Occurs on mainland China	*Crocidura attenuata*
b.	Occurs on Taiwan	*Crocidura tanakae*

References: Fang et al. (1997); Heaney and Timm (1983); Jenkins (1976); Jiang and Hoffmann (2001); Motokawa et al. (1997a; 2000; 2001b).

Southeast Asian Shrew

Crocidura fuliginosa (Blyth, 1855) PLATE 29 MAP 260
长尾大麝鼩 Changweida Shequ

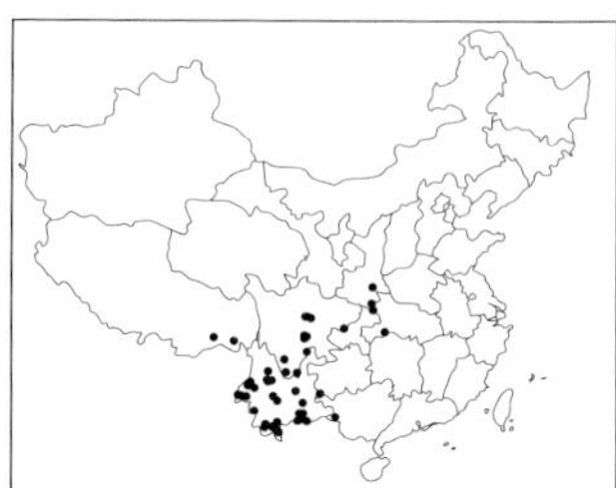

MAP 260. SOUTHEAST ASIAN SHREW, *Crocidura fuliginosa*

Distinctive Characteristics: HB 79–105; T 62–89; HF 15–19; E 10; GLS 22–25; Wt 13 g. A very large, long-tailed shrew; tail usually more than 80% of HB length, longest about 90% of HB length. Dorsal pelage smoky brown to dark grayish black, gradually merging into dark gray on the ventrum; tail dark drown above and lighter below, but the contrast is not strong.
Distribution: Central S China; extending to N India, Myanmar, peninsular Malaysia, and Vietnam. Chinese subspecies: *C. fuliginosa dracula* Thomas, 1912.
Natural History: This species tends to be found below 3,000 m and "appears to be restricted to river valleys and foothills where hot, dry weather shows an obvious effect on the environment" (Allen 1938).
Comments: Specimens identified as *C. fuliginosa* from Zhejiang (Zhuge 1993) probably represent an undescribed species (Jiang and Hoffmann 2001).
Conservation Status: China RL—LC.
References: Allen (1938); Jenkins (1976); Jiang and Hoffmann (2001); Ruedi and Vogel (1995).

Gmelin's Shrew

Crocidura gmelini (Pallas, 1811) MAP 261
北小麝鼩 Beixiao Shequ

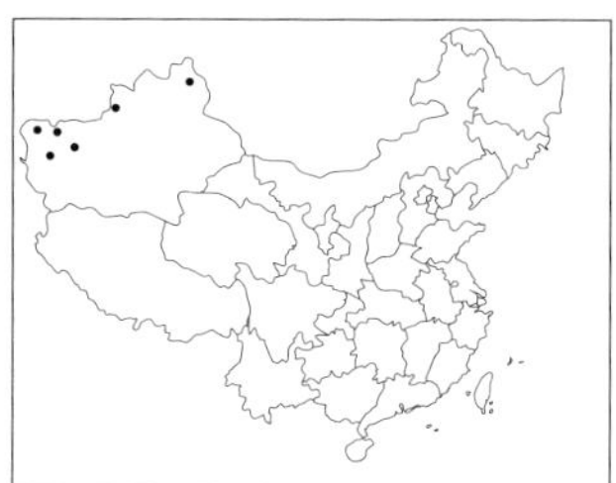

MAP 261. GMELIN'S SHREW, *Crocidura gmelini*

Distinctive Characteristics: HB 52–72; T 25–42; HF 11–14; GLS 17–18. Nearly as small as *C. shantungensis*, but allopatric in distribution, being restricted in China to western Xinjiang (as far as is currently known); ventral pelage lighter gray than in *C. shantungensis;* tail often shorter.
Distribution: NW Xinjiang; extending through Mongolia, Kazakhstan, Uzbekistan, Afghanistan, Pakistan, Turkmenistan, Iran, and to Israel. While

several subspecies have been named (*lar, ilensis, lignicolor, mordeni*), these are best considered synonyms of *gmelini*.

Natural History: Gmelin's Shrew is adapted to arid habitats, including salt-grass plain and sand dunes; tamarisk shrubs growing on low mounds in sandy blow-outs; and ecotones between tamarisk and salt-grass, and sand-dune shrub (*Nitraria*). It also is known to inhabit thick riparian vegetation along the Yarkand River and arid grassy steppe environments.

Comments: Both *shantungensis* and *gmelini* were long considered to be subspecies of *C. suaveolens*, but Hoffmann (1996) seperated these two out as a single species under the older name *gmelini*. This view was subsequently revised by Jiang and Hoffmann (2001), who recognized both taxa as separate species.

Conservation Status: China RL—VU B1ab(i, ii, iii).

References: Hoffmann (1996); Jiang and Hoffmann (2001).

Indochinese Shrew

Crocidura indochinensis
Robinson and Kloss, 1922 — MAP 262
南小麝鼩 Nanxiao Shequ

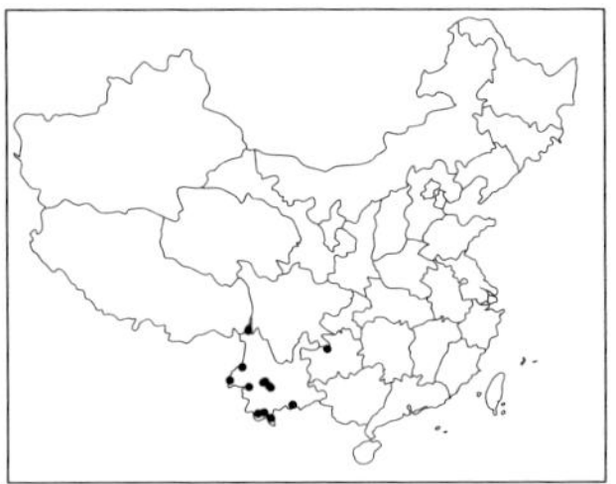

MAP 262. INDOCHINESE SHREW, *Crocidura indochinensis*

Distinctive Characteristics: HB 66; T 47–50; HF 12–13; E 9–11; GLS 17–18. Similar to *C. wuchihensis*, but larger and with different skull proportions.

Distribution: S China (Yunnan, Fujian, Sichuan); extending to Myanmar, N. Thailand, and Vietnam.

Natural History: Inhabits montane forests from 1,200 to 2,400 m.

Comments: Previously included as a synonym of *C. horsfieldii*, but following Lunde et al. (2003a) *C. horsfieldii* is restricted to Sri Lanka and peninsular India, with *indochinensis* and *wuchihensis* representing separate species. See Lunde et al. (2003a; 2004) for further descriptions and comparative measurements of C. *wuchihenisis* and *C. indochinensis*. The species, as currently treated, may still represent a complex of more than one species.

Conservation Status: China RL—VU A3c; B1ab(i, ii, iii).

References: Heaney and Timm (1983); Jameson and Jones (1977); Jenkins (1976); Jiang and Hoffmann (2001); Lunde et al. (2003a; 2004).

Ussuri White-Toothed Shrew

PLATE 29
Crocidura lasiura Dobson, 1890 — MAP 263
大麝鼩 Da Shequ

Distinctive Characteristics: HB 68–104; T 28–47; HF 15–23. A large blackish to dark brown shrew merging into brownish gray on lateral surface; dorsal pelage long and dense; ventrum slate-gray; tail thick and nearly mono-colored. Size largest and tail relatively the shortest in this genus—tail about 45% of HB length. Sagittal crest and lambdoidal crest of skull well developed; condyloincisive length 21.5–25 mm.

Distribution: NE China; a Palaearctic species restricted to NE Asia. Two subspecies in China: (1) *C. l. campuslincolnensis* Sowerby, 1945; Jiangsu, Shanghai, Sichuan; (2) *C. l. lasiura* Dobson, 1890; Heilongjiang, Jilin, Nei Mongol.

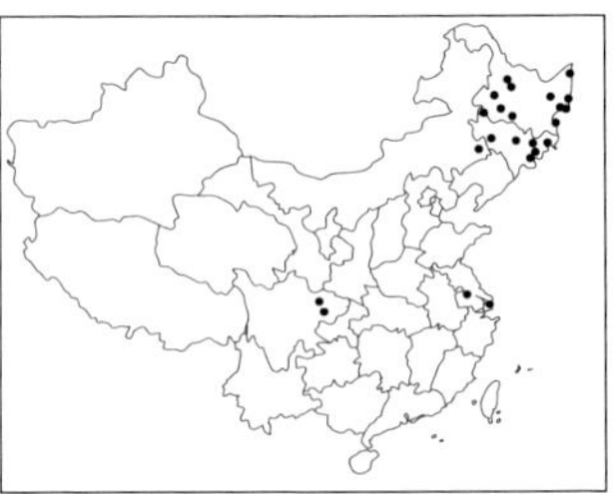

MAP 263. USSURI WHITE-TOOTHED SHREW, *Crocidura lasiura*

Natural History: Occupies broadleaf forest, forest glades, bogs, dry meadows, and shrubby thickets along the banks of rivers and lakes; also in agricultural fields and roadside verges overgrown with sagebrush. Nutrition is based on animal foods. Its diet is predominantly insects and other invertebrates, and small vertebrate animals. Females may produce litters containing as many as 10 embryos, and it is believed that they reproduce throughout the spring-summer period.

Conservation Status: China RL—VU B1ab(i, ii, iii).

References: Motokawa et al. (2000); Ohdachi et al. (2004); Zima et al. (1998).

Chinese White-Toothed Shrew

PLATE 29
Crocidura rapax Allen, 1923 — MAP 264
华南中麝鼩 Huananzhong Shequ

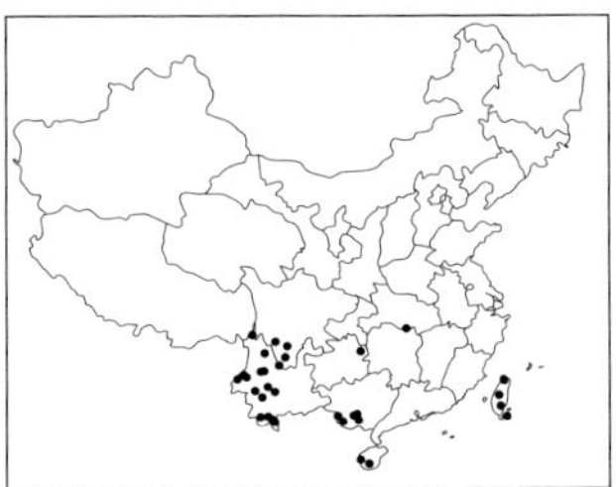

MAP 264. CHINESE WHITE-TOOTHED SHREW, *Crocidura rapax*

Distinctive Characteristics: HB 56–70; T 38–47; HF 11–13; GLS 17.4–18.3. Similar in general form to *C. vorax*, but dorsal pelage much darker brown and ventral pelage nearly as dark, but grayish brown; tail not bicolored, dark brown over entire length, or nearly so; long sensory hairs sparse, restricted to basal third of tail.
Distribution: SE China; extending to India and other bordering countries. Four subspecies in China: (1) *C. r. kurodai* Jameson and Jones, 1977; Taiwan; (2) *C. r. lutaoensis* Fang and Lee, 2002; Green Island; (3) *C. r. rapax* Allen 1923; S China, including Hainan Island; (4) *C. r. tadae* Tokuda and Kano, 1936; Orchid Island.
Natural History: Information lacking.
Comments: The classification history of this species is similar to that of *C. vorax*. Once thought to be subspecies of *C. gueldenstaedtii* or *C. pullata*. Includes taxa from Taiwan and nearby islands that were previously included in *C. horsfieldii* or regarded as separate species.
Conservation Status: China RL—LC.
References: Fang et al. (1997); Fang and Lee (2002); Jiang and Hoffmann (2001).

Asian Lesser White-Toothed Shrew PLATE 29

Crocidura shantungensis Miller, 1901 MAP 265
山东小麝鼩 Shandong Xiaoshequ

MAP 265. ASIAN LESSER WHITE-TOOTHED SHREW, *Crocidura shantungensis*

Distinctive Characteristics: HB 51–65; T 35–43; HF 10–13; GLS 15.5–17. Smallest white-toothed shrew in Eurasia, similar in size to *C. wuchihensis*, but pelage lighter than that species, and distributed further to the north; tail very short, less than 70% HB length, and broad at base, tapering to tip, bearing a scattering of long sensory hairs.
Distribution: Widely distributed from C to E China; extending to E Russia and Korea. Four subspecies in China: (1) *C. s. hosletti* Jameson and Jones, 1977; Taiwan; (2) *C. s. orientis* Ognev, 1922; Heilongjiang, Liaoning, Jilin; (3) *C. s. phaeopus* G. Allen, 1923; Sichuan, Yunnan, Guizhou, Hebei, Shaanxi, Gansu, Qinghai; (4) *C. s. shantungensis* Miller, 1901; Hebei, Beijing, Shandong, Shanxi, Anhui, Zhejiang, Jiangsu.
Natural History: With such an extensive range, this species has been recorded in a wide variety of habitats. In the western section of its distribution, it is found in semi-desert grasslands, while farther to the north it occupies steppe biotopes, and the southern fringe of coniferous forest and mixed broadleaf forest. In the south-central portion of its range it occurs in montane forests, while along the south-eastern edge it occupies the heavily agricultural Yangtze River valley.
Comments: This species was once thought to be a subspecies of *C. sauveolens*; but see Jiang and Hoffmann (2001).
Conservation Status: China RL—LC. IUCN RL—DD ver 2.3 (1994).
References: Jiang and Hoffmann (2001); Motokawa et al. (2003); Ohdachi et al. (2004).

Siberian Shrew

Crocidura sibirica Dukelsky, 1930 MAP 266
西伯利亚麝鼩 Xiboliya Shequ

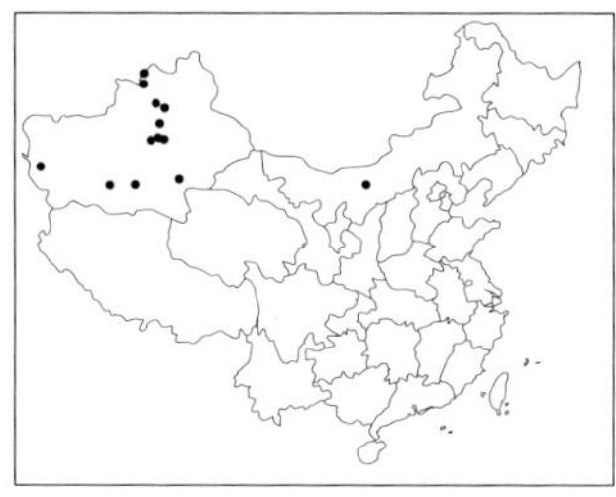

MAP 266. SIBERIAN SHREW, *Crocidura sibirica*

Distinctive Characteristics: HB 58–80; T 30–39; HF 10–13; GLS 18–20; Wt 50–96 g. Size medium, but tail quite short, usually less than half of HB length; tail uniformly colored dark brown; color of pelage lighter than other white-toothed shrews; dorsum dark brownish gray, ventrum whitish gray, sharply delineated.
Distribution: NW China; extending to Mongolia and Central Asia.
Natural History: The Siberian Shrew occupies a variety of habitats within its rather limited range, due to the range of altitudes it occupies. These habitats include montane coniferous forest, streamside meadows with thickets of willow, birch, and aspen groves, dark taiga with ground cover of diverse herbaceous plants, swampy lakeshores and flooded meadows, and creek valleys. Known to occupy mole tunnels. As with other white-toothed shrews, its principal foods are insects; stomach contents have contained a variety of beetles and orthopterans.
Comments: Once thought to be subspecies of *C. leucodon*.
Conservation Status: China RL—VU A3c; B1ab(i, ii, iii); B2ab(i, ii, iii).
References: Han et al. (2002); Ohdachi et al. (2004); Zaitsev (1993).

Taiwanese Gray Shrew

Crocidura tanakae Kuroda, 1938 MAP 267
台湾麝鼩 Taiwan Shequ
Distinctive Characteristics: HB 70–86; T 47–62; HF 12–14.5; E 8–10; GLS 20–22. Very similar to *C. attenuata*, but with a different chromosome number.
Distribution: Taiwan. Endemic.

Natural History: A common species occuring in grass-land, secondary forest, bamboo thickets, and pastures from sea level to 2,200 m. Females with one or two embryos have been found in March and August, and with two or three embryos in February.

MAP 267. TAIWANESE GRAY SHREW, *Crocidura tanakae*

Comments: Originally described as a species, then synonomized with *C. attenuata* (Fang et al. 1997) only to be ressurected as a valid species (Fang and Lee 2002) when differences in karyotype became apparent (Motokawa et al. 1997a; 2001).
Conservation Status: China RL–LC.
References: Fang et al. (1997); Fang and Lee (2002); Motokawa et al. (1997a; 2001).

Voracious shrew

Crocidura vorax Allen, 1923 MAP 268
西南中麝鼩 Xinanzhong Shequ

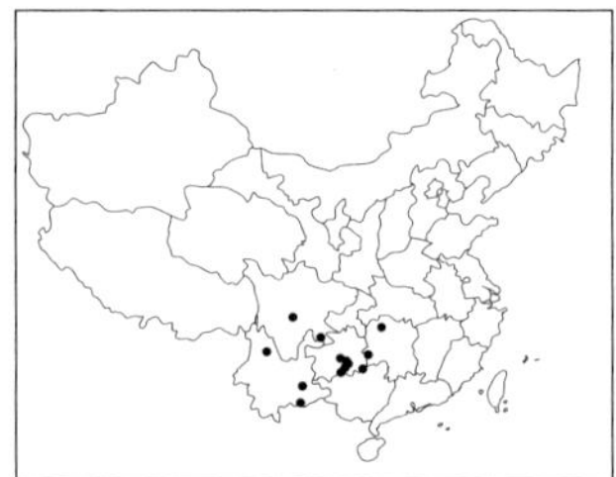

MAP 268. VORACIOUS SHREW, *Crocidura vorax*

Distinctive Characteristics: HB 54–90; T 41–51; HF 11–14; GLS 18.8. Similar to *C. rapax*, but larger and much paler in both dorsal and ventral coloration; paler dorsal fur due to subterminal gray band in *vorax* that is lacking in *rapax*. Dorsal hair tricolor, not distinct from ventrum, which is only slightly lighter than dorsum; dorsum light grayish brown; venter gray; tail distinctly bicolor.
Distribution: Central S China (Yunnan, Sichuan, Guizhou); extending to India, Thailand, Laos, and Vietnam.
Natural History: A highland species. The holotype was captured in timberline forest on Ssu Shan (Snow Mountain) at 4,000 m. Poorly known.
Comments: Once thought to be subspecies of *C. russula, C. gueldenstaedtii,* or *C. pullata*.
Conservation Status: China RL–VU B1ab(i, ii, iii) + 2ab(i, ii, iii).
References: Jiang and Hoffmann (2001).

Wuchi Shrew

Crocidura wuchihensis Wang, 1966 MAP 269
五指山麝鼩 Wuzhishan Shequ

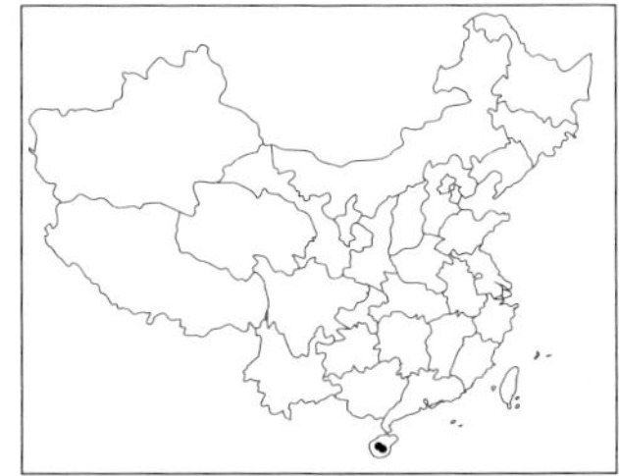

MAP 269. WUCHI SHREW, *Crocidura wuchihensis*

Distinctive Characteristics: HB 55–65; T 35–42; HF 10–13; E 6–9; GLS 15–17; Wt 3.5–6 g. Dorsal pelage dark grayish brown, individual hairs slate gray at base but brownish near their ends and sometimes tipped with silvery gray; ventral pelage somewhat grayer; dorsal surfaces of hands and feet whitish with brown pigmentation evident laterally; tail brown with long bristles along the proximal half. Similar to *C. indochinensis*, but smaller and with a narrower braincase.
Distribution: Described from Hainan Island, and since discovered in Vietnam, Laos, and Yunnan (specimens collected by Lunde, and specimens in Chinese Academy of Sciences).
Natural History: Little known; specimens have been captured in forests between 1,300 and 1,500 m.
Comments: Previously included as a synonym of *C. horsfieldii*, but following Lunde et al. (2003a) *C. horsfieldii* is restricted to Sri Lanka and peninsular India, with *indochinensis* and *wuchihensis* representing separate species. See Lunde et al. (2003a; 2004) for further descriptions and comparative measurements of *C. wuchihensis* and *C. indochinensis*.
Conservation Status: China RL–VU A3c; B1ab(i, ii, iii) (as *C. horsefieldii*).
References: Lunde et al. (2003a; 2004).

Genus *Suncus*—Musk Shrews

臭鼩属 Chouqu Shu—臭鼩 Chouqu

Either larger or smaller than typical size of Soricidae; four unicuspids in upper jaw, 1 unicuspid in lower jaw, unicuspid dental formula: 1.4.1.3/1.1.1.3 = 30. Distributed in Old World tropical and subtropical zones. Of 18 species of *Suncus*, 2 are reported from China.

Key to the Chinese Species of *Suncus*

1.a. Size very large; HB > 118 mm; tail length > 59 mm; hind foot length > 18 mm; four unicuspid teeth in upper jaw — *Suncus murinus*
b. Size tiny; HB length < 54 mm; tail length < 32 mm; hind foot length < 10 mm — *Suncus etruscus*

Etruscan Shrew

PLATE 29
MAP 270

Suncus etruscus (Savi, 1822)
小臭鼩 Xiao Chouqu

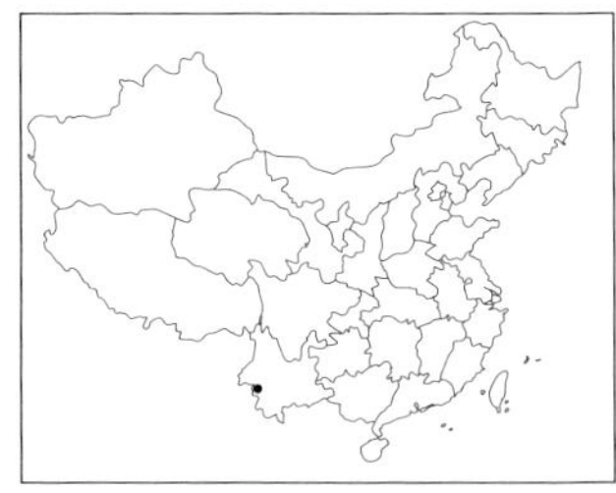

MAP 270. ETRUSCAN SHREW, *Suncus etruscus*

Distinctive Characteristics: HB 43–53; T 20–31; HF 6–9; E 4.5–6; GLS 13–14; Wt 2–3 g. This species is the smallest of the known mammals in China. Dorsal pelage dark grayish brown, ventral, pale gray; fur short, velvety; tail bicolored, darker above.
Distribution: SW Yunnan (known only from Gengma County); extending throughout Indochina, India, and Sri Lanka, across Central Asia, to Europe and N Africa.
Natural History: The Etruscan Shrew is poorly known in China. Observations from throughout its range indicate that it occupies open grasslands, scrub, and deciduous woodlands where it occurs under logs and rocks, or similar crevices. It also frequents human habitations. Diet consists of small insects, such as termites.
Conservation Status: China RL—CR B1ab (i, iii); B2ab(i, ii, iii).
References: Feiler and Nadler (1997); Smith et al. (1998).

Asian House Shrew

PLATE 29
MAP 271

Suncus murinus (Linnaeus, 1766)
臭鼩 Chouqu

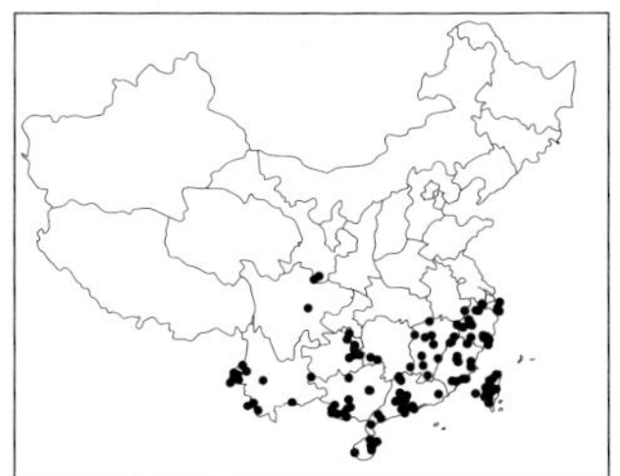

MAP 271. ASIAN HOUSE SHREW, *Suncus murinus*

Distinctive Characteristics: HB 119–147; T 60–85; HF 19–22; GLS 30. Largest shrew in China. Snout long, with profuse, soft vibrissae; ear naked, prominently "crumpled" in appearance; fur short, dense, and velvety, usually ash-gray in color, but darker morphs are sometimes seen. Body pelage varies from blackish to brownish to light bluish gray dorsally, with underparts slightly paler; tail long and heavy with long, coarse hairs thinly scattered along its length; scent glands on the flanks are surrounded by stiff hairs pointing inward, most prominent in the breeding season. Skull large with prominent sagital crest.
Distribution: SE China, including Hainan and Taiwan; extending to Japan, continental and peninsular Indomalayan region, Myanmar, Bhutan, Nepal, Sri Lanka, India, Pakistan, and Afghanistan.
Natural History: The commensal forms of this species are usually found in or near human habitation, in grain storehouses, and in cultivated fields. Wild forms, in contrast, occupy sparse vegetation, both shrubs and forest, often far from a significant human presence. They seem to favor moist habitats, being especially abundant in swamps and around ponds. House shrews are omnivorous, eating seeds and fruit as well as insects and other invertebrates. They occasionally attack large frogs and snakes (up to 46 cm length), but they concentrate on insects such as crickets, cockroaches, and dipterans (taken in flight). There are two breeding seasons per year, the first premonsoonal, and the second toward the end of the monsoon (roughly April–June and August–October). Litter size is one to five, averaging three or four young. Young are weaned in about three weeks but remain with the mother for another two to three weeks, moving about by "caravaning."
Comments: Numerous synonyms and subspecies have been described.
Conservation Status: China RL—LC.
References: Ruedi et al. (1996); Yoshida (1985).

Subfamily Soricinae—Red-toothed Shrews

鼩鼱亚科 Qujing Yake—鼱 Qujing

A subfamily characterized by having the articular facets of the mandibular condyle often widely separated but merged along the labial side and forming a distinct lingual notch on the articular surface; mental foramen located posterior to the anterior root of m1; p4 with a posterio-lingual basin; tooth pigment absent in *Anourosorex, Chimarrogale,* and *Nectogale*, but present in the remaining genera. Mainly distributed in Asia, Europe, and North America (i.e., Holarctic realm). The Soricinae can be divided into six tribes, four of which are represented in China. In all, there

Key to the Chinese Genera of Soricinae

1.a. Tooth cusps without any trace of chestnut red pigmentation — 2
b. Tooth cusps with chestnut red pigmentation — 4
2.a. Basal one-third of tail square in cross-section, with four distinct ridges of stiff hairs present along each of the corners — *Nectogale*
b. Not as above — 3
3.a. Tail length ≤ hind foot length; two unicuspid teeth in upper jaw — *Anourosorex*
b. Tail length > hind foot length; three unicuspid teeth in upper jaw — *Chimarrogale*
4.a. Hind feet and under surface of tail with fringes of silvery hair; four unicuspid teeth in upper jaw — *Neomys*
b. Not as above — 5
5.a. Fewer than five unicuspid teeth in upper jaw; first lower incisor with only one proximal lobe on upper margin — 6
b. Five unicuspid teeth in upper jaw; first lower incisor with more than one proximal lobe on upper margin — 8
6.a. Skull with three unicuspid teeth — *Chodsigoa*
b. Skull with four unicuspid teeth — 7
7.a. Tail length > 50% HB length, foreclaws short (1–2 mm) — *Episoriculus*
b. Tail length < 50% HB length, foreclaws long (2.5–4 mm) — *Soriculus*
8.a. Fourth and fifth unicuspid teeth in upper jaw very small, usually not visible from side; only from below — *Blarinella*
b. Fourth and fifth unicuspid teeth in upper jaw small, but usually visible from side as well as from below — *Sorex*

are 12 genera and 148 species; 9 genera and 39 species occur in China.

Genus *Anourosorex*—Mole Shrews

短尾鼩属 Duanweiqu Shu—短尾鼩 Duanwei Qu

This genus is the only one of the Soricinae that is fully adapted to a life underground, although *Blarinella* and *Soriculus nigrescens* are partially so. Rostrum blunt and projecting; forefeet with well-developed claws; tail very short, shorter than hind feet; tail with no hair but covered with scales; eyes and external ears very reduced; ear pinnae hidden in pelage; skull solid, with well-developed sagittal and lambdoidal crests. Unicuspid dental formula: 1.2.1.3/1.1.1.3 = 26; third molars in both upper and lower jaws very reduced. Mainly distributed in SE Asia. Of four species, two occur in China.

Chinese Mole Shrew — PLATE 29

Anourosorex squamipes
Milne-Edwards, 1872 — MAP 272
短尾鼩 Duanwei Qu

Distinctive Characteristics: HB 74–110; T 8–19; HF 11–16; E 0; GLS 23–26. Body fur dense and lax, color dark grayish brown, uniform dorsally and laterally; ventral surface only slightly lighter; tail extremely short and thin; forefeet have somewhat lengthened claws.
Distribution: Central S China; extending to N Vietnam, Thailand, Myanmar, Bhutan, E India.
Natural History: A fossorial species found at intermediate altitudes (1,200–3,000 m) in montane forests of various kinds. Tunnels in friable soils, but probably forages on the ground surface under leaf litter.
Comments: Included *yamashinai* until recently, see comments in that account.

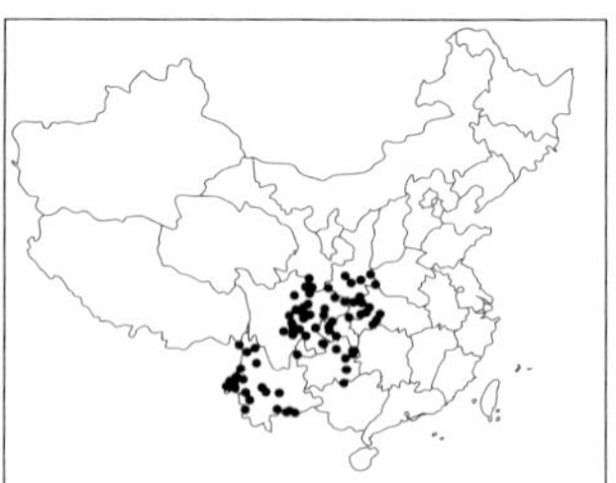

MAP 272. CHINESE MOLE SHREW, *Anourosorex squamipes*

Conservation Status: China RL—LC.
References: Motokawa and Lin (2002); Motokawa et al. (2004).

Taiwanese Mole Shrew

Anourosorex yamashinai Kuroda, 1935 — MAP 273
台湾短尾鼩 Taiwanduanwei Qu

Distinctive Characteristics: HB 50–98; T 7–13; HF 13–16; E 0; GLS 23–26. Similar to *A. squamipes,* but separable based on its smaller body size, shorter tail, and different karyotype.
Distribution: Taiwan. Endemic.
Natural History: Range from 300 m to more than 3,000 m in the mountains, including subtropical forests through mixed deciduous to coniferous, and above timberline to alpine tundra. They are most

abundant in deciduous forests between 1,500 and 2,500 m but have also been captured in agricultural fields, riparian woodlands, and dwarf bamboo.
Comments: Described as a subspecies of *A. squamipes*, and long regarded as such, *A. yamashinai* is a separate species differing from the mainland species by smaller body size, shorter tail, and a distinct karyotype.

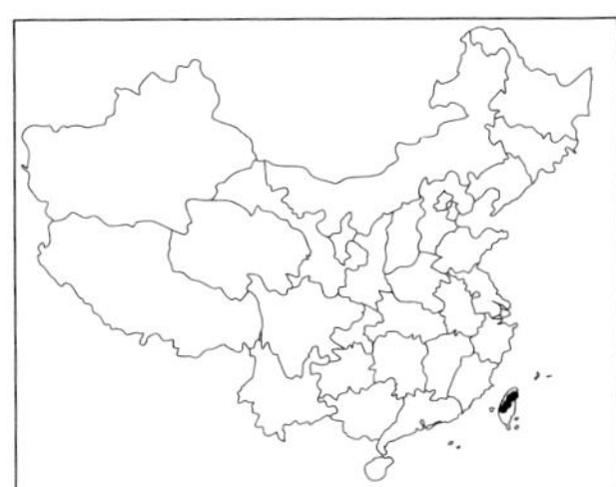

MAP 273. TAIWANESE MOLE SHREW, *Anourosorex yamashinai*

Conservation Status: China RL—NE.
References: Jameson and Jones (1977); Motokawa and Lin (2002); Motokawa et al. (2004).

Genus *Blarinella*—Asiatic Short-tailed Shrews

川鼩属 Chuanqu Shu—川鼩 Chuanqu

Size fairly large for shrews; tail relatively short, less than half HB length; external ears vestigial; forefeet with strong claws skull fairly robust; braincase broad and flat; interterygoid foramen walls netlike. Unicuspid dental formula: 1.5.1.3/1.1.1.3 = 32; lower incisor shorter than in *Sorex*, curving upward, with two low scalloped cusps on upper cutting edge; fourth upper unicuspid very small; fifth upper unicuspid especially tiny; these two teeth usually not visible from side. This genus is one of only a few species adapted to an underground digging life in the subfamily Soricinae. The genus contains three species, all occurring in China.

Indochinese Short-Tailed Shrew

Blarinella griselda Thomas, 1912 MAP 274

甘肃川鼩 Gansu Chuanqu

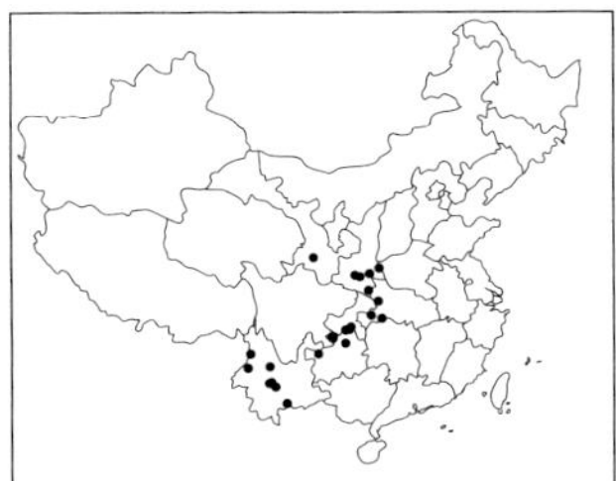

MAP 274. INDOCHINESE SHORT-TAILED SHREW, *Blarinella griselda*

Distinctive Characteristics: HB 52–79; T 31–42; HF 8–14; E 6; GLS 19–21; Wt 8 g. Size medium; color of venter slightly lighter than dorsum, which is dark gray-brown, with lighter grayish highlights; tail lighter than dorsum, dorsal surfaces of hands and feet brownish.
Distribution: Range consists of large part of SW Yunnan, south of the range of *B. quadraticauda;* extending to N Vietnam.
Natural History: Specimens from Vietnam were collected in bamboo forest between 1,500 and1,700 m elevation.
Comments: This species averages intermediate in body size, tail length, and fur color when compared to the other two species of *Blarinella,* and its distribution is between those two as well. In the past this has been considered evidence of intergradation, and *griselda* and *wardi* have been regarded as subspecies of *B. quadraticauda* (Hoffmann 1987), but recent evidence indicates that the three species are morphologicaly distinct and show no evidence of intermediacy (Jiang et al. 2003).
Conservation Status: China RL—LC.
References: Hoffmann (1987); Jiang et al. (2003); Lunde et al. (2003a); Thomas (1912d).

Key to the Chinese Species of *Blarinella*

1.a. Tail long relative to HB length (HB 60–80 mm; T 46–60 mm) *Blarinella quadraticauda*
b. Tail short relative to HB length (HB 60–80 mm; T 30–40 mm) 2
2.a. Dorsal pelage dark brown with grayish highlights and tail slightly paler; upper fourth unicuspid tooth subequal to half of height of upper third unicuspid tooth; skull broader, 8.57–9.63 (average 9.12) mm; interorbital distance wider, 4.06–4.83 (average 4.39) mm; postpalate deeper, 3.29–3.65 (average 3.46) mm; upper toothrow longer, 7.78–8.85 (average 8.30) mm *Blarinella griselda*
b. Dorsal pelage dark brown, tail slightly darker; upper fourth unicuspid tooth subequal to three fourths height of third unicupsid tooth; skull narrower, 7.84–8.72 (average 8.39) mm; interorbital distance narrower, 3.89–4.32 (average 4.03) mm; postpalate shallower, 3.07–3.34 (average 3.20) mm; upper toothrow shorter, 6.98–7.97 (average 7.63) mm *Blarinella wardi*

Asiatic Short-Tailed Shrew

Blarinella quadraticauda (Milne-Edwards, 1872)
黑齿鼩鼱 Heichi Qujing

PLATE 29
MAP 275

MAP 275. ASIATIC SHORT-TAILED SHREW, *Blarinella quadraticauda*

Distinctive Characteristics: HB 65–81; T 40–60; HF 13–16; GLS 20–22. Size relatively large; dorsal and ventral fur uniform dark brown without any gray-brown highlights; tail color and dorsal surfaces of hands and feet as dark as, or darker than that of the dorsal pelage. Of the three species of *Blarinella, quadricaudata* is the largest and has the longest tail.
Distribution: Sichuan. Endemic.
Natural History: These terrestrial shrews are most commonly found in riparian growth along streams in montane coniferous forest, and upward to the alpine zone; but may also occur in secondary forest away from streams. Like the very similar Northern Short-tailed Shrew (*Blarina brevicauda*) from Noth America, this species may also be semifossorial, burrowing through leaf litter or grassy ground cover when foraging for invertebrates.
Conservation Status: China RL—NT; although it nearly met the criteria for VU B1ab(i, iii).
References: Jiang et al. (2003); Lunde et al. (2003a).

Burmese Short-Tailed Shrew

Blarinella wardi Thomas, 1915
云南川鼩 Yunnan Chuanqu

MAP 276

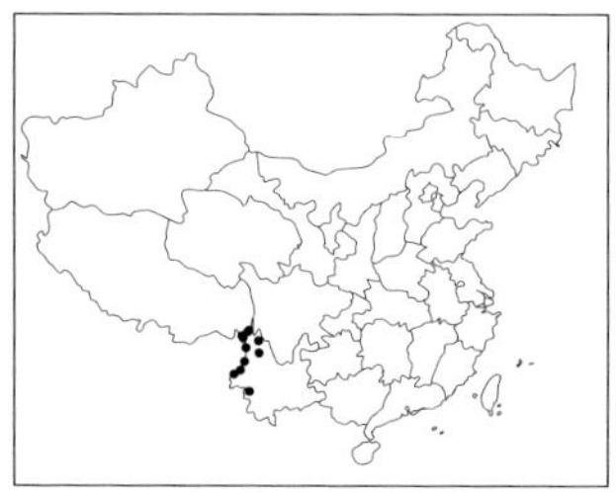

MAP 276. BURMESE SHORT-TAILED SHREW, *Blarinella wardi*

Distinctive Characteristics: HB 60–69; T 32–43; HF 10–13; GLS 18–20. Smallest of the Asian short-tailed shrews; dorsal fur uniformly dark brown, as in *quadraticauda*, but venter visibly lighter, grayish. Feet whitish, while other two *Blarinella* species have dark feet. The skull is much narrower than either *B. quadraticauda* or *B. griselda*, its greatest breadth being less than 9 mm.
Distribution: Central S China; Yunnan, SW Sichuan; extending into Myanmar.
Natural History: Temperate forests, including openings and edges, between 1,600 and 3,000 m elevation; forages in cool, damp ground cover.
Conservation Status: China RL—NT; although it nearly met the criteria for VU B1ab(i, iii). IUCN RL—LR/nt ver 2.3 (1994).
References: Anthony (1941); Jiang et al. (2003); Lunde et al. (2003a).

Genus *Chimarrogale*—Oriental Water Shrews

水鼩属 Shuiqu Shu—水鼩 Shuiqu

A large shrew adapted to aquatic life. Guard hairs slender and soft; rump has long and slender hairs; tail length about equal to HB length; hind feet with a fringe of stiff hairs along sides of toes; skull relatively wide and flat, gradually narrowing anteriorly. Unicuspid dental formula: 1.3.1.3/1.1.1.3 = 28; posterior cusps of incisors in upper jaw weakly developed; anterior tips sharp; three unicuspids in upper jaw about equal in length; tooth crowns wholly white. Occurs throughout mainland East Asia; includes six species, two of which occur in China.

Himalayan Water Shrew

Chimarrogale himalayica (Gray, 1842)
喜马拉雅水鼩 Ximalaya Shuiqu

PLATE 30
MAP 277

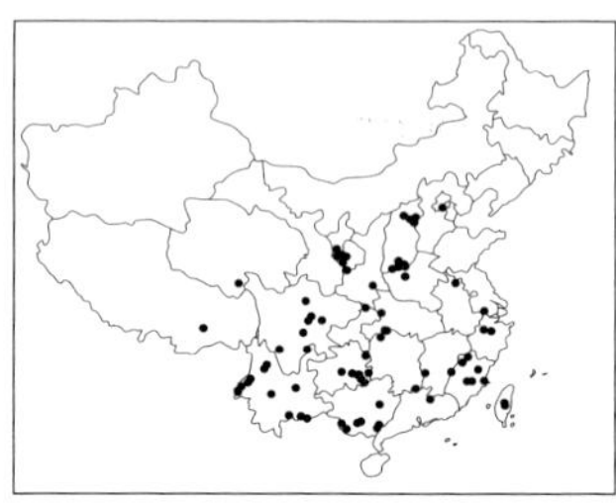

MAP 277. HIMALAYAN WATER SHREW, *Chimarrogale himalayica*

Distinctive Characteristics: HB 115–132; T 79–112; HF 17–30; E 0; GLS 25–28; Wt 23–56 g. In Taiwan only:

Key to the Chinese Species of *Chimarrogale*

1.a. Dorsal pelage sharply distinct from light grayish ventral surface	*Chimarrogale styani*
b. Dorsal pelage merges gradually with light grayish ventral surface	*Chimarrogale himalayica*

HB 109–130, T 80–101, HF 23–26. Pelage blackish brown; ventral surface somewhat lighter, not sharply differentiated laterally; whole body, especially dorsum and rump, have scattered coarse white hairs; fringe of whitish hairs along margin of fore and hind feet and toes; tail long, fringe of white mid-vental hairs along basal 1/3 to 1/2 of tail. Three or four pairs of upper unicuspid teeth; cusps of teeth unpigmented.
Distribution: Widespread throughout C to SE China; extending through SE Asia to Indochina. Three subspecies in China: (1) *C. h. leander* Thomas, 1902; Zhejiang, Fujian, Guangdong, Guangxi, Jiangsu, Guizhou, Taiwan; (2) *C. h. himalayica* (Gray, 1842); Beijing, Hebei, Shanxi, Shaanxi, Hubei Guizhou, Yunnan, Sichuan, Ningxia; (3) *C. h. varennei* Thomas, 1927; E and S Yunnan.
Natural History: Inhabits clear streams flowing through evergreen forest from 250 to 2,000 m altitude. Reported to feed on both fish and aquatic insects.
Conservation Status: China RL—LC.
References: Abe (1971; 1982); Jones and Mumford (1971); Lunde and Musser (2002).

Chinese Water Shrew

PLATE 30
MAP 278

Chimarrogale styani de Winton, 1899
斯氏水鼩 Sishi Shuiqu

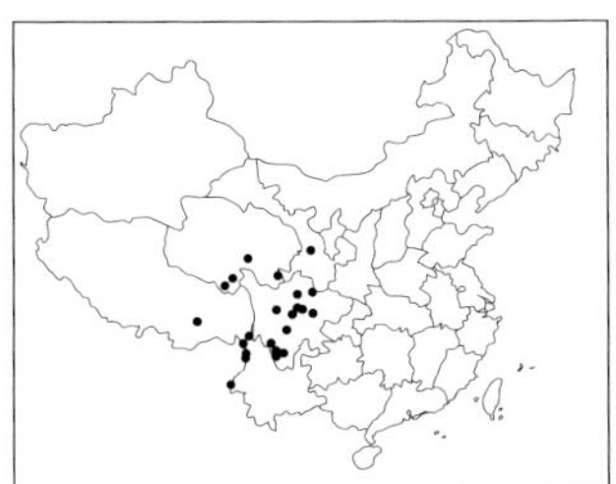

MAP 278. CHINESE WATER SHREW, *Chimarrogale styani*

Distinctive Characteristics: HB 96–108; T 61–85; HF 20–23; GLS 23–25. Similar to the Himalayan water shrew, but slightly smaller. Dorsal pelage darker, almost black, and sharply delineated from the wholly white ventral surface.
Distribution: Xizang, Yunnan, Sichuan, Qinghai, Gansu; extending to N Myanmar.
Natural History: Occurs in high-altitude areas between 1,700 and 3,500 m, where it is found in or adjacent to cool mountain streams. Very little is known about this species, but it is likely to be altitudinally allopatric with the Himalayan Water Shrew, although they are geographically sympatric.
Conservation Status: China RL—NT; although it nearly met the criteria for VU B1ab(iii).
References: Anthony (1941).

Genus *Chodsigoa*—Asiatic Shrews

亚洲鼩属 Yazhouqu Shu—洲鼩 Yazhouqu

Originally named as a subgenus of *Soriculus*, Thomas (1908) subsequently elevated *Chodsigoa* to full generic rank, and this arrangement is followed by Allen (1938). Although numerous authors continued to include it in *Soriculus*, *Chodsigoa* is now almost universally regarded as a distinct genus following Hutterer (1994) and Motokawa (1997b; 1998). Members of the genus *Chodsigoa* are most noticeably distinguished in having only three unicuspids in the upper dentition and a more concave posterior margin of P4–M2. As in *Soriculus*, the cusps of the teeth are tipped with red and the tail is rather thin. Known from China and countries bordering to the south. There are eight known species, seven of which occur in China.

Key to the Chinese Species of *Chodsigoa*

1.a.	Tail > HB; hind foot larger, usually > 17 mm	2
b.	Tail < HB; hind foot smaller, usually < 17 mm	4
2.a.	Size very large, condyloincisor length about 25 mm; tail > 110 mm, hind foot > 21 mm; N Sichuan	*Chodsigoa salenskii*
b.	Size smaller	3
3.a.	Size medium; condyloincisor length 21.1–23.3 mm; skull robust, rostrum long, abruptly narrowing anteriorly	*Chodsigoa smithii*
b.	Size smaller; condyloincisor length 18.9–20.9 mm; skull more lightly built; rostrum short, gradually tapering anteriorly	*Chodsigoa parca*
4.a.	Size larger; condyloincisor length of skull > 19.0 mm	*Chodsigoa hypsibia*
b.	Size smaller; condyloincisor length of skull < 19.0 mm	5
5.a.	Found on Asian mainland; skull flattened in profile	6
b.	Found only on Taiwan; skull not flattened in profile	*Chodsigoa sodalis*
6.a.	Size larger; hind foot 15 mm	*Chodsigoa lamula*
b.	Size smaller; hind foot < 12 mm	*Chodsigoa parva*

De Winton's Shrew

PLATE 31
MAP 279

Chodsigoa hypsibia (de Winton, 1899)
川西长尾鼩 Chuanxi Changweiqu

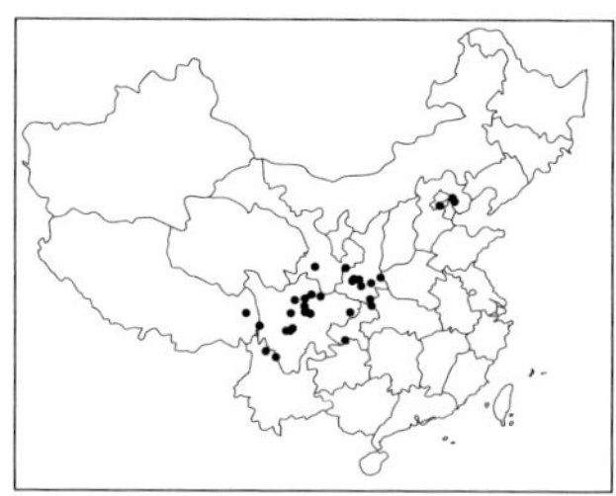

MAP 279. DE WINTON'S SHREW, *Chodsigoa hypsibia*

Distinctive Characteristics: HB 73–99; T 60–80; HF 15–18; GLS 19–22. Dorsal pelage brownish gray, ventral pelage more brownish; tail indistinctly bicolored, grayish above and whitish below, usually just shorter than HB; dorsal surfaces of hands and feet whitish. Skull markedly flattened in profile.
Distribution: C China. Endemic. Two subspecies: (1) *S. h. hypsibia* (de Winton, 1899); Sichuan, Yunnan, Shaanxi, E Xizang; (2) *S. h. larvarum* Thomas, 1911; a disjunct population occurring in Hebei.
Natural History: This species' main area of occurrence is in the Hengduan Shan montane region of SW China, where the natural geography is very complicated and marked with high mountains and deep valleys, and highly diversified, altitudinally zoned vegetation. This core region is surrounded by peripheral populations in E Xizang, the Qinling Shan mountains in Shaanxi , and the isolated Eastern Tombs population in Hebei. With the exception of the last locality, altitude of which is 300 m, the other populations occupy mid- and high-montane areas at altitudes of 1,200–3,500 m.
Conservation Status: China RL—LC.
References: Hoffmann (1985a).

Lamulate Shrew

PLATE 31
MAP 280

Chodsigoa lamula Thomas, 1912
甘肃长尾鼩 Gansu Changweiqu

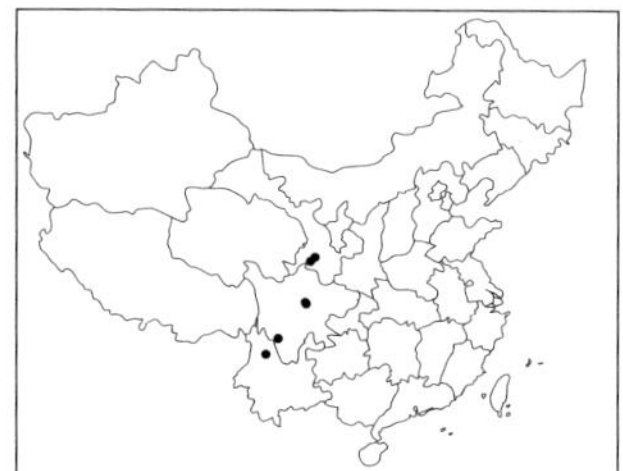

MAP 280. LAMULATE SHREW, *Chodsigoa lamula*

Distinctive Characteristics: HB 54–75; T 43–66; HF 11–16; GLS 17–19. Very similar to *C. hypsibia*, but smaller.
Distribution: Central S China. Endemic.
Natural History: Very little information has been published on the Lamulate Shrew. Apparently it lives in montane forests at high elevations (ca. 3,000 m).
Comments: Once thought to be subspecies of *C. hypsibia;* but size smaller, and these forms are sympatric in distribution.
Conservation Status: China RL—LC.
References: Hoffmann (1985); Lunde et al. (2003a); Thomas (1912d).

Lowe's Shrew

MAP 281

Chodsigoa parca Allen, 1923
云南缺齿鼩 Yunnan Quechiqu

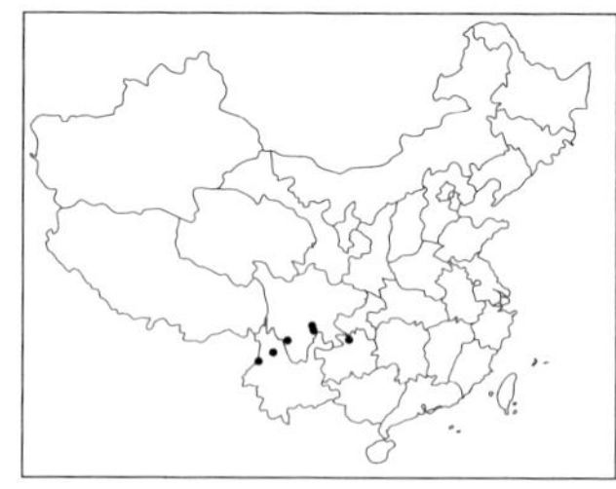

MAP 281. LOWE'S SHREW, *Chodsigoa parca*

Distinctive Characteristics: HB 68–84; T 74–108; HF 15–20; E 8–10; GLS 19–21; Wt 7–9.5 g. Dorsal pelage slate gray with brownish tinges; ventral pelage similarly colored, but slightly lighter; tail longer than HB and distinctly bicolored brown above and creamy white below; dorsal surfaces of hands and feet appear creamy white with a faint browning tinge. Skull with well-domed braincase. Similar to *Chodsigoa smithii,* but smaller; rostrum narrower, tapering more gradually in premaxillary region.
Distribution: Central S China; extending to N Myanmar, Thailand, Vietnam.
Natural History: Specimens collected from near the China border in Vietnam were from montane bamboo forests between 1,500–2,000 m elevation, and in western Yunnan they have been recorded up to 3,000 m.
Comments: Largely allopatric in distribution with *C. smithii*, although these forms are known to occur together in at least one locality.
Conservation Status: China RL—NT; although it nearly met the criteria for VU B1ab(i, ii, iii).
References: Allen (1923a); Hoffmann (1985); Lunde et al. (2003a).

Pygmy Red-Toothed Shrew

MAP 282

Chodsigoa parva Allen, 1923
滇北长尾鼩 Dianbei Changweiqu
Distinctive Characteristics: Not available.
Distribution: Known only from the type locality in the Likiang range, W Yunnan.
Natural History: Little known. Specimens have been collected around 3,000 m elevation.

Comments: Has been synonymized with *C. lamula* (Hoffmann 1985; Corbet and Hill 1992), but Lunde et al. (2003a) showed clearly that *parva* is distinctive from, and smaller than, *C. lamula*.

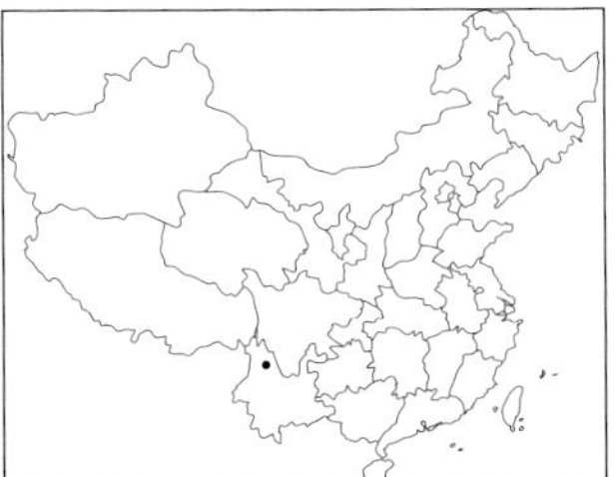

MAP 282. PYGMY RED-TOOTHED SHREW, *Chodsigoa parva*

Conservation Status: China RL—NE.
References: Hoffmann (1985); Lunde et al. (2003a).

Salenski's Shrew

Chodsigoa salenskii (Kastschenko, 1907) MAP 283
大长尾鼩 Da Changweiqu

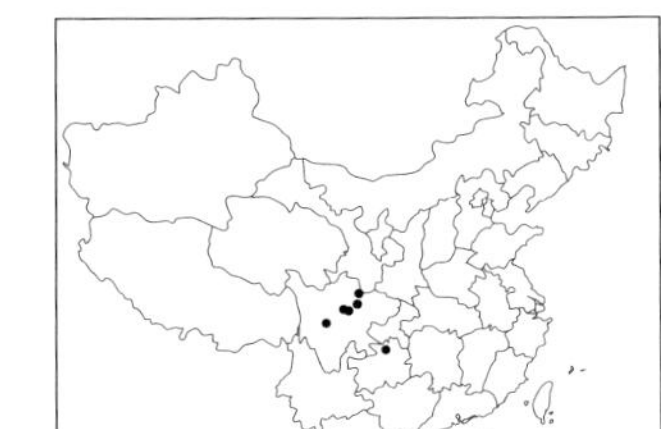

MAP 283. SALENSKI'S SHREW, *Chodsigoa salenskii*

Distinctive Characteristics: HB 78; T 110; HF 22; GLS 25. Very similar to *C. smithii*, but larger.
Distribution: Guizhou and Sichuan. Endemic.
Natural History: Unknown.
Comments: Hoffmann (1985) examined the holotype of this species and strongly suggested that it will prove to be conspecific with *C. smithii*.
Conservation Status: China RL—EN A2c + D2. IUCN RL—CR B1 + 2c ver 2.3 (1994).
References: Gureev (1971); Hoffmann (1985).

Smith's Shrew

PLATE 31
Chodsigoa smithii Thomas, 1911 MAP 284
缺齿鼩 Quechi Qu

Distinctive Characteristics: HB 72–96; T 92–108; HF 16–19; GLS 21–23. Dorsal pelage dark grayish brown; underside somewhat lighter; tail pale brown above, white below; dorsal surfaces of hands and feet brownish white. Similar to *C. salenskii* and *C. parca* but intermediate in size between these two.
Distribution: C China (C Sichuan, Chongqing, S Shaanxi). Endemic.
Natural History: Few specimens of this species have been captured, and information on their biology is scarce. Most have come from forested mountains at high altitudes (3,000+ m). Their morphology, long tail, and large hind feet suggest that they may be more agile climbers than some other members of the subgenus. Their range is widely sympatric with *C. hypsibia*.

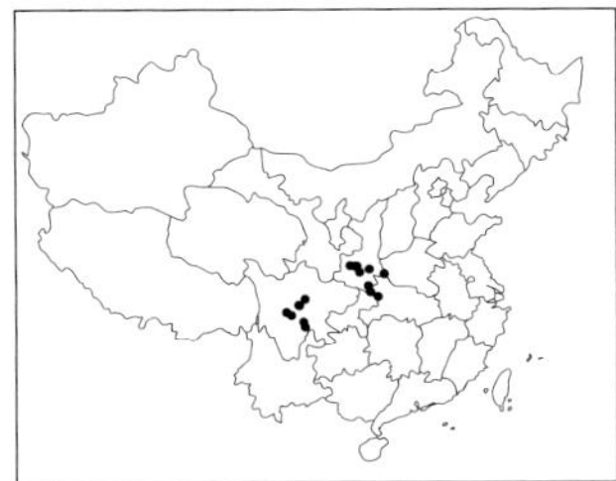

MAP 284. SMITH'S SHREW, *Chodsigoa smithii*

Comments: Once thought to be subspecies of *C. salenskii*.
Conservation Status: China RL—VU B1ab(i, ii, iii) + 2ab(i, ii, iii).
References: Hoffmann (1985).

Lesser Taiwanese Shrew

Chodsigoa sodalis Thomas, 1913 MAP 285
阿里山长尾鼩 Alishan Changweiqu

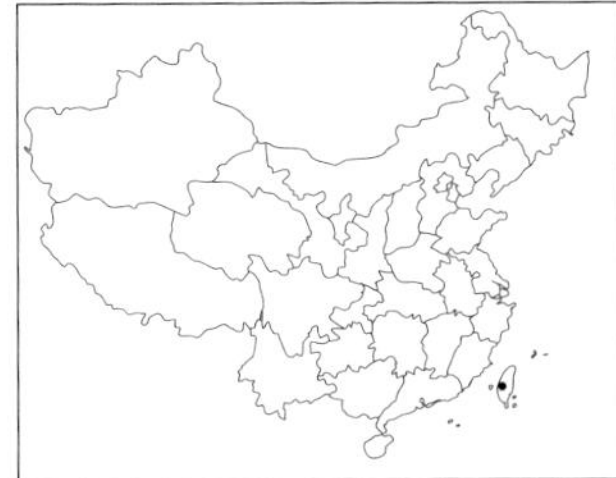

MAP 285. LESSER TAIWANESE SHREW, *Chodsigoa sodalis*

Distinctive Characteristics: HB 65–71; T 64–73; HF 13–15; Wt 4.2–5.6 g. A small, slender form; body covered with long (4–5 mm) hairs. Dorsal pelage dark gray-brown gradually blending into dark gray ventrum; winter pelage without a distinct boundary between the dorsal and ventral coloration; tail dark olive-brown above and below, about the same length as HB, fore- and hind feet relatively large and covered with short whitish hairs.
Distribution: Taiwan. Endemic.
Natural History: This species was recently rediscovered in broadleaf forest at 1,560 m (Yu 1993). In contrast, *Episoriculus fumidus*, which is geographically sympatric with *sodalis*, appears to have a broader niche, being found in either broadleaf or conifer forest, and also dwarf bamboo and subalpine shrubs, and at higher elevations (to 3,200 m).
Comments: This species was long confused with *Episoriculus fumidus*, but Motokawa et al. (1997b) point out many differences between the two species.
Conservation Status: China RL—EN C2a(i, ii).
References: Motokawa et al. (1997b); Yu (1993).

Key to the Species of *Episoriculus*

1.a.	Size large, condyloincisor length usually > 18.8 mm; tail length ≥ HB length	*Episoriculus leucops*
b.	Size small, condyloincisor length usually < 18.8 mm (except on Taiwan); tail variable	2
2.a.	Upper unicuspid teeth quadrate, or wider than long; rostrum broad	*Episoriculus macrurus*
b.	Upper unicuspid teeth longer than wide; rostrum slender	3
3.a.	Ratio of maxillary breadth to palatoincisor length usually > 0.65; found in mainland Asia	*Episoriculus caudatus*
b.	Ratio of maxillary breadth to palatoincisor length usually < 0.65; found on Taiwan	*Episoriculus fumidus*

Genus *Episoriculus*—Long-tailed Asiatic Shrews

长尾亚洲鼩属 Changweiyazhouqu Shu—
长尾亚洲鼩 Changweiyazhouqu

Once included as a subgenus within *Soriculus*, members of *Episoriculus* are distinguished in having a longer tail, shorter claws, and a much narrower coronoid process with a smaller, less oval articular facet. All four species of *Episoriculus* occur in China.

Hodgson's Red-Toothed Shrew

PLATE 31
MAP 286

Episoriculus caudatus (Horsfield, 1851)
长尾鼩鼱 Changwei Qujing

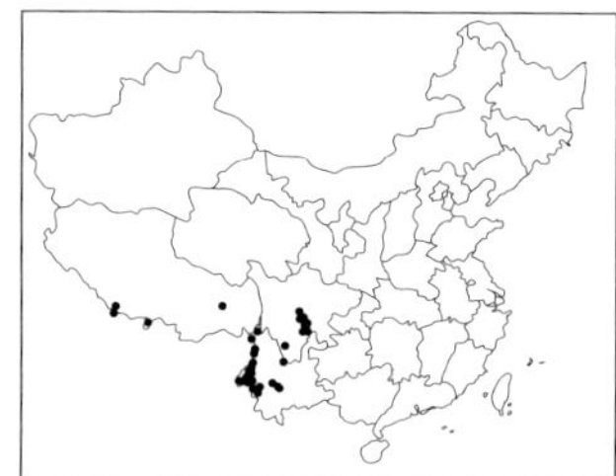

MAP 286. HODGSON'S RED-TOOTHED SHREW, *Episoriculus caudatus*

Distinctive Characteristics: HB 58–74; T 48–69; HF 12–16; GLS 17–19. Dorsal pelage cinnamon brown with faint gray tinges; ventral pelage paler; tail about equal to, or shorter than, HB length and either monocolored or bicolored brown above, whitish below; dorsal surfaces of hands and feet whitish with scattered brown hairs in center; tips of upper incisors separated by noticeable gap; four upper unicuspid teeth usually present. Conformation and skull size similar to *E. macrurus*; tail shorter, about equal to or less than HB length; rostrum long and slender; upper unicuspids (especially second) longer than wide; while rostrum of *E. macrurus* is shorter and wider; skull breadth and interorbital breadth smaller.
Distribution: SW China; extending to India (Kashmir) and N Myanmar. Three subspecies in China: (1) *S. c. caudatus* Horsfield, 1851; Xizang (*soluensis* Gruber, 1969 is a synonym); (2) *S. c. sacratus* (Thomas, 1911) (pelage brown; tail bicolored, dark above, light below; Sichuan, Gansu; (3) *S. c. umbrinus* (Allen, 1923) (hair dark brown; tail monocolored); SW Yunnan.
Natural History: This shrew is widespread at middle elevations, above 2,200 m, frequenting dense oak-rhododendron forest and, higher up, subalpine and alpine meadows. It is also common at the edge of rhododendron and coniferous forests and is attracted to riparian habitats with rich ground litter, or to rocky ground supporting grasses and mosses. It is frequently found near human habitation and cultivated fields. There are two breeding seasons; litters of five or six young are produced during April–June, and litters ranging from three to five are born during the August–October period.
Conservation Status: China RL—LC.
References: Abe (1971); Hoffmann (1985); Mitchell (1977).

Taiwanese Red-Toothed Shrew

MAP 287

Episoriculus fumidus (Thomas, 1913)
台湾长尾鼩鼱 Taiwanchangwei Qujing

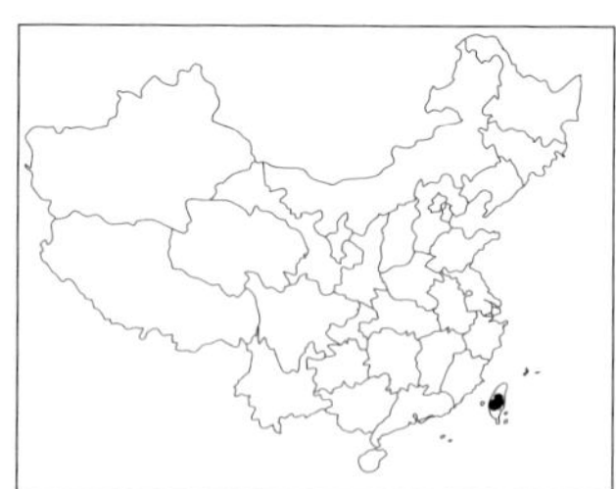

MAP 287. TAIWANESE RED-TOOTHED SHREW, *Episoriculus fumidus*

Distinctive Characteristics: HB 53–71; T 37–52; HF 11–14.5; GLS 18–19. Dorsal pelage brownish above, with a sharp transition to the grayish ventrum; tail relatively short, about half of HB length, dark above, light below. Four upper unicuspid teeth, the fourth very small, and wedged in front of first premolar; posterior margin of fourth premolar and both molars not strongly concave.
Distribution: Taiwan. Endemic.
Natural History: This small shrew prefers dense ground cover in both broadleaf and coniferous forest, and subalpine shrublands in high mountains of central Taiwan, between 1,560 and 2,438 m elevation. It is active both day and night. The breeding season is between March and June, the dry season in Taiwan. Mean litter size is 3.4 young (range 2–4).

Whether more than one breeding season occurs per year has not been determined. The species is sympatric with *C. sodalis* at Tsuifeng (2,300 m) and on Mt. Ali Shan (2,438 m) (Motokawa et al. 1997a).
Comments: Once thought to be subspecies of *E. caudatus* but has a distinct geographic range and distinctive discriminating characters: skull and rostrum short and narrow; angular and coronoid processes of inferior maxilla long; size larger than that of *S. caudatus*. *C. sodalis* was listed as synonym of this species by Jameson and Jones (1977), later repeated by Hoffmann (1985b). Additional specimens, however, demonstrated the independent species status of *C. sodalis* (Motokawa et al. 1997a).
Conservation Status: China RL—NT; although it nearly met the criteria for VU D2.
References: Hoffmann (1985a); Jameson and Jones (1977); Motowaka et al. (1997b; 1998); Yu (1993).

Long-Tailed Red-Toothed Shrew

PLATE 31
MAP 288

Episoriculus leucops (Horsfield, 1855)
印度长尾鼩 Yindu Changweiqu

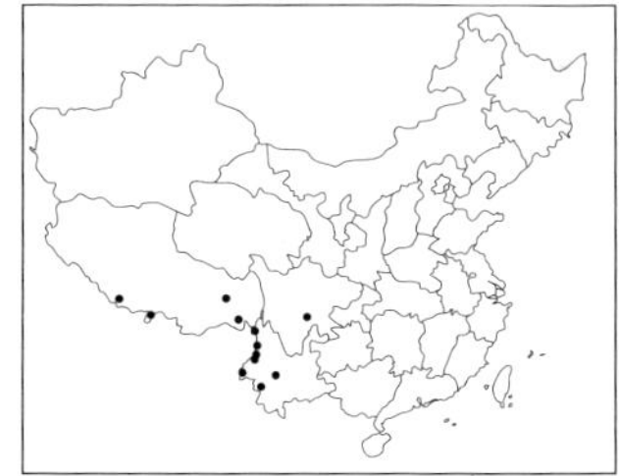

MAP 288. LONG-TAILED RED-TOOTHED SHREW, *Episoriculus leucops*

Distinctive Characteristics: HB 53–81; T 58–83; HF 12–19; GLS 18–21. Size large; pelage uniform dark blackish brown to slate gray both dorsally and ventrally; tail only slightly longer than HB length; four upper unicuspids. Body structure of this species shows fossorial adaptations.
Distribution: SW China; Sechuan, Yunnan, Xizang; extending along E Himalayas from C Nepal eastward through Sikkim, Bhutan, India (Assam), N Myanmar, N Vietnam. Chinese subspecies: *E. l. baileyi* (Thomas, 1914).
Natural History: The Long-tailed Red-toothed Shrew apparently favors moist conifer, rhododendron, and broadleaf deciduous forests at altitudes between 3,000 and 3,500 m. It can also be found in moist stands of dwarf bamboo, shrubs, and grasses, and is known to inhabit villages and cultivated fields. It is sympatric with the smaller *E. caudatus*. Diet consists of earthworms, and they may produce litters of six young.
Comments: Status of this name has been chaotic. It had been thought to be a medium-size grayish species with a very long tail; i.e, *E. macrurus*. Hoffmann (1985) found that the holotype in the British Museum was a large dark brown species of *Episoriculus* with a tail only slightly longer than HB length. Since this name had long been assigned to *E. macrurus*, Red-toothed shrews of this species had been named *baileyi*, *gruberi*, or *caudatus*.
Conservation Status: China RL—LC.
References: Abe (1971; 1982); Hoffmann (1985); Mitchell (1977).

Long-Tailed Mountain Shrew

PLATE 31
MAP 289

Episoriculus macrurus (Blanford, 1888)
缅甸长尾鼩 Miandian Changweiqu

MAP 289. LONG-TAILED MOUNTAIN SHREW, *Episoriculus macrurus*

Distinctive Characteristics: HB 47–73; T 76–101; HF 14–18; GLS 17–19. Pelage light gray. HB length moderate, but tail very long, usually more than 1.5 times as long as HB; four upper unicuspid teeth; upper unicuspids quadrate to wider than long at base; rostrum broad, hind feet large.
Distribution: Central S China; extending to Nepal, India, Myanmar, and Vietnam. Chinese subspecies: *E. m. irene* (Thomas, 1911).
Natural History: This species appears to have semiarboreal habits, as its morphology also suggests (long tail, large hind feet). Primarily occupies temperate broadleaf evergreen forests to lower rhododendron forests, where it is adapted to a life on the ground in closed evergreen forests with scanty undergrowth. Occasionally it is found in bushes near water. It is sympatric with *E. caudatus*.
Comments: Previously referred to incorrectly under the name *leucops*.
Conservation Status: China RL—LC.
References: Abe (1982); Hoffmann (1985); Mitchell (1977).

Genus *Nectogale* (monotypic)

蹼足鼩属 Puzuqu Shu—蹼足鼩 Puzuqu

Elegant Water Shrew

PLATE 30
MAP 290

Nectogale elegans Milne-Edwards, 1870
蹼麝鼩 Pu Shequ

Distinctive Characteristics: HB 90–115; T 100–104; HF 25–27; GLS 25–27. Of all the Soricidae, this shrew is most adapted to aquatic life, in terms of body conformation: external ear pinnae valvate; middle and sides of tail with fringes of stiff, short hairs; which, because of different lengths of stiff hairs, change the cross section of tail from quadrangular at the base to triangular, and finally, flat at the tip; feet fully webbed;

fringe of stiff hairs along sides of toes; long white hairs mixed in pelage. Dorsal pelage dark slaty gray, with scattered white-tipped hairs, especially on the rump; sharply demarcated from the grayish white sides and ventrum; feet dark above and fringed with stiff white hairs. Skull flat; braincase wide and flat, skull becoming narrow and more pointed anteriorly; skull breadth 15–16 mm, Dental formula: 1.3.1.3/1.1.1.3 = 28; upper unicuspids very long, basal cusps weakly developed; first and second unicuspids about equal in size; third (canine) smaller; size similar to that of *Chimarrogale himalayica*, but tail longer, and feet larger. The webbed feet and uniquely haired tail make this species unmistakable.

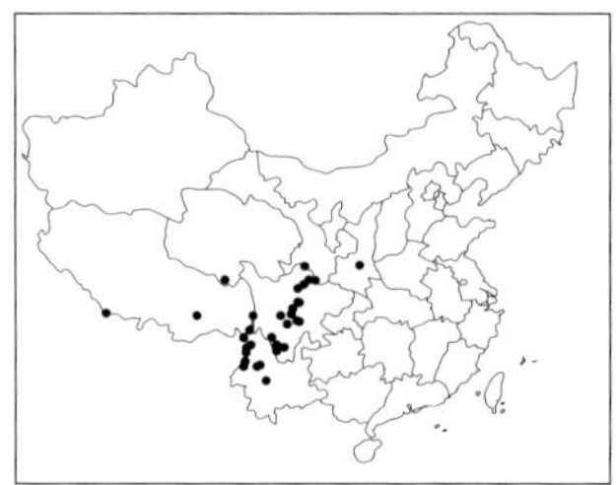

MAP 290. ELEGANT WATER SHREW, *Nectogale elegans*

Distribution: Central S China; extending to Nepal, India (Sikkim), Bhutan, N Myanmar. Two subspecies in China: (1) *N. e. elegans* Milne-Edwards, 1870; Shaanxi, Gansu, Qinghai, Sichuan, Yunnan; (2) *N. e. sikhimensis* de Winton, 1899; Xizang.
Natural History: This is the only fully aquatic shrew; it is, moreover, active during the day, and it may be observed foraging for aquatic invertebrates and small fish in rapidly flowing streams in mountainous regions. One foraging technique is for the shrew to work its way upstream at the water's edge, exploring under rocks, sticks, and stream bank vegetation for some tens of meters, and then to swim out into swift water, where it allows itself to float downstream, and seems to forage in this deeper water, diving down periodically.
Conservation Status: China RL—NT; although it nearly met the criteria for VU B1ab(iii)c.
References: Hoffmann (1987); Hutterer (1993).

Genus *Neomys*—Water Shrews

水鼩鼱属 Shuiqujing Shu—水鼩鼱 Shui Qujing

Semiaquatic; hind feet and undersurface of tail have fringes of silvery hair; cusps heavily pigmented. Unicuspid dental formula: 1.4.1.3/1.1.1.3 = 30. Of three species, one occurs in China.

Eurasian Water Shrew

PLATE 30
MAP 291

Neomys fodiens (Pennant, 1771)
水鼩鼱 Shui Qujing

Distinctive Characteristics: HB 69–94; T 44–80; HF 17–21; Wt 8–26 g. Four pairs of upper unicuspid teeth, progressively smaller posteriorly; sharply bicolored in pelage, dark brown above, grayish buff on sides and belly; mid-ventral line of silvery hairs on tail; short, silvery hairs fringe digits of fore-and hind limbs. Tail long, more than half of HB length; ears and eyes small, covered in hairs; feet large, toes edged with fringes of long, stiff hairs.
Distribution: NE and NW China; extending from Europe (British Isles) across Asia to N Korea and Sakhalin Island.

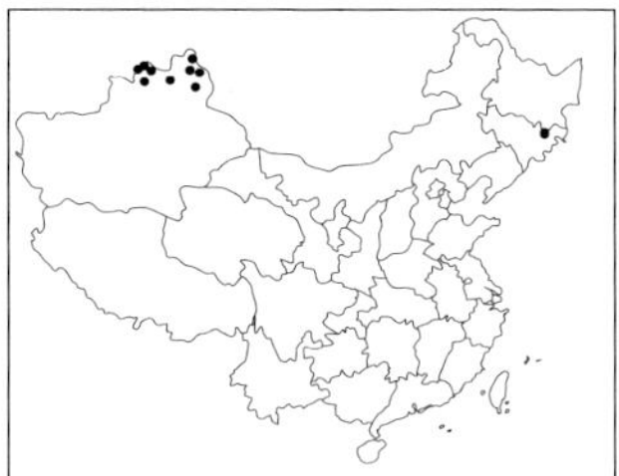

MAP 291. EURASIAN WATER SHREW, *Neomys fodiens*

Natural History: Generally lives close to water and seems to prefer less turbid, fast-flowing streams; mostly found in forests, but may also visit woodlands, grasslands, or even alpine heaths; has been found up to 2,500 m in the European Alps. Forages both on the ground surface and below, in tunnels that it excavates or remodels from those of moles. The tunnel system may have several entrances, either under ground litter, or underwater. It feeds on insect larvae of many kinds, mollusks, crustaceans, small fish and amphibians, earthworms, and terrestrial insects such as beetles. Whether it feeds on small mammals is uncertain, but submaxillary glands secrete venom that in other shrew species enables the shrew to immobilize a small rodent. The breeding season is in the spring and summer months, and the litter size averages 6 young (range 3–15); two litters per year may be produced, depending on favorable weather.
Conservation Status: China RL—VU D2.
References: Hoffmann (1987); Yudin (1989).

Genus *Sorex*—Holarctic Shrews

鼩鼱属 Qujing Shu—鼩鼱 Qujing

Size small; greatest body mass less than 16 g; length of hind foot less than 17 mm; GLS less than 23.3 mm; dorsum color generally grayish to reddish brown, darker mid-dorsally; venter usually paler; head long and rostrum pointed; tail nearly half of HB length; limbs slender; both forefeet and hind feet with five toes; skull fragile and thin; braincase broad and flat. Unicuspid dental formula usually: 1.5.1.3/1.1.1.3 = 32; first upper and lower incisors especially enlarged, procumbent; first upper incisor has two cusps, front and hind; five unicuspids behind; first two developed, size about equal to hind cusp of first upper incisor; later three successively smaller; fourth premolar and first two molars quite developed, and have perfect "W" tooth crown structure; their protocone and

Key to the Chinese Species of *Sorex*

1.a.	Black stripe running down spine from neck to rump; may be conspicuous or inconspicuous	2
b.	No black stripe running down spine	3
2.a.	Tail about 80% of HB length; mid-dorsal stripe conspicuous; GLS > 19 mm	*Sorex cylindricauda*
b.	Tail usually > 80% of HB length, often about equal to it; mid-dorsal stripe inconspicuous; GLS < 19 mm	*Sorex bedfordiae*
3.a.	Body size very small, tail ≤ 32 mm; GLS < 15 mm	*Sorex minutissimus*
b.	Not as above	4
4.a.	Forefeet with large claws > 3mm in length; size large, GLS ≤ 19 mm	*Sorex unguiculatus*
b.	Foreclaws not enlarged < 3 mm long; body size small to large	5
5.a.	Size small; GLS 15.5–18.5 mm, usually < 17.8 mm; second upper unicuspid smaller than first and third unicuspids, which are about equal in size	6
b.	Size small to large; GLS > 17.2 mm, usually > 17.5 mm (except *S. gracillimus*, in which < 17 mm); second upper unicuspid larger than third and usually smaller than first unicuspid	7
6.a.	Size smaller, GLS < 16.3 mm; unworn upper unicuspid teeth with base longer than height	*Sorex minutus*
b.	Size larger, GLS 16.0–18.5 mm; unworn upper unicuspid teeth with base < height	8
7.a.	HB length 51–63.5 mm; GLS 15.8–17.3 mm; skull more inflated, rounder	*Sorex thibetanus*
b.	HB length 51–74 mm; GLS 16.4–17.6 mm; skull flat	*Sorex planiceps*
8.a.	Size very large; GLS > 22.7 mm; third unicuspid < fourth; large accessory tine on medial surface of first upper incisor	*Sorex mirabilis*
b.	Not as above	9
9.a.	Pelage uniformly dark, dorsal color merging gradually with ventral color, which is, if any, only slightly lighter; unicuspid teeth decreasing in size gradually and evenly	10
b.	Light venter separated from dark dorsum by distinct line	11
10.a.	Size larger; tail relatively long, about 80% of HB length; GLS > 20.3 mm; narrow braincase and long rostrum	*Sorex sinalis*
b.	Size smaller; tail relatively short, about 60% of HB length; GLS < 20.4 mm; wide braincase and short rostrum	*Sorex isodon*
11.a.	Teeth very heavily pigmented, the pigment extending into the basins of the molariform teeth	*Sorex daphaenodon*
b.	Not as above	12
12.a.	Size large, GLS > 20.5 mm; posterior margins of molariform teeth deeply excavated	*Sorex roboratus*
b.	Not as above	13
13.a.	Size moderate; GLS 18.5–20.2 mm; second upper unicuspid larger than, as large as, or only a little smaller than, first unicuspid; third unicuspid distinctly smaller than second	14
b.	Size smaller; GLS < 18.8 mm; second upper unicuspid usually < first	15
14.a.	Restricted to the Tian Shan region	*Sorex asper*
b.	Restricted to C China	14
15.a.	Restricted to Yunnan and Sichuan	*Sorex excelsus*
b.	Restricted to Gansu	*Sorex cansulus*
16.a.	Indistinct light side stripe often present (especially in winter adults); unicuspid teeth in occlusal view quadrate to wider than long; rostrum relatively wide and short	*Sorex tundrensis*
b.	No side stripe; unicuspid teeth in occlusal view longer than wide; rostrum relatively long and narrow	17
17.a.	Size larger, GLS > 17 mm	*Sorex caecutiens*
b.	Size smaller, GLS < 16.5 mm	*Sorex gracillimus*

hypocone both developed (hypocone of fourth premolar may be weakly developed); first incisors of lower jaw extend forward horizontally; its dental ridge has three distinct cusps. This is the commonest genus of Soricinae and is widely distributed in N Asia, Europe, and North America. Of 77 *Sorex*, 18 occur in China.

Tian Shan Shrew

Sorex asper Thomas, 1914 MAP 292
天山鼩鼱 Tianshan Qujing

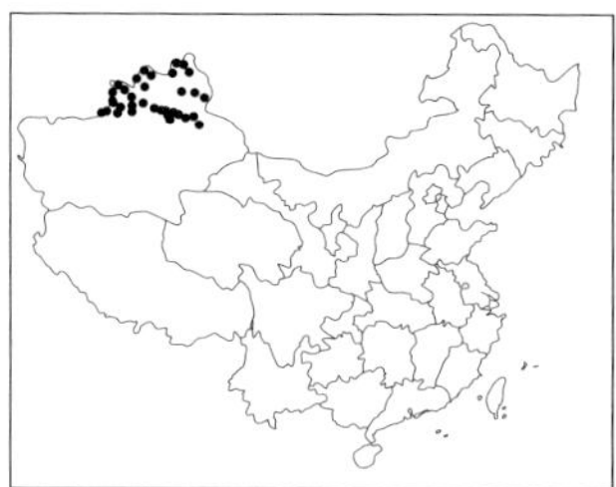

MAP 292. TIAN SHAN SHREW, *Sorex asper*

Distinctive Characteristics: HB 55–77; T 32–47; HF 10–14; GLS 19–20; Wt 5–12 g. Medium-large size; second unicuspid larger than both first and third; fourth much smaller than third; unicuspids tend to point backwards, their tips forming a convex line; rostrum long, upper first incisors and unicuspids unusually massive.

Once thought to be subspecies of *S. araneus*; very similar to *S. excelsus* and *S. tundrensis*. These two species, like *asper*, have relatively slender rostra; upper unicuspids high and conelike, but second unicuspid of this species about equal to or larger than first; third equal to or slightly smaller than first; skull breadth 9.1–9.5 mm.
Distribution: NW Xinjiang; extending to Kazakhstan.
Natural History: Poorly known. The Tian Shan Shrew is probably an alpine specialist, as are *cansulus* and *excelsus*. The species is known to inhabit spruce forests, moist alpine meadows, and stands of shrubs and reeds, generally at elevations of 2,000–3,000 m. It favors cluttered places with a thick layer of friable litter. It is active throughout the year. Most of its activity is during twilight and night, but it is occasionally encountered during the day. Its diet is diverse but is predominantly composed of insects. Breeding begins at the end of March or early in April. At this time the testes of males enlarge to 6 mm. They remain in this condition to the end of July and then regress to their original dimensions, 1–2 mm. Litter size: 1–8 (average 5.3). Independent young are first noticed in early July.
Comments: Once thought to be a subspecies of *A. araneus*, and has also been linked taxonomically with *excelsus* and *tundrensis* (Hoffmann 1987). Recent molecular studies have shown that these species are not closely related (Fumagalli et al. 1999).
Conservation Status: China RL—NA.
References: Fumagalli et al. (1999); Hoffmann (1987).

Lesser Striped Shrew

PLATE 30
Sorex bedfordiae Thomas, 1911 MAP 293
小纹背鼩鼱 Xiaowenbei Qujing
Distinctive Characteristics: HB 50–72; T 48–66; HF 11–15; GLS 17–19. A black mid-dorsal stripe runs from the base of the neck to the base of the tail in most individuals (less conspicuous than that of *S. cylindricauda*); both dorsal and ventral pelages are dark brown, almost monotone, or the venter slightly lighter. Length of upper toothrows 7.1–7.8 mm; first, second and third upper unicuspids about equal in size; fourth and fifth upper unicuspids decreasing in size gradually or about equal in size; compared with *S. cylindricauda*, fifth upper unicuspid much smaller; body size distinctly smaller; and proportion of tail length to HB length longer.
Distribution: Central S China; extending to Myanmar and Nepal. Three subspecies in China: (1) *S. b. bedfordiae* Thomas, 1911; C Sichuan; (2) *S. b. gomphus* Allen, 1923; W Yunnan; (3) *S. b. wardi* Thomas, 1911; S Gansu, Shaanxi.

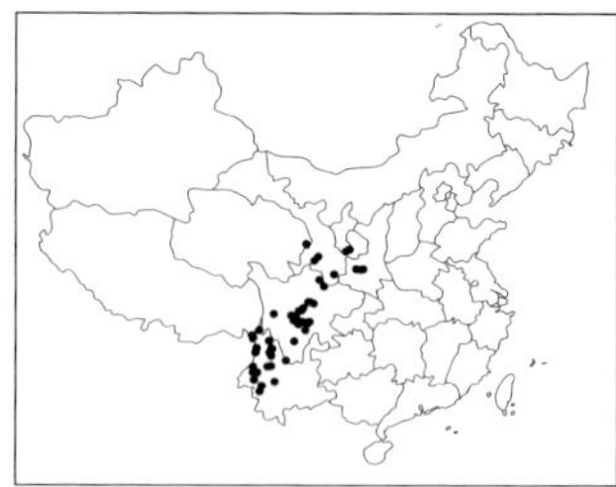

MAP 293. LESSER STRIPED SHREW, *Sorex bedfordiae*

Natural History: This species has been studied in Nepal (as "*cylindricauda*"). There it occupies the alpine zone above 4,000 m, but it may also be found somewhat lower (3,500 m) in the rhododendron-conifer zone. In China it occurs between 2,135 and 4,270 m (higher, on average, than *S. cylindricauda* that occurs about 2,500 m). It lives in the ground litter and forages on insects. It shares this niche with its congener, *S. minutus*, but the two appear to be allopatric in distribution. In addition, *Soriculus nigrescens* and *S. caudatus* are taken in association with *S. bedfordiae*.
Comments: Once thought to be a subspecies of *Sorex cylindricauda*.
Conservation Status: China RL—NT; although it nearly met the criteria for VU A2c.
References: Hoffmann (1987).

Laxmann's Shrew

PLATE 30
Sorex caecutiens Laxmann, 1788 MAP 294
中鼩鼱 Zhong Qujing

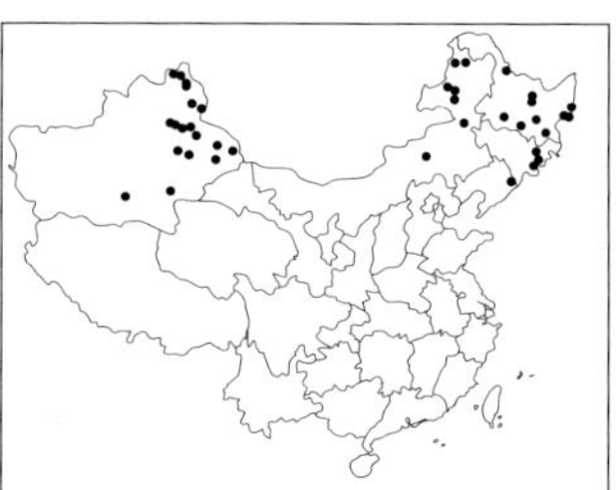

MAP 294. LAXMANN'S SHREW, *Sorex caecutiens*

Distinctive Characteristics: HB 52–65; T 30–38; HF 11–13. Rostrum long and narrow; no light stripe on side. Size relatively small; tail length more than half of HB length, usually 65% or more; condyloincisive length of skull 16.4–18.1 mm; length of upper toothrows 6.8–8.1 mm; first and second upper unicuspids about equal in size; third and fourth upper unicuspids also about equal in size and smaller than first and second; fifth tiny; tooth crown of first lower unicuspid short, height less than half of length. Overlaps with *S. tundrensis* in distribution; the two species are relatively difficult to distinguish. Chromosome numbers of these two species are quite different. *S. caecutiens* has natural XY chromosomes; 2N=42; FN = 68. *S. tundrensis* has male chromosomes of X, Y_1, and Y_2; chromosome number of males 31–39; chromosome number of females 30–38; FN = 52–56.
Distribution: NW and NE China; extending from E Europe across Asia to Korea, Sakhalin Island, and Japan. Three subspecies in China: (1) *S. c. altaicus* Ognev, 1922; Altai mountain region, Xinjiang; (2) *S. c. koreni* Allen, 1914; Heilongjiang, Nei Mongol; (3) *S. c. macropygmaeus* Miller, 1901; NE China.
Natural History: *S. caecutiens* represents still another boreally adapted species that inhabits the Eurasian portion of the circumpolar taiga zone. It is widespread in both lowland and montane taiga forest and also ventures onto adjacent tundra. It is partial to damp ground that supports berry bushes and small trees, and extends along the shores of swamps and streams in moorlands. Foods are mainly insects, especially beetles, a few spiders, millipedes, and earthworms, and also conifer seeds. Breeding season is June to August, and up to four litters may be produced in that time. Litter size ranges from 2 to11, with a mean of 7 to 8.
Conservation Status: China RL—NT; although it nearly met the criteria for VU A2c.
References: Hoffmann (1987); MacDonald and Barrett (1993); Ohdachi et al. (2001); Okhotina (1993).

Gansu Shrew

Sorex cansulus Thomas, 1912 MAP 295
甘肃鼩鼱 Gansu Qujing

MAP 295. GANSU SHREW, *Sorex cansulus*

Distinctive Characteristics: HB 62–64; T 38–43; HF 12. Once thought to be a subspecies of *S. caecutiens*; small-sized *Sorex*; dorsal pelage dust-color to grayish brown; sides buffy; ventral pelage hazel; forefeet and hind feet white brown; dorsum of tail dark brown; venter of tail slightly lighter. Posterior cusps and anterior tips of upper incisors about equal size; size slightly larger than S. *caecutiens*; condyloincisive length 18.5–19.2 mm; length of upper toothrows 8.1 mm; first upper unicuspid larger than second; third unicuspid distinctly smaller than second.
Distribution: Restricted distribution in C China; S Gansu. Endemic.
Natural History: Nothing appears to be known about the biology of this rare species, except that specimens have been found at high altitudes (2,600–3,000 m).
Comments: For many years this taxon was known only from the type locality, and another location close by in S Gansu. Several additional specimens have now been taken in SW Gansu, adjacent Qinghai, and one from E Xizang. Moreover, these new specimens are from localities where *S. caecutiens* also occurs, thus supporting the independent species status of *S. cansulus*.
Conservation Status: China RL—VU D2. IUCN RL—CR B1 + 2c ver 2.3 (1994).
References: Hoffmann (1987); Thomas (1912d).

Stripe-Backed Shrew

Sorex cylindricauda Milne-Edwards, 1872 PLATE 30 MAP 296
纹背鼩鼱 Wenbei Qujing

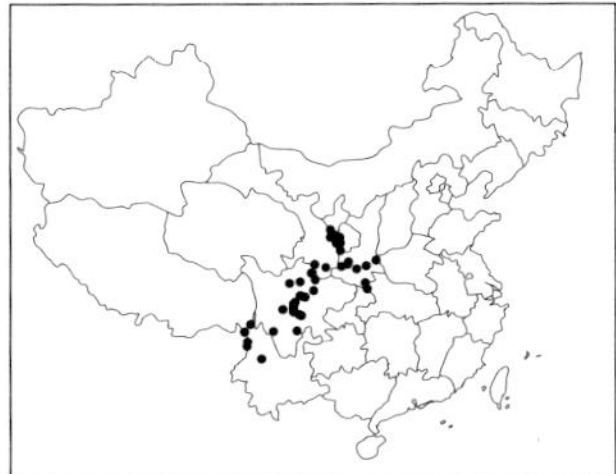

MAP 296. STRIPE-BACKED SHREW, *Sorex cylindricauda*

Distinctive Characteristics: HB 67–77; T 55–62; HF 15–16; GLS 17–21. Dorsal pelage cinnamon-brown; venter dark gray-brown, nearly as dark as dorsum. Conformation similar to that of *Sorex caecutiens*, but larger; conspicuous dark stripe running down spine from neck to rump; tail about equal to HB length or slightly shorter (about 80%). Length of upper toothrows 8.75 mm; first, second, and third upper unicuspids about equal in size; fourth and fifth upper unicuspids decreasing in size gradually or about equal in size; fifth unicuspid relatively larger than that of other *Sorex*.
Distribution: Central China (NW Yunnan, C Sichuan, S Gansu, Shaanxi). Endemic.
Natural History: Since this species has consistently been confused with *S. bedfordiae*, it is not possible to separate statements made about the biology of "*cylindricauda*" except to note that their habitat must include montane forests that surround the type locality, Moupin, Sichuan.

Conservation Status: China RL–LC. IUCN RL–EN B1 + 2c ver 2.3 (1994).
References: Hoffmann (1987).

Large-Toothed Siberian Shrew

PLATE 30
MAP 297

Sorex daphaenodon Thomas, 1907
栗齿鼩鼱 Lichi Qujing

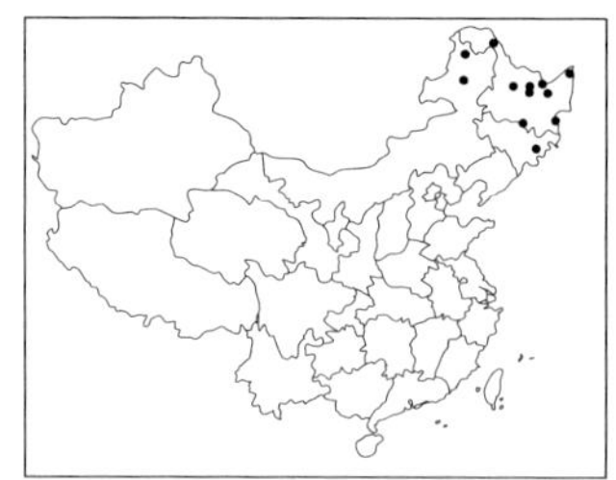

MAP 297. LARGE-TOOTHED SIBERIAN SHREW, *Sorex daphaenodon*

Distinctive Characteristics: HB 48–76; T 25–39; HF 10–13. Pelage dark brown dorsally and lighter gray-brown ventrally; separated by a distinct line; soles of feet dark brown; reddish brown pigment of teeth much more extensive and deeper in color than in other species of *Sorex;* teeth more massive than those of other large shrews, dark pigment spreads into basins of anterior molars; hypocone of upper premolars (P4) well developed, also heavily pigmented. Size larger than *S. caecutiens*; tail about half of HB length; condyloincisive length 17.5–18.5 mm; length of upper toothrows 7.6–7.9 mm.
Distribution: Heilongjiang, Nei Mongol, Jilin; extending across Asia from Sakhalin Island to Kazakhstan and the Ural mountains.
Natural History: This large species occupies mixed forest (conifer and broadleaf types) over much of its range, and it may also occupy birch groves in the wooded steppe. In the Altai region *daphaenodon* may be sympatric with *S. minutus, caecutiens* and *araneus*, as well as *Crocidura sibirica*. Diet consists of earthworms, spiders, millipedes, and insects (lepidoptera, orthoptera, crickets, diptera, and a variety of beetles). Breeding occurs in the summer months, and pregnant females are encountered in June–August. Litter size ranges from four to nine (average seven). Males with enlaged gonads have been recorded from June to the middle of September. The Large-toothed Siberian Shrew is preyed on by nocturnal and diurnal birds of prey and mammalian carnivores (Sable, Siberian Weasel, Ermine).
Conservation Status: China RL–DD.
References: Hoffmann (1987); Yudin (1971).

Chinese Highland Shrew

PLATE 30
MAP 298

Sorex excelsus Allen, 1923
云南鼩鼱 Yunnan Qujing

Distinctive Characteristics: HB 60–73; T 44–51; HF 16–13; GLS 18–20; Wt 5–10 g. Brown back, buff sides, and gray belly (the dorsal and ventral color differentiate distinctly); tail sharply bicolored, brown above, white below; feet white to silvery gray. Size medium; once thought to be subspecies of *S. araneus*; very similar to *S. asper, S. cansulus,* and *S. tundrensis*. These three species all have relatively slender rostra; upper unicuspids high and cone like. The first two unicuspids of similar size, third and fourth also similar, but distinctly smaller than second unicuspid. Size of unicuspids more like those of *S. tundrensis*. Skull breadth 8.6–9.0 mm.
Distribution: C China (N Yunnan, Sichuan, Xizang, S Qinghai); possibly extending into Nepal.

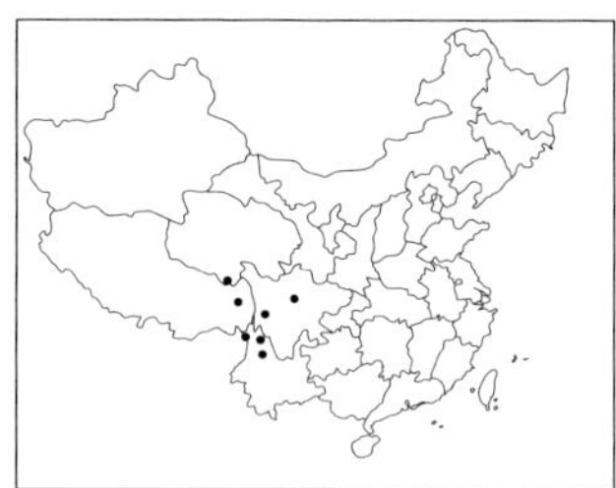

MAP 298. CHINESE HIGHLAND SHREW, *Sorex excelsus*

Natural History: This species appears to be of regular occurrence in alpine and montane forest regions, up to 4,000 m elevation. In S Qinghai it has been captured along small streams with shrubby banks and moist litter on the soil surface.
Conservation Status: China RL–VU B1ab(i, ii, iii) + 2ab(i, ii, iii); C1. IUCN RL–DD ver 2.3 (1994).
References: Allen (1923a); Fumagalli et al. (1999); Hoffmann (1987).

Slender Shrew

PLATE 30
MAP 299

Sorex gracillimus Thomas, 1907
细鼩鼱 Xi Qujing

MAP 299. SLENDER SHREW, *Sorex gracillimus*

Distinctive Characteristics: HB 48–52; T 37–43; HF 10–11; GLS < 17. Second upper unicuspids larger than third and usually smaller than first unicuspids; braincase nearly round rather than oval, as in most members of the *S. minutus* group, and rising abruptly from the base of the rostrum.
Distribution: Nei Mongol, Heilongjiang, Jilin; extending to NE Asia (Hokkaido Island, Sakhalin Island, N Korea, Russia).
Natural History: Throughout its range the Slender Shrew primarily occupies coniferous forest habitat in

mountainous areas. It may also occur in riparian willows, tall-grass sections of buckwheat, and large bamboo stands. Maximum densities are attained in mixed coniferous-broadleaf forests and riparian willows. It avoids fields and meadows. Density of animals is higher in secondary woodland than in deep, continuous taiga. Diet primarily consists of invertebrates living in the surface litter and upper soil horizon. Breeding occurs between May and October. Litter size: one to eight (average five to six).
Comments: The range of *S. gracillimus* is entirely allopatric with respect to *S. minutus*, and the two species seem to occupy the same ecological niches.
Conservation Status: China RL—NA.
References: Dolgov and Lukyanova (1966); George (1988); Hoffmann (1987); Hutterer (1979); Ohdachi et al. (2001); Okhotina (1993); Orlov and Bulatova (1983); Yudin (1971)

Taiga Shrew

Sorex isodon Turov, 1924 MAP 300
远东鼩鼱 Yuandong Qujing

MAP 300. TAIGA SHREW, *Sorex isodon*

Distinctive Characteristics: HB 65–83; T 40–48; HF 13–15; GLS 19–21. Once thought to be subspecies of *S. araneus* or *S. sinalis*. *S. isodon* is somewhat smaller, with a relatively shorter tail, shorter rostrum, and wider cranium than *sinalis*. Size large; ventral pelage hazel to dark brownish gray, slightly lighter than dorsal pelage; these gradually blend laterally. Upper unicuspids decrease in size gradually from first to fifth.
Distribution: Restricted distribution in NE China; Heilongjiang and E Nei Mongol; extending across Eurasia from Scandinavia to the Pacific (Kamchatka, Sakhalin Island, Korea).
Natural History: Throughout its range the Taiga Shrew occupies low-lying evergreen-forested country. Its very large range overlaps three other large *Sorex*: *araneus, roboratus,* and *unguiculatus,* the last two also occurring in China. The ability of *isodon* to co-exist with these two potential competitors is attributed to its specialized diet of fly larvae and pupae.
Conservation Status: China RL—NA.
References: Hoffmann (1987); Sulkava (1990).

Eurasian Least Shrew

Sorex minutissimus Zimmermann, 1780 MAP 301
姬鼩鼱 Ji Qujing

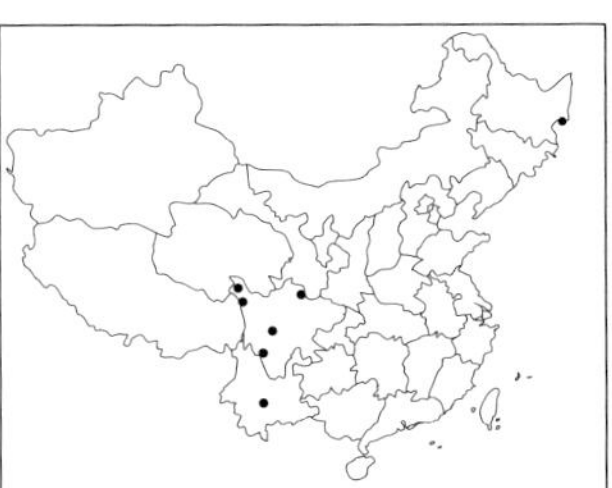

MAP 301. EURASIAN LEAST SHREW, *Sorex minutissimus*

Distinctive Characteristics: HB 39–55; T 20–35; HF 7–11; GLS 12.4–14.2; Wt 1.4–2.9 g. By far the smallest soricid shrew found in China. Similar in size to the crocidurine *Suncus etruscus*, from which it can be separated on the basis of tooth pigmentation. Pelage somewhat tricolor, brownish dorsally, and lighter gray ventrally, separated by brownish gray flanks.
Distribution: Central S and NE China; extending from Scandinavia to E Siberia, South Korea, and the islands of Sakhalin and Hokkaido. At least 16 subspecies have been described, although no name has been given to the isolated population in Yunnan and Sichuan. *S. m. tscherskii* Ognev, 1913, occurs in Heilongjiang.
Natural History: The biology of this tiny shrew is poorly known because it is so hard to capture and observe. What data there are suggest it ranges across a wide variety of habitats, evidenced by the large geographic range it occupies. It apparently avoids open tundra, preferring taiga forests. Because of its very small size its food requirements are less than with larger *Sorex*, and it is capable of survival in low-productivity habitats.
Conservation Status: China RL—LC.
References: Hoffmann (1987); Ohdachi et al. (1997a; 1997b).

Eurasian Pygmy Shrew

Sorex minutus Linnaeus, 1766 MAP 302
小鼩鼱 Xiao Qujing

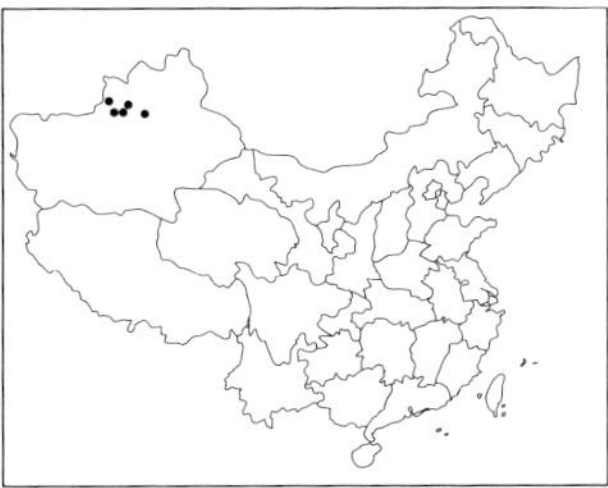

MAP 302. EURASIAN PYGMY SHREW, *Sorex minutus*

Distinctive Characteristics: HB 46–52; T 35–36; HF 10–11; GLS 15–17. Dorsal pelage medium brown, contrasting with gray-white venter; tail relatively thick

and hairy. First and third upper unicuspids about equal in size; second upper unicuspid smaller than first and third; unworn upper unicuspid teeth with base longer than height of tooth crown.
Distribution: NW Xinjiang; extending from Europe to Lake Baikal.
Natural History: Little is known of the biology of this species. Apparently it occupies coniferous forests, although it may also occur in rocky habitats at high elevation. It lives on a diet of arthropods and beetles.
Comments: Once thought to include *thibetanus, kozlovi, planiceps* and *gracillimus*; later divided into four species; *buchariensis*, *thibetanus* (incl. *kozlovi*), *planiceps,* and *gracillimus.* Only the first does not occur in China, being restricted to Pamir mountains of Tadzhikistan; the remaining three are included in the Chinese fauna.
Conservation Status: China RL–NA.
References: Dolgov and Hoffmann (1977); Hoffmann (1987; 1996a;1996b); Hutterer (1979).

Ussuri Shrew

Sorex mirabilis Ognev, 1937 PLATE 31 MAP 303
大鼩鼱 Da Qujing

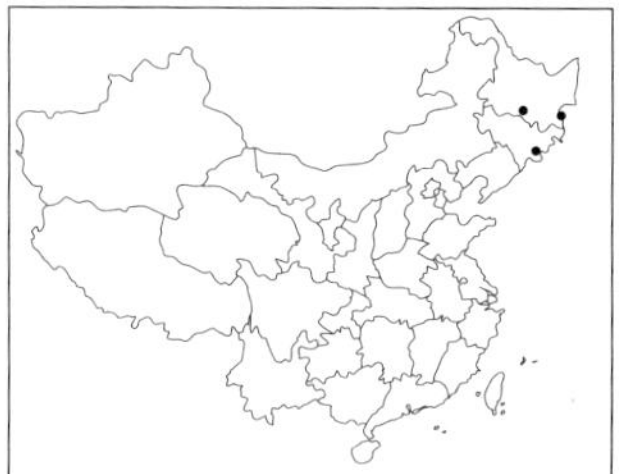

MAP 303. USSURI SHREW, *Sorex mirabilis*

Distinctive Characteristics: HB 74–97; T 63–73; HF 16–18; Wt 11–14 g. The largest species of *Sorex*; dorsal hair iron-gray, not distinct from gray ventral surface; condyloincisive length more than 23 mm; length of upper toothrows 10 mm; anterior cusps of upper first incisors tiny; second unicuspid larger or smaller than first; fourth unicuspid larger than third but smaller than first and second unicuspids.
Distribution: NE China; Heilongjiang and Jilin; extending to Korea and E Russia.
Natural History: A poorly known and rarely encountered species. Apparently its preferred habitat consists of primary broadleaf and coniferous-broadleaf forest. Here it inhabits valleys and the slopes of hills. Demonstrates a higher level of activity than in other red-toothed shrews. Apparently this activity is related to the lesser nutritional value of its primary foodstuffs—earthworms, other invertebrates, and flesh of rodents that this shrew consumes. It consumes 214.2% of its body weight daily. Breeding occurs once a year, with young beginning to appear in traps only at the end of August. In favorable years two litters are possible. Young first become sexually mature in the following warm season.
Conservation Status: China RL–VU B1ab(i, iii); D2.
References: Hoffmann (1987); Hutterer (1982b); Zima et al. (1998).

Kashmir Pygmy Shrew

Sorex planiceps Miller, 1911 MAP 304
克什米尔鼩鼱 Keshimi'er Qujing

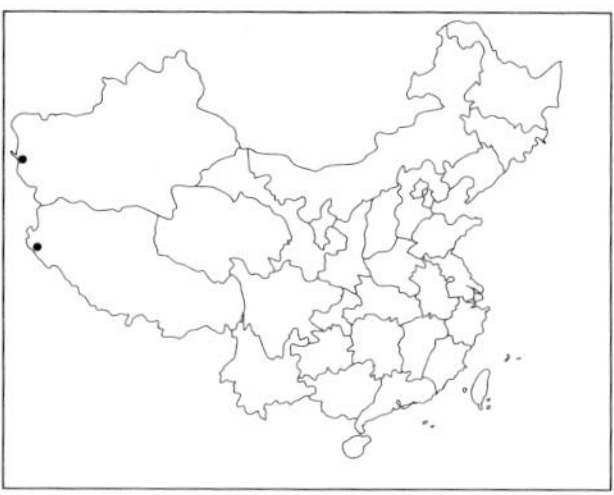

MAP 304. KASHMIR PYGMY SHREW, *Sorex planiceps*

Distinctive Characteristics: HB 57–75; T 37–48; HF 10–14. Dorsal pelage is brown, shading gradually into grayish on the venter. Feet are light and tail is bicolored, brown on top and light gray to white below. As in other taxa of the *minutus* group, the 2nd unicuspid is smaller than either the 1st or 3rd unicuspids flanking it. Somewhat larger than *S. minutus* and *S. thibetanus,* with a less expanded braincase, and thus a flatter skull profile.
Distribution: Far W Xinjiang; extending to N Pakistan and India (Kashmir).
Natural History: The Kashmir Pygmy Shrew lives in coniferous forest and alpine rocky habitats (up to 3,600 m) that may be covered with snow for up to eight months of the year. Presumably lives on various species of arthropods, woodlice, and beetles.
Comments: The relationship of *S. planiceps* to *S. buchariensis* in the Pamir mountains to its northeast, and to what Hutterer (1979) considers to be typical *S. minutus* in the Himalayas to the west, and also *S. thibetanus* on the Tibetan Plateau, is controversial and requires additional data to clarify.
Conservation Status: China RL–DD.
References: Hutterer (1979); Roberts (1997).

Flat-Skulled Shrew

Sorex roboratus Hollister, 1913 MAP 305
扁颅鼩鼱 Bianlu Qujing

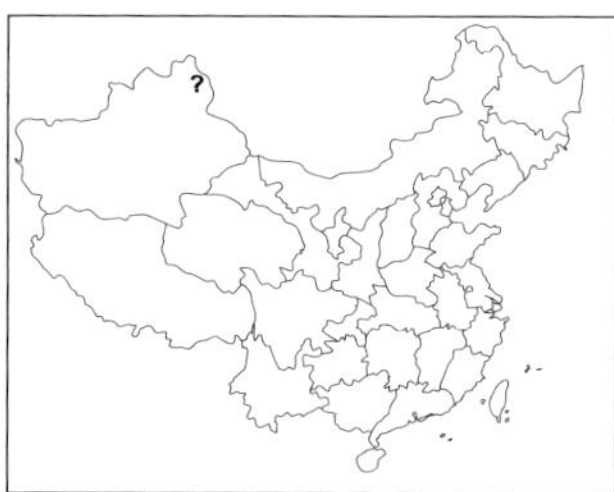

MAP 305. FLAT-SKULLED SHREW, *Sorex roboratus*

Distinctive Characteristics: HB 58–87; T 31–43; HF 12–15.5; GLS 20–22. Dorsal pelage very dark brown, sides lighter, ventral pelage buffy gray. Tail sharply bicolored, dark brown above, pale below.
Distribution: Xinjiang (Altai mountains); extending from N Mongolia west to the Ob River.
Natural History: Inhabits tundra and northern Taiga.
Comments: Previously called *vir*, but *roboratus* has priority.
Conservation Status: China RL—NE.
References: Hoffmann (1985b; 1987); Zaitsev (1988).

Chinese Shrew

PLATE 31
MAP 306

Sorex sinalis Thomas, 1912
陕西鼩鼱 Shaanxi Qujing

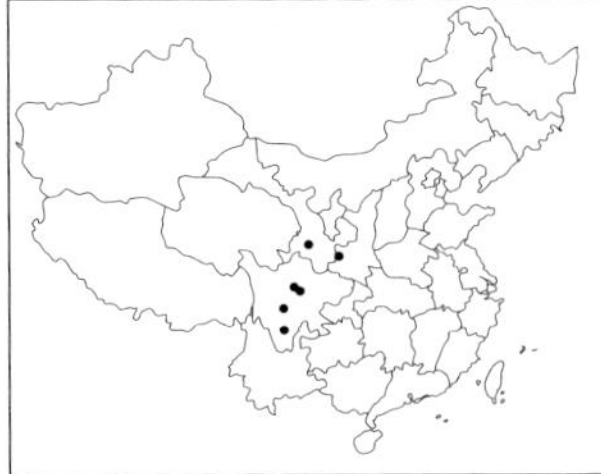

MAP 306. CHINESE SHREW, *Sorex sinalis*

Distinctive Characteristics: HB 64–85; T 49–68; HF 13–17; GLS 20–22. A large, long-tailed shrew, long rostrum; pelage uniformly gray-brown to drab brown pelage both dorsally and ventrally; once thought to be a subspecies of *S. araneus*; similar to *S. isodon*; ventral pelage hazel, only slightly lighter than dorsum; rostrum longer than that of *S. isodon*; skull breadth narrower (8.6–9.6 mm); small tine on middle medial surface of each first incisor; upper unicuspids gradually decreasing in size from first to fifth (as also seen in *S. isodon*).
Distribution: C China; Gansu, Sichuan, S Shaanxi. Endemic.
Natural History: The Chinese Shrew occupies rocky mossy mountain-top habitat at elevations ranging from 2,700 to 3,000 m. It coexists with another large shrew, *S. cylindricauda*.
Comments: Formerly regarded as conspecific with *S. isodon*.
Conservation Status: China RL—VU A2c; D2. IUCN RL-VU B1 + 2c ver 2.3 (1994).
References: Hoffmann (1987); Thomas (1912d).

Tibetan Shrew

MAP 307

Sorex thibetanus Kastschenko, 1905
藏鼩鼱 Zang Qujing

Distinctive Characteristics: HB 51–64; T 32–54; HF 12–13; GLS 16–18. First and third upper unicuspids about equal in size; second upper unicuspid smaller than first and third; once thought to be subspecies of *S. minutus*, but size larger; unworn upper unicuspid teeth with base shorter than height of tooth crown.
Distribution: C China. Endemic. Two subspecies in China: (1) *S. t. kozlovi* Stroganov, 1952; Qinghai (S of Kunlin mountains); (2) *S. t. thibetanus* Kastschenko, 1905; Sichuan, Qinghai, Xizang.
Natural History: Unknown.
Comments: The Tibetan Shrew has been at the center of controversy concerning the status of several forms of Chinese shrew. For details, see comments in Hutterer (2005).

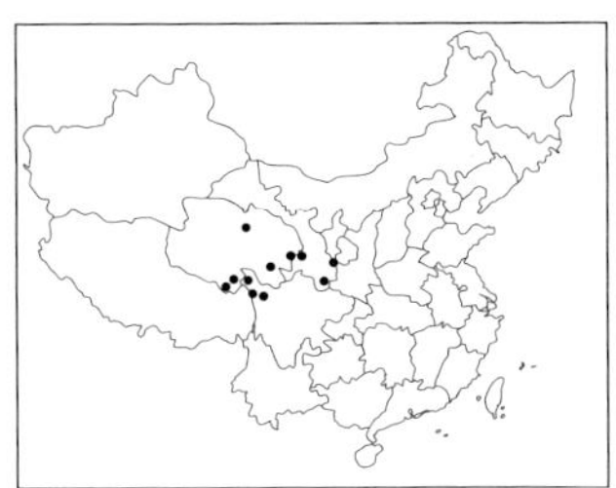

MAP 307. TIBETAN SHREW, *Sorex thibetanus*

Conservation Status: China RL—LC.
References: Hoffmann (1987); Hutterer (2005).

Tundra Shrew

PLATE 31
MAP 308

Sorex tundrensis Merriam, 1900
苔原鼩鼱 Taiyuan Qujing

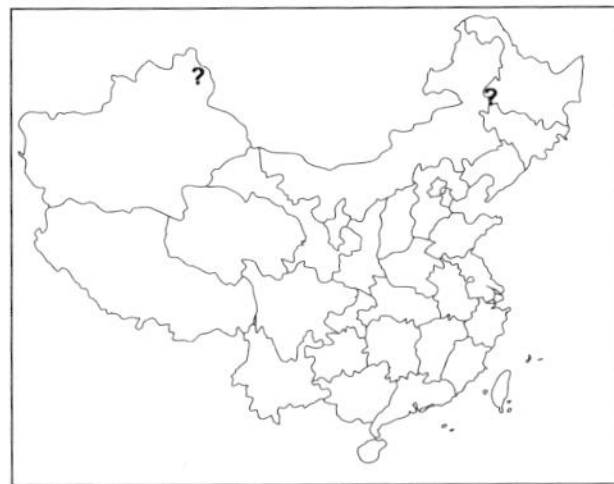

MAP 308. TUNDRA SHREW, *Sorex tundrensis*

Distinctive Characteristics: HB 60–85; T 22–36; Wt 5–10 g. Summer pelage is tricolored; dark brown above, pale gray-brown on the sides, and pale gray on the underside. Winter pelage bicolored, dark brown above, pale gray below.
Distribution: NE China (Altai mountains, Xinjiang); extending across the Bering Strait into Alaska and N Canada.
Natural History: Inhabits dense vegetation of grasses and shrubs.
Conservation Status: China RL—NE.
References: Hoffmann (1987); van Zyll de Jong (1983).

Long-Clawed Shrew

MAP 309

Sorex unguiculatus Dobson, 1890
长爪鼩鼱 Changzhao Qujing

Distinctive Characteristics: HB 70–91; T 41–51; HF 12–14; GLS 19–21; Wt 6–10 g. Size large. Pelage color dark brown, both dorsal and ventral, but ventrum slightly paler and grayer than dorsum. Forefeet broad, claws of forefeet more than 3 mm long, much longer than claws on hind feet. First, second, and

third upper unicuspids gradually decreasing in size, or second unicuspid slightly smaller than first and third; first three distinctly larger than fourth and fifth unicuspids.
Distribution: NE China; Heilongjiang and E Nei Mongol; extending to E Russia and Hokkaido Island.

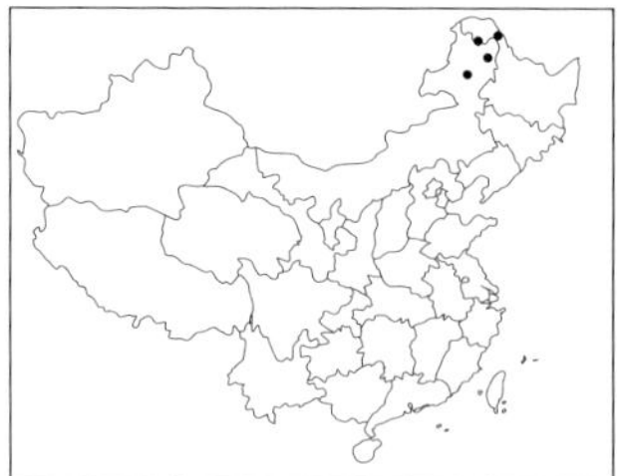

MAP 309. LONG-CLAWED SHREW, *Sorex unguiculatus*

Natural History: Very common in grasslands and open field of plains or low mountains. In some parts of its range, occupies bamboo groves or riparian willows. Burrows with its strong broad forefeet and enlarged claws. Forages in tunnels and in litter on surface. Main foods are earth-worms, insects, centipedes, and snails. Its distribution is connected to thick stands of coniferous and mixed pine-broadleaf forest. It is sympatric with *S. caecutiens* and *S. isodon*, to which it is often subordinate. Reproduction occurs during the warm season; litter size ranges from one to seven.
Conservation Status: China RL—NA.
References: Hoffmann (1971).

Genus *Soriculus* (monotypic)

长尾鼩鼱属 Changweiqujing Shu

Himalayan Shrew

PLATE 31
MAP 310

Soriculus nigrescens (Gray, 1842)
大爪长尾鼩 Dazhua Changweiqu

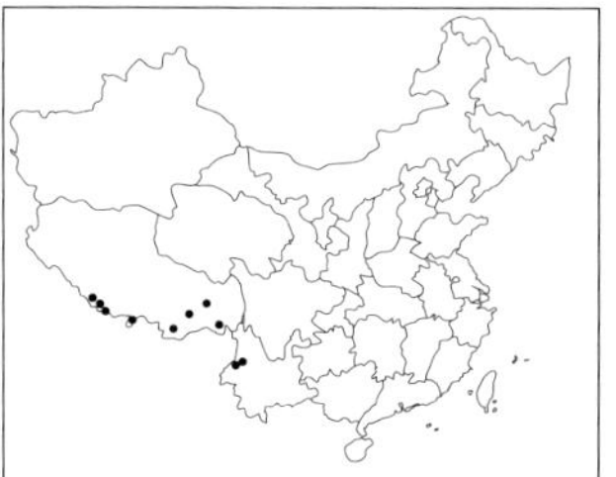

MAP 310. HIMALAYAN SHREW, *Soriculus nigrescens*

Distinctive Characteristics: HB 70–94; T 32–48; HF 12–17; GLS 20–23; Wt 17.5–25.5 g. Pelage dust color; forefeet and claws enlarged, larger than hind feet; tail short, not more than 3/4 of HB length. Third lower molar tiny; first lower molar possesses tooth crown that links entoconid with metaconid, and small shovellike coronoid process. Cusps of teeth dark red-brown, skull with four unicuspids, foreclaws enlarged.
Distribution: SW China; extending to Nepal, Bhutan, India (Assam). Two subspecies in China: (1) *S. n. minor* Dobson 1890; Xizang, Yunnan; (2) *S. n. nigrescens* (Gray, 1842); Xizang.
Natural History: Common in three of the altitudinal zones in the Himalayas, in ascending order; mixed deciduous-coniferous forest, conifer-rhododendron forest, and above timberline, the alpine zone. Insects (beetles, flies, bees) and especially earthworms constitute the primary food. The Himalayan Shrew has a primary (June–July) and a secondary (August–October) breeding season. Average litter size in spring is 6; and in autumn is 4.5; overall litter sizes range from 3 to 9. Young males born in spring may mature rapidly, attaining breeding condition toward the end of their first summer. Young are born into a nest formed of dry grasses and other fiber, about 12–15 cm in diameter, and placed under stones.
Comments: This genus once included *Chodsigoa* and *Episoriculus* as subgenera; however, elevating these to full genus rank leaves *Soriculus* a monotypic genus. *S. n. minor*, the form occurring in SW China, is much smaller and may represent a separate species for which the name *radulus* has been often applied, but Motokawa (2003) showed that *minor* has priority over *radulus*.
Conservation Status: China RL—NA.
References: Abe (1971); Hoffmann (1985b); Mitchell (1977); Motokawa (2003).

Family Talpidae—Moles and Shrew Moles

鼹科 Yan Ke—鼹类 Yan Lei

Moles are highly adapted for fossorial life, or in some cases semiaquatic life, having a cylindrical body, pointed rostrum, and enlarged, outward-turned forefeet with thick sharp claws for digging through loose soil. The eyes are minute and hidden in the pelage, and there is a complete absence of external ears. The fur is soft and lustrous; almost all of the hairs are the same length and will lie in any direction. Shrew moles comprise a lineage basal to moles (Motokawa 2004; Shinohara et al. 2003) and, while having a molelike skull and dentition, retain a more shrewlike external appearance (feet not enlarged for digging, external ears present) and have a more ambulatory life-style. In all members of the family the skull is long and tapering; sutures are obliterated early in life, and there are no ridges or crests for muscle attachments; zygomatic arch slender but complete, auditory bulla low and round; teeth with cutting edges, upper molars possess W-shaped cusps, number of teeth 34–44. Habits terrestrial, mostly subterranean; some are aquatic; feeding habits insectivorous or polyphagous. The family Talpidae has been traditionally divided into three subfamilies comprising moles, shrew moles, and the aquatic desmans; however, we follow Hutterer (2005) in dividing the family into three subfamilies of a somewhat different composition, with the various molelike animals divided between two different subfamilies, the scalopinae and the talpinae, and with the desmans (which do not occur in China) included in the latter. Talpids occur in the Palaearctic, Nearctic, and Indo-Malayan realms; with species from all three subfamilies (Scalopinae, Talpinae, and Uropsilinae) occurring in China (Hutterer 2005).

Subfamily Scalopinae—American Moles

美洲鼹亚科 Meizhouyan Yake—美洲鼹 Meizhouyan

The subfamily Scalopinae comprises seven species from five genera. Most occur in North America, but one monotypic genus is endemic to central China.

Genus *Scapanulus* (monotypic)

甘肃鼹属 Gansuyan Shu

Gansu Mole

PLATE 32
MAP 311

Scapanulus oweni Thomas, 1912
甘肃鼹 Gansu Yan

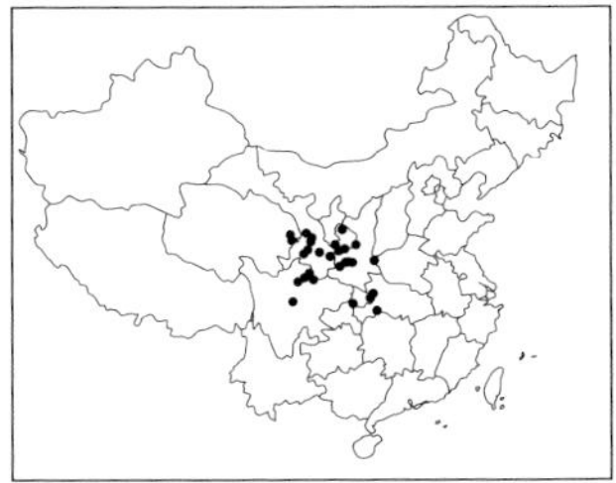

MAP 311. GANSU MOLE, *Scapanulus oweni*

Distinctive Characteristics: HB 108–136; T 37–41; HF 14–20; E 0; GLS 27–32. Form molelike, but readily distinguished from all other Chinese talpids by the first toe of the hind foot, which is set outward at a slight angle to the remaining toes and is stouter and more sharply curved than in other moles. A number of craniodental characters further distinguish the species, with the most field observable among these being the large, bladelike first upper incisors, which taper down to a sharp point and are much longer that the second upper incisors; and the presence of a gap between the first and second upper incisors. In all other Chinese moles the first incisors are smaller than the canine and the first and second incisors are in contact. Pelage drab brownish gray; tail about twice the length of the hind foot, stout and densely haired. Only *Scaptonyx fusicaudus* has a tail that measures longer relative to hind foot, but this species is smaller and distinguished by the characters described above. Dental formula: 2.1.3.3/2.1.3.3 = 36.

Distribution: Shaanxi, Gansu, Sichuan, Qinghai. Endemic.

Natural History: Gansu Moles have been captured in the mossy undergrowth of montane fir forest. The species thus occupies habitats similar to *Scaptonyx*; however, *Scapanulus* is significantly larger than *Scaptonyx*, and it may excavate larger, deeper tunnel systems and differ in foraging modes, since the two species are geographically sympatric over a wide area.

Comments: Forms a monophyletic clade with the North American genera *Condylura*, *Parascalops*, *Scalopus*, and *Scapanus* (the remaining members of the subfamily) (Shinohara et al. 2003). See Motokawa (2004) for a matrix and descriptions of characters distinguishing the Gansu Mole from other members of the family. The Gansu Mole is known from just a few museum specimens, but this is most certainly a consequence of the very few faunal surveys that have been conducted within its range and by historical under sampling of insectivores in general and moles in particular.

Conservation Status: China RL—VU A1bc.

References: Motokawa (2004); Shinohara et al. (2003); Thomas (1912d).

Subfamily Talpinae—True Moles

鼹亚科 Yan Yake—鼹类 Yanlei

The subfamily Talpinae comprises a group of predominantly Old World moles and desmans but also includes one North American form. Most are modified for burrowing, although the desmans, a group not occurring in China, are aquatic. Of all the moles occurring in China, all but one (the Gansu Mole) belong to the Talpinae. The subfamily comprises 11 genera and 28 species; of these, 5 genera and 10 species are found in China (Hutterer 2005).

Key to the Chinese Subfamilies of Talpidae

1.a.	Body molelike, forefeet broadened and foreclaws lengthened for digging; ear pinnae absent	2
b.	Body shrewlike, forefeet and claws not modified for digging; ear pinnae well developed	Uropsilinae
2.a.	First upper incisors very large, much larger than the greatly reduced canines; second upper incisor not in contact with the first upper incisor	Scalopinae
b.	Upper incisors not greatly enlarged and much smaller than canines; second upper incisor in contact with the first upper incisor	Talpinae

Key to the Chinese Genera of Talpinae

1.a.	Total number of teeth in skull and mandibles 44	*Euroscaptor*
b.	Total number of teeth in skull and mandibles < 44	2
2.a.	Total number of teeth in skull and mandibles 40	*Scaptochirus*
b.	Total number of teeth in skull and mandibles 42	3
3.a.	Upper toothrow with 10 teeth	*Parascaptor*
b.	Upper toothrow with 11 teeth	4
4.a.	Size large, GLS > 25; tail much shorter then HF	*Mogera*
b.	Size small, GLS < 25; tail much longer than HF	*Scaptonyx*

Key to the Chinese Species of *Euroscaptor*

1.a.	Size large, GLS > 35 mm	*Euroscaptor grandis*
b.	Smaller, GLS < 35 mm	2
2.a.	Molars reported to be noticeably smaller than in other *Euroscaptor* (measurements unavailable); 4th upper premolar with well-developed anterior cingulum	*Euroscaptor parvidens*
b.	Molars larger (M1–M3 / 5.1–5.3 mm); 4th upper premolar lacks cingulum or if present poorly developed	3
3.a.	Aperture to auditory bulla small, < 2 mm	*Euroscaptor longirostris*
b.	Aperture to auditory bulla large, > 2 mm	4
4.a.	Tail > 10 mm	*Euroscaptor klossi*
b.	Tail < 10 mm	*Euroscaptor micrura*

Genus *Euroscaptor*—Oriental Moles

东方鼹属 Dongfangyan Shu—东方鼹 Dongfangyan

Euroscaptor is sometimes considered a subgenus of the European genus *Talpa*. The species-level taxonomy of the group is still uncertain, with most species known from very few specimens. Dental formula: 3.1.4.3/3.1.4.3 = 44. Five of six species of *Euroscaptor* occur in China.

Greater Chinese Mole

Euroscaptor grandis Miller, 1940 MAP 312

巨鼹 Ju Yan

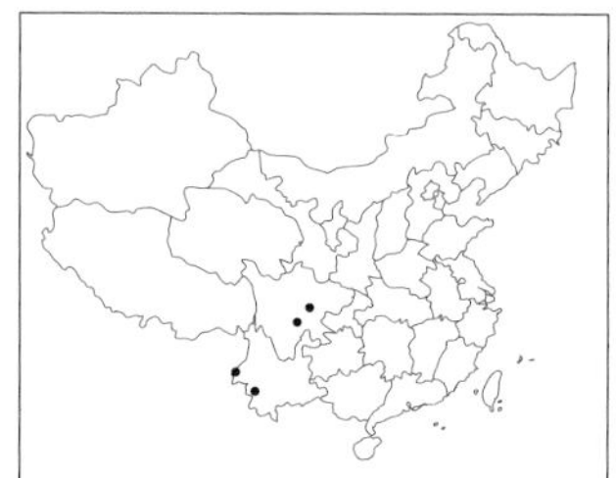

MAP 312. GREATER CHINESE MOLE, *Euroscaptor grandis*

Distinctive Characteristics: HB 150; T 10; HF 18; E 0; GLS 37. Size very large, much larger than the sympatric *Euroscaptor longirostris*. Pelage dark brown, not black, as in *E. longirostris*. Tail short and swollen at the end and sparsely covered with long brown hairs.

Distribution: C Sichuan, W Yunnan. Probably extending into adjacent Myanmar, but not yet recorded from this area. Endemic.

Natural History: Occupies forest habitat.

Comments: Records of this species from N Vietnam are based on specimens of *E. klossi* reported in Osgood (1932); but, Miller (1940b) identified these as *E. longirostris*, not *E. grandis*. Wang (2003) reported specimens from Yunnan as "*Euroscaptor grabdis yunnanensis*"; an apparent *nomen nudum*.

Conservation Status: China RL—VU B1ab(i, ii, iii).

References: Miller (1940b).

Kloss's Mole

Euroscaptor klossi (Thomas, 1929) MAP 313

克氏鼹 Keshi Yan

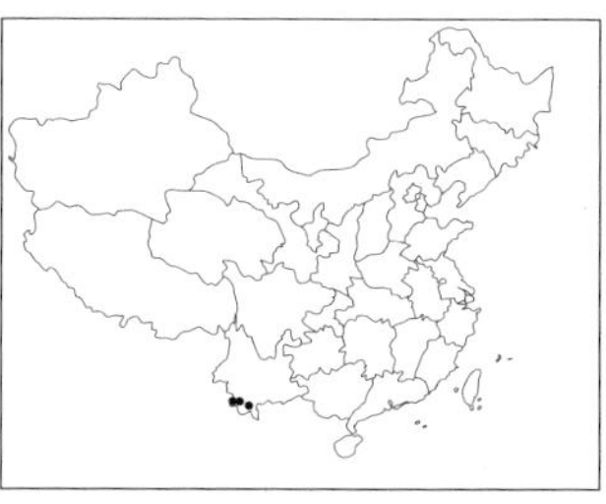

MAP 313. KLOSS'S MOLE, *Euroscaptor klossi*

Distinctive Characteristics: HB 123–138; T 11–16.5; HF 16; E 0; GLS 30–32. Pelage dark blackish brown.

Tail about as long as the hind foot. Similar to *E. micrura*, but with a longer tail.
Distribution: S Yunnan; extending to Thailand, Laos, and peninsular Malaysia.
Natural History: Occupies forest habitat.
Comments: Previously included as a synonym of *micrura*, but see Yoshiyuki (1988b).
Conservation Status: China RL–NA.
References: Thomas (1929); Yoshiuki (1988).

Long-Nosed Mole

PLATE 32

Euroscaptor longirostris (Milne-Edwards, 1870)

MAP 314

长吻鼹 Changwen Yan

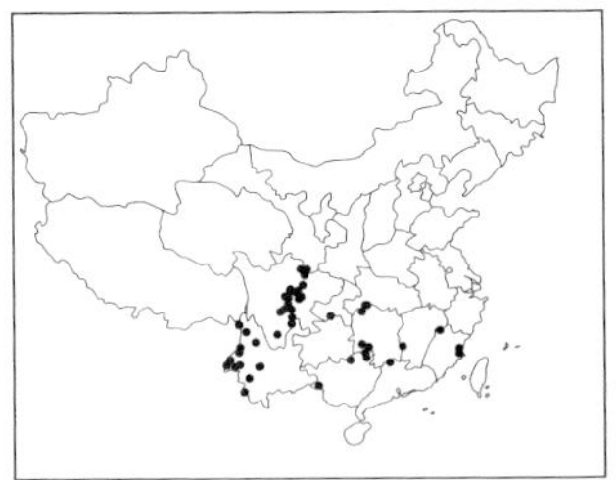

MAP 314. LONG-NOSED MOLE, *Euroscaptor longirostris*

Distinctive Characteristics: HB 90–145; T 11–25; HF 14–23; E 0; GLS 30–33. Body dark gray to black, sometimes with slightly brownish tinge; tail sparsely haired except toward the tip, where white hairs may be up to 12.5 mm long. Rostrum longer and narrower than any of the larger moles in China; head appears long and narrow. Aperture to auditory bulla small, less than 2 mm.
Distribution: Widely distributed in S China (W Sichuan, N Yunnan, SE Guizhou, Fujian). Apparently extending into NW Vietnam; see comments below.
Natural History: Thought to be a montane species, ranging between 1,800 and 2,900 m in elevation. Occupies mesic mossy habitat in alpine birch forests. This species also co-occurs widely with another small, blackish mole, *Mogera insularis latouchei*, in S China. Poorly known.
Comments: Two specimens originally identified as *Talpa klossi* from NW Vietnam by Osgood (1932) were later assigned to *E. longirostris* by Miller (1940b).
Conservation Status: China RL–VU A1acd.
References: Motokawa (2004).

Himalayan Mole

Euroscaptor micrura (Hodgson, 1841)

MAP 315

短尾鼹 Duanwei Yan

Distinctive Characteristics: HB 128–135; T 5–9; HF 15–16; E 0; GLS 30–34; Wt 44–72. Similar to *E. klossi*, but with a shorter, club-shaped tail.
Distribution: W Yunnan; extending to E Himalaya and peninsular Malaysia.
Natural History: Occupies forest habitat, where it usually uses surface tunnels. Does not construct large mounds or dig deeply into the ground.

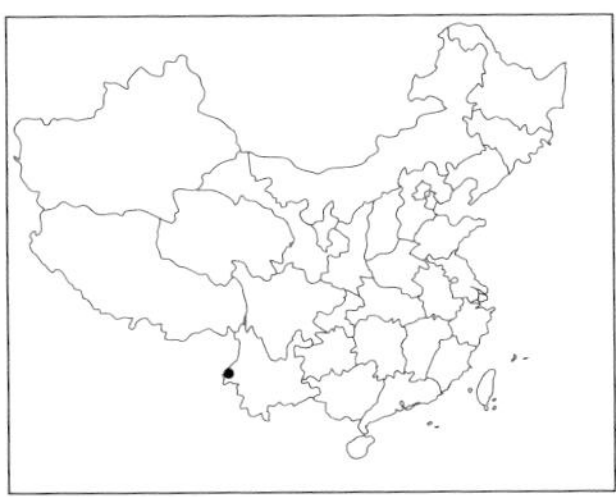

MAP 315. HIMALAYAN MOLE, *Euroscaptor micrura*

Conservation Status: China RL–NA.
References: Kawada et al. (2003); Motokawa (2004).

Small-Toothed Mole

Euroscaptor parvidens (Miller, 1940)

MAP 316

小齿鼹 Xiaochi Yan

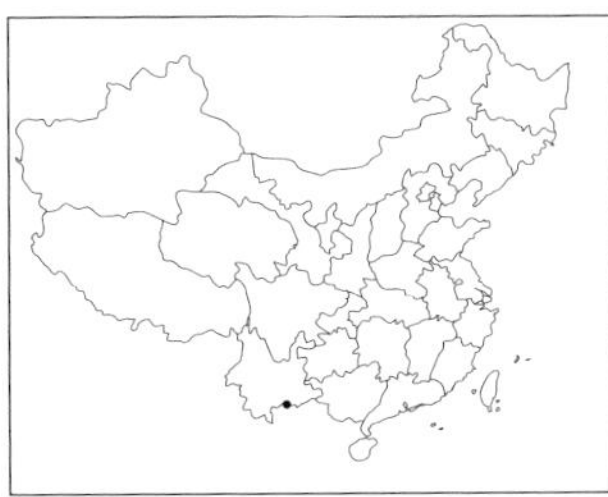

MAP 316. SMALL-TOOTHED MOLE, *Euroscaptor parvidens*

Distinctive Characteristics: HB 140; T 6; HF 18; E 0; GLS 34. Similar to *E. klossi* and *E. micrura* in external appearance, but with a more slender skull and smaller molars. Fourth upper premolar with a well-developed anterior cingulum.
Distribution: S Yunnan; extending to Vietnam.
Natural History: Little known; the holotype was collected near a stream at 800 m elevation.
Conservation Status: China RL–NA.
References: Miller (1940a).

Genus *Mogera*—East Asian Moles

缺齿鼹属 Quechiyan Shu—缺齿鼹 Quechiyan

Size small or very large; HB length varies in individuals, longest about 220 mm, shortest less than 100 mm; lower canines absent. Dental formula: 3.1.4.3/3.0.4.3 = 42; tail thickset. The five species of *Mogera* range widely across E Asia; two species occur in China.

Key to the Chinese Species of *Mogera*

1.a.	Smaller, HB length < 140 mm, GLS < 35 mm	*Mogera insularis*
b.	Larger, HB length > 170 mm, GLS > 35 mm	*Mogera robusta*

Insular Mole

PLATE 32
MAP 317

Mogera insularis (Swinhoe, 1863)
华南缺齿鼹 Huanan Quechiyan

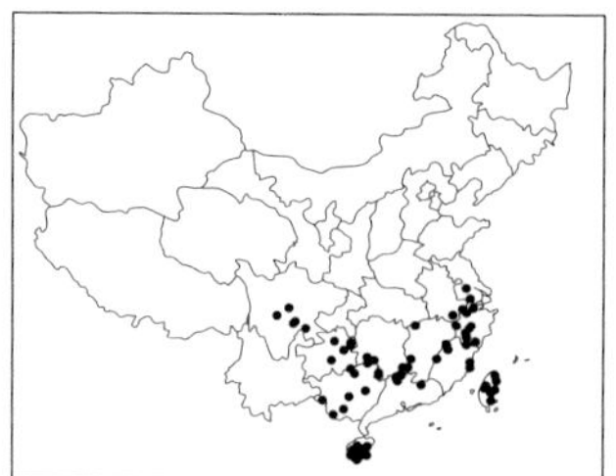

MAP 317. INSULAR MOLE, *Mogera insularis*

Distinctive Characteristics: HB 87–137; T 3–14; HF 5–18; E 0; GLS 27–33. Size very small; pelage slate black both dorsally and ventrally, except for whitish hair scattered on feet and tip of tail. The only species of mole to occur on Taiwan and Hainan; however, in S China, it occurs with *Euroscaptor longirostris*, another small, dark-colored mole. Externally, *M. insularis* has a shorter, broader rostrum than *E. longirostris*, and the enlarged claws of its forefeet are narrower than the broad claws of *longirostris*. Their tooth formulas also distinguish them, since *Mogera* lacks a lower canine tooth. The three subspecies vary in size, the largest being *insularis* proper on Taiwan, and the smallest, *latouchei* of the mainland, with *hainana* intermediate in size.
Distribution: S China; C Sichuan to Zhejiang and south to Taiwan and Hainan Island. Endemic. Three subspecies: (1) *M. i. hainana* Thomas, 1910; Hainan; (2) *M. i. insularis* (Swinhoe, 1863); Taiwan; (3) *M. i. latouchei* Thomas, 1907; Fujian, Guizhou, Guangxi, Hunan, Sichuan, Anhui.
Natural History: Reported to be common in the hill country of S China, as well as in high mountains.
Comments: Although ranges of the three subspecies are now separated, in the last Ice Age (Pleistocene) the sea level was much reduced, and both Taiwan and Hainan were joined with the mainland. With the melting of glacial ice at the end of the last glacial period, sea level rose, and both islands became isolated from the mainland and each other. This isolation may have played a role in the differentiation of the modern populations. As noted above, the greatest difference is between larger, but highly variable, *insularis* of Taiwan and the very small *latouchei* of S China, which might be considered separate allospecies.
Conservation Status: China RL—NT; although it nearly met the criteria for VU A1abcd.
References: Abe (1995); Lin et al. (2002a); Motokawa et al. (2001c).

Large Mole

PLATE 32
MAP 318

Mogera robusta Nehring, 1891
大缺齿鼹 Da Quechiyan

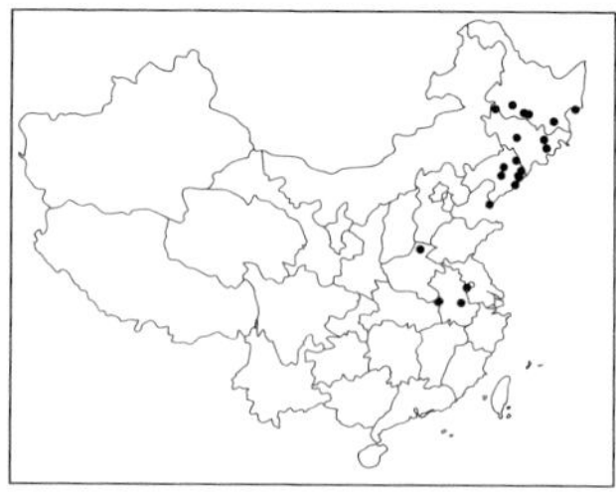

MAP 318. LARGE MOLE, *Mogera robusta*

Distinctive Characteristics: HB 170–220; T 19–23; HF 22–24; E 0; GLS 37–48; measurements from nominate subspecies. By far the largest mole in China. Hairs on dorsum brownish mixed with gray, metallic sheen; anterior portion of nose paler and yellower; ventral pelage shiny silvery yellow hue, on chest a weakly defined pale gray region; feet and claws yellow. Tail relatively short but well-haired; forefeet very large, with long thick claws. Skull stout, rostrum broad, nasal region wide and somewhat elevated; first lower premolar greatly enlarged, triangular, double rooted.
Distribution: NE China; extending into Russia and Korea. Two subspecies in China: (1) *M. r. coreana* Thomas, 1907; Liaoning, Henan, Anhui; (2) *M. r. robusta* Nehring, 1891; Heilongjiang, Liaoning, Jilin.
Natural History: Habitat is montane woodland, forest, grassland, and farmland. Rarely found on steep slopes with rocky soils. Little else is known about its biology.
Comments: This form has generated considerable systematic confusion. Hutterer (2005) considers *robusta* as a synonym of *M. wogura* of Japan. Many have proposed raising *coreana* to full species status because of its much smaller size and lack of evidence for intergradation with *robusta*; the two forms are parapatric in distribution in Liaoning (Jones and Johnson 1960; Zhang et al. 1997). In *coreana* HB length = 140–150 mm, tail length about 15 mm, hind foot length about 16 mm; and the GLS = 37.5 mm or less. Moreover, some authors have united *M. kobeae*

Thomas, 1905, the largest of the Japanese moles, with *robusta* (Corbet 1978), and although Japanese authors continue to consider them separate species, they share many characteristics.
Conservation Status: China RL—NT; although it nearly met the criteria for VU A1c.
References: Abe (1995); Jones and Johnson (1960).

Genus *Parascaptor* (monotypic)

白尾鼹属 Baiweiyan Shu

White-Tailed Mole

PLATE 32
MAP 319

Parascaptor leucura (Blyth, 1850)
白尾鼹 Baiwei Yan

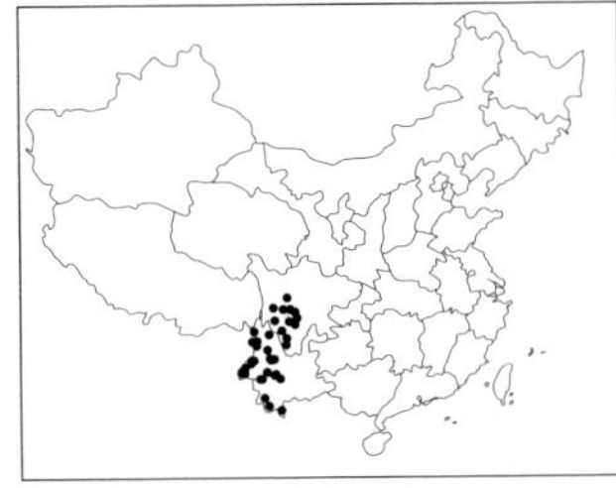

MAP 319. WHITE-TAILED MOLE, *Parascaptor leucura*

Distinctive Characteristics: HB 100–112; T 10–15; HF 15–16; E 0; GLS 27–30. Pelage dark blackish brown; tail very short and club-shaped, usually with white hairs. Dental formula: 3.1.3.3/3.1.4.3 = 42.
Distribution: Yunnan and Sichuan; extending to Myanmar and India (Assam).
Natural History: Inhabits montane forests and scrub-grassland between 1,000 and 3,000 m.
Conservation Status: China RL—LC.
References: Motokawa (2004).

Genus *Scaptochirus* (monotypic)

麝鼹属 Sheyan Shu

Short-Faced Mole

PLATE 32
MAP 320

Scaptochirus moschatus Milne-Edwards, 1867
麝鼹 She Yan

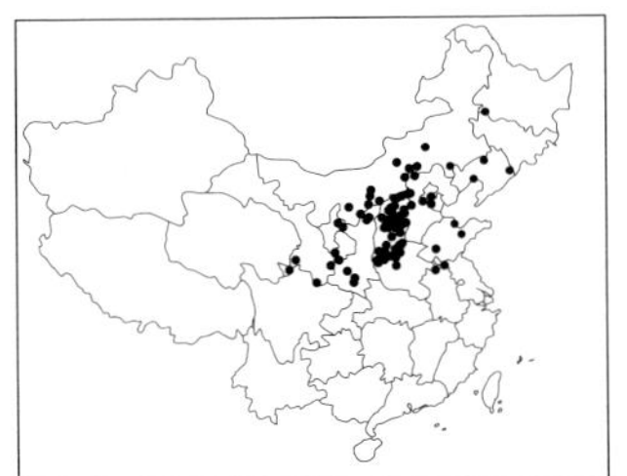

MAP 320. SHORT-FACED MOLE, *Scaptochirus moschatus*

Distinctive Characteristics: HB 100–126; T 14–23; HF 15–19; E 0; GLS 30–36. A medium-sized mole. Pelage clear grayish brown; paler around mouth and forearms. Tail slender, subequal in length to hind feet, sparsely covered with hairs and with a small tuft at the tip. Skull large, rostrum short and broad. Dental formula: 3.1.3.3./3.1.3.3 = 40. Thus, the upper and lower premolars are reduced to three or two on each side; the only other Chinese mole with such reduction is *Scapanulus oweni*, but this form also has an incisor reduction from three to two, while *Scaptochirus* maintains the usual three incisors.
Distribution: C to NE China. Endemic. Wang (2003) recognized three subspecies: (1) *S. m. gilliesi* Thomas, 1910; Ningxia, Gansu, Shaanxi, Hubei, Shanxi; (2) *S. m. grandidens* (Stroganov, 1941); E Nei Mongol, Heilongjiang, Liaoning; (3) *S. m. moschatus* Milne-Edwards 1867; Beijing, C Nei Mongol, Hebei, Shandong, Henan, Jiangsu.
Natural History: This species occupies the cold, dry northeastern quadrant of China and is adapted to arid conditions to a much greater extent than other moles. These include sandy grasslands and meadows, loess regions, and even the borders of deserts, such as the Ordos. The scarcity of earthworms, a staple of mole diet in more mesic regions, has resulted in the short-faced mole feeding on larvae of beetles and other arthropods.
Conservation Status: China RL—NT; although it nearly met the criteria for VU A1c.
References: Kawada et al. (2002); Motokawa (2004).

Genus *Scaptonyx* (monotypic)

长尾鼩鼹属 Changweiquyan Shu

Long-Tailed Mole

PLATE 32
MAP 321

Scaptonyx fusicaudus Milne-Edwards, 1872
长尾鼩鼹 Changwei Quyan

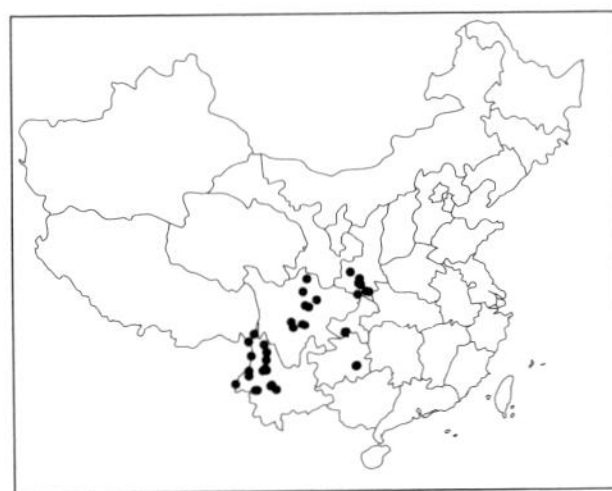

MAP 321. LONG-TAILED MOLE, *Scaptonyx fusicaudus*

Distinctive Characteristics: HB 72–90; T 26–45; HF 17; E 0; GLS 23; Wt 12 g. Small, long-tailed moles, the pelage is dark gray-brown, both dorsally and ventrally, with scattered white hairs; tail surface covered with black hairs. Dental formula: 3.1.4.3/2.1.4.3 = 42.
Distribution: Central S China; extending to Myanmar and N Vietnam. At least two subspecies in China: (1) *S. f. affinis* Thomas, 1912; Yunnan, Guizhou; (2) *S. f. fusicaudus* Milne-Edwards, 1872; Sichuan, Shaanxi, Guizhou.

Natural History: Although small, like *Uropsilus*, this is a true mole and is apparently fully fossorial. It appears to be restricted to high altitude (2,000–4,100 m), in montane coniferous forests with damp, friable soils. Here it digs shallow burrows, recognizable because of their small diameter compared to those of other larger Chinese moles. *Scaptonyx* is geographically sympatric with all four species of *Uropsilus*, but this is not surprising, since the former forages below the soil surface, while the latter seek food on the surface in leaf litter.
Comments: Specimens from Shaanxi have been assigned to *S. f. affinis* by Zhang (1997), but these are disjunct from the nominate Yunnan populations and are closer to *fusicaudus* populations in Sichuan. Wang (2003) refers to additional specimens from Yunnan as "*Scaptonyx fusicaudus gaoligongensis* Wang 2002"; an apparent *nomen nudum*.
Conservation Status: China RL—NT; although it nearly met the criteria for VU A1c.
References: Lunde et al. (2003a); Motokawa (2004); Thomas (1912c).

Subfamily Uropsilinae

Genus *Uropsilus*—Shrew Moles

鼩鼹亚科 Quyan Yake; 鼩鼹属 Quyan Shu—鼩鼹 Quyan

A basal lineage within the Talpidae (Motokawa 2004; Shinohara et al. 2003), differing from other talpids in having a shrewlike external form not modified for burrowing. Fur long and directed backwards, not short and velvety as in moles; snout long and thin; external ear present; forefeet small, not broadened for digging; tail long. Skull rather molelike with complete zygomatic arches. Tooth formulas and total numbers of teeth variable; this variation was once interpreted as evidence of three genera (*Uropsilus*, *Rhynchonax*, and *Nasillus*); or, conversely, as intraspecific variation within one species, *Uropsilus soricipes*. The natural history of shrew moles is very poorly known. All seem to have similar habits, foraging on the ground surface among leaf litter for small invertebrates. They may form faint trails along the surface, where ground cover is sparse, but apparently do not burrow into the soil. The current taxonomy follows Hoffmann (1984) in recognizing one genus for all known species, except we recognize *U. investigator* as a separate species following Hutterer (2005), whereas Hoffmann (1984) included it in *U. gracilis*. All four species of *Uropsilus* are found in China.

Anderson's Shrew Mole

Uropsilus andersoni (Thomas, 1911) MAP 322
峨眉鼩鼹 Emei Quyan

Distinctive characteristics: HB 65–83; T 59–72; HF 14–17.5; GLS 21–22. This species is darker than its congeners and has a unique dental formula: two lower incisors and three lower premolars. Number of teeth is 38; upper third incisors absent, lower first incisors and third premolars absent; upper teeth 10 each side, lower teeth 9 each side.
Distribution: Only known from Emei Mountain and adjacent small area of China, where it is in limited geographic sympatry with *U. gracilis* and *U. soricipes*. Endemic.

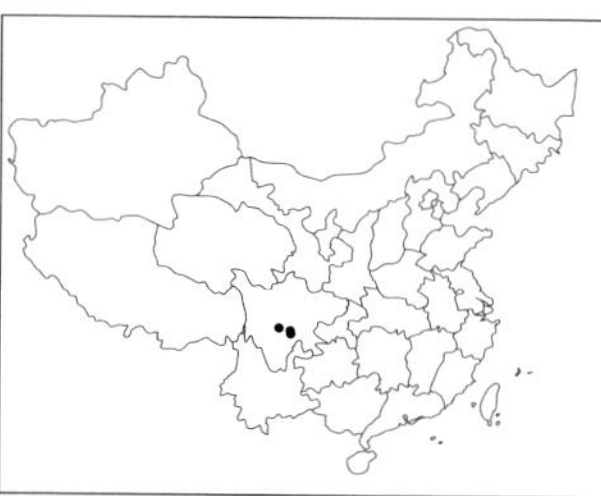

MAP 322. ANDERSON'S SHREW MOLE, *Uropsilus andersoni*

Natural History: Presumed similar to its congeners, but very little is known.
Comments: The type species of *Rhynchonax*. Wang (2003) classifies as belonging to the genus *Nasillus*.
Conservation Status: China RL—EN B2ab(i, ii, iii); C2a(i, ii).
References: Hoffmann (1984); Motokawa (2004).

Gracile Shrew Mole

Uropsilus gracilis (Thomas, 1911) MAP 323
长吻鼩鼹 Changwen Quyan

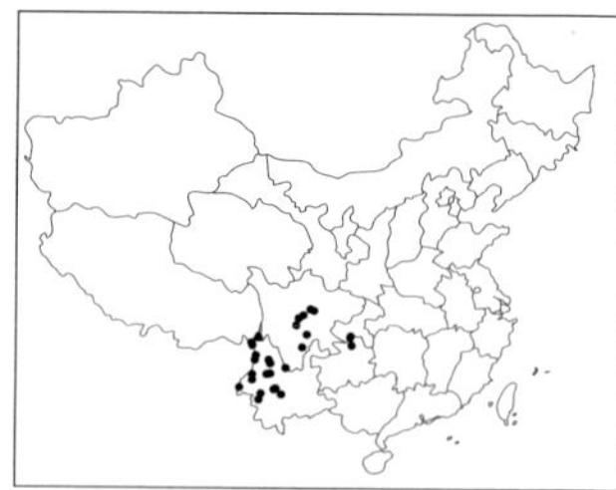

MAP 323. GRACILE SHREW MOLE, *Uropsilus gracilis*

Distinctive characteristics: HB 69–84; T 67–78; HF 15–18; GLS 22–23. Total number of teeth 38; but distinguished from *U. andersoni* in having only one lower incisor and four premolars. Similar to *U. investigator*, but smaller and occurring at lower elevations.
Distribution: Mainly occurs in SW China; extending to N Myanmar. Wang (2003) recognizes a number of described and undescribed subspecies; however, the status of these needs to be addressed in the context of a systematic revision.
Natural History: This species inhabits mixed deciduous-coniferous forests, usually above the rhododendron zone and up to timberline (3,000–4,000 m, depending on topographic conditions). Unlike its congeners, it occupies alpine tundra habitats, at least in the Likiang range.
Comments: Wang (2003) classifies as belonging to the genus *Nasillus*. Both *atronates* and *nivatus* were

Keys to *Uropsilus*

1.a.	Dental formula: 2.1.3.3/1.1.3.3 = 34	*Uropsilus soricipes*
b.	Total number of teeth 38	2
2.a.	Dental formula: 2.1.4.3/2.1.3.3 = 38	*Uropsilus andersoni*
b.	Dental formula: 2.1.4.3/1.1.4.3 = 38	3
3.a.	Size larger, occurs at elevations > 3,000 m	*Uropsilus investigator*
b.	Size smaller, occurs at lower elevations, down to 1,000 m	*Uropsilus gracilis*

named as subspecies of *andersoni*, but Hoffmann (1984) assigned them to *U. gracilis*.
References: Hoffmann (1984); Motokawa (2004).

Inquisitive Shrew Mole

Uropsilus investigator (Thomas, 1922) MAP 324
怒江鼩鼹 Nujiang Quyan

MAP 324. INQUISITIVE SHREW MOLE, *Uropsilus investigator*

Distinctive Characteristics: HB 67–83; T 54–75; HF 13–16; GLS 20–22. Very similar to *U. gracilis*, and once regarded as a subspecies within it, *U. investigator* is distinguished by its larger size, darker, almost black pelage color, and distribution at higher altitudes.
Distribution: NW Yunnan. Endemic.
Natural History: Occurs in open alpine meadows or perhaps fir forests at high altitudes (3,600–4,600 m).
Comments: Once considered a subspecies of *U. gracilis*, Wang and Yang (1989) held that *investigator* differed from *U. gracilis* in both form and distribution.
Conservation Status: China RL—EN C2a(i, ii) + D. IUCN RL—EN B1 + 2c ver 2.3 (1994).
References: Hoffmann (1984); Wang and Yang (1989).

Chinese Shrew Mole

Uropsilus soricipes Milne-Edwards, 1871 PLATE 32 MAP 325
鼩鼹 Qu Yan

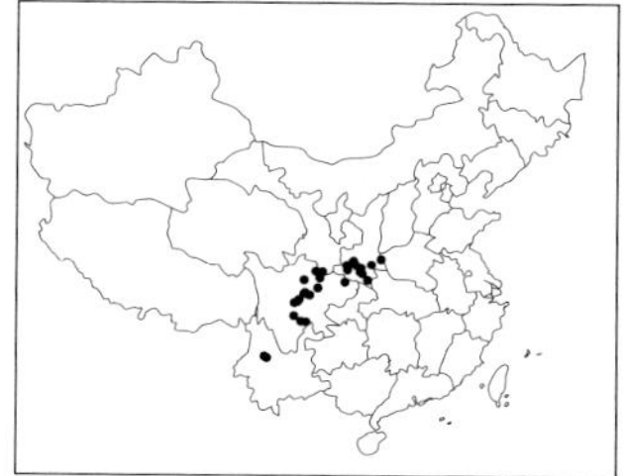

MAP 325. CHINESE SHREW MOLE, *Uropsilus soricipes*

Distinctive Characteristics: HB 66–80; T 50–69; HF 14–17; GLS 20–21.5. Second and third incisors and third premolars in upper and lower jaws absent; nine upper teeth each side, eight lower teeth each side; total number of teeth = 34; dorsum dark brown, ventral surface dark slate gray, back of feet same color as upper tail and dorsum.
Distribution: Gansu, Sichuan, Yunnan, Shaanxi. Endemic.
Natural History: Very poorly known, as is the case with all shrew moles. *U. soricipes* is geographically sympatric with *U. gracilis* in the vicinity of Wenchuan, Sichuan, but is segregated altitudinally; *U. soricipes* is found below 2,200 m, while *U. gracilis* is found higher, above 3,000 m.
Conservation Status: China RL—VU A1c. IUCN RL—EN B1 + 2c ver 2.3 (1994).
References: Hoffmann (1984); Motokawa (2004).

ORDER CHIROPTERA—Bats

翼手目 Yishou Mu—蝙蝠 Bianfu

Don E. Wilson

The order Chiroptera contains the only mammals capable of true flight. Characters include specialized forelimbs; phalanges especially elongated; radii longer than humeri; ulnae reduced; patagium between phalanges linked with hind legs; hind legs and tail also linked by uropatagium; uropatagium usually possesses cartilagenous calcania, which function as stays; and almost complete fusion of skull bones with most sutures inconspicuous. Most species are insectivorous with cusps and dental ridges of molar crowns arranged in primitive W-shaped ectoloph. A few species are frugivorous with relatively flat molar crowns, a well-developed pectoral girdle with a keeled sternum, and a reduced pelvic girdle.

Bats are nocturnal and possess highly developed ears. For most species the flight path and prey capture completely depend on emitting and retrieving ultrasonic vocalizations, but Pteropodidae rely on vision.

The order is distributed throughout both Eastern and Western hemispheres except in polar regions. Most forms are found in tropical and temperate zones, with diversity inversely related to latitude. Relationships of higher categories are sufficiently unclear to argue against recognition of traditional suborders Megachiroptera (including the single family Pteropodidae) and Microchiroptera (all

Key to the Chinese Families of Chiroptera

1.a.	Second digit of forelimb free to some extent, with three phalanges, usually with claw; ear structure simple, without tragus or antitragus, ear edge ovoid to round in shape; incisor number 2/2	Pteropodidae
b.	Second digit of forelimb not free, with two or fewer phalanges, never with claws; ear structure complicated, usually with tragus or antitragus; ear edge not round in shape; incisor number not 2/2	2
2.a.	Rostrum with projecting leaflike outgrowth, which forms noseleaf	3
b.	Rostrum without projecting leaflike outgrowth	5
3.a.	Tragus dichotomous, without antitragus; nose leaf simple; premaxilla absent	Megadermatidae
b.	Tragus absent, antitragus developed; nose leaf complicated; premaxilla dissociated	4
4.a.	Toes with two phalanges; nose leaf with transverse, elongate apical lobe; two premolars on each side of lower jaw	Hipposideridae
b.	Toes with three phalanges (except first); nose leaf with vertical and sellate top leaf; three premolars on each side of lower jaw	Rhinolophidae
5.a.	Tail contained in uropatagium	Vespertilionidae
b.	Tail extends beyond uropatagium	6
6.a.	Second digit of forelimb without phalanx; tail extends dorsally from uropatagium; skull with postorbital processes	Emballonuridae
b.	Second digit of forelimb with phalanges; tail extends beyond uropatagium; skull without postorbital processes	Molossidae

Key to the Chinese Genera of Pteropodidae

1.a.	Size large; forearm length more than 90 mm; tail absent	*Pteropus*
b.	Size small; forearm length less than 90 mm; tail short	2
2.a.	Five cheek teeth (premolars and molars) on each side of upper jaw; rear of skull not deflected	3
b.	Four cheek teeth (premolars and molars) on each side of upper jaw; rear of skull deflected	5
3.a.	Tongue normal, not particularly extensible	*Rousettus*
b.	Tongue elongated, extensible	4
4.a.	Second digit without claw	*Eonycteris*
b.	Second digit with claw	*Macroglossus*
5.a.	Short tail present; postorbital foramen large	*Cynopterus*
b.	Tail absent; postorbital foramen absent	*Sphaerias*

remaining families). Of 18 families, 7 occur in China. Our taxonomic arrangement is based on the treatment of Simmons (2005). The global status and conservation action plans for bats are presented in Hutson et al. (2001; microchiropera) and Mickleburgh et al. (1992; megachiroptera).

Family Pteropodidae—Old World Fruit Bats

狐蝠科 Hufu Ke—狐蝠 Hufu

Size medium to very large; tragus absent; ear edges form a complete ring; second digit free, with three phalanges and usually with claw; tail reduced or absent; both skull and rostrum relatively elongated; premaxilla dissociated, without palatine; bony palate extended backward beyond posterior edge of last molar; postorbital process distinctly developed; basioccipital and basisphenoid not abnormally narrow; angular process in lower jaw wide and low, or completely absent.

Tooth structure specialized for frugivory; cusps undeveloped; tooth crowns flat, with linear mesosulcus; two blunt cusps on the anterior crowns of upper and lower molars; protocones and anterior tips on upper molars; protoconids and metaconids on lower molars; incisor number of each side of lower jaw less than two.

Distributed in tropical and subtropical zones of the Eastern Hemisphere; range extends eastward to Australia but not to New Zealand; of 42 genera, 6 occur in China.

Genus *Cynopterus*—Short-nosed Fruit Bats

犬蝠属 Quanfu Shu—犬蝠 Quanfu

Size medium; forearm length 55–92 mm; nostrils noticeable and nearly proboscis-like; upper lip with deep vertical grooves in middle; second digit with developed claws; tail short but conspicuous, distal half separated from uropatagium; calcar short, length about equal to breadth of hind foot; ears with pale edges. Rostrum short; postorbital process developed; cerebral cranium of skull distinctly turns toward ventral surface, occiput proboscis-like. Dental formula: 2.1.3.1/2.1.3.2 = 30; canines with cusplets on inner side; first lower premolar small; second lower premolar large; crowns of premolars and molars possess dental ridges, with shallow vertical grooves in middle. Widely distributed in tropical and subtropical zones of Indo-Malayan Realm. Of seven species, two occur in China.

Lesser Short-Nosed Fruit Bat

Cynopterus brachyotis (Müller, 1838) MAP 326

短耳犬蝠 Duan'er Quanfu

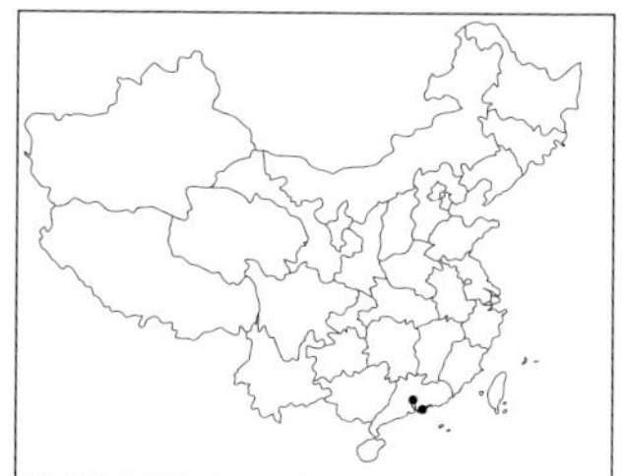

MAP 326. LESSER SHORT-NOSED FRUIT BAT, *Cynopterus brachyotis*

Distinctive Characteristics: HB 70–84; T 9–12; HF 13–15; E 13–18; FA 54–72; GLS 27–31. Externally quite similar to *Cynopterus sphinx*, but slightly smaller and paler in color; ears shorter, about 13–18 mm. Fur color ranges from light grayish through dark or bright brown; breeding adults may have orange or yellow area on throat and shoulders; basal third of ear hairy, margins pale or whitish; fingers whitish in contrast to dark brown wing membranes. *C. brachyotis* has been confused with *C. sphinx* in the past, and the identity of some literature records is in doubt.

Distribution: Guangdong; Wang (2003) lists additional records from Xizang (Medog) and S Yunnan; extending to the Indian subcontinent and through S Malayan region. Chinese subspecies: *C. b. hoffeti* Bourret, 1944.

Natural History: Little is known from China, but some information is available from other areas. Common in both secondary forests and agricultural areas, this bat is also taken in small villages. Normally roosts in pairs or small colonies in the foliage but may also use dimly lighted regions of caves. Feeds on fruit, nectar, and pollen of at least 10 families of plants. Marked animals moved from 0.2 to 1.3 km, and recaptures suggested a population den-sity of 0.2–0.3 animals per hectare. Females appear to be polyestrous and are thought to produce a single young twice per year. The gestation period is 3.5–4 months, and lactation lasts six to eight weeks. Documented longevity is five years in the wild and is likely considerably more than that.

Conservation Status: China RL—VU B1ab(i, ii, iii).

References: Heideman and Heaney (1989).

Greater Short-Nosed Fruit Bat

Cynopterus sphinx (Vahl, 1797) PLATE 33 MAP 327

犬蝠 Quanfu

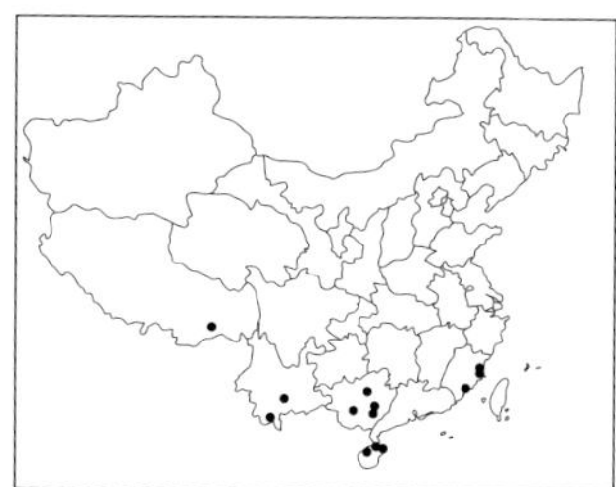

MAP 327. GREATER SHORT-NOSED FRUIT BAT, *Cynopterus sphinx*

Distinctive Characteristics: HB 80–90; T 7–12; HF 16–19; E 18–21; FA 66–83; GLS 30–38. Size medium; wingspan averages 380 mm; dorsal hair olive brown; body sides reddish brown; ventral surface rusty yellow to greenish brown; female pelage distinctly paler; ears with pale edges. Rostral length (from anterior border of orbit to nostril) about equal to or more than 1/4 GLS; dental alveoli extend backwards, nearly under cerebral cranium; crowns of fourth premolars and first molars in lower jaw without conspicuous cusps.

Distribution: Occurs in southern China from Tibet to Fujian; Wang (2003) lists it from Guangxi, Yunnan, Hainan, Guangdong, Hong Kong, and Fujian;

Key to the Chinese Species of *Cynopterus*

1.a. Ears long, about 18–24 mm; distance between anterior border of orbit and nostril about 1/4 GLS — *Cynopterus sphinx*

b. Ears short, about 13–18 mm; distance between anterior border of orbit and nostril less than 1/4 GLS — *Cynopterus brachyotis*

extending from Indian subcontinent across Southeast Asia. Chinese subspecies: *C. s. angulatus* Miller, 1898, whose size is small, with forearm length 65–72 mm and GLS 30.5–33.2 mm.
Natural History: Primarily an inhabitant of lowland forested regions and agricultural areas, *C. sphinx* is known to feed on a variety of fruits, flowers, and even leaves. In doing so, it is likely to be an important pollinator and seed disperser of various plants. Plucks small fruits without landing, and carries them to feeding roosts a short distance away. Shuttle back and forth between fruiting trees and feeding roosts several times per night. Roosts are most often in the foliage, and it is known to modify leaves, stems, and clusters of fruit into "tents" that serve as shelters. Colonies are usually small, and composition within roosts suggests a harem structure, with males defending roosts containing various numbers of females and young. The reproductive system is one of bimodal polyestry with females undergoing postpartum estrus, and producing a single young twice per year. The gestation period is 115–125 days. The young weigh about 11 g at birth and grow rapidly to about 25 g by the time they are weaned at about one month. Adult dimensions are attained by about two months of age.
Comments: The form *angulatus* was transferred to *C. sphinx* from *C. brachyotis* by Hill and Thonglaya (1972).
Conservation Status: China RL—NT; although it nearly met the criteria for VU A1cd.
References: Storz and Kunz (1999).

Genus *Eonycteris*—Dawn Bats

大长舌果蝠属 Dachangsheguofu Shu—大长舌果蝠 Dachangsheguofu

Tongue long and pointed, quite extensible; second digit without claws; metacarpals of fifth digit much shorter than those of third; tail length about equal to hind foot length (with claw); size medium or small; forearm length 60–80 mm; skull noticeably deflected; anterior premaxillae in contact or slightly divided. Dental formula: 2.1.3.2/2.1.3.3 = 34. Distributed in Indian and Malayan realms. Of three species, only one occurs in China.

Lesser Dawn Bat

PLATE 33
MAP 328

Eonycteris spelaea (Dobson, 1871)
长舌果蝠 Changsheguofu

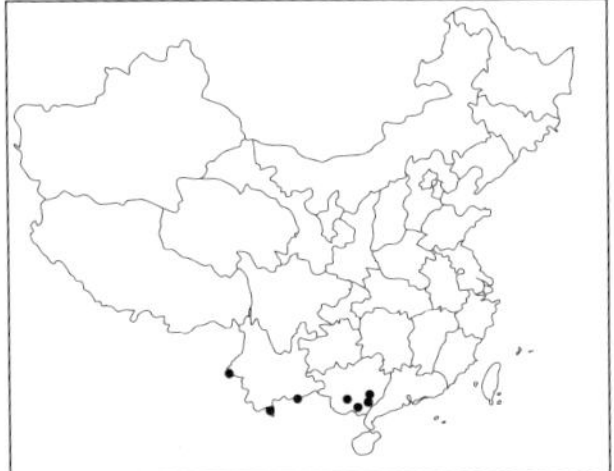

MAP 328. LESSER DAWN BAT, *Eonycteris spelaea*

Distinctive Characteristics: HB 80–130; T 11–23; HF 17–24; E 17–24; FA 61–73; GLS 35–37. Compound hairs short and thick; dorsal hair dark brown or blackish brown; ventral surface paler and taupe colored; anal glands well developed; third molar in upper jaw tiny.
Distribution: SW Guangxi and Yunnan; extending from Indian subcontinent to Malaysia and Indonesian archipelago. Chinese subspecies is nominate form.
Natural History: Dawn bats roost primarily in caves, making them vulnerable to disturbance. Colonies of tens of thousands have been reported from areas outside China. They are more often found in disturbed and agricultural areas, although they do occur in primary forest as well. These are nectar-feeding bats and have adapted to using the flowers of many important agricultural and orchard crops. They are particularly abundant in banana plantations. This species has been known to travel up to 38 km to reach feeding areas. Females become sexually mature at six months, but males mature later, at one year or more of age. Reproductive cycle in China unknown, but reported to breed asynchronously and aseasonally in India.
Conservation Status: China RL—VU A1acd; B1ab(i, ii, iii).
References: Bhat et al. (1980).

Genus *Macroglossus*—Long-nosed Fruit Bats

小长舌果蝠属 Xiaochangsheguofu Shu—小长舌果蝠 Xiaochangsheguofu

Premaxillaries proclivous and solidly fused together anteriorly; middle upper premolar and cheek teeth reduced in size. Second digit with claw, but tail vestigial or absent. Upper incisors minute; lower incisors subequal in size, resembling simple widely spaced pegs. Dental formula: 2.1.3.2/2.1.3.3 = 34. Third and fifth metacarpals subequal in size. Distributed from Myanmar to the Solomon Islands and northern Australia. One of two species is found in China.

Greater Long-Nosed Fruit Bat

MAP 329

Macroglossus sobrinus Andersen, 1911
安氏长舌果蝠 Anshi Changsheguofu

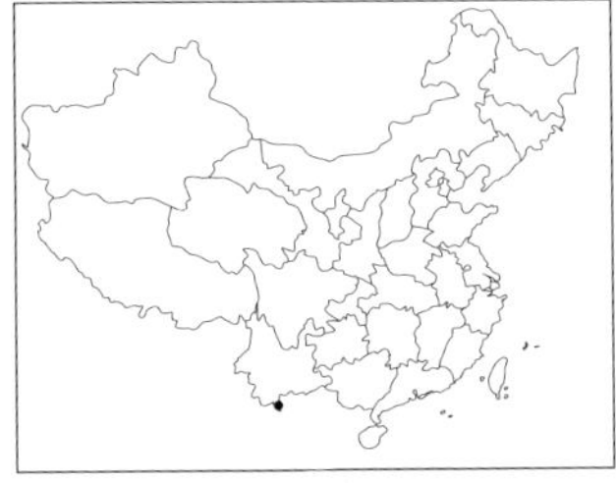

MAP 329. GREATER LONG-NOSED FRUIT BAT, *Macroglossus sobrinus*

Distinctive Characteristics: HB 70–89; T 0–6; HF 10–18; E 14–19; FA 38–52; GLS 28–29. Rostrum elongated and slender, clearly adapted for nectar feeding. Ears medium-sized, brown, with small antitragus and narrow, rounded tips. Pelage soft and fine, uniformly clay brown dorsally, and buffy brown ventrally. Forearms and inner part of wing membranes haired, as are the upper surface of the tibiae and interfemoral membrane. Wing membranes insert at base of fourth toe; calcar reduced. Eight undivided palatal ridges, five of which are interdental.

Distribution: Mengla, Xishuangbanna, Yunnan; extending to Myanmar, NE India, S Laos, C and S Thailand, and Vietnam. Chinese subspecies is the nominate form.

Natural History: Nothing known for China. Elsewhere known to occur in evergreen forest up to about 2000 m in montane and lowland forests, and in mangrove swamps. They have been found roosting in palm trees in small groups of 5–10 individuals. May roost outside of buildings in NE India. Feeds on nectar and pollen of wild bananas and other plants. Home ranges are thought to be small, with typical movements of 1–2 km per night. They may breed year-round, but few data are available.

Conservation Status: China RL—NA.

References: Lekagul and McNeely (1977).

Genus *Pteropus*—Flying Foxes

狐蝠属 Hufu Shu—狐蝠 Hufu

Size largest in the Chiroptera; forearm length more than 90 mm; second digit with well-developed claw (fig. 9); hind foot with well-developed calcar; tail absent; uropatagium rather narrow; skull noticeably turned downward; palatal surface and basal skull form a conspicuous angle; rostrum elongated, longer than lacrymal breadth; middle occiput tubular and extending backwards. Dental formula: 2.1.3.2/2.1.3.3 = 34; premolar (P2) in upper jaw extremely reduced; posterior upper molar (M2) small; premolars and posterior molars in lower jaw also reduced. Distributed in Indo-Malayan Realm, eastward to Australia; in China restricted to the south, but collected once in southern Qinghai; of 65 species, 4 are reported from China.

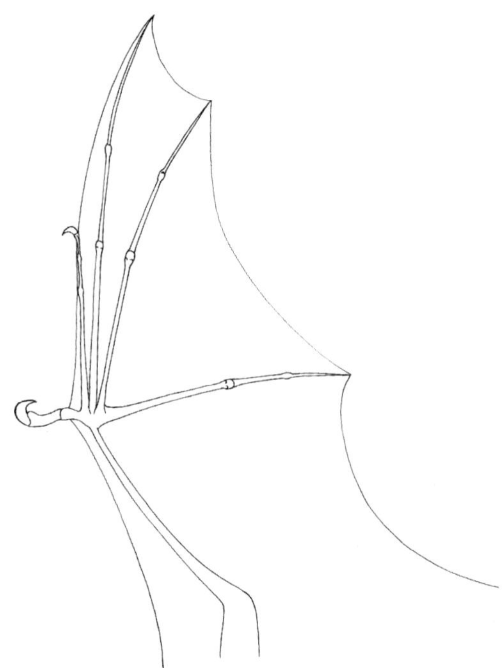

Figure 9. Wing of a flying fox (*Pteropus*) showing the second digit with a well-developed claw and an enlarged thumb.

Key to the Chinese Species of *Pteropus*

1.a.	Forearm length 125–137 mm; GLS 59–63 mm	*Pteropus dasymallus*
b.	Forearm length > 140 mm	2
2.a.	Forearm length > 180 mm; GLS 72–91 mm	*Pteropyus vampyrus*
b.	Forearm length 137–180 mm	3
3.a.	Underparts buffy brown, paler than back; mantle yellowish	*Pteropus giganteus*
b.	Underparts blackish brown, sometimes brighter; mantle ochraceous buff	*Pteropus lylei*

Ryukyu Flying Fox

PLATE 33

Pteropus dasymallus Temminck, 1825 MAP 330

琉球狐蝠 Liuqiu Hufu

Distinctive Characteristics: HB 186–227; HF 40–55; E 20–28; FA 124–141; GLS 60–65. Size smaller than *Pteropus giganteus*; upper part of tibia with hairs; entire body with long, compound hairs, giving fur an almost woolly aspect; color reddish brown with yellowish white nape.

Distribution: Taiwan; extending to Ryukyu and Philippine islands. Chinese subspecies: *P. d. formosus* Sclater, 1873.

Natural History: Little is known of the natural history of this species. Hunted for food in the past, populations have been reduced to the point that it is considered endangered. Limited data available on food habits for other subspecies in Japan.

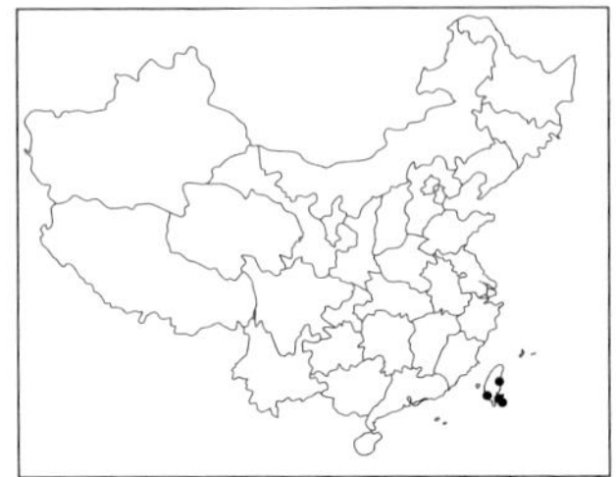

MAP 330. RYUKYU FLYING FOX, *Pteropus dasymallus*

Comments: *P. dasymallus* belongs to the *subniger* species group.

Conservation Status: China RL—EN A1acd; B1ab(i, ii, iii). CITES—II. IUCN RL—EN A1ce ver 2.3 (1994).

References: Mickleburgh et al. (1992).

Indian Flying Fox

Pteropus giganteus (Brünnich, 1782) MAP 331

大狐蝠 Dahu Fu

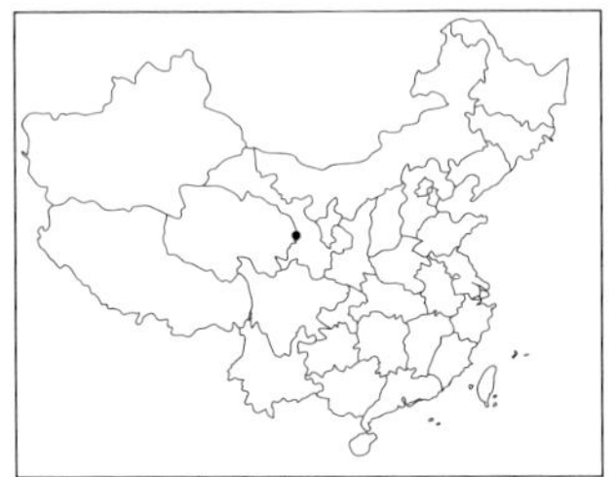

MAP 331. INDIAN FLYING FOX, *Pteropus giganteus*

Distinctive Characteristics: HB 198–300; HF 43–58; E 33–45; FA 152–186; GLS 63–78. Size very large; forearm length 186 mm on Chinese specimens; ear long and sharp; breadth of uropatagium 28 mm; head and dorsal hair dark taupe; shoulder and nape rusty brown, separated from dorsal color by a black stripe; chin, throat, and upper chest blackish brown; venter paler than dorsum.

Distribution: Qinghai; extending across the Indo-Malayan realm. Chinese subspecies: *P. g. chinghaiensis* Wang and Wang, 1962.

Natural History: Nothing known from China. In other areas, this species forms large, conspicuous colonies in the canopy of large forest trees. Feeds on a wide variety of fruits, including some orchard crops. Females are monoestrous and bear a single young after a gestation period of 140–150 days.

Comments: *P. giganteus* belongs to the *vampyrus* species group.

Conservation Status: China RL—NA. CITES—II.

References: Wang and Wang (1962).

Lyle's Flying Fox

Pteropus lylei Andersen, 1908 MAP 332

泰国狐蝠 Taiguo Hufu

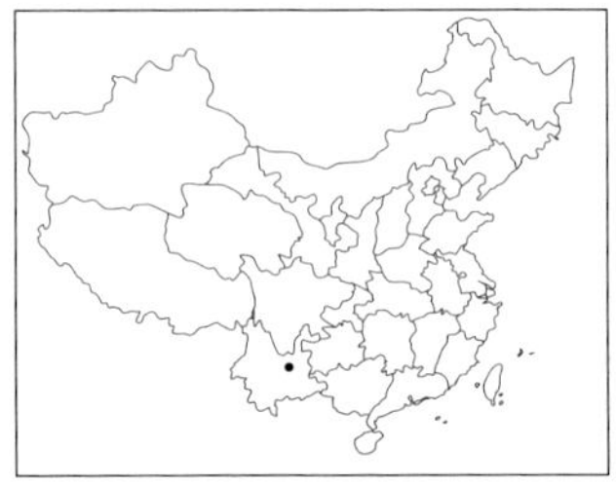

MAP 332. LYLE'S FLYING FOX, *Pteropus lylei*

Distinctive Characteristics: HB 200–250; HF 40–45; E 35–39; FA 145–160; GLS 61–67. Medium-sized flying fox, with dark brown rostrum becoming paler between the ears, yellowish mantle, and black dorsum and wings. Ventrally, the chin is dark, throat varies from yellowish to reddish, and venter black. Fur on mantle somewhat softer than other areas. Nostrils separated by deep groove, rendering them almost tubular in appearance. Dentition relatively weak, with premolars lacking posterior ridge.

Distribution: Yunnan; extending to Cambodia, Thailand, and Vietnam.

Natural History: Nothing known from China. In other areas, it is known to form large colonies in trees that can become stripped of leaves by the bats' activity. They are thought to be pests on some fruit crops.

Comments: *P. lylei* belongs to the *vampyrus* species group.

Conservation Status: China RL—NA. CITES—II.

References: Lekagul and McNeely (1977).

Large Flying Fox

Pteropus vampyrus (Linneaus, 1758) MAP 333

马来大狐蝠 Malaida Hufu

Distinctive Characteristics: HB 259–340; HF 44–65; E 28–57; FA 190–210; GLS 75–87. Externally similar to *P. giganteus*, but larger. Also, the venter tends to be darker than that of *P. giganteus*. Throat dark russet brown, chest and abdomen blackish brown, with

occasional paler tips. Braincase appears protuberant posteriorly, with basicranial axis deflected downward. Dentition robust, with the first upper molar particularly well developed.
Distribution: Shaanxi (Xi'an); extending to Myanmar, Indonesia, Malaysia, Philippines, and Vietnam. Chinese subspecies is the nominate form.

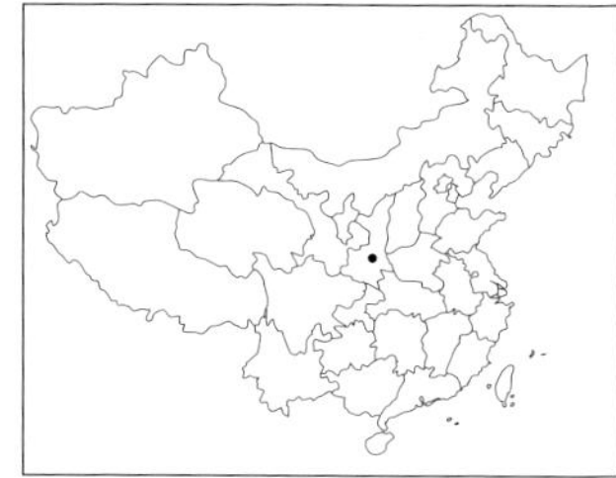

MAP 333. LARGE FLYING FOX, *Pteropus vampyrus*

Natural History: Nothing known from China. Forms large colonies in forest canopy, including primary and secondary forest, agroecosystems, and mangroves along the coast. Reported to feed on a wide variety of fruits, and may fly 10–20 km from roosts to foraging sites. Heavily hunted in some areas, where its large size makes it a useful food item. Ranges from sea level up to 1,300 m. Females give birth to a single young, varying seasonally depending on location. Young remain with mothers for two or three months, and the lifespan may exceed 15 years.
Comments: *P. vampyrus* belongs to the *vampyrus* species group.
Conservation Status: China RL—NA. CITES—II.
References: Bates and Harrison (1997).

Genus *Rousettus*—Rousette Fruit Bats

果蝠属 Guofu Shu—果蝠 Guofu

Size medium; length of forearm 73–103 mm; second digit with claw; has tail and calcar; occiput of skull turned downward; anterior extremities of left and right premaxillas touching or nearly so; rostrum slightly elongated. Dental formula: 2.1.3.2/2.1.3.3 = 34; cusps of molars weakly developed. Distributed in Africa and southern Asia, to Indonesia islands. Two of nine species are found in China.

Geoffroy's Rousette

Rousettus amplexicaudatus
(Geoffroy Saint-Hilaire, 1810) MAP 334
抱尾果蝠 Baowei Guofu

Distinctive Characteristics: HB 105–115; T 15–17; HF 20–23; E 18–20; FA 79–87; GLS 35–40. Slightly smaller than *R. leschenaulti*, but with considerable overlap in size. *R. amplexicaudatus* is darker in color than *R. leschenaulti* and tends to be a uniform dull grayish brown. The underparts are gray-brown, the neck is pale gray, and the wings are uniformly dark brown. The ears tend to be a bit narrower (12–13 mm) than those of *R. leschenaulti* (14–15 mm). Cranium rounded and rostrum relatively short. Maxillary tooth row averages slightly smaller (13–14 mm) than in *R. leschenaulti* (14–16 mm). The last lower molar tends to be more oval in shape than in *R. leschenaulti*.
Distribution: Yunnan; extending to Cambodia, Thailand, Myanmar, and Laos; Malay Peninsula through Indonesia, Java, and Bali; Philippines; New Guinea; and Bismarck archipelago to Solomon Islands. Chinese subspecies is the nominate form.

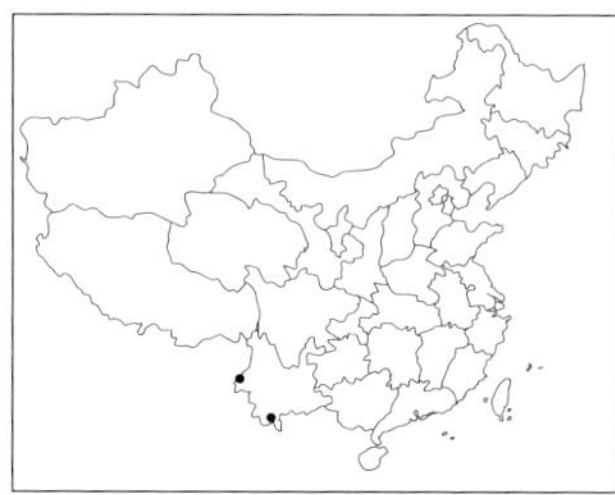

MAP 334. GEOFFROY'S ROUSETTE, *Rousettus amplexicaudatus*

Natural History: This species has been recorded from sea level up to 2,200 m elevation. Roosts are known from caves, rock crevices, and old tombs. They may travel long distances each night, in search of appropriate fruit. *Rousettus* are known to use a primitive form of echolocation while foraging. Gestation is thought to be about 15 weeks, and lactation about three months.
Comments: *R. amplexicaudatus* belongs to the subgenus *Rousettus*.
Conservation Status: China RL—NA.
References: Lekagul and McNeely (1977).

Leschenault's Rousette

PLATE 33
Rousettus leschenaultii (Desmarest, 1820) MAP 335
棕果蝠 Zong Guofu

Distinctive Characteristics: HB 95–120; T 10–18; HF 19–24; E 18–24; FA 80–99; GLS 34–40. Medium-sized species, with pollex 23–31 mm and second phalanx of third digit 41–51 mm; breadth of jugal about 23 mm; dorsal hair uniformly dark brown; nape and ventral surface relatively pale, grayish brown; occiput of skull distinctly turns downward; anterior extremities of left and right premaxillas touch; premolars in upper jaw little reduced; premolars in

Key to the Chinese Species of *Rousettus*

1.a.	Color darker; lower last molar subcircular	*Rousettus amplexicaudatus*
b.	Color paler, lower last molar elliptical	*Rousettus leschenaulti*

lower jaw much larger than incisors; third lower molar 1.5–2 times longer than wide.
Distribution: Across S China, including S Fujian, S Guangdong, Hainan Island, S Guangxi, S Yunnan, and Guizhou (Wang 2003 also lists it from Xizang [Medog], Sichuan, and Jiangxi); extending to Sri Lanka, Pakistan, Vietnam, and Malay Peninsula plus Sumatra, Java, Bali, and Mentawai islands (Indonesia). Chinese subspecies is the nominate form.

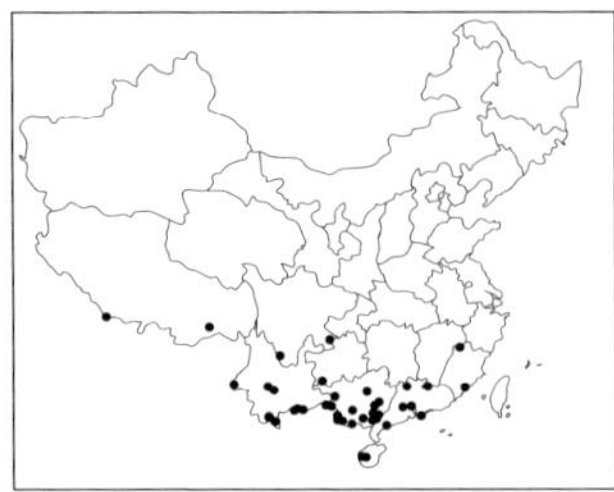

MAP 335. LESCHENAULT'S ROUSETTE, *Rousettus leschenaultii*

Natural History: Generally found in forested areas where it roosts in colonies of up to 2,000 individuals in caves and manmade structures. Colonies may shift depending on food availability. Roosts containing both sexes are known, as are male-only and female-only colonies. The breeding system appears to be bimodal polyestry, with the females having postpartum estrus after the birth of a single young twice each year. Lactation lasts about two months, and females become sexually mature at about five months, in time to participate in the second breeding cycle of their birth year. Both sexes reach full adult size after one year, and males become sexually mature at about 15 months.
Comments: *R. leschenaultii* is in the subgenus *Rousettus*.
Conservation Status: China RL—LC.
References: Khan (1985).

Genus *Sphaerias* (monotypic)

球果蝠属 Qiuguofu Shu

Blanford's Fruit Bat

Sphaerias blanfordi (Thomas, 1891). PLATE 33 MAP 336
布氏球果蝠 Bushi Qiuguofu

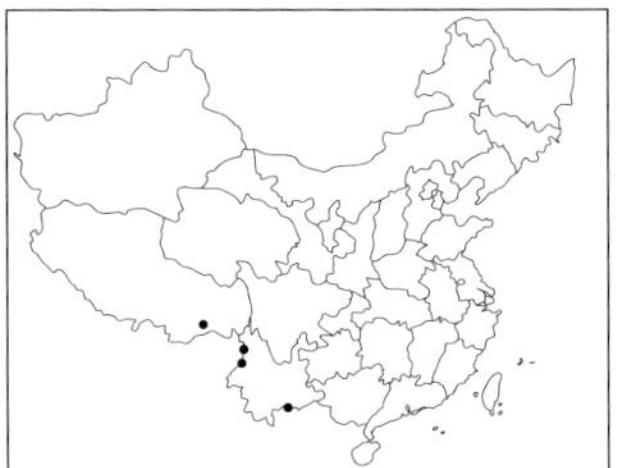

MAP 336. BLANFORD'S FRUIT BAT, *Sphaerias blanfordi*

Distinctive Characteristics: HB 80–90; HF 11–12; E 16–20; FA 50–61; GLS 27–28. Body dull grayish brown; pelage long and dense; fur extends onto tibia and underside of forearm; anterior margin of ears edged in white; antitragus small and triangular; tail absent; interfemoral membrane very narrow, with no calcar; wing membrane inserts on distal half of first phalanx of outer toe; lower incisors with four conspicuous serrations. Postorbital foramen lacking; incisors proclivous, with pointed, triangular crowns; cheek teeth narrow; uropatagium reduced. Dental formula: 2.1.3.1/2.1.3.2 = 30.
Distribution: S Xixang and E Yunnan; extending to N India and Bhutan through Myanmar, N Thailand, and Vietnam. Two subspecies in China: (1) *S. b. blanfordi* (Thomas, 1891); Yunnan; (2) *S. b. motuoensis* Cai and Zhang, 1980; Xizang (but this form is poorly marked and probably not sufficiently distinct from the nominate form to warrant recognition).
Natural History: This species is very poorly known but thought to be most common in lower montane forests.
Conservation Status: China RL—EN B1ab(i, ii, iii) + 2ab(i, ii, iii).
References: Lekagul and McNeely (1977).

Family Rhinolophidae—Horseshoe Bats

菊头蝠科 Jutoufu Ke—菊头蝠 Jutoufu

Ears wide and long, without tragus; rostrum with complicated leaflike skin outgrowth—the nose leaf; first toe with only two phalanges, others each with three; second digit of forelimb with metacarpal bone only, lacking phalanx; third digit with two phalanges. Premaxilla of skull undeveloped, only left palatine remains, which is disassociated, not linked with maxillas, and embedded with a tiny incisor in the anterior extremity; without postorbital process; both anterior and posterior parts of palate distinctly sunken, so palate very short, length of its center less than the smallest breadth between toothrows.

Distributed widely in the Eastern Hemisphere; east to Philippines, New Guinea, and northeastern Australia; mainly occurs in tropical and temperate zones. Only one genus is known—*Rhinolophus* Lacépède, 1799.

Genus *Rhinolophus*—Horseshoe Bats

菊头蝠属 Jutoufu Shu—菊头蝠 Jutoufu

External characters as in Rhinolophidae (see above); sagittal crest of skull well developed; auditory bullae very small and cochlea very large; basisphenoid pits absent; dental formula: 1.1.2.3/2.1.3.3 = 32; upper incisors tiny; canines strong but without styles; second upper premolars tiny; lower canines small. Twenty of 77 species are known to occur in China, most of which are in the south. See Csorba et al. (2003).

Key to the Chinese Species of *Rhinolophus*

1.a. Extension of conjoined leaf near or higher than level of top sellar leaf; sellar leaf small, its basal part with no leaflike transverse process, and no pterygoid or cup-shaped large leaf 2

b. Extension of conjoined leaf distinctly lower than horizontal line of top sellar leaf; sellar leaf larger, its basal part with leaflike transverse processes on either side, forming a pterygoid or cup-shaped large leaf, which covers nostrils 12

2.a. Conjoined leaf completely round in side view; size large; forearm length > 44 mm 3

b. Conjoined leaf acute in side view; size relatively small; forearm length < 44 mm 7

3.a. Lateral margins of sellar leaf parallel; metacarpal bones of third, fourth, and fifth digits about equal in size; second phalanx of third digit about ≤ 1.5 times of first phalanx in size 4

b. Lateral margins of sellar leaf sunken; metacarpal bones of third, fourth, and fifth digits different in size, usually those of third digit shortest; second phalanx of third digit > 1.5 times of first 6

4.a. Size slightly smaller; forearm length 45–46 mm; length of metacarpal bones of third digit 30–31 mm; GLS about 18 mm; second upper premolar lies outside toothrow; lancet reduced, tip short and rudimentary *Rhinolophus thomasi*

b. Size slightly larger; forearm length 45–53 mm; length of metacarpal bones of third digit 34–40 mm; GLS 20–24 mm; second upper premolar lies in toothrow; lancet normal, not reduced 5

5.a. Larger, wingspan 290–326 mm, GLS 21.5–23.5 mm *Rhinolophus rouxii*

b. Smaller, wingspan 264–296 mm, GLS 20.2–21.5 mm *Rhinolophus sinicus*

6.a. Size slightly larger; forearm length 56–64 mm; palatal spine of skull long, about 1/3 of length of upper toothrow (from anterior canine to posterior molar); second upper premolar lies outside toothrow *Rhinolophus ferrumequinum*

b. Size smaller; forearm length 50–56 mm; palatal spine of skull relatively short, about 1/4 of length of upper toothrow or shorter; second upper premolar lies in toothrow *Rhinolophus affinis*

7.a. Conjoined leaf bends forward in form of acute angle 8

b. Conjoined leaf in form of right-angled triangle 9

8.a. Smaller; forearm 31–34 mm, maxillary toothrow length 5.1–5.4 mm *Rhinolophus subbadius*

b. Larger; forearm 34–39 mm, maxilillary toothrow length 5.4–5.7 mm *Rhinolophus monoceros*

9.a. Skull wide, about 8 mm; forearm length 40–44 mm; GLS usually not < 16 mm 10

b. Skull relatively narrow, about 6.8–7.2 mm; forearm length < 40 mm; GLS < 17.5 mm 11

10.a. Sella widest at base; connecting process triangular and pointed; lancet extremely hastate *Rhinolophus shortridgei*

b. Sella parallel-sided; connecting process more rounded; lancet less hastate *Rhinolophus osgoodi*

11.a. Size slightly larger; forearm length about 39 mm; tibia length about 16.2–17.4 mm; basal part of middle rictus of horseshoe-shaped anterior lobe without small mamillary process; sellar leaf relatively wide *Rhinolophus cornutus*

b. Size slightly smaller; forearm length about 37 mm; tibia length about 13.5–15 mm; basal part of middle rictus of horseshoe-shaped anterior lobe with two small mamillary processes; sellar leaf relatively narrow *Rhinolophus pusillus*

12.a. Breadth of zygomatic process > mastoidal breadth 13

b. Breadth of zygomatic process < mastoidal breadth 17

13.a. Basal sellar leaf not winglike; conjoined leaf grows out from top of sellar leaf 14

b. Basal sellar leaf winglike; conjoined leaf grows out from middle back of sellar leaf 15

14.a. Smaller; forearm 48–57 mm, maxillary toothrow length 11–12 mm *Rhinolophus pearsonii*

b. Larger; forearm 55–60 mm, maxillary toothrow length 12–14 mm *Rhinolophus yunanensis*

15.a. Found on Taiwan *Rhinolophus formosae*

b. Found on mainland 16

16.a. Smaller; forearm 46–54 mm, maxillary toothrow length 8–9.4 mm; upper incisors minute, widely separated *Rhinolophus trifoliatus*

b. Larger; forearm 54–78 mm, maxillary toothrow length 9.5–12.3 mm; upper incisors moderate, their tips convergent *Rhinolophus luctus*

17.a. Size small; forearm length 43–48 mm; GLS about 20 mm; sellar leaf and apical lobe about equal in height 18
b. Size larger; forearm length 54–63 mm; GLS 23–24 mm; sellar leaf distinctly higher than apical lobe and hides it from view completely 19
18.a. Smaller, forearm 43–45 mm *Rhinolophus siamensis*
b. Larger, forearm 46–48 mm *Rhinolophus macrotis*
19.a. Smaller, forearm 53–55 mm *Rhinolophus paradoxolophus*
b. Larger, forearm 59–63 mm *Rhinolophus rex*

Intermediate Horseshoe Bat

Rhinolophus affinis Horsfield, 1823 PLATE 34 MAP 337
中菊头蝠 Zhong Jutoufu

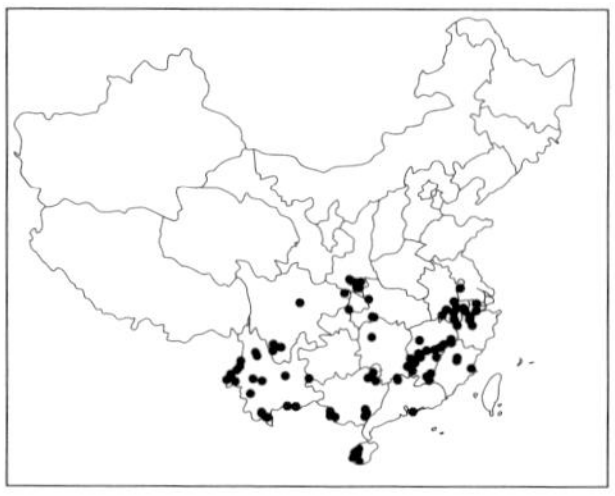

MAP 337. INTERMEDIATE HORSESHOE BAT, *Rhinolophus affinis*

Distinctive Characteristics: HB 58–63; T 20–35; HF 11–13; E 15–21; FA 46–56; GLS 22–24. Size smaller than that of *Rhinolophus ferrumequinum*; tibia length 20–25 mm; tail length about 1.5 times of that of tibia; wing membrane long; fourth and fifth metacarpal bones about equal in length, both slightly longer than third; horseshoe lobe of nose leaf large, accessory lobe very reduced; sellar leaf slightly fiddlelike, its lateral margins a little sunken; conjoined leaf low and round; apical lobe cuneal; hair color brown or taupe, ventral surface slightly paler; palatal bridge of skull very short, about 1/4 of length of upper toothrow (C-M3); premolar (P2) in upper jaw small, and lies in toothrow; canines and large premolar (P4) nearly join; premolar (p3) in lower jaw also tiny, and leans to outside of toothrow, so canines and large premolar (p4) sometimes in contact.
Distribution: SW, S, C China; extending widely in the Indo-Malayan realm. Three subspecies in China: (1) *R. a. hainanus* Allen, 1906 (horseshoe lobe slightly wider; hair color rust brown); Hainan Island; (2) *R. a. himalayanus* Andersen, 1905 (forearm length 50–53 mm; tibia length 20–21.4 mm; skull narrow, breadth around 10–10.6 mm; tympanic bullae narrow); Hunan, Shanxi, Hubei, Guizhou, Sichuan, Yunnan (and a specimen in the British Museum from Heilongjiang, listed by Csorba et al. [2003], is allocated provisionally to this subspecies); (3) *R. a. macrurus* Andersen, 1905 (horseshoe lobe slightly narrower than that of previous subspecies; tibia length 22.8– 23.8 mm; skull wide, around 10.4–11.9 mm; tympanic bullae slightly larger); Zhejiang, Fujian, Jiangxi, Hunan, Guangdong, Hong Kong, Guangxi, Jiangsu, Anhui.

Natural History: Found both in wet western highlands and in more tropical eastern lowlands. Occurs from sea level up to at least 2,000 m, and roosts in caves. Roosts contain both sexes, with little or no spatial segregation. Forages near ground level, as evidenced by frequent capture in mist nets. Echolocation frequencies from 73 to 80 kHz have been recorded. Reproductive habits unknown in China, but there is some indication of bimodal polyestry from other areas. Females bear only a single young at a time.
Comments: *R. affinis* is a member of the *megaphyllus* species group.
Conservation Status: China RL—NT; although it nearly met the criteria for VU B1ab(i, ii, iii).
References: Bates and Harrison (1997); Francis and Habersetzer (1998).

Little Japanese Horseshoe Bat

Rhinolophus cornutus Temminck, 1835 MAP 338
角菊头蝠 Jiao Jutoufu

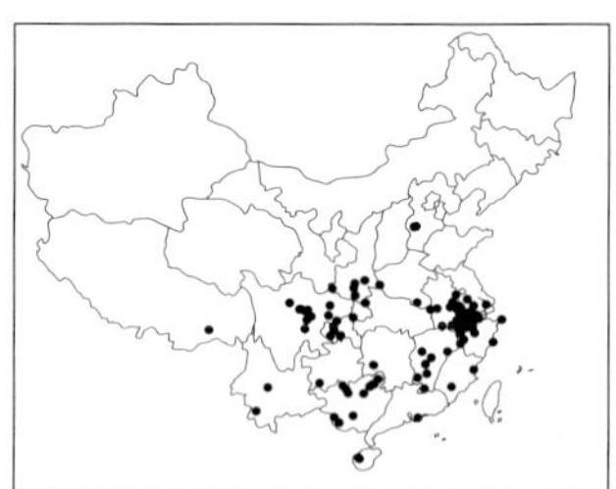

MAP 338. LITTLE JAPANESE HORSESHOE BAT, *Rhinolophus cornutus*

Distinctive Characterstics: HB 38–44; T 17–27; HF 7–8; E 16–19; FA 38–41; GLS 16. Size very small; condyloincisive length about 14.8 mm; tibia long, around 16.2–17.4 mm; tail distinctly longer than tibia; ears very large, wing membrane not very prolonged; middle rictus of horseshoe lobe without small mamillary process; sellar leaf wide, tending to be narrow from basal part to upper section; conjoined leaf in sharp triangle form, higher than the top level of sellar leaf; pelage color blackish brown, with off white basal parts; skull narrow; breadth of zygomatic bone 7.9–8.0 mm; small premolar (P2) in upper jaw lies in toothrow; position of small premolar (p3) in lower jaw variable. *R. cornutus* is a member of the *pusillus* species group.
Distribution: SW China; extending to Japan and the Ryukyu islands.

Natural History: Allen (1938) reported several specimens from the higher country of W China. Some were taken from caves or rock crevices, and this species is not common in houses. A variety of moth wings have been found beneath their roosts. However, many of those specimens were later referred to *R. pusillus* (see Corbet and Hill 1992), making the true occurrence of *R. cornutus* from China difficult to determine. It is likely that the species *R. cornutus* is restricted to Japan, and the Chinese records actually pertain to *R. pusillus*.
Comments: *R. cornutus* belongs to the *pusillus* species group. According to Wang (2003), the Chinese subspecies is *R.c. pumilus* Andersen, 1905. However, *pumilus* is otherwise known only from the Ryukyu Islands. Csorba et al. (2003) suggested restricting *cornutus* to Japan and other islands, and calling all of the mainland animals *R. pusillus*. Thus, the inclusion of *cornutus* in the Chinese fauna is provisional, based on Wang (2003).
Conservation Status: China RL—NT; although it nearly met the criteria for VU A1bcd. IUCN RL—LR/nt ver 2.3 (1994).
References: Yoshiyuki (1989).

Greater Horseshoe Bat

PLATE 34

Rhinolophus ferrumequinum (Schreber, 1774)

MAP 339

马铁菊头蝠 Matie Jutoufu

MAP 339. GREATER HORSESHOE BAT, *Rhinolophus ferrumequinum*

Distinctive Characteristics: HB 56–79; T 25–44; HF 10–14; E 18–29; FA 53–64; GLS 21–25. Size large; length of tibia 23–26.6 mm; wing membrane long; metacarpal bones of third, fourth, and fifth digits increasing in length gradually; horseshoe lobe of nose leaf very wide, its accessory lobe small and inconspicuous; lateral margins of sellar leaf sunken and slightly fiddle-shaped; conjoined leaf low and round; tip of apical lobe sharp, long, and narrow; only a medium vertical groove left in underlip, two lateral grooves have disappeared; pelage color smoky gray brown; palatal bridge of skull long, about 1/3 of length of upper toothrow (C-M3); small premolar (P2) in upper jaw lies outside toothrow or absent, so basal edges of canines in contact with large premolar (P4); small premolar (p3) in lower jaw also lies outside toothrow or absent, so small premolar (p2) also in contact with large premolar (p4).

Distribution: Occurs throughout SE China; extending across the Palaearctic realm. Two subspecies in China: (1) *R. f. nippon* Temminck, 1835 (forearm length 49–59 mm; tibia length less than 25 mm); Jilin, Liaoning, Hebei, Beijing, Shanxi, Henan, Shandong, Jiangsu, Shanghai, Zhejiang, Anhui, Sichuan, Guangxi, Hunan, Guizhou, Yunnan, Hubei, Shaanxi, Gansu, Ningxia, and Fujian; (2) *R. f. tragatus* Hodgson, 1835 (forearm length 58–64 mm; tibia length more than 25 mm); Yunnan and Guizhou.
Natural History: This is the most northern species in the genus, and it occupies a wide range of habitats. They are active year-round in southern parts of the range but hibernate during the northern winters. Adult bats forage up to 2–3 km from the roost each night, feeding on beetles and a variety of other insects. Like other hibernators, they have a long lifespan and have been recorded living to 26 years of age. This species appears to have a long prepubertal period of three to seven years, with females averaging five years of age when they first give birth. Individual females may give birth only every other year in some cases. Although a single young is more common, twins are produced on occasion. Lactation lasts about 45 days, with the young beginning to fly and forage on their own before weaning.
Comments: *R. ferrumequinum* belongs to the *ferrumequinum* species group.
Conservation Status: China RL—LC. IUCN RL—LR/nt ver 2.3 (1994).
References: Jones et al. (1995).

Formosan Woolly Horseshoe Bat

Rhinolophus formosae Sanborn, 1939

MAP 340

台湾菊头蝠 Taiwan Jutoufu

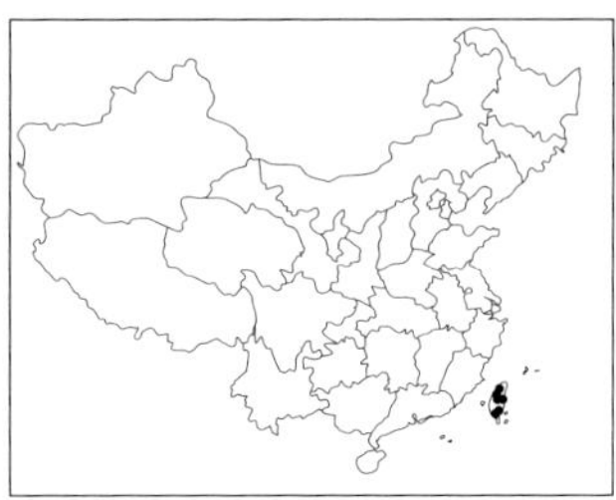

MAP 340. FORMOSAN WOOLLY HORSESHOE BAT, *Rhinolophus formosae*

Distinctive Characteristics: HB 90; T 28–39; HF 16–17; E 28–33; FA 56–61; GLS 24–28. Similar to *R. luctus*, but smaller; length of tibia 28–33 mm; zygomatic breadth 11–13 mm; fur silky and glossy; length of second phalanx of third digit less than 1.5 times that of first phalanx; third, fourth, and fifth metacarpal bones increase gradually in length; nose leaf with posterior part tapered into lancet; intermediate part with circular lateral lappets at base of sella; connecting process low; anterior part horseshoe-shaped with deep notch in lower margin; ear, nose leaf, and wing membranes blackish; skull robust, similar to *R. luctus*, but smaller; zygomatic breadth

greater than mastoidal breadth; sagittal crest well developed in older adults; palate more than 1/3 of upper toothrow; interorbital region narrow; upper anterior premolar (P2) minute, but in toothrow.
Distribution: Taiwan Island (Taipei, Hsinchu, Taichung, Hualien, Taitung, Pingtung, and Nantou counties). Endemic.
Natural History: Poorly known, rare, form. Individuals have been found roosting in caves, buildings, tunnels, and irrigation conduits at low to middle altitudes. Reported from primary forest in the central part of Taiwan.
Comments: *Rhinolophus formosae* is a member of the *trifoliatus* species group. It was formerly considered a subspecies of *R. luctus*, but Yoshiyuki and Harada (1995) considered it distinct.
Conservation Status: China RL—VU B1ab(i, ii, iii) + 2ab(i, ii, iii).
References: Yoshiyuki and Harada (1995).

Woolly Horseshoe Bat

PLATE 34
Rhinolophus luctus Temminck, 1835
MAP 341
大菊头蝠 Da Jutoufu

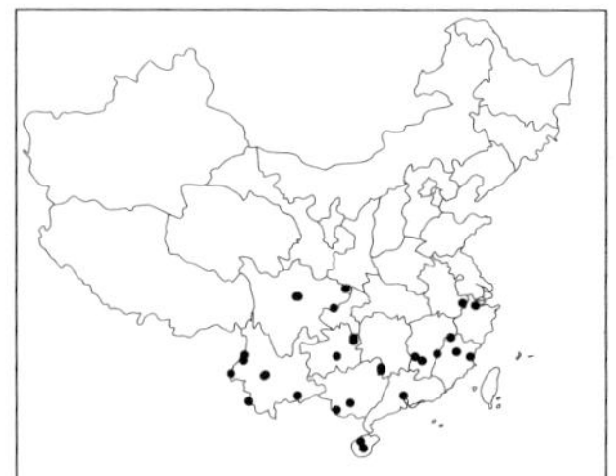

MAP 341. WOOLLY HORSESHOE BAT, *Rhinolophus luctus*

Distinctive Characteristics: HB 75–95; T 36–61; HF 16–18; E 28–44; FA 58–81; GLS 28–33. Size very large, largest of Chinese *Rhinolophus*; length of tibia 34–36 mm; breadth of zygomatic process 14–16 mm; compound hairs slender, soft, and slightly curly; wing membrane not very elongated; length of second phalanx of third digit less than 1.5 times of that of first phalanx; third, fourth, and fifth metacarpal bones increasing in length gradually; anterior horseshoe lobe of nose leaf noticeably expanded, covering rostrum and without small adhering leaf on sides; inner and outer edges of nostrils protrude, and derive into internasal leaf; basal sellar leaf conspicuously expands into aliform toward either side, so whole sellar leaf takes on trefoil form; conjoined leaf very low and round, growing out from very underside of top of back sellar leaf; apical lobe narrow, long, and tonguelike, with round top; pelage brown or smoky gray; hair tips with light rings, hence a little gray; both ear and flying membrane heavily pigmented; breadth of zygomatic process greater than mastoidal breadth; sagittal crest developed; length of palatal bridge more than 1/3 of that of upper toothrow; relatively small; postnasal aperture deep; interorbital region very narrow; coronoid process in lower jaw high; teeth all small; small premolars in upper and lower jaws all lie in toothrow.
Distribution: SE China; extending to India and Nepal eastward to Vietnam and islands in the South China Sea. Three subspecies in China: (1) *R. l. lanosus* Andersen, 1905; Zhejiang, Jiangxi, Guangdong, Guizhou, Sichuan, Fujian, Guangxi and Anhui; (2) *R. l. perniger* Hodgson, 1843; Yunnan (Wang 2003); (3) *R. l. spurcus* Allen, 1928; Hainan Island.
Natural History: Appears to be solitary or living in pairs and favoring tunnels and old mine shafts in China. They have been taken in hollow trees and under thick bark in other areas. They emerge early in the evening and fly near ground level. Most have been collected in forested areas. This is a widespread species, with little ecological information available.
Comments: *Rhinolophus luctus* belongs to the *trifoliatus* species group.
Conservation Status: China RL—NT; although it nearly met the criteria for VU A1cd.
References: Bates and Harrison (1997).

Big-Eared Horseshoe Bat

PLATE 34
Rhinolophus macrotis Blyth, 1844
MAP 342
大耳菊头蝠 Da'er Jutoufu

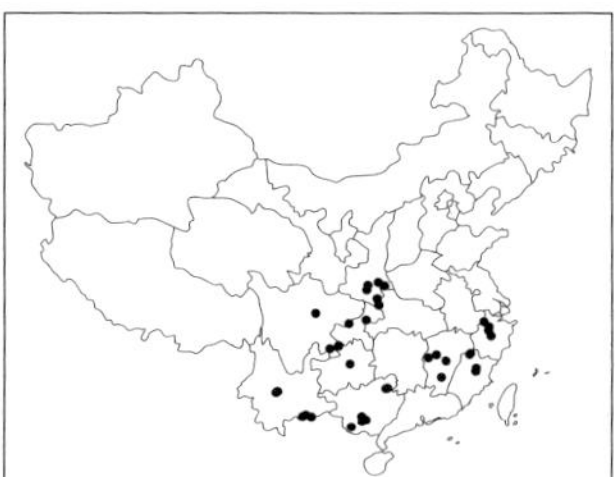

MAP 342. BIG-EARED HORSESHOE BAT, *Rhinolophus macrotis*

Distinctive Characteristics: HB 47–51; T 12–32; HF 9–10; E 18–27; FA 39–48; GLS 20. Size small; ears especially large; antitragus relatively small; condyloincisive length 16.5–18.2 mm; tibia length about 18 mm; first three metacarpal bones of forelimbs short, fourth and fifth about equal in length; length of second phalanx of third digit less than 1.5 times of that first phalanx; first phalanges of fourth and fifth digits both a little shorter than their second phalanges; pelage color brown; basal hair off white; ventral surface pale; horseshoe lobe of nose leaf very wide, with obvious indentation in middle and a small adhering leaf on both front sides; sellar leaf very wide, breadth about half of its length, two lateral margins parallel, basal part enlarged and forms a simple cup-shaped lobe with internasal leaf; conjoined leaf especially low and in simple arc form, growing out from underside of top of back sellar leaf; apical leaf about equal to sellar leaf in length, with slightly recessed lateral margins and blunt top; lower lip with three vertical grooves; sagittal crest inconspicuous; length of palatal bridge more than 1/3 of that of upper toothrow; interorbital region distinctly atrophied; breadth of zygomatic process about equal

to or a little greater than mastoidal breadth; coronoid process of lower jaw low; small premolar (P2) of upper jaw developed and lies in toothrow; small premolar (p3) in lower jaw leans to outside of toothrow.
Distribution: SE China; extending from Pakistan through Indochina to the Philippines. Two subspecies in China: (1) *R. m. caldwelli* Allen, 1923 (hair color dark taupe; forearm length 43 mm); Zhejiang, Jiangxi, Guangdong, Guizhou, Guangxi, Fujian; (2) *R. m. episcopus* Allen, 1923 (hair color smoky gray; forearm long, length about 48 mm); Sichuan, Shaanxi.
Natural History: Known to hibernate in caves, but otherwise little is known about this species in China. They have been collected above 1,500 m in India and probably get above that elevation in China as well.
Comments: *R. macrotis* belongs to the *philippinensis* species group, and although Wang (2003) considered *R. siamensis* to be a subspecies of *R. macrotis*, we treat it as a full species (Hendrichsen et al. 2001).
Conservation Status: China RL–LC.
References: Hendrichsen et al. (2001).

Formosan Lesser Horseshoe Bat

Rhinolophus monoceros Andersen, 1905 MAP 343
单角菊头蝠 Danjiao Jutoufu

Distinctive characteristics: HB 40–50; T 15–27; HF 7–9; E 16–17; FA 34–40; GLS 14–16. Size relatively small, similar to *Rhinolophus cornutus*, but conjoined leaf of nose leaf very sharp and slender, and projecting forward; apical lobe nearly in equilateral triangle form; basal part of sellar leaf wide; small premolars in upper jaw tiny, and lie in toothrow; small premolars in lower jaw lie outside toothrow, in contact with large ones.
Distribution: Taiwan. Endemic.
Natural History: This common form roosts in large colonies in caves and tunnels at low elevations. It is occasionally found roosting with other species but segregates from them inside the cave.

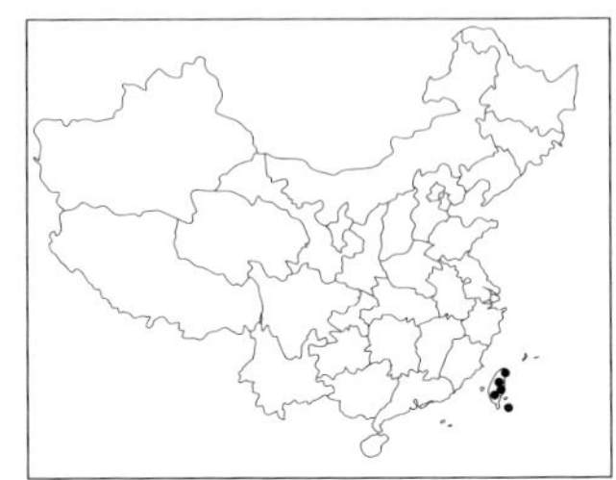

MAP 343. FORMOSAN LESSER HORSESHOE BAT, *Rhinolophus monoceros*

Comments: *R. monoceros* is a monotypic species belonging to the *pusillus* species group. In the past, this species has been considered conspecific with both *cornutus* and *pusillus* (Corbet and Hill 1992). We follow Csorba et al. (2003) in recognizing it as a distinct species.
Conservation Status: China RL—VU A1cd; B1ab(i, ii, iii). IUCN RL—LR/nt ver 2.3 (1994).
References: Lin et al. (1997).

Osgood's Horseshoe Bat

Rhinolophus osgoodi Sanborn, 1939 MAP 344
奥氏菊头蝠 Aoshi Jutoufu

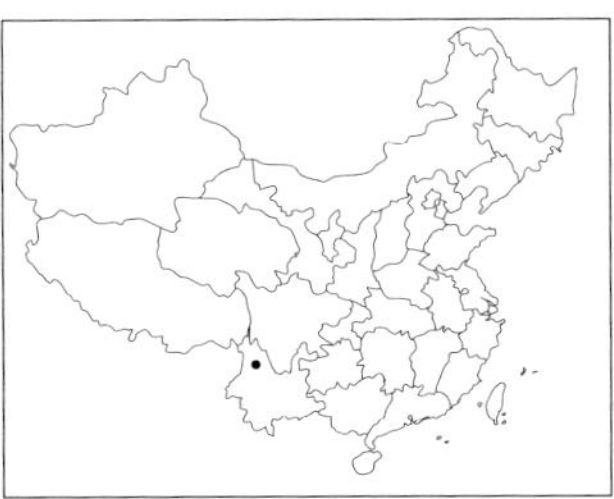

MAP 344. OSGOOD'S HORSESHOE BAT, *Rhinolophus osgoodi*

Distinctive Characteristics: HB 52–54; T 17–21; HF 8–9; E 12–20; FA 41–46; GLS 15–16. Size medium; horseshoe wide (6.4 mm), covering most of rostrum; sella broad with rounded tip and parallel sides; connecting process varies from pointed to blunt triangle; lancet straight sided; metacarpals roughly equal in size; pelage pale brown with gray bases above, paler gray below. Skull small, but strong; mastoid width greater than zygomatic breadth; weak saggital crest; frontal depression shallow, with sharp bordering ridges; second upper premolar in toothrow; third lower premolar displaced halfway outside toothrow.
Distribution: Known only from type series, from Nguluko, Yunnan. Endemic.
Natural History: Nothing is known about this species, and apparently it has not been collected since the original type series.
Comments: Osgood (1932) originally referred the 10 specimens in the type series to *R. lepidus*, and later Sanborn (1939) described them. *Rhinolophus osgoodi* is in the *pusillus* species group.
Conservation Status: China RL—EN A2cd; B1ab(i, ii, iii) + 2ab(i, ii, iii). IUCN RL—DD ver 2.3 (1994).
References: Osgood (1932); Sanborn (1939).

Bourret's Horseshoe Bat

Rhinolophus paradoxolophus (Bourret, 1951) MAP 345
高鞍菊头蝠 Gao'an Jutoufu

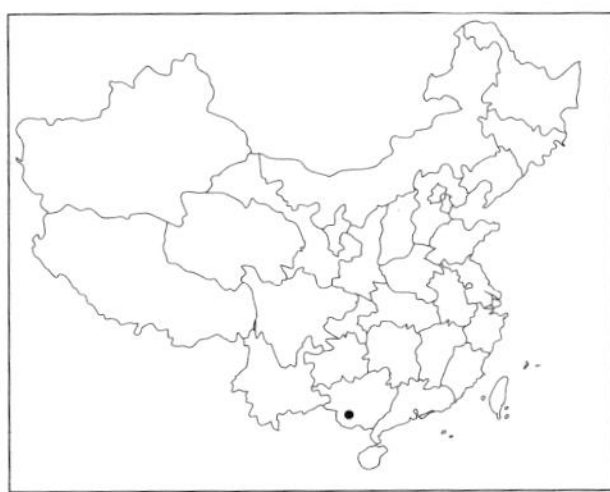

MAP 345. BOURRET'S HORSESHOE BAT, *Rhinolophus paradoxolophus*

Distinctive Characteristics: HB 47; T 24; HF 10; E 26–39; FA 50–63; GLS 19–22. Similar to *R. rex*, but

smaller. Ears wide, about 21 mm, and very long; antitragus large, 17 × 8 mm; nose leaf sella broad and lacking lappets; internarial cup broad, subcircular, and enclosing the base of the sella; lancet low and rounded; skull slender, rostrum and infraorbital canal long; mastoid width greater than zygomatic width; low, but sharp, sagittal crest; both upper and lower small premolars are in toothrow.
Distribution: Guangxi (Zhao et al. 2002); extending to Vietnam, Thailand, Laos.
Natural History: This is a rare species, only recently reported from China. One specimen from Thailand was taken in a dry pine forest, near open plains. Other trees in the area included *Shorea, Pentacme, Xylia*, and *Ficus*. Several parasites were obtained from that animal, including trombiculid mites, nycteribiid flies, and flies in the genus *Ascodipteron*, which were embedded in the ear and wing membranes (Thonglongya 1973). These bats roost in caves, in limestone areas of lowland rainforest. Relative to other rhinolophids, *R. paradoxolophus* uses lower frequency echolocation sounds (22–43 kHz).
Comments: *R. paradoxolophus* belongs to the *philippinensis* species group. It may be conspecific with *rex* (Corbet and Hill 1992), but Eger and Fenton (2003) considered it a distinct species.
Conservation Status: China RL—LC.
References: Eger and Fenton (2003); Thonglongya, (1973); Zhao et al. (2002).

Pearson's Horseshoe Bat

Rhinolophus pearsonii Horsfield, 1851 PLATE 34 MAP 346
皮氏菊头蝠 Pishi Jutoufu

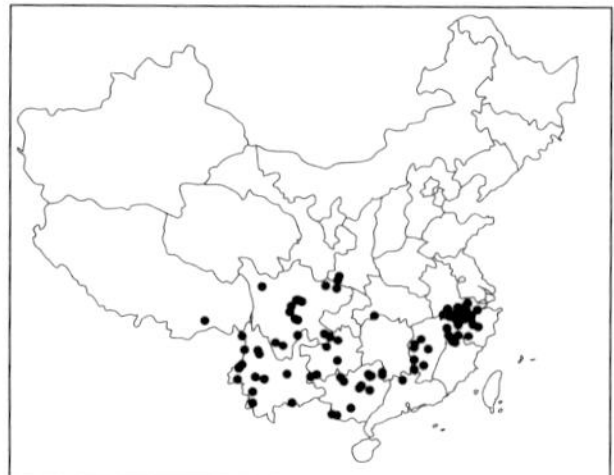

MAP 346. PEARSON'S HORSESHOE BAT, *Rhinolophus pearsonii*

Distinctive Characteristics: HB 61–68; T 16–29; HF 12–13; E 23–29; FA 47–56; GLS 24. Similar to *Rhinolophus yunnanensis*, but size smaller; tail slightly shorter than tibia; third, fourth, and fifth, metacarpal bones of wing membrane slightly increasing in length by turns; sellar leaf high, with blunt lateral margins; basal nose leaf not expanded into aliform; conjoined leaf low and round, extending downwards from top of sellar leaf in shape of round arc, and conspicuously lower than the top level of sellar leaf; apical lobe sharp; paralabral groove single; hairs long and thick, dark brown; dorsum color not distinct from ventral surface; sagittal crest high; palatal bridge short; premolars in upper jaw very small, but lie in toothrow.
Distribution: SE and C China; extending across S Asia. Two subspecies in China: (1) *R. p. chinensis* Andersen, 1905 (skull relatively small; tibia short, length about 26 mm); Zhejiang, Anhui, Fujian, Jiangxi, Guangdong, Guangxi, Hunan; (2) *R. p. pearsonii* Horsfield, 1851 (skull large; tibia long, length about 29 mm); Xizang, Sichuan, Guizhou, Yunnan, Shaanxi, Hubei.
Natural History: This species has been taken from a very broad elevational range, from 600 to over 3,000 m. It is also known to hibernate in caves and bomb shelters, even when other species of *Rhinolophus* do not. Individuals were observed using feeding perches, from which they made short sallies, in bamboo thickets in Thailand. Young have been recorded in May and June. Echolocation calls are around 65 kHz.
Comments: The validity of *chinensis* as a subspecies was questioned by Csorba et al. (2003). This species is a member of the *pearsonii* group.
Conservation Status: China RL—LC.
References: Csorba et al. (2003); Robinson (1995).

Least Horseshoe Bat

Rhinolophus pusillus Temminck, 1834 MAP 347
菲菊头蝠 Fei Jutoufu

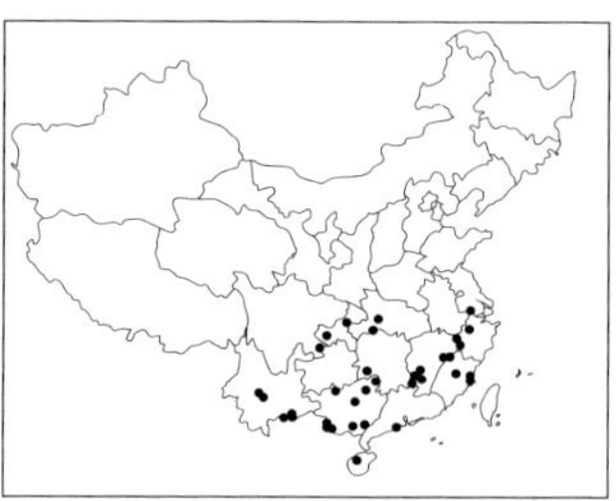

MAP 347. LEAST HORSESHOE BAT, *Rhinolophus pusillus*

Distinctive Characteristics: HB 38–42; T 13–26; HF 6–8; E 13–20; FA 33–40; GLS 14.8–16.8. Very similar to *Rhinolophus cornutus*, but size even smaller; tibia short, length 13.5–15 mm; wing membrane not very long; length of second digit of third digit less than 1.5 times of that of first digit; basal part of middle rictus of horseshoe lobe with two small mamillary process; sellar leaf narrow, its basal part distinctly wider than top; connecting process triangular or hornlike; lancet hastate, varying from equilateral to elongate; hair color brown, with off-white basal parts; small premolar (P2) in upper jaw lies in toothrow, clearly with small cusps; most premolars in lower jaw also lie in toothrow.
Distribution: S and SW China; extending across S Asia. Four subspecies in China: (1) *R. p. calidus* Allen, 1923 (pelage color lighter, bright brown); Fujian, Guangxi, Guangdong, Guizhou; (2) *R. p. lakkhanae* Yoshiyuki, 1990; Wang (2003) allocates specimens from Yunnan to this subspecies; (3) *R. p. parcus* Allen, 1928 (pelage color darker, rust brown); Hainan Island; (4) *R. p. szechwanus* Andersen, 1918 (pelage color dark brown); Sichuan, Guizhou, Hubei (Wang 2003 also lists it from Xizang).

Natural History: Little known from China, but in other parts of SE Asia most specimens have come from between 1,000 and 1,500 m. They are known to roost in caves in numbers up to 1,500 and in smaller colonies in houses. They have been noted foraging low over bamboo clumps in limestone areas and have also been taken in primary forest. Echolocation calls of 90–95 kHz were recorded in Thailand.
Comments: A member of the *pusillus* species group. The taxonomy of this species remains somewhat confused (Csorba et al. 2003). Subspecies limits are not clear, and likely to be modified with additional study.
Conservation Status: China RL—NT; although it nearly met the criteria for VU B1ab(i, ii, iii).
References: Robinson (1995); Robinson et al. (1996).

King Horseshoe Bat

Rhinolophus rex Allen, 1923 MAP 348
贵州菊头蝠 Guizhou Jutoufu

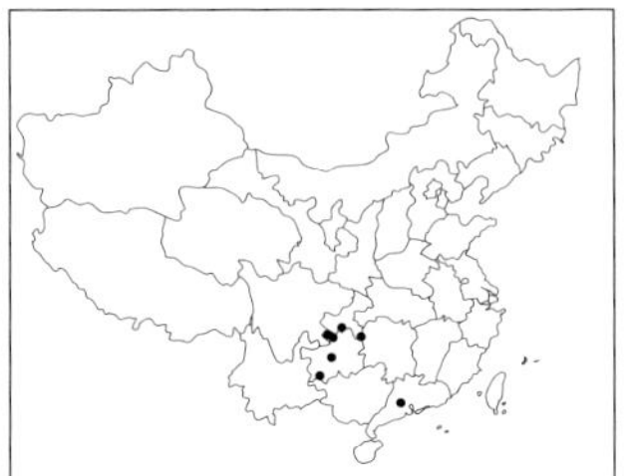

MAP 348. KING HORSESHOE BAT, *Rhinolophus rex*

Distinctive Characteristics: HB 50; T 32–38; HF 9; E 29–35; FA 55–63; GLS 23–24. Similar to *Rhinolophus paradoxolophus*, but size noticeably larger; tibia length about 21 mm; antitragus well developed; third, fourth, and fifth metacarpal bones about equal in size; length of second phalanx of third digit less than 1.5 times that of first phalanx; horseshoe lobe of nose leaf very wide, breadth 3–4 mm more than that rostrum, with a deep indentation in middle; sides of basal part without small adhering leaf; inner edges of nostrils linked with aliform lateral leaf of basal sellar leaf to form cup-shaped lobe; sellar leaf tall, with slightly protruding lateral margins and round top; conjoined leaf undeveloped, low and of simple arc form, growing out from very underside of top of back sellar leaf; apical lobe very short and completely covered by sellar leaf, its lateral margins slightly protruding, length about 1/3 of that of sellar leaf; compound hairs very long, length of dorsal hairs 16 mm; dorsal pelage brown and ventral surface light; tympanic bullae well developed; breadth of skull wider than that of zygomatic process; palatal bridge very long; small premolars in upper and lower jaw all in toothrow.
Distribution: Sichuan, Guangxi, Guangdong, and Guizhou. Endemic.
Natural History: Little known other than Allen's (1928) report of individuals hibernating in a cave in Sichuan.
Comments: Monotypic species in the *philippinensis* group.
Conservation Status: China RL—EN A2cd + 3cd; B2b(i, ii, iii)c(i, ii, iii). IUCN RL—VU B1 + 2c ver 2.3 (1994).
References: Allen (1928).

Rufous Horseshoe Bat

Rhinolophus rouxii Temminck, 1835 MAP 349
鲁氏菊头蝠 Lushi Jutoufu

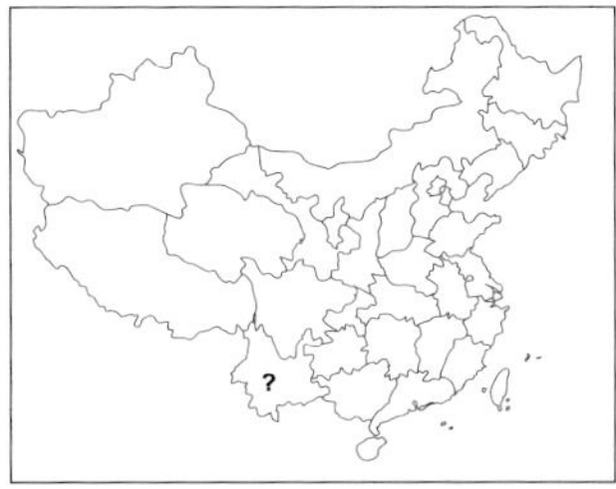

MAP 349. RUFOUS HORSESHOE BAT, *Rhinolophus rouxii*

Distinctive Characteristics: HB 59; T 20–33; HF 22; E 14–22; FA 44–53; GLS 20–23. Similar to *Rhinolophus sinicus*, but slightly larger; metacarpals increase slightly in size from third to fifth; horseshoe narrow (7–9 mm), with small secondary leaflet; sella parallel-sided with round summit; connecting process rounded; lancet hastate with narrow tip; soft, silky pelage brown to rufous dorsally and slightly paler below; length of palatal bridge of skull about 1/3 of upper toothrow; small premolar (P2) in upper jaw lies inside toothrow, so anterior premolar (P2) and posterior premolar (P4) separated.
Distribution: Wang (2003) recorded a single record from W Yunnan (Gaoligong mountain); extending from Sri Lanka through India to Vietnam.
Natural History: Nothing known of this species from China. In India, the species is restricted to forested areas with high rainfall below 1,500 m. Colonies of dozens to hundreds of individuals are known from caves, tunnels, hollow trees, wells, and temples. Females may form maternity colonies while males scatter. They have been reported to feed on grasshoppers, moths, beetles, termites, mosquitoes, and other diptera. In India, copulation occurs in December and parturition in May and June. Apparently, young are born in October in Sri Lanka. Echo-location calls range from 73 to 85 kHz.
Comments: *R. rouxii*, a member of the *rouxii* species group, is included in the fauna of China solely on the basis of Wang's (2003) single record. Otherwise, the closest known locality is in Myanmar. This species is remarkably similar to *Rhinolophus sinicus*, which is relatively common in China.
Conservation Status: China RL—NA.
References: Brosset (1962); Phillips (1980); Wang (2003).

Shortridge's Horseshoe Bat

PLATE 34
MAP 350

Rhinolophus shortridgei Anderson, 1918
短翼菊头蝠 Duanyi Jutoufu

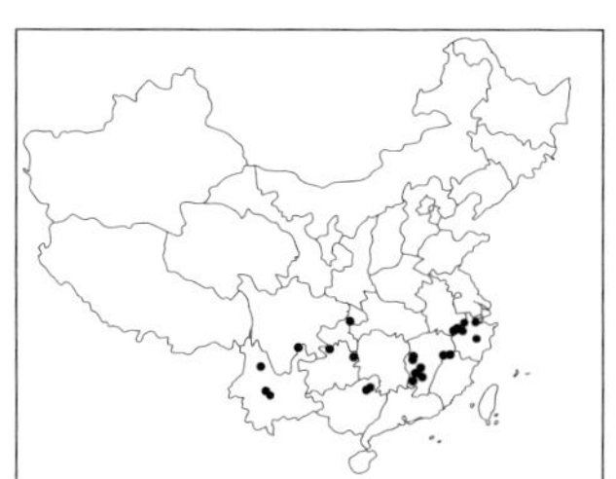

MAP 350. SHORTRIDGE'S HORSESHOE BAT, *Rhinolophus shortridgei*

Distinctive Characteristics: HB 51–59; T 18–25; HF 9; E 16–20; FA 39–43; GLS 16.8–18.7. Size medium; tail slightly longer than tibia; wing membrane not very elongated; length of second phalanx of third digit less than two times that of first phalanx; third metacarpal bone also not elongated, its length about equal to that of fourth and fifth; nostril not completely covered by nose leaf, which possesses an indentation in the middle with a small depression on either side; basal sellar leaf wider than top, middle part slightly recessed; lower lip with three vertical grooves; hair color brown; basal hair black gray; ventral surface relatively pale; mandible of skull long, its length more than 1/4 and a little less than 1/3 that of upper toothrow; breadth of zygomatic process roughly equal to, or slightly exceeding, mastoidal breadth; small premolar (P2) in upper jaw lies in toothrow; small premolar (p3) in lower jaw variable but frequently lies outside toothrow; anterior premolar not in contact with large premolar.

Distribution: SW China (Yunnan, Sichuan, Guizhou, Hunan, Guangxi, and Fujian; Wang 2003 also lists it from Hubei, Hainan, and Guangdong); extending to India and Myanmar.

Natural History: Although it has been collected in seasonally dry dipterocarp forest in Myanmar (specimen in USNM), little is known of the natural history of this species.

Comments: *R. shortridgei* is a member of the *pusillus* species group. It was formerly thought to be a subspecies of *R. lepidus*, but we (DEW) collected the two in sympatry in Myanmar.

Conservation Status: China RL–LC.

References: Csorba et al. (2003).

Thai Horseshoe Bat

MAP 351

Rhinolophus siamensis Gyldenstolpe, 1917
泰国菊头蝠 Taiguo Jutoufu

Distinctive Characteristics: HB 38; T 14; HF 8–9; E 19–22; FA 36–41; GLS 17–18. Size small; ears large in relation to head; antitragus small; zygomatic breadth 8.2 mm; maxillary length 6–7 mm; third metacarpal slightly shorter than fourth and fifth; fur short, but not woolly; upperparts pale brown and venter buffy; nose leaf large and covers the upper lip; sella broad and rounded, well-haired; lancet triangular; connecting process rounded on top; lower lip with three grooves; first upper premolar in toothrow and with cusp; lower p3 small and outside toothrow.

Distribution: Yunnan; extending to Thailand, Laos, and Vietnam.

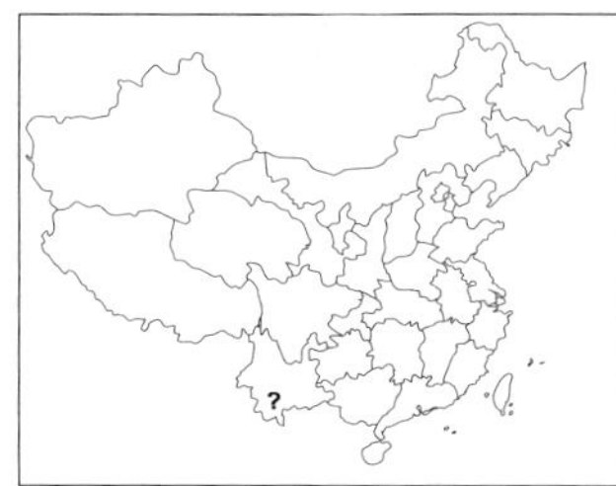

MAP 351. THAI HORSESHOE BAT, *Rhinolophus siamensis*

Natural History: Echolocation calls have been recorded at 51 kHz (Francis and Habersetzer 1998).

Comments: *Rhinolophus siamensis* is a member of the *philippinensis* species group. Frequently considered a subspecies of *R. macrotis*, but the two have been taken in sympatry in Laos (Francis et al. 1996).

Conservation Status: China RL–LC.

References: Francis and Habersetzer (1998); Francis et al. (1996).

Chinese Rufous Horseshoe Bat

PLATE 34
MAP 352

Rhinolophus sinicus Andersen, 1905
中华菊头蝠 Zhonghua Jutoufu

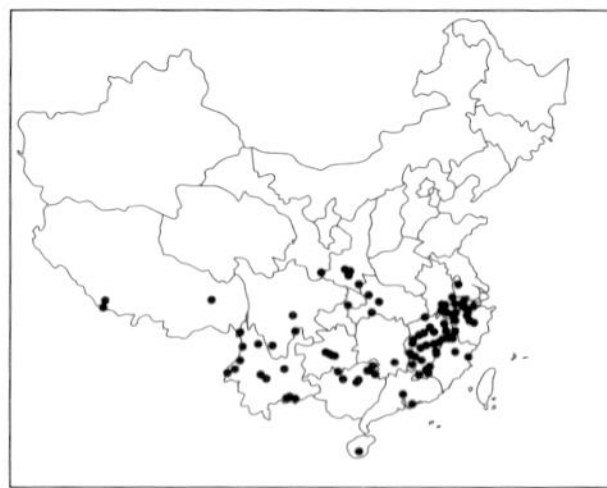

MAP 352. CHINESE RUFOUS HORSESHOE BAT, *Rhinolophus sinicus*

Distinctive Characteristics: HB 43–53; T 21–30; HF 7–10; E 15–20; FA 43–56; GLS 18–23. Size medium; similar to *R. rouxii* and *R. thomasi*, but with relatively longer wings than *rouxii*; slightly larger than *R. thomasi*; second phalanx of third digit smaller than or close to 1.5 times of first phalanx in size; wing membrane attaches at heel; metacarpal bones long, third about 33–38 mm; either side of horseshoe nose leaf with an adhering, secondary leaf; horseshoe nose leaf breadth 8–9.2 mm; lateral margins of sellar leaf nearly parallel, its top wide and round; connecting process low and round; upper part of apical lobe slender; 2/3 section of basal dorsal hair brownish white, hair tip reddish brown; ventrum brownish white; length of palatal bridge of skull about 1/3 of upper toothrow; small premolar (P2) in upper jaw lies outside toothrow; cingula of lower anterior premolar (p2) and posterior

premolar (p4) usually in contact with each other, or only a little separated.
Distribution: C, S and SW China; extending across the Indo-Malayan realm. Two subspecies in China: (1) *R. s. septentrionalis* Sanborn, 1939; Yunnan; (2) *R. s. sinicus* Anderson, 1905; Anhui, Zhejiang, Jiangsu, Hubei, Guangdong, Guizhou, Xizang, Fujian, Sichuan.
Natural History: This species is reasonably common in S China and occurs as high as 2,800 m in India, where it is also know to hibernate. Colony size is variable, ranging from a few individuals to several hundred, and females form maternity colonies during the reproductive season.
Comments: *Rhinolophus sinicus* is a member of the *rouxii* group. Andersen (1905) described *sinicus* as a small subspecies of *R. rouxii*. Thomas (2000) separated *sinicus* as a distinct species based on both phenetic and molecular data. Wang (2003) lists *sinicus* as a subspecies of *rouxii*, and *septentrionalis* as a subspecies of *thomasi*.
Conservation Status: China RL–LC.
References: Bates and Harrison (1997); Wroughton (1914).

Little Nepalese Horseshoe Bat

Rhinolophus subbadius Blyth, 1844 MAP 353
浅褐菊头蝠 Qianhe Jutoufu

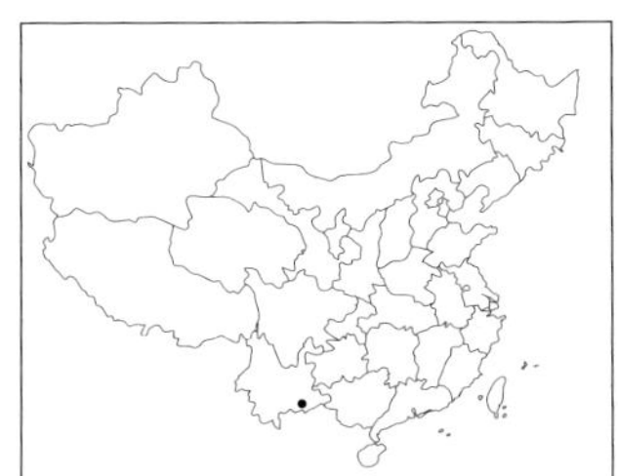

MAP 353. LITTLE NEPALESE HORSESHOE BAT, *Rhinolophus subbadius*

Distinctive Characteristics: HB 35–37; T 16–19; HF 7–8; E 14–18; FA 33–38; GLS 14–15. Size small, smallest species of *Rhinolophus*; ears small to medium; sella like *R. pusilla*, but superior connecting process more hornlike; lancet short and broad; lower lip with three grooves; third metacarpal slightly shorter than fourth and fifth; pelage cinnamon brown dorsally, with grayish bases and brownish tips; underparts slightly paler. Skull small and narrow; upper toothrow length short; first upper premolar small, but in toothrow.
Distribution: Yunnan; extending to India, Nepal, Vietnam, and Myanmar.
Natural History: This species is poorly known, and nothing is known of its habits in China. Extralimitally, they are known from lowland forests.
Comments: Hill (1962) referred a specimen in the British Museum to this species, and it remains the only record from China. *R. subbadius* belongs to the *pusillus* species group.
Conservation Status: China RL–DD.
References: Bates and Harrison (1997); Csorba et al. (2003).

Thomas's Horseshoe Bat

Rhinolophus thomasi Andersen, 1905 MAP 354
托氏菊头蝠 Tuoshi Jutoufu

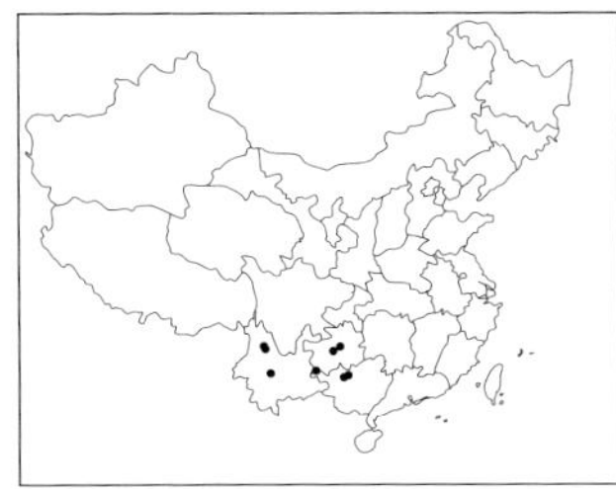

MAP 354. THOMAS'S HORSESHOE BAT, *Rhinolophus thomasi*

Distinctive Characteristics: HB 48–50; T 18–28; HF 8–10; E 16–20; FA 40–48; GLS 18–20. Similar to *Rhinolophus sinicus*, but size slightly smaller; metacarpal bones short, length of third 30–34 mm; second phalanx of third digit longer than 1/2 of the length of first phalanx; horseshoe lobe medium, breadth 7.2–8.9 mm; apical lobe short; lateral margins of sellar leaf parallel; both upper premolar (P2) and lower premolar (p3) small and outside toothrow; hence, canine and large premolar (P4) in upper jaw contact, as do small premolar (p2) and large premolar (p4) in lower jaw.
Distribution: SW China; extending down the Indochina Peninsula.
Natural History: Nothing is known from China, but this species is known to roost in caves, and with other species of *Rhinolophus* in other areas.
Comments: A member of the *rouxii* group, *R. thomasi* is monotypic. Wang (2003) assigns Chinese material to the subspecies *R. t. latifolius*, but we follow Csorba et al. (2003) in relegating *latifolius* as a synonym of the nominate form.
Conservation Status: China RL–VU A1cd. IUCN RL–LR/nt ver 2.3 (1994).
References: Duckworth et al. (1999); Lekagul and McNeely (1977); Van Peenen et al. (1969).

Trefoil Horseshoe Bat

Rhinolophus trifoliatus Temminck, 1834 MAP 355
三叶菊头蝠 Sanye Jutoufu

Distinctive Characteristics: HB 62–65; T 30–35; HF 13; E 22–27; FA 50–54; GLS 21–25. Medium-sized and most similar to *R. luctus*, from which it differs in having a yellowish nose leaf. Base of ear also yellowish; nose leaf broad (10.5–12.4 mm); sella narrow with basal lappets; connecting process low; lancet long and emarginated; lower lip with single groove; metacarpals increase in size from third through fifth; fur long and somewhat woolly, pale buff or brownish above, and grayish brown below. Skull robust with zygomatic breadth exceeding mastoid breadth; distinct supraorbital and sagittal crests; palatal bridge about 1/3 of upper toothrow length; upper P2 small and variably placed in toothrow; lower p2 lies outside toothrow or is missing.
Distribution: Included on the basis of a single specimen from Guizhou (Jinsha) listed by Wang

(2003); extending to NE India, Myanmar, Thailand, Malay Peninsula, Borneo, Sumatra, and outlying islands.
Natural History: Nothing known from China, but known primarily from lowland evergreen forests in other areas. Echolocation calls were recorded at 51.2 kHz in Malaysia.

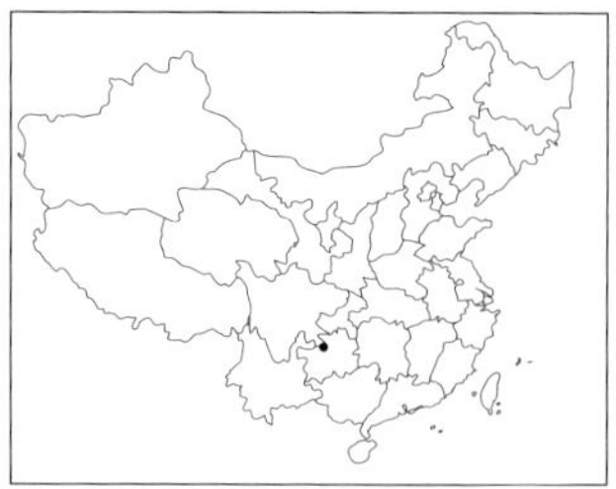

MAP 355. TREFOIL HORSESHOE BAT, *Rhinolophus trifoliatus*

Comments: A member of the *trifoliatus* species group, the Chinese population is presumably referable to *R. t. edax*.
Conservation Status: China RL—EN C2a(i, ii).
References: Francis and Habersetzer (1998); Koopman (1994).

Dobson's Horseshoe Bat

Rhinolophus yunanensis Dobson, 1872 MAP 356
云南菊头蝠 Yunnan Jutoufu

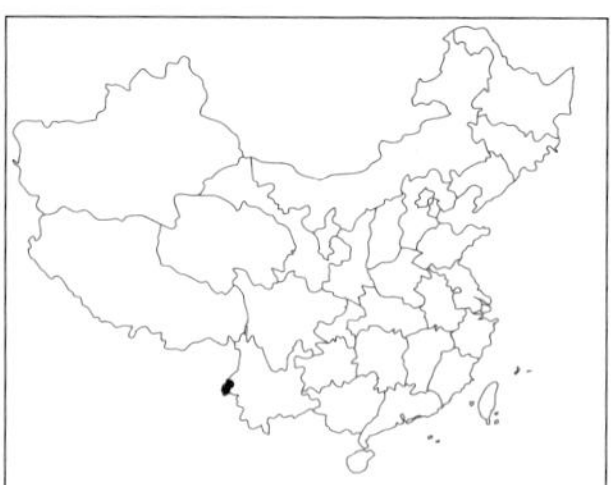

MAP 356. DOBSON'S HORSESHOE BAT, *Rhinolophus yunanensis*

Distinctive Characteristics: HB 60–68; T 18–26; HF 12–14; E 23–32; FA 54–60; GLS 24–28. Size large for genus. Most similar to *R. pearsonii*, but larger. Horseshoe broad (12.5–14 mm); sella wide at base and tapering toward tip; lancet long and triangular; lower lip with single groove; third metacarpal shortest and fifth longest; fur woolly and dense, pale brown or gray dorsally and paler ventrally. Skull similar to *pearsonii*, with zygomatic width greater than mastoid breadth; dentition heavy, with massive canines and posterior premolars; anterior upper premolar large and in toothrow; p2 extends slightly outside the toothrow.
Distribution: Yunnan; extending to Thailand, Myanmar, and India.
Natural History: Apparently most common at middle elevations from about 600 to 1,300 m, this species has been collected from bamboo thickets, and also from thatched roofs.
Comments: *R. yunanensis* is a member of the *pearsonii* species group. It was formerly considered a subspecies of *pearsonii*, but recent workers have separated it as a distinct species.
Conservation Status: China RL—EN A2abc; B1ab(i, ii, iii) + 2ab(i, ii, iii). IUCN RL—LR/nt ver 2.3 (1994).
References: Bates and Harrison (1997); Hill (1986); Lekagul and McNeely (1977); Yoshiyuki (1990).

Family Hipposideridae—Old World Leaf-nosed Bats

蹄蝠科 Tifu Ke—蹄蝠 Tifu

Very similar to Rhinolophidae, but nose-leaf structure different; nose leaf includes a horseshoe anterior lobe, with a few leaflets on either side of its anterior extremity; behind horseshoe lobe is a transversely protuberant middle lobe (corresponding to sellar leaf of Rhinolophidae), further behind it is a transversal apical lobe (corresponding to apical lobe of Rhinolophidae), which is sometimes separated into four sections by a longitudinal ridge; also without tragus. Dental formula: 1.1.1–2.3 / 2.1.2.3 = 28–30; second digit of wing only possesses metacarpal bones, other digits each with two phalanges; each toe with two phalanges. Distributed in tropical and subtropical zones of the Eastern Hemisphere,

Key to the Chinese Genera of Hipposideridae

1a. Tail very reduced or absent, length < 2 mm; incisors and canines in lower jaw not touching; cusps of upper molars strongly developed — *Coelops*
b. Tail normal; incisors and canines in lower jaw closely touching; cusps of upper molars normal — 2
2a. Apical lobe of nose leaf separated into three narrow and sharp leaflets; cusps of upper incisors dichotomous; posterior zygomatic arch extremely developed, forming a high, vertical layer, its length equal to distance from third molar to glenoid cavity of jaw — *Aselliscus*
b. Apical lobe of nose leaf with different structure; cusps of upper incisors not dichotomous; posterior zygomatic arch extremely developed, forming a vertical layer, its length conspicuously less than distance from third molar to glenoid cavity of jaw — *Hipposideros*

east to Oceania; in China restricted to southern regions, including southwestern, southern, and central China. Of nine genera, three are known to occur in China.

Genus *Aselliscus*—Old World Leaf-nosed Bats

三叶蹄蝠属 Sanyetifu Shu—三叶蹄蝠 Sanyetifu

Size similar to that of *Hipposideros*; tail normal; structure of nose leaf different, upper edges of apical lobe noticeably recessed, forming three linked sharp leaflets; skull and teeth as in *Hipposideros*; posterior of zygomatic arch especially developed, forming a high and vertical layer, its height about equal to distance from third molar to glenoid cavity of mandible; cusps of upper incisors dichotomous. Of two species, only one occurs in China.

Stoliczka's Asian Trident Bat

PLATE 35
MAP 357

Aselliscus stoliczkanus (Dobson, 1871)

三叶蹄蝠 Sanye Tifu

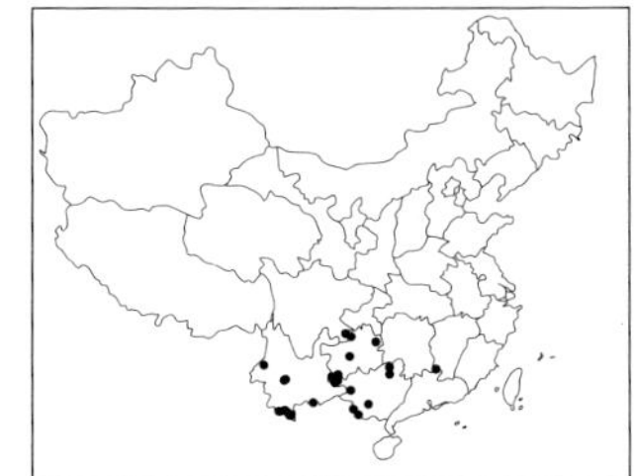

MAP 357. STOLICZKA'S ASIAN TRIDENT BAT, *Aselliscus stoliczkanus*

Distinctive Characteristics: HB 40–50; T 30–40; HF 9–10; E 10–14; FA 39–44; GLS 16. Size very small; fur long; basal part of dorsal hairs nearly white; hair tip brown; ventral surface paler than dorsum; upper margin of nose leaf with three distinct points; two accessory lateral leaflets on each side of nose leaf. Braincase low, rostrum deep, and sagittal crest well developed; postorbital processes lacking; first upper premolar lies in toothrow.
Distribution: Yunnan, Guangxi, and Guizhou (known records few); monotypic.
Natural History: A colony in Thailand roosted in loose association in limestone caves, with individuals at least 30 cm from one another. Reproductively active females have been collected in May and June in Laos and Vietnam.
Comments: Allen (1938) listed this species as *Triaenops wheeleri*.
Conservation Status: China RL—NT; although it nearly met the criteria for VU A1c.
References: Phillips (1967); Sanborn (1952); U Tun Yin (1993).

Genus *Coelops*—Tailless Leaf-nosed Bats

无尾蹄蝠属 Wuweitifu Shu—无尾蹄蝠 Wuweitifu

Tail especially reduced; well-developed antitragus; horseshoe lobe of nose leaf very wide, separated into two broad parts by a crevice in middle, and with a long and narrow leaflet on either side of basal part. Skull as in *Hipposideros*; rostrum not bulging. Dental formula as in *Hipposideros*: 1.1.2.3/2.1.2.3 = 30; upper canines with conspicuous cingula; inner sides of crowns of upper molars contracted; tooth edges developed; lower jaw with a small diastema between outer incisors and canines. Of two species, only one occurs in China.

East Asian Tailless Leaf-Nosed Bat

PLATE 35
MAP 358

Coelops frithii Blyth, 1848

无尾蹄蝠 Wuwei Tifu

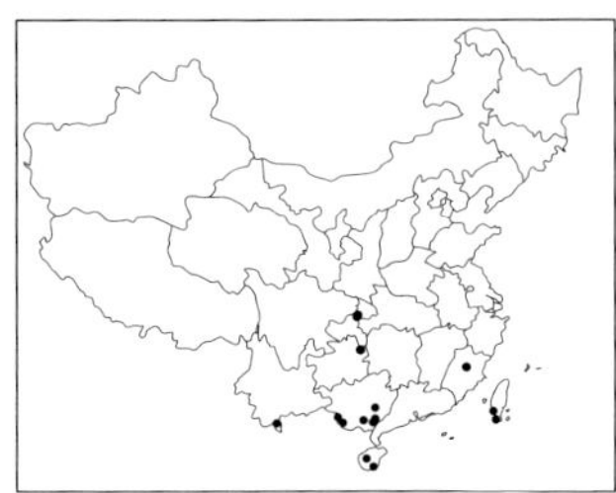

MAP 358. EAST ASIAN TAILLESS LEAF-NOSED BAT, *Coleops frithii*

Distinctive Characteristics: HB 38–50; T 0; HF 5–9; E 11–15; FA 35–42; GLS 16. Size very small; compound hairs slender and thick, basal part grayish black and tip brown; tips of ventral hairs slightly brownish white; rostrum of skull bulging, but not as distinctly as in *Hipposideros bicolor*; interorbital region conspicuously contracted; skull very inflated, its lateral sides extrude over zygomatic arch.
Distribution: SE China; extending across Indochina. Three subspecies in China: (1) *C. f. formosanus* Horikawa, 1928; Taiwan; (2) *C. f. inflatus* Miller, 1928; Fujian, Guangdong, Guangxi, Hainan; (3) *C. f. sinicus* Allen, 1923; Yunnan, Sichuan.
Natural History: The holotype of *sinicus* was found in a warm cave where it seemed to be hibernating. In Taiwan, this species is found in manmade structures, such as old pillboxes. Basically a forest species, it has been found in small colonies in hollow trees extralimitally. Breeding females are known from January and March in Java.
Comments: All three subspecies were named originally as species. Subspecies limits are poorly understood in this widespread, but rare, species.
Conservation Status: China RL—VU A1cd.
References: Bates and Harrison (1997); Nowak (1994).

Key to the Chinese Species of *Hipposideros*

1.a.	Size large; forearm length ≥ 70 mm	2
b.	Size small; forearm length < 70 mm	5
2.a.	Forearm > 80 mm	3
b.	Forearm < 80 mm	4
3.a.	Basal horseshoe lobe of nose leaf with four leaflets on either side; skull rises gradually from rostrum to front	*Hipposideros armiger*
b.	Basal horseshoe lobe of nose leaf with two leaflets on either side; rostrum of skull flat, not rising	*Hippodideros pratti*
4.a.	Transverse accessory bilobed structure behind posterior leaf	*Hippodideros lylei*
b.	No transverse accessory bilobed structure	*Hipposideros turpis*
5.a.	Forearm length > 50 mm	6
b.	Forearm length < 50 mm	7
6.a.	Ear length ≥ 23 mm	*Hippodideros grandis*
b.	Ear length ≤ 23 mm	*Hipposideros larvatus*
7.a.	Vomer with thick posterior projection	*Hipposideros pomona*
b.	Vomer with thin, bladelike posterior projection	*Hipposideros fulvus*

Genus *Hipposideros*—Old World Leaf-nosed Bats

蹄蝠属 Tifu Shu—蹄蝠 Tifu

Form similar to that of *Rhinolophus*, but structure of nose leaf very different (see above, Hipposideridae); each toe only with two phalanges; external ears well developed; tragus absent; basal parts of anterior ears with large antitragi on outer side; tail developed, longer than femur; rostrum of skull rounded; interorbital region contracted; sagittal crest low; interorbital without sagittal crest; auditory bullae small; cochleas large; skull rises abruptly from rostrum to braincase; posterior zygomatic arch extends upwards, forming a vertical layer, its length conspicuously less than distance from third molar (M3) to glenoid cavity. Dental formula: 1.1.2.3/2.1.2.3 = 30; M3 smaller than that of *Rhinolophus*; one fewer lower small premolar than *Rhinolophus*; lower jaw with four incisors, tightly arranged between canines without spaces. Geographical distribution matches that of *Rhinolophus*; of 67 species of *Hipposideros*, 8 are known to occur in China.

Great Leaf-Nosed Bat

PLATE 35
MAP 359

Hipposideros armiger (Hodgson, 1835)
大蹄蝠 Da Tifu

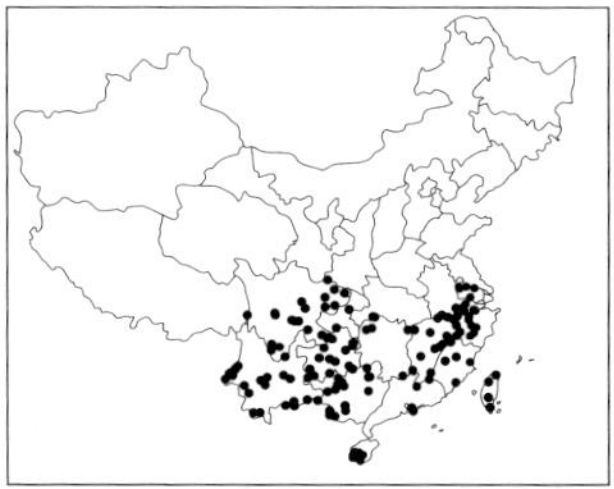

MAP 359. GREAT LEAF-NOSED BAT, *Hipposideros armiger*

Distinctive Characteristics: HB 80–110; T 48–70; HF 13–17; E 26–35; FA 82–99; GLS 31–33. Size very large; third and fourth metacarpal bones about equal in length, fifth slightly shorter; calcar half as long as tibia; ears large and sharp, with recessed posterior edges; large horseshoe anterior lobe of nose leaf without indentation in middle, but with four leaflets on either side of basal part; behind it is a transverse middle lobe, which possesses a protuberant vertical ridge; behind middle lobe is apical lobe, with three vertical ridges; behind apical lobe of adult male are two thickened dermal lobes, with a frontal gland in middle; wing membrane starts at anterior extremity of tibia. Rostrum of skull distinctly slopes up from anterior to posterior, and links with well-developed sagittal crest in interorbital region; posterior of zygomatic arch vertically expanded, but its length less than distance from third upper molar to glenoid cavity of jaw.
Distribution: C and SE China, S of the Yangtze River; widely distributed in the Indo-Malayan realm. Three subspecies in China: (1) *H. a. armiger* (Hodgson, 1835); Jiangxi, Zhejiang, Guangdong, Hong Kong, Macao, Guangxi, Hainan, Hunan, Jiangsu, Anhui, Yunnan, Sichuan, Shaanxi, Guizhou; (2) *H. a. fujianensis* Zhen, 1987; Fujian; (3) *H. a. terasensis* Kishida, 1924; Taiwan.
Natural History: *Hipposideros armiger* is a widespread, colonial species found in a variety of habitats. They are known to inhabit caves and a variety of manmade structures. Colonies can number in the hundreds of individuals, and they co-occur with species of *Rhinolophus* and others. They forage both close to the ground and occasionally above the canopy of the forest. Breeding activity tends to be in the summer, and two young are born at a time.
Comments: A member of the *armiger* species group, this is one of the largest species of the genus. *H. a. swinhoei* Peters, 1871 is considered a synonym of the

nominate form. Some recent workers have considered *terasensis* a separate species.
Conservation Status: China RL—LC.
References: Hendrichsen et al. (2001); Lin et al. (1997); Yoshiyuki (1991a).

Fulvus Leaf-Nosed Bat

Hipposideros fulvus Gray, 1838 MAP 360
大耳小蹄蝠 Da'er Xiaotifu

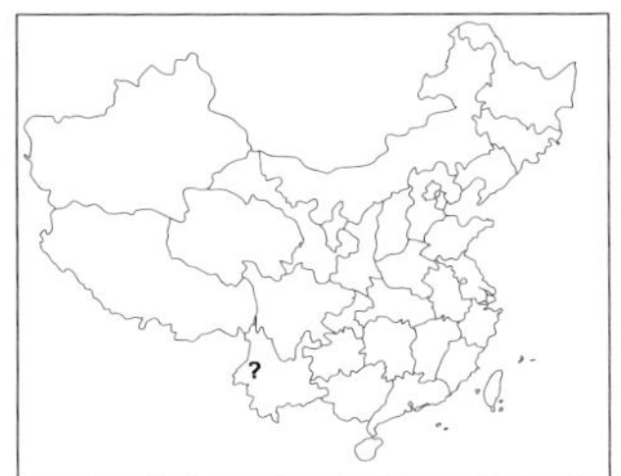

MAP 360. FULVUS LEAF-NOSED BAT, *Hipposideros fulvus*

Distinctive Characteristics: HB 40–50; T 24–35; HF 6–10; E 19–26; FA 38–44; GLS 15–16; Wt 8–9 g. Size medium; ears large, with rounded tips; third metacarpal shorter than fourth; feet small; nose leaf about 5 mm wide; pelage color variable, ranging from dull yellow through pale gray to golden orange. Rostrum robust, but braincase fragile; frontal depression lacking; zygoma flared posterio-laterally.
Distribution: W Yunnan (Wang 2003); extending from Afghanistan to Vietnam.
Natural History: Nothing is known from China, but elsewhere it is common in a variety of habitats, ranging from dry plains to upland forests. It is also found in both wet and dry areas. Roosts include wells and buildings, as well as caves. Colonies may range from a few individuals to several hundred. Flight is slow and maneuverable, and they sometimes forage close to the ground, in addition to the canopy. Breeding begins in November, and parturition occurs in April and May.
Comments: A member of the *bicolor* species group, *H. fulvus* has been confused with that species in the literature.
Conservation Status: China RL—NA.
References: Bates and Harrison (1997).

Grand Leaf-Nosed Bat

Hipposideros grandis Allen, 1936 MAP 361
缅甸蹄蝠 Miandian Tifu

Distinctive Characteristics: HB 60–80; T 30–45; HF 10–15; E 20–23; FA 52–65; GLS 20–22. Size large; two color phases, dark brown and reddish brown; ventral hairs smoky gray with brownish tips; mantle pale brown; ears, nose leaf, and wings brown; glandular frontal sac on throat, most prominent in males; ears large and triangular; nose leaf with three supplementary leaflets on each side; anterior leaf simple, with medial notch; skull large, with slender zygomatic arches and slight supraorbital ridges; first upper premolar tightly compressed between canine and second premolar.
Distribution: Yunnan; extending to Myanmar, Thailand, and Vietnam.
Natural History: Nothing is known that is unequivocally attributable to this species.
Comments: Member of the *larvatus* species group, and previously thought to be conspecific with *larvatus*.

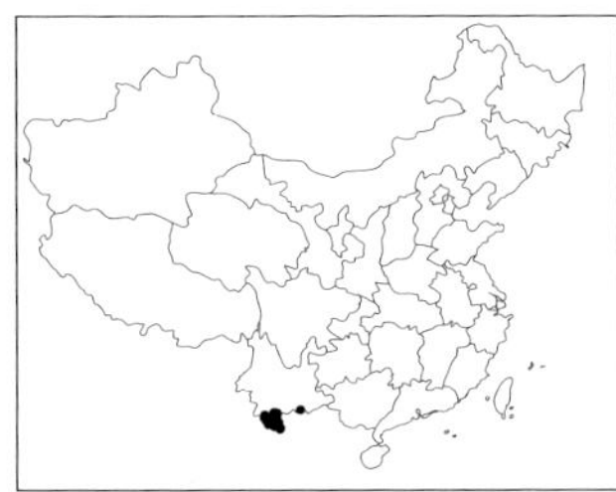
MAP 361. GRAND LEAF-NOSED BAT, *Hipposideros grandis*

Conservation Status: China RL—NA.
References: Kitchener and Maryanto (1993).

Intermediate Leaf-Nosed Bat

PLATE 35
Hipposideros larvatus (Horsfield, 1823) MAP 362
中蹄蝠 Zhong Tifu

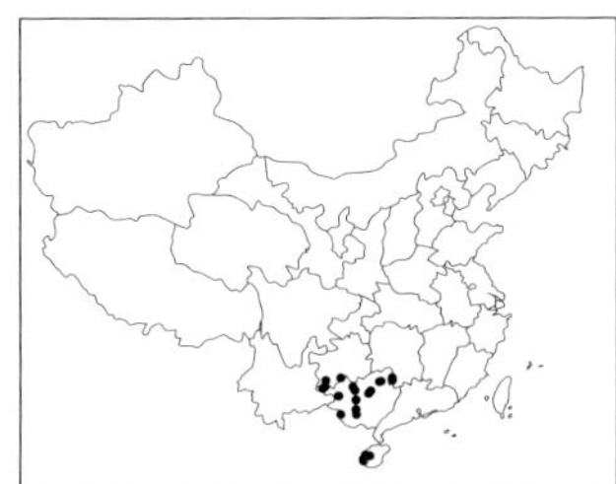
MAP 362. INTERMEDIATE LEAF-NOSED BAT, *Hipposideros larvatus*

Distinctive Characteristics: HB 74–78; T 37–44; HF 10–15; E 23–26; FA 56–69; GLS 23. Size medium; ears very large; horseshoe lobe of nose leaf with indentations in middle, outer sides of its basal part with three leaflets and frontal glands; wing membrane starts at the 1/5 section of anterior tibia; pelage color nearly grayish puce; ventral surface slightly paler; basal hair pale brown gray; rostrum of skull slightly rounded; sagittal crest developed; supraorbital ridge inconspicuous; interorbital region long and narrow; canines without grooves and cingula.
Distribution: Hainan Island, Guangdong, Guangxi, and Guizhou; extending from India across Indochina. Chinese subspecies: *H. l. poutensis* Allen, 1906.
Natural History: This species has been taken from sea level up to 1,000 m. It occupies diurnal roosts in caves, mine shafts, and pagodas. Little is known of its habits in China.

Comments: A member of the *larvatus* species group, this species does not include *grandis*, with which it has been confused in the literature. Wang (2003) lists both *grandis* and *alongensis* (actually *H. turpis*) as subspecies of *larvatus*.
Conservation Status: China RL—VU A2abcd + 3abcd.
References: Hill (1963); Kitchener and Maryanto (1993); Sinha (1999); Topál (1993).

Shield-Faced Leaf-Nosed Bat

Hipposideros lylei Thomas, 1913 MAP 363
鞘面蹄蝠 Qiaomian Tifu

MAP 363. SHIELD-FACED LEAF-NOSED BAT, *Hipposideros lylei*

Distinctive Characteristics: HB 72–95; T 48–55; HF 16–21; E 30; FA 78–84; GLS 28–29. Size large; color brownish or grayish, with buffy venter; nose leaf brownish pink; ears and wings pale brown; ears wide and triangular, without antitragus; frontal sac with winglike projections, prominent in males; lateral margins of anterior and posterior nose leaves continuous; skull large with moderate zygomata and low sagittal crest.
Distribution: Yunnan; extending to Myanmar, Thailand, Malaysia, and Vietnam.
Natural History: The type specimen was taken from a cave, but little else known about this species.
Comments: This species is a member of the *pratti* species group and has been considered a subspecies of that species in the past.
Conservation Status: China RL—NA.
References: Hendrichsen et al. (2001); Robinson et al. (2003).

Pomona Leaf-Nosed Bat

Hipposideros pomona Andersen, 1918 PLATE 35 MAP 364
双色蹄蝠 Shuangse Tifu

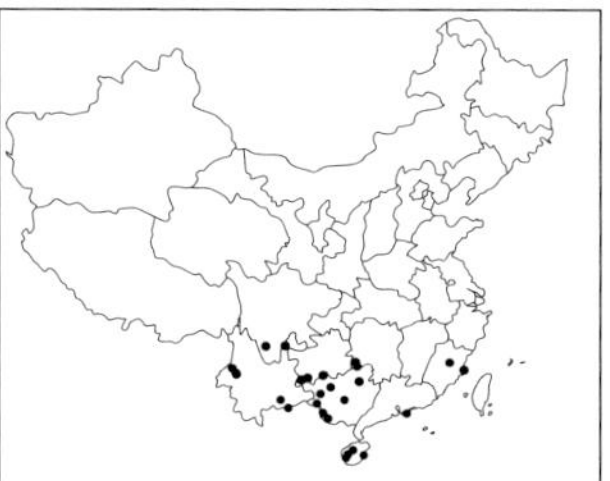

MAP 364. POMONA LEAF-NOSED BAT, *Hipposideros pomona*

Distinctive Characteristics: HB 36–52; T 28–35; HF 6–9; E 18–25; FA 38–43; GLS 17–18. Size small; ears very large and blunt, with protruding anterior edges, recessed posterior edges and a pair of small and low antitragi; nose-leaf structure simple, without leaflets on sides; horseshoe anterior lobe narrow, without indentation in middle; dorsal hair reddish brown; venter brownish white. Skull small, long, and narrow; rostrum slightly expanded; interorbital region narrow; skull wide; zygomatic arch protuberant, low and small; P2 very small, lying outside upper toothrow.
Distribution: Yunnan, Guangxi, Guangdong, Fujian, Hunan, and Hainan Island; extending from India to China, and also found in Malaysia, the Philippines, Sumatra, Java, and neighboring islands. Chinese subspecies: *H. p. sinensis* Andersen, 1918.
Natural History: Information on the life history of this species is lacking. Because of confusion over taxonomy, it is difficult to allocate published information to the proper species in many cases. Although *H. pomona* is widespread, it remains poorly known.
Comments: A member of the *bicolor* species group, *H. pomona* was once thought to be conspecific with *H. bicolor*. Wang (2003) lists *H. bicolor* from several localities in China, and those specimens may represent *H. gentilis* Andersen, 1918, a form now considered to be a subspecies of *H. pomona*. If both *gentilis* and *sinensis* prove to be valid subspecies, then it is possible that both forms occur in China. At present, there is insufficient material from China to make that determination.
Conservation Status: China RL—NT; although it nearly met the criteria for VU A2abc + 3abc.
References: Bates and Harrison (1997); Corbet and Hill (1992); Hill et al. (1986).

Pratt's Leaf-Nosed Bat

Hipposideros pratti Thomas, 1891 PLATE 35 MAP 365
普氏蹄蝠 Pushi Tifu

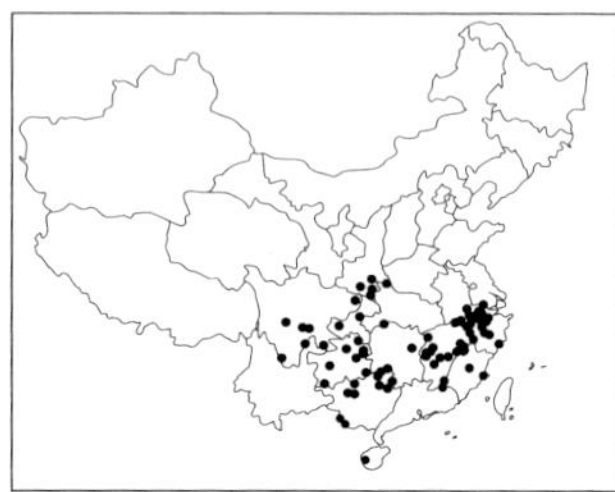

MAP 365. PRATT'S LEAF-NOSED BAT, *Hipposideros pratti*

Distinctive Characteristics: HB 91–110; T 50–62; HF 15–22; E 33–38; FA 75–90; GLS 28–35. Size similar to that of *Hipposideros armiger*; ears large and wide; antitragi low and small; horseshoe anterior lobe of nose leaf with only two leaflets on either side, and with concavity in middle; middle of apical lobe higher than sides; behind apical lobe are two large leaflets, with a bundle of long and straight hairs, especially developed in adult males; pelage color

brown or dark smoky brown; ventral surface light. Sagittal crest of skull developed; rostrum low and wide, not sloping from anterior to posterior; hence skull vertically declines forward from sagittal crest.
Distribution: SE China; extending to Myanmar, Thailand, Malaysia, and Vietnam.
Natural History: *Hipposideros pratti* is a cave-roosting species and has been found roosting in the same caves as *H. armiger*. Other than that, little is known of its natural history.
Comments: *H. pratti* is a member of the *pratti* species group.
Conservation Status: China RL—NT; although it nearly met the criteria for VU A1abc. IUCN RL—LR/nt ver 2.3 (1994).
References: Hendrichsen et al. (2001); Robinson et al. (2003).

Lesser Leaf-Nosed Bat
Hipposideros turpis Bangs, 1901 MAP 366
丑蹄蝠 Chou Tifu

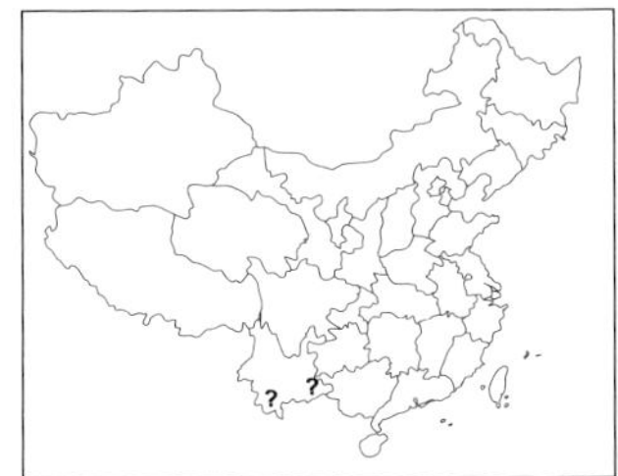

MAP 366. LESSER LEAF-NOSED BAT, *Hipposideros turpis*

Distinctive Characteristics: HB 66–88; T 44–59; HF 13–18; E 26–34; FA 66–80; GLS 26–27. Size large; nose leaf simple, with four lateral leaflets; ears large, triangular, with pointed tips; wings broad, attached to ankle; color brownish; individual hairs paler basally with darker tips. Skull robust; infraorbital foramen semicircular, with anterior margin anterior to center of first upper molar; interorbital region constricted and pentagonal.
Distribution: Included in Chinese fauna only through Wang (2003), who listed it under *H. larvatus*; also known from Japan (Ryukyu islands), Vietnam, and Thailand. Chinese subspecies: *H. t. alongensis* Bourret, 1942.
Natural History: This species has been netted in forested areas and collected from caves, but nothing is known of its life history.
Comments: *H. turpis* is a member of the *armiger* species group. It was considered by some to be conspecific with *armiger*. The subspecies *alongensis* was previously aligned with *H. larvatus*.
Conservation Status: China RL—VU A2abcd + 3abcd.
References: Hendrichsen et al. (2001); Hill (1963); Topál (1993); Yoshiyuki (1989).

Family Megadermatidae—False Vampire Bats
假吸血蝠科 Jiaxixuefu Ke—假吸血蝠 Jiaxixuefu

Ears especially large, with tragi divided; rostrum with projecting skin outgrowths, which form simple, long narrow nose leaf; second digit with a developed phalanx; third digit with two phalanges; tail lacking; premaxilla of skull reduced; orbital process very short, sometimes absent; upper jaw without incisors; canines projecting forward; metaconules developed. Dental formula: 0.1–1–2.3/2.1.2.3 = 26–28. Distributed in southern Asia, Africa, and Australia; of three genera, only one occurs in China.

Genus *Megaderma*—False Vampire Bats
假吸血蝠属 Jiaxixuefu Shu—假吸血蝠 Jiaxixuefu

Rostrum slightly shorter than half of greatest length of skull; its rear portion a little sunken, but braincase relatively flat; basisphenoid high and conspicuous; sagittal crest low and inconspicuous, its anterior extremity bifurcates and projects to undeveloped postorbital process; auditory bullae small, length less than breadth of basioccipital between them; canines in upper jaw developed with anterior and posterior cingulae; a small premolar between canine and posterior premolar in upper jaw slightly outside of toothrow; mesostyles all reduced; hypocones all absent, so "W" form of tooth crown slightly lost; incisors in lower jaw all slightly trifurcate, and arranged in a projecting arc; cusps of molars in lower jaw very close, inner cusps undeveloped; third lower molar without inner posterior cusp. Dental formula: 0.1.2.3/2.1.2.3 = 28. Distributed in southern Asia, including Sumatra, Kalimantan, and the Philippines. Of two species, only one occurs in China.

Greater False Vampire Bat
PLATE 34
Megaderma lyra
Geoffroy Saint-Hilaire, 1810 MAP 367
印度假吸血蝠 Yindu Jiaxixuefu

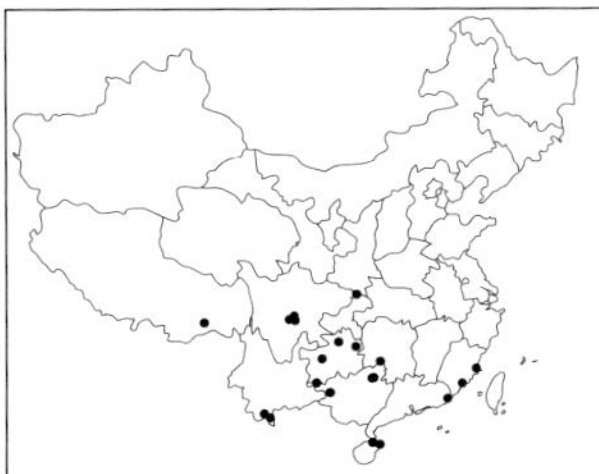

MAP 367. GREATER FALSE VAMPIRE BAT, *Megaderma lyra*

Distinctive Characteristics: HB 70–95; T 0; HF 14–20; E 31–45; FA 56–72; GLS 30. Size medium; ears very large and ovoid; inner edges of ears join on top of forehead; nose leaf large, protuberant and ovoid, with simple structure, length about 10 mm; tail reduced or absent; dorsum mouse-brown; ventrum paler; basal

hair dark gray and hair tip white; tibia longer than half of forearm length.
Distribution: C and S China; extending from the Indian subcontinent through Indochina to China. Chinese subspecies: *M. l. sinensis* Andersen and Wroughton, 1907; Fujian, Sichuan, Guangdong, Hainan, Xizang, Yunnan, Guizhou, Guangxi, Hunan.
Natural History: Tends to occupy more arid areas but is found in a variety of habitats. Frequently forages less than 1 m from the ground among trees and undergrowth in tropical forested habitats. Uses a variety of day roosts, including caves, pits in the ground, buildings, and hollow trees. Mating occurs from November through January, with one, or sometimes two, young born from April to June, after a gestation period of 150–160 days. Females form maternity colonies prior to parturition; otherwise both sexes occupy the same roost sites. The sex ratio is balanced at birth, and males are sexually mature by 15 months, females at 19 months. Young are nursed for two to three months, by which time they are capable of flight and foraging on their own. Females may carry the young with them during foraging until the pups are two ro three weeks old, at which point they leave them behind in the day roost, or in a special night roost. These bats are highly social animals, forming colonies of a few to dozens of animals. A seasonal colony of 1,500–2,000 was reported in India. Most individuals roost with some space between them. Mothers and offspring, however, frequently roost together more tightly. *Megaderma lyra* is mostly carnivorous, feeding on small vertebrates such as bats, birds, rodents, and fish, but also taking large insects and spiders. They detect their prey either by passive listening for sounds made by the prey itself, or using echolocation. Usually, they take the prey from the leaves or ground and retreat to a night roost where they consume the items at their leisure. They have been known to enter houses to take lizards and insects directly from the walls.
Comments: *Megaderma lyra* is a member of the subgenus *Lyroderma* Peters, 1872.
Conservation Status: China RL–VU A1cd.
References: Bates et al. (1994); Bates and Harrison (1997); Goymann et al. (2000); Lekagul and McNeely (1977); Nowak (1994); Rajan and Marimuthu (1999); Schmidt et al. (2000).

Family Emballonuridae—Sheath-tailed Bats

鞘尾蝠科 Qiaoweifu Ke—鞘尾蝠 Qiaoweifu

Ears with well-developed tragus; inner edges of ears usually joined at the vertex; rostrum without skin outgrowths; tail traverses through the septum femorale intermedium of the dorsum; tail tip slightly exceeds posterior edges of septum femorale intermedium; second digit with metacarpal bones but lacking phalanx; third digit with two phalanges, which fold toward the back of metacarpal bones at rest. Many species of Emballonuridae have glandular sacs on the anterior edges of propatagium. Premaxillaries unfused and not meeting dorsal to nasal aperture; postorbital process strongly developed; posterior edges of hard palate end at third molar or slightly posterior; tooth structure is insectivorous type, with sharp cusps. Dental formula: 2.1.2.3/3.1.2.3 = 30–34. Distributed in tropical zones of Eastern and Western hemispheres; but not known from Australia and New Zealand. There are two subfamilies, Emballonurinae (11 genera) and Taphozoinae (2 genera), but only Taphozoinae occurs in China, where only one genus is known to occur.

Genus *Taphozous*—Tomb Bats

墓蝠属 Mufu Shu—墓蝠 Mufu

Size medium; ears large and straight; tragus nearly rectangular; lower lip separated by medium vertical grooves; calcaria very long; septum femorale intermedium short; tail traverses the dorsum of septum femorale intermedium; forearm length 50–80 mm. Front of skull hollow and nearly disklike; postorbital process developed and slender, its tip sharp and longer than wide by about four times; crowns of first and second upper molars distinctly reduced. Dental formula: 1.1.2.3/2.1.2.3 = 30. Mainly distributed in tropical zones of the Eastern Hemisphere; of 14 species, 2 occur in China.

Black-Bearded Tomb Bat

PLATE 34
MAP 368

Taphozous melanopogon Temminck, 1841
黑髯墓蝠 Heiran Mufu

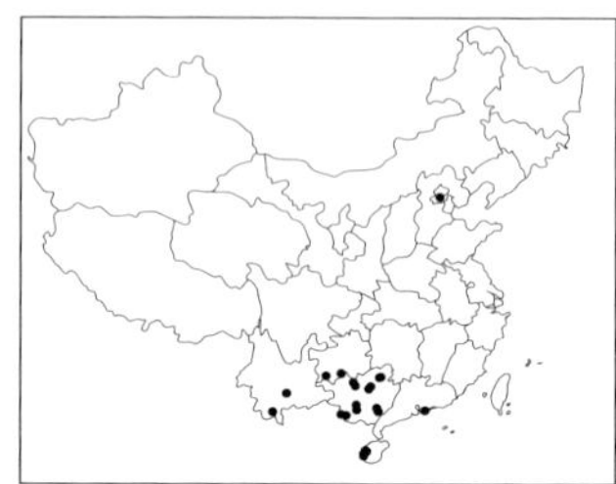

MAP 368. BLACK-BEARDED TOMB BAT, *Taphozous melanopogon*

Distinctive Characteristics: HB 67–86; T 20–32; HF 8–15; E 16–23; FA 55–68; GLS 19.4–21.9. Size small; chin with a small tuft of black beard; tail thickened toward

Key to the Chinese Species of *Taphozous*

1.a. Size small, forearm ≤ 69 mm	*Taphozous melanopogon*
b. Size large, forearm ≥ 69 mm	*Taphozous theobaldi*

tip and laterally compressed; wings attach to tibia, above ankle; both dorsal and ventral hairs black brown; basal hairs all white.
Distribution: S Yunnan, S Guangxi, Guangdong, and Hainan Island; extending throughout the tropical areas of S Asia. In addition, the type series of *T. solifer* Hollister, 1913, is purportedly from Beijing. We allocate all Chinese material to *T. m. philippinensis* Waterhouse, 1845.
Natural History: This species is known from a wide variety of forested habitats in tropical regions. It forms colonies of up to 15,000 or more individuals in caves, temples, and ruins. The sexes may roost in separate colonies, or spatially separated within the same colony. The breeding season seems to be well defined, and a single young is normally born after a gestation period of 120–125 days, although twins have been recorded as well.
Comments: *T. melanopogon* is a member of the subgenus *Taphozous*. There are several available names for this widespread species, and a definitive study of geographic variation has not been done. Wang (2003) allocates the records from S China to *T. m. fretensis* Thomas, 1916. However, *fretensis* is from islands in the straits of Malacca. In addition, he recognizes *T. m. solifer* Hollister, 1913, based on the type series that is listed as from "Peking, China." We have examined the type of *solifer* in the USNM and find it differs in no substantial way from *T. m. philippinensis* Waterhouse, 1945, from the Philippines. Futhermore, the provenance of *solifer* has been questioned, as Beijing is a most unlikely locality for this otherwise tropical species. The accession number for this material in the USNM is 38826 in the Mammal Catalog, but there is no record for that number in the accession files. The material catalogued immediately following the *T. solifer* series is accession number 38896 and is a collection of mammals collected by W. Abbott from Sumatra and nearby islands. Awaiting a more definitive study of geographic variation in *T. melanopogon*, we believe the conservative approach is to allocate all Chinese material to *T. m. philippinensis*.
Conservation Status: China RL—VU A1acd.
References: Allen (1938); Bates and Harrison (1997); Heaney et al. (1998).

Theobald's Tomb Bat

Taphozous theobaldi Dobson, 1872 MAP 369
大墓蝠 Da Mufu
Distinctive Characteristics: HB 88–95; T 25–35; HF 11–18; E 21–28; FA 70–76; GLS 22–24. Size large; color variable, dark brown dorsally and paler ventrally; adult males with a reddish brown beard; uropatagium hairless; muzzle nearly naked; wings attach above the ankle; wings with well-developed radio-metacarpal pouch; inner edge of nostrils raised; ears large and rounded, with a small round tragus; tail with a few long hairs at tip. Braincase narrower than that of *T. melanopogon*.
Distribution: Included in China solely on the basis of Wang (2003), who lists a record from Yunnan; extending from C India to Vietnam.

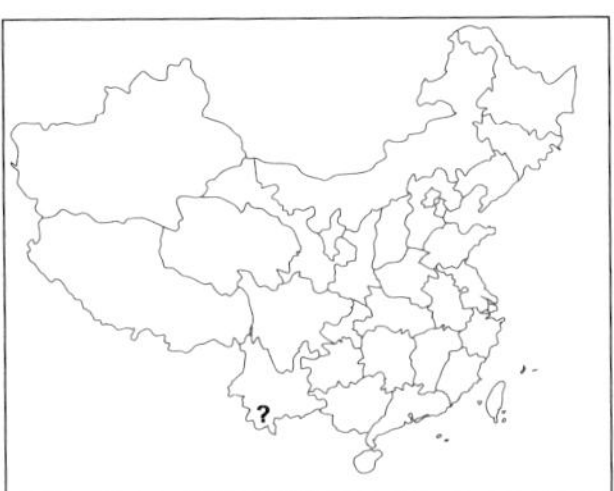

MAP 369. THEOBALD'S TOMB BAT, *Taphozous theobaldi*

Natural History: *Taphozous theobaldi* is a forest species, normally found roosting in caves. These colonies may number from a few hundred to several thousand individuals. Guano from this insectivorous species is mined and used as fertilizer in some areas.
Comments: *T. theobaldi* is a member of the subgenus *Taphozous*. Chinese specimens are referable to the nominate form on geographic grounds.
Conservation Status: China RL—NA.
References: Bates and Harrison (1997).

Family Molossidae—Free-tailed Bats

犬吻蝠科 Quanwenfu Ke—犬吻蝠 Quanwenfu

Hairs slender and soft, slightly fluffy; ears small, nearly quadrate, with thickened inner edges; ears sometimes join at front; tragi reduced and antitragi developed; upper lip plump and crumpled, without nose leaf; uropatagium narrow, short and plump, second half of tail protrudes from its posterior edges; hind legs dumpy; wing membrane long and narrow; fifth digit slightly longer than metacarpal bones of third digit; skull without postorbital process. Distributed in tropical and subtropical regions of the Eastern and Western hemispheres. There are two subfamilies, Molossinae (15 genera) and Tomopeatinae (1 genus), but only Molossinae, represented by 2 genera, is known to occur in China.

Key to the Chinese Genera of Molossidae

1.a.	Ears joined by broad band of skin; palatal emargination slight	*Chaerephon*
b.	Ears separated; deeply notched anterior palate	*Tadarida*

Genus *Chaerephon*—Lesser Free-tailed Bats

小犬吻蝠属 Xiaoquanwenfu Shu—
小犬吻蝠 Xiaoquanwenfu

Size medium; tail extends beyond interfemoral membrane; tibia short; wing membranes long and narrow, but with relatively broad tips; ears joined by band over nose; jaw relatively slender and delicate; mandibular condyle elevated; palatal emargination constricted; posterior commisure on upper third molar moderately developed. Dental formula: 1.1.2.3/2.1.2.3 = 30. Distributed broadly in Africa and Eurasia, but only a single species out of 18 occurs in China.

Wrinkle-Lipped Free-Tailed Bat

PLATE 35
MAP 370

Chaerephon plicatus (Buchanan, 1800)
犬吻蝠 Quanwenfu

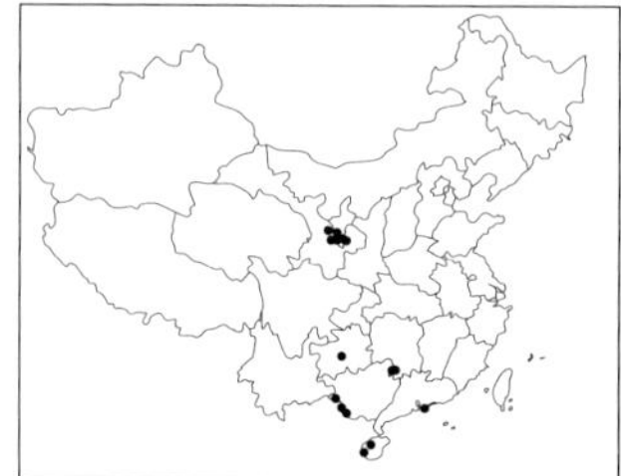

MAP 370. WRINKLE-LIPPED FREE-TAILED BAT, *Chaerephon plicatus*

Distinctive Characteristics: HB 65–75; T 30–40; HF 9–12; E 16–21; FA 40–50; GLS 18–21. Size medium; zygomatic width about 11–12 mm; ears join at front; upper lip with conspicuous crimps; pelage color dark brown; tips of ventral hairs slightly hoary; rostrum of skull low and flat; sagittal crest and lambdoidal crest very low; anterior palate without conspicuous small indenture.
Distribution: Gansu, Yunnan, Hainan, Guangxi, Guangdong, Hong Kong, and Guizhou; extending throughout the tropical regions of S Asia. Chinese population belongs to nominate subspecies.
Natural History: Colonies ranging from a few hundred to more than 200,000 have been reported, roosting in caves and buildings. Insectivorous, they forage high and fast, and the guano deposits under large colonies are mined and used for fertilizer in some regions.
Comments: *C. plicatus* is a member of the *plicatus* species group.
Conservation Status: China RL–VU A2abcd.
References: Bates and Harrison (1997); Lekagul and McNeely (1977).

Genus *Tadarida*—Free-tailed bats

犬吻蝠属 Quanwenfu Shu—犬吻蝠 Quanwenfu

Size medium or smaller; terminal half of tail protrudes from uropatagium; tibia short; wing membrane long and narrow; premaxilla of skull either complete or lacking a nasal branch, hence with a small indentation in anterior extremity; interorbital region of rostrum with a shallow vertical groove; skull wide and slightly flat; anterior occiput slightly recessed; sagittal crest undeveloped; supraorbital ridge low and inconspicuous; two premolars in upper jaw; two or three pairs of incisors in lower jaw. Dental formula: 1.1.1–2.3/1–3.1.2.3 = 26–32. Geographical distribution of this genus is widest of the Molossidae, occurring throughout the tropical and subtropical regions of both the Eastern and Western hemispheres. Of 10 species, only 2 are known from China.

East Asian Free-Tailed Bat

PLATE 35
MAP 371

Tadarida insignis Blyth, 1862
宽耳犬吻蝠 Kuan'er Quanwenfu

Distinctive Characteristics: HB 84–94; T 48–60; HF 10–15; E 31–34; FA 57–65; GLS 22–24. Size larger; posterior margin of ear concave in center; 24–26 horny excrescences on rhinarium; hairs bicolored, paler at base, giving frosted appearance to otherwise uniform pale drab dorsum; keeled calcar; plagiopatagium attached between one fourth and one third the length of tibia; tragus fringed with hair anteriorly and dorsally; braincase high; palatal emargination deep, longer than wide.
Distribution: Yunnan, Sichuan, Fujian, Anhui, Guangxi, Taiwan, Guizhou; extending to Japan and Korea. We do not recognize subspecies in this species.

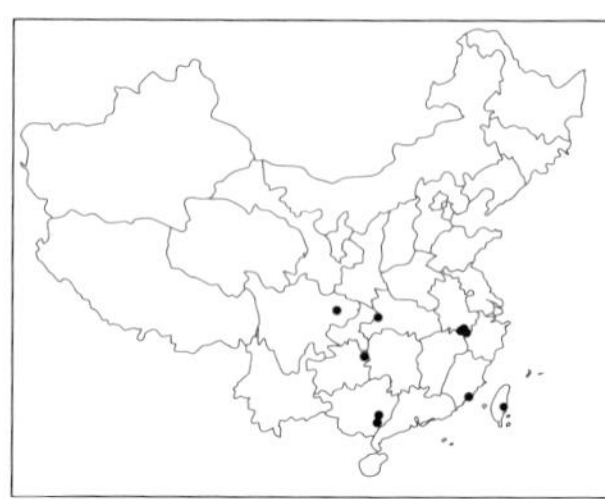

MAP 371. EAST ASIAN FREE-TAILED BAT, *Tadarida insignis*

Natural History: Specimens have been taken from caves, but little else is known about this species.
Comments: *Tadarida insignis* is a member of the *teniotis* species group. This group is poorly understood, and badly in need of systematic revision. For the most part, *T. insignis* languished in the synonymy of *T. teniotis* since Dobson (1874), until resurrected by

Key to the Chinese Species of *Tadarida*

1.a. Forearm length > 57 mm	*Tadarida insignis*
b. Forearm length < 57 mm	*Tadarida latouchei*

Imaizumi and Yoshiyuki (1965). We are including *T. coecata* Thomas, 1922, as a synonym of *T. insignis*; hence the records from Yunnan and Sichuan may warrant reexamination should that allocation change. Wang (2003) listed *insignis*, *coecata*, and *latouchei* all as subspecies of *teniotis*. We believe that *insignis* and *latouchei* are best considered species separate from *teniotis*, but the status of *coecata* is more difficult to determine, as pointed out by Kock (1999).
Conservation Status: China RL—VU A2cd.
References: Dobson (1874); Funakoshi and Kunisaki (2000); Helgen and Wilson (2002); Imaizumi and Yoshiyuki (1965); Kock (1999); Yoshiyuki (1989); Yoshiyuki et al. (1989).

La Touche's Free-Tailed Bat

Tadarida latouchei Thomas, 1920 MAP 372
华北犬吻蝠 Huabei Qunwenfu

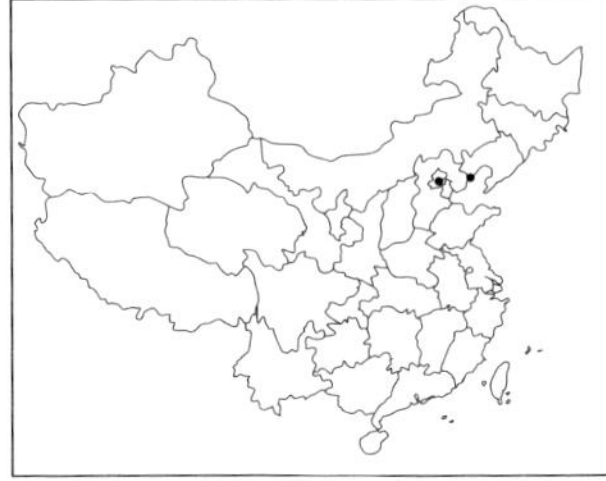

MAP 372. LA TOUCHE'S FREE-TAILED BAT, *Tadarida latouchei*

Distinctive Characteristics: HB 67–72; T 41–46; HF 12–13; E 22–25; FA 53–57; GLS 20–22. Size smaller; ears large; ears join at front; upper lip with vertical crimples; pelage color blackish brown; basal hair nearly white; tips of ventral hairs relatively light; plagiopatagium attached to basal third of tibia; fur soft and dense; ears thinner, smaller, and rounder than those of *T. insignis*.
Distribution: Hebei, Beijing, Nei Mongol, and Heilongjiang; also known from Thailand, Laos, and Japan.
Natural History: Nothing is known of the natural history of this species.
Comments: *Tadarida latouchei* is a member of the *teniotis* species group. The geographic distribution of this species, with one or possibly more species intervening in southern China, suggests the need for further study of the entire species group (see account for *T. insignis*). That *T. latouchei* represents a species distinct from *T. teniotis* and *T. insignis* seems clear. However, the species limits of all three forms, plus the enigmatic *T. coecata* (which we allocate to *T. insignis*), need further study.
Conservation Status: China RL—DD. IUCN RL—DD ver 2.3 (1994).
References: Funakoshi and Kunisaki (2000); Helgen and Wilson (2002); Kock (1999).

Family Vespertilionidae—Vesper Bats

蝙蝠科 Bianfu Ke—蝙蝠 Bianfu

Most common, widespread, and speciose family of Chiroptera; has many widely distributed species; development of ears normal; ears usually separated, only join at front in a few species; tragi developed, with sharp or blunt tips; rostrum without special dermal outgrowths; second digit with normally developed metacarpal bones and a small phalanx; third digit with three phalanges, the terminal one cartilaginous except at base; uropatagium complete, wholly encloses tail, or only tip slightly protrudes; skull without postorbital process; premaxilla without palatal branch, hence anterior palate fenestrate; teeth with normally developed cusps, typically insectivorous. Dental formula: 1–2.1.1–3.3/2–3.1.2–3.3 = 28–38.

Widely distributed in Eastern and Western hemispheres and many large islands, except polar regions; 6 subfamilies and 48 genera; 18 genera representing 5 subfamilies occur throughout China. Wang (2003) also included the genus *Scotozous*, based on a record from Taiwan, but that record is erroneous (Koopman 1994).

Subfamily Vespertilioninae

蝙蝠亚科 Bianfu Yake—蝙蝠 Bianfu

Size medium to very small; length of ear medium, ears not funnel-shaped, lacking a keel, but with an obvious anterior basal lobe; anterior and middle upper premolars, when present, small and simpler than posterior premolar; second phalanx of third digit not elongated; nostrils not tubular; seventh cervical vertebra free from first thoracic; sternum slender, twice as long as presternum is wide and presternum with small median lobe; sternum with six or seven ribs connected; coracoid process of scapula curved outward. Distributed worldwide; of 38 total genera, 13 occur in China.

Genus *Arielulus*—Sprites

金背伏翼属 Jinbeifuyi Shu—金背伏翼 Jinbeifuyi

Size small to medium; muzzle short, broad, and blunt; ears large, rounded, with blunt tips; ears and tragus edged with dull or yellowish white; pelage blackish brown, with individual hairs frosted with yellowish, orange, russet, copper, or brown. Braincase high and globose; postorbital region wide; small supraorbital projections; rostrum short and wide; cranial profile almost straight; zygomata strong; interdental palate longer than wide. Dental formula: 2.1.2.2/3.1.2.3 = 34. Contains five species that are widely distributed in SE Asia, with two species known from China. *Arielulus* is a member of the tribe Eptesicini and was formerly thought to be a subgenus of *Pipistrellus*.

Key to the Chinese Subfamilies of Vespertilionidae

1.a. Anterior premolars in upper jaw (P2 and P3) not especially reduced, their sizes at least half of posterior premolar (P4); nostrils prolonged into small tubes — Murininae
b. Anterior premolars reduced; nostrils not tubular — 2
2.a. Ears tubiform — Kerivoulinae
b. Ears not tubiform — 3
3.a. Second phalanx of third digit especially prolonged, length about three times of that of first phalanx — Miniopterinae
b. Second phalanx of third digit not especially prolonged, length < three times of that of first phalanx — 4
4.a. Six cheek teeth behind canine on either side of upper or lower jaw; dental formula: 2.1.3.3/3.1.3.3 = 38 — Myotinae
b. Less than six cheek teeth behind canine on either side of upper or lower jaw; dental formula different from above — Vespertilioninae

Key to the Chinese Genera of Vespertilioninae

1.a. Two premolars on each side of upper jaw — 2
b. One premolar on each side of upper jaw — 7
2.a. Ears very large, distinctly longer than head; three premolars on each side of lower jaw — *Plecotus*
b. Ears normal, not much longer than head; two premolars on each side of lower jaw — 3
3.a. Height of upper outer incisor (I3) not > edges of inner incisor (I2) — 4
b. Height of upper outer incisor (I3) distinctly > edges of inner incisor (I2) — 5
4.a. Crown of upper outer incisor flat, not forming conspicuous cusps; size very large; forearm length about 72 mm — *Ia*
b. Upper outer incisor with sharp cusp; size very small; forearm length about 33 mm — *Scotozous*
5.a. Fifth digit shortened, slightly longer than third or fourth metacarpal bone — *Nyctalus*
b. Fifth digit normal, length > total length of third or fourth metacarpal bone plus first phalanx — 6
6.a. Rostrum of skull recessed; ears joined in front — *Barbastella*
b. Rostrum of skull protruding; ears not joined in front — 11
7.a. Two incisors on each side of upper jaw — 8
b. One incisor on each side of upper jaw — 10
8.a. Skull distinctly low and flat, height of occiput < 1/3 of GLS — *Tylonycteris*
b. Skull normal, height of occiput > 1/3 of GLS — 9
9.a. Sides of rostrum protruding; narial emargination < half of distance from rostrum tip to narrow part of interorbital region; anterior palatal emargination longer than wide — *Eptesicus*
b. Sides of rostrum recessed; narial emargination equal to half of distance from rostrum tip to narrow part of interorbital region; anterior palatal emargination wider than long — *Vespertilio*
10.a. Mesostyles of first and second upper molars reduced, which makes W-shaped ectoloph incomplete; second triangle structure of first and second lower molars smaller than first triangle structure; hair color khaki or brown, without white spots — *Scotophilus*
b. Mesostyles of first and second upper molars with normal cusps and ridges, W-shaped ectoloph complete; second triangle structure of first and second lower molars larger than first triangle structure; hair color dark brown, inlayed with large white spots — *Scotomanus*
11.a. Braincase relatively high and rounded — *Pipistrellus*
b. Braincase relatively low and flatter — 12
12.a. Braincase longer; maxillary toothrows convergent; palate longer than wide; anterior upper premolar normal — *Falsistrellus*
b. Braincase shorter; maxillary toothrows parallel; palate wider than long; anterior upper premolar reduced or absent — *Hypsugo*

Key to the Chinese Species of *Arielulus*

1.a. Occurring on mainland — *Arielulus circumdatus*
b. Occurring on Taiwan — *Arielulus torquatus*

Bronze Sprite

PLATE 36
MAP 373

Arielulus circumdatus (Temminck, 1840)
大黑伏翼 Da Heifuyi

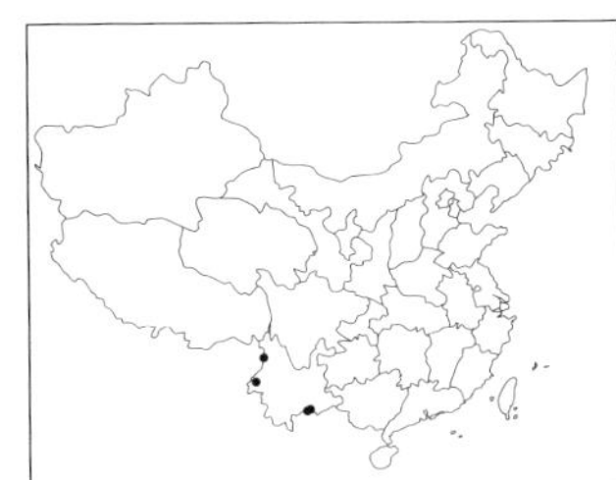

MAP 373. BRONZE SPRITE, *Arielulus circumdatus*

Distinctive Characteristics: HB 95; T 40; HF 10; E 15; FA 41–44; GLS 15–16. Size medium; dorsal pelage black with some orange tips, giving an almost orange sheen to the head and back; hairs are soft and long; ventral surface uniform brown, paler than dorsal; hairs slightly bicolored, with the roots slightly darker than the tips; ears dark brown-black with pale anterior and posterior margins in some specimens; tragus broad with pale margins; membranes uniform dark brown and essentially naked. Skull large with distinct frontal depression; rostrum broad and short.
Distribution: Yunnan; extending across SE Asia.
Natural History: This species appears to be widespread, but uncommon, as few specimens are known. It has been collected from 2,000 m in elevation in Nepal and appears to be a highland species, but nothing is known of its natural history.
Comments: Wang (2003) allocates the Chinese material to *A. c. drungicus* Wang, 1982, but it differs only in minor dental characters from the nominate form. This species should be regarded as monotypic until additional material allows a more thorough study of geographic variation.
Conservation Status: China RL—EN A2C + 3C; C2a(i,ii).
References: Corbet and Hill (1992); Heller and Volleth (1984); Hill and Francis (1984).

Necklace Sprite

Arielulus torquatus Csorba and Lee, 1999 — MAP 374
黄喉黑伏翼 Huanghou Heifuyi
Distinctive Characteristics: FA 43–46; GLS 16–17; other external measurements not published. Size medium; dorsal pelage black tipped with bronze; ventral pelage dark tipped with silver; throat with bright ochraceous collar; ears triangular, black and without pale edging; tragus short and curved; muzzle short and broad; proximal half of uropatagium furred; plagiopatagium inserts at base of fifth toe. Skull massive with strong supraorbital and lacrimal processes; frontal depression distinct; narial emargination V-shaped; palatal emargination wide and shallow.
Distribution: Taiwan. Endemic.
Natural History: The type locality is at 1,800 m elevation, and the only two other known specimens are also from the highlands. Nothing else is known of the life history.

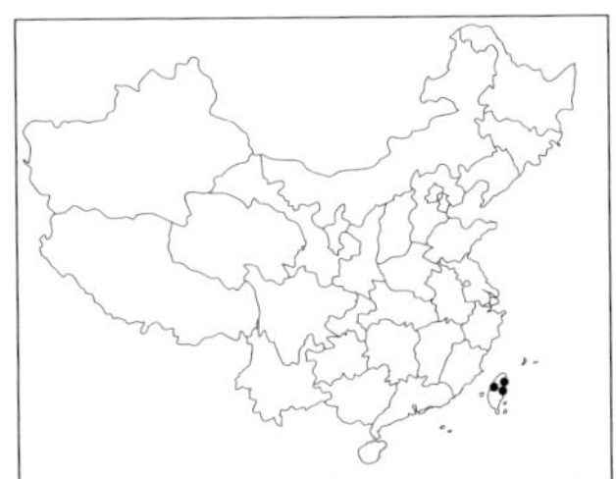

MAP 374. NECKLACE SPRITE, *Arielulus torquatus*

Comments: First collected in 1992, there is an excellent color photograph of this species in Lin et al. (1997).
Conservation Status: China RL—EN C2a(i,ii); D.
References: Csorba and Lee (1999); Lin et al. (1997).

Genus *Barbastella*—Barbastelles

宽耳蝠属 Kuan'erfu Shu—宽耳蝠 Kuan'erfu

Ears wide and short, joined at front; nostrils lie behind nasal pad, directed upward; dorsal hair dark, with paler tips; interfemoral membrane near body sides covered with short hair. Skull with long, round cranium; rostrum elongate, and distinctly recessed on mid-dorsal surface; zygomatic arch also extenuated, not protruding in middle. Dental formula: 2.1.2.3/3.1.2.3 = 34; small premolar in upper jaw tiny, lying in internal angle between canine and large premolar (P4). There is no small style behind upper canine, while there is one in front of the main cusp of lower canine. Upper molars without hypocone; crown of third upper molar larger than half that of first or second. Distributed across C and SE Asia, Europe, and N Africa. Of two species in the genus, one occurs in China. *Barbastella* is a member of the tribe Plecotini.

Eastern Barbastelle

PLATE 36
MAP 375

Barbastella leucomelas (Cretzschmar, 1826)
宽耳蝠 Kuan'erfu
Distinctive Characteristics: HB 47–51; T 40–47; HF 7–8; E 15–17; FA 38–45; GLS 14–16. Size small; muzzle short, flat, and broad, with glandular swellings; upper

lip densely fringed with hair; ears nearly square, with no antitragal lobe; wings attach to base of outer toe; tail long. Pelage color gray, with whiter tips; compound hairs on ventral surface near uropatagium white. Skull relatively small; weak zygomata and supraorbital ridges; tympanic bullae small; basioccipital broad.
Distribution: Known from Yunnan, Sichuan, Gansu, Shanxi, Qinghai, Nei Mongol, Xinjiang, and Taiwan; extending widely from N Africa and the Caucasus to Japan. Chinese subspecies: *B. l. darjelingensis* (Dobson, 1855).

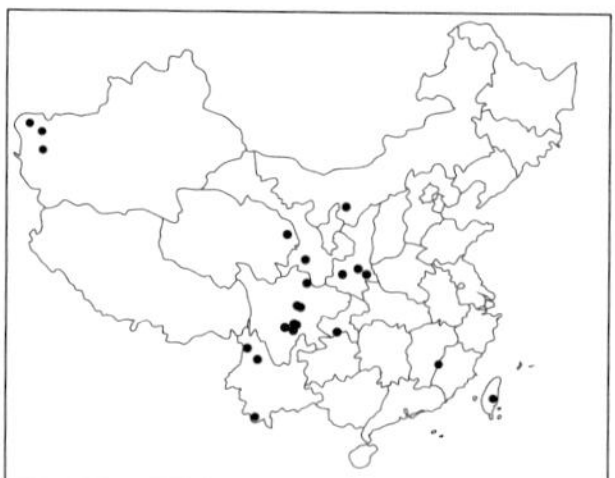

MAP 375. EASTERN BARBASTELLE, *Barbastella leucomelas*

Natural History: These are insectivores with slow and maneuverable flight, frequently seen flying low. They roost in caves, trees, and buildings. Most colonies are relatively small. In Taiwan, they are found at mid- to high elevations in oak and conifer forests. They are known from similar ecological zones in India.
Comments: Some have suggested that the nominate form of *B. leucomelas* may actually be conspecific with the Western Barbastelle, *B. barbastella.* Should that prove to be the case, the Chinese population would be known as *B. darjelingensis*. Wang (2003) listed *B. formosanus* as a Taiwan endemic. However, this name is a *nomen nudum*.
Conservation Status: China RL–VU A1acd.
References: Bates and Harrison (1997); Horácek et al. (2000); Lin et al. (1997); Lin et al. (2002b).

Genus *Eptesicus*—Serotines

棕蝠属 Zongfu Shu—棕蝠 Zongfu

Form similar to that of *Pipistrellus*, but rostrum slightly thicker; tragus long and straight, its tip slightly acute; rostrum of skull relatively flat or slightly thick, without conspicuous long groove; nasal sinus not distinctly enlarged, not extending to center between rostrum tip and interorbital region. Dental formula: 2.1.1.3/3.1.2.3 = 32; structure of tooth cusps normal; upper inner incisor large, with a main cusp and a small style; outer incisor small, separated from canine by small diastema; basal part of canine without cingulum; upper molars with distinguishable hypocones. *Eptesicus* belongs to the tribe Eptesicini. Distributed in temperate and tropical zones of Eastern and Western hemispheres. Of 23 species, 4 occur in China.

Gobi Big Brown Bat

PLATE 36
MAP 376

Eptesicus gobiensis Bobrinskii, 1926
戈壁北棕蝠 Gebi Beizongfu

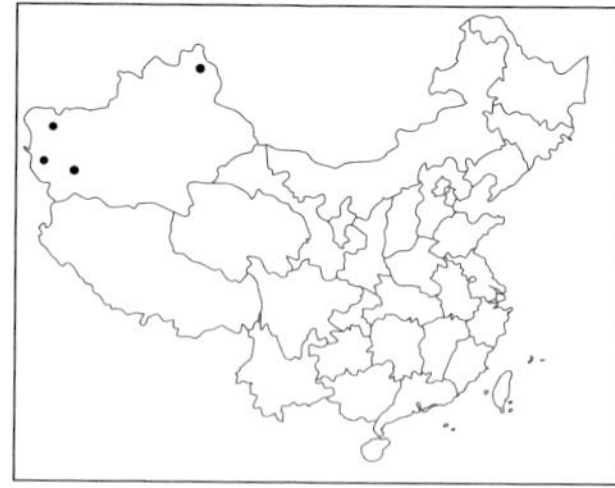

MAP 376. GOBI BIG BROWN BAT, *Eptesicus gobiensis*

Distinctive Characteristics: HB 57–65; T 40–45; HF 9–10; E 10–15; FA 38–42; GLS 16. Size small; dorsal pelage reddish yellow, its basal part dark brown; ventral surface brownish white; skull relatively low; supraorbital ridge extenuated; rostrum, palate, and zygomatic arches all narrow; in upper jaw outer incisor distinctly lower than inner incisor.
Distribution: NW China; extending from Iran to Mongolia. Two subspecies in China: (1) *E. g. centrasiaticus* Bobrinskii, 1926; (2) *E. g. kashgaricus* Bobrinskii, 1926; both have been recorded from Xinjiang.
Natural History: *E. gobiensis* is a pale desert species originally described from the Altai mountains in the Gobi Desert. It ranges eastward in arid mountain and desert regions as far as Iran. It is known to inhabit both caves and abandoned buildings.
Comments: *E. gobiensis* is a member of the subgenus *Eptesicus*. It has been considered a subspecies of *E. nilssonii* in the past (e.g., Wang 2003), but most recent workers treat it as a distinct species. The limits of the two named subspecies, *kashgaricus* and *centrasiaticus*, are unknown at

Key to the Chinese Species of *Eptesicus*

1.a.	Upper surface of rostrum transversely convex	2
b.	Upper surface of rostrum flat	3
2.a.	Outer upper incisors > half the length of the inner incisors	*Eptesicus nilssonii*
b.	Outer upper incisors about half the length of the inner incisors	*Eptesicus gobiensis*
3.a.	Size large; forearm length 49–57 mm; GLS > 20 mm	*Eptesicus serotinus*
b.	Size small; forearm length 38–42 mm; GLS about 16 mm	*Eptesicus pachyotis*

present. In fact, the relationships of *E. gobiensis*, *nilssonii*, and *pachyotis* are badly in need of revision.
Conservation Status: China RL–NA.
References: Bates and Harrison (1997); Corbet and Hill (1992); Horácek et al. (2000); Strelkov (1986); Yoshiyuki (1989).

Northern Bat

PLATE 36
Eptesicus nilssonii
(Keyserling and Blasius, 1839) MAP 377
北棕蝠 **Beizongfu**

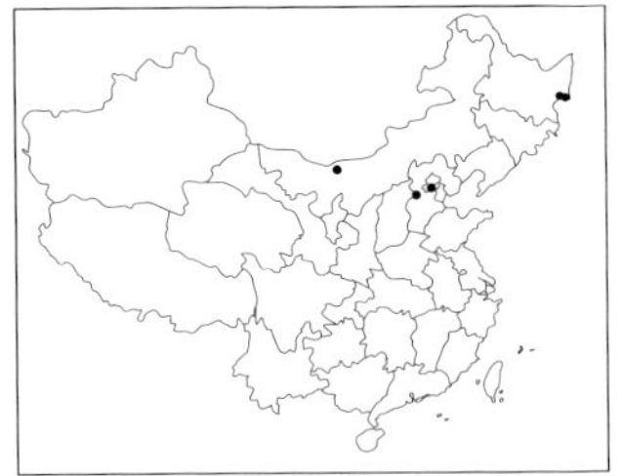

MAP 377. NORTHERN BAT, *Eptesicus nilssonii*

Distinctive Characteristics: HB 54–64; T 35–50; HF 10–12; E 13–18; FA 37–44; GLS 14–16. Size small; ears short, round, and fleshy; tragus short and round, curving inward; fur dark brown or blackish dorsally, with some golden tipped hairs; venter yellowish brown; wings long and broad with short, rounded tips; calcar extends half the length of uropatagium; tail extends slightly beyond uropatagium; wing membrane attaches at base of toe. Skull delicate and braincase low; little or no sagittal crest; dentition robust.
Distribution: Nei Mongol, Heilongjiang, Jilin, and Shandong; extending from Europe through E Russia. Chinese subspecies: *E. n. parvus* Kishida, 1932.
Natural History: The Northern Bat frequents boreal coniferous forests in much of its range. Diet consists mainly of diptera, but feeds on moths and beetles as well. Frequently roosts in buildings, including the attics of occupied houses. Gives birth in June and July. Litter size is one in the north, but twins are more frequent in southerly regions. The young are volant at two or three weeks of age. Females form maternity colonies in the summer, and most are philopatric. Known to live for 15 years.
Comments: *E. nilssonii* is a member of the subgenus *Eptesicus*. It is closely related to *E. gobiensis*, and recent molecular work suggests that it is much closer to *E. serotinus* than previously suspected.
Conservation Status: China RL–LC. IUCN RL–LR/nt ver 2.3 (1994).
References: Mayer and von Helversen (2001); Rydell (1993); Yoshiyuki (1989).

Thick-Eared Bat

Eptesicus pachyotis (Dobson, 1871) MAP 378
肥耳棕蝠 **Fei'er Zongfu**
Distinctive Characteristics: HB 55–56; T 40–41; HF 8–9; E 13–14; FA 38–40; GLS 21. Size small; ears triangular with rounded tips, and quite thick and fleshy; tragus short and round with inward curve; head flat and muzzle short; wings attached to base of toes; color dark brown dorsally and paler ventrally. Dorsal profile of skull rises smoothly to lambdoid crests; zygomata robust with small dorsal projection from jugal; tympanic bullae small, subequal to space between them; first upper incisor bifid and much longer than second; canine with cingulum but lacking accessory cusplets; lacks small upper premolar (P2).
Distribution: C China; extending to Bangladesh and India.

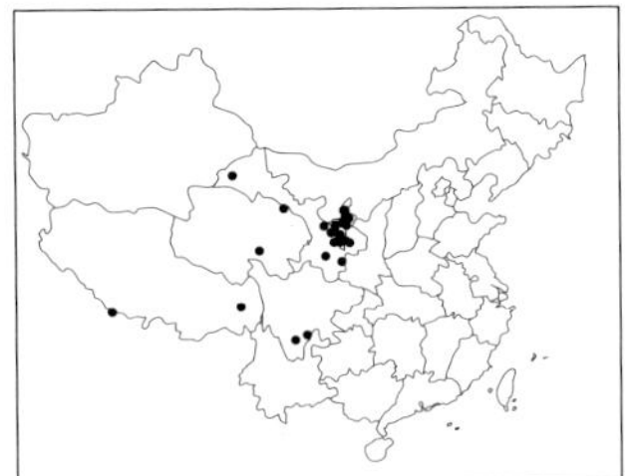

MAP 378. THICK-EARED BAT, *Eptesicus pachyotis*

Natural History: This is a poorly known species, with nothing known about its natural history.
Comments: *E. pachyotis* is a member of the subgenus *Eptesicus*.
Conservation Status: China RL–LC.
References: Bates and Harrison (1997); Lekagul and McNeely (1977).

Common Serotine

PLATE 36
Eptesicus serotinus (Schreber, 1774) MAP 379
大棕蝠 **Da Zongfu**

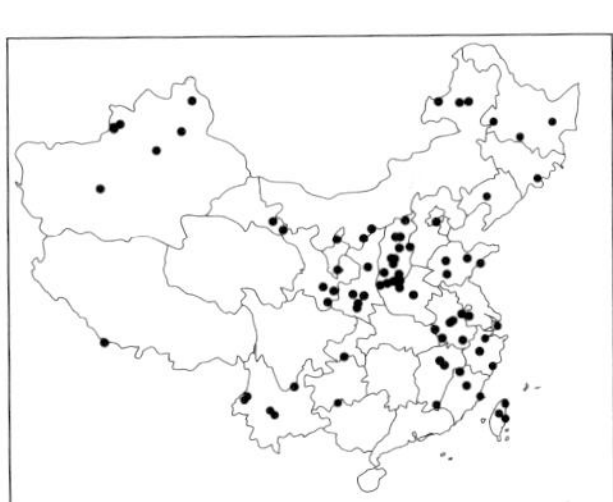

MAP 379. COMMON SEROTINE, *Eptesicus serotinus*

Distinctive Characteristics: HB 70–80; T 52–58; HF 10–18; E 14–18; FA 49–57; GLS > 20. Size large; dorsal pelage dark brown, with gray spots; ventral surface black to brownish white; skull relatively wide and flat; postorbital process of zygomatic arch developed; occiput with projecting ridge; supraorbital ridge developed; main cusp of inner incisor with posterior style; main cusp of outer incisor about equal in size with style behind inner incisor.
Distribution: Widely distributed across China; extending across N Asia and through Europe. Four subspecies in China: (1) *E. s. andersoni* Dobson, 1871; Sichuan, Guizhou, Hunan, Jiangxi, Shanghai,

Zhejiang, Fujian, Jiangsu, Anhui, Yunnan; (2) *E. s. horikawai* Kishida, 1924; Taiwan; (3) *E. s. pallens* Miller, 1991; Heilongjiang, Gansu, Sichuan, Ningxia, Shanxi, Nei Mongol, Shaanxi, Hebei, Beijing, Tianjin, Shandong, Henan, Anhui, Jiangsu, Hubei, Shanxi, Liaoning, Jilin; (4) *E. s. turcomanus* Eversmann, 1840; Xinjiang.

Natural History: The Common Serotine is one of the largest species of *Eptesicus* and frequently is one of the first to appear in the evening, often emerging while there is still daylight. The broad wings and a leisurely, highly maneuverable flight with occasional short glides or steep descents are distinctive. Flies at about tree-top height (to about 10 m) often close to vegetation and will sometimes land, wings outstretched, on the foliage to catch large insects. Feeds around street lamps and even catches prey from the ground on occasion. Breeding season is usually in September and October. In the spring, females form maternity colonies, and the young are born in June and July. The young are weaned at about six weeks of age. Colonies, frequently in buildings, are small. Individuals may live up to 19 years of age. Favored feeding areas include pasture, parkland, open woodland edge, tall hedgerows, gardens, suburban areas, and forested regions. Most foraging activity is within 2 km of the roost although they may range up to 6 km. Having caught a large insect, will fly around slowly, chewing and dropping the wings and legs. Sometimes carries prey to a feeding perch, where it hangs and eats it at its leisure. Roosts mainly in buildings, including houses and churches, but is found less frequently in modern buildings. Access to the roost is usually at or near the highest point or through the eaves. This is one of the most building-oriented species and is hardly ever found roosting in trees. Echolocation calls range from 15–65 kHz, with a peak at 25–30 kHz.

Comments: *E. serotinus* is a member of the subgenus *Eptesicus*.

Conservation Status: China RL—LC.

References: Bates and Harrison (1997); Horácek et al. (2000); Jones (1975).

Genus *Falsistrellus*—False Pipistrelles

假伏翼属 Jiafuyi Shu—假伏翼 Jiafuyi

Size small to medium; similar to *Pipistrellus*, but larger; braincase relatively narrow in relation to length; dorsal profile of skull flatter; both sagittal and lambdoidal crests present; posterior apex of skull projects beyond supraoccipital; prominent supraorbital tubercles; first upper incisor unicuspid; second upper incisor very small; first and second upper molars with hypocone; upper canine with lingual cingulum and cusplets; lower incisors imbricate and in close contact. Dental formula: 2.1.2.3/3.1.2.3 = 34. *Falsistrellus* is broadly distributed in SE Asia and Australia. Of five species, two are known from China. *Falsistrellus* is a member of the tribe Vespertilionini and was formerly considered a subgenus of *Pipistrellus*.

Chocolate Pipistrelle

Falsistrellus affinis (Dobson, 1871) MAP 380

茶褐伏翼 Cahe Fuyi

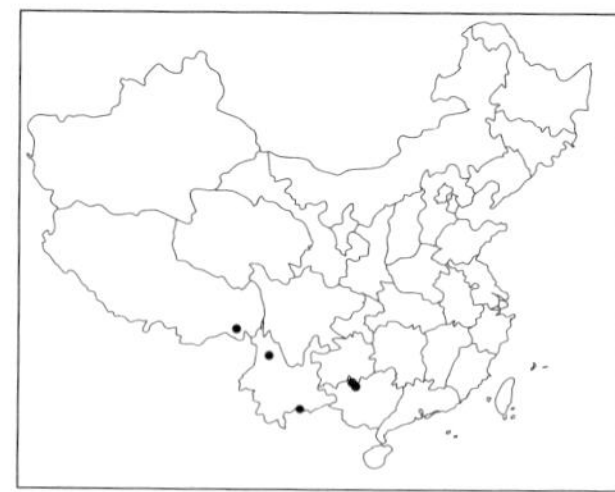

MAP 380. CHOCOLATE PIPISTRELLE, *Falsistrellus affinis*

Distinctive Characteristics: HB 43–51; T 30–41; HF 7–8; E 12–15; FA 38–40; GLS 15.5. Size medium; zygomatic width about 9.6 mm; hair color brown; hair tips gray; ventral surface grayish white; skull long; cranium low; basisphenoid absent; zygomatic arch relatively thick, with postorbital process; palate relatively narrow; small premolar (P2) in upper jaw not smaller than outer incisor, and slightly leaning to inner side of toothrow, hence large premolar (P4) and canine touching.

Distribution: Xizang, Yunnan, and Guangxi; extending NE Myanmar, Nepal, India, and Sri Lanka; monotypic species.

Natural History: This species roosts in trees and buildings. It frequently can be seen foraging on small flying insects around human habitations, fairly low to the ground. Occurs from sea level up to 2,000 m elevation.

Comments: *F. affinis* is closely related to *F. mordax*, and the two may yet prove conspecific. Wang (2003) lists this species as *Pipistrellus affinis*.

Conservation Status: China RL—NT; although it nearly met the criteria for VU A1bc.

References: Bates and Harrison (1997); Corbet and Hill (1992).

Key to the Chinese Species of *Falsistrellus*

1.a. Smaller, forearm 38–40 mm	*Falsistrellus affinis*
b. Larger, forearm 40–42 mm	*Falsistrellus mordax*

Pungent Pipistrelle

Falsistrellus mordax (Peters, 1866) MAP 381
大灰蝠翼 Dahui Fuyi

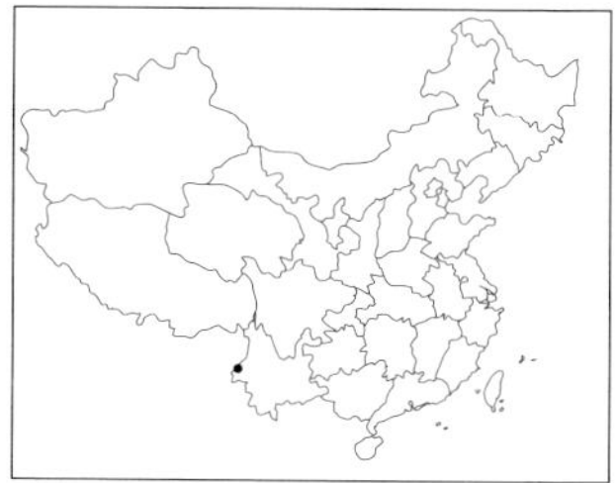

MAP 381. PUNGENT PIPISTRELLE, *Falsistrellus mordax*

Distinctive Characteristics: HB 47–56; T 37–42; HF 6–9; E 14–16; FA 40–42. Size medium; dorsum rust-brown with paler tips; venter black-brown with pale brown tips; anal region pale brownish yellow; tragus medium long; wing membrane attached to base of toes; tail projects beyond uropatagium; terminal cartilage of fourth digit divided into a "T."
Distribution: Known only from Java. Included in the fauna of China based on Wang (2003), who listed it from Yingjiang, Yunnan.
Natural History: Nothing is known about the natural history of this species.
Comments: The Chinese record is likely based on a specimen in the American Museum of Natural History (44565), which is actually *F. affinis*. Otherwise, the species is known only from Java, Indonesia. However, the two species may be conspecific, in which case the earliest name is indeed *mordax*. Wang (2003) lists this species as *Pipistrellus mordax*.
Conservation Status: China RL—NA.
References: Corbet and Hill (1992); Hill and Harrison (1987); Tate (1942).

Genus *Hypsugo*—High Pipistrelles

高级伏翼属 Gaojifuyi Shu—高级伏翼 Gaojifuyi

Size small; skull low; median groove in frontal region; deep lateral depression anterior to suproorbital ridge; basioccipital pits lacking; anterior upper premolar absent or minute; dorsal fur often grizzled or yellow-tipped; baculum short and stout, with expanded base and tip. *Hypsugo* is found in Asia and Africa. Of 18 species, 3 are found in China. It is a member of the tribe Vespertilionini and was formerly considered a subgenus of *Pipistrellus*.

Alashanian Pipistrelle

Hypsugo alaschanicus (Bobrinskii, 1926) MAP 382
阿拉善伏翼 Alashan Fuyi

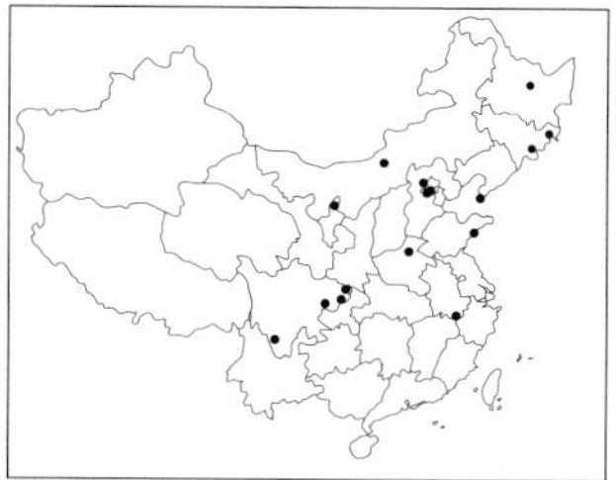

MAP 382. ALASHANIAN PIPISTRELLE, *Hypsugo alaschanicus*

Distinctive Characteristics: HB 38; T 39–40; HF 8; E 13; FA 36–38; GLS 14. Size small; color brownish dorsally, but with tips paler; venter paler, but with hairs dark brown basally; outer edge of wing with distinct pale border; tragus narrow with clearly defined basal lobe; tip of tail protrudes slightly beyond uropatagium; upper incisors about equal in length; skull slightly convex above the interorbital region.
Distribution: C and N China (Nei Mongol, Gansu, Ningxia, Sichuan, Henan, Anhui, Shandong, Liaoning, Jilin, and Heilongjiang); extending to Mongolia, Russia, and Korea.
Natural History: Originally described from desert mountain ranges in northern China, this species is now known from a variety of habitats. In spite of this, little is known of its natural history, other than that it roosts in caves.
Comments: The relationships of this species are not clearly understood. It was long thought to be a subspecies of *H. savii*, and Wang (2003) lists it as *Pipistrellus savii alaschanicus*.
Conservation Status: China RL—LC.
References: Allen (1938); Horácek et al. (2000).

Chinese Pipistrelle

PLATE 36
Hypsugo pulveratus (Peters, 1871) MAP 383
灰伏翼 Hui Fuyi

Distinctive Characteristics: HB 44–47; T 37–38; HF 7–8; E 12–14; FA 33–36; GLS 14–15. Size about equal to that of *Pipistrellus abramus* or slightly larger; zygomatic width 7–9 mm; ears larger; tragus short and wide; wing membrane attaches to basal part of toe; dorsal hair dark, nearly blackish brown; ventral surface relatively pale, nearly brown; hair tips a little off-white; skull low and long, but cranium protruding; zygomatic arches and supraorbital processes well developed; crown of small premolar (P2) in upper jaw about equal in size to that of outer incisor; inner upper incisors bicuspid.

Key to the Chinese Species of *Hypsugo*

1.a.	Anterior upper premolar (P2) not greatly reduced	*Hypsugo pulveratus*
b.	Anterior upper premolar greatly reduced	2
2.a.	Tragus widest near base, with one basal lobe	*Hypsugo alaschanicus*
b.	Tragus widest above the middle, with two basal lobes	*Hypsugo savii*

Distribution: Originally described from China; found in Anhui, Shanghai, Fujian, Guangdong, Hong Kong, Hainan, Yunnan, Sichuan, Shaanxi, Hunan, Guizhou, and Jiangsu; extending to Vietnam, Laos, and Thailand; monotypic species.

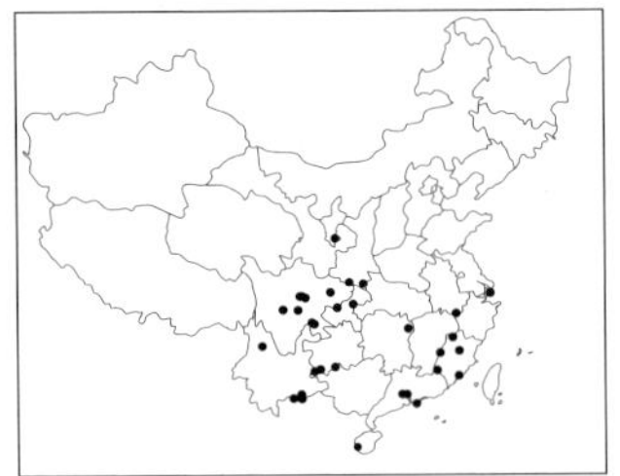

MAP 383. CHINESE PIPISTRELLE, *Hypsugo pulveratus*

Natural History: This species appears to inhabit forested regions but has also been found roosting in houses. Little is known of its natural history.
Comments: Corbet and Hill (1992) placed *H. pulveratus* in a *pulveratus* subgroup of their *savii* group. Wang (2003) lists it as *Pipistrellus pulveratus*.
Conservation Status: China RL—NT; although it nearly met the criteria for VU A1bcd. IUCN RL—LR/nt ver 2.3 (1994).
References: Bates et al. (1997); Hendrichsen et al. (2001).

Savi's Pipistrelle

Hypsugo savii (Bonaparte, 1837) MAP 384
萨氏伏翼 Sashi Fuyi

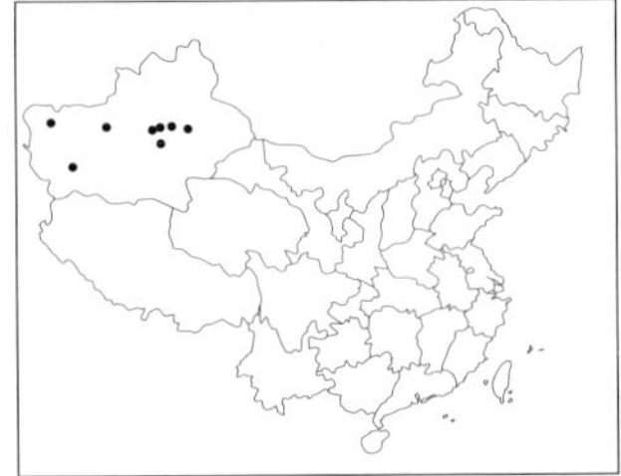

MAP 384. SAVI'S PIPISTRELLE, *Hypsugo savii*

Distinctive Characteristics: HB 47–60; T 30–35; HF 6–8; E 10–14; FA 32–36; GLS 13.1–14.2. Medium-sized for group; zygomatic width 8.9–9.3 mm; ear and tragus wide and short; wing membrane attaches to heel; tail extends from posterior margins of uropatagium about 5 mm; dorsal hair dark brown; ventral surface taupe; rostrum of skull flat; cranium wide and low; zygomatic arch slightly thick, with slender supraorbital process; inner incisors bicuspid; crowns of outer incisors a little smaller than those of inner incisors; small premolar (P2) relatively reduced, its size about 1/6–1/4 of that of outer-incisor crown; occasionally it is absent on one or both sides.
Distribution: Xinjiang; extending across Asia and N Europe. Chinese subspecies: *H. s. caucasicus* Satunin, 1901.

Natural History: The diet is small flying insects, which are pursued throughout the night. Occurs from sea level up to high mountain valleys across a wide range in southern Europe and Asia. Roosts have been found in cracks and crevices, both natural and in buildings. May be migratory in some areas. Becomes sexually mature at about one year of age. One or two young are born in maternity roosts and are weaned at about seven to eight weeks.
Comments: Wang (2003) lists this species as *Pipistrellus savii*, and placed the Chinese population in *P. s. pallescens* (Bobrinskii, 1926), which is a junior synonym of *caucasicus*.
Conservation Status: China RL—LC.
References: Bates and Harrison (1997); Horácek et al. (2000); Richarz and Limbrunner (1993).

Genus *Ia* (monotypic)

南蝠属 Nanfu Shu

Great Evening Bat

Ia io Thomas, 1902 PLATE 36 MAP 385
南蝠 Nanfu

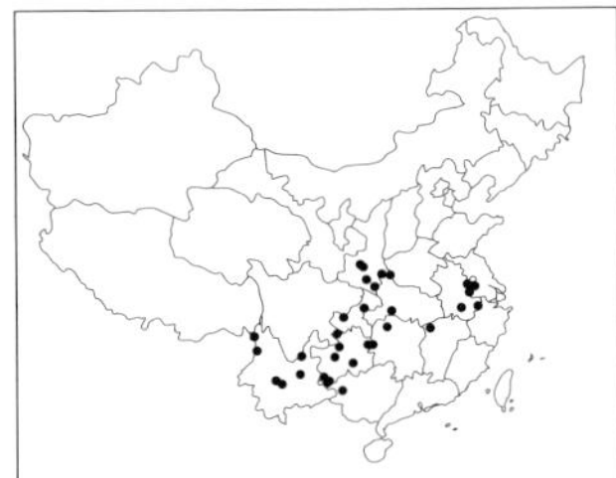

MAP 385. GREAT EVENING BAT, *Ia io*

Distinctive Characteristics: HB 89–104; T 61–83; HF 13–18; E 22–29; FA 71–80; GLS 27. Very similar to *Pipistrellus*, but size very large; fifth digit very short, its tip only reaching about 1/2 or 2/3 of first phalanx of third digit; skull strong; sagittal crest developed; occiput noticeably protruding up and back; palate narrow; basisphenoid longer than wide. Dental formula: 2.1.2.3/3.1.2.3 = 34; outer incisor in upper jaw relatively reduced, its crown flat, height only to inner incisor edges, and lacking cusp in middle; canine and large premolar (P4) join closely; small premolar (P2) lies in the internal angle of canine and premolar; mesostyles of first and second upper molars inconspicuous, not extending outward to the part outside the line connecting style and posterior style. Size large; zygomatic width 16.7–17.0 mm; pelage color dark smoky brown dorsally and dark grayish brown ventrally; face hairless; ears densely haired; tip of tail extends slightly beyond uropatagium.
Distribution: Sichuan, Guizhou, Anhui, Jiangxi, Hunan, Guangxi, Jiangsu, Yunnan, Shaanxi, and Hubei; extending to Nepal, India, Thailand, Laos, and Vietnam. *Ia* is a monotypic genus in the tribe Vespertilionini.
Natural History: This species is known to roost in caves and occurs at elevations to at least 1,700 m. They forage early and sometimes return to the caves

early as well. They may also be migratory in some areas. They have been taken in pine forests in China.
Comments: *Ia longimana* Pen, 1962, is a synonym.
Conservation Status: China RL–NT; although it nearly met the criteria for VU A2abcd. IUCN RL–LR/nt ver 2.3 (1994).
References: Bates and Harrison (1997); Csorba (1998); Hendrichsen et al. (2001); Topál (1970a).

Genus *Nyctalus*—Noctules

山蝠属 Shanfu Shu—山蝠 Shanfu

Size medium, but sturdy; ears short and wide; tragus short and curved; third digit very short, its length about equal to or a little more than length of metacarpal bone of third or fourth digit; nostrils enlarged, extending half the distance from rostrum tip to interorbital region; rostrum slightly high; zygomatic arch relatively extenuated; basisphenoid developed; lambdoidal crest conspicuous; incisors in upper jaw with one main cusp, and behind main cusp of outer incisor is another small style; canine and large premolar (P4) touch closely; small premolar (P2) pushed to inner side of toothrow; canines without small posterior cusp; styles of first and second upper molar small; posterior cusp of third upper molar developed. Dental formula: 2.1.2.3/3.1.2.3 = 34. Distributed in N Eastern Hemisphere. Of eight species known, three have been recorded from China. *Nyctalus* is a member of the tribe Pipistrellini.

Birdlike Noctule

PLATE 37
MAP 386

Nyctalus aviator (Thomas, 1911)
大山蝠 Dashan Fu

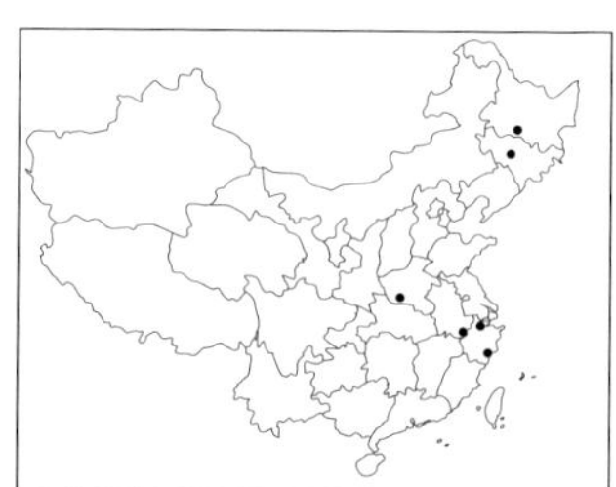

MAP 386. BIRDLIKE NOCTULE, *Nyctalus aviator*

Distinctive Characteristics: HB 80–106; T 45–62; HF 12–17; E 16–23; FA 58–64. Size large; thumb short, but with strong claw; calcar keeled; fur dense and velvety; color deep yellowish brown; upper inner incisor longer than outer incisor; muzzle broad with gland between eye and nostril; tragus short and stubby; antitragus long and low; fifth finger shortest, third longest; wing membrane attached to ankle; tip of tail barely extends past uropatagium; skull broad and robust; postorbital process weak; teeth large, with low cusps.
Distribution: Heilongjiang, Jilin, Henan, Zhejiang, and Anhui; extending to Japan, Korea, and probably Russia.
Natural History: This species inhabits mountainous areas, where it forages in deciduous forests. They leave the roost early in the evening and forage actively for flying insects fairly high off the ground. Diurnal roosts are frequently in tree cavities.
Comments: Sometimes considered a subspecies of *N. lasiopterus*, with which it is allopatric. *Vespertilio molossus* Temminck, 1840 is a synonym but is also an unavailable homonym of *V. molossus* Pallas 1767.
Conservation Status: China RL–NT; although it nearly met the criteria for VU A1acd. IUCN RL–LR/nt ver 2.3 (1994).
References: Corbet (1978); Wallin (1969); Yoshiyuki (1989).

Noctule

PLATE 37
MAP 387

Nyctalus noctula (Schreber, 1774)
褐山蝠 Heshan Fu

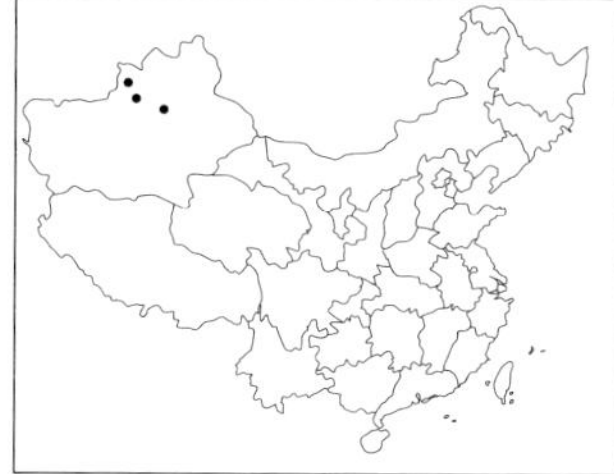

MAP 387. NOCTULE, *Nyctalus noctula*

Distinctive Characteristics: HB 60–82; T 41–61; HF 12–14; E 16–21; FA 47–60; GLS 17–19.4. Size small; pelage thick, extending onto wing membrane between 1/3 section of basal part of fifth digit and knees; rostrum of skull relatively high and wide; front not recessed; lambdoidal crest undeveloped; zygomatic arch extenuated; upper outer incisor larger than inner incisor; crown of small premolar (P2) about half of or nearly equal to outer incisor in size.
Distribution: Xinjiang; widely distributed throughout the Eastern Hemisphere. Chinese subspecies: *N. n. mecklenburzevi* Kuzyakin, 1934.
Natural History: This species is widespread in Eurasia and is primarily an inhabitant of lowland deciduous forests. It frequently roosts in buildings and tree hollows. It has adapted readily to human habitations and can be seen flying in cities and suburbs as well.

Key to the Chinese Species of *Nyctalus*

1.a.	Size large; forearm length 61–68 mm	*Nyctalus aviator*
b.	Size small; forearm length < 60 mm	2
2.a.	Single pair of basal pits; individual hairs unicolored	*Nyctalus noctula*
b.	Two pairs of basal pits; individual hairs bicolored	*Nyctalus plancyi*

The females form maternity colonies in summer. One or two young are born after a gestation period of a little over two months. They are weaned after a further two months and become sexually mature at one or two years of age. They are known to live for up to twelve years. The diet is large flying insects such as moths and larger beetles.
Comments: Wang (2003) lists *N. n. plancei* as a subspecies, but these animals should be referred to *Nyctalus plancyi velutinus.*
Conservation Status: China RL–NA.
References: Bates and Harrison (1997); Harrison and Bates (1991); Horácek et al. (2000); Richarz and Limbrunner (1993).

Chinese Noctule

Nyctalus plancyi Gerbe, 1880 MAP 388
中华山蝠 Zhonghua Shanfu

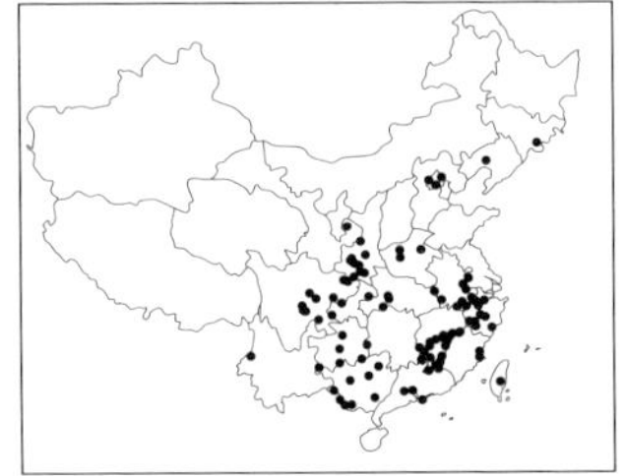

MAP 388. CHINESE NOCTULE, *Nyctalus plancyi*

Distinctive Characteristics: HB 65–75; T 36–52; HF 10–11; E 15–18; FA 47–50; 17–19. Size small; smaller and darker than *N. noctula*; bases of individual hairs fuscous, with brownish tips, paler ventrally; fur extends onto plagiopatagium along proximal half of humerus and onto uropatagium to midtibia. Infraorbital foramen large; lacrimal foramen on orbital ridge; deep basial pits; upper outer incisor low, not extending beyond cingulum of inner incisor.
Distribution: Throughout SE China, as far north as Jilin Province, and on Taiwan. Endemic. Two subspecies in China: (1) *N. p. plancyi* Gerbe, 1880; Beijing, Shandong, Henan, Shanxi, Shaanxi, Gansu, Liaoning, Jilin; (2) *N. p. velutinus* Allen, 1923; Fujian, Anhui, Jiangsu, Shanghai, Zhejiang, Jiangxi, Guangdong, Hong Kong, Guangxi, Hunan, Hubei, Guizhou, Yunnan, Sichuan, Taiwan.
Natural History: This form enters hibernation in early–mid-November and ovulates at the end of March–early April. They exhibit delayed fertilization, and twins are normally produced in late June following a 50–60 day gestation.
Comments: *N. plancyi* has been considered a subspecies of *N. noctula* in the past, as has *N. p. velutinus. N. p. velutinus* has also been considered a distinct species at times in the past.
Conservation Status: China RL–LC.
References: Liang and Dong (1985); Tate (1942); Yoshiyuki (1989); Zhang (1990).

Genus *Pipistrellus*—Pipistrelles

伏翼属 Fuyi Shu—伏翼类 Fuyilei

Form similar to that of *Myotis*, but generally size smaller, rostrum wider, cranium also lower than that of *Myotis*; ears smallish; tragus short and blunt, unlike the narrow, long, and sharp ones of *Myotis*, and tips slightly turning forward; hind foot smallish; tail entirely enclosed in uropatagium, with only the tip slightly protruding in some species; fifth digit not contracted; skull relatively broad. Dental formula: 2.1.2.3/3.1.2.3 = 34; inner incisor in upper jaw usually possesses mesostyle, outer incisor a little smaller than inner incisor, but distinctly higher than cingulum of inner incisor; canines developed, sometimes with mesostles in posterior root; small premolar (P2) in upper jaw leans to inner side of toothrow, or squeezed out of toothrow. Widely distributed in the Eastern Hemisphere and most areas of northern Western Hemisphere; Chinese distribution also very broad. Of 31 species, 8 are known from China. *Pipistrellus* is a member of the tribe Pipistrellini.

Japanese Pipistrelle

PLATE 37
Pipistrellus abramus (Temminck, 1840) MAP 389
东亚伏翼 Dongya Fuyi

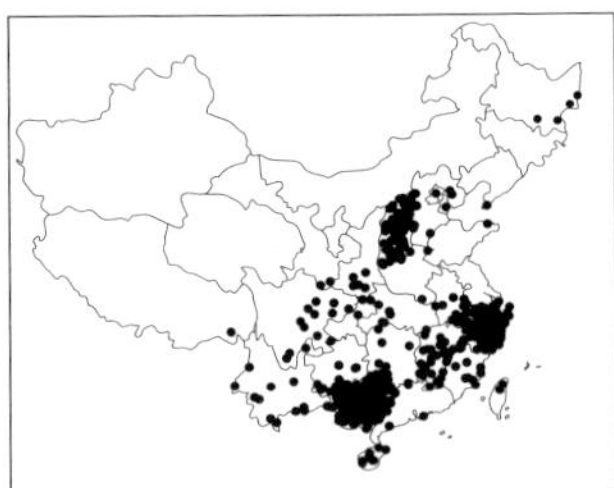

MAP 389. JAPANESE PIPISTRELLE, *Pipistrellus abramus*

Distinctive Characteristics: HB 38–60; T 29–45; HF 6–10; E 8–13; FA 31–36; GLS 12.2–13.4. Size small; zygomatic width 8.3–9.0 mm; wing membrane starts from basal part of toe; length of baculum about 10 mm; dorsal hair taupe or brown; skull very wide; zygomatic arch slender; rostrum wide and flat; crown of inner incisor in upper jaw dichotomous; size of small premolar (P2) about equal to that of outer incisor, but smaller than inner incisor; there is a small cusp behind each canine.
Distribution: Widely distributed across eastern half of China including Nei Mongol, Heilongjiang, Liaoning, Hebei, Tianjin, Shanxi, Jiangsu, Gansu, Sichuan, Yunnan, Shandong, Anhui, Zhejiang, Hubei, Hunan, Guangxi, Fujian, Taiwan, Jiangxi, Guangdong, Hong Kong, Macao, Guizhou, Xizang, Shaanxi, and Hainan; extending across E Asia.
Natural History: Common throughout its range in China, *P. abramus* is frequently found in buildings and around human habitations. It regularly forms small colonies in attics or between the walls of

Key to the Chinese Species of *Pipistrellus*

1.a. Inner upper incisor unicuspid; outer small, crown area less than half that of inner, tip extends barely beyond cincugulum of inner; crown of anterior upper premolar < half that of inner upper incisor — *Pipistrellus kuhlii*
b. Inner upper incisor bicuspid; outer large, crown area equal to inner, tip extends to half or more of inner, crown of anterior upper premolar equal to that of inner upper incisor — 2
2.a. Anterior upper premolar in toothrow and visible laterally; upper canine separated from posterior premolar — *Pipistrellus pipistrellus*
b. Anterior upper premolar in lingual recess and invisible laterally; upper canine in contact with posterior premolar labially, obscuring all but tip of anterior premolar — 3
3.a. Larger; forearm > 35 mm; condylobasal length > 14 mm; cranial profile convex over frontal region — *Pipistrellus ceylonicus*
b. Smaller; forearm < 35 mm; condylobasal length < 14 mm; cranial profile straight from anterior to posterior — 4
4.a. Supraorbital region broad; rostrum broad, dorsally flattened; palate strongly domed — 5
b. Supraorbital region narrow; rostrum narrow, not dorsally flattened; palate weakly domed — 7
5.a. Skull smaller; condylobasal length < 11.6 mm; upper canine without posterior cusp — *Pipistrellus paterculus*
b. Skull larger; condylobasal length > 11.6 mm; upper canine with tiny posterior cusp — 6
6.a. Braincase barely inflated (convex) above frontal region; rostrum wider; palate narrower; upper molars less robust — *Pipistrellus abramus*
b. Braincase slightly convex above frontal region; rostrum narrower; palate broader; upper molars more robust — *Pipistrellus javanicus*
7.a. Condylobasal length > 11.4 mm; width across upper molars more than 5.3 mm — *Pipistrellus coromandra*
b. Condylobasal length < 11.4 mm; width across upper molars less than 5.3 mm — *Pipistrellus tenuis*

houses and other buildings. An aerial insectivore, it can be seen feeding in open areas around lights and in disturbed habitats of various types. In spite of being widespread and abundant, little is known of its natural history.
Comments: A member of the subgenus *Pipistrellus*, *P. abramus* was sometimes considered a subspecies of *P. javanicus* in the past.
Conservation Status: China RL–LC.
References: Hill and Harrison (1987); Yoshiyuki (1989).

Kelaart's Pipistrelle

PLATE 37
MAP 390

Pipistrellus ceylonicus (Kelaart, 1852)
锡兰伏翼 Xilan Fuyi

Distinctive Characteristics: HB 45–64; T 30–45; HF 6–11; E 9–14; FA 33–42; GLS 14.7–15.8; Wt 9–10 g. Size large; zygomatic width 10–10.9 mm; hair color dark brown or brown, without gray hair tip; skull relatively large; rostrum wide and short; cranium low; zygomatic arch slender, without supraorbital process; upper toothrow short (length 5.7–6.0 mm); there is a mesostyle behind each upper canine; in upper jaw small premolar (P2) and outer incisor about equal in size.
Distribution: S Guangxi, Hainan Island; extending across Indo-Malayan realm. Two subspecies in China: (1) *P. c. raptor* Thomas, 1904; S Guangxi; extending to Vietnam; (2) *P. c. tongfangensis* Wang, 1966; Hainan.

MAP 390. KELAART'S PIPISTRELLE, *Pipistrellus ceylonicus*

Natural History: Although the range in China is limited, this species occupies a variety of habitats and can be locally common. It is a frequent inhabitant of populated areas, where it roosts in buildings of all types. Colonies from a few to more than a hundred individuals have also been noted in caves, tree holes, wells, and similar areas. They fly early in the evening, close to the ground, and are quite maneuverable. Beetles and other small insects make up the diet. Females have been shown to store sperm, and the gestation period is just under two months. Twins are the rule, although singles and triplets are also known. Lactation lasts for a little over a month.
Comments: A member of the subgenus *Pipistrellus; P. ceylonicus* is widespread and abundant eastward to India and Pakistan.
Conservation Status: China RL–NA.
References: Bates and Harrison (1997).

Indian Pipistrelle

PLATE 37
MAP 391

Pipistrellus coromandra (Gray, 1838)
印度伏翼 Yindu Fuyi

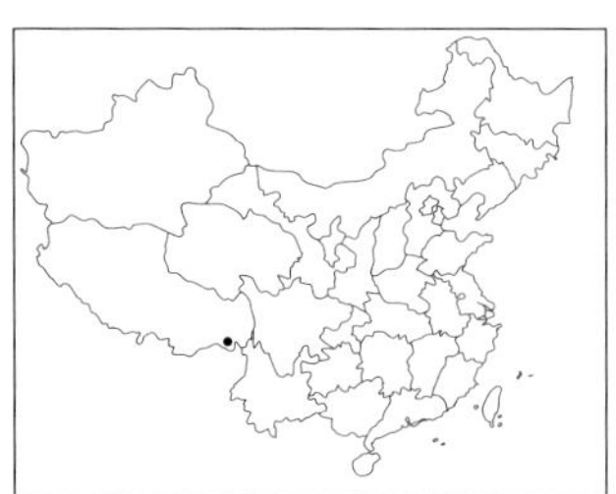

MAP 391. INDIAN PIPISTRELLE, *Pipistrellus coromandra*

Distinctive Characteristics: HB 34–49; T 22–39; HF 3–8; E 7–14; FA 25–35; GLS 10.6–11.9. Size small; dorsal pelage uniformly mid- to dark brown, ranging from chestnut to dark clove brown; ventral surface paler, with beige brown or cinnamon brown tips and dark roots; ears and membranes mid- to dark brown and essentially naked, with a few hairs on the uropatagium next to the body and tail, above and below. Skull slightly larger than *P. tenuis* and slightly smaller than *P. javanicus*. Very similar to *P. tenuis*.
Distribution: Xizang; extending to Afghanistan.
Natural History: Small colonies of a few to dozens of individuals roost in buildings and tree holes and under the bark of trees. Foraging begins at dusk, and individuals occasionally return to the diurnal roost for varying periods during the night. Flight is slow and maneuverable, as the bats feed on small diptera and other insects, close to the ground. Twins are the norm, although singles are also known. They may also breed more than once per year, depending on the locality.
Comments: A member of the subgenus *Pipistrellus*, *P. coromandra* barely penetrates westward into China. Wang (2003) included *P. tramatus* and *portensis* in this species, but those populations actually belong with *P. tenuis*.
Conservation Status: China RL—NT; although it nearly met the criteria for VU A1bc.
References: Corbett and Hill (1992); Bates and Harrison (1997).

Javan Pipistrelle

PLATE 37
MAP 392

Pipistrellus javanicus (Gray, 1838)
爪哇伏翼 Zhaowa Fuyi

Distinctive Characteristics: HB 40–55; T 26–40; HF 3–8; E 5–15; FA 30–36. Size medium; dorsal coloration reddish brown to darker brown, sometimes with frosting of paler tipped hairs; venter paler; wings and tail membranes darker brown, and essentially hairless; skull robust; rostrum broad and flat; dorsal profile more or less straight; palate broad and concave; basisphenoid pits moderate; first upper premolar displaced inward, but canine and second premolar not quite in contact.
Distribution: Xizang, Yunnan; extending broadly across SE Asia and eastward to Afghanistan. Chinese subspecies: *P. j. peguensis* Sinha, 1969.
Natural History: Uncommon resident of both forested and disturbed habitats. This species is known to roost in buildings and other manmade structures. It occurs through a wide elevational range extralimitally, but little is known of its natural history in China.

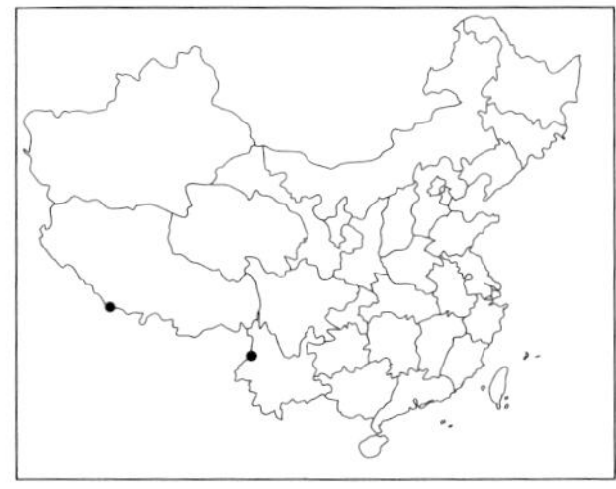

MAP 392. JAVAN PIPISTRELLE, *Pipistrellus javanicus*

Comments: A member of the subgenus *Pipistrellus*, *P. javanicus* was previously known as *P. tralatitius*.
Conservation Status: China RL—NA.
References: Allen (1938); Corbet and Hill (1992); Kock (1996); Bates and Harrison (1997).

Kuhl's Pipistrelle

MAP 393

Pipistrellus kuhlii (Kuhl, 1817)
古氏伏翼 Gushi Fuyi

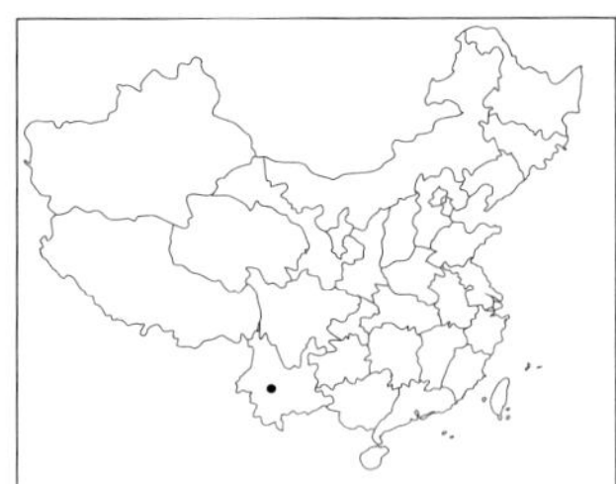

MAP 393. KUHL'S PIPISTRELLE, *Pipistrellus kuhlii*

Distinctive Characteristics: HB 35–49; T 30–45; HF 6–8; E 10–13; FA 31–36; GLS 13–14. Size medium; ears short and round; tragus parallel-sided; trailing edge of wing membrane frequently with whitish border; hair color variable, but dark basally; wings narrow. Rostrum long and slightly flattened; dorsal profile straight; palate longer than broad; basisphenoid pits shallow; first upper premolar minute and displaced lingually.
Distribution: This species is included in the Chinese fauna solely on the basis of a single record in Yunnan from Wang (2003); extending from Kazakhstan and India eastward to central Europe. Presumably, the Chinese subspecies would be *P. k. lepidus* Blyth, 1845.
Natural History: Nothing is known from China, but in Europe this species is known to bear twins normally. They live to about eight years and become sexually mature at about one year of age. Like other pipistrelles, they feed on small flying insects. They enjoy a wide elevational range and are frequently encountered near human settlements.

Comments: Verification of this species' presence in China is needed. It is a member of the subgenus *Pipistrellus*.
Conservation Status: China RL–DD.
References: Wang (2003).

Mount Popa Pipistrelle

PLATE 37
Pipistrellus paterculus Thomas, 1915 MAP 394
棒茎伏翼 Bangjing Fuyi

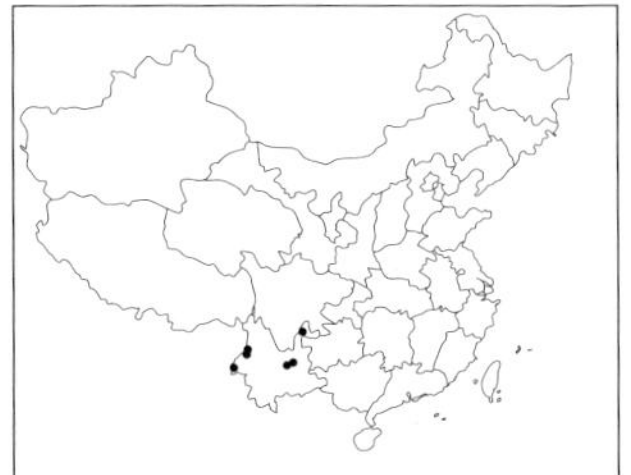

MAP 394. MOUNT POPA PIPISTRELLE, *Pipistrellus paterculus*

Distinctive Characteristics: HB 42–48; T 31–38; HF 6–7; E 10–13; FA 29–34; GLS 13–14. Size small; dark brown dorsally, and bicolored ventrally with hair tips paler; uropatagium furred for proximal one-third. Rostrum broad; braincase robust, and slightly distinct from rostrum; dentition robust; first upper premolar small, and slightly displaced; canine and second premolar not quite in contact.
Distribution: Yunnan; extending to India. Chinese subspecies: *P. p. yunnanensis* Wang, 1982.
Natural History: Nothing is known of the habits of this species in China, and very little from elsewhere. They are known from sea level up to 2,400 m. Specimens have been collected from clearings in forested regions.
Comments: *P. paterculus* is a member of the subgenus *Pipistrellus*. At one time this species was thought to be included in *P. abramus*.
Conservation Status: China RL–VU D2. IUCN RL–LR/nt ver 2.3 (1994).
References: Lunde et al. (2003b).

Common Pipistrelle

Pipistrellus pipistrellus (Schreber, 1774) MAP 395
伏翼 Fuyi

Distinctive Characteristics: HB 40–48; T 29–35; HF 6–7; E 10–12; FA 30–32; GLS 10.5; Wt 4–5 g. Size small; interorbital breadth 3.3 mm; occipital width 6.2 mm; length of upper toothrow (C-M3) 3.8 mm; calcar slightly keeled; pelage color blackish gray, paler near sides of body; basal part of hair jet-black. Skull narrow; cranium slightly elevated; small premolar (P2) in upper jaw slightly lower than outer incisor, lying on inner side of toothrow, touching canine and large premolar (P4).
Distribution: Widely distributed in SE China and Taiwan, and also found in Xinjiang; extending widely across both Asia and Europe. Chinese subspecies: *P. p. aladdin* Thomas, 1905.
Natural History: Common Pipistrelles feed on small flying lepidoptera and diptera, which they catch by foraging in set patterns. They occupy a wide range of habitats but roost primarily in houses. One or two young are born after a gestation period of about a month and a half. The young begin to fly at about one month and are fully weaned by six to seven weeks of age. They first breed in the year following their birth, and individuals are known to live for up to 17 years.

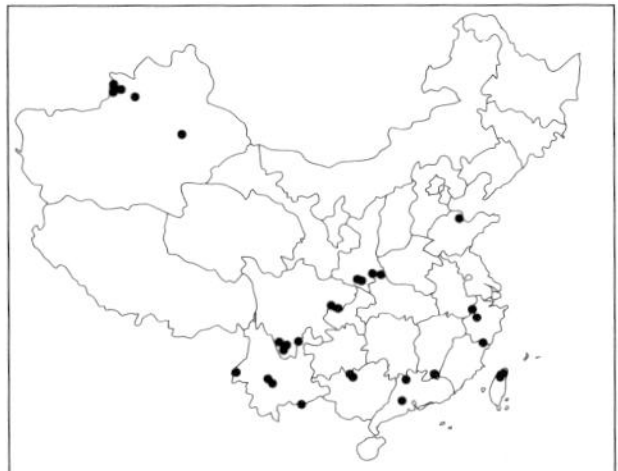

MAP 395. COMMON PIPISTRELLE, *Pipistrellus pipistrellus*

Comments: A member of the subgenus *Pipistrellus*, this species was recently shown to be composite, with *P. pygmaeus* designated as a separate species. The limits of *P. pipistrellus* and *P. pygmaeus* remain to be determined, as the two are separable only on molecular and echolocation characters.
Conservation Status: China RL–LC.
References: International Commission on Zoological Nomenclature (2003).

Least Pipistrelle

Pipistrellus tenuis (Temminck, 1840) MAP 396
小伏翼 Xiao Fuyi

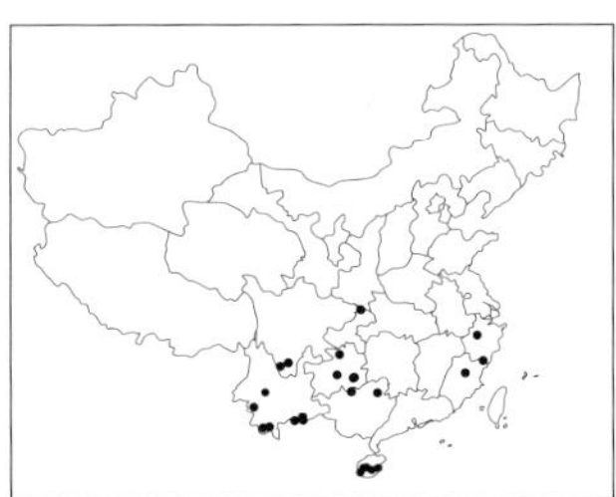

MAP 396. LEAST PIPISTRELLE, *Pipistrellus tenuis*

Distinctive Characteristics: HB 33–45; T 20–35; HF 3–7; E 5–11; FA 25–31; GLS 9–11; Wt 2 g. Size small; dorsal color varies from medium to dark brown, ventral color paler and hair tips are buffy with dark brown bases. Skull delicate; braincase small with broad postorbital constriction; first upper incisor bicuspid, second incisor well developed; both upper and lower first premolars slightly outside toothrow.
Distribution: SE China, including Hainan Island; extending westward to Afghanistan. Chinese subspecies: *P. t. portensis* Allen, 1906.

Natural History: This is a widespread species that occurs in a variety of habitats and is also partial to towns and villages. These bats roost in attics, under roofs, in holes and crevices of walls, in tree holes, and occasionally in the foliage. Colony size is usually small, with no more than a dozen or two individuals. They fly early in the evening and feed on tiny flying insects both in forests and over clearings and fields. Pregnant females have been collected throughout the year, but in most tropical regions there are probably two peaks of activity. From one to three young are born, and weaned at 30–40 days of age.
Comments: A member of the subgenus *Pipistrellus*, *P. tenuis* is poorly understood taxonomically and may prove to be a composite. Wang (2003) includes *P. mimus* as a separate species, but *mimus* is likely just a subspecies of *tenuis*. It is possible that some mainland populations of *P. tenuis* belong to *P. t. mimus*, rather than to *P. t. portensis*, which was named from Hainan Island.
Conservation Status: China RL–LC.
References: Corbett and Hill (1992); Bates and Harrison (1997).

Genus *Plecotus*—Long-eared Bats

大耳蝠属 Da'erfu Shu—大耳蝠 Da'erfu

Size small; ear extremely large, its length much more than head length; ears joined at front; tragus relatively long; nostrils upturned; wing membrane attached to base of toes; tail length about equal to HB length; tail wholly enclosed in uropatagium; cranium of skull long and round; auditory bullae large and round, diameter about two times the distance between auditory sacs; rostrum very narrow; two premolars (P2 and P4) in upper jaw, three premolars (p2–p4) in lower jaw. Dental formula: 2.1.2.3/3.1.3.3 = 36. Distributed in N Asia, Europe, and N Africa; in China mainly distributed in northern regions, and Taiwan. *Plecotus* is a member of the tribe Plecotini. Of eight species in the genus, three occur in China.

Brown Long-Eared Bat

PLATE 37
Plecotus auritus (Linnaeus, 1758) MAP 397
褐长耳蝠 He Chang'erfu

Distinctive Characteristics: HB 40–45; T 48–50; HF 7–8; E 39–41; FA 36–46; GLS 16.5–18.8. Size small; zygomatic width 8.9–10.2 mm; length of hind foot about half of tibia length; calcar unkeeled; dorsal hair taupe; ventral surface off-white; ears very large, almost equal in surface area to the head and body; ears joined across forehead by narrow band; tail long, exceeding HB length.

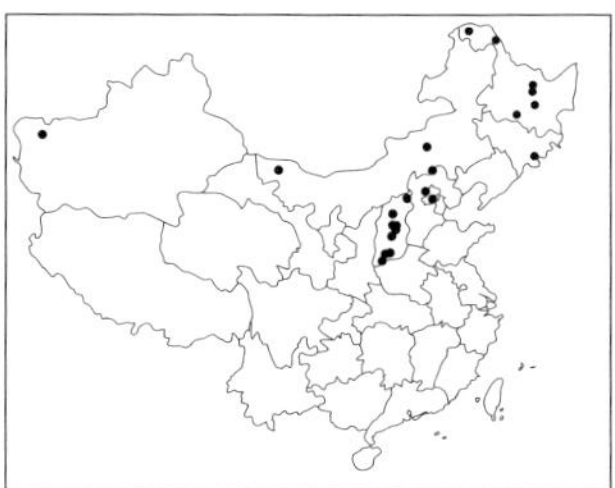

MAP 397. BROWN LONG-EARED BAT, *Plecotus auritus*

Distribution: Across N China, but Wang (2003) lists a record from Yunnan; extending across N Asia and to W Europe. Chinese subspecies: *P. a. sacrimontis* Allen, 1908, but Wang (2003) attributes the Yunnan record to *P. a. homochrous* Hodgson, 1847.
Natural History: Brown Long-eared Bats feed primarily on medium-sized moths and other insects. This wide-spread species occurs in forested areas at low and moderate elevations. These bats also frequent inhabited areas. They roost in tree holes and a variety of buildings, as well as caves and tunnels. They have a slow, maneuverable foraging flight, and they occasionally glean prey from the foliage. A single young is the norm, but occasional twins have been reported. They are weaned at about six to seven weeks of age and become sexually mature in their second year. The maximum recorded lifespan is 22 years.
Comments: Allocation of Chinese subspecies is uncertain, and the species may be composite. The Yunnan record is particularly interesting, as *P. p. homochrous* may deserve recognition as a separate species.
Conservation Status: China RL–NT; although it nearly met the criteria for VU A1bcd.
References: Horácek et al. (2000); Wang (2003); Yoshiyuki (1991b).

Gray Long-Eared Bat

PLATE 37
Plecotus austriacus (Fischer, 1829) MAP 398
灰长耳蝠 Hui Chang'erfu

Distinctive Characteristics: HB 41–58; T 37–55; HF 7–10; E 37–42; FA 37–45. Size medium; ears conspicuously long; muzzle long and pointed; fur long and

Key to the Chinese Species of *Plecotus*

1.a.	Width of tragus 5.4 mm or less; upper canine height 1.7 mm or less; dorsal pelage buffy or gray; ventral hairs with dark brown or buff bases	2
b.	Width of tragus 5.4 mm or more; upper canine height 1.7 mm or more; dorsal pelage gray, ventral hairs with black bases	*Plecotus austriacus*
2.a.	On the Chinese mainland	*Plecotus auritus*
b.	On Taiwan	*Plecotus taivanus*

gray in color, with hair dark basally; tips of dorsal hairs vary from buff to brown; ventral hair tips are paler and whitish. Skull slightly larger and longer than *P. auritus*; tympanic bullae large and basioccipital region narrow.

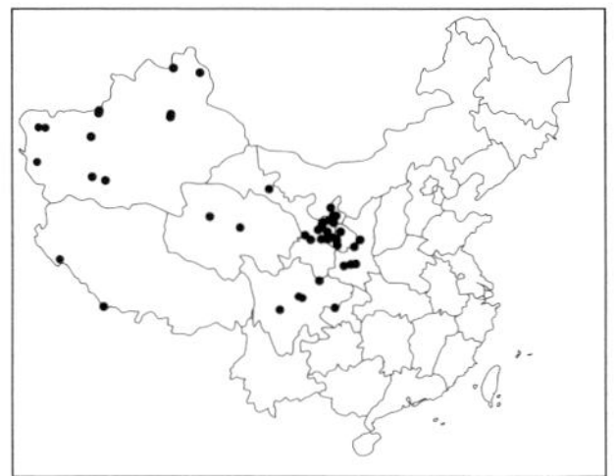

MAP 398. GRAY LONG-EARED BAT, *Plecotus austriacus*

Distribution: C and W China; extending eastward to Mongolia and to Europe. Two subspecies in China: (1) *P. a. ariel* Thomas, 1911; Sichuan, Qinghai, Nei Mongol, Gansu, Ningxia; (2) *P. a. wardi* Thomas, 1911; Xinjiang, Xizang.
Natural History: This widespread species is frequently found around human habitations. They forage low and slowly, feeding on a variety of small lepidoptera, coleopteran, and diptera. Roosts are known from buildings, as well as caves. Colonies tend to be small, and single individuals are common as well.
Comments: As in *P. auritus*, subspecies limits are not always clear in *P. austriacus*. Wang (2003) recognized *P. a. kozlovi* Bobrinski, 1926, and *P. a. mordax* Thomas, 1926 from China as well, but we consider *kozlovi* a synonym of *ariel* and *mordax* a synonym of *wardi*.
Conservation Status: China RL-LC.
References: Horácek et al. (2000); Wang (2003); Yoshiyuki (1991b).

Taiwan Long-Eared Bat

Plecotus taivanus Yoshiyuki, 1991 MAP 399
台湾长耳蝠 Taiwan Chang'erfu

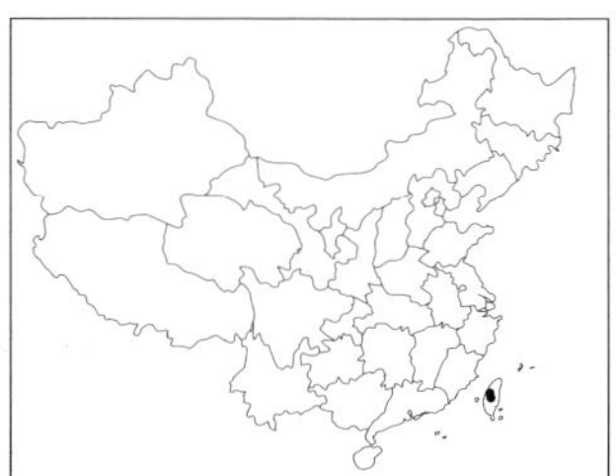

MAP 399. TAIWAN LONG-EARED BAT, *Plecotus taivanus*

Distinctive Characteristics: HB 48–50; T 47–49; HF 9–11; E 36–39; FA 37–38. Size small; fur rough and long, but with shorter hairs in mid-dorsal region; color blackish with buffy-brown hair tips, giving a golden sheen; ears about the same length as forearms; tragus long and wide, with prominent basal lobe; wings wide; calcar unkeeled; tail completely enclosed in uropatagium. Skull fragile; supraorbital region ridged; rostrum narrow and flattened with medial concavity; zygomatic arches weak; braincase relatively broad.
Distribution: Taiwan. Endemic.
Natural History: The holotype was collected in forest at an elevation of 2,250 m in the central mountainous region of Taiwan. Nothing is known of the life history of this species.
Comments: The original description suggested closest similarity to *P. homochrous* and *P. puck* Barrett-Hamilton, 1907, both of which are now considered subspecies of *P. auritus*.
Conservation Status: China RL-EN B2ab(i, ii, iii). IUCN RL–VU A2c ver 2.3 (1994).
References: Lin et al. (1997); Yoshiyuki (1991b).

Genus *Scotomanes* (monotypic)

斑蝠属 Banfu Shu—斑蝠 Banfu

Harlequin Bat

PLATE 38
Scotomanes ornatus (Blyth, 1851) MAP 400
斑蝠 Banfu

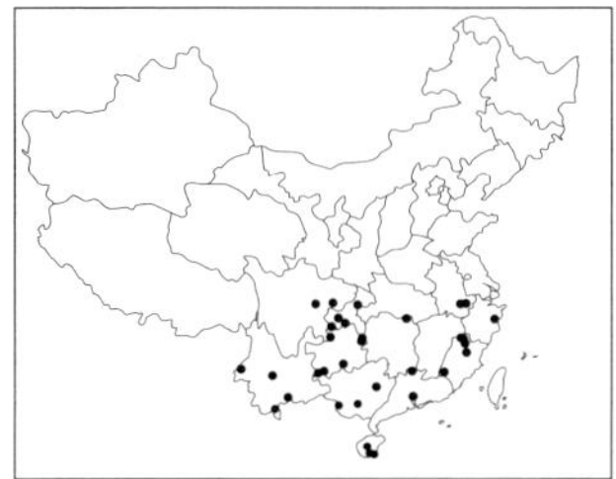

MAP 400. HARLEQUIN BAT, *Scotomanes ornatus*

Distinctive Characteristics: HB 64–85; T 52–66; HF 12–15; E 19–23; FA 50–62; GLS 20. Size large; pelage color orange-brown or nearly reddish brown; ventral surface slightly lighter; front, shoulder, and back all with white sploches or long spots; ears large; tragus broad and crescent-shaped. Skull robust and broad; prominent lacrimal processes and supraorbital ridges; zygomatic arches strong. Form similar to that of *Scotophilus*, but with unique pelage color, brown and with white stripes; tragus shape similar to that of *Pipistrellus*; rostrum of skull very short; palatal sinus very small, its depth nearly half of width between canines; lacrimal relatively expanded; braincase low; sagittal and lambdoidal crests both extenuated. Dental formula same as in *Scotophilus*: 1.1.1.3/3.1.2.3 = 30; third upper molar not distinctly reduced as in *Scotophilus*.
Distribution: Sichuan, Yunnan, Guizhou, Anhui, Fujian, Hunan, Guangxi, Guangdong, and Hainan; extending eastward to India. Chinese subspecies: *S. o. sinensis* Thomas, 1921.
Natural History: The striking color pattern is likely an adaptation for roosting in the foliage, where most

roosts have been found. It seems to be an inhabitant of lowland forests, but little has been recorded of its natural history.
Comments: *Scotomanes* is a member of the tribe Nycticeiini. Wang (2003) recognizes some specimens from Yunnan and Guizhou as *S. o. imbrensis* Thomas, 1921 and others from the same region as *S. emarginatus* Dobson, 1841. Although *imbrensis* is the recognized subspecies for populations in India, we consider all Chinese populations to be *S. o. sinensis*. *Scotomanes emarginatus* is a junior synonym of *S. ornatus* and was named from an indeterminate locality in India.
Conservation Status: China RL–LC. IUCN RL–LR/nt ver 2.3 (1994).
References: Bates and Harrison (1997); Corbet and Hill (1992); Wang (2003).

Genus *Scotophilus*—Yellow House Bats

黄蝠属 Huangfu Shu—黄蝠 Huangfu

Size quite similar to that of *Eptesicus*; form sturdy; ears short and blunt; tragus crescent-shaped; hind foot very large; calcar thick, with a narrow keel; tail tip slightly projects from posterior margins of uropatagium; skull strong; sagittal crest developed; well-developed lambdoidal crest protruding from posterior of occiput. Dental formula: 1.1.1.3/3.1.2.3 = 30; mesostyles of molars in upper jaw reduced, hence occlusion of molars in incomplete "W" form; hypoconids and entoconids of lower molars relatively normal. Distributed in S Asia and Africa; of 12 species in the genus, 2 are known from China. *Scotophilus* is a member of the tribe Nycticiinae.

Greater Asiatic Yellow House Bat

PLATE 38
Scotophilus heathii (Horsfield, 1831) MAP 401
大黄蝠 Da Huangfu

Distinctive Characteristics: HB 67–93; T 43–71; HF 9–15; E 13–21; FA 55–66; GLS 21–26. Size large; zygomatic width 16–18 mm; pelage short and fine; dorsal hair snuff-colored; ventral surface light, brownish, or khaki but frequently with a distinct yellowish tint; tail tip protrudes slightly beyond uropatagium; muzzle short and broad. Skull robust; lambdoidal crest well developed, protruding back and upwards; prominent lacrimal processes; anterior emargination of palate deep and broad; tympanic bullae small.
Distribution: Across S China, including Hainan Island; extending through S and SE Asia. Chinese subspecies: *S. h. insularis* Allen, 1906.
Natural History: *Scotophilus heathii* is a common house bat. They forage in clearings and over fields and along forest edges. They are known from sea level up to at least 1,500 m. Colony size is small, usually less than 50 individuals occupying a single roost. Males form harems of two to six females during the breeding season, but the sexes roost separately otherwise. There is evidence of sperm storage in the females. One or two young are born after a gestation period of 115 days.

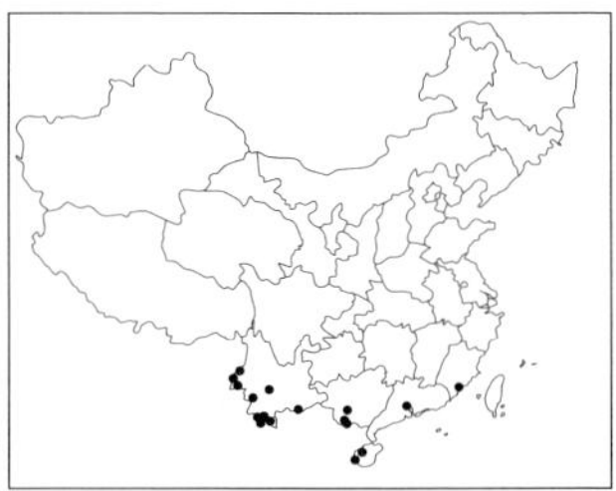

MAP 401. GREATER ASIATIC YELLOW HOUSE BAT, *Scotophilus heathii*

Comments: Subspecific allocation of Chinese specimens is tentative. Wang (2003) calls animals from the mainland *S. h. belangeri* Geoffroy, 1834, but that name is a synonym of the nominate form. Because there is an intervening subspecies in Thailand, *S. h. watkinsi* Sanborn, 1952, we are inclined to regard all Chinese populations as *S. h. insularis*.
Conservation Status: China RL–LC.
References: Bates and Harrison (1997); Wang (2003).

Lesser Asiatic Yellow House Bat

Scotophilus kuhlii Leach, 1821 MAP 402
小黄蝠 Xiao Huangfu

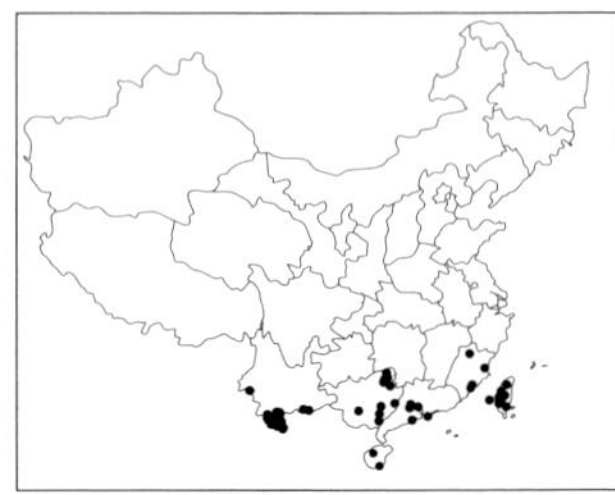

MAP 402. LESSER ASIATIC YELLOW HOUSE BAT, *Scotophilus kuhlii*

Key to the Chinese Species *Scotophilus*

1.a.	Size large; forearm length 55–69 mm; GLS > 21 mm; ventral pelage usually yellowish	*Scotophilus heathii*
b.	Size small; forearm length 44–55 mm; GLS < 21 mm; ventral pelage brownish	*Scotophilus kuhlii*

Distinctive Characteristics: HB 60–78; T 40–65; HF 8–13; E 9–17; FA 44–55; GLS 16–20. Size small; zygomatic width 12–14 mm; dorsal hair chestnut brown; ventral surface paler, but without yellowish hue. Skull less robust than that of *Scotophilus*; lambdoidal crest undeveloped, not protruding back and upward; upper toothrow 6.1–6.8 mm.
Distribution: The distribution is approximately the same as that of *Scotophilus heathii*. In China the distribution includes Taiwan, Fujian, Guangdong, Hong Kong, Hainan, Guangxi, and Yunnan; extending from Pakistan to W Malaysia and the Philippines. Chinese subspecies: *S. t. consobrinus* Allen, 1906.
Natural History: The similarity between *S. kuhlii* and *S. heathii* has led to confusion over their habits. They seem to be quite similar in roosting habits and foraging strategies. Colonies of up to a few hundred are known from houses, other manmade structures, and hollow trees. They forage early in the evening and fly low to the ground. They can be seen foraging in inhabited areas, as well as over water sources.
Comments: Similarity between these two species of *Scotophilus* has led to a plethora of named forms that have moved back and forth between the two species. The uncertainty of subspecific allocations makes it difficult to treat the Chinese material authoritatively. Wang (2003) used *S. k. gairdneri* Kloss, 1917, for animals from Yunnan, and it is certainly possible that those animals may be more closely related to Thai populations than to Hainan Island forms, but until the intervening populations are documented and allocated, such usage seems premature. Similarly, Wang (2003) used the name *S. k. swinhoei* for all other mainland forms, restricting *S. k. consobrinus* to the insular populations on Hainan and Taiwan. However, Blyth's (1860) description of *Nycticejus*(?) *swinhoei* is not identifiable, and the type specimen appears to have been lost. Therefore, we have employed the conservative approach of using a single subspecific name (*consobrinus*) for all Chinese populations.
Conservation Status: China RL—LC.
References: Bates and Harrison (1997).

Genus *Tylonycteris*—Bamboo Bats

扁颅蝠属 Bianlufu Shu—扁颅蝠 Bianlufu

Size very small; HB length 35–45 mm; head wide and flat; ear length about equal to head length; tragus short, with blunt tip. There are round pads at base of thumbs and on soles of hind feet (fig. 10); skull extremely low and flat; length of cranium only half of width; back of skull forms a very flat inclined plane from cranium to rostrum; rostrum short and wide; zygomatic arch extenuated. Dental formula same as in *Eptesicus*: 2.1.1.3/3.1.2.3 = 32; inner upper incisor bicuspid; upper canines with a small style behind main cusp. Distributed in S Asia and neighboring islands. Both species occur in China. *Tylonycteris* belongs to the tribe Vespertilionini.

Lesser Bamboo Bat

PLATE 38
MAP 403

Tylonycteris pachypus (Temminck, 1840)
扁颅蝠 Bianlufu

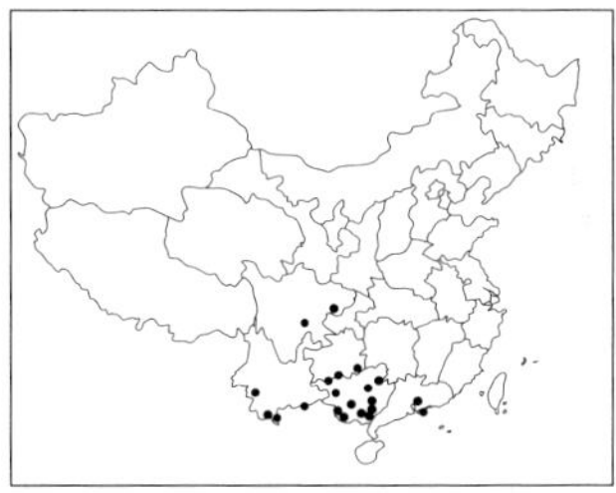

MAP 403. LESSER BAMBOO BAT, *Tylonycteris pachypus*

Distinctive Characteristics: HB 34–46; T 26–33; HF 5–7; E 9–10; FA 25–29; GLS 11. Size very small; hair bases yellowish brown; hair tips dark brown; ventral surface brownish yellow; wing membrane attached to base of toes; ears broadly rounded; tragus short and broad. Skull remarkably flattened; supraorbital process of skull undeveloped; lambdoidal crest developed, lower incisors tricuspidate.
Distribution: Yunnan, Sichuan, Guizhou, Guangxi, Guangdong, and Hong Kong; extending throughout

Key to the Chinese Species of *Tylonycteris*

1.a.	Pelage color dark brown; GLS 10.5–11.6 mm	*Tylonycteris pachypus*
b.	Pelage color relatively light, snuff-colored; GLS about 12.5 mm	*Tylonycteris robustula*

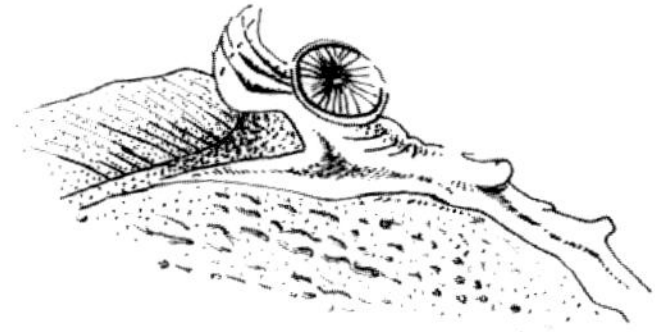

Figure 10. Feet of bamboo bats (*Tylonycteris*) showing the round pads at base of their thumbs and on the soles of the hind feet.

the S Indo-Malayan realm. Chinese subspecies: *T. p. fulvidus* (Blyth, 1859).
Natural History: These tiny bats are found roosting in the internodes of larger species of bamboo. The flattening of the skull and the pads on the feet are presumably adaptations to allow it to use this unique roosting habitat. They form colonies of up to 40 individuals and may form harems. The gestation period is about three months and usually results in twins. The young are weaned at about weeks of age. Bamboo bats are known to feed on swarming termites.
Comments: This is the smallest species of bat in China.
Conservation Status: China RL–NT; although it nearly met the criteria for VU A1acd.
References: Bates and Harrison (1997); Nowak (1994).

Greater Bamboo Bat

PLATE 38
Tylonycteris robustula Thomas, 1915 MAP 404
褐扁颅蝠 He Bianlufu

MAP 404. GREATER BAMBOO BAT, *Tylonycteris robustula*

Distinctive Characteristics: HB 40–44; T 26–31; HF 5–6; E 8–11; FA 26–29; GLS 11.8–12.5. Size slightly larger than that of *T. pachypus*; forearm length usually 28 mm or more. Pelage color dark brown, darker than that of *T. pachypus*; throat and venter somewhat paler. Rostrum and braincase of skull even broader than that of *T. pachypus*; supraorbital process of skull developed; lambdoidal crest undeveloped; nasal notch extends to level of infraorbital foramen.
Distribution: Yunnan and Guangxi; extending throughout SE Asia.
Natural History: Apparently this species has habits quite similar to those of *T. pachypus*. In addition to roosting in bamboo, they are reported to use crevices in rock. Colony size is usually small; colonies consist of a single adult male and few adult females with attendant young. This species is also reported to feed on swarming termites.
Comments: Allen (1938) recognized both species of *Tylonycteris* from China, although he questioned their distinctness. Tate (1942) provided useful discussion which led to our current understanding. If *T. malayana* Chasen, 1940 is recognized as a valid subspecies of *T. robustula*, that name might apply to the Chinese material.
Conservation Status: China RL–VU A1acd.
References: Allen (1938); Tate (1942).

Genus *Vespertilio*—Particolored Bats

蝙蝠属 Bianfu Shu—蝙蝠 Bianfu

Size small to medium; HB length 55–75 mm; very similar to *Eptesicus*, but ears shorter and wider; pelage with bright gray spots; rostrum of skull relatively low and flat, with a long recessed groove on each side of back; nasal sinus very large, extending backwards to middle part between rostrum tip and interorbital region; palatal sinus (indentation in anterior palate) large and laterally expanded, its width much greater than depth; dental structure same as in *Eptesicus*. Dental formula: 2.1.1.3/3.1.2.3 = 32. Mainly distributed in N Europe and Asia. Both species occur in China. *Vespertilio* is a member of the tribe Vespertilionini.

Particolored Bat

Vespertilio murinus Linnaeus, 1758 MAP 405
双色蝙蝠 Shuangse Bianfu

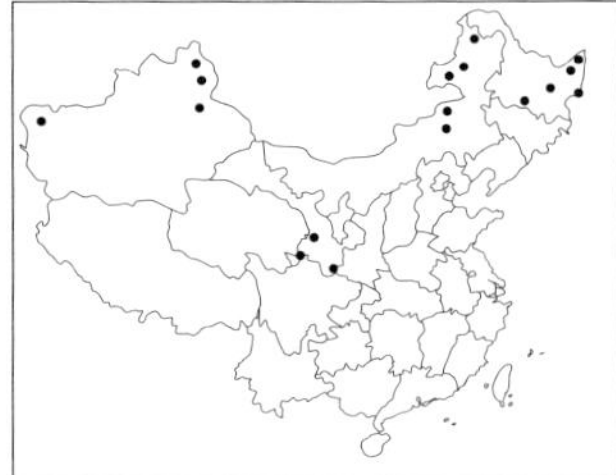

MAP 405. PARTICOLORED BAT, *Vespertilio murinus*

Distinctive Characteristics: HB 55–66; T 40–48; HF 8–10; E 14–16; FA 41–46; GLS 16.5. Size small; zygomatic width 9.1–10.9 mm; two pairs of nipples; basal parts of dorsal and ventral hairs blackish brown; hair tips white; white tips of ventral hairs more distinct than those of dorsal hairs; hairs on lateral venter and throat all white.
Distribution: C and NW China; extending across N Asia and throughout Europe. Two subspecies in China: (1) *V. m. murinus* Linnaeus, 1758; Xinjiang, Gansu; (2) *V. m. ussuriensis* Wallin, 1969; Nei Mongol, Heilongjiang.
Natural History: This species is widely distributed, and frequently found in and around manmade structures. Roosts are often in cracks and crevices, both natural ones in cliffs and caves, and also in attics, behind

Key to the Chinese Species of *Vespertilio*

1.a.	Size small; forearm length 41–46 mm; GLS usually < 17 mm; zygomatic width < 10.8 mm	*Vespertilio murinus*
b.	Size large; forearm length 46–54 mm; GLS usually > 17 mm; zygomatic width > 10.8 mm	*Vespertilio sinensis*

shutters, and under joists. Colonies are small, and single individuals are frequently encountered. They forage late in the evening and fly fast and high. They produce audible calls while foraging, in addition to high-frequency echolocation pulses. They feed on medium-sized beetles and moths and other insects. Two and sometimes three young are born, and lactation lasts about six or seven weeks. They breed in the year following their birth and live for up to five years.
Conservation Status: China RL–LC.
References: Baagøe (2001); Horácek et al. (2000).

Asian Particolored Bat

PLATE 38
Vespertilio sinensis (Peters, 1880) MAP 406
东方蝙蝠 Dongfang Bianfu

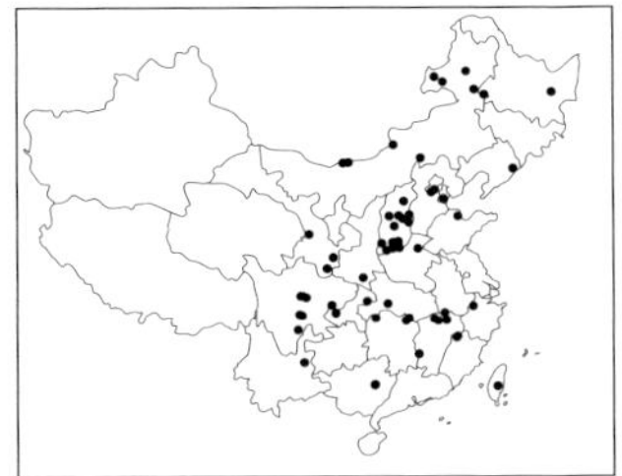

MAP 406. ASIAN PARTICOLORED BAT, *Vespertilio sinensis*

Distinctive Characteristics: HB 58–80; T 34–54; HF 9–16; E 14–21; FA 43–55; GLS 17.3–18. Size slightly larger than *V. murinus*; zygomatic width 10.8–11.7 mm; one pair of nipples; basal parts of dorsal and ventral hairs all blackish brown; hair tips off-white or white; ventral surface a little paler than dorsum; hair color of lower venter wholly white.
Distribution: Widely distributed across C and E China; extending mainly across E Asia. Three subspecies occur in China (Wang 2003): (1) *V. s. andersoni* Wallin, 1963; Nei Mongol; (2) *V. s. orientalis* (Wallin, 1969); Fujian, Shanxi, Gansu, Sichuan, Taiwan; (3) *V. s. sinensis* (Peters, 1880); Heilongjiang, E Nei Mongol, Hebei, Beijing, Tianjin, Shandong, Hubei, Hunan, Jiangxi, Guangxi, Yunnan.
Natural History: Little is known of the natural history of this species. It has been reported roosting in the foliage and is known from both mountainous and steppe regions.
Comments: This species was called *V. superans* in earlier literature. Subspecies limits are quite unclear and await examination of all available material.
Conservation Status: China RL–LC.
References: Horácek (1997); Wallin (1969).

Subfamily Myotinae

Genus *Myotis*—Little Brown Bats

鼠耳蝠亚科 Shu'erfu Yake; 鼠耳蝠属 Shu'erfu Shu—鼠耳蝠 Shu'erfu

Size medium to very small; HB length 35–80 mm; ears well developed, long, and narrow; tragus straight and slender, with sharp tip; tail length 40–60 mm, contained in uropatagium; uropatagium large, its basal part covered with hairs; skull long and narrow; rostrum and cranium about equal in length; sagittal crest low and cranium high; anterior palate with a deep indentation; auditory bullae well developed, their diameter equal to width of basioccipital between auditory bullae. Dental formula: 2.1.3.3/3.1.3.3 = 38; third premolars in upper and lower jaws large, others all small; first and second molars both with well-developed cusps and ridges arranging in W-shaped ectoloph, and with protocones and hypocones on inner side; third molars in upper and lower jaws both small, their hypocones relatively reduced. This subfamily and genus is the most widely distributed of terrestrial mammals, with more than 100 species worldwide, 23 of which are widely distributed in China.

Large-Footed Myotis

Myotis adversus (Horsfield, 1824) MAP 407
爪哇大足鼠耳蝠 Zhaowadazu Shu'erfu

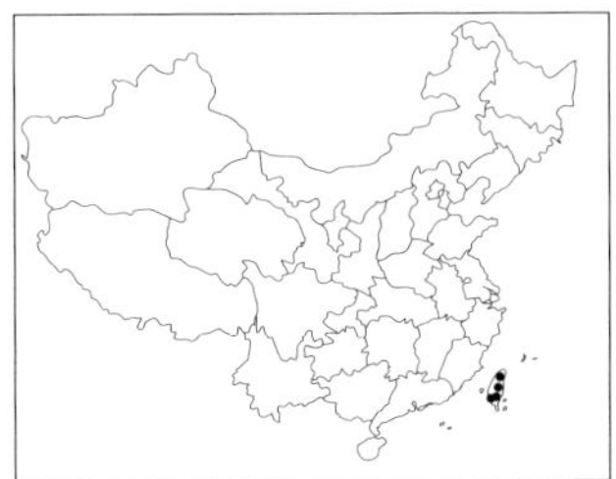

MAP 407. LARGE-FOOTED MYOTIS, *Myotis adversus*

Distinctive Characteristics: HB 51–53; T 33–48, HF 10–13; E 14–18; FA 38–45; GLS 15.5. Size very small; tibia length 18 mm, less than two times hind foot length; wing membrane stops at ankles; length of tail less than HB length; calcar long; ears short, length less than head length; dorsal hair reddish brown; ventral surface dark brown; small premolars in upper and lower jaws visible from outer side of toothrow; second and fourth premolars separated.
Distribution: Taiwan; extending down Malay Peninsula to New Guinea and to Solomon islands, Vanuatu, and E and N coastal Australia. Chinese subspecies: *M. a. taiwanensis* Arnback-Christie Linde, 1908.
Natural History: In Taiwan this species occurs mainly at low to middle elevations and is known to roost in caves and tunnels. Extralimitally, they are known to feed over water, where they catch insects. The large feet and aquatic feeding habitat have led to speculation that this species might occasionally feed on fish.
Comments: Wang (2003) considered *taiwanensis* to be a full species.
Conservation Status: China RL–NT; although it nearly met the criteria for VU A2cd; B1abc(i, ii, iii); D2.
References: Bates et al. (1999); Ellerman and Morrison-Scott (1951); Findley (1972).

Key to the Chinese Species of *Myotis*

1.a.	Membranes multicolored, black, red, orange, or yellow	*Myotis formosus*
b.	Membranes normally black	2
2.a.	Hind foot length equal to tibia length	3
b.	Hind foot length < tibia length	4
3.a.	Larger, forearm > 50mm	*Myotis pilosus*
b.	Smaller, forearm < 50 mm	*Myotis dasycneme*
4.a.	Hind foot length ½–¾ tibia length	5
b.	Hind foot length less than half tibia length	10
5.a.	Outer margin of tibia fringed with hair	6
b.	Outer margin of tibia without fringe of hair	7
6.a.	Shallow lateral depressions on each side of rostrum	*Myotis longipes*
b.	Pronounced lateral depressions on each side of rostrum	*Myotis fimbriatus*
7.a.	Small upper premolar in toothrow	8
b.	Small upper premolar intruded from toothrow	9
8.a.	Larger, HB length > 43 mm	*Myotis daubentonii*
b.	Smaller, HB length < 43 mm	*Myotis laniger*
9.a.	Wing inserted on metatarsus	*Myotis horsfieldii*
b.	Wing inserted on ankle	*Myotis adversus*
10.a.	Ears relatively large	11
b.	Ears relatively small	16
11.a.	Larger, forearm > 53 mm, condylobasal length > 18.6 mm, maxillary toothrow length > 8 mm	12
b.	Smaller, forearm < 53 mm, condylobasal length < 18.6 mm, maxillary toothrow length < 8 mm	13
12.a.	Smaller, forearm usually < 60 mm, condylobasal length usually < 22 mm, maxillary toothrow length usually < 9.2 mm, outer upper incisor barely larger than inner in crown area	*Myotis blythii*
b.	Larger, forearm usually > 60 mm, condylobasal length usually > 22 mm, maxillary toothrow length usually > 9.2 mm, outer upper incisor about twice crown area of inner	*Myotis chinensis*
13.a.	Smaller, forearm < 45 mm, condylobasal length < 15.4 mm, maxillary toothrow length < 7 mm	14
b.	Larger, forearm > 45 mm, condylobasal length > 15.4 mm, maxillary toothrow length > 7 mm	*Myotis pequinius*
14.a.	Larger, forearm > 42 mm	*Myotis altarium*
b.	Smaller, forearm < 42 mm	*Myotis bombinus*
15.a.	Smaller, forearm usually ≤ 40 mm; condylocanine length usually ≤14 mm	16
b.	Larger, forearm usually ≥ 40 mm; condylocanine length usually ≥ 14 mm	22
16.a.	Braincase domed, rising abruptly from rostrum	17
b.	Braincase flatter, not rising abruptly from rostrum	18
17.a.	Larger, forearm > 37 mm	*Myotis frater*
b.	Smaller, forearm < 37 mm	*Myotis siligorensis*
18.a.	Dorsal pelage brownish, tipped with shiny, paler, ochraceous hairs; ventral pelage whitish, tipped with creamy white hairs	19
b.	Dorsal pelage darker, hair tips less shiny; ventral pelage black at base, tipped with ochraceous brown or pale gray	20
19.a.	Smaller, forearm usually < 34 mm	*Myotis davidii*
b.	Larger, forearm usually > 34 mm	*Myotis brandtii*
20.a.	Larger, forearm usually > 34 mm	*Myotis nipalensis*
b.	Smaller, forearm usually < 34 mm	21
21.a.	Hind foot smaller, 7 mm or less	*Myotis muricola*
b.	Hind foot longer, 7 mm or more	*Myotis ikonnikovi*
22.a.	Antorbital foramen widely separated from rim of orbit	*Myotis montivagus*
b.	Antorbital foramen narrowly separated from rim of orbit	*Myotis annectans*

Szechwan Myotis
PLATE 38
MAP 408

Myotis altarium Thomas, 1911
西南鼠耳蝠 Xinan Shu'erfu

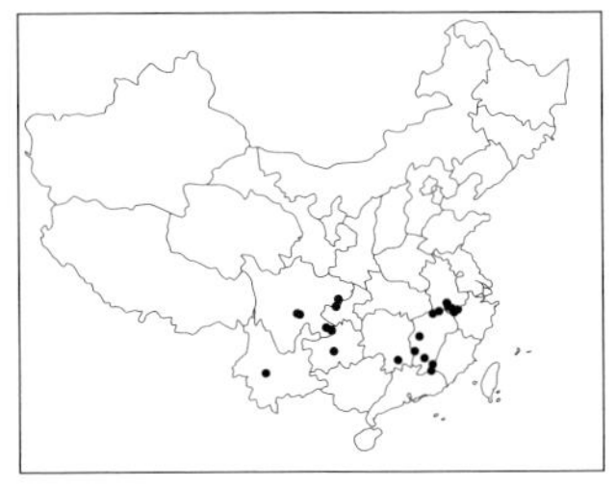

MAP 408. SZECHWAN MYOTIS, *Myotis altarium*

Distinctive Characteristics: HB 55–60; T 48–50; HF 11–12; E 22–24; FA 42–46; GLS 15–16. Size medium; tail length less than HB length; hind foot large; calcar very long, length more than half of tibia length, with narrow and small keel; ears long and narrow; laid forward, ears extend beyond rostrum tip; exterior margins of uropatagium without fringe; rostrum short and wide; cranium distinctly protruding; small premolars in upper and lower jaws lie in toothrows; hair color black brown, ventral surface paler, but without off-white tips.
Distribution: SE China (Sichuan, Yunnan, Guangxi, Jiangxi, Fujian, Anhui, and Guizhou); extending to Thailand; monotypic species.
Natural History: All of the known specimens of *M. altarium* have been collected from caves. Other than this roosting habitat, nothing is known of the natural history of this species.
Conservation Status: China RL—NT; although it nearly met the criteria for VU A2ac + 3ac.
References: Blood and McFarlane (1988); Stager (1949).

Hairy-Faced Myotis
MAP 409

Myotis annectans (Dobson, 1871)
缺齿鼠耳蝠 Quechi Shu'erfu

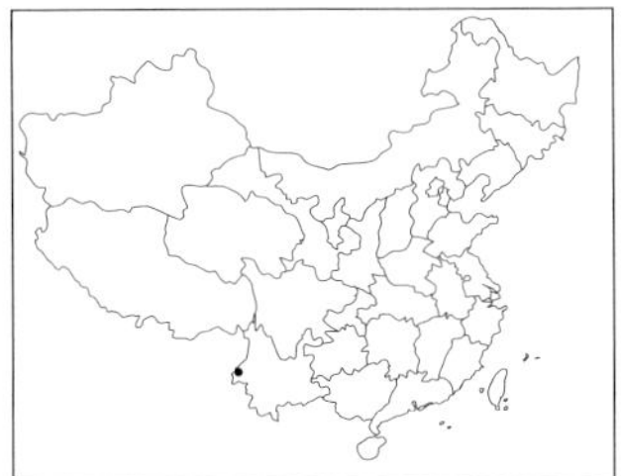

MAP 409. HAIRY-FACED MYOTIS, *Myotis annectans*

Distinctive Characteristics: HB 45–55; T 39–48; HF 10; E 14–16; FA 45–48; GLS 15–17. Size medium; pelage long, dense, and soft; dorsally dark brown and ventrally the hairs have paler tips; face covered with dark brown hair; ears small and rounded, with relatively broad tragus; skull robust, rostrum broad; second upper premolar minute and completely intruded from toothrow.
Distribution: Yunnan (known from a single record; Wang 2003); extending from India to Vietnam.
Natural History: Most of the known specimens have come from midelevations. In Vietnam, one was taken in second growth along a river valley. Little is known of the life history of this species.
Comments: Prior to 1970, *M. annectans* was considered a member of the genus *Pipistrellus*.
Conservation Status: China RL—NA.
References: Bates and Harrison (1997); Lunde et al. (2003); Topál (1970b).

Lesser Mouse-Eared Myotis
PLATE 38
MAP 410

Myotis blythii (Tomes, 1857)
狭耳鼠耳蝠 Xia'er Shu'erfu

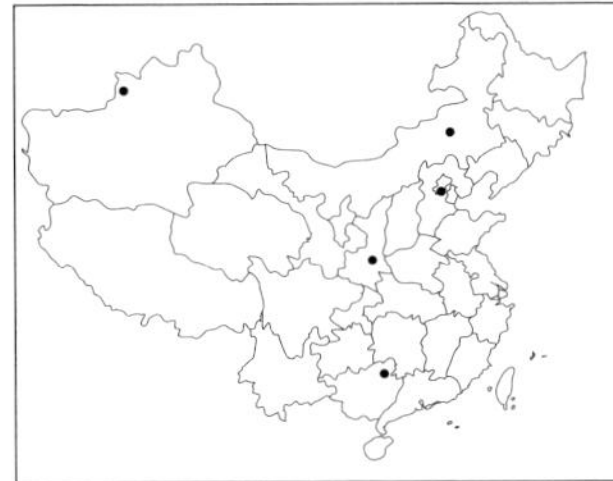

MAP 410. LESSER MOUSE-EARED MYOTIS, *Myotis blythii*

Distinctive Characteristics: HB 65–89; T 53–81; HF 11–17; E 19–22; FA 53–70; GLS 21–23. Size large; skull width 9.4–10.8 mm; dorsal hair black brown or taupe; ventral surface brown gray or off-white, with gray hair tips; ears long and narrow; tragus slender; wing membrane attached at ankles; calcar slender and unkeeled; skull long and narrow, with slight sagittal crest; cranium low and round; first two premolars in upper jaw both lie in toothrow, not intruded.
Distribution: Scattered localities in China including Xinjiang, Nei Mongol, Shaanxi, Shanxi, and Guangxi; extending across continental Asia and Europe. Two subspecies in China (Wang 2003): (1) *M. b. ancilla* Thomas, 1910; Shanxi, Shaanxi, Guangxi; (2) *M. b. omari* Thomas, 1906; Xinjiang, Nei Mongol.
Natural History: This species is known to inhabit a wide variety of habitats, including disturbed areas of various types. They roost in attics of buildings and also in caves, and occasionally in tree holes as well. They may be migratory in some areas. They feed on medium to large insects, including beetles and moths. They may take occasional prey items directly from the ground. They have one or sometimes two young at a time, which are weaned at six to seven weeks of age. Maximum recorded longevity is 13 years.
Comments: Earlier literature sometimes confused this species with *M. myotis*. Subspecific allocations need confirmation, as *M. b. omari* is otherwise known only from W Asia. Both *M. b. omari* and *M. b. ancilla* might actually represent distinct species, once species limits are better defined in this group.
Conservation Status: China RL—VU B1ab(i, ii, iii).
References: Horácek et al. (2000); Strelkov (1972).

Far Eastern Myotis

PLATE 38
MAP 411

Myotis bombinus Thomas, 1906
远东鼠耳蝠 Yuandong Shu'erfu

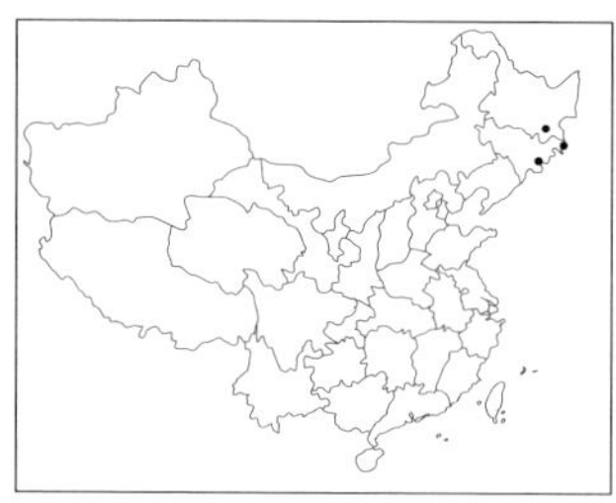

MAP 411. FAR EASTERN MYOTIS, *Myotis bombinus*

Distinctive Characteristics: HB 41–52; T 38–45; HF 8–12; E 14–19; FA 37–42; GLS 14. Size slightly small; ears long and narrow, with narrow tips; tragus narrow and markedly recurved; border of stiff bristles on free edge of uropatagium straight or very slightly curved; pelage soft, woolly, and dark, with basal part of dorsal hairs fuscous, with paler tips; ventral coloration paler than that of the dorsum; wings attached to base of toes; calcar long and unkeeled. Skull long and robust, with shorter rostrum and longer braincase; upper P3 in toothrow or slightly intruded.
Distribution: Heilongjiang and Jilin; extending to Japan, Korea, SE Russia. Chinese subspecies: *M. b. amurensis* Ognev, 1927.
Natural History: This species is very poorly known in China. They roost in caves, in small colonies, and may be at least partially migratory.
Comments: Earlier literature sometimes considered this species a subspecies of *M. nattereri.* Wang (2003) listed them as *M. nattereri* and includes Nei Mongol in the distribution. He also listed *M. bombinus* from Jilin, indicating that additional study is needed to determine species limits and ranges in these forms. *M. nattereri* is otherwise unknown east of Turkmenistan.
Conservation Status: China RL—NA. IUCN RL—LR/nt ver 2.3 (1994).
References: Horácek and Hanak (1984); Horácek et al. (2000); Kawai et al. (2003); Yoon (1990); Yoshiyuki (1989).

Brandt's Myotis

MAP 412

Myotis brandtii (Eversmann, 1845)
埃氏鼠耳蝠 Aishi Shu'erfu

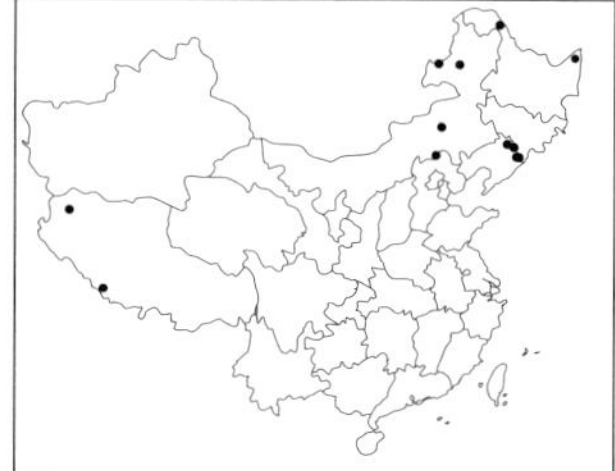

MAP 412. BRANDT'S MYOTIS, *Myotis brandtii*

Distinctive Characteristics: HB 39–51; T 32–44; HF 7–9; E 12–17; FA 33–39; GLS 14. Size small; pelage long; dorsum pale brown with golden sheen; venter paler gray, sometimes with yellowish tinge; wing membrane attaches at base of outer toe; ear moderately long; tragus narrow and pointed, about half as long as ear; skull slender and delicate; upper P3 slightly intruded from toothrow.
Distribution: Disjunct distribution in China (NE—Nei Mongol, Heilongjiang, Jilin; and SW—Xizang); widely distributed in Europe and Asia. Chinese subspecies: *M. b. gracilis* Ognev, 1927.
Natural History: Primarily a forest species, *M. brandtii* has been collected along water courses. Summer maternity colonies are found in buildings, where the individuals frequently hide in cracks and behind beams. Winter roosts are known from caves, tunnels, cellars, and mine shafts. Northern populations hibernate, and some populations are partially migratory as well. They forage on small insects at low altitudes and have quick, maneuverable flight. One, and occasionally two, young are born in early summer, and they are able to fly at about a month of age. Maximum known longevity is nearly 20 years.
Comments: *M. brandtii* was considered a subspecies of *M. mysticinus* in the earlier literature. Wang (2003) considered *meinertzhageni* Thomas, 1926 a synonym of *M. brandtii*, but it should be placed in the synonymy of *M. nipalensis.*
Conservation Status: China RL—DD.
References: Benda and Tsytsulina (2000); Horácek et al. (2000); Won and Smith (1999).

Large Myotis

PLATE 38
MAP 413

Myotis chinensis (Tomes, 1857)
中华鼠耳蝠 Zhonghua Shu'erfu

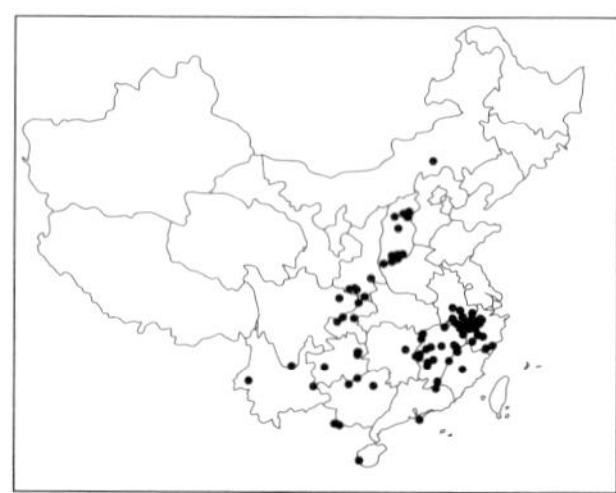

MAP 413. LARGE MYOTIS, *Myotis chinensis*

Distinctive Characteristics: HB 91–97; T 53–58; HF 16–18; E 20–23; FA 64–69; GLS 23. Size large; dorsal coloration dark olive brown, with lateral taupe or blackish brown striations in transition to dark gray ventral pelage with hair tips slightly paler; calcar long and slender, unkeeled; skull slender, but robust; upper P3 slightly intruded from toothrow.
Distribution: C and SE China (Jiangsu, Jiangxi, Guangdong, Hong Kong, Guangxi, Fujian, Hainan, Hunan, Zhejiang, Sichuan, Guizhou, Yunnan); extending to Thailand, Myanmar, and Vietnam.
Natural History: This species is found in a wide range of habitats from lowlands through the hill country. It is known to hibernate in caves.

Comments: Zhang et al. (1997) included this species in *M. myotis*, but it is clearly distinct. Wang (2003) recognized two subspecies in China, the nominate form and *luctuosus*, but geographic variation throughout the range needs further study.
Conservation Status: China RL—VU A1abc.
References: Bates et al. (1999); Lekagul and McNeely (1977); Zhang et al. (1997).

Pond Myotis

Myotis dasycneme Boie, 1825 MAP 414
沼泽鼠耳蝠 Zhaoze Shu'erfu

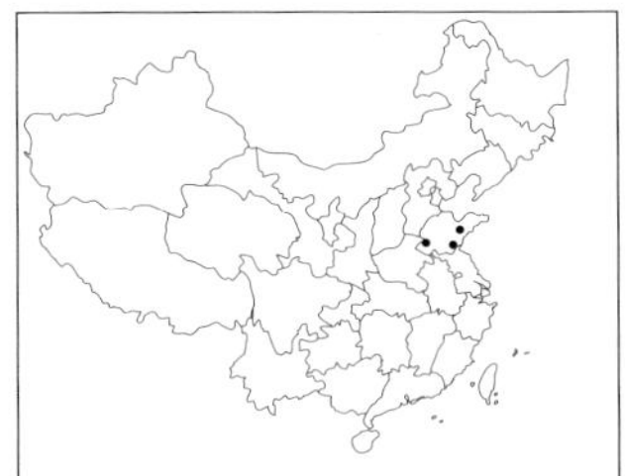

MAP 414. POND MYOTIS, *Myotis dasycneme*

Distinctive Characteristics: HB 57–67; T 46–51; HF 11–12; E 17–18; FA 43–49. Size medium; dorsal coloration yellowish brown; venter slaty black; tragus short, less than half length of ear; uropatagium lacking fringe; skull large and robust; little or no sagittal crest; lachrymal ridge developed; upper P3 intruded from toothrow.
Distribution: Shandong; Wang (2003) lists it from Nei Mongol and Heilongjiang as well; extending across Russia to W Europe.
Natural History: Known from lowlands and foothills, this species frequents areas with abundant water. They are known to roost in caves and tunnels, as well as buildings and hollow trees. They may migrate between summer and winter roosts. They leave the roost to forage early and have another foraging bout just before dawn. They feed on a variety of small insects, such as craneflies, other diptera, and small lepidoptera, over the surface of the water, and may take them right off the water surface as well. One, and occasionally two, young are born after a gestation period of about two months. They are weaned after a further two months, and individuals have been known to live for almost 20 years.
Comments: *M. dasycneme* is one of the large-footed species of *Myotis* frequently associated with foraging over water.
Conservation Status: China RL—DD. IUCN RL—VU A2c ver 2.3 (1994).
References: Miller (1912); Richarz and Limbrunner (1993).

Daubenton's Myotis

PLATE 39
Myotis daubentonii (Kuhl, 1819) MAP 415
水鼠耳蝠 Shui Shu'erfu

Distinctive Characteristics: HB 44–58; T 27–41; HF 9–12; E 11–15; FA 34–39; GLS 14. Size small; tibia length about 17 mm; length of hind foot more than half of tibia length, about 11 mm; wing membrane attached at middle part of ankle; tail short, length less than HB length; calcar slender and long, without keel; ear length medium; if turned forward, ears can exceed rostrum tip 1–2 mm; length of tragus about half of ear length; pelage short and thick; dorsal hair dark brown; ventral surface brownish gray or off-white; rostrum relatively wide; width of cranium greater than half of GLS; canines in lower jaw low and small; small premolar (P3) in upper jaw lies in toothrow; upper molars with small protocones.
Distribution: NE China (Heilongjiang, Jilin, Nei Mongol); extending across the Palaearctic realm. Chinese subspecies: *M. d. loukashkini* Shamel, 1942. Wang (2003) also lists *M. d. volgensis* from Xinjiang, and a "Tibet form" from Xizang.

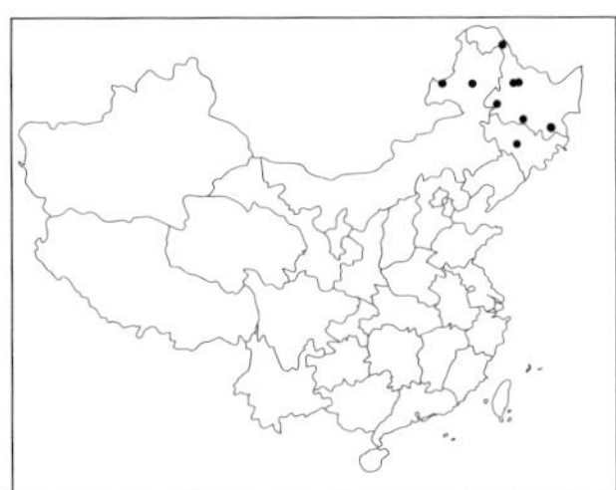

MAP 415. DAUBENTON'S MYOTIS, *Myotis daubentonii*

Natural History: This is another species that forages extensively over water and frequently roosts nearby. They are known to inhabit caves, mine tunnels, cellars, wells, and under rubble on the floor of caves. They hibernate in winter and migrate to summer nursery roosts in tree holes, attics, steeples, and under bridges. They fly early in the evening and fly fast and erratically. They feed on small flying insects like diptera and lepidoptera, frequently over water. One or sometimes two young are born after a 50–55-day gestation period, and they are weaned about two months later. Neonates weigh about 2.3 g. Maximum known longevity is more than 20 years.
Comments: *Myotis laniger* was considered a subspecies of *daubentonii* in earlier literature. Wang (2003) includes *M. laniger* as a subspecies of *daubentonii*, but we consider it a distinct species. This species may prove composite, with eastern forms representing a species distinct from European *daubentonii*. Subspecies limits are very poorly understood.
Conservation Status: China RL—LC.
References: Bates et al. (1999); Horácek et al. (2000); Ruedi and Mayer (2001); Yoshiyuki (1989).

David's Myotis

PLATE 38
Myotis davidii (Peters, 1869) MAP 416
须鼠耳蝠 Xushu'erfu

Distinctive Characteristics: HB 41–44; T 30–43; HF 7–9; E 12–15; FA 31–35. Size very small; tibia length 12–13 mm; length of hind foot more than half of tibia length; tail short, barely less than HB length; wing membrane attaches to basal part of toe; calcar long,

its length slightly more than half of distance to tail tip; dorsal hair dark brown; hair tips a little paler; ventral hair color same as that of dorsal hair, but tips grayish; rostrum of skull very short; small premolar (P3) in upper jaw leans to inner side of toothrow, which leaves anterior and posterior premolars (P2 and P4) in contact; premolar (p3) in lower jaw also small, and leans to inner side of toothrow too, but the anterior premolar does not touch the posterior one because they are small and intruded as well.
Distribution: Beijing, Hebei, Gansu, Jiangxi, Fujian, Guizhou, and Hainan; Endemic; monotypic species.

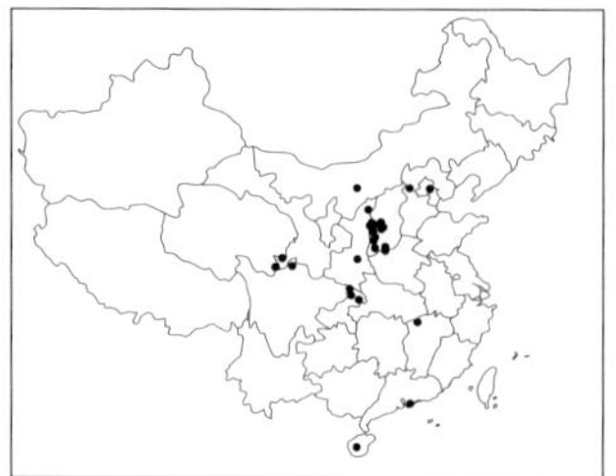

MAP 416. DAVID'S MYOTIS, *Myotis davidii*

Natural History: Nothing is known of the natural history of this species.
Comments: Formerly considered a subspecies of *M. mysticinus*, and listed as such by Wang (2003).
Conservation Status: China RL—NT; although it nearly met the criteria for VU A1bc.
References: Kawai et al. (2003).

Fringed Long-Footed Myotis

Myotis fimbriatus (Peters, 1871) MAP 417
毛腿鼠耳蝠 Maotui Shu'erfu

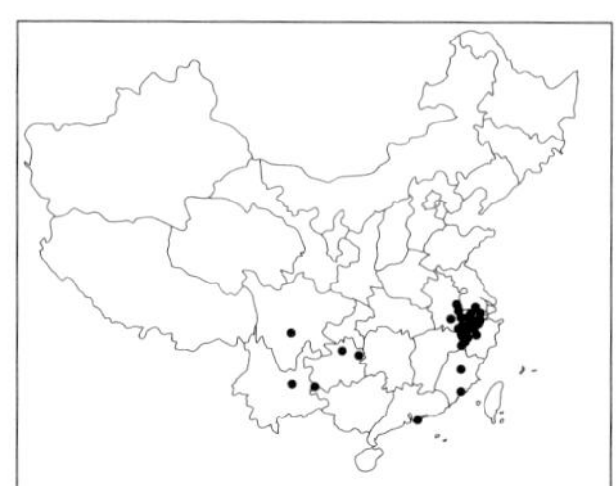

MAP 417. FRINGED LONG-FOOTED MYOTIS, *Myotis fimbriatus*

Distinctive Characteristics: HB 42–52; T 37–48; HF 8–10; E 14–16; FA 37–40; GLS 15. Size small; tibia length about 17 mm; length of hind foot more than half of tibia length; wing membrane attaches at ankles; ventral uropatagium covered with short hairs, its exterior margin also covered with comb-shaped short hairs; length of tail less than HB length; calcar unkeeled; ears about equal in length with head; pelage very short and thick; dorsal hairs black brown and gray; ventral surface taupe, with slightly off-white hue; basal part of tail with white spots; front of skull lower and flatter than that of *M. daubentonii*; small premolars in upper jaw lie in toothrow, or sightly lean to its inner side.
Distribution: S C and SE China. Endemic.
Natural History: Collected material suggests that this is a colonial, cave-dwelling species, but aside from that, nothing is known of the natural history.
Comments: Various authors have suggested relationships with *M. mysticinus*, *M. macrodactylus*, or *M. capaccinii*, but *M. fimbriatus* seems best considered a Chinese endemic species.
Conservation Status: China RL—VU A4cd; B1ab(i, ii, iii).
References: Corbet (1978); Corbet and Hill (1992); Findley (1972).

Hodgson's Myotis

PLATE 39
Myotis formosus (Hodgson, 1835) MAP 418
绯鼠耳蝠 Fei Shu'erfu

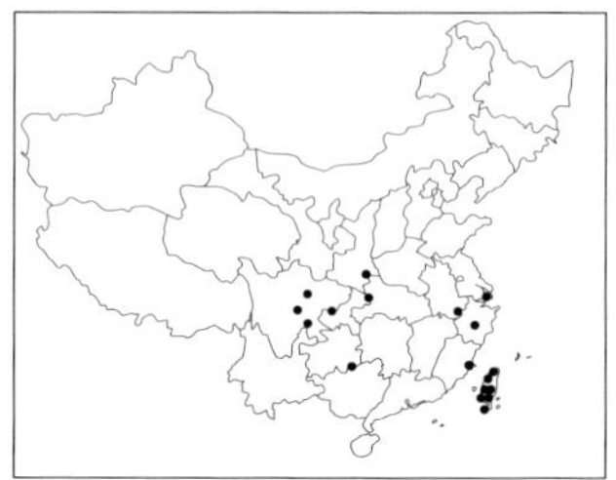

MAP 418. HODGSON'S MYOTIS, *Myotis formosus*

Distinctive Characteristics: HB 45–70; T 43–52; HF 10–12; E 16–17; FA 45–50. Size large; wing membrane attaches at basal part of toe; ears long and narrow, slightly egg-shaped; tragus sharp, long, and narrow; wing membrane along humerus and body sides covered with sparse and short hairs; hair color bright; dorsal hair brown; ventral surface, wing membrane, and most of uropatagium all bright rufous; but wing membrane between phalanxes brown black; back of skull relatively flat; cranium not very protruding; upper outer incisor (I3) smaller than inner incisor (I2); first upper premolar (P2) larger than second premolar (P3).
Distribution: E and S China; extending widely in the Indo-Malayan realm. Two subspecies in China: (1) *M. f. rufoniger* (Tomes, 1858); Sichuan, Zhejiang, Anhui, Shanghai, Hubei, Shaanxi, Jiangsu, Fujian, Taiwan, Guangxi, Guizhou; (2) *M. f. watasei* Kishida, 1924; Taiwan.
Natural History: This brightly colored little bat is known to roost in the foliage, which probably accounts for the striking color pattern. They have been taken from sea level up to the foothills of the Himalayas. They hibernate in caves during the winter.
Comments: This widespread and striking species is poorly understood in terms of geographic variation.
Conservation Status: China RL—VU A1acd.
References: Bates and Harrison (1997); Findley (1972); Swinhoe (1862); Won and Smith (1999).

Fraternal Myotis

PLATE 39
MAP 419

Myotis frater Allen, 1923
长尾鼠耳蝠 Changwei Shu'erfu

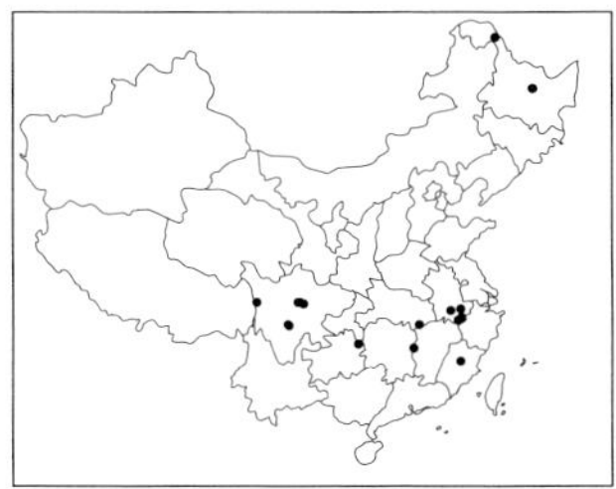

MAP 419. FRATERNAL MYOTIS, *Myotis frater*

Distinctive Characteristics: HB 43–57; T 38–47; HF 7–12; E 11–14; FA 36–42; GLS 13.5. Size slightly small; zygomatic width about 7.8 mm; ears short, not reaching rostrum tip when laid forward; wing membrane attached at heel; length of tibia about 20 mm; hind foot length less than half of tibia length; tail length equal to or slightly less than HB length; calcar with small keel; hair dark brown; rostrum a little upturned; interorbital region recessed; cranium not especially protruding; second upper premolar (P3) small, leaning to inner side of toothrow; hence first and third upper premolars in contact; lower small premolar (p3) slightly leans to inner side of toothrow.
Distribution: NE, C, and S China; extending across E Asia. Two subspecies in China: (1) *M. f. frater* Allen, 1923; Fujian, Jiangxi, Sichuan, Anhui; (2) *M. f. longicaudatus* Ognev, 1927; Nei Mongol, Heilongjiang.
Natural History: The type series was taken from holes in bamboo stems at an elevation of 760 m. Otherwise, nothing is known of the natural history.
Comments: The wide geographic separation and presumed habitat differences of the two subspecies in China argues for a reexamination of variation in this species. Tsytsulina and Strelkov (2002) examined geographic variation in the northern forms but did not include the nominate form.
Conservation Status: China RL—VU A1acd. IUCN RL—LR/nt ver 2.3 (1994).
References: Tsytsulina and Strelkov (2002); Wang (1959).

Horsfield's Myotis

PLATE 39
MAP 420

Myotis horsfieldii (Temminck, 1840)
郝氏鼠耳蝠 Haoshi Shu'erfu

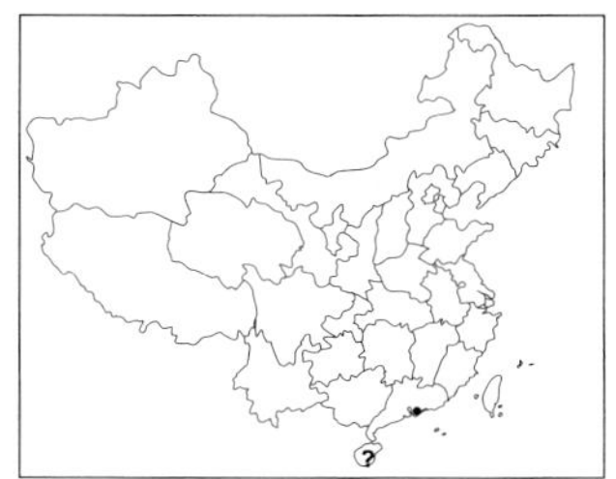

MAP 420. HORSFIELD'S MYOTIS, *Myotis horsfeldii*

Distinctive Characteristics: HB 49–59; T 34–42; HF 7–11; E 13–15; FA 36–42. Size medium; dorsal coloration dark brown to black; ventral coloration deep brown with grayish tips near tail; wings attached to outer metatarsal; ears rounded and naked; tragus short and relatively broad; hind foot length more than half tibia length. Skull delicate with shallow gradient in dorsal profile; rostrum robust with shallow depression in midline; upper P3 in toothrow or only slightly intruded.
Distribution: Guangdong, Hainan, Hong Kong; extending across SE Asia. Chinese subspecies: *M. h. deignani* Shamel, 1942 (Corbet and Hill 1992).
Natural History: This species frequents wooded areas and is often found near water. It roosts in abandoned tunnels, caves, buildings, and bridges, as well as occasionally in foliage. Colonies are small, with groups over 100 individuals known, but uncommon.
Comments: Specimens from Vietnam were referred to *M. h. horsfieldii*, suggesting that subspecies limits need additional attention.
Conservation Status: China RL—VU A1acd.
References: Bates and Harrison (1997); Bates et al. (1999); Corbet and Hill (1992); Hill (1983).

Ikonnikov's Myotis

PLATE 39
MAP 421

Myotis ikonnikovi Ognev, 1912
伊氏鼠耳蝠 Yishi Shu'erfu

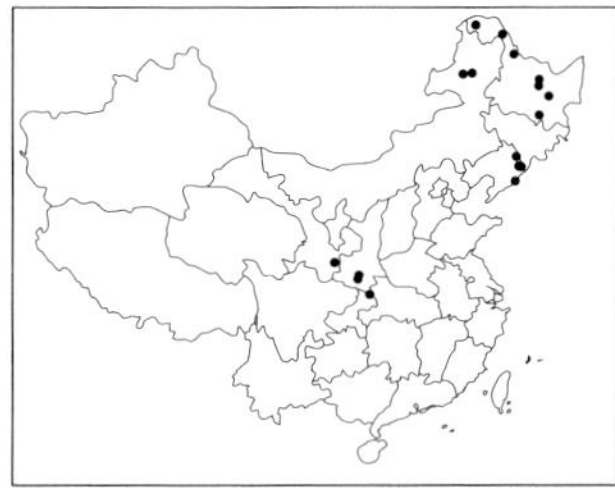

MAP 421. IKONNIKOV'S MYOTIS, *Myotis ikonnikovi*

Distinctive Characteristics: HB 36–52; T 30–38; HF 7–9; E 11–13; FA 30–36; GLS 12.7. Size very small; ears short, turning forward nearly to rostrum tip and not distinctly beyond it; wing membrane attached at basal part of toe; exterior margins of uropatagium without comb-shaped fuzz; calcar keeled; dorsal hair dark brown; ventral surface brown; rostrum of skull pointed; interorbital breadth greater than distance between canines; second upper premolar (P3) slightly smaller than first premolar (P2), lying in toothrow and not leaning to inner side.
Distribution: Nei Mongol, Heilongjiang, Jilin, Liaoning, Shaanxi, and Gansu; extending to Russia, Mongolia, Korea, and Japan.
Natural History: Aside from an individual found hibernating in a cave, nothing is known of the natural history of this species.
Comments: See Tsytsulina (2001) for a taxonomic review of this species.
Conservation Status: China RL—LC.
References: Tsytsulina (2001); Yoshiyuki (1989).

Chinese Water Myotis

Myotis laniger (Peters, 1871) MAP 422
华南水鼠耳蝠 Hua'nanshui Shu'erfu

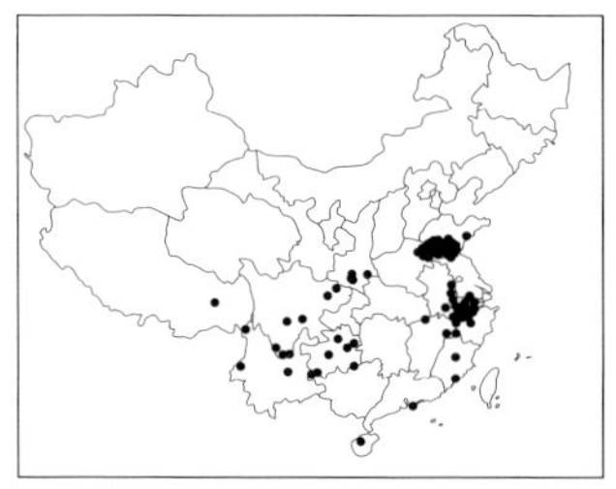

MAP 422. CHINESE WATER MYOTIS, *Myotis laniger*

Distinctive Characteristics: HB 40–42; T 38–40; HF 8–11; E 12–16; FA 34–36. Size small; dorsal coloration dark brown, ventral hairs dark at base, with paler brown or gray tips; pelage short; face densely haired; hind foot length slightly more than half tibia length; unkeeled calcar; wing membrane attached to base of toes. Skull delicate; upper molars with distinct protoconule; small premolars wholly in toothrow; upper canine with small cingulum.
Distribution: Widespread in C and SE China; extending to India and Vietnam.
Natural History: Other than the fact that most specimens have been collected from caves, nothing is known of the habits of this species.
Comments: Formerly included in *M. daubentonii*, but considered distinct by Topál (1997). Wang (2003) listed it as a subspecies of *M. daubentonii*.
Conservation Status: China RL—LC.
References: Allen (1938); Bates et al. (1999); Topál (1997).

Kashmir Cave Myotis

Myotis longipes (Dobson, 1873) MAP 423
长指鼠耳蝠 Changzhi Shu'erfu

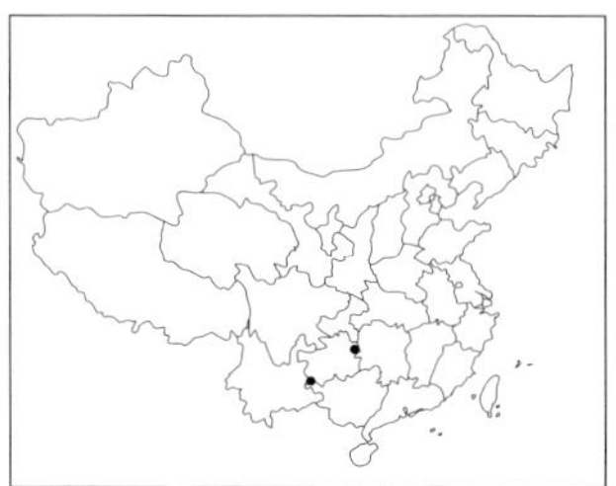

MAP 423. KASHMIR CAVE MYOTIS, *Myotis longipes*

Distinctive Characteristics: HB 43–46; T 37–42; HF 9–10; E 10–15; FA 36–39. Size small; pelage soft and dense; dorsally grayish brown with paler tips; ventrally brownish black with creamy white tips; hind foot length exceed half tibia length; ears long and narrow; tragus long and narrow, about half the ear length; third metacarpal barely exceeds fourth and fifth in length; wing attached to distal end of metatarsal; skull robust; braincase rounded, with little or no sagittal crest; zygomata flared; upper P3 tiny and intruded from toothrow.
Distribution: Included in Chinese fauna solely on the basis of Wang (2003), who lists it from Guizhou; otherwise known only from India, Nepal, and Afghanistan. Vietnamese records may be incorrect.
Natural History: Large colonies in caves and underground canals have been described extralimitally.
Comments: Formerly considered a subspecies of *M. capacinnii*.
Conservation Status: China RL—VU D2. IUCN RL—VU B1 + 2c, D2 ver 2.3 (1994).
References: Bates and Harrison (1997); Bates et al. (1999).

Burmese Whiskered Myotis

PLATE 39
Myotis montivagus (Dobson, 1874) MAP 424
山地鼠耳蝠 Shandi Shu'erfu

MAP 424. BURMESE WHISKERED MYOTIS, *Myotis montivagus*

Distinctive Characteristics: HB 56–62; T 42–48; HF 9–10; E 14–16; FA 40–49. Size medium; dorsal pelage dark brown, with darker roots and paler tips; ventrally similar, with tips paler brown; ears short and blunt; tragus short; wings attached to base of toe; hind foot length less than half tibia length; skull robust; rostrum broad and flat; braincase elevated and lacking sagittal crest; P3 small and intruded.
Distribution: Yunnan and central E China; extending to India, Myanmar, and the Malay Peninsula.
Natural History: This species is known primarily from low to midelevations, but details of its life history are lacking.
Comments: Chinese populations belong to the nominate subspecies and are considerable smaller than other subspecies to the west, suggesting that a complete study of geographic variation might be rewarding.
Conservation Status: China RL—VU A1bcd. IUCN RL—LR/nt ver 2.3 (1994).
References: Bates et al. (1999); Findley (1972); Hill (1962).

Nepalese Whiskered Myotis

Myotis muricola (Gray, 1846) MAP 425
南洋鼠耳蝠 Nanyang Shu'erfu
Distinctive Characteristics: HB 41–47; T 25–39; HF 4–7; E 6–13; FA 31–37. Size small; pelage thick and soft; dorsal hairs black basally with paler tips; ventrally slightly paler tips; ears large and pointed; tragus narrow and half the ear length; wing attached to base of metatarsal; hind foot length less than half tibia

length; skull delicate with elevated braincase; posterior part of rostrum with concavity; P3 in toothrow and contacting other premolars.
Distribution: Taiwan, central S China; widely distributed in SE Asia. Three subspecies in China: (1) *M. m. caliginosus* Tomes, 1859; Xizang; (2) *M. m. latirostris* Kishida, 1932; Taiwan; (3) *M. m. moupinensis* (Milne-Edwards, 1872); Sichuan, Yunnan.

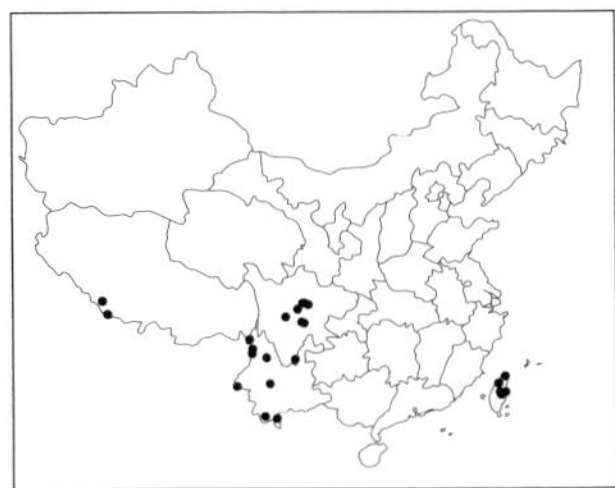

MAP 425. NEPALESE WHISKERED MYOTIS, *Myotis muricola*

Natural History: This species has been taken in a variety of habitats, including scrub and second growth, from sea level to moderately high elevations. Small colonies are known from caves, and it has also been recorded roosting in rolled banana leaves. Foraging begins early in the evening, and the bats fly high and fast.
Comments: This widespread species may be composite. Wang (2003) lists *M. m. blanfordi* from Xizang and Yunnan, but *blanfordi* is a synonym of *M. m. caliginosus*. He also lists *M. m. orii* from Taiwan, but *orii* is a synonym of *M. m. latirostris*, which he lists as a distinct species.
Conservation Status: China RL—VU A1c.
References: Bates and Harrison (1997); Findley (1972); Hill (1983); Kock (1996).

Nepalese Myotis

Myotis nipalensis (Dobson, 1871) MAP 426
尼泊尔须鼠耳蝠 Nibo'erxu Shu'erfu

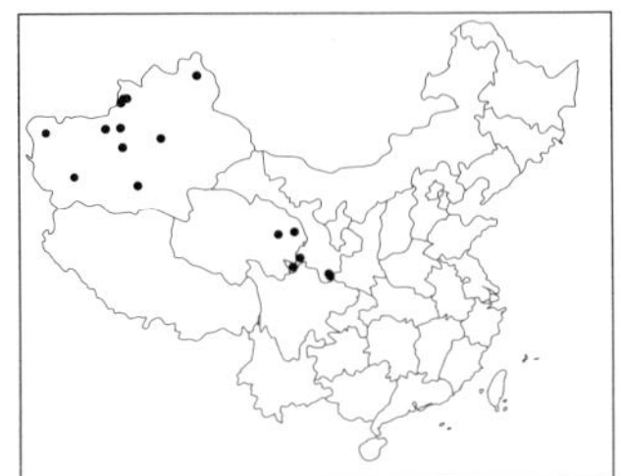

MAP 426. NEPALESE MYOTIS, *Myotis nipalensis*

Distinctive Characteristics: HB 38–47; T 32–40; HF 7–8; E 12–14; FA 34–37. Size small; dorsal pelage dark basally with brown tips, or sometimes more reddish gray; ventral pelage also dark basally but with paler grayish tips; ears small; tragus long and narrow, half as long as ear; hind foot small, less than half tibia length; wing membrane attached to distal end of metatarsal; braincase bulbous; rostrum narrow; upper premolars in toothrow.
Distribution: C and NW China; extending from Iran to Siberia. Two subspecies in China: (1) *M. n. kukunoriensis* Bobrinskii, 1929; Qinghai, Gansu; (2) *M. n. przewalski* Bobrinskii, 1926; Xinjiang.
Natural History: *M. nepalensis* inhabits both low and high elevation areas. It occurs in desert and mountainous habitats. It has been reported to feed on lepidoptera.
Comments: Previous inclusion of this species in *M. mystacinus* makes it difficult to interpret earlier literature. Wang (2003) included these forms, along with *M. davidii*, in *M. mystacinus*.
Conservation Status: China RL—LC.
References: Benda and Tsytsulina (2000).

Peking Myotis

Myotis pequinius Thomas, 1908 PLATE 39 MAP 427
北京鼠耳蝠 Beijing Shu'erfu

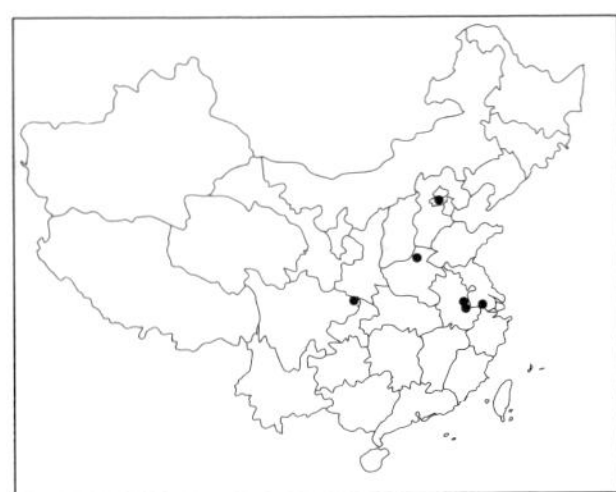

MAP 427. PEKING MYOTIS, *Myotis pequinius*

Distinctive Characteristics: HB 62; T 42; HF 12; E 18; FA 48–50. Size large; jaw length about 14.5 mm; zygomatic width 12.2 mm; compound hairs long and delicate; when turned forward, ears do not go beyond rostrum tip; tragus relatively short, about half length of ears; wing membrane attached at ankle; exterior margins of uropatagium hairless or lightly fringed; tail slightly shorter than HB length; length of hind foot more than half tibia length; fur rather short and velvety; dorsal hair gray reddish brown; ventral surface off-white; rostrum of skull short and upturned; front very low and flat; small premolars in upper and lower jaws both very small, lying in toothrows and occasionally absent.
Distribution: Hebei, Beijing, Shandong, Sichuan, Henan, Jiangsu. Endemic; monotypic species.
Natural History: The type and one other were collected from a cave that also contained *Miniopterus*. Otherwise, nothing is known of the habits of this Chinese endemic.
Comments: Earlier literature placed this species in the subgenus *Leuconoe*. Recent workers have suggested relationships with the *nattereri* group of Findley (1972).
Conservation Status: China RL—NT; although it nearly met the criteria for VU A1bcd. IUCN RL—LR/nt ver 2.3 (1994).
References: Findley (1972); Horácek et al. (2000).

Rickett's Big-Footed Myotis

PLATE 39
MAP 428

Myotis pilosus (Peters, 1869)
大足鼠耳蝠 Dazu Shu'erfu

MAP 428. RICKETT'S BIG-FOOTED MYOTIS, *Myotis pilosus*

Distinctive Characteristics: HB 65; T 45–54; HF 15–17; E 15–18; FA 53–56; GLS 21. Size large; ears well developed; hind foot long; length of calcar 18–21.5 mm; compound hairs short and closely appressed to skin; entire hind legs and feet, and basal part of septum uropatagium all covered with short hairs; dorsal hair reddish brown; ventral surface nearly off-white, with black gray hair tips; hind foot length with claw equal to tibia length; wing membrane attached at midtibia; skull long and narrow; sagittal crest low; auditory bullae small; zygomatic arch slender and attenuated; hypocones of upper molars undeveloped, without small protocones; outer incisors in upper jaw possess developed cusps.
Distribution: E China (Beijing, Shanxi, Zhejiang, Guangdong, Hong Kong, Guangxi, Yunnan, Fujian, Anhui, Shandong). Endemic.
Natural History: This large-footed *Myotis* feeds on fish and aquatic insects. They have been captured foraging over water, and at cave entrances, in second-growth forest, and in limestone regions. Biweekly studies of fecal samples from animals captured near Beijing documented a diet of fish (*Zacco platypus*, *Carassius auratus*, and *Phoxinus lagowskii*), and insects (Coleoptera, Lepidoptera, Homoptera, Ephemeroptera, Hemiptera, Diptera, and Hymenoptera). A single species of fish (*Z. platypus*) made up 60% of the diet, and beetles composed 13%.
Comments: The name *Myotis pilosus* was supplanted by *Myotis ricketti* Thomas, 1894 because in Peters' original description, he listed the type locality as Uruguay. However, Allen (1936) demonstrated clearly that the locality was erroneous, and that the descriptions of *pilosus* and *ricketti* both applied to the same taxon. Accepting that, the name *pilosus* Peters, 1869 clearly has priority.
Conservation Status: China RL—LC. IUCN RL 2003: LR/nt ver 2.3 (1994).
References: Allen (1936); Bates et al. (1999); Corbet and Hill (1992); Findley (1972); Horácek et al. (2000); Ma et al. (2006).

Himalayan Whiskered Myotis

PLATE 39
MAP 429

Myotis siligorensis (Horsfield, 1855)
高颅鼠耳蝠 Gaolu Shu'erfu

Distinctive Characteristics: HB 40–41; T 25–38; HF 6–8; E 8–13; FA 31–36; GLS 13. Size small; tail slightly shorter than HB length; wing membrane attached at basal part of toe; length of hind foot about half of tibia length; calcar with obvious keel; dorsal hair dark smoky gray; ventral surface taupe; wing membrane black; upper canines very undeveloped; lower canines about equal in length with large premolar (p4); second upper premolar (P3) very small, lying in toothrow.
Distribution: E and SE China, including Hainan Island; extending widely across the Indo-Malayan realm. Chinese subspecies: *M. s. sowerbyi* Howell, 1926 (although Wang [2003] lists specimens from Yunnan as *M. s. alticraniatus* Osgood, 1932).

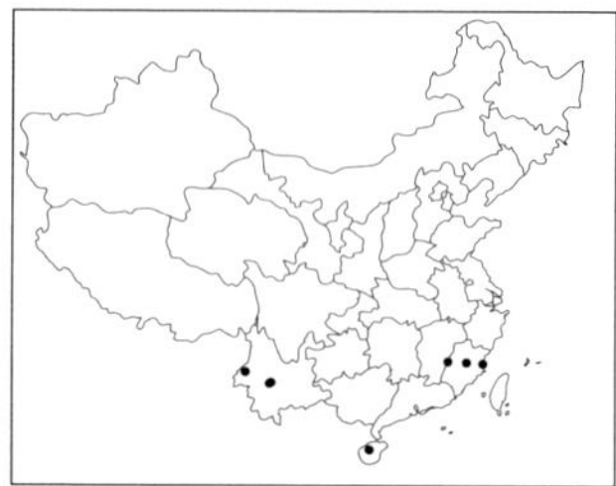

MAP 429. HIMALAYAN WHISKERED MYOTIS, *Myotis siligorensis*

Natural History: This species has been collected in lowland second-growth forests over streams and at the mouth of caves. They inhabit a variety of both lowland and upland habitats. Colonies of up to 1,200 individuals have been reported from caves. They are reported to forage fairly high in the air, but also to enter houses to feed on insects. They are active both at dusk and dawn.
Comments: Wang (2003) reported a "Kunming form" from Yunnan. Subspecies allocations are tentative because of considerable size variation in animals from Vietnam.
Conservation Status: China RL—NT; although it nearly met the criteria for VU D2.
References: Bates and Harrison (1997); Bates et al. (1999).

Subfamily Miniopterinae

Genus *Miniopterus*—Long-fingered Bats

长翼蝠亚科 Changyifu Yake; 长翼蝠属 Changyifu Shu—长翼蝠 Changyifu

Ears short and wide; tragus slender, with tip slightly turned forward; wing membrane long and narrow; third metacarpal bone relatively short; length of second phalanx of third digit three times that of first phalanx; compound hairs short and thick; rostrum of skull low and slightly wide, with tip slightly upturned,

Key to the Chinese Species of *Miniopterus*

1.a.	Condylobasal length < 14 mm	*Miniopterus pusillus*
b.	Condylobasal length > 14 mm	2
2.a.	Width across M3–M3 7.3 mm or less	*Minipterus schreibersii*
b.	Width across M3–M3 7.4 mm or more	*Miniopterus magnater*

slightly recessed in middle; cranium high, large, and round; preorbital fossa relatively far from orbit, approximately lying above canines; sagittal and lambdoidal crests both relatively low; coronoid process of mandible very low. Dental formula: 2.1.2.3/3.1.3.3 = 36; incisors in upper jaw about equal in height, crown of small premolar (P2) not very reduced, P2 lies on inner side of toothrow, its height about half of that of large premolar (P4); third upper molar not very reduced; first two premolars (p2 and p3) in lower jaw about equal in size, and smaller than posterior premolar (p4). Widely distributed in tropical and subtropical regions of Asia, S Europe, and N Africa. Of 19 species, 3 occur in China. Wang (2003) lists *M. fuscus* from Fujian and Taiwan with "(?)," a notation suggesting that he was following Maeda (1982). The *Miniopterus* on Taiwan is *M. schreibersii*, and more recent authorities (Corbet and Hill 1992; Hill 1983; Yoshiyuki 1989) have allocated the Fujian specimens to *M. schreibersii* as well.

Western Long-Fingered Bat

Miniopterus magnater Sanborn, 1931 MAP 430
几内亚长翼蝠 Jineiya Changyifu

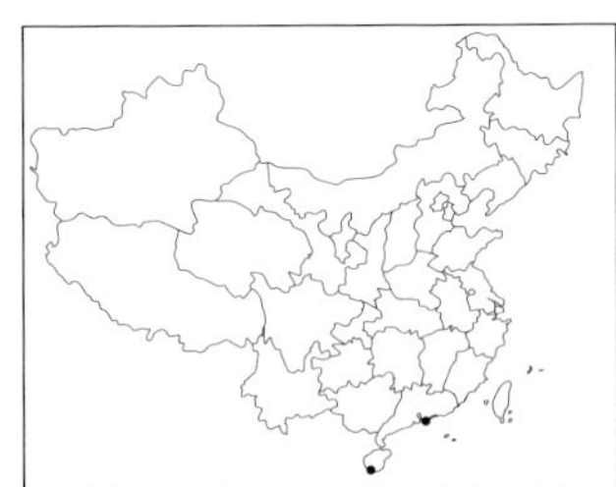

MAP 430. WESTERN LONG-FINGERED BAT, *Miniopterus magnater*

Distinctive Characteristics: HB 58–75; T 52–64; HF 9–13; E 11–17; FA 47–54; GLS > 17. Size large; dorsal pelage long, soft, and blackish brown in color; ventral pelage dark brown, with paler tips. Skull long, braincase considerably higher than rostrum, and broad, with a central concavity; rostrum broad.
Distribution: Fujian, Guangdong, Hong Kong, and Hainan Island; widely distributed in SE Asia. Chinese subspecies: *M. m. macrodens* Maeda, 1982.
Natural History: *Miniopterus magnater* roosts in caves. It occupies both primary and secondary forested areas in lowlands, and is common around human habitations. It forages for high-flying insects above the forest canopy and can also be seen around street lights in settlements.
Comments: Wang (2003) listed *macrodens* as a full species, but all other recent authors have considered *macrodens* a subspecies of *M. magnater*.
Conservation Status: China RL—VU A2bc; B2ab(i, ii, iii)
References: Bonaccorso (1998); Corbet and Hill (1992); Hill (1983); Koopman (1994); Maeda (1982).

Small Long-Fingered Bat

Miniopterus pusillus Dobson, 1876 MAP 431
南长翼蝠 Nan Changyifu

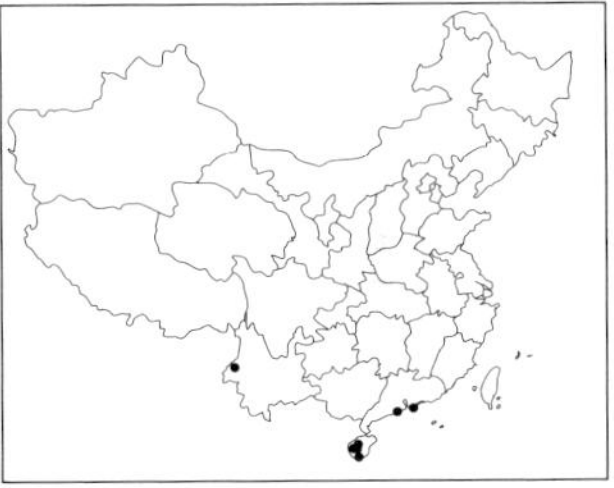

MAP 431. SMALL LONG-FINGERED BAT, *Miniopterus pusillus*

Distinctive Characteristics: HB 45–48; T 40–48; HF 7–8; E 10–11; FA 39–42; GLS 13.5–14.5. Size small; zygomatic width 7.5–7.6 mm; pelage color dark brown, but slightly lighter than that of *Miniopterus schreibersii*; fur extends slightly onto uropatagium; muzzle relatively long; skull without sagittal crest; palate relatively narrow.
Distribution: Hong Kong, Guangdong, Hainan Island, and Yunnan; distributed throughout the Indo-Malayan realm.
Natural History: Nothing is known of the life history of this species.
Comments: Although widespread in distribution, this species is known from relatively few localities. Its relationship to *M. australis* and *M. macroneme* needs clarification.
Conservation Status: China RL—A2bc; B2ab(i, ii, iii).
References: Bates and Harrison (1997); Corbet and Hill (1992); Hill (1983).

Schreiber's Long-Fingered Bat

PLATE 40
Miniopterus schreibersii (Kuhl, 1819) MAP 432
长翼蝠 Changyifu

Distinctive Characteristics: HB 67–78; T 50–62; HF 9–12; E 12–14; FA 47–50; GLS 15.7–17.2. Size large; zygomatic width 8.7–9.8 mm; dorsal pelage color dark brown or reddish brown; venter similar, but tips paler; tail, uropatagium, and wings long; sagittal crest of skull low and slender; rostrum slender and small, but palate relatively broad.

Distribution: N, SE, and S China; extending in a very broad distribution across Europe and Asia. Three subspecies in China: (1) *M. s. chinensis* Thomas, 1908; Hebei, Henan, Zhejiang, Anhui; (2) *M. s. fuliginosus* (Hodgson, 1835); Yunnan, Sichuan; (3) *M. s. parvipes* Allen, 1923; Fujian, Taiwan, Guangdong.
Natural History: This is basically a cave-roosting species, but occasionally individuals or small numbers are found in buildings or tree crevices. They begin to forage early in the evening and have a characteristic rapid, erratic flight. They catch flying beetles and other small insects, frequently 10 m or more off the ground. In the north, they hibernate in cool caves in the winter. Some populations may also undergo seasonal migrations. They are highly gregarious, and some roosts have tens of thousands of individuals. A single young is born, and the females leave them behind in communal nurseries when they leave to forage.

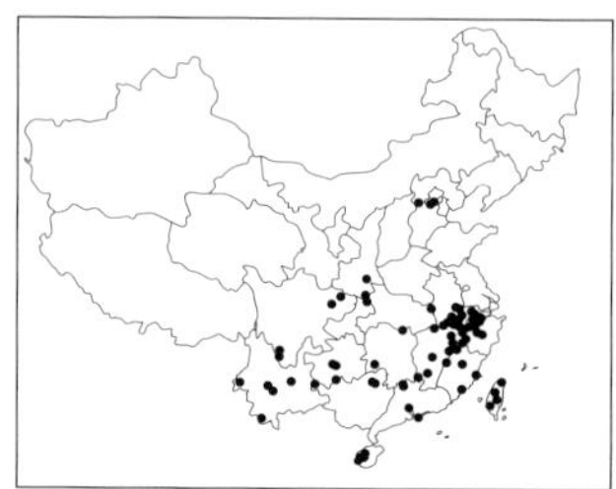

MAP 432. SCHREIBER'S LONG-FINGERED BAT, *Miniopterus schreibersii*

Comments: There are lots of available names and recognized subspecies within this wide-ranging and common species. Wang (2003) recognized *M. fuliginosus* as a distinct species, with *chinensis* and *parvipes* as subspecies. He also recognized *M. oceanensis* Maeda, 1982, based on Maeda's contention that two broken skulls from Yunnan represented that taxon.
Conservation Status: China RL—LC. IUCN RL—LR/nt ver 2.3 (1994).
References: Hill (1983); Horácek et al. (2000); Koopman (1994); Maeda (1982).

Subfamily Murininae—Hairy-winged Bat and Tube-nosed Bats

管鼻蝠亚科 Guanbifu Yake—管鼻蝠 Guanbifu

Nostrils elongated into tubular structures; ears more or less funnel-shaped; second phalanx of third digit not particularly elongated. Dental formula: 2.1.2.3/3.1.2.3 = 34; anterior upper premolar not particularly reduced, nor simpler than posterior upper premolar. Occurring from Pakistan and Ceylon to the Philippines, New Guinea, Australia, and northward to Siberia and Japan. Both genera of Murininae are found in China.

Genus *Harpiocephalus* (monotypic)

毛翅蝠属 Maochifu Shu

Lesser Hairy-Winged Bat — PLATE 40, MAP 433

Harpiocephalus harpia (Temminck, 1840)
毛翼管鼻蝠 Maoyi Guanbifu

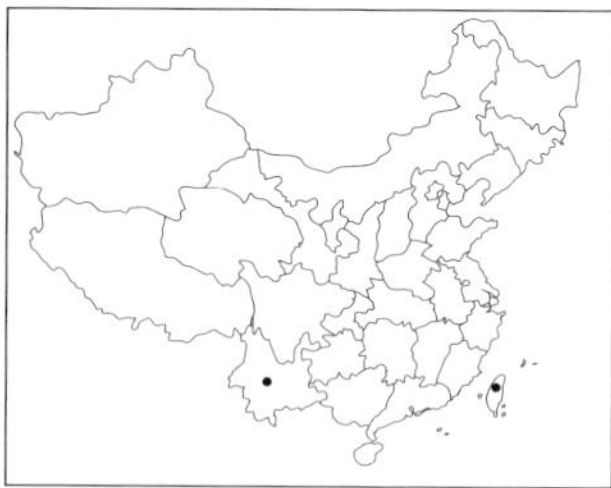

MAP 433. LESSER HAIRY-WINGED BAT, *Harpiocephalus harpia*

Distinctive Characteristics: HB 60–75; T 40–50; HF 11–14; E 17–18; FA 44–50; GLS 23. Size large; pelage thick and soft; dorsal hair orange brown; ventral surface light brown; ears rounded; tragus long with a basal notch; nostrils protuberant. Form very similar to that of *Murina*; hind legs, wing membrane and uropatagium covered with hair in part. Skull robust, with conspicuous sagittal crest; rostrum short and wide, recessed in middle; zygomatic arches long and expanded at jugal. Dental formula: 2.1.2.3/3.1.2.3 = 34; upper incisors large, with low crowns, and conspicuous small styles on posterior part; lower incisors low, long and trifurcate; canines also low; anterior premolars in upper and lower jaws slightly smaller than posterior premolars; first and second molars in upper jaw similar to premolars in shape, only posterior cusps developed, protocones and anterior tips very reduced, mesostyles absent, prestyles and posterior styles also developed; third upper molar reduced and close to posterior outer side of second upper molar, its length less than 1/4 crown length of second upper molar; lower molars also reduced, only one protoconid remains.
Distribution: Yunnan, Guangdong, Fujian, and Taiwan; extending across SE Asia. Chinese subspecies: *H. h. rufulus* Allen, 1923.
Natural History: This species is very poorly known. They are known to feed on beetles. They have been taken at elevations from sea level up to about 1,500 m.

Key to the Chinese Genera of Murininae

1.a.	Forearm < 44 mm	*Murina*
b.	Forearm > 44 mm	*Harpiocephalus*

Comments: Wang (2003) refers the mainland material to *H. h. rufulus*, and the Taiwan population to the nominate form. The Taiwan material has not been allocated to subspecies, but given that the nominate type locality is on Java, and the type locality for *rufulus* is in Vietnam, that seems highly unlikely. Awaiting a complete study of geographic variation, we assume all of the Chinese material is referable to *H. h. rufulus*.
Conservation Status: China RL—VU A2abcd + D2.
References: Bates and Harrison (1997); Corbet and Hill (1992).

Genus *Murina*—Tube-nosed Bats

管鼻蝠属 Guanbifu Shu—管鼻蝠 Guanbifu

Form similar to that of *Myotis*, but nostrils prolonged into short tubes; feet small; ears wide and short; uropatagium covered with hairs; skull shape also similar to that of *Myotis*, relatively long and narrow, and rising gradually from rostrum to cranium. Dental formula: 2.1.2.3/3.1.2.3 = 34; upper incisors without posterior cusp, outer incisor larger than inner one, small premolar (P2) between canine and posterior premolar (P4) sometimes strongly developed; first and second upper molars with quadrate crowns, hypocone absent, anterior styles on inner side relatively reduced, hence "W" structure of occlusal surfaces incomplete; third upper molar short and narrow. Distributed in C, E, and S Asia. Of 18 species known, 8 occur in China.

Little Tube-Nosed Bat

PLATE 40
Murina aurata Milne-Edwards, 1872
MAP 434
小管鼻蝠 Xiao Guanbifu

Distinctive Characteristics: HB 33–35; T 29–31; HF 7–8; E 10–12; FA 28–32; GLS 15.6–15.9. Size small, smallest of the *Murina*; nasal tube somewhat long, projecting forwards and outward; ears short, wide, and round; wing membrane attached to base of toes; uropatagium covered with spindly hairs; base of dorsal hair grayish black, hair tips with golden hue; base of ventral hair also grayish black, tips off-white; rostrum of skull very low; anterior premolar (P2) in upper jaw much smaller than posterior premolar (P4); crowns of lower canines relatively low, about equal in height with anterior premolar (p2).
Distribution: Sichuan, Gansu, Hainan, Yunnan, Guizhou, and Xizang; extending across E and S Asia.

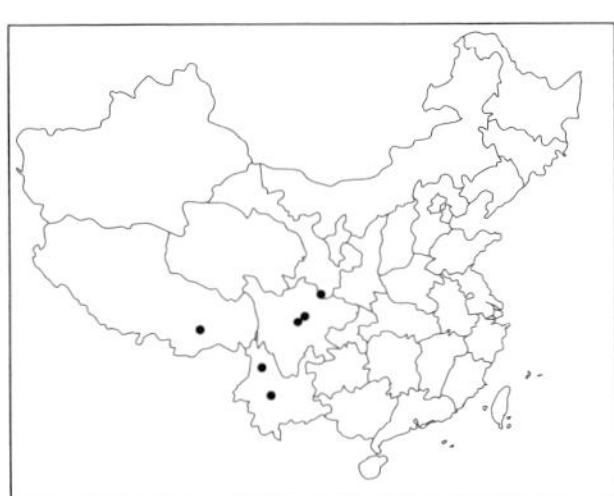

MAP 434. LITTLE TUBE-NOSED BAT, *Murina aurata*

Natural History: This widely distributed species remains poorly known. It has been collected as high as 4,000 m. It does not seem to inhabit caves and may use foliage roosts.
Comments: Wang (2003) lists *M. a. feae* Thomas, 1891 as a subspecies for animals from Xizang and Yunnan, but Maeda (1980) regarded it as a synonym of *M. aurata*. The holotype of *M. aurata* was sent to Paris by Père David in 1871.
Conservation Status: China RL—VU D2. IUCN RL—LR/nt ver 2.3 (1994).
References: Allen (1938); Bates and Harrison (1997); Hill (1983); Maeda (1980).

Key to the Chinese Species of *Murina*

1.a.	Small premolar in upper jaw slightly smaller than posterior premolar; left and right toothrows do not noticeably close up in the forepart; space between canines (C-C) about 80% of that between molars	2
b.	Small premolar in upper jaw much smaller than posterior premolar; left and right toothrows noticeably close up in the forepart; space between canines (C-C) about 65-70% of that between molars	4
2.a.	Size small; forearm length 30–33 mm	*Murina cyclotis*
b.	Size middle; forearm length 34–38 mm	3
3.a.	Found on the mainland	*Murina huttoni*
b.	Found on Taiwan	*Murina puta*
4.a.	Size very small; forearm length about 28–32 mm	5
b.	Size slightly larger; forearm length 40–43 mm	6
5.a.	Smaller, GLS < 14.7 mm	*Murina aurata*
b.	Larger, GLS > 14.7 mm	*Murina ussuriensis*
6.a.	Size small, HB length about 50 mm	*Murina hilgendorfi*
b.	Size larger, HB length > 55 mm	7
7.a.	Occipital region projects backward	*Murina leucogaster*
b.	Occipital region less backwardly projecting	*Murina fusca*

Round-Eared Tube-Nosed Bat

PLATE 40
MAP 435

Murina cyclotis Dobson, 1872
圆耳管鼻蝠 Yuan'er Guanbifu

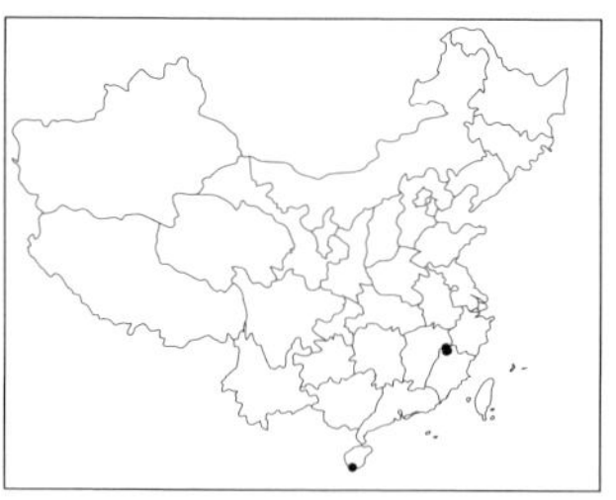

MAP 435. ROUND-EARED TUBE-NOSED BAT, *Murina cyclotis*

Distinctive Characteristics: HB 38–50; T 32–42; HF 7–10; E 12–15; FA 30–35. Size small; nostrils tubular; ears nearly round, width close to length; tragus wiry; wing membrane attaches to base of toes along lateral margins of hind foot; tail tip dissociated; uropatagium with hairs; back of hind foot also with short hairs; base of dorsal hair dark brown, tips smoky brown; ventral surface light brown; in upper jaw large premolar (P4) slightly larger than anterior premolar (P2).
Distribution: Jiangxi and Hainan Island; extending to Zhongnan Peninsula, Philippines, and Sri Lanka. Chinese subspecies is the nominate form.
Natural History: This species inhabits agroforestry areas at intermediate elevations. They roost in the foliage, where their color pattern makes them difficult to detect. They have also been taken in small caves or rock shelters. They forage near the ground and are quite maneuverable in vegetated areas.
Comments: A widespread distribution combined with relatively few specimens makes assessment of geographic variation difficult for this species.
Conservation Status: China RL—VU B2ab(i,ii,iii); D2.
References: Bates and Harrison (1997); Hill (1983).

Dusky Tube-Nosed Bat

PLATE 40
MAP 436

Murina fusca Sowerby, 1922
暗色管鼻蝠 Anse Guanbifu

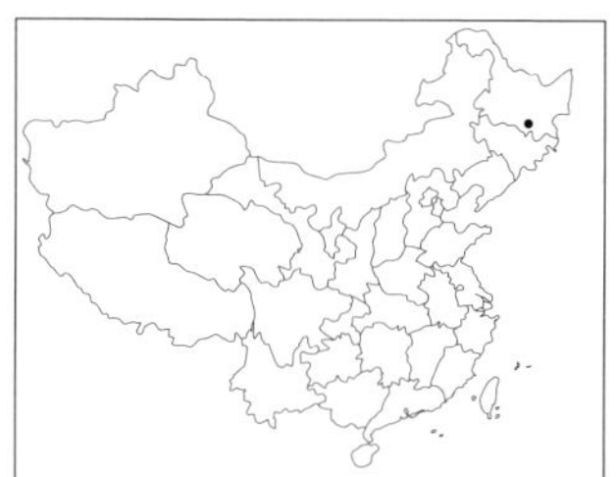

MAP 436. DUSKY TUBE-NOSED BAT, *Murina fusca*

Distinctive Characteristics: HB 58; T 34; HF 8; E 18; FA 40; GLS 17. Size medium; pelage dusky brown with numerous longer whitish hairs interspersed; dorsally the effect is almost grayish; venter paler; fur extends onto uropatagium and hind feet are also quite hairy; skull robust; no sagittal crest; occiput not noticeably projecting backward.
Distribution: Known only from the type locality in Heilongjiang. Endemic.
Natural History: The type specimen was collected in the house of a Russian peasant in late September, suggesting that the species might hibernate in the area.
Comments: Originally described as a subspecies of *M. huttoni*, this species has also been associated with *M. hilgendorfi* and *M. leucogaster*. The holotype in the USNM is quite different from those and all other species of *Murina*.
Conservation Status: China RL—NA. IUCN RL—DD ver 2.3 (1994).
References: Wallin (1969); Wang (1959).

Hilgendorf's Tube-Nosed Bat

MAP 437

Murina hilgendorfi (Peters, 1880)
东北管鼻蝠 Dongbei Guanbifu

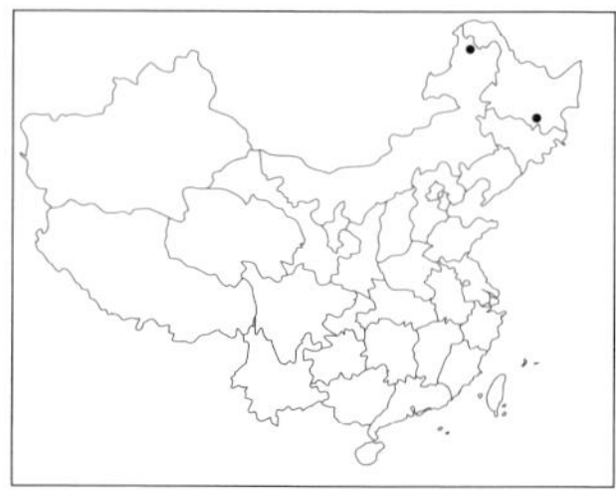

MAP 437. HILGENDORF'S TUBE-NOSED BAT, *Murina hilgendorfi*

Distinctive Characteristics: HB 46–70; T 32–45; HF 10–15; E 14–20; FA 40–45; GLS 16–19. Size large; fur soft, woolly, and glossy; dorsal hair four-banded, dark grayish brown basally, then paler grayish brown, then olive to orange brown, with golden buff tips; ventral hairs dark brown basally, with silvery tips; dorsal surface of uropatagium, plagiopatagium, and thumb covered with hair; ear with two concavities on margin; tragus deflected outward; skull robust; rostrum short and stout; braincase low and narrow.
Distribution: Great Xing'an Mountain, Nei Mongol, and Heilongjiang; extending to Japan, Kazakhstan, and Russia.
Natural History: Nothing is known of the natural history of this species.
Comments: The systematic status of this species has been confused. Wang (2003) considered it a subspecies of *fusca*, but the name *hilgendorfi* clearly antedates *fusca*. Others have included it in *M. leucogaster*, but it seems distinct.
Conservation Status: China RL—NA.
References: Wang (1959); Yoshiyuki (1989).

Hutton's Tube-Nosed Bat

PLATE 40
MAP 438

Murina huttoni (Peters, 1872)
中管鼻蝠 Zhong Guanbifu

Distinctive Characteristics: HB 47–50; T 31–39; HF 6–10; E 16–18; FA 29–38; GLS 15–18. Size medium; pelage thick, soft, and brown; ventral surface slightly paler than dorsal hair, but not distinct from it; uropatagium and feet hairy. Skull robust and narrow; patate broad and parallel-sided; upper anterior premolar (P2) somewhat smaller than posterior premolar (P4). **Distribution:** Fujian, Jiangxi, and Guangxi; extending from India through Indochina and SE Asia. Chinese subspecies: *M. h. rubella* Thomas, 1914.

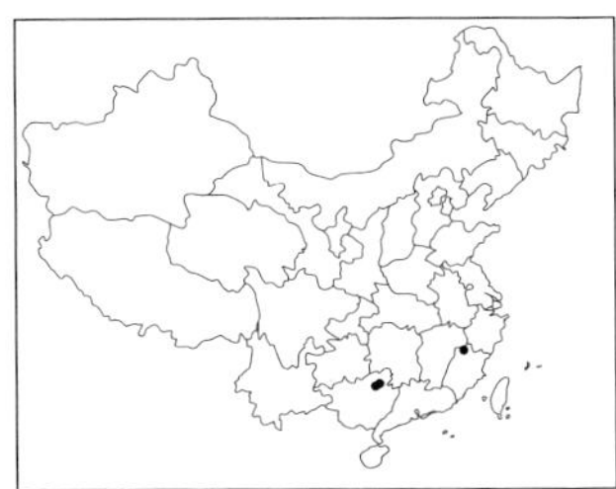

MAP 438. HUTTON'S TUBE-NOSED BAT, *Murina huttoni*

Natural History: *Murina huttoni* appears to be a bat of midelevations, adapted to a variety of habitats. No details are available on the natural history, however. **Comments:** *M. huttoni* is another wide-ranging species whose systematic relationships are poorly understood.
Conservation Status: China RL—VU A2bc + D2. IUCN RL—LR/nt ver 2.3 (1994).
References: Bates and Harrison (1997); Hill (1983); Sinha (1999).

Greater Tube-Nosed Bat

Murina leucogaster Milne-Edwards, 1872 PLATE 40 MAP 439
白腹管鼻蝠 Baifu Guanbifu

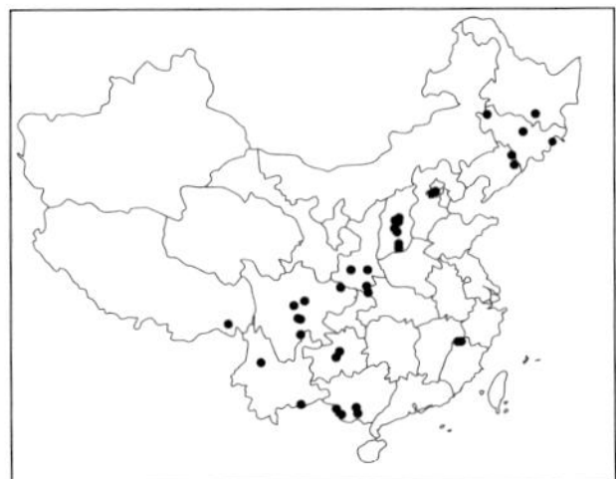

MAP 439. GREATER TUBE-NOSED BAT, *Murina leucogaster*

Distinctive Characteristics: HB 47–49; T 35–45; HF 9–10; E 14–15; FA 40–43; GLS 18–19. Size relatively large; zygomatic width 10.2–11.5 mm; ears relatively narrow and short; wing membrane attached to toes; fifth metacarpal bone slightly longer than fourth, so wing membrane very wide; both uropatagium and back of hind foot covered with hairs; pelage color reddish brown or brownish gray; dorsal hair mingled with off-white slender and long hairs; ventral surface white and blackish white; rostrum of skull relatively wide; with sagittal and lambdoidal crests, but inconspicuous; anterior premolar (P2) distinctly less than half of posterior premolar (P4) in size.
Distribution: Widely spread across E China; also extending widely across Asia. Chinese subspecies is the nominate form.
Natural History: This species is known to roost in caves, trees, and houses. They forage in both forested and open areas.
Comments: Wang (2003) recorded *M. rubex* from Xizang, but *rubex* is an Indian subspecies of *M. leucogaster*. The conservative approach is to consider all Chinese specimens to be *M. l. leucogaster*, as the type locality is in Sichuan.
Conservation Status: China RL—LC.
References: Bates and Harrison (1997); Yoshiyuki (1989).

Taiwanese Tube-Nosed Bat

Murina puta Kishida, 1924 MAP 440
台湾管鼻蝠 Taiwan Guanbifu

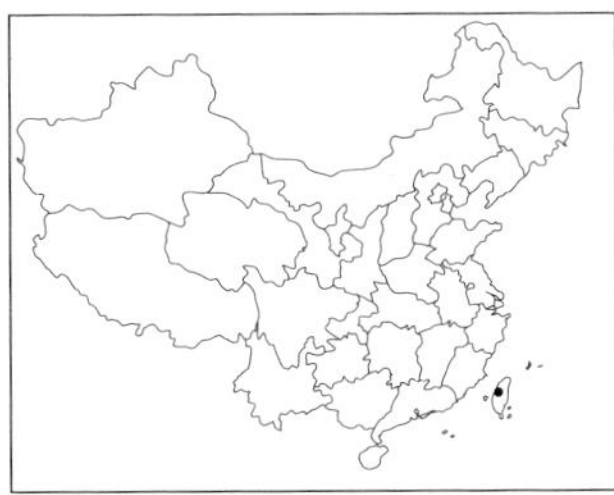

MAP 440. TAIWANESE TUBE-NOSED BAT, *Murina puta*

Distinctive Characteristics: HB 59–61; T 32–36; HF 10–11; E 17–19; FA 34–35. Size medium; pelage long and soft; dorsal color reddish brown, hairs tricolored with dark bases, tan intermediate zone, and reddish tips; venter paler; legs, hind feet, dorsal surface of uropatagium and tail furred; skull robust and broad; P2 slightly smaller than P4.
Distribution: Taiwan. Endemic.
Natural History: This Taiwan endemic is uncommon and apparently restricted to mountainous regions with temperate forest.
Comments: This species appears to be the insular equivalent of the mainland *M. huttoni*.
Conservation Status: China RL—EN B2ab(i, ii, iii); D2. IUCN RL—VU A2c ver 2.3 (1994).
References: Lin et al. (1997); Yoshiyuki (1989).

Ussurian Tube-Nosed Bat

Murina ussuriensis Ognev, 1913 MAP 441
乌苏里管鼻蝠 Wusuli Guanbifu
Distinctive Characteristics: HB 40; T 25; HF 10; E 13; FA 27; GLS 15. Size small; pelage short and soft; individual hairs dark basally, with pale intermediate band, and reddish brown tips; venter paler with grayish cast; uropatagium, legs, and hind feet hairy dorsally; skull somewhat delicate; P2 much smaller than P4; upper toothrows divergent front to back.

Distribution: Nei Mongol, Jilin, and Heilongjiang; extending to E Russia and Korea.
Natural History: Three specimens from Korea were removed from the stomach of a snake. Nothing is known of the natural history in China.
Comments: Formerly considered a subspecies of *M. aurata*, *M. ussuriensis* seems to be distinct.

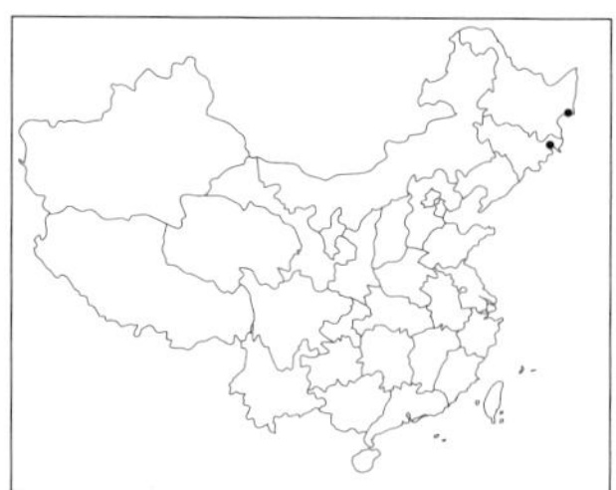

MAP 441. USSURIAN TUBE-NOSED BAT, *Murina ussuriensis*

Conservation Status: China RL—NA. IUCN RL—EN A2c ver 2.3 (1994).
References: Maeda (1980); Yoshiyuki (1989).

Subfamily Kerivoulinae

Genus *Kerivoula*—Woolly Bats

彩蝠亚科 Caifu Yake; 彩蝠属 Caifu Shu—彩蝠 Caifu

Size small; length of ear medium; ears turned forward slightly exceed rostrum tip, not joined, and slightly funnel-shaped; tragus long and slender; nostrils normal; whole body with slender and soft hairs; wing membrane attaches to base of toe; calcar unkeeled; skull relatively long and narrow, similar to that of *Myotis*; cranium high and round, without occipital crest, abruptly declining from cranium to interorbital region; rostrum sharp and narrow; nasal sinus narrow; palatal sinus also small; palate long and narrow; pterygoid process very short; small auditory bullae and large cochleae. Dental formula: 2.1.3.3/3.1.3.3 = 38; premolars not very different in size, and all in toothrows. Of 19 *Kerivoula*, 2 occur in China.

Hardwicke's Woolly Bat PLATE 40
Kerivoula hardwickii (Horsfield, 1824) MAP 442
哈氏彩蝠 Hashi Caifu

Distinctive Characteristics: HB 39–55; T 35–43; HF 5–10; E 11–15; FA 31–36; GLS 15. Size very small; dorsal hair smoky brown; ventral surface grayish ochre, with brownish gray base; cranium of skull slightly low and flat; size difference between first two premolars (P2 and P3) in upper jaw and posterior premolar (P4) a little more conspicuous than in *Kerivoula picta*.
Distribution: SE China; extending across S Asia, Indonesia, and the Philippines.
Natural History: This species is widely distributed through subtropical and tropical areas. It has been collected in both forested and agricultural areas. It sometimes forages around houses and villages. It roosts in buildings and under tile roofs on occasion.

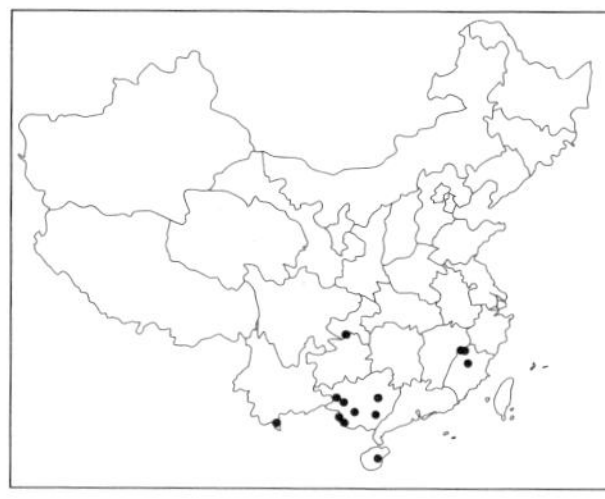

MAP 442. HARDWICKE'S WOOLLY BAT, *Kerivoula hardwickii*

Comments: Wang (2003) and others have used the name *depressa* Miller, 1906 as the Chinese subspecies, but recent work argues against recognition of subspecies.
Conservation Status: China RL—VU A2abc + 3abc.
References: Bates and Harrison (1997); Corbet and Hill (1992); Hendrichsen et al. (2001).

Painted Woolly Bat PLATE 40
Kerivoula picta (Pallas, 1767) MAP 443
彩蝠 Caifu

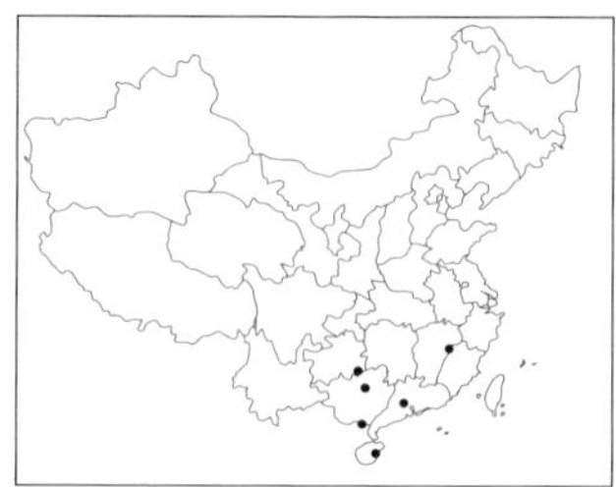

MAP 443. PAINTED WOOLLY BAT, *Kerivoula picta*

Distinctive Characteristics: HB 40–48; T 43–48; HF 4–8; E 13–16; FA 31–38; GLS 15. Size medium; compound hairs slender and soft; striking coloration unique; body hair orange; wing membrane also orange, but its interdigital membrane brownish black.
Distribution: SE China; extending across S Asia. Chinese subspecies: *K. p. bellissima* Thomas, 1906.

Key to the Chinese Species of *Kerivoula*

1.a.	Forearm length about 37–39 mm; pelage color orange and black brown	*Kerivoula picta*
b.	Forearm length about 34 mm; hair smoky brown	*Kerivoula hardwickii*

Natural History: This strikingly colored bat roosts in the foliage, frequently among dried leaves or flowers that allow it to blend in well. They apparently estivate during the day, as they are relatively sluggish when disturbed. The fluttering, erratic flight resembles a large moth.
Comments: In contrast to the situation with *K. hardwickii*, the northern subspecies of *K. picta*, *K. p. bellissima*, seems to be a well-marked, larger form.
Conservation Status: China RL—VUA2abcd.
References: Bates and Harrison (1997); Corbet and Hill (1992).

ORDER PHOLIDOTA
Family Manidae
Genus *Manis*—Pangolins
鳞甲目 Linjia Mu; 穿山甲科 Chuanshanjia Ke; 鲮鲤属 Lingli Shu—穿山甲 Chuanshanjia

Andrew T. Smith

Body covered with scales that are arranged in overlapping rows; with sparse hairs between dorsal scales (Asian forms); venter and inner sides of limbs without scales, but covered with sparse hairs; each limb with five toes; claws long, claws on middle toes of fore- and hind feet especially developed; claws of forefeet turning backward; usually walk on back feet; tail long and flat. Head small and rostrum pointed, acute, and cone-shaped; without teeth; nasal bone and supraoccipital bone large; without jugal; mandible reduced, without angular or coronoid processes. Keenly adapted to their behavior of living on ants and termites. This order only contains one family, Manidae, and one genus, *Manis*. Pangolins are distributed in southern Asia and tropical and subtropical areas of Africa. There are eight species, two of which occur in China.

Indian Pangolin
Manis crassicaudata Gray, 1827 MAP 444
印度穿山甲 Yindu Chuanshanjia

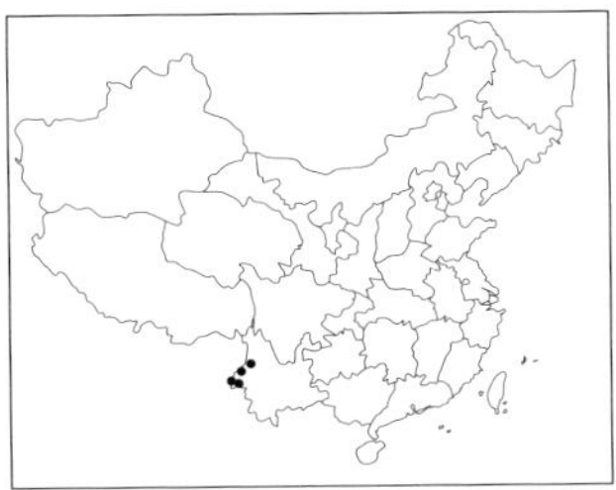

MAP 444. INDIAN PANGOLIN, *Manis crassicaudata*

Distinctive Characteristics: HB 450–750; T 330–460; HF to 100; GLS 101; Wt 4.7–9.5 kg. Generally similar to the Chinese Pangolin in form, but the external ear is smaller and the underside of the tail tip is well covered with scales (fig. 11). Also, the hind feet are covered with more scales. There are 11–13 rows of body scales and 14–16 scales along edge of tail. Anal glands secrete a foul-smelling yellow fluid that is apparently used as a defense mechanism. The nasal bones are the same width throughout, unlike in the Chinese Pangolin.
Distribution: W Yunnan; extending through India, Pakistan, and Sri Lanka.
Natural History: Occupies forest and scrub habitat. Nocturnal. While terrestrial, it is also an agile climber using its prehensile tail. The diet is almost exclusively of ants and termites, which it procures using its long sticky tongue (which may be as long as

Key to the Chinese Species of *Manis*

1.a. Ear pinna pronounced; ventral midline of tail tip with no scales (fig. 11); 15–18 rows of body scales; posterior part of nasal bone wider than its anterior extremity *Manis pentadactyla*
b. Ear pinna small; ventral midline of tail tip covered with scales (fig. 11); 11–13 rows of body scales; anterior and posterior parts of nasal bone about equal in width *Manis crassicaudata*

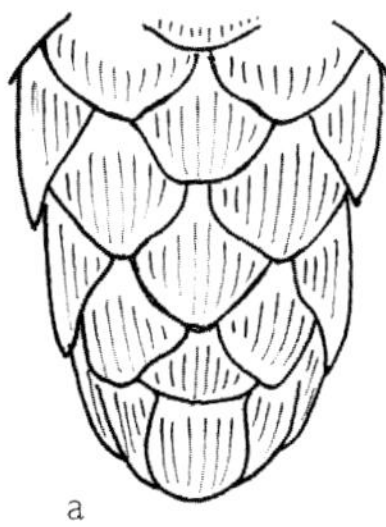

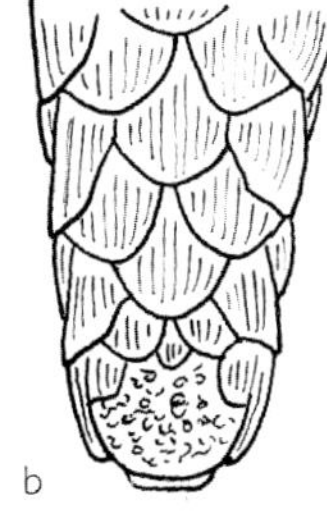

Figure 11. Comparative scale patterns on the tails of Indian (*Manis crassicaudata*; a) and Chinese (*M. pentadactyla*; b) pangolins.

30 cm). The powerful forefeet assist in digging for food and in constructing burrows that may extend 150–600 cm deep. Burrow entrances are closed when they are occupied. When alarmed, it curls up into a ball for defense. Usually a single young is produced (occasionally two); births have been reported during all seasons. Young ride on the base of the mother's tail.
Conservation Status: China RL—NA. CITES—II.
References: Heath (1995).

Chinese Pangolin

Manis pentadactyla Linnaeus, 1758 PLATE 1
穿山甲 Chuanshanjia MAP 445

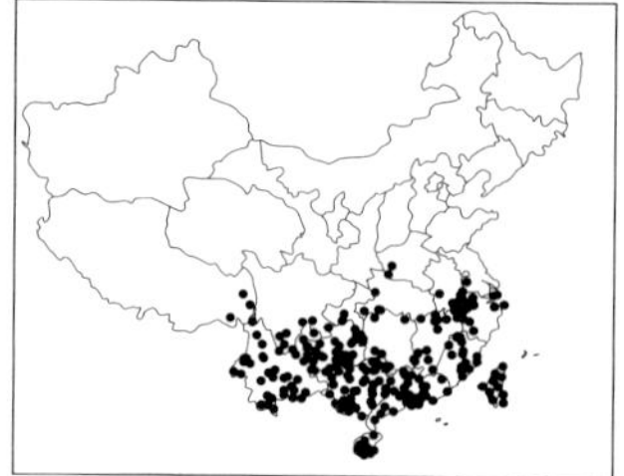

MAP 445. CHINESE PANGOLIN, *Manis pentadactyla*

Distinctive Characteristics: HB 423–920; T 280–350; HF 65–85; E 20–26; GLS 72–94; Wt 2.4–7 kg. Dorsum, sides of limbs, and tail all covered with brown scales; only the ventral midline of the tail tip without scales (fig. 11). There are 15–18 rows of body scales and 16–19 scales along edge of tail; scales smaller than in the Indian Pangolin. Ventral surface off-white, without scales. Has a postanal depression in the skin. Head and ears small, limbs short with long claws (claws of hind feet less than twice as long as those on forefeet); each limb with five toes. Skull coniform and flat, mandible without anular process; auditory sacs small and open; posterior of nasal bone wider than its anterior, and its middle posterior margin sharp. Lacks pads on the soles of its feet—a characteristic that separates it from a third species, *M. javanica*, which it overlaps south of China. 2N = 38.
Distribution: Throughout SE China and Taiwan; extending into Nepal and N Indochina. Two subspecies in China: (1) *M. p. aurita* Hodgson 1836, throughout SE China including Hainan Island; (2) *M. p. pentadactyla* Linnaeus, 1758; Taiwan.
Natural History: Prefers environments with a thick layer of shrub and herbs growing under a tree canopy. Generally similar to the Indian Pangolin. Diet consists almost entirely of ants and termites, which are procured with a long sticky tongue following active digging using strongly built fore claws. Nocturnal and solitary burrowing animals, that roll into a ball for defense when threatened. Adept at climbing trees. Chinese Pangolins spend winter months in burrows as deep as 3–4 m. Reproduction occurs in late summer to early fall; generally a single young is born.
Comments: Some believe that the Hainan forms represent a third subspecies, *M. p. pusilla* J. Allen, 1906.
Conservation Status: Has undergone a drastic decline and may have been extirpated in some areas due to heavy poaching for food, traditional Chinese medicine, and other products. China RL—EN A2cd + 3cd. China Key List—II. CITES—II. IUCN RL—LR/nt ver 2.3 (1994).
References: Heath (1992); Ke et al. (1999); Wu et al. (2003).

ORDER CARNIVORA—Carnivores

食肉目 Shirou Mu—食肉类 Shiroulei

W. Chris Wozencraft

Many of the animals in this order, usually called beasts of prey, are famous for preying on other animals—but not all. Some specialize in eating fruit, insects, bamboo, or shellfish. Although body forms and sizes differ among various species, all the mammals in this order are rather robust and vigorous, with a rather high development of sense organs (hearing, sight, sense of smell). All the terrestrial species have four or five toes with sharp, curved claws on each foot, and are generally quick and agile. Some species are very well adapted to aquatic lifestyles, and the seals rarely even come to land.

Many species of this order are of very high economic value. Some are important furbearers, such as sables, otters, seals, weasels, and ferret-badgers. Other species such as tigers and bears have been used for traditional medicines. Recently, members of

Key to the Chinese Suborders of Carnivora

1.a. Many species with spots, stripes, or other markings on the body. Postglenoid foramina reduced or absent; paroccipital process broad and cupping the auditory bullae; condyloid foramen usually in common fossa with posterior lacerate foramen; alisphenoid canal absent. M2 reduced/absent; simple, deep, narrow, "slitlike" carnassial notch in P4; large P4 parastyle. Baculum small or absent — Feliformia

b. Most species without spots or stripes over the body. Postglenoid foramina present; paroccipital process long and pendulant; condyloid foramen separated from posterior lacerate foramen; alisphenoid canal absent or present. M2 large and complex; carnassial notch on P4 is V-shaped or absent; P^4 parastyle reduced or absent. Baculum prominent — Caniformia

the civet and weasel families have been found to have a connection with infectious diseases acquired by humans, although the exact nature of this connection is unclear. Perhaps the most famous Chinese animal is the Giant Panda (*Ailuropoda*), an endemic rare animal of China.

Carnivores are found on every continent except Antarctica and in nearly every type of habitat, with species found in the oceans, the Arctic, tropical rainforests, prairies, temperate forests, deserts, high mountains, and even the urban environment. They are rarely a common or abundant part of any ecosystem, usually because they are relatively large and near the top of the food chain. They are the only order of mammals that have ocean-going, terrestrial, arboreal, and semifossorial species. The order Carnivora contains 285 species in 15 families and 2 suborders. The suborder Caniformia contains the "doglike" carnivores (dogs, foxes, bears, weasels, Red Panda, sea lions, and seals) whereas the suborder Feliformia contains the "catlike" carnivores (cats, mongooses, and civets). Fifty-eight species and 38 genera in 9 families from both suborders occur nearly all over China and the adjacent seas.

Carnivores have adapted in a variety of ways for feeding on everything from large mammals to bamboo and fruit. The single most important feature, and the one that is most often cited as uniting the entire order, is a unique modification of the teeth for eating meat. Carnivores have the last premolar (P4) in upper jaw and first molar (m1) in the lower jaw normally modified to form two vertical sharp cutting surfaces, which slide against each other in a scissorlike manner. At this location on the skull the jaws have their greatest force, making this pair of teeth—called the carnassial pair—extremely efficient as shears. However, although this is a distinguishing feature, some carnivores have further modified these teeth to best utilize different food resources. Plant-eating and fruit-eating carnivores have more horizontal crushing surfaces, and insect-eating carnivores have reduced teeth with tiny bladelike cusps that can pierce the exoskeleton of insects and get to the food inside. The incisors are relatively small, and the canines are almost always strong and sharp and adapted especially for capturing. The premolars and molars usually have sharp cusps and are hence called sectorial teeth.

The wrist bones are also uniquely modified: the centrale, scaphoid, and lunar bones are fused in all carnivores. Other unique skeletal features include the baculum, which is well developed in the suborder Caniformia and is distinctively different among families. It is much reduced or absent in the suborder Feliformia. In the skull, the dentary condyle and the squamosal's glenoid fossa fit together in such a way that allows the jaw only limited transverse motion. In the weasels (Mustelidae) this articulation can form a very tight locking mechanism. Females have a bicornuate or symmetrical uterus, and their nipples are on the ventral surface. Delayed implantation is found in many species.

Most terrestrial species of this order are nocturnal and solitary, although some species become more diurnal away from human disturbances. Only a few species show any social organization beyond pair bonding. Carnivores are well noted for being highly adaptable and opportunistic and can modify their behavior, home ranges, habits, and feeding to be successful in a variety of situations. For this reason, most are found in a variety of habitats. Carnivores have the most highly developed brain of any order of mammals outside of Primates. Although the majority live on the ground and are good at running and chasing, some are highly arboreal (Binturong) or semiaquatic (otters), with the seals (Phocidae) being pelagic (ocean going).

Suborder Feliformia—Catlike Carnivores

猫亚目 Mao Yamu—猫 Mao

This suborder includes six families, three of which—the cats (Felidae), civets (Viverridae), and mongooses (Herpestidae)—are found in China. Not found in China are the hyenas (Hyaenidae), the African Palm Civet (Nandinidae), and the newly created Eupleridae, a family of endemic Malagasy carnivores. The Feliformes are principally united on morphological and molecular characters (see key above).

Family Felidae—Cats

猫科 Mao Ke—猫 Mao

Of all terrestrial carnivores, the felids are clearly the most carnivorous. Some species can overcome prey several times their own weight and regularly kill prey in their own weight class. Cats cannot crush food very well; their teeth consist almost entirely of sharp, scissorlike blades, without flat surfaces for crushing. Two distinguishing features of felids are the horny papillae on the tongue and the presence of only one molar in each jaw (M2/2 absent). They have short faces, forward-pointing eyes, and highly domed or vaulted heads. They do not show the diversity of body form prevalent in other carnivore families. The cats of China all have completely retractile claws and webbing between the toes. A black tail tip is common in most species of cats. The first toe on the forefoot is raised above the level of the others, and it is missing on the hind foot. Cats' binocular vision, unique dentition, and other modifications have been successfully adapted to a wide variety of environments, from high mountain deserts to tropical rain forests. All cats have some ability to climb trees, and all Chinese cats are stalkers or ambush killers. Most cats have good color vision and hunt principally by sight, in spite of the fact that most hunting occurs at night.

The skull of cats can easily be separated from other carnivores by the rounded appearance, forward pointing orbits, and short rostrum. There is no alisphenoid canal, and the posterior palatine foramina are located on the maxilla-palatine suture. The canines are large and sharp, and the carnassial pair

Key to the Chinese Families of Feliformia

1.a. Rounded head with short rostrum and forward-pointing orbits; tongue covered with horny papillae; claws retractile; feet digitigrade, manus = 5; pes = 4. Nasals protrude posteriorly past the anterior border of the orbits; posterior palatine foramina at the maxilla/palatine suture. P1/1 absent; carnassials large and well developed; M1 vestigial; M2/2 absent; middle lower incisor at the same level of the other two — Felidae

b. Elongated head with pointed rostrum; tongue without horny papillae; claws nonretractile or semiretractile; feet may or may not be digitigrade, manus and pes = 5. Nasals do not protrude posteriorly past the anterior border of the orbits; posterior palatine foramina anterior to the maxilla/palatine suture. P1/1 present; carnassials may be large or small; M1 well developed; M2/2 usually present; middle lower incisor raised above the level of the other two — 2

2.a. No spots or stripes on back or tail; long tapering tail; ears do not protrude above the head profile; ear bursa lost; anal sac with two or more laterally located anal glands; no perineal scent glands. Postorbital processes elongate and often connecting with the zygomatic process to form a postorbital bar; medial lacerate foramen ventrally exposed; mastoid enlarged; ectotympanic inflated and near equal in size to entotympanic; external division between ento- and ectotympanic well defined and perpendicular to the skull midline. P3 with lingual cusp — Herpestidae

b. Spots or stripes on back or tail (except *Arctictis* which is completely black); long cylindrical tail (except *Arctictis* where it is tapering); ears protrude above the head profile; ear bursa present; anal glands not noticeable; perineal scent glands present. Postorbital processes reduced; medial lacerate foramen not ventrally exposed; mastoid not enlarged; ectotympanic small, not well inflated, entotympanic many times larger than ectotympanic; external division between ento- and ectotympanic well defined and at an oblique angle. P3 without lingual cusp in all but one species — Viverridae

Key to the Chinese Subfamilies of Felidae

1.a. Pelage spotted, striped, or of one color; small, HB length 600–1,400 mm. Short paroccipital process; palate width ≥ length; jugal usually reaches the lacrimal; mastoid not greatly expanded; frontal-nasal midline suture depression absent, or only slightly developed; palatal length < 45% of condylobasal length; condylobasal length < 150 mm. P4 length < 18 mm. Hyoid apparatus ossified — Felinae

b. Pelage spotted or striped; large, HB length 700–2,800 mm. Long descending paroccipital process; palate width < length; jugal does not reach the lacrimal; large bulbous mastoid; prominent circular depression along midline at frontal-nasal suture; palatal length > 45% of condylobasal length; condylobasal length > 140 mm. P4 length > 18 mm. Hyoid apparatus partly cartilagineous — Pantherinae

is especially developed. P1/1 is absent and M1 is small and vestigial. The lower first molar is dominated by the shearing blade composed of the paraconid and protoconid cusps–the metaconid cusp is absent. P4 is also highly modified with a well-developed parastyle that along with the paracone and metastylar blade give a continuous cutting blade. The protocone is comparatively small (especially when compared with other Chinese feliforms). Dental formula: 3.1.3.1/3.1.3.2 = 30.

There have been various classifications of the cat family proposed over the last half century, and they have varied from taxonomies that include nearly all species in the genus *Felis*, to those that show a high degree of separation of taxa into monotypic genera. The classification below attempts to follow the most current thinking along monophyletic lines (Wozencraft 2005). Only two subfamilies are recognized: the Pantherinae, or large roaring cats, and the Felinae, or small purring cats. There are 39 species of felids found worldwide, 12 of which are found in China. All species of the Felidae are listed on CITES Appendix I or II, and the status and conservation of cats has been thoroughly reviewed by Nowell and Jackson (1996).

Subfamily Felinae—Purring Cats

猫亚科 Mao Yake—猫 Mao

The Felinae have a completely ossified hyoid, which, by vibrating these bones, can produce a purring sound; in the Pantherinae it is not completely ossified. Feline skulls are also more rounded than pantherine skulls and have a shorter rostrum. The jugal usually contacts the lacrimal. The postorbital processes are well developed, often connecting to

Key to the Chinese Genera Felinae

1.a. HB length > 700. Condylobasal length > 110 mm; zygomatic width > 80 mm; mastoid protrudes laterally considerably beyond squamosal. P4 length > 15 mm — 2

b. HB length < 850. Condylobasal length < 110 mm; zygomatic width < 80 mm; mastoid does not protrude laterally beyond squamosal. P4 length < 15 mm — 3

2.a. Tail short (< 350 mm), its length only equal to length of hind foot; ear tipped with long hair tufts; long-haired fringe on throat; tail not bicolored and tip usually black. Nasals > 20 mm at greatest width; entotympanic not well inflated. M1 width < 5 mm; P2 absent; C1 (from tip to alveolus) considerably longer than P4 length; toothrow width ≥ 45% of condylobasal length — *Lynx*

b. Tail long (> 350 mm), its length more than two times the length of hind foot; ear without long hair tufts or fringe on throat; tail distinctly bicolored and tip usually white. Nasals < 20 mm at greatest width; entotympanic well inflated. M^1 width > 5 mm; P2 present; C1 (from tip to alveolus) equal to or slightly longer than P4 length; toothrow width < 45% of condylobasal length — *Catopuma*

3.a. Tail length near equal to HB length; body pattern clouded or marbled. Postorbital processes complete and form a postorbital bar. Nasal width ≥ 14 mm. P4 length ≥ 13 mm — *Pardofelis*

b. Tail length considerably less than HB length (near equal or less than half HB length); body pattern spotted or without spots. Postorbital processes long, and may be complete in old animals; mesopterygoid edge truncate, or perpendicular to midline. Nasal width ≤ 14 mm. P4 length ≤ 13 mm — 4

4.a. Color of the back of the ear dark or same as ground color. Mesopterygoid palate short (width > length, length < length of P3); intraorbital width ≥ 20% of condylobasal length; infraorbital canal large (> 3 mm) — *Felis*

b. Color of the back of the ear with a distinct white patch. Mesopterygoid palate long (width = length, length ≥ length of P3); intraorbital width ≤ 20% of condylobasal length; infraorbital canal small (< 3 mm) — *Prionailurus*

form a postorbital bar. Of 11 genera of Felinae, 5 are found in China.

Genus *Catopuma*—Golden Cats

金猫属 Jinmao Shu—金猫 Jinmao

The two species of Catopuma are restricted to SE Asia. There appears to be a great deal of uncertainty as to the relationship of the Asian Golden Cat (*Catopuma temmincki*; the form found in China), and its sister species–the Bay Cat of Borneo (*C. badia*)–to other felids. Some have placed the Asian (*Catopuma*) and African (*Profelis aurata*) golden cats in the genus, *Profelis*. They share the interesting feature of occurring in many different color phases throughout their respective ranges. Recent molecular studies suggest that the African Golden Cat is more closely related to the Caracal (*Caracal*) (Johnson and O'Brien 1997; Mattern and McLennan 2000).

Asian Golden Cat — PLATE 41

Catopuma temminckii

(Vigors and Horsfield, 1827) — MAP 446

金猫 Jinmao

Distinctive Characteristics: HB 710–1,050; T 400–560; HF 165–180; E 60–70; GLS 98–131; Wt 9–16 kg. The Asian Golden Cat shows two distinctive color patterns: the golden pattern–from which it derives its name–ranges from very dark brown to red, gold, or gray with occasional melanistic individuals. The normal color pattern is that in which the neck and back are a reddish or golden color, with the sides of the body distinctly paler. In this phase the head always shows the distinctive Golden Cat pattern (see below). The second pattern is the spotted pattern, resembling that found in the Leopard Cat (*Prionailurus bengalensis*). The head coloration is distinctive: sharply contrasting longitudinal white interocular eye patches; and a lighter coloration stripe, running from a point medial to the interocular patches between the eyes to the crown, which are bordered laterally with black lines. There are usually broad white cheek patches running from just below the eyes to the cheeks, and the area below the rhinarium and the lower lips are white. The backs of the ears are dark colored (black to dark brown), with a fainter coloration in the center. The tail is long (50–66% of HB length) and distinctly bicolored, dark above and whitish below, especially in the distal half of the tail. In the spotted phase, the tail may have 12–15 black bars but retains the bicolored nature of the golden phase pattern.

The skull can only be confused with the Eurasian Lynx (*Lynx lynx*) in terms of size, for these are the only two Chinese cat species in which skull size would regularly fall between 100 and 150 mm. The Jungle Cat (*Felis chaus*), which can approach this size, can be distinguished by the shallow depressions in the rostral process of the maxilla and by a relatively flat mastoid that is closely applied to the bullae. In the Golden Cat and Lynx, the depression is absent and the mastoid is much more produced laterally.

The Lynx has a relatively large inflation of the ectotympanic bullae, a distinct depression in the intraorbital region of the frontal, and a distinct frontal/nasal depression along the midline (these are missing in the Golden Cat). In the Golden Cat there is a well-developed lateral flange on the side of the pterygoid. Males have a distinctive sagittal crest, whereas in females the crest is often lyre-shaped and smaller in outline. Dental formula: 3.1.2–3.1/3.1.2.1 = 28–30.

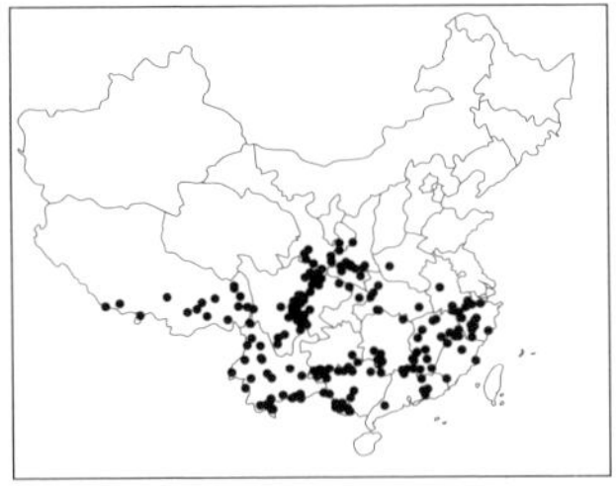

MAP 446. ASIAN GOLDEN CAT, *Catopuma temminickii*

Distribution: Widely distributed in C and SE China; extending through SE Asia, west to Nepal and south to Sumatra. Three subspecies in China: (1) *C. t. bainsei* (Sowerby, 1924); SE Yunnan; (2) *C. t. dominicanorum* (Sclater, 1898); Anhui, Fujian, Guangdong, Guangxi, Guizhou, Hubei, Hunan, Jiangxi, Zhejiang (includes *badiodorsalis* (Howell, 1926); *dominicorum* (Howell, 1929); melli (Matschie, 1922); *mitchelli* (Lydekker, 1908)); (3) *C. t. tristis* (Milne-Edwards, 1872); Gansu, Ningxia, Shaanxi, Sichuan, Xizang, NW Yunnan (includes *semenoi* Satunin, 1904).
Natural History: The Golden Cat is found in dry deciduous forests, tropical rainforests, tropical savanna, and grasslands. It has also occasionally been reported from shrub and grassland and as high as 3,170 m in NW Yunnan. It appears to be a carnivore that focuses on medium-sized vertebrates, including small mammals, lagomorphs, small deer, birds, and lizards. Has been known to kill some livestock, including sheep, goats, gorals, and calves of domestic water buffalo. It is a solitary nocturnal hunter and hunts mostly on the ground but is also a good climber. It breeds in tree hollows or in burrows in the ground. No specific breeding season is known. Gestation is about 85–95 days and a litter of one or two kittens is produced. Males play a role in the rearing of the young. They are sexually mature at 18–24 months.
Comments: There is some confusion as to the assignment of subspecies because of the distribution of the two color phases: the "golden" phase and the "spotted" phase. Pocock (1939) classified those specimens with a spotted pattern from Sichuan as *C. t. tristis*, and many have followed this for the assignment of subspecies. However, it appears as though this is a pattern that randomly occurs throughout China, N Myanmar, N India, and Nepal. The golden phase appears to be more prevalent as one goes south, with the spotted phase not reported from Indochina, Malaysia, or Sumatra. It is most likely that the nominate type from Sumatra is the same population as found in S Yunnan. If one restricts the nominate form to Sumatra, then the next available name for Indochina-Malaysian forms is *bainsei* (Sowerby, 1924) which is here also applied to S Yunnan populations. There appears to be little question that all SE Chinese specimens belong to *dominicanorum*. Most probably, plateau specimens from Sichuan, Yunnan, Gansu, Shaanxi, and Ningxia belong to *tristis*. Xizang specimens are here also assigned to *tristis*, although it is probable that *moormensis* (Hodgson, 1831) from Nepal is the correct name to apply to populations from S Xizang and perhaps NW Yunnan and W Sichuan (thereby restricting *tristis* to E Sichuan, Gansu, Ningxia, and Shaanxi). Corbet and Hill (1992) and Wang (2003) perhaps took the best route and did not recognize subspecies.
Conservation Status: There are an estimated 3,000–5,000 left in China (Sheng 1998a). China RL—CR A3cd; C2a(i). China Key List—II. CITES—I. IUCN RL—VU C2a(i) ver 3.1 (2001).
References: Allen (1938); Biswas and Ghose (1982); Corbet and Hill (1992); Guggisberg (1975); Johnson and O'Brien (1997); Lekagul and McNeely (1977); Louwman and Van Owen (1968); Mattern and McLennan (2000); Pocock (1939); Sheng (1998a); Wang (2003); Wozencraft (2005).

Genus *Felis*—Cats

猫属 Mao Shu—猫 Mao

The genus *Felis* is perhaps most familiar to people as it includes the domestic house cat (*Felis catus*), and indeed, all members of this genus can be mistaken for house cats. *Felis* is represented by small cats with rounded heads, short rostrums, pointed ears, and long tails. Most have spots on the back and stripes on the tail. They have small rounded skulls with short rostrums; a palate as wide or wider than long; relatively well-inflated ectotympanic bullae; distance from preorbital margin to rostrum smaller than the biggest diameter of orbit; postorbital process long and sharp. The genus *Felis* contains six species and is widely distributed in Europe, Asia, the Americas, and Africa. There are four species in China. There is considerable controversy over the exact relationship between the European *Felis catus* and the Eurasian and African *Felis silvestris*, with some authors considering them conspecific (Ragni and Randi 1986).

Chinese Mountain Cat

PLATE 41
MAP 447

Felis bieti Milne-Edwards, 1892
漠猫 Mo Mao

Distinctive Characteristics: HB 600–850; T 290–350; E 58–67; GLS 94–100; Wt 5.5–9 kg. About twice the size of a domestic cat, the Chinese Mountain Cat is one of the least-known cats. Pelage is a uniform color but may have indistinct stripes on the legs and sides, and the basic color varies from a yellow-gray to dark brown, with the belly white to light gray. There are two indistinct brownish stripes on the cheeks, and the chin and lower lips are white. The distal portion of the relatively short tail has three or four dark rings

Key to the Chinese Species of *Felis*

1.a. Ears rounded and set very wide apart and low down on the sides of the head, so that their rims hardly rise above the profile of the head; forehead with black spots; fur throughout body very thick; eyes with distinct white ocular rings. Ectotympanic bullae larger than entotympanic; anterior rim of jugal with sharp edge, no horizontal expansion; frontal greatly inflated, a very high domed rounded skull. P2 absent; P4 paracone vestigial *Felis manul*

b. Ears pointed; ears not wide apart and stand above the head profile; forehead with dark longitudinal lines; fur throughout body of normal length; ocular coloration does not completely encircle eye. Ectotympanic bullae considerably smaller than entotympanic; anterior rim of jugal with or without sharp edge, horizontal expansion maybe present; frontal slightly inflated. P2 present; P4 paracone normal 2

2.a. Small tuft of black hair on ears; tail length about 1/3 of HB length; faint stripes on legs; spots and stripes absent from most of the head and body. Skull is relatively long and narrow with long rostrum (> 29 mm); distinctive depression in the rostral process of the maxilla; condylobasal length > 90 mm; zygomatic width < 75% of condylobasal length, and > 65 mm; tooth row width > 45 mm; length > 33 mm. P4 > 11 mm, P4 paracone wide *Felis chaus*

b. Small tuft of red hair on ears, or no tuft; tail length near equal to HB length; no stripes on legs; spots and stripes absent or present from most of the head and body. Skull is relatively short and wide with noticeably short rostrum (< 29 mm); distinctive depression in the rostral process of the maxilla absent; condylobasal length < 90 mm; zygomatic width > 75% of condylobasal length, and < 65 mm; toothrow width < 45 mm; length < 33 mm. P4 < 11 mm, P4 paracone narrow 3

3.a. Ear tuft absent; ear back similar to ground color to dark brown; pattern of dorsal stripes and of lateral spots conspicuous; the same size as a house cat; spinal crest and stripe hardly differentiated. Jugal touches lacrimal without sharp edge, horizontal expansion present; nasal suture length > 18 mm; width of auditory bullae < 15 mm; postorbital width > 25 mm *Felis silvestris*

b. Reddish ear tuft present; ear back reddish; no spots or stripes (although some indistinct faint vertical stripes may be present); about twice the size of a house cat; no spinal stripe. Jugal does not reach lacrimal, anterior rim of jugal, with sharp edge, without horizontal expansion; nasal suture length < 18 mm; width of auditory bullae > 15 mm; postorbital width < 25 mm *Felis bieti*

and a black tip. The backs of the ears are close to the same color as the body, and there is a small ear tuft of dark reddish hairs. At the base of the ear is a pale reddish brown area. Very rounded skull (with short nasals) with well-inflated auditory bullae measuring about 25% of GLS. The auditory bullae are noticeably larger than those found in other *Felis*. Nasals are concave in middle third and convex upward distally. The anterior orbital rim is sharp, with no horizontal expansion, resembling in this respect *Felis manul*. Unlike other Felis, the jugal does not touch the lacrimal. Dental formula: 3.1.3.1/3.1.2.1 = 30.
Distribution: Widely but apparently sparsely distributed in C China. Endemic. Chinese subspecies:
F. b. bieti Milne-Edwards, 1892; Gansu, E Qinghai, NW Sichuan (includes *pallida* Büchner, 1892; and *subpallida* Jacobi, 1923).
Natural History: The Chinese Mountain Cat is found at high elevations (2,800–4,100 m) in alpine meadow, alpine bush, edges of coniferous forests, grassy meadows, and steppe. Its diet consists predominately of mole-rats, voles (*Microtus*), pikas (*Ochotona*), and hares (*Lepus*). It also captures birds, especially pheasants. Like most cats, it is solitary and nocturnal. Males and females live separately. They breed from January to March and have a 60-day gestation with an average litter size of two.

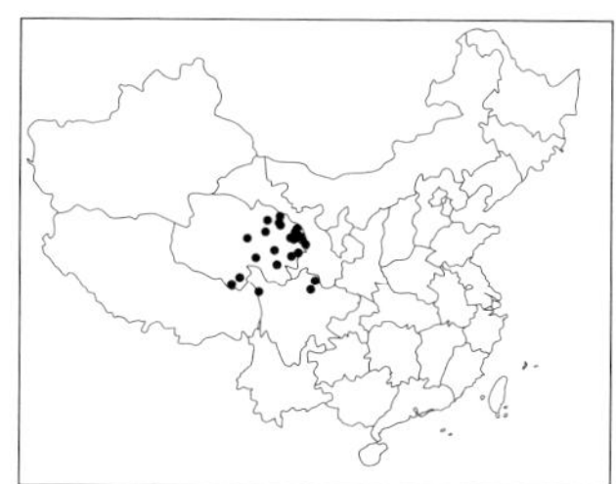

MAP 447. CHINESE MOUNTAIN CAT, *Felis bieti*

Comments: Only a few specimens of the Chinese Mountain Cat are available for study in the world's museums. Many reports have confused *F. bieti* with *F. silvestris*. The subspecies *chutuchta* and *vellerosa* have been assigned to *F. bieti* by some authors but are here assigned to *F. silvestris* following Haltenorth (1953). Although there are reports in the literature of the Chinese Mountain Cat from other provinces, He et al. (2004) reviewed the records, distribution, and conservation status of this species and found that the records from Gansu, Xinjiang, Ningxia, and Nei Mongol either could be assigned to *F. silvestris* or could not be confirmed.

Conservation Status: China RL—CR A2abc; C1 + 2a(i). China Key List—II. CITES—II. IUCN RL—VU C2a(i) ver 3.1 (2001).

References: Haltenorth (1953); He et al. (2004); Liao (1988); Pocock (1951); Ragni and Randi (1986).

Jungle Cat

PLATE 41
MAP 448

Felis chaus Schreber, 1777
丛林猫 Conglin Mao

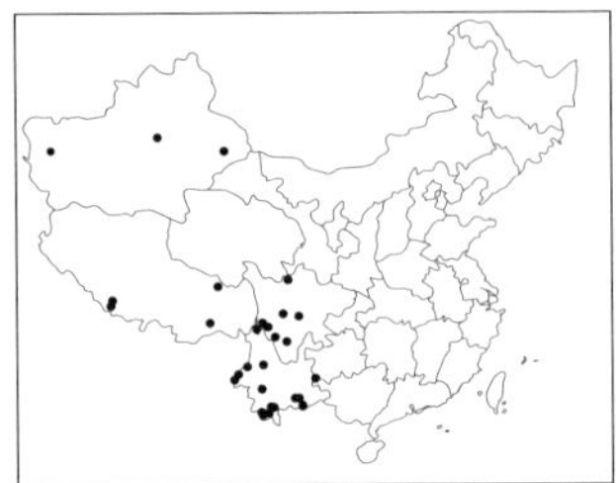

MAP 448. JUNGLE CAT, *Felis chaus*

Distinctive Characteristics: HB 580–760; T 218–270; HF 108–145; E 45–80; GLS 100–120; Wt 5–9 kg. Jungle Cats are light brown, reddish, or brownish gray cats and have no distinctive pattern throughout the body except for some stripes on the legs. Melanistic individuals have been reported from several areas. There is a uniform mixture of dark-tipped hairs throughout the body except the head, which is usually a rusty color, and there is a distinct spinal crest. The chin and upper throat, the chest between the legs, and the inguinal region are white to light gray. Ears are generally reddish, set close together, with a small dark brown to black tufts beyond the ear tips. Eyes and rostrum highlighted with white patches, and a dark patch rostral to the eyes. The tail is usually around 40% of HB length, with a black tip and distinctive dark rings on the distal half. Males are significantly larger than females. Winter coat is darker than the summer coat. The skull of the Jungle Cat is more oblong and less rounded than that of other *Felis*. The nasals are concave; anterior rim of jugal with a distinctive horizontal expansion; mastoid flat and oppressed against bullae. Rostrum with concave maxilla giving the rostrum a "pinched in" appearance. P4 paracone is developed more than in other *Felis*, being at least 50% of the size and height of the parastyle. Dental formula: 3.1.2-3.1/3.1.2.1 = 28–30.

Distribution: Scattered localities throughout C and W China; extending from Egypt through the Middle East, Central Asia, India, and Indochina. Two subspecies in China: (1) *F. c. affinis* Gray, 1830; Guizhou, Sichuan, Yunnan, Xizang (includes *erythrotus* (Hodgson, 1836); *jacquemontii* I. Geoffroy Saint-Hilaire, 1844); (2) *F. c. chaus* Schreber, 1777; Xinjiang (includes *catolynx* Pallas, 1811; *shawiana* Blanford, 1876 [in part]; *typica* de Winton, 1898).

Natural History: The name "Jungle Cat" is a misnomer as they are found in a wide variety of habitat types, but rarely in tropical rainforests. They prefer tall grass, swamps, and reeds throughout most of China but also can be found in dry environments along riparian ecosystems. Some consider this cat typical of reed and cattail thickets and wet lowland forests around lakes. They are also found in tropical deciduous forests and shrubs, and as high as 2,400 m in the Himalayas. They are very adaptable to a variety of habitat types and often found in agricultural areas. In the southern part of their range, they are often associated with sugarcane plantations. They are usually found near water and prefer dense cover, although they have been reported from desert areas with only sparse cover. The increase in the development of irrigation systems has resulted in an increase in Jungle Cat populations in arid regions. They have been reported to be associated with gardens, hedgerows, barns, and around dwellings. Jungle Cats feed mostly on small vertebrates usually less than 1 kg (lagomorphs, birds, amphibians, fish, and reptiles) but depend primarily on rodents. They eat bird's eggs and occasionally take the young of small ungulates such as a wild pigs, gazelle, and chital fawns. Where they live next to humans, they will take chickens, ducks, and geese. They are good swimmers and will go after fish. One study found that hares, rodents, and birds made up the largest percent occurrence in the diet (rodents 85–92%, birds 12–44%, hares 10–17%). They can climb and often escape humans by swimming, although they chiefly hunt on the ground. While they can be found at all times of the day or night, they are more diurnal than most cat species. Normally solitary, their home ranges are around 5–6 km^2. Breeding normally takes place from January to February, with the gestation lasting 60–70 days; however kittens have been observed year round. Their average litter size is two or three, and they usually have only one litter a year. Jungle cats become sexually mature at 1–1.5 years.

Comments: *F. chaus* Güldenstädt, 1776, is invalid (Allen 1920). Corbet and Hill (1992) cast doubt on the validity of the subspecies as most of the characteristics used to delineate subspecies have been shown to vary widely. The division between *affinis* Gray, 1830, from the southern slopes of the Himalayas, and *fulvidina* Thomas, 1928, from Vietnam, is based principally on a more uniformly bright reddish color in *fulvidina*, something that varies considerably throughout the range of *F. chaus*. S Yunnan specimens may be more appropriately assigned to *fulvidina*. Wang (2003) did not include Xinjiang specimens.

Conservation Status: China RL—EN A1c; B1ab(i, iii). China Key List—II. CITES—II.

References: Allen (1920); Corbet and Hill (1992); Guggisberg (1975); Heptner and Sludskii (1972); Ishunin (1965); Khan and Beg (1986); Pocock (1939); Rathore and Thapar (1984); Roberts (1977); Schaller (1967); Sunquist and Sunquist (2003); Tikader (1983); Vereshchagin (1959); Wang (2003).

Pallas' Cat

Felis manul Pallas, 1776 PLATE 41 MAP 449
兔狲 Tusun

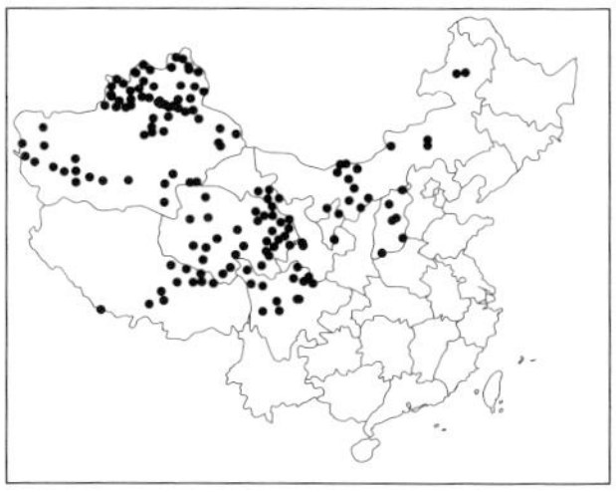

MAP 449. PALLAS' CAT, *Felis manul*

Distinctive Characteristics: HB 450–650; T 210–350; HF 120–140; E 40–50; GLS 82–92; Wt 2.3–4.5 kg. Pallas' Cat is a short-legged cat about the same size as the Wildcat. However, it has very dense and thick fur, a bushy tail, and a broad forehead with the ears widely spaced apart so that the ears appear to sit on the sides of the head. Its coat is the longest of any species of wildcat and is a grayish color, with white tips to the hairs, which creates a frosted appearance. The eyes are set forward. Forehead with randomly scattered small black spots. Six or seven narrow transverse stripes across the back extend into the sides to various degrees. The backs of the ears are similar to the ground color. White rings surround the eyes, and there are three small black bands extending under eyes through cheeks and two continue toward neck and ears. A black line outlines eye patches. The tail is uniformly gray above and below with a very small black tip. The skull is the most distinctive of the genus *Felis*, with complete orbits, highly domed skull (inflated frontals); short rostrum; ectotympanic portion of the bullae inflated more than the entotympanic portion; anterior rim of the orbit has a sharp edge, without any horizontal expansion of the jugal; orbits are displaced forward increasing the binocular overlap; plane of the orbits is more vertical than in most cats; suture between ecto- and entotympanic distinct; the nasals are depressed along the midline but have no constriction. P4 paracone is vestigial; the canine is longer than P4; and P2 is absent. Dental formula: 3.1.2.1/3.1.2.1 = 28. 2N = 38.
Distribution: Found throughout C, N, and W China; ranging to Mongolia, Russia, Central Asia, and the Middle East and as far west as Armenia. Two subspecies in China: (1) *F. m. manul* Pallas, 1776; Beijing, Gansu, Hebei, Heilongjiang, Nei Mongol, Ningxia, Shansi, N Xinjiang (includes *mongolica* Satunin, 1905; *satuni* Lydekker, 1907); (2) *F. m. nigripecta* Hodgson, 1842; Gansu, Qinghai, Sichuan, S Xinjiang, Xizang.
Natural History: Pallas' Cats live on the slopes of low mountains, hilly deserts, and steppes with rock outcrops. They can be found in Central Asia as high as 4,000 m. They generally inhabit dry high mountain regions of low rainfall and shallow snow cover. They apparently cannot negotiate deep snow cover in capturing prey, as a continuous snow cover of 15–20 cm or less marks a good boundary for the range of this species. Exposed rock outcrops, talus, and south-facing slopes represent their characteristic habitat. They feed predominantly on pikas (*Ochotona*), small rodents (*Alticola, Meriones, Cricetulus*), birds (*partridge-Pyrrhocorax*), hares (*Lepus*), and marmots (*Marmota*) and appear to be most numerous where pikas and voles are abundant and not living under deep snow cover. Pallas' Cats are nocturnal and crepuscular, solitary, and hunt by ambush. They are not fast runners and are most active at dusk and dawn. They breed in February, with a gestation of 65 to 70 days. The average litter size is 3–6. They usually have one litter a year and are sexually mature at 12–18 months.
Comments: With the widely spaced ears, highly domed skull, greatly inflated ectotympanic, and the loss of P2, some have argued that Pallas' Cat should be placed in a separate genus (= *Otocolobus*)(Birula 1917; Pocock 1951; Severtzov 1858). However, recent DNA studies indicate that its closest ancestors are in the domestic cat lineage (Collier and O'Brien 1985).
Conservation Status: China RL—EN A1cd; B1ab(i, ii, iii). China Key List—II. CITES—II. IUCN RL—NT ver 3.1 (2001).
References: Birula (1917); Collier and O'Brien (1985); Pocock (1951); Severtzov (1858); Sunquist and Sunquist (2003).

Wildcat

Felis silvestris Schreber, 1777 MAP 450
野猫 Ye Mao

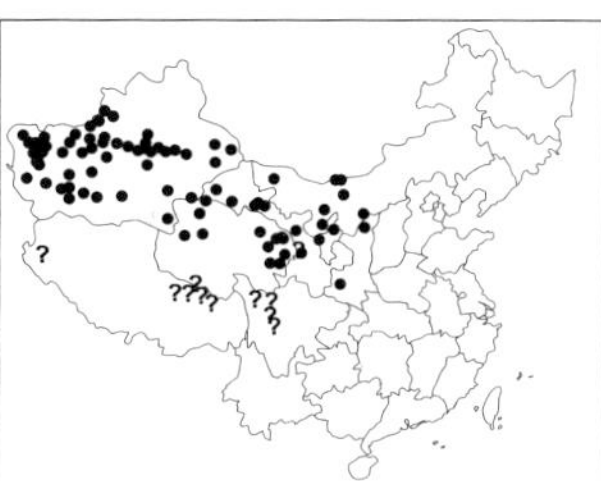

MAP 450. WILDCAT, *Felis silvestris*

Distinctive Characteristics: HB 630–700; T 230–330; HF 120–160; E 60–70; GLS 80–106; Wt 3–8 kg. The domestic cat (*Felis catus*) and Wildcat populations are similar in behavior and appearance, and these forms are known to interbreed. Many have suggested that they are conspecific (see comments). The pelage color is extremely variable from a grayish yellow to red, with many irregular black or red-brown spots and two small brown stripes on the cheek. The body is covered with small solid spots that are sometimes fused into stripes. The throat and ventral surfaces are usually whitish to light gray. The forehead has a pattern of four well-developed black bands that contrast against a background color that is light; and the eyes and rostrum are usually highlighted with white to light gray patches. There are white or light-colored fringes on edges of the ears; and the hairs on inner surface of ears are yellowish white. The backs of the ears vary from being similar to ground color to a dark brown. The tip of tail is black with some black transverse rings on tail. The tail length is more than 50% of the HB length. They have four pairs of teats.

In the grassland and arid regions of NW China, this is the only species that resembles the common house cat in the wild. It is easily distinguished from Pallas' Cat, which is stockier, with lower set ears; or from the Chinese Mountain Cat, which is considerably larger with red ear tufts. The skulls of the Wildcat are indistinguishable from domestic or feral domestic cat skulls. They have a short rostrum, and the palate is as wide as long. Within the genus *Felis*, only *F. chaus* and *F. silvestris* have the horizontal expansion of the jugal. *F. silvestris* can be separated from *F. chaus* on several features: (1) absence of rostral depression of the maxilla (present in *F. chaus*); (2) height of P4 paracone (small in *F. silvestris*); and (3) short rostrum (long in *F. chaus*).

Distribution: NW China; ranging across Asia and Africa. Four subspecies in China: (1) *F. s. chutuchta* Birula, 1917; C Nei Mongol, Ningxia; (2) *F. s. issikulensis* Ognev, 1930; Tian Shan range in Xinjiang; (3) *F. s. shawiana* Blanford, 1876 (in part); Gansu, W Nei Mongol, Qinghai, Sichuan, Xinjiang, Xizang (includes *kozlovi* Satunin, 1905); (4) *F. s. vellerosa* Pocock, 1943; Shaanxi.

Natural History: The Wildcat lives in an extremely wide variety of habitats and prefers to live close to fresh-water sources in more arid regions. It is not found in any area with a snow cover over 20 cm. Common in plains and steppe, deserts, and semideserts and is often associated with shrub desert. Often colonizes oases, gardens, and settlements, and has been found as high as 2,500 m. It feeds opportunistically on small vertebrates, prefering rodents. In some areas Wildcat activities closely match those of the hare (*Lepus yarkandensis*). Wildcats will raid agricultural areas for poultry. Small mammals compose 60–70% of diet, with ground squirrels (*Spermophilus*), gerbils (*Meriones*), and jerboas (*Allactaga*) being the most common prey items. Birds constitute the next most common (11–30% occurrence), with passerines (especially *Rhodopechys*, *Scotocerca*, and *Streptopelia*) being the most common type. Reptiles and insects are also common in the diet (15–25%). They are mostly nocturnal but sometimes have been observed during the daytime. They are solitary and appear to be territorial. Home ranges are generally around 3–4 km^2. They live year-round in burrows excavated by other mammals. They can have one or two litters a year and initiate breeding in January and February, with a gestation of 56–65 days. The average litter size is three, and they become sexually mature at 18–24 months. Breeding between the Wildcat and domestic cats is common.

Comments: There is considerable controversy as to the correct scientific name for the Wildcat. The four basic divisions (European [*catus*], African [*lybica*], Asian [*silvestris*], and domestic [*domestica*?]) are so similar that some have proposed placing them all in one species. Although molecular differences are small, the African-Asian populations (including China) appear to be more closely related and are here both considered in *Felis silvestris*. European and some domestic populations appear to represent a separate radiation. To make matters more confusing, the International Commission on Zoological Nomenclature declared *silvestris* as the specific name for the European Wildcat (with the understanding that *F. catus* and *F. silvestris* are usually considered conspecific). It is most probable that domesticated cats came independently from European, African, and Asian populations. Furthermore, the closely related *F. bieti* is often confused with *F. silvestris*, and the two subspecies *chutuchta* and *vellerosa* have been sometimes assigned to *F. bieti*. These subspecies are placed here in *silvestris*.

Ognev (1962) also recognized the subspecies *kozlovi* Satunin, 1904 and *shawiana* (Blanford, 1876) as occurring in China. However, there is some confusion as to the type of *shawiana*. This specimen consists of a skull (which is actually *F. chaus*) and a skin (which is actually *F. constantina* = *F. s. caudata*) purchased in Kashgar. Earlier, Ognev (1930) used *shawiana* for specimens from E Kazahstan and continuing throughout the Tarim Basin. He described *F. ornata issikulensis* from the Issyk-Kul region of Kazakstan and believed that its distribution continued eastward through the Tian Shan mountains, where it merged with *F. s. kozlovi* (= *shawiana*). The existence of *kozlovi*, however, also appears to be questionable. Pocock (1951) cast doubt on the validity of *kozlovi* (from the Turpan depression), indicating that it was probably a domestic house cat. Wozencraft (2005) placed *issikulensis* and *shawiana* in *caudata* Gray, 1874. The confusion between domestic cats, feral cats, and Asian Wildcats, and interbreeding among these populations of the same species has lead to most of the confusion in the identification and distribution of these subspecies in China.

Conservation Status: Feng (1998) estimated the Chinese population at more than 10,000. China RL—CR A1a. China Key List—II. CITES—II. IUCN—LC.

References: Allayarov (1963); Feng (1998); Haltenorth (1953); Heptner and Sludskii (1972); Ognev (1930; 1962); Pocock (1951); Roberts (1977); Wozencraft (2005).

Genus *Lynx*

猞猁属 Sheli Shu—猞猁 Sheli

The lynx are easily distinguishable from other felids by their long tufted ears and their bobbed tail. They have a ruff of long fur around the sides of their head, giving them a distinctive appearance. The four species in the genus are distributed throughout the Holartic, with two species in North America, and two in Eurasia—one of which occurs in China. Lynx give the appearance of being rather short-bodied animals with extremely long legs (the hind limbs are longer than the forelimbs). All lynx lack the first and second premolars.

Lynx PLATE 41
Lynx lynx (Linnaeus, 1758) MAP 451
猞猁 She Li

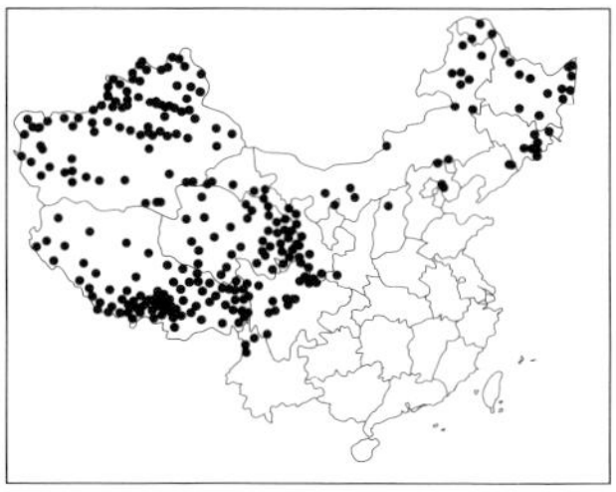

MAP 451. LYNX, *Lynx lynx*

Distinctive Characteristics: HB 800–1,300; T 110–250; HF 225–250; E 80–95; GLS 145–160; Wt 18–38 kg. The largest of all lynxes, they have a ground color that runs from a grizzled gray to a gray brown. Spotting on pelage is quite variable and ranges from a few indistinct spots to large, well-defined spots. Himalayan Lynxes are very pale in coloration and often lack the distinct spotting seen in the more typical European Lynx. The throat and undersides are a white to light gray color. Lynx are noted for having the finest silky fur of any of the cat species, with a reported 9,000 hairs per cm^2 on their back. Lynxes have distinctly long legs with hind limbs appearing longer than forelimbs. The manus and pes are wide with well-developed webbing between the toes, and in winter the undersides of the feet are covered with long, dense hair. The lightness of the weight load on a track (weight/cm^2) is one of the best for any species of cat and can support three times that of *Felis*. Ears have distinctively long ear tufts and the backs of the ears have a central light gray spot. There is a wide fringe of long hair from ears to throat. The inside of the ears is always covered with white hairs. The tail is very short–about equal to the hind foot length and always with a black tip. There are three pairs of teats. In the distinctive auditory bullae, the ectotympanic (anteriolateral portion) is well inflated. The mastoid is large and bulbous, and the frontal is not well inflated. There is a distinct depression between postorbital processes, and these processes are relatively small. The jugal protrudes rostrally to the infraorbital canal. The rostral processes of the premaxilla and frontal either meet or nearly do. P2 is absent; canine much longer than P4 length. Dental formula: 3.1.2.1/3.1.2.1 = 28.
Distribution: Widely distributed in all but SE China; extending to Europe, North America, and N Asia. Three subspecies in China: (1) *L. l. isabellinus* (Blyth, 1847); Gansu, Hebei, C Nei Mongol, Qinghai, Shaanxi, Shanxi, Sichuan, Xinjiang, Xizang, Yunnan (includes *kamensis* (Satunin, 1905); *tibetanus* (Gray, 1863); *wardi* (Lydekker, 1904)); (2) *L. l. stroganovi* Heptner, 1969; Heilongjiang, Jilin, Liaoning, E Nei Mongol; (3) *L. l. wardi* (Lydekker, 1904); N. Xinjiang (Altai mountains; see Comments for its inclusion here).
Natural History: Principally a creature of dense, thick, boreal forests, but also occurs in deciduous forest, steppe, mountains, and alpine regions. The favorite summer range of the Lynx in the Tian Shan mountains includes steep slopes with rock outcrops and talus slopes overgrown with forests. In the Altai mountains they are found in the taiga zone with snow cover not deeper than 40–50 cm. To a great extent, hare and small ungulate distribution determine lynx distribution. Lynx feed predominately on hares, marmots, pikas, small ungulates, and birds. Throughout most of their range, small ungulates are the most important part of their diet. One study, when ungulates were scarce, gave occurrence in their diet as 65% hare and 21% rodents (many of which were marmots, particularly in the spring). During the winter in the Altai, their diet was more focused on small ungulates: 14% Roe Deer (*Capreolus capreolus*); 59% Siberian Musk Deer (*Moschus moschiferus*). They occasionally kill deer ranging from 15 to 220 kg. They will also actively seek out and kill foxes. Solitary and nocturnal, they usually they avoid water, and may travel up to about 10 km per day. They are ambush predators, and are known to migrate up and down slopes following ungulates and hares to areas of lesser snow cover. Lynx are rare where wolves are numerous. They are excellent tree climbers and use forest trails, logs, and rock outcroppings when hunting. They usually have one litter a year, with an average size of two or three. The gestation is 63–74 days.
Comments: Lydekker (1904) proposed the name *wardi* for the Altai Lynx. Although most authors considered this form synonymous with *isabellinus*, Stroganov (1952) supported it as a separate subspecies.
Conservation Status: Chinese population is estimated at around 70,000 (Feng and Ma 1998). China RL—EN A1cd. China Key List—II. CITES—II. IUCN RL—NT ver 3.1 (2001).
References: Ellerman and Morrison-Scott (1951); Feng and Ma (1998); Heptner (1992); Lydekker (1904); Stroganov (1952).

Genus *Pardofelis* (monotypic)

云猫属 Yunmao Shu

Marbled Cat PLATE 41
Pardofelis marmorata (Martin, 1837) MAP 452
云猫 Yunmao

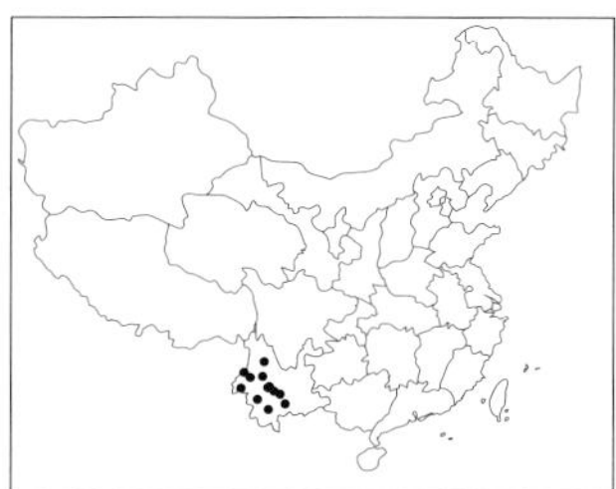
MAP 452. MARBLED CAT, *Pardofelis marmorata*

Distinctive Characteristics: HB 400–660; T 450–560; HF 115–120; E 35–40; GLS 79–91; Wt 3–5.5 kg. The Marbled Cat has features that it shares with the Clouded Leopard (*Neofelis*) and Snow Leopard (*Uncia*), and it appears to be intermediate between the two forms. A little larger than a domestic cat, the general body shape is more elongated. The background color varies from dark gray to yellowish gray to red-brown. The legs and venter are patterned with black dots, and there are longitudinal stripes on the neck. The ground color is usually a brownish gray to reddish brown with large, irregular dark-edged blotches on the flanks and back. The feet of the Marbled Cat are unusually large, resembling pantherines more than other felines. The ears are marked with white bars on the back. There are black stripes on the head, neck, and back, and distinctive white eye patches around the eyes. Spots are scattered on the forehead, rostrum, legs, and tail. The tail is very long and bushy, about as long as the HB. Skull is often with a complete postorbital bar and very wide zygomatic arches. In the Felinae the only other species that average over 70 mm in zygomatic width (usually > 80% of condylobasal length) are the much larger *Lynx* and *Catopuma*. Also distinctive are the P3 with a medial expansion; P4 length between 13–15 mm; and the canines longer than P4 length. Dental formula: 3.1.3.1/3.1.2.1 = 30.
Distribution: Yunnan; extending from the southern edge of the Himalayas, throughout Indochina, the Malay Peninsula, and Indonesia (Sumatra and Borneo). Two subspecies in China: (1) *P. m. charltonii* (Gray, 1846); NW Yunnan (includes *dosul* Gray, 1863; *duvaucellii* (Hodgson, 1863); *ogilbii* (Hodgson, 1847)); (2) *P. m. marmorata* (Martin, 1837); C Yunnan (includes *diardii* (Jardine, 1834) [preoccupied]; *longicaudata* (de Blainville, 1843)).
Natural History: The Marbled Cat is closely associated with lowland tropical forest, although it has been noted in recently logged forests as well. In the eastern Himalayan foothills it is associated with moist deciduous and semievergreen forest habitats between 1,500–3,000 m. It can be considered a small vertebrate feeder on squirrels, rats, lizards, frogs, rodents, and birds. Birds are thought to be a major part of the diet. It is nocturnal and solitary, and perhaps more arboreal than most cats. The gestation is 81 days, with an average litter size between one and four young. They are sexually mature at two years.
Comments: There is considerable controversy over the correct placement of this genus. Many have placed it as the first outgroup to the pantherines, and perhaps just as many have suggested a relationship with felines while recognizing similarities with *Panthera*. It is unlikely that the subspecies reported from Sumatra would be the same subspecies for N Indochina and S China (i.e., *marmorata*), however, systematic studies are lacking.
Conservation Status: China RL—CR A1c; B1ab(i, iii). CITES—I. IUCN RL—VU C2a(i) ver 3.1 (2001).
References: Bininda-Emonds et al. (1999); Biswas and Ghose (1982); Collier and O'Brien (1985); Hemmer (1978); Janczewski et al. (1995); Mattern and McLennan (2000).

Genus *Prionailurus*—Southeast Asian Spotted Cats

豹猫属 Baomao Shu—豹猫 Baomao

Prionailurus contains five species of small SE Asian cats (all about the same size as a house cat), only one of which is found in China. The Fishing Cat, *Prionailurus viverrinus* (Bennett, 1833), has been reported by various authors as occurring in China. This account is based on an 1862 paper by Swinhoe who reported skins, believed to be the Fishing Cat, bought in the market in Taiwan, but this is a dubious record at best. The Fishing Cat has not been reported from Taiwan since 1862. The range of the Fishing Cat borders China/Indochina and probably does occasionally go into China.

Leopard Cat

PLATE 41
MAP 453

Prionailurus bengalensis (Kerr, 1792)
豹猫 Baomao

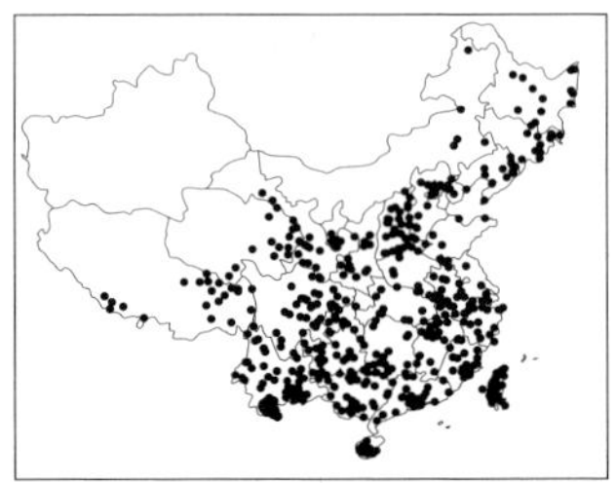

MAP 453. LEOPARD CAT, *Prionailurus bengalensis*

Distinctive Characteristics: HB 360–660; T 200–370; HF 80–130; E 35–55; GLS 75–96; Wt 1.5–5 kg. The Leopard Cat is also known in China as "Qian Mao" or money cat because its spots are said to look like Chinese coins. It is the size of a small house cat but is more slender and with longer legs. Pelage has a light brown or yellowish ground color in the south, and a more grayish ground color in the northern areas with dark brown spots over the body. The pattern is always distinct and usually consists of four main stripes running back from the head onto the shoulders, where they are broad and conspicuous, but down the spine they are broken up. The sides of the body are marked with spots that never fuse to form vertical stripes. Prominent white stripes run from the nose, by the medial corner of the eyes, and often up over the head. The ears are large and pointed, and the backs of the ears are black with a white spot. Two prominent dark stripes run from the inner corner of each eye to the base of the ear. There is a white streak that extends from the inner corner of each eye toward the nose, and the rostrum is white. The long tail (around 40–50% of HB length) is spotted with some rings toward the black tip. In the skull, the nasal bones are not everted; there is a concave rostral process of the maxilla, and the postorbital bar is sometimes complete in skulls that have just reached maturity. The width of the mesopterygoid is approximately equal to its length, and the mastoid is flat and closely applied to the surface of the bullae. P1 is often missing and P2 is vestigal. The skull of *Prionailurus* could be confused with *Felis silvestris*, and differentiating among the forms may be difficult as hybrids are known. *Prionailurus* will usually have a narrower mesopterygoid palate (in *Felis*, it is generally wider than long); the intraorbital width is narrower (16–20% of condylobasal length in *Prionailurus*, 19–24% in *Felis*); the skull is narrower, with the zygomatic breadth generally < 75% of the condylobasal length (in *Felis* it is usually greater). Dental formula: 3.1.3.1/3.1.2.1 = 30.

Distribution: Widely distributed across China, except for the arid N and W; extending from Afghanistan through the Indian subcontinent, SE Asia, Russia, and Korea. Five subspecies in China: (1) *P. b. alleni* Sody, 1949; Hainan Island (includes *hainanus* Xu and Liu, 1980); (2) *P. b. bengalensis* (Kerr, 1792); SW Guangxi, SW Guizhou, Sichuan, S Xizang, Yunnan (includes *ellioti* (Gray, 1842); *herschelii* (Gray, 1869); *jerdoni* Blyth, 1863; *nipalensis* (Horsfield and Vigors, 1829); *servalinus* Gray, 1843; *tenasserimensis* (Gray, 1867); *undatus* Desmarest, 1816; *wagati* (Gray, 1867)); (3) *P. b. chinensis* (Gray, 1837); S Anhui, Fujian, Guangdong, Guangxi, Guizhou, Hubei, Hunan, Jiangsu, Jiangxi, Shanghai, Shaanxi, E Sichuan, Taiwan, Yunnan, Zhejiang (includes *decoloratus* (Milne-Edwards, 1872); *ingrami* (Bonhote, 1903); *microtis* (Milne-Edwards, 1872); *minutus* (Temminck, 1824) [preoccupied]; *reevesii* (Gray, 1843); *ricketti* (Bonhote, 1903); *sinensis* (Shih, 1930); *undatus* (Radde, 1862)); (4) *P. b. euptilurus* (Elliot, 1871); N Anhui, Beijing, Hebei, Heilongjiang, Henan, N Jiangsu, Jilin, Liaoning, Nei Mongol, Shandong, Shanxi (includes *manchuricus* (Mori, 1922); *raddei* (Trouessart, 1904)); (5) *P. b. scripta* (Milne-Edwards, 1870); N Yunnan, W Sichuan, Qinghai, Gansu, Ningxia, Shaanxi, E Xizang (includes *anastaseae* (Satunin, 1905)).

Natural History: Leopard Cats occur in a broad variety of habitat types from the tropical rainforests of Southeast Asia to the conifer forests of the Amur region. They also occur in shrub forests, but not in grasslands or steppe (except marginal areas and riparian ecosystems), and usually avoid areas of deep and continuous snow cover over 10 cm. They can be found in dense second growth, logged areas, tree plantations, and agricultural areas and can live close to rural settlements. They have been found at elevations from 1,000 to 3,000 m in the Himalayas. Small vertebrate feeders, they feed on hares, birds, reptiles, amphibians, fish, rodents, as well as occasional carrion. They are nocturnal and solitary and are good climbers and excellent swimmers. The average home range size for males tracked in Thailand was 3.5 km^2. They are often found in pairs, and the male may help in the rearing of young. They are aseasonal breeders with a gestation of 60–70 days. The average litter size is two or three, and young become sexually mature at 18–24 months.

Comments: The Leopard Cat closely resembles the domestic cat and the Wildcat. The Leopard Cat and the Wildcat are the two smallest felids in China. They have been known to interbreed with feral domestic cats and produce fertile viable offspring. Subspecies assignment in SW China is problematic. It is unlikely that Nepal/S Xizang populations are the same subspecies as the reported Guangxi/Guizhou/Sichuan populations of *bengalensis*. Assignment of subspecies in Sichuan, Yunnan, and Xizang should be viewed as tentative. Although some place *scripta* and *anastaseae* in *chinensis*, we have followed Pocock (1939) and separated the SW plateau specimens into *scripta*.

Conservation Status: China RL—VU A1acd. CITES—II.

References: Ellerman and Morrison-Scott (1951); Gao et al. (1987); Lekagul and McNeeley (1977); Pocock (1939); Rabinowitz (1990); Swinhoe (1862); Wang (2003); Wozencraft (2005).

Subfamily Pantherinae—Roaring Cats

豹亚科 Bao Yake—豹 Bao

The Pantherinae subfamily of large cats is appropriately named: they are the largest members of the Felidae and contain the only carnivore known to feed on humans—the tiger. All three genera are represented in China. They are all ambush predators and represent some of the most endangered carnivores in the world. They are morphologically very similar, and several authors have suggested placing all the members of this subfamily in the genus *Panthera*. There appears to be no single uniting factor on their pelage coloration; however, they share several morphological features of the skull. Although the subfamily Felinae all have well-developed postorbital processes, often forming a complete postorbital bar, the pantherines have comparatively weakly developed processes. With the exception of the Snow Leopard (*Uncia*), the ectotympanic portion of the bullae is very reduced, and in the Snow Leopard, it is only moderately developed. The skull is larger (all are over 150 mm), and the rostrum is comparatively longer than in the felines. The intraorbital width is approximately equal to or greater than the postorbital width (in felines, the postorbital width is considerably greater). The jugal does not touch the lacrimal. All of the pantherines have a very distinct circular depression along the midline of the frontal, near the frontal/nasal suture.

Genus *Neofelis* (monotypic)

云豹属 Yunbao Shu

Clouded Leopard

PLATE 42
MAP 454

Neofelis nebulosa (Griffith, 1821)

云豹 Yun Bao

Distinctive Characteristics: HB 700–1,080; T 550–915; HF 200–225; E 45–60; GLS 150–200; Wt 16–32 kg. The Clouded Leopard is noted for the distinctive cloud-shaped markings on the back and sides. Its pelage has a ground color uniformly light yellowish to gray, with large, cloud-shaped spots on sides; two intermittent black stripes running down spine to tail base. There are six longitudinal stripes on the neck,

Key to the Chinese Genera of Pantherinae

1.a. Size large; HB length usually > 1 m; body pattern not clouded or marbled; no distinct broad longitudinal stripes on neck; tail spotted or ringed, but not both. Rostral length > 60 mm; palatal midline length > 75 mm; greatest width of nasals > 28 mm; zygomatic width > 130 mm. Postcanine diastema similar to other felids; P3 has two roots; C1 (from tip to alveolus) less than three times as long as the basal width (C1 usually slightly longer than P4) 2

b. Size small; HB length usually < 1 m; body pattern clouded or marbled; distinct broad black longitudinal stripes on neck; tail spotted, but has black rings toward tip. Rostral length < 60 mm; palatal midline length < 75 mm; greatest width of nasals < 28 mm; zygomatic width < 130 mm. Large postcanine diastema; P3 has three roots; C1 (from tip to alveolus) about three times as long as the basal width (C1 longer than P3 + P4) *Neofelis*

2.a. Ear back white, noticeable supraocular eye patch; black spots or rings distinct; tail not thick and especially long. Skull elongated; length between postglenoid fossa and occipital condyles > 49 mm (≥ 30% of condylobasal length); palatal midline length > 80 mm; intraorbital width < 25% of condylobasal length; paroccipital process does not extend beyond auditory bulla; ectotympanic not well inflated; lower margin of mandible curved. M1 width nearly twice its length (and > 6 mm) *Panthera*

b. Ear back gray, supraocular eye patch indistinct if present; black spots or rings indistinct; tail thick and much longer than HB length. Skull noticeably domed; length between postglenoid fossa and occipital condyles < 49 mm (< 30% of condylobasal length); palatal midline length < 80 mm; intraorbital width > 25% of condylobasal length; paroccipital process extends beyond auditory bulla; anterior width of nasals nearly equal to length; ectotympanic well inflated; lower margin of mandible straight. M1 width nearly equal to length (and < 6 mm) *Uncia*

starting behind the ears. The limbs and ventral surface are marked with large black ovals. Crown spotted; rostrum white; dark stripes from the eye and the corner of the mouth along the sides of the head. Ears are short and rounded, and the ear back is black with a light gray spot. Posteriorly the black eyering continues as a black strip across the cheek. The tail is thick and plush, covered proximally with spots and becoming encircled with black rings toward the tip. Length of tail nearly equivalent to HB length. The auditory bullae of *Neofelis* resembles that of felines, in that the ventralmost expansion is small (< 10 mm) below the external auditory meatus (in *Panthera* and *Uncia*, it is posterior and > 10 mm); the paraoccipital processes project posteriorly. The nasals are relatively narrow (16% of condylobasal length); the zygomatic breadth is < 130 mm; toothrow length < 60 mm; the rostrum is the shortest among the pantherines both in real length (< 58 mm) and proportionally (< 36% of condylobasal length). The most distinctive feature about the teeth is the canine–the longest of any felid. The upper canines are about as long as the combined length of P3 + P4. The second upper premolar is usually absent. Dental formula: 3.1.2–3.1/3.1.2.1 = 28–30.

Distribution: Found across S China; extending to Indochina, SE Asia, and the Indian subcontinent. Three subspecies in China : (1) *N. n. brachyura* (Swinhoe, 1862); Taiwan; (2) *N. n. macrosceloides* (Hodgson, 1853); S Xizang (*macrocelis* (Tickell, 1843) [preoccupied]); (3) *N. n. nebulosa* (Griffith, 1821); Anhui, Fujian, Guangdong, Guangxi, Guizhou, Hainan, Hubei, Hunan, Jiangxi, Shaanxi, Sichuan, E Xizang, Yunnan, Zhejiang (includes *melli* (Matschie, in *Mell* 1922)).

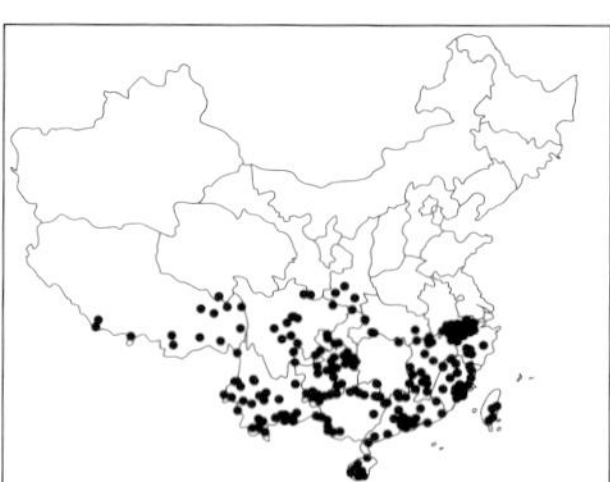

MAP 454. CLOUDED LEOPARD, *Neofelis nebulosa*

Natural History: Clouded Leopards are closely associated with primary evergreen tropical rainforest but have also been found in secondary and logged forests. They have been recorded in the Himalayas up to 1,450 m and have been found in coniferous forests up to 3,000 m in Taiwan. Although less common, they have been found in grassland and scrub, dry tropical forests, and mangrove swamps. Clouded Leopards have been reported to feed on Palm Civets (*Paradoxurus*), pigs, pheasants, macaques (*Maccaca*), gibbons (*Hylobates*), small mammals, and birds, and have also been known to raid chicken coops. Nocturnal and solitary, most of their hunting appears to occur on the ground, although they are one of the most highly arboreal felids. They can climb down head first, traverse

branches upside down, and hang from branches with their hind feet. They are good swimmers and may hunt in pairs. They are sexually mature at two years of age and have a gestation of 94 days. Average litter size is three.
Comments: The position of *Neofelis* is uncertain; it has been placed in Pantherinae, in the Neofelinae, as the most primitive member of the Pantherinae, and in the Felinae. Some have even considered this monotypic genus a synonym of *Pardofelis*. It resembles the larger pantherines in body shape and build but is about the size of some of the smaller leopards. Its coloration is similar to the Marbled Cat. Most have considered Xizang specimens as *nebulosa*; however, those collected along the Nepal-Xizang border are probably better considered as *macrosceloides*.
Conservation Status: China RL—EN A1cd; C1. China Key List—I. CITES—I. IUCN RL—VU C2a(i) ver 3.1 (2001).
References: Biswas et al. (1985); Davies (1990); Davis (1962); Hemmer (1968); Lekagul and McNeeley (1977); Mattern and McLennan (2000); Prater (1971); Rabinowitz and Walker (1991); Rabinowitz et al. (1987); Santiapillai and Ashby (1988).

Genus *Panthera*—Panthers

豹属 Bao Shu—豹 Bao

The largest catlike mammals, with the body distinctly striped or spotted in Asian species. The tail is longer than half of HB length; legs are large and muscular, especially the front legs. The rostrum is relatively long compared to the length of the skull; nasals are broad and taper only very slightly. Whereas most felines appear to have a rounded skull, skulls of *Panthera* appear to be "flattened." The basicranial region is also long and drawn out so that the auditory bullae are well separated from the postglenoid process. Dental formula: 3.1.3.1/3.1.3.2 = 30. The genus *Panthera* is distributed on all the continents of the world and contains four species, two of which widely occur in China.

Leopard

PLATE 42
MAP 455

Panthera pardus Linnaeus, 1758
豹 Bao

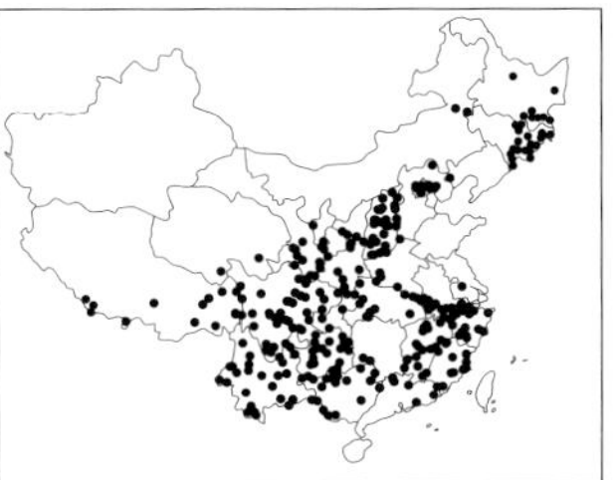
MAP 455. LEOPARD, *Panthera pardus*

Distinctive Characteristics: HB 1,000–1,910; T 700–1,000; HF 220–245; E 63–75; GLS 175–221; Wt 37–90 kg. The ground color of the Leopard is generally light brown to yellowish gray with head, limbs, and tail all covered with black rosettes—with single black spots on the head, legs, and ventral surfaces. The ears appear wide-set on the head, short and rounded. Ventral surfaces are white. Melanistic individuals are relatively common. Leopards have comparatively short legs, and they are the largest spotted cat in Asia. Their tail is about 60–75% of the HB length. Males are 30–50% heavier than females. In nearly all proportions, the Leopard skull is smaller than the Tiger. Proportionally, the skull is narrower, with the zygomatic width < 70% of the condylobasal length (> 70% in Tigers); toothrow length (< 75 mm) is < 40% of condylobasal length. Males with well-developed sagittal crest, which is nearly absent in females. Width of M1 < 10 mm, and P4 length < 30 mm. Dental formula: 3.1.2–3.1/3.1.2.1 = 28–30.
Distribution: Widely distributed in E, C, and S China; Leopards have the widest distribution of any Old World cat. They are found throughout Africa, the Middle East, Central Asia, Indian subcontinent, Indochina, SE Asia, and Russia. Three subspecies in China: (1) *P. p. fusca* (Meyer, 1794); Anhui, Fujian, Guangdong, Guangxi, Guizhou, Henan, Hubei, Hunan, Jiangxi, Qinghai, S Shaanxi, Shanxi, Sichuan, S Xizang, Yunnan, Zhejiang (includes *antiquorum* Fitzinger, 1868; *centralis* (Lönnberg, 1917); *chinenesis* (Brass, 1904); *iturensis* Allen, 1924; *longicaudata* (Valenciennes, 1856); *melas* (Pousargues, 1896);

Key to the Chinese Species of *Panthera*

1.a. Pattern on pelage consisting mainly of irregularly arranged rosettes; HB length < 1.6 m. Condylobasal length < 250 mm; width of tooth row < 100 mm; zygomatic breadth < 160 mm; intraorbital breadth > 40 mm; nasals do not project posteriorly much beyond maxilla; length of median suture of nasal bone < 1.5 times of its maximal width, nasal midline length < 55 mm; intraorbital width ≥ postorbital width — *Panthera pardus*

b. Pattern on pelage consisting of vertical black stripes; HB length > 1.6 m. Condylobasal length >250 mm; width of tooth row > 100 mm; zygomatic breadth < 160 mm; intraorbital breadth > 40 mm; nasals project posteriorly much beyond maxilla; length of median suture of nasal bone > 1.5 times of its maximal width, nasal midline length > 55 mm; intraorbital width > postorbital width — *Panthera tigris*

millardi Pocock, 1930; *pernigra* (Gray, 1863); *variegata* (Allen, 1912)); (2) *P. p. japonensis* (Gray, 1862); Beijing, Hebei, N Shaanxi, Shanxi (includes *bedfordi* Pocock, 1930; *chinensis* (Gray, 1867); *fontanierii* (Milne-Edwards, 1867); *grayi* (Trouessart, 1904); *hanensis* Matschie, 1907); (3) *P. p. orientalis* (Schlegel, 1857); Heilongjiang, Jilin, Nei Mongol (includes *villosa* (Bonhote, 1903)).

Natural History: Very adaptable, Leopards are found in a wide variety of habitat types, from open areas with rocks and shrubs to dense tropical forests. They are absent from true deserts but are found in just about any other habitat. Leopards are most commonly associated with some type of forest cover, woodlands, scrub jungles, or rocky hills. They have been found at elevations up to 5,000 m. Leopards are predators principally of large ungulates, wild goats, Argali (*Ovis ammon*), and sheep. They are opportunistic feeders and have the amazing ability to survive even on small prey. Leopards eat a much wider range of prey than most other large cats, including rodents, rabbits, deer, antelope, pigs, foxes, monkeys, birds, partridges, and amphibians. Near humans they will eat dogs, cats, sheep, and calves. They usually focus on ungulates weighing less than 50 kg. Whatever is the most locally abundant species of ungulate prey appears to be the most important prey item in the diet. Leopards are very powerful predators and can kill prey two to three times their own weight. They will kill humans and will break into homes to eat humans. Leopards are solitary and nocturnal. They easily climb trees and swim well. They are superb climbers and can descend trees headfirst. In the tropical rainforest they will move in the daytime as well as night. Most hunt on the ground and range 3–5 km per day in areas of abundant prey and 10–20 km in areas of scarce prey. Home ranges of females have been reported to be 6–8 km^2 and males 17–76 km^2. They breed in February, and after a gestation of 90-105 days they have a litter of two or three.

Comments: Although not recorded from China, *P. p. delacouri* Pocock, 1930, is found in N Vietnam and probably in S Yunnan and perhaps Guizhou. Wang (2003) recognized Hebei, Beijing, Shanxi, and Shaanxi populations as *fontanierii*.

Conservation Status: Ma (1998a) estimated Chinese populations at less than 10,000. China RL—CR A1acd; C1. China Key List—I. CITES—I. IUCN RL—*P. p. japonensis*: EN C2a; *P. p. orientalis*: CR A2c; D ver 3.1 (2001).

References: Heptner and Sludskii (1972); Ma (1998a); Miththapala et al. (1996); Ognev (1962); Rabinowitz (1989); Wang (2003).

Tiger

PLATE 42
MAP 456

Panthera tigris (Linnaeus, 1758)

虎 Hu

Distinctive Characteristics: HB 140–280 cm; T 910–1,100; HF 234–420; E 95–130; GLS 252–333; Wt 90–306 kg. One of the world's largest carnivores and the largest of all extant cats, the tiger is the only carnivore that regularly feeds on humans. Perhaps no other carnivore has played such a prominent role in the history and culture of China. Widely believed to be a symbol of power and strength, it is used not only by the Chinese culture, but by other cultures as well. According to the *I Ching*, the Tiger represents yin, or evil. Killing or capturing a Tiger is thought to bring the highest honor to the hunter. It is the most easily recognizable cat, being the only striped cat, and the largest. The pelage is reddish orange to red-brown or orange-yellow with a series of narrow black transverse stripes. The stripes differ on each side of the body, and continue onto the ventral surface. The ventral surface is white; with a light white region above the eye; the tail usually has about ten black rings. The hind legs are slightly longer than the front legs, and the tail is longer than half the HB and very cylindrical. The skull of the Tiger is easily distinguishable from other felid skulls on size alone, being the only one over 250 mm in length. Other features to distinguish the Tiger are intraorbital region wider than postorbital region; jugal that does not touch lacrimal; distinct depression at frontal/nasal suture; small postorbital processes; toothrow length > 80 mm; zygomatic breadth > 200 mm; and length of P4 > 30 mm and with strong ectoparastyle; width of M1 > 10 mm; m1 with distinct hypoconid; p4 with a large hypoconid that is larger than paraconid. Dental formula: 3.1.3.1/3.1.2.1 = 30.

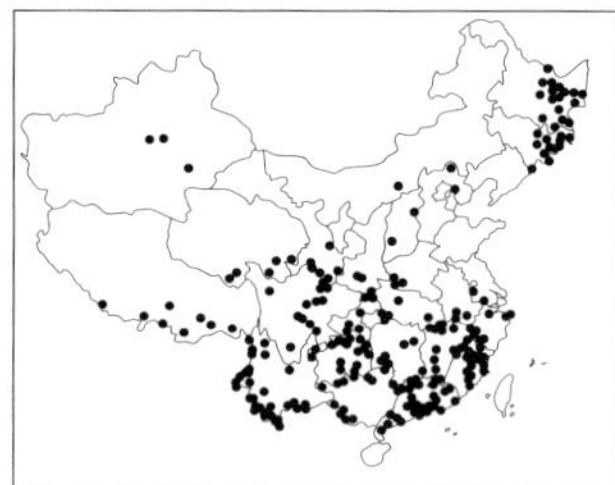

MAP 456a. TIGER, *Panthera tigris* (historical distribution)

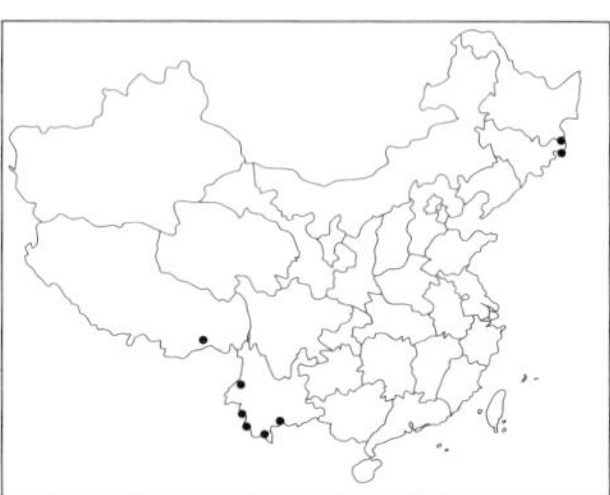

MAP 456b. (current distribution)

Distribution: Tigers were originally distributed widely in China, primarily in the NE and SE; the worldwide distribution includes the Indian subcontinent, Indochina, and Russia. Five allopatric subspecies are known to have occurred in China: (1) *P. t. altaica* Temminck, 1844; Heilongjiang, Jilin (extirpated: Nei Mongol, Gansu, Hebei, Henan, Shanxi; includes *amurensis* (Dode, 1871); *coreensis* (Brass,

1904); *longipilis* (Fitzinger, 1868); *mandshurica* (Baykov, 1925); *mikadoi* (Satunin, 1915)); (2) *P. t. amoyensis* (Hilzheimer, 1905); Fujian, Guangdong, Hunan, Jiangsu, Jiangxi (extirpated: Anhui, Gansu, NW Guangxi, Guizhou, Henan, Hubei, Shandong, Shaanxi, Sichuan, NE Yunnan, Zhejiang; includes *styani* (Pocock, 1929)); (3) *P. t. corbetti* Mazak, 1968; S Guangxi, S Yunnan (extirpated: SE Guangdong); (4) *P. t. tigris* (Linnaeus, 1758); S Xizang, Yunnan (extirpated: *fluviatilis* (Sterndale, 1884); *montana* (Sterndale,1884); *regalis* (Gray, 1842); *striata* (Severtzov,1858)); (5) *P. t. virgata* (Illiger, 1915); (extinct: originally occurred in Xinjiang; includes *leoqi* Schwarz, 1916; *septentrionalis* (Satunin, 1904); *trabata* (Schwarz, 1916)).

Natural History: Tigers have historically been found in a wide variety of habitats from scrub forests to tropical rainforests to mangrove swamps. From some of the coldest areas in Sibera, to the tropical rainforests of SE Asia, Tigers are clearly very adaptable to a wide variety of habitats. In China they are found in tropical evergreen, deciduous, coniferous, scrub oak, and birch forests, mangrove swamps, and dry thorn forests. They range as high as 3,900 m. Although Tigers are opportunistic, like most carnivores, they feed mainly on large mammals, especially ungulates. They can prey on Sambar (*Cervus unicolor*) or buffalo that weigh 160–400 kg, but they usually take species that weigh between 10 and 100 kg. They are one of the few carnivores that appear to rely on prey that is many times their own size. Tigers are infamous for their strength, and there are accounts of Tigers moving large prey such as cows or horses, and one account of moving a 770 kg Gaur. Wild Boar (*Sus scrofa*), Roe Deer (*Capreolus*), and Red Deer (*Cervus*) appear to be principal components of their diet, but they have been known to kill the Asiatic Black Bear (*Ursus thibetanus*) and the Brown Bear (*Ursus arctos*). One study in the Russian Far East showed that Wild Boar and deer constituted over 60% of their diet. They are considered ambush predators, springing onto their prey and taking them down with their muscular front limbs. Tigers kill small prey by a bite to the back of the head and neck. They kill large prey by a throat bite causing suffocation. They may spend several days feeding on a large prey item, covering it up with leaves and grass each time they depart. Tigers forage over a large area and may range over 15–30 km in a single night of hunting. Unlike other cats, Tigers will enter water without hesitation and are excellent swimmers. Their impact on their prey is substantial, and it is estimated that they take 10% of the available prey biomass. In undisturbed areas Tigers will hunt at any time of the day or night, but in areas disturbed by human activites they become principally nocturnal. Although Tigers are usually solitary except when in heat, mating, and rearing the young, there are reports of males associating with females and cubs. Seldom found in pairs, the usual group consists of a mother and her young. They coexist throughout most of their range with other large carnivores (Leopards and Dholes, *Cuon*), although Tigers are clearly the dominant carnivore. The average home range size varies depending on cover and prey availability but ranges from 15 to 51 km^2 with little overlap (< 10%) between individuals in tropical areas of high prey abundance, to 300–1000 km^2 in the Amur region (low prey abundance) where home ranges may overlap nearly completely (but not at the same time). Tigers breed in January and February and have a gestation of 90–105 days. The litter size is one to six, but two or three is more common. They are sexually mature at one to two years.

Conservation Status: Three of the original eight subspecies of Tigers are extinct, including one in China, the far western Caspian Tiger of Xinjiang (*P. t. virgata*). As four of the remaining five Tiger subspecies have occurred in China, conservation efforts in China are critical to the species' survival. Tilson et al. (1997) believed *P. t. amoyensis* to be the antecedent of all tigers, and shortly after World War II it was believed that there were 4,000 left. Today, the population level for all of S China is estimated at below 30 individuals. Extensive surveys for South China Tigers over the last 10 years have failed to find direct evidence of their existence (Tilson et al. 2004). The total population of all Chinese Tigers is estimated at less than 200. This dramatic drop in numbers is principally due to habitat destruction and hunting. Tiger bone has been an important ingredient in traditional Chinese medicine, and one Tiger on the black market can result in as much as ten year's income for the poacher. China RL—CR D. China Key List—I. CITES—I. IUCN RL—EN C2a(i) ver 3.1 (2001); *P. t. altaica*: CR C2a(ii); *P. t. amoyensis*: CR D; *P. t. virgata*: EX ver 3.1 (2001).

References: Karanth and Sunquist (1995); Lekagul and McNeeley (1977); Li et al. (2001); Luo et al. (2004b); Ma (1998b); Matyushkin et al. (1980); Mazák (1981); Miquelle et al. (1996); Nowell and Jackson (1996); Pocock (1929); Prater (1971); Schaller (1967); Sheng et al. (1999); Seidensticker and McDougal (1993); Sunquist (1981); Tilson et al. (1997); Tilson et al. (2004).

Genus *Uncia* (monotypic)

雪豹属 Xuebao Shu

Snow Leopard

PLATE 42
MAP 457

Uncia uncia (Schreber, 1776)

雪豹 Xue Bao

Distinctive Characteristics: HB 1,100–1,300; T 800–1,000; HF 265; E 61; GLS 155–173; Wt 38–75 kg. The pelage ground color of Snow Leopards is a uniformly light gray scattered with black rings or spots. Although there is variation throughout the range of the Snow Leopard, it appears to be mostly in gray-black-and white combinations. The venter is white. The spots on the head and neck are solid, whereas on the body they are broken up into irregular circles. The spots on the back coalesce to form two black lines that go from the neck to the base of the tail. The ears are short, rounded, and set on the sides of the head and wide apart. The backs of the ears are black with a pale grayish center. The eyes are distinctive among felids in that the iris is always a pale green or gray. Tail is very long and quite thick, at least 75% of the HB length, and legs seem disproportionably short. The fur is highly valued for its luxurious condition, measured at 5 cm along the back and 12 cm along the belly in winter pelage, and with a hair density of up to 4,000 hairs per cm^2. The front feet are larger than the hind feet. This is a large felid with a distinctively highly domed or vaulted and rounded skull. This is reflected in the relatively short basicranial distance, and this species is the only pantherine with the distance between the postglenoid processes and the occipital condyles being less than 30% of the condylobasal length. Ectotympanic portion of the bullae nearly as large as the entotympanic, and the paraoccipital processes extend considerably beyond the auditory bullae. The nasal cavities appear larger than one would expect in a skull of this size. The height of the mandible before the third premolar is at least as great as, or even greater than, the height behind the first molar. The nasals are wider than in any other pantherine, with the nasal suture length only being between 5% and 20% longer than the width and not extending as far posteriorly as the maxilla. The intraorbital breadth is wider than the postorbital breadth and is proportionally wider than in any other pantherine (> 25% of condylobasal length). The first upper molar is more quadrate than in other pantherines, and the width is less than 6 mm. Dental formula: 3.1.3.1/3.1.3.1 = 30.

Distribution: Gansu, W Nei Mongol, Qinghai, Shanxi, W Sichuan, Xinjiang, S and W Xizang, Yunnan (includes *baikalensis-romanii* Medvedev, 2000; *irbis* (Ehrenberg, 1830); *schneideri* (Zukowsky, 1950); *uncioides* (Horsfield, 1855). Subspeciation of Snow Leopards is not clear, although two subspecies have been described. The insular distribution of Snow Leopards within their high mountain habitat, coupled with their tendency to migrate up to 600 km, make any assignment of subspecies tentative at this time (Heptner and Sludskii 1972). The Snow Leopard extends into Afghanistan, Bhutan, India, Kazakhstan, Kyrgyzstan, Mongolia, Nepal, Pakistan, Russia, Tajikistan, and Uzbekistan.

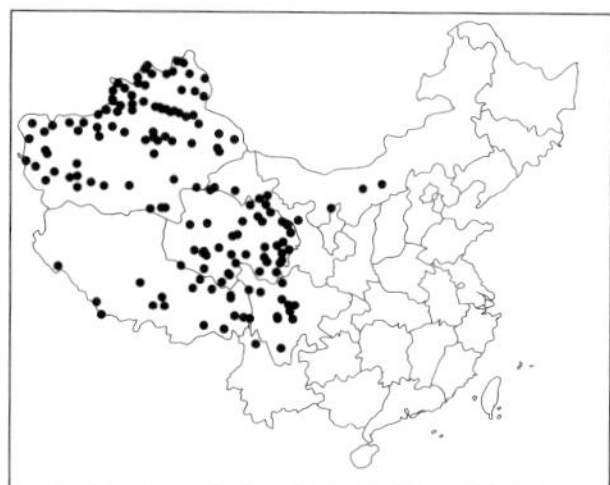

MAP 457. SNOW LEOPARD, *Uncia uncia*

Natural History: Snow Leopards are found in high mountains, generally between 3,000 and 4,500 m and occasionally as high as 5,500 m. They prefer cliffs, rocky outcrops, and broken terrain, and terrain where the slope exceeds 40°. They will, however, use wide, flat valleys (for example, in the Kunlun Shan mountains). Normally they are found in grassland, steppe, and high-mountain arid shrubland. Snow Leopards can kill prey up to three times their own weight. Most common prey items are wild sheep, wild goats, pikas, hares, marmots, and gamebirds; they appear to be specialist predators on Blue Sheep (*Pseudois nayaur*) and the Ibex (*Capra ibex*). In one study in the Taxkorgan Reserve, a spring survey yielded scats with 60% Blue Sheep remains and 29% marmot. They will kill a large prey animal every two weeks and will occasionally take livestock. There are several accounts that Snow Leopards appear to take advantage of snow, fog, and rain and may hunt more intensively during those times. They occasionally eat vegetation, and a high incidence of tamarix has been reported in their scats. May remain in a small area for several days, then shift 1–7 km to a new part of their home range. Solitary and generally nocturnal, although they will hunt at any time of the day or night. Home ranges have been recorded from 14 to 142 km^2 in Mongolia. They can leap up to 15 m horizontally and 6 m vertically. They pair during the mating season and apparently breed during a very short interval. Birth records of over 400 captive Snow Leopards show that 89% of births occurred in April, May, and June, with 54% in May alone. Gestation lasts 90–100 days, and average litter size consists of two or three young.

Comments: Although some have proposed placing this species in *Panthera*, features of the skull, skin, habits, and ecology suggest a very different animal. Morphological features of the skull resemble in some respects those of the feline more than other pantherines. It "purrs," similar to felines, in spite of having a pantherine hyoid. Rather than having the long, drawn-out rostrum, its skull is more rounded with a short rostrum, again like the feline cats. Yu et al. (1996) considered *Uncia* congeneric with *Panthera*.

Conservation Status: Endangered in Xinjiang (Abdukadir 2002b). Total Chinese population estimated at 2,000–2,500 (Yang and Feng 1998). China RL—CR A1cd. China Key List—I. CITES—I. IUCN RL—EN C2a(i) ver 3.1 (2001).

References: Abdukadir (2002b); Fox (1989); Fox (1994); Hemmer (1972); Heptner and Sludskii (1972); Jackson and Ahlborn (1988); Schaller (1977); Schaller et al. (1988a); Schaller et al. (1988b); Stroganov (1962); Wang (2003); Wozencraft (2005); Yang and Feng (1998); Yu et al. (1996); Zhirjakov (1990).

Family Viverridae—Civets, Linsangs and Binturongs

灵猫科 Lingmao Ke—灵猫，狸，熊狸 Lingmao, Li, Xiongli

The general body form of civets displays wide variation, however, almost all have extremely long cylindrical tails, which usually exceed 90% of the HB length. Chinese viverrids include the smallest

Key to the Chinese Subfamilies of Viverridae

1.a. Large, well-defined, and sharply contrasting spots, more or less in rows from the head to the tail; scent glands absent; HB length < 450 mm and weight < 1 kg. Condylobasal length 70–80 mm. M2 absent; m1 with vestigal or reduced talonid — Prionodontinae

b. Most without large, well-defined, sharply contrasting spots in rows (one contains sharply contrasting bands across the back); scent glands present in one or both sexes; HB length > 450 mm and weight > 1 kg. Condylobasal length > 80 mm. M2 present; m1 talonid well developed — 2

2.a. Terrestrial in mode, six or more rings on tail; metatarsal pads absent; digitigrade. Buccal lobes of M2 asymmetrical (parastyle more developed than metastyle); m1 trigonid longer than wide; trigonid cusps on m1 much higher than cusps on talonid; P4 without posterolingual cingulum; P4-m1 with well-developed shearing surface — Viverrinae

b. Semiarboreal/arboreal in mode, no well-developed rings on tail; metatarsal pads present; semiplantigrade. Buccal lobes of M1 approximately equal in size; m1 trigonid wider than long; trigonid cusps on m1 similar in height to cusps on talonid; P4 with a wide posterolingual cingulum; P4-m1 with poorly retained vertical shearing surface — 3

3.a. Pelage monocolored, or with small spots in rows, but never in transverse bars; paroccipital process extends past the ventralmost expansion of the bullae; Steno's foramen absent; entotympanic portion of bulla well inflated and with midventral ridge. Vestigial or absent anterolingual cingulum on P4; P3 without lingual cusp — Paradoxurinae

b. Pelage with transverse bars across the back; paroccipital process does not extend past the ventralmost expansion of the bullae; large Steno's foramen present; entotympanic portion of bulla not well inflated and without midventral ridge. Wide anterolingual cingulum on P4; P3 with large lingual cusp — Hemigalinae

(*Prionodon pardicolor*) as well as one of the largest (*Arctictis binturong*) species of the family. Civets generally have eyes that protrude from their orbits, giving them a "bulging eye" appearance. All civets have five toes on each foot and at least some webbing between the toes. Sexual dimorphism is not pronounced within the group, males being slightly (< 5%) larger, except for the some of the palm civets where females are larger. The feet are plantigrade or digitigrade, and the claws are semiretractile. Nearly all species have a perineal scent gland located near the genital and anal orifices. Tail rings occur in all viverrines and are reduced or absent in the other subfamilies. The paradoxurine palm civets are slightly more robust but resemble the viverrine body plan without the spots and with longer tails; the Binturong has a heavy, robust, bearlike body and a thick, prehensile, tapering tail.

Civet skulls can be generally described as having a long rostrum, distinct supraorbital processes, narrow postorbital constriction and an elongated auditory bulla. The posterior palatine foramina are rostral to the maxillo-palatine suture. Premolars are large, and m1 has a talonid. Dental formula: 3.1 4.2/3.1.4.2 = 40.

The word "civet" comes from the Arabic word "zabat," which was used to describe the peculiar scent obtained from the glands of these animals. Civets have been important in the perfume industry since at least the time when King Solomon imported civet oil from Africa. The "civet" secretion comes from a pouchlike perineal gland situated anterior to the anal region. The civet oil is sometimes collected by scraping around five grams of yellowish greasy liquid from the pouch and was originally stored in antelope horns and stomachs for shipment to the perfume industry in France. Civets do not have the capacity to squirt the secretion as do the New World skunks. The liquid, once refined, is cherished by the perfume industry because of its odor and its long-lasting properties. Civet oil is based on an alcohol compound that has been labeled "civetone" and is chemically different from the musk oil found in other carnivores.

Traditionally the Viverridae has included 20 genera and 34 species. Recent morphological and molecular studies have separated some of the species into other families. The Viverridae as understood here, includes the subfamilies Viverrinae, Paradoxurinae, Hemigalinae, and Prionodontinae, with a total of 14 genera and 35 species found worldwide. Although Gaubert et al. (2004) concluded that the subfamily Prionodontinae should be elevated to the family level, here it is provisionally kept at the subfamily level. There are 8 genera and 9 species of viverrids found in China, organized into 4 subfamilies, mainly occurring in provinces south of the Huang He watershed.

Subfamily Hemigalinae—Hemigaline Civets

带狸亚科 Daili Yake—带狸 Daili

The hemigaline civets are among the rarest of all carnivores, and little is known of their natural history, ecology, or behavior. They are restricted to primary-growth forests in the Sunda Shelf and Indochinese region. As a group, they are more terrestrial than the paradoxurines, but not as cursorial as *Viverra.* All are semiarboreal, and even the Otter Civet (*Cynogale*) will take refuge by climbing when chased. However, the extent to which they are arboreal is unknown and all information is anecdotal. The civet gland is present in all species, but the group is also distinguished by the development of large anal glands. Some have speculated that the aposematic coloration pattern of *Chrotogale* might indicate a noxious protective secretion of the anal glands.

At present there are no reliable records of the Otter Civet (*Cynogale bennettii*) as occurring in China. It is known from northern parts of Vietnam. Pocock (1933) described another species, *Cynogale lowei* from North Vietnam based on a single incomplete juvenile specimen; however, here it is considered synonymous with *C. bennettii.* Two sight records are noteworthy: Sheng (1999) recorded *Cynogale* from the "Red River Valley of Southern Yunnan," and Schreiber et al. (1989) report that a skin of *C. lowei* was found in a fisherman's house near Yilong lake in southern Yunnan in 1973. Thus, of the four genera in the Hemigalinae, only one is known definitively from China.

Genus *Chrotogale* (monotypic)

带狸属 Daili Shu

Owston's Palm Civet

Chrotogale owstoni Thomas, 1912 — PLATE 43, MAP 458

长颌带狸 Changhe Daili

MAP 458. OWSTON'S PALM CIVET, *Chrotogale owstoni*

Distinctive Characteristics: HB 400–660; T 350–490; HF 70–90; GLS 102–113; Wt 2.4–3.4 kg. The pelage of Owston's Palm Civet is uniformly yellowish brown, with five blackish brown wide and transverse stripes on back. The venter and limbs have blackish brown spots, and the nape has two dark black longitudinal hands. The distal half of the tail is black with its base having two white rings. There are rows of small black spots on its neck, sides, and limbs.

The skull is narrow and long; rostrum is also long with the premaxilla projecting forward, hence there is a space between incisors and canines; supraorbital process short and blunt; the anterior root of the zygomatic arch is above the molars rather than the carnassial; Steno's foramen large and elongated; rostrum constricted posterior to canines; external auditory meatus expanded laterally into a bowl-shaped lip. The teeth appear small for a skull of this size; upper incisors form a distinctive C-shaped pattern and are spatulate; M2 near equal in size to M1; P1 surrounded by wide diastemas—especially between C1 and P1. Lower incisors spatulate and procumbent, occluding with lingual sides of upper incisors. Dental formula: 3.1.4.2/3.1.4.2 = 40.

Distribution: Guangxi, Yunnan; extending into Laos and Vietnam. Chinese subspecies: *C. o. owstoni* Thomas, 1912.

Natural History: Owston's Palm Civet prefers densely vegetated habitats near water sources in both primary and secondary forests below 500 m. They feed principally on the ground but will climb trees in search of food. They are nocturnal and solitary and nest in large trees or dense brush. Although very little is known of their diet, anecdotal information indicates that it principally consists of earthworms. However, they may also eat small vertebrates (squirrels), invertebrates, and some fruit. Dens are constructed under large tree trunks and in dense brush or may be located in natural holes in trees, rocks, or the soil. Their scent secretion may also be used in predator defense. They breed between January and March, and after a gestation of 60 days have an average litter of three. Breeding may occur twice a year.

Comments: Although Corbet and Hill (1992) considered the *Chrotogale* synonymous with *Hemigalus*, there are strong morphological and molecular studies to support its separation (Veron and Heard 2000).

Conservation Status: *C. owstoni* occurs in several protected areas in China (the Dawei Mountain National Reserve, Jinping Divide National Reserve, and Huanlian Mountain National Reserve). Chinese population estimated at 300 (Wang 1998). China RL—EN B1ab(v); D. IUCN RL—VU A1cd ver 2.3 (1994).

References: Corbet and Hill (1992); Dang et al. (1992); Gaubert et al. (2004); Nowak (1999); Prater (1971); Schreiber (1989); Veron and Heard (2000); Wang (1998); Wozencraft (2005).

Subfamily Paradoxurinae—Palm Civets

长尾狸亚科 Changweili Yake—长尾狸 Changweili

The paradoxurines are medium to large civets with an elongated body, short legs, and an extremely long tail. The tail is equal to or longer than the HB and is cylindrical except for the Binturong (*Arctictis*), which has a tapering, muscular tail. This subfamily contains one of the largest civets (Binturong) and one of the most widely distributed (Common Palm Civet, *Paradoxurus hermaphroditus*). They occur throughout the Indo-Malayan realm, primarily in tropical forests. The Paradoxurinae comprises five genera, four of which occur in China; of these, three are monotypic (*Arctictis, Arctogalidia, Paguma*).

The head has a long rostrum and pointed, catlike ears. The rhinarium is large and connected to the lip by a medial groove. The vibrissae are prominent and

Key to the Chinese Genera of Paradoxurinae

1.a. Prehensile tail; ear tufted; pelage of long, blackish hair. Intraorbital region greatly inflated. Procumbent incisors; P4 metastyle reduced, and protocone medial to paracone *Arctictis*

b. Tail not prehensile; ear not tufted; pelage with or without distinct markings. Intraorbital region not well inflated. Incisors not procumbent; P4 metastyle long, protocone medial to paracone 2

2.a. Scent gland absent in males; female scent gland with well-developed labia; first digit of each foot far from others; three brown-black stripes running down the back. Deeply emarginate postpalatal notch; constricted, tubular mesopterygoid with ventrolateral flanges; mesopterygoid more than twice as long as wide; elongation of supraorbital processes; ectotympanic and endotympanic portions of the bulla not clearly divided externally; the width of the palate as measured from the buccal edges of M2 > the width as measured from the buccal edges of M1. M2 displaced laterally, teeth noticeably reduced and widely spaced *Arctogalidia*

b. Scent gland present in males; female scent gland without well-developed labia; first digit of each foot not removed from others; back pattern never consisting of three brown stripes. Postpalatal notch small, if present; mesopterygoid not tubular; mesopterygoid as wide or wider than long; supraorbital processes short; ectotympanic and entotympanic portions of the bulla clearly divided externally; the width of the palate as measured from the buccal edges of M2 < the width as measured from the buccal edges of M1. M2 not displaced laterally; teeth not reduced nor spaced apart 3

3.a. Prominent black-and-white striped face mask; rest of body monocolored without traces of spots or bands; two pair of mammae. Postorbital constriction broad, its width > than the intraorbital width; frontal sinus slightly expanded; mesopterygoid as wide as long; palate elongated beyond tooth row. Canines laterally compressed with blade on posterior edge; P3 lingual cusp vestigial; M2 reduced to small, peglike tooth; P4 asymmetrical with some shearing surface left, protocone posterior to parastyle, no posterior cingulum *Paguma*

b. Face without noticeable striped mask; back with lateral body spots arranged in rows; three pair of mammae. Postorbital constriction narrow, its width < intraorbital width; frontal sinus not expanded; mesopterygoid wider than long; palate not elongated beyond toothrow. Canines not laterally compressed and without blade on posterior edge; P3 lingual cusp present; M2 with more than one cusp; P4 symmetrical with shearing surface left, protocone posterior to parastyle, posterior cingulum present *Paradoxurus*

can be either white or black or a combination of both. The young have pale or white eyespots located above and/or below the orbits. The eyespots disappear in some species with age. The development of the scent gland (a saclike depression surrounded by two labia) varies slightly from species to species. The feet in the paradoxurines have extensive hairless interdigital webbing and are subplantigrade.

Palm civets are opportunistic frugivores, a feeding style that is reflected in their derived dentition. They have bunodont teeth with little or no functional carnassial shear. The trigonid on m1 is rotated to a narrower acute angle, which increases the crushing surfaces of the talonid. P1 is reduced and usually lost with age. The palatal surface is increased by the divergence of the toothrows and a posterior palatal extension beyond the toothrow, into the orbital region. This extension is limited to the posterolateral portions of the palate. The mesopterygoid is elongate, separating the air passages during the crushing process: in the Small-toothed Palm Civet (*Arctogalidia*) it is long and tubular, while the Binturong has the widest mesopterygoid region, which is slightly concave.

Genus *Arctictis* (monotypic)

熊狸属 Xiongli Shu—熊狸 Xiongli

Binturong PLATE 43

Arctictis binturong (Raffles, 1821) MAP 459

熊狸 Xiong Li

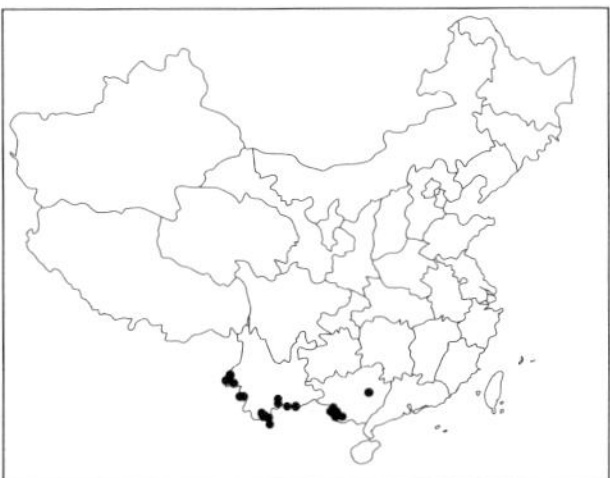

MAP 459. BINTURONG, *Arctictis binturong*

Distinctive Characteristics: HB 522–900; T 520–890; HF 100–135; E 45–65; GLS 113–155; Wt 9–14 kg. The Binturong is the largest viverrid in Asia. A stout, bear-like animal with long, shaggy hair, usually black. The ears are tipped with long, tufted hairs that extend beyond the ears. The Binturong is the only placental mammal in the Old World with a true prehensile tail, although other palm civets use their tail as an accessory limb. Its form is stout and strong with a body color of black, mixed with light brown hairs. Females are normally 20% heavier and larger than the males. Anterior margin of the ear is often white. Their eyes are usually a reddish brown. 2N = 42.

The skull is distinctive in the extraordinarily large frontal sinuses that give the skull a "domed" appearance and inflate the intraorbital region (although there is considerable individual variation). Teeth are reduced and peglike. p1 and M2 very small or absent. The incisors are slightly curved and are separated from each other. They project anteriorly from the premaxilla and are blunt, rather than having the spatulate condition more typical of carnivores. Dental formula: 3.1.4.2/ 3.1.4.2 = 40.

Distribution: Yunnan and Guangxi; ranging throughout SE Asia. Chinese subspecies: *A. b. menglaensis* Wang and Li, 1987.

Natural History: Binturongs are arboreal animals that live in dense tropical and monsoon rainforests below 800 m. They subsist primarily on fruit, especially that of the fig (*Ficus* spp.). They also eat eggs, young shoots, and leaves, and hunt birds, rodents, and other small animals. Binturongs will dive into water to pursue fish. They are critical seed dispersers in Southeast Asia. Binturongs are slow-moving nocturnal, arboreal animals that live alone or in small groups of adults with immature offspring. Almost always, the female is dominant. Males sometimes stay with the females after mating, even after they have given birth. Young can suspend themselves by their tail. Binturongs are awkward on the ground and spend most of their time in trees. They are aseasonal breeders, usually with one litter a year of two or three. Their gestation is 90–92 days, and they are sexually mature at 2–2.5 years.

Conservation Status: Population in China estimated at 200 in S and SW Yunnan (Wang 1998). China RL—CR A1cd; B1ab(i,ii,iii); C1. China Key List—I.

References: Ewer (1973); Kleiman (1974); Macdonald (1987); Medway (1969); Nowak (1991); Wang (1998); Wemmer and Murtaugh (1981).

Genus *Arctogalidia* (monotypic)

小齿狸属 Xiaochili Shu

Small-Toothed Palm Civet

PLATE 43
MAP 460

Arctogalidia trivirgata (Gray, 1832)

小齿狸 Xiao Chi Li

Distinctive Characteristics: HB 440–600; T 510–690; HF 74–80; E 38–42; GLS 100–118; Wt 2–2.5 kg. Head and back is brownish gray, with the venter a light brown. There is a white stripe running from the nose tip to the forehead. The back has three distinct black or dark brown stripes running along the length of the body. This civet is also known by the name "Three-striped Palm Civet." The median stripe is complete, but the lateral stripes are discontinued, alternating with broken spots or absent. Feet and tail tip blackish brown. The Small-toothed Palm Civet has short fur that is generally tawny or buff. Only the females have the perineal scent gland, located near the vulva. The tail is longer than the HB.

The skull has a highly constricted intraorbital and postorbital region. The mesopterygoid is tubular and elongated, with distinctive ventrolaterally directed flanges protruding from the palatal surface. The divergent nature of the toothrows of the upper palate is unique within the Carnivora. The first and second upper molars are displaced laterally to the carnassial pair. This results in the last pair of upper molars being the farthest apart in the toothrow. The Small-toothed Palm Civet is appropriately named, for the atrophy of the size and cusps on the teeth have considerably reduced the occlusal surface. The smaller teeth are widely spaced and demonstrate no shearing function.

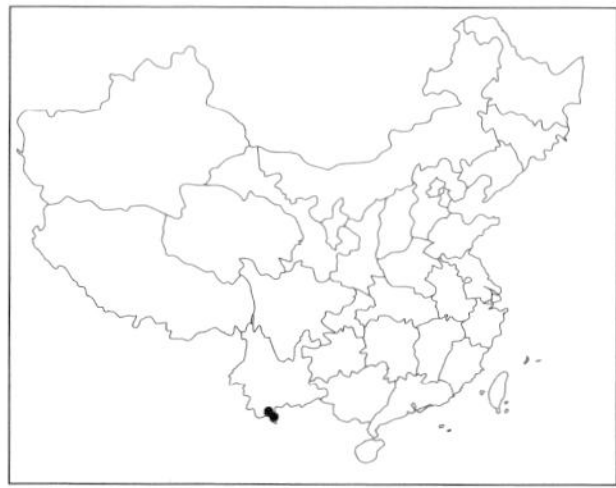

MAP 460. SMALL-TOOTHED PALM CIVET, *Arctogalidia trivirgata*

Distribution: S Yunnan; extending to India, Myanmar, Bangladesh, Thailand, Laos, Vietnam, Indonesia, and Malaysia. Chinese subspecies: *A. t. millsi* Wroughton, 1921.

Natural History: Small-toothed Palm Civets inhabit tropical rainforests at altitudes below 1,200 m. They are nocturnal and solitary and found in primary and secondary growth forests, and even in areas where there is considerable logging. They generally stay away from human habitation, although they have been reported from coconut plantations. Lack of records may be the result of their confinement to the top layers of the evergreen forest canopy. Little is known about their food habits; based on their highly modified dentition, fruit must be the most important item. They will also eat insects, small mammals, birds, frogs, and lizards. They are aseasonal breeders, with some having two litters a year of two to three young. The gestation has been reported to be 45 days.

Comments: *A. t. leucotis* is listed by Zhang et al. (1997) as occurring in China, although Pocock (1933) limited the distribution to S Myanmar. Zhang et al. also included *A. t. major*, found elsewhere in S Thailand. Most likely, these subspecies are not represented in China. Wroughton's *A. t. millsi*, found elsewhere in N Indochina, would be the logical choice for S Yunnan populations. Corbet and Hill

(1992) took a different approach and only recognized three subspecies: *leucotis* (Indochina); *trivirgata* (Malaya, Sumatra, and Borneo); and *trilineata* (Java).
Conservation Status: Probably extinct in China. China RL—NA.
References: Corbet and Hill (1992); Duckworth et al. (1999); Lekagul and McNeely (1977); Pocock (1933); Sheng et al. (1999); Wang (1998); Zhang et al. (1997).

Genus *Paguma* (monotypic)

花面狸属 Huamianli Shu

Masked Palm Civet

PLATE 43
Paguma larvata (Hamilton-Smith, 1827) MAP 461
花面狸 Hua Mian Li

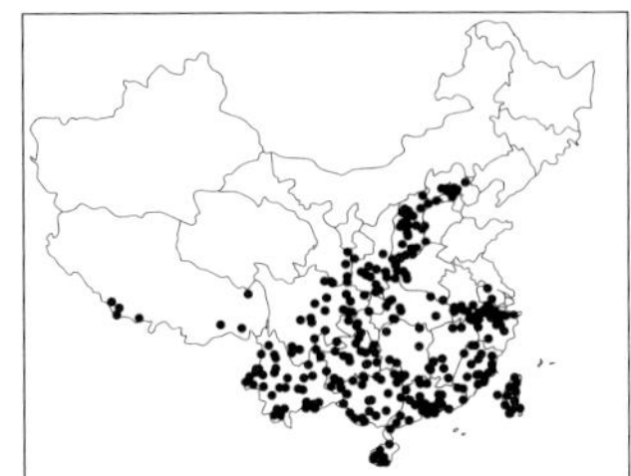

MAP 461. MASKED PALM CIVET, *Paguma larvata*

Distinctive Characteristics: HB 400–690; T 350–600; HF 65–120; E 40–60; GLS 100–130; Wt 3–7 kg. The distinctive face mask of the Masked Palm Civet varies geographically but usually consists of a medial longitudinal stripe from the forehead to the rhinarium, a small white or pale eyespot below the eye, and a larger, more distinctive white patch above the eye that may extend to the base of the ear. The rostrum is black. There are no traces of spots on the body and the guard hairs are rusty brown to dark brown, with the underwool generally light brown to gray. In some young juveniles, a faint spotting pattern can be detected. The tail is the same color as the body, with the distalmost portion often dark. Females, which have two pairs of mammae, are slightly larger than males.

The Masked Palm Civet skull is, in some respects, intermediate between the Binturong and the Common Palm Civet. The frontal sinus is expanded, but not to the extent seen in the Binturong. In the Masked Palm Civet, the postorbital constriction is equal in width to the intraorbital breadth, and the supraorbital processes are small. The upper incisors are not tightly packed. The teeth are rounded and not as spatulate as in the Common Palm Civet. The canines are straight and laterally compressed. P1 is simple and often lost in old adults. P2 and P3 are single cusped without lingual lobes. P4 has the protocone slightly posterior to the parastyle, but not as posterior as in the Binturong, and the protocone lobe is rounded with a wide posterolingual cingulum.
Distribution: Widespread across SE China; extending to Bangladesh, Myanmar, Cambodia, India (and S Andaman islands), Indonesia (Kalimantan, Sumatra), Japan (introduced), Laos, Malaysia (Sabah, Sarawak, West), Nepal, Pakistan, Singapore, Thailand, Vietnam. Five subspecies in China: (1) *P. l. grayi* (Bennett, 1835); S Xizang (includes *lanigera* (Hodgson, 1836); *nipalensis* (Hodgson, 1836)); (2) *P. l. hainana* Thomas, 1909; Hainan; (3) *P. l. intrudens* Wroughton, 1910; SW Guangxi, S Guizhou, SW Sichuan, E. Xizang, Yunnan (includes *chichingensis* Wang, in Peng and Wang, 1981; *vagans* Kloss, 1919; *yunalis* Thomas, 1921); (4) *P. l. larvata* (Hamilton-Smith, 1827); Anhui, Beijing, Fujian, Guangdong, Guangxi, Jiangxi, Hebei, Hubei, N Hunan, Shanghai, Shaanxi, Shanxi, Sichuan, Zhejiang (includes *rivalis* Thomas, 1921, *reevesi* Matschie, 1907); (5) *P. l. taivana* Swinhoe, 1862; Taiwan.
Natural History: Masked Palm Civets can be found in a variety of forest habitats, from primary growth evergreen to second-growth deciduous forest, and they frequent agricultural areas. They eat mostly fruits but will also eat birds, rodents, insects, and roots. They will attack chickens and waterfowl in farmland. They are arboreal, solitary, and nocturnal and spend the daytime sleeping in a den in a tree. They dwell in burrows and live in small family groups of 2–10. They have a home range of around 3.7 km^2. The litter size varies from one to five, with a gestation of 70–90 days. They are sexually mature at one year.
Comments: There is much confusion as to the subspecies of *Paguma* in the SW plateau region of China. Five subspecies have been described for this geographically complex region, and most of the characteristics used to differentiate the subspecies do not hold when a larger series of specimens is examined. We have tentatively placed *lanigera* (Hodgson, 1836) within *grayi*, as the only known specimen is "an imperfect, no doubt immature skin, without skull." Most of the SW plateau specimens are tentatively placed in *intrudens* Wroughton, 1910, as the principal differences appear to be individually variable. Wang (2003) separated Shanghai, Anhui, Hubei, Hunan, Sichuan, Shaanxi, Shanxi, Hebei, and Beijing forms into *P. l. reevesi*. Any assignment of subspecies in this region must be viewed as tentative.
Conservation Status: China RL—NT; although it nearly met the criteria for VU A2cd + 3cd.
References: Rabinowitz (1991); Wang (2003).

Genus *Paradoxurus*—Palm Civets

椰子狸属 Yezili Shu—椰子狸 Yezili

Paradoxurus contains three species, of which only one occurs in China.

Common Palm Civet

PLATE 43
Paradoxurus hermaphroditus (Pallas, 1777) MAP 462
椰子狸 Ye Zi Li
Distinctive Characteristics: HB 470–570; T 470–560; HF 67–85; E 42–58; GLS 90–118; Wt 2.4–4 kg. The Common Palm Civet is similar in size to the domestic cat, with the tail about equal to the HB length. The pelage contains at least five rows of spots; however,

the spots are indistinct and usually lost in adults and in some geographical subspecies. The color is mostly light brown, with several dark brown long stripes on back; sides with spots; white spots on face; most of the tail is black (although there may be faint traces of tail rings). The feet are also black. There are three pairs of mammae.

The skull has a long rostrum with a tightly constricted intraorbital region. The postorbital constriction is usually narrower than the intraorbital constriction. P4 has a blunt shearing edge and a broad posterior cingulum. M2, although rounded and modified from the primitive condition, still retains the trigon basin. Dental formula: 3.1.4.2/3.1.4.2 = 40.

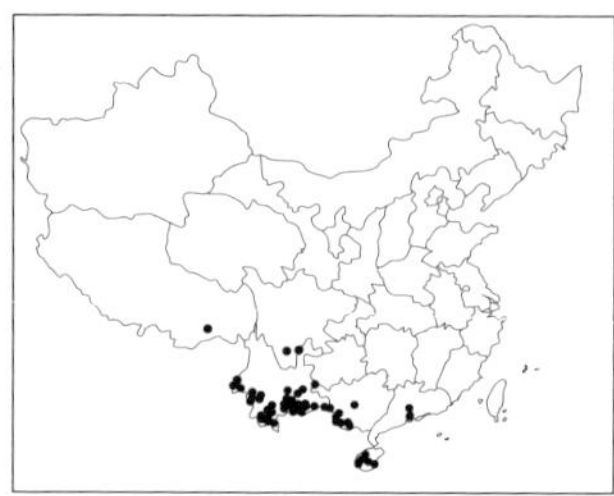

MAP 462. COMMON PALM CIVET, *Paradoxurus hermaphroditus*

Distribution: S China; extending to Bhutan, Myanmar, Cambodia, India, Indonesia, Laos, Malaysia, Nepal, New Guinea, Philippines, Singapore, Sri Lanka, Thailand, Vietnam; scattered records in Sulawesi, Moluccas, and Aru islands, probably resulting from introductions. Four subspecies in China: (1) *P. h. dongfangensis* Corbet, 1992; Hainan Island; (2) *P. h. exitus* Schwarz, 1911; Guangdong (extirpated); (3) *P. h. laotum* Gyldenstolpe, 1917; Guangdong, Guangxi, Sichuan, Yunnan, Xizang (includes *birmanicus* Wroughton, 1917); (4) *P. h. pallasii* Gray, 1832; W Yunnan (includes *nigrifons* Gray, 1864; *prehensilis* Desmarest, 1820 [preoccupied]; *quadriscriptus* Horsfield (Hodgson, 1855 MS); *strictus* Wroughton, 1917; *vicinus* Schwarz, 1910).

Natural History: Common Palm Civets are found in montane, tropical, and subtropical forests. They are also abundant in second growth and plantations (coconut, coffee, mango, pineapple, bananas). One study reported a home range of 17 km^2 and a daily movement of 1 km; there is considerable overlap of home ranges among individuals. They are nocturnal and solitary and seek out the largest trees in an area to nest. They may use the same nesting trees or holes for several days in a row. Their affinity for the fleshy hull of coffee beans and palm sap is well known. Palm sap is sometimes made into a drink called "toddy," and sometimes the Common Palm Civet is referred to as the "Toddy Cat" because of its affinity for palm sap. An expensive coffee is sometimes marketed from the beans collected from Common Palm Civet scats. It is believed that the Common Palm Civet selects the best and most ripe beans to eat; this coffee can sell for more than $100 per pound. They are opportunistic omnivores but depend heavily on nuts, berries, and fruits. Local hunters often set snares for *Paradoxurus* and *Paguma* by placing them at the bases of freshly ripe *Ficus* or palm trees. In Thailand they are known as rat-catchers around plantations. Palm Civets will also feed on small vertebrates, eggs, and insects. They are sexually mature at one year and breed year round. Average litter size is three, born after a 60-day gestation. They are considered pests to fruit and coffee plantations.

Comments: Wang (2003) separated populations from SW Guangxi and S Yunnan into the "Xishuangbanna form" and those from S Yunnan and SW Sichuan into the "Hekou form." *P. h. hainana* Wang and Xu, 1981 was recognized by Wang (2003). However, Corbet and Hill (1992) pointed out that Wang and Xu's name is preoccupied.

Conservation Status: China RL—VU A2cd+3cd.

References: Corbet and Hill (1992); Joshi et al. (1995); Rabinowitz (1991); Wang (2003).

Subfamily Prionodontinae

Genus *Prionodon*—Linsangs

灵狸亚科 Lingli Yake; 灵狸属 Lingli Shu—灵狸 Lingli

Pocock (1933) placed *Poiana* and *Prionodon* in the Prionodontinae, considered a sister group to the remaining viverrines. Although there still appears to be some uncertainty as to the relationship of *Prionodon* to the African linsang (*Poiana*), recent studies concluded that *Prionodon* should be excluded from the Viverrinae and perhaps placed in a separate family (Gaubert et al. 2004). Of the two species within the subfamily and genus, only one is represented in China.

Spotted Linsang PLATE 43
Prionodon pardicolor Hodgson, 1842 MAP 463
斑灵猫 Ban Lingmao

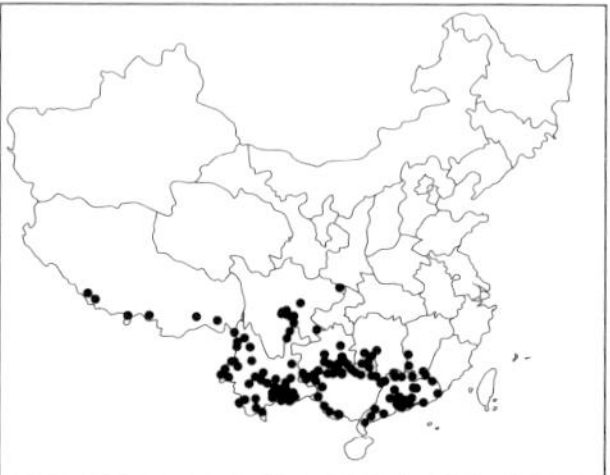

MAP 463. SPOTTED LINSANG, *Prionodon pardicolor*

Distinctive Characteristics: HB 350–400; T 300–375; HF 60–68; E 30–35; GLS 65–75; Wt 4.1–8 kg. Distinguished from all other Viverridae by the absence of the scent glands in both sexes The Spotted Linsang is the smallest viverrid in China. The only animal that this could be confused with is the Banded Linsang (*Prionodon linsang*), which does not occur in China (it occurs in Indonesia and Malaysia). The Banded Linsang is also easily distinguished externally by having broad transverse bands rather than the spots found in the Spotted Linsang. m2 length in *P. pardicolor* is greater than the length of p1; in *P. linsang*, the reverse is true. The general body form of the Spotted Linsang is distinctly slender with short limbs; thin short, and dense fur; and a very long neck. The color pattern on the sides consists of large spots with two black longitudinal stripes running down from forehead to shoulder. The ground color tends to be lighter than in the Banded Linsang, and the spots do not form transverse bands. There are two rows of spots adjacent to the middle of the back, which sometimes fuse into a mid-dorsal line near the tail. Each side of the body has three to four rows of spots. The tail is long (nearly as long as the HB), with eight to ten tail rings and a white tip. The Spotted Linsang has completely retractile claws and hairy claw sheaths.

The palate is short and does not extend over the mesopterygoids. M2 is absent; the trigonid on m1 is much longer than wide with a very reduced talonid; and m2 is modified so that it has large central cusps. Dental formula: 3.1.4.1/3.1.4.2 = 38. The Spotted Linsang is the smallest viverrid in China and can be distinguished from all other viverrids on skull size.

Distribution: S China; extending to Bhutan, Myanmar, India, Laos, Nepal, Thailand, Vietnam. Two subspecies in China: (1) *P. p. pardicolor* Hodgson, 1842; Xizang, NW Yunnan (includes *pardochrous* Gray, 1863; *perdicator* (Schinz 1844)); (2) *P. p. presina* Thomas, 1925; Guangdong, Guangxi, Guizhou, Hunan, Jiangxi, Sichuan, Yunnan.

Natural History: The Spotted Linsang prefers evergreen broadleaf rainforests, subtropical evergreen forests, and monsoon forests below 2,700 m. Linsangs have also been reported hunting in disturbed forests and forest-edge habitats. They feed mainly on small vertebrates (frogs, rodents, lizards), bird's eggs, insects and berries. They are arboreal, solitary, and nocturnal and appear to be rare throughout their range. They spend a large part of their time in the hollows of trees and will come to the ground in search of food. They breed from February to August and have an average litter size of two to four young.

Comments: The boundary between *P. p. pardicolor* and *P. p. presina* in Yunnan and Sichuan has not been well defined. Wang (2003) did not recognize subspecies.

Conservation Status: China RL—VU A2cd. China Key List—II. CITES—I.

References: Gaubert et al. (2004); Gregory and Hellman (1939); Hunt (2001); Lekagul and McNeely (1977); Lim (1973); Pocock (1933); Wang (2003).

Subfamily Viverrinae—Civet Cats

灵猫亚科 Lingmao Yake—灵猫 Lingmao

This subfamily has the widest distribution among the Viverridae, being found throughout all of Africa (excluding the Saharan region), in southern Europe (southwest of the Rhine river), from the western edge of the Indian subcontinent eastward throughout most of Southeast Asia, and north into central China (including Taiwan). Of the five genera, two occur in China.

The terrestrial civets are all nocturnal solitary foragers inhabiting dense vegetation or open woodland. They are ambush killers and occupy an ecological niche similar in certain aspects of food habits and behavior to that of some of the smaller canids (e.g., *Canis latrans*, *C. mesomelas*, *C. aureus*), the foxes (*Vulpes*), or the Procyonid coati (*Nasua*). All foraging is done on the ground, although most will climb trees when threatened. They do not form established nesting sites but live in burrows, rock crevices, or thick vegetation during the day. They are all general omnivores and eat small mammals, birds, eggs, frogs, toads, lizards, carrion, fruit, insects, and snails. Because of their opportunistic foraging, they may chance upon temporary abundant food sources such as termite mounds, carrion, or ripening fruit, upon which they will concentrate for limited periods of time.

Genus *Viverra*—Civet Cats

大灵猫属 Dalingmao Shu—大灵猫 Dalingmao

Viverra species are about the size of domestic dogs. Their general color is gray, and they have a black spinal stripe running from behind the shoulders to

Key to the Chinese Genera of Viverrinae

1.a. Dorsal crest of hair along the back at least from the shoulders; forehead wide between the anterior edges of the ears; black-and-white pattern on side of face; second and fourth toes of forelimbs with skin sheath on tip; size large. GLS > 130 mm; auditory bullae small, its length < interval between external margins of occipital condyles; alisphenoid canal present; infraorbital foramen directly above P3–P4; cerebellum part of braincase not externally constricted, low sagittal crest; rostrum long — *Viverra*

b. No dorsal crest of hair; forehead narrow between the anterior edges of the ears, which are set comparatively close together; no black-and-white pattern on side of face; feet without claw sheaths; size small; GLS < 130 mm; auditory bullae large, its length > interval between external margins of occipital condyles; alisphenoid canal absent; infraorbital foramen directly above P2–P3; cerebellum part of braincase noticeably constricted with high sagittal crest; rostrum short — *Viverricula*

Key to the Chinese Species of *Viverra*

1.a. With two black transverse stripes under neck; tail with four black rings; tail is 30–50% of HB length; toes without skin lobes protecting the claws; feet comparatively naked beneath between the pads. Vestigial or blunt supraorbital processes; mesopterygoid region wide. Length of m2 about equal to its width *Viverra megaspila*

b. With three black transverse stripes under neck; tail with six black rings; tail is 55–60% of HB length; at least the third and fourth toes of the forefoot with well-developed sheaths protecting the claws; feet thickly hairy between the pads. Sharp supraorbital processes; mesopterygoid region narrow. m2 longer than wide *Viverra zibetha*

the root of the tail. The front of the rostrum on each side has a whitish patch. The rostrum, chin, and throat are blackish. The sides and lower surface of the neck are conspicuously banded with black stripes set off by white interspaces. Tail with variable number of complete black-and-white rings; black much broader than the white.

Zygomatic arch of the skull thick; upper carnassial narrow, long and triangular; buccal margin of M1 longer than lingual margin, M2 small and elliptic; p2–p4 in lower jaw about equal in size. Dental formula: 3.1.4.2/3.1.4.2 = 40. The genus *Viverra* is distributed in southern Asia and contains four species, two of which occur in China.

Large-Spotted Civet

Viverra megaspila Blyth, 1862 MAP 464

大斑灵猫 Daban Lingmao

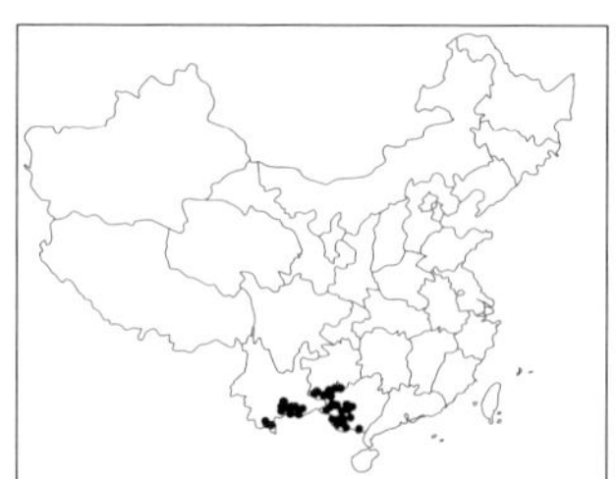

MAP 464. LARGE-SPOTTED CIVET, *Viverra megaspila*

Distinctive Characteristics: HB 770–900; T 320–400; HF 70–80; E 40–50; GLS 130–135. The Large-spotted Civet can be distinguished from the Large Indian Civet by two black neck stripes, larger spots, four black tail rings, and m_2 width approximating its length. Form and size similar to those of *Viverra zibetha*, but with two black transverse stripes under the neck; back gray-brown, a black stripe running down from shoulder to rump, with large dark brown spots on its sides; complete absence of the skin lobes on the third and fourth digits on the forefoot. The posterior portion of the body has well-defined round to quadrangular spots, which are arranged in rows and appear pale in the center of the spot. The mid-dorsal stripe is black and distinctly separate from the spots. Tail with four black rings, and the distal section of the tail is black.

Skull is similar to that of *Viverra zibetha*, but teeth are larger and mandible longer. The sagittal crest is vestigial or absent, the occipital crest being much more strongly developed. The supraorbital processes are vestigial "bumps" and do not protrude from the intraorbital region. The intraorbital and frontal regions are swollen. The rostrum is lengthened so that the supraorbital processes are approximately at the midpoint of the skull. The palate is wide and long and extends over the mesopterygoids. The trigonid on m1 is long, and the talonid is equal to it or smaller. m2 is smaller than the m1 talonid. Dental formula: 3.1.4.2/3.1.2.4 = 40.

Distribution: Guangxi, Yunnan; extending to Myanmar, Cambodia, Laos, W Malaysia, Thailand, Vietnam. Chinese subspecies: *V. m. megaspila* Blyth, 1862.

Natural History: The Large-spotted Civet has not been studied in the wild. It is believed that its natural history and diet closely resemble those of the Malabar Large-spotted Civet (*V. civettina*) and the Large Indian Civet (*V. zibetha*). It seems to prefer subtropical and monsoon forests with thick vegetation and riparian ecosystems. It is nocturnal and solitary and has not been observed in trees.

Comments: Although some have considered this civet conspecific with the Malabar Civet, their populations are widely allopatric, and the only systematic studies have placed them in separate species. The Malabar Civet lives in the Western Ghats region of India and is found in evergreen rainforests.

Conservation Status: Only eight furs have been obtained in China since the 1970s (Wang 1998). China RL—NA.

References: Bothma (1965); Ewer (1973); Kingdon (1977); Lekagul and McNeeley (1978); Maberly (1955); Prater (1981); Rand (1935); Rosevear (1974); Wang (1998).

Large Indian Civet

Viverra zibetha Linnaeus, 1758 PLATE 43 MAP 465

大灵猫 Da Lingmao

Distinctive Characteristics: HB 500–950; T 380–590; HF 90–145; E 35–65; GLS 135–150; Wt 3.4–9.2 kg. The Large Indian Civet can be distinguished from the Large Spotted Civet by three black neck stripes, absence of large spots, seven to nine black tail rings, and m2 width greater than length. The Large Indian Civet is the largest terrestrial civet in Asia. The ground color is gray to gray-brown, with numerous black spots on the body and legs. The facial region is unmarked except for a small dorsal eyespot and a large white rhinarial patch. The neck stripes on this civet have the most contrast of any civet. The two broad, pure white bands reach from ear to ear around the throat, and these are surrounded by broad black bands. There is a black mid-dorsal stripe that runs from the back of the external pinnae to the base of the tail. The four to seven black tail rings are separated by smaller, complete white rings. The third and fourth digits of the manus have protecting claw sheaths (absent from the pes).

The skull has a sagittal crest that starts at the postorbital constriction and becomes somewhat higher at the junction with the occipital crest. The supraorbital processes are blunt and small and are located in the anterior half of the skull. The metastyle of P4 is rotated to be more parallel to the midline than in other members of the genus. The protocone of P4 is greatly reduced and forms part of the shearing blade. m1 has a trigonid that is longer than wide with a reduced metaconid that is approximately at the same level as the talonid. The talonid of m1 is long and approximately equal in length to the length of m2.

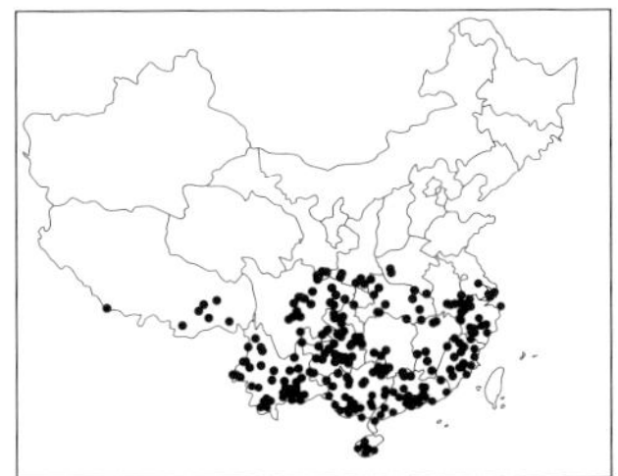

MAP 465. LARGE INDIAN CIVET, *Viverra zibetha*

Distribution: Widespread throughout C and SE China; extending to Myanmar, Cambodia, India, Indonesia, Laos, W Malaysia, Nepal, Thailand, and Vietnam. Four subspecies in China: (1) *V. z. ashtoni* Swinhoe, 1864; Anhui, Fujian, Gansu, Guangdong, Guangxi, Guizhou, Hubei, Hunan, Jiangsu, Jiangxi, Shaanxi, Sichuan, N Yunnan, Zhejiang (includes *expectata* Corbert and Hooijer, 1953; *filchneri* Matschie, 1907); (2) *V. z. hainana* Wang and Xu, 1983; Hainan Island; (3) *V. z. picta* Wroughton, 1915; SW Guangxi, SW Guizhou, Xizang, Yunnan (includes *surdaster* Thomas, 1927; *tainguensis* Sokolov et al., 1997); (4) *V. z. zibetha* Linnaeus, 1758; S Xizang (includes *civettoides* Hodgson, 1842; *melanurus* Hodgson, 1842; *orientalis* Hodgson, 1842; *undulata* Gray, 1830).

Natural History: Large Indian Civets are found in forests, scrub, and agricultural lands. They are mostly carnivorous and will eat birds, frogs, snakes, small mammals, eggs, crabs, fish, fruit, and roots. They are solitary and nocturnal. Although they spend most of their time on the ground, they can climb in search of food. They spend much of their time during the day sleeping in burrows that have been dug by other animals and abandoned. They are territorial and mark their territories with excretions from their anal glands. One Thai study reported a home range of 12 km^2 and a daily movement of 1.7 km. They are often found adjacent to villages and agricultural areas. Like *Viverricula*, this civet has been used as a source of civetone, an oil-like substance secreted by the perineal gland. Civetone has been used in the production of perfume for centuries. They are more active during the day than most civets. Large Indian Civets are aseasonal breeders and can have two litters a year of one to five young.

Comments: Specimens along the Xizang-Nepal border should be considered as *V. z. zibetha*.

Conservation Status: Formerly abundant in China, but since the 1950s the population has declined in most areas by 94–99%. Based on the rate of decline, the total population is probably around 3,000 (Wang 1998). China RL—EN A2acd. China Key List—II.

References: Prater (1988); Rabinowitz (1991); Wang (1998).

Genus *Viverricula* (monotypic)

小灵猫属 Xiaolingmao Shu

Small Indian Civet

PLATE 43
MAP 466

Viverricula indica Desmarest, 1817

小灵猫 Xiao Lingmao

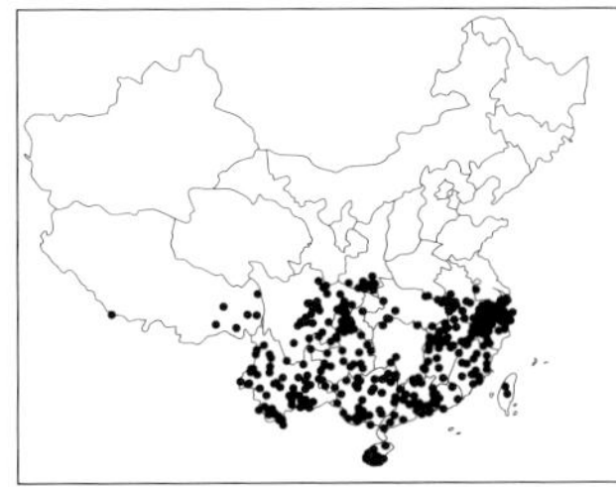

MAP 466. SMALL INDIAN CIVET, *Viverricula indica*

Distinctive Characteristics: HB 500–610; T 280–390; HF 65–120; E 25–43; GLS 90–105; Wt 1.6–4 kg. The body hair is short, coarse, and dense and lacks an erectile dorsal hair crest. The head is small with a short, acutely pointed muzzle and large, rounded external pinnae. Because of the narrow skull, the external pinnae are close set on top of the head. The ground color is gray to brown with dark brown or black feet. The lateral neck stripes are not as pronounced as in *Viverra*. The two black stripes are very narrow and not always clearly separated from the body spotting pattern. The mid-dorsal line is black and there are four to five rows of small spots on each side. The spots run together toward the midline and are more distinct ventrally. The tail has six to nine complete black tail rings, and the tip is usually white. There are no skin lobes over the semiretractile claws. The interdigital webbing is extensive and sparsely covered with hair. There are three pairs of mammae. The skull has a short rostrum and the rostral extensions of the maxilla are concave. The infraorbital

foramen is located above the P2–P3 diastema. There is no alisphenoid canal. The cerebellum portion of the cranium is restricted and externally distinct from the cerebrum portion. The sagittal crest over the cerebellum is high. The m_1 trigonid is longer than wide and much longer than the talonid. 2N = 36.
Distribution: Widespread throughout C and SE China; extending from Yemen and Afghanistan to the Malay Peninsula and Indonesia; also found on many islands in SE Asia (many of these populations have been introduced). Four subspecies in China: (1) *V. i. malaccensis* (Gmelin, 1788); Hainan Island; (2) *V. i. pallida* (Gray, 1831); Anhui, Fujian, Guangdong, Guangxi, Guizhou, Hubei, Hunan, S Jiangsu, Jiangxi, Shaanxi, Sichuan, Yunnan, Zhejiang (includes *hanensis* Matschie, 1907); (3) *V. i. taivana* Schwarz, 1911; Taiwan; (4) *V. i. thai* Kloss, 1919; Guizhou, S Yunnan.
Natural History: The Small Indian Civet is found in grassland and scrub, but also often in agricultural areas and near villages. This civet will feed on rats, squirrels, small birds, lizards, insects, grubs, and fruit. If given the opportunity they will eat domestic poultry. They are solitary and nocturnal, although they will occasionally hunt by day. They prefer to seek for food on the ground, though they can climb trees with agility. They dig readily and prefer to sleep in burrows. They are aseasonal breeders, with the average litter size two to five. A Thai study reported a home range of 3.1 km^2. The Small Indian Civet is often kept in captivity for the purpose of harvesting the secretion of the perineal gland. This yellowish fluid can be collected by scooping out the gland. The secretion has been used as the basis of perfume for centuries.
Comments: Wang (2003) proposed *V. i. peni* for the SW and W Yunnan populations but did not give a valid description. The subspecies status for Taiwan and Hainan is provisional. Allen (1929) believed Hainan animals were smaller in size and more grayish in color than mainland Chinese forms, although Pocock (1933) could not support this distinction. Zhang et al. (1997) considered Hainan populations in *malaccensis* (followed here), whereas Wang (2003) listed Taiwan and Hainan populations in *taivana*, but this is unlikely unless mainland forms are included as well. Pocock (1933) and others considered Taiwan populations to be *pallida* because Schwarz's skin characters could not be used to unambiguously separate Taiwanese from S Chinese specimens. We have provisionally chosen to keep insular populations as separate subspecies.
Conservation Status: China RL—VU A2cd. China Key List—II.
References: Allen (1929); Ellerman and Morrison-Scott (1951); Pocock (1933); Rabinowitz (1991); Wang (1998); Wozencraft (2005); Zhang et al. (1997).

Family Herpestidae—Mongooses

獴亚科 Meng Yake—獴类 Menglei

Once considered a subfamily of the Viverridae, the mongooses are now generally separated into their own family (Wozencraft 2005). They are small carnivores with grizzled fur and a long, tapering tail. They are terrestrial in nature and have nonretractile claws. They are distributed throughout Asia and Africa. Some species are famous for their rat-catching abilities and have been introduced throughout the world in the hope of controlling populations of *Rattus*. This has always had disastrous effect on the ecosystem, especially on ground-nesting birds. This is a large family represented by 14 genera; of these only 1 genus and 2 species are found in China.

Genus *Herpestes*—Mongooses

獴属 Meng Shu—獴类 Menglei

Herpestes are small, weasel-like animals with grizzled fur, conical heads, and short ears without ear bursa. The rounded ears do not protrude above the head profile. They have a well-developed anal sac around the anus and in some species can squirt this secretion in defense. Mongooses have the general form of a slender animal with a pointed head, short rounded ears, and short legs with a long, tapering tail. Except for distinguishing features around the throat, they are generally of one color. Mongooses, at quick glance, have a general appearance similar to some weasels of the family Mustelidae. The skin can be distinguished from that of typical viverrids by the lack of spots or stripes or facial masks, and the lack of protruding ears. Their skull can be distinguished from a viverrid skull by its shortened rostrum, postorbital bar, and the uniquely shaped auditory bullae. The auditory bullae have nearly equal inflated ectotympanic and

Key to the Chinese Species of *Herpestes*

1.a. Size small; HB length < 400 mm; monocolored without spots or stripes; tail more than 66% of HB length; legs the same color as body. Ectotympanic portion of bullae larger than entotympanic portion; length of mesopterygoid portion of palate longer than wide; intraorbital constriction about equal to postorbital constriction; GLS < 80 mm — *Herpestes javanicus*

b. Size large; HB length > 400 mm; cheek with a white longitudinal stripe that goes to the shoulder; tail less than 66% of HB length; legs darker than body color. Ectotympanic portion of bullae smaller than entotympanic portion; length of mesopterygoid portion of palate wider than long; intraorbital constriction usually greater than postorbital constriction; GLS > 80 mm — *Herpestes urva*

entotympanic portions that are clearly separated by a line perpendicular to the skull's midline.

Terrestrial in nature, all are very poor tree climbers, and all can swim well when forced to do so. The Crab-eating Mongoose spends more time in the water than most and can be considered semiaquatic. The genus *Herpestes* is widely distributed in tropical and subtropical areas of Asia and contains 10 species, 2 of which occur in China. Some authors have included African mongooses in this genus, herein they are separated following Wozencraft (2005).

Small Indian Mongoose

PLATE 47

Herpestes javanicus

Geoffroy Saint-Hilaire, 1818

MAP 467

红颊獴—Hongjia Meng

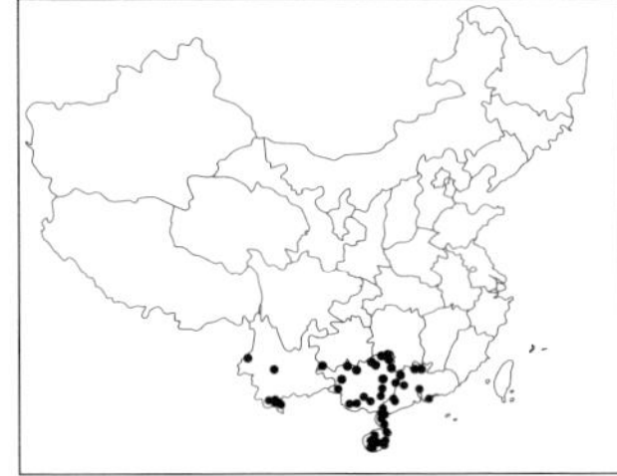

MAP 467. SMALL INDIAN MONGOOSE, *Herpestes javanicus*

Distinctive Characteristics: HB 250–370; T 240–270; HF 50–65; E 12–27; GLS 66–77; Wt 0.6–1.2 kg. The Small Indian Mongoose is the smallest mongoose in Asia. Form small and slender; back, limbs, and tail all brownish gray; ventral surface chestnut. It can be distinguished from the Crab-eating Mongoose by body and skull size. Tail length about equal to HB length; no distinctive tail tip. The skull is narrow and with a short rostrum; postorbital constriction is less than the intraorbital constriction; postorbtial processes usually forming a postorbital bar; hammular processes of the pterygoid extend posterior to the postglenoid process; P3 with lingual cusp; upper incisors in a straight line; width of toothrow < 25 mm; M1 width < 7 mm. Dental formula: 3.1.4.2/3.1.4.2 = 40.

Distribution: SE China; extending to Afghanistan, Bangladesh, Bhutan, Myanmar, Cambodia, India, Indonesia, Malaysia, Nepal, Pakistan, Thailand, and Vietnam, and widely introduced worldwide. Two subspecies in China: (1) *H. j. auropunctatus* Hodgson, 1836; W Yunnan (includes *birmanicus* Thomas, 1886; *nepalensis* Gray, 1837); (2) *H. j. rubrifrons* Allen, 1909; Guangdong, Guangxi, Hainan.

Natural History: Often found in dry forests, grasslands, and secondary scrub forests; also around human habitation and agricultural areas. It digs and lives in burrows, hedgerows, thickets, groves of trees, and cultivated fields. Several large field studies have revealed the Small Indian Mongoose to be primarily an insectivore, though it also feeds opportunistically on small vertebrates. An early field study of the amount and type of food eaten by a mongoose was done on the island of Trinidad. In this study, the nature of their foodstuffs depended largely on the opportunities available. An examination of the stomachs of 180 individuals revealed (in order of occurrence) grasshoppers, beetles, spiders, miscellaneous insects, rodents, birds, snakes, lizards, frogs, centipedes, fish, and fruit. Small Indian Mongooses are diurnal animals. Contrary to popular belief, mongooses are not immune to snake venom; instead, they rely on their skill, agility, and thick fur to avoid being bitten. However, the Small Indian Mongoose appears to be highly resistant to cobra venom. The Small Indian Mongoose is easily tamed and is often kept as a pet and a destroyer of household vermin. It lives in holes burrowed by itself in bushes, hedges, and cultivated fields. It is a cautious diurnal creature that generally remains around cover. Aseasonal breeders, they have a gestation of 50 days, with litter size averaging between two and six. They usually have one litter a year and are sexually mature at 6–12 months.

Comments: Eastern Asian subspecies can be distinguished from the Indian subcontinent subspecies based on a phenetic analysis of skull measurements (Taylor and Matheson 1999). Wang (2003) proposed *H. j. nerubrifons* for S Yunnan populations, but he did not provide a valid description. If this form proves to be distinct from *rubrifrons*, then it may represent *H. j. exilis* Eydoux, 1841, found throughout Indochina.

Conservation Status: China RL—VU A1cd.

References: Bechthold (1939); Cavallini and Serafini (1995); Hinton and Dunn (1967); Lekagul and McNeeley (1977); Pocock (1941); Taylor and Matheson (1999); Wang (2003); Williams (1918); Wozencraft (1993; 2005).

Crab-Eating Mongoose

PLATE 47

Herpestes urva (Hodgson, 1836)

MAP 468

食蟹獴 Shixie Meng

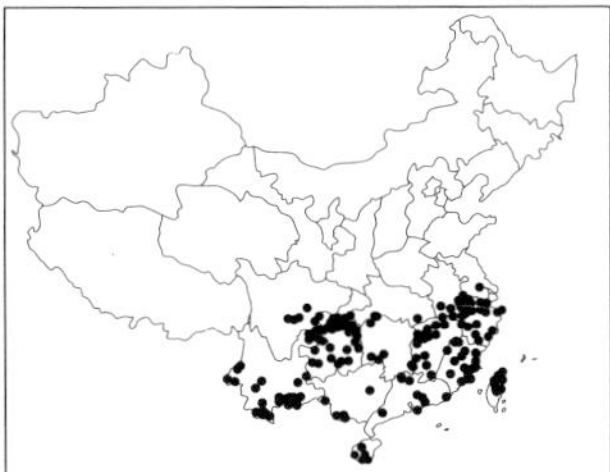

MAP 468. CRAB-EATING MONGOOSE, *Herpestes urva*

Distinctive Characteristics: HB 360–520; T 240–336; HF 80–102; E 20–30; GLS 88–100; Wt 1–2.3 kg. Size larger than *Herpestes javanicus*. Fur is long, coarse, and somewhat ragged; wool underfur dark brown at the base and pale brownish yellow at the tips. Back is gray, mixed with yellowy white color; two white longitudinal striations on the region from cheek to shoulder; all four legs dark brown. Tail-tip pale; tail short, length up to 2/3 HB length. Skull robust with short rostrum; postorbital processes usually complete;

hammular processes of the pterygoid extend about even to the postglenoid process; toothrow width > 30 mm; teeth robust; P3 with lingual cusp; upper incisors in a slightly curved line; M1 width > 8 mm.
Distribution: Widely distributed in SE China; extending to Myanmar, India, Laos, Malaysia, Nepal, Thailand, Vietnam. Two subspecies in China: (1) *H. u. formosanus* Bechthold, 1936; Taiwan; (2) *H. u. sinensis* Bechthold, 1936; Anhui, Fujian, Guangdong, Guangxi, Guizhou, Hainan, Hunan, Jiangsu, Jiangxi, Sichuan, Yunnan, Zhejiang (includes *hanensis* (Matschie, 1907)).
Natural History: Very little is known about the Crab-eating Mongoose. Commonly found in evergreen forests near streams and terraced rice fields at low altitudes. In Laos there are reports from more mountainous areas. More aquatic than most species, it is an expert swimmer and diver. It feeds mainly on frogs, fish, and crabs and hunts along the banks of streams. Despite its name, its food habits have never been extensively studied, and it is unknown how important crabs are to its diet. Recent records indicate that it is crepuscular and diurnal. Normally solitary, it can squirt out a fetid fluid from its anal gland as a means of defense.
Comments: Several authors have not recognized subspecies because they could not find distinctive skin characteristics to separate populations across its range.
Conservation Status: China RL—NT; although it nearly met the criteria for VU A1cd.
References: Pocock (1941); Wang (2003).

Suborder Caniformia—Doglike Carnivores

犬亚目 Quan Yamu—犬 Quan

This suborder includes nine families, six of which—the dogs (Canidae), bears (Ursidae), eared seals (Otariidae), earless seals (Phocidae), Red Panda (Ailuridae), and weasels (Mustelidae)—are found in China. Not found in China are the raccoons (Procyonidae), Walrus (Odobenidae), and skunks (Mephitidae). The caniformes are principally united on morphological and molecular characteristics (see key above).

Family Canidae—Canids

犬科 Quan Ke—犬 Quan

Medium-sized carnivores with a long rostrum; limbs are slender and adapted for fast running; digitigrade stance with nonretractile claws. The forefoot has five digits, but the pollex is small and set high above the rest; four digits on pes. Rostrum relatively long; paroccipital processes are applied to the auditory bullae; postpalatine foramina are situated on the maxilla-palatine suture; mesopterygoid palate absent; M1 wider than long; canines large. Dental formula: usually 3.1.4.2/3.1.4.3 = 42.

Olfaction and auditory senses well developed; lives on animal foods, but also usually eats plants. This order presently contains 13 genera and 35 species—4 genera and 6 species occur in China. Wild species of this family are distributed widely in China except for Taiwan and Hainan. They inhabit the mountains, forest regions, deserts, and grasslands. The conservation status of the Canidae has been reviewed by Sillero-Zubiri et al. (2004).

Genus *Canis*—Dogs and Wolves

犬属 Quan Shu—犬，狼 Quan, Lang

The genus *Canis* includes animals that are strong and vigorous and similar in appearance to the domestic dog (included in this genus). Their front shoulder and head are held relatively high; ears are upstanding, and tail extents to about 66% the HB length. These are the largest representatives of the Canidae. Dental formula: 3.1.4.2/3.1.4.3 = 42. The distribution of this genus extends nearly all over the world and contains six species. Only one wild species occurs in China, although the Golden Jackal (*C. aureus indicus*) is reported from several localities directly adjacent to the southern Chinese border (Nepal, Sikkim, Bhutan, N Myanmar, N Thailand).

Wolf

PLATE 44
MAP 469

Canis lupus Linnaeus, 1758
狼 Lang

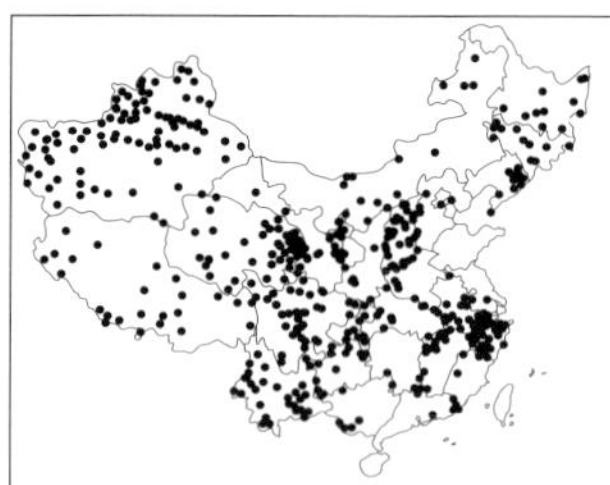

MAP 469. WOLF, *Canis lupus*

Distinctive Characteristics: HB 1,000–1,600; T 330–550; HF 200–250; E 90–120; GLS 214–250; Wt 28–40 kg. The wolf is the largest species of the Canidae. The common dog was domesticated from this form and is considered the same species. Color generally grayish yellow, brownish gray, or grizzled gray, but varies widely. The winter coat can conserve body heat so well that wolves can function below −40°C. Wolves are characterized by relatively thin bodies on long legs with a long rostrum and forward-pointing ears and eyes. The baculum is pointed, with a ventral groove. The skull has an orbital angle of 40°–45° as compared to 53°–60° in domestic dogs; nasals depressed along entire length; M1 cingulum with a noticeable gap. Dental formula: 3.1.4.2/3.1.4.3 = 42. Not easily confused with other canids; only wolves have a condylobasal length > 200 mm; P4 length > 20 mm;

Key to the Chinese Families of Caniformia

1.a. Feet modified into flippers; aquatic. Lacrimal foramen absent; posterior lacerate foramen greatly enlarged. Teeth nearly homodont; i3 absent; all teeth with one or two roots 5

b. Feet not modified into flippers; plantigrade or digitigrade; terrestrial, arboreal, aquatic and semiaquatic. Lacrimal foramen present. Teeth complex, many with accessory cusps; i3 present; all teeth with one to four roots 2

2.a. Five well-developed toes on each foot, plantigrade. Toothrows parallel; auditory bullae flat or only moderately inflated; lacrimal greatly reduced in size and confined within the orbital rim; posterior lacerate foramen enlarged; low ridge of bone connecting the paroccipital process with the mastoid process; postglenoid foramen large. M1-2 enlarged and quadrate with the development of a hypocone and accessory cusps 3

b. Hind foot usually with four or five toes; digitigrade. Toothrows divergent; auditory bullae inflated; lacrimal not reduced and participates in the orbital rim; posterior lacerate foramen not enlarged; paroccipital and mastoid process not connected by ridge of bone; postglenoid foramen not enlarged. M1-2 not quadrate without hypocone and accessory cusps 4

3.a. Tail much shorter than hind foot; no stripes; rostrum and ear color similar to ground color; rostrum long. Palate flat and not grooved medially. P1-3 rudimentary, often lost in old animals; P4 without hypocone; the P4 paracone is located about the middle of the lingual tooth length Ursidae

b. Tail much longer than hind foot, marked with stripes; rostrum and ears white and distinctly set off from reddish ground color; rostrum short. Palate highly arched and grooved medially; alisphenoid canal present. P3 strong with well-developed paracone and hypocone, P4 with a well-developed hypocone; the P4 paracone is located at the anterior-lingual border of the tooth Ailuridae

4.a. Head round, ears do not protrude much, if any beyond head profile; legs dramatically short for body length; manus and pes always five; digitigrade, plantigrade, and semiplantigrade; anal glands well developed into scent glands that can emit fluid; baculum long and hooked. Postglenoid process long and wraps around mandibular condyle; alisphenoid canal absent; stylomastoid foramen double. M2 absent; P4 without carnassial notch; M1 often in hourglass shape; m1 without bicuspid talonid Mustelidae

b. Head elongated, ears long and pointed and protrude above head profile; legs long for body length; pes always four; digitigrade; anal glands not well developed; grooved baculum. Postglenoid process long but does not wrap around mandibular condyle; alisphenoid canal present; stylomastoid foramen single. M2 present; P4 with carnassial notch; M1 never in hourglass shape; m1 with a bicuspid talonid Canidae

5.a. Small external pinnae; tail distinct and free; males much larger than females; can support body on front legs; testes scrotal; brown. Auditory bullae flat, not inflated; tooth rows parallel; alisphenoid canal present; frontal bones project anteriorly between the nasal bones; mastoid fused to jugular process; supraorbital processes present; jugal-squamosal joint overlapping. I1-2 transversely notched Otariidae

b. External ear pinnae absent; tail enclosed in a web of skin; males about the same size as females; cannot support body on front legs; testes abdominal; brown or spotted or ringed. Auditory bullae inflated; diverging tooth rows; alisphenoid canal absent; nasal bones project posteriorly between the frontal bones; mastoid not fused to jugular process; supraorbital processes absent; jugal-squamosal joint interlocking. I1–2 not notched Phocidae

large M2 (length × width of M2 exceeds 100 mm^2 only in *Canis lupus*).

Distribution: Wolves have been recorded across China, and the largest populations are in NE China. It is still widely distributed in China except for Taiwan, Hainan, and Shandong. This species was formerly widely distributed in Europe, Asia, and America. Four subspecies in China, although there is some confusion as to the correct placement of subspecies (see Comments): (1) *C. l. campestris* Dwigubski, 1804; Xinjiang (includes *bactrianus* Laptev, 1929; *cubanenesis* Ognev, 1923; *desertorum* Bogdanov, 1882); (2) *C. l. chanco* Gray, 1863; Anhui, Beijing, Fujian, Gansu, Guangdong, Guangxi, Guizhou, Hebei, Heilongjiang, Henan, Hubei, Hunan, Jiangsu, Jiangxi, Jilin, Liaoning, E Nei Mongol, Ningxia, Qinghai, Shandong, Shaanxi, Shanxi, Sichuan, Xizang, Yunnan, Zhejiang (includes *coreanus* Abe, 1923; *dorogostaiskii* Skalon, 1936; *karanorensis* (Matschie, 1907); *niger* Sclater, 1874; *tschiliensis* (Matschie, 1907)); (3) *C. l. filchneri* (Matschie, 1907); Gansu, Qinghai, Xizang, and probably S Xinjiang (includes *ekloni* Przewalski, 1883; *laniger* (Hodgson, 1847) [preoccupied]); (4) *C. l. lupus* Linnaeus, 1758; N Xinjiang (Altai); (includes *altaicus* (Noack, 1911); *argunensis* Dybowski, 1922; *canus* de Sélys Longchamps, 1839;

Key to the Chinese Genera of Canidae

1.a. Reddish color; back of ear also reddish. Vaulted palate; zygomatic breadth > 62% of condylobasal length; sphenopalatine foramen more than 4 × posterior palatine foramen; nasals noticeably expanded in the posterior half. Only one large diastema in toothrow—between C1 and P1; m3 absent; m1 with only one cusp on talonid *Cuon*

b. Color yellowish gray or reddish yellow or brown; back of ear black or brown, darker than body. Palate flat; zygomatic breadth < 62% of condylobasal length; sphenopalatine foramen less than 3 × posterior palatine foramen; nasals not expanded in the posterior half. C1–P4 teeth spaced apart; m3 present; m1 with more than one cusp on talonid. 2

2.a. Hairs on the sides of head long, forming a ruff; cheek colored black; tail < 33% of HB length. Basal margin of dentary forms a large and rounded subangular process; maxilla-jugal suture straight; posterior margin of mesopterygoid behind posterior margin of molars. m1–p4 without overlap *Nyctereutes*

b. Hairs on the sides of head short, no ruff; cheek not black; tail > 33% of HB length. Basal margin of dentary without a conspicuous subangular process; maxilla-jugal suture V-shaped; posterior margin of mesopterygoid rostral to posterior margin of molars. m1–p4 with overlap 3

3.a. Size large; HB length > 900 mm; GLS > 200 mm. Intraorbital region distinctly ridged and swollen; rostrum relatively short and thick. P4 > 20 mm; M1 buccal cingulum with gap *Canis*

b. Size small; HB length < 900 mm; GLS < 200 mm. Intraorbital region not distinctly ridged and swollen; rostrum narrow and long. P4 < 20 mm; M1 buccal cingulum without gap *Vulpes*

communis Dwigubski, 1804; *deitanus* Cabrera, 1907; *flavus* Kerr, 1792; *fulvus* de Sélys Longchamps, 1839; *italicus* Altobello, 1921; *kurjak* Bolkay, 1925; *lycaon* Trouessart, 1910; *major* Ogérien, 1863; *minor* Ogerien, 1863; *niger* Hermann, 1804; *orientalis* (Wagner 1841); *orientalis* Dybowski, 1922; *signatus* Cabrera, 1907).

Natural History: The Wolf's habitat range is very wide, including mountainous regions, tundra, forests, plains, deserts, alpine zone, and agricultural areas. It is abundant on the Tibetan Plateau and found at very high altitudes. However, it is not found in rainforests. One of the few carnivores in China that feeds mainly on large mammals–Red Deer (*Cervus*), Roe Deer (*Capreolus*), sheep (*Ovis*)–but will also feed on small animals such as lagomorphs and marmots (*Marmota*). Most food habit studies have shown that wolves consume mostly the young, old, and other susceptible members of the prey. Highly adaptable, they will also eat fruit, game birds, fish, and large rodents. Wolves are social animals and usually run in family groups called "packs" of five to eight, or larger. They mark their territory by scent marking, scratching, and howling. The order within the pack is maintained by a dominance hierarchy centered around the alpha male and alpha female. Wolves are good swimmers and do not hesitate to swim. They travel extensively, mostly at night, within their home range, which can vary from 130 to 13,000 km^2. They are monogamous, and both parents help raise the young. The gestation period is 60–63 days, and the young are born in late spring. The normal litter size is six. Sexual maturity reached at two years of age.

Comments: This species includes the domestic dog. The widespread variability and geographic distribution has made subspecies designations tentative at best. Mech and Boitani (2004a) place all Chinese populations in *C. l. lupus*. Wang (2003) recognized five populations for China. He placed Altai/Tian Shan populations in *C. d. desertorum*. We consider *desertorum* as a junior synonym of *campestris* and have placed Altai populations in *C. l. lupus*. Ellerman and Morrison-Scott (1951) placed *desertorum*/*campestris* in *lupus*, but most have followed Novikov (1956) and kept it separate (followed herein). Wang (2003) placed populations in Qinghai, Gansu, and Xizang in *filchneri*, and populations in C and N China in *chanco*, and this arrangement is followed here. Wang also distinguished two unnamed forms from S China and Nei Mongol.

Conservation Status: Gao (1998) stated that the Wolf is now mainly restricted to NE China, Nei Mongol, and the Tibetan Plateau, with a population estimated at 6,000. China RL—VU A2abc. CITES—II.

References: Gao (1998); Mech (1974); Mech and Boitani (2004a; 2004b); Nowak (1995); Schaller (1998); Sheng et al. (1999); Wozencraft (2005).

Genus *Cuon* (monotypic)

豺属 Chai Shu—豺 Chai

Dhole

PLATE 44
MAP 470

Cuon alpinus (Pallas, 1811)

豺 Chai

Distinctive Characteristics: HB 880–1,130; T 400–500; HF 70–90; E 95–105; GLS 150–170; Wt 10–20 kg. Similar to *Canis*, but with shorter rostrum and shorter tail. Color can range from a deep red to a grayish brown or yellowish red, with white on the throat, legs, and face. Ears are large, rounded, and filled with white hair. The tail tip is almost always black and < 50% of HB length. Males and females are approximately the same size. Six or seven pairs of mammae. Skull

similar to the Wolf's, but frontal bone is low (frontal sinus not well inflated), and rostrum is shorter (toothrow width is > 75% of palatal length). M3/3 absent; only one cusp on talonid of m1; M2 small in comparison to M1 (length × width of M2 < 40mm^2). P2 and P3 have a small posterior cusp in addition to the cingulum cusp. Dental formula: 3.1.4.2 /3.1.4.2 = 40.
Distribution: Occurs across China; extending to Indonesia (Java, Sumatra), Malaysia, India, Pakistan, Indochina, Korea, Mongolia, and Russia. Five subspecies in China: (1) *C. a. adustus* Pocock, 1941; Yunnan; (2) *C. a. alpinus* (Pallas, 1811); Heilongjiang, Jilin, Liaoning, E Nei Mongol (includes *antiquus* Matthew and Granger, 1923); (3) *C. a. fumosus* Pocock, 1936; Gansu, Qinghai, Shaanxi, NW Sichuan; (4) *C. a. laniger* Pocock, 1936; Xinjiang, S Xizang (includes *grayiformis* Hodgson, 1863; *primaevus* (Hodgson, 1833)); (5) *C. a. lepturus* Heude, 1892; Anhui, Fujian, Guangdong, Guangxi, Guizhou, Hubei, Hunan, Jiangsu, Jiangxi, Zhejiang (includes *clamitans* Heude, 1892).

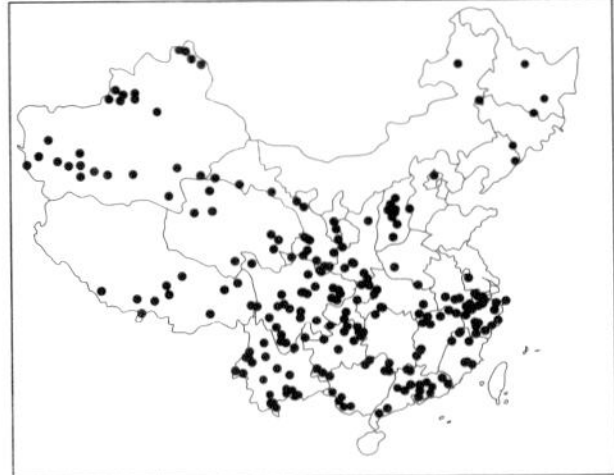

MAP 470. DHOLE, *Cuon alpinus*

Natural History: Dholes are found in nearly every habitat (except desert), from open country in Xizang to dense forests and thick scrub jungles as high as 2,100 m. Dhole packs focus on large prey and will eat Wild Boar (*Sus scrofa*), muntjacs (*Muntaicus*), Sambar (*Rusa unicolor*), wild sheep (*Ovis*), wild goat (*Capra*) small deer, rodents, and lagomorphs. They hunt in packs and can kill animals up to 10 times their own size. Dholes hunt in packs of 5–12 individuals, but groups of 40 have been reported. Dhole home range can be from 40 to 84 km^2, the size of which is determined by the availability of food and water. They are primarily diurnal and crepuscular but are occasionally active at night. In many packs that have been studied, there were twice as many males as females in the pack. The dens are usually ones that were occupied by other animals. All members of the pack care for the cubs and carry food back for them from a hunt. The gestation period is 60–62 days; births occur in spring with four to six cubs in a litter that are sexually mature in one year.
Comments: Cohen (1978) followed Afanasiev and Zolotarev (1935) and only recognized two subspecies worldwide: *alpinus* (including *javanicus*, *dukhunensis*, *primaevus*, *rutilans*, *sumatrensis*, *grayiformes*, *lepturus*, *clamitans*, *infuscus*, *laniger*, *adustus*) and *hesperius* (restricted to Russian Turkistan).

Conservation Status: China RL—EN A2abcde. China Key List—II. CITES—II. IUCN RL—VU C2a ver 2.3 (1994).
References: Cohen (1978); Davidar (1975); Durbin et al. (2004); Fox (1984); Iyengar et al. (2005); Johnsingh (1982); Venkataraman and Johnsingh (2004).

Genus *Nyctereutes* (monotypic)

貉属 He Shu

Raccoon Dog

PLATE 44
MAP 471

Nyctereutes procyonoides (Gray, 1834)

貉 He

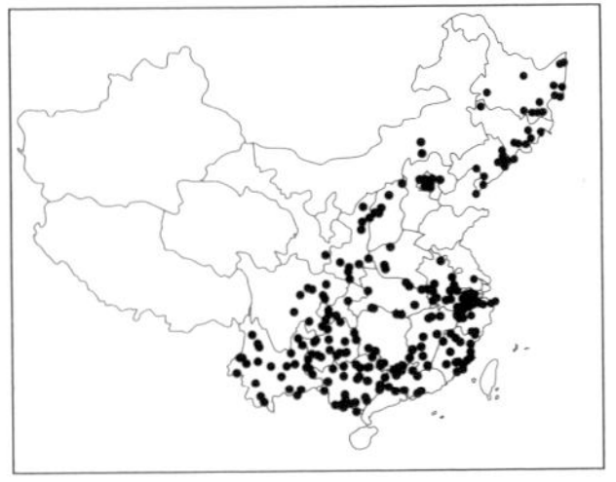

MAP 471. RACCOON DOG, *Nyctereutes procyonoides*

Distinctive Characteristics: HB 450–660; T 160–220; HF 75–120; E 35–60; GLS 100–130; Wt 3–6 kg. A small canid with disproportionally short legs, foxlike in appearance. They have a distinctive facemask like a North American Raccoon (*Procyon lotor*). The forehead and muzzle are white while the eyes are surrounded by a black ocular region. The cheeks are covered with shaggy, long hairs forming a ruff; there is a cross-shaped pattern on the anterior part of the back; chest and legs and feet are dark brown. Their general form is relatively stout, with the tail < 33% of HB and covered with shaggy hairs. Dorsal and distal hairs of tail tipped in black; dorsal hair brownish gray, mingled with black tips. Skull profile flat; sharp and sudden depression at the proximal third of the nasals; parietals rugose and with a crest closing up to the sagittal crest on posterior part of skull; adults with noticeable lambdoidal crest; distinctively large subangular process on mandible; mesopterygoid fossa extends beyond toothrows. Dental formula: 3.1.4.2/3.1.4.3 = 42.
Distribution: C, S, and E China; extending to Japan, Mongolia, North and South Korea, Russia; introduced into Europe. Three subspecies in China: (1) *N. p. orestes* Thomas, 1923; Gansu, Guizhou, Shaanxi, Sichuan, Yunnan; (2) *N. p. procyonoides* (Gray, 1834); Anhui, Fujian, Guangdong, Guangxi, Hubei, Hunan, Jiangsu, Jiangxi, Zhejiang (includes *kalininensis* Sorokin, 1958; *sinensis* Brass, 1904; *stegmanni* Matschie, 1907); (3) *N. p. ussuriensis* Matschie, 1907; Hebei, Heilongjiang, Jilin, Liaoning, E Nei Mongol (includes *amurensis* Matschie, 1907).
Natural History: Raccoon Dogs inhabit open broadleaf forests near water or open meadows, thick bushy areas, and reeds. They are seldom found in

dense forests of high mountains and are usually associated with water. Raccoon Dogs prefer to forage in woodlands with an abundant understory—especially ferns. Their diet consists of amphibian, mollusks, insects, fish, small mammals, birds and their eggs, fruit and grains. Rodents form the bulk of their diet, although they rely more heavily on plants than most canids and eat roots, stems, leaves, bulbs, berries, seeds, and nuts. They are nocturnal and solitary but sometimes live in family groups and will often forage in pairs. Home ranges vary from 5 to 10 km^2. They are the only canid that hibernates in the northern parts of their range. Raccoon Dogs use latrine sites, and a study in Japan showed that each animal used at least 10 different latrines. Raccoon Dogs are monogamous and are established as a permanent pair when mating begins in February to March. The gestation period is 59–64 days. There are 5–8 young per litter, but sometimes as many as 12.
Conservation Status: Once thought to occur widely; today it is not well known and may be in danger of local extinction. China RL—VU A2abcd.
References: Ikeda (1984; 1987); Kauhala and Saeki (2004); Kauhala et al. 1993; Novikov (1956); Ward and Wurster-Hill (1990).

Genus *Vulpes*—Foxes

狐属 Hu Shu—狐狸 Huli

These are long, slender, doglike canids with a thick tail that is > 50% of HB length. The hairs on the tail are dense and shaggy. Limbs are relatively short and usually darker than the body color. The rostrum is noticeably slender. The distance from preorbital fossa to rostrum ≥ the width between molars; postorbital process low and flat; intraorbital space wider than muzzle above the canines; upper canines slender; lower canines longer than edge of alveolus of upper canines when jaw is closed. Dental formula: 3.1.4.2 / 3.1.4.3 = 42. Widely distributed in Asia, Africa, Europe, and North America. This genus contains 12 species, 3 of which occur in China.

Corsac Fox

PLATE 44
MAP 472

Vulpes corsac (Linnaeus, 1768)
沙狐 Sha Hu

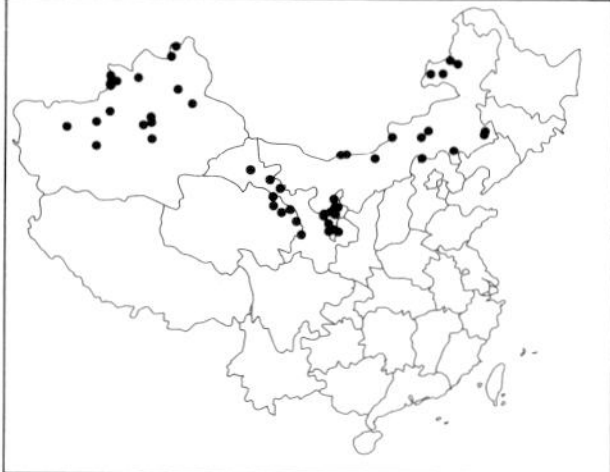

MAP 472. CORSAC FOX, *Vulpes corsac*

Distinctive Characteristics: HB 450–600; T 240–350; HF 90–120; E 50–70; GLS 95–118; Wt 1.8–2.8 kg. Smaller than *V. vulpes* but with longer legs; chest and groin white; dorsal hair brownish gray; ears short; color of the back of the ears and tail base the same as that of the back. The tail tip is black, which can be used to distinguish it from the Tibetan Fox, which has a white tail tip. Tail approximately 50% of HB length. Temporal ridges on the skull uniting posteriorly but extending forward in lyrate form; distance from front of I1 to back edge of infraorbital foramen exceeds width across molars. Upper canine scarcely or only a little exceeds combined length of P4 and M1; outer incisor is separated by a slight space.
Distribution: Found across N China; extending to N Afghanistan, Kazakhstan, Kyrgyzstan, Mongolia, Russia. Two subspecies in China: (1) *V. c. corsac* (Linnaeus, 1768); Gansu, Nei Mongol, Ningxia, Qinghai, Xinjiang (includes *corsak* Ognev, 1935; *nigra*

Key to the Chinese Species of *Vulpes*

1.a. Size small; HB length < 700 mm; tail tip black; back of ears gray. GLS < 130 mm; zygomatic width < 70 mm; distance from preorbital fossa to rostrum ≈ to width between buccal margins of molars; nasals protrude posteriorly to the level of the orbits; nasals do not extend posteriorly to the level of the maxilla's posteriormost extension; nasal suture length < 40% of condylobasal length; sagittal crests parallel/lyre shape; postorbital width > 20% of condylobasal length — *Vulpes corsac*

b. Size large; HB length > 700 mm; tail tip white; back of ears black or similar to body. GLS > 130 mm; zygomatic width > 70 mm; distance from preorbital fossa to rostrum > width between buccal margins of molars; nasals protrude posteriorly past the level of the orbits; nasals do not extend rostrally to the level of the maxilla's posteirormost extension; nasal suture length > 40% of condylobasal length; single sagittal crest; postorbital width < 20% of condylobasal length — 2

2.a. Body uniformly reddish brown; back of ears black or brown, distinct from nape. Rostrum not distinctly narrowed behind canines, mostly parallel sided; toothrow length about 1.5 times the width between buccal margins of molars — *Vulpes vulpes*

b. Body uniformly yellowish brown; back of ears similar to nape. Rostrum distinctly narrowed behind canines; toothrow length nearly twice as long as rostrum width between buccal margins of molars — *Vulpes ferrilata*

Kastschenko, 1912; *skorodumovi* Dorogostaiski, 1935); (2) *V. c. turcmenicus* Ognev, 1935; Gansu, Nei Mongol, Ningxia, Qinghai, Xinjiang.
Natural History: Inhabits open steppes and semi-deserts and does not live in forests, areas of dense brush, or cultivated lands. It is not found in mountainous regions or in areas where snow depth exceeds 150 mm. The Corsac Fox feeds chiefly on pikas (*Ochotona*), rodents, birds, insects and lizards. One study reported a percent occurrence in scats of pika (55%), vole (22%), hamster (16.5%), marmot (44%), other rodents (85%), carnivores (5.5%), other mammals (16.5%), birds (5.5%), and insects (22%). Apparently well adapted to deserts, Corsac Foxes can go without water for extensive periods of time. They live in burrows, and several individuals may share dens. Foxes may form small packs in winter and inhabit burrows abandoned by marmots. Home ranges have been reported from 1 to 3.7 km^2 in Russia. They are nocturnal in habit, and mating occurs from January to March. Gestation lasts 50–60 days, and the young are born in late spring and early summer. Females produce one litter of three to six pups per year; sexual maturity is attained at the age of two.
Comments: Wang (2003) and Poyarkov and Ovsyanikov (2004) have separated *V. c. scorodumovi* Dorogostajski, 1935, for Chinese populations, although most have placed it in *V. c. corsac* (followed here).
Conservation Status: China RL—VU A2cd. IUCN RL—DD ver 2.3 (1994).
References: Ellerman and Morrison-Scott (1951); Heptner et al. (1967a); Novikov (1956); Poyarkov and Ovsyanikov (2004); Sidorov and Botvinkin (1987); Wozencraft (2005).

Tibetan Fox

PLATE 44
MAP 473

Vulpes ferrilata Hodgson, 1842
藏狐 Zang Hu

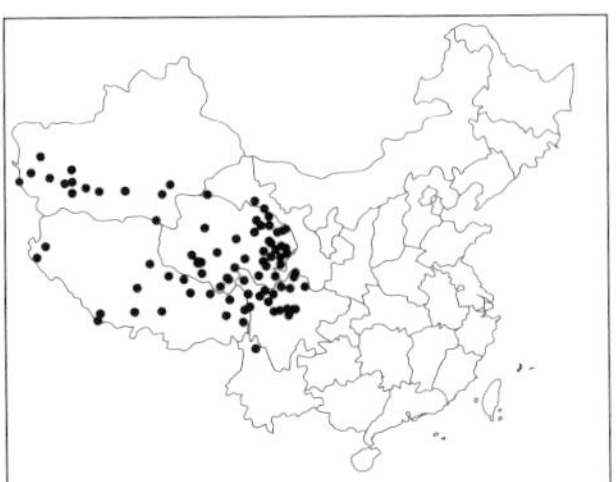
MAP 473. TIBETAN FOX, *Vulpes ferrilata*

Distinctive Characteristics: HB 490–650; T 250–300; HF 110–140; E 52–63; GLS 138–150; Wt 3.8–4.6 kg. Size similar to *V. vulpes*, but with brownish red back and white venter; body sides with grayish broad bands; distinct from back and venter. The Tibetan Fox has a conspicuously narrow reddish muzzle and reddish color on crown, neck, back, and lower legs. The backs of the small ears are tan and the insides white; undersides are whitish to light gray. The tail is bushy and gray except for a white tip. Tail < 50% of HB length. Distance from anterior margin of preorbital fossa to rostrum tip conspicuously longer than width between left and right molars. Upper canine clearly larger than combined length of P4 and M1 in upper jaw.
Distribution: Gansu, Qinghai, Sichuan, Xinjiang, Xizang; includes the form *ekloni* (Przewalski, 1883); extending to Nepal. No subspecies are recognized.
Natural History: Found in semiarid to arid areas of alpine meadow, alpine steppe, and desert steppe and hills from about 2,000 to 5,200 m. The principal diet of the Tibetan Fox consists of pikas and rodents. One study showed a percent occurrence of 95% pika (*O. curzoniae*) and small rodents (*Pitymus*, *Alticola*, *Cricetelus*); and the remainder insects, feathers, and berries (Schaller 1998). Other studies have noted lizard species (*Phrynocephalus*), hares (*Lepus oiostolus*), marmot (*Marmota himalayana*), musk deer (*Moschus* spp.), blue sheep (*Pseudois nayaur*), and livestock as prey items. They are diurnal and solitary, although they can be seen together in family groups of a mated pair with young. Tibetan Foxes are most active in the morning and evening but can be seen out during the day. Burrows are found at the base of boulders, along old beach lines, low on slopes, and at other such sites. There may be one to four entrances to a den, the entrance about 25–35 cm in diameter. Mating occurs in late February, and litters of two to five young appear in April to May.
Conservation Status: China RL—EN A4d.
References: Feng et al. (1986); Piao (1989); Schaller (1998); Schaller and Ginsberg (2004); Wang (2003); Wozencraft (2005); Wu et al. (2002); Zheng (1985).

Red Fox

PLATE 44
MAP 474

Vulpes vulpes (Linnaeus, 1758)
赤狐 Chi Hu

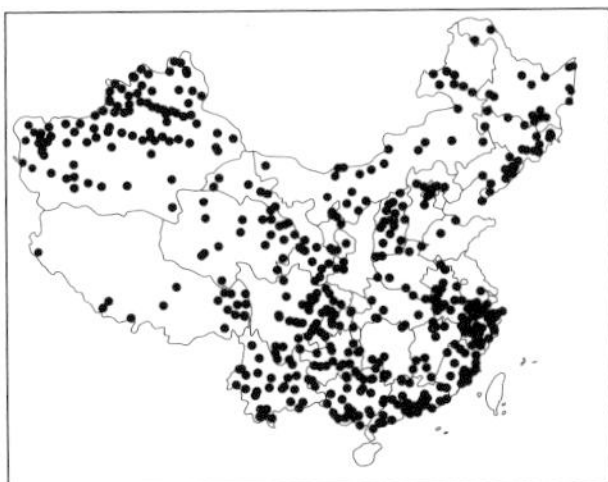
MAP 474. RED FOX, *Vulpes vulpes*

Distinctive Characteristics: HB 500–800; T 350–450; HF 115–155; E 74–102; GLS 130–150; Wt 3.6–7 kg. The largest fox in the genus, the Red Fox is usually reddish brown with long, slender black legs. The dorsal hair is normally reddish brown, with shoulders and body sides more yellowish; backs of ears are black or brown; venter is white. The color variance is very large, ranging from yellow to brown to crimson, etc. The bushy tail is 60–70% of HB length and the same color as the body, with a white tip. A 20 mm-long subcaudal gland on the upper portion of the tail gives off a foxy odor. Flat intraorbital and frontal region; postorbital processes have a well-marked

fossae on the dorsal side. Lower canines project markedly beyond alveoli of the upper canines.
Distribution: Occurs nearly all over China; distribution extends widely across Asia and Europe. Five subspecies in China: (1) *V. v. daurica* Ognev, 1931; Heilongjiang, Jilin, Liaoning, E Nei Mongol (includes *ussuriensis* Dybowski, 1922); (2) *V. v. hoole* Swinboe, 1870; Anhui, Fujian, Guangdong, Guangxi, Guizhou, S Henan, Hubei, Hunan, Jiangsu, Jiangxi, Shaanxi, Shanxi, E Sichuan, Yunnan, Zhejiang (includes *aurantioluteus* Matschie, 1907; *lineiventer* Swinhoe, 1871); (3) *V. v. karagan* (Erxleben, 1777); Gansu, C Nei Mongol, Ningxia, Qinghai, Shaanxi, N Xinjiang (includes *ferganensis* Ognev, 1926; *melanotus* (Pallas, 1811); *pamirensis* Ognev, 1926; *tarimensis* Matschie, 1907);(4) *V. v. montana* (Pearson, 1836); S Xinjiang, Xizang, NW Yunnan (includes *alopex* Blanford, 1888; *himalaicus* (Ogilby, 1837); *ladacensis* Matschie, 1907; *nepalensis* Gray, 1837; *waddelli* Bonhote, 1906); (5) *V. v. tschiliensis* Matschie, 1907; Beijing, Hebei, N Henan, Shandong (includes *huli* Sowerby, 1923).
Natural History: The Red Fox lives in all kinds of habitats, from deserts and forests to major metropolitan areas. They prefer brushy habitats with a mix of open areas and cover. They are found in semideserts, high mountain tundra, forests, and farmland. They are predators of ecotonal environments and do well in fragmented agricultural and urban areas. Their diet consists principally of small ground dwelling mammals, lagomorphs, and sciurids. Other items taken are galliformes, birds, frogs, snakes, insects, berries, and vegetables. Carrion may be seasonally important to some populations. The Red Fox is very mobile, often covering 10 km per day with nonoverlapping territories. Territories are larger in winter than in summer. Dispersal occurs in the fall, with the males generally dispersing further than females. The basic Red Fox unit is a monogamous pair, with the male helping with parental care. It is nocturnal and will cache surplus food. Mating occurs from late December to late March. The young are born from March to May. Litter size 1–10, occasionally up to 13.
Conservation Status: China RL—NT; although it nearly met the criteria for VU A2abcd.
References: Allen and Sargeant (1993); Blumstein and Robertson (1995); Catling and Burt (1995); Larivière and Pasitschniak-Arts (1996); Macdonald (1977); Macdonald and Reynolds (2004); Sheng et al. (1999); Voigt (1987); Weber and Aubry (1993).

Family Ursidae—Bears

熊科 Xiong Ke—熊 Xiong

Representatives of the bear family exceed in size all other species of the Carnivora, and they have among the largest distributions for any species. Bears are strong, possess a very short tail, have large heads with a projecting rostrum, and display relatively small eyes. They are plantigrade, with five digits on each foot. The front feet have long and inflexible claws. In the skull the auditory bullae are flat and the lacrimal foramen is double. The teeth are large and blunt; there has been an almost total loss of the shearing function of the carnassial. P4 is anterior to the infraorbital foramen and has only two roots. Dental formula: 3.1.3-4.2/3.1.3-4.3 = 38 or 42.

Bears are terrestrial and can climb trees and swim. They are generally herbivorous by nature but are also opportunists and will take advantage of nearly any source of food: carrion, small mammals, large herbivores, and fish. They are solitary and nocturnal. There are five genera and eight species of bears worldwide, three genera and four species of which occur in China. Conservation and the status of bears have been reviewed comprehensively by Servheen et al. (1999).

Key to the Chinese Genera of Ursidae

1.a. Body mainly white; with black legs; black ears, and black ocular patches. Palate does not extend posteriorly beyond the toothrow; frontal region reduced, postorbital processes vestigal; very pronounced sagittal crest; postglenoid process well developed and wraps around condylar process of mandible. P3 and P4 with three buccal cusps; P4 length > 25 mm — Ailuropoda

b. Body mostly dark brown/back; legs same color as body. Palate extends posteriorly beyond the toothrow; frontal and postorbital processes inflated; sagittal crest small or absent; postglenoid process not well developed and does not lock around condylar process of mandible; P3 with one cusp or absent. P4 with two buccal cusps; P4 length < 20 mm — 2

2.a. Size small; HB length < 1.5 m; ears short, their length about 50 mm. Auditory bulla inflated below the level of the basioccipital; mastoid processes not well developed; skull wide and short; mastoid width > palatal length; distance between P4 and C1 ≈ length of P4 — Helarctos

b. Size large; HB length > 1.5 m; ears tall, their length > 50 mm. Auditory bullae not well inflated, hardly produced below the level of the basioccipital; mastoid processes well developed; skull narrow and long; mastoid width < palatal length; distance between P4 and C1 > than length of P4 — Ursus

Genus *Ailuropoda* (monotypic)

大熊猫属 Daxiongmao Shu

Giant Panda

PLATE 45
MAP 475

Ailuropoda melanoleuca (David, 1869)
大熊猫 Da Xiong Mao

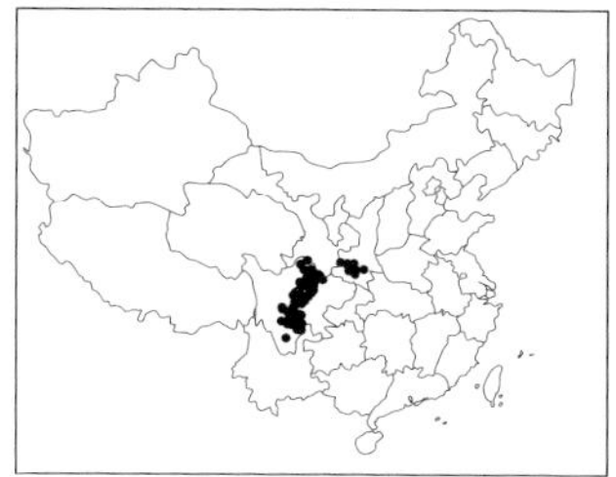

MAP 475. GIANT PANDA, *Ailuropoda melanoleuca*

Distinctive Characteristics: HB 1,500–1,800; T 120–150; HF 140–200; E 70–110; GLS 280–300; Wt 85–125 kg. Perhaps there is no other mammal that is so identified with China as the Giant Panda. It is a bear with a wide and massive head with a short rostrum. The body is uniformly white; the limbs and shoulders are black; a pair of upstanding round black ears, large black eyes and ocular patches, and sharply contrasting black nose. Males are larger than females. A notable feature on these animals is an extra, opposable sesamoid structure in the manus (manus and pes = 5; pes is semiplantigrade). Skull is the most robust of the bear family, with a distinctively massive sagittal crest and robust zygomatic arches; intraorbital/postorbital region distinctly narrowed; supraorbital processes vestige, and the alisphenoid canal is absent. P4 with large protocone, parastyle, and hypocone; P4 and M1 are quadrate; P2 and P3 well developed; M1 and M2 massive, covered with many cusps and tubercles. Dental formula: 3.1.4.2/3.1.4.3 = 42.
Distribution: Distributed in S Gansu, Shaanxi, N, C, S Sichuan. Endemic. Their former range covered almost all of the entire southern half of China and some of Myanmar, but their numbers have been reduced significantly to six distinct populations (includes *fovealis* Matthew and Granger, 1923).
Natural History: Giant Pandas inhabit montane forests (generally mixed coniferous and broadleaf forests) at elevations of 1,200–3,900 m where bamboo stands (*Sinarundinaria*) are present. They sometimes descend to lower elevations during the winter. They feed on gentle slopes with a high forest canopy. Giant Pandas feed almost entirely on the leaves of 30 or more species of bamboo, and bamboo can account for up to 99% of their diet. The digestive tract is extremely muscular and covered with a thick layer of mucus to help digest the woody diet and protect against splinters. Other foods eaten include fruits, fir bark, vines, small mammals, fish, insects, and leaves. Adults consume 12-15 kg of food per day. Giant Pandas take shelter in trees and caves. They are primarily terrestrial, although also good climbers and capable of swimming. They are solitary, nocturnal, and crepuscular. Home ranges of females do not overlap, while male home ranges may overlap several females. Home range size is 4–8.5 km^2 and is largely dependent on the quantity and quality of bamboo resources. Sexual maturity occurs at 4.5–6 years, and the breeding season extends from March to May. There is a delayed implantation of 45–120 days, followed by a gestation of 112–163 days. Although up to three cubs may be born in a litter, normally only one cub survives to adulthood.
Comments: Since the first "black and white bear" was described by the French missionary Père David in 1869, there has been some confusion as to the Giant Panda's taxonomic position, perhaps because of its highly specialized adaptations for feeding on bamboo. However, it is now generally agreed that it belongs in the bear family as its most primitive member, a view supported by both molecular and morphological evidence (Davis 1964; Hendey 1980a, 1980b; Mayr 1986; O'Brien et al. 1985; Wozencraft 1989a).
Conservation Status: Total population estimated at < 1,000 (Hu 1998a). China RL—EN A2c + 3c; E. China Key List—I. CITES—I. IUCN RL—EN B1 + 2c, C2a ver 2.3 (1994). U.S. ESA—Endangered.
References: Chorn and Hoffmann (1978); Davis (1964); Hendey (1980a, b); Hu (1998a); Liu et al. (1998); Lu and Schaller (2002); Mayr (1986); Milius (2001); O'Brien et al. (1985); Reid and Gong (1999); Schaller et al. (1985); Schaller (1993); Servheen et al. (1999); Ward and Kynaston (1995); Wozencraft (1989a); Zhang et al. (2002).

Genus *Helarctos* (monotypic)

马来熊属 Malaixiong Shu

Sun Bear

PLATE 45
MAP 476

Helarctos malayanus (Raffles, 1821)
马来熊 Malaixiong

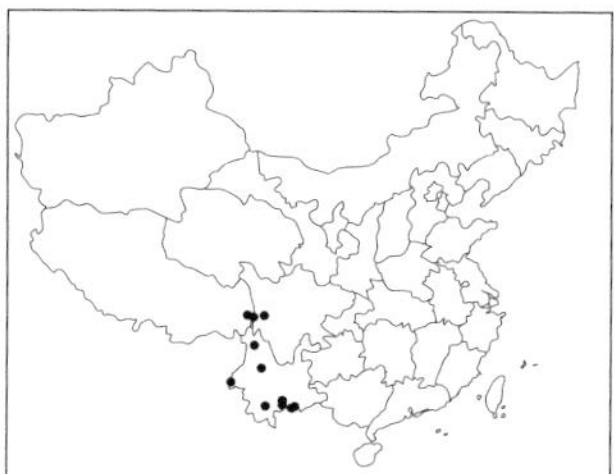

MAP 476. SUN BEAR, *Helarctos malayanus*

Distinctive Characteristics: HB 1,000–1,400; T 30–70; HF 180–210; E 40–60; GLS 230–290; Wt 25–65 kg. The Sun Bear is the smallest living bear species in the world and the only bear characteristic of the tropical forests of SE Asia. Its name comes from the tan crescent shape mark (shape is variable) on its chest.

This sharply constrasting crescent is white, tan, or orange and stands out against the almost pure black background. Males are generally 20% larger than the females. They have a very short, dense coat that is jet black with light markings on their face. They have very small, rounded ears set low on their heads. The muzzle is shorter and a lighter in color than body color; muzzle color varies from orangish tan to gray or a silver color. The rhinarium continues downward and unites with the lips. Forelimbs are distinctively bowed and the manus is turned inward. Rostrum of the skull is very short. The length of the nasals about equal to the width across the first upper molars with a steeply convex frontal profile; mastoid width greater than the length of the palate–and the mastoids flare out laterally; the auditory bullae are swollen. P1 and P2 are often lost at a very early age; M1 quadrate; canines distinctively stout and large. Dental formula: 3.1.3.2/3.1.3.3 = 38, although the number of premolars is usually two in adults (fig.12).

Distribution: May be extinct in China. Historic distribution in Sichuan, NW Yunnan, SE Xizang; extending to Indochina, Sumatra, and Borneo. Chinese subspecies: *H. m. anmamiticus* Heude, 1901; (includes *wardi* (Lydekker, 1906)–see Comments).

Natural History: Sun Bears, the most arboreal bear, live predominantly in lowland tropical dipterocarp rainforests but have also been reported from coconut plantations, low montane, and swamp forests up to 2,400 m. They have been reported to eat termites, fruits, insects, bees, earthworms, small mammals, birds, coconuts, and the heart and growing tips of coconut palms. They will sometimes cause damage to coconut plantations. They are known in some areas as the "honey bear" for their attraction to bee nests. Sun Bears are normally solitary. They are usually nocturnal in disturbed areas and largely diurnal in undisturbed areas. They are aseasonal breeders, with a gestation of 95–96 days. Litters of 1–2 cubs.

Comments: The phylogenetic position of the Sun Bear remains unsettled. Zhang and Ryder (1994) suggested a close relationship with the American Black Bear (*Ursus americanus*), whereas Waits et al. (1999) suggested a sister relationship with the Brown Bear (*U. arctos*) and Polar Bear (*U. maritimus*). Most have retained the Sun Bear in a monotypic genus. The correct subspecies for the Chinese Sun Bear also is in question. The type of *H. m. malayanus* is from Sumatra, and it is unlikely for the Chinese subspecies to be of the same population. *H. anmamiticus* (Heude, 1901) certainly represents the same population as those Chinese bears found along the Vietnam-Yunnan border. Less certainty can be assigned to Sun Bears from E Xizang, Sichuan, and NW Yunnan. Lydekker described a new subspecies for China supposedly from "Tibet." However, the exact type locality of his *H. m. wardi* is unknown, and it appears that Lydekker accidentally based the description on a skull of *Helarctos* and a skin–reported from Tibet–of *Ursus thibetanus*. We are restricting *malayanus* to

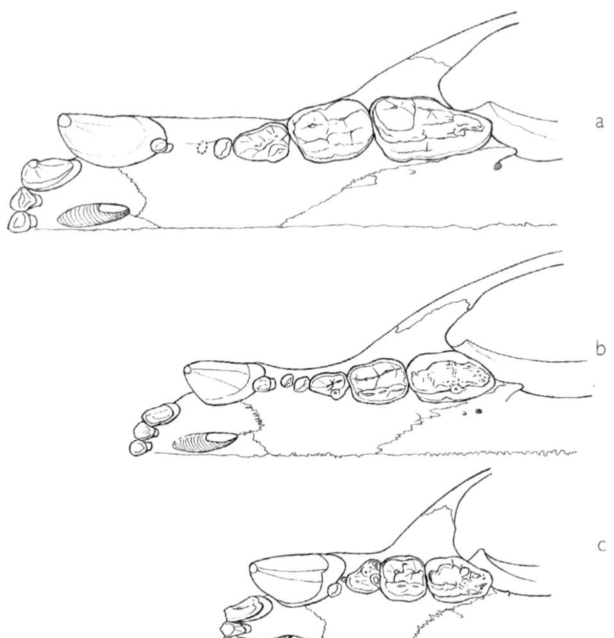

Figure 12. Comparative dentition of Brown (a), Asian Black (b) and Sun (c) bears.

Sumatra, and the next available name would be *annamiticus* (Heude, 1901) for Chinese populations.
Conservation Status: The Sun Bear's existence in China today is doubtful. No Chinese bears are reported from the wild or have been kept in captivity since the 1970s, although it has been reported in Laos directly across the border (Ma 1998). China RL—EN D. China Key List—I. CITES—I. IUCN RL—DD ver 2.3 (1994).
References: Fitzgerald and Krausman (2002); Lekagul and McNeely (1977); Ma (1981; 1998d); Pocock (1932); Servheen (1990; 1993; 1999); Waits et al. (1999); Wang (2003); Wong et al. (2004); Wozencraft (2005); Zhang and Ryder (1994).

Genus *Ursus*—Bears

棕熊属 Zongxiong Shu—熊 Zongxiong

The genus *Ursus* contains the world's largest terrestrial carnivores. Chinese *Ursus* are massive and are usually brown, dark brown, or black. The heads are robust and the rostrum is very long. Ears are proportionally small. Cubs have a V-shaped light stripe on breast, which usually disappears in adults. Skull rostrum long; suture of nasal bone longer than width between first molars; length of M1 + M2 > width of palate. Of the four *Ursus* species, two occur in China.

Brown Bear

PLATE 45
MAP 477

Ursus arctos Linnaeus, 1758
棕熊 Zongxiong

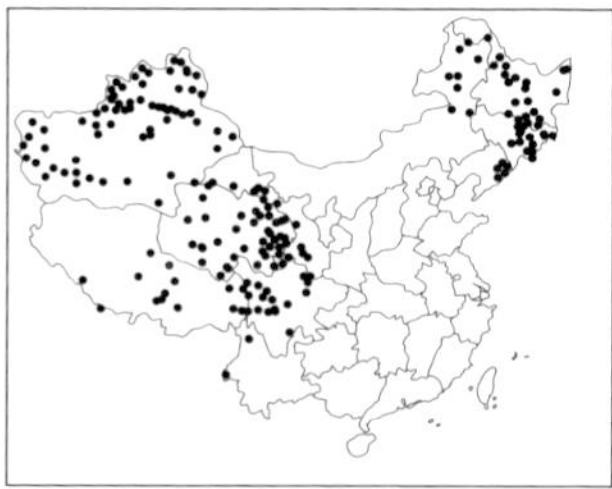

MAP 477. BROWN BEAR, *Ursus arctos*

Distinctive Characteristics: HB 1,150–1,190; T 80–130; HF 190–280; E 100–170; GLS 250–380; Wt 125–225 kg. The Brown Bear is the world's largest terrestrial carnivore, with massive head and shoulders and a dish-shaped face with a long rostrum. They have a Holarctic distribution and represent one of the most widely distributed land mammals. There is considerable variability in the size of Brown Bears from different populations, depending on the food available and the habitat. Brown Bears show the greatest variation in color and size of any ursid—from shades of blond to black to red—and this has led to the assignment of over 200 synonyms for this one species. The ears are small and project laterally; males are larger than females. The front foot pad is about half the size of that in the Asiatic Black Bear (fig. 13). Mastoid width > half the condylobasal length. P1-3 have only one root; M2 length ≤ the lengths of M1 + P4; length of two upper molars not greater than width of bony palate between first molars; M1 length > 20.4 mm; M2 length > 31 mm; m3 narrows posteriorly. Dental formula: 3.1.4.2/3.1.4.3 = 42 (fig. 12).
Distribution: At one time, the Brown Bear was one of the most widely distributed land mammals on earth. Today, their populations are greatly reduced and fragmented. They were widespread across C, W, and NE China, extending across most of the Holarctic. Brown Bears have the confusing characteristic of highly polymorphic skin color and physical size, varying sometimes from valley to valley. Because of their highly variable physical traits, there has been an abundance of species and subspecies identified over the years. Brown Bear subspecies taxonomy is in great need of revision, and the four subspecies recognized below should be considered tentative (see Comments for discussion): (1) *U. a. isabellinus* Horsfield, 1826; Xinjiang (Tian Shan mountains); W Xinjiang; W and SW Xizang (includes *leuconyx* Severtzov, 1873; *pamirensis* Ognev, 1924); (2) *U. a. jeniseensis* Ognev, 1924; Xinjiang (Altai populations); (includes *yeniseensis* Ognev, 1924); (3) *U. a. lasiotus* Gray, 1867; Heilongjiang, Jilin, Liaoning (includes *mandchuricus* Heude, 1898; *baikalensis* Ognev, 1924; *cavifrons* Heude, 1901; *ferox* Temminck, 1844 [preoccupied]; *macneilli* Lydekker, 1909; *melanarctos* Heude, 1898; *yesoensis* Lydekker, 1897);

Key to the Chinese Species of *Ursus*

1.a. Color brown; manus with two small carpal pads surrounded by fur, considerably smaller than plantar pad. Long rostrum such that the postorbital processes are about at the skull midpoint; a vertical line drawn between M1 and M2 passes anterior to the anterior rim of the orbit; length of nasal bone longer than width between external margins of left and right M1. M2 length > 35 mm, width > 20 mm; P4 length > 22 mm; posterior edge of M2 is triangular ... *Ursus arctos*

b. Color black; manus with one large carpal pad nearly equal in size to plantar pad. Short rostrum such that the postorbital processes are in the rostral half of the skull; a vertical line drawn between M1 and M2 passes posterior or approximately the same as the anterior rim of the orbit; length of nasal bone equal to width between external margins of left and right M1. M2 length < 30 mm, width < 16 mm; P4 length < 20 mm; posterior edge of M2 is square ... *Ursus thibetanus*

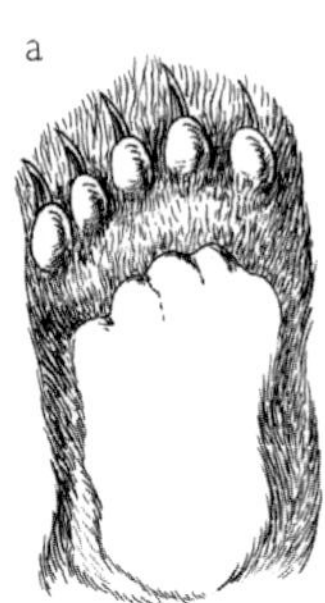

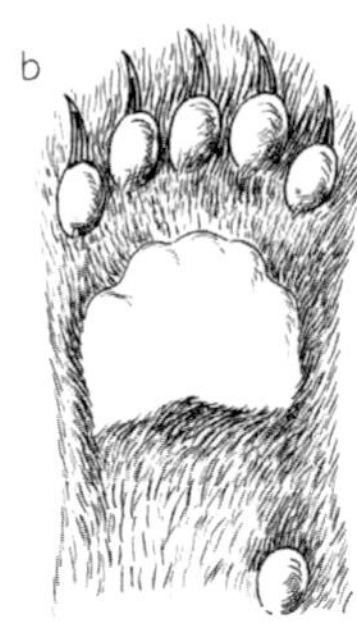

Figure 13. Comparative front paws of Asian Black (a) and Brown (b) bears.

(4) *U. a. pruinosus* Blyth, 1854; W Gansu, Qinghai, Shaanxi, W Sichuan, S Xinjiang, Xizang, NW Yunnan; Pocock (1931) included *lagomyiarius* Przewalski, 1883; *clarki* Sowerby, 1920.

Natural History: Brown Bears occupy a wide range of habitats including dense forests, subalpine mountain areas, and tundra. Brown Bears mainly eat vegetation—such as grasses, sedges, bulbs, roots, tubers, herbaceous plants, corns, berries, fruits, and nuts —which compose 60–90% of their diet. Common animal matter consumed includes insects, rodents, hoofed mammals, fish, and carrion. In some areas they have become significant predators of large hoofed mammals such as moose (*Alces*), caribou (*Rangifer*), and Red Deer (*Cervus*). In spite of their large size, Brown Bears can sprint at almost 50 km/h. They are nocturnal and crepuscular. Under most circumstances, they are solitary, except for females accompanied by their cubs and during the breeding season. Brown Bears are distributed in overlapping home ranges, and male home ranges are larger than those occupied by females; there is no territorial defense. In the northern parts of their range they will hibernate six or seven months. They have been known to cache food. Sexual maturity occurs at 4.5–7 years of age. Mating occurs from early May to July, but implantation does not occur until about October or November. The young are born from about January to March. The litter size averages two. Female bears are induced ovulators. A male bear may father more than one litter of cubs a year.

Comments: Brown Bear taxonomy has been plagued with a duplicity of subspecies as they appear to vary greatly depending on their immediate habitat, rather than on geography. Therefore, any taxonomy based on a few scattered specimens has to be viewed as tentative. The following four subspecies deserve further comment. (1) The Altai Bear, *U. a. jeniseensis* Ognev, 1924: When Ognev recognized the Altai populations as a distinct subspecies, he did not mention *collaris* Cuvier and Geoffroy Saint-Hilaire (1824). Pocock (1932:794) guessed that they might be the same, but no systematic study was done. Ma (1981) placed this form in *U. a. arctos*. Based on the lack of any systematic work showing synonymy of *collaris* and *jeniseensis*, they are here kept separate. (2) The Tian Shan or Kashmir Bear, *U. a. isabellinus* Horsfield, 1826: This bear is known under various common names, including Isabelline Bear, Red Bear, Kashmir Bear, and Tian Shan Bear—a sure indication of the variability of coat color, with whitish grey and red color variants occasionally appearing. (3) The Manchurian Bear: *U. a. lasiotus* Gray, 1867: There is much uncertainty as to the boundary between typical Chinese populations and populations to the northeast in Russia. See Ognev's (1962b [1931]) and Pocock's (1932) extensive analysis of the eastern Siberian-Manchurian bears. (4) Tibetan Bear/Blue Bear: *pruinosus* Blyth, 1854: Although some separate this form into a separate species (one account even into a separate subgenus, *Mylarctos*), Pocock's (1931) analysis could only support subspecies recognition. The general color varies from a dark brown or blackish-brown, to a pale brown or grayish-white (perhaps the source of the name, "Blue Bear"). The claws of the Tibetan Bear are typically pale and only lightly pigmented, as opposed to the more typical condition of dark brown to black found in other Brown Bear subspecies.

Conservation Status: Total Chinese population estimated at 7,000–8,000 (Ma 1998). China RL—VU C1. China Key List—II. CITES—I.

References: Allen (1938); Bunnell and McCann (1993); Ellerman and Morrison-Scott (1951); Feng et al. (1986); Ma (1981; 1998); Ognev (1962b); Pasitschniak-Arts (1993); Pocock (1931; 1932).

Asian Black Bear

PLATE 45

Ursus thibetanus Cuvier, 1823

MAP 478

黑熊 Heixiong

Distinctive Characteristics: HB 1,160–1,750; T 50–160; HF 190–340; E 115–180; GLS 206–413; Wt 54–240 kg. This medium-sized, black-colored bear has a lightish muzzle and ears, which appear large in proportion to the rest of its head, especially when compared with other species of bears. There is a distinct white patch on the chest, which is sometimes in the shape of a V, and white on the chin. Although the chest crescent patch can occur in Brown Bears (especially in the young), it is never as distinctive in the adult as in the Asiatic Black Bear and is usually absent in adult Brown Bears. A brown color phase also occurs. Hairs on sides of neck rather are long and form a distinctive crest of hairs down each side of the neck. The front foot pad is large compared with that of the Brown

Bear (fig. 13). In the skull, the sagittal crest is inconspicuous; length of the nasals are about the same as the width of the molars, and the bullae are flat. m1 hypoconid and entoconid are oblique to each other. Dental formula: 3.1.4.2/3.1.4.2 = 42 (fig. 12). 2N = 74.

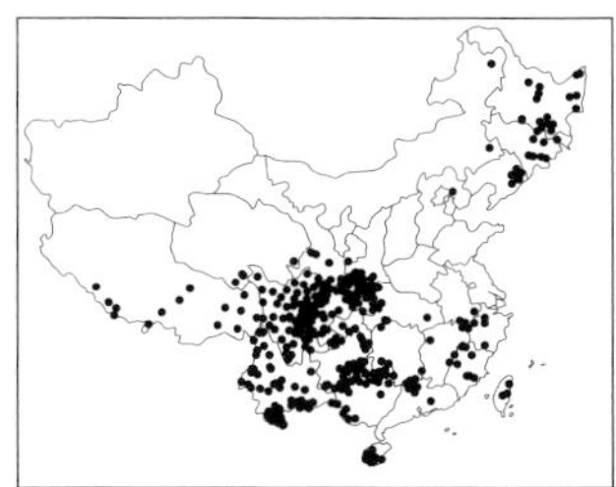

MAP 478. ASIAN BLACK BEAR, *Ursus thibetanus*

Distribution: Widespread in C, S, and NE China; extending to Afghanistan, India, Indochina, Japan, Korea, Laos, Nepal, Pakistan, Thailand, Russia (SE Primorski Krai), Vietnam. Five subspecies in China: (1) *U. t. formosanus* Swinboe, 1864; Zhejiang, Guangdong, Hainan, Taiwan (includes *melli* Matschie, 1922); (2) *U. t. laniger* (Pocock, 1932); S Xizang; (3) *U. t. mupinensis* (Heude, 1901); Anhui, Fujian, Gansu, Guangdong, Guangxi, Guizhou, Henan, Hubei, Hunan, Jiangxi, N Qinghai, Shaanxi, Sichuan, SE Xizang, Yunnan, Zhejiang (includes *kokeni* Matthew and Granger, 1923; *clarki* Sowerby, 1920; *leuconyx* (Heude, 1901); *macneilli* Lydekker, 1909) (4) *U. t. thibetanus* Cuvier, 1823; S Qinghai, NW Sichuan, SE Xizang, NW, W Yunnan (includes *labiatus* Blanford, 1876; *torquatus* Wagner, 1841); (5) *U. t. ussuricus* (Heude, 1901); Hebei, Heilongjiang, Jilin, Liaoning, NE Nei Mongol (includes *torquatos* Blanford, 1892 in part; *wulsini* Howell, 1928).
Natural History: Asian Black Bears are reported to occupy oak, broadleaf, and mixed forests and prefer forested hills and mountains. They are well adapted to tropical rainforests and oak forests. In summer, they have been reported at altitudes over 3,000 m, descending to lower elevations during winter. They are principally herbivorous, with one study showing that 89% of food consists of plant matter. In the spring, there was a greater reliance on bark, lichen and moss, nuts and acorns (21%). During the summer a diet shift occurs toward berries, buds, invertebrates, and small vertebrates, and at this time they enlarge their home ranges, moving to ripe patches of berries. They are also known to eat carrion. In the Wolong Reserve they have been reported to feed on early spring bamboo shoots. They occasionally kill domestic livestock, but the amount to which they prey on wild hoofed mammals is unknown. In fall they frequently climb nut-bearing trees and pull down branches to feed on the acorns and nuts, then deposit the branches in the tree to serve as a crude platform for further feeding. Asian Black Bears are solitary and nocturnal, although they are often seen in the daytime when fruits are ripening. Apparently, they den for winter sleep in the northern parts of their range. It has been suggested that in the southern limits of their range, where it is quite hot, they do not undergo winter sleep, but this has not been confirmed. In Russia the home range is reported to be 10–20 km^2; an adult male in Tangjiahe, China, had a home range of 37 km^2. Gestation lasts seven or eight months; on average they give birth to two cubs. Sexual maturity of females is thought to occur at three to four years of age. In Russia, mating is reported to occur in June and July, with births occurring between December and March.
Conservation Status: Total population in China estimated at 12,000–18,000 (Ma 1994). This species is commonly kept in bear farms throughout China to provide bile for use in traditional Chinese medicine. China RL—VU C1. China Key List—II. CITES—I. IUCN RL—VU A1cd ver 2.3 (1994).
References: Ma (1981); Ma and Li (1999); Mills et al. (1995); Ying (1999).

Family Otariidae—Eared Seals

海狮科 Haishi Ke—狮 Haishi

This is the family of aquatic carnivores normally referred to as sea lions and fur seals. All living species fall into two monophyletic groups: the Arctocephalinae or fur seals and the Otariinae or sea lions (Berta and Deméré 1986). However, the differences among the members of this family are not great, as intergeneric hybrids have been observed between *Zalophus* and *Eumetopias*; *Callorhinus* and *Arctocephalus*; and *Callorhinus* and *Zalophus*.

Otariids can be distinguished from seals in the family Phocidae based on a variety of external morphological features and features of the skeleton and skull. Also known as the eared seals, otariids retain a small external pinnae. As a group, they are more littoral than phocids, have the ability to support the front half of their body on their pectoral girdle, can turn

Key to the Chinese Genera of Otariidae

1.a. First digit of fore flipper shorter than second; digits of hind flippers approximately equal in length; forelimbs naked. Infraorbital canal small; interorbital region usually greater than 20% of condylobasal length; tympanic bullae concave. P4-M1 diastema < length of P4 — *Callorhinus*

b. First digit of fore flipper longer than second; outer digits of hind flipper distinctly longer than middle three; forelimbs well furred. Infraorbital canal large; supraorbital process quadrate. P4-M1 diastema > length of P4 — *Eumetopias*

their hind feet forward, and have a basicranial region that is very similar to that of the ursids. They use their front limbs as the principle means of locomotion in the water. Of seven genera within the Otariidae, two are present in China. Reijnders et al. (1993) reviewed the conservation and status of the world's seals, fur seals, and sea lions.

Genus *Callorhinus* (monotypic)

海狗属 Haigou Shu

Northern Fur Seal

Callorhinus ursinus (Linnaeus, 1758) PLATE 46 MAP 479

海狗 Hai Gou

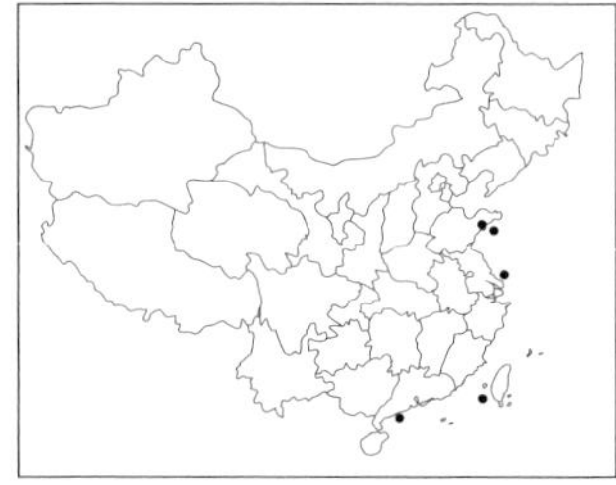

MAP 479. NORTHERN FUR SEAL, *Callorhinus ursinus*

Distinctive Characteristics: HB 1.4–2.5 m; Wt 175–275 kg (males), 30–50 kg (females). Adult males are a rich dark brown to gray; females are more grayish dorsally and a lighter gray ventrally. There is a light colored patch on the chest; the ears are almost hidden beneath the fur; the flippers have sparse hair; and the inner sides are naked. Newborn pups are entirely black. Postcanine teeth usually with one prominent cusp, although molars and premolars are indistinguishable and are usually referred to as postcanine teeth (= 5). Dental formula: 3.1.3.2/2.1.3.2 = 34.
Distribution: Vagrant populations reported off the coasts of Guangdong, Jiangsu, Shandong, and Taiwan; extending broadly across N Pacific coastal regions from the United States and Canada to Japan; the primary breeding grounds are on the Pribilof Islands, USA. Most recent authors do not recognize subspecies. However, Wang (2003) identified the Chinese forms as *C. u. curilensis* Jordan and Clark, 1899.
Natural History: This is the animal that has been used most extensively for seal fur coats. They spend most of the year at sea and rarely come ashore during the nonbreeding period. They migrate south during the winter. During migration they do not travel in large herds, but in small groups of 1–10 animals. Northern Fur Seals feed at sea during the evening, night, and early morning and sleep during the day. Deep-water "seal fish" (*Bathylagus callorhinus*) have been found in stomach contents. The most common food items are squid, herring, pollack, lantern fish, and mollusks. Predators include sharks, Arctic Fox (*Vulpes alopex*), Killer Whale (*Orcinus orca*), and Steller Sea Lion (*Eumetopias jubatus*). Breeding rookeries are generally near the continental slope and are rocky. Males arrive first in May and establish territories eventually occupied by 10–50 cows. The females arrive in mid-June and give birth within two days of arrival. Nearly all seals are infected with nematodes, and the hookworm (*Uncinaria lucasi*) is one of the chief causes of pup death. Mating occurs within one week of giving birth, followed by a delayed implantation of three to four months, yielding a total gestation period of one year. Females become sexually mature at age 3; males at 5–6. They breed at about 8 years of age but do not establish harems until around 12. Adult females normally migrate south in late October–November.
Conservation Status: Over three thousand fur seals are caught and drowned annually in Japanese gill nets, and the Japanese fishing industry uses some 7,000 animals for food. China RL—VU A2cd + 3cd. IUCN RL—VU A1b ver2.3 (1994).
References: Berta and Deméré (1986); Ichihara and Yoshida (1972); Keyes (1965); Lander (1979); Rice (1998); Taylor et al. (1955).

Genus *Eumetopias* (monotypic)

北海狮属 Beihaishi Shu—北海狮 Beihaishi

Steller's Sea Lion

Eumetopias jubatus (Schreber, 1776) PLATE 46 MAP 480

北海狮 Bei Haishi

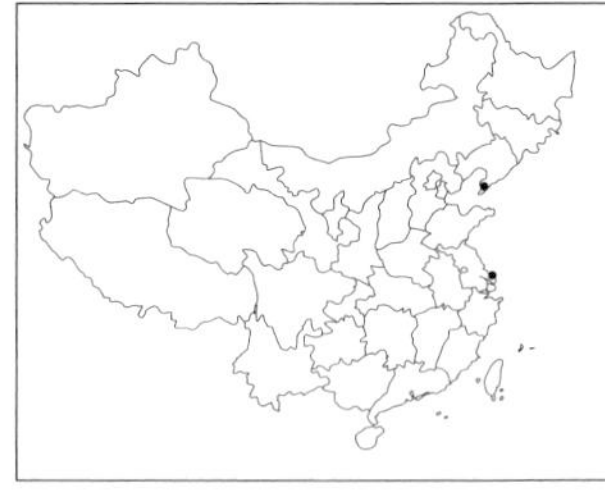

MAP 480. STELLER'S SEA LION, *Eumetopias jubatus*

Distinctive Characteristics: HB 2.3–3.3 m; GLS 325–400; maximum Wt 350 kg (females), 1,120 kg (males). The largest otariid and with marked sexual dimorphism. Yellowish brown to reddish brown and slightly darker on the chest and abdomen; pups are dark brown to black; adult males have long coarse hair on the chest shoulders and back of the neck; neck is narrow and slim in females. Conspicuous diastema between the upper fourth and fifth postcanines; palate is slightly concave; upper postcanine 5 is double rooted. Dental formula: 3.1.3.2/2.1.3.2 = 34.
Distribution: Vagrant populations found off the coasts of China reported from the coasts of Jiangsu, Liaoning, and Shangdong. An abundant, widely distributed sea lion of the cooler regions of the N Pacific, the worldwide distribution includes the N Pacific coastal regions of Canada, Japan, Russia, and the United States. The center of abundance is probably the Aleutian Islands.

Natural History: Steller's Sea Lions are opportunistic feeders, foraging mostly near the shore and over the continental shelf for fish and cephalopods. They are very gregarious and will form rafts of several hundred individuals while floating on the water. Their diet consists of squid, herring, halibut, flounder, rockfish, cod, and lamprey. Food is normally swallowed whole. Cephalopods are a major portion of the diet, but they will occasionally take Northern Fur Seal pups. Most usual cause of death of young pups is drowning, however, nematodes are a serious problem. Pups are born between May and July and stay close to mothers for about a week, then gather in groups and play and sleep together. Pups will not voluntarily go into the open ocean. Bulls arrive at the rookery first and become sexually mature three to eight years (females between two to eight). Mating occurs in late May and early July. During the breeding season females remain on land during the day and feed principally at night. They are gregarious and polygynous and use traditional rookeries and haul-out sites, usually on remote islands.
Conservation Status: China RL—EN A1b + 2cd + 3cd. IUCN RL—EN A1b ver 2.3 (1994).
References: Kenyon and Rice (1961); Loughlin et al. (1987).

Family Phocidae—True Seals

海豹科 Haibao Ke—海豹 Haibao

The earless seals are the most highly aquatic carnivores, with little ability to walk on land. Their hind limbs are modified into flippers and extend backward and cannot be bent forward. On land they move with a wriggling motion by forelimbs and body. They propel themselves through the water principally with their hind limbs. The skull is without a supraorbital process, and the teeth are simple and conical-shaped. Both the premolars and molars have two roots. They are all carnivorous and distributed in sea areas of the Northern Hemisphere. All Chinese phocids are considered members of the subfamily Phocinae. *Phoca* and *Pusa* are often placed in the tribe Phocini. The separation of *Pusa* from *Phoca* follows Rice (1998), who reviewed the taxonomy of this group. Three of the 13 genera of Phocidae are found in Chinese waters.

Genus *Erignathus* (monotypic)

髯海豹属 Ranhaibao Shu

Bearded Seal

PLATE 46
MAP 481

Erignathus barbatus Erxleben, 1777
髯海豹 Ran Haibao

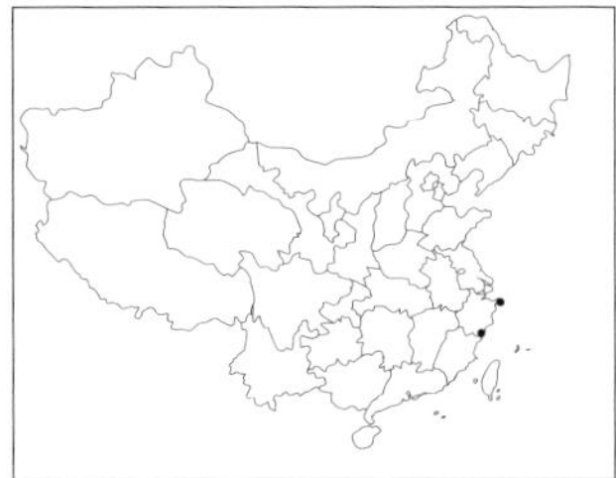

MAP 481. BEARDED SEAL, *Erignathus barbatus*

Distinctive Characteristics: HB 2.1–2.3 m; Wt 200–250 kg. The largest phocid in Chinese waters. No sexual dimorphism in color. Gray, slightly darker down the midline, brownish on the proportionally small head; lighter ventrally; great profusion of long, very sensitive glistening white vibrissae; four mammary teats; square shape of the fore flippers; the third digit is slightly longer than the others. 2N = 34.
Distribution: Vagrant populations of *E. b. nautica* (Pallas, 1811) have been reported from Zhejiang. Worldwide, Bearded Seals are circumpolar in their distribution and are found in all circumpolar Arctic seas and coastal regions, with vagrant populations wandering as far south as Japan, Spain, and the USA.

Key to the Chinese Genera of Phocidae

1.a. Third digit of fore flipper longest. Jugal bone short and wide—width > 1/3 its greatest diagonal length; spaces between postcanines almost as long as tooth width *Erignathus*

b. Third digit of fore flipper shorter than first or second. Jugal bone longer and narrower—width < 1/3 its greatest diagonal length; spaces between postcanines less than tooth width or absent 2

2.a. Pelage with dark spots on a light background. Condylobasal length > 187 mm; postcanine teeth often crowded out of line and overlapping; inner side of mandible between middle postcanines convex; posterior palatine foramina anterior to maxillo-palatine suture; nasals short and broad; infraorbital foramen small—diameter 2/3 to 1/3 that of the alveolus of the canine. First lower postcanines usually with four cusps *Phoca*

b. Spotted. Condylobasal length ≤ 187 mm; mandibular teeth always aligned with jaw, never crowded; inner side of mandible between middle postcanines concave; posterior palatine foramina posterior to maxillo-palatine suture; nasals narrow and long; infraorbital foramen same diameter as the alveolus of the canine. First lower postcanines usually with three cusps *Pusa*

Natural History: Bearded Seals prefer shallow waters near coasts that are free of fast ice in winter. Mostly found in seasonally ice-covered waters less than 200 m deep. They prefer to inhabit areas of broken pack ice and drifting ice floes but are quite versatile and also occur in areas of shorefast ice and thick ice, where they are able to maintain breathing holes. Many of the seals move long distances to follow the receding ice in the summer. Bearded Seals feed on decapod crustaceans (such as shrimps and crabs), holothurians, molluscs (such as clams and whelks), octopus, and bottom fish. Bearded Seals prefer to feed at the bottom in areas with water depths of less than 130 m. They are solitary and are not found in very large numbers in any one locality. They do not concentrate during breeding; pups are born in the open on ice floes. Implantation of 2 months; gestation about 11 months. Most pups are born from mid-March to early May, later in the north than in the south.
Conservation Status: China RL—NA.

Genus *Phoca*—Common Seals

海豹属 Haibao Shu 海豹 Haibao

Some have considered *Pusa hispida* in this genus, but the forms are separated here, following Rice (1998). There are only two species in Phoca, *P. largha*, and *P. vitulina*, which some have included as conspecific, and there is much confusion in the literature concerning these two species; however, the arrangement here follows Rice (1998), Shaughnessy and Fay (1977), and Wozencraft (2005).

Spotted Seal

Phoca largha Pallas, 1811 PLATE 46
斑海豹 Ban Haibao MAP 482

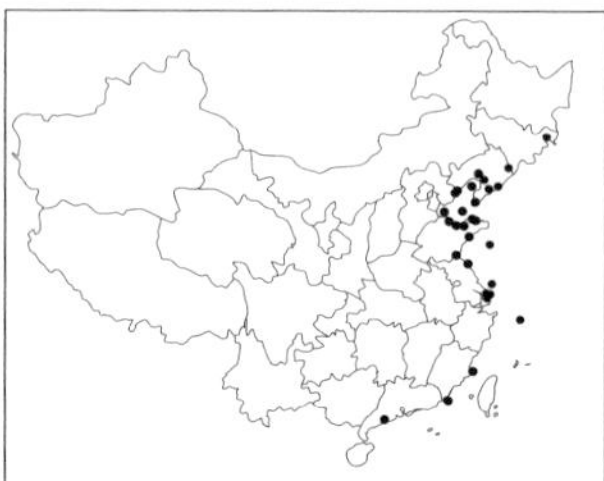

MAP 482. SPOTTED SEAL, *Phoca largha*

Distinctive Characteristics: HB 1.4–1.7 m; GLS 218; Wt 85–150 kg. Tail is short; pelage is grayish yellow or dark gray with numerous spots; pelage has a pale silver background with a darker gray area along the dorsal surface; superimposed on the pale and dark areas is a scattering of brown-black oval spots. Round head and large eyes; fingers of the hand decrease very slightly in length from first to fifth. Skull broad and flat; rostrum short; occipital wide and thick, extending upward to region between parietals. Differentiation of premolar and molar extremely inconspicuous—they are about equal in shape and size; cusps of all teeth slightly tilted; lower incisors are reduced to two on each side; molars to one in both jaws; P2–P4 two-rooted. Dental formula: 3.1.4.1/2.1.4.1 = 34.
Distribution: Fujian, Guangdong, Hebei, Jiangsu, Jilin, Liaoning, Shandong, Shanghai, Zhejiang; worldwide associated with pack ice in coastal N Pacific off Canada, Japan, Russia (Bering and Okhotsk seas), USA (Alaska).
Natural History: Spotted Seals are the only phocid that breeds in China (Bohai Sea), where some give birth on land; this is the most southerly latitude of its breeding areas. There is an annual migration in the fall and winter to the edge of the pack ice, where the seals haul out on floes. They may ascend rivers, possibly including the Yangtze. Usually breed in association with pack ice (*P. vitulina* does not). Feed on fish, squid, crustaceans. The diet of the Spotted Seal is known to include crustaceans, cephalopods, and fish such as herring, capelin, pollock, eelpout, sand lance, and cod. Known predators are sharks, Killer Whale, Walrus, Steller's Sea Lion, Brown Bear, Wolf, foxes, and some large birds. Mating occurs in March. In the beginning of November the seals enter Liaodong Bay in pairs. A single pup is born from January to February after a gestation of 11–12 months (2–3 months delayed implantation). Females sexually mature at two years, males at four to five years.
Comments: The confusion in taxonomy between *largha* and *vitulina* has led to mixed reports on distribution, ecology, and natural history. *P. largha* is normally pagophilic and usually hauls out on sea ice floes to mate. *P. vitulina* is pagophobic and usually hauls out on beaches, sandbars, and reefs. However, in more southerly latitudes (e.g., China), they may both use beaches. Spotted Seals are monomorphic with a pattern somewhat like the light phase of Harbor Seals. Genetic isolation of the two taxa was confirmed by a study of their mtDNA (O'Corry-Crowe and Westlake 1997). *P. v. stegnegeri* Allen, 1902 is found along the coasts of the western N Pacific from SE Kamchatka, SW around the sea of Okhotsk to the Pacific coast of Hokkaido, and would be the southernmost population of *vitulina*. Shaughnessy and Fay (1977) suggested *incertae sedis* for assignment of these populations to species. We follow Rice (1998) and consider vagrant populations off the coast of China as *P. largha*.
Conservation Status: China RL—EN C2a(i, ii); E.
References: O'Corry-Crowe and Westlake (1997); Rice (1998); Shaughnessy and Fay (1977); Sheng (1999).

Genus *Pusa*—Ringed Seals

环斑海豹属 Huanbanhaibao Shu—
环斑海豹 Huanbanhaibao

This genus includes three allopatric species: the Ringed Seal, the Caspian Seal, and the Baikal Seal, of which only one is represented in China. Globally, their distribution includes the Arctic Ocean, going south in vagrant populations to Japan, China, Europe, and USA.

Ringed Seal PLATE 46
Pusa hispida (Schreber, 1775) MAP 483
环斑海豹 Huanban Haibao

MAP 483. RINGED SEAL, *Pusa hispida*

Distinctive Characteristics: HB 1.4–1.5 m; Wt 45–90 kg. Light gray background spotted with black; many of the spots are surrounded by ring-shaped lighter marks. Appropriately named because of these ring-shaped marks on its coat. 2N = 32.
Distribution: Vagrant populations of *P. h. ochotensis* (Pallas, 1811) appear in Shandong and Jiangsu; generally found only N of 35°.
Natural History: Animals of inshore waters, Ringed Seals are rarely encountered in the open sea or on floating pack ice. They may remain in contact with drifting pack ice or shorefast ice for much of the year. During winter they may dig caves into snow that has gathered above breathing holes. They are opportunistic feeders, feeding on fish (cod, smelt, herring), pelagic crustaceans and invertebrates, and squid. It is believed that they can go as deep as 91 m when feeding. Normally fairly solitary, but one of the most common seals of the Arctic. Killer Whales, Polar Bears, and Arctic Foxes (sometimes Walruses) eat pups. Pups are born in March and April after a delayed implantation of 2–3 months (total gestation about 11 months). Males are mature at five years; females at four to seven. They are born with a pure white coat, which they shed within four to six weeks. Mating takes place about a month after parturition.
Conservation Status: China RL—EN C2a(i, ii); E.
References: King (1983b).

Family Mustelidae—Weasels, Badgers, Martens, and Otters

鼬科 You Ke—鼬类, 獾类, 貂类, 水獭 Youlei, Huanlei, Diaolei, Shuita

Mustelids are small to medium-sized carnivores and make up the largest family of carnivores, with 22 genera and 59 species; of these, 10 genera and 19 species occur in China. They are found on all continents except Australia and Antarctica. Their form is either slender and short legged (otters, weasels) or robust and stout (badgers, Wolverine). There is a wide amount of variation within the family, but they all share the loss of the alisphenoid canal, the loss of the carnassial notch on P4, and the loss of molars (molar formula is M 1/2). The palate is extended considerably beyond the toothrow in most species. All have five toes on each foot. They all have well-developed anal glands that give them a powerful and distinctive odor called musk. The usual condition is to have two glands that empty into a sac that can be discharged through the anus. Some mustelids can discharge the fluid as a reflex reaction as a secondary defense function. Most are highly carnivorous, but some specialize in eating insects and fruit. In most species, the sexes live separately throughout the year and sexual dimorphism is the rule, rather than the exception. They have large, distinctive bacula, and copulation is vigorous and usually associated with induced ovulation. Many mustelids have delayed implantation of the developing embryo.

Few have questioned the distinctiveness of the otters, the Lutrinae, but the traditionally recognized Melinae (badgerlike) and Mustelinae (martens and weasels) appear to be paraphyletic (Bininda-Emonds et al. 1999; Bryant et al. 1993). For these reasons, only two subfamilies are recognized here, the Lutrinae and the Mustelinae (provisionally including taxa traditionally placed in Melinae, Guloninae, Taxidiinae, and Mellivorinae). The Ferret Badger, *Melogale*, may be ancestral to Lutrinae and Mustelinae (Bryant et al. 1993). Most mustelids are valuable fur bearers, with species such as the Wolverine, martens, Ermine, and otter having a high economic value. The Mink, *Neovison vison* (Schreber, 1777), has been introduced to China for economic purposes (but will not be covered in these accounts).

Key to the Chinese Subfamilies of Mustelidae

1.a. Highly aquatic; fur waterproof; pes wider than manus; tail thick and muscular; external pinnae conspicuously small. Rostral process of premaxilla only with narrow contact with nasal; posterior lacerate foramen large; mastoid region inflated posteriolateral to auditory bullae. P1/1 usually absent; P4 talon with wide basin without accessory cusps; M1 not transversely elongated, but quadrate in appearance ... Lutrinae

b. Not especially adapted for aquatic lifestyle; width of pes ≈ manus; tail without muscular base; external pinnae normal size. Rostral process of premaxilla with wide contact with nasal; posterior lacerate foramen small; mastoid region not inflated posteriolateral to auditory bullae. P1/1 absent or present; P4 talon either absent, or with accessory cusps (but not the condition found in Lutrinae with a wide basin); M1 either transversely elongated, or rhomboidal in outline ... Mustelinae

Subfamily Lutrinae—Otters

水獭亚科 Shuita Yake—水獭 Shuita

Adapted to semiaquatic habits, the 13 species of otters are the only truly aquatic members of the Mustelidae. Of the seven genera, three occur in China. They have long, cylindrical bodies and a thick muscular tail used in swimming that is fully haired. The pes is wider than manus, and both have well-developed webbing. The fur is thick, smooth, and waterproof; facial vibrissae are noticeably long and stiff; muzzle short and blunt; nostrils and ears are valvular and can be closed underwater. The postpalatine foramen is in front of maxilla-palatine suture; the braincase is distinctively flattened and the postorbital region very narrow; cavity of bulla undivided externally. The P4 is massive; M1 nearly as large as P4 and rectangular. Foster-Turley et al. (1990) reviewed the conservation status and distribution of otters.

Genus *Aonyx*—Small-clawed Otters

非洲小爪水獭属 Feizhouxiaozhuashuita Shu—小爪水獭 Xiaozhuashuita

Aonyx is distributed in S Asia and Africa. It contains two species, one of which occurs in China. Recent molecular studies have shown that *Aonyx* is congeneric with *Amblonyx* (Koepfli and Wayne 1998); however, some previous morphological studies considered them separate (Harris 1968; Medway 1977; van Zyll de Jong 1972; 1987).

Asian Small-Clawed Otter PLATE 47

Aonyx cinerea (Illiger, 1815) MAP 484

小爪水獭—Xiaozhua Shuita

Distinctive Characteristics: HB 400–610; T 290–350; HF 75–95; E20–25; GLS 84–94; Wt 2–4 kg. The Asian Small-clawed Otter is the smallest species of otter, however, it is relatively stouter than other otter species. Its color is uniformly brown with a light throat and venter; long, dense vibrissae; small rounded ears on sides of head (which is more rounded than in other otters); eyes are proportionally larger (when compared to head size in other otters); rhinarium profile with two concavities on the upper border; manus is partially webbed with vestigal claws; base of tail is thick but tapers quickly to a narrow tip and flattened dorsoventrally; female with two pairs of mammae. Skull small, short, and wide; although the teeth are similar in size to *Lutra* and *Lutrogale*, the skull size is significantly smaller (<90 mm); supraorbital process sharp and thin; auditory bullae inflated; zygomatic width > 60% of condylobasal length. P1/1 usually absent; m1 has a wide buccal cingulum. Dental formula: 3.1.3.1/3.1.3.2 = 34. 2N = 38.

Distribution: S China; extending to Bangladesh, Myanmar, India, Indonesia (Sumatra, Java, Kalimantan), Laos, Malaysia (West, Sarawak, Sabah), Philippines (Palawan Island), Thailand, Vietnam. Chinese subspecies: *A. c. concolor* (Rafinesque, 1832); Fujian, Guangdong, Guangxi, Guizhou, Hainan, Sichuan, Taiwan, Xizang, Yunnan (includes *swinhoei* Gray, 1867; *fulvus* (Pohle, 1919); *sikimensis* Horsfield 1855; *indigitatus* Hodgson, 1839; *leptonyx* Anderson, 1879).

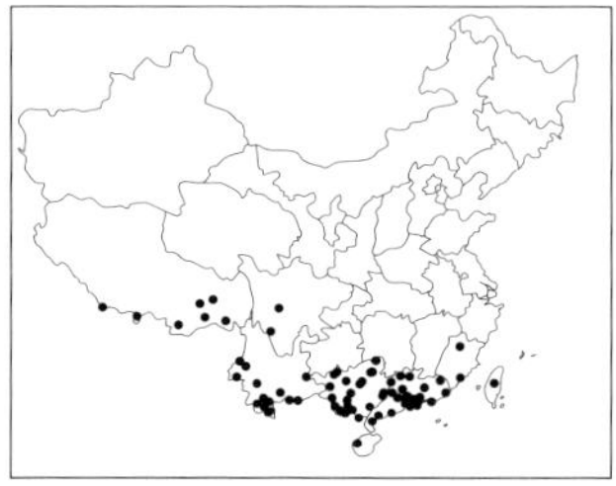

MAP 484. ASIAN SMALL-CLAWED OTTER, *Aonyx cinerea*

Natural History: Asian Clawless Otters are found in small streams, ponds, rice paddies, marshes, swamps, mangroves, and freshwater wetlands up to 2,000 m.

Key to the Chinese Genera of Lutrinae

1.a. Size small; HB length < 500 mm; claws small and undeveloped, digits only partially webbed. Condylobasal length ≈ 75–90 mm; zygomatic breadth > 65% of condylobasal length; toothrow wider than long; length of postorbital region short. P1/1 usually absent; m1 with wide buccal cingulum, m1 width ~ 60% of length *Aonyx*

b. Size large; HB length > 600 mm; claws developed, digits fully webbed. Condylobasal length > 90 mm; zygomatic breadth < 65% of condylobasal length; toothrow longer than wide; length of postorbital region long. P1/1 present; m1 with narrow or absent buccal cingulum; m1 width ≤ 50% of length 2

2.a. Upper margin of nasal pad with concavities; tail without lateral keel. Straight dorsal profile of braincase; postorbital constriction 50–75% of intraorbital constriction; toothrow length < 35% of condylobasal length; palatal midline length < 500 mm; anterior margin of orbit directly vertical to the P3–P4 diastema. m1 length < 12 mm *Lutra*

b. Upper margin of nasal pad straight; tail with lateral keel. Rounded convex dorsal profile of braincase; postorbital constriction 80–110% of intraorbital constriction; toothrow length > 35% of condylobasal length; palatal midline length > 500 mm; anterior margin of orbit directly vertical to the P2-P3 diastema. m1 length > 12 mm *Lutrogale*

They can coexist with the Eurasian Otter (*Lutra lutra*) and the Smooth-coated Otter (*Lutrogale perpicillata*), but they are more frequent in smaller bodies of water than the other species. They regularly scent mark distinct territories and are principally diurnal and crepuscular. They feed on aquatic animals such as crabs, snails, shellfish, crayfish, insects, and frogs and are mainly known as crab eaters. They leave shellfish in the sun to bake and will eat them after the shells have opened. They forage in groups of 12–15, although 4–12 appears to be normal. They are monogamous and mate for life, and both parents help to raise their offspring. Young may stay with the family unit for more than one year, and unrelated individuals may join the group. Gestation is 60 days, and they may have two litters a year. Average litter size is four. Age at sexual maturity is 2.5 years.
Comments: Populations in Xizang and Sichuan are found at lower elevations along river courses.
Conservation Status: China RL—EN A2cd. China Key List—II. CITES—II. IUCN RL—LR/nt ver 2.3 (1994).
References: Bininda-Emonds et al. (1999); Bryant et al. (1993); Davis (1978); Ellerman and Morrison-Scott (1951); Foster-Turley (1992); Foster-Turley and Engfer (1988); Foster-Turley and Santiapillai (1990); Johnson et al. (2000); Koepfli and Wayne (1998); Kruuk et al. (1994); Larivière (2003); Melisch et al. (1994); Shariff (1984); Timmis (1971).

Genus *Lutra*—Otters

水獭属 Shuita Shui—水獭 Shuita

Of the three species of *Lutra*, only one is present in China (*Lutra*, as here understood, does not include species previously assigned to *Lutrogale*, *Hydrictis*, or *Lontra*). The genus is widely distributed in Asia, Europe, and Africa.

Eurasian Otter

PLATE 47
MAP 485

Lutra lutra (Linnaeus, 1758)
水獭 Shui Ta

MAP 485. EURASIAN OTTER, *Lutra lutra*

Distinctive Characteristics: HB 490–840; T 243–440; HF 88–125; E 15–30; GLS 90–120; Wt 2.5–9 kg. The Eurasian Otter has an elongated body on short legs with dense, thick, brownish fur. Their color is lighter on the neck and venter. They have a conical, thick, muscular tail; feet are webbed with well-developed claws; large nasal pad facing forward and upward with dorsal profile with noticeable concavities; anal glands are present. Rostrum of skull very short; postorbital region narrow and nearly parallel sided; postorbital constriction much smaller than interorbital constriction; cranium noticeably flat and large. Infraorbital foramen more than twice the diameter of the canines. P1, when present, usually medial to canines; M1 rectangular, the buccal and lingual sides each have two cusps, which are separated by a groove. Dental formula: 3.1.4.1/3.1.3.2 = 36.
Distribution: Distributed across China; extending throughout Eurasia. Four subspecies in China: (1) *L. l. chinensis* Gray, 1837; Anhui, Fujian, Gansu, Guangdong, Guangxi, Guizhou, Henan, Hubei, Hunan, Jiangsu, Jiangxi, Qinghai, Shanghai, Shaanxi, Sichuan, Taiwan, Yunnan, Zhejiang (includes *sinensis* Trouessart, 1897; *hanensis* Matschie, 1907); (2) *L. l. hainana* Xu and Lu, in Xu et al., 1983; Hainan Island; (3) *L. l. kutab* Schinz, 1844; W Xizang; (4) *L. l. lutra* (Linnaeus, 1758); Heilongjiang, Jilin, Liaoning, Nei Mongol, N Xinjiang (Altai); (includes *vulgaris* (Erxleben, 1777); *piscatoria* (Kerr, 1792); *marinus Billberg*, 1827; *nudipes* Melchior, 1834; *roensis* Ogilby, 1834; *whiteleyi* Gray, 1867; *japonica* Nehring, 1887).
Natural History: Eurasian Otters live in freshwater areas such as rivers, lakes, ponds, streams, marshes, swamps, and rice fields, from sea level up to 4,120 m. They avoid areas of deep water. Otters eat two or three times a day, sometimes consuming up to 25% of their own body weight. They feed principally on fish, which sometimes makes up more than 80% of their diet. Other occasional food items include frogs, birds, crustaceans, crabs, waterfowl, lagomorphs, and rodents. The Eurasian Otter is solitary, nocturnal, and crepuscular, with males and females coming together only to mate. They are territorial, marking the boundaries of their home ranges with their anal glands. Males have larger home ranges than females. The population density is around one otter per 1–5 km of river. These aseasonal breeders, with delayed implantation, reach sexual maturity at two to three years. Gestation lasts 63 days, and litter sizes range from two to three. Eurasian Otters are sometimes used to herd fish into nets.
Comments: Ellerman and Morrison-Scott (1951) restricted *L. l. nair* to S India and Sri Lanka. Allen (1938), Xu (in Gao 1987), Wang (2003), and Zhang et al. (1997) considered W Yunnan specimens in this subspecies, which would give *nair* allopatric populations. We have provisionally left Yunnan populations in *chinensis*. *L. l. monticolus* Hodgson, 1839, occurs in Nepal and Sikkim and may also occur in S Xizang.
Conservation Status: China RL—EN A2cd. China Key List—II. CITES—I. IUCN RL—VU A2cde ver 2.3 (1994).
References: Allen (1938); Foster-Turley and Santiapillai (1990); Harris (1968); Novikov (1956); Webb (1975); Wozencraft (2005); Xu (in Gao 1987).

Genus *Lutrogale* (monotypic)

印度水獭属 Yindushuita Shu

Smooth-Coated Otter

PLATE 47

Lutrogale perspicillata

(Geoffroy Saint-Hilaire, 1826)

MAP 486

江獭 Jiang Ta

MAP 486. SMOOTH-COATED OTTER, *Lutrogale perspicillata*

Distinctive Characteristics: HB 650–750; T 400–450; HF 100–140; E 20–30; GLS 122–128; Wt 5–12 kg. The Smooth-coated Otter is the largest species of otter in Asia. It has smooth and sleek pelage of a deep blackish brown color; pale neck and venter; small rounded ears that are set low on the head; white lips; flat upper margin of nasal pad (in *Lutra* there are noticeable concavities); higher domed head than in *Lutra*. Feet are large with webbing that extends to the second joint of each digit; males are significantly larger than the females; females have two pairs of mammae; tail > 50% of HB length and flattened toward the tip. In the skull the elongated postorbital area is noticeably inflated (unlike *Lutra*) and nearly parallel sided, and usually about 80–110% of the intraorbital constriction. Although the toothrow length is > 35% of the CBL, the rostrum is short (~ 20% of CBL) and almost on the same plane as the braincase; the palate extends caudad and is > 500 mm in length; anterior rim of orbit above P2-3. Dental formula: 3.1.4.1/3.1.3.2 = 36.

Distribution: S China; extending throughout S and SE Asia, India, and Indonesia. Chinese subspecies: *L. p. perspicillata* Geoffory Saint-Hilaire, 1826; Guangdong, Yunnan (includes *simung* (Lesson, 1827); *tarayensis* (Hodgson, 1839); *macrodus* (Gray, 1865); *ellioti* (Anderson, 1879)).

Natural History: Smooth-coated Otters are found in many different kinds of lowland habitats: mangroves, wetlands, rivers, swamps, and rice fields. They usually require forest cover adjacent to the water and are excellent swimmers; they are able to swim underwater for long distances. Rice fields appear to be one of the best habitats for Smooth-coated Otters. They do not hesitate to travel long distances over land. The Smooth-coated Otter feeds predominantly on fish and uses its large vibrissae to help find prey. They are principally piscivorous, and in some populations fish make up 90% or more of their diet. Although they are primarily fish-eaters, other items found in scats include small mammals, crustaceans, frogs, turtles, and birds. They hunt in wetlands, streams, rivers, and open ocean. Depending on the habitat, Smooth-coated Otters may hunt by day or by night. Cooperative hunting techniques have been observed; a typical group consists of the dominate male and female and three to five young. They are monogamous and aseasonal breeders. Males and females jointly raise the altricial young.

Comments: Most recent studies place *perspicillata* in the monotypic *Lutrogale*, considered a subgenus by Pohle (1919).

Conservation Status: China RL—EN A2cd + 3cd. CITES—II. IUCN RL—VU A1acd ver 2.3 (1994). There are no recent records from China.

References: Anoop and Hussain (2005); Foster-Turley (1992); Hussain (1996); Mason and Macdonald (1986); Pocock (1941), Prater (1971); Tiler et al. (1989); van Zyll de Jong (1987; 1991).

Subfamily Mustelinae—Weasels, Wolverine, Martens, and Badgers

鼬亚科 You Yake—

类, 獾类, 貂类 Youlei, Huanlei, Diaolei

The weasels, martens, Wolverine, and badgers are provisionally included here in the Mustelinae. They are generally long-bodied and short-limbed carnivores with dense fur. They have five well-developed digits and claws on all feet. The Chinese mustelines fall naturally into two groups: (1) the weasels, wolverine, and martens (with a characteristically hour-glass-shaped M1); and (2) the badgerlike mustelids (with a more quadrate M1).

The weasels represent some of the smallest carnivores—all weighing less than 2 kg, and the Least Weasel (*Mustela nivalis*) is the smallest species of carnivore. They are principally terrestrial hunters and are purely carnivorous. They feed on small vertebrates, bird's eggs, and insects. Males are considerably larger than females.

The martens are arboreal counterpart to the weasels. They are medium-sized carnivores and spend a great deal of time hunting in the trees. They are solitary predators and are opportunistic hunters that focus on small vertebrates, carrion, and sometimes fruits and nuts.

The Wolverine is the largest mustelid and will eat large prey—even caribou and deer. They are adept scavengers and sometimes rely on carrion. They are generally restricted to more northern latitudes, and they use the high snow levels to their advantage in capturing prey.

The badgerlike mustelids are well represented in China with three genera. They are more omnivorous than the other mustelines and correspondingly have a more crushing dentition. They are powerfully built and have a long snout and short tail. They eat a variety of food and have well-developed musk glands. Badgers rely more on roots, fruit, invertebrates, and nuts than do other mustelines.

Although there is little disagreement that weasels, martens, and the Wolverine are closely related, there is considerable controversy over the relationships among the badgerlike mustelids. Recent molecular

Key to the Chinese Genera of Mustelinae

1.a. Form slender; foot palm covered with hairs; rostrum without longitudinal stripes; claws flexible. Auditory bullae length ≥ width. P4 narrow and long, only one lingual lobe; M1 usually has a distinctive hour-glass shape and is always wider than long — 2—weasels and martens

b. Form robust; foot palm bare with long claws adapted for digging; longitudinal white or black stripes on rostrum. Auditory bullae as wide or wider than long, often with long external meatal tube. P4 wide with two lingual cusps; M1 is usually as long, or longer than wide, never with hour-glass shape — 5—badgerlike mustelids

2.a. Hairs on body sides longer than back; HB length ≈ 750–850 mm. Condylobasal length ≈ 135–150 mm; mastoid processes produced laterally beyond the external auditory meatus. No cusplet behind main cusp of P4; buccal side of P4 and posterior side of M1 are at right angles — *Gulo*

b. Hairs on body sides same as back; HB length < 750 mm. Condylobasal length < 110 mm; mastoid processes not produced laterally beyond the external auditory meatus. Cusplet present behind main cusp of p4; buccal side of P4 and posterior side of M1 are not at right angles — 3

3.a. Hind foot length > 70 mm; HB length > 300 mm. Condylobasal length > 75 mm; wall of auditory bullae thin; toothrow width ≈ 70% of its length; coronoid processes of mandible do not come to a sharp point. P1/1 present; M1 width > 7 mm — *Martes*

b. Hind foot length < 70 mm; HB length < 400 mm. Condylobasal length < 75 mm; wall of auditory bullae spongy; toothrow width ≈ its length; coronoid processes of mandible come to a sharp point. P1/1 absent; M1 width < 7 mm — 4

4.a. Back without variegated pattern; tail color similar to head-body color. Foramen ovale well in advance of bulla; hamular process distinct from auditory bullae. Metaconid on m1 absent — *Mustela*

b. Back variegated with black and yellow irregular lines; tail all white with dark tip. Foramen ovale close to bullae; hamular process attached to auditory bullae. m1 with distinct metaconid — *Vormela*

5.a. HB length > 520 mm; white throat; pale claws; rhinarium continues to upper lip. Mesopterygoid palate reaches the level of the glenoid fossa and its length > P4–M1 combined length and laterally inflated; distance from antorbital rim to tip of rostrum ~ 45% of condylobasal length; frontal region inflated; angular process of mandible absent; auditory bullae very low and flat — *Arctonyx*

b. HB length < 520 mm; black or dark brown throat; dark claws; rhinarium separated from upper lip. Mesopterygoid palate does not reach the level of the glenoid fossa, and its length ≅ P4– M1 combined length, and there is no lateral inflation; distance from antorbital rim to tip of rostrum <42% of condylobasal length; frontal region not inflated; angular process of mandible small; auditory bullae well inflated — 6

6.a. HB length > 400 mm; tail < 30% of HB length; white ear tufts; white median stripe (sometimes broken) from rostrum to occiput; venter dark. Condylobasal length > 100 mm; sagittal crest single; paraoccipital process not applied to caudal surface of bullae. m1 trigonid < talonid length — *Meles*

b. HB length < 400 mm; tail > 35% of HB length; no white ear tufts; white median stripe from rostrum to back; venter light. Condylobasal length < 100 mm; sagittal crest double; paraoccipital process applied to caudal surface of bullae. m1 trigonid > talonid length — *Melogalee*

studies indicate that *Melogale* may be primitive to weasels and not closely related to the group including *Meles* and *Arctonyx*. Because of this uncertainty, taxa are listed here simply by genus.

Genus *Arctonyx* (monotypic)

猪獾属 Zhuhuan Shu

Hog Badger — PLATE 48

Arctonyx collaris Cuvier, 1825 — MAP 487

猪獾 Zhu Huan

Distinctive Characteristics: HB 317–740; T 90–220; HF 55–135; E 21–45; GLS 80–140; Wt 9.7–12.5 kg. The Hog Badger receives its name from its piglike snout; otherwise, it is similar to the Asian Badger (*Meles lecurus*), although usually larger. In fact, the Hog Badger is the largest badger in China. The head is elongate and conical in shape and the face is mostly white, with two black stripes extending from the nose, over the eyes, and over the whitish ears to the neck. Feet, legs, and venter dark brown to black; throat white (in *Meles* it is black); claws on their front feet are white (in *Meles* these are also black); the tail is whitish in color. The skull is relatively narrow and high; rostrum is long; temporal crests do not close up as a sagittal crest; the mesopterygoid palate nearly reaches the level of the glenoid fossa; infraorbital foramen is noticeably large; auditory

bullae are flat; mastoid breadth nearly equal to the zygomatic breadth; lower incisors are procumbent. Dental formula: 3.1.4.1/3.1.3.2 = 36.
Distribution: Widespread in C and E China; ranges from Assam (India) and Myanmar to Indochina, Thailand, Sumatra, and probably Perak in Malaysia. Four subspecies occur in China: (1) *A. c. albogularis* (Blyth, 1853); S Anhui, Fujian, Gansu, Guangdong, Guangxi, Guizhou, Hubei, Hunan, S Jiangsu, Qinghai, Shaanxi, Shanxi, Sichuan, Yunnan, Zhejiang (includes *incultus* Thomas, 1922; *obscurus* (Milne-Edwards, 1871); *orestes* Thomas, 1911);
(2) *A. c. collaris* Cuvier, 1825; Xizang, W Yunnan (includes *isonyx* Horsfield, 1856; *taraiyensis* (Gray, 1863); *taxoides* (Blyth, 1853)); (3) *A. c. dictator* Thomas, 1910; Yunnan (includes *annaeus* Thomas, 1921); (4) *A. c. leucolaemus* (Milne-Edwards, 1867); N Anhui, Beijing, N Hebei, N Heilongjiang, Henan, N Jiangsu, N Jilin, N Liaoning, N Nei Mongol, N Shanxi (includes *milne-edwardsii* Lönnberg, 1923).

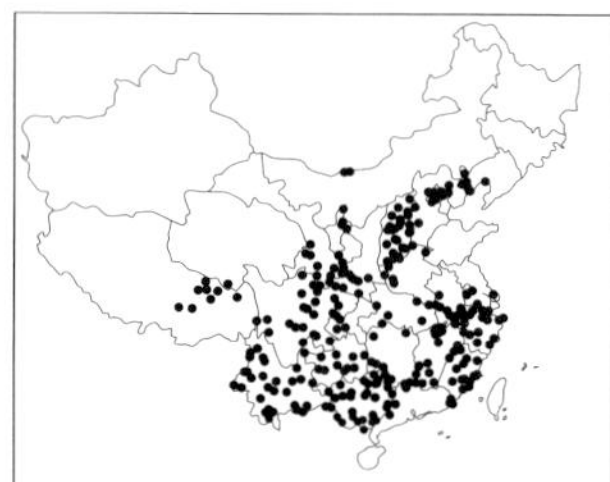

MAP 487. HOG BADGER, *Arctonyx collaris*

Natural History: The Hog Badger in China has been principally reported from forested areas of its range, from lowland jungles to wooded highlands 3,500 m in elevation. In India it has been reported as common in grasslands. It is solitary, crepuscular, and terrestrial. It is omnivorous, with a diet that consists principally of tubers, roots, earthworms, snails, and insects; occasionally will feed on small mammals. As with the Asian Badger, earthworms appear to be the principal item in its diet. It uses its long, hoglike nose to root through the forest floor. Little is known of its behavior or ecology. Adult females have been observed foraging with offspring. The Hog Badger is preyed upon by Tiger and Leopard. Hog Badgers will dig their own burrows. Females will have their young in a burrow and produce one litter per year in February or March of two to four young.
Comments: The distribution of *A. c. collaris* Cuvier, 1825, is Sikkim, Bhutan, Assam, and the SE foothills of the Himalayas. W Yunnan populations are provisionally assigned to this subspecies.
Conservation Status: China RL—VU C1; A2c.
References: Feng et al. (1986); Wang and Fuller (2003).

Genus *Gulo* (monotypic)

狼獾属 Langhuan Shu

Wolverine

PLATE 47
MAP 488

Gulo gulo (Linnaeus, 1758)
貂熊 Diao Xiong

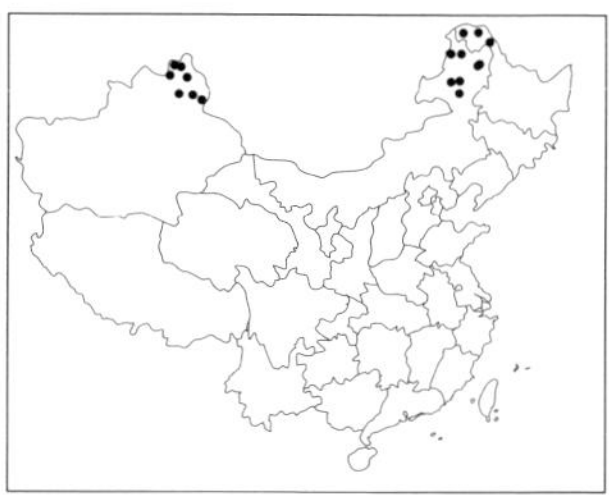

MAP 488. WOLVERINE, *Gulo gulo*

Distinctive Characteristics: HB 675–780; T 180–195; HF 180–195; E 45–55; GLS 140–165; Wt 6.5–14 kg. The Wolverine is the largest and most powerfully built mustelid (females are 10–12% smaller than males). It has proportionally short limbs and tail with the hairs on body sides conspicuously longer than dorsal ones. The body is uniformly dark brown; limbs and venter blackish brown, and there is a broad, light-colored stripe from neck to base of tail on sides of body. Variable white patches on the chest are common. There are four pairs of mammae, and anal, abdominal, and plantar scent glands. Wolverines have short, round ears. The plantigrade feet are large, with powerful, bearlike semiretractile claws. The skull is robust; the zygomatic arch is extremely well developed, with a breadth > 85 mm and > 65% of the condylobasal length. The rostrum and nasals are short and broad. Infraorbital foramen < half the diameter of canines. The sagittal crest is well developed, its posterior portion distinctly protuberant. The teeth and mandibles are extremely robust and capable of crushing most of the larger bones of adult ungulates; width of palate > 70% of length of palate. M1 is displaced medially from the palate, and the carnassial pair is extremely large. Dental formula: 3.1.4.1/3.1.4.2 = 38.
Distribution: NE and NW China; distribution Holarctic. Chinese subspecies: *G. g. gulo* (Linnaeus, 1758); Heilongjiang, Jilin, Liaoning, Nei Mongol, N Xinjiang (includes *arcticus* Desmarest, 1820; arctos Kaup, 1829; *biedermanni* Matschie, 1918; *borealis* Nilsson, 1820; *kamtschaticus* Dybowsky, 1922; *luscus* Trouessart, 1910; *sibirica* Pallas, 1780; *vulgaris* Oken, 1816; *wachei* Matschie, 1918).
Natural History: Wolverines are major predators in the mixed conifer, larch (*Larix*), and taiga forests. They are opportunistic feeders that focus on carrion, large ungulates (*Rangifer*, *Capreolus*, *Cervus*), rodents (*Marmota*, *Myodes*), lagomorphs, and forest game birds. They will eat small quantities of berries, nuts, and fungus. Carrion is an important part of their diet, and their massive teeth are adapted for crushing

bones and obtaining bone marrow. For a stocky animal, they are very swift when attacking prey and can reach speeds of 45 kph. They are mostly nocturnal (although in some areas will be active at any time) and solitary, and they can climb and swim readily. They do not appear to be hindered by deep snow and are active year round. The fur of Wolverines is especially valued because of its frost-resisting properties and is often used to line parkas. They have a very light loading factor on snow, with a weight load of 27–35g/cm^2, which gives them an advantage in attacking ungulates in deep snow cover. They are highly territorial and practice food caching. Sexually mature at 2.5 years, they normally breed in May–August and average one litter every two years of two to four altricial young between January and April. Wolverines have delayed implantation.
Comments: Placed in subfamily Guloninae by some authors; however, molecular data suggest that Wolverines are closely allied to *Martes* (see below; Stone and Cook 2002).
Conservation Status: Total population in China estimated at < 400 (Ma 1998). (China RL—EN A1acd; D. China Key List–I. IUCN RL—VU A2c ver 2.3 (1994).
References: Hash (1987); Ma (1998); McKenna and Bell (1997); Novikov (1956); Pasitschniak-Arts and Larivière (1995); Stone and Cook (2002).

Genus *Martes*—Martens

貂属 Diao Shu—貂 Diao

The eight species of marten have a principally Holarctic distribution; three species occur in China. Their tail is bushy and its length is usually > 50% of HB length. Their limbs are short and the feet are semidigitigrade. The skull has an elongated rostrum; the infraorbital foramen is approximately equal to the canine diameter. The inflated auditory bullae and mastoid process protrude slightly. The width of M1 > 7 mm; P1 often lost with age. Dental formula: 3.1.4.1/3.1.4.2 = 38.

There is some controversy regarding the relationship of martens to the Wolverine. Cytochrome *b* data suggest that the recognition of *Martes* as here understood (to the exclusion of *Gulo*) would make the genus paraphyletic (Stone and Cook 2002).

Yellow-Throated Marten

PLATE 48
MAP 489

Martes flavigula (Boddaert, 1785)
青鼬 Qing You

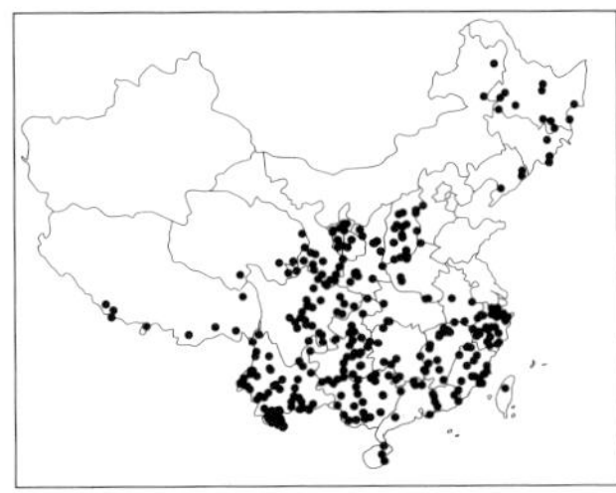

MAP 489. YELLOW-THROATED MARTEN, *Martes flavigula*

Distinctive Characteristics: HB 325–630; T 250–480; HF 70–130; E 24–53; GLS 90–103; Wt 0.8–2.8 kg. The Yellow-throated Marten is distinctly different from other martens in body proportions, giving the appearance of a remarkably elongated body with a long neck and a long, slim tail. Anterior half of body is light brown to yellowish brown; posterior half

Key to the Chinese Species of *Martes*

1.a. Tail 60–75% of HB length; tail not bushy; dark line above pale throat; distinctly contrasting bright yellow throat and dark head separated by distinct line; upper lip without medial groove; rump and tail very dark. Condylobasal length > 90 mm; length of auditory bullae > 19 mm; zygomatic breadth > 50 mm; intraorbital width ≥ postorbital width; length between condyles and postglenoid process > 35 mm; length from condyles to mesopterygoid fossa exceeding length of palate. M1 width > 8 mm. Baculum with 3–4 prongs on tip — *Martes flavigula* (Subgenus *Charronia*)

b. Tail 40–65% of HB length; tail bushy; dark line above pale throat absent; basic throat color similar to head color, with irregularly shaped white or pale patches, division between throat and head; upper lip with medial groove; rump and tail same color as body. Condylobasal length < 90 mm; length of auditory bullae < 19 mm; zygomatic breadth < 50 mm; intraorbital width ≤ postorbital width; length between condyles and postglenoid process < 35 mm; length from condyles to mesopterygoid fossa less than length of palate. M1 width < 8 mm. Baculum without 3–4 prongs on tip — 2 (Subgenus *Martes*)

2.a. Tail < 50% of HB length; brown body color with head lighter in color; white neck patch vestigal. Length of P4 < 9 mm; P3 with outer and inner edges straight; M1 length of lingual lobe > length of labial lobe; M1 width ≈ buccal length of P4; M1 labial border convex — *Martes zibellina*

b. Tail ≈ 50% of HB length; head same color as body; distinctive white chest patch. Length of P4 > 9 mm; P3 with outer and inner edges lightly convex; M1 length of lingual lobe ≈ length of labial lobe; M1 width < buccal length of P4; M1 labial border emarginated (not convex) — *Martes foina*

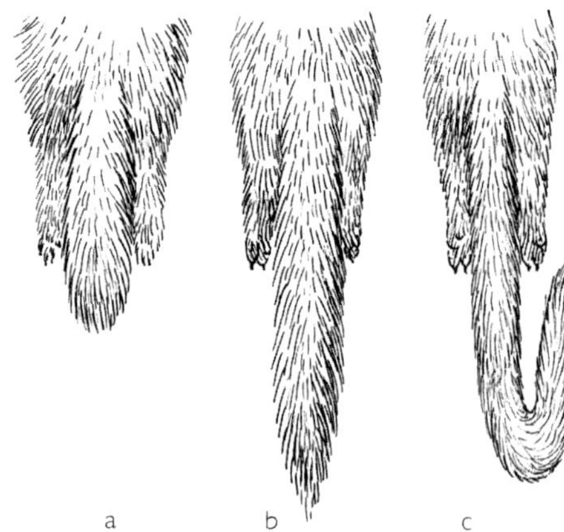

Figure 14. Comparative tail lengths and bushiness of the Sable (a), Beech Marten (b), and Yellow-throated Marten (c).

blackish brown; throat distinctively bright yellow; limbs and tail black; darker hair on head and backside; venter is light yellow. The long tail is all black, not bushy, and 60–75% of the HB length (fig. 14). There is hair between the rhiniarium and upper lip (medial rhiniarial groove is lacking); a dark stripe runs along the side of the neck. Females have four mammae. The basicranial region is long—length from condyles to mesopterygoid fossa exceeding the length of the palate. Males have considerably larger canines than females; M1 > 8 mm. Dental formula: 3.1.4.1/3.1.4.2 = 38.

Distribution: Widely distributed in S and E China; extending across to India, Indonesia (Sumatra, Java, and Borneo), North and South Korea, Pakistan, E Russia, Vietnam. Four subspecies in China: (1) *M. f. aterrima* (Pallas, 1811); Heilongjiang, Jilin, NE Nei Mongol; (2) *M. f. chrysospila* Swinhoe, 1866; Taiwan (includes *xanthospila* Swinhoe, 1870); (3) *M. f. flavigula* (Boddaert, 1785); Anhui, Fujian, Gansu, Guangdong, Guangxi, Guizhou, Henan, Hubei, Hunan, Jiangxi, Shaanxi, Shanxi, Sichuan, S Xizang, Yunnan, Zhejiang (includes *chrysogaster* (Smith, 1842); *hardwickei* (Horsfield, 1828); *kuatunensis* (Bonhote, 1901); *leucotis* (Bechstein, 1800); *melina* (Kerr, 1792); *melli* (Matschie, 1922); *quadricolor* (Shaw, 1800); *szetchuensis* (Hilzheimer, 1910); *typica* (Bonhote, 1901); *tyranus* Colbert and Hooijer, 1953; *yuenshanensis* (Shih, 1930); (4) *M. f. hainana* Xu and Wu, 1981; Hainan Island.

Natural History: Found in forests of *Cedrus*, *Quercus*, tropical pine, coniferous, and moist deciduous forests at altitudes of 200–3,000 m. Diet consists of rodents, pikas, game birds, snakes, lizards, insects, eggs, frogs, fruit, nectar, and berries. In some places it has been reported that they prey on musk deer (*Moschus*), and the young of wild boar, deer, and gorals. May hunt in pairs or small family groups. Mostly crepuscular and diurnal, but become nocturnal near human habitations. A mean annual range size of 7.2 km^2 was reported in one study in Thailand. Average number of young per litter is two or three. They have a gestation of 220–290 days.

Conservation Status: China RL—NT; although it nearly met the criteria for VU A1cd. China Key List—II. CITES—III.

References: Grassman et al. (2005); Novikov (1956); Roberts (1977).

Beech Marten

Martes foina (Erxleben, 1777) PLATE 48
石貂 Shi Diao MAP 490

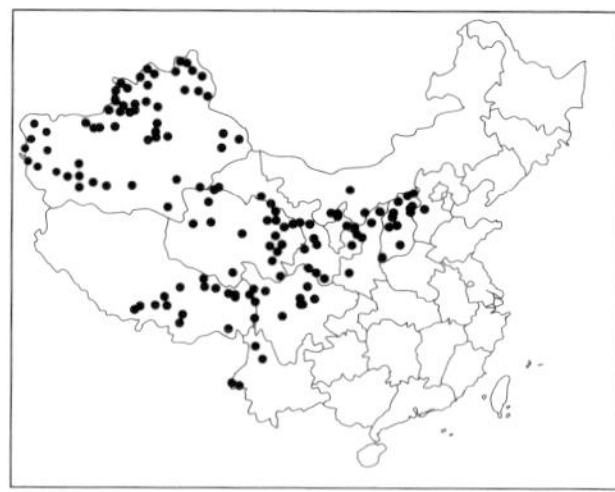

MAP 490. BEECH MARTEN, *Martes foina*

Distinctive Characteristics: HB 340–480; T 220–330; HF 45–100; E 18–25; GLS 75–90; Wt 0.8–1.6 kg. The general coloration of the Beech Marten is a solid pale grayish brown to dark brown with a bushy tail about half of HB length (fig. 14), and most specimens have a prominent white or pale neck patch. The upper lip has medial rhinarial groove. Tail and limbs are darker than the back. Sexual dimorphism is not noticeable. In the skull the lateral edge of the nasals has a noticeable constriction. P3 with outer and inner edges lightly convex; greatest diameter of M1 exceeds the outer length of P4; M1 length of lingual lobe ≈ buccal lobe.

Distribution: C through NW China; extending from Europe and some islands of the Mediterranean eastward to the Middle East, Kazakhstan, Mongolia, and Russia. Two subspecies in China: (1) *M. f. intermedia* (Severtzov, 1873); Gansu, Hebei, W Liaoning, Nei Mongol, Ningxia, Qinghai, Shaanxi, Shanxi, Xinjiang (includes *altaica* Satunin, 1914; *leucolachnaea*

Blanford, 1879; (2) *M. f. kozlovi* Ognev, 1931; SE Qinghai, W Sichuan, S Xizang, NW Yunnan.
Natural History: Beech or Stone Martens prefer rocky and open areas in the mountains up to 4,000 m, and they are generally found in more open environments than other martens. In more lowland areas, they prefer highly fragmented forests, hedgerows, and cultivated areas and are often found around human habitations. They appear to avoid conifer forests. They will use rocky crevices, stone heaps, abandoned burrows of other animals, and hollow trees for resting. The Beech Marten is opportunistic, and its diet consists of rodents, birds, eggs, and berries. In France, voles (*Microtus*) make up 30–53% of its total diet, but it shows strong seasonality, with microtines utilized most heavily in winter and spring. Another study in the Caucasus revealed martens relying almost exclusively on murine rodents (occurrence 85%) during the summer. Vegetable matter forms a major part of the late summer and early fall food in some areas (in Ukraine, 90% occurrence), and they are fond of Russian olives (*Elaeagnus*). The Beech Marten is a good climber but rarely goes high in trees. It is active at all times away from human habitations, but primarily nocturnal and crepuscular. Male territories overlap those of females. They breed once a year in midsummer with litters usually containing three or four, but as many as eight, altricial young that are cared for by the female. They have delayed implantation.
Conservation Status: China RL—EN A2cd + 3cd. China Key List—II.
References: Anderson (1970); Delibes (1978); Heptner et al.(1967b); Lode (1994); Novikov (1956); Sacchi and Meriggi (1995); Stone and Cook (2002).

Sable

PLATE 48
MAP 491

Martes zibellina (Linnaeus, 1758)
紫貂 Zi Diao

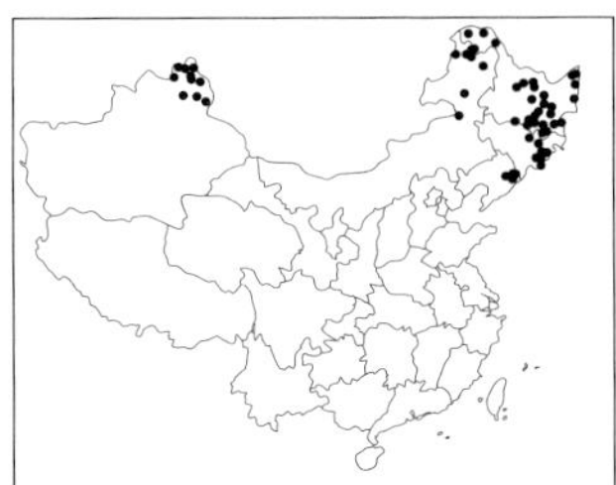

MAP 491. SABLE, *Martes zibellina*

Distinctive Characteristics: HB 340–460; T 110–180; HF 60–90; E 32–50; GLS 68–85; Wt 0.4–1.1 kg. The winter pelage of the Sable is long, silky, and luxurious. Its silky full appearance has made the Sable one of the most highly prized furs in the fur industry. Its color varies, but is generally yellowish brown to dark black-brown. Legs and tail color similar to back, but usually darker. Sometimes there is an ill-defined light patch on chest. Top of head usually lighter than back. The summer pelage is shorter, coarser, duller, and darker than the winter coat. They have a short, bushy tail (length ≈ 1/3 HB; fig. 14). The skull is long and narrow, with the width of the palate < 26 mm and the width of the zygoma < 45 mm; nasals sharply constricted. Length of P4 about equal to the width of M1; the labial and lingual lobes of M1 are expanded, giving the tooth a distinctive hour-glass shape with the labial border convex in outline. The lingual lobe is considerably larger than the labial lobe; a large posterior accessory cusp on m1.
Distribution: NW and NE China; extending across N Asia. Four subspecies in China: (1) *M. z. altaica* Kuznetzov, 1941; NE Xinjiang (includes *averini* Bashanov, 1943; *jurgensoni* Rossolimo and Pavlinov, 1987; (2) *M. z. camtschadalica* (Birula, 1919); SE Heilongjiang, E Jilin, and E Liaoning (includes *coreensis* Kishida, 1927; *hamgyenensis* Kishida, 1927; *hangiengensis* Kishida and Mori, 1931; *kamtschatica* (Dybowski, 1922); (3) *M. z. linkouensis* Ma and Wu, 1981; Heilongjiang; (4) *M. z. princeps* (Birula, 1922); NE Nei Mongol, N Heilongjiang (includes *baicalensis* (Dybowski, 1922); *vitimensis* Timofeev and Nadeev, 1955).
Natural History: The Sable dwells in both coniferous and deciduous forests, sometimes high in the mountains, and preferably near streams. It prefers dense tree canopy of mixed species, but with a high density of larch. The diet consists mostly of rodents (one study reported 72% occurrence in summer), but also includes pikas, birds, fish, insects, honey, nuts, vegetation, and berries. Nuts and berries become more important in its diet during the winter. It is mainly terrestrial but can also climb. An individual may have several permanent and temporary dens, located in holes among or under rocks, logs, or roots. A burrow several meters long may lead to the enlarged nest chamber, which is lined with dry vegetation and fur. The Sable hunts either by day or by night. It tends to remain in one part of its home range for several days and then move on. There may be migrations to higher country in summer and also large-scale movements associated with food shortage. Reported population densities vary from one Sable per 1.5 km^2 in some pine forests to one per 25 km^2 in larch forests. Individual home range is usually several hundred ha but may be as great as 3,000 ha. Mating occurs from June to August, and young are usually born April or May; because of delayed implantation, the total period of pregnancy is 250–300 days. The number of young per litter ranges from one to five , with sexual maturity at 15–16 months.
Comments: This species may be conspecific with *americana*, *martes*, and *melampus*. The subspecies for NE China are in need of revision and should be considered provisional. Heptner and Sludskii (1972) recognized *M. z. arsenjevi* Kusnetzov, 1941, for the Ussuri Valley, and the relationship of this form to *camtschadalica* is unclear.
Conservation Status: Estimated population in China of 6,000 (Ma 1998c). China RL—EN A2acd. China Key List—I.
References: Anderson (1970); Bao et al. (2003); Buskirk et al. (1996); Hagmeier (1961); Ma (1998c); Novikov (1956).

Key to the Eurasian Species of *Meles*

1.a. Narrow blackish brown stripe runs over the eye and above the ear (but does not include it); white facial stripe is narrow and does not reach the back of the head. P1 absent; p2 one-rooted (< 4 mm); posterior buccal edge of M1 has a concave notch — *Meles leucurus*

b. Wide black or dark brown stripes run from the snout, over the eyes and ears; between them, a white facial stripe extends partially onto the neck. P1 usually present; p2 two-rooted (≥ 4 mm); posterior buccal edge of M1 is convex in outline — *Meles meles* (not reported from China)

Genus *Meles*—Badgers

獾属 Huan Shu—獾类 Huanlei

Meles and *Arctonyx* have a superficial resemblance to each other, with their long, narrow heads and extended nose rhinarium, and few have questioned their close relationship. However, there has been considerable controversy over the years as to the number of species of *Meles* in Eurasia. The traditional approach considered *Meles* monotypic. However, most recent studies support the position that European and Asian badgers are not conspecific. Recent morphological studies support the separation of *Meles* into several species (Abramov 2001; 2002; 2003; Abramov and Medvedev 2003; Abramov and Puzachenko 2006), and this alignment is followed here.

Meles is widely distributed in the Palaearctic realm except N Africa. In China it occurs in the north as well as regions to the south of the Yangtze River, but there are no records from Taiwan and Hainan. Although it might be possible for the Eurasian Badger (*Meles meles*) to occur along the far western border of Xinjiang; there are no reliable records in China. A key to the identification of the two species is included, although a species account is included only for the Asian Badger, *Meles lecurus*. The line of demarcation between the closest population of the Eurasian Badger, *M. meles canescens*, distributed in Pamir-Altai mountain system (Kyrgyzstan), and *Meles lecurus tianschanensis* from Yining (W Xinjiang), is not clear. In the ecologically and geologically complex region of the W Tian Shan ranges, these boundaries are not well established.

Asian Badger

PLATE 48
MAP 492

Meles leucurus (Hodgson, 1847)

狗獾 Gouhuan

MAP 492. ASIAN BADGER, *Meles leucurus*

Distinctive Characteristics: HB 495–700; T 130–205; HF 85–110; E 35–50; GLS 110–128; Wt 3.5–9 kg. The Asian Badger is a stout, large mustelid with a pronounced long nose ending in a large external nose pad. The stout body is set on short, thick legs, with a short and thick tail. The face is elongated and cone-shaped, with small, round white-tipped ears set low to the sides of the head. The fur is coarse, dense, and of medium length. It is grizzled gray on the body, a darker gray to almost black on the legs. Asian Badgers have distinct markings on their heads– the majority of their face is white, with two black stripes, one on each side of the head, running longitudinally across the face, from the nose, over the eyes, to the base of the ears. The white face markings contrast with the all-black throat and venter. The rostrum is long and has a cartilaginous nasal pad, and the region between nasal pad and upper lip is covered with hairs. Musk glands are present just outside the anal opening underneath the tail, which is used for scent marking. The feet are digitigrade, with five toes on each foot, and the soles of the feet are devoid of hair. Long, black, curved claws are present on all toes, being longer on the manus. Three pairs of mammae are present. The skull is narrow, with the distance from the anterior margin of orbit to rostrum tip about a third of the condylobasal length; infraorbital foramen larger than diameter of canine; extremely large mastoid process. M1 quadrate, with two cusps on outer margin and a longitudinal ridge composed of three cusps at middle;between its inner margin and the longitudinal ridge there is a concavity; m1 long, its talonid with four cusps. Dental formula: 3.1.3.1/3.1.3.2 = 34.

Distribution: Distributed across China; extending to Kazakhstan, North and South Korea, Russia (from the Volga River through Siberia). Five subspecies in China: (1) *M. l. amurensis* Schrenck, 1859; Heilongjiang, Jilin, Liaoning, NE Nei Mongol (includes *melanogenys* Allen, 1913; *schrenkii* Nehring, 1891); (2) *M. l. blanfordi* Matschie, 1907; W Xinjiang; (3) *M. l. leucurus* (Hodgson, 1847); Anhui, Beijing, Fujian, Gansu, Guangdong, Guangxi, Guizhou, Hebei, Henan, Hubei, Hunan, Jiangsu, Jiangxi, Nei Mongol, Qinghai, Shaanxi, Shandong, Shanxi, Sichuan, Yunnan, Zhejiang (includes *chinensis* Gray, 1868; *hanensis* Matschie, 1907; *leptorhynchus* Milne-Edwards, 1867; *siningensis* Matschie, 1907; *tsingtauensis* Matschie, 1907); (4) *M. l. sibiricus* Kastschenko, 1900; N Xinjiang (Altai mountains; includes *aberrans* Stroganov, 1962; *altaicus* Kastschenko, 1902; *enisseyensis* Petrov, 1953;

eversmanni Petrov, 1953; *raddei* Kastschenko, 1902); (5) *M. l. tianschanensis* Hoyningen-Huene, 1910; N Xinjiang (Tian Shan mountains; includes *talassicus* Ognev, 1931).

Natural History: Most of the information below is taken from studies of the Eurasian Badger (*Meles meles*). It is presumed that there are few differences in basic natural history between these species. They occupy a large range of habitats throughout their range and prefer densely forested areas adjacent to areas of wide open fields up to 1,600–1,700 m. They are found in deciduous, mixed, and coniferous woodland, hedges, scrub, riverine habitat, agricultural land, grassland, steppes, and semideserts. They are also occasionally found in suburban areas. They live in social groups of 2–23 animals, with an average of 6. In warmer climates, they tend to be solitary or live in pairs. In colder climates, the clans are larger and more closely knit. The group is lead by a dominant pair, a male and a female. Badgers live in large underground catacombs called "setts," usually constructed in wooded areas. Setts are interlocking tunnels that contain the nesting chambers, and they often have around 20 entrances and exits to the ground above. Badgers will often take over marmot burrows. They are very territorial and will defend their home range from other badgers. Distribution of setts varies depending on soil and landscape. Deciduous and mixed woodland are preferred for digging setts, followed by hedgerow/scrub and coniferous woodland, and sometimes under buildings. They prefer to live in areas with well-drained soil that is easy to dig, has minimal disturbance by humans and their animals, and a good food supply. Badgers are opportunistic feeders and will feed on invertebrates (earthworms, insects, mollusks, beetle, and wasp larvae), small mammals (mice, rabbits, rats, voles, shrews, moles, hedgehogs), ground-nesting birds, small reptiles, frogs, carrion, plant matter (acorns, nuts, berries, fruits, seeds, cereal grains, tubers, roots, bulbs), and mushrooms. In many areas of their range, earthworms are a staple in their diet. They are nocturnal or crepuscular. They only have one litter per year, and females take sole responsibility for the care of the young. They are induced ovulators and experience delayed implantation, which usually occurs in December or early January. Gestation lasts for seven weeks after a delayed implantation.

Comments: Ellerman and Morison-Scott (1951) separated *leptorhynchus* from *leucurus*. Wozencraft (2005) listed *blanfordi* from Kashgar as a junior synonym of *leucurus* from Lhasa.

Conservation Status: China RL—CR A2cd.

References: Abramov (2001; 2002; 2003); Aristov and Baryshnikov (2001); Baryshnikov and Potapova (1990); Ellerman and Morrison-Scott (1951); Heptner et al. (1967); Kastschenko (1902); Kurose et al. (2001); Long and Killingley (1983); Neal (1948); Novikov (1956); Ognev (1931); Satunin (1914); Stroganov (1962).

Genus *Melogale*—Ferret Badgers

鼬獾属 Youhuan Shu—鼬獾 Youhuan

A more robust form than *Mustela*, the Ferret Badgers have a face with white stripes; a cartilaginous, long nose and a snout that projects considerably beyond the lower jaw; their rostrum is terminated by a large subcircular rhinarium that has no philtrum; claws relatively well developed; tail ≈ 50% of HB length. The two temporal crests on the skull are quite conspicuous and parallel, extending well to the nuchal crest; the molars are nearly parallelogram-shaped. Dental formula: 3.1.4.1/3.1.4.2 = 38. The subtropical genus *Melogale* is distributed throughout S Asia. It contains four species, two of which occur in China.

Chinese Ferret Badger

PLATE 48
MAP 493

Melogale moschata (Gray, 1831)

鼬獾 You Huan

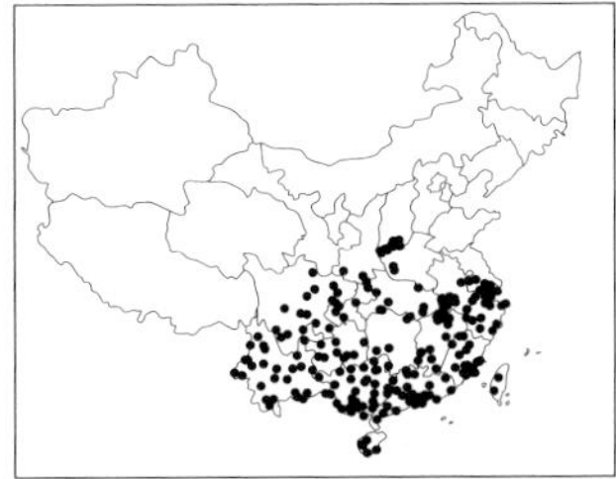

MAP 493. CHINESE FERRET BADGER, *Melogale moschata*

Distinctive Characteristics: HB 305–430; T 115–215; HF 45–65; E 20–40; GLS 70–84; Wt 0.5–1.6 kg. The Chinese Ferret Badger is smaller and more slender than true badgers, but more heavily built than weasels. The limbs are short and the snout is long and cartilaginous and projects well beyond the lower jaw. There is no philtrum dividing the upper lip. The manus and pes have five digits and long, nonretractile claws, and the soles are naked to the heel. They have a face that is basically dark in color (grayish or

Key to the Chinese Species of *Melogale*

1.a. Tail > 50% of HB length; tail hair all dark color. Auditory bullae length > 12 mm. P4 labial margin is convex; P4 length and M1 width > 8 mm (P4 is approximately equal to one third the length of the cheek teeth); P1 is disproportionately smaller than P2 — *Melogale personata*

b. Tail < 50% of HB length; white hairs on end of tail. Auditory bullae length < 12 mm. P4 labial margin is straight or concave; P4 length and M1 width < 8 mm (P4 is approximately equal to one quarter the length of the cheek teeth); P1 is slightly smaller than P2 — *Melogale moschata*

brownish), but with large, whitish patches on the cheeks, and a white band between the eyes. There is considerable variation in white facial coloration. A small black spot is present on each cheek; a pale stripe runs from the top of the head between the ears to the shoulders and then gets thinner and fades out toward the middle of the back; black band across the rostrum; and another across the forehead. The body color is dark gray or brown; venter yellow; long, bushy tail with white tip. The tail is short (≤ 1/2 HB length), bushy, and brown with a white tip. There are two anal glands and four inguinal mammae. There are two distinct temporal ridges, which are low and are either parallel or slightly bowed out over the braincase. Labial edge of P4 slightly concave; P4 length < 6 mm; P1 slightly smaller than P2; m1 talonid without distinct cusps.
Distribution: C and SE China; extending to India (Assam), N Laos, N Vietnam. Six subspecies in China: (1) *M. m. ferreogrisea* (Hilzheimer, 1905); Anhui, Fujian, Hubei, Hunan, Jiangsu, Jiangxi, Shanghai, Shaanxi, Sichuan, Zhejiang; (2) *M. m. hainanensis* Zheng and Xu, 1983; Hainan Island; (3) *M. m. millsi* (Thomas, 1922); NW Yunnan; (4) *M. m. moschata* (Gray, 1831); Guangdong, Guangxi, and Guizhou; (5) *M. m. subaurantiaca* (Swinhoe, 1862); Taiwan (includes *modesta* (Thomas, 1922); (6) *M. m. taxilla* (Thomas, 1925); Guangdong, Guangxi, S Yunnan.
Natural History: Chinese Ferret Badgers live in subtropical forest, grasslands, and agricultural areas. They are omnivorous and their diet includes small mammals, birds, bird eggs, frogs, insects, snails, earthworms, fruit, and carrion. They use their probing snouts to dig for roots and earthworms. In one study in Taiwan, invertebrates had a relative importance index of 89%. They are nocturnal, solitary, and have a home range of 4–9 ha. They usually live in preexisting burrows and are terrestrial, although they will occasionally forage in trees. Mating occurs from May to October; gestation from 60 to 80 days; average litter size of two; no delayed implantation. In China the fur of Chinese Ferret Badgers is used for collars and jackets.
Conservation Status: China RL—NT nearly met VU A2cd + 3cd.
References: Everts (1968); Long (1978); Neal (1986); Sheng (1982); Storz and Wozencraft (1999); Wu (1999); Zheng and Yu (1981; 1983).

Burmese Ferret Badger

Melogale personata.
Geoffroy Saint-Hilaire, 1831 MAP 494
缅甸鼬獾 Miandian Youhuan

Distinctive Characteristics: HB 390–410; T 175–180; HF 60–70; E 30–35; GLS 80–85; Wt 0.9–1.6 kg. In general appearance, the Burmese Ferret Badger is very similar to the Chinese Ferret Badger. Head color is also similar, except the forehead black band is thinner. The back is grayish brown to blackish. The key external feature that distinguishes this species is a white dorsal stripe that runs all the way to the base of the tail (in the Chinese Ferret Badger, it runs from the top of the head to the shoulders). The tail is dark, bushy, and with a white tip, however, it is considerably longer (> 1/2 HB) than in the Chinese Ferret Badger. The key skull feature is in the pattern of dentition. *Melogale personata* has a massive P4 (> 8 mm), and P1 is significantly smaller than P2.
Distribution: Guangdong, Yunnan; extending to Myanmar, Nepal, India (Assam), W Malaysia, Thailand, Vietnam. Chinese subspecies: *M. p. tonquinia* Thomas, 1922.

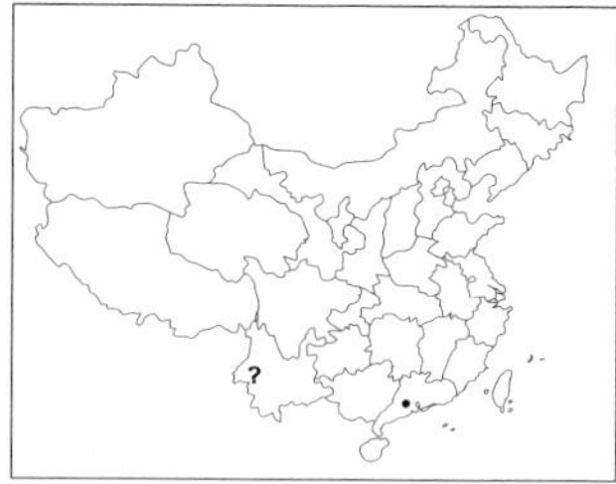

MAP 494. BURMESE FERRET BADGER, *Melogale personata*

Natural History: Little is known about the Burmese Ferret Badger's natural history. It has been reported to live in forests, grasslands, and agricultural areas throughout its range. It forages principally on the ground, and males are believed to have home ranges that enclose several female home ranges. It is principally insectivorous and eats cockroaches, grasshoppers, earthworms, and snails. It also preys upon small vertebrates (lizards, frogs, rodents, small birds) and consumes fruits and nuts. It is nocturnal, crepuscular, and believed to be solitary. During daylight hours it stays in preexisting burrows or natural shelters, which it may then enlarge. It can climb trees readily, which is assisted by the rough ridges on the soles of its feet.
Conservation Status: China RL—NA.
References: Chakraborty and Bhattacharya (1999); Lekagul and McNeely (1977); Long (1978).

Genus *Mustela*—Weasels and Ferrets

鼬属 You Shu—鼬类 Youlei

Weasels are characterized by a very long, slender body with exceptionally short limbs and ears that do not protrude above the head profile. They are all terrestrial and highly carnivorous. Rostrum of skull short: Dental formula: 3.1.3.1/2.1.3–4.2 = 34–36. Seventeen species occur worldwide on all continents except Australia. Abramov (2000) recently evaluated the relationships within the genus and organized the species diversity around nine subgenera, five of which, including seven species, occur in China: *Mustela* (includes *M. erminea*); *Gale* (includes *M. nivalis*, *M. altaica*, and *M. kathiah*); *Putorius* (includes *M. eversmanii*); *Kolonokus* (includes *M. sibirica*); and *Cryptomustela* (includes *M. strigidorsa*).

Key to the Chinese Species of *Mustela*

1.a. Feet blackish brown; venter darker than dorsum. Cranium wide; occipit breadth (as measured from the mastoid processes) > than the distance from the glenoid fossa to the occipital condyles; mastoid processes distinct and well-produced laterally; auditory bullae width near equal to length. Buccal edges of P3 and P2 are nearly at right angles because P3 is anteriorly deflected medially *Mustela eversmanii*

b. Foot color same as that of body; venter lighter than dorsum. Cranium narrow; occipit breadth (as measured from the mastoid processes) < than the distance from the glenoid fossa to the occipital condyles; mastoid processes not distinct and may not be visible from the dorsal aspect of the skull; auditory bullae width much less than length. Buccal edges of P3 and P2 are nearly in line 2

2.a. Venter pale or white; dorsal hair color changes to white in winter. Skull relatively short and broad; occipit breadth about half of condylobasal length; condylobasal length < 50 mm; toothrow length < 16 mm. M1 width < 4 mm 3

b. Venter not pale or white; hair color does not change to white in winter. Skull narrow and long; occipit breadth < than half of condylobasal length; condylobasal length > 50 mm; toothrow length >16 mm. M1 width > 4 mm 4

3.a. Tail long, its length about two times hind foot length; tail < ½ HB length; distal third of tail always black; forepaws conspicuously white and contrasted with the rest of the legs in summer pelage. Width of rostrum at canines < intraorbital constriction; intraorbital constriction ~ postorbital constriction; infraorbital foramen diameter larger than canine diameter; m1 usually has additional root in lingual side *Mustela erminea*

b. Tail short, its length only slightly larger than hind foot length; tail and its tip wholly white in winter. Width of rostrum at canines ≌ intraorbital constriction; intraorbital constriction > postorbital constriction; infraorbital foramen diameter approximately equal to canine diameter; m1 usually without additional root in lingual side *Mustela nivalis*

4.a. Size small; HB length 200–340 mm; manus conspicuously white and contrasted with the rest of the legs. Postorbtial region contracted, its bilateral margins unparallel *Mustela altaica*

b. Size large; HB length 250–400 mm; manus not contrasted with the rest of the legs. Postorbital region relatively wide, its bilateral margins nearly parallel 5

5.a. Dorsal surface monocolored with venter; pelage uniformly light brown; manus same color as with the rest of the legs. Postorbital region very long and parallel-sided; postorbital process relatively short and blunt; zygomatic arch flat; length of auditory bullae > 15 mm *Mustela sibirica*

b. Dorsal hair dark, noticeably different from lighter venter. Postorbital region short; postorbital process relatively sharp and long; zygomatic arch arc-shaped; length of auditory bullae < 16 mm 6

6.a. White stripe running down spine from head to rump; venter yellowish; tail < 50% of HB. Condylobasal length > 55 mm; auditory bullae noticeably flat, not inflated; medial lacerate foramen at anterior edge of bullae; length of toothrow > 18 mm. Length of P4 > 5 mm *Mustela strigidorsa*

b. Dorsum with no white stripe; venter orange; tail > 50% of HB. Condylobasal length < 55 mm; auditory bullae inflated; medial lacerate foramen not at anterior edge of bullae; length of toothrow < 18 mm. Length of P4 < 5 mm *Mustela kathiah*

Mountain Weasel
Mustela altaica Pallas, 1811
香鼬 Xiang You

PLATE 49
MAP 495

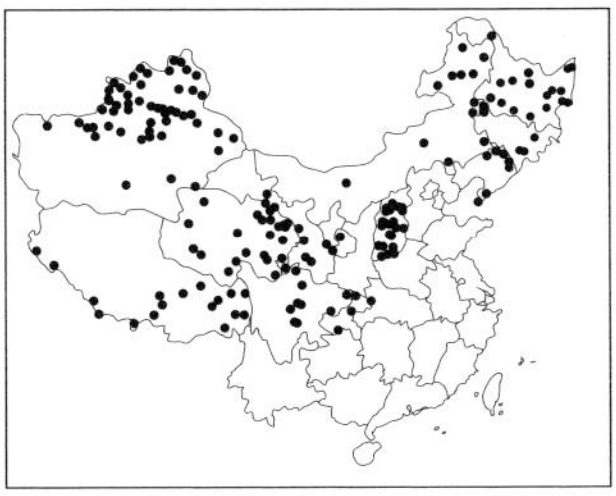

MAP 495. MOUNTAIN WEASEL, *Mustela altaica*

Distinctive Characteristics: HB 105–270; T 66–162; HF 22–47; E 11–28 GLS 36–50; Wt 80–280 g. Similar to *M. sibirica* in general color but smaller; back and tail a pale brownish yellow or reddish brown; venter yellow to yellow-white and sharply contrasted from the back. Head grayish brown with lips and chin white. Mountain Weasels have a spring and autumn molt, with the summer coat being darker brown than the lighter; winter coat pale or straw-colored. Tail > 40% of HB length and is not bushy nor tipped with black; limbs like the back but with the feet white contrasted with the back and legs. Short rostrum and long cranium; auditory bullae long, inner margins straight and nearly parallel; posterior lacerate foramen concealed. Postorbital region contracted;

infraorbital foramen ≤ diameter of canine. The two smallest weasels in China are the Least Weasel and the Mountain Weasel. They can be externally distinguished from each other based on the length of the tail (Least Weasel tail < 33% of HB).

Distribution: Throughout China except SE; extending across Asia. Four subspecies in China: (1) *M. a. altaica Pallas,* 1811; Gansu, Nei Mongol, Qinghai, Shanxi, N Xinjiang (includes *alpina* (Gebler, 1823); *sacana* Thomas, 1914; Heptner et al. (1967) placed in Russia only); (2) *M. a. raddei* (Ognev, 1928); Heilongjiang, Jilin, Liaoning, Nei Mongol; (3) *M. a. temon* Hodgson, 1857; Qinghai, W Sichuan, S Xizang (includes *astutus* (Milne-Edwards, 1870); *longstaffi* Wroughton, 1911); (4) *M. a. tsaidamensis* (Hilzheimer, 1910); Qinghai, N Sichuan, E Xizang.

Natural History: Mountain Weasels prefer alpine meadow, live among the rocky slopes, and have been found from 1,500 to 4,000 m. They may live near human habitation and occasionally attack domestic fowl. They feed mainly on pikas (*Ochotona*), hamsters (*Cricetulus*), and voles (*Alticola*), and their numbers are positively correlated with the density of pikas. They also eat a variety of small vertebrates, including rodents, rabbits, birds, lizards, frogs, fish, and insects. They occasionally eat berries. They may undergo extreme fluctuations in populations from year to year, perhaps related to variability in food supply. They are principally nocturnal; however, they may hunt during the day as well. They can climb and swim well. It is believed that they are polygynous breeders. Gestation of 35–50 days. There is no direct evidence of delayed implantation. Altricial young appear in early July, and only the female cares for the young.

Comments: Ellerman and Morrison-Scott (1951) and Wozencraft (2005) considered *M. a. tsaidamensis* (Hilzheimer, 1910) as a junior synonym of *Mustela kathiah kathiah*. Allen (1938) maintained that it is unclear as to which species this form belonged.

Conservation Status: China RL—NT; although it nearly met the criteria for VU A2cd. CITES—III.

References: Novikov (1956); Roberts (1977); Stroganov (1969); Wei et al. (1994).

Ermine

Mustela erminea Linnaeus, 1758 MAP 496

白鼬 Bai You

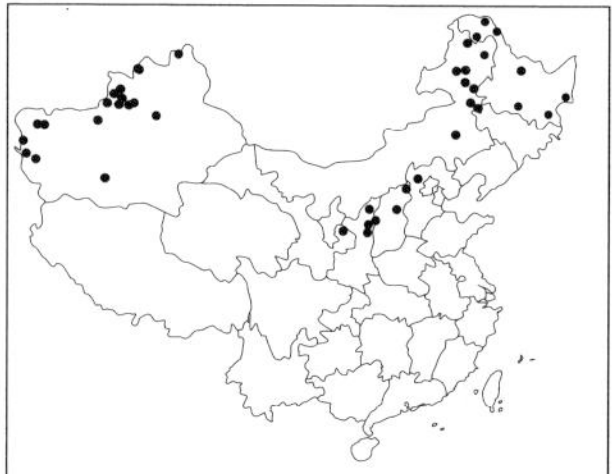

MAP 496. ERMINE, *Mustela erminea*

Distinctive Characteristics: HB 190–220; T 42–80; HF 30–40; E 12–20; GLS 38–45; Wt 60–110 g. The Ermine is widely valued for the characteristics of its fur, the color of which changes along with seasons. The summer coat is reddish brown or yellowish brown, but the feet are whitish and contrasted—there is a sharp demarcation between venter and dorsal surface. The foot pad is totally covered with fur. The winter coat is all white in northern areas—in more southern areas it may stay a yellowish brown with white venter. Size sexual dimorphism large, with males weighing up to 150% of females. Tail is greater than 33% of HB length with terminal 1/3 black; four or five pairs of teats. Rostrum of skull very short; nasals sharply constricted; mastoid width ≥ 50% of condylobasal length; mesopterygoid extends posteriorly over half of distance from molars to the end of pterygoids; width of rostrum at canines narrower than the intraorbital width; infraorbital foramen diameter > diameter of canine.

Distribution: NW and NE China; extending widely across Europe, Asia, and North America. Three subspecies in China: (1) *M. e. ferghanae* Thomas, 1895; S Xinjiang (includes *shnitnikovi* Ognev, 1935; *whiteheadi* Wroughton, 1908); (2) *M. e. kaneii* (Baird, 1857); Heilongjiang, Jilin, Liaoning, Nei Mongol (includes *baturini* Ognev, 1929; *digna* Hall, 1944; *kamtschatica* (Dybowski, 1922); *kanei* Allen, 1914; *naumovi* Jurgenson, 1938; *orientalis* Ognev, 1928; *transbaikalica* Ognev, 1928; Heptner et al. (1967) considered this subspecies absent outside of Russia and considered *transbaikalica* separate); (3) *M. e. mongolica* Ognev, 1928; Xinjiang; may be a synonym of *ferghanae*.

Natural History: The Ermine has a wide habitat range from tundra, alpine meadow, woodland (coniferous, mixed), marsh, mountains, and riverbanks, to farmland and hedgerows. Key components for habitat appear to be prey abundance and ground cover. Found up to 2,000–3,000 m year round. They have voracious appetites and will eat up to 40% of their own weight in a single day. Their diet consists of lagomorphs, microtine rodents, squirrels, rats, birds, eggs, lizards, frogs, snakes, insects, earthworms, and fruit. Mostly nocturnal and solitary; may be more diurnal in winter; climb and swim well; male territory may include several female territories. During winter they may hunt under the snow. There may be considerable flucuations in population numbers from year to year. Males and females have separate territories that they defend against members of the same sex. They will use hollow logs, rocks, and rodent burrows for dens and will cache surplus prey. A delayed implantation of 9–10 months is followed by a four-week gestation. Ermines mate once a year, producing litters of four to nine altricial young. Average natural lifespan of 1.5 years. Ermines are preyed upon by raptors and other carnivores.

Conservation Status: China RL—EN A2cd + 3cd.

References: Day (1968); King (1983a; 1990); Novikov (1956); Ognev (1962).

Steppe Polecat

PLATE 49
MAP 497

Mustela eversmanii Lesson, 1827
艾鼬 Ai You

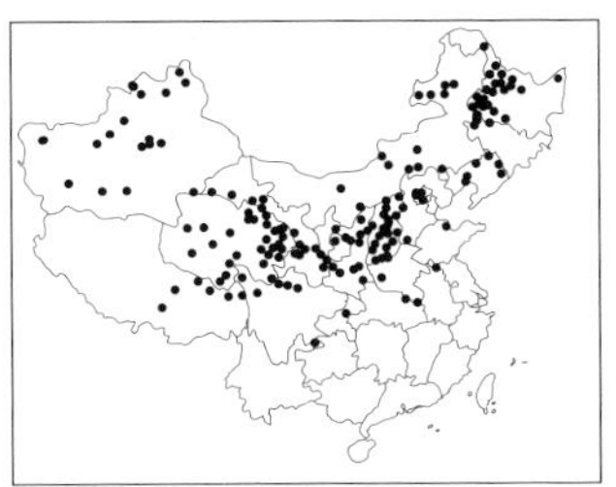

MAP 497. STEPPE POLECAT, *Mustela eversmanii*

Distinctive Characteristics: HB 315–460; T 90–200; HF 45–68; E 15–35; GLS 62–73; Wt 460–1,198 g. The Steppe Polecat is the largest species of the genus *Mustela* in China and the only member of the genus for which the feet, tail, and venter are black. The body has long black guard hairs against a yellowish brown underfur. There is a dark brown mask on the light-colored muzzle. Tail tip dark brown to black (may be 1/2 of tail); tail about 1/3 of HB. Skull robust; rostrum short; auditory bullae flat, wide, and diverging inner borders (giving the bullae a triangular appearance). Width of auditory bullae > 12 mm; width of skull at canines < interorbital width; infraorbital foramen size much greater than diameter of canine; skull with mastoid width exceeding the length between the lower edge of the foramen magnum and the anterior edge of the mesopterygoid fossa (mastoid width > 1/2 GLS); length of P4 ≈ 7–9 mm.
Distribution: C, NW, and NE China; extending widely across Asia and through E Europe. Four subspecies in China: (1) *M. e. admirata* (Pocock, 1936); Hebei, Liaoning, Nei Mongol; (2) *M. e. amurensis* (Ognev, 1930); Heilongjiang; (3) *M. e. larvatus* (Hodgson, 1849); C Qinghai, NW Sichuan, Xinjiang, E and S Xizang (includes *tibetanus* Horsfield, 1851); (4) *M. e. michnoi* (Kastschenko, 1910); Gansu, Guizhou, Heilongjiang, Henan, Jiangsu, Jilin, Liaoning, Nei Mongol, Ningxia, W Qinghai, Shaanxi, Shanxi, Sichuan, Xinjiang (includes *dauricus* (Stroganov, 1958); *lineiventer* Hollister, 1913; *sibiricus* (Kastschenko, 1912); *triarata* Hollister, 1913; *tuvinicus* (Stroganov, 1958)).
Natural History: The Steppe Polecat occupies open steppe environments through most of its range and avoids forests. It is primarily nocturnal but can also be seen active during the day in areas away from humans. Steppe Polecats are solitary and occupy burrows made by other animals. They may use a single burrow year round and enlarge it and refurnish it daily. They are small vertebrate feeders and eat murine rodents, ground squirrels, voles, birds and bird eggs, reptiles, and insects, consuming 100–150 g of meat daily. On the Tibetan Plateau it is a dietary specialist on Plateau Pikas (*Ochotona curzoniae*). Year-to-year population fluctuations can be considerable. Mating occurs early such that young are born in early spring (April–May). Gestation is around 36–40 days. Litter size ranges from 4 to 10 young.
Comments: Ellerman and Morrison-Scott (1951) considered *eversmanii* a subspecies of *Mustela putorius*.
Conservation Status: China RL—NT; although it nearly met the criteria for VU A2cd. IUCN RL—*M. e. amurensis* VU A2cd ver 2.3 (1994).
References: Novikov (1956); Sheng et al. (1999); Stroganov (1962).

Yellow-Bellied Weasel

PLATE 49
MAP 498

Mustela kathiah Hodgson, 1835
黄腹鼬 Huangfu You

Distinctive Characteristics: HB 205–334; T 65–182; HF 22–46; E 12–21; GLS 43–54; Wt 168–250 g. In external measurements and skull size, the Yellow-bellied Weasel is the largest member of the subgenus *Gale*. Back and tail dark brown, venter and mandible yellow-white, forming a distinct division from head to rump on sides of body. Edge of upper lip, the chin, and a little of the throat whitish, but the rest of the underside a deep yellow; tail about 66% of HB length. The foot pads are well developed and exposed. The medial lacerate foramen is in the anterior half of the auditory bullae. *Mustela altaica*, *M. kathiah*, and *M. nivalis* are the Chinese members of the subgenus *Gale* Wagner, 1841. They are most easily identified based on external characteristics (see key above); however, there is considerable overlap in skull features that is further confused by size sexual dimorphism. For this reason, below is a key to the skulls of the Chinese *Mustela* in the subgenus *Gale* (however, species accounts in the genus are listed in alphabetical order).
Distribution: C and SE China; extending to S Asia. Chinese subspecies: *M. k. kathiah* Hodgson, 1835; Anhui, Fujian, Guangdong, Guangxi, Guizhou, Hainan, Hubei, Hunan, Jiangxi, Jiangsu, Shaanxi, Sichuan, Taiwan, Yunnan, Zhejiang (includes *auriventer* Hodgson, 1837; *dorsalis* (Trouessart, 1895); *tsaidamensis* (Hilzheimer, 1910); *melli* (Matschie, 1922).
Natural History: Yellow-bellied Weasels are relatively unknown, and most information is anecdotal in nature. They eat rodents, birds, birds eggs, lizards, frogs, fruit, and insects. They are nocturnal, solitary, and territorial. Mating occurs in late spring or early summer. Births occur in April and May, with litter sizes ranging from 3 to 18. Adults are sexually mature in one year.

Key to the Chinese Species in *Mustela* Subgenus *Gale*

1.a. CBL < 40 mm; width at zygomatic arches < 21 mm; toothrow length < 11.5 mm. Length of M1 < 2 mm — *Mustela nivalis*
b. CBL > 40 mm; width at zygomatic arches > 20 mm; toothrow length > 11 mm. Length of M1 ≥ 2 mm — 2
2.a. Rostral length > 12 mm. Length of M1 < 3 mm; width of M1 < 5 mm — *Mustela kathiah*
b. Rostral length < 12.5 mm. Length of M1 > 3 mm; width of M1 > 5 mm — *Mustela altaica*

Comments: The Yellow-bellied Weasel was photographed near Hong Kong by camera traps in the Pat Sin Leng area.

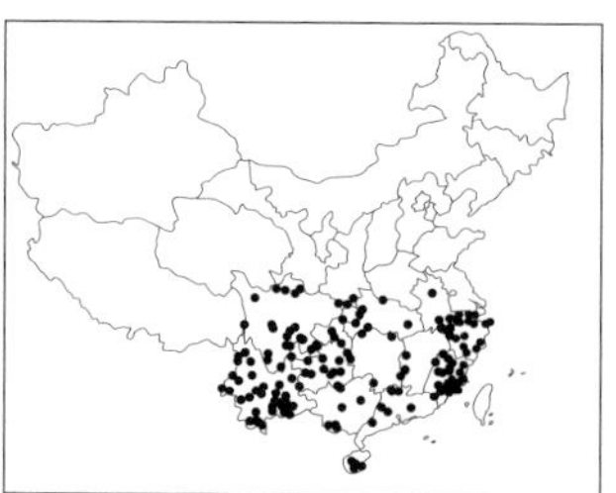

MAP 498. YELLOW-BELLIED WEASEL, *Mustela kathiah*

Conservation Status: China RL—NT; although it nearly met the criteria for VU A2cd. CITES —III.
References: Hussain (1999); Jha (1999); Nowak (1999); Sterndale (1992).

Least Weasel

PLATE 49
MAP 499

Mustela nivalis Linnaeus, 1766
伶鼬 Ling You

Distinctive Characteristics: HB 130–190; T 20–53; HF 16–25; E 9–13; GLS 27–37; Wt 28–70 g. The Least Weasel is the smallest carnivore. Males are about twice the size of females. Hair color changes seasonally; summer coat is brownish red and venter sharply offset as white or pale; winter coat pelage is uniformly white in northern parts of the range, paler than summer coat in southern parts. Tail tip same as body color (in some specimens, the very tip of the tail is black); tail < 35% of HB length; females with 3–4 pairs of mammae. Rostrum of skull extremely short; cerebral cranium large and long; width of rostrum at canines approximates intraorbtial width. Diameter of the infraorbital foramen is about equal to diameter of the canine.
Distribution: NW, C, and NE China; extending widely across Asia, Europe, and North America. Five subspecies in China: (1) *M. n. aistoodonnivalis* (Wu and Kao, 1991); S Shaanxi, NW Sichuan, Gansu (not listed in Wozencraft 2005) (2) *M. n. nivalis* Linnaeus, 1766; Hebei, Heilongiang, Jilin, Liaoning, Nei Mongol (includes *kamtschatica* (Dybowski, 1922); *punctata* Domaniewski, 1926); (3) *M. n. pallida* (Barrett-Hamilton, 1900); W Xinjiang (Tian Shan and Pamir mountains); (4) *M. n. russelliana* Thomas, 1911; Sichuan; (5) *M. n. stoliczkana* Blanford, 1877; S Xinjiang.
Natural History: Found in a wide range of habitats: forests, steppe, meadows, mountains (up to 4,000 m), villages, gardens, and farmlands. However, generally avoids any habitat that lacks good cover. May spend the whole winter under snow. Prey abundance and dense cover determines distribution. Feeds principally on microtine rodents, but also rats, hares, birds, and bird's eggs. They must eat frequently, about a third of their body weight per day. They store food for winter. Do not make their own burrows. Solitary and primarily nocturnal, although they can be active during the day. Separate territories for males and females. *M. nivalis* and *M. erminea* display character displacement. When prey numbers are high, both species can coexist. Home range of males varies from 0.5 to 25 ha, and the population may fluctuate seasonally in response to microtine abundance. Climbs trees and swims well. Mate from February–August and may have two litters of four to six annually. No delayed implantation; gestation of 34–37 days.

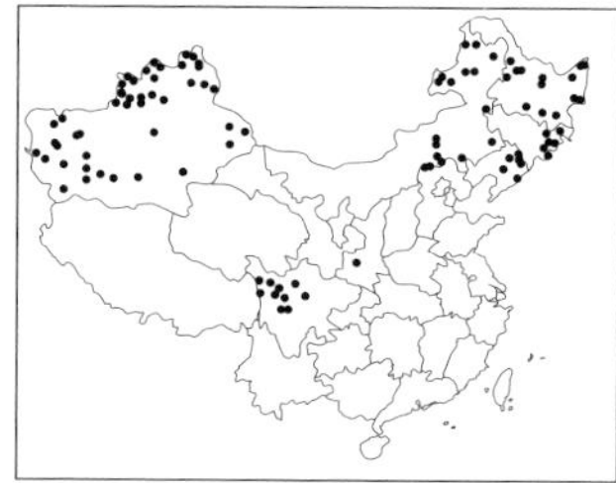

MAP 499. LEAST WEASEL, *Mustela nivalis*

Comments: Although Allen (1938) recognized *russelliana* as a full species, it is here placed in *M. nivalis* following Abramov and Baryshinkov (2000). Wu and Kao (1991) described *Mustela aistoodonnivalis* from Shaanxi Province. They distinguished their species from *M. nivalis* based on the lack of m2 in four specimens collected, a variable feature in other populations of *nivalis*, and probably should be considered as *russelliana*, but here is provisionally kept separate. Wang (2003) considered Gansu, Sichuan, and Shaanxi populations in *Mustela aistoodonivalis* Wu and Kao, 1991. Reviewed by Abramov and Baryshinkov (2000).
Conservation Status: China RL—VU A2cd+3cd.
References: Abramov and Baryshnikov (2000); Allen (1938); King (1990); Novikov (1956); Sheffield and King (1994); Stroganov (1962); van Zyll de Jong (1992); Wu and Kao (1991).

Siberian Weasel

PLATE 49
MAP 500

Mustela sibirica Pallas, 1773
黄鼬 Huang You

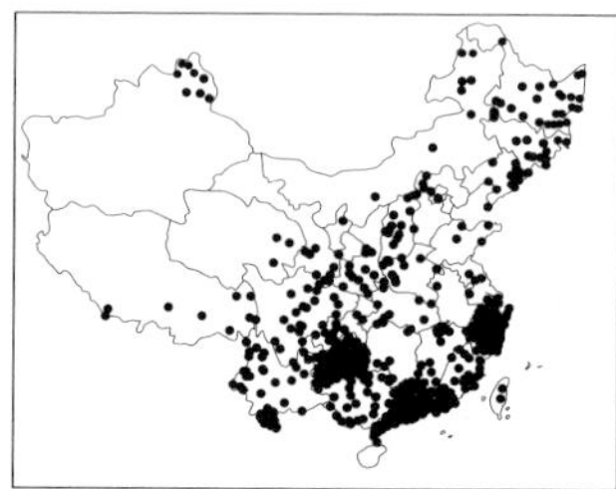

MAP 500. SIBERIAN WEASEL, *Mustela sibirica*

Distinctive Characteristics: HB 220–420; T 120–250; HF 45–65; E 15–25; GLS 50–72; Wt 500–1,200 g. Body color reddish brown to dark brown, gradually changing to a yellowish brown venter; face and front dark brown; upper lip white; an indistinct dark mask, tail about 50% of HB length, may have darker tip; size sexual dimorphism. Postorbtial constriction noticeably elongated; infraorbital foramen < diameter of

canines; bullae width less than 1/2 length. Dental formula: 3.1.3.1/3.1.3.2 = 34.
Distribution: Widespread in C and E China and the NW; extending across Asia. Six subspecies in China: (1) *M. s. canigula* Hodgson, 1842; S Xizang; (2) *M. s. davidiana* (Milne-Edwards, 1871); Anhui, Fujian, Guangdong, Taiwan, Guangxi, E Guizhou, S Hubei, Hunan, Jiangxi, Shaanxi, S Sichuan, Zhejiang (includes *melli* (Matschie, 1922); *noctis* (Barrett-Hamilton, 1904); *taivana* Thomas, 1913); (3) *M. s. fontanierii* (Milne-Edwards, 1871); Anhui, Beijing, Hebei, Henan, Hubei, Jiangsu, W Liaoning, C Nei Mongol, Shaanxi, Shandong, Shanghai, Shanxi (includes *stegmanni* (Matschie, 1907)); (4) *M. s. manchurica* Brass 1911; Heiliongjiang, Jilin, E Liaoning (includes *charbinensis* Lowkashkin, 1934); (5) *M. s. moupinensis* (Milne-Edwards, 1874); Gansu, Guizhou, W Hubei, SE Qinghai, S Shaanxi, W Sichuan, Xizang, Yunnan (includes *hamptoni* Thomas, 1921; *major* (Hilzheimer, 1910); *tafeli* (Hilzheimer, 1910)); (6) *M. s. sibirica* Pallas, 1773; NE Nei Mongol, N Xinjiang (includes *australis* (Satunin, 1911); *miles* Barrett-Hamilton, 1904).
Natural History: Found in dense primary and secondary forests, forest steppe, and mountains from 1,500 to 5,000 m. Often found in river valleys, near swamps and areas with dense ground vegetation. Also found around villages and in cultivated areas. Feeds principally on small mammals, especially murine rodents. Also reported to eat rice-field rats (*Rattus argentiventer*), domestic fowl, amphibians, birds, fish berries, nuts, and invertebrates. May store prey for later consumption. Nocturnal and crepuscular, but may be active during the day in thick vegetation. They are solitary and maintain territories. They have been observed moving up to 8 km in a single night and swim well. They will often swim in pursuit of water voles. Mating occurs in March and April. Gestation period is 33–37 days. Young are born in late May; usually five or six individuals per litter.
Conservation Status: China RL—NT; although it nearly met the criteria for VU A2cd + 3cd. CITES—III.
References: Novikov (1956); Sheng et al. (1999); Wu (1999).

Back-Striped Weasel

PLATE 49
MAP 501

Mustela strigidorsa Gray, 1853
纹鼬 Wen You

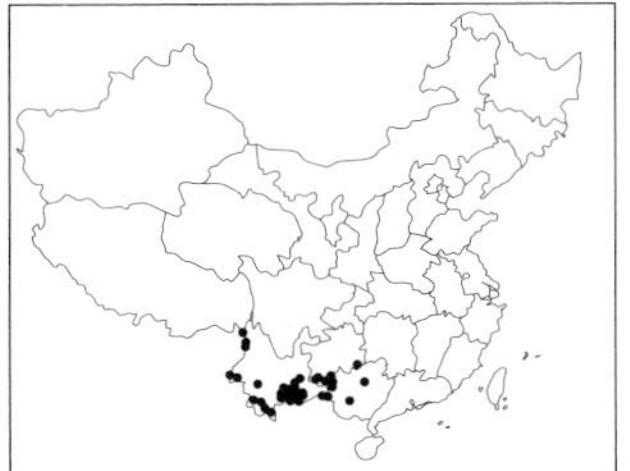

MAP 501. BACK-STRIPED WEASEL, *Mustela strigidorsa*

Distinctive Characteristics: HB 275–340; T 145–205; HF 47–54; E 20–23; GLS 57–65; Wt 443–1,200 g. The Back-striped Weasel is the only representative of the subgenus *Cryptomustela*. Basic body color is brown with a thin, whitish to silvery median dorsal stripe that goes from head to base of tail; bushy tail < 50% of HB length; lip, cheeks, chin, and throat pale yellowish. There are two pairs of mammae. The skull is most easily distinguished by the auditory bullae. In most *Mustela*, the auditory bullae is well inflated, and the medial lacerate foramen is located on the medial side. In the Back-striped Weasel, the auditory bullae is flattened, and the medial lacerate foramen is located at the anterior edge of the bullae. There is no sagittal crest on the skull, and the postorbital region is constricted (parallel-sided in *sibirica*). The length of P4 > 5.5 mm. Dental formula: 3.1.3.1/3.1.4.2 = 36.
Distribution: S China (Guangzi, Yunnan); extending throughout SE Asia. Monotypic species.
Natural History: Almost nothing is known about the Back-striped Weasel's habits. All information is anecdotal. It has been reported to live in river valleys at altitudes between 1,200 and 2,200 m. It has also been found in evergreen forests, farmland, and around villages.
Conservation Status: Total Chinese population estimated at 10,000 (Sheng 1998b). China RL—EN A2cd + 3cd. IUCN RL—VU C2a ver 2.3 (1994).
References: Sheng (1998b); Sheng et al. (1999).

Genus *Vormela* (monotypic)

虎鼬属 Huyou Shu

Marbled Polecat

PLATE 49
MAP 502

Vormela peregusna (Güldenstäedt, 1770)
虎鼬 Hu You

Distinctive Characteristics: HB 300–400; T 150–210; HF 24–88; E 15–30; GLS 52–65; Wt 370–700 g. The Marbled Polecat has a back that is basically a yellowy white color mixed with a mosaic of brown and white stripes and spots. The face, limbs, and venter all blackish brown; tail all white with blackish brown tip; tail long, its length up to half of HB length. The Marbled Polecat has noticeably large ears. The underparts are dark brown, and the facial mask is dark brown. Females have five pairs of mammae. Skull more solid than in species of *Mustela*; the nasal bones fork posteriorly; the hamulus of pterygoid in contact with triangular auditory bullae; infraorbital foramen diameter < canine diameter. M1 does not have the more typical hour-glass shape of most mustelines, and m1 has a well-developed trigonid.
Distribution: NW and NC China; extending widely across Asia and Europe. Chinese subspecies: *V. p. negans* Miller 1910; Gansu, Nei Mongol, Ningxia, Qinghai, Shaanxi, Shanxi, Xinjiang.
Natural History: Most commonly found in steppe and dry open hill and valley habitats. Has been found as high as 2,100 m. Like most mustelids, *Vormela* possesses anal scent glands, from which a noxious substance is emitted. When threatened, it throws its head back, erects its body hairs, curls its tail over its back, and emits musk from the anal glands. It excavates deep, roomy burrows and is nocturnal and

crepuscular. It has been reported to be a good climber, although it is the most fossorial of weasels. It preys on rodents and focuses on *Meriones* colonies. It will also eat birds (including poultry), reptiles, and lagomorphs. Solitary except during the breeding season. Births occur from February to March after a gestation period of about nine weeks.

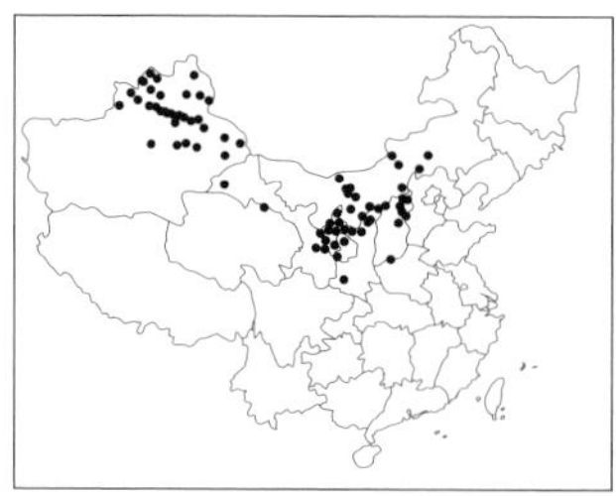
MAP 502. MARBLED POLECAT, *Vormela peregusna*

Conservation Status: China RL—VU A2cd+3cd.
References: Abdukadir (2002a); Ben-David et al. (1991); Novikov (1956); Rozhnov and Abramov (2006).

Family Ailuridae

Genus *Ailurus* (monotypic)

小熊猫科 Xiaoxiongmao Ke;
小熊猫属 Xiaoxiongmao Shu

The Red Panda has been placed in the Ursidae, Procyonidae, in a family by itself, and in a family with the Giant Panda. Recent morphological, biochemical, and molecular evidence suggests that *Ailurus* is most closely related to a group that contains the mephitids and procyonids (Decker and Wozencraft 1991; Flynn et al. 2000). The resemblances to the Giant Panda could perhaps be convergences due to their similar dietary habits. There are at least six unambiguous shared derived features in the procyonids, all of which are lacking in *Ailurus* (Decker and Wozencraft 1991). There is strong molecular support for a musteloid clade consisting of *Ailurus*, Mephitidae, Mustelidae, and Procyonidae (Flynn et al. 2000). For these reasons, the Red Panda is placed in its own family and separate from the Giant Panda.

Red Panda PLATE 45
Ailurus fulgens Cuvier, 1825 MAP 503
小熊猫 Xiaoxiongmao

Distinctive Characteristics: HB 510–730; T 370–480; HF 95–115; E 50–80; GLS 100–120; Wt 2.5–5 kg. Form as stout as that of a domestic cat; pelage uniformly reddish brown; rostrum white; cheek, brow, and ear margin all covered with white hairs; ears are large, erect, and pointed; tail long, thick, and shaggy, with 12 alternating red and dark rings; tail tip dark brown. Head round; rostrum shortened; four pairs of mammae; plantigrade; manus and pes = 5; no sexual dimorphism. Skull high and round; bullae relatively flat; postorbital process vestigal or absent; sagittal crest low; alisphenoid present; palate highly arched and grooved medially; mesopterygoid palate constricted; coronoid process is strongly hooked. Each upper premolar with more than one cusp; p1 absent; P4 with five cusps: Dental formula: 3.1.3.2/3.1.4.2 = 38.

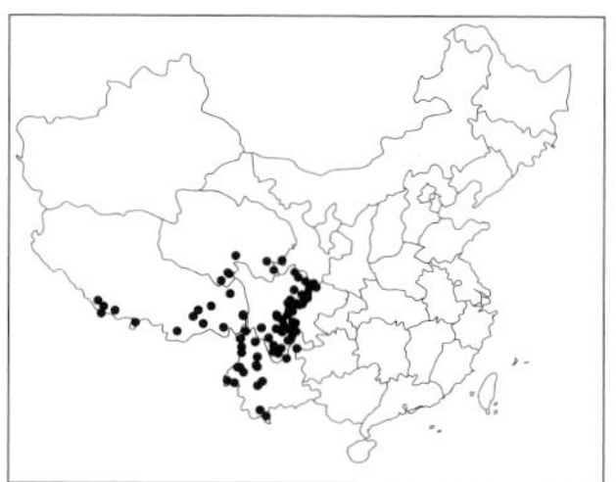
MAP 503. RED PANDA, *Ailurus fugens*

Distribution: C and SW China; extending to N Myanmar, Nepal, India (Sikkim). Two subspecies in China: (1) *A. f. fulgens* F. Cuvier, 1825; S and SE Xizang, NW Yunnan; recently extinct or absent in Guizhou, Gansu, Shaanxi, and Qinghai (Wei et al. 1999) (includes *ochraceus* Hodgson, 1847; *refulgens* Milne-Edwards, 1874); (2) *A. f. styani* Thomas, 1902; N Yunnan, W Sichuan.
Natural History: Found in the temperate forest zone of the Himalayan ecosystem at heights of 1,500–4,000 m in mixed forest habitat with a dense understory of bamboo. It lives in evergreen broadleaf, evergreen mixed, and coniferous forests, but mainly in bamboo scrub near valleys and ranges with temperatures lower than 20° C in summer and 0° C in winter. One of the ways that Red Pandas cope with a low-temperature environment is to lower their own metabolic rate; they have one of the lowest metabolic rates of any carnivore. In a study of Giant Pandas and Red Pandas in the Qionglai mountains, it was found that Red Pandas prefer south-and west-facing steep slopes in conifer forests with a high amount of logs and stumps (Giant Pandas were found on gentler slopes with a higher canopy). They focus on places where the basal diameter of bamboo is small and the humidity is high. The bulk of the diet consists of bamboo (*Chimonobambusa, Giongzhuea, Phyllostachys, Sinarundinaria,* and *Thamnocalamus*); and they focus on the tender and young shoots and leaves. They may also eat small vertebrates, eggs, blossoms, berries, and seeds (*Acer, Fagus, Morus*). They are solitary and nocturnal. Sometimes Red Pandas will form small groups of two to five individuals. They can rapidly climb high trees and move through trees when a threat appears; foraging, however, often occurs on the ground. Adults rarely interact with one another outside of the mating season, and latrines are used to mark territories. Breeding is seasonal (February and March), and gestation is 120–150 days. One litter averaging one to four is produced annually.
Comments: Hu (1998b) recognized both subspecies as occurring in China, with *A. f. fulgens* restricted to small populations in Xizang and Yunnan. More recent studies cannot support the recognition of two

Key to the Chinese Species of *Equus*

1.a. Ear short, its length < 170 mm; mane upstanding, long and exceeding anterior margin of ear base; tail wholly covered with long hairs; hoof wide and round; zygomatic arch relatively flattened and straight; coronoid process of mandible straight *Equus caballus*

b. Ear long, its length > 170 mm; mane short, not extending to anterior margin of ear base; tail base with no long hair; hoof narrow and high; zygomatic arch protruding outward; coronoid process of mandible bent 2

2.a. Size small; height of shoulder about 1.3 m; color sandy brown; color demarcation line of back and venter along upper part of lateral venter; distributed in Nei Mongol, Gansu, and Xinjiang *Equus hemionus*

b. Size large; height of shoulder about 1.4 m; color reddish brown; color demarcation line of back and venter on lower part of lateral venter; distributed in Qinghai and Xizang *Equus kiang*

subspecies in Yunnan and Sichuan. *A. refulgens* was a *lapsus calami* for *A. fulgens*.
Conservation Status: The Chinese population has been estimated between 3,500 and 7,000 (Wei et al. 1999). China RL—VU A2acd. China Key List—II. CITES—I. IUCN RL—EN C2a ver 2.3 (1994).
References: Allen (1938); Decker and Wozencraft (1991); Flynn et al. (2000); Glatston (1994); Han et al. (2004); Hu (1998b); Roberts and Gittleman (1984); Su et al. (2001); Wei et al. (1999); Wozencraft (1989b); Zhang et al. (2002).

ORDER PERISSODACTYLA
Family Equidae

Genus *Equus*—Horses, Zebras, and Asses
奇蹄目 Qiti Mu; 马科 Ma Ke; 马属 Ma Shu—
马, 斑马, 驴 Ma, Banma, Lü

Andrew T. Smith

Perissodactyls are large animals possessing an odd number of toes, with hooves on the tip—essentially these animals support their body weight on the median third toe of their feet, and their limbs are unguligrade. The skulls tend to be elongated. Unlike the artiodactyls (even-toed ungulates), they possess a third trochanter on their femur. The dentition is dominated by large cheek teeth with complex grinding surfaces (lophodont), and the canine teeth, if present, are small. All forms are herbivorous and have a simple stomach and large caecum. Once a flourishing order, the Perissodactyla are now represented by only 3 families, 6 genera, and 17 species. Only 1 family, the Equidae, occurs in China, although 2 species of rhinoceros (family Rhinocerotidae) come close to the southern border. The Equidae, all genus *Equus*, includes 8 species, distributed across Asia and Africa, although domesticated forms have been introduced worldwide; 3 species occur in China. Equids are the most cursorial of the perissodactyls. Their neck is long and laterally compressed, with long forelocks on the forehead and manes on the neck in some species; ears are sharp and upstanding; tail long, with tail hairs even extending to the middle part of the hind leg. Dental formula: 3.0–1.3–4.3/3.0–1.3.3 = 36–42.

Horse (Przewalski's Horse)

PLATE 50
MAP 504

Equus caballus Linnaeus, 1758
野马 Yema

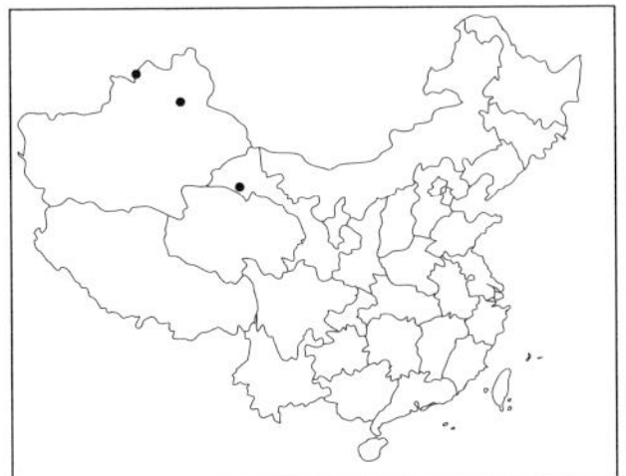

MAP 504. (PRZEVALSKI'S) HORSE, *Equus caballus* (current reintroduced localities)

Distinctive Characteristics: HB 180–280 cm; SH 120–146 cm; T 38–60 cm (without hair); E 140–180; GLS 471–540; Wt 200–350 kg. This account addresses a single subspecies of horse, the wild horse or Przewalski's Horse, *E. c. przewalskii* Poliakov, 1881. Compared with domestic horses, the head is large, legs thicker; pelage uniformly light brown in summer, and lighter in winter; ventral surface yellowish; long hair on forehead absent; manes brown, short, and upstanding; rostrum milk white; a blackish brown stripe runs down spine from middle back to base of tail; several inconspicuous transverse striations visible on limbs in summer. Front of anterior palatine straight; nasal bone long and narrow, its anterior edge extremity sharp; zygomatic arch slightly straight; posterior margin of mandible stops at anterior margin of third molar. 2N = 64–66 (64 = lineage of domesticated forms; 66 = lineage of wild horses, including Przewalski's Horse, which apparently has not contributed to the domesticated lineage)
Distribution: Formerly E Xinjiang, W Nei Mongol, NW Gansu; extending into Mongolia and Central Asia.
Natural History: Przewalski's Horse apparently survived in the wild longer than any other of the lineages of horse, largely because it inhabited remote areas in Central Asia. The morphology of Przewalski's Horse indicates that it evolved adaptations for cold climate in tundra and steppe environments—thus that its last known habitat in the semidesert steppes of Central Asia represents an environment to which it was not

well adapted. It frequently had to survive draught conditions, digging holes with its hooves to access water or migrating to areas with potential water sources. The social order of wild horses probably matches that of feral domestic horses: there is a dominant male who remains close to five or six females in a haremlike association, and separate groups of bachelor males. Mating occurs in August–September, and parturition in May–July. Only one foal is normally produced.

Comments: This form has often been treated as an independent species (*E. przewalskii*); also known as *E. ferus przewalskii*.

Conservation Status: The general history of this species has been one of spread of domesticated forms and gradual elimination by interbreeding or persecution of wild forms. The last subspecies to hold out was *przewalskii* due to its remote locale. They were rare at the time the first specimens were made available to science, and it is now felt that they are extinct in the wild. The last confirmed sighting, in Mongolia just N of the Chinese border, occurred in 1969. Between these events 12 founders were successfully brought into captivity and bred. The breeding program was rife with problems, from inbreeding, undesirable artificial selection, and introgression with nonpure lineages. Conservation geneticists have been cleaning up this captive population, and the form is now being reintroduced to parts of its former range in the Dzungarian Basin and near Dunhuang in the Gansu corridor. The Dzungarian population is being managed in the Kalamaili Reserve, where 27 horses were released in 2001, and an additional 10 in 2004. China RL—EW. China Key List—I. CITES—I. IUCN RL—EW ver 2.3 (1994) as *Equus ferus przewalskii*.

References: Bennett and Hoffmann (1999); Boyd and Houpt (1994); Breining (2006); Ryder (1993); Wakefield et al. (2002).

Kulan

PLATE 50
MAP 505

Equus hemionus Pallas, 1775
蒙古野驴 Menggu Yelu

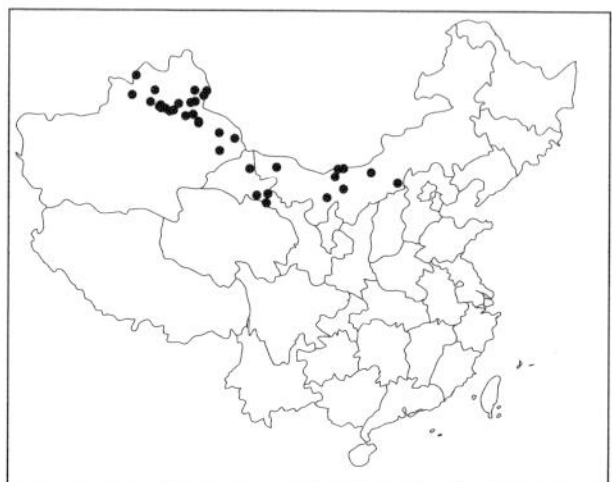

MAP 505. KULAN, *Equus hemionus*

Distinctive Characteristics: HB 200–220 cm; SH 126–130 cm; T 43–48 cm; HF 58 cm; E 178; GLS 489–544; Wt 200–260 kg. Similar to the horse, but ear larger. In winter, dorsal pelage light brown, with sand-yellow color; short erect mane; ventral surface yellowish white; inner sides of all four legs milk white; rostrum white; a brown median dorsal stripe runs down from shoulder to base of tail; shoulder blade with brown transverse pectoral stripe. Summer fur dark brown. Anterior extremity of premaxilla round; zygomatic arch bent; posterior margin of mandible stops at anterior margin of the second molar.

Distribution: Xinjiang and Nei Mongol as the nominate subspecies *E. h. hemionus* including the form *luteus*; extending into Mongolia and formerly Kazahstan, S Russia, to Syria, N Iraq, Iran, Afghanistan, Pakistan, NW India; now survives in isolated populations in India, Turkmenistan, and C Iran.

Natural History: Occupies xeric steppes and mountainous areas. Diurnally active. Kulans are primarily grazers when grass is abundant but may also feed on a variety of desert shrubs; they apparently can go for long periods without water. Normally a single male controls access to a small harem; occasionally found in large groups. The birthing season begins in May, and mating extends to the end of September; in any one population births normally extend over a two- or three-month period. Gestation lasts 11 months and may result in twins.

Comments: Known by a number of common names, including Asiatic Wild Ass and Onager.

Conservation Status: The Kulan is severely depleted throughout its range; the most extensive population resides in S Mongolia (see Reading et al. 2001) and extends into N China. Here it is perceived that they cause rangeland damage. They are also heavily poached for meat and hides (Li et al. 2002). China RL—EN A1acd. China Key List—I. CITES—I. IUCN RL—VU A3bcd; C1 ver 3.1 (2001).

References: Feh et al. (2001); Feh et al. (2002); Gao and Gu (1989); Li et al. (2002); Reading et al. (2001).

Kiang

PLATE 50
MAP 506

Equus kiang Moorcroft, 1841
藏野驴 Zang Yelu

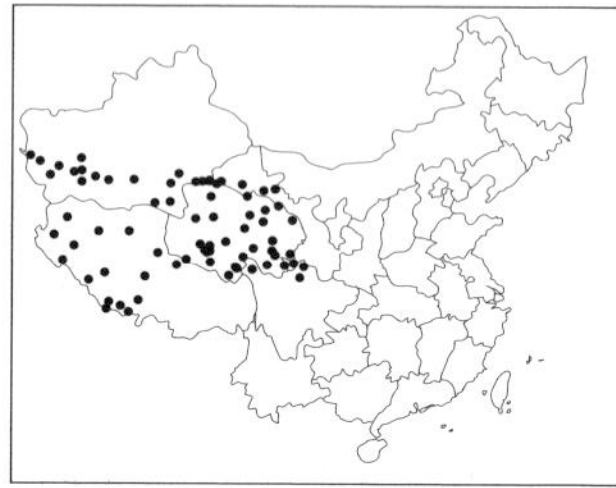

MAP 506. KIANG, *Equus kiang*

Distinctive Characteristics: HB 182–214 cm; SH 132–142 cm; T 32–45 cm; HF 41–54 cm; E 220; GLS 473–547; Wt 250–400 kg. Typical equid with large head and blunt muzzle; nose convex. The short main is held upright. The pelage is a rich chestnut color, becoming darker brown in winter and assuming a more reddish hue in late summer. Legs and undersides are

Key to the Chinese Families of Artiodactyla

1.a. Upper incisor present; shape of lower canine different from that of lower incisor 2
b. Upper incisor absent; shape of lower canine same as that of lower incisor 3
2.a. Cannon bone not present; upper canines directed upward and outward; metacarpals of 2nd and 5th digits complete Suidae
b. Cannon bone present; upper canines straight and directed down; toe pads soft (digitigrade); metacarpals of 2nd and 5th digits absent Camelidae
3.a. Small size (HB length normally < 1 m); no horns or antlers; prominent canines 4
b. Large size (HB length normally > 1 m); with horns or antlers in males of most species; canines not prominent 5
4.a. Four prominent digits (side toes well developed) Tragulidae
b. Two prominent digits (side toes absent or reduced to dew claws); males with distinctive musk glands (preputial scent gland) Moschidae
5.a. Antlers present on males (except *Hydropodes*); cheek teeth relatively short-crowned with roots; upper canine present Cervidae
b. Nondeciduous horns present on males and most females (although smaller); cheek teeth high-crowned and more or less rootless; upper canine absent Bovidae

white. There is a dark dorsal stripe that extends from the mane to the terminus of the tail. Ear tips are black, as is a narrow band along the margin of the hooves.
Distribution: W C China; extending into Ladak and Sikkim (India), and Nepal. Three subspecies in China: (1) *E. k. holdereri* Matschie, 1911; Qinghai, NW Sichuan, W Gansu; (2) *E. k. kiang* Moorcroft, 1841; S Xinjiang, C and W Xizang; (3) *E. k. polyodon* Hodgson 1847; S Xizang.
Natural History: Kiang inhabit the open country of the high Tibetan Plateau. They may range as high as 5,300 m but are also found in adjoining desert steppe as low as 2,700 m. In China their diet consists almost entirely of grasses and sedges, primarily *Stipa* spp.; forbs are rarely eaten. Their social dynamics are variable; many Kiang are seen alone, but they may also be seen in small groups or in extremely large assemblages of hundreds of animals. The mating season usually commences in late July and may extend to September; young are born from mid-July to August following a 355-day gestation.
Comments: Kiang have historically been included in *Equus hemionus*; recent analyses clarify their morphological and genetic distinctness. Further, there is a 350 km gap between the current distributional ranges of the two species.
Conservation Status: Populations are becoming increasingly fragmented and negatively impacted by current development priorities, primarily fencing, on the plateau. China RL—EN A1acd. China Key List—I. CITES—II. IUCN RL—*E. k. polyodon* DD ver 2.3 (1994).
References: Gao and Gu (1989); Schaller (1998); Shah (2002).

ORDER ARTIODACTYLA—Even-toed Ungulates
偶蹄目 Outi Mu—偶蹄类 Outilei

John MacKinnon

Artiodactyls comprise medium-to-large hoofed animals. All four legs possess an even number of toes, nearly equal in size, that are arranged around the axis formed by the highly developed third and fourth toes; the limb axis supports the body on these two toes. Toes two and five, or rudiments thereof, are smaller and face backward. Most species are strictly herbivorous (except the omnivorous pigs), fast running, and social living. Some species have horns or antlers growing from the frontal bone. Canines are reduced in most species that have horns or antlers and highly developed in those that do not. Stomachs complex with two to four chambers; several families possess a ruminant three-or four-chambered stomach. Face or other external secreting glands are a common characteristic. Skeletal characteristics include the astragalus of the ankle with its two pulley-shaped surfaces that accommodate a springing ligament used to give flexibility and speed to their gait. Additionally they do not have a third trochanter on the femur (as do perissodactyls); the nasals are not wide posteriorly; there is no alisphenoid canal; and premolars are smaller than molars.

The Artiodactyla represents a diverse lineage composed of 10 families (6 of which occur in China), 87 genera, and over 220 species. They are distributed throughout the world, naturally or through introduction. Recent molecular analyses link the artiodactyls closely with the whales (cetaceans); and thus some classifications place them in the order Cetartiodactyla.

Family Suidae—Pigs

猪科 Zhu Ke—猪 Zhu

The Suidae represents an Old World family of nonruminant ungulates comprising pigs and the Babirusa and is closely related to families of peccaries and hippos. Pigs are medium-sized with thickset bodies and sparse bristly hair. The rostrum is long, and its anterior extremity forms a bare nasal disk or snout. The lower canine is large and tusklike, being constantly sharpened by wear against upper canine. In the Babirusa the upper canine is unusually curled up over forehead. Stomach is simple and two- chambered; females bear three to six pairs of nipples. Young are striped, and pigs live in small social herds. There are five genera, of which only one, *Sus*, occurs in China.

Genus *Sus*—Pigs

猪属 Zhu Shu—猪 Zhu

Among the eight species of *Sus* is the ubiquitous Wild Boar, *S. scrofa*, the form that ranges across most of China. Other species of pig, for example, the warty pigs, occur in Indochina and the Sundaic and Wallacean regions. The pygmy hog (*Sus salvinus*) occurs in grasslands on the north side of the Brahmaputra River in Assam very close to the border claimed by China (but in fact well inside territory controlled by India). All pigs live in herds that roam forests and wild lands as well as raiding farmland in search of worms, fruits, and other foods. They have a unique snout designed to root about under the surface of the ground, both sniffing out and digging up their favored foods.

Wild Boar

Sus scrofa Linnaeus, 1758 PLATE 51 MAP 507

野猪 Ye Zhu

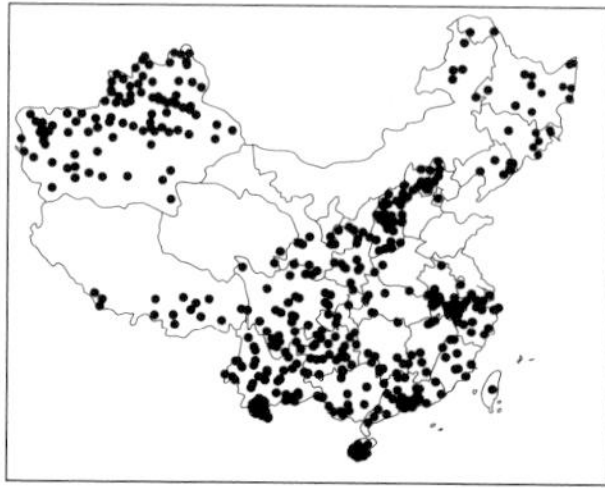

MAP 507. WILD BOAR, *Sus scrofa*

Distinctive Characteristics: HB 900–1,800; SH 590–1,090; T 200–300; HF 250–350; E 114; GLS 295–350; Wt 50–200 kg. Distinctive brown or blackish heavy-set pig with coarse hair. Male has ridge of hair from crown down back of neck. Northern races are long-haired, those in tropics rather sparsely haired. Hind toes generally leave prints, contrary to deer, on most substrates. Toes sometimes rather blunt compared to those of deer, and associated rooting signs and sloppy black dung are diagnostic signs. Skull long and slender. Dental formula: 3.1.4.3/3.1.4.3 = 44; upper incisors laterally compressed and nearly level; molars with many small, rounded protuberances among cusps. Males have prominent tusks. 2N = 36.

Distribution: Occurs across China except the driest deserts and high plateau areas; extending to Europe, N Africa, through Asia to the Malay Peninsula, Sumatra, and Java. Seven subspecies occur in China: (1) *S. s. chirodontus* Heude, 1888; S of Yangtze River; (2) *S. s. cristatus* Wagner, 1839; SW China; (3) *S. s. moupinensis* Milne-Edwards, 1871; C China; (4) *S. s. nigripes* Blanford, 1875; NE China; (5) *S. s. taininensis* Heude, 1888; Yunnan; (6) *S. s. taivanus* Swinhoe, 1863; Taiwan; (7) *S. s. ussuricus* Heude, 1888; NE China.

Natural History: Wild Boars are found in all wild habitats from forest to scrub, grasslands, and swamps, raiding cultivation areas and ranging far into mountains. Mainly crepuscular and nocturnal. Omnivorous, feeding on plant material, mushrooms, seeds, and fruit, especially acorns, but also worms, snails, insects, small vertebrates, and carrion. When feeding, Wild Boars rummage through the topsoil with their flat sensitive snout, sniffing out delicacies. Can become predatory, sometimes attacking snakes upon encounter. Male canine teeth rub together to give very sharp tusks used in defense and aggressive status fighting. Travel in small herds, although some males are solitary. Wild Boars are known to be good swimmers. Makes piles of broken off saplings as a nursery nest. One litter of four to eight young is born in spring following a four-month gestation.

Conservation Status: Much reduced in numbers due to hunting but still widespread, sometimes common and even becomes an agricultural pest in some areas. In Taiwan hunting of Wild Boars to prevent crop damage has severely reduced their population. China RL—LC.

References: Oliver et al. (1993).

Family Camelidae—Camels

骆驼科 Luotuo Ke—骆驼 Luotuo

The Camelidae is a small South American, African, and Asian family comprising the camels, vicuñas, guanacos, alpacas, and llamas. These are large ungulates with no horns and a long neck. Their muzzle is split to form a harelip. Toes two and five are absent, and the end of toes three and four is expanded into a broad pad (they do not possess hoofs) to allow effective movement in sand and on rocks; the foot posture is digitigrade. The upper incisor is tusk-shaped, and molar teeth are selenodont. The stomach has three chambers. Several species have been domesticated. Of three genera, only *Camelus* occurs in the Old World and in China.

Genus *Camelus*—Old World Camels

骆驼属 Luotuo Shu—骆驼 Luotuo

Large camelid with one or two large dorsal humps. Dental formula: 1.1.3.3/3.1.2.3 = 34. Two species occur, of which only one occurs in China.

Bactrian Camel

PLATE 51
MAP 508

Camelus bactrianus Linnaeus, 1758
双峰驼 Shuangfeng Tuo

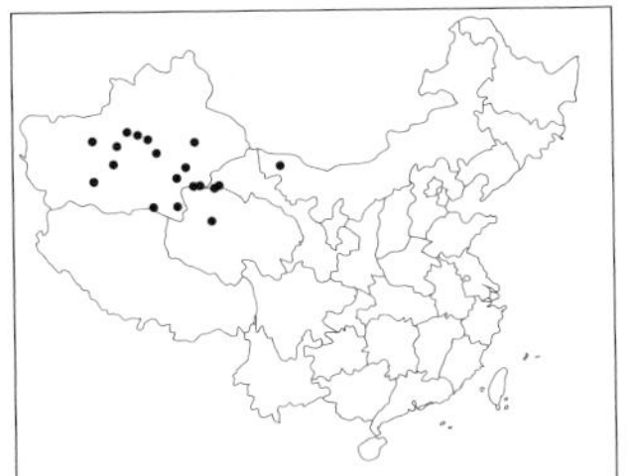

MAP 508. BACTRIAN CAMEL, *Camelus bactrianus*

Distinctive Characteristics: HB 3.2–3.5 m; SH 1.6–1.8 m; Wt 450–680 kg. Very large ungulate with two prominent humps on back. Head small, neck long and curved upward. Color golden to bark brown, darkest on thighs. In winter has long, shaggy hair on neck and humps. Has double row of long eyelashes and hair in ears to protect it from sandstorms. Its slitlike nostrils can close during dust storms. The wild Bactrian Camel is relatively small and lithe when compared to the domesticated form; its humps appear significantly smaller and are more conical in shape. Its fur coat is not as thick.
Distribution: Taklamakan Desert of SE Xinjiang, NW Qinghai, and NW Gansu, and into the Gobi Desert; extending into Mongolia and Central Asia.
Natural History: Occupies steppe grassland, montane desert, semidesert, and arid scrub. Can occur up to 4,000 m in altitude. Domesticated for over 4,000 years, and more domesticated animals now remain than wild. Eats a wide variety of desert plants and leaves of thorn trees and bushes. Can eat salty halophytic plants. In times of food scarcity will eat bones, meat, shoes, canvas, etc. The humps store fat and enable the camel to live for many days without food. Water-filled chambers surround the stomach and enable the camel to live for several weeks without water. The camel can drink slightly saline water and can urinate concentrated salt. It can hold over 100 liters of water. The camel can vary its body temperature facultatively, so it does not need to sweat or expend energy to thermoregulate. The overall suite of adaptations of the Bactrian Camel allows it to withstand winter temperatures many degrees below zero and extremely hot summer temperatures. Lives in small herds of 6–20 animals; seasonal migrants. During the mating season, males fight, bite, spit, snort and try to push each other to the ground. Gestation is about 400 days, and one or two young are born per litter. Young stay with the mother for three to five years. Adults live up to 30 years.
Conservation Status: Only about 500–1,500 wild Bactrian Camels remain globally, about half in China. These herds are threatened by habitat alteration, illegal hunting, and hybridization with domestic camels. China RL—EN A1acd. China Key List—I. IUCN RL—CR A3de + 4ade ver 3.1 (2001).
References: Hare (1997); Schaller (1998).

Family Tragulidae—Chevrotains and Mouse-deer

鼷鹿科 Xilu Ke—鼷鹿 Xilu

The Tragulidae are the world's smallest deer. They show several primitive features such as lacking antlers or horns, having large canines (in males the canine is a well-developed long, curving, narrow sharp tusk; in females the upper canine is very small), and retaining slender but well-formed second and fifth digits. They are mostly nocturnal and frugivorous, feeding on fallen fruits in forest. They possess a three-part stomach. Dental formula: 0.1.3.3/3.1.3.3 = 34. Of three genera, only *Tragulus* reaches SE Asia and China.

Genus *Tragulus*—Mouse-deer

鼷鹿属 Xilu Shu—鼷鹿 Xilu

The mouse-deer have short forelegs and long hind legs, and usually sport light spots on their throat and breast. The rostrum is slender and laterally compressed; the premaxilla and nasal bone are about equal in length. *Tragulus* is a SE Asian genus composed of two (Grubb 2005) to six (Meijaard and Groves 2004a) species ranging from Indochina to Borneo. This discrepancy in treatments of *Tragulus* honestly reflects the confusion surrounding the taxonomy of this ancient group. Only a few specimens have been recorded in China at the southern tip of Xishuangbanna in SW Yunnan, and correspondingly the taxonomy of these forms remains unclear. Below we attribute these specimens following Grubb (2005); but see Comments.

Java Mouse-Deer

PLATE 51
MAP 509

Tragulus javanicus (Osbeck, 1765)
小鼷鹿 Xiao Xilu

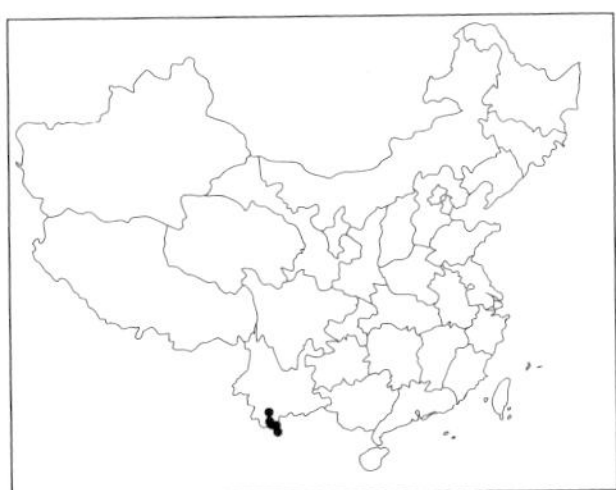

MAP 509. JAVA MOUSE-DEER, *Tragulus javanicus*

Distinctive Characteristics: HB 430–500; SH 350; T 65–80; E 35–50; GLS 92–103; Wt 2.5–4.5 kg. Tiny deer lacking antlers and having long, curved canines in both sexes–reflecting the general trend in deer for males to possess either antlers or large canines. General pelage reddish brown with characteristic three white bars under the throat joined under the chin in a neat "T" shape. Underparts yellowish white. Footprints and dung are tiny compared to those of other Chinese ungulates.
Distribution: Found in China only in Xishuangbanna prefecture of S Yunnan; ranging to the Greater Sundas and Indochina. The form *williamsoni* is now recognized as a separate species (see below), confined to S Yunnan and N Indochina, but its exact limits remain unknown.
Natural History: Inhabits tropical evergreen lowland forests, using crown-gap areas with dense undergrowth as foraging sites and ridge areas as resting sites. Feeds largely on fallen fruits, especially figs, but also eats young shoots. Once thought to be nocturnal; recent studies have shown it to be diurnally active and to rest at night (Matsubayashi et al. 2003). Solitary. Eyes very reflective at night. Runs to water when chased by dogs. Hunters can attract mousedeer by patting the ground in imitation of the female's thumping behavior. Makes shrill, squeaky whistle on contact. Runs with jerky, stiff-legged gait and sits hunched on haunches. Gestation is five or six months, and pregnancy may almost immediately follow birth of the single (sometimes two) young, so that the reproductive rate is high.
Comments: Specimens found to the west of the Mekong River could be referred to the rather large form *williamsoni*. Specimens from the east could be *kanchil*. These have now been separated as distinct species from *javanicus* by Meijaard and Groves (2004a), but given the doubt as to which form occurs in Xishuangbanna (*williamsoni* has been described on the basis of only a single specimen from N Thailand), it is safer to retain the older classification for the time being.
Conservation Status: Rare and restricted in China; widespread and fairly common elsewhere, although their densities seem to be reduced significantly in areas of logged forest (Heydon and Bulloh 1997). China RL—CR A1cd; B1ab(i,ii,iii); D. China Key List—I.
References: Grubb (2005); Heydon and Bulloh (1997); Matsubayashi et al. (2003); Meijaard and Groves (2004a).

Family Moschidae

Genus *Moschus*—Musk Deer

麝科She Ke; 麝属She Shu—麝 She

These are small deer without antlers; instead, both genders sport prominent canines. Their lower incisor has a linguiform crown. Dental formula: 0.1.3.3/3.1.3.3 = 34. Their hair is very stiff and bristly. Most forms live in mountains. Musk deer are very agile and can jump out of walled pens 2 m high, as well as into trees where they balance on small branches. Toes long and sharp. While they lack infaorbital glands, male musk deer have a preputial scent gland on their underbelly that is extremely valued both in the perfume industry and for traditional Chinese medicine. This has led to severe persecution and snaring of all species, driving them close to extinction (Yang et al. 2003). However, musk deer can be farmed with moderate success, although captive animals remain very wild and nervous (Yang et al. 2003; Zhou et al. 2004). The conservation status of musk deer has been reviewed by Wemmer (1998). Of a total of seven *Moschus* species, six are recognized in China.

Anhui Musk Deer

Moschus anhuiensis
Wang, Hu, and Yan, 1982 MAP 510
安徽麝 Anhui She
Distinctive Characteristics: HB 696–765; SH < 500; T 18–32; HF 192–195; GLS 141–151; Wt 7.1–9.7 kg. Body gray-brown; lower hind legs nearly black. The ear is

Key to the Chinese Species of *Moschus*

1.a.	Small and dark with no lateral spotting in adult and no contrasting pale marks on neck	*Moschus fuscus*
b.	Some pale or contrasting marks on neck and lower mandible	2
2.a.	Pale yellowish spots on sides of adult	3
b.	No pale spots on sides of adult	4
3.a.	Height at shoulder < 530 mm	*Moschus anhuiensis*
b.	Height at shoulder > 530 mm	*Moschus moschiferus*
4.a.	Back of neck in whorls giving banded appearance; ear fringe rufous	5
b.	Back of neck not whorled; ear fringes white or yellow	*Moschus berezovskii*
5.a.	Pelage light brown with sandy hue; distinctive orange eyering; throat with noticeable white stripes or a single broad creamy band	*Moschus chrysogaster*
b.	Pelage dark brown, throat dark; eyering poorly expressed; only an indistinct yellowish stripe up front of neck	*Moschus leucogaster*

fringed with white and blackish on the back; the black coloration extends to the cheeks and forehead. The chin and throat are white, and a white stripe extends up to the cheek while two white stripes run backward along the underside of the neck, forming a ring on the upper breast. Young (one to two years old) possess 13 orange stripes crossing the body between the shoulder and the hip, although these gradually disappear, becoming many spots that form three lines on sides of the back in adults. The rump is dusky brown, and the rump patch insignificant.
Distribution: Found locally only in Mt. Dabie area of W Anhui Province. Endemic.

MAP 510. ANHUI MUSK DEER, *Moschus anhuiensis*

Natural History: This species is poorly known, but its natural history is likely similar to that of *M. berezovskii* and *M. moschiferus* (see Comments). It is more likely to produce twins than single births. Females mature rapidly and are capable of breeding in their first year of life.
Comments: Formerly treated as a subspecies of *M. berezovskii* and *M. moschiferus*, but now regarded as a separate sister species.
Conservation Status: Threatened in China due to restricted distribution. China RL—EN B1ab(i,ii,iii) + 2ab(i,ii,iii). China Key List—II. CITES—II.
References: Groves and Feng (1986); Su et al. (1999); Wang et al. (1982); Wang et al. (1993).

Forest Musk Deer

Moschus berezovskii Flerov, 1929 — PLATE 52, MAP 511

林麝 Lin She

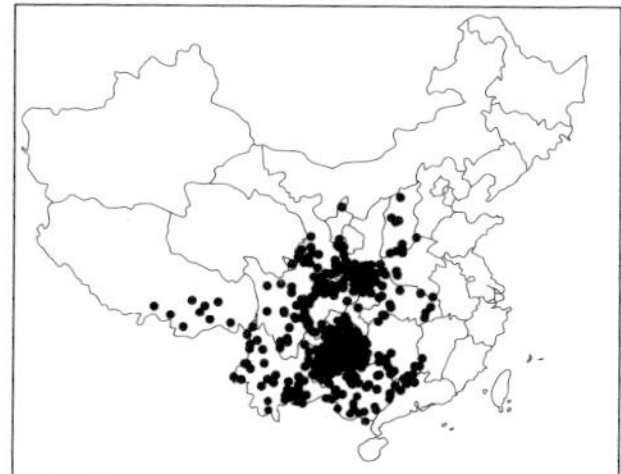

MAP 511. FOREST MUSK DEER, *Moschus berezovskii*

Distinctive Characteristics: HB 630–800; SH < 500; T 40; GSL 102–146; Wt 6–9 kg. Pelage dark olive brown without spotting on back of adult; nearly black on the rump; legs and venter yellow to orange-brown. Inside of ears and eyebrows whitish; ears black at tip and orange-brown at their base. Lower jaw with cream stripe; cream patches on side of throat join to two broad cream stripes running down the front sides of neck to breast; contrasting band up median of neck dark brown. Juveniles spotted. Races vary in details: *berezovskii* is larger and darker brown with orange-yellow underparts and brownish yellow neck stripes; *caobangis* is the smallest and palest form with more fulvous pelage; *yunguiensis* is intermediate in color and also small; and *bijiangensis* is large in size, paler brown on the back and with grayish white neck stripe and spot.
Distribution: Widely distributed in C and S China; extending to the eastern Himalayas and into NE Vietnam. Four subspecies in China: (1) *M. b. berezovskii* Flerov, 1929; Sichuan, Qinghai, Xizang; (2) *M. b. bjiangensis* Wang and Li, 1993; NW Yunnan; (3) *M. b. caobangis* Dao, 1969; S Yunnan, Guangxi, Guangdong; (4) *M. b. yunguiensis* Wang and Ma, 1993; Yunnan-Guizhou highland, Hunan, Jiangxi; Wang (2003) lists an unnamed form as occurring in S Gansu, Ningxia, S Shaanxi, W Hubei, and W Henan.
Natural History: Inhabits coniferous or broadleaf forests, or mixed forests at high elevations (2,000–3,800 m). Most active between dusk and dawn, alternately resting and feeding. Animals share communal latrines, leaving large piles of tiny pellets. These animals are shy, sedentary, and remain within a defined home range throughout the year. Males utilize their large musk gland to defend their territory and attract mates. When alarmed they make great leaps with wild changes of direction. Forest Musk Deer eat leaves, grasses, moss, lichens, shoots, twigs. They can adroitly jump into trees to forage. Their main predators include leopard, marten, fox, wolf, lynx, and especially humans. Gestation lasts 6.5 months, after which one or two young are born. During the first two months, the young deer lie hidden in secluded areas, independent of their mother except at feeding times. They are weaned within 3–4 months and reach sexual maturity by 24 months. Animals may live up to 20 years.
Comment: Has included the form *anhuiensis*, which herein is treated as an independent species.
Conservation Status: China RL—EN A1cd. China Key List—II. CITES—II. IUCN RL—LR/nt ver 2.3 (1994).
References: Wang et al. (1993); Wemmer (1998).

Alpine Musk Deer

Moschus chrysogaster (Hodgson, 1839) — PLATE 52, MAP 512

马麝 Ma She

Distinctive Characteristics: HB 800–900; SH 500–600; T 40–70; HF 270; GSL 140–170; Wt 9.6–13 kg. A large musk deer. Pelage light brown with sandy yellow hue and hair on back of neck distinctively whorled, giving a banded appearance. Juvenile has white spots on back, but these are rarely visible in adults. Throat with noticeable white stripes or single broad creamy band; throat pelage often a red-gold color. Inside ears lined with long sandy hairs; distinctive orange eye ring. Skull tends to be long and slender.

Distribution: Highlands of C China and south to the Himalayas; extending to Nepal, India (Sikkim), and Bhutan. Two subspecies in China: (1) *M. c. chrysogaster* (Hodgson, 1839); SE Xizang, E Qinghai; (2) *M. c. sifanicus* Büchner, 1891; Qinghai, Gansu, Ningxia, W Sichuan, and NW Yunnan. There is no clear delineation between these forms.

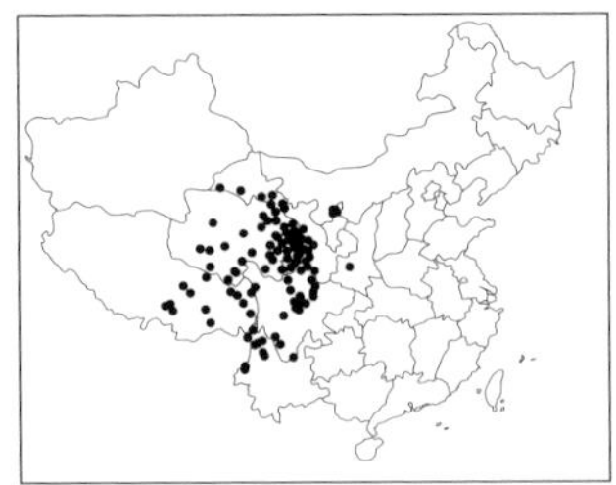

MAP 512. ALPINE MUSK DEER, *Moschus chrysogaster*

Natural History: An animal of barren plateaus at high altitudes, where it occupies meadows, fell-fields, shrublands, or fir forests. In W Sichuan, where it overlaps the distribution of *M. berezovskii*, the Alpine Musk Deer inhabits the higher elevations (above 3,000 m), compared with the 1,000–2,500 m altitudinal range of the Forest Musk Deer. Feeds mainly on grasses and shrubs. Solitary and crepuscularly active. Densities in Qinghai may be as low as two to three animals per km^2. One to two young (normally one) are born in June following a six-month gestation.
Comments: The form *sifanicus* has been included in *M. moschiferus* and as an independent species. Until recently the form *leucogaster* was included in *chrysogaster*, but here it is treated independently.
Conservation Status: This species has been heavily poached for its musk. China RL—EN A1d + 2cd + 3cd. China Key List—II. CITES—II. IUCN RL—LR/nt ver 2.3 (1994).
References: Green (1986); Harris (1991); Wang et al. (1993).

Black Musk Deer

Moschus fuscus Li, 1981 PLATE 52 MAP 513
黑麝 Hei She

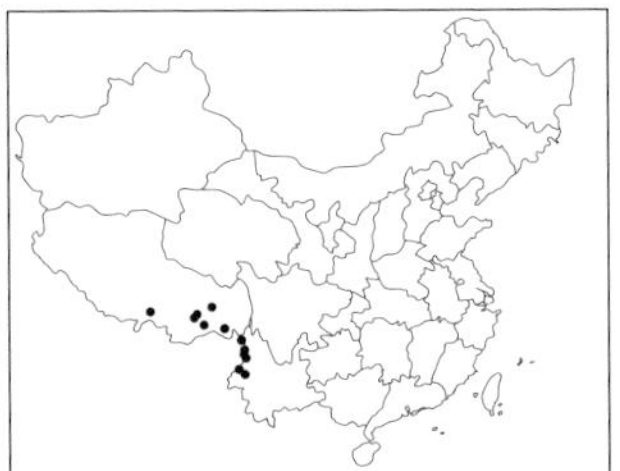

MAP 513. BLACK MUSK DEER, *Moschus fuscus*

Distinctive Characteristics: SH < 500; GLS < 150; Wt 8 kg. Small, dark musk deer; smaller and darker than the similar *berezovskii*. Unspotted with no white markings on face or neck. Sometimes lighter brown patch on shoulders. Throat dark, frequently with two incomplete yellow collars. Limbs black, and hind limbs longer than forelimbs.
Distribution: E Himalayas (east of Chumbi divide in SE Xizang to NW Yunnan); extending to Bhutan.
Natural History: Occurs in coniferous forests, forest edge, and rocky ridges at high elevations (2,600–4,200 m). Poorly known form; all life-history attributes are likely similar to those of the Alpine Musk Deer (see Comments).
Comments: Considered by many authorities to be a subspecies of *M. chrysogaster*.
Conservation Status: China RL—EN A2cd+3cd. China Key List—II. CITES—II. IUCN RL—LR/nt ver 2.3 (1994).
References: Green (1986); Groves et al. (1995); Wang et al. (1993).

Himalayan Musk Deer

Moschus leucogaster Hodgson, 1839 MAP 514
喜马拉雅麝 Ximalaya She

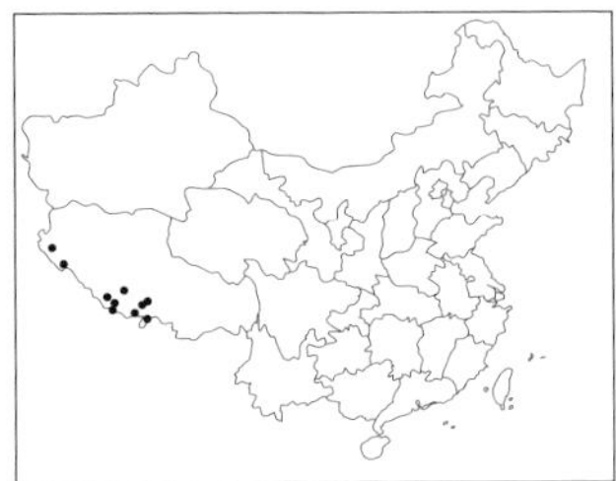

MAP 514. HIMALAYAN MUSK DEER, *Moschus leucogaster*

Distinctive Characteristics: HB 860–1,000; SH 510–530; T 40–60; GLS 150–180; Wt 11–16 kg. Similar to the Alpine Musk Deer; hair on back of neck distinctively whorled. Dorsal pelage a grizzled dark brown, rump paler, with only an indistinct yellowish stripe up front of neck and onto lower jaw; throat dark. Ears are long and rounded, lined white inside and with yellowish tips and edges at rear; eyering poorly expressed.
Distribution: SW Xizang; extending in the western Himalayas to west of Chumbi divide, on south side of Himalayas.
Natural History: Inhabits high alpine environments; while poorly known, its natural history is likely to be similar to that of the Alpine Musk Deer (see Comments).
Comments: Variously treated as a Himalayan subspecies of *M. chrysogaster*, but separated by Groves et al. (1995) on the basis of different skull proportions.
Conservation Status: Rare in China. China RL—NE. China Key List—II. CITES—I. IUCN RL—NE.
References: Groves et al. (1995); Wang et al. (1993).

Siberian Musk Deer PLATE 52
Moschus moschiferus Linnaeus, 1758 MAP 515
原麝 Yuan She

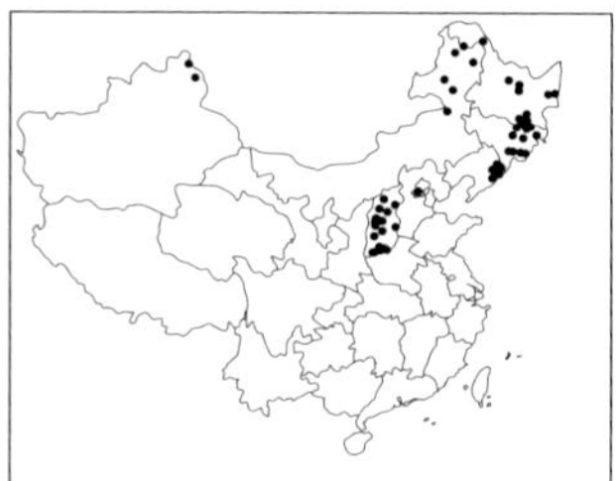

MAP 515. SIBERIAN MUSK DEER, *Moschus moschiferus*

Distinctive Characteristics: HB 650–900; SH 560–610; T 40–60; GLS 130–160; Wt 8–12 kg. Soft pelage is dark brown with rufous tinge; many distinctive pale yellow spots on back. The lower jaw is white, and there are two white stripes running down from neck to shoulder. Skull lightly built; lacrymal bone is higher than long; nasals long and slender, of equal width throughout.
Distribution: NE and NW China; extending to Siberia, Korea, Mongolia. Two subspecies in China: (1) *M. m. moschiferus* Linnaeus, 1758; Xinjiang (Altai mountains); Nei Mongol, Heilongjiang; (2) *M. m. parvipes* Hollister, 1911; Lesser Xing'an and Changbai mountain ranges, also as far west as Ordos Plateau.
Natural History: Occupy broadleaf and coniferous forests, or mixed forests, where they are solitary and primarily active at dusk and dawn. Diet consists of leaves, herbs, and lichens. Generally two young (1–3) are born in May–June following a six-month gestation.
Conservation Status: The form *moschiferus* disappeared from Xinjiang by the end of the 19th century, and the species has generally retracted throughout its range in China. China RL—EN A1cd. China Key List—II. CITES—II. IUCN RL—VU A1acd ver 2.3 (1994).
References: Wang et al. (1993); Wemmer (1998).

Family Cervidae—Deer
鹿科 Lu Ke—鹿 Lu

The Cervidae is a large family in which males typically have branched, bony antlers with no horny sheath that are shed periodically. Females of some species have smaller antlers, but usually these are absent. Males of small species or species without antlers have long, tusklike upper canines. Otherwise, the upper canine is reduced or absent. There is a distinct lacrimal depression present, and two lacrimal foramina are present. Many species have external secretion glands–infraorbital, digital, and/or inguinal. Wemmer (1998) has reviewed the conservation status of the cervids in China. There are three subfamilies worldwide, all of which are represented in China.

Subfamily Capreolinae—Deer, Moose, and Reindeer
狍亚科 Pao Yake—鹿，驼鹿，驯鹿 Lu, Tuolu, Xun Lu

The Capreolinae is comprised of nine genera found throughout the Holarctic and Neotropical realms. In China it is comprised of three genera of northern cervids, all characterized by at least partly hairy noses and irregular antler form.

Genus *Alces*—Moose
驼鹿属 Tuolu Shu—驼鹿 Tuolu

Moose are the largest members of the deer family. Adult males have wide, sweeping, upturned palmate antlers with many tines. Their nose is large and camel-like. A moose's lifespan can exceed 20 years. Predators include humans, tigers, wolves, and bears. A home range varies in size from 20–40 km^2 to a maximum of 300 km^2. In winter, when much of their diet consists of branches and other dry woody materials, the scat is in pellet form. Both moose

Key to the Chinese Subfamilies of Cervidae

1.a.	Male lacking antlers, upper canines long	Hydropotinae
b.	Males with antlers, canines absent to long	2
2.a.	Brow tine absent or irregular, rostrum wholly or partly covered in hair or nose with black moustache stripe	Capreolinae
b.	Brow tine normal or reduced, rostrum bare	Cervinae

Key to the Chinese Genera of Capreolinae

1.a.	Size small (HB < 150 cm), tail insignificant, nose with black moustache stripe	*Capreolus*
b.	Size large (HB > 150 cm), tail longer, no black moustache stripe	2
2.a.	Size huge (SH > 1.7 m), females lack antlers, male antlers lateral and palmate	*Alces*
b.	Size smaller (SH < 1.5 m) females have antlers, backward-sweeping antlers not palmate	*Rangifer*

species can be found in China. The skull tends to be narrow and long; nasal bone short; maxilla narrow; frontal bone wide and concave in the middle. Dental formula: 0.0.3.3/3.1.3.3 = 32.

Eurasian Elk

PLATE 53
MAP 516

Alces alces (Linnaeus, 1758)
驼鹿 Tuo Lu

MAP 516. EURASIAN ELK, *Alces alces*

Distinctive Characteristics: HB 2.0–2.9 m; SH 1.7–2.1 m; T 7–10 cm; Wt 320–450 kg (male), 275–375 kg (female). Huge deer with a short neck, and which rises much higher at the shoulder than the rump. The lip is inflated, and the nose is large and camel-like. The face is long and narrow. Bulls carry antlers that become palmated (flat and extended) after the third year; a front tine branches from the trunk, which is then flattened to form a wide palm with many upward-pointing small tines. Antlers can spread up to 2 m wide. These are shed in January-February. Bulls have a small, beardlike tassel on throat. Pelage is rich reddish brown above, grayer on flanks and underside; browner in summer; grayer and woollier in winter.
Distribution: Xinjiang (Altai); extending to W Siberia and to Scandinavia.
Natural History: In the spring and summer Eurasian Elk eat branches, shoots, and leaves from various broadleaf trees—birch, ash, mountain ash, and willow, as well as clover, rape, grain, and different herbs and water-lily roots. During the autumn and winter the elk changes its diet to blueberry bushes and heather, and later to mostly pine branches as well as juniper, the bark and branches from broadleaf trees (ash, willow, mountain ash) and occasionally the bark from spruce trees. Eurasian Elk have long legs and spreading hooves that help them in marshes and deep snow. They have poor eyesight, but great senses of smell and hearing. They are also excellent swimmers and have been known to cross lakes more than 1 km wide. During winter they form small family groups of four to eight individuals. The cow is in heat from the later half of September to the middle of October, and gestation lasts eight months. Cows usually give birth to one or two calves weighing 8–15 kg at birth. Calves start to browse at three weeks and are fully weaned at five months, staying with their mother until they are a year old. They become sexually mature after 2 years, and the life span is 20–25 years.
Conservation Status: Very rare with a limited distribution in China, though widespread and common across boreal Eurasia. China RL—EN A2acde. China Key List—II. IUCN RL—*A. a. cameloides* LR/nt ver 2.3 (1994).
References: Sheng and Ohtaishi (1993).

Moose

MAP 517

Alces americanus (Clinton, 1822)
美洲驼鹿 Meizhou Tuolu

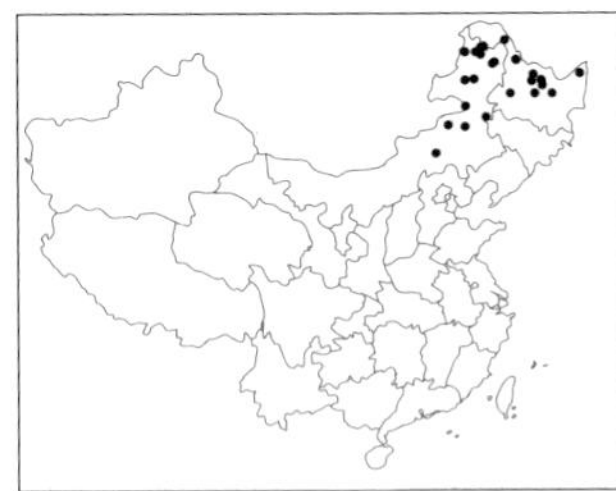

MAP 517. MOOSE, *Alces americanus*

Distinctive Characteristics: HB 2.4–3.1 m; SH 1.7–2.2 m; T 8–12 cm; Wt 360–600 kg (male); 270–400 kg (female). Similar to Eurasian Elk with which it was formerly classified, but slightly larger, redder, and with a more prominent neck tassel (dewlap).
Distribution: NE China (Greater and Lesser Xing'an mountains); extending to E Siberia, Canada, United States. Chinese subspecies: *A. a. cameloides* (Milne-Edwards, 1867).
Natural History: An animal of the boreal evergreen and mixed hardwood forests. Moose is an Algonquin (American Indian) word meaning twig-eater, and indeed the big mammal eats a massive amount of twigs and other browse. Most aspects of its natural history are similar to those of the Eurasian Elk.
Conservation Status: Extremely rare and of limited distribution in China. Common in Siberia and North America. China RL—EN A2acde.
References: Piao et al. (1995); Sheng and Ohtaishi (1993); Yu et al. (1993).

Genus *Capreolus*—Roe Deer

狍属 Pao Shu—狍类 Paolei

Capreolus represents an ancient northern genus of only two species, one of which occurs in China. Roe deer are small. The antler is unusual, lacking a brow tine, but having a forward tine on the upper half of the main trunk of the antler. The main trunk has a further simple fork giving a maximum of three tines. The entire antler is covered in many small protuberances. The nose has a black moustache stripe that contrasts with two white nose spots. The tail is short and concealed by hair. The upper canine is absent, and the lacrimal foramen is shallow. Roe deer are unique among ungulates in employing delayed implantation to ensure birthing at the optimal time of year. Fertilized embryos remain unattached in uterus for up to five months.

Siberian Roe

PLATE 53
MAP 518

Capreolus pygargus (Pallas, 1771)
西伯利亚狍 Xiboliya Pao

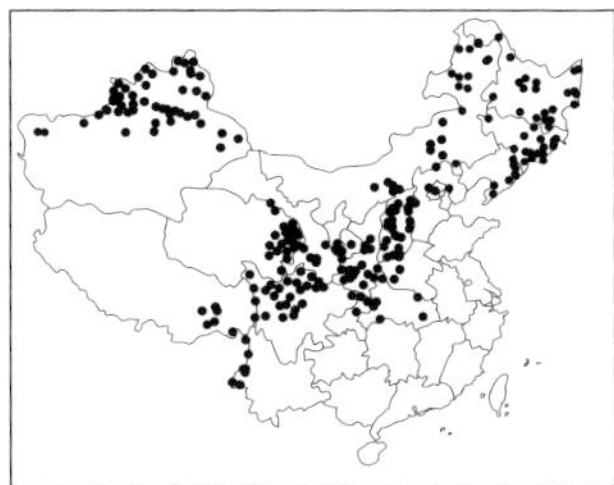

MAP 518. SIBERIAN ROE, *Capreolus pygargus*

Distinctive Characteristics: HB 95–140 cm; SH 65–95 cm; T 20–40; E 128–140; GLS 210–250; Wt 20–40 kg. Small, stocky deer. Back horizontal, neck vertical. Male antlers are compact and vertical with three tines. The form *pygargus* is larger than *bedfordi*. Pelage in winter is gray brown, becoming more yellow-brown to red in summer; underparts yellowish. White on chin contrasts with their black muzzle. Rump and undertail white, and tail is raised when alarmed.
Distribution: Widespread throughout C, NW, and NE China; extending to the Ural mountains, eastward across Siberia, Mongolia, and to Korea, and south into NE Myanmar. Two subspecies in China: (1) *C. p. bedfordi* Thomas, 1908 (including *mantchuricus* and *melanotis*); C and NE China; (2) *C. p. pygargus* (Pallas, 1771) (= *tianshanicus* Satunin, 1906); N Xinjiang.
Natural History: A deer of dark woodlands that feeds on open meadows and farmland at night.Diet includes grass, browse, and tree bark. Normally solitary, or found in small feeding parties. A shy, retiring, mostly crepuscular and nocturnal species. Mating takes place in August and September. Gestation is 294 days including the period of delayed implantation of 4–5 months. Calves (normally twins) are dropped in June. Maturity is reached by 13 months, and adults live 10–12 years.
Conservation Status: China RL—VU A2bcd.
References: Sheng and Ohtaishi (1993).

Genus *Rangifer* (monotypic)

驯鹿属 Xunlu Shu

Reindeer

PLATE 53
MAP 519

Rangifer tarandus (Linnaeus, 1758)
驯鹿 Xun Lu

Distinctive Characteristics: HB 1.2–2.2 m; SH 94–127 cm; T 7–21 cm; Wt 91–272 kg. *Rangifer* is an old northern genus of deer adapted to life in tundra conditions. These are compact, medium-sized deer with antlers in both sexes. Antlers variable, sometimes complex, rarely symmetrical. Front tines long and horizontal, often palmate. Pelage gray and woolly, browner and finer in summer; under parts whiter. Has long, beard-like hair below throat. Nasal bone large; bottom of postorbital process augmented with a short accessory process.
Distribution: Nei Mongol (extreme north of Greater Xing'an mountains); extending to Alaska, Canada, Greenland, and across the N Palearctic from E Siberia to Europe. Chinese subspecies: *R. t. fennicus* Lönnberg, 1909; *phylarchus* a synonym.

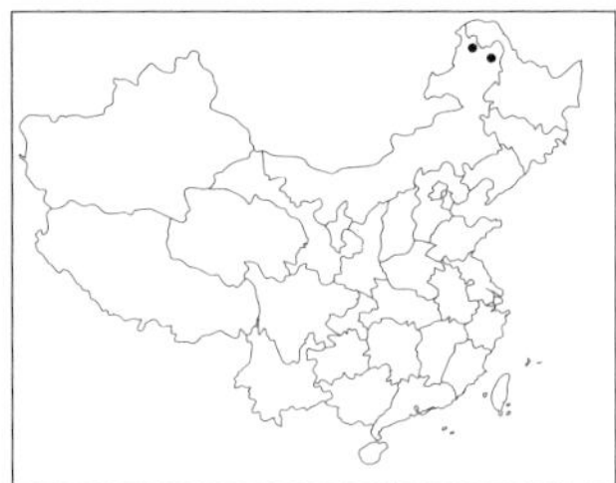

MAP 519. REINDEER, *Rangifer tarandus*

Natural History: Reindeer live in taiga forest and tundra where they eat mostly browse, bark and mosses, lichens, grasses, herbs, and ferns. A social deer; forms large herds. Able to make long migrations between summer and winter feeding areas. Rutting takes place about October. Young are born in May and June after a gestation of about 228 days. One or two young born that reach maturity at 2.5–3.5 years. Thick fur and short tail are adaptations to extreme cold winters. Ability to smell and find lichens and other food under snow is a special adaptation.
Conservation Status: Rare; only a few hundred animals remain in China. Most of its habitat was burned in great fires in 1986. China RL—NA.
References: Ma et al. (1993); Sheng and Ohtaishi (1993).

Subfamily Cervinae—Deer and Muntjacs

鹿亚科 Lu Yake—鹿，麂 Lu, Ji

The Cervinae represents a group of small to large deer ranging in size from small muntjacs to the huge Red Deer. All males bear antlers, and many boast a fine spread. Eld's deer and Pere David's deer are extinct in the wild, but releases of the latter may be now creating new wild breeding populations. Most species are now rare and threatened due to hunting pressure. Meijaard and Groves (2004b) reviewed the evolutionary and biogeographic relationships among SE Asian deer. Of nine genera in the Cervinae, eight are found in China.

Key to the Chinese Genera of Cervinae

1.a.	Size small (HB < 1.3 m), GLS< 25 cm), upper canines absent or tusklike	2
b.	Size larger (HB > 1.3 m), GLS > 25 cm), male upper canine usually present but not tusk-shaped	4
2.a.	Upper canines large and tusklike, lacrimal foramen large	3
b.	Upper canines absent, lacrimal foramen small	*Axis*
3.a.	Lacrimal foramen very large, its diameter larger than eye socket; male antlers tiny and unbranched	*Elaphodus*
b.	Lacrimal foramen large, but diameter less than eye socket; male antlers simple with up to three tines held on long bony pedicle	*Muntiacus*
4.a.	Antlers with brow tine; trunk branching at least once; tail rarely longer than ankle bone	5
b.	Antlers lack brow tine, trunk divides into front and back branches a short distance from base; both branches usually forked into multiple tines; tail generally longer than ankle bone	*Elaphurus*
5.a.	Anal spot lacking; brow tine of antler at obtuse angle forming arc with antler trunk	*Rucervus*
b.	With pale anal spot; brow tine of antler at acute angle or right angle to antler trunk	6
6.a.	With white or yellow anal spot; brow tine of antler at right angle or acute angle with trunk	7
b.	Body very large; side of nose and underlip white, browtine close to antler base	*Przewalskium*
7.a.	Antler spot rusty; front tine of antler acute, antlers trifurcate	*Rusa*
b.	Front tine of antlers at almost right angle to trunk, generally more than three tines	*Cervus*

Genus *Axis*—Axis Deer

豚鹿属 Tunlu Shu—豚鹿 Tunlu

A genus of smallish deer with trifurcate antlers and obtusely angled front tine. Very similar to *Cervus* with which they are sometimes combined (the primary difference being lack of an upper canine in *Axis*). Of three species, only one occurs marginally in China.

Hog Deer

Axis porcinus (Zimmermann, 1780) PLATE 55 MAP 520

豚鹿 Tun Lu

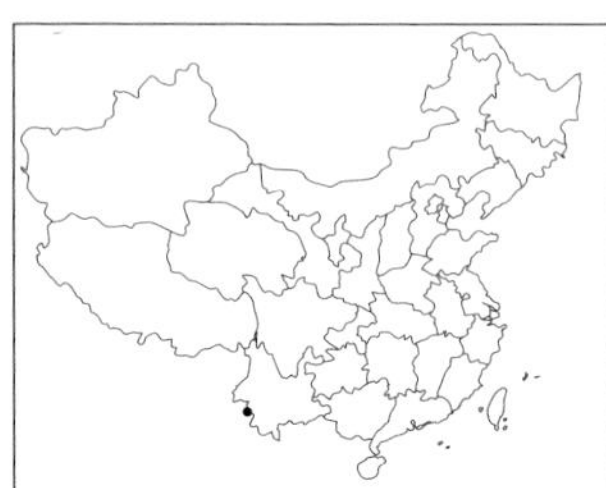

MAP 520. HOG DEER, *Axis porcinus*

Distinctive Characteristics: HB 105–115 cm; SH 60–72 cm; T 20 cm; Wt 36–50 kg. Smallish, short-legged, dark brown deer, becoming grayer in winter. Under parts are paler, throat and long hairs inside ears are white. Antlers three-tined as in the Sambar, but smaller and more gracile, and the brow tine meets beam at more acute angle. Male lacks mane of Sambar, and young are always spotted. Lateral rows of small white spots may persist in some adults. Male has dark band across lower forehead and on hocks. Lacks upper canines.

Distribution: Recorded only in lowest valleys of Xishuangbanna in S Yunnan; extending to N India, Assam, Myanmar, and N Indochina; introduced to Sri Lanka. Chinese subspecies: *A. p. annamiticus* (Heude, 1888).

Natural History: Hog Deer prefer low lying rather open grassy habitat, especially along river banks, on floodplains, and in swamps. Much more a grazer and less a browser than the Sambar. Originally diurnal and herd forming, now they have become usually nocturnal and solitary as a response to hunting pressure. They run like a pig through brush with their head held low, rather than leaping as other deer; hence their common name. They rut between September and February in China, and one to two fauns are born between April and October.

Conservation Status: Now certainly extinct in wild in China; although they may occur as a trade item from neighboring Myanmar and Laos. China RL—CR D. China Key List—I. CITES—I (*A. p. annamiticus*). IUCN RL—*A. p. annamiticus* DD ver 2.3 (1994).

References: Sheng and Ohtaishi (1993).

Genus *Cervus*—Red Deer and Elk

鹿属 Lu Shu—鹿 Lu

Cervus are typically medium- to large-sized deer, with many-tined antlers. Antler length more than twice the length of skull. Possess an infraorbital gland, but not digital gland. Both lacrimal foramena noticable; posterior end of nasal bone wider than anterior; with canine in upper jaw, not tusk shaped, or upper canine absent. They tend to live in large herds with serious fighting of stags during a rut period over access to harems of females. Both *Cervus* species occur in China.

Key to the Chinese Species of *Cervus*

1.a. Antlers with the second tine considerably above the brow tine; size small (HB < 170 cm); coat spotted with white in adults — *Cervus nippon*

b. Antlers with the second tine coming off close above the brow tine; size large (HB > 170 cm); coat not spotted in adults — *Cervus elaphus*

Red Deer

PLATE 54
MAP 521

Cervus elaphus Linnaeus, 1758
马鹿 Ma Lu

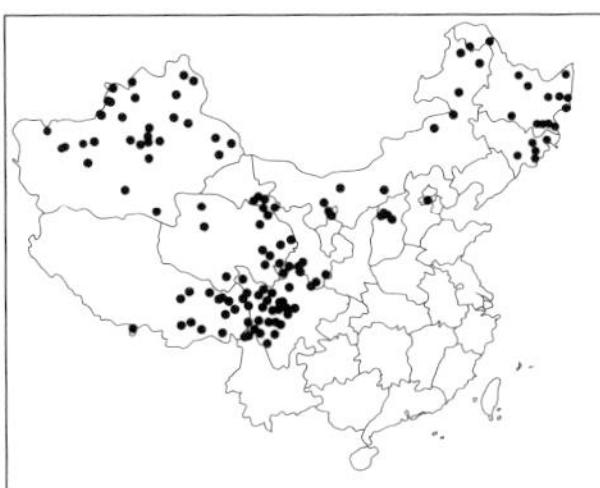

MAP 521. RED DEER, *Cervus elaphus*

Distinctive Characteristics: HB 165–265 cm; SH 100–150 cm; T 10–22 cm; GLS 40–45 cm; Wt 75–240 kg. Large, stately deer with wide antlers sporting many (up to six per antler) tines. Large gap between first and second tine. Pelage varies with season, being reddish brown in summer and darker brown and thicker furred in winter. Rump patch large, conspicuous, and light reddish yellow; its upper margin dark brown. Nasal bone long; inner side of face high; lacrimal bone triangular; upper canine small.
Distribution: Widespread in temperate mountain ranges of NE, NW, and C China, and Xinjiang; extending through most of the northern Holarctic (across Siberia and Europe to Canada and W USA), and NW Africa. Various subspecies of Red Deer have been described in China, and there is controversy concerning their validity; here we provisionally list seven described forms: (1) *C. e. alashanicus* Bobrinskii and Flerov, 1935; Ningxia (Helan Shan mountains); (2) *C. e. kansuensis* Pocock, 1912; Gansu, Qinghai, N Sichuan; (3) *C. e. macneilli* Lydekker, 1909; W Sichuan, SE Xizang (with white anal spot with black edge and a black dorsal stripe); (4) *C. e. songaricus* Severtzov, 1875; N Xinjiang (Tian Shan and Altai mountains; golden narrow anal spot not including tail base); (5) *C. e. wallichi* Cuiver, 1823 (*affinis* a synonym); S Xizang (white anal spot and antler trunk swept almost vertically); (6) *C. e. xanthopygus* Milne-Edwards, 1867; NE China and Nei Mongol (ochre yellow anal spot, yellowish hue on neck, large hooves); (7) *C. e. yarkandensis* Blanford, 1892; S Xinjiang (Tarim Basin). In addition, the form *C. e. hanglu* Wagner, 1844, could have occurred in SW Xizang (although it may be endemic to the Kashmir valley, N India), and *C. e. affinis* may be found in small numbers in SE Xizang.

Natural History: A deer of temperate woodlands, moorlands, and grassy meadows. Mostly found in mountain ranges with combination of conifer forests and open alpine meadows. Found in China up to 5,000 m. Animals come lower into valleys in winter. Eats grass, herbs, lichens, mosses, and bark of trees. Lives in small herds of females and young, gathering into larger herds in winter. Stags live singly or form all-male herds in summer but gather harems in rut season in late summer, without obvious territories. Antlers are shed before winter. New antlers are grown by summer in time for the next rutting season. Males rub trees to strip off velvet. Natural lifespan is about 15 years, but a captive animal lived up to almost 27 years. Stags give deep roars and fight with clashing antlers, sometimes blinding or otherwise injuring one other in dominance disputes over females. Calving occurs in June–July following a gestation of 235 days. Females drop single calves in late spring. Young are mature at 1.5–2.5 years.
Conservation Status: Very rare and restricted in China. The form *yarkandensis* has a declining population of about 4,000–5,000, and it has been feared that *wallichi* may be extinct. However, recently Schaller et al. (1996) discovered several small and one substantial (c. 200) populations of *wallichi* north of the Yarlung Tsampo River. The Helan Shan race in Ningxia (*alashanicus*) is rare. China RL—VU A2cd + 3cd. China Key List—II. IUCN RL—*C. e. yarkandensis*: EN; *C. e. alashanicus*, *C. e. wallichi*, *C. e. macneilli*: DD ver 2.3 (1994).
References: Chen et al. (1993); Clutton Brock et al. (1982); Geist (1982); Schaller et al. (1996); Wemmer (1998).

Sika Deer

PLATE 54
MAP 522

Cervus nippon Temminck, 1838
梅花鹿 Meihua Lu

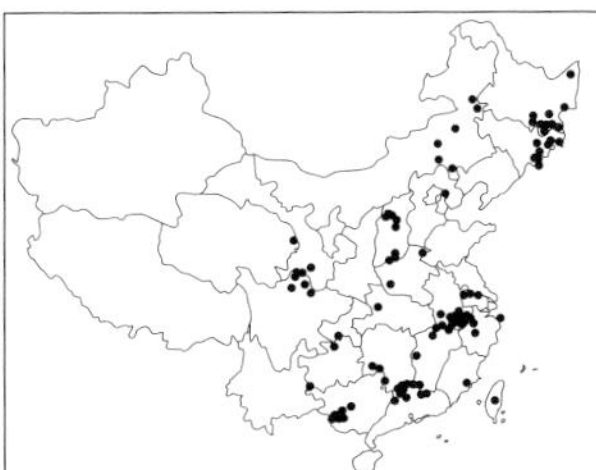

MAP 522. SIKA DEER, *Cervus nippon*

Distinctive Characteristics: HB 105–170 cm; SH 64–110 cm; T 80–180; GLS 260–290; Wt 40–150 kg.

Smallish, elegant deer with rich, reddish pelage and many irregular rows of white spots along dorsum and on sides. The lower jaw is white, and the undertail and sides of tail are white. There is a dark brown line down the back broadening into a dark patch above tail. Center of tail is reddish brown. In winter the coat is thicker and more chestnut and the white spots are less conspicuous. Male antlers generally sport only three to four tines. Nasal bone quite long, its posterior margin nearly on the same line with the anterior margin of orbit; upper canine small. Regional variation includes: *grassianus* tall and dark with black edged white patch on outer side of hind feet; *hortulorum* taller with no white spots on neck and spots on body more conspicuous in winter; *kopschi* with inconspicuous dark dorsal line and spots on neck inconspicuous; *mandarinus* similar to *hortulorum* but darker brown, white spots on neck and dark dorsal stripe; and *taiouanus* shorter with reddish hue on neck, spots in winter inconspicuous.
Distribution: Widespread across E China; extending to SE Siberia, Japan, Ryukyu, Korea, and formerly N Vietnam; introduced to Europe, United States and New Zealand. Six subspecies in China: (1) *C. n. grassianus* (Heude, 1884); Shanxi; (2) *C. n. hortulorum* Swinhoe, 1864; NE China; (3) *C. n. kopschi* Swinhoe, 1873; SE China south of the Yangtze River; (4) *C. n. mandarinus* Milne-Edwards, 1871; Hebei, Beijing; (5) *C. n. sichuanicus* Guo, Chen, and Wang, 1987; Sichaun, SW Gansu, E Qinghai; (6) *C. n. taiouanus* Blyth, 1860; Taiwan.
Natural History: Prefers woods and forest with dense understory but forages in open grassy areas. Eats grass, some browse, and even fruit. Crepuscular, but sometimes active by day and night. Forages singly or in small herds. Adults can live up to 25 years. Herds move down to lower valleys in winter. Large males are territorial and mark territory with urine and ground thrashing. Lesser males are driven out during the rut by fights involving both antlers and hooves. Dominant males round up females into a harem. Mating occurs in autumn and gestation is about 210–223 days with young being born in April and May. Stags drop antlers soon after the rut.
Conservation Status: Heavily depleted in the wild, and several of the Chinese subspecies may be extinct in the wild (*mandarinus, grassianus*), and others are endangered. The form *taiouanus* was extirpated on Taiwan in 1969 but was reintroduced in 1988 from captivity to Kenting National Park. It is thought that only 400–500 *sichuanicus* exist in the wild; and *kopschi* occurs in only five isolated small populations. Large herds exist in captivity to meet the demand for velvet antlers used in traditional Chinese medicine. China RL—EN A2cd + 3cd. China Key List—I. IUCN RL—*C. n. sichuanicus, C. n. kopschi*: EN; *C. n. grassianus, C. n. taiouanus, C. n. mandarinus*: CR; *C. n. mantchuricus*: DD; *C. n. taiouanus*: CR D ver 2.3 (1994).
References: Feldhamer (1980); Groves and Grubb (1987); Miura (1984); Sheng and Ohtaishi (1993); Wemmer et al. (1998).

Genus *Elaphodus* (monotypic)

毛冠鹿属 Maoguanlu Shu

Tufted deer PLATE 55

Elaphodus cephalophus
Milne-Edwards, 1872 MAP 523
毛冠鹿 Maoguan Lu

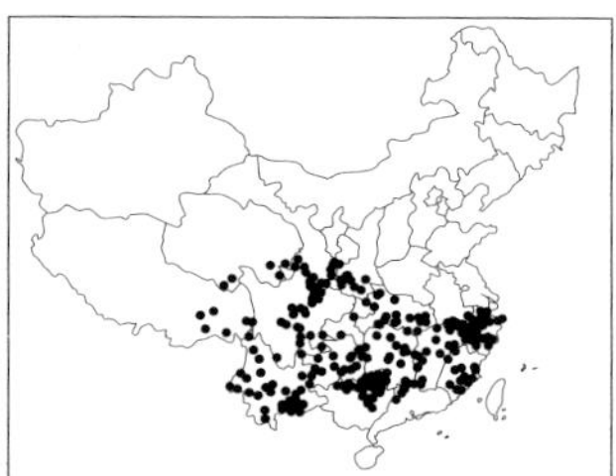

MAP 523. TUFTED DEER, *Elaphodus cephalophus*

Distinctive Characteristics: HB 85–170 cm; SH 49–72 cm; T 70–130; HF 440; E 80; GLS 166–190; Wt 15–28 kg. These small deer possess long canines in males, prominent suborbital glands, and a bushy, dark tuft of hair on the forehead that hides the short, thin pedicels and tiny antlers of the male. The fur is very coarse, almost spinelike, giving a shaggy appearance. Undertail is white, and there are white hairs on ear tips, base of ears, and sides of muzzle. Characterized by a short head and exceptionally large lacrimal foramen; auditory bullae small. Tufted deer do not have incisors in the upper jaw; instead they have a callous pad that presses against the lower jaw's incisors, allowing the deer to tear off vegetation as it feeds. Form *cephalophus* is large with uniform dark chocolate brown pelage, darkest in winter and somewhat reddish in summer, *ichangensis* is smaller but also dark brown, *michianus* is smaller but grayish black. Young show line of faint white spots along median dorsum.
Distribution: Widespread in SE China; extending to N Myanmar. Three subspecies in China: (1) *E. c. cephalophus* Milne-Edwards, 1872; Qinghai, W Sichuan, Guizhou, Yunnan; (2) *E. c. ichangensis* Lydekker, 1904; Shanxi, E. Sichuan, Hubei; (3) *E. c. michianus* (Swinhoe, 1874); SE China.
Natural History: Lives in high, damp forests up to the treeline and close to water. Lives between 300 and 800 m in SE China; between 1,500 and 2,600 m in the middle of its range; and to as high as 4,750 m in W Sichuan. Diet is grass, some browse, and fruits. Secretive and crepuscular; usually solitary or found in pairs. Feeds on grassy meadows above treeline in early morning. Lives within a well-defined home territory where it travels along well-established paths, rendering it vulnerable to snares. Barks like a muntjac when alarmed and in the mating season. Rut occurs between September and December. Single or twin fawns are born in April to July after about a six-month gestation.

Comments: The Tufted Deer is closely related to the muntjacs, and the separate genus is questionable.
Conservation Status: China RL–VU A2bcd + 3bcd. IUCN RL–DD ver 2.3 (1994).
References: Sheng and Lu (1982).

Genus *Elaphurus* (monotypic)

麋鹿属 Milu Shu

Père David's Deer

PLATE 55
MAP 524

Elaphurus davidianus Milne-Edwards, 1866
麋鹿 Mi Lu

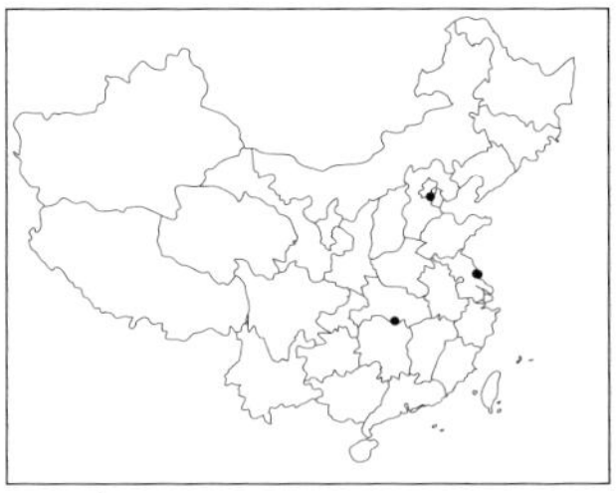

MAP 524. PÈRE DAVID'S DEER, *Elaphurus davidianus* (introduced localities)

Distinctive Characteristics: HB 150–200 cm; SH 114 cm; T 500; GLS 400–420; Wt 150–200 kg. A large, elegant, rufous brown deer with long, wavy guard hairs and unique antler formation. The antler lacks a brow tine but has a long rear branch almost parallel to the back. All tines of both branches are swept backward. Antlers are sometimes dropped more than once per year. The summer antlers are the larger set and are dropped in November, after the June–August rut. The second set, if they appear, are fully grown by January and are dropped a few weeks later. Summer coat ochre to reddish tan throughout the year. Winter coat is woollier, duller gray, with the undersides a bright cream. There is a darker stripe along the shoulders and down the spine. Head is long and slender with large eyes and small pointed ears. Males have a throat mane. The long tail ends in a black tuft, with long hairs drooping over the back of the hind legs. Skull narrow and long; lacrimal foramen conspicuous; nasal bones narrow; upper canine very small.
Distribution: Marshy habitats of NE China. Endemic.
Natural History: Formerly lived in low-lying grasslands and reed beds often in seasonally flooded areas such as the lower Yangtze River valley and coastal marshes. Eats grass, reeds, and leaves of bushes. Lives in single sex or maternal herds. Fond of water and can swim well and spend long periods in water. Rather tame. During the breeding season, stags fast as they spar for the right to mate. When fighting, males not only use their antlers and teeth but also rear up on their hind legs and "box." Animals reach maturity during second year. Gestation is 270–300 days. One, rarely two, young are born. These are weaned in 10–11 months. Adults live up to 18 years. Long legs and hooves adapted to walk on wet marshy land.
Conservation Status: Père David's Deer became extinct in the wild in China about 1900, and today they remain entirely conservation dependent. The first captive herd was maintained by the Chinese emperor at Nanhaizi Park. French missionary Père Armand David saw this herd and obtained specimens for description of the species. The Chinese herd was destroyed by a combination of flood and insurgents associated with the Boxer Rebellion, but by that time several animals had been sent as gifts to Europe. A captive herd was assembled at Woburn Abbey, U. K. The Duke of Bedford donated this founder stock back to the Chinese government in three groups between 1985 and 1987. These were reintroduced to the Beijing Milu Park and at Dafeng. Both captive herds are thriving, and a few accidental and deliberate releases to the wild have taken place. China RL–EW. China Key List–I. IUCN RL–CR D ver 2.3 (1994).
References: Butzler (1990); Cao (1993); Hu and Jiang (2002); Jiang et al. (2000); Liang et al. (1993).

Genus *Muntiacus*—Muntjacs

麂属 Ji Shu—麂类 Jilei

Muntjacs are small deer. Males have small, simple antlers that emerge from long pedicles. Females have small bony pedicles only, covered with tufts of hair. Both sexes have long canine teeth in their upper jaw that protrude when the mouth is closed. Dental formula: 0.1.3.3/3.1.3.3 = 34. In males the upper canine is tusk-shaped, but not as slender as the tusks of *Moschus* or *Hydropotes* species. The skull is somewhat triangular, and the lacrimal foramen noticeable.

Key to the Chinese Species of *Muntiacus*

1.a.	Color of upperparts reddish brown	2
b.	Color of upperparts dark brown to black	3
2.a.	Size small, dark stripe down back of neck	*Muntiacus reevesi*
b.	Size larger, no dark stripe on nape	*Muntiacus muntjak*
3.a.	Size large, back and tail blacker, long tuft of orange hair on forehead	*Muntiacus crinifrons*
b.	Size small, back and tail dark brown, no tuft on forehead	*Muntiacus gongshanensis*

Muntjacs forage just before sunrise and in the late evening. They are browsers feeding on twigs, grasses, leaves of trees, herbs, and fallen fruit. They regularly visit salt licks in search of minerals. Muntjacs travel alone, in pairs, or occasionally in groups of up to four animals. They are territorial and use secretion from a gland located in front of their eyes to scent-mark territorial boundaries. They can live to be more than 10 years old. Muntjacs are constantly on the lookout for predators. When alarmed, they give a series of deep, barklike sounds; hence the name "barking deer." The female makes high-pitched mewing sounds and the male barks during the mating season. Hunters imitate these calls to lure males within gunshot range.

Of 11 species of *Muntiacus*, 4 apparently occur in China, although much confusion remains as to how many forms may actually occur in China. Two species, Roosevelt's Muntjac (*M. rooseveltorum*) and the Leaf Muntjac (*M. putaoensis*), are known from N Laos and NE Myanmar, respectively, and may extend marginally into China although never recorded. The Yunnan species (*M. gongshanensis*) is doubted as a species by some authors and may in fact be a western race of the Black Muntjac (*M. crinifrons*), but it has also been described as a northern form of Fea's Muntjac (*M. feae*). Reeve's, Black, and Red muntjac are better documented.

Black Muntjac

PLATE 56

Muntiacus crinifrons (Sclater, 1885) MAP 525

黑麂 **Hei Ji**

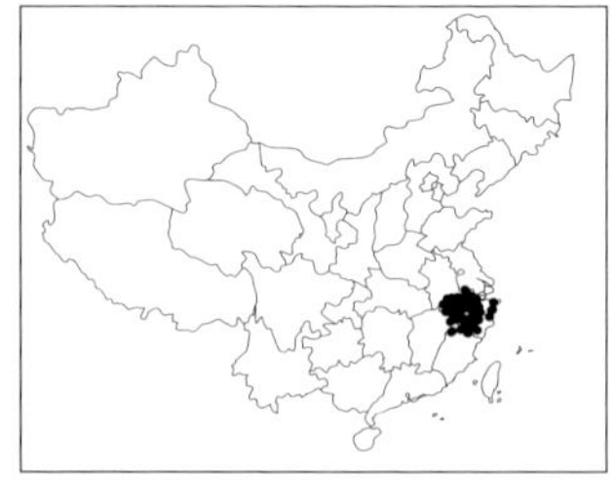

MAP 525. BLACK MUNTJAC, *Muntiacus crinifrons*

Distinctive Characteristics: HB 98–132 cm; SH 62–78 cm; T 165–240; HF 280; E 105; GLS 200–235; Wt 21–28.5 kg. A large, dark muntjac. Body color dark blackish brown with yellowish orange on sides of nose, top of head, ears, crown tuft, and long-haired pedicles. Inside of ears are white. Sometimes yellowish hairs appear on shoulders. Tail is long and black and contrasts sharply with white undertail. Both antlers and pedicles are of medium length. Antler single or two-tined. 2N = 9 (male), 8 (female).
Distribution: Confined to a small area of S Anhui and W Zhejiang and adjacent Mt. Huaiyuan in E Jiangxu and Mt. Wuyi in N Fujian. Endemic.
Natural History: Occupies rolling hills in mountainous areas at about 1,000 m in a variety of forest formations. Eats twigs, leaves of trees, herbs, and grasses; also some fruit, but less fruit than Reeve's Muntjac. Single fauns are born following a six- or seven-month gestation. The reproductive cycle is aseasonal, and some females conceive new litters while still lactating. Gestation 210 days.
Comments: Discovery of similar looking muntjacs in W Yunnan and Myanmar are here attributed to *M. gongshanensis*, but these may prove to be an eastern population of *crinifrons*.
Conservation Status: Rare and persecuted with a limited distribution. China RL—EN A2bcd. China Key List—I. CITES—I. IUCN RL—VU C1 ver 2.3 (1994).
References: Lu and Sheng (1984); Ma et al. (1986); Sheng and Lu (1980).

Gongshan Muntjac

Muntiacus gongshanensis Ma, 1990 MAP 526

贡山麂 **Gongshan Ji**

MAP 526. GONGSHAN MUNTJAC, *Muntiacus gongshanensis*

Distinctive Characteristics: HB 95–105 cm; SH 55–57 cm; T 90–160; GLS 190–205; Wt 16–24 kg. A medium-sized, dark muntac. Coloration is similar to the Black Muntjac, being dark brown with pale orange on head; but the animal differs in various ways. It is smaller, less black, has longer hooves, has a shorter tail, has a short thick pedicle, lacks a crown tuft, and has white sock rings around its feet. 2n = 9 (male), 8 (female).
Distribution: Gong Shan mountain region of extreme NW Yunnan; extending into N Myanmar.
Natural History: Believed to be similar to that of the Black Muntjac.
Comments: There is confusion with the forms *feae* and *rooseveltorum* in the literature, and it is possible more than one taxon of smallish dark muntjacs occur in W Yunnan, thus sympatric with *gongshanensis*.
Conservation Status: China RL—EN A2cd + 3cd; B1ab(i, ii, iii). IUCN RL—DD ver 2.3 (1994).
References: Ma et al. (1990).

Red Muntjac

PLATE 56

Muntiacus muntjak (Zimmermann, 1780) MAP 527

赤麂 **Chi Ji**

Distinctive Characteristics: HB 98–120 cm; SH 50–72 cm; T 170–200; GLS 176–220; Wt 17–40 kg. Medium-sized reddish-colored muntjac with long, narrow pedicle. Has very large preorbital gland. Different races vary as to size and extent of black marking on outer foreleg, but all have black on forehead and front side of pedicles. Undertail is white, and top side of tail is reddish as the body. Usually has white socklets. There is no dark dorsal stripe down neck. 2N = 7 (male), 6 or 8 (female).

Distribution: S China; extending into India, Pakistan, Indochina, Greater Sundas. Two subspecies in China: (1) *M. m. nigripes* Allen, 1930; Hainan Island; (2) *M. m. vaginalis* (Boddaert, 1785); SE China extending to S Xizang.
Natural History: Red Muntjacs occupy mountain forests where they live singly or sometimes in small groups of two to four individuals. Their diet consists of flowers, buds, and leaves of woody plants. Like other muntjacs, reproduction is aseasonal, and females mate shortly after giving birth to a single young.

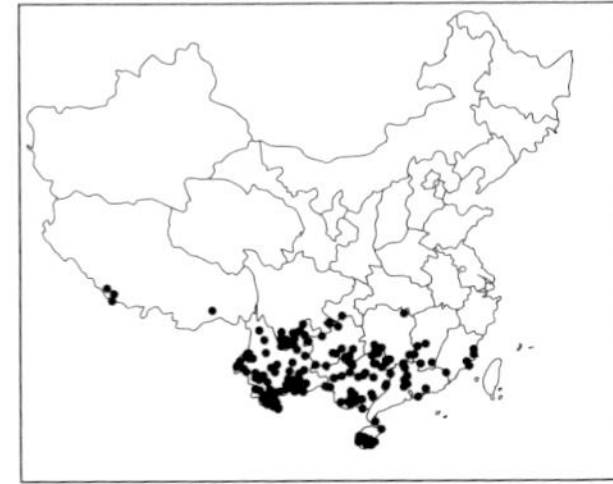

MAP 527. RED MUNTJAC, *Muntiacus muntjak*

Comments: Adding to the systematic confusion throughout the genus, the Red Muntjac is sometimes classified as *M. vaginalis*, including up to five subspecies including *nigripes* (Wang 2003).
Conservation Status: China RL—VU A2bcd + 3bcd.
References: Ma et al. (1986).

Reeve's Muntjac

PLATE 56
MAP 528

Muntiacus reevesi (Ogilby, 1839)
小麂 Xiao Ji

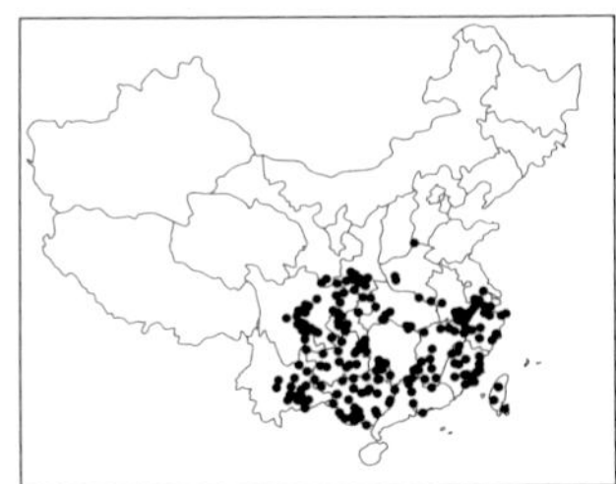

MAP 528. REEVE'S MUNTJAC, *Muntiacus reevesi*

Distinctive Characteristics: HB 64–90 cm; SH 40–49 cm; T 86–130; HF 210–223; E 85; GLS 146–164; Wt 11–16 kg. Reeve's Muntjac is reddish chestnut in color with blackish brown limbs. The forehead is rufous in color, and a distinct black stripe generally is present along the nape of the neck onto back. The throat, chin, and underside of the tail are white. The tail is short and reddish; undertail white. Pedicle is short and antler medium length. The subspecies (*micrurus*) living on Taiwan is darker and richer in color than the mainland China forms. 2N = 46.
Distribution: C, S, and SE China and Taiwan. Endemic. Four subspecies: (1) *M. r. jiangkouensis* Gu and Xu, 1998; Guizhou; (2) *M. r. micrurus* (Sclater, 1875); Taiwan; (3) *M. r. reevesi* (Ogilby, 1939); Guangdong, Guangxi, Jiangxi, Hunan; (4) *M. r. sinensis* Hilzheimer, 1905; Anhui, Zhejiang.
Natural History: Natural history similar to that of other muntjacs. Reeve's Muntjacs occupy brush-clad rocky places and open woodlands of pine and oak. They seek cover in steep ravines and usually have well-defined areas to which they retreat. Head and neck are carried low when running. They are basically solitary, although sometimes found in pairs or small family groups. Home ranges average about 100 ha, overlap considerably, and do not vary in size by gender. Female core areas also overlap, indicating they are not territorial, whereas male core areas overlap minimally, suggesting territoriality. Females mature within first year. In the wild, mating takes place throughout the year. The gestation period lasts 209–220 days. Fawns remain hidden in dense vegetation until they can move around with their mother. They have spots to aid in their camouflage, which slowly disappear as they reach adult size.
Conservation Status: China RL—VU A2bcd.
References: McCullough et al. (2000); Ma et al. (1986).

Genus *Przewalskium* (monotypic)

白唇鹿属 Baichunlu Shu

White-Lipped Deer

PLATE 54
MAP 529

Przewalskium albirostris (Przewalski, 1883)
白唇鹿 Baichun Lu

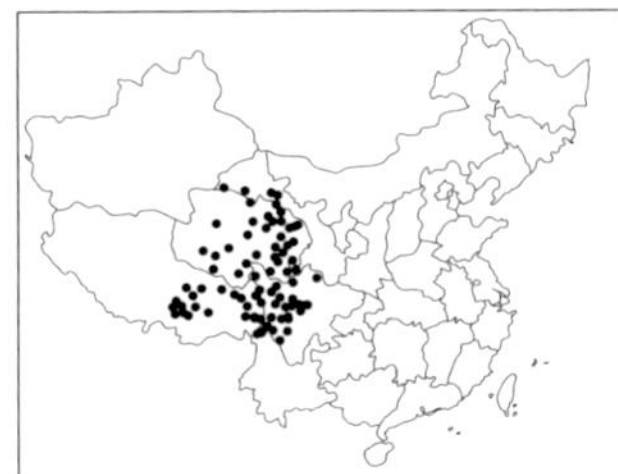

MAP 529. WHITE-LIPPED DEER, *Przewalskium albirostris*

Distinctive Characteristics: HB 155–210 cm; SH 120–140 cm (male), 115 cm (female); T 100–130; HF 330–520; E 210–280; GLS 340–404; Wt 180–230 kg (male), < 180 kg (female). *Przewalskium* is a large, robust deer, very similar to *Cervus*. Pelage is grayish brown with a dark ridge from the crown and down the back; underparts creamier. Tail is short; fringe of ears, nose, lips (giving rise to the common name), chin, and rump patch are white. Fur becomes dense, woolly, and paler in winter. The large antlers are strongly flattened toward the top; large stags have a brow tine branching from close to the base, and normally three branches originating from farther up the beam; these in turn may also fork. The nasal bone is short and wide, and the convex brain case with large lacrimal foramen occupying the whole of lacrimal bone (these pits are almost twice the size of those in

the Red Deer). Stout hooves and limbs are adaptations for high altitudes.
Distribution: Confined to eastern edge of the Tibetan Plateau in E Xizang, E Qinghai, SW Gansu, and W Sichuan. Endemic.
Natural History: Inhabits conifer forest, rhododendron and willow scrub, and alpine grasslands from 3,500 to 5,100 m; somewhat lower in winter. Compared with other cervids on the plateau, the White-lipped Deer is most likely to be found in open habitats. Feeds on grass, herbs, lichens, leaves and bark of trees and bushes. Typical of large social cervids, it lives in small groups, but seasonally it can be found in herds of 200–300 animals. Males and females live separately except during the breeding season. The species has been heavily depleted due to hunting for young antlers. Extensively farmed in China (and in other countries, such as New Zealand). The single young are born between late May and late June following a seven- to eight-month gestation; animals mature at an age of three years.
Comments: Has been included in the genus *Cervus* in many treatments.
Conservation Status: Lost from much of its former range. China RL—EN A2cd + 3cd. China Key List—I. IUCN RL—VU C1 ver 2.3 (1994).
References: Cai (1988); Groves and Grubb (1987); Kaji et al. (1993); McTaggart-Cowan and Holloway (1978); Miura et al. (1993); Schaller (1998); Sheng and Ohtaishi (1993).

Genus *Rucervus*—Deer

坡鹿属 Polu Shu—坡鹿 Polu

Small Asian genus containing three species of large cervids with complex antlers spreading from a very short beam. Includes the extinct Schomburgk's Deer (*R. schomburgki*; original range primarily in Thailand, although one specimen has been recorded from Yunnan, and it may still occur in Laos), and the Indian Barasingha *(R. duvaucelii)*. *Rucervus* is closely related to *Cervus* and sometimes included in that genus. A single species occurs in China.

Eld's Deer

Rucervus eldii (M'Clelland, 1842) PLATE 54 MAP 530
坡鹿 Po Lu

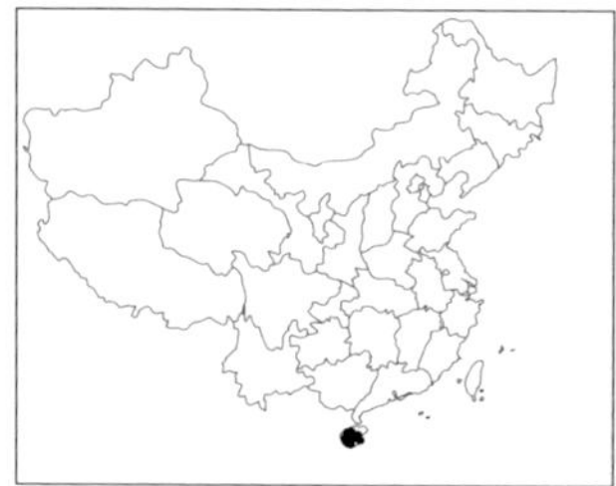

MAP 530. ELD'S DEER, *Rucervus eldii* (captive distribution)

Distinctive Characteristics: HB 150–170 cm; SH 120–130 cm; T 220–250; E 136–170; HF 350–400; GLS 290; Wt 64–100 kg. Large, reddish brown, elegant, long-headed deer with no anal spot, light spots along median dorsum and characteristic male antlers in which the front brow tine joins the main bream at an obtuse angle to form a sweeping continuous curve. Anterior of frontal bone flattened, its posterior slightly ridged in the middle; lacrimal foramen conspicuous.
Distribution: Formerly distributed in tropical zone of SW Yunnan and S China (but now extinct there), survives in China only in captive herds at western end of Hainan Island (Chinese form: *R. e. hainanus* Thomas, 1918); extending to Myanmar, Cambodia, N India, Laos, Thailand, and Vietnam; *siamensis* a synonym.
Natural History: Formerly lived in rather open, seasonal forests at low altitude. The Chinese form occupies seasonally dry grasslands, although some other forms may be secondarily specialized to life in swampy terrain. Feeds on grass and some browse; also fallen fruits and flowers. Will raid rice fields. Lives in small to large herds. Outside of the breeding season male groups form. In the breeding season males fight for dominance and collect harems of females. Males give barking grunt or roar during this period, and many suffer eye injuries during fighting. Although Eld's Deer can live without water for several days, males are fond of wallowing in mud. Regularly visit salt licks. Rutting is in the spring (unlike other large Chinese deer that rut in autumn), and a single young is born about eight months later. Unusually broad antlers are effective for fighting but appear to be a liability in forested terrain (thus its preference for open country).
Conservation Status: Extinct in the wild in China. Several hundred exist in captive herds in Datian and Bangxi nature reserves in large fenced compounds. There is little suitable habitat remaining and no protection from hunting, so wild releases not currently planned. China RL—CR A3e; B1ab(i, ii, iii). China Key List—I. CITES—I (as *Cervus eldii*). IUCN RL—VU A2c ver 2.3 (1994).
References: Sheng and Ohtaishi (1993); Song (1993); Yuan et al. (1993).

Genus Rusa—Deer

水鹿属 Shuilu Shu—水鹿 Shuilu

A small genus of four large Indomalayan deer centered mostly on Malaysia and the Philippines. Very closely related to *Cervus* and sometimes included in that genus. A single species is found in China.

Sambar

Rusa unicolor (Kerr, 1792) PLATE 54 MAP 531
水鹿 Shui Lu

Distinctive Characteristics: HB 180–200 cm; SH 140–160 cm; T 250–280; E 180–220; GLS 370–390; Wt 185–260 kg. Large brown deer with sparse, coarse hair and usually three tines on male antlers. Adult males develop longish hair as mane on neck and forequarters.

Ears large and broad; and tail densely covered with black shaggy long hair making it look thick. Undertail is white and flashed in alarm. Bare glandular patch on throat. Fawns generally not spotted. Females lack antlers, and young males may have a single tined almost straight antler. Antlers are stouter than in most cervids. They are cast annually, breaking from a short pedicel that grows into a broad, roseate base. Nasal and frontal bones well-developed, occupying nearly 3/4 the surface of the skull; lacrimal foramen conspicuous; upper canine short and blunt.
Distribution: Through tropical and subtropical zones of SE China, including Hainan and Taiwan; extending to E India and Sri Lanka along southern Himalayas, through Indochina to Borneo and Sumatra, and north into the Philippines. Four subspecies in China: (1) *R. u. dejeani* Pousargues, 1896; W Sichuan, Qinghai; (2) *R. u. equina* (Cuvier, 1823); Yunnan, Guizhou, Hunan, Guangxi, Guangdong, Jiangxi; (3) *R. u. hainana* (Xu, 1983); Hainan Island; (4) *R. u. swinhoii* (Sclater, 1862); Taiwan.

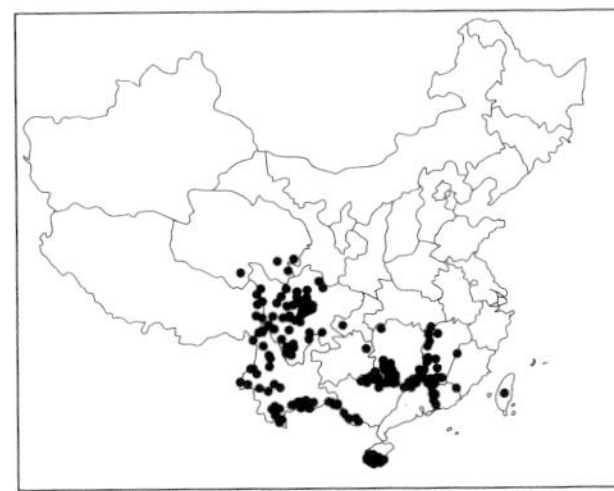

MAP 531. SAMBAR, *Rusa unicolor*

Natural History: Sambar live in tropical forests, scrub, hills, and secondary growth marshes up to 3,700 m, also venturing into agricultural fields. Eats grass, browse, ferns, leaves of small trees, and some fruits; more of a browser than grazer. Crepuscular and nocturnal, it is a generalized deer in a wide range of wooded habitats; hiding up in dense vegetation by day and feeding in more open areas at night. Generally solitary, or mother with young in small parties. Uses salt licks, especially when growing new antlers. Males roar and rut in winter months; a single fawn is born after about eight months. In Hainan, the reproductive cycle may be aseasonal.
Conservation Status: Widely hunted, but still widespread. China RL—VU A2cd + 3cd. China Key List—II.
References: Legakul and McNeely (1977); Schaller (1967); Sheng and Ohtaishi (1993).

Subfamily Hydropotinae

Genus *Hydropotes* (monotypic)

獐亚科 Zhang Yake; 獐属 Zhang Shu

Chinese Water Deer PLATE 55
Hydropotes inermis Swinhoe, 1870 MAP 532
獐 Zhang

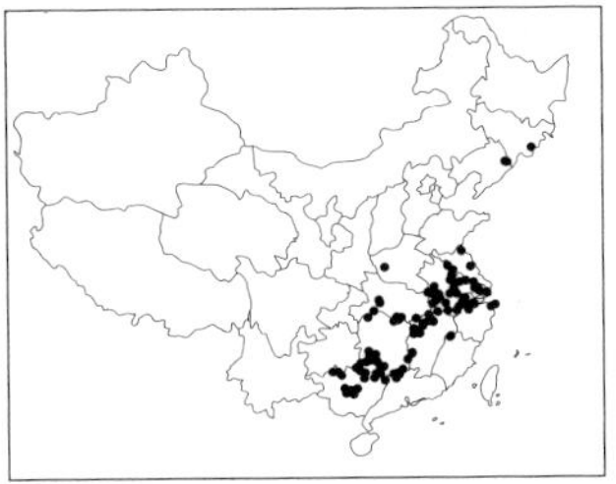

MAP 532. CHINESE WATER DEER, *Hydropotes inermis*

Distinctive Characteristics: HB 89–103 cm; SH 45–57 cm; T 60–70; GLS 150–170; Wt 14–17 kg. The Chinese Water Deer is a small cervid with no antlers in either sex. The male upper canines are long and laterally compressed; fur is dense and thick; the tail is very short. Pelage is rich reddish brown. Young with two rows of small white spots on sides. Skull is long and narrow; lacrimal bone has small deep hole; posterior margin of palate is V-shaped.
Distribution: E China; extending to Korea. Two subspecies in China: (1) *H. i. argyropus* (Heude, 1884); Jilin and Liaoning; (2) *H. i. inermis* Swinhoe, 1870; Zhejiang, Jiangsu, Hubei, Henan, Anhui, Guangdong, Fujian, Jiangxi, Shanghai, Guangxi.
Natural History: Lives in low-lying grasslands and reed beds, often in seasonally flooded areas such as the lower Yangtze River valley and coastal marshes. Feeds on grass, reeds, and leaves of bushes. Can swim well. Rather tame. Occurs at low densities (0.5–3.2/km^2) and may either be solitary or found in small groups. Mates in winter to give birth to two to five young (usually two to three) in May to June.
Conservation Status: Known population approximates 10,000 individuals and is increasingly fragmented, mostly distributed along the lower reaches of the Yangtze River and its associated lake system. China RL—VU A2bcd. China Key List—II. IUCN RL—LR/nt ver 2.3 (1994).
References: Ni et al. (1993); Sheng and Ohtaishi (1993); Wemmer et al. (1998); Xu et al. (1998).

Key to the Chinese Subfamilies of Bovidae

1.a.	Size very large; horns not annulated; infraorbital, digital, and inguinal glands absent	Bovinae
b.	Size not large; horns annulated; infraorbital, digital, or inguinal glands present	2
2.a.	Horns long, rather erect and partly bending forward or inward, neck long and slender	Antilopinae
b.	Horns short to long, always initially recurved and maybe spiraling outward, neck shorter and thicker	Caprinae

Key to the Chinese Genera of Antilopinae

1.a.	Horn is nearly straight, its end bending slightly forward; rostrum inflated	*Saiga*
b.	Horn curved, tip not bending forward and rostrum not inflated	2
2.a.	Tail length < 11 cm; inner and external margins of nasal bone not parallel, its anterior extremity sharp; lacrimal foramen inconspicuous, auditory bulla small; inguinal gland absent	*Procapra*
b.	Tail length > 12 cm; inner and external margins of nasal bone nearly parallel; lacrimal foramen conspicuous, auditory bulla large; infraorbital and inguinal glands developed	*Gazella*

Family Bovidae—Antelope, Cattle, Bison, Buffalo, Goats, and Sheep

牛科 Niu Ke—羚羊，牛，野牛，水牛，山羊，绵羊 Lingyang, Niu, Yeniu, Shuiniu, Shanyang, Mianyang

The bovids represent a large family of herbivorous ungulates ranging from small to large and from stocky to gracefully elongate. Rostrum tip hairy except for *Bos*; lateral toes (2 and 5) reduced or replaced by hooflets; phalanx replaced by anomalous small condyles. Both sexes with horns, but absent among some females; horns grow from frontal bone, are never branched or shed and are sheathed in a corneous theca with osseous marrow inside. Surface of horn may be smooth or annulated, and may be curved or twisted but never forked. Lacrimal bone complete, with no gap between it and nasal and frontal bones. Dental formula: 0.0.3.3/3.1.3.3 = 32; upper incisors and canines absent; cheek teeth uniform; premolars with two condyles; molars with four. Ruminant stomach with four chambers; some species have infraorbital glands; possess one to two pairs of nipples. Widely distributed in North America and the Old World; of eight subfamilies worldwide, only three are found in China. Shackleton (1997) and Jiang and Wang (2001), respectively, review the conservation and status of Chinese bovids and antelopes.

Subfamily Antilopinae—Gazelles and Saiga

羚羊亚科 Lingyang Yake—羚羊 Lingyang

A diverse subfamily of smaller antelopes and gazelles. Antilopinae tend to be slender and agile animals. They are mostly social grazers. The horns are placed near the back of the skull and are heavily annulated. Of 15 genera in the Antilopinae, 3 occur in China. The genus *Panthalops* is sometimes placed in this subfamily, but herein is included within the Caprinae on the basis of DNA studies (Grubb 2005; Lei et al. 2003a). Lei et al. used molecular studies to elucidate the phylogenetic relationships among Chinese antelopes.

Genus *Gazella*—Gazelles

羚羊属 Lingyang Shu—羚羊 Lingyang

Medium-sized antelopes; both sexes with horns, except absent in females of *G. subgutturosa*. Tail short but not < 12 cm; infraorbital gland conspicuous, and digital and inguinal glands present. Has stripes on face; nasal bone short, with external margins parallel, its anterior extremity with conspicuous indenture; lacrimal foramen distinct. Social herd-living grazers of open grassland and deserts of Africa, E Europe, and Asia. Of 10 species of *Gazella*, only 1 occurs in China.

Goitered Gazelle

PLATE 57
MAP 533

Gazella subgutturosa (Guldenstaedt, 1780)

鹅喉羚 E'houling

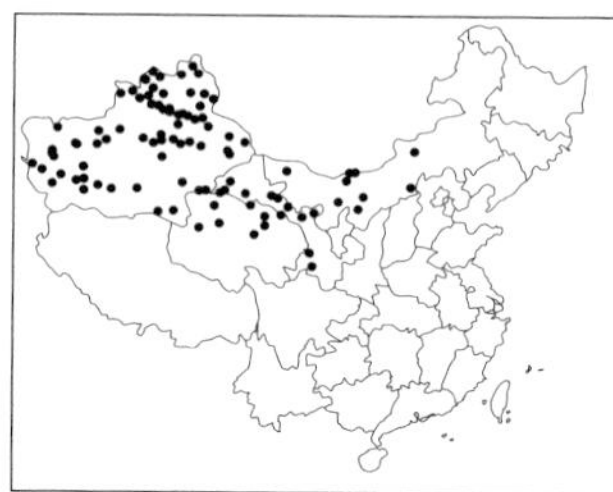

MAP 533. GOITERED GAZELLE, *Gazella subgutturosa*

Distinctive Characteristics: HB 88–109 cm; SH 60–70 cm; T 120–175; GLS 170–215; Wt 29–42 kg. Elegant gazelle with pale head, underparts, and inner legs, and a white rump. Dorsal pelage brown, including contrasting tail. Some races with prominent dark facial stripes. The strongly annulated horns divide and sweep backward before curving slightly forward at tips (fig. 15). Lump at front of neck gives the species its English name. Subspecies differ in details: *yarkandensis*—large with bold facial stripes and front and rostrum brown; *sairensis*—large but with shorter

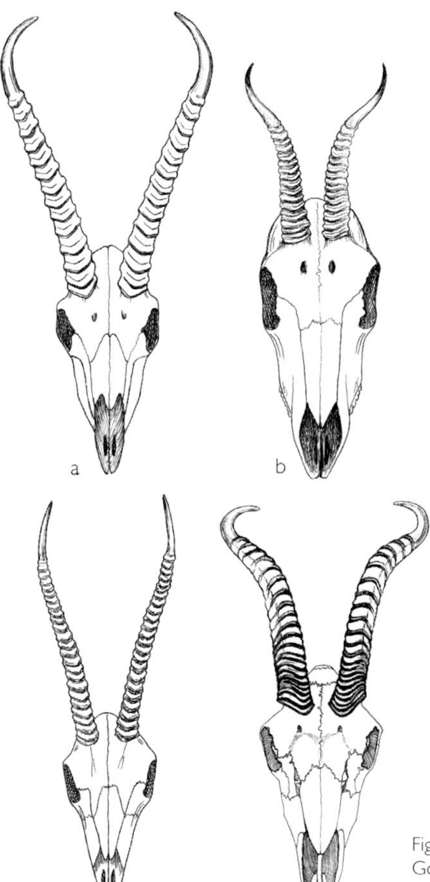

Figure 15. Skull and horn profiles of Goitered (a), Mongolian (b), Tibetan (c), Przewalski's (d) gazelles.

horns c. 27 cm; *hilleriana*–smaller, brown facial stripes below eyes, gray brown front, and white rostrum; *reginae*–larger with horns ca. 30 cm and pelage sandier color.

Distribution: Confined to lower altitude deserts of N and NW China; extending to Mongolia, Pakistan, and Arabia. Four subspecies in China: (1) *G. s. hillieriana* Heude, 1894; Nei Mongol, Gansu, N Shaanxi; (2) *G. s. reginae* Adlerberg, 1931; Qinghai (Qaidam Basin); (3) *G. s. sairensis* Lydekker, 1900; N Xinjiang (Dzungarian Basin); (4) *G. s. yarkandensis* Blanford, 1875; Xinjiang (Tarim Basin).

Natural History: Inhabits steppes, alpine grasslands, and semidesert vegetation at low to moderate altitudes. Feeds on many herbs and grasses including halophytic vegetation. Lives in small herds of 1–12 animals wandering over large areas seasonally. Larger herds of up to 30 may form in winter. Mates in winter, and single or twin calves are dropped in May or June after a gestation of 5–6 months.

Conservation Status: While the Goitered Gazelle used to be an important game species, its range and numbers have declined as a result of uncontrolled hunting and habitat degradation. Extirpated from parts of former range such as Ordos Plateau. China RL–EN A1d + 2cd + 3cd. China Key List–II. IUCN RL–NT ver 3.1 (2001).

References: Gao et al. (1996); Jiang and Wang (2001); Wang and Schaller (1996).

Genus *Procapra*—Central Asian Gazelles

原羚属 Yuanling Shu—原羚 Yuanling

Medium-sized antelopes with short tail; no facial vein; slender legs; only some species have inguinal and/or infrorbital glands. Only males have horns, and these are long and slender. Orbit well developed; lacrimal foramen inconspicuous; nasal bone sharp. These are herd-living grazers of open grasslands and deserts. Some treatments consider *Procapra* a subgenus of *Gazella*. All three *Procapra* species are found in China.

Key to the Chinese Species of *Procapra*

1.a. Size large (HB > 1.1 m); infraorbital and inguinal glands present; horns shorter, < 30 cm, rise almost parallel before spreading apart near tip; condyloincisive length > 22 cm — *Procapra gutturosa*
b. Size smaller (HB < 1.1 m); infraorbital and inguinal glands absent; horns > 30 cm; condyloincisive length < 20 cm — 2
2.a. Horns curved back sharply, the tips bending inward and upward like hooks; condyloincisive length up to 20 cm; rear end of premaxilla does not extend to margin of nasal bone — *Procapra przewalskii*
b. Horns long and slender with tips bending slightly backward and upward; condyloincisive length < 20 cm; rear end of premaxilla contacts external margin of nasal bone — *Procapra picticaudata*

Mongolian Gazelle

PLATE 57
MAP 534

Procapra gutturosa (Pallas, 1777)
黄羊 Huang Yang

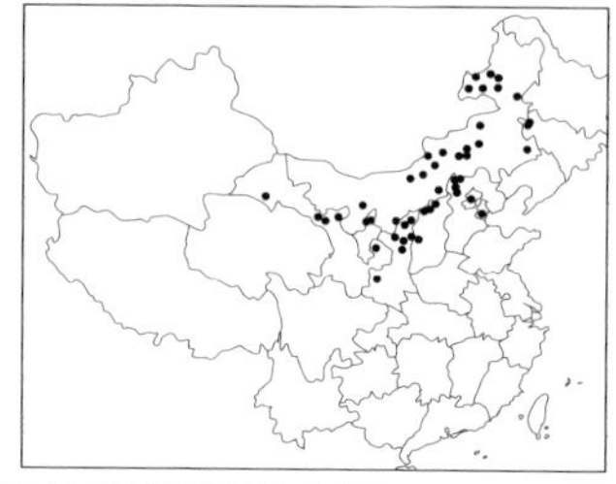

MAP 534. MONGOLIAN GAZELLE, *Procapra gutturosa*

Distinctive Characteristics: HB 108–160 cm; SH 54–84 cm; T 50–120; E 97; GLS 220–270; Wt 25–45 kg. Medium-sized, elegant gazelle with male horns short (20 cm) and reclined, bending backward then turned upward and inward at the tip (fig. 15). Pelage is orange buff in summer with cinnamon sides; much richer in color than the pale sandy of the Goitered Gazelle. White underparts and a white rump patch. Dark tail contrasts conspicuously when wagged from side to side. Pelage is paler in winter.
Distribution: Dry steppes and semidesert of central N China; extending into Mongolia and adjacent parts of Siberia and grasslands of N China. Two subspecies in China: (1) *P. g. altaica* Hollister, 1913; NW Xinjiang (Altai; most likely extinct, if indeed it ever occurred in China in historical times); (2) *P. g. gutturosa* (Pallas, 1777); Nei Mongol, Jilin, Hebei, Shaanxi, Shanxi, Ningxia, Gansu.
Natural History: Inhabits dry grassy steppe, semidesert, and formerly moister northeastern grasslands. Feeds on mostly grasses with some browse. Lives in large herds. Has been observed to gather in even larger herds (6,000–8,000) for the spring northern migration. Males separate from herds on summer pastures. Mates in late autumn and winter. Males develop a swollen throat at this time. Single or twinned young are dropped in June after a gestation of 186 days. Young reach maturity at two years, and captive animals live up to seven years.
Conservation Status: Persecuted by hunters and limited by fencing and farming of grasslands. The herds of C and W Mongolia have largely vanished. Endangered in Russia and rare in China. The range of Mongolian Gazelles in China is about 25% of what it was in the 1950s–1970s (they are now found only in E Nei Mongol), and the population has decreased dramatically during that interval from approximately 2,000,000 to 250,000 (only about 85,000 of which reside permanently in China and do not migrate into Mongolia; Jiang and Wang 2001; see also Olson et al. 2005). China RL—VU A2cd + 3cd. China Key List—II.
References: Jiang and Wang (2001); Schaller (1998); Sokolov and Lushchekina (1997); Wang et al. (1997).

Tibetan Gazelle

PLATE 57
MAP 535

Procapra picticaudata Hodgson, 1846
藏原羚 Zang Yuanling

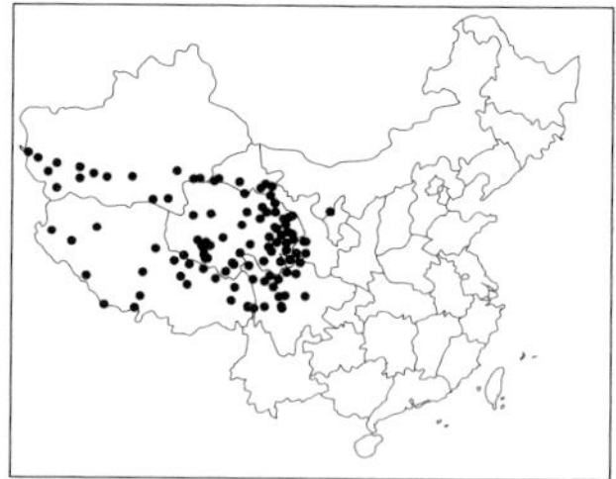

MAP 535. TIBETAN GAZELLE, *Procapra picticaudata*

Distinctive Characteristics: HB 91–105 cm; SH 54–65 cm; T 80–100; GLS 170–190; Wt 13–16 kg. Smallish, stocky gazelle. Pelage gray brown with thick saddle-like hair on the back. Underparts and rump patches are white. Lacks conspicuous facial marking and a lateral stripe. Small tail is fluffy and black; it is raised when alarmed. Male horns grow upward then sweep backward before rising again toward the tip (fig. 15). The heavily annulated horns are almost parallel to each other, not splaying as in other gazelles.
Distribution: Tibetan Plateau. Endemic.
Natural History: The Tibetan Gazelle inhabits cold northern deserts, semideserts, grasslands, and mountain shrublands at high altitudes (up to 5,750 m). Occupies more mountainous habitat than Przewalksi's Gazelle in their area of range overlap. Feeds mostly at dusk and dawn on grasses, forbs, and lichens. Generally found in small herds of 3–20 animals, gathering in larger herds during migrations to higher summer pastures. A wary and speedy animal.

Scrapes out a depression for shelter in bad weather. Mating takes place in winter, and single (or occasionally twin) young are dropped in June.
Conservation Status: Formerly very common, and huge herds used to migrate with the seasons across the Tibetan Plateau. Today the Tibetan Gazelle is much reduced in numbers due to uncontrolled hunting and deterioration of habitat caused by domestic herds. They mostly remain where humans and livestock are scarce. China RL—VU A2cd + 3cd. China Key List—II.
References: Jiang and Wang (2001); Schaller (1998).

Przewalski's Gazelle

PLATE 57
MAP 536

Procapra przewalskii (Büchner, 1891)
普氏原羚 Pushi Yuanling

MAP 536. PRZEWALSKI'S GAZELLE, *Procapra przewalskii*

Distinctive Characteristics: HB 109–160 cm; SH 50–70 cm; T 70–120; GLS 185–220; Wt 17–32 kg. Medium-sized, rather stocky gazelle with sandy brown pelage, white underparts, and white rump patch divided into two spots by dark median line. Male horns relatively stubby, bowed backward and splayed apart before growing upward and toward each other near tips (fig. 15).
Distribution: Central N China; now largely confined to the area near Qinghai Lake (1997). Formerly was more widespread in N Qinghai, Gansu (Loess Plateau), and Nei Mongol (W Ordos Plateau). Endemic.
Natural History: Inhabits high-altitude steppe plateau including open valleys, undulating terrain, dunes, and some wetland grasslands. Eats mostly grass and reed tips, and a few other herbs such as the legume *Astragulus* spp., which is poisonous to most domestic animals. Behavior similar to that of other steppe gazelles. Lives in small herds; exhibits a polygynous mating system typical of most ungulates. Age at first reproduction is two years. The single young (sometimes twins) are born in May and June.
Conservation Status: Critically endangered as a result of hunting and heavy domestic grazing and disturbance on its habitat. Only 114 animals estimated in 1997 compared with 200 in 1994 and 350 in 1984; currently confined to four subpopulations near Qinghai Lake. Additionally, grassland fencing in 1999 has led to further dramatic declines in the population and calving rate. China RL—CR A2bce + 3bce; C1; D. China Key List—I. IUCN RL—CR C1 ver 3.1 (2001).
References: Hoffmann (1991); Jiang and Wang (2001); Jiang et al. (2000); Lei et al. (2003b); Li and Jiang (2002); Liu and Jiang (2002).

Genus *Saiga* (monotypic)

高鼻羚羊属 Gaobilingyang Shu

Steppe Saiga

PLATE 58
MAP 537

Saiga tatarica (Linnaeus, 1766)
赛加羚羊 Saijia Lingyang

Distinctive Characteristics: HB 100–140 cm; SH 60–80 cm; T 60–120; GLS 190–240; Wt 26–69 kg. The Steppe Saiga is a medium-sized, ungainly antelope with greatly inflated and downturned nostrils lending to a mulelike profile. Pelage a dull brown. The heavily annulated horns are quite short, nearly straight, and with forward-bending tips; they are amber or whitish in contrast to the black horns of other antelopes. Infraorbital gland is small and both digital and branchial glands are present. Premaxilla and nasal bone short; nasal cavity large; lacrimal foramen shallow.
Distribution: NW Xinjiang (Dzungarian Basin); current distribution now restricted to S Ukraine, E Kazakhstan, and SW Mongolia. Formerly widespread from grasslands of Europe and Central Asia to Mongolia and Siberia (in the Pleistocene to Alaska). Chinese subspecies: *S. t. mongolica* Bannikov, 1946.

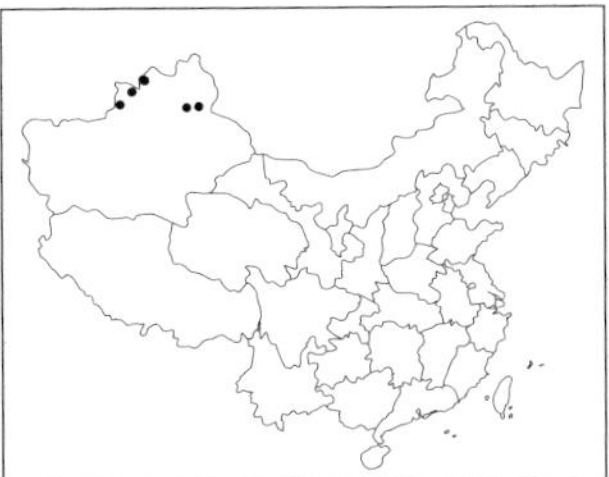

MAP 537. STEPPE SAIGA, *Saiga tatarica*

Natural History: Inhabits temperate grassy plains, often in arid areas. Eats mostly grass with mosses, lichens, some browse, and tree bark. Active throughout the day, never observed far from water. Runs at high speed. Some populations undertake large seasonal migrations. Summer herds may consist of 30–40 animals, but migration herds formerly numbered hundreds of thousands. In mating season in early winter males become territorial and fight to gather a harem. Many males die in fights or of exhaustion by end of winter. Single or twin young are dropped in April and May after gestation of 139–152 days. Young mature after their first year, but captive animals can live up to 12 years. The strange nose with down-pointing nostrils and extensive internal convolutions and membranes seems to serve a temperature regulation function, as well as giving the animal exceptional olfactory ability.

Key to the Chinese Species of *Bos*

1.a. Size large with body weight up to 1,500 kg and SH up to 2 m; legs white below knees; with dewlap; short hair; horns thick and arc-shaped — *Bos frontalis*
b. Size smaller with body weight about 500 kg; SH about 1.6 m; no white socks; no dewlap; hair long and straggly; horns slender and bending forward — *Bos grunniens*

Conservation Status: The horns are believed to have strong medicinal properties, and trade of these items has caused the species to become endangered. The Steppe Saiga is now considered extinct in the wild in China, although some animals may cross the border from Kazakhstan. Neighboring populations in Kazakhstan and Mongolia are extremely rare and declining. Additionally, the sex ratio is highly skewed, and most herds remaining in Central Asia are nearly all female due to heavy harvesting of males for their horns; correspondingly, breeding has been sharply curtaled (Milner-Gulland et al. 2003). Reintroduction efforts are being made. China RL—RW. China Key List—I. CITES—II. IUCN RL—CR A2a ver 3.1 (2001).
References: Bannikov et al. (1961); Jiang and Wang (2001); Milner-Gulland et al. (2003); Sokolov (1974).

Subfamily Bovinae—Wild Cattle and Spiral-horned Antelope

牛亚科 Niu Yake—牛 Niu

Generally large animals with massive or spiral horns including cows, buffalo, and spiral horned African antelope, Indian Nilgai, and the aberrant Indochinese Saola. Horns are not annulated; muzzle broad; nostrils lateral, and without face glands. The tall upper molars have inner columns. Of nine genera, only one occurs in China. Wild buffalo (*Bubalus arnee*) may formerly have roamed into S Yunnan and SE Xizang.

Genus *Bos*—Cattle and Yak

野牛属 Yeniu Shu—野牛 Yeniu

Large size and stubby legs; long tail with tip covered with long hairs; infraorbital, digital, and inguinal glands absent; both sexes with smooth-surfaced, outward-then upward-sweeping horns; skull thick; nasal bone long; highest part of skull situated between the two horns. Of six species of *Bos*, two occur in the wild in China. Both have been domesticated and cross-bred with domestic cattle. There is at least one skull of a third species (*B. javanicus*), reportedly recovered from Xishuangbanna and S Simao in Yunnan, but since this is far north of the species' northern distribution in Laos, and these skulls are often traded as trophies, we are ignoring these records until further evidence arises.

Gaur

PLATE 58
MAP 538

Bos frontalis Lambert, 1804
野牛 Ye Niu

Distinctive Characteristics: HB 250–330 cm; SH 165–220 cm; T 70–105 cm; E 30–35 cm; GLS 500; Wt 650–1,500 kg. Large, dark, wild cattle with grayish or yellow-white "socks" on lower legs; no whitish rump patch. Both sexes are mostly blackish brown; calf is brown. Inside of ears are white. Male has heavy horns that sweep outward then curve upward, growing from massive pale colored crown hump. Male has a dewlap. Female has more delicate horns. A stouter version of Gaur with massive outspreading horns is sometimes traded from Myanmar across the W Yunnan border. This is the Mythan or Gayal (*B. f. frontalis*), a domesticated animal sometimes also crossed with domestic cattle.
Distribution: Central S China; extending to the Indian subcontinent through Myanmar and Indochina to the Malay Peninsula. Two subspecies in China: (1) *B. f. gaurus* Lambert, 1804; SE Xizang (Mishmi hills); (2) *B. f. laosiensis* Heude, 1901; S Yunnan.

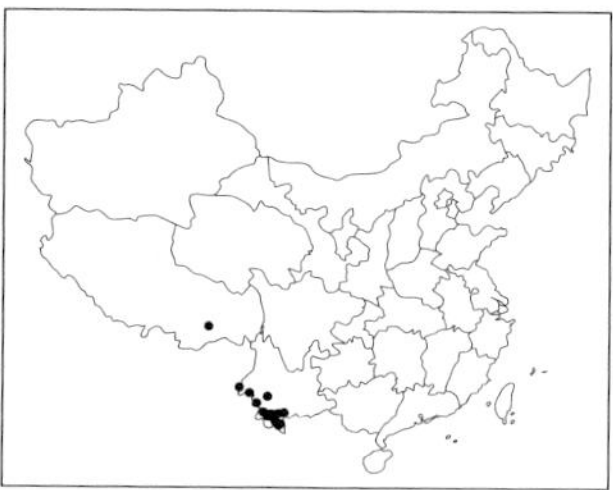

MAP 538. GAUR, *Bos frontalis*

Natural History: Inhabits dense to open tropical forests at low to moderate altitudes. Lives in denser forest than other Asian cattle. Feeds on grass and browse, favors bamboo shoots and the leaves of dwarf bamboo *Arundinella*. Diurnal and nocturnal but rests in shady places during the heat of the day. Can sleep standing but usually lies down like a domestic cow. Lives in small herds and regularly visits salt licks. Gaur emit an oily sweat, which they rub on trees in a form of scent marking. In breeding season males fight like bulls for dominance with much roaring and snorting. Gestation is almost 10 months. Single young are born to each female in the herd, and they come back into heat a few weeks later.
Comments: The form *gaurus* a common synonym, where in *frontalis* is sometimes considered the domestic (yet interbreeding) form.
Conservation Status: In China, rare, restricted in range, and endangered by hunting and habitat loss. China RL—EN A1bc; B1ab(i, ii, iii); D. China Key List—I. CITES—I. IUCN RL—VU A1cd + 2cd, C1 + 2a ver 2.3 (1994).
References: Lekagul and McNeely (1977).

Yak PLATE 58
Bos grunniens Linnaeus, 1776 MAP 539
野牦牛 Ye Maoniu

Distinctive Characteristics: HB 305–380 cm; SH 170–200 cm (males), 137–156 cm (females); T 100 cm; GLS 50 cm; Wt 535–821 kg (male), 306–338 kg (female). Large, black cattle with long, shaggy hair that almost reaches the ground; long wisp of hair on tail (over 100 cm long). Long, sharp horns, colored gray to black, spread laterally then twist upward and backward at tips. Horns of males longer, wider, and more massive than those of females.

Distribution: Tibetan Plateau; extending to N India (Ladakh), Nepal; apparently in Kazakhstan, Mongolia, and S Russia until the 13th–18th centuries.

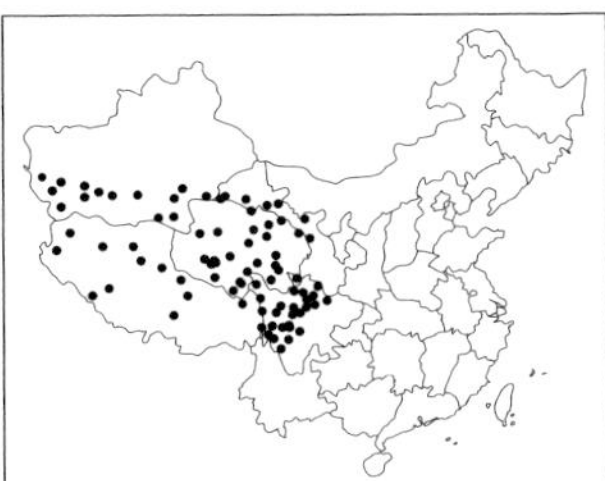

MAP 539. YAK, *Bos grunniens*

Natural History: Inhabits high altitude grasslands and cold desert from 4,000–6,100 m. Descends into lower valleys in winter. Feeds mostly on grass with some herbs and mineral rich soil. Lives in small groups of two to six animals. Most Yak on the plateau today are domesticated, and some are crossed with cattle; wild Yak are much larger. Runs with a jerky, bouncing gait. Single young are dropped in May and June after 258 days of gestation. Females give birth at only two-year intervals but can live for 25 years. The stout compact body, thick woolly coat, and richness of milk are all adaptations to the harsh conditions in which this species lives. Bushy tail is an adaptation to flick away summer flies. The Tibetans became pastoralists around their yak herds that provide meat, milk, cheese, leather, bones for carvings, and jewelry. The sheared hair is woven into coarse cloth and rope and used to make tents. The dung is used for fuel.

Comments: The form *mutus* a synonym.

Conservation Status: Rather rare and much restricted from its former range into W Sichuan. China RL—EN A1c; B1ab(i,ii,iii); C2a(ii). China Key List—I. CITES—I. IUCN RL—VU A1cd + 2cd, C1 ver 2.3 (1994).

References: Schaller (1998); Schaller and Liu (1996).

Subfamily Caprinae—Goats and Sheep

羊亚科 Yang Yake—山羊，绵羊 Shanyang, Mianyang

Caprinae is a diverse subfamily of goat antelopes, musk ox, goats, and sheep. Horns usually carried by both sexes, but those of females are small. Members of the group vary considerably in length, from just over 1 m for a goral to almost 2.5 m for a Musk Ox. Muzzle narrow and hairy; upper molar teeth have narrow crowns lacking a distinct inner column. Their social dynamics range from solitary territorial species with daggerlike horns that use scent marking for territorial defense of small home ranges to social grazers that live in large herds, have butting horns, establish dominance hierarchies, and wander over large tracts of open land. Of 13 genera of Caprinae, 8 are recognized in China.

Key to the Chinese Genera of Caprinae

1.a.	Horn long, almost straight, slightly bent forward at tip	*Pantholops*
b.	Legs sturdy, horns strongly recurved or twisted	2
2.a.	Horns of sexes about of equal size	3
b.	Horns of males much larger than those of females	6
3.a.	Horn longer than head, extending directly upward, then bending outward and backward; infraorbital and digital glands absent	*Budorcas*
b.	Horn shorter than head and strongly recurved	4
4.a.	Size large; horn triangular in cross section	*Hemitragus*
b.	Size small to largish; horns circular in cross section with basal rings	5
5.a.	Size larger (SH up to 100 cm); infraorbital gland large	*Capricornis*
b.	Size smaller (SH < 80 cm); infraorbital gland small	*Naemorhedus*
6.a.	No beard below jaw; conspicuous infraorbital gland; horn thick, spiraling backward, with transverse ridges on horn surface; lacrimal bone hollow	*Ovis*
b.	With or without beard; infraorbital gland absent	7
7.a.	Males with beard below jaw; back with black stripe; horns scimitar-shaped, rising high and arching backward and slightly outward. Horn with high transverse ridges and rectangular in cross section	*Capra*
b.	Neither sex with beard; no black stripe down back; horn twists widely outward with small ridge and nearly triangular in cross section	*Pseudois*

Genus *Budorcas* (monotypic)

羚牛属 Lingniu Shu

Takin

PLATE 58
MAP 540

Budorcas taxicolor Hodgson, 1850
羚牛 Ling Niu

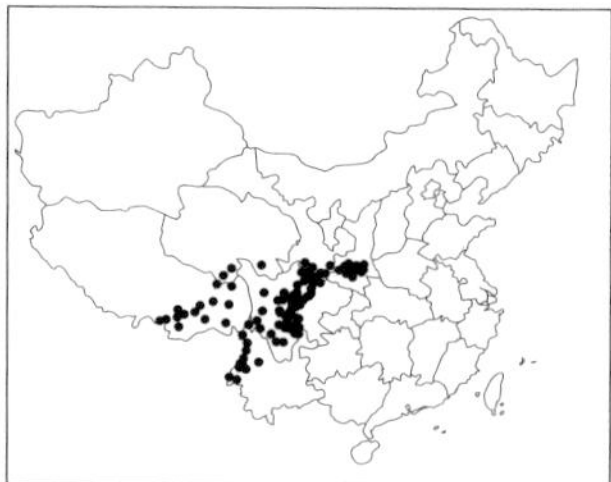

MAP 540. TAKIN, *Budorcas taxicolor*

Distinctive Characteristics: HB 170–220 cm; SH 107–140 cm; T 100–216; HF 267–444; E 101–149; GLS 350–460; Wt 250–600 kg. The Takin is a large, sturdy goat antelope that appears rather like a musk ox with stocky legs, broad hoofs, and strong dew claws. The coat is dense and shaggy, with a stripe along the back. Coat color varies with race, age, and sex from whitish yellow, reddish gray, darker brown, or gold. The tail is short and bushy. A bull's face is often dark, while only the nose is dark on females and calves. All Takin have an arched nose and hairy snout. Males are much larger than females. Profile of face convex. Both sexes have horns that arise from the midsection of their massive head, quickly curve outward, and then sweep backward and upward to a point. Horns may reach up to 64 cm in length. Horn bases may show transverse ridges. Infraorbital and digital glands absent; nasal bone short; premaxilla slender; rostrum ridged; flat lacrimal bone without foramen and at posterior end bending to form anterior margin of orbit. Different subspecies are based largely on coat color: *tibetana* being darkish brown; *taxicolor* being grayish (winter) or light brown (summer) with a buff mane; and *bedfordi* being rich golden yellow.
Distribution: Central S China; extending to the eastern Himalayas (Bhutan, Sikkim) and through N Myanmar. Four subspecies in China: (1) *B. t. bedfordi* Thomas, 1911; S Shaanxi; (2) *B. t. taxicolor* Hodgson, 1850; SE Xizang, NW Yunnan; (3) *B. t. tibetana* Milne-Edwards, 1874; W Sichuan, S Gansu; (4) *B. t. whitei* Lydekker, 1907; S Xizang (Yarlung Zanbo valley).
Natural History: In summer, Takin feed in alpine meadows up to 4,000 m. In winter they descend into the valleys and forests to as low as 1,000 m. They feed on a variety of grasses, bamboo shoots, forbs, and leaves of shrubs and trees. Takin forage in early morning and late afternoon and regularly visit salt-licks, which renders them very vulnerable to poachers who lay in ambush. Although Takin are mostly slow moving, they can move quickly over short distances when required. They can leap from rock to rock on steep slopes as a means of escape. If cornered they can fiercely attack their pursuers with their dangerous horns. Surprised at close range, they can charge humans, and some hunters have been killed by Takin. Takin may nibble the walls of deserted buildings for minerals and have been known to enter and climb into the second floor of buildings. They emit a loud warning cough in alarm. Rutting males give a low bellow. Takins seasonally migrate to preferred habitats. During spring and early summer months, they begin to gather in large herds of up to 100 animals at the uppermost limits of treeline. During cooler autumn months, when food is less plentiful at higher elevations, herds disband into smaller groups of up to 20 individuals and move to forested valleys at lower elevations. Groups mainly comprise females, subadults, young, and some adult males. Older males usually remain solitary throughout most of the year but gather with females during the rutting season. Sexually mature at about 3.5 years of age. Rutting occurs in late summer, followed by a gestation of 200 to 220 days. Single young are born in March or April. Longevity is about 16–18 years. Although Takin have no skin glands, their entire body secretes an oily, strong-smelling substance that serves as a moisture barrier on the animal's coat, protecting it from fog and rain.
Conservation Status: Increasingly rare as a result of hunting, forest loss, bamboo die-off after flowering, road construction, and disturbance from tourism. Some races are more endangered than others. China RL—*B. t. bedfordi*, *B. t. taxicolor*, *B. t. tibetana*: EN A1bcd + 2bcd; *B. t* C1; *B. t. whitei*: CR A1bcd+2bcd; C1. China Key List—I. CITES—II. IUCN RL—*B. t. bedfordi*: EN A2cd, C2a, D; *B. t. taxicolor*: EN A2cd; *B. t. tibetana*: VU A2cd; *B. t. whitei*: VU A2cde ver 2.3 (1994).
References: Ge et al. (1989); Neas and Hoffmann (1987); Schaller et al. (1986); Zeng et al. (2003).

Genus *Capra*—Goats

羊属 Yang Shu—羊 Yang

The true goats, *Capra* are of medium size and both sexes have horns, although the male's is much longer, some reaching over 1 m. Horn surface with broad transverse ridges in males but smooth in females. Infraorbital gland absent; only forefoot has digital gland. Crown of skull protruding with frontal area flat and inclined; lacrimal bone lacks foramen and is on almost same plane as nasal bone. There are eight species of *Capra* found in arid and mountainous regions of N Africa, Europe, Central Asia, the Indian subcontinent, China, and Siberia. Only one species occurs in China.

Key to the Chinese Species of *Capricornis*

1.a. Size small; SH ca. 60 cm; no long mane on nape — *Capricornis swinhoei*
b. Size large; SH ca. 100 cm; long mane on nape — 2
2.a. General color black with black or whitish mane and almost no red hair on body apart from lower legs — *Capricornis milneedwardsii*
b. Back black but extensive red in tail, lower legs and face — *Capricornis thar*

Siberian Ibex

PLATE 59
MAP 541

Capra sibirica (Pallas, 1776)
北山羊 Bei Shanyang

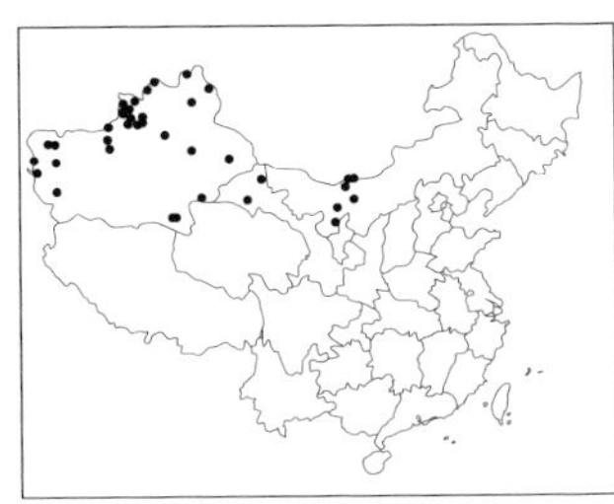
MAP 541. SIBERIAN IBEX, *Capra sibirica*

Distinctive Characteristics: HB 115–170 cm; SH 65–105 cm; T 100–200; GLS 230–306; Wt 80–100 kg (male), 30–50 kg (female). Large goat with spectacular, large, back-curved horns. Male horns up to 100 cm long. Pelage is light brown with pale underparts; with a black longitudinal stripe along midline of dorsum. Fronts of legs with dark brown stripes. Males have long beard; females short. In winter color becomes yellowish white or pure white, and the venter gray-brown.
Distribution: NW China; extending to Central Asia, N India, N Pakistan, S and W Mongolia, Russia (S Siberia). Four subspecies in China: (1) *C. s. alaiana* Noack, 1902; W Xinjiang; (2) *C. s. dementievi* Tzalkin, 1949; eastern Kunlun mountains; (3) *C. s. hagenbecki* Noack, 1903; N Xinjiang, Gansu, Nei Mongol; (4) *C. s. sibirica* (Pallas, 1776); N Xinjiang (Altai mountains).
Natural History: The Siberian Ibex occupies mountainous regions from 3,000 to 6,000 m in bare rocky terrain and open meadows. Its diet consists of alpine grasses and herbs, and it feeds in early morning and evenings. Lives in small parties of 4–10 but sometimes forms large herds. Uniquely massive recurved horns used in territorial fights between males. Mates in winter months with a gestation of 147–180 days. Usually one, sometimes two, kids are born in spring. Mature at two to three years.
Comments: Early treatments considered these forms synonyms of *C. ibex*, and many contemporary treatments have retained this classification.
Conservation Status: Highly threatened by poaching, habitat degradation, and competition from domestic stock (Bagchi et al. 2004). Extirpated from E Kunlun, Qiling (Qinghai), and W Gansu; vulnerable elsewhere. China RL—EN A2cd+3cd. China Key List—I. IUCN RL—LR/nt ver 2.3 (1994).
References: Bagchi et al. (2004); Roberts (1977); Schaller (1977).

Genus *Capricornis*—Serows

鬣羚属 Lieling Shu—Lieling

Serows are tall, dark-colored goats with short body and tall legs; hind legs longer than front legs; coat coarse with little underwool; some species have a long mane of hair on the neck. The horns are recurved and narrowly annulated basally. Of six species of *Capricornis*, three exist in China.

Chinese Serow

PLATE 60
MAP 542

Capricornis milneedwardsii David, 1869
甘南鬣羚 Gannan Lieling

Distinctive Characteristics: HB 140–170 cm; SH 90–100 cm; T 115–160; E 175–205; GLS 280–320; Wt 85–140 kg. A tall, long-legged, dark goat-antelope with short, recurved horns and a long, shaggy mane down back of neck extending as ridge of coarse hair down back. Ears are large, and there are prominent glands in front of eye. Tail is short and bushy. Pelage is blackish with grayish or reddish grizzling, especially on the long mane and legs. The hair is coarse and rather thin. The horns are longer, stouter, and more heavily annulated than those of any goral. The Chinese Serow is much larger than a goral and much smaller than a Takin. Form *milneedwardsii* has a black mane; the form *argyrochaetes* has a grayish white mane.
Distribution: Widespread across C and SE China; extending through the Himalayas to Indochina, but replaced in N Myanmar by *C. rubidus*. Two subspecies in China: (1) *C. m. argyrochaetes* Heude, 1888; SE China south of the Yangtze River; (2) *C. m. milneedwardsii* David, 1869 (including *maritimus* and *montinus*); through the Himalayas and eastern parts of Tibetan Plateau and through Sichuan, Yunnan, S Gansu, S Shaanxi to Hubei.

MAP 542. CHINESE SEROW, *Capricornis milneedwardsii*

Natural History: Inhabits rugged steep hills and rocky places, especially limestone regions up to 4,500 m. They normally winter in the forest belt and move to higher-elevation cliffs during summer. Feeds on a wide range of leaves and shoots; visits saltlicks. Mostly nocturnal and solitary. Has regular sleeping scrapes and sometimes rests on promontories with a good view.
Comments: Formerly included in *C. sumatraensis*. This form has commonly been included in the genus *Naemorhedus*.
Conservation Status: China RL—VU A2cd + 3cd. IUCN RL—VU A2cd ver 2.3 (1994) as *C. sumatraensis milneedwardsii*.
References: Groves and Grubb (1985); Shackleton (1997).

Taiwan Serow

Capricornis swinhoei Gray, 1862 MAP 543
台湾鬣羚 Taiwan Lieling
Distinctive Characteristics: HB 80–114 cm; SH 50–60 cm; T 70–120; Wt 17–25 kg. Smaller and more goral-like than mainland serow; with brown fur. Has shorter mane than mainland serow, but this is more erectile. Has pale creamy patch extending from chin to throat. Horns smaller and more gracile than mainland serow.
Distribution: Taiwan. Endemic.
Natural History: Inhabits rugged forest and rocky slopes along the main mountain chain on Taiwan between 1,000 and 3,000 m. Feeds on grass and browse, young twigs, and some fruits. Generally solitary. Uses rock shelters. Crepuscular. Single young born after seven months of gestation. Mating takes place in October and November.

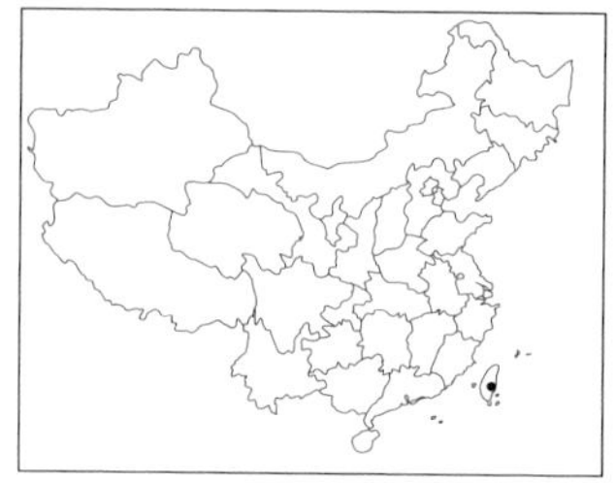

MAP 543. TAIWAN SEROW, *Capricornis swinhoei*

Comments: Formerly included under Japanese Serow (*C. crispus*). This form has commonly been included in the genus *Naemorhedus*.
Conservation Status: China RL—EN A2cd. China Key List—I. IUCN RL—VU A2cd ver 2.3 (1994).
References: Groves and Grubb (1985).

Himalayan Serow

Capricornis thar (Hodgson, 1831) MAP 544
尼泊尔鬣羚 Nibo'er Lieling
Distinctive Characteristics: Similar to the Chinese Serow, but some specimens reddish.
Distribution: Xizang on southern Himalayan slopes in region of Mt. Everest, in the Chumbi Valley, and in Medog County; extending into the Himalayas, Bhutan, Bangladesh, parts of Assam, Sikkim. Includes the form *jamrachi*.

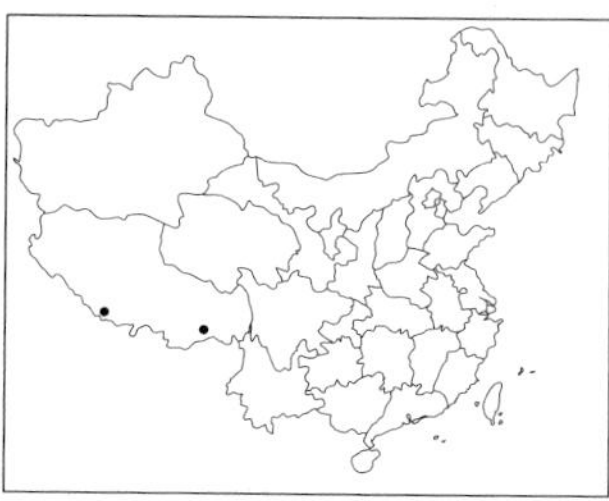

MAP 544. HIMALAYAN SEROW, *Capricornis thar*

Natural History: Similar to that of the Chinese Serow, although it is normally found at lower elevations (2,000–3,000 m) in the forested belt of high mountains.
Comments: Formerly treated as a subspecies of *C. sumatraensis*.
Conservation Status: China RL—NE; China Key List—II; CITES I (as *C. sumatraensis*); IUCN RL-VU A2cd (as *C. s. thar*).
References: Feng et al. (1986).

Genus *Hemitragus*—Thars

塔尔羊属 Ta'eryang Shu—塔尔羊 Ta'eryang

The thars are a small genus of three goatlike species, living in barren rocky or mountainous areas of Arabia, Nilgiri Hills of India, and the Himalayas. Legs are relatively short; head small, ears small and pointed; eyes large; horns found in both sexes are triangular in cross-section. Only one species occurs marginally in China.

Himalayan Thar

PLATE 59
Hemitragus jemlahicus (Hamilton Smith, 1826) MAP 545
喜马拉雅塔尔羊 Ximalaya Ta'eryang

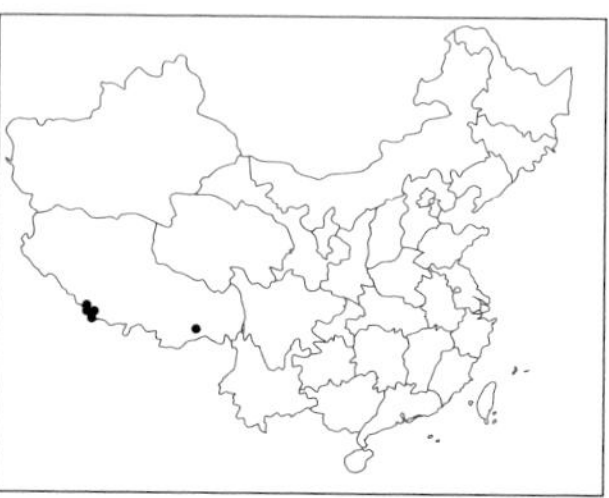

MAP 545. HIMALAYAN THAR, *Hemitragus jemlahicus*

Distinctive Characteristics: HB 130–170 cm; SH 62–106 cm; T 90–120; Wt 50–108 kg. Medium-sized goatlike animal with reddish to dark brown hair; males have a shaggy mane around the neck extending to knees, especially long in winter. Males lack a beard, have a bare muzzle, and possess digital glands. Small horns in both sexes sweep upward and backward then inward, later-

Key to the Chinese Species of *Naemorhedus*

1.a.	General color foxy red; ear length < 115 mm	*Naemorhedus baileyi*
b.	General color gray or brown; ear length > 115 mm	2
2.a.	Hair gray and shaggy, tail distally black and not bushy	*Naemorhedus goral*
b.	Color brown, tail bushy	3
3.a.	Tail long and very bushy, color light gray brown without black overlay	*Naemorhedus caudatus*
b.	Tail shorter and bushy, color darker brown with some black overlay, broad dorsal stripe	*Naemorhedus griseus*

ally flattened to give triangular cross section; not twisted and not ringed. Horn length up to 45 cm. 2N = 48.
Distribution: Found in only in a few spots along the S Xizang border near Qubuo River; extending south into the Himalayas and can be expected in extreme W Xizang adjacent to known populations in India. Introduced into New Zealand.
Natural History: Inhabits steep rocky mountain sides between 3,000 and 4,000 m with woods and rhododendron scrub. Eats grass, other herbs, and some fruits. Lives in small parties of 2–20 animals. Mating occurs from October to January. Males lock horns in dominance fights. One or occasionally two kids are born in June and July after a gestation of 180–242 days, depending on delayed implantation. Animals become mature after 1.5 years. A captive animal lived up to 22 years. Extreme agility in jumping among steep rocks.
Conservation Status: Endangered within China, threatened by small range, heavy hunting pressure, and competition and disturbance from domestic grazers. China RL—EN D. China Key List—I. IUCN RL—VU A2cde ver 2.3 (1994).
References: Schaller (1977).

Genus *Naemorhedus*—Gorals

斑羚属 Banling Shu—斑羚 Banling

Naemorhedus includes several small goat antelope species: the gorals. These have coarse, shaggy hair with a woolly undercoat. They are stockier than serows, with smaller horns; front legs and back legs of similar length; infraorbital glands small. Nasal bones are free for most of their length, and lacrimal bones lack a deep depression. The genus is found through the Himalayas and from Siberia to N India and Indochina. All four species occur in China, although some past authors have treated three gorals as forms of a single species or as forms of two species. All live in rugged mountainous terrain.

Red Goral

PLATE 60

Naemorhedus baileyi Pocock, 1914

MAP 546

红斑羚 Hong Banling

Distinctive Characteristics: HB 930–1,070; SH 570–610; T 80–100; E 95–106; HF 200–250; GLS 168–199; Wt 20–30 kg. Small goral with small, slender recurved horns. Distinguished from other species by foxy red pelage with no black ticking. Narrow, dark brown stripe runs down back to the short, blackish tufted tail. Sometimes pale on forehead. Lacks pale throat patch. Ears shorter than in other gorals.
Distribution: SE Xizang and extreme NW Yunnan; extending into NE Assam and N Myanmar.

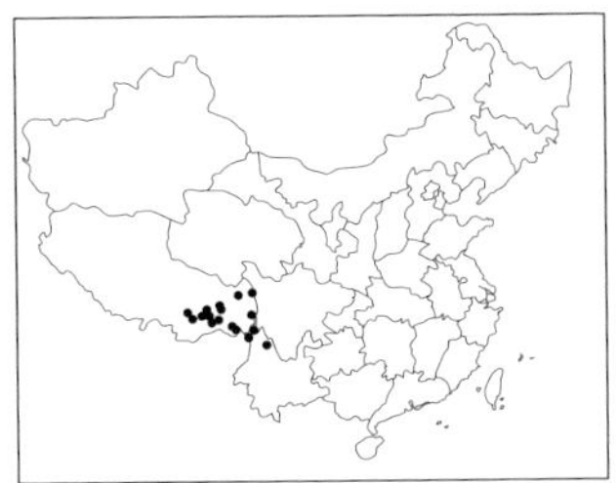

MAP 546. RED GORAL, *Naemorhedus baileyi*

Natural History: Inhabits forest, ragged crags, scrub, and meadows from 2,000 m up to 4,500 m in summer. Most aspects of their natural history are similar to those of other gorals, although they are supposedly rather tame. Mates in December, and young are born in June after a six-month pregnancy.
Comments: Treated as a subspecies of *N. caudatus* by some authors; *cranbrooki* a synonym.
Conservation Status: Uncommon within narrow distribution and much threatened by hunting and forestry operations. China RL—EN A1cd. China Key List—I. CITES—I. IUCN RL—VU A2cd ver 2.3 (1994)
References: Feng et al. (1986); Rabinowitz (1999).

Long-Tailed Goral

PLATE 60

Naemorhedus caudatus

Milne-Edwards, 1867

MAP 547

中华鬣羚 Zhonghua Lieling

Distinctive Characteristics: HB 1,060–1,200; SH 690–750; T 130–160; E 130–170; HF 270–320; Wt 32–42 kg. Gray, goatlike antelope with a pale throat patch. Pelage mostly gray-brown with no black overlay. Much smaller and paler than serows and lacking a long mane, although it does have an inconspicuous dark dorsal stripe. Legs paler than body, but with less sharp transition than in *N. griseus*. Distinguished from *N. goral* by its bushier tail and black stripes of foreleg passing to outer leg below knee rather than down median. Recurved black horns are basally annulated, but more gracile than in serows; horn length short (127–178 mm typical, but as long as 235 mm). Has inconspicuous glands in front of eyes. Undercoat more woolly than in serow. The throat is particularly broadly white, this color extending to the chin; tail is long and appears longer as it is bushy throughout. Skull is shorter and higher than in serows.

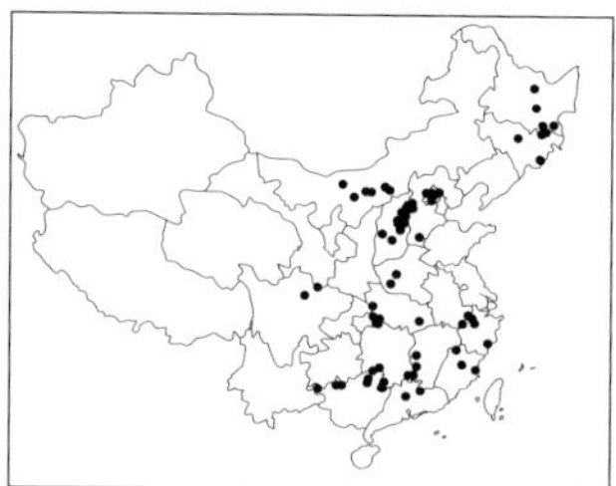

MAP 547. LONG-TAILED GORAL, *Naemorhedus caudatus*

Distribution: E China; extending to E Russia and Korea.
Natural History: Inhabits steep and rocky terrain in evergreen and deciduous forests, especially with exposed grassy ridges from about 500–2,000 m altitude. Eats a wide range of plant material: grass, herbs and shoots, leaves of small trees, and even some fruit. Lives singly or in small groups. Diurnal and crepuscular. Keeps to steeper slopes where it is very agile over rocky crags and cliffs. Has resting scrapes in sheltered places under rock sides also rests on rock ledges. Visits salt licks. Gives hissing sneeze call when alarmed. Mates in early winter, and one or two kids born about six months later. Small, rather vertical toes allow for great agility and good grip on steep, rocky slopes.
Comments: Here treated as an independent species separate from *N. goral* (see also Grubb 2005).
Conservation Status: Much reduced by hunting, snares, habitat degradation, and grazing competition. China RL—VU A2cd + 3cd. China Key List—II. CITES—I. IUCN RL—VU A2cd ver 2.3 (1994).
References: Groves and Grubb (1985); Mead (1989).

Himalayan Goral

Naemorhedus goral (Hardwicke, 1825) MAP 548
斑羚 Banling

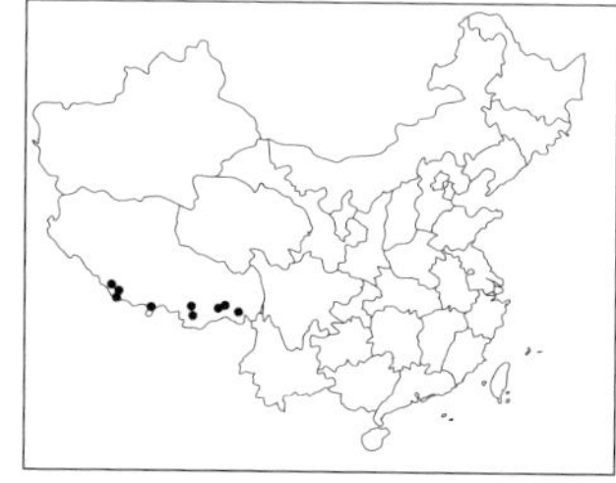

MAP 548. HIMALAYAN GORAL, *Naemorhedus goral*

Distinctive Characteristics: HB 1,000–1,200; SH 590; T 80–150; HF 240–275; GLS 196–214; Wt 35–42 kg. Large, grizzled gray to brownish gray goral with thick woolly undercoat, covered by longer, coarser black guard hairs and a short, semi-erect mane on male. Coat becomes shaggy in winter. Legs light brown or tan; even white on forelegs; dark dorsal stripe weak or absent; throat generally variably white; underparts grayish white. Distal half of tail is black and not bushy. Includes form *hodgsoni*. Horns 12–18 cm in length.
Distribution: Only marginally present in China along the northern flanks of the Himalayas; extending from Kashmir to the Changbi Valley between Sikkim and Bhutan.
Natural History: Feeds on grassy ridges and steep rocky slopes but hides in forest or rock crevices; shelters under rock overhangs. Eats grasses, herbs, and twigs with some fruits. Males usually single; otherwise found in pairs or small parties. Active in early morning and at dusk; resting through mid-day, but more active in cloudy weather. Usually finds drinking water in small streams. Gives a hissing sneeze in alarm. One or two young are born after a gestation of six to eight months. Young are weaned by eight months of age, and mature by three years. May live up to 15 years.
Comments: Some authors treat as *N. caudatus hodgsoni*.
Conservation Status: China RL—EN A2cd + 3cd. China Key List—I. CITES—I. IUCN RL—LR/nt ver 2.3 (1994).
References: Feng et al. (1986); Mead (1989).

Chinese Goral

Naemorhedus griseus
(Milne-Edwards, 1871) MAP 549
川西斑羚 Chuanxi Banling

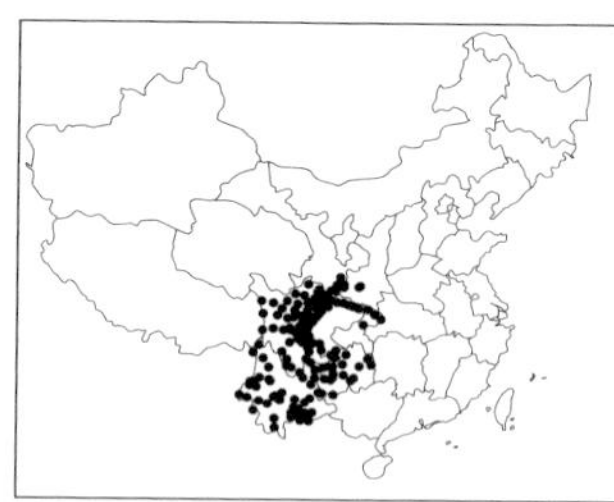

MAP 549. CHINESE GORAL, *Naemorhedus griseus*

Distinctive Characteristics: HB 880–1,180 cm; SH 610–680; T 115–200; E 117–150; HF 235–285; GLS 184–225; Wt 22–32 kg. Tallish, dark brown, fawn, or grayish goral with some black overlay. Has short, dark crest and clear, thick, dark dorsal stripe. Legs are sharply paler than body. Forelegs sometimes reddish with black stripe; pale patch on throat is edged orange; chin is dark. Underparts light gray. Tail not long but bushy. Form *arnouxianus* is a darker brown, and its throat patch is buff-edged reddish yellow; *griseus* is darker with a reddish brown edge to a whitish throat patch and a brown tail base.
Distribution: Central S China; extending to NE India, W Myanmar, NE Thailand, E Bangladesh (unconfirmed in N Laos and NW Vietnam). Two subspecies

in China: (1) *N. g. arnouxianus* Heude, 1888; C China; (2) *N. g. griseus* (Milne-Edwards, 1871); Yunnan.
Natural History: Similar to other gorals.
Conservation Status: China RL—EN A2cd + 3cd. China Key List—II. CITES—I.
References: Groves and Grubb (1985); Mead (1989); Shackleton (1997).

Genus *Ovis*—Sheep

盘羊属 Panyang Shu—盘羊 Panyang

Ovis includes domestic sheep and their wild allies. Five species are distributed in the Palaearctic and Nearctic regions (Grubb 2005). These are stocky caprines with shortish legs. Both sexes with horns, those of males much larger and usually spiraling, roughly circular in cross section and ribbed with many rings; with infraorbital, digital and inguinal glands. Skull shaped with obtuse angle when viewed from rear; rostrum short; orbit protruding distinctly sideways; lacrimal foramen shallow. Only one species occurs in China.

Argali

PLATE 59
MAP 550

Ovis ammon (Linnaeus, 1758)
盘羊 Panyang

Distinctive Characteristics: Male: HB 180–200 cm; SH 110–125 cm; T 10–18; HF 43–50; E 10–15; GLS 290–360; Wt 95–140 kg, rarely up to 180 kg. Females much smaller, with weight about 1/3 that of males (68 kg). Very large sheep with small ears and tail, and long, silky fur. Pelage grayish brown with yellowish breast and white underparts, lower legs, and rump patch. Males carry massive horns up 100–170 cm long with heavy annuli and broad base that increase in length and mass with age. The horns curve down and forward for more than 360 degree. Female horns are much smaller and only slightly curved. 2N = 56.
Distribution: Widespread in mountains of W China; extending to Pakistan, N India, Nepal, Central Asia, Mongolia, and S Siberia. Many subspecies (some dubious) have been recognized; herein we follow Shackleton (1997): (1) *O. a. ammon* (Linnaeus, 1758); N Xinjiang (Altai mountains); (2) *O. a. darwini* Przevalski, 1883; N Xinjiang, Nei Mongol, and NW Gansu; (3) *O. a. hodgsoni* Blyth, 1841; widespread across Tibetan Plateau (the form *dalailamae* found along the northern edge of the Arjin mountains is likely a synonym); (4) *O. a. jubata* Peters, 1876; C Nei Mongol and Ningxia (Helan Shan, Yabraishan, Langshan and Daqinshan ranges); (5) *O. a. karelini* Severtzov, 1873; N and C Xinjiang (some split this form into four separate subspecies including the forms *adametzi, littledalei, sairensis*—see Shackleton 1997); (6) *O. a. polii* Blyth, 1841; Pamir Plateau along W Xinjiang border.
Natural History: Lives on alpine grasslands between 3,000 and 5,000 m, descending lower in winter. Prefers to occupy open areas with a gentle slope; females occupy steeper (cliff) terrain following lambing. Feeds on grasses and some herbs and lichens, and regularly drinks from open springs and rivers. Where sympatric with Blue Sheep they are more likely to occur in forb-dominated communities compared to the grass-dominated communities occupied by Blue Sheep. Populations are reported to be small and sporadically distributed across their range. They are gregarious and live in groups of 2–150 individuals. One, rarely two, lambs are born in May and June after a 150–160-day gestation. Massive horns are used for head-butting fights during the rut and for protection. The thick, woolly coat provides protection during cold winters.

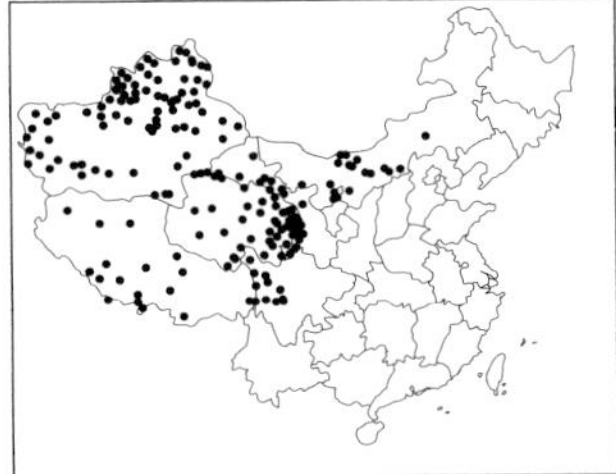

MAP 550. ARGALI, *Ovis ammon*

Conservation Status: Endangered in China; most populations are small and severely fragmented. China RL—EN A2cd + 3cd. China Key List—II. CITES—*O. a. hodgsoni*: I; other subspecies: II. IUCN RL—VU A2cde; *O. a. ammon*: VU A2cde, C1; *O. a. darwini*: EN C1; *O. a. hodgsoni*: VU A2cde; *O. a. jubata*: CR C2a; *O. a. karelini*: VU A2cde, C1 + 2a; *O. a. polii*: VU A2cde, C1 ver 2.3 (1994)
References: Bunch et al. (2000); Fedosenko and Blank (2005); Harris and Loggers (2004); Namgail et al. (2004); Schaller (1977; 1998); Shackleton (1997).

Genus *Pantholops* (monotypic)

藏羚属 Zangling Shu

Tibetan Antelope

PLATE 57
MAP 551

Pantholops hodgsonii (Abel, 1826)
藏羚 Zang Ling

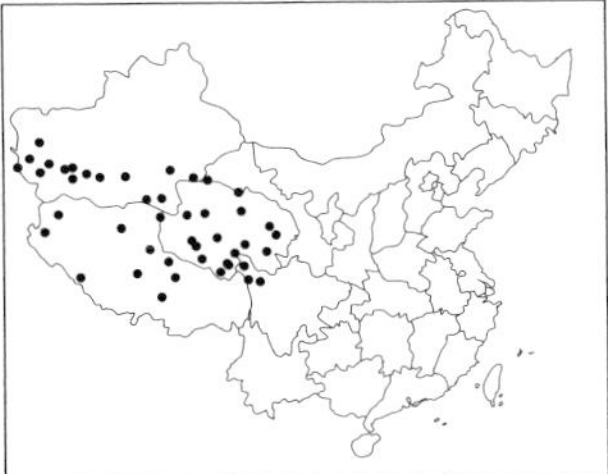

MAP 551. TIBETAN ANTELOPE, *Pantholops hodgsonii*

Distinctive Characteristics: HB 100–140 cm; SH 79–94 cm; T 130–140; E 120–150; GLS 216–278; Wt 24–42 kg. The Tibetan Antelope is the single representative of a rather aberrant caprine genus (*Pantholops*). They are sometimes classified with the antilopines on account of their general appearance and horn structure, and sometimes placed within their own subfamily. Molecular evidence and some morphological traits indicate that this form belongs within the Caprinae (Grubb 2005; Lei et al. 2003a). This is a largish antelope with sandy brown to reddish fawn pelage and white underparts. The coat is dense and woolly. Males have black markings on front of their face, with a contrasting white patch on the upper lip. A black patch is found on the front of their neck. In winter the pelage lightens, such that at a distance males may appear white. Males have diagnostic very tall horns (50–71 cm) held almost vertically, but curving slightly forward at tips. Unlike other caprines, females are hornless. Both males and females possess large inguinal glands in the groin, with an opening 5 cm long and a pouch 6 cm deep; this pouch contains a smelly, peanut-butter-like waxy yellow substance (Schaller 1998).

Distribution: Tibetan Plateau; extending to Ladakh and Kashmir.

Natural History: Inhabits cold deserts and alpine grasslands of the Tibetan Plateau, including the lower-altitude Qaidam Basin. Feeds on grass, herbs, and lichens. Lives in large herds. Males and females almost completely segregate during their seasonal migration; females move long distances, whereas males may travel only a short distance from their wintering areas. Single calves are born in June after a gestation of six to seven months. It is believed that females first reproduce at 1.5–2.5 years of age. The fleecy undercoat so prized for making shatoosh wool is an adaptation for extreme cold winters.

Conservation Status: Seriously endangered by poaching for its valuable soft shatoosh wool. Tibetan Antelope are also vulnerable to the railroad and highway corridors that disrupt their migration path. Population size has undergone a drastic decline in recent decades. China RL—EN A2cd + 3cd. China Key List—I. CITES—I. IUCN RL—EN A2d ver 3.1 (2001).

References: Harris and Loggers (2004); Jiang and Wang (2001); Li et al. (2000b); Ruan et al. (2005); Schaller (1998); Schaller et al. (1991).

Genus *Pseudois*—Blue Sheep

岩羊属 Yanyang Shu—岩羊 Yanyang

A small genus of medium-sized sheep found in China and the Himalayas; both species occur in China. Similar to *Ovis*, but differ in horn structure and some morphological characteristics. Their horn does not spiral, but rather twists outward from the head, roughly triangular in cross section and with a ridge on the inner margin. Inguinal and digital glands are poorly developed, and the infraorbital gland is absent; back end of nasal bone is wide, gradually becoming sharp; lacrimal bone lacks a foramen and lies nearly on top of the face; eye orbit is extended laterally and is tube-shaped.

Blue Sheep

Pseudois nayaur (Hodgson, 1833) PLATE 59 MAP 552

岩羊 Yanyang

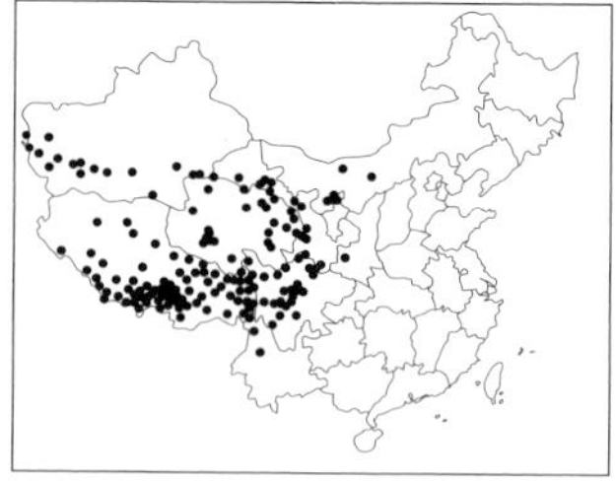

MAP 552. BLUE SHEEP, *Pseudois nayaur*

Distinctive Characteristics: Male: HB 120–165 cm; SH 69–91 cm; T 130–200; E 90–130; HF 70–100 cm; GLS 198–258; Wt 50–70 kg. Females are smaller (wt 35–45 kg). Winter pelage is thick and woolly; shorter and finer in summer. Upperparts brownish gray with slaty blue tinge; whitish underparts and inner legs. Outer legs marked with black. *Pseudois* has a broad, flat tail with a bare central surface, large dewclaws, no inguinal glands, no preorbital glands, and usually no pedal glands. The rounded, smooth horns curve backward over the neck then flare outward with a twist. Both sexes have horns, but those of males are much larger, reaching up to 82 cm.

Distribution: Tibetan Plateau extending into W Sichuan, S Gansu, and as far east as C Nei Mongol; extending south into Bhutan and N Myanmar and across the Himalayas into Nepal, N India, Pakistan, and Tajikistan (Pamir mountains). Two subspecies occur in China (although their validity has been questioned): (1) *P. n. nayaur* (Hodgson, 1833); S Xizang; (2) *P. n. szechuanensis* Rothschild, 1922; Yunnan, Sichuan, Qinghai, Gansu, Ningxia, Shaanxi, Nei Mongol.

Natural History: Blue Sheep inhabit open grassy slopes in high mountains from 2,500 to 5,500 m. They feed on grass, alpine herbs, and lichens and live in small to rather large herds, alternately resting and feeding on steep grassy slopes of alpine meadows.

Key to the Species of *Pseudois*

1.a.	Smaller; wt 28–39 kg (male); 25 kg (female); horns thinner and with less of an inward curve	*Pseudois schaeferi*
b.	Larger; wt 50–70 kg (male); 35–45 kg (female); horns thicker and more of an inward curve	*Pseudois nayaur*

Key to the Chinese Families of Cetacea

1.a.	Rostrum projecting and cone-shaped, its length about 1/6 of HB length; tooth root flat and wide; suture in lower jaw long, greater than half as long as lower jaw; live in freshwater	Iniidae
b.	Rostrum short, its length < 1/10 of HB length; tooth root sharp; suture in lower jaw short and less than half as long as lower jaw; live in open seas	2
2.a.	Rostrum short and not projecting; teeth laterally compressed and shovel-shaped	Phocoenidae
b.	Rostrum usually conspicuous; teeth coniform	Delphinidae

Males sometimes form all male herds, and sometimes mix with family herds. Sentinels watch out for snow leopards, their primary predator. Mates during winter followed by a 160-day gestation. Single lambs (rarely twins) are born in early summer; weaning occurs in six months, and young reach maturity 1.5 years.
Conservation Status: China RL—VU A2cd + 3cd. China Key List—II. IUCN RL—LR/nt ver 2.3 (1994).
References: Namgail et al. (2004); Oli and Rogers (1996); Schaller (1998); Schaller and Gu (1994); Wang and Hoffmann (1987).

Sichuan Blue Sheep

Pseudois schaeferi Haltenorth, 1963 MAP 553
矮岩羊 **Ai Yanyang**

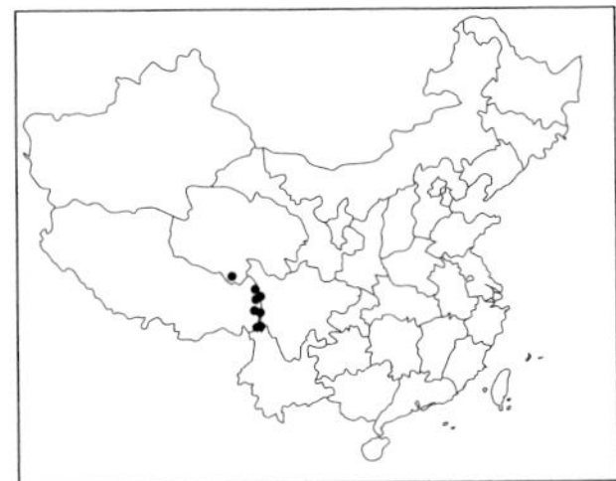

MAP 553. SICHUAN BLUE SHEEP, *Pseudois schaeferi*

Distinctive Characteristics: HB 109–160 cm; SH 50–80 cm; T 7–12 cm; GLS 208–247; Wt 28–65 kg (male), 17–40 kg (female). Similar to Blue Sheep of which it was formerly regarded a subspecies, but generally smaller than *P. nayaur* and has a drabber coloration with a silvery sheen. Horn thinner and with less of a curl.
Distribution: Confined to a narrow area along the Jingshajiang Valley in the upper reaches of the Yangtze River in Batang and Bayu counties of Sichuan and a small part of Muking and Markam counties on the other side of the river in E Xizang. It possibly also occurs in SW Sichuan (Derong County) and NW Yunnan (Deqen County). Endemic.
Natural History: Lives among very steep rocky slopes between 2,700 and 3,200 m; occasionally range into conifer forest and forest clearings. Blue Sheep may live in same region at higher altitudes. Diet consists of grasses, low shrubs, club moss, and lichens. Feed and rest alternately throughout the day on the grassy slopes of mountains. Groups formerly of 10–36 animals, but now usually less than 15 as a result of overhunting. Males sometimes form all-male groups or sometimes mix with females and young. Usually single young (rarely twins) are born in May or June after a gestation of 160 days. Young are weaned within six months and reach maturity at 1.5 years. Males may take seven years to reach full size.
Comments: The separation of *schaeferi* into an independent species is controversial. While some believe that it is clearly an independent taxa, others claim that it should be designated as a subspecies of *P. nayaur* (Feng et al. 2001). Recent molecular evidence (Zhou et al. 2003) did not support the independent species status of *schaeferi*.
Conservation Status: Population has drastically declined as a result of hunting, with group size dropping from a former range of 10–36 to only 3–8 by 1990. Protected on religious grounds by Baiyu minority in Sichuan. China RL—CR B1ab (i, ii, iii, v). China Key List—II. IUCN RL—EN A2d, B1 + 2e ver 2.3 (1994).
References: Feng et al. (2001); Groves (1978); Wang et al. (2000); Wang and Hoffmann (1987); Wu et al. (1990); Zhou et al. (2003).

ORDER CETACEA—Whales, Porpoises, and Dolphins

鲸目 **Jing Mu—鲸, 海豚 Jing, Haitun**

Andrew T. Smith

The Cetacea are completely aquatic mammals. Both form and structure are highly adapted for aquatic life; body pisciform; neck inconspicuous; body surface with no hair or scales; forelimb finlike (flipper); hind limbs absent; most have dorsal fins; tail very long, ending in two flat fins; both dorsal fin and fluke composed of connective tissue, without bone or fin ray; tail is the main locomotor organ; head without external ear; auditory sensation very developed; both smell and vision reduced; nostrils elevated, with valves that can open and close; eyes very small.

All members of this group live in seas except a few freshwater species; usually gregarious; food habits carnivorous, living on invertebrates, fish, and plankton; classified into two suborders: Odontoceti, with teeth in mouth; and Mysticeti, no teeth, but with long strips of baleen. At times these two suborders have been treated as independent orders, but now their close relationship is recognized. Recent classifications have shown the close affinity of cetaceans with artiodactyls, and some treatments combine them into the order Cetartiodactyla. Others believe that the hippopotamuses should be combined with the Cetacea.

Mysticeti includes about 13 species; size generally large or very large; HB length more than 10 m; the largest Blue Whale is about 30 m long and weighs more than 180,000 kg; with hundreds of inserted corneous baleen strips in upper jaw, which filter plankton in the water; nostril with two openings; forelimb with four digits.

Odontoceti includes about 72 species; tooth number usually very large (about 100, or 260 the most numerous), the smallest with only a pair of homodont teeth; HB length generally only several meters; nostril with one opening; skull asymmetrical; forelimb with five fingers.

Cetaceans are distributed over all seas and many rivers. Of about 11 families, 40 genera, and 85 species, approximately 8 families, 24 genera, and 35 species may occur in coastal waters of China (appendix I). As most of these species have wide distributions and are commonly treated, here we present only those three species, belonging to separate odontocete families, that occur commonly in China's inland waters.

Family Dephinidae—Dolphins

海豚科 Haitun Ke—海豚 Haitun

The Delphinidae is the most diverse family of whales with 35 species in 17 genera. Dolphins are small to medium-sized cetaceans that are gregarious and form large social groups. Most species have a dorsal fin and a distinctive beak (a snout that is sharply differentiated from the forehead) or a long snout. The skull is concave and slightly asymmetrical; a "melon" (a lens-shaped fatty deposit) lies in the facial depression. Up to 18 species of dolphin are known from the coastal waters of China.

Genus *Sousa*—Humpback Dolphins

白海豚属 Zhonghuabai Shu

Sousa are characterized by a sloping "forehead" and a double-step dorsal fin marked by a smaller fin that sits on an elongated hump on the dolphin's back. The beak is long and slender and is usually exposed when surfacing. Of two species of *Sousa*, one occurs in China; the other occurs in the Atlantic Ocean.

Indo-Pacific Humpback Dolphin — PLATE 61

Sousa chinensis (Osbeck, 1765) — MAP 554

中华白海豚 Zhonghuabai Haitun

Distinctive Characteristics: HB 2.5 m; GLS 575; Wt 250 kg. The robust body of the Indo-Pacific Humpback Dolphin is uniformly white or off-white, sometimes almost reddish in hue; may have some black spots on body, particularly males. Young are a deep gray and conspicuously darker than adults. The sexual dimorphism (males larger) found throughout much of the species range is not evident in Chinese populations. The species is characterized by a distinctive hump at the base of the small dorsal fin, although this is not as pronounced or may be lacking in Chinese forms. They have a relatively long, slender beak, clearly set off from the melon. Possesses many homodont teeth (tooth counts = 30–36 upper jaws; 24–37 lower jaws).

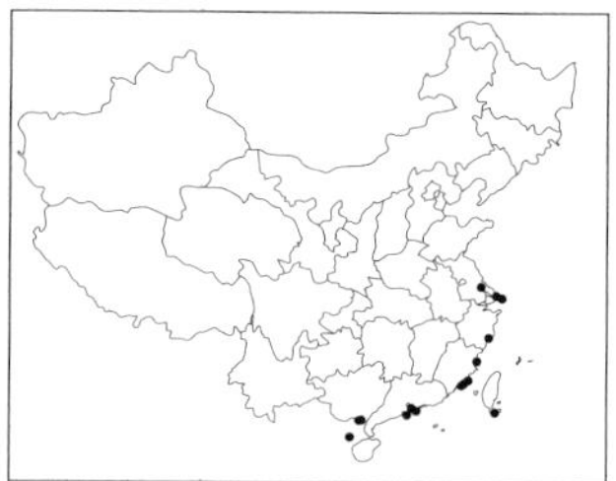

MAP 554. INDO-PACIFIC HUMPBACK DOLPHIN, *Sousa chinensis*

Distribution: Found in SE sea area of China, in major river mouths from the Yangtze River south; extending to coastlines along N and W Australia to India, and all the way to the tip of South Africa.
Natural History: Generally occur in shallow, nearshore waters less than 20 m in depth. They swim up into fresh water in Chinese rivers and as far out as 50 km into the ocean where depths remain shallow. Normally swim in pods of fewer than 10 individuals; the maximum group size appears to be 20–30. Strong social bonds among pod members are uncommon. Diet consists primarily of fish and cephalopods. While the single calves may be born year-round, calving is most common in the spring to summer months following a gestation of 10 to 12 months.
Conservation Status: Population numbers are very small in China and appear to be negatively affected by marine pollution, major development projects, and fishing activity. In 1996, 60 individuals were spotted in the Xiamen area, but these have been decreasing with subsequent comprehensive surveys. Only 1,000 are known to live in the Pearl River estuary region. China RL—EN A1ac. China Key List—I. CITES—I. IUCN RL—DD ver 2.3 (1994).
References: Huang and Liu (2000); Jefferson (2000); Jefferson and Karczmarski (2001); Liu and Hills (1997); Reeves et al. (2003); Zhou et al. (2001); Zhou et al. (2003).

Family Phocoenidae—Porpoises

鼠海豚科 Shuhaitun Ke—海豚 Haitun

Porpoises are small cetaceans that largely occupy Northern Hemisphere seas and coastlines. The teeth are laterally compressed and spadelike; the head has short jaws and no beak. There are distinctive bumps on the premaxillae immediately in front of the external nares. The dorsal fin is not prominent, being short or absent. There are six species represented in three genera, only one of which is found in Chinese waters.

Genus *Neophocaena* (monotypic)

江豚属 Jiangtun Shu

Finless Porpoise

PLATE 61
MAP 555

Neophocaena phocaenoides (Cuiver, 1829)
江豚 Jiang Tun

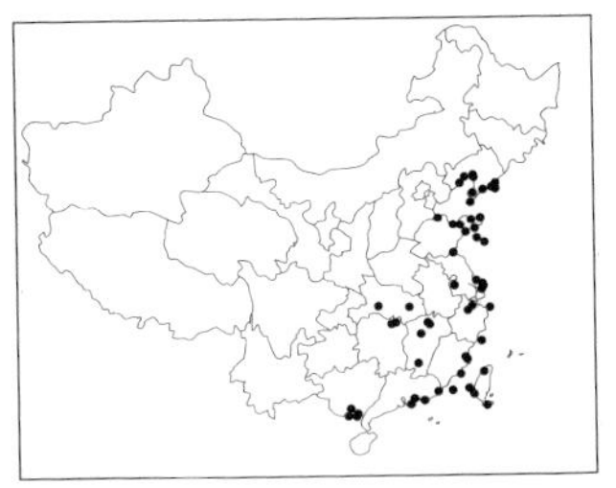

MAP 555. FINLESS PORPOISE, *Neophocaena phocaenoides*

Distinctive Characteristics: HB 1.0–2.3 m; Wt 25–50 kg. Anterior body thicker than posterior; head rounded; protruding forward; no fin on back; flipper sicklelike; whole body pale gray with a bluish tinge on the back and sides; 15–21 shovel-shaped teeth on each side of the jaw.
Distribution: In China found along coastal waters and in bays from the Korean Peninsula to Vietnam; extending throughout Indo-Pacific shorelines from the Persian Gulf to Japan. Three subspecies in China: (1) *N. p. asiaeorientalis* Pilleri and Gihr, 1972; the truly Chinese form that lives in the Yangtze River; (2) *N. p. phocaenoides* (G. Cuiver, 1829); S East China Sea, South China Sea, and Indian Ocean; (3) *N. p. sunameri* Pilleri and Gihr, 1975; Yellow Sea and East China Sea.
Natural History: Occupies warm seas and coastal inland waters, with a freshwater population that inhabits the middle-lower reaches of the Yangtze River and its adjacent lake systems. Prefers sandy areas with reedy swamps for feeding. Diet of fish and squid. Swims alone or in pairs, although groups of 12–15 individuals have been observed. Can swim upstream for a very long distance. The Finless Porpoise produces a characteristic vocalization with a narrow sonar band that can be used to accurately census populations with detection devices rather than direct observation. In the Yangtze River population, mating occurs from May through June, and normally a single calf is born during late April of the following year.
Conservation Status: Thought to be seriously depleted due to heavy fisheries bycatch; the decline of the ocean-dwelling subspecies may be as great as 95% in some areas. The total Yangtze River population has been estimated at 2,000–3,000, and there is every indication that it is declining precipitously. China RL—EN A1acd. CITES—I. IUCN RL—DD; *N. p. asiaeorientalis*: EN C2b ver 2.3 (1994).
References: Barros et al. (2002); Gao and Zhou (1993); Jefferson et al. (2002); Reeves et al. (2003); Wei et al. (2002); Xiao and Zhang (2002); Yu et al. (2005).

Family Iniidae—River dolphins

河豚科 Hetunke—河豚 Hetun

The river dolphins were at one time lumped together in the family Platanistidae. More recently the Platanistidae, including only *Platanista* and its two species (the Ganges and Indus River dolphins), was determined to be unrelated to the other river dolphins, herein assigned to the Iniidae (Mead and Brownell 2005). Others have gone further and split the Iniidae into three monotypic families, including the Lipotidae (the Yangtze River Dolphin). These forms all have long rostrums and many repetitive teeth, reduced eyes, and ability to locate food by echolocation. Of the three genera in Iniidae, only one occurs in China.

Genus *Lipotes* (monotypic)

白暨豚属 Baijitun Shu

Yangtze River Dolphin

PLATE 61
MAP 556

Lipotes vexillifer Miller, 1918
白暨豚 Baiji Tun

Distinctive Characteristics: HB to 2.2 m (males), to 2.5 m (females); Wt 135–160 kg (males), 240 kg (females). Rostrum narrow and long, its tip slightly upturned; dentition of uniform cone-shaped teeth ranges from 32–34 above and 31–34 below; roots laterally compressed; eyes small; flipper relatively wide, with blunt tip; dorsal fin low and triangular; blowhole longitudinal and somewhat rectangular; back light blue or off-white; ventral surface white.
Distribution: Currently found in the middle and lower reaches of the Yangtze River between two large tributary lakes, Dongting and Poyang. In the past it occupied these lakes and extended as far as 1,900 km up the Yangtze River, and occurred in the separate drainages of the Qiantang and Fuchun rivers. Endemic.
Natural History: Inhabits fresh water, including major rivers and tributaries; prefers sandy substrates to estuarine habitats. Historically swam in small groups of 2–6 individuals, with a maximum pod size of 15. Now that they are becoming increasingly difficult to find, most sightings are of solitary Yangtze River Dolphins, and maximum group size approaches 4 individuals. Commonly swims with fin exposed above water surface; breathes at intervals of 10–30 seconds. Swims at a speed of 7.5–9.7 km/hr, and has been known to range up to 200 km. Diet of fish. Vocalizations consist of whistles as well as broadband sonar signals. Reproductive season February–April; interbirth interval two years; gestation 10–11 months; a single young is born.

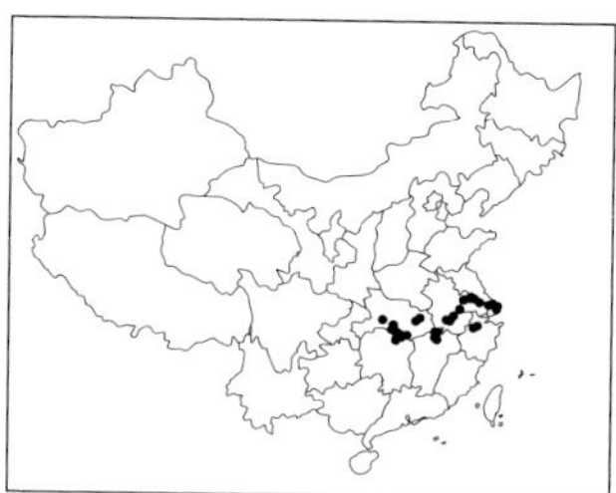

MAP 556. YANGTZE RIVER DOLPHIN, *Lipotes vexillifer*

Comments: Also commonly knows as Baiji.
Conservation Status: Likely the most endangered of all cetaceans. It is believed that there may be only 30–80 alive today; although one recent comprehensive survey concluded that the minimum number of individuals could be as low as 13 (Zhang et al. 2003a). The species is likely to be further impacted by construction of the Three Gorges Dam along the Yangtze River. Recently the Yangtze River Dolphin disappeared from the Qiantang and Fuchun rivers following construction of a high dam in 1957. Conservation options are controversial, involving debates over whether or not to manage the species within its native habitat or to move a breeding population to seminatural but controlled conditions (Reeves and Gales 2006; Wang et al. 2006; Yang et al. 2006). China RL—CR A1acd; C2b; D. China Key List—I. CITES—I. IUCN RL—CR A1bc, C2b, D ver 2.3 (1994).
References: Brownell and Herald (1972); Reeves and Gales (2006); Reeves et al. (2003); Wang et al. (2006); Yang et al. (2006); Zhang et al. (2003b); Zhou et al. (1994); Zhou et al. (1998).

Appendix I

Cetaceans Found Off the Coast of China (not covered in text)

ORDER CETACEA

Suborder Mysticeti

Family Balaenidae

Eubalaena japonica (Lacépède, 1818)—**North Pacific Right Whale**

Family Balaenopteridae

Balaenoptera acutorostrata Lacépède, 1804—**Common Minke Whale**

Balaenoptera borealis Lesson, 1828—**Sei Whale**

Balaenoptera edeni Anderson, 1879—**Bryde's Whale**

Balaenoptera musculus (Linnaeus, 1758)—**Blue Whale**

Balaenoptera physalus (Linnaeus, 1758)—**Fin Whale**

Megaptera novaeangliae (Borowski, 1781)—**Humpback Whale**

Family Eschrichtiidae

Eschrichtius robustus (Lilljeborg, 1861)—**Gray Whale**

Suborder Odontoceti

Family Delphinidae

Delphinus delphis Linnaeus, 1758—**Short-beaked Common Dolphin**

Feresa attenuata Gray, 1874—**Pygmy Killer Whale**

Globicephala macrorhynchus Gray, 1846—**Short-finned Pilot Whale**

Grampus griseus (Cuvier, 1812)—**Risso's Dolphin**

Lagenodelphis hosei Fraser, 1956—**Fraser's Dolphin**

Lagenorhynchus obliquidens Gill, 1865—**Pacific White-sided Dolphin**

Orcinus orca (Linnaeus, 1758)—**Killer Whale**

Peponocephala electra (Gray, 1846)—**Melon-headed Whale**

Pseudorca crassidens (Owen, 1846)—**False Killer Whale**

Stenella attenuata (Gray, 1846)—**Pantropical Spotted Dolphin**

Stenella coeruleoalba (Meyen, 1833)—**Striped Dolphin**

Stenella longirostris (Gray, 1828)—**Spinner Dolphin**

Steno bredanensis (Cuvier in Lesson, 1828)—**Rough-toothed Dolphin**

Tursiops truncatus (Montagu, 1821)—**Bottlenose Dolphin**

Family Physeteridae

Koiga breviceps (Blainville, 1838)—**Pygmy Sperm Whale**

Koiga sima (Owen, 1866)—**Dwarf Sperm Whale**

Physeter catodon Linnaeus, 1758—**Sperm Whale**

Family Ziphiidae

Berardius bairdii Stejneger, 1883—**Baird's Beaked Whale**

Mesoplodon densirostris (Blainville, 1817)—**Blainville's Beaked Whale**

Mesoplodon ginkgodens Nishiwaki and Kamiya, 1958—**Ginkgo-toothed Beaked Whale**

Ziphus cavirostris Cuvier, 1823—**Cuvier's Beaked Whale**

Appendix II

Hypothetical Mammals (those found close to China but without known representation in the Chinese Mammal Fauna)

ORDER PRIMATES

Family Cercopithecidae

Trachypithecus geei Khajuria, 1956—**Gee's Golden Langur**

Trachypithecus pileatus (Blyth, 1843)—**Capped Langur**

ORDER RODENTIA

Family Sciuridae

Eupetaurus cinereus Thomas, 1888—**Woolly Flying Squirrel**

Petaurista nobilis (Gray, 1842)—**Bhutan Giant Flying Squirrel**

Spermophilus fulvus (Lichtenstein, 1823)—**Yellow Ground Squirrel**

Family Dipodidae

Pygeretmus platyurus (Lichtenstein, 1823)—**Lesser Fat-tailed Jerboa**

Salpingotus thomasi Vinogradov, 1928—**Thomas's Pygmy Jerboa**

Stylodipus sungorus Sokolov and Shenbrot, 1987—**Mongolian Three-toed Jerboa**

Family Spalacidae

Myospalax myospalax (Laxmann, 1773)—**Altai Zokor**

Family Cricetidae

Alticola barakshin Bannikov, 1947—**Gobi Altai Mountain Vole**

Myodes regulus (Thomas, 1907)—**Korean Red-backed Vole**

Family Muridae

Apodemus rusiges Miller, 1913—**Kashmir Field Mouse**

Hapalomys longicaudatus Blyth, 1859—**Greater Marmoset Rat**

ORDER SORICOMORPHA

Family Soricidae

Crocidura hilliana Jenkins and Smith, 1995—**Hill's Shrew**

Crocidura pergrisea Miller, 1913—**Pale Gray Shrew**

Chodsigoa caovansunga Lunde, Musser and Son, 2003—**Van Sung's Shrew**

Suncus stoliczkanus (Anderson, 1877)—**Anderson's Shrew**

ORDER CHIROPTERA

Family Vespertilionidae

Hesperoptenus tickelli (Blyth, 1851)—**Tickell's Bat**

Miniopterus medius Thomas and Wroughton, 1909—**Intermediate Long-fingered Bat**

Murina tubinaris (Scully, 1881)—**Scully's Tube-nosed Bat**

ORDER CARNIVORA

Family Canidae

Canis aureus Linnaeus, 1758—**Golden Jackal**

Family Felidae

Prionailurus viverrinus (Bennett, 1833)—**Fishing Cat**

Family Viverridae

Cynogale bennettii Gray, 1837—**Otter Civet**

ORDER PERISSODACTYLA

Family Rhinocerotidae

Dicerorhinus sumatrensis (Fischer [von Waldheim], 1814)—**Sumatran Rhinoceros**

Rhinoceros sondaicus Desmarest, 1822—**Javan Rhinoceros**

Rhinoceros unicornis Linnaeus, 1758—**Indian Rhinoceros**

ORDER ARTIODACTYLA

Family Suidae

Sus salvanius (Hodgson, 1847)—**Pygmy Hog**

Family Tragulidae

Tragulus napu (Cuvier, 1922)—**Greater Mouse-deer**

Family Cervidae

Rucervus schomburgki (Blyth, 1863)—**Schomburgk's Deer**

Family Bovidae

Bos javanicus d'Alton, 1823—**Banteng**

Appendix III

Introduced Alien, Feral, or Free-ranging Domestic Mammals

ORDER RODENTIA

Family Cricetidae

Ondatra zibethicus (Linnaeus, 1776)—**Common Muskrat**

Family Muridae

Mus musculus Linnaeus, 1758—**House Mouse**

Rattus rattus (Linnaeus, 1758)—**Roof Rat**

Family Myocastoridae

Myocastor coypus (Molina, 1782)—**Coypu**

ORDER CARNIVORA

Family Felidae

Felis catus Linnaeus, 1758—**Domestic Cat**

Family Canidae

Canis lupus familiaris Linnaeus, 1758—**Domestic Dog**

Family Mustelidae

Neovison vison (Schreber, 1777)—**American Mink**

ORDER PERISSODACTYLA

Family Equidae

Equus asinus Linnaeus, 1758—**Ass**

Equus caballas Linnaeus, 1758—**Horse (domesticated)**

ORDER ARTIODACTYLA

Family Suidae

Sus scrofa vittatus Boie, 1828—**Wild Boar (domesticated)**

Family Camelidae

Camelus bactrianus Linnaeus, 1758—**Bactrian Camel (domesticated)**

Family Bovidae

Bos grunniens Linnaeus, 1766—**Yak (domesticated)**

Bos taurus Linnaeus, 1758—**Aurochs (domesticated cattle)**

Bubalus bubalis (Linnaeus, 1758)—**Water Buffalo**

Capra hircus Linnaeus, 1758—**Goat (domesticated)**

Ovis aries Linnaeus, 1758—**Red Sheep (domesticated sheep)**

Glossary

abdominal cavity. The largest body cavity in mammals, holding most of the internal organs and separated from the thoracic cavity by a muscular diaphragm.
aliform. Shaped like a wing.
alisphenoid canal. Hole in the base of the alisphenoid bone through which a blood vessel passes.
allopatric. Geographical separation of populations; occurring in different places.
alveoli. Holes; dental alveoli are tooth sockets.
anterocone. Small cusp on the front of upper teeth.
anteroconid. Small cusp on the front of lower teeth.
antitragus. Small lobe at the base of the ear, opposite to the tragus (*plural* antitrogi).
apical. At the tip, as in apical lobe of a nose leaf (on some bats).
aposematic coloration. Advertisement of dangerous or defensive mechanisms involving bright coloration or conspicuous morphological structures.
astralagus. Ankle bone; its pullylike surface limits motion to a single plane in some ungulates.
auditory bullae. The inflated (hollow) structure that encloses the middle ear chamber.
axillary. The portion of the body supported by the spinal column and rib cage.
baculum. A bone found in the penis of certain mammals; also called *os penis*.
baleen. Keritinized plates forming from the upper jaw of mysticete whales used for straining marine organisms from water.
basioccipital. Basal part of the back of the skull.
basisphenoid. Base of the cranium between the basioccipital and the presphenoid.
brachyodont. Cheek teeth with low crowns; typical of omnivorous mammals.
brow tine. The first tine above the base of an antler.
buccal. In dendition, the "outside" of the teeth, toward the cheeks; same as labial.
bullae. *See* auditory bullae.
calcar. A bony or cartilaginous medial projection from the ankle of microchiropteran bats, used to support the uropatagium.
callosities. Thick, hardened areas of the skin.
canine. Cuspid, or eye tooth, situated between incisors and premolars.
cannon bone. Fused metacarpals or metatarsals.
carnassial. Scissorlike teeth of carnivores specialized for shearing flesh; last upper premolar and first lower molar.
cingulum. An enamel shelf that borders the margin of an upper tooth.
cochlea. The conical labyrinth that forms the anterior part of the inner ear.
commisure. Any sharp, crescent-shaped projection on a cheek tooth.
condylar process. Smoothly rounded projection from the rear of the dentary where the lower jaw articulates with the skull.
condylobasal length. Distance from the anterior border of the premaxillae to the plane of posterior border of the occipital condyles.
condylocanine length. Distance from the anterior edge of the alveoli of the upper canines to the posterior plane of the condylar process.
condyloincisive length. Distance from the anterior edge of the upper incisors to the posterior plane of the condylar process.
coronoid process. The back part of the lower jaw that rises up.
cranium. Skull.
crown. Occlusal surface of a tooth.
cuneal. Wedge-shaped.
cusp. Any of the points on a premolar or molar tooth.
cusplet. Small accessory cusp.
denticle. Toothlike projection.
diastema. A long, natural gap in a row of teeth, particularly that between the incisors (or canines) and the cheek teeth of herbivores.
digit. Finger or toe.
digitigrade. Pertains to walking on the digits, with the wrist or heel held off the ground.
ectoloph. An enamel ridge running along the outer margin of an upper molar.
ectotympanic. Bone in the middle ear that supports the tympanic membrane or eardrum.
endemic. A species found in a given geographic region and not found elsewhere.

entocone. A cusp on the anterior, lingual side of the talon in upper cheek teeth.
entoconid. A cusp on the anterior, lingual side of the talonid in lower cheek teeth.
entotympanic. A bone surrounding the middle ear and sometimes fused with the tympanic.
external auditory meatus. The canal leading from the surface of the head into the tympanic membrane.
fenestrae. Small perforations or openings.
fenestrated. Having fenestrae.
foramen. Small hole in a bone of the skull, for passage of nerves and blood vessels.
foramen magnum. A large opening in the back of the skull, through which the spinal cords leaves the brain; bracketed by the occipital condyles.
fossorial. Pertains to an animal that burrows and conducts most of its activity underground.
frontal. Bones that comprise the front part of the braincase, situated between the orbits.
frugivorous. Feeding on fruit.
glenoid cavity (fossa) . Depression in the scapula into which the head of the humerus articulates.
hastate. Like a spear point, with flaring pointed lobes at the base.
heterodont. Teeth that vary in structure in different parts of the jaw; in mammals represented by the different morphologies of the canines, incisors, premolars, and molars.
homodont. Teeth that are repetitive in morphology.
humerus. Upper arm bone, connecting the forearm to the shoulder.
hypocone. A cusp on the posterior lingual side of the crown in upper cheek teeth.
hypoconid. The main cusp on the labial side of the talonid of the lower molars.
hypsodont. Teeth with high crowns; usually rootless and continuously growing.
incisive foramina. Paired openings in the anterior palate behind the incisors; at the junction of the premaxillae and maxillae (*also* palatal foramina).
incisor. Tooth adapted for cutting or gnawing, located at the front of the mouth along the apex of the dental arch.
Indo-Malayan realm. Biogeographic region encompassing India, southern China, the Malay Peninsula, the Philippine islands, and the islands of Indonesia to Wallace's line (*also* Oriental realm).
infraorbital foramen. A large hole in the side of the maxilla, usually in front of or below the orbit.
inguinal. Pertaining to the region of the groin.
insectivorous. Feeding on insects.
interfemoral membrane. Membrane stretching between the thighs.
internarial. Between the nostrils.
interorbital breadth. Minimum distance between the orbits (*also* interorbital constriction).
interparietal. An unpaired bone at the rear of the cranium, lying between the parietal bones and above and anterior to the occipital bone.
interpterygoid fossa. The depression formed by the divergence posteriorly of the plates of the pterygoid process of the sphenoid bone.
ischial swelling. A patch of thickened hairless and often brightly colored skin on the buttocks of many apes.
jugal. The bone that forms the midsection of the zygomatic arch.
labial. On the side proximal to the lips.
lacrimal. Paired bone of the cranium lying between the jugal and frontal bones at the anterior portion of the orbit; contains the opening for the tear (lacrimal) duct.
lambdoidal crest. A transverse bony ridge across the rear of the cranium formed where the occipital and parietal bones join.
lancet. Tip of *Rhinolophus* nose leaf, projecting upward between the eyes.
lappet. Small flap on lobe of *Rhinolophus* nose leaf.
lingual. On the side proximal to the tongue.
loph. A ridge on the occlusal surface of a tooth.
mammae. Milk-producing glands.
mammillary. Breastlike, or breast-shaped.
mandible. The lower jaw as formed by the paired dentary bones.
manus. The forefoot or hand.
mastoid process. The exposed portion of the petromastoid bone, most of which is concealed within the auditory bulla; if present it is located posterior to the auditory bulla.
maxilla. Bones forming the upper jaw and holding the upper teeth.

meatus. External opening to the auditory bullae.

mesopteroid fossa. Shallow area behind the internal nares and between the pterygoid bones.

mesostyle. Middle stylar cusp along the buccal margin of an upper molar.

mesosulcus. Median groove on a tooth.

metacarpal. Any bone in the manus between the carpals and phalanges; only one metacarpal per digit.

metacone. The posterior, outer cusp of an upper molar.

metaconid. The posterior, outer cusp of a lower molar.

metastyle. Stylar cusp near the buccodistal corner of an upper molar.

metatarsal. Any bone in the pes between the tarsals and phalanges; only one metatarsal per digit.

molars. Teeth with broad crowns used to grind food, located behind the premolars.

monstrous. Having a single estrous cycle per year.

nasal. Paired bones forming the upper surface of the rostrum.

nose leaf. Accessory flap attached to top of nostrils.

occipital. Bone forming the back of the skull; contains the foramen magnum.

occipital condyles. Smooth, rounded knobs on each side of the foramen magnum, where the skull articulates with the first vertebrae; two in mammals.

occipital crest. A ridge formed where the parietal bones join the occipital bone, across the top, back part of the skull.

occiput. The back of the head, or skull; also occipital region.

occlusal surface. The chewing, or grinding, surface of a tooth.

oestrus. The period during which a female is receptive to copulation.

optic foramen. Opening in the medial wall of the orbit through which pass nerves and arteries.

pagophilic. Ice loving, as in seals that breed on ice.

pagophobic. Ice avoiding, as in seals that breed on land.

Palaearctic realm. Biogeographic region encompassing northern Africa, Europe, the Middle East, and northern Asia.

palatal foramina. *See* incisive foramina.

palate. The roof of the mouth.

palatine. Bone on the palate between the maxilla and the pterygoid process of the sphenoid.

palatoincisive. Length from posterior palate to tip of incisors.

paraconid. A cusp on the anterior, lingual side of the trigonid portion of the crown in lower cheek teeth.

paralabral. Beside the lips.

parastyle. The anterior cusp on the stylar shelf.

paroccipital process. Bony projection extending ventrally from or located ventrally on the paroccipital bone.

parietal. Paired bones forming the top, back part of the skull; situated posterior to the frontal and dorsal to the squamosal.

patagium. A thin membrane of skin between the limbs that provides a gliding surface; forms the wing membranes of bats.

pectoral girdle. The bones or cartilaginous structures in the trunk that articulate with the forelimb.

pelvic girdle. The bones or cartilaginous structures in the trunk that articulate with the hind limb.

perineal. Pertaining to the anogenital region.

pes. The hind foot.

phalanges. The bones of the fingers or toes.

phalanx. Any one of the fingers or toes.

philtrum. The area from below the nose to the upper lip.

pinna. External ear (*plural* pinnae).

piscivorous. Fish eating.

plagiopatagium. The membrane of a bat wing that extends between the body and hind limbs to the arm and fifth digit.

plantar pad. The soft portion on the sole of the foot.

plantigrade. A form of locomotion in which the entire foot touches the ground.

pollex. The first (most medial) digit on the manus; the thumb of primates.

polyestrous. Having several estrous cycles during a single breeding season.

postglenoid foramina. Small holes in posterior part of the temporal bone.

postglenoid fossa. Indentation in posterior part of the temporal bone.

postorbital. Bone situated behind or around the eye socket.

postorbital processes. Projection from the frontal bone that marks the rear, upper edge of the eye socket.

postpartum. After birth; postpartum estrous is a cycle beginning shortly after giving birth.

premaxilla. A pair of small cranial bones at the very tip of the jaws bearing teeth; connected to the maxilla and the nasals.

premolars. Bicuspids, or the teeth between canine and molars.

presphenoid. The anterior part of the body of the sphenoid bone in front of the basisphenoid.

proboscis. Long, tubular snout.

proclivous. Having the incisor teeth directed forward.

procumbent. Pertaining to teeth that slant forward.

protocone. The principal cusp of the upper molar, on the inner central part of the tooth.

protoconid. The principal cusp of the lower molar, on the inner central part of the tooth.

pterygoid. Paired bone on ventral surface of cranium, posterior to palatine and anterior to alisphenoid; forms border of internal nares.

pterygopalatine fossa. Depression between the pterygoid processes and the rear surface of the maxilla.

quadritubercular. An upper cheek tooth with four major cusps: paracone, metacone, protocone and hypocone.

radius. One of the two bones of the forearm.

rhinarium. The area of hairless skin surrounding the nostrils.

rhombic dental leaves. Cusp pattern resembling an oblique equilateral parallelogram.

rostrum. Beaklike projection of the anterior part of the head or skull.

sagittal crest. Ridge running lengthwise along the top of the braincase.

sella. The characteristic posterior nose leaf of bats of the genus *Rhinolophus.*

sellate. Saddle-shaped.

septum femorale intermedium. Middle section of extraperitoneal fatty tissue surrounding the femoral ring.

sesamoid structure. A bone formed in a tendon where it passes over a joint.

sphenoid. Compound bone with winglike processes, situated at the base of the skull.

sphenopalatine foramen. Small hole in the skull connecting the nasal cavity with the pterygopalatine fossa.

squamosal. Bone forming the major portion of the lateral wall of the braincase.

squamosal ridge. Small ridge on squamosal part of the temporal region of the skull.

Steno's foramen. Small hole between the incisive foramena.

style. Minor cusp on a tooth.

stylomastoid foramen. Small hole between the tyloid and mastoid processes of the temporal bone.

superciliary arch. Ridge on the frontal bone above the orbit, or eye socket.

supraoccipital. *See* occipital.

supraorbital process. Bony projection above the orbit on the frontal.

sympatric. Area of overlap in the distribution of two species; occurring in the same place.

synonym. Each of two or more names applied to the same taxon.

talonoid. An extension of the posterior cingulum of a lower cheek tooth.

tapetum lucidum. A reflective choroid layer in the eyes of nocturnal mammals aiding in night vision; yields "eye shine."

tarsules. Toe bones.

temporal fossa. The large space behind the orbit bounded by the zygomatic arch and the postorbital processes.

tibia. The shin bone; the more medial of the two bones between the knee and the ankle.

tragus. The cartilaginous projection anterior to the external opening of the ear in microchiropteran bats (*plural* tragi).

transverse lophs. Linear cusps across cheek teeth.

trefoil. A three-lobed leaf, on *Rhinolophus* nose leaf.

tribosphenic tooth. An upper molar with three main cusps in a triangular pattern, or a lower molar with a triangular arrangement of the trigonid and an adjacent talonid.

tribubercular tooth. An upper tribosphenic molar or premolar.

trigonid. A triangle formed by three mains cusps of an lower molar.

trochanter. One of two processes near the head of the femur, the outer being called the great trochanter, and the inner the small trochanter.

tubercules. A small elevation on the surface of a tooth.

tympanic bullae. *See* auditory bullae.

type specimen. A specimen from which a nominal species or subspecies has been or may be named.

ulna. One of the two bones of the forearm.

ultrasonic. Wavelengths above the frequencies of audible sound, normally any wavelengths over 20,000 Hz.

unicuspid. A tooth with a single, well-developed cusp.

uropatagium. The flap of skin found between the hind legs and the tail of most bats.

vestigial. Reduced, atrophied, remnant.

vibrissae. Enervated long, stiff hairs found on the snout of most mammals.

viviparous. Giving birth to live young.

vomer. Unpaired bone of the cranium that may form the septum in the nasal passage.

zygomatic arch. The curved bone forming an arch along the side of the skull below the orbit; the cheekbone.

zygomatic plate. Platelike extension—expanded and flattened—of the lower maxillary process.

References

Includes all literature cited in the text, as well as general mammal sources and Chinese provincial and regional guides that are not cited.

Abdukadir, A. 2002a. [A checklist of the mammals in Xinjiang, China]. *Arid Zone Research* 19 (Supplement):1–75 (in Chinese).

——. 2002b. [*General Introduction of Felidae in Xinjiang, China. Part 1*]. Xinjiang Scientific, Technological and Sanitary Press: Urumqi, China (in Chinese).

Abe, H. 1971. Small mammals of central Nepal. *Journal of the Faculty of Agriculture*, Hokkaido University, Sapporo, Japan, 56:367–423.

——. 1982. Ecological distribution and faunal structure of small mammals in central Nepal. *Mammalia* 46:477–503.

——. 1983. Variation and taxonomy of *Niviventer fulvescens* and notes on *Niviventer* group of rats in Thailand. *Journal of the Mammalogical Society of Japan* 9:151–161.

——. 1995. Revision of the Asian moles of the genus *Mogera*. *Journal of the Mammalogical Society of Japan* 20:51–68.

Abramov, A. V. 2000. A taxonomic review of the genus *Mustela* (Mammalia, Carnivora). *Zoosystematica Rossica* 8:357–364.

——. 2001. [Notes on the taxonomy of the Siberian badgers (Mustelidae: *Meles*)]. *Proceedings of the Zoological Institute Russian Academy of Sciences*, St. Petersburg, 288:221–233 (in Russian).

——. 2002. Variation of the baculum structure of the Palaearctic badger (Carnivora, Mustelidae, *Meles*). *Russian Journal of Theriology* 1:57–60.

——. 2003. The head colour pattern of the Eurasian badgers (Mustelidae, *Meles*). *Small Carnivore Conservation* 29:5–7.

Abramov, A. V., and G. F. Baryshnikov. 2000. Geographic variation and intraspecific taxonomy of weasel *Mustela nivalis* (Carnivora, Mustelidae). *Zoosystematica Rossica* 8:365–402.

Abramov, A. V., and S. G. Medvedev. 2003. Notes on zoogeography and taxonomy of the badgers (Carnivora: Mustelidae: *Meles*) and some of their fleas (Siphonaptera: Ceratophyllidae: *Paraceras*). *Zoosystematica Rossica* 11:397–402.

Abramov, A. V., and A. Yu. Puzachenko. 2006. Geographical variability of skull and taxonomy of Eurasian badgers (Mustelidae, *Meles*). *Zoologicheskii Zhurnal* 85 (5): 641–655 (in Russian).

Adler, G. H. 1995. Habitat relations within lowland grassland rodent communities in Taiwan. *Journal of Zoology*, London, 237:563–576.

——. 1996. Habitat relations of two endemic species of highland forest rodents in Taiwan. *Zoological Studies* 35:105–110.

Afanasiev, A. V., and N. T. Zolotarev. 1935. [New data on the systematics and distribution of the Siberian dhole (*Cuon alpinus hesperius* Afanasiev et Zolotarev)]. *Izvestiya AN SSR* 7:3 (in Russian).

Agrawal, V. C. 2000. Taxonomic studies on Indian Muridae and Hystricidae (Mammalia: Rodentia). *Records of the Zoological Survey of India*, Occasional Paper No. 180:1–177.

Ågren, G., Q. Zhou, and W. Zhong. 1989a. Ecology and social behaviour of Mongolian gerbils, *Meriones unguiculatus*, at Xilinhot, Inner Mongolia, China. *Animal Behaviour* 37:11–27.

——. 1989b. Territoriality, cooperation and resource priority: Hoarding in the Mongolian gerbil, *Meriones unguiculatus*. *Animal Behaviour* 37:28–32.

Allayarov, A.M. 1963. [Information on the ecology and geographical distribution of the spotted cat in Uzbekistan]. *Voprosy Biologii I Kraevoi Meditsiny* 4:315–321 (in Russian).

Allen, G. M. 1923a. New Chinese insectivores. *American Museum Novitates* 100:1–11.

——. 1923b. New Chinese bats. *American Museum Novitates* 85:1–8.

——. 1924. Microtines collected by the Asiatic expeditions. *American Museum Novitates* 133:1–13.

——. 1926. Rats (genus *Rattus*) from the Asiatic expeditions. *American Museum Novitates* 217:1–16.

——. 1927. Murid rodents from the Asiatic expeditions. *American Museum Novitates* 270:1–12.

——. 1929. Mustelids from Asiatic expeditions. *American Museum Novitates* 358:1–12.

——. 1936. The status of *Vespertilio pilosus* Peters. *Journal of Mammalogy* 17:168–169.

——. 1937. Second preliminary report on the results of the second Dolan expedition to west China and Tibet: A new race of *Ochotona*. *Proceedings Academy Natural Sciences Philadelphia* 89:341–342.

——. 1938–1940. *The Mammals of China and Mongolia (Natural History of Central Asia)*. W. Granger, editor. Central Asiatic Expeditions of the American Museum of Natural History, New York, 11:part 1:1–620[1938]; part 2:621–1350[1940].

Allen, J. A. 1920. Note on Gueldenstaedt's names of certain species of Felidae. *Journal of Mammalogy* 1:90–91.

Allen, J. A., and R. C. Andrews. 1913. Mammals collected in Korea. *Bulletin of the American Museum of Natural History* 32:427–436.

Allen, S. H., and A. B. Sargeant. 1993. Dispersal patterns of red foxes relative to population density. *Journal of Wildlife Management* 57:526–533.

Andersen, K. 1905. On some bats of the genus *Rhinolophus* with remarks on their mutual affinities, and descriptions of twenty-six new forms. *Proceedings of the Zoological Society of London* 2: 75–145.

Anderson, E. 1970. Quaternary evolution of the genus *Martes* (Carnivora, Mustelidae). *Acta Zoologica Fennica* 130:1–132.

Anderson, S., and J. K. Jones, Jr. 1984. *Orders and Families of Recent Mammals of the World*. John Wiley and Sons: New York.

Angermann, R. 1966. Beiträge zur Kenntnis der Gattung *Lepus* (Lagomorpha, Leporidae) II. Der taxionomische Status von *Lepus brachyurus* Temminck und *Lepus mandshuricus* Radde. *Mitteilungen aus dem Zoologische Museum in Berlin* 42:321–335.

Anoop, K. R., and S. A. Hussain. 2005. Food and feeding habits of smooth-coated otters (*Lutra perspicillata*) and their significance to the fish population of Kerala, India. *Journal of Zoology*, London, 266:15–23.

Anthony, H. E. 1941. Mammals collected by the Vernay-Cutting Burma Expedition. *Field Museum of Natural History, Zoological Series* 27:37–123.

Aoki, B., and R. Tanaka. 1938. Biostatistical research on *Rattus losea* (Swinhoe, 1870), a Formosan wild rat, with special reference to its diagnostic characters for taxonomy. *Memoirs of the Faculty of Science and Agriculture*, Taihoku Imperial University, 23:1–74

——. 1941. The rats and mice of Formosa illustrated. *Memoirs of the Faculty of Science and Agriculture*, Taihoku Imperial University, 23:121–191.

Aplin, K. P., P. R. Brown, J. Jacob, C. J. Krebs, and G. R. Singleton. 2003. *Field Methods for Rodent Studies in Asia and the Indo-Pacific*. Australian Centre for International Agricultural Research: Canberra.

Aristov, A. A., and G. F. Baryshnikov. 2001. [*Mammals of Russia and Adjacent Territories. Carnivores and Pinnipeds*]. Russian Academy of Sciences: St. Petersburg (in Russian).

Asakawa, M., K. Hagiwara, L. F. Liao, W. Jiang, S. S. Yan, J. J. Chai, Y. Oku, and M. Ito. 2001. Collection record of small mammals in Xinjiang-Uygur, 1998 and 1999 with brief review of its mammalian fauna. *Biogeography* (Japan) 3:13–31.

Asher, R. J., M. C. McKenna, R. J. Emry, A. R. Tabrum, and D. G. Kron. 2002. Morphology and relationships of *Apternodus* and other extinct, zalambdodont, placental mammals. *Bulletin of the American Museum of Natural History* 273:1–117.

Baagøe, H. J. 2001. *Vespertilio murinus* Linnaeus, 1758–Zweifarbfledermaus. Pp. 473–514. In *Handbuch der säugetiere Europas. Band 4: Fledertiere. Teil I: Chiroptera I, Rhinolophidae, Vespertilionidae I.* J. Niethammer and F. Krapp, editors. Aula Verlag: Wiebelsheim.

Bagchi, S., C. Mishra, and Y. V. Bhatnagar. 2004. Conflicts between traditional pastoralism and conservation of Himalayan ibex (*Capra siberica*) in the Trans-Himalayan mountains. *Animal Conservation* 7:121–128.

Bannikov, A. G., L. V. Zhirnov, L. S. Lebedeva, and A. A. Fandeev. 1961. [*Biology of Saiga*]. Selskokchozyajstvennaya Literature Publishers: Moscow (in Russian).

Bao, X., and Y. Zhuge. 1986. [An ecological study on *Eothenomys melanogaster*]. *Acta Theriologica Sinica* 6:297–305 (in Chinese).

Bao, X. K., J. Z. Ma, and Y. M. Zhang. 2003. [Analysis of seasonal diet composition of sable (*Martes zibellina*) in Daxinganling Mountains, northeastern China]. *Acta Theriologica Sinica* 23:203–207 (in Chinese).

Barros, N. B., T. A. Jefferson, and E. C. M. Parsons. 2002. Food habits of finless porpoises (*Neophocaena phocaenoides*) in Hong Kong waters. *Raffles Bulletin of Zoology*, Supplement 10:115–123.

Baryshnikov, G. F., and O. R. Potapova. 1990. [Variability of the dental system in badgers (*Meles*, Carnivora) in the USSR fauna]. *Zoologicheskii Zhurnal* 69:84–97 (in Russian).

Bates, P.J.J., and D. L. Harrison. 1997. *Bats of the Indian Subcontinent*. Harrison Zoological Museum: Kent, U.K.

Bates, P.J.J., D. L. Harrison, and M. Mundi. 1994. The bats of western India revisited. Part 2. *Journal of the Bombay Natural History Society* 91:224–240.

Bates, P.J.J., D. L. Harrison, P. D. Jenkins, and J. L. Walston. 1997. Three rare species of *Pipistrellus* (Chiroptera: Vespertilionidae) new to Vietnam. *Acta Zoologica Academiae Scientiarum Hungaricae* 43:359–374.

Bates, P.J.J., D. K. Hendrichsen, J. L. Walston, and B. Hayes. 1999. A review of the mouse-eared bats (Chiroptera: Vespertilionidae: *Myotis*) from Vietnam with significant new records. *Acta Chiropterologica* 1:47–74.

Bechthold, G. 1939. Die asiatischen Formen der Gattung *Herpestes*. *Zeitschrift für Säugetierkunde* 14:113–219.

Bekenov, A., and Z. H. Myrzabekov. 1977. [Reproduction of the small five-toed jerboa (*Allactaga elater*) in the northern Kyzyl-Kum desert and Ustyurt plateau Kazakh-SSR]. *Zoologicheskii Zhurnal* 56:769–778 (in Russian).

Benda, P., and K. A. Tsytsulina. 2000. Taxonomic revision of *Myotis mystacinus* group (Mammalia: Chiroptera) in the western Palearctic. *Acta Societatis Zoologicae Bohemoslovenicae* 64:331–398.

Ben-David, M., S. Pellis, and V. Pellis. 1991. Feeding habits and predatory behaviour in the marbled polecat, *Vormela peregusna syriaca*: 1. Killing methods with relation to prey size and prey behaviour. *Behaviour* 118:127–143.

Bennett, D., and R. S. Hoffmann. 1999. Equus caballus. *Mammalian Species* 628:1–14.

Berman, C. M., C. S. Ionica, and J. H. Li. 2004. Dominance style among *Macaca thibetana* on Mt. Huangshan, China. *International Journal of Primatology* 25: 1283–1312.

Berta, A., and T. A. Deméré. 1986. *Callorhinus gilmorei* nov. sp. (Carnivora: Otariidae) from the San Diego Formation (Blancan) and its implications for otariid phylogeny. *Transactions of the San Diego Society of Natural History* 21:111–126.

Bhat, H. R., M. A. Sreenivasan, and P. G. Jacob. 1980. Breeding cycle of *Eonycteris spelaea* (Dobson, 1871) (Chiroptera, Pteropidae, Macroglossinae) in India. *Mammalia* 44:343–347.

Bininda-Emonds, O.R.P., J. L. Gittleman, and A. Purvis. 1999. Building large trees by combining phylogenetic information: A complete phylogeny of the extant Carnivora (Mammalia). *Biological Reviews* 74:143–175.

Birula, A. 1916 [1917]. Contributions à la classification et à la distribution géographique des mammifères. VI. Sur la position de l'*Otocolobus manul* (Pallas) dans le systéme de la fam. Felidae et sur ses rasses. *Annuaire du Musée Zoologique de l'Académie Impériale des Sciences de St. Pétersbourg* 21:130–163.

Biswas, B., and R. K. Ghose. 1982. *Progress Report of Pilot Survey of the World Wildlife Fund–India/Zoological Survey of India Collaborative Project on the Status Survey of the Lesser Cats in Eastern India.* IUCN (Project 1357): Calcutta.

Biswas, B., R. K. Ghose, and D. K. Ghosal. 1985. *Progress Report Two on Pilot Survey of the WWF-India/Zoological Survey of India Collaborative Project on the Status Survey of the Lesser Cats in Eastern India.* Zoological Survey of India: Calcutta.

Blandford, W. T. 1888–91. *The Fauna of British India, Mammalia.* Taylor and Francis: London.

Bleisch, W. V. 1995. Conservation of Guizhou golden monkeys, *Rhinopithecus brelichi.* Pp. 150–156. In *Primate Research and Conservation.* Proceedings of the Second International Conference of the China Primatological Society. W. Xia and Y. Zhang, editors. China Forestry Publishing House: Beijing.

Bleisch, W. V., and N. Chen. 1990. Conservation of the black-crested gibbon: The Wu Liang and Ai Lao Mountain Reserves of Yunnan Province, China. *Oryx* 24:147–156.

——. 1991. Ecology and behavior of wild black-crested gibbon (*Hylobates concolor*) in China with a reconsideration of evidence for polygyny. *Primates* 32:539–548.

Bleisch, W. V., A. S. Cheng, X. D. Ren, and J. H. Xie. 1993. Preliminary results from a field study of wild Guizhou snub-nosed monkeys (*Rhinopithecus brelichi*). *Folia Primatologica* 60:72–82.

Blood, B. R., and D. A. McFarlane. 1988. Notes on some bats from northern Thailand. *Zeitschrift für Säugetierkunde* 53:276–280.

Blumstein, D. T., and W. Arnold. 1998. Ecology and social behavior of golden marmots (*Marmota caudata aurea*). *Journal of Mammalogy* 79:873–886.

Blumstein, D. T., and M. Robertson. 1995. Summer diets of Tibetan red foxes in Khunjerab National Park, Pakistan. *Zeitschrift für Säugetierkunde* 60:243–245.

Bonaccorso, F. J. 1998. *Bats of Papua New Guinea.* Conservation International Tropical Field Guide Series, Conservation International: Washington, DC.

Borries, C., E. Larney, A. M. Derby, and A. Koenig. 2004. Temporary absence and dispersal in Phayre's leaf monkeys (*Trachypithecus phayrei*). *Folia Primatologica* 75:27–30.

Bothma, J. du P. 1965. Random observations on the food habits of certain Carnivora (Mammalia) in southern Africa. *Fauna Flora* (Pretoria) 16:18–22.

Boyd, L., and K. Houpt (editors). 1994. *Przewalski's Horse: The History and Biology of an Endangered Species.* State University of New York Press: Albany.

Brandon-Jones, D., A. A. Eudey, T. Geissmann, C. P. Groves, D. J. Melnick, J. C. Morales, M. Shekelle, and C. Stewart. 2004. Asian primate classification. *International Journal of Primatology* 25:97–164.

Breining, G. 2006. The wildest horse. Wildlife Conservation 109:32–39.

Brosset, A. 1962. The bats of central and western India. Part II. *Journal of the Bombay Natural History Society* 59:583–624.

Brownell, R. L., Jr., and E. S. Herald. 1972. Lipotes vexillifer. *Mammalian Species* 10:1–4.

Bryant, H. N., A. P. Russell, and W. D. Fitch. 1993. Phylogenetic relationships within the extant Mustelidae (Carnivora): Appraisal of the cladistic status of the Simpsonian subfamilies. *Zoological Journal of the Linnean Society* 108:301–334.

Bunch, T. D., S. Wang, R. Valdez, R. S. Hoffmann, Y. Zhang, A. Liu, and S. Lin. 2000. Cytogenetics, morphology and evolution of four subspecies of the giant sheep argali (*Ovis ammon*) of Asia. *Mammalia* 64:199–207.

Bunnell, F. L., and R. K. McCann. 1993. The brown or grizzly bear. Pp. 88–95. In *Bears: Majestic Creatures of the Wild.* I. Stirling, editor. Rodale Press: Emmaus, PA.

Buskirk, S. W., Y. Ma, L. Xu, and Z. Jiang. 1996. Winter habitat ecology of sables (*Martes zibellina*) in relation to forest management in China. *Ecological Applications* 6:318–325.

Butzler, W. 1990. Pere David's deer (Genus *Elaphurus*). Pp. 161–164. In *Grzimek's Encyclopedia of Mammals.* S. P. Parker, editor. McGraw-Hill: New York.

Cai, G. Q. 1988. [Notes on white-lipped deer (*Cervus albirostris*) in China]. *Acta Theriologica Sinica* 8:7–12 (in Chinese).

Cai, G. Q., and Z. J. Feng. 1982. [A systematic revision of the subspecies of highland hare (*Lepus oiostolus*), including two new subspecies]. *Acta Theriologica Sinica* 2:167–182 (in Chinese).

Caldarini, G., E. Capanna, M. V. Civitelli, M. Corti, and A. Simonetta. 1989. Chromosomal evolution in the subgenus *Rattus* (Rodentia, Muridae): Karyotype analysis of two species from the Indian subregion. *Mammalia* 53:77–84.

Cao, J., E. B. Yang, J. J. Su, Y. Li, and P. Chow. 2003. The tree shrews: Adjuncts and alternatives to primates as models for biomedical research. *Journal of Medical Primatology* 32:123–130.

Cao, K. Q. 1993. Selection of a suitable area for re-introduction of wild Père David's deer in China. Pp. 297–300. In *Deer of China: Biology and Management.* N. Ohtaishi and H. L. Sheng, editors. Elsevier: Amsterdam.

Carleton, M. D., and G. G. Musser. 1984. Muroid rodents. Pp. 289–379. In *Orders and Families of Recent Mammals of the World.* S. Anderson and J. K. Jones, Jr., editors. John Wiley and Sons: New York.

——. 2005. The rodents. Pp. 745–752. In *Mammal Species of the World*, third edition. D. E. Wilson and D. M. Reeder, editors. Johns Hopkins University Press: Baltimore.

Carleton, M. D., G. G. Musser, and I. Ya. Pavlinov. 2003. *Myodes* Pallas, 1811, is the valid name for the genus of Red-backed voles. Pp. 96–98. In *Systematics, Phylogeny and Paleontology of Small Mammals.* Proceedings International Conference, Devoted to the 90th Anniversary of Prof. I. M. Gromov. St. Petersburg.

Catling, P. C., and R. J. Burt. 1995. Why are red foxes absent from some eucalypt forests in eastern New South Wales? *Wildlife Research* 22:535–546.

Cavallini, P., and P. Serafini. 1995. Winter diet of the small Indian mongoose, *Herpestes auropunctatus,* on an Adriatic island. *Journal of Mammalogy* 76:569–574.

Chakraborty, R., and S. Chakraborty. 1999. Feeding behaviour of the large Bandicoot Rat *Bandicota indica*

(Bechstein) [Rodentia: Muridae]. *Records of the Zoological Survey of India* 97:45–72.

Chakraborty, S., and U. Bhattacharya. 1999. Burmese ferret-badger, *Melogale personata* Geoffroy (Carnivora: Mustelidae) in Jalpaiguri district, West Bengal. *Tigerpaper* 26:17–18.

Chan, B.P.L., and J. R. Fellowes. 2003. *Hainan Gibbon Status Survey and Conservation Action Plan*. Kadoorie Farm and Botanic Garden: Hong Kong.

Chen, H. P., J. Z. Ma, F. Li, Y. H. Wang, H. Wang, and F. Li. 1993. Regional variation in winter diets of red deer in Heilongjiang, northeastern China. Pp. 181–186. In *Deer of China: Biology and Management*. N. Ohtaishi and H. L. Sheng, editors. Elsevier: Amsterdam.

Chen, J. S. 1969. [*Vertebrate Fauna of Taiwan*]. Commercial Shanwu Press of Taiwan: Taipei (in Chinese).

Chen, J. X. 1991. [Life table and reproduction of Alashan ground squirrel]. *Acta Theriologica Sinica* 11:138–142 (in Chinese).

Chen, Z. P. , R. Q. Liu, C. Y. Li, and Y. X. Wang. 1996. [Studies on the chromosomes of three species of wood mice]. *Zoological Research* 17:347–352 (in Chinese).

Cheng, J. Z. 1999. Status and management of bears in Heilongjiang, China. Pp. 123–125. In *Bears: Status Survey and Conservation Action Plan*. C. Servheen, S. Herrero, and B. Peyton, editors. IUCN: Gland, Switzerland.

Chorn, J., and R. S. Hoffmann. 1978. Ailuropoda melanoleuca. *Mammalian Species* 110:1–6.

Cifelli, R. L. 2001. Early mammalian radiations. *Journal of Paleontology* 75:1214–1226.

CITES. 2006. The Convention on International Trade in Endangered Species of Wild Fauna and Flora. http://www.cites.org/.

Clutton-Brock, T. H., F. E. Guinness, and S. D. Albon. 1982. *Red Deer: Behavior and Ecology of Two Sexes*. University of Chicago Press: Chicago.

Cohen, J. A. 1978. Cuon alpinus. *Mammalian Species* 100:1–3.

Colak, E., and N. Yigit. 1998. Ecology and biology of *Allactaga elater*, *Allactaga ruphratica* and *Allactaga williamsi* (Rodentia: Dipodidae) in Turkey. *Turkish Journal of Zoology* 22:105–117.

Collier, G. E., and S. J. O'Brien. 1985. A molecular phylogeny of the Felidae: Immunological distance. *Evolution* 39:473–487.

Cook, J. A., A. M. Runck, and C. J. Conroy. 2004. Historical biogeography at the crossroads of the northern continents: Molecular phylogenetics of red-backed voles (Rodentia: Arvicolinae). *Molecular Phylogenetics and Evolution* 30:767–777.

Corbet, G. B. 1978. *The mammals of the Palaearctic region: A taxonomic review*. British Museum (Natural History): London.

—— 1988. The family Erinaceidae: A synthesis of its taxonomy, phylogeny, ecology and zoogeography. *Mammal Review* 18:117–172.

Corbet, G. B., and J. E. Hill. 1992. *Mammals of the Indomalayan Region. A Systematic Review*. Oxford University Press: Oxford.

Courant, F., P. Brunet-Lecomte, V. Volobouev, J. Chaline, J.-P. Quérér, A. Nadachowski, S. Montuire, G. Bao, L. Viriot, R. Rausch, M. Erbajeva, D. Shi, and P. Giraudoux. 1999. Karyological and dental identification of *Microtus limnophilus* in a large focus of alveolar echinococcosis (Gansu, China). *Compte Rendu Academie des Sciences, Paris, Sciences de la Vie* 322:473–480.

Csorba, G. 1998. The distribution of the great evening bat *Ia io* in the Indomalayan region. *Myotis* 36:197–201.

Csorba, G., S. V. Kruskop, and A. V. Borissenko. 1999. First and new records of bats (Chiroptera) from Nepal, with remarks on their natural history. *Mammalia* 63:61–78.

Csorba, G., and L. L. Lee. 1999. A new species of vespertilionid bat from Taiwan and a revision of the taxonomic status of *Arielulus* and *Thianycteris* (Chiroptera: Vespertilionidae). *Journal of Zoology*, London, 248:361–367.

Csorba, G., P. Ujhelyi, and N. Thomas. 2003. *Horseshoe Bats of the World*. Alana Books: Bishop's Castle, U.K.

Cui, Q. H., and Q. K. Zhao. 1999. [Supplementary observation to father-infant behavior of *Macaca thibetana* at Mt. Emei, China]. *Zoological Research* 20:196–200 (in Chinese).

Dang, N. X., P. T. Anh, and D. H. Huynh. 1992. The biology and status of Owston's palm civet in Vietnam. *Small Carnivore Conservation* 6:5–6.

Dannelid, E. 1998. Dental adaptations in shrews. Pp. 157–174. In *Evolution of Shrews*. J. M. Wójcik and M. Wolsan, editors. Mammal Research Institute, Polish Academy of Sciences: Bialowieza.

Dao, V. T. 1993. On the north Indochinese gibbons (*Hylobates concolor*) (Primates, Hylobatidae) in North Vietnam. *Journal of Human Evolution* 12:367–372.

Davidar, E. R. C. 1975. Ecology and behaviour of the dhole or Indian wild dog (*Cuon alpinus* Pallas). Pp. 109–119. In *The Wild Canids*. M. W. Fox, editor. Van Nostrand Reinhold: New York.

Davies, R. G. 1990. Sighting of a clouded leopard (*Neofelis nebulosa*) in a troop of pigtail macaques (*Macaca nemestrina*) in Khao Yai National Park, Thailand. *Natural History Bulletin of the Siam Society* 28:95–96.

Davis, D. D. 1962. Mammals of the lowland rainforest of north Borneo. *Bulletin of the National Museum of Singapore* 31:1–129.

—— 1964. The giant panda: A morphological study of evolutionary mechanisms. *Fieldiana: Zoology, Memoirs* 3:1–339.

Davis, J. A. 1978. A classification of otters. Pp. 14–33. In *Otters*. N. Duplaix, editor. IUCN (New Series): Morge, Switzerland.

Day, M. G. 1968. Food habits of British stoats (*Mustela erminea*) and weasels (*Mustela nivalis*). *Journal of Zoology*, London, 155:485–497.

Decker, D. M., and W. C. Wozencraft. 1991. Phylogenetic analysis of Recent procyonid genera. *Journal of Mammalogy* 72:42–55.

de Grammont, P. C., and A. D. Cuarón. 2006. An evaluation of threatened species categorization systems used on the American continent. *Conservation Biology* 20:14–27.

Delibes, M. 1978. Feeding habits of Stone marten, *Martes foina* (Erxleben 1777) in northern Burgos, Spain. *Zeitschrift für Säugertierkunde* 43:282–288.

Deng, X. B., P. Y. Ren, J. Y. Gao and Q. J. Li. 2004. The striped squirrel (*Tamiops swinhoei hainanus*) as a nectar robber of ginger (*Alpina kwangsiensis*). *Biotropica* 36:633–636.

Deng, X. Y., Q. Feng, and Y. X. Wang. 2000. [Differentiation of subspecies of Chinese white-bellied rat (*Niviventer confucianus*) in southwestern China with descriptions of two new subspecies]. *Zoological Research* 5:375–382 (in Chinese).

DePutte, B. L. 1982. Duetting in male and female songs of the white-cheeked gibbon (*Hylobates concolor leucogenys*). Pp. 67–93. In *Primate Communication*. C. T. Snowdon, C. H. Brown, and M. R. Petersen, editors. Cambridge University Press: Cambridge.

Ding, W., and Q. K. Zhao. 2004. *Rhinopithecus bieti* at Tacheng, Yunnan: Diet and daytime activities. *International Journal of Primatology* 25:583–598.

Dobson, F. S., A. T. Smith, and X. G. Wang. 1998. Social and ecological influences on dispersal and philopatry in the plateau pika. *Behavioral Ecology* 9: 622–635.

—— 2000. The mating system and gene dynamics of plateau pikas. *Behavioural Processes* 51:101–110.

Dobson, G. E. 1874. On the Asiatic species of Molossi. *Journal of the Asiatic Society of Bengal* 43:142–144.

Dolgov, V. A., and R. S. Hoffmann. 1977. [The Tibetan shrew–*Sorex thibetanus* Kastschenko, 1905 (Soricidae, Mammalia)]. *Zoologicheskii Zhurnal* 56:1687–1692 (in Russian).

Dolgov, V. A., and I. V. Lukyanova. 1966. [The genital structure of Palaearctic shrews (Insectivora, Soricidae)]. *Zoologicheskii Zhurnal* 45:1852–1861 (in Russian).

Douzery, E.J.P., and D. Huchon. 2004. Rabbits, if anything, are likely Glires. *Molecular Phylogenetics and Evolution* 33:922–935.

Duckworth, J. W., and S. Hedges. 1998. *Tracking Tigers: A Review of the Status of Tiger, Asian Elephant, Guar and Banteng in Vietnam, Lao, Cambodia and Yunnan (China), with Recommendations for Further Conservation Action*. WWF Indochina Program: Hanoi.

Duckworth, J. W., R. E. Salter, and K. Khounboline. 1999. *Wildlife in Lao PDR: 1999 Status Report*. IUCN, WCS, CPAWM: Ventiane, Laos.

Durbin, L. S., A. Venkataraman, S. Hedges, and W. Duckworth. 2004. Dhole. Pp. 210–219. In *Canids: Foxes, Wolves, Jackals and Dogs: Status Survey and Conservation Action Plan*. C. Sillero-Zubiri, M. Hoffmann, and D. Macdonald, editors. IUCN: Gland, Switzerland.

Eger, J. L., and M. B. Fenton. 2003. Rhinolophus paradoxolophus. *Mammalian Species* 731:1–4.

Ellerman, J. R., and T. C. S. Morrison-Scott. 1951. *Checklist of Palaearctic and Indian Mammals 1758 to 1946*. Trustees of the British Museum (Natural History): London.

Emelyanova, L.G. 1994. [Spatial distribution and abundance of wood lemming populations in their north-eastern portion of their range]. *Byulleten Moskovskovo Obshchestva Ispytatelei Prirody, Otdel Biologicheskii* 99:37–43 (in Russian).

Erlinge, S. 1981. Food preference, optimal diet and reproductive output in stoats *Mustela erminea* in Sweden. *Oikos* 36:303–315.

Everts, W. 1968. Beitrag zur Systematik der Sonnendachse. *Zeitschrift für Säugetierkunde* 33:1–19.

Ewer, R. F. 1973. *The Carnivores*. Cornell University Press: Ithaca, NY.

Fan, F. L. 1984. Preliminary observation on the life habits of the steppe lemming (*Lagurus lagurus*). *Chinese Journal of Zoology* 5:29–37.

Fan, L. S., and H. J. Liu (editors). 1996. *Mammals in Shanxi*. China Forestry Publishing House: Beijing.

Fan, N. C., and S. Gu. 1981. [The structure of the tunnel system of the Chinese zokor]. *Acta Theriologica Sinica* 1:67–72 (in Chinese).

Fan, N. C., and Y. Z. Shi. 1982. [A revision of the zokors of subgenus *Eospalax*]. *Acta Theriologica Sinica* 2: 183–199 (in Chinese).

Fang, Y. P., and L. L. Lee. 2002. Re-evaluation of the Taiwanese white-toothed shrew, *Crocidura tadae* Tokuda and Kano, 1936 (Insectivora: Soricidae) from Taiwan and two offshore islands. *Journal of Zoology, London*, 257:145–154.

Fang, Y. P., L. L. Lee, F. H. Yew, and H. T. Yu. 1997. Systematics of white-toothed shrews (*Crocidura*) (Mammalia: Insectivora: Soricidae) of Taiwan: Karyological and morphological studies. *Journal of Zoology*, London 242:151–166.

Fedosenko, A. K., and D. A. Blank. 2005. Ovis ammon. *Mammalian Species* 773:1–15.

Feh, C., B. Munkhtuya, S. Enkhbold, and T. Sukhbaatar. 2001. Ecology and social structure of the Gobi khulan *Equus hemionus subsp.* in the Gobi B National Park, Mongolia. *Biological Conservation* 101:51–61.

Feh, C., N. Shah, M. Rowen, R. Reading, and S. P. Goyal. 2002. Status and action plan for the Asiatic Wild Ass (*Equus hemionus*). Pp. 62–71. In *Equids: Zebras, Asses and Horses: Status Survey and Conservation Action Plan*. P. D. Moehlman, editor. IUCN: Gland, Switzerland.

Feiler, A., and T. Nadler. 1997. Erstnachweis der Etruskerspitzmaus, *Suncus etruscus* (Savi, 1822) für Vietnam (Mammalia: Insectivora: Soricidae). *Faunistische Abhandlungen Staatliches Museum für Tierkunde Dresden* 21:161–162.

Feldhamer, G. A. 1980. Cervus nippon. *Mammalian Species* 128:1–7.

Feng, J., C. Lajia, D. J. Taylor, and M. S. Webster. 2001. Genetic distinctiveness of endangered dwarf blue sheep (*Pseudois nayaur schaeferi*): Evidence from mitochondrial control region and Y-linked ZFY intron sequences. *Journal of Heredity* 92:9–15.

Feng, L. M., and L. Zhang. 2005. [Habitat selection by Asian Elephant (*Elephas maximus*) in Xishuangbanna, Yunnan, China]. *Acta Theriologica Sinica* 25:229–236 (in Chinese).

Feng, Z. J. 1973. [A new species of *Ochotona* (Ochotonidae, Mammalia) from the Mount Jolmo-lungma area]. *Acta Zoologica Sinica* 19:69–75 (in Chinese).

Feng, Z. J., G. Q. Cai, and C. L. Zheng. 1986. [*The Mammals of Xizang. The Comprehensive Scientific Expedition to the Qinghai-Xizang Plateau*]. Science Press, Academia Sinica: Beijing (in Chinese).

Feng, Z. J., and Y. T. Kao. 1974. [Taxonomic notes on the Tibetan pika and allied species–including a new subspecies]. *Acta Zoologica Sinica* 20:76–87 (in Chinese).

Feng, Z. J., and Y. Q. Ma. 1998. *Lynx lynx*. Pp. 105–106. In *China Red Data Book of Endangered Animals. Mammalia*. S. Wang, editor. Science Press: Beijing (in Chinese and English).

Feng, Z. J., and C. L. Zheng. 1985. [Studies on the pikas (genus *Ochotona*) of China—taxonomic notes and distribution]. *Acta Theriologica Sinica* 5:269–289 (in Chinese).

Feng, Z. J., C. L. Zheng, and J. Y. Wu. 1983. [A new subspecies of *Apodemus peninsulae* from Qinghai-Xizang (Tibet) Plateau, China]. *Acta Zootaxonomica Sinica* 8:108–112 (in Chinese).

Findley, J. S. 1972. Phenetic relationships among bats of the genus *Myotis*. *Systematic Zoology* 21:31–52.

Fitzgerald, C. S., and P. R. Krausman. 2002. Helarctos malayanus. *Mammalian Species* 696:1–5.

Flux, J.E.C., and R. Angermann. 1990. The hares and jackrabbits. Pp. 61–94. In *Rabbits, Hares and Pikas: Status Survey and Conservation Action Plan*. J. A. Chapman and J.E.C. Flux, editors. IUCN/WWF: Gland, Switzerland.

Flynn, J. J., M. A. Nedbal, J. W. Dragoo, and R. L. Honeycutt. 2000. Whence the red panda? *Molecular Phylogenetics and Evolution* 17:190–199.

Flynn, L. T. 1990. The natural history of Rhizomid rodents. Pp. 155–183. In *Evolution of Subterranean Mammals at the Organismal and Molecular Levels*. E. Nevo and O. A. Reid, editors. Wiley-Liss: New York.

Fooden, J. 1975. Taxonomy and evolution of liontail and pigtail macaques (Primates: Cercopithecidae). *Fieldiana: Zoology* 67:1–169.

—— 1982. Taxonomy and evolution of the *sinica* group of macaques: 3. Species and subspecies accounts of *Macaca assamensis*. *Fieldiana: Zoology*, new series, 10:v–vii, 1–52.

—— 1983. Taxonomy and evolution of the *sinica* group of macaques: 4. Species and subspecies accounts of *Macaca thibetana*. *Fieldiana: Zoology*, new series, 17:1–20.

—— 1990. The bear macaque, *Macaca arctoides*: A systematic review. *Journal of Human Evolution* 19:607–686.

—— 2000. Systematic review of the rhesus macaque, *Macaca mulatta* (Zimmermann, 1780). *Fieldiana: Zoology*, new series, 96:i–vi, 1–180.

Fooden, J., G. Q. Quan, Y. Z. Zhang, M. C. Wu, and M. Y. Liang. 1994. Southward extension of the range of *Macaca thibetana*. *International Journal of Primatology* 15:623–627.

Formozov, A. N. 1966. Adaptive modifications of behavior in mammals of the Eurasian steppes. *Journal of Mammalogy* 47:208–223.

Formozov, N. A. 1997. Pikas (*Ochotona*) of the world: Systematics and conservation. *Giber Faune Sauvage (Game and Wildlife)* 14:506–507.

Formozov, N. A., I. Yu. Baklushinskaya, and Y. Ma. 2004. Taxonomic status of the Helan-shan pika, *Ochotona argentata*, from the Helan-shan ridge (Ningxia, China). *Zoologicheskii Zhurnal* 83:995–1007.

Foster-Turley, P. 1992. Conservation aspects of the ecology of Asian small-clawed and smooth otters on the Malay Peninsula. IUCN, *Otter Specialist Group Bulletin* 7:26–29.

Foster-Turley, P., and S. Engfer. 1988. The species survival plan for the Asian Small-clawed Otter, *Aonyx cinerea*. *International Zoo Yearbook* 27:79–84.

Foster-Turley, P., S. Macdonald, and C. Mason (editors). 1990. *Otters: An Action Plan for their Conservation*. IUCN: Gland, Switzerland.

Foster-Turley, P., and C. Santiapillai. 1990. Action plan for Asian otters. Pp. 52–63. In *Otters: An Action Plan for Their Conservation*. P. Foster-Turley, S. Macdonald, and C. Mason, editors. IUCN: Gland, Switzerland.

Fox, J. L. 1989. *A Review of the Status and Ecology of the Snow Leopard (Panthera uncia)*. International Snow Leopard Trust: Seattle.

——. 1994. Snow leopard conservation in the wild—comprehensive perspective on a low density and highly fragmented population. *Proceedings of the International Snow Leopard Symposium* 7:3–15.

Fox, M. W. 1984. *The Whistling Hunters: Field Studies of the Asiatic Wild Dog (Cuon alpinus)*. State University of New York Press: Albany.

Francis, C. M. 2001. *A Photographic Guide to the Mammals of South-east Asia*. Ralph Curtis Books: Sanibel Island, FL.

Francis, C. M., and J. Habersetzer. 1998. Interspecific and intraspecific variation in echolocation call frequency and morphology of horseshoe bats, *Rhinolophus* and *Hipposideros*. Pp. 169–179. In *Bat Biology and Conservation*. T. Kunz and P. A. Racey, editors. Smithsonian Institution Press: Washington, DC.

Francis, C. M., K. Khounboline and N. Aspey. 1996. *Report on 1996 Survey of Bats and Small Mammals in the Nakai-Nam Theun NBCA and Nearby Areas*. Wildlife Conservation Society: Vientiane.

Frost, D. R., W. C. Wozencraft, and R. S. Hoffmann. 1991. Phylogenetic relationships of hedgehogs and gymnures (Mammalia: Insectivora: Erinaceidae). *Smithsonian Contributions to Zoology* 518:1–69.

Fumagalli, L., P. Taberlet, D. T. Stewart, L. Gielly, J. Hausser, and P. Vogel. 1999. Molecular phylogeny and evolution of *Sorex* shrews (Soricidae: Insectivora) inferred from mitochondrial DNA sequence data. *Molecular Phylogenetics and Evolution* 11:222–235.

Funakoshi, K., and T. Kunisaki. 2000. On the validity of *Tadarida latouchei*, with references to morphological divergence among *T. latouchei*, *T. insignis* and *T. teniotis* (Chiroptera, Molossidae). *Mammal Study* 25:115–123.

Gao, A. L., and K. Y. Zhou. 1993. [Notes on classical literatures and contemporary researches on the finless porpoise (*Neophocaena phocaenoides*)]. *Acta Theriologica Sinica* 13:223–234 (in Chinese).

Gao, X. Y., and J. H. Gu. 1989. [The distribution and status of equidae in China]. *Acta Theriologica Sinica* 9:269–274 (in Chinese).

Gao, X. Y., K. F. Xu, J. Yao, and Z. X. Jia. 1996. [The population structure of goitered gazelle in Xinjiang]. *Acta Theriologica Sinica* 16:14–18 (in Chinese).

Gao, Y. T. 1981. [On the present status, historical distribution and conservation of wild elephants in China]. *Acta Theriologica Sinica* 1:19–26 (in Chinese).

——. 1983. Current studies on the Chinese Yarkand hare. *Acta Zoologica Fennica* 174:23–25.

—— (editor). 1987. [*Fauna Sinica, Mammalia: Carnivora*]. Science Press: Beijing (in Chinese).

Gao, Y. T., and Z. J. Feng. 1964. [On the subspecies of the Chinese gray-tailed hair, *Lepus oiostolus* Hodgson]. *Acta Zootaxonomica Sinica* 1:19–30 (in Chinese).

Gao, Z. X. 1998. *Canis lupus*. Pp. 87–89. In *China Red Data Book of Endangered Animals. Mammalia.* S. Wang, editor. Science Press: Beijing (in Chinese and English).

Gardenfors, U. 2001. Classifying threatened species at national versus global levels. *Trends in Ecology and Evolution* 16:511–516.

Gardenfors, U., C. Hilton-Taylor, G. M. Mace, and J. P. Rodriguez. 2001. The application of IUCN Red List criteria at regional levels. *Conservation Biology* 15:1206–1212.

Gaubert, P., M. Tranier, A. S. Delmas, M. Colyn, and G. Veron. 2004. First molecular evidence for reassessing phylogenetic affinities between genets (*Genetta*) and the enigmatic genet-like taxa *Osbornictis*, *Poiana* and *Prionodon* (Carnivora, Viverridae). *Zoologica Scripta* 33:117–129.

Ge, T. A., J. C. Hu, M. D. Jiang, and Q. T. Deng. 1989. [The herd compositions, numbers and distribution of Sichuan takin (*Budorcas taxicolor tibetana*) in Tangjiahe Natural Reserve]. *Acta Theriologica Sinica* 9:262–268 (in Chinese).

Geissmann, T. 1989. A female black gibbon, *Hylobates concolor* ssp., from northeastern Vietnam. *International Journal of Primatology* 10:455–476.

——. 1995. Gibbon systematics and species identification. *International Zoo News* 42:467–501.

Geissmann, T., C. P. Groves, and C. Roos. 2004. The Tenasserim Lutung, *Trachypithecus barbei* (Blyth, 1847) (Primates: Cercopithecidae): Description of a live specimen, and a reassessment of phylogenetic affinities, taxonomic history, and distribution. *Contributions to Zoology* 73:271–282.

Geist, V. 1982. Adaptive behavioral strategies. Pp. 219–277. In *Elk of North America: Ecology and Management.* J. W. Thomas and D. E. Toweill, editors. Stackpole Books: Harrisburg, PA.

George, S. B. 1988. Systematics, historical biogeography, and evolution of the genus *Sorex*. *Journal of Mammalogy* 69:443–461.

Glatston, A. R. (editor). 1994. *Status Survey and Conservation Action Plan for Procyonids and Ailurids: The Red Panda, Olingos, Coatis, Raccoons and Their Relatives*. IUCN: Gland, Switzerland.

Gong, Z. D., Y. X. Wang, Z. H. Li, and S. Q. Li. 2000. [A new species of pika: Pianma black pika, *Ochotona nigrita* (Lagomorpha: Ochotonidae) from Yunnan, China]. *Zoological Research* 21:204–209 (in Chinese).

Goodwin, G. G. 1934. Two new mammals from Kazakstan. *American Museum Novitates* 742:1–2.

Gould, G. C. 1995. Hedgehog phylogeny (Mammalia, Erinaceidae)—the reciprocal illumination of the quick and the dead. *American Museum Novitates* 3131:1–45.

Goymann, W., D. Leippert, and H. Hofer. 2000. Sexual segregation, roosting, and social behavior in a free-ranging colony of Indian false vampires (*Megaderma lyra*). *Zeitschrift für Säugetierkunde* 65:138–148.

Grassman, L. I., M. E. Tewes, and N. J. Silvy. 2005. Ranging, habitat use and activity patterns of binturong *arctictis binturong* and yellow-throated marten *Martes flavigula* in north-central Thailand. *Wildlife Biology* 11:49–57.

Green, M.J.B. 1986. The distribution, status and conservation of the Himalayan musk deer *Moschus chryogaster*. *Biological Conservation* 35:347–375.

Gregory, W. K., and M. Hellman. 1939. On the evolution and major classification of the civets (Viverridae) and allied fossil and recent Carnivora: Phylogenetic study of the skull and dentition. *Proceedings of the American Philosophical Society* 81:309–392.

Gromov, I. M., and M. A. Erbajeva. 1995. [*The Mammals of Russia and Adjacent Territories. Lagomorphs and Rodents*]. Russian Academy of Sciences, Zoological Institute St. Petersburg (in Russian).

Gromov, I. M., and I. Ya. Polyakov. 1992. *Fauna of the USSR, Mammals, Voles (Microtinae)*, Volume III, No. 8. English translation; originally published in Russian, 1977, Nauka: Moscow-Leningrad. D. Siegel-Causey and R. S. Hoffmann, scientific editors. Smithsonian Institution Libraries and the National Science Foundation: Washington, DC.

Groves, C. P. 1971. Systematics of the genus *Nycticebus*. *Proceedings of the Third International Congress of Primatology* (Zürich, 1970) 1:44–53.

——. 1978. The taxonomic status of the dwarf blue sheep (Artiodactyla: Bovidae). *Säugetierkunde Mitteilungen* 26:177–183.

——. 1998. Systematics of tarsiers and lorises. *Primates* 39:13–27.

——. 2001. *Primate Taxonomy*. Smithsonian Institution Press: Washington, DC.

——. 2005. Order Primates. Pp. 111–184. In *Mammal Species of the World*, third edition. D. E. Wilson and D. M. Reeder, editors. Johns Hopkins University Press: Baltimore.

Groves, C. P., and Z. J. Feng. 1986. The status of Musk deer from Anhui province, China. *Acta Theriologica Sinica* 6:101–106 (in Chinese and English)

Groves, C. P., and P. Grubb. 1985. Reclassification of the serows and gorals (*Nemorhaedus*: Bovidae). Pp. 45–50. In *The Biology and Management of Mountain Ungulates*. S. Lovari, editor. Croon Helm: London.

——. 1987. Relationships of living deer. Pp. 21–59. In *Biology and Management of the Cervidae*. C. M. Wemmer, editor. Smithsonian Insitution Press: Washington, DC.

Groves, C. P., and Y. X. Wang. 1990. The gibbons of the sub-genus *Nomascus* (Primates, Mammalia). *Zoological Research* 11:147–154.

Groves, C. P., Y. X. Wang, and P. Grubb. 1995. Taxonomy of musk-deer, genus *Moschus* (Moschidae, Mammalia). *Acta Theriologica Sinica* 15:181–197.

Grubb, P. 2005. Order Artiodactyla. Pp. 637–722. In *Mammal Species of the World*, third edition. D. E. Wilson and D. M. Reeder, editors. Johns Hopkins University Press: Baltimore.

Gruber, U. F. 1969. Tiergeographische, ökologische und bionomische Untersuchungen an kleinen Säugetieren in Ost-Nepal. *Khumbu Himal* 3:197–312.

Guggisberg, C. A. W. 1975. *Wild Cats of the World.* Taplinger: New York.

Gulotta, E. F. 1971. Meriones unguiculatus. *Mammalian Species* 3:1–5.

Guo, C., Y. Wang, A. G. Chen, B. Li, M. W. Zhang, and Z. J. Wu. 1997. [Studies on the migration of *Microtus fortis* in Dongting lake area]. *Acta Theriologica Sinica* 17:279–286 (in Chinese).

Gureev, A. A. 1971. [*Shrews of the World Fauna*]. Nauka: Leningrad (in Russian).

Gurung, K. K., and R. Singh. 1996. *Field Guide to the Mammals of the Indian Subcontinent.* Academic Press: San Diego.

Haimoff, E. H. 1984. The organization of song in the Hainan Black Gibbon (*Hylobates concolor hainanus*). *Primates* 25:225–235.

Haltenorth, T. 1953. *Die Wildkatzen der Alten Welt; eine über-sicht über die Untergatung.* Geest and Portig: Leipzig.

Han, S. H., M. A. Iwasa, S. D. Ohdachi, H. S. Oh, H. Suzuki, K. Tsuchiya, and H. Abe. 2002. Molecular phylogeny of *Crocidura* shrews in northeastern Asia: A special reference to specimens on Cheju Island, South Korea. *Acta Theriologica* 47:369–379.

Hanski, I. K., P. C. Stephens, P. Ihalempia, and V. Selonen. 2000. Home range size, movements, and nest-site use in the Siberian flying squirrel, *Pteromys volans*. *Journal of Mammalogy* 81:798–809.

Hare, J. 1997. The wild Bactrian camel *Camelus bactrianus ferus* in China: The need for urgent action. *Oryx* 31:45–48.

Harris, C. J. 1968. *Otters: A Study of the Recent Lutrinae.* Weidenfeld and Nicolson: London.

Harris, R. B. 1991. Conservation prospects for musk deer and other wildlife in southern Qinghai, China. *Mountain Research and Development* 11:353–358.

Harris, R. B., and C. O. Loggers. 2004. Status of Tibetan plateau mammals in Yeniugou, China. *Wildlife Biology* 10:91–99.

Harrison, D. L., and P. J. J. Bates. 1991. *The Mammals of Arabia,* second edition. Harrison Zoological Museum: Sevenoaks, U.K.

Harrison, R. G., S. M. Bogdanowicz, R. S. Hoffmann, E. Yensen, and P. W. Sherman. 2003. Phylogeny and evolutionary history of the ground squirrels (Rodentia: Marmotinae). *Journal of Mammalian Evolution* 10:249–276.

Hash, H. S. 1987. Wolverine. Pp. 575–585. In *Wild Furbearer Management and Conservation in North America.* M. Novak, J. A. Baker, M. E. Obbard, and B. Malloch, editors. Ontario Ministry of Natural Resources: Ontario.

He, H. 1958. [*Report on Mammalian Survey in Northeast China*]. Science Press: Beijing (in Chinese).

He, L., R. Garcia-Perea, M. Li, and F. W. Wei. 2004. Distribution and conservation status of the endemic Chinese mountain cat *Felis bieti*. *Oryx* 38:55–61.

He, X. R. 1984. [A preliminary observation on the structure of the tunnel system of the Chinese bamboo rat (*Rhizomys sinensis*)]. *Acta Theriologica Sinica* 4: 196, 206 (in Chinese).

He, X. R., and X. D. Yang. 1982. [Preliminary study on the biology of *Presbytis phayrei*]. *Zoological Research* 3 (Supplement):349–354 (in Chinese).

He, X. R., X. D. Yang, and T. Li. 1991. [A preliminary study on the ecology of the lesser bamboo rat (*Cannomy badius*) in China]. *Zoological Research* 12:41–47 (in Chinese).

Heaney, L. R., D. S. Balete, M. L. Dolar, A. C. Alcala, A. T. L. Dans, P. C. Gonzales, N. R. Ingle, M. V. Lepiten, W. L. R. Oliver, P. S. Ong, E. A. Rickart, B. R. Tabaranza, Jr., and R. C. B. Utzurrum. 1998. A synopsis of the mammalian fauna of the Philippine Islands. *Fieldiana: Zoology*, new series, 88:1–61.

Heaney, L. R., and R. M. Timm. 1983. Systematics and distribution of shrews of the genus *Crocidura* (Mammalia: Insectivora) in Vietnam. *Proceedings of the Biological Society of Washington* 96:115–120.

Heath, M. E. 1992. Manis pentadactyla. *Mammalian Species* 414:1–6.

——. 1995. Manis crassicaudata. *Mammalian Species* 513:1–4.

Heideman, P. D., and L. R. Heaney. 1989. Population biology and estimates of abundance of fruit bats (Pteropodidae) in Philippine submontane rainforest. *Journal of Zoology*, London, 218:565–586.

Helgen, K. M. 2005. Family Castoridae. Pp. 842–843. In *Mammal Species of the World,* third edition. D. E. Wilson and D. M. Reeder, editors. Johns Hopkins University Press: Baltimore.

Helgen, K. M., and D. E. Wilson. 2002. The bats of Flores, Indonesia, with remarks on Asian *Tadarida*. *Breviora* 511:1–12.

Heller, K. G., and M. Volleth. 1984. Taxonomic position of "*Pipistrellus societatis*" Hill, 1972 and the karyological characteristics of the genus *Eptesicus* (Chiroptera: Vespertilionidae). *Zeitschrift für Zoologische Systematik und Evolutionsforschung* 22:65–77.

Hemmer, H. 1968. Untersuchungen zur Stammesgeschichte der Pantherkatzen (Pantherinae). Teil II. Studien zur Ethologie des Nebelparders *Neofelis nebulosa* (Griffith 1821) und des Irbis *Uncia uncia* (Schreber 1775). *Veröffentlichungen der Zoologischen Staatssammlung München* 12:155–247.

——. 1978. The evolutionary systematics of living Felidae: Present status and current problems. *Carnivore* 1:71–79.

Hendey, Q. B. 1980a. *Agriotherium* (Mammalia: Ursidae) from Langebaanweg, South Africa, and relationships of the genus. *Annals of the South African Museum* 81:1–109.

——. Q. B. 1980b. Origin of the giant panda. *South African Journal of Science* 76:179–180.

Hendrichsen, D. K., P.J.J. Bates, B. D. Hayes, and J. L. Walston. 2001. Recent records of bats (Mammalia: Chiroptera) from Vietnam with six species new to the country. *Myotis* 39:35–122.

Heptner, V. G., N. P. Naumov, P. B. Yurgenson, A. A. Sludskii, A. F. Chirkova, and A. G. Bannikov. 1967a. [*The Mammals of the Soviet Union. Sirenia and Carnivora*]. Vysshaya Shkola: Moscow, Volume II, Part 1a:1–734 (in Russian). English translation (1988), R. S. Hoffmann, editor. Smithsonian Institutions Libraries and the National Science Foundation: Washington, DC.

——. 1967b. [*The Mammals of the Soviet Union. Carnivora (Weasels, Additional Species)*]. Vysshaya Shkola: Moscow, Volume II, Part 1b:735–1552 (in

Russian). English translation (2001), R. S. Hoffmann, editor. Smithsonian Institutions Libraries and the National Science Foundation: Washington, DC.

Heptner, V. G., and A. A. Sludskii. 1972. [*The Mammals of the Soviet Union. Carnivora (Hyaenas and Cats)*]. Vysshaya Shkola: Moscow, Volume II, Part 2:1–784 (in Russian). English translation (1992), R. S. Hoffmann, editor. Smithsonian Institutions Libraries and the National Science Foundation: Washington, DC.

Herron, M. D., T. A. Chase, and C. L. Parkinson. 2004. Sciurid phylogeny and the paraphyly of Holarctic ground squirrels (*Spermophilus*). *Molecular Phylogenetics and Evolution* 31:1015–1030.

Heske, E. J., G. I. Shenbrot, and K. A. Rogovin. 1995. Spatial organization of *Stylodipus telum* (Dipodidae, Rodentia) in Dagestan, Russia. *Journal of Mammalogy* 76:800–808.

Heydon, M. J., and P. Bulloh. 1997. Mousedeer densities in a tropical rainforest: The impact of selective logging. *Journal of Applied Ecology* 34:484–496.

Hill, J. E. 1962. Notes on some insectivores and bats from Upper Burma. *Proceedings of the Zoological Society of London* 139:119–137.

——. 1963. A revision of the genus *Hipposideros*. *Bulletin of the British Museum (Natural History)*, Zoology Series, 11:1–129.

——. 1983. Bats (Mammalia: Chiroptera) from Indo-Australia. *Bulletin of the British Museum (Natural History)*, Zoology Series, 43:103–208.

——. 1986. A note on *Rhinolophus pearsoni* Horsfield, 1851 and *Rhinolophus yunanensis* Dobson, 1872 (Chiroptera: Rhinolophidae). *Journal of the Bombay Natural History Society* 83 (supplement):12–18.

Hill, J. E., and C. M. Francis. 1984. New bats (Mammalia: Chiroptera) and new records of bats from Borneo and Malaya. *Bulletin of the British Museum (Natural History)*, Zoology Series, 47:303–329.

Hill, J. E., and D. L. Harrison. 1987. The baculum in the Vespertilioninae (Chiroptera: Vespertilionidae) with a systematic review, a synopsis of *Pipistrellus* and *Eptesicus*, and the description of a new genus and subgenus. *Bulletin of the British Museum (Natural History)*, Zoology Series, 52:225–305.

Hill, J. E., and K. Thonglongya. 1972. Bats from Thailand and Cambodia. *Bulletin of the British Museum (Natural History)*, Zoology Series, 22:171–196.

Hill, J. E., A. Zubaid, and G. W. H. Davison. 1986. The taxonomy of leaf-nosed bats of the *Hipposideros bicolor* group (Chiroptera: Hipposideridae) from southeastern Asia. *Mammalia* 50:535–540.

Hinton, H. E., and A. M. S. Dunn. 1967. *Mongooses: Their Natural History and Behavior*. Oliver & Boyd Publishers: Edinburgh.

Hinton, M. A. C. 1923. On the voles collected by Mr. G. Forrest in Yunnan; with remarks upon the genera *Eothenomys* and *Neodon* and upon their allies. *Annals and Magazine of Natural History*, Series 9, Vol. 11:145–162.

Hoffmann, R. S. 1971. Relationships of certain Holarctic shrews, genus *Sorex*. *Zeitschrift für Säugetierkunde*, 36:193–200.

——. 1984. A review of the shrew-moles (genus *Uropsilus*) of China and Burma. *Journal of the Mammalogical Society of Japan* 10:69–80.

——. 1985a [1986]. A review of the genus *Soriculus* (Mammalia: Insectivora). *Journal of the Bombay Natural History Society* 82:459–481.

——. 1985b. The correct name for the Palearctic brown, or flat-skulled, shrew is *Sorex roboratus*. *Proceedings of the Biological Society of Washington* 98:17–28.

——. 1987. A review of the systematics and distribution of Chinese red-toothed shrews (Mammalia: Soricinae). *Acta Theriologica Sinica* 7:100–139.

——. 1991. The Tibetan Plateau fauna. A high altitude desert associated with the Sahara-Gobi. Pp. 285–297. In *Mammals in the Palaearctic Desert: Status and Trends in the Sahara-Gobian Region*. J. McNeely and V. M. Neronov, editors. Russian Academy of Sciences: Moscow.

——. 1996. Noteworthy shrews and voles from the Xizang-Qinghai Plateau. Pp. 155–168. In *Contributions in Mammalogy: A Memorial Volume Honoring Dr. J. Knox Jones Jr.* Museum of Texas Tech University: Luboch, TX.

——. 2001. The southern boundary of the Palaearctic Realm in China and adjacent countries. *Acta Zoologica Sinica* 47:121–131.

Hoffmann, R. S., and A. T. Smith. 2005. Order Lagomorpha. Pp. 185–211. In *Mammal Species of the World*, third edition. D. E. Wilson and D. M. Reeder, editors. Johns Hopkins University Press: Baltimore.

Holden, M. E. 2005. Family Gliridae. Pp. 819–841. In *Mammal Species of the World*, third edition. D. E. Wilson and D. M. Reeder, editors. Johns Hopkins University Press: Baltimore.

Holden, M. E., and G. G. Musser. 2005. Family Dipodidae. Pp. 871–893. In *Mammal Species of the World*, third edition. D. E. Wilson and D. M. Reeder, editors. Johns Hopkins University Press: Baltimore.

Hollister, N. 1912. New mammals from the highlands of Siberia. *Smithsonian Miscellaneous Collections* 60:1–6.

Horácek, I. 1997. The status of *Vesperus sinensis* Peters, 1880 and remarks on the genus *Vespertilio*. *Vespertilio, Revúca-Praha* 2:59–72.

Horácek, I., and V. Hanák. 1984. Comments on the systematics and phylogeny of *Myotis nattereri* (Kuhl, 1818). *Myotis* 21–22:20–29.

Horácek, I., V. Hanák, and J. Gaisler. 2000. Bats of the Palearctic region: A taxonomic and biogeographic review. Pp 11–157. In *Proceedings of the VIIIth European Bat Research Symposium*. Vol I. *Approaches to Biogeography and Ecology of Bats*. B. W. Woloszyn, editor. Chiropterological Information Center, Institute of Systematics and Evolution of Animals Poland Academy of Science: Krakow, Poland.

Hou, L. X., S. L. Xue, L. X. Ma, X. F. Wang, and Kamili. 1995. [New record of mammals in China—*Alticola barakshin*]. *Acta Theriologica Sinica* 15:105 (in Chinese).

Howell, A. B. 1928. New Asiatic mammals collected by F. R. Wulsin. *Proceedings of the Biological Society of Washington* 32:105–110.

Hrdy, S. B. 1974. Male-male competition and infanticide among the langurs (*Presbytis entellus*) of Abu Rajasthan. *Folia Primatologica* 22:19–58.

Hu, G., X. Dong, Y. Wei, Y. Zhu, and X. H. Duan. 2004. Evidence for a decline of Francois' langur

Trachypithecus francoisi in Fusui Nature Reserve, southwest Guangxi, China. *Oryx* 38:48–54.

Hu, H. J., and Z. G. Jiang. 2002. Trial release of Père David's deer *Elaphurus davidianus* in the Dafeng Reserve, China. *Oryx* 36:196–199.

Hu, J. C. 1998a. *Ailuropoda melanoleuca*. Pp. 158–165. In *China Red Data Book of Endangered Animals. Mammalia*. S. Wang, editor. Science Press: Beijing (in Chinese and English).

——. 1998b. *Ailurus fulgens*. Pp. 166–170. In *China Red Data Book of Endangered Animals. Mammalia*. S. Wang, editor. Science Press: Beijing (in Chinese and English).

Hu, J. C., and Y. Wang (editors). 1984. [*Sichuan Fauna Economica*, Volume 2: *Mammals*]. Sichuan Science and Technology Publishing House: Chengdu (in Chinese).

Huang, B. M., L. K. Lin, and P. S. Alexander. 1997. Annual reproductive cycle of the Formosan Wood Mouse, *Apodemus semotus*. *Zoological Studies* 36:17–25.

Huang, C. M., F. Ren, and L. Lu. 1995. [Night-staying cave selecting strategy of white-headed langur]. *Chinese Journal of Zoology* 30:36–37 (in Chinese).

Huang, C. M., F. W. Wei, M. Li, G. Q. Quan, and H. H. Li. 2002. Current status and conservation of white-headed langur (*Tachypithecus leucocephalus*) in China. *Biological Conservation* 104:221–225.

Huang, C. M., F. W. Wei, M. Li, Y. B. Li, and R. Y. Sun. 2003. Sleeping cave selection, activity pattern and time budget of white-headed langurs. *International Journal of Primatology* 24:813–824.

Huang, W. J., Y. X. Chen, and Y. X. Wen. 1987. [*Glires of China*]. Fudan University Press: Shanghai (in Chinese).

Huang, X. L., Z. J. Wang, J. S. Wu, and L. X. Liu. 1986. [The breeding biological characteristics of *Marmota himalayana* in Reshuitan and Wulannaotan, Haiyan County, Qinghai Province]. *Acta Theriologica Sinca* 6:307–311 (in Chinese).

Huang, Z., and W. Liu. 2000. [*Chinese White Dolphin and Other Cetaceans*]. Xiamen University Press: Xiamen (in Chinese).

Hunt, R. M., Jr. 2001. Basicranial anatomy of the living linsangs *Prionodon* and *Poiana* (Mammalia, Carnivora, Viverridae), with comments on the early evolution of Aeluroid Carnivorans. *American Museum Novitates* 3330:1–24.

Husar, S. L. 1978. Dugong dugong. *Mammalian Species* 88:1–7.

Hussain, S. A. 1996. Group size, group structure and breeding in smooth-coated otter *Lutra perspicillata* Geoffroy (Carnivora, Mustelidae) in National Chambal Sanctuary. *Mammalia* 60:289–297.

Hutson, A. M., S. P. Mickleburgh, and P. A. Racey. 2001. *Microchiropteran Bats: Global Status Survey and Conservation Action Plan*. IUCN/SSC Chiroptera Specialist Group. IUCN: Gland, Switzerland.

Hutterer, R. 1979. Verbreitung und Systematik von *Sorex minutus* Linnaeus, 1766 (Insectivora; Soricidae) im Nepal- Himalaya und angrenzenden Gebieten. *Zeitschrift für Säugetierkunde* 44:65–80.

——. 1982. Biologische und morphologische Beobachtungen an Alpenspitzmäusen (*Sorex alpinus*). *Bonner Zoologische Beiträge* 33:3–18.

——. 1993. Ein Lebensbild der tibetanischen Wasserspitzmaus (*Nectogale elegans*). Pp. 39–51. In *Semiaquatische Säugetiere*. M. Stubbe, editor. Wissenschaftliche Beiträge der Universität Halle: Wittenberg.

——. 1994. Generic limits among neomyine and soriculine shrews (Mammalia: Soricidae). *Neogene and Quaternary Mammals of the Palaearctic*. Conference in honor of Professor Kamimierz Kowalski. Krakow, Poland. Abstracts 32:17–21.

——. 2005. Order Soricomorpha. Pp. 220–311. In *Mammal Species of the World*, third edition. D. E. Wilson and D. M. Reeder, editors. Johns Hopkins University Press: Baltimore.

Ichihara, T., and K. Yoshida. 1972. Diving depth of northern fur seals in the feeding time. *Scientific Reports, Whales Research Institute* 24:145–148.

Ikeda, H. 1984. Raccoon dog scent-marking by scats and its significance in social behaviour. Journal of Ethology, Tokyo, 2:77–84.

——. 1987. Social behaviour and social system of raccoon dogs. Abstract. In *XVIIIth Congress of the International Union of Game Biologists:* Krakow, Poland.

Imaizumi, Y., and M. Yoshiyuki. 1965. [Taxonomic studies on *Tadarida insignis* from Japan]. *Journal of the Mammalogical Society of Japan* 2:105–108 (in Japanese).

International Commission on Zoological Nomenclature. 2003. Opinion 2028 (Case 3073). *Vespertilio pipistrellus* Schreber, 1774 and *V. pygmaeus* Leach, 1825 (currently *Pipistrellus pipistrellus* and *Pipistrellus pygmaeus*; Mammalia, Chiroptera): Neotypes designated. *Bulletin of Zoological Nomenclature* 60:85–87.

Ishunin, G. I. 1965. [On the biology of *Felis chaus chaus* Güldenstädt in south Uzbekistan]. *Zoologicheskii Zhurnal* 44:630–632 (in Russian).

IUCN. 1994. *IUCN Red List Categories*. Prepared by the IUCN Species Survival Commission. IUCN: Gland, Switzerland.

——. 2001. *IUCN Red List Categories and Criteria: Version 3.1*. IUCN Species Survival Commission: Gland, Switzerland and Cambridge, UK.

——. 2003. *Guidelines for Application of IUCN Red List Criteria at Regional Levels: Version 3.0*. IUCN Species Survial Commission: Gland, Switzerland and Cambridge, UK.

Iyengar, A., V. N. Babu, S. Hedges, A. B. Venkataraman, N. Maclean, and P. A. Morin. 2005. Phylogeography, genetic structure, and diversity in the dhole (*Cyon alpinus*). *Molecular Ecology* 14:2281–2297.

Jackson, R., and G. Ahlborn. 1989. Snow leopards (*Panthera uncia*) in Nepal—home range and movements. *National Geographic Research* 5:161–175.

Jameson, E. W., and G. S. Jones. 1977. The Soricidae of Taiwan. *Proceedings of the Biological Society of Washington* 90:459–482.

Janczewski, D. N., W. S. Modi, J. C. Stephens, and S. J. O'Brien. 1995. Molecular evolution of mitochondrial 12S RNA and cytochrome b sequences in the pantherine lineage of Felidae. *Molecular Biology and Evolution* 12:690–707.

Jansa, S., and M. Weksler. 2004. Phylogeny of muroid rodents: Relationships within and among major lineages as determined by IRBP gene sequences. *Molecular Phylogenetics and Evolution* 31:256–276.

Jefferson, T. A. 2000. Population biology of the Indo-Pacific hump-backed dolphin in Hong Kong waters. *Wildlife Monographs* 144:1–67.

Jefferson, T. A., S. K. Hung, L. Law, M. Torey, and N. Tregenza. 2002. Distribution and abundance of finless porpoises in Hong Kong and adjacent waters of China. *Raffles Bulletin of Zoology Supplement* 10:43–55.

Jefferson, T. A., and L. Karczmarski. 2001. Sousa chinensis. *Mammalian Species* 655:1–9.

Jenkins, P. D. 1976. Variation in Eurasian shrews of the genus *Crocidura* (Insectivora: Soricidae). *Bulletin of the British Museum (Natural History)*, Zoology Series, 30:271–309.

Jenkins, P. D., and M. F. Robinson. 2002. Another variation on the gymnure theme: Description of a new species of *Hylomys* (Lipotyphla, Erinaceidae, Galericinae). *Bulletin of the Natural History Museum, London (Zoology)*, 68:1–11.

Jha, A. J. 1999. Status of the weasel family in Sikkim. *Tigerpaper* 26:2–3.

Ji, W. Z., and X. L. Jiang. 2004. Primatology in China. *International Journal of Primatology* 25:1077–1092.

Jiang, J. Q., Y. Ma, and Z. X. Luo. 1993. [On the classification of the subspecies of *Clethrionomys rufocanus* in China]. *Acta Zootaxonomica Sinica* 18:114–122 (in Chinese).

Jiang, X. L., and R. S. Hoffmann. 2001. A revision of the white-toothed shrews (*Crocidura*) of southern China. *Journal of Mammalogy* 82:1059–1079.

Jiang, X. L., and Y. X. Wang. 2000. [The field mice (*Apodemus*) in Wuliang Mountain with a discussion of *A. orestes*]. *Zoological Research* 21:473–478 (in Chinese).

Jiang, X. L., Y. X. Wang, and R. S. Hoffmann. 2003. A review of the systematics and distribution of Asiatic short-tailed shrews, genus *Blarinella* (Mammalia: Soricidae). *Mammalian Biology* 68:193–204.

Jiang, X. L., Y. X. Wang, and S. L. Ma. 1991. [Taxonomic and subspecies of rhesus monkey (*Macaca mulatta*) in China]. *Zoological Research* 12:241–246 (in Chinese).

Jiang, X. L., Y. X. Wang, and Q. Wang. 1996. [Taxonomy and distribution of Tibetan macaque (*Macaca thibetana*)]. *Zoological Research* 17:361–369 (in Chinese).

Jiang, Y. J., and Z. W. Wang. 1991. Social behavior of *Ochotona cansus*: adaptation to the alpine environment. *Acta Theriologica Sinica* 11:23–40.

Jiang, Z. G., D. Q. Li, and Z. W. Wang. 2000. Population declines of Przewalski's gazelle around Qinghai Lake, China. *Oryx* 34:129–135.

Jiang, Z. G., and S. Wang. 2001. China. Pp. 168–177. In *Antelopes: Global Survey and Regional Action Plans;* Part 4: *North Africa, the Middle East, and Asia*. D. P. Mallon and S. C. Kingwood, editors. IUCN: Gland, Switzerland.

Jiang, Z. G., C. Q. Yu, Z. J. Feng, L. Y. Zhang, J. S. Xia, Y. H. Ding, and N. Lindsay. 2000. Père David's deer in China. *Wildlife Society Bulletin* 28:681–687.

Johnsingh, A. J. T. 1982. Reproductive and social behaviour of the dhole, *Cuon alpinus* Canidae. *Journal of Zoology*, London, 198:443–463.

Johnson, W. E., and S. J. O'Brien. 1997. Phylogenetic reconstruction of the Felidae using 16S rRNA and NADH-5 mitochondrial genes. *Journal of Molecular Evolution* 44 (supplement 1):S98–S116.

Jones, G. S. 1975. Catalogue of the type specimens of mammals of Taiwan. *Quarterly Journal of the Taiwan Museum* 28:183–217.

Jones, G. S., P. L. Duverge, and R. D. Ransome. 1995. Conservation biology of an endangered species: Field studies of greater horseshoe bats. Pp. 309–323. In *Ecology, Evolution and Behaviour of Bats*. P. A. Racey and S. M. Swift, editors. Zoological Society of London Symposia 67, Oxford Science Publications: Oxford.

Jones, G. S., and R. E. Mumford. 1971. *Chimarrogale* from Taiwan. *Journal of Mammalogy* 52:228–232.

Jones, J. K., and D. H. Johnson. 1960. Review of the insectivores of Korea. University of Kansas, *Publications of the Museum of Natural History* 9:549–578.

——. 1965. Synopsis of the lagomorphs and rodents of Korea. University of Kansas, *Publications of the Museum of Natural History* 16:357–407.

Joshi, A. R., J.L.D. Smith, and F. J. Cuthbert. 1995. Influence of food distribution and predation pressure on spacing behavior in palm civets. *Journal of Mammalogy* 76:1205–1212.

Kaji, K., N. Ohtaishi, S. Miura, T. Koizumi, K. Tokida, and J. Wu. 1993. Distribution and status of white-lipped deer and associated ungulate fauna in the Tibetan plateau. Pp. 147–158. In *Deer of China: Biology and Management*. N. Ohtaishi and H. L. Sheng, editors. Elsevier: Amsterdam.

Kaneko, Y. 1987. Skull and dental characters, and skull measurements of *Microtus kikuchii* Kuroda, 1920 from Taiwan. *Journal of the Mammalogical Society of Japan* 12:31–39.

——. 1990. Identification and some morphological characters of *Clethrionomys rufocanus* and *Eothenomys regulus* from USSR, northeast China, and Korea in comparison with *C. rufocanus* from Finland. *Journal of the Mammalogical Society of Japan* 14: 129–148.

——. 1992. Identification and morphological characteristics of *Clethrionomys rufocanus*, *Eothenomys shanseius*, *E. inez* and *E. eva* from the USSR, Mongolia, and northern and central China. *Journal of the Mammalogical Society of Japan* 16:71–95.

——. 1996. Morphological variation, and latitudinal and altitudinal distribution of *Eothenomys chinensis*, *E. wardi*, *E. custos*, *E. proditor*, and *E. olitor* (Rodentia, Arvicolidae) in China. *Mammal Study* 21:89–114.

——. 2002. Morphological variation and geographical and altitudinal distribution in *Eothenomys melanogaster* and *E. mucronatus* (Rodentia, Arvicolinae) in China, Taiwan, Burma, India, Thailand, and Vietnam. *Mammal Study* 27:31–63.

Kaneko, Y., K. Nakata, T. Saitoh, N. C. Stenseth, and O. N. Bjornstad. 1998. The biology of the vole *Clethrionomys rufocanus*: A review. *Research in Population Ecology* 40:21–37.

Karanth, K. U., and M. E. Sunquist. 1995. Prey selection by tiger, leopard and dhole in tropical forests. *Journal of Animal Ecology* 64:439–450.

Kastschenko, N. F. 1902 [1901]. [About the sandy badger (*Meles arenarius* Satunin) and about the Siberian races of badger]. *Ezhegodnik Zoologicheskogo muzeya Imperatorskoi Akademii Nauk* 6:609–613 (in Russian).

Kauhala, K., M. Kaunisto, and E. Helle. 1993. Diet of the raccoon dog, *Nyctereutes procyonoides*, in Finland. *Zeitschrift für Säugetierkunde* 58:129–136.

Kauhala, K., and M. Saeki. 2004. Raccoon Dog. Pp. 136–142. In *Canids: Foxes, Wolves, Jackals and Dogs: Status Survey and Conservation Action Plan*. C. Sillero-Zubiri, M. Hoffmann, and D. Macdonald, editors. IUCN: Gland, Switzerland.

Kawada, S., M. Harada, K. Koyasu, and S. Oda. 2002. Karyological note on the short-faced mole, *Scaptochirus moschatus* (Insectivora, Talpidae). *Mammal Study* 27:91–94.

Kawada, S., A. Shinohara, M. Yasuda, S. Oda, and Lim Boo Liat. 2003. The mole of peninsular Malaysia: Notes on its identification and ecology. *Mammal Study* 28:73–77.

Kawai, K., M. Nikaido, M. Harada, S. Matsumura, L. K. Lin, Y. Wu, M. Hasegawa, and N. Okada. 2003. The status of the Japanese and East Asian bats of the genus *Myotis* (Vespertilionidae) based on mitochondrial sequences. *Molecular Phylogenetics and Evolution* 28:297–307.

Kawamichi, M. 1996. Ecological factors affecting annual variation in commencement of hibernation in wild chipmunks (*Tamias sibiricus*). *Journal of Mammalogy* 77:731–744.

Kawamichi, T. 1971. Daily activities and social pattern of two Himalayan pikas, *Ochotona macrotis* and *O. roylei*, observed at Mt. Everest. *Journal of the Faculty of Science*, Hokkaido University, Japan, Ser. VI, Zool. 17:587–609.

Ke, Y. Y., H. Chang, S. B. Wu, Q. Liu, and G. X. Fong. 1999. [A study on Chinese pangolin's main food nutrition]. *Zoological Research* 20:394–395 (in Chinese).

Kenyon, K. W., and D. W. Rice. 1961. Abundance and distribution of the Steller sea lion. *Journal of Mammalogy* 42:223–234.

Keyes, M. C. 1965. Pathology of the northern fur seal. *Journal of the American Veterinary Medical Association* 147:1091–1095.

Khan, A. A., and M. A. Beg. 1986. Food of some mammalian predators in the cultivated areas of Punjab. *Pakistan Journal of Zoology* 18:71–79.

Khan, R. 1985. *Mammals of Bangladesh*. Nazma Reza: Dhaka.

Kim, S. W., and W. K. Kim. 1974. *Avi-mammalian Fauna of Korea*. Wildlife Population Census in Korea No. 5. Office of Forestry, Forest Research Institute: Beijing.

King, C. M. 1983a. Mustela erminea. *Mammalian Species* 195:1–8.

——. 1990. *The Natural History of Weasels and Stoats*. Christopher Helm Publishers: London.

King, J. E. 1983b. *Seals of the World*, second edition. Cornell University Press: Ithaca, NY.

Kingdon, J. 1977. *East African Mammals: An Atlas of Evolution in Africa. (Carnivores)*. Academic Press: New York.

Kirkpatrick, R. C. 1995. The natural history and conservation of the snub-nosed Monkeys (Genus *Rhinopithecus*). *Biological Conservation* 72:363–369.

Kirkpatrick, R. C., H. J. Gu, and X. P. Zhou. 1999. A preliminary report on Sichuan snub-nosed monkeys (*Rhinopithecus roxellana*) at Baihe Nature Reserve. *Folia Primatologica* 70:117–120.

Kirkpatrick, R. C., and Y. C. Long. 1994. Altitudinal ranging and terrestriality in the Yunnan snub-nosed monkey (*Rhinopithecus bieti*). *Folia Primatologica* 63:102–106.

Kitchener, D. J., and I. Maryanto. 1993. Taxonomic reappraisal of the *Hipposideros larvatus* species complex (Chiroptera: Hipposideridae) in the Greater and Lesser Suns Islands, Indonesia. *Records of the Western Australian Museum* 16:119–173.

Kleiman, D. G. 1974. Scent marking in the binturong, *Arctictis binturong*. *Journal of Mammalogy* 55:224–227.

Klingener, D. 1984. Gliroid and dipodoid rodents. Pp. 381–388. In *Orders and Families of Recent Mammals of the World*. S. Anderson and J. K. Jones, Jr., editors. John Wiley and Sons: New York.

Kock, D. 1996. Fledermäuse aus Nepal (Mammalia: Chiroptera). *Senkenbergiana Biologica* 75:15–21.

——. 1999. *Tadarida (Tadarida) latouchei*, a separate species recorded from Thailand with remarks on related Asian taxa (Mammalia, Chiroptera, Molossidae). *Senkenbergiana Biologica* 78:237–240.

Koenig, A., E. Larney, A. Lu, and C. Borries. 2004. Agonistic behavior and dominance relationships in females Phayre's leaf monkeys—preliminary results. *American Journal of Primatology* 64:351–357.

Koepfli, K. P., and R. K. Wayne. 1998. Phylogenetic relationships of otters (Carnivora: Mustelidae) based on mitochondrial cytochrome b sequences. *Journal of Zoology*, London, 246:401–416.

Koh, H. S., T. Y. Chun, H. S. Yoo, Y. Zhang, J. Wang, M. Zhang, and C. Wu. 2001. Mitochondrial Cytochrome b gene sequence diversity in the Korean hare, *Lepus coreanus* Thomas (Mammalia, Lagomorpha). *Biochemical Genetics* 39:417–429.

Koh, H. S., and W. J. Lee. 1994. Geographic variation of morphometric characters in three subspecies of Korean field mice, *Apodemus peninsulae* Thomas, in China and Korea. *Korean Journal of Zoology* 37:33–39.

Koopman, K. R. 1994. *Chiroptera: Systematics. Handbook of Zoology*. Vol 8, Part 60: *Mammalia*. Walter de Gruyter: Berlin.

Krapp, V. F., and J. Niethammer. 1982. *Microtus agrestis* (Linnaeus, 1761)—Erdmaus. Pp. 349–373. In *Handbuch der Säugetiere Europas*. J. Niethammer and F. Krapp, editors. Akademische Verlagsgesellschaft (Wiesbaden) 2/I:1–649.

Kruuk, H., B. Kanchanasaka, S. O'Sullivan, and S. Wanghongsa. 1994. Niche separation in three sympatric otters, *Lutra perspicillata*, *L. lutra*, and *Aonxy cinerea*, in Huai Kha Khaeng, Thailand. *Biological Conservation* 69:115–120.

Kuo, C. C., and L. L. Lee. 2003. Food availability and food habits of Indian giant flying squirrels (*Petaurista philippensis*) in Taiwan. *Journal of Mammalogy* 84:1330–1340.

Kurose, N., Y. Kaneko, A. V. Abramov, B. Siriaroonrat, and R. Masuda. 2001. Low genetic diversity in Japanese populations of the Eurasian badger *Meles meles* (Mustelidae, Carnivora) revealed by mitochondrial cytochrome b gene sequences. *Zoological Science*, Tokyo, 18:1145–1151.

Lai, C. H., and A. T. Smith. 2003. Keystone status of plateau pikas (*Ochotona curzoniae*): effect of control on biodiversity of native birds. *Biodiversity and Conservation* 12:1901–1912.

Lander, R. H. 1979. Alaskan or Northern fur seal. In *Mammals in the Seas*, Vol. 2: *Pinniped Species Summaries and Report on Sireniams*. FAO Fisheries Series, No: 5: 19–23

Larivière, S., 2003. Amblonyx cinereus. *Mammalian Species* 720:1–5.

Larivière, S., and M. Pasitschniak-Arts. 1996. Vulpes vulpes. *Mammalian Species* 537:1–11.

Lawrence, M. A. 1982. Western Chinese arvicolines (Rodentia) collected by the Sage Expedition. *American Museum Novitates* 2745:1–19.

——. 1991. A fossil *Myospalax* cranium (Rodentia: Muridae) from Shanxi, China, with observations on zokor relationships. Pp. 261–286. In *Contributions to Mammalogy in Honor of Karl F. Koopman*. T. A. Griffiths and D. Klingener, editors. *Bulletin of the American Museum of Natural History* 206:1–432.

Lazell, J., W. H. Lu, W. Xia, S. Y. Li, and A. T. Smith. 1995. Status of the Hainan hare (*Lepus hainanus*). *Species* 25:61–62.

Lee, P. F., Y. S. Lin, and D. R. Progulske. 1993a. Reproductive biology of the red giant flying squirrel, *Petaurista petaurista*, in Taiwan. *Journal of Mammalogy* 74:982–989.

Lee, P. F., D. R. Progulske, and Y. S. Lin. 1993b. Spotlight counts of giant flying squirrels (*Petaurista petaurista* and *P. alborufus*) in Taiwan. *Bulletin of the Institute of Zoology, Academia Sinica* 32:54–61.

Lei, R. H., Z. Hu, Z. G. Jiang, and W. L. Yang. 2003b. Phylogeography and genetic diversity of the critically endangered Przewalski's gazelle. *Animal Conservation* 6:361–367.

Lei, R. H, Z. G. Jiang, Z. Hu, and W. L Yang. 2003a. Phylogenetic relationships of Chinese antelopes (subfamily Antilopinae) based on mitochondrial ribosomal RNA gene sequences. *Journal of Zoology*, London, 261:227–237.

Lekagul, B., and J. A. McNeely. 1977. *Mammals of Thailand*. Association for the Conservation of Wildlife, Sahakarnbhat Co.: Bangkok.

Li, B. G., and F. G. Chen. 1987. [A comparative study of the karyotypes and LDH isoenzymes from some zokors of the subgenus *Eospalax* Genus *Myospalax*]. Acta Theriologica Sinica 7:275–282 (in Chinese).

——. 1989. [A taxonomic study and new subspecies of the subgenus *Eospalax*]. *Acta Zoologica Sinica* 35: 89–95 (in Chinese).

Li, B. G., C. Chen, W. H. Ji, and B. P. Ren. 2000a. Seasonal home range changes of the Sichuan snub-nosed monkey (*Rhinopithecus roxellana*) in the Qinling Mountains of China. *Folia Primatologica* 71:375–386.

Li, C. W., Z. G. Jiang, J. D. Zhou, and Y. Zeng. 2002. [Distribution, numbers and conservation of Mongolian wild ass (*Equus hemionus hemionus*) in west Inner Mongolia]. Acta Theriologica Sinica 22:1–6 (in Chinese).

Li, C. Y., S. L. Ma, Y. X. Wang, and G. C. Lu. 1987. [Mammals from Honghe region]. Pp. 26–27. In [*Report on the Biological Resources of Honghe Region, Southern Yunnan*. Vol. 1. *Land Vertebrates*]. Yunnan National Press: Kunming (in Chinese).

Li, D. H. (editor). 1989. [*Qinghai Fauna Economica*]. Qinghai People's Press: Xining (in Chinese).

Li, D. Q., and Z. G. Jiang. 2002. Population viability analysis for the Przewalski's gazelle. *Russian Journal of Ecology* 33:115–120.

Li, M., F. W. Wei, C. M. Huang, R. L. Pan, and J. de Ruiter. 2004. Phylogeny of snub-nosed monkeys inferred from mitochondrial DNA, Cytochrome B, and 12S rRNA sequences. *International Journal of Primatology* 25:861–873.

Li, T., J. S. Jiang, Z. G. Wu, X. D. Han, J. C. Wu, and X. J. Yang. 2001. [Survey on Amur tigers in Jilin Province]. *Acta Theriologica Sinica* 21:1–6 (in Chinese).

Li, W. D. 1997. [An endangered species of Lagomorpha—Ili pika (*Ochotona iliensis*)]. *Chinese Biodiversity* 5 (supplement):23–28 (in Chinese).

Li, W. D., H. Li, X. Hamit, and J. Ma. 1991a. [A preliminary study on the distribution and habitat of *Ochotona iliensis*]. *Chinese Journal of Zoology* 26:28–30 (in Chinese).

Li, W. D., and Y. Ma. 1986. [A new species of Ochotonidae, Lagomorpha]. *Acta Zoologica Sinica* 32:375–379 (in Chinese).

Li, W. D., and A. T. Smith. 2005. Dramatic decline of the threatened Ili pika (*Ochotona iliensis*) (Lagomorpha: Ochotonidae) in Xinjiang, China. *Oryx* 39:30–39.

Li, W. D., and W. Zhao. 1991. [The component species of Genus *Ochotona* and its distribution areas in Xinjiang]. *Chinese Journal of Vector Biology and Control* 2:305–308 (in Chinese).

Li, W. D., W. Zhao, X. Hamit, and J. Ma. 1991b. [A preliminary study on ecology of the Ili pika and its relationship with the plague natural foci]. *Chinese Journal of Vector Biology and Control* 2:202–205 (in Chinese).

Li, X. C., and T. Z. Wang. 1995. [Discussion of taxonomy of Vernaya's climbing mouse]. *Zoological Research* 16:325–328 (in Chinese).

Li, Y. B., C. M. Huang, Z. Tang, Z. M. Huang, and L. Wei. 2005a. Conservation status of Francois's Leaf Monkey *Trachypithesus francoisi* in Guangxi. *Living Forests* 9:46–49 (in Chinese and English).

Li, Y. M. 2001. The seasonal diet of the Sichuan snub-nosed monkey (*Rhinopithecus roxellana*) in Shennongjia Nature Reserve, China. *Folia Primatologica* 72:40–43.

——. 2004. The effect of forest clear-cutting on habitat use in Sichuan snub-nosed monkey (*Rhinopithecus roxellana*) in Shennongjia Nature Reserve, China. *Primates* 45:69–72.

Li, Y. M., Z. X. Gao, X. H. Li, S. Wang, and J. Niemela. 2000b. Illegal wildlife trade in the Himalayan region of China. *Biodiversity and Conservation* 9:901–918.

Li, Z., and N. Wang. 2003. An initial study on habitat conservation of Asian elephant (*Elephas maximus*), with a focus on human elephant conflict in Simao, China. *Biological Conservation* 112:453–459.

Li, Z. C., L. Xia, Q. S. Yang, and M. Y. Liang. 2005b. Population genetic structure of the Yarkand hare (*Lepus yarkandensis*). *Acta Theriologica Sinica* 25:224–228.

Li, Z. Y. 1993. Preliminary investigation of the habitats of *Presbytis francoisi* and *Presbytis leucocephalus*, with notes on the activity pattern of *Presbytis leucocephalus*. *Folia Primatologica* 60:83–93.

Li, Z. Y., and S. Ma. 1980. [A revision of the white-headed langur]. *Acta Zootaxonomica Sinica* 5:440–442 (in Chinese).

Li, Z. Y., and E. Rodgers. 2004a. Habitat quality and activity budgets of white-headed langurs in Fusui, China. *International Journal of Primatology* 25:41–54.

——. 2004b. Social organization of white-headed langurs *Tachypithecus leucocephalus* in Fusui, China. *Folia Primatologica* 75:97–100.

Li, Z. Y., Y. Wei, and E. Rodgers 2003. Food choice of white-headed langurs in Fusui, China. *International Journal of Primatology* 24:1189–1205.

Liang, B., S. Y. Zhang, and L. X. Wang. 2000. Development of sexual morphology, physiology and behaviour in Sichuan golden monkeys, *Rhinopithecus roxellana*. *Folia Primatologica* 71:413–416.

Liang, C. Q., Y. H. Din, J. Lu, and H. Shen. 1993. Population dynamics of the Milu herd in the Dafeng reserve. Pp. 301–308. In *Deer of China: Biology and Management*. N. Ohtaishi and H. L. Sheng, editors. Elsevier: Amsterdam.

Liang, R., and Y. Dong. 1985. [On the ecology of *Nyctalus velutinus*]. *Acta Theriologica Sinica* 5:11–15 (in Chinese).

Liao, Y. F. 1988. [Some biological information on the desert cat in Qinghai, China]. *Acta Theriologica Sinica* 8:128–131 (in Chinese).

Lim, B. K., and P. D. Ross. 1992. Taxonomic status of *Alticola* and a new record of *Cricetulus* from Nepal. *Mammalia* 56:300–302.

Lim Boo Liat. 1973. The banded linsang and the banded musang of west Malaysia. *Malay Nature Journal* 26: 105–111.

Lin, L. K., L. L. Lee, and H. C. Cheng. 1997. *Bats of Taiwan*. National Museum of Natural Science: Taichung.

Lin, L. K., M. Motokawa, and M. Harada. 2002a. Karyotype of *Mogera insularis* (Insectivora, Talpidae). *Mammalian Biology* 67:176–178.

Lin, L. K., M. Motokawa, M. Harada, and H. C. Cheng. 2002b. New record of *Barbastella leucomelas* (Chiroptera: Vespertilionidae) from Taiwan. *Mammalian Biology* 67:315–319.

Liu, B. W., and Z. G. Jiang. 2002. Quantitative analysis of the habitat selection by *Procapra przewalskii*. *Acta Theriologica Sinica* 22:15–21.

Liu, C. S., W. N. Wu, S. K. Guo, and J. H. Meng. 1991. [A study of the subspecies classification of *Apodemus agrarius* in eastern continental China]. *Acta Theriologica Sinica* 11:294–299 (in Chinese).

Liu, J. H., and P. Hills. 1997. Environmental planning, biodiversity and the development process: The case of Hong Kong's Chinese white dolphins. *Journal of Environmental Management* 50:351–367.

Liu, L. G. 2000. [Mammal diversity and conservation in Taiwan]. *Biological Diversity* 2000:106–115 (in Chinese).

Liu, X. M., F. W. Wei, M. Li, and Z. J. Feng. 2002. [A review of the phylogenetic study on the genus *Apodemus* of China]. *Acta Theriologica Sinica* 22:46–52 (in Chinese).

Lode, T. 1994. Feeding habits of the stone marten *Martes foina* and environmental factors in western France. *Zeitschrift für Säugeteirkunde* 59:189–191.

Long, C. A. 1978. A listing of Recent badgers of the world, with remarks on taxonomic problems in *Mydaus* and *Melogale*. *Reports on the Fauna and Flora of Wisconsin*. University of Wisconsin, Steven's Point, Museum of Natural History, 14:1–6.

Long, C. A., and C. A. Killingley. 1983. *The Badgers of the World*. Charles C. Thomas: Springfield IL.

Long, Y. C. 1992. A preliminary report on the Yunnan snub-nosed monkey (*Rhinopithecus bieti*). *Asian Primates* 1:1–3.

Long, Y. C., R. C. Kirkpatrick, Zhongtai, and Xiaolin. 1994. Report on the distribution, population and ecology of the Yunnan snub-nosed monkey (*Rhinopithecus bieti*). *Primates* 35:241–250.

Loughlin, T. R., M. A. Perez, and R. L. Merrick. 1987. Eumetopias jubatus. *Mammalian Species* 283:1–7.

Loukashkin, A. S. 1943. On the hares of northern Manchuria. *Journal of Mammalogy* 24:73–81.

Louwman, J.W.W., and W. G. Van Owen. 1968. A note on breeding Temminck's golden cat at Wassenaar Zoo. *International Zoo Yearbook* 8:47–49.

Lovari, S. (editor). 1985. *The Biology and Management of Mountain Ungulates*. Croom Helm: London.

Lu, C. K., T. Y. Wang, G. Q. Quan, S. K. Gin, T. H. Ma, and T.H. Yang. 1965. [On the mammals from the Lin-Tsang area, western Yunnan]. *Acta Zootaxonomica Sinica* 2:279–295 (in Chinese).

Lu, H. G., and H.L. Sheng. 1984. Status of the black muntjac, *Muntiacus crinifrons*, in eastern China. *Mammal Review* 14:29–36.

Lu, L. R. 2000. Survival crisis for the White-headed Leaf Monkeys in Guangxi. *Living Forests* 1:12–14 (in Chinese and English).

Lu, L. R., and Z. Li. 1991. On the taxonomy of the *Presbytis francoisi leucocephalus*: Discussion with Ma Shilai. *Journal of Guangxi Normal University* 9:67–70 (in Chinese).

Lu, Z., and G. B. Schaller. 2002. *Giant Pandas in the Wild*. Aperture: New York.

Lunde, D. P., and G. G. Musser. 2002. The capture of the Himalayan water shrew (*Chimarrogale himalayica*) in Vietnam. *Mammal Study* 27:137–140.

Lunde, D. P., G. G. Musser, and N. T. Son. 2003a. A survey of small mammals from Mt. Tay Con Linh II, Vietnam, with the description of a new species of *Chodsigoa* (Insectivora: Soricidae). *Mammal Study* 28:31–46.

Lunde, D. P., G. G. Musser, and P. D. Tien. 2003b. Records of some little known bats (Chiroptera: Vespertilionidae) from Vietnam. *Mammalia* 67:459–461.

Lunde, D. P., G. G. Musser, and T. Ziegler 2004. Description of a new species of Crocidura (Soricomorpha: Soricidae, Crocidurinae) from Ke Go Nature Reserve, Vietnam. *Mammal Study* 29:27–36.

Lunde, D., and N. T. Son. 2001. *An Identification Guide to the Rodents of Vietnam*. Center for Biodiversity and Conservation, American Museum of Natural History: New York.

Luo, J., D. M. Yang, H. Suzuki, Y. X. Wang, W. J. Chen, K. L. Campbell, and Y. P. Zhang. 2004a. Molecular phylogeny and biogeography of Oriential voles: Genus *Eothenomys* (Muridae, Mammalia). *Molecular Phylogenetics and Evolution* 33:349–362.

Luo, R. (editor). 1993. [*The Mammalian Fauna of Guizhou*]. Guizhou Science and Technology Publishing House: Guiyang (in Chinese).

Luo, S. J., J. H. Kim, W. E. Johnson, J. van der Walt, J. Martenson, N. Yuhki, D. G. Miquelle, O. Uphyrkina, J. M. Goodrich, H. B. Quigley, R. Tilson, G. Brady, P. Martelli, V. Subramaniam, C. McDougla, S. Hean, S. Q. Huang, W. Pan, U. K. Karanth, M. Sunquist, J. L. D. Smith, and S. J. O'Brien. 2004b. Phylogeography and genetic ancestry of tigers (*Panthera tigris*). *Public Library of Science: Biology* 2(12)e442:2275–2293.

Luo, Z. X. 1981. [A systematic review of the Chinese cape hare, *Lepus capensis* Linnaeus]. *Acta Theriologica Sinica* 1:149–157 (in Chinese).

——. 1982. [On a new subspecies of cape hare from Qinghai, China]. Sinozoologica 2:3–6 (in Chinese).

——. 1988. [*The Chinese Hare*]. China Forestry Publishing House: Beijing (in Chinese).

——. 2001. A new Mammaliaform from the Early Jurassic and evolution of mammalian characteristics. *Science* 292:1535–1540.

Luo, Z. X., W. Chen and W. Gao (editors). 2000. [*Fauna Sinica, Mammalia*, Vol 6, *Rodentia, Part III: Cricetidae*]. Science Press: Beijing (in Chinese).

Lydekker, R. 1904. The coloration of the lynxes. *The Field* 1904:576.

Ma, J., J. S. Zhang, B. Liang, L. Zhang, S. Y. Zhang, and W. Metzner. 2006. Dietary characteristics of *Myotis ricketti* in Beijing, North China. *Journal of Mammalogy* 87:339–344.

Ma, J. Z., H. P. Chen, Z. X. Gao, Z. B. Zhao, F. Li, J. P. Wu, J. C. Chang, and G. Y. Liu. 1993. Impacts of super-intensive forest fire on the deer population in the northern Great Xing'an Mountains. Pp. 319–324. In *Deer of China: Biology and Management*. N. Ohtaishi and H. L. Sheng, editors. Elsevier: Amsterdam.

Ma, S. L., X. F. Ma, and W. Y. Shi. 2001. [*A Guide to Mammal Tracking in China*]. China Forestry Publishing House: Beijing (in Chinese).

Ma, S. L., and Y. X. Wang. 1986. [The taxonomy and distribution of the gibbons in southern China and its adjacent region–with description of three new subspecies]. *Zoological Research* 7:393–410 (in Chinese).

Ma, S. L., Y. X. Wang, X. L. Jiang, J. X. Li, and R. L. Xian. 1989. [Study on the social behavior and habitual specialty of Yunnan golden monkey]. *Acta Theriologica Sinica* 9:161–167 (in Chinese).

Ma, S. L., Y. X. Wang, and F. E. Poirier. 1988. Taxonomy, distribution, and status of gibbons (*Hylobates*) in southern China and adjacent areas. *Primates* 29: 277–286.

Ma, S. L., Y. X. Wang, and L. H. Xu. 1986. [Taxonomic and phylogenetic studies on the genus *Muntiacus*]. *Acta Theriologica Sinica* 6:191–209 (in Chinese).

Ma, S. L., Y. Xiang, and L. M. Shi. 1990. [A new species of genus *Muntiacus* from Yunnan, China]. *Zoological Research* 11: 47–53 (in Chinese).

Ma, Y. 1964. [A new species of hedgehog from Shansi Province, *Hemiechinus sylvaticus* sp. n.]. *Acta Zootaxonomica Sinica* 1:31–36 (in Chinese).

——. 1965. [A new subspecies of narrow-skulled vole from Inner Mongolia, China]. *Acta Zootaxonomica Sinica* 2:183–186 (in Chinese).

Ma, Y., and J. Q. Jiang. 1996. [The reinstatement of the status of genus *Caryomys* (Thomas, 1911) (Rodentia: Microtinae)]. *Acta Zootaxonomica Sinica* 21:493–498 (in Chinese).

Ma, Y., and S. Li. 1979. [A new subspecies of the long-eared jerboa from Xinjiang]. *Acta Zootaxonomica Sinica* 4:301–303 (in Chinese).

Ma, Y., Y. Lin, and S. Li. 1980. [A new subspecies of Pallas's pika from the Inner Mongolia, China]. *Acta Zootaxonomica Sinica* 5:212–214 (in Chinese).

Ma, Y., F. G. Wang, S. K. Jin and S. H. Li. 1987. [*Glires (Rodents and Lagomorphs) of Northern Xinjiang and Their Zoogeographical Distribution*]. Science Press, Academia Sinica: Beijing (in Chinese).

Ma, Y. Q. 1981. [On the distribution of bears in China]. *Acta Theriologica Sinica* 1:138–144 (in Chinese).

——. 1986. [*Fauna Heilongjiangica: Mammalia*]. Heilongjiang Science and Technology Publishing Press: Harbin (in Chinese).

——. 1998a. *Panthera pardus*. Pp. 114–118. In *China Red Data Book of Endangered Animals. Mammalia*. S. Wang, editor. Science Press: Beijing (in Chinese and English).

——. 1998b. *Panthera tigris*. Pp. 119–125. In *China Red Data Book of Endangered Animals. Mammalia*. S. Wang, editor. Science Press: Beijing (in Chinese and English).

——. 1998c. *Martes zibellina*. Pp. 148–150. In *China Red Data Book of Endangered Animals. Mammalia*. S. Wang, editor. Science Press: Beijing (in Chinese and English).

——. 1998d. *Helarctos malayanus*. Pp. 171–172. In *China Red Data Book of Endangered Animals. Mammalia*. S. Wang, editor. Science Press: Beijing (in Chinese and English).

Ma, Y. Q., and X. M. Li. 1999. Status and management of the Asiatic black bear in China. Pp. 200–202. In *Bears: Status Survey and Conservation Action Plan*. C. Servheen, S. Herrero, and B. Peyton, editors. IUCN: Gland, Switzerland.

Maberly, C. T. A. 1955. The African civet. *African Wildlife* 9:55–58.

Macdonald, D. W. 1977. On food preference in the red fox. *Mammal Review* 7:7–23.

——. (editor). 1987. *The Encyclopedia of Mammals*. Facts on File Inc.: New York.

Macdonald, D. W., and P. Barrett. 1993. *Mammals of Britain and Europe*. Harper Collins: London.

Macdonald, D. W., and J. C. Reynolds. 2004. Red fox. Pp. 129–136. In *Canids: Foxes, Wolves, Jackals and Dogs: Status Survey and Conservation Action Plan*. C. Sillero-Zubiri, M. Hoffmann, and D. Macdonald, editors. IUCN: Gland, Switzerland.

Macholán, M. 2001. Multivariate analysis of morphometric variation in Asian *Mus* and Sub-Saharan *Nannomys* (Rodentia: Muridae). *Zoologischer Anzeiger* 240:7–14.

MacKinnon, J., and N. Hicks. 1996. *Wild China*. The MIT Press: Cambridge, MA.

MacKinnon, J., and K. Phillipps. 2000. *A Field Guide to the Birds of China*. Oxford University Press: Oxford.

MacKinnon, J., M. Sha, C. Cheung, G. Carey, Z. Xiang, and D. Melville. 1996. *A Biodiversity Review of China*. WWF International China Programme: Hong Kong.

Maeda, K. 1980. Review on the classification of little tube-nosed bats, *Murina aurata* group. *Mammalia* 44:531–551.

——. 1982. Studies on the classification of *Miniopterus* in Eurasia, Australia, and Melanesia. *Honyurui Kagaku (Mammalian Science)*, supplement 1:1–176.

Malygin, V. M., V. N. Orlov, and V. N. Yatsenko. 1990. [Species independence of *Microtus limnophilus*, its relations with *M. oeconomus* and distribution of these species in Mongolia]. *Zoologicheskii Zhurnal* 69: 115–127 (in Russian).

Marsh, H., H. Penrose, C. Eros, and J. Hugues. 2002. *Dugong: Status Reports and Action Plans for Countries and Territories*. UNEP: Nairobi.

Marshall, J. T., Jr. 1977a. Family Muridae: Rats and mice. Pp. 396–487. In *Mammals of Thailand*. B. Lekagul and J. A. McNeely, editors. Association for the Conservation of Wildlife, Sahakarnbhat Co.: Bangkok.

——. 1977b. A synopsis of Asian species of *Mus* (Rodentia, Muridae). *Bulletin of the American Museum of Natural History* 158:173–220.

Mason, C. F., and S. M. Macdonald. 1986. *Otters–Ecology and Conservation*. Cambridge University Press: Cambridge.

Masui, K., Y. Narita, and S. Tanaka. 1986. Information on the distribution of Formosan monkeys (*Macaca cyclopis*). *Primates* 27:383–392.

Matsubayashi, H., E. Bosi, and S. Kohshima. 2003. Activity and habitat use of lesser mouse-deer (*Tragulus javanicus*). *Journal of Mammalogy* 84:234–242.

Mattern, M. Y., and D. A. McLennan. 2000. Phylogeny and speciation of felids. *Cladistics* 16:232–253.

Matyushkin, E. N. 1979. [Lynx of the Holarctic]. Pp. 76–162. In [*Mammals: Investigations on the Fauna of the Soviet Union*]. O. L. Rossolimo, editor. Sbornik Trudov Zoologicheskogo Muzeia MGU 13:1–279 (in Russian).

Matyushkin, E. N., V. I. Zhivotchenko, and E. N. Smirnov. 1980. *The Amur Tiger in the USSR*. IUCN: Gland, Switzerland.

Mayer, F., and O. von Helversen. 2001. Cryptic species diversity in European bats. *Proceedings of the Royal Society of London*, B 268:1825–1832.

Mayr, E. 1986. Uncertainty in science: Is the giant panda a bear or raccoon? *Nature* 323:769–771.

Mazák, V. 1981. Panthera tigris. *Mammalian Species* 152:1–8.

McCullough, D. R., C. J. Pei-Kurtis, and Y. Wang. 2000. Home range, activity patterns, and habitat relations of Reeves' muntjacs in Taiwan. *Journal of Wildlife Management* 64:430–441.

McKenna, M. C., 1962. *Eupetaurus* and the living Petauristine sciurids. *American Museum Novitates* 2104:1–38.

McKenna, M. C., and S. K. Bell. 1997. *Classification of Mammals above the Species Level*. Columbia University Press: New York.

McLaughlin, C. A. 1984. Protrogomorph, sciuromorph, castorimorph, myomorph (geomyoid, anomaluroid, pedetoid, and ctenodactyloid) rodents. Pp. 267–288. In *Orders and Families of Recent Mammals of the World*. S. Anderson and J. K. Jones, Jr., editors. John Wiley and Sons: New York.

McTaggart-Cowan, I., and C. W. Holloway. 1978. Geographical location and current conservation status of the threatened deer of the world. Pp. 11–22. In *Threatened Deer: Proceedings of a Working Meeting of the IUCN Survival Service Commission*. IUCN: Morges, Switzerland.

Mead, J. G., and R. L. Brownell, Jr. 2005. Order Cetacea. Pp. 723–743. In *Mammal Species of the World*, third edition. D. E. Wilson, and D. M. Reeder, editors. Johns Hopkins University Press: Baltimore.

Mead, J. I. 1989. Nemoraedus goral. *Mammalian Species* 335:1–5.

Mech, D. L. 1974. Canis lupus. *Mammalian Species* 37:1–6.

Mech, L. D., and L. Boitani. 2004a. Wolf. Pp. 124–129. In *Canids: Foxes, Wolves, Jackals and Dogs: Status Survey and Conservation Action Plan*. C. Sillero-Zubiri, M. Hoffmann and D. W. Macdonald, editors. IUCN: Gland, Switzerland.

——. 2004b. *Wolves: Behavior, Ecology and Conservation*. University of Chicago Press: Chicago.

Medway, L. 1967. Observations on breeding of the pencil-tailed tree mouse, *Chiropodomys gliroides*. *Journal of Mammalogy* 48:20–26.

——. 1969. *The Wild Mammals of Malaya and Offshore Islands Including Singapore*. Oxford University Press: London.

——. 1977. *Mammals of Borneo: Field Keys and an Annotated Checklist*, second edition. Monograph, Malay Branch of the Royal Asiatic Society 7:1–172.

Meijaard, E., and C. P. Groves. 2004a. A taxonomic revision of the *Tragulus* mouse-deer (Artiodactyla). *Zoological Journal of the Linnean Society* 140:63–102.

——. 2004b. Morphometrical relationships between south-east Asian deer (Cervidae, tribe Cervini): Evolutionary and biogeographic implications. *Journal of Zoology*, London, 263:179–196.

Melisch, R., P. B. Asmoro, and L. Kusumawardhani. 1994. Major steps taken towards otter conservation in Indonesia. *IUCN, Otter Specialist Group Bulletin* 10: 21–24.

Melnick, D. J., G. A. Hoelzer, R. Absher, and M.V. Ashley. 1993. mtDNA diversity in rhesus monkeys reveals overestimates of divergence time and paraphyly with neighbouring species. *Molecular Biology and Evolution* 10:282–295.

Mercer, J. M., and V. L. Roth. 2003. The effects of Cenozoic global change on squirrel phylogeny. *Science* 299:1568–1572.

Mezhzherin, S. V. 1997a. [Revision of mouse genus *Apodemus* (Rodentia, Muridae) of northern Eurasia]. *Vestnik Zoologii* 31:29–41 (in Russian).

——. 1997b. Biochemical systematics of the wood mouse, *Sylvaemus sylvaticus* (L., 1758) sensu lato (Rodentia, Muridae) from eastern Europe and Asia. *Zeitschrift für Säugetierkunde* 62:303–311.

Mi, J. C., L. X. Xia, L. F. Wang, D. Y. Zhang, and X. Z. Han. 1998. [The spatial patterns of rodents in the north desert steppe of Inner Mongolia]. *Acta Theriologica Sinica* 18:314–316 (in Chinese).

Michaux, J., A. Reyes, and F. Catzeflis. 2001. Evolutionary history of the most speciose mammals: Molecular phylogeny of muroid rodents. *Molecular Biology and Evolution* 18:2017–2031.

Mickleburgh, S. P., A. M. Hutson, and P. A. Racey. 1992. *Old World Fruit Bats: An Action Plan for Their Conservation*. IUCN/SSC Chiroptera Specialist Group. IUCN: Gland, Switzerland.

Miller, G. S., Jr. 1912. *Catalogue of the Mammals of Western Europe (Europe Exclusive of Russia) in the Collection of the British Museum*. British Museum (Natural History): London.

——. 1940a. A new mole from Annam. *Journal of Mammalogy* 21:203–204.

——. 1940b. Notes on some moles from southeastern Asia. *Journal of Mammalogy* 21:442–444.

Mills, J. A., S. Chan, and A. Ishihara. 1995. *The Bear Facts: The East Asian Market for Bear Gall Bladder*. TRAFFIC International: Cambridge, UK.

Milius, S. 2001. The lives of pandas. *Science News* 159:61.

Milner-Gulland, E. J., O. M. Bukreeva, T. Coulson, A. A. Lushchekina, M. V. Kholodova, A. B. Bekenov, and I. A. Grachev. 2003. Reproductive collapse in saiga antelope harems. *Nature* 422:135.

Miquelle, D. G., E. N. Smirnov, H. G. Quigley, M. G. Hornocker, I. G. Nikolaev, and E. N. Matyushkin. 1996. Food habits of Amur tigers in Sikhote-Alin Zapovednik and the Russian Far East, and implications for conservation. *Journal of Wildlife Research* 1:138–147.

Mitchell, R. M. 1977. Accounts of Nepalese Mammals and Analysis of the Host-ectoparasite Data by Computer Techniques. Ph.D. Dissertation, Iowa State University: Ames.

Miththapala, S., J. Seidensticker, and S. J. O'Brien. 1996. Phylogeographic subspecies recognition in leopards (*Panthera pardus*): Molecular genetic variation. *Conservation Biology* 10:1115–1132.

Mittermeier, R. A., C. G. Mittermeier, and P. R. Gil. 1997. *Megadiversity: Earth's Biologically Wealthiest Nations*. CEMEX, S. A.: Agrupación Sierra Madre, Mexico.

Miura, S. 1984. Social behaviour and territoriality in male sika deer (*Cervus nippon* Temminck 1838) during the rut. *Zeitschrift für Tierpsychologie* 64:33–73.

Miura, S., K. Kaji, N. Ohtaishi, T. Koizumi, K. Tokida, and J. Wu. 1993. Social organization and mating behavior of white-lipped deer in the Qinghai-Xizang Plateau, China. Pp. 220–234. In *Deer of China: Biology and Management*. N. Ohtaishi and H. L. Sheng, editors. Elsevier: Amsterdam.

Montgelard, C., C. A. Matthee, and T. J. Robinson. 2003. Molecular systematics of dormice (Rodentia: Gliridae) and the radiation of *Graphiurus* in Africa. *Proceedings of the Royal Society of London* B 270:1947–1955.

Moore, J. C., and G.H.H. Tate. 1965. A study of the diurnal squirrels, Sciurinae, of the Indian and Indochinese subregions. *Fieldiana: Zoology* 48:1–351.

Motokawa, M. 2003. *Soriculus minor* Dobson, 1890, senior synonym of *S. radulus* Thomas, 1922 (Insectivora, Soricidae). *Mammalian Biology* 68: 178–180.

——. 2004. Phylogenetic relationships within the family Talpidae (Mammalia: Insectivora). *Journal of Zoology, London* 263:147–157.

Motokawa, M., M. Harada, L. K. Lin, H. C. Cheng, and K. Koyasu. 1998. Karyological differentiation between two *Soriculus* (Insectivora: Soricidae) from Taiwan. *Mammalia* 62:541–547.

Motokawa, M., M. Harada, L. K. Lin, K. Koyasu, and S. Hattori. 1997a. Karyological study of the gray shrew *Crocidura attenuata* (Mammalia: Insectivora) from Taiwan. *Zoological Studies* 36:70–73.

Motokawa, M., M. Harada, L. K. Lin, and Y. Wu. 2004. Geographic differences in karyotypes of the mole-shrew *Anourosorex squamipes* (Insectivora, Soricidae). *Mammalian Biology* 69:197–201.

Motokawa, M., M. Harada, Y. Wu, L. K Lin, and H. Suzuki. 2001b. Chromosomal polymorphism in the Gray Shrew *Crocidura attenuata* (Mammalia: Insectivora). *Zoological Science* 18:1153–1160.

Motokawa, M., and L. K. Lin. 2002. Geographic variation in the mole-shrew *Anourosorex squamipes*. *Mammal Study* 27:113–120.

Motokawa, M., L. K. Lin, H. C. Cheng, and M. Harada. 2001c. Taxonomic status of the Senkaku mole, *Nesoscaptor uchidai*, with special reference to variation in *Mogera insularis* from Taiwan (Mammalia: Insectivora). *Zoological Science* 18:733–740.

Motokawa, M., L. K. Lin, M. Harada, and S. Hattori. 2003. Morphometric geographic variation in the Asian lesser white-toothed shrew *Crocidura shantungensis* (Mammalia, Insectivora) in East Asia. *Zoological Science* 20:789–795.

Motokawa, M., K. Lu, M. Harada, and L. K. Lin. 2001a. New records of the Polynesian rat *Rattus exulans* (Mammalia: Rodentia) from Taiwan and the Ryukyus. *Zoological Studies* 40:299–304.

Motokawa, M., H. Suzuki, M. Harada, L. K. Lin, K. Koyasu, and S. I. Oda. 2000. Phylogenetic relationships among East Asian *Crocidura* (Mammalia: Insectivora) inferred from mitochondrial cytochrome b gene. *Zoological Science* 17:497–504.

Motokawa, M., H. T. Yu, Y. P. Fang, H. C. Cheng, L. K. Lin, and M. Harada. 1997b. Re-evaluation of the status of *Chodsigoa sodalis* Thomas, 1913 (Mammalia: Insectivora: Soricidae). *Zoological Studies* 36:42–47.

Musser, G .G. 1970. Species-limits of *Rattus brahma*, a murid rodent of northeastern India and northern Burma. *American Museum Novitates* 2406:1–27.

——. 1972. The species of *Hapalomys* (Rodentia, Muridae). *American Museum Novitates* 2503:1–27.

——. 1973a. Notes on additional specimens of *Rattus brahma*. *Journal of Mammalogy* 54:267–270.

——. 1973b. Species-limits of *Rattus cremoriventer* and *Rattus langbianis*, Murid rodents of Southeast Asia and the Greater Sunda Islands. *American Museum Novitates* 2525:1–65.

——. 1979. Results of the Archbold expeditions. No. 102. The species of *Chiropodomys*, arboreal mice of Indochina and the Malay Archipelago. *Bulletin of the American Museum of Natural History* 162: 377–445.

——. 1981. Results of the Archbold expeditions. No. 105. Notes on systematics of Indo-Malayan murid rodents, and descriptions of new genera and species from Ceylon, Sulawesi, and the Philippines. *Bulletin of the American Museum of Natural History* 168:225–334.

——. 1987. The occurrence of *Hadromys* (Rodentia: Muridae) in early Pleistocene Siwalik strata in northern Pakistan and its bearing on biogeographic affinities between Indian and northeastern African murine faunas. *American Museum Novitates* 2883:1–36.

Musser, G. G., and E. M. Brothers. 1994. Identification of bandicoot rats from Thailand (*Bandicota*, Muridae, Rodentia). *American Museum Novitates* 3110:1–56.

Musser, G. G., E. M. Brothers, M. D. Carleton, and R. Hutterer. 1996. Taxonomy and distributional records of Oriental and European *Apodemus*, with a review of the *Apodemus-Sylvaemus* problem. *Bonner Zoologische Beiträge* 46:143–190.

Musser, G. G., and M. D. Carleton. 2005. Superfamily Muroidea. Pp. 894–1531. In *Mammal Species of the World*, third edition. D. E. Wilson and D. M. Reeder, editors. Johns Hopkins University Press: Baltimore.

Musser, G. G., and S. Chiu. 1979. Notes on taxonomy of *Rattus andersoni* and *R. excelsior*, murids endemic to western China. *Journal of Mammalogy* 60:581–592.

Musser, G. G., and L. R. Heaney. 1985. Philippine *Rattus*: A new species from the Sulu Archipelago. *American Museum Novitates* 2818:1–32.

Musser, G. G., and C. Newcomb. 1983. Malaysian Murids and the giant rat of Sumatra. *Bulletin of the American Museum of Natural History* 174:327–598.

——. 1985. Definitions of Indochinese *Rattus losea* and a new species from Vietnam. *American Museum Novitates* 2814:1–32.

Nadler, T. 1996. Verbreitung und status von delacour-, tonkin-, und goldshopf-languren (*Trachypithecus delacouri, Trachypithecus francoisi,* und *Trachypithecus poliocephalus*) in Vietnam. *Zoologische Garten* 66: 1–12.

Namgail, T., J. L. Fox, and Y. V. Bhatnagar. 2004. Habitat segregation between sympatric Tibetan argali *Ovis ammon hodgsoni* and blue sheep *Pseudois nayaur* in the Indian trans-Himalaya. *Journal of Zoology*, London, 262:57–63.

Naumov, N. P., and V. S. Lobachev. 1975. Ecology of desert rodents of the U.S.S.R. (Jerboas and Gerbils). Pp. 465–598. In *Rodents in Desert Environments*. I. Prakash and P. K. Ghosh, editors. Dr. W. Junk Publishers: The Hague.

Neal, E. 1948. *The Badger*. Collins: London.

——. 1986. *The Natural History of Badgers*. Facts on File Publications: New York.

Neas, J. F., and R. S. Hoffmann. 1987. Budorcas taxicolor. *Mammalian Species* 277:1–7.

Ni, B., H. M. Cao, and H. L. Sheng. 1993. A morphological study of scent glands of Chinese water deer and forest musk deer. Pp. 80–84. In *Deer of China: Biology and Management*. N. Ohtaishi and H. L. Sheng, editors. Elsevier: Amsterdam.

Niethammer, J., and F. Krapp. 1982. *Microtis arvalis* (Pallas, 1779)—Feldmaus. Pp. 284–318. In *Handbuch der Säugetiere Europas*. Vol. 2/I. J. Niethammer and F. Krapp, editors. Akademische Verlagsgesellschaft: Wiesbaden.

Niu, Y. D. 2002. [Molecular Systematics and Evolution of Genus *Ochotona* in the World]. Ph.D. Dissertation, Institute of Zoology, Academia Sinica: Bejjing (in Chinese).

Niu, Y. D., F. W. Wei, M. Li, and Z. J. Feng. 2001. [Current status on taxonomy and distribution of subgenus *Pika* in China]. *Acta Zootaxonomica Sinica* 26:394–400 (in Chinese).

Niu, Y. D., F. W. Wei, M. Li, X. M. Liu, and Z. J. Feng. 2004. Phylogeny of pikas (Lagomorpha, *Ochotona*) inferred from mitochondrial cytochrome *b* sequences. *Folia Zoology* 53:141–155.

Novikov, G. A. 1956. [*Carnivorous Mammals of the Fauna of the USSR*]. Akademii Nauk SSSR: Moscow. (in Russian). English translation (1962) Program for Scientific Translations, Jerusalem, Israel [available from the Office of Technical Services, U.S. Department of Commerce, Washington, DC].

Nowak, R. M. 1991. *Walker's Mammals of the World*, fifth edition. Johns Hopkins University Press: Baltimore.

——. 1994. *Walker's Bats of the World*. Johns Hopkins University Press: Baltimore.

——. 1995. Another look at wolf taxonomy. Pp. 375–397. In *Ecology and Conservation of Wolves in a Changing World: Proceedings of the Second North American Symposium on Wolves*. L. N. Carbyn, S. H. Fritts, and D. R. Seip, editors. Canadian Circumpolar Institute, University of Alberta: Edmonton, Canada.

——. 1999. *Walker's Mammals of the World*, sixth edition. Johns Hopkins University Press: Baltimore.

Nowell, K., and P. Jackson. 1996. *Wild Cats: Status Survey and Conservation Action Plan*. IUCN: Gland, Switzerland.

O'Brien, S. J., W. G. Nash, D. E. Wildt, M. E. Bush, and R. E. Benveniste. 1985. A molecular solution to the riddle of the gaint panda's phylogeny. *Nature* 317: 140–144.

O'Corry-Crowe, G. M., and R. L. Westlake. 1997. Molecular investigation of spotted seals (*Phoca largha*) and harbor seals (*P. vitulina*) and their relationship in areas of sympatry. Pp. 291–304. In *Molecular Genetics of Marine Mammals*. A. E. Dixon, S. J. Chivers, and W. F. Perrin, editors. Special Publication No. 3. Society for Marine Mammalogy: Lawrence, KS.

Ognev, S. I. 1930. Übersicht der russischen Kleinkatzen. *Zeitschrift für Säugeteirkunde* 5:48–85.

——. 1931. [*Mammals of Eastern Europe and Northern Asia: Carnivorous Mammals*]. Glavnauka: Moscow 2: 1–776 (in Russian).

——. 1962a. *Mammals of Eastern Europe and Northern Asia: Insectivora and Chiroptera* [A translation of S. I. Ognev, 1928, Zveri vostochnoi Evropy i severnoi

Azii: Nasekomoyadnye i letychie myshi]. Program for Scientific Translations: Jerusalem, Israel 1:1–487.
——. 1962b. *Mammals of Eastern Europe and Northern Asia: Carnivora (Fissipedia)* [A translation of S. I. Ognev, 1931, Zveri vostochnoi Evropy i severnoi Azii: Khishchnye mlekopitayushchie]. Program for Scientific Translations: Jerusalem, Israel 2:1–590.
——. 1962c. *Mammals of the USSR and Adjacent Countries: Fissipedia and Pinnipedia* [A translation of S. I. Ognev, 1935, Zveri SSSR i prilezhashchikh stran. Khishchnyei i lastonogie (Zveri vostochnoi Evropy i severnoi Azii)]. Program for Scientific Translations: Jerusalem, Israel 3:1–641.
——. 1963a. *Mammals of the USSR and Adjacent Countries: Rodents (continued).* (Mammals of Eastern Europe and Northern Asia) [A translation of S. I. Ognev, 1947, Zveri SSSR i prilezhashchikh stran: Gryzuny (prodolzhenie). (Zveri vostochnoi Evropy i severnoi Azii)]. Program for Scientific Translations: Jerusalem, Israel 5:1–662.
——. 1963b. *Mammals of the USSR and Adjacent Countries: Rodents (continued).* (Mammals of Eastern Europe and Northern Asia) [A translation of S. I. Ognev, 1948, Zveri SSSR i prilezhashchikh stran: Gryzuny (prodolzhenie). (Zveri vostochnoi Evropy i severnoi Azii)]. Program for Scientific Translations: Jerusalem, Israel 6:1–508.
——. 1964. *Mammals of the USSR and Adjacent Countries: Rodents (continued).* (Mammals of Eastern Europe and Northern Asia) [A translation of S. I. Ognev, 1950, Zveri SSSR i prilezhashchikh stran: Gryzuny (prodolzhenie). (Zveri vostochnoi Evropy i severnoi Azii)]. Program for Scientific Translations: Jerusalem, Israel 7:1–626.
——. 1966. *Mammals of the USSR and Adjacent Countries: Rodents* (Mammals of Eastern Europe and Northern Asia) [A translation of S. I. Ognev, 1940, Zveri SSSR i prilezhashchikh stran: Gryzuny. (Zveri vostochnoi Evropy i severnoi Asii)]. Program for Scientific Translations: Jerusalem, Israel 4:1–429.
Ohdachi, S. D., N. E. Dokuchaev, M. Hasegawa, and K. Masuda. 2001. Intraspecific phylogeny and geographical variation of six species of northeastern Asiatic *Sorex* shrews based on the mitochondrial cytochrome *b* sequences. *Molecular Ecology* 10: 2199–2213.
Ohdachi, S. D., M. A. Iwasa, V. A. Nesterenko, H. Abe, R. Masuda, and W. Haberl. 2004. Molecular phylogenetics of Crocidura shrews (Insectivora) in east and central Aisa. *Journal of Mammalogy* 85:396–403.
Ohdachi, S. D., R. Masuda, H. Abe, J. Adachi, N. E. Dokuchaev, V. Haukisalmi, and M. C. Yoshida. 1997b. Phylogeny of Eurasian soricine shrews (Insectivora, Mammalia) inferred from the mitochondrial cytochrome *b* gene sequences. *Zoological Science* 14: 527–532.
Ohdachi, S. D., R. Masuda, H. Abe, and N. E. Dokuchaev. 1997a. Biogeographical history of northeastern Asiatic soricine shrews (Insectivora, Mammalia). *Researches on Population Ecology* 39:157–162.
Okhotina, M. V. 1993. [Subspecies taxonomic revision of Far East shrews (Insectivora, *Sorex*) with the description of new subspecies]. *Trudy Zoologicheskogo Instituta* 242 [1991]:58–71 (in Russian).
Oli, M. K., and M. E. Rogers. 1996. Seasonal pattern in group size and population composition of blue sheep in Manang, Nepal. *Journal of Wildlife Management* 60:797–801.
Oliver, W. L. R., I. Brisbin, and S. Takahashi. 1993. The Eurasian wild pig (*Sus scrofa*). Pp. 112–121. In Pigs, Peccaries, and Hippos. W.L.R. Oliver, editor. IUCN: Gland, Switzerland.
Olson, K. A., T. K. Fuller, G. B. Schaller, D. Odonkhuu, and M. G. Murray. 2005. Estimating the population density of Mongolian gazelles *Procaptra gutturosa* by driving long-distance transects. *Oryx* 39:164–169.
Orlov, V. N., and N. Sh. Bulatova. 1983. [*Comparative Cytogenetics and Karyosystematics of Mammals*]. Nauka: Moscow (in Russian).
Orlov, V. N., and N. Davaa. 1975. [On the systematic position of the Alashan ground squirrel *Citellus alashanicus* Buch. (Sciuridae, Rodentia)]. Pp. 8–9. In Systematics and Cytogenetics of Mammals. V. N. Orlov, editor. Nauka: Moscow (in Russian).
Orlov, V. N., and V. M. Malygin. 1988. [A new species of hamster—*Cricetulus sokolovi* sp. n. (Rodentia, Cricetidae) from the People's Republic of Mongolia]. *Zoologicheskii Zhurnal* 67:304–308 (in Russian).
Osgood, W. H. 1932. *Mammals of the Kelley-Roosevelt and Delacour Asiatic Expedition.* Publication 312, Field Museum of Natural History, Zoological Series 18: 193–339.
Oshida, T., Y. Obara, L. K. Lin, and M. C. Yoshida. 2000. Comparison of banded karyotypes between two subspecies of the red and white giant flying squirrel *Petaurisa alborufus* (Mammalia, Rodentia). *Caryologia* 53:261–267.
Pan, R. L., Y. Z. Peng, Z. Z. Ye, H. Wang, and F. H. Yu. 1993. Classification and relationships of the macaque population on Hainan Island, China. *Folia Primatologica* 59:39–43.
Panteleyev, P. A. 2000. [*Species of the Fauna of Russia and Contiguous Countries. The Water Vole: Mode of the Species*]. Nauka: Moscow (in Russian).
Parr, J. W. K. 2003. *A Guide to the Large Mammals of Thailand.* Sarakadee Press: Bangkok.
Pasitschniak-Arts, M. 1993. Ursus arctos. *Mammalian Species* 439:1–10.
Pasitschniak-Arts, M., and S. Larivière. 1995. Gulo gulo. *Mammalian Species* 499:1–10.
Pavlinov, I. Ya., Yu. A. Dubrovsky, O. L. Rossolimo, and E. G. Potapova. 1990. [*Gerbils of the World*]. Nauka: Moscow (in Russian).
Pavlinov, I. Ya., and O. L. Rossolimo. 1987. [*Systematics of the Mammals of the USSR*]. Moscow University Press: Moscow (in Russian).
Pen, H. S., Y. T. Kao, C. K. Lu, Z. C. Feng, and C. X. Chen. 1962. [Report on mammals from southwestern Szechwan and northwestern Yunnan]. *Acta Zoologica Sinica* 14 (supplement):105–133 (in Chinese).
Peng, Y. Z., R. L. Pan, F. H. Yu, Z. Z. Ye, and H. Wang. 1993. [Cranial comparison between the populations of rhesus monkeys (*Macaca mulatta*) distributed in China and India]. *Acta Theriologica Sinica* 13:1–10, 24 (in Chinese).
Peng, Y. Z., Z. Z. Ye, Y. P. Zhang, and R. L. Pan. 1988. [The classification of snub-nosed monkey (*Rhinopithecus*

spp.) based on gross morphological characters]. *Zoological Research* 9:239–248 (in Chinese).
Pfister, O. 2004. *Birds and Mammals of Ladakh*. Oxford University Press: New Delhi.
Phillips, C. J. 1967. A collection of bats from Laos. *Journal of Mammalogy* 48:633–636.
Phillips, W. W. A. 1980. *Manual of the Mammals of Sri Lanka*. Part I. Wildlife and Nature Protection Society of Sri Lanka: Colombo.
Piao, R. 1989. [Surveying the abundance of Tibetan sand fox in Tibet]. *Chinese Wildlife* 6:22–26 (in Chinese).
Piao, R. Z., G. S. Guan, and M. H. Zhang. 1995. [Population size and distribution of Moose in China]. *Acta Theriologica Sinica* 15:11–16 (in Chinese).
Pocock, R. I. 1929. Tigers. *Journal of the Bombay Natural History Society* 33:505–541.
——. 1931. The black and brown bears of Europe and Asia. Part I. European and Asiatic representatives of the brown bear. *Journal of the Bombay Natural History Society* 35:771–823.
——. 1932. The black and brown bears of Europe and Asia. Part II. The sloth bear (*Melursus*), the Himalayan black bear (*Selenarctos*) and the Malayan bear (*Helarctos*). *Journal of the Bombay Natural History Society* 36:101–138.
——. 1933. The civet-cats of Asia. *Journal of the Bombay Natural History Society* 36:421–449.
——. 1939. The Fauna of British India, including Ceylon and Burma. Mammalia. Vol. I. *Primates and Carnivora (in part), Families Felidae and Viverridae*. Taylor & Francis: London.
——. 1941. *The Fauna of British India, including Ceylon and Burma*. Mammalia. Vol. II. *Carnivora (Suborders Aeluroidae (part) and Arctoidae)*. Taylor & Francis: London.
——. 1951. *Catalogue of the Genus Felis*. British Museum (Natural History): London.
Pohle, H. 1919. Die Unterfamilie der Lutrinae. *Archiv für Naturgeschichte* 85A:1–247.
Poyarkov, A., and N. Ovsyanikov. 2004. Corsac. Pp. 142–148. In *Canids: Foxes, Wolves, Jackals and Dogs: Status Survey and Conservation Action Plan*. C. Sillero-Zubiri, M. Hoffmann, and D. Macdonald, editors. IUCN: Gland, Switzerland.
Prakash, I., P. Singh, and A. Saravanan. 1995a. Small mammals of the Abu Hill, Aravalli Ranges in Rajasthan, India. A comprehensive taxonomic and ecological study. *Journal of Pure and Applied Zoology* 5:55–64.
——. 1995b. Ecological distribution of small mammals in the Aravalli Ranges. *Proceedings of the Indian Natural Science Academy* 61B:137–148.
Prater, S. H. 1971. *The Book of Indian Animals*, third edition. Bombay Natural History Society: Bombay.
——. 1980. *The Book of Indian Animals*, third edition, corrected. Bombay Natural History Society: Bombay.
Qi, X. G., B. G. Li, C. L. Tan, and Y. F. Gao. 2004. [Spatial structure in a Sichuan golden snub-nosed monkey *Rhinopithecus roxellana* group in Qingling Mountains while being in no-locomotion]. *Acta Zoologica Sinica* 50:697–705 (in Chinese).
Qian, Y. W., J. Zhang, S. Wang, B. L. Zheng, G. X. Guan, and X. Z. Shen. 1965. [*Birds and Mammals of Southern Xinjiang*]. Science Press: Beijing. (in Chinese).
Qin, C Y. 1984. [An investigation of ecology of gerbil]. *Acta Theriologica Sinica* 4:43–51 (in Chinese).
——. 1991. [On the faunistics and regionalization of glires in Ningxia Autonomous Region]. *Acta Theriologica Sinica* 11:143–151 (in Chinese).
Qu, W., Y. Zhang, M. David, and C. H. Southwick. 1993. Rhesus monkey (*Macaca mulatta*) in the Taihang Mountains, Jiyuan County, Henan China. *International Journal of Primatology* 14:607–621.
Qui, Y. H. 1989. [A systematic cluster for the Chinese cape hare, *Lepus capensis*]. *Acta Theriologica Sinica* 9:168–172 (in Chinese).
Rabinowitz, A. R. 1989. The density and behavior of large cats in a dry tropical forest mosaic in Huai Kha Khaeng Wildlife Sanctuary, Thailand. *Natural History Bulletin of the Siam Society* 37:235–251.
——. 1990. Notes on the behavior and movements of leopard cats, *Felis bengalensis*, in a dry tropical forest mosaic in Thailand. *Biotropica* 22:397–403.
——. 1991. Behaviour and movements of sympatric civet species in Huai Kha Khaeng Wildlife Sanctuary, Thailand. *Journal of Zoology*, London, 223:281–298.
——. 1999. Notes on the rare red goral (*Naemorhedus baileyi*) of north Myanmar. *Mammalia* 63:119–123.
Rabinowitz, A. R., P. Andau, and P. P. K. Chai. 1987. The clouded leopard in Malaysian Borneo. *Oryx* 21: 107–111.
Rabinowitz, A. R., and S. R. Walker. 1991. The carnivore community in a dry tropical forest mosaic in Huai Kha Khaeng Wildlife Sanctuary, Thailand. *Journal of Tropical Ecology* 7:37–47.
Ragni, B., and E. Randi. 1986. Multivariate analysis of craniometric characters in European wild cat, domestic cat, and African wild cat (genus *Felis*). *Zeitschrift für Säugetierkunde* 51:243–251.
Rajan, K. E., and G. Marimuthu. 1999. Localization of prey by the Indian false vampire bat, *Megaderma lyra*. *Mammalia* 63:149–158.
Rand, A. L. 1935. On the habits of some Madagascar mammals. *Journal of Mammalogy* 16:89–104.
Rathore, F. S., and V. Thapar. 1984. Behavioral observations of leopard and jungle cat in Ranthambhor National Park and Tiger Reserve, Rajasthan. Pp 136–139. In *The Plight of the Cats: Proceedings of the Meeting and Workshop of the IUCN/SSC Cat Specialist Group at Kanha National Park, Madhya Pradesh, India, 9–12 April 1984*. IUCN/SSC Cat Specialist Group: Bougy-Villars, Switzerland.
Rayfield, D. 1976. *The Dream of Lhasa: The Life of Nikolay Przhevalsky (1839–88) Explorer of Central Asia*. Ohio University Press.
Reading, R. P., H. M. Mix, B. Lhagvasuren, C. Feh, D. P. Kane, S. Dulamtseren, and S. Enkhbold. 2001. Status and distribution of khulan (*Equus hemionus*) in Mongolia. *Journal of Zoology*, London, 254:381–389.
Reeves, R. B., and N. J. Gales. 2006. Realities of Baiji conservation. *Conservation Biology* 20:626–628.
Reeves, R. B., B. D. Smith, E. A. Crespo, and G. Notabartolo di Sciara. 2003. *Dolphins, Whales and Porpoises: 2002–2010 Conservation Action Plan for the World's Cetaceans*. IUCN: Gland, Switzerland.
Reid, D. G., and J. Gong. 1999. Giant Panda Conservation Action Plan. Pp. 241–254. In *Bears: Status Survey and*

Conservation Action Plan. C. Servheen, S. Herrero, and B. Peyton, editors. IUCN: Gland, Switzerland.

Reijnders, P., S. Brasseur, J. van der Toorn, P. van der Wolf, I. Boyd, J. Harwood, D. Lavigne, and L. Lowry. 1993. *Seals, Fur Seals, Sea Lions, and Walrus: Status Survey and Conservation Action Plan*. IUCN: Gland, Switzerland.

Repenning, C. A. 1967. Subfamilies and genera of the Soricidae. *Geological Survey Professional Paper* 565: 1–74.

Rice, D. W. 1998. Marine mammals of the world: systematics and distribution. *Society for Marine Mammalogy, Special Publication* 4:1–230.

Richarz, K., and A. Limbrunner. 1993. *The World of Bats*. TFH Publications: Neptune, NJ.

Roberts, M. S., and J. L. Gittleman. 1984. Ailurus fulgens. *Mammalian Species* 222:1–8.

Roberts, T. J. 1977. *The Mammals of Pakistan*. Ernest Benn Limited: London.

——. 1997. *The Mammals of Pakistan* (revised edition). Oxford University Press: Oxford.

Robinson, M. F. 1995. A relationship between echolocation calls and noseleaf widths in bats of the genera *Rhinolophus* and *Hipposideros*. *Journal of Zoology*, London, 239:389–393.

Robinson, M. F., S. Bumrungsri, and J. E. Hill. 1996. Chiroptera from Thung Yai Naresuan and Huai Kha Khaeng Wildlife Sanctuaries. *Natural History Bulletin of the Siam Society* 44:243–247.

Robinson, M. F., P. D. Jenkins, C. M. Francis, and A. J. C. Fulford. 2003. A new species of the *Hipposideros pratti* group (Chiroptera, Hipposideridae) from Lao PDR and Vietnam. *Acta Chiropterologica* 5:31–48.

Rodrigues, A. S. L., J. D. Pilgrim, J. F. Lamoreux, M. Hoffmann, and T. M. Brooks. 2006. The value of the IUCN Red List for conservation. In *Trends in Ecology and Evolution* 21: 71–76.

Rogovin, K. A. 1992. Habitat use by two species of Mongolian marmots (*Marmota sibirica* and *M. baibacina*) in a zone of sympatry. *Acta Theriologica* 37:345–350.

Rogovin, K. A., E. J. Heske, and G. I. Shenbrot. 1996. Patterns of social organization and behaviour of *Pygeretmus pumilio* Kerr, 1792 (Dipodidae, Rodentia): radiotelemetry study in the Dagestan desert, Russia. *Journal of Arid Environments* 33:355–366.

Roos, C., and T. Geissmann. 2001. Molecular phylogeny of the major hylobatid divisions. *Molecular Phylogenetics and Evolution* 19:486–494.

Rosevear, D. R. 1974. *The Carnivores of West Africa*. Trustees of the British Museum (Natural History): London.

Ross, P. D. 1988. The taxonomic status of *Cansumys canus* (Rodentia, Cricetinae). Abstract. In *Symposium of Asian-Pacific Mammalogy*. A. T. Smith, R. S. Hoffmann, W. Z. Lidicker, Jr., and D. A. Schlitter, editors. American Society of Mammalogists and Mammalogical Society of China: Huirou, Beijing.

Ross, P. D. 1994. Phodopus roborovskii. *Mammalian Species* 459:1–4.

Ross, P. D. 1995. Phodopus campbelli. *Mammalian Species* 503:1–7.

Rossolimo, O. L. 1989. [Revision of Royle's high-mountain vole *Alticola* (*A.*) *argentatus* (Mammalia: Cricetidae)]. *Zoologicheskii Zhurnal* 68:104–114 (in Russian).

Rossolimo, O. L., and I. Ya. Pavlinov. 1992. Species and subspecies of *Alticola* s. str. (Rodentia: Arvicolidae). Pp. 149–176. In Prague Studies in Mammalogy. I. Horáček and V. Vohralik, editors. Charles University Press: Prague.

Rossolimo, O. L., I. Ya. Pavlinov, and R. S. Hoffmann. 1994. Systematics and distribution of the rock voles of the subgenus *Alticola* S. Str. in the People's Republic of China (Rodentia: Arvicolinae). *Acta Theriologica Sinica* 14:86–99.

Rozhnov, V. V., and A.V. Abramov. 2006. Sexual dimorphism of marbled polecat *Vormela peregusna* (Carnivora: Mustelidae). *Biology Bulletin* 33:144–148.

Ruan, X. D., P. J. He, J. L. Zhang, Q. H. Wan, and S. G. Fang. 2005. Evolutionary history and current population relationships of the Chiru (*Panthelops hodgsonii*) inferred from mtDNA variation. *Journal of Mammalogy* 86:881–886.

Ruedi, M., M. Chapuisat, and D. Iskandar. 1994. Taxonomic status of *Hylomys parvus* and *Hylomys suillus* (Insectivora: Erinaceidae): Biochemical and morphological analyses. *Journal of Mammalogy* 75:965–978.

Ruedi, M., C. Courvoisier, P. Vogel, and F. M. Catzeflis. 1996. Genetic differentiation and zoogegraphy of Asian *Suncus murinus* (Mammalia: Soricidae). *Biological Journal of the Linnean Society* 57:307–316.

Ruedi, M., and L. Fumagalli. 1996. Genetic structure of gymnures (genus *Hylomys*; Erinaceidae) on continental islands of southeast Asia: Historic effects of fragmentation. *Journal of Zoological Systematics and Evolutionary Research* 34:153–162.

Ruedi, M., and F. Mayer. 2001. Molecular systematics of bats of the genus *Myotis* (Vespertilionidae) suggests deterministic ecomorphological convergences. *Molecular Phylogenetics and Evolution* 21:436–448.

Ruedi, M., and P. Vogel. 1995. Chromosomal evolution and zoogeographic origin of southeast Asian shrews (genus *Crocidura*). *Experientia* 51:174–178.

Rydell, J. 1993. Eptesicus nilssonii. *Mammalian Species* 430:1–7.

Ryder, O. A. 1993. Przewalski's horse: Prospects for reintroduction into the wild. *Conservation Biology* 7:13–15.

Sacchi, O., and A. Meriggi. 1995. Habitat requirements of the stone marten (*Martes foina*) on the Tyrrhenian slopes of the Northern Apennines. *Hystrix* 7:99–104.

Saiful, A. A., A. H. Idris, Y. N. Rashid, N. Tamura, and F. Hayashi. 2001. Home range size of sympatric squirrel species inhabiting a lowland dipterocarp forest in Malaysia. *Biotropica* 33:346–351.

Sanborn, C. C. 1939. Eight new bats of the genus *Rhinolophus*. *Field Museum of Natural History, Zoological Series* 24:37–43.

——. 1952. The status of "*Triaenops wheeleri*" Osgood. *Chicago Academy of Sciences, Natural History Miscellanea* 97:1–3.

Santiapillai, C., and K. R. Ashby. 1988. The clouded leopard in Sumatra. *Oryx* 22:44–45.

Santiapillai, C., and P. Jackson. 1990. *The Asian Elephant: An Action Plan for Its Conservation*. IUCN: Gland, Switzerland.

Satunin, K. A. 1914. [Guide to the mammals of Imperial Russia]. *Tiflis* 1:1–410 (in Russian).

Schackleton, D. M. 1997. *Wild Sheep and Goats and Their Relatives: Status Survey and Conservation Action Plan for Caprinae*. IUCN: Gland, Switzerland.

Schafer, E. H. 1963. The Golden Peaches of Samarkand: A Study of T'ang Exotics. University of California Press: Berkeley.

Schaller, G. B. 1967. *The Deer and the Tiger*. University of Chicago Press: Chicago.

——. 1977. *Mountain Monarchs: Wild Sheep and Goats of the Himalaya*. University of Chicago Press: Chicago.

——. 1993. *The Last Panda*. University of Chicago Press: Chicago.

——. 1998. *Wildlife of the Tibetan Steppe*. University of Chicago Press: Chicago.

Schaller, G. B., and J. R. Ginsberg. 2004. Tibetan fox. Pp. 148–151. In *Canids: Foxes, Wolves, Jackals and Dogs: Status Survey and Conservation Action Plan*. C. Sillero-Zubiri, M. Hoffmann, and D. Macdonald, editors. IUCN: Gland, Switzerland.

Schaller, G. B., and B. Gu. 1994. Comparative ecology of ungulates in the Aru basin of northwest Tibet. *National Geographic Research* 10:266–293.

Schaller, G. B., J. C. Hu, W. S. Pan, and J. Zhu. 1985. *The Giant Pandas of Wolong*. University of Chicago Press: Chicago.

Schaller, G. B., H. T. Li, J. Ren, and M. Qiu. 1988a. Distribution of snow leopard in Xinjiang, China. *Oryx* 22:197–204.

Schaller, G. B., and W. L. Liu. 1996. Distribution, status, and conservation of wild yak *Bos grunniens*. *Biological Conservation* 76:1–8.

Schaller, G. B., W. L. Liu, and X. M. Wang. 1996. Status of Tibet red deer. *Oryx* 30:269–274.

Schaller, G. B., J. R. Ren, and M. J. Qiu. 1988b. Status of the snow leopard *Panthera uncia* in Qinghai and Gansu provinces, China. *Biological Conservation* 45:179–194.

——. 1991. Observations on the Tibetan antelope *Pantholops hodgsoni*. *Applied Animal Behavioral Science* 29:361–378.

Schaller, G. B., Q. T. Teng, W. S. Pan, Z. S. Qin, X. M. Wang, J. C. Hu, and H. M. Shen. 1986. Feeding behavior of Sichuan takin *(Budorcas taxicolor)*. *Mammalia* 50: 311–22.

Schmidt, S., S. Hanke, and J. Pillat. 2000. The role of echolocation in hunting terrestrial prey—new evidence for an underestimated strategy in the gleaning bat, *Megaderma lyra*. *Journal of Comparative Physiology* 186:975–988.

Schreiber, A., R. Wirth, M. Riffel, and H. van Rompaey. 1989. *Weasels, Civets, Mongooses and Their Relatives: An Action Plan for the Conservation of Mustelids and Viverrids*. IUCN: Gland, Switzerland.

Section of Mammalogy, Institute of Zoology, Chinese Academy of Sciences. 1958. [*Report on Mammalian Survey in Northeastern China*]. Science Press: Beijing (in Chinese).

Seidensticker, J., and C. McDougal. 1993. Tiger predatory behaviour, ecology and conservation. *Symposium of the Zoological Society of London* 65:105–125.

Servheen, C. 1993. The sun bear. Pp. 124–127. In *Bears: Majestic Creatures of the Wild*. I. Stirling, editor. Rodale Press: Emmaus, PA.

——. 1999. Sun bear conservation action plan. Pp. 219–224. In *Bears: Status Survey and Conservation Action Plan*. C. Servheen, S. Herrero, and B. Peyton, editors. IUCN: Gland, Switzerland.

Servheen, C., S. Herrero, and B. Peyton (editors). 1999. *Bears: Status Survey and Conservation Action Plan*. IUCN: Gland, Switzerland.

Setoguchi, M. 1991. Nest site selection and nest building behavior of red-bellied tree squirrels on Tomogashima Island, Japan. *Journal of Mammalogy* 72:163–170.

Severtzov, M. N. 1857–1858. Notice sur la classification multiseriale des Carnivores, specialement des Felides, et les etudes de zoologie generale que s'y rattachment. *Revue et Magasin de Zoologie*, ser. 2, 9:387–391; 433–439; 10:3–8; 145–150; 193–196.

Shah, N. 2002. Status and action plan for the Kiang (*Equus kiang*). Pp. 72–81. In *Equids: Zebras, Asses and Horses: Status Survey and Conservation Action Plan*. P. D. Moehlman, editor. IUCN: Gland, Switzerland.

Shariff, S. M. 1984. Some observations on otters at Kuala Gula, Perak, and National Park, Pahang. *Journal of Wildlife and Parks* 3:75–88.

Shaughnessy, P. D., and F. H. Fay. 1977. A review of the taxonomy and nomenclature of north Pacific harbour seals. *Journal of Zoology*, London, 182:385–419.

Sheffield, S. R., and C. M. King. 1994. Mustela nivalis. *Mammalian Species* 454:1–10.

Shen, L. T., L. R. Lu, and F. Z. Zeng. 1988. [*Distribution List of Land Vertebrates of Guangxi: Mammalia*]. Guangxi Normal University Press: Guilin (in Chinese).

Sheng, H. L. 1982. [Daily rhythmic behavior of the Chinese ferret badger]. *Acta Theriologica Sinica* 2:132 (in Chinese).

——. 1998a. *Catopuma temmincki*. Pp. 93–95. In *China Red Data Book of Endangered Animals. Mammalia*. S. Wang, editor. Science Press: Beijing (in Chinese and English).

——. 1998b. *Mustela strigidorsa*. Pp. 151–152. In *China Red Data Book of Endangered Animals. Mammalia*. S. Wang, editor. Science Press: Beijing (in Chinese and English).

Sheng, H. L., and H. J. Lu. 1980. Current studies on the rare Chinese black muntjac. *Journal of Natural History* 14:803–807.

——. 1982. [Distribution, habits and resource status of the tufted deer (*Elaphodus cepholophus*)]. *Acta Zoologica Sinica* 28:307–310 (in Chinese).

Sheng, H. L., and N. Ohtaishi. 1993. The status of the deer in China. Pp. 1–11. In *Deer of China: Biology and Management*. N. Ohtaishi and H. L. Sheng, editors. Elsevier: Amsterdam.

Sheng, H. L., N. Ohtaishi, and H. J. Lu. 1999. *The Mammalian of China*. China Forestry Publishing House: Beijing.

Sheng, H. L., H. F. Xu, and E. D. Zhang. 1990. [Xinjiang beaver and castorium]. *Acta Theriologica Sinica* 10:263–267 (in Chinese).

Shinohara, A., K. L. Campbell, and H. Suzuki. 2003. Molecular phylogenetic relationships of moles, shrew moles, and desmans from the new and old worlds. *Molecular Phylogenetics and Evolution* 27:247–258.

Shoshani, J. 2005. Order Proboscidea. Pp. 90–91. In *Mammal Species of the World*, third edition. D. E. Wilson and D. M. Reeder, editors. Johns Hopkins University Press: Baltimore.

Shou, Z. H. 1936. [*The Birds of Hopei Province*]. 2 vols. Fan Memorial Institute of Biology: Peking [Beijing] (in Chinese).

—— (editor). 1962. [*Economic Fauna of China: Mammals*]. Science Press: Beijing (in Chinese).

Shrestha, T. K. 1981. *Wildlife of Nepal*. Bimala Shrestha: Kathmandu, Nepal.

Shubin, I. G. 1972. Reproduction and numbers of steppe lemming in northern Balkhash area. *Soviet Journal of Ecology* 3:450–452.

——. 1974. [Ecology of *Lagurus luteus* in the Zaisan Hollow]. *Zoologicheskii Zhurnal* 53:272–277 (in Russian).

Sidorov, G. N., and A. D. Botvinkin. 1987. [Corsac fox (*Vulpes corsac*) in southern Siberia]. *Zoologicheskii Zhurnal* 66:914–927 (in Russian).

Sillero-Zubiri, C., M. Hoffmann, and D. W. Macdonald (editors). 2004. *Canids: Foxes, Wolves, Jackals and Dogs: Status Survey and Conservation Action Plan*. IUCN: Gland, Switzerland.

Simmons, N. B. 2005. Order Chiroptera. Pp. 312–529. In *Mammal Species of the World*, third edition. D. E. Wilson and D. M. Reeder, editors. Johns Hopkins University Press: Baltimore.

Sinha, Y. P. 1999. Contribution to the knowledge of bats (Mammalia; Chiroptera) of North East Hills, India. *Records of the Zoological Survey of India*, Occasional Papers 174:1–52.

Smith, A. L., M. F. Robinson, and M. Webber. 1998. Notes on a collection of shrews (Insectivora: Soricidae) from Lao PDR. *Mammalia* 62:585–588.

Smith, A. T., and J. M. Foggin. 1999. The plateau pika (*Ochotona curzoniae*) is a keystone species for biodiversity on the Tibetan plateau. *Animal Conservation* 2:235–240.

Smith, A. T., A. N. Formozov, R. S. Hoffmann, C. L. Zheng, and M. A. Erbajeva. 1990. The pikas. Pp. 14–60. In *Rabbits, Hares and Pikas: Status Survey and Conservation Action Plan*. J. A. Chapman and J.E.C. Flux, editors. IUCN/WWF: Gland, Switzerland.

Smith, A. T., H. J. Smith, X. G. Wang, X. C. Yin, and J. X. Liang. 1986. Social behavior of the steppe-dwelling black-lipped pika (*Ochotona curzoniae*). *Acta Theriologica Sinica* 6:13–43 (in Chinese and English).

Smith, A. T., and X. G. Wang. 1991. Social relationships of adult black-lipped pikas (*Ochotona curzoniae*). *Journal of Mammalogy* 72:231–247.

Smorkatcheva, A. V. 1999. The social organization of the mandarin vole *Lasiopodomys mandarinus*, during the reproductive period. *Zeitschrift für Säugetierkunde* 64:344–355.

Sokolov, V. E. 1974. Saiga tatarica. *Mammalian Species* 38:1–4.

Sokolov, V. E., and N. V. Bashenina (editors). 1994. [*Species of the Fauna of Russia and the Contiguous Countries. Common Vole, the Sibling Species: Microtus arvalis Pallis, 1779, M. rossiaemeridionalis Ognev, 1924*]. Nauka: Moscow (in Russian).

Sokolov, V. E., and A. A. Lushchekina. 1997. Procapra gutturosa. *Mammalian Species* 571:1–5.

Sokolov, V. E., and V. N. Orlov. 1980. [*Guide to the Mammals of the Mongolian People's Republic*]. Nauka: Moscow (in Russian).

Sokolov, V. E., O. L. Rossolimo, I. Ya. Pavlinov, and O. I. Podtyazhkin. 1981. [Comparative characteristics of two species of jerboas from Mongolia–*Allactaga bullata* Allen, 1925 and *A. nataliae* Sokolov, 1981]. *Zoologicheskii Zhurnal* 60:895–906 (in Russian).

Song, K., and R. T. Liu. 1984. [The ecology of midday gerbil (*Meriones meridanus* Pallas)]. *Acta Theriologica Sinica* 4:291–300 (in Chinese).

Song, S. 1985. [A new subspecies of *Cricetulus triton* from Shaanxi, China]. *Acta Theriologica Sinica* 5: 137–139 (in Chinese).

Song, Y. L. 1993. Diurnal activity rhythms of Eld's deer on Hainan Island, China. Pp. 214–219. In *Deer of China: Biology and Management*. N. Ohtaishi and H. L. Sheng, editors. Elsevier: Amsterdam.

Sowerby, A. de C. 1933. The rodents and lagomorphs of China. *The China Journal* 19:189–207.

Stager, K. E. 1949. Notes on the mammal of Kweichow Province, China. *Journal of Mammalogy* 30:68–71.

Stanhope, M. J., V. G. Waddell, O. Madsen, W. de Jong, S. B. Hedges, G. C. Cleven, D. Kao, and M. Springer. 1998. Molecular evidence for multiple origins of Insectivora and for a new order of endemic African insectivore mammals. *Proceedings of the National Academy of Science* 95:9967–9972.

Stein, B. R. 2000. Morphology of subterranean rodents. Pp. 19–61. In *Life Underground: The Biology of Subterranean Rodents*. E. A. Lacey, J. L. Patton, and G. Cameron, editors. University of Chicago Press: Chicago.

Steppan, S. J., R. Adkins, and J. Anderson. 2004. Phylogeny and divergence-date estimates of rapid radiations in Muroid rodents based on multiple nuclear genes. *Systematic Biology* 53:533–553.

Steppan, S. J., M. R. Akhverdyan, E. A. Lyapunova, D. G. Fraser, N. N. Vorontsov, R. S. Hoffmann, and M. J. Braun. 1999. Molecular phylogeny of the marmots (Rodentia: Sciuridae): tests of evolutionary and biogeographic hypotheses. *Systematic Biology* 48: 715–734.

Steppan, S. J., B. L. Storz, and R. S. Hoffmann. 2004. Nuclear DNA phylogeny of the squirrels (Mammalia: Rodentia) and the evolution of arboreality from c-myc and RAG1. *Molecular Phylogenetics and Evolution* 30:703–719.

Sterndale, R. M. 1992. *Natural History of the Mammalia of India and Ceylon*, new unabridged edition. Himalayan Books: New Delhi.

Stone, K. D., and J. A. Cook. 2002. Molecular evolution of Holarctic martens (genus *Martes*, Mammalia: Carnivora: Mustelidae). *Molecular Phylogenetics and Evolution* 24:169–179.

Stone, R. D. (compiler). 1995. *Eurasian Insectivores and Tree Shrews: Status Survey and Conservation Action Plan*. IUCN: Gland, Switzerland.

Storz, J. F., and T. H. Kunz. 1999. Cynopterus sphinx. *Mammalian Species* 613:1–8.

Storz, J. F., and W. C. Wozencraft. 1999. Melogale moschata. *Mammalian Species* 631:1–4.

Strelkov, P. P. 1972. [*Myotis blythi* (Tomes, 1857): Distribution, geographical variability and differences from *Myotis myotis* (Borkhausen, 1797)]. *Acta Theriologica* 17:355–380 (in Russian).

——. 1986. [The Gobi bat (*Eptesicus gobiensis* Bobrinskii 1926), a new species of chiropteran of the Palearctic fauna]. *Zoologicheskii Zhurnal* 65:1103–1108 (in Russian).

Stroganov, S. U. 1962. [*Animals of Siberia. Carnivores*]. Akademii Nauk SSSR: Moscow (in Russian). English translation (1969) Program for Scientific Translations, Jerusalem, Israel [available from the U.S. Dept. of Commerce, Clearinghouse for Federal Scientific and Technical Information, Springfield, VA. TT 68-50349].

Su, B., Y. X. Fu, Y. X. Wang, J. Li, and R. Chakraborty. 2001. Genetic diversity and population history of the red panda *Ailurus fulgens* as inferred from mitochondrial DNA sequence variations. *Molecular Biology and Evolution* 18:1070–1076.

Su, B., Y. X. Wang, H. Lan, W. Wang, and Y. P. Zhang. 1999. Phylogenetic study of complete cytochrome *b* gene in musk deer (Genus *Moschus*) using museum samples. *Molecular Phylogenetics and Evolution* 12:241–249.

Su, J. P. 2001. [A Comparative Study on the Habitat Selection of Plateau Pika (*Ochotona curzoniae*) and Gansu Pika (*Ochotona cansus*)]. Ph.D. thesis, Northwest Plateau Institute of Biology; Xining, Qinghai (in Chinese).

Sugiyama, Y. 1965. On the social change of Hanuman Langurs (*Presbytis entellus*) in their natural condition. *Primates* 6:381–418.

Sukumar, R. 1989. *The Asian Elephant: Ecology and Management*. Cambridge University Press: Cambridge.

Sulkava, S. 1990. *Sorex caecutiens* Laxmann, 1788–Maskenspitzmaus; *Sorex isodon* Turov, 1924–Taigaspitzmaus. Pp. 215–236. In *Handbuch der Säugetiere Europas*. J. Niethammer and F. Krapp, editors. Aula-Verlag: Wiesbaden.

Sunquist, M. E. 1981. The social organization of tigers (*Panthera tigris*) in Royal Chitawan National Park, Nepal. *Smithsonian Contributions to Zoology* 336:1–98.

Sunquist, M., and F. Sunquist. 2003. *Wild Cats of the World*. University of Chicago Press: Chicago.

Suzuki, H., J. J. Sato, K. Tsuchiya, J. Luo, Y. P. Zhang, Y. X. Wang, and X. L. Jiang. 2003. Molecular phylogeny of wood mice (*Apodemus*, Muridae) in East Asia. *Biological Journal of the Linnaean Society* 80:469–481.

Swinhoe, R. 1862. Note on a species allied to *Kerivoula formosa*. *Proceedings of the Zoological Society of London* 1862:356.

——. 1862 [1863]. On the mammals of the island of Formosa (China). *Proceedings of the Zoological Society of London* 1862:347–356.

Tamura, N. 1995. Postcopulatory mate guarding by vocalization in the Formosan squirrel. *Behavioral Ecology and Sociobiology* 36:377–386.

Tan, C. L., and J. H. Drake. 2001. Evidence of tree gouging and exudate eating in pygmy slow lorises (*Nycticebus pygmaeus*). *Folia Primatologica* 72:37–39.

Tate, G. H. H. 1942. Review of the vespertilionine bats, with special attention to genera and species of the Archbold collections. *Bulletin of the American Museum of Natural History* 80:221–297.

——. 1947. *Mammals of Eastern Asia*. MacMillan: New York.

Taylor, F. H. C., M. Fujinaga, and F. Wilke. 1955. *Distribution and Food Habits of the Fur Seals of the North Pacific Ocean; Report of Cooperative Investigations by the Governments of Canada, Japan, and the United States of America, February–July 1952*. United States Fish and Wildlife Service: Washington, DC.

Taylor, M. E., and J. Matheson. 1999. A craniometric comparison of the African and Asian mongooses in the genus *Herpestes* (Carnivora: Herpestidae). *Mammalia* 63:449–464.

Thomas, J. W., and D. E. Toweill. 1982. *Elk of North America: Ecology and Management*. Stackpole Books: Harrisburg, PA.

Thomas, N. M. 2000. Morphological and mitochondrial-DNA variation in *Rhinolophus rouxii* (Chiroptera). *Bonner Zoologisches Beitragen* 49:1–18.

Thomas, O. 1908. The Duke of Bedford's zoological exploration in eastern Asia. X. List of mammals from the provinces of Chih-li and Shan-si, northern China. *Proceedings of the Zoological Society of London*: 635–646.

——. 1909. A collection of mammals from northern and central Manchuria. *Annals and Magazine of Natural History*, Series 8, Vol. 4:500–505.

——. 1911. Mammals collected in the provinces of Kansu and Sze-chewan, western China, by Mr. Malcom Anderson, for the Duke of Bedford's exploration of eastern Asia. *Abstracts of the Proceedings of the Zoological Society of London* 90:3–5.

——. 1912a. Two new Asiatic Voles. *Annals and Magazine of Natural History*, Series 8, Vol. 9:348–350.

——. 1912b. On mammals from central Asia, collected by Mr. Douglas Carruthers. *Annals and Magazine of Natural History*, Series 8, Vol. 9:391–408.

——. 1912c. On Insectivores and Rodents collected by Mr. F. Kingdon Ward in N.W. Yunnan. *Annals and Magazine of Natural History*, Series 8, Vol. 9:513–519.

——. 1912d. On a collection of small mammals from the Tsin-ling Mountains, Central China, presented by Mr. G. Fenwick Owen to the National Museum. *Annals and Magazine of Natural History*, Series 8, Vol. 10: 395–403.

——. 1921. On small mammals from the Kachin Province, Northern Burma. *Journal of the Bombay Natural History Society* 27:499–505.

——. 1922a. On mammals from the Unnan highlands collected by Mr. George Forrest and presented to the British Museum by Col. Stephenson R. Clarke, D.S.O. *Annals and Magazine of Natural History*, Series 9, Vol. 10:391–406.

——. 1922b. On some new forms of *Ochotona*. *Annals and Magazine of Natural History*, Series 9, Vol. 9: 187–193.

——. 1923. On mammals from the Li-kiang Range, Yunnan, being a further collection obtained by Mr. George Forrest. *Annals and Magazine of Natural History*, Series 9, Vol. 11:655–663.

——. 1929. A new mole from Western Siam. *Annals and Magazine of Natural History* 3:206–207.

Thomas, O., and M. A. C. Hinton. 1922. The mammals of the 1921 Mount Everest expedition. *Annals and Magazine of Natural History*, Series 9, Vol. 9:178–186.

Thorington, R. W., Jr., D. Pitassy, and S. A. Jansa. 2002. Phylogenies of flying squirrels (Pteromyinae). *Journal of Mammalian Evolution* 9:99–135.

Thorington, R. W., and R. S. Hoffmann. 2005. Family Sciuridae. Pp. 754–818. In *Mammal Species of the World*, third edition. D. E. Wilson and D. M. Reeder, editors. Johns Hopkins University Press: Baltimore.

Thonglongya, K. 1973. First record of *Rhinolophus paradoxolophus* (Bourret, 1951) from Thailand, with the description of a new species of the *Rhinolophus philippensis* group (Chiroptera: Rhinolophidae). *Mammalia* 37:587–597.

Tikader, B. K. 1983. *Threatened Animals of India*. Zoological Survey of India: Calcutta.

Tiler, C., M. Evans, C. Heardman, and S. Houghton. 1989. Diet of the smooth Indian otter (*Lutra perspicillata*) and of fish eating birds; a field survey. *Journal of the Bombay Natural History Society* 86:65–70.

Tilson, R., D. F. Hu, J. Muntifering, and P. J. Nyhus. 2004. Dramatic decline of wild South China tigers *Panthera tigris amoyensis*: Field survey of priority tiger reserves. *Oryx* 38:40–47.

Tilson, R., K. Traylor-Holzer and M. Qiu. 1997. The decline and impending extinction of the South China tiger. *Oryx* 31:243–252.

Timmis, W. H. 1971. Observations on breeding the oriental short-clawed otter *Amblonyx cinerea* at Chester Zoo. *International Zoo Yearbook* 11:109–111.

Topál, G. 1970a. The first record of *Ia io* Thomas, 1902 in Vietnam and India, and some remarks on the taxonomic position of *Parascotomanes beaulieui* Bourret, 1942, *Ia longimana* Pen, 1962, and the genus *Ia* Thomas, 1902 (Chiroptera: Vespertilionidae). *Opuscula Zoologica*, Budapest, 10:341–347.

——. 1970b. On the systematic status of *Pipistrellus annectans* Dobson, 1871 and *Myotis primula* Thomas, 1920 (Chiroptera: Vespertilionidae). *Annales Historico-Naturales Musei Nationalis Hungarici*, Budapest, 62:373–379.

——. 1993. Taxonomic status of *Hipposideros larvatus alongensis* Bourret, 1942 and the occurrence of *H. turpis* Bangs, 1901 in Vietnam (Mammalia, Chiroptera). *Acta Zoologica Academiae Scientiarum Hungarica* 39:267–288.

——. 1997. A new mouse-eared bat species, from Nepal, with statistical analyses of some other species of subgenus *Leuconoe* (Chiroptera, Vespertilionidae). *Acta Zoologica Academiae Scientiarum Hungaricae* 43:375–402.

Tosi, A. J., J. C. Morales, and D. J. Melnick. 2000. Comparison of Y chromosome and mtDNA phylogenies leads to unique inferences of macaque evolutionary history. *Molecular Phylogenetics and Evolution* 17:133–144.

——. 2003. Paternal, maternal, and biparental molecular markers provide unique windows onto the evolutionary history of macaque monkeys. *Evolution* 57:1419–1435.

Trout, R. C. 1978. A review of studies on populations of wild harvest mice [*Micromys minutus* (Pallas)]. *Mammal Review* 8:143–58.

Tsytsulina, K. 2001. *Myotis ikonnikovi* (Chiroptera, Vespertilionidae) and its relationships with similar species. *Acta Chiropterologica* 3:11–19.

Tsytsulina, K., and P. P. Strelkov. 2001. Taxonomy of the *Myotis frater* species group (Vespertilionidae, Chiroptera). *Bonner Zoologische Beiträge* 50:15–26.

U Tun Yin. 1993. *Wild Mammals of Myanmar*. Forest Department: Yangon.

Van Peenen, P. F. D., P. F. Ryan, and R. H. Light. 1969. *Preliminary Identification Manual for Mammals of South Vietnam*. United States National Museum, Smithsonian Institution: Washington, DC.

van Zyll de Jong, C. G. 1972. A systematic review of the Nearctic and Neotropical river otters (genus *Lutra*, Mustelidae, Carnivora). *Royal Ontario Museum, Life Sciences, Contribution* 80:1–104.

——. 1983. A morphometric analysis of North American shrews of the *Sorex arcticus* group, with special consideration of the taxonomic status of *S. a. maritimensis*. *Nature Canada*, Quebec, 110:373–378.

——. 1987. A phylogenetic study of the Lutrinae (Carnivora; Mustelidae) using morphological data. *Canadian Journal of Zoology* 65:2536–2544.

——. 1991. A brief review of the systematics and a classification of the Lutrine. Pp. 79–83. In *Proceedings of the V International Otter Colloquium*. C. Reuther and R. Röchert, editors. Habitat 6: Hankensbüttel.

——. 1992. A morphometric analysis of cranial variation in Holarctic weasels (*Mustela nivalis*). *Zeitschrift für Säugeteirkunde* 57:77–93.

Venkataraman, A. B., and A. J. T. Johnsingh. 2004. The behavioural ecology of dholes in India. Pp. 323–356. In *The Biology and Conservation of Wild Canids*. D. W. Macdonald and C. Sillero-Zubiri, editors. Oxford University Press: Oxford.

Vereshchagin, N. K. 1959. [*The Mammals of the Caucasus: A history of the Evolution of the Fauna*]. Nauka: Moscow (in Russian). English translation (1967) Program for Scientific Translations: Jerusalem, Israel.

Veron, G., and S. Heard. 2000. Molecular systematics of the Asiatic Viverridae (Carnivora) inferred from mitochondrial cytochrome b sequence analysis. *Journal of Zoological Systematics and Evolutionary Research* 38:209–217.

Voigt, D. R. 1987. Red fox. Pp. 379–392. In *Wild Furbearer Management and Conservation in North America*. M. Nowak, J. A. Baker, M. E. Obbard, and B. Malloch, editors. Ontario Ministry of National Resources: Ontario.

Vorontsov, N. N., and E. Yu. Ivanitskaya. 1973. Comparative karyology of north Palaearctic pikas (*Ochotona*, Ochotonidae, Lagomorpha). *Caryologia* 26:213–223.

Waits, L. P., J. Sullivan, S. J. O'Brien, and R. H. Ward. 1999. Rapid radiation events in the Family Ursidae indicated by likelihood phylogenetic estimation from multiple fragments of mtDNA. *Molecular Phylogenetics and Evolution* 13:82–92.

Wakefield, S., J. Knowles, W. Zimmermann, and M. van Dierendonck. 2002. Status and action plan for the Przewalski's Horse (*Equus ferus przewalskii*). Pp. 82–92. In *Equids: Zebras, Asses and Horses: Status Survey and Conservation Action Plan*. P. D. Moehlman, editor. IUCN: Gland, Switzerland.

Wallin, L. 1969. The Japanese bat fauna. *Zoologiska Bidrage Fran Uppsala* 37:223–440.

Wang, D., X. F. Zhang, K. X. Wang, Z. Wei, B. Würsig, G. T. Braulik, and S. Ellis. 2006. Conservation of the Baiji: No simple solution. *Conservation Biology* 20:623–625.

Wang, F. 1985a. [Preliminary study of the ecology of *Trogopterus xanthipes*]. *Acta Theriologica Sinica* 5:103–110 (in Chinese).

Wang, G. M., Q. Q. Zhou, W. Q. Zhong, and G. H. Wang. 1992. [Food habits of Brandt's vole (*Microtus brandti*)]. *Acta Theriologica Sinica* 12:57–64 (in Chinese).

Wang, P. L. 1999. [*Chinese Cetaceans*]. Ocean Business Limited Company: Hong Kong (in Chinese).

Wang, P. L., and J. Y. Sun. 1986. [Distribution of the dugong off the coast of China]. *Acta Theriologica Sinica* 6:175–181 (in Chinese).

Wang, Q. S. (editor). 1990. [*The Mammal Fauna of Anhui*]. Anhui Publishing House of Science and Technology: Hefei (in Chinese).

Wang, Q. S., X. L. Hu, and Y. H. Yan. 1982. [On a new subspecies of Siberian musk-deer (*Moschus moschiferus anhuiensis* subsp. nov.) from Anhui, China]. *Acta Theriologica Sinica* 2:133–138 (in Chinese).

Wang, Q. Y., J. H. Bian, and Y. Z. Shi. 1993. [Influence of plateau zokor mounds on the vegetation and soil nutrients in an alpine meadow]. *Acta Theriologica Sinica* 13:31–37 (in Chinese).

Wang, Q. Y., W. Y. Zhou, W. H. Wei, Y. M. Zhang, and N. C. Fan. 2000. The burrowing behavior of *Myospalax baileyi* and its relation to soil hardness. *Acta Theriologica Sinica* 20:277–283.

Wang, S. 1959. [Further report on the mammals of northeastern China]. *Acta Zoologica Sinica* 11:344–352 (in Chinese).

——. 1964. [New species and subspecies of mammals from Xinjiang, China]. *Acta Zootaxonomica Sinica* 1: 6–15. (in Chinese).

—— (editor). 1998. *China Red Data Book of Endangered Animals: Mammalia*. Science Press: Beijing (in Chinese and English).

Wang, S., and Y. Xie (editors). 2004. [*China Species Red List*. Volume 1. *Red List*]. Higher Education Press: Beijing (in Chinese).

Wang, S., Y. Xie, and J. Wang (editors). 2001. [*A Dictionary of Mammalian Names (Latin, Chinese, English)*]. Hunan Educational Press: Changsha (in Chinese).

Wang, S., and C. L. Zheng. 1973. [Notes on Chinese hamsters (Cricetinae)]. *Acta Zoologica Sinica* 19:61–68 (in Chinese).

——. 1981. [On the subspecies of the Chinese sulphur-bellied rat - *Rattus niviventer* Hodgson]. *Sinozoologia* 1:1–8 (in Chinese).

Wang, S. B., and G. Y. Yang. 1981. [A new record of Chinese rodent from Xinjiang]. *Acta Zootaxonomica Sinica* 6:112 (in Chinese).

——. 1983. [*Rodent Fauna of Xinjiang*]. Xinjiang People's Publishing House: Urumqi (in Chinese).

Wang, T. Z., and X. Li. 1993. [Study on reproductive characteristics of the Gansu zokor and Chinese zokor]. *Acta Theriologica Sinica* 13:153–155 (in Chinese).

Wang, T. Z., and W. X. Xu. 1992. [*Glires (Rodentia and Lagomorpha) Fauna of Shaanxi Province*]. Shaanxi Normal University Press: Xi'an (in Chinese).

Wang, T. Z., J. K. Liu, M. M. Shao, S. Liu, and B. Zhou. 1992. [Studies on the population characteristics of Daurian ground squirrels (*Spermophilus dauricus*)]. *Acta Theriologica Sinica* 12:147–152 (in Chinese).

Wang, W., M. R. J. Forstner, Y. P. Zhang, Z. M. Liu, Y. Wei, H. Q. Huang, H. G. Hu, Y. X. Xie, D. H. Wu, and D. J. Melnick. 1997. A phylogeny of Chinese leaf monkeys using mitochondrial ND3-ND4 gene sequences. *International Journal of Primatology* 18:305–320.

Wang, W., and K. P. Ma. 1999. [Predation and dispersal of *Quercus liaotungensis* acorns by Chinese rock squirrels and Eurasian jays]. *Acta Botanica Sinica* 41:1142–1144 (in Chinese).

Wang, X. M., and R. S. Hoffmann. 1987. Pseudosis nayaur *and* Pseudosis schaeferi. *Mammalian Species* 278:1–6.

Wang, X. M., J. T. Peng, and H. M. Zhou. 2000. Preliminary observations on the distribution and status of dwarf blue sheep *Pseudois schaeferi*. *Oryx* 34:21–26.

Wang, X. M., and G. B. Schaller. 1996. Status of large mammals in western Inner Mongolia, China. *Journal of East China Normal University* 1996(12):93–104.

Wang, X. M., H. L. Sheng, J. Bi, and M. Li. 1997. Recent history and status of the Mongolian gazelle in Inner Mongolia, China. *Oryx* 31:120–126.

Wang, X. T. (editor). 1990. [*Vertebrate Fauna of Ningxia*]. Ningxia People's Publishing House: Yinchuan (in Chinese).

——. 1991. [*Vertebrate Fauna of Gansu*]. Gansu Science and Technology Publishing House: Lanzhou (in Chinese).

Wang, Y., A. G. Chen, B. Li, C. Guo, and S. B. Li. 1994. [Studies on the characteristics of reproduction of striped field mouse (*Apodemus agrarius ningpoensis*) in Dongting Plain]. *Acta Theriologica Sinica* 14:138–146 (in Chinese).

Wang, Y. X. 1987. [Taxonomic research in Burma-Chinese tree shrew, *Tupaia belangeri* (Wagner), from southern China]. *Zoological Research* 8: 213–230 (in Chinese).

——. 1998. *Arctogalidia trivirgata* and *Chrotogale owstoni*. Pp. 185–189. In *China Red Data Book of Endangered Animals. Mammalia*. S. Wang, editor. Science Press: Beijing (in Chinese and English).

——. 2003. [*A Complete Checklist of Mammal Species and Subspecies in China: A Taxonomic and Geographic Reference*]. China Forestry Publishing House: Beijing (in Chinese).

Wang, Y. X., Z. D. Gong, and X. D. Duan. 1988. [A new species of *Ochotona* (Ochotonidae, Lagomorpha) from Mt. Gaoligong, northwest Yunnan]. *Zoological Research* 9:201–207 (in Chinese).

Wang, Y. X., X. L. Jiang, and D. Li. 1998. Classification and distribution of the extant subspecies of golden snub-nosed monkey (*Rhinopithecus roxellana*). Pp. 53–54. In *The Natural History of the Doucs and Snub-nose Monkeys*. N. G. Jablonski, editor. World Scientific: Singapore.

Wang, Y. X., C. Y. Li, and Z. P. Chen. 1996. [Taxonomy, distribution and differentiation on *Typhlomys cinereus* (Platacanthomyidae, Mammalia)]. *Acta Theriologica Sinica* 16:54–66 (in Chinese).

Wang, Y. X., Z. X. Luo., and Z. J. Feng. 1985. [Taxonomic revision of Yunnan hares, *Lepus comus* with description of two new subspecies]. *Zoological Research* 6:101–109 (in Chinese).

Wang, Y. X., S. L. Ma, and C. G. Li. 1993. The taxonomy, distribution and status of forest musk deer in China. Pp. 22–30. In *Deer of China: Biology and Management*. N. Ohtaishi and H. L. Sheng, editors. Elsevier: Amsterdam.

Wang, Y. X., and L. H. Xu. 1981. [A new subspecies of Palm civet (Carnivora: Viverridae) from Hainan, China]. *Acta Zootaxonica Sinica* 6:446–448 (in Chinese).

Wang, Y. Z. 1985b. [A new genus and species of Gliridae *Chaetocauda sichuanensis* gen. and sp. nov.]. *Acta Theriologica Sinica* 5:67–75 (in Chinese).

——. 1985c. Subspecific classification and distribution of *Apodemus agrarius* in Sichuan, China. Pp. 86–89. In *Contemporary Mammalogy in China and Japan*. T. Kawamichi, editor. Mammalogical Society of Japan: Osaka.

Wang, Y. Z., and J. C. Hu. 1999. [*The Intimately-colored Pictoral Handbook of the Mammals in Sichuan*]. China Forestry Publishing House: Beijing (in Chinese).

Wang, Y. Z., J. C. Hu, and C. Ke. 1980. [A new species of Murinae - *Vernaya foramena* sp. nov.]. *Acta Zoologica Sinica* 26:393–397 (in Chinese).

Wang, Y. Z., Y. R. Tu, and S. Wang. 1966. [Notes on some small mammals from Szechuan Province with description of a new subspecies]. *Acta Zootaxonomica Sinica* 3:85–91 (in Chinese and English).

Wang, Y. Z., and G. Yang. 1989. [Insectivores]. Pp. 202–210. In [*A List of Medical Animals in Yunnan*]. Yunnan Office for Endemic Disease Control and Yunnan Sanitation and Antiepidemic Station, editors. Yunnan Science and Technology: Kunming (in Chinese).

Wang, Z. Y., and S. Wang. 1962. [The discovery of a flying fox (*Pteropus giganteus* Brunnich) from Ching-Hai Province, northwestern China]. *Acta Zoologica Sinica* 14:494 (in Chinese).

Ward, O. G., and D. H. Wurster-Hill. 1990. Nyctereutes procyonoides. *Mammalian Species* 358:1–5.

Ward, P., and S. Kynaston. 1995. *Bears of the World*. Blandford: London.

Weber, J. M., and S. Aubry. 1993. Predation by foxes, *Vulpes vulpes*, on the fossorial form of the water vole, *Arvicola terrestris* Scherman, in western Switzerland. *Journal of Zoology*, London, 229:553–559.

Wei, F. W., J. Z. Feng, Z. W. Wang, and J. C. Hu. 1999. Current distribution, status and conservation of wild red pandas *Ailurus fulgens* in China. *Biological Conservation* 89:285–291.

Wei, W. H., W. Y. Zhou, N. C. Fan, and D. E. Biggins. 1994. [Habitat selection, feeding and caring for the young of alpine weasel]. *Acta Theriologica Sinica* 14:184–188 (in Chinese).

Wei, Z., D. Wang, X. N. Kuang, K. X. Wang, X. Q. Wang, J. Q. Xiao, Q. Z. Zhao, and X. F. Zhang. 2002. Observations on behavior and ecology of the Yangtze finless porpoise (*Neophocaena phocaenoides asiaeorientalis*) group at Tian-e-Zhou Oxbow of the Yangtze River. *Raffles Bulletin of Zoology Supplement* 10:97–103.

Wemmer, C. (editor). 1987. *Biology and Management of the Cervidae*. Smithsonian Institution Press: Washington, DC.

——. 1998. *Deer: Status Survey and Conservation Action Plan*. IUCN: Gland, Switzerland.

Wemmer, C., and J. Murtaugh. 1981. Copulatory behavior and reproduction in the binturong, *Arctictis binturong*. *Journal of Mammalogy* 62:342–352.

Wessels, W. 1998. Gerbillidae from the Miocene and Miocene of Europe. *Mitteilungen-Bayerische Staatssummlung für Palaontologie und Historische Geologie* 38:187–207.

Williams, C. B. 1918. The food of the mongoose in Trinidad. *Trinidad Tobago Bulletin* 7:167–188.

Wilson, D. E., and D. M. Reeder. 1993. *Mammal Species of the World: A Taxonomic and Geographic Reference*, second edition. Smithsonian Insitution Press: Washington, DC.

Wilson, D. E., and D. M. Reeder. 2005. *Mammal Species of the World: A Taxonomic and Geographic Reference*, third edition. Johns Hopkins University Press: Baltimore.

Won, C. M., and K. G. Smith. 1999. History and current status of mammals of the Korean Peninsula. *Mammal Review* 29:3–33.

Wong, H. M. 1994. Asiatic beavers last stand. *China Explorer* 6:16–19.

Wong, S. T., C. W. Servheen, and L. Ambu. 2004. Home range, movement and activity patterns, and bedding sites of Malayan sun bears *Helarctos malayanus* in the rainforest of Borneo. *Biological Conservation* 119: 169–181.

Wozencraft, W. C. 1989a. The phylogeny of the Recent Carnivora. Pp. 495–535. In *Carnivore Behavior, Ecology and Evolution*. J. L. Gittleman, editor. Cornell University Press: Ithaca, NY.

——. 1989b. Classification of the Recent Carnivora. Pp. 569–593. In *Carnivore Behavior, Ecology and Evolution*. J. L. Gittleman, editor. Cornell University Press: Ithaca, NY.

——. 1993. Order Carnivora. Pp. 279–348. In *Mammal Species of the World*, second edition. D. E. Wilson and D. M. Reeder, editors. Smithsonian Institution Press: Washington, DC.

——. 2005. Order Carnivora. Pp. 532–628. In *Mammal Species of the World*, third edition. D. E. Wilson and D. M. Reeder, editors. Johns Hopkins University Press: Baltimore.

Wroughton, R. C. 1914. Report No. 15: Kumaon. Bombay Natural History Society's Mammal Survey of India. *Journal of the Bombay Natural History Society* 22: 282–301.

Wu, B. 1994. Patterns of spatial dispersion, locomotion and foraging behavior in three groups of Yunnan snub-nosed langur (*Rhinopithecus bieti*). *American Journal of Primatology* 33:253.

Wu, C. H., J. P. Wu, T. D. Bunch, Q. W. Li, Y. X. Wang, and Y. P. Zhang. 2005. Molecular phylogenetics and biogeography of *Lepus* in eastern Asia based on mitochondrial DNA sequences. *Molecular Phylogenetics and Evolution* 37:45–61.

Wu, D. L. 1982. [On subspecific differentiation of brown rat (*Rattus norvegicus* Berkenhout) in China]. *Acta Theriologica Sinica* 2:107–112 (in Chinese).

Wu, D. L., and X. F. Deng. 1984. [A new species of tree mice from Yunnan, China]. *Acta Theriologica Sinica* 4:207–212 (in Chinese).

Wu, D. L., X. F. Deng, G. H. Wang, and Z. P. Gan. 1987. [Home range of *A. draco* (Barrett-Hamilton)]. *Acta Theriologica Sinica* 7:140–146 (in Chinese).

Wu, D. L., J. Luo, and B. J. Fox. 1996b. A comparison of ground-dwelling small mammal communities in primary and secondary tropical rainforests in China. *Journal of Tropical Ecology* 12:215–230.

Wu, D. L., and G. H. Wang. 1984. [A new subspecies of *Typhlomys cinereus* from Yunnan, China]. *Acta Theriologica Sinica* 4:213–215 (in Chinese).

Wu, H. 1995. [Variation in the population and distribution of stump-tailed macaques in Fujian Wuyishan Nature research]. Pp. 276–280. In [*Primate Research and Conservation*]. W. Xia and Y. Zhang, editors. China Forestry Publishing House: Beijing (in Chinese).

Wu, H. Y. 1999. Is there current competition between sympatric Siberian Weasels (*Mustela sibirica*) and Ferret Badgers (*Melogale moschata*) in a subtropical forest ecosystem of Taiwan? *Zoological Studies* 38:443–451.

Wu, J. Y., and Y. T. Kao. 1991. [A new species of mammal in China—lackedteeth pygmy weasel (*Mustela aistoodonnivalis* sp. nov.]. *Journal of Northwest University* 21:87–94 (in Chinese).

Wu, L., M. W. Zhang, and B. Li. 1998. [Studies on the food composition of *Microtus fortis* in Dongting lake area]. *Acta Theriologica Sinica* 18:282–291 (in Chinese).

Wu, S. B., N. F. Liu, G. Z. Ma, Z. R. Xu, and H. Chen. 2003. Habitat selection by Chinese pangolins (*Manis pentadactyla*) in winter in Dawuling Natural Reserve. *Mammalia* 67:493–501.

Wu, W., X. M. Wang, and Z. H. Wang. 2002. [Tibetan Fox]. *Chinese Wildlife* 23:45–46 (in Chinese).

Wu, Y., C. G. Yuan, J. C. Hu, J. T. Peng, and P. L. Tao. 1990. [A biological study of the dwarf blue sheep]. *Acta Theriologica Sinica* 10:185–188 (in Chinese).

Wu, Z. J. , A. G. Chen, B. Li, C. Guo, Y. Wang, and M. W. Zhang. 1996a. [Studies on the breeding characteristics of Yangtze vole (*Microtus fortis*) in Dong Lake area]. *Acta Theriologica Sinica* 16:142–150 (in Chinese).

Wyss, A. 2001. Digging up fresh clues about the origin of mammals. *Science* 292:1496–1497.

Xia, W. P. (editor). 1963. [*Illustrated Books of Chinese Animals—Mammalia*]. Science Press: Beijing (in Chinese).

Xia, W. P., and X. Feng. 1964. [A new subspecies of *Allactaga bullata* G. Allen (Dipodidae)]. *Acta Zootaxonomica Sinica* 1:16–18 (in Chinese).

Xiao, W., and X. F. Zhang. 2002. [Distribution and population size of Yangtze Finless Porpoise in Poyang Lake and its branches]. *Acta Theriologica Sinica* 22: 7–14 (in Chinese).

Xiao, Z. H. (editor). 1988. [*Fauna of Liaoning: Mammalia*]. Liaoning Science and Technology Press: Shenyang (in Chinese).

Xie, Y., Z. Y. Li, W. P. Gregg, and D. M. Li. 2001. Invasive species in China—An overview. *Biodiversity and Conservation* 10:1317–1341.

Xie, Y., J. MacKinnon, and D. M. Li. 2004a. Study on biogeographical divisions of China. *Biodiversity and Conservation* 13:1391–1417.

Xie, Y., S. Wang, and P. Schei. 2004b. *China's Protected Areas*. Tsinghua University Press: Beijing.

Xiang, Y. 2004. [Molecular systematics of the Genus *Lepus* in China]. MS thesis. Chinese Academy of Sciences, Beijing (in Chinese).

Xiong, C. P. 1998. [Sexual behavioral pattern in the female Thibetan monkeys (*Macaca thibetana*)]. *Acta Theriologica Sinica* 18:247–253 (in Chinese).

Xu, H. F., X. Z. Zhang, and H. J. Lu. 1998. [Impact of human activities and habitat changes on distribution of Chinese Water Deer along the coast area in northern Jiangsu]. *Acta Theriologica Sinica* 18:161–167 (in Chinese).

Xu, L. H. 1984. [Studies on the biology of the hoary bamboo rat (*Rhizomys pruinosis* Blyth)]. *Acta Theriologica Sinica* 4:99–105 (in Chinese).

Xu, Z. H., and W. J. Huang. 1982. [On the karyotypes of three species of *Cricetulus*]. *Acta Theriologica Sinica* 2:201–210 (in Chinese).

Xu, L. H., Z. H. Liu, and S. M. Yu. 1983. [*Birds and Mammals of Hainan Island*]. Science Press: Beijing (in Chinese).

Xu, L. H., and S. M. Yu. 1985. [A new subspecies of Edward's rat from Hainan Island, China]. *Acta Theriologica Sinica* 5:131–135 (in Chinese).

Yan, Z. T., and M. M. Zhong. 1984. [Analysis of the population dynamics of gray hamster (*Cricetulus migratorius*) and house mouse (*Mus musculus*) in Xinjiang]. *Acta Theriologica Sinica* 4:283–290 (in Chinese).

Yang, D. H. (editor). 1983. [*Fauna of Xishuangbanna*]. Yunnan University Press: Kunming (in Chinese).

Yang, D. H., and Y. Xu. 1988. [Observation of white-cheeked gibbon in Xishuangbanna, southern Yunnan]. *Sichuan Journal of Zoology* 7:36–38 (in Chinese).

Yang, G. A., M. W. Bruford, F. W. Wei, and K. Y. Zhou. 2006. Conservation options for the Baiji: Time for realism. *Conservation Biology* 20:620–622.

Yang, G. R. 1985. [Some biological notes on the southwest Chinese vole (*Eothenomys custos*)]. *Acta Theriologica Sinica* 5:24, 34 (in Chinese).

Yang, G. R., and Y. X. Wang. 1987. [A new subspecies of *Hadromys humei* (Muridae, Mammalia) from Yunnan, China]. *Acta Theriologica Sinica* 11:118–125 (in Chinese).

Yang, G. R., and D. I. Wu. 1979. [Two new records of Chinese rodents]. *Acta Zootaxonomica Sinica* 4: 192–193 (in Chinese).

Yang, Q. S., and Z. J. Feng. 1998. *Uncia uncia*. Pp. 132–135. In *China Red Data Book of Endangered Animals. Mammalia*. S. Wang, editor. Science Press. Beijing (in Chinese and English).

Yang, Q. S., X. X. Meng, L. Xia, and Z. J. Feng. 2003. Conservation status and causes of decline of musk deer (*Moschus* spp.) in China. *Biological Conservation* 109:333–342.

Yang, Y. H., and H. Q. Lu. 1998. [The comparative study on morphological and biochemical indexes of striped field mouse (*Apodemus agrarius*) in eastern China]. *Acta Theriologica Sinica* 18:50–53 (in Chinese).

Yates, T. L. 1984. Insectivores, elephant shrews, tree shrews, and dermopterans. Pp. 117–144. In *Orders and Families of Recent Mammals of the World*. S. Anderson and J. K. Jones, Jr., editors. John Wiley and Sons: New York.

Ye, X. D., Y. Ma, J. S. Zhang, Z. L. Wang, and Z. K. Wang. 2002. [A summary of *Eothenomys* (Rodentia: Cricetidae: Microtinae)]. *Acta Zootaxonomica Sinica* 27:173–182 (in Chinese).

Yin, B. G., and W. L. Liu. 1993. [*Wildlife and Its Conservation in Xizang*]. China Forestry Publishing House Beijing (in Chinese).

Ying, W. 1999. Status and management of the Formosan black bear in Taiwan. Pp. 213–215. In *Bears: Status Survey and Conservation Action Plan*. C. Servheen, S. Herrero, and B. Peyton, editors. IUCN: Gland, Switzerland.

Yo, S. P., Y. S. Lin, and W. E. Howard. 1992. Home range dynamics of red-bellied tree squirrels (*Callosciurus erythraeus*) in Chitou. *Bulletin of the Institute of Zoology, Academia Sinica* 31:119–211.

Yoon, M. H. 1990. Taxonomical study on four *Myotis* (Vespertilionidae) species in Korea. *Korean Journal of Systematic Zoology* 6:173–191.

Yoshita, H. T. 1985. The evolution and geographic differentiation of the house shrew karyotypes. *Acta Zoologica Fennica* 170:31–34.

Yoshiyuki, M. 1988. Notes on Thai mammals 1. Talpidae (Insectivora). *Bulletin of the National Science Museum*, Tokyo, Series A, 14:215–222.

——. 1989. *A Systematic Study of the Japanese Chiroptera*. National Science Museum: Tokyo.

——. 1990. Notes on Thai mammals. 2. Bats of the *pusillus* and *philippinensis* groups of the genus *Rhinolophus*. *Bulletin of the National Science Museum*, Tokyo, Series A, 16:21–40.

——. 1991a. Taxonomic status of *Hipposideros terasensis* Kishida, 1924 from Taiwan (Chiroptera, Hipposideridae). *Journal of the Mammalogical Society of Japan* 16:27–35.

——. 1991b. A new species of *Plecotus* (Chiroptera, Vespertilionidae) from Taiwan. *Bulletin of the National Science Museum*, Tokyo, Series A, 17:189–195.

Yoshiyuki, M., and M. Harada. 1995. Taxonomic status of *Rhinolophus formosae* Sanborn, 1939 (Mammalia, Chiroptera, Rhinolophidae) from Taiwan. *Special Bulletin of the Japanese Society of Coleopterology* 4:497–504.

Yoshiyuki, M., S. Hattori, and K. Tsuchiya. 1989. Taxonomic analysis of two rare bats from the Amami Islands (Chiroptera, Molossidae and Rhinolophidae). *Memoirs of the National Science Museum*, Tokyo, 22:215–225.

Yu, D. P., J. Wang, G. Yang, and X. Zhang. 2005. [Primary analysis on habitat selection of Yangtze finless porpoise in spring in the section between Hukou and Digang]. *Acta Theriologica Sinica* 25:302–306 (in Chinese).

Yu, F. R., F. H. Yu, J. F. Pang, C. W. Kilpatrick, P. M. McGuire, Y. X. Wang, S. Q. Lu, and C. A. Woods. 2006. Phylogeny and biogeography of the *Petaurista philippensis* complex (Rodentia: Sciuridae), inter- and intraspecific relationships inferred from molecular and morphometric analysis. *Molecular Phylogenetics and Evolution* 38: 755–766.

Yu, H. T. 1993. Natural history of small mammals of subtropical montane areas in central Taiwan. *Journal of Zoology*, London, 231:403–422.

——. 1994. Distribution and abundance of small mammals along a subtropical elevational gradient in central Taiwan. *Journal of Zoology*, London, 234:577–600.

——. 1995. Patterns of diversification and genetic population structure of small mammals in Taiwan. *Biological Journal of the Linnaean Society* 55:69–89.

Yu, H. T., Y. P. Fang, C. W. Chou, S. W. Huang, and F. H. Yew. 1996. Chromosomal evolution in three species of murid rodents of Taiwan. *Zoological Studies* 35:195–1999.

Yu, M. Z. 1991. [*A Synopsis of the Vertebrates of Taiwan*, revised, Volume III, *Mammalia*]. Taiwan Commercial Publishing House: Taipei (in Chinese).

Yu, N., and C. L. Zheng. 1992a. [A taxonomic revision of Nubra pika (*Ochotona nubrica* Thomas, 1922)]. *Acta Theriologica Sinica* 12:132–138 (in Chinese).

——. 1992b. [A revision of the Huanghe pika–*Ochotona huangensis* (Matschie, 1907)]. *Acta Theriological Sinica* 12:175–182 (in Chinese).

Yu, N., C. L. Zheng, and L. M. Shi. 1997. Mitochondrial DNA variation and phylogeny of six species of pika (genus *Ochotona*). *Journal of Mammalogy* 78:387–396.

Yu, N., C. L. Zheng, X. L. Wang, G. X. He, Z. H. Zhang, A. J. Zhong, W. Q. Lu, and F. Tang. 1996. [A revision of genus *Uncia* Gray, 1854 based on mitochondrial DNA restriction site maps]. *Acta Theriologica Sinica* 16: 105–108 (in Chinese).

Yu, N., C. L. Zheng, Y. P. Zhang, and W. H. Li. 2000. Molecular systematics of pikas (Genus *Ochotona*) inferred from mitochondrial DNA sequences. *Molecular Phylogenetics and Evolution* 16:85–95.

Yu, X. C., Q. Z. Xiao and Y. M. Lu. 1993. Selection and utilization ratio of winter diet, and seasonal changes in feeding and bedding habitat selection by moose in northeastern China. Pp. 172–180. In *Deer of China: Biology and Management*. N. Ohtaishi and H. L. Sheng, editors. Elsevier: Amsterdam.

Yuan, X. C., B. W. Lu, W. C. Chen, Z. H. Liu, C. H. Lu, D. X. Yun, and K. Chen. 1993. Population dynamics of Hainan Eld's deer in the State Datian Nature Reserve, Hainan Island. Pp. 249–257. In *Deer of China: Biology and Management*. N. Ohtaishi and H. L. Sheng, editors. Elsevier: Amsterdam.

Yudin, B. S. 1971. [*Insectivorous Mammals of Siberia*]. Nauka: Novosibirsk (in Russian).

——. 1989. [*Insectivorous Mammals of Siberia*, second edition]. Nauka: Novosibirsk (in Russian).

Zaitsev, M. V. 1988. [On the nomenclature of red-toothed shrews of the genus *Sorex* in the fauna of the USSR]. *Zoologicheskii Zhurnal* 67:1878–1888 (in Russian).

——. 1993. [Species composition and questions of systematics of white-toothed shrews (Mammalia, Insectivora) of the fauna of USSR]. *Proceedings of the Zoological Institute, Russian Academy of Sciences* 243:3–46 (in Russian).

Zeng, Z. G., W. Q. Zhong, Y. L. Song, J. S. Li, L. G. Zhao, and H. S. Gong. 2003. [Present status of studies on eco-biology of Takin]. *Acta Theriologica Sinica* 23: 161–167 (in Chinese).

Zeng, Z. Y., W. J. Ding, Y. M. Yang, M. S. Luo, J. S. Liang, R. K. Xie, Y. G. Dai, and Z. M. Song. 1996a. Population ecology of *Rattus nitidus* in the western Sichuan Plain I. Population dynamics and body size. *Acta Theriologica Sinica* 16:202–210.

——. 1996b. Population ecology of *Rattus nitidus* in the western Sichuan Plain II. Survival and movement. *Acta Theriologica Sinica* 16:278–284.

Zeng Z. Y., Y. M. Yang, M. S. Luo, J. S. Liang, R. K. Xie, and Z. M. Song. 1999. Population ecology of *Rattus nitidus* in the western Sichuan plain III. Reproduction. *Acta Theriologica Sinica* 19:183–196.

Zhang, C. L. 1989. [Mammalia]. Pp. 709–720. In *Qinghai Fauna Economica*. D. H. Li, editor. Qinghai People's Press: Xining (in Chinese).

Zhang, D. C., N. C. Fan, and H. Yin. 2002. [Comparative analysis of behaviour between *Ochotona daurica* and *Ochotona curzoniae* in sympatric coexistence]. *Journal of Hebei University*, Natural Science Edition, 21:71–77 (in Chinese).

Zhang, J. 1986. [Studies on the population reproduction ecology of striped hamsters in Daxing County, Beijing]. *Acta Theriologica Sinica* 6:45–56 (in Chinese).

——. 1989. [On the population age and reproduction of *Apodemus agrarius* in Beijing area]. *Acta Theriologica Sinica* 9:41–48 (in Chinese).

Zhang, L., and N. Wang. 2003. An initial study on habitat conservation of Asian elephant (*Elephas maximus*), with a focus on human elephant conflict in Simao, China. *Biological Conservation* 112:453–459.

Zhang, R., and K. Zhou. 1978. Revision of Chinese animal geographic divisions. *Acta Zoologica Sinica* 24:196–202 (in Chinese).

Zhang, W. 1990. [A study of karyotype and C-banding pattern of *Nyctalus velutinus*]. *Journal of Anhui Normal University* 4:58–63 (in Chinese).

Zhang, X. F., D. Wang, R. Liu, Z. Wei, Y. Hua, Y. Wang, Z. Chen, and L. Wang. 2003b. The Yangtze River dolphin or baiji (*Lipotes vexillifer*): Population status and conservation issues in the Yangtze River, China. *Aquatic Conservation–Marine and Freshwater Ecosystems* 13:51–64.

Zhang, Y. M., and J. K. Liu. 2003. Effects of plateau zokors (*Myospalax fontanierii*) on plant community and soil in an alpine meadow. *Journal of Mammalogy* 84:644–651.

Zhang, Y. M., Z. B. Zhang, and J. K. Liu. 2003. Burrowing rodents as ecosystem engineers: The ecology and management of plateau zokors *Myospalax fontanierii* in alpine meadow ecosystems on the Tibetan plateau. *Mammal Review* 33:284–294.

Zhang, Y. P., and O. A. Ryder. 1994. Phylogenetic relationships of bears (the Ursidae) inferred from mitochondrial DNA sequences. *Molecular Phylogenetics and Evolution* 3:351–359.

Zhang, Y. Z., S. K. Jin, G. Q. Quan, S. H. Li, Z. Y. Ye, F. G. Wang, and M. L. Zhang. 1997. *Distribution of Mammalian Species in China*. China Forestry Publishing House: Beijing (in Chinese and English).

Zhang, Y. Z., and Y. L. Lin. 1981. [On the development of mammalian zoogeography in China for the past thirty years]. *Acta Theriologica Sinica* 1:3–18 (in Chinese).

Zhang, Z. B., R. Pech, S. Davis, D. H. Shi, X. R. Wang, and W. Q. Zhong. 2003a. Extrinsic and extrinsic factors determine the eruptive dynamics of Brandt's voles *Microtus brandti* in Inner Mongolia, China. *Oikos* 100:299–310.

Zhang, Z. B., J. Zhu, H. F. Yang, S. Q. Wang, S. S. Hao, F. S. Wang, and X. P. Cao. 1977. [The distribution of rat-like hamster (*Cricetulus triton*) caves in farmland and the study of their seasonal dynamic]. *Chinese Journal of Zoology* 32:32–34 (in Chinese).

Zhang, Z. Q. 2001. *Mammals of China: A Faunistic Analysis and Checklist*. Magnolia Press: Bellevue, WA.

Zhang, Z. Y., and M. S. Zhao. 1984. [A new subspecies of the sulphur-bellied rat from Jilin - *Rattus niviventer naoniuensis*]. *Acta Zoologica Sinica* 30:99–102 (in Chinese).

Zhao, H. H., S. Y. Zhang, J. Zhou, and Z. M. Liu. 2002. [New record of bats from: *Rhinolophus paradoxolophus*]. *Acta Theriologica Sinica* 22:74–76 (in Chinese).

Zhao, K. 1984. [Observation on the ecology of Mongolian steppe lemming (*Lagurus przewalskii*)]. *Acta Theriologica Sinica* 4:217–222 (in Chinese).

Zhao, K. T., P. Li, G. Wang, and L. Fung. 1981. [*Rodents of Inner Mongolia*]. Inner Mongolian Press: Hoh-hot (in Chinese).

Zhao, X. F., and H. Q. Lu. 1986. [Comparative observations of several biochemical indexes of *Apodemus agrarius pallidior* and *Apodemus agrarius ninpoensis* of the striped backed field mice]. *Acta Theriologica Sinica* 6:57–62 (in Chinese).

Zheng, C. L. 1979. [A study on the mammal fauna of Ngari and a preliminary discussion on faunal development in Qinghai-Xizang (Tibet) Plateau]. Pp. 191–227. In [*Expedition Report of Animals and Plants in the Area of Ngari, Xizang (Tibet)*]. Science Press: Beijing (in Chinese).

——. 1986. [Recovery of Koslov's pika (*Ochotona koslowi* Büchner) in Kunlun mountains of Xinjiang Uygur Autonomous Region, China]. *Acta Theriologica Sinica* 5:285 (in Chinese).

Zheng, C. L., and S. Wang. 1980. [On the taxonomic status of *Pitymys leucurus* Blyth]. *Acta Zootaxonomica Sinica* 5:106–112 (in Chinese).

Zheng, S. H., and C. K. Li. 1990. Comments on fossil arvicolids of China. Pp. 431–442. In *International Symposium Evolution, Phylogeny and Biostratigraphy of Arvicolids (Rodentia, Mammalia)*. O. Fejfar and W. D. Heinrich, editors. Geological Survey: Prague.

Zheng, S. W. 1985. [Data on the foods of the Tibetan sand fox]. *Acta Theriologica Sinica* 5:222, 240 (in Chinese).

Zheng, Y. L., and L. H. Yu. 1981. [New record of ferret-badger in China]. *Acta Theriologica Sinica* 1:158 (in Chinese).

——. 1983. [Subspecific study on the ferret-badger (*Melogale moschata*) in China, with description of a new species]. *Acta Theriologica Sinica* 3:165–171 (in Chinese).

Zhirjakov, V. A. 1990. On the ecology of the snow leopard in the Zailiskky-Alatau (Northern Tien Shan). *International Pedigree Book of Snow Leopards* 6:25–30.

Zhong, W. Q., M. J. Wang, and X. R. Wan. 1999. Ecological management of Brandt's vole (*Microtus brandti*) in Inner Mongolia, China. Pp. 199–214. In *Ecologically-based Rodent Management.* G. Singleton, L. Hinds, H. Leirs, and Z. B. Zhang, editors. Australian Centre for International Agricultural Research: Canberra.

Zhou, C. Q., K. Y. Zhou, and J. C. Hu. 2003. The validity of the dwarf bharal (*Pseudois schaeferi*)(Bovidae, Artiodactyla) species status: Inferred from mitochondrial Cyt-b gene. *Acta Zoologica Sinica* 49:578–584.

Zhou, K. Y., S. Ellis, S. Leatherwood, M. Bruford, and U. Seal. 1994. *Baiji (Lipotes vexillifer) Population and Habitat Viability Assessment.* IUCN–CBSG Report.

Zhou, K. Y., J. Sun, A. Gao, and B. Würsig. 1998. Baiji (*Lipotes vexillifer*) in the lower Yangtze River: Movements, numbers, threats and conservation needs. *Aquatic Mammals* 24:123–132.

Zhou, K. Y., P. Xie, D. Li, P. Wang, D. Wang, and L. Zhou. 2001. *Marine Mammals of China.* FAO: Rome.

Zhou, K. Y., X. R. Xu, and J. S. Tang. 2003. [Survey of the status of the Dugong in the Beibu Gulf, China, with remarks on the Indian Humpbacked Dolphin (*Sousa plumbea*)]. *Acta Theriologica Sinica* 23:21–26 (in Chinese).

Zhou, L. Z., Y. Ma, and D. Q. Li. 2000. [Distribution of great gerbil (*Rhombomys opimus*) in China]. *Acta Zoologica Sinica* 46:130–137 (in Chinese).

Zhou, Y. J., X. X. Meng, J. C. Feng, Q. S. Yang, L. Xia, and L. Bartos. 2004. Review of the distribution, status and conservation of musk deer in China. *Folia Zoologica* 53:129–140.

Zhu, G. Y. (editor). 1989. [*Fauna of Zhejiang: Mammalia*]. Zhejiang Science and Technology Publishing House: Hangzhou (in Chinese).

Zhu, S. K., and Z. H. Qin. 1991. [Studies on the population dynamics of ratlike hamster and striped hamster in rural districts of norther Huaihe River, Anhui]. *Acta Theriologica Sinica* 11:99–108 (in Chinese).

Zhuge, Y. 1993. *Crocidura* (Insectivora: Soricidae). Pp. 19–23. In [*Fauna of Zhejiang: Mammalia*]. Y. Zhuge and H. Q. Gu, editors. Zhejiang Science and Technology Publishing House: Hangzhou (in Chinese).

Zima, J., L. Lukácová, and M. Macholán. 1998. Chromosomal evolution in shrews. Pp. 175–218. In *Evolution of Shrews.* J. M. Wójcik and M. Wolsan, editors. Mammal Research Institute, Polish Academy of Sciences: Bialowieza.

Zorenko, T. A., V. Smorkacheva, and T. G. Aksenova. 1994. [Reproduction and postnatal ontogenesis of mandarin vole *Lasiopodomys mandarinus* (Rodentia, Arvicolinae)]. *Zoologischeskii Zhurnal* 73:120–129 (in Russian).

Zou, R., W. Ji, L. Sha, J. Lu, Y. Yan, and K. Yang. 1987. [Reproduction in tree shrews (*Tupaia belangeri chinensis*)]. *Zoological Research Sinica* 8:231–237 (in Chinese).

Index to Scientific Names

Numbers in bold refer to species plates

Index to Common Names

Numbers in bold refer to species plates

DATE DUE
DISCARDED
LIBRARY
GAYLORD
PRINTED IN U.S.A.